THE SAGES

EPHRAIM E. URBACH

THE SAGES

THEIR CONCEPTS AND BELIEFS

Translated from the Hebrew by
ISRAEL ABRAHAMS

Harvard University Press
Cambridge, Massachusetts
and London, England
1987

Printed in the United States of America

10 9 8 7 6 5 4 3 2 1

Published by arrangement with the Magnes Press, The Hebrew University, Jerusalem

Library of Congress Cataloging-in-Publication Data

Urbach, Efraim Elimelech, 1912–
The sages, their concepts and beliefs.

Translation of: Ḥazal, pirḳe emunot ṿe-de ʻot.
Bibliography: p.
Includes indexes.
1. Talmud — Theology. I. Title.
BM504.3.U713 1987 296.1′206 87-8415
ISBN 0-674-78523-1 (pbk.)

To the memory of my son
AVRAHAM YEHUDA
who gave his life
in defence of the Land of Israel
18 Tevet 5728
19 January 1968

TRANSLATOR'S FOREWORD

In my rendering of Prof. Ephraim E. Urbach's work, *The Sages — Their Concepts and Beliefs*, I have endeavoured to keep as close to the Hebrew original as English usage would permit.

My reason for adopting this course was not only the desire for fidelity, although this was, needless to say, a major consideration, but the nature of Prof. Urbach's work and the qualities of his style. The author is essentially a scholar; he is not only eminently objective in his approach, but he writes with exemplary precision and economy of expression. Thus the basic structure and aims of the book made it vitally necessary for the translator to observe the greatest care in reflecting the exactitude and nuances of the Hebrew; any deviation from this standard would have distorted Prof. Urbach's presentation of his subject.

It must not, however, be supposed that the exigencies of scientific scholarship have voided *The Sages* of literary distinction. While remaining true to its genre, the work makes a notable contribution to modern Hebrew literature by its classical, idiomatic patina and by its streamlined, architectonic construction.

I must regretfully admit that, for a number of reasons, I could not reproduce these characteristics in my translation. But I did attempt to preserve one dominant feature of the work. On almost every page three — or at the very least two — literary strata are discernible: Biblical quotations, Rabbinic dicta, and the author's own comments, analysis, and general discussion. To reflect this threefold literary tapestry, I have employed Elizabethan English (I had recourse mainly, though not invariably, to The Jewish Publication Society version, *The Holy*

Scriptures) for the Biblical citations; the Rabbinic passages I translated myself in a slightly antiquated English (but without the use of 'thou', 'thee', or 'ye'); and for the writer's own discourse I used the modern English idiom. By this means I have sought to convey, in a modest — and admittedly imperfect — measure, the stylistic characteristics of the original.

Translators are often stigmatized — and not altogether without warrant — as traitors (*traduttori, traditori*). But curiously enough in the present instance the translation has one distinct advantage of which, I would hope, even Hebrew scholars will avail themselves. The spectrum of Prof. Urbach's quotations from Talmudic and Midrashic literature is unusually wide and inevitably includes a number of obscure passages. Whereas the Hebrew work cites these dicta in their original form, without necessarily adding elucidatory annotations, the translator has consistently been compelled, by his rendering, to interpret them, since every translation is also, by its very nature, a commentary. All my translations of Rabbinic dicta have, like the rest of the English version, the approval of the author.

Consideration for the needs of the English (and perhaps non-Jewish) reader has necessitated, at times, the addition of a few explanatory notes. To avoid overloading the book, these annotations have been kept to an absolute minimum. They will be found in square brackets. The round brackets, on the other hand, where these do not reproduce the writer's own parenthesis, indicate, as a rule, additions in the translation required to make sense in the English.

The renderings of extracts from Philo and Josephus follow the translation of the Loeb Classical Library, which was considered the most suitable for the purpose.

Generally the retention of Hebrew words has been avoided. But this could not be done in the case of personal (or place-) names, technical terms, and the titles of Hebrew books. For this purpose transcription was used wherever possible. However, in quoting variant readings and in exceptional instances where transliteration would not fully convey the Hebrew spelling, the Hebrew characters were retained.

The question of transcription presented a number of problems, which I endeavoured to solve with due regard to the convenience of the English reader. Biblical names are given the accepted spelling found in the majority of English versions. In the case of Rabbinic references, a compromise plan was adopted: the well-known names are spelt according to the most popular convention (e.g. Akiba, Joḥanan). But in the case of the less familiar names the transliteration is more (though not always completely) scientific. The transcription of technical terms and book titles accords with the rules given in the 'Key to the Transliteration'. The signs for the vowels are used for fully transliterated words, but are often omitted if the word is frequently repeated.

The titles of Hebrew works cited in the Text are generally translated (in square brackets) on their occurrence. But book names that are essentially of a poetic character and would, if translated, only serve to puzzle the English reader, are left in their original Hebrew form. Likewise Hebrew books referred to in the notes are not rendered into English; translation, in this case, would have made the annotations far too unwieldy.

The old Rabbinic teaching that 'All sacrifices will ultimately be abolished, except the thanksgiving offering' comes spontaneously to mind when I consider those who have helped in various ways to bring this work of translation to fruition.

First, I wish to recall, with abiding gratitude, that the late Mr. Silas S. Perry ז"ל made this publication possible not only by his financial generosity, but also by his life-long, loving interest in Jewish scholarship, which he fervently believed would ultimately spread the light and wisdom of Jewish knowledge among the broad masses of the Jewish (and non-Jewish) laity. His constant encouragement to me personally in my work for the Perry Foundation I can never forget.

My translation of *The Sages* could never have achieved its present form without the careful attention given to the translation in all its stages by Prof. Urbach. He has been a veritable tower of strength to me, and I record my appreciation of his friendship and inspiring erudition with deepfelt thanks.

Mrs. Yvonne Glickson (a daughter of Mr. Perry) has, with true filial piety, made a noteworthy contribution to the project by her valuable suggestions in matters of styling and presentation. Her association with the work will, I am sure, be a source of gratification to the entire Perry family.

I wish also to acknowledge, with appreciative thanks, my indebtedness to Mr. Ch. Toren, the director of the Magnes Press, for his unfailing interest in the progress of the translation and its publication; to the staff of the Central Printing Press, for the care and devotion with which they carried out their tasks.
Jerusalem

Nisan, 5733 ISRAEL ABRAHAMS
April, 1973

AUTHOR'S PREFACE TO THE ENGLISH EDITION

The English translation of this book is based on the second Hebrew edition without additions or changes. The printing started in spring of 1973. It was still in progress when to the great sorrow of his friends and all who knew him, Professor Israel Abrahams passed away after a brief illness on 26 October 1973. He managed to read most of the chapters in proof before he became ill.

The publication schedule had to be postponed because of his untimely death and also because of delays following the Yom Kippur War.

While working on the translation, Professor Abrahams used to pass to me drafts of each chapter; we would then meet to clarify any problems that had arisen. These hours we spent together discussing and studying the text, trying to achieve the most correct renderings of words, idioms and terminology, gave me great pleasure and will remain in my memory.

Mrs. Yvonne Glickson undertook an additional reading of the proofs; she suggested a few stylistic and linguistic alterations which I have accepted and which, I believe, would have been approved by the translator. The exacting task of proofreading was undertaken by Miss Susan Corb and Mrs. Janet Shvili. Dr. Yosef (Alan) Unterman prepared the indices and Mrs. E. Even Shoshan helped in compiling the bibliography. The publishers and staff of the Hebrew University's Magnes Press and the Central Press, Jerusalem, devoted a great deal of time and effort to complete the work in difficult conditions. To all of these I am most grateful.

10 Kislev, 5735
24 November, 1974 EPHRAIM E. URBACH

An index of non-rabbinic sources was added to the second English edition. I am most grateful to Dr. Robert Brody for his help in preparing the index.

13 Tevet 5739
12 January 1979

KEY TO THE TRANSLITERATION OF THE HEBREW

Consonants

א	= ’	ל	= l
בּ	= b	מ, ם	= m
ב	= v	נ, ן	= n
גּ	= g	ס	= s
ג	= gh	ע	= ‘
דּ	= d	פּ	= p
ד	= dh	פ, ף	= ph
ה	= h	צ, ץ	= ṣ
ו	= w	ק	= q
ז	= z	ר	= r
ח	= ḥ	שׂ	= ś
ט	= ṭ	שׁ	= š
י	= y	תּ	= t
כּ, ךּ	= k	ת	= th
כ, ך	= kh		

Note: (1) Unsounded ה at the end of a word is not represented in the transcription;

(2) the customary English spelling is retained for Biblical names and rabbinic works and authorities.

Vowels

Long			*Short*		
ָ	(*Qāmeṣ gādhōl*)	= ā	ַ		= a
ִי, ִ	(*Ḥīreq gādhōl*)	= ī	ֶ		= e
ֵי, ֵ		= ē	ִ	(*Ḥīreq qāṭān*)	= i
ֹ, וֹ		= ō	ָ	(*Qāmeṣ qāṭān*)	= o
וּ		= ū	ֻ		= u

ְ	(*Šewā’*)	= ĕ
ֲ		= ă
ֳ		= ŏ
ֱ		= ĕ

CONTENTS

Chapter VI: Magic and Miracle

Chapter VII: The Power of the Divine Name

Chapter VIII: The Celestial Retinue

Chapter IX: He Who Spoke and the World Came into Being

Chapter X: Man

Chapter XI: On Providence

Chapter XII: The Written Law and the Oral Law

Chapter XIII: The Commandments

Chapter XIV: Acceptance of the Yoke of the Kingdom of Heaven. Love and Reverence

Chapter XV: Man's Accounting and the World's Accounting

and the preservation of the principle of reward and punishment — theodicean methods of interpreting harsh Scriptural episodes — past events explained by later events — the selling of Josephus and the martyred Sages — 'What have you to do with the mysteries of the All-Merciful?' pp. 511–523

Chapter XVI: The People of Israel and its Sages

1. *Election and Reality*

The idea of election in the Bible — the derision of the Gentiles at the Jewish claim to election in times of oppression — the Sages' replies to the sectarians — the answer they gave to their own people — the concept of election as a cosmic act — the twofold election — Israel chose its God — the choosing people became the chosen people — the nation's destiny is determined by its attitude to its God since the acceptance of the Torah — the implications of mutual suretyship. pp. 525–541

2. *Election and Proselytization*

The function of spreading Israel's faith among the Gentiles — the effect of the destruction of the Temple — explanations of the Jewish people's dispersion — the attitude to Christians and pagans — the struggle on two fronts — the laws governing the acceptance of proselytes — the attitude to proselytes in the post-Hadrianic period — the attitude of the Amoraim — the strength of the consciousness of election — its expression in prayers and benedictions. pp. 541–554

3. *Indictment and Defence of the Congregation of Israel*

The attitude to the episode of the golden calf — the assessment of the work of the prophets among their people — the function of reproof and defence. pp. 554–564

4. *The Status of the Sages in the Days of the Hasmoneans*

The cessation of prophecy — the Great Synagogue — Scribes and Sages — Ben Sira's description — Joḥanan the High Priest — Simeon b. Sheṭaḥ — Shemaʿya and Avṭalion. pp. 564–576

5. *Hillel's Character and Work*

Hillel and the Sons of Bathyra — the attitude to tne Holy Spirit — the enactments of Hillel — his influence on the institutions of the Temple and Sanhedrin — his attitude to the masses of the people — the laws of purity and impurity — the differences between the associations of the Pharisees and the Essenes and the Qumran Covenanters — the changed meaning of the term *ʿam ha-'areṣ* and the consequences in the relationship between them and the *ḥăvērîm* [associates] — Hillel's attributes and conduct. pp. 576–593

6. *The Régime of the Sages after the Destruction of the Temple*

The School of Shammai and the School of Hillel — the Zealots in the period of the Revolt — the work of R. Joḥanan b. Zakkai — the episode of ʿAqaviah b. Mahalalel — the dynasty of the Patriarchs of the House of Hillel — the struggle for freedom of Halakhic decision — the problem of the livelihood of the Sages — the clash between ideals and reality. pp. 593–603

CHAPTER I

THE STUDY OF THE BELIEFS AND CONCEPTS OF THE SAGES

The term 'Sages' is customarily used to denote the Sages of the Oral Law, who are mentioned in its literary sources: the Mishna, Tosefta, Halakhic Midrashim, Talmuds and Haggadic Midrashim. The earliest of the scholars lived in the era preceding the Maccabean revolt, and the last, when the Mediterranean countries were conquered by the Arabs — that is, their activities extended over a period of more than nine hundred years. This long interval was rich in events and acts that changed the face of the world. The beginning of this epoch witnessed the Hellenization of the lands of the East Mediterranean. After Alexander the Great had destroyed the Persian empire, the eastern countries, including Eretz-Israel, were opened to Greek culture, but at the same time the Orient — its beliefs and cultures — also began to influence Greek culture, and the synthesis, known as Hellenistic civilization, was formed. This civilization determined the physiognomy of Egypt, Syria, some of the lands of the Euphrates and Asia Minor even after their political conquest by the Romans. The Jewish people, whose country was conquered by Alexander the Great in 332 B.C.E., was also drawn into the process of Hellenization. After the wars of the Diadochi, it was subject for a century to the dominion of the Ptolemies, and only the victory of Antiochus III over the Ptolemies in 200–198 B.C.E. brought it under the rule of the Seleucids. Then for the first time there broke out an open clash between internal forces of the nation — between the Hellenistic party, who forsook the ancestral customs and found an ally in Antiochus IV, Epiphanes, and the Hasidim ('Pietists'), who were opposed to them.

The revolt, begun by the Hasidim, led to the establishment of the Maccabean state. The Greek cities were destroyed, and in the era of the Hasmoneans there arose within the nation movements that contended for leadership of the people. In this struggle religious, political and social elements were interlinked, and it continued after political independence had been lost and the Roman empire had spread the tentacles of its dominion over the whole country, until the destruction of the Temple. The Destruction did not end the struggle for political sovereignty, and the national centre remained in the Land for a long period, but the Jewish Diaspora and its centres acquired increased importance. The beginning of the Babylonian, and also of the Egyptian, dispersion dates back to the destruction of the First Temple, but the Diaspora was subsequently reinforced both by the cultural and commercial ties that grew between Eretz-Israel and the Hellenistic kingdoms, and by the stream of emigration from the Land in the wake of the internal disputes, rebellions, and wars, as well as by the conversion of many Gentiles who accepted Israel's Torah in some measure. One of the sectarian groups that sprang up in the last century before the destruction of the Temple, and also remained linked — at least in part — to the corporate nation for some time after the Destruction, penetrated primarily the Jewish communities in the Greek Diaspora, and as a result of proselytization, complete and partial, in which it widely engaged, it infiltrated also into the Gentile world. From being a persecuted and tolerated religion, Christianity became the dominant faith in the Roman empire. On the one hand it is clear that the events enumerated — and many others besides — left their mark on the thought and doctrines of their times; but on the other, the Sages, in each generation, introduced, by their beliefs and concepts, a ferment into the ranks of the nation, and by waging a constant struggle they achieved the crystallization and formulation of ideas and sentiments that were accepted as credal principles and were held in common by the scholars and the nation as a whole. These principles are few in number, but actually enter into many spheres of life and encompass them from various aspects, both large and small. Alongside the matters that formed common ground, there also remained subjects and issues on which the views of the Sages were not identical with the beliefs and views prevailing among the people, while on many matters even the scholars were divided among themselves.

These differences of opinion are explicable, apparently, in the light of the divergence of political, economic, and social background, when Sages living in different periods are spoken of. If the reference is to members of the same generation, the disagreements would be indicative of individual disparities between diverse religious types. But such differentiations are very difficult to determine, on account of the particular character of the sources with which we are dealing. Not only are there many dicta, the names of whose authors are unknown to us, but even in cases where they are attributed to Sages whom we know, there is no assurance whatsoever that these statements are the product of their thinking, for conceivably they were only transmitted by these scholars while their source is much older; thus they do not represent the individual opinion of this or that Rabbi but a generally accepted view. Attention must also be paid to the literary form of the source. The Talmuds and Midrashim contain sayings in which the Sages expressed religious and ethical ideas. These dicta are distinguished by their lapidary form, by their felicitous abstract formulation, by their pithiness, which is capable of condensing in a few words complete and complicated themes. With sayings and aphorisms of this kind there are bound up exegetical problems, but it cannot be doubted that they pertain to our subject. The position is different in respect of other literary forms: parables, homilies, narratives, and prayers; here we have to enquire how much weight should be given to the ideas that we tend to find in them, and what should be credited to the rhetorical-homiletic tendency and the artistic aspiration of the authors and editors.

We shall add one more source, which has been little used in relation to our subject, namely the Halakha. The Halakha does not openly concern itself with beliefs and concepts; it determines, in practice, the way in which one should *walk*, that which is permitted and forbidden, obligatory and exempted, clean and unclean. Nevertheless beliefs and concepts lie at the core of many Halakhot; only their detection requires exhaustive study of the history of the Halakha combined with care to avoid fanciful conjectures and unfounded explanations.

Common to all the sources is the fact that none of them provides systematic treatment of the subject of beliefs and conceptions, and there are almost no continuous discourses dealing with a single theme. In most instances we have to integrate and arrange the scattered material into one unit of thought. A great fund of terms and concepts was created in the era of the Sages, some of which are not known — at least in their present formulation — in the Bible, and some, although found in Scripture, have acquired a different meaning and content. It will suffice to mention the following concepts: 'this world' and 'the next world', 'good inclination' and 'evil inclination', 'penitence' and 'redemption', 'resurrection of the dead', 'reward' and 'punishment', *miṣwā* ('precept', 'good deed') and transgression, 'the kingdom of Heaven', 'the bestowal of lovingkindness', 'Gehinnom' ('Hell') and 'the Garden of Eden' ('Paradise'); likewise the new epithets and designations of God, such as: the Omnipresent (*Māqôm*, literally: 'Place'), 'Sovereign of the universe', 'the Holy One, blessed be He', 'the All-Merciful', 'the Almighty', 'Heaven'. The signification of these concepts is not defined or discussed in detail in the sources, and no attempt has been made to relate them or to reveal their common elements. Such attempts on our part are likely to show contradictions between the conclusions drawn from one set of ideas and those derived from another. It is just this lack of consistency and system that provided subsequent generations with a great measure of freedom in defining the principles of faith. The teachings of the Sages were accepted by them as a source of the highest authority, challenged by none, but the freedom allowed in the interpretation of its truths opened up multi-faceted possibilities. The philosophers of the Middle Ages, the Cabbalists, and the Hasidim all based themselves on Rabbinic dicta in expounding their systems.

Since their respective systems were of primary importance to these thinkers, the original meaning of the words of the Sages was dimmed and even set aside, especially as their modes of expression and literary form made them a tree of many boughs and branches, on which extraneous ideas could easily be appended. This method is prevalent also in our days in a particular category of books that is widely disseminated, especially in non-Hebrew languages, and whose theme is the presentation of 'Judaism'. They appear under the general title

'Judaism' or bear more piquant names. The authors largely make use of the sayings of the Rabbis — their parables and stories — but place upon them the interpretation given to them by Maimonides or Judah ha-Levi, by the Cabbalists and the Hasidic leaders, and even introduce into them modern concepts that are current in the philosophical and theological systems of our times. Needless to say, each writer quotes what seems to him to approximate to his own views, while disregarding other sources. Undoubtedly we may not completely deny the value of works of this nature as reading matter for those who are interested in them and in their authors' outlook — if, indeed, they have a view and outlook of their own — but they are of no value for our study, which is concerned with the history of *the beliefs and concepts of the Sages against the background of the reality of their times and environment*.

Modern Jewish scholarship ('Wissenschaft des Judentums') has paid but little attention to our subject. The scholars who were interested in philosophical thought and doctrine devoted their talents to medieval philosophy. They had an affinity with its rationalistic trends and succeeded in adapting to its study the accepted methods employed in the field of medieval philosophy, both Arabic and Christian scholastic. Here and there the introductions to general works on the Jewish philosophy of the Middle Ages incorporate brief surveys of Rabbinic thought. The best of them is that in Julius Guttmann's book, *Philosophies of Judaism*,[1] I, 3, 'The Religious Ideas of Talmudic Judaism'. But apart from several pertinent notes, this chapter contains only a summary survey that skims lightly over a number of problems. Research on the Talmud and Midrash was mainly concerned with literary and exegetical questions. It is true that a few monographs have been written, but this does not amount to a compendious account, unless we are prepared to regard as such the presentation of Isaac Hirsch Weiss in his *Dor Dor we-Doreshaw* ('Zur Geschichte der jüdischen Tradition'),[2] published in 1871.

Solomon Schechter's work, *Some Aspects of Rabbinic Theology*,[3] 1909, is certainly a fine book. But Schechter himself emphasized that the circumstances in which he began to write his work — the lack of preliminary monographic treatises — prevented him from writing the history of Jewish theology and its development, and consequently he confined himself to giving a general account of a few themes. He also admitted that in his treatment of the subject he had in mind principally the ideas that had become an integral part of the religious consciousness of the bulk of the Jewish people, or, as he terms it, of 'Catholic Israel'. Schechter did not, in truth, ignore the actual existence of differences of opinion, but he posited that views that failed to receive general approval — the particular time being irrelevant — were not of particular importance even in their own day. Hence he was also prepared to forgo the exposition of beliefs and concepts that show a special resemblance to those found in the Pseudepigrapha. He regarded them as chaff that somehow got mixed up with the wheat. But despite these prefatory remarks about his guiding principles and notwithstanding that sixty years have elapsed since the publication of the work, many of its sections have not lost their significance.

Kaufmann Kohler's *Jewish Theology Systematically and Historically Considered,* 1928, largely belongs to the class of general books on 'Judaism'. He himself defined his task thus: to provide 'a Jewish Theology by which the Jew can comprehend his own religious truths in the light of modern thought and at the same time defend them against the aggressive attitude of the ruling religious sects.'[4]

Studies in Christianity devoted special attention to the world of Jewish faith in the period close to the time of Jesus, at the outset in order to entrench and reinforce the polemic against the Pharisees found in the Gospels and in ancient Christian literature, and to stress the superiority of Christianity and its dogmas over Judaism. An outstanding example of this approach is found in Wilhelm Bousset's *Die Religion des Judentums in neutestamentlichen Zeitalter*, Berlin 1903. This title of the first edition is indicative of the trend to regard Judaism as merely the background of Christianity. In the second edition, revised by Hugo Gressmann, which appeared in 1926, the name of the book was changed to *Die Religion des Judentums im späthellenistischen Zeitalter*. The Jewish religion is described in this treatise primarily on the basis of external sources — the apocryphal literature and the Hellenistic literature — and relies only to a small extent on Rabbinic works, and even this was done without sufficient knowledge and with the help of secondary authorities, with the result that some gross errors have been perpetrated.

One of the sources used by Bousset, as by other Christian scholars — until the publication of the work by Strack and Billerbeck[5] — was Weber's book, *Jüdische Theologie auf Grund des Talmud und verwandten Schriften* (2 verb. Aufl. hrg. von F. Delitzsch und G. Schnederman, Leipzig 1897). Despite the reservation expressed by Bousset and Gressmann[6] about Weber's lack of historical discernment, they nevertheless preserved his aim, an aim that is reflected even in the order of the chapters, which seeks to underscore the legalistic character of Judaism. Felix Perles devoted an entire volume to a comprehensive critique of Bousset's work.[7] Bousset replied to this in a brochure entitled *Volksfrömmigkeit und Schriftgelehrtentum*, 1903. This polemic, which was waged sixty years ago, is itself a historic document. Perles was easily able to demonstrate Bousset's gross ignorance in dealing with Rabbinic sources as well as the tendentiousness of his book, which was partly conscious and partly the result of Christian education and the belief that Judaism was only a preparation for Christianity, combined, to put it mildly, with a lack of sympathy for existing Judaism. On the other hand, Perles's rejoinder is marked by a distinctly apologetic tone, which spoils the case. Actually Perles often adopts Bousset's method, only he uses it for his own purposes. The opinions and concepts of Christianity are also accepted by him as a criterion, only he finds them already in Judaism. His contention against Bousset that, whenever the latter finds in Christianity good and noble features and also objectionable and surprising elements, he regards the good things as the creation of Christianity, and the bad things as the heritage from Judaism, can almost be reversed in his own case. Perles wished to find in Judaism everything that appeared good and proper in the estimation of the humanitarian Christian liberalism of Germany at the beginning of the present century and to exclude, as alien to its spirit, whatever was not to his liking.

Perles's approach is characteristic of an entire generation of Jewish scholars. In the same year that Perles published his book against Bousset, another learned savant, Benno Jacob, wrote: 'Judaism must protest, if she is indiscriminately charged with responsibility for the pseudepigraphical literature.... Judaism can no more be portrayed by the *Book of Enoch*, or *Jubilees*, or *Ezra IV*, and similar writings, than Christianity can be depicted on the basis of the apocryphal gospels, spurious "acts", or Gnostic fantasies.' However, Jacob admits that it is difficult to find clear criteria in Judaism as to what is of its essence and what is not, for no dogmas were formulated in it as in Christianity; but on the pseudepigrapha — he declares — source-true Judaism has already passed judgment and rejected them; hence they are primarily a witness to Christianity, which preserved them. 'If a more fitting epithet cannot be found for what is contained in the pseudepigraphical works than the term "Jewish", then the study must avoid giving the impression that what is quoted from these writings is "Judaism". The latter can be depicted not only by means of the Haggada, but even better by having recourse to the Halakha, and to this end a beginning has not yet been made.'[8] It is a pity that Perles, Jacob, and other Jewish scholars like them did not write, in place of polemics, the history of the beliefs and opinions of the Sages. They would undoubtedly have arrived at a less uniform and monochromatic view of all the periods, at a different evaluation of the function of the trends that they term sub-currents, and of phenomena with which they have no sympathy, and which they find for some reason only in the marginal trends. Instead of showing that the pseudepigraphical works do not represent 'Judaism', they would have found them a great help in discovering the ideas and emotions that stirred Judaism from within, in uncovering the processes and struggles that preceded the formulation of the dicta and rulings of the Sages. But, unhappily, these Jewish scholars ally themselves with Christian scholars (whom they criticize in their writings) in positing that Judaism is fossilized, devoid of dynamism or vitality. Thus Benno Jacob writes that parallels to Christian teachings in Talmudic-Midrashic literature cannot be regarded as sources for Christianity, for they were composed later than the Christian writings, and should research prove the antiquity of a source, then, if the subject is not to be found in the Bible, the question arises whether the parallel passages do not have a common source. The premise is that spiritual life and religious thinking were extinguished among the Jewish people with the close of the Bible, and that outside Scripture and after it nothing was created, no emotions were felt, no thinking was done.

Bousset's tendentiousness and one-sidedness are manifest, and almost require no proof; but at the same time we must not wrong him, for he presented quite a number of problems in a form and mode acceptable to religious research. No less tendentious are most of the studies that treat Judaism as the background to Christianity or as the soil upon which it grew.

A change came about with the publication of the work of G. Foot Moore, *Judaism in the First Centuries of the Christian Era — The Age of the Tannaim* (vols. I–II, 1927; Notes, 1930). Moore does not portray Judaism merely as the background to the understanding of Christian origins, and his portrayal is based chiefly on Rabbinic literature and not on apocryphal and Hellenistic literature. The author's objectivity and his moderation and caution deserve commendation. He also made greater use than any of his predecessors of the researches of Jewish writers, and was not averse to learning from them. The influence of Schechter's work is discernible in many places. Christian scholars considered Pharisaic Judaism, as they are accustomed to call it, the Judaism of legalistic Halakha and the antithesis of prophetic Judaism, which became the heritage of apocalyptic Judaism. The consolidation of legalistic Judaism and its separation from other elements took place, according to some, with the rise of Christianity, and according to others, upon the destruction of the Temple. Some writers argue that in the Judaism preceding the Destruction there was evidence of universalistic elements and the desire to transcend the boundaries of people and country. But the Destruction, followed by rebellions among Diaspora Jewry in the reign of Trajan and the revolt of Bar Kokhba in Eretz-Israel in the time of Hadrian, led to the triumph of the nationalist elements, to the narrowing of horizons and to petrifaction; thereafter Christianity replaced Judaism as a missionary and universalistic religion. Another view[9] holds that the development took the opposite course. Judaism of the first century, with which Jesus, his apostles, and disciples dispute, was less spiritual. Only the destruction of the Temple and the consequences of the revolt brought about its spiritualization.

Against these and similar views, Foot Moore emphasizes the continuity of the teaching of 'normative Judaism', that is, of Judaism as it is reflected in the Tannaitic literature of the second century. In his opinion there is no antithesis between 'ethical-prophetic' and legalistic religion. The particular literary character of the apocalyptic literature and its kinship with prophetic literature does not yet make it the opponent of Halakhic literature; nor may we ignore the ethical instruction contained in Tannaitic literature. The restriction of proselytization, especially in the days of Hadrian, did not affect the essential character of the teaching of the Tannaim. The wars of 66–72 brought about changes in the social structure. The Sadducees and the priestly aristocracy left the stage of history. The Zealots perished in the course of the fighting, and the voice of the Essenes was also stilled immediately afterwards. The revival of Judaism after the Destruction was the work of the Pharisees. Judaism, which had been splintered into various sects, achieved, in the two generations after the Destruction, a homogeneity and authority that characterize it to this day. Although a ramified development in the details of the Halakha took place in the schools of the Tannaim in the second century, yet this unfoldment does not evince different principles or new features in relation to the earlier epochs, nor are such to be found in the fundamentals of the religion and ethic. The basic tenets and principles had been fixed long ago and it was necessary to emphasize them and to make each generation more fully conscious of them, but not to search for them and reveal them.

Caution and moderation, which rightly appeared to Moore essential after the fanciful expositions that he had encountered in the writings of his predecessors, caused him to confine himself to a presentation of normative Judaism (a parallel expression to Schechter's 'Catholic Judaism') in the epoch of the Tannaim. He admits that he bypassed the problems of 'the history of religion' (*religionsgeschichtliche Probleme*), that is to say, the question of the origin of beliefs and concepts found among Jews and known also to others, because he considered that these problems belong to the general history of religion and not specifically to the history of Judaism. But this is not the main defect. Moore did not always go deeply enough into the essence of the problems that he discussed. He failed to give an account of the origin of the beliefs and concepts, of their struggles and evolution, of their entire chequered course till their crystallization, of the immense dynamism and vitality of the spiritual life of the Second Temple period, of the tension in the relations between the parties and sects, and between the various sections of the Sages themselves. The character and status of the Rabbis are not elucidated.

The very concept of normative Judaism as finally crystallized is untenable from many aspects. There are Halakhot and concepts that were crystallized at an early period, and others that reached their accepted formulation only at the end of the era of the Sages, and not a few of them never attained even to that. The close of the Tannaitic epoch certainly cannot be regarded as a turning point or termination. The argument voiced by Moore against the scholars who set a boundary at the time of the destruction of the Temple, or against those who draw a distinction between ethical-prophetic and legalistic religion, applies equally to the line of demarcation that he set. A literary boundary is by no means of itself a demarcation or turning point in respect to the content of that literature. It is a well-known fact that Amoraic literature comprises topics and dicta for which there are parallels in the apocryphal literature and these prove to be much older than the age of the Tannaim, although their works contain no mention of them. The religious significance of the Halakha and its place among the spiritual treasures of Judaism did not receive adequate treatment and suitable exposition, despite Moore's recognition, in principle, of the importance of the phenomenon.[10]

These criticisms could already be levelled when Moore's book first appeared. But in the course of the decades that have elapsed since its publication, new sources have become available — it will suffice to mention the Qumran Scrolls — and the Rabbinic sources themselves have been equipped with critical commentaries based on a more reliable examination of the texts, while a long series of monographs has been added on specific subjects. These alone necessitate and justify renewed study of the history of the beliefs and concepts of the Sages. Such research is required no less by the recent studies in the Jewish history of the period and the new approaches that have come to light in them. The fresh data — archaeological, epigraphic and papyrological — have enriched our knowledge of the material and social life of the era, and also of the extent to which the Halakha controlled it. The more thorough use of external sources has changed considerably the picture of the relationship between the world of the Sages and that round about them — the Hellenistic-pagan and Christian worlds combined. This added information also brought in its train novel general insights.

Yitzhak Baer[11] presented a comprehensive, overall view of the course of Jewish history. The decisive era, to his mind, for laying the foundations of Judaism was the period between the conquest of the Orient by Alexander the Great and the Diadochi and the rise of the Hasmonean state. In this interval the special character of Judaism and of the Jewish people assumed the form it was destined to have for generations to come. At its commencement — in the Hellenistic, pre-Hasmonean period — there were created socio-religious ideals of an ascetic, spiritual, and martyrological nature, on the basis of which the society of the First Hasidim was built. This was followed by the epoch of the earlier Hasmoneans in which the attempt was made to establish a theocratic state according to these ideals, and which ended in a ruthless struggle between the Hasidim and the secular rulers. The circles of the Hasidim and the Sages were divested of their official influence in politics, but in practice they remained dominant in religious and social life. The attempt to restore a complete theocracy during the war against Rome failed, and the renewal of the regime of the spiritually-minded Sages came as a result of the recurrent collapse of the natural foundations of society. The spiritual-ascetic and eschatological trends continued also after the Destruction and even after the close of the Mishna, but in the closing of the Mishna there was implicit a conscious feeling of the continuous decline of creative power. The Jewish Hasid-Sage was born, according to Baer, by the meeting of the Hebrew prophetic tradition with Greek culture. Common elements in the ethical aims of the types of Sages and Pietists are to be found in Judea and in Greece: to live in accordance with the laws of nature and to maintain in the social order the ideals of natural life. Baer sets the contact between Judaism and Hellenism in the first generations of the spread of Hellenism, in the third century B.C.E., or at latest in the second. The Jewish Hasidim and Sages sought to realize ideals similar to the political ideals of Plato, only the concepts that appeared in an intellectual guise in the West, assumed among them a completely religious character, both in content and in form. These Sages and Hasidim were identical, according to Baer, with the Essenes as they are known to us from works of Philo and Josephus. They are even to be regarded as the prototype of the later Christian monks.

They were ascetics, inspired by the highest religious idealism, who, in the Hasmonean revolt, set an example of self-sacrifice for the sake of religion to all the monotheistic faiths. The Sages of the Mishna who lived after the destruction of the Temple were, in Baer's view, weak types in comparison with the Sages and the Hasidim who preceded the Hasmonean state. The latter, although they remained mostly anonymous, acted historically as creative forces far stronger than the later Sages, who wished merely to walk in the footsteps of their predecessors. The spiritual outlook that prevailed in the time of the Second Temple served as the starting point in the history of Christianity, and above all remained authoritative among the Jewish people for all generations. This outlook is marked by unity of ideas and teachings — a complete *Weltanschauung*, religious ideas that were generated and developed according to laws well known in the history of religion. They came into being through living contact with prophetic teaching, on the one hand, and also, on the other, as a result of the living encounter with the Western world.

There is a common aspect to Baer's approach and to Moore's. Baer also postulates continuity from the earliest period (of Judaism) to the close of the Mishna, but while Moore sets the epoch of creativity and crystallization at the end of this era, in the second century C.E., Baer places it specifically at the beginning, that is in the second century B.C.E. Another feature common to Moore and Baer is that both of them minimize the importance of the external tradition and of the problem of the sects; only in this regard, too, the motivating factors are different. Moore dates the crystallization of Judaism to the time when these factions had already passed away and ceased to exert any influence. Baer, on the contrary, states that the Halakha, in its basic aspects and with most of its details, was formed before the secession and schism of the sects. These sects were the result of external and internal decline and disintegration, and contrary to the express testimonies of Josephus and the Talmudic sources, this historian is inclined to transfer them from the days of the earlier Hasmoneans to the last period before the Destruction.[12]

The comprehensive, overall view of Baer, which represents the Sages and Hasidim as a creative factor on the stage of ancient history, is attractive and enticing. But it calls for a thorough and unbiased examination of the sources, and this, it would seem, leads to different results not only in details, but also in the general conception. One must admit, however, that Baer has restored a historic dimension to problems that require discussion and has raised questions that cannot be evaded.

Another attempt to give a general picture of the world of the Sages was made in our time by Louis Finkelstein in his English work *The Pharisees — The Sociological Background of their Faith.*[13]

Since Max Weber gave us his large tomes on the sociology of religion, no one doubts the importance of elucidating the relationship between socio-economic data and religious teachings, and undoubtedly there is need for an exposition of this kind in the sphere of the history of the Jewish religion regarding the centrality of the Halakha, which deals expressly with civil law, torts and the like. But, regrettably, the two volumes of Finkelstein do not advance our knowledge or understanding of the subject. The book is an ingenious amalgam of fanciful and far-fetched conjectures, of construction on unproven suppositions and premises, together with apologetical arguments. The apologetic orientation compels the author to explain away everything, or, more correctly, to 'sweeten' everything and make it plausible. This type of apologetic differs from that which was customary in 'Wissenschaft des Judentums' in Europe. The aim of the latter was to demonstrate that 'the teaching of Judaism' is in no way inferior to Christianity, and even transcends it. But it never claimed that the teaching of Judaism had been realized. As against this Finkelstein states that Pharisaism became the cornerstone of modern civilization. Judaism, Christianity, and Islam are the product of the Pharisaic party and its activity. 'Fully half of the world adheres to Pharisaic faiths.'[14] Christianity is only a facet of Pharisaism. Paul was a propagator of Pharisaism; the Gentile peoples that abandoned idolatry were won over by 'Pharisaism', which is common to both religions — to Judaism and to Christianity.[15] Finkelstein discovers a close resemblance between the Puritan movement of England and of New England and Pharisaism. Although Milton decried the Pharisees, his plea for intellectual freedom is the basis of Pharisaism. The persistent social conflict between Town and Country and the clear tendency towards urbanization with its problems can find a course of instruction, in his opinion, in the synthesis of urban and rural life that he discovers in Pharisaism. In the Foreword to the second edition Finkelstein seeks to allay somewhat the astonishment aroused by his presentation of Christianity as a part of Pharisaism by distinguishing between the Pharisaic Order and the acceptance of the principles of their teaching. He attributes to the Pharisees the desire to disseminate primarily their philosophic truth and to receive affirmation of their universal ethic. In the addenda to the third edition Finkelstein identifies the Pharisees with the Hasidim. The difference between the Pharisees and Sadducees was not primarily one of economic standing, the difference between rich and poor (a theory that he himself maintained in his book on R. Akiba). He also rejects Geiger's thesis that the Pharisees were innovators and reformers. The Pharisees, in Finkelstein's opinion, were burghers of Jerusalem, market people, traders and artisans, while the Sadducees were priests, owning great estates in the neighbourhood of Jericho and in Galilee. The Pharisees possessed ancient Jerusalem traditions, and the Sadducees provincial traditions. Many of the disputes between them had already originated in the time of the First Temple. Nowadays Finkelstein frequently uses such terms as 'Proto-Sadducees', 'Proto-Pharisees', and even 'Proto-Hillelites'. It was actually the Pharisees, or 'Proto-Pharisees', who guarded the written word of the Torah, whereas it was the Sadducees who deviated from the Scriptural text. On the other hand, the divergences of opinion among the Pharisees centred on the texts that could be interpreted in various ways. 'Difference of opinion ... was, at least in the early ages of Pharisaism, the glory of the whole movement.'[16] The Pharisees inherited their views from the Prophets, and the Sadducees from the tradition of the priests and the aristocracy, and many of their ideas have their origin in the last centuries of the First Temple period. Finkelstein seeks to prove all this by delving into the inner reasons of the Halakhot. But most of his interpretations and theories are not sufficiently grounded in the sources. Finkelstein wrote his book in the hope that it would help to shed light on our contemporary problems,[17] but we are not exempt from enquiring whether this hope serves to illumine the teaching of the Pharisees. The truth is that Pharisaic Judaism did not become a world religion, but remained a world on its own; and it is the image of this world that arouses our curiosity.

The desire to underscore the universal significance of Rabbinic teaching and to present it as a practical source of instruction for the solution of contemporary problems is understandable. 'The State of our Sages', writes Baer,[18] 'is part of the great historic world, which embraces and unites East and West. It is impossible to comprehend ancient history — including Christianity — unless we understand this determinant factor.... an organic chain links the different generations together. The epoch of the Second Temple is essentially and ultimately the period when the foundation of all facets of our Tradition was laid. In the measure that this structure is revealed to us as a true and actual reality of its time, in the same measure there are dispersed and forgotten, before the grandeur of the subject, all thoughts of concrete political or dogmatic religious connection with the present, and the structure remains standing before us as an ideal and as a testament for generations to come.' The words do honour to the author. But when we come to make generalizations of this nature, we must bear in mind the possibility that they may only be the result of inner conviction. It is just the person who holds that historical research is not intended to be merely an interesting pastime, but must fulfil a function, yet at the same time does not seek to pretend that it is possible to dispense with all evaluations, who may not overlook the difference between the researcher and the preacher. The historian is also permitted to be a mentor and preacher, but he must distinguish between these two functions for the benefit of both.

Our critical observations serve to outline our own approach. It is not our aim to portray Judaism of the Second Temple and of the centuries following the Destruction. We wish to describe the beliefs and concepts of the Sages, realizing that there were other trends, too, whose traces have been left not only in the pseudepigraphical literature and in the Qumran Scrolls, but also in the words of the Sages themselves, whether these ideas were rebutted in polemic or accepted by integration. Hence, in our discussions we have to take into account external and sectarian sources. Comparison of the external and internal sources shows that not every idea and teaching appearing in the writings of a sect represent an original concept belonging to it specifically. Sometimes they are only a part of older traditions that were adopted for tendentious reasons. In Rabbinic sources, too, there are to be found beliefs and concepts and even Halakhot that first germinated and became current in altogether different circles. Our method will be philological-historical. Main attention will be devoted to the elucidation of the sources on the basis of a reliable and clarified text against the historic background in which they originated and grew. Only if they yield sufficient evidence and proof, shall we permit ourselves to draw inferences relative to earlier periods. The primary basis of the Sages' teaching is the Bible. The work of the Sages is to be viewed as a protracted process aimed at the realization of the Torah and the ideals of the prophets in the reality and framework of their time. This reality influenced not only the Rabbis' manner of preaching and exposition, and determined to no small extent the formulation of their dicta and their underlying reasons, but also stamped their content. Just as we must clarify the nature and compass of the effect exerted by religious beliefs on social phenomena, so we must trace the influence of political and social forces on religious conceptions. Israel's contact with the world around them not only subjected them to various influences, but also gave rise to struggles and polemics. We shall rigorously eschew any trace of apologetics. We shall learn from the sources what is to be learnt from them by the methods developed by Talmudic research, which are simply the accepted philological techniques. This research has produced enduring results both in exegesis and in identifying and analysing the sources. The philological basis set bounds to conjectures and homiletical interpretations, for which the very type and nature of our sources provided ample opportunity. Careful attention must also be given both to the exegetical and homiletical methods used by the Sages in their Halakhot and Haggadot and to the artistic form that they gave to their own words.[19] Only the study of these aspects can teach us what weight to attach to a dictum, a homily, or a Halakhic discussion as expressing a substantive idea, and what must be put down to method, form, and formulation. Without philological examination and form — criticism of the sources it is impossible to give a historical account of religious ideas.[20]

The aim of our work is to give an epitome of the beliefs and concepts of the Sages as the history of a struggle to instil religious and ethical ideals into the every-day life of the community and the individual, while preserving at the same time the integrity and unity of the nation and directing its way in this world as a preparation for another world that is wholly perfect. In discussing the beliefs and concepts of the Sages, we shall not lose sight of the Sages themselves. Although their image and character were moulded by the Torah, which was their heritage, yet the world of the Sages was diversified and rich in varied types, who left the impress of their individuality upon their thinking and teaching. The author of the *Letter of Aristeas* writes (§§ 140–141): 'Hence the leading Egyptian priests... call us "men of God". This is a title which does not belong to the rest of mankind, but only to those who worship the true God. The rest are men (not of God), but of meats and drinks and clothing. For their whole disposition leads them to find solace in these things. Among our people such things are reckoned of no account, but throughout their whole life their main consideration is the sovereignty of God.' Certainly the words befit the majority of the Tannaim and Amoraim.

Their eyes and their hearts were turned Heavenward, yet one type was not to be found among them — not even among those who occupied themselves with the 'Work of the Chariot' and the 'Work of Creation' — namely the mystic who seeks to liberate himself from his ego, and in doing so is preoccupied with himself alone. They saw their mission in work here in the world below. There were Sages who inclined to extremism in their thoughts and deeds, and there were those who preached the way of compromise, which they did not, however, determine on the basis of convenience. Some were severe and exacting, while others demonstrated an extreme love of humanity and altruism. The vast majority of them recognized the complexities of life with its travail and joy, its happiness and tragedy, and this life served them also as a touchstone for their beliefs and concepts.

Without doubt our account will be found lacking in continuity, and at times the lacunae will preponderate, but we have preferred to acknowledge our ignorance and to reveal our doubts rather than take the way of facile and attractive generalizations.

CHAPTER II

THE BELIEF IN ONE GOD

The monotheistic concept of One God, beside whom there is no other, was at the beginning of our epoch the heritage of the whole Jewish people. It was not given a new formulation as a dogma, but the duty was introduced to read the verse Deuteronomy vi 1 ('Hear, O Israel', etc.) twice a day, and this very act implied the establishment of the belief in the Unity of God as the supreme creed. When was this practice made obligatory? We have no tradition on the subject. The Mishna assumes the existence of the custom as something well known, as though it were Scriptural, and asks 'From what time is the *Shĕma*ʿ ('Hear') to be read in the evening?' 'From what time is the *Shĕma*ʿ to be read in the morning?'[1] With regard to the details of the recital of the *Shĕma*ʿ, the Tannaim who lived about the time of the destruction of the Temple — namely the School of Shammai and the School of Hillel, and R. Eliezer and R. Joshua — hold different views. In the Mishna describing the order of service in connection with the daily sacrifice in the Temple it is stated 'They read the Decalogue, *Shĕma*ʿ, *wĕ-hāyā 'im shāmōa*ʿ ("And it shall come to pass, if ye shall hearken"), and *wa-yō'mer* ("And [the Lord] spoke").'[2] This combination of the Decalogue and the *Shĕma*ʿ is found in the Nash Papyrus, about whose exact date scholars are divided. Some date it as early as the second century B.C.E., and others as late as the first century C.E. The abolition of the recital of the Ten Commandments we shall discuss in another context. The precedence given to the recitation of the Decalogue, which obtained not only in the Temple but also outside Jerusalem, apparently points to the fact that it antedated the recital of the *Shĕma*ʿ. To the question 'Why are these two sections recited every day?' the Amora R. Levi already replied 'Because the Ten Commandments are comprised in them.'[3] The recitation of the content of the Sinaitic Revelation at the time when the sacrifice was being offered up constituted a renewal, as it were, of the covenant made by the Lord with His people. Now this section — unique in character and as a historic occurrence — is given prominence even in the Torah. When, however, was the section of the *Shĕma*ʿ added? We may possibly find a clue to the time, if we note what its first verse adds to the opening commandments of the Decalogue. In the Decalogue it is stated that God is the God of Israel, whom He brought forth from Egypt, and Israel is commanded 'Thou shalt have no other gods before Me', 'Thou shalt not make unto Thee a graven image, nor any likeness'. But they contain no express negation of the existence of other gods, such as find expression in the sharp polemic of the prophets, and emerges clearly from the proclamation 'The Lord is our God, the Lord is One.' In the Persian period the Jews encountered a religion (Hebrew, *dat*, which is, incidentally, of Persian origin) that was different in many respects from the religions that they had known hitherto, a religion that did not recognize idols.[4] Even if the Achaemenidian kings did not accept the teaching of Zarathustra, but held to the ancient Persian religion, or to the conception that Ahura-Mazda is the god of both day and night and transcends the antithesis of good and evil, yet he is still the father of the twins (*mainyū*),[5] between whom exists perpetual antagonism; it is clear, therefore, that to people from without the dualistic principle was more in evidence than the distinctions that present-day scholars point out. If in the eyes of Herodotus, the Greek, the Iranian gods, in contradistinction to the Greek deities, appeared far removed from human nature, to the Jews they were gods. The daily proclamation in the one Temple at Jerusalem, 'The Lord is our God, the Lord is One', expressed the great difference. The verse preceding 'Hear, O Israel' in the Bible is, 'Hear therefore, O Israel, and observe to do it; that it may be well with thee, and that ye may increase mightily, as the Lord, the God of thy fathers, hath promised unto thee — a land flowing with milk and honey.' But in the Septuagint we have the following addition: 'And these are the statutes and the ordinances that the Lord commanded the children of Israel in the wilderness, when they went forth from the land of Egypt.' This addition is found in the Nash Papyrus, and the probability is that it was interpolated into the Septuagint from the liturgy and not *vice versa*.[6] The recital of the verse amounted to a proclamation *vis-à-vis* the world, that the God of Israel is the God of the universe and there is none beside Him, which is the sense, in truth, that the Tannaim gave to the text: ' "The Lord is our God" — over us, "the Lord is One" — over all mankind.'[7]

The concept of Absolute Unity was deemed climactic in the understanding of God. To attain to the comprehension of this concept was not considered a simple matter in so far as 'all mankind' was concerned; the Sages regarded it as the outcome of a process of evolution, and found the various stages thereof in Scriptural verses. In a homiletical interpretation, which is not later than the second century, it is stated: ' "Now I know that the Lord is greater than all the gods": the Rabbis declared that Jethro did not omit to worship a single idol in the world, hence he said "than all the gods". Rahab said, "for the Lord your God, He is God in heaven above, and on earth beneath." Naaman acknowledged even more than they did, for it is stated: "Behold now, I know that there is no God in all the earth, but in Israel." '[8] Jethro attributed substance to idolatry, and acknowledged only the supremacy of the God of Israel over other divinities; Rahab set Him in heaven and on earth, but did not say that there was no other deity beside Him; Naaman went further and said, 'there is no God in all the earth, but in Israel'; but he did not say 'in heaven and on earth'. The concept of the Oneness and Uniqueness of God was expressed by Moses: 'that the Lord, He is God in heaven above and upon the earth beneath; there is none else'; in a still later Midrash the Sages interpreted this to mean: 'even throughout the expanse of the universe.'[9]

The belief in the One God finds expression in the complete negation of every other deity — in Rabbinic phraseology, of 'strange service' (i.e. idolatry) — that is to say, of any form of worship that is not unqualified 'service', which means service of the Lord. This thought was formulated in the dictum 'Whoever acknowledges idolatry disavows the whole Torah, and whoever disavows idolatry acknowledges the whole Torah.'[10] He who disavows idolatry does not deny its existence, but its reality;[11] he who acknowledges it acknowledges its reality. To whom is the dictum directed? It is addressed to those people who do not observe the whole of the Torah, but disavow idolatry, and also to another group who acknowledge the Torah but also idolatry. These circles were to be found among 'those who fear Heaven' — semi-proselytes — in the Jewish Exile. However, the prevailing view of the Sages in the third century was that the craving for idolatry had been uprooted and removed from Israel already at the beginning of the Second Temple period,[12] and there is parallel testimony for this in the Book of Judith: 'For there arose none in our age, neither is there any of us today, tribe, or kindred, or family, or city, which worship gods made with hands, as was done in the former days.'[13] This statement is corroborated by external evidence. Hecataeus of Abdera, a contemporary of Alexander the Great, deemed the essence of Judaism to lie in the fact that Moses introduced no image in the service of God on account of the dogma that God has no form.[14] He also noted the devotion with which the Jews of his day guarded their faith. The Jews of Babylonia refused to participate in the rebuilding, enjoined by Alexander the Great, of the ruined temple of Bel, and accepted severe afflictions and punishments in consequence; while the Jews of Eretz-Israel broke down the sanctuaries and altars erected by aliens who entered the country, without heeding the penalties imposed upon them.[15] Without doubt, in the period of Hellenization, which preceded the Hasmonean revolt, regression had set in in this sphere, too, a fact to which the account in Maccabees also bears witness:[16] 'Next day [after the battle with Gorgias], when the troops of Judas went — as it was high time they did — to pick up the corpses of the slain, in order to bring them home, to lie with their kinsfolk in their fathers' sepulchres, they discovered under the shirts of every one of the dead men amulets of the idols of Jamnia — a practice forbidden the Jews by law. All saw at once, that this was why they had perished.' The last part of the statement points to the activity of the earlier Maccabees in removing idolatry from the Land. Their conquests and mass proselytization were connected with the eradication of foreign cults and the destruction of their sanctuaries. But under the rule of the House of Herod and the Roman procurators these cities became Hellenistic cities again in all respects. Following upon the attempt of the Jews of Jabneh [Jamnia] to destroy a pagan altar, the Emperor issued an edict ordering them, according to Philo's account,[17] to set up a costly image and an altar in the Temple of Jerusalem. This incident serves to explain R. Joḥanan b. Zakkai's warning: 'Be not hasty to destroy the high places of the Gentiles lest you rebuild them with your own hand; lest you destroy structures of brick and they say to you, Make them of stone; of stone, and they say to you, Make them of wood!'[18] We may assume that it was in the time of the Maccabees that the Mishnaic benediction was composed: 'If one sees... a place from which idolatry has been rooted out, one should say: Blessed be He that rooted out idolatry from our land.'[19] In the Tosefta there is added the prayer: 'May it be Thy will, O Lord our God, that idolatry be rooted out from all Jewish places, and that Thou restore the hearts of their worshippers to worship Thee.'[20] Evidently this prayer belongs to a later period, when the Jews were no longer able to destroy Gentile idols, and it was even necessary to formulate a benediction for one who sees an idolatrous object — 'Blessed be He who is slow to anger'.[21] To a period of much proselytization — whether by compulsion or persuasion — or to a time when many of these 'dragged-in' converts reverted to paganism we must attribute the saying: 'Whoever acknowledges idolatry disavows the whole Torah, and whoever disavows idolatry acknowledges the whole Torah.'

The repudiation of idolatry became the common heritage of the Jewish people in the days of the Hasmoneans, and with the limitation of proselytization the feeling prevailed that idolatry presented no danger, since it had no substance; and this view was so deeply rooted that it even posited that actually even the Gentiles cannot believe in the reality of idolatry.[22] In truth there were many pagans in the second and third century, who regarded the images and idols not as having intrinsic worth, but as symbols. But the Sages, needless to say, looked even upon such a cult as a form of idolatry, and certainly did not accept the view that the idols were only the work of demons who are active through the medium of representations and images, a view that was widely current in Hellenistic literature and in the writings of the Church Fathers (in the Septuagint the word δαίμονες frequently occurs instead of idols). This notion is reported by Amoraim in the third century, but there is no evidence that they agreed with this explanation and did not look upon the Gentiles who credited it as fetishists. This also emerges explicitly from the source where this belief is mentioned: 'It has been stated: If an idol was broken of its own accord, R. Joḥanan said that (its broken parts) are prohibited, but Resh Laqish said that they are permitted. R. Joḥanan said that they are prohibited, because (the idolater) had not annulled it; and Resh Laqish said that they are permitted, because it may be assumed that (the idolater) certainly annulled it, saying to himself, It could not save itself, how then can it save me?... R. Joḥanan put an objection to Resh Laqish; (it is written:) "And the head of Dagon and both the palms of his hands lay cut off", and it is written: "Therefore the priests of Dagon do not tread... on the threshold of Dagon in Ashdod", etc. He answered him: Can proof be brought from there? In that instance, they abandoned Dagon and served the threshold, for they argued thus: Dagon's genius has left him and come to dwell upon the threshold' (*T.B. 'Avoda Zara* 41b).

Resh Laqish merely reports the argument of the pagans.[23] But in later Midrashim this notion also took root.[24] The difference becomes evident when we compare two narratives, in which this motif is developed. Even the sceptics among the Gentiles were won over by the facts, namely the miracles — particularly, the healing of the sick — that were wrought in the temples, especially in those of Asklepios.[25] In a story from the period of the Tannaim it is recounted: 'Zonin said to R. Akiba, We both know in our hearts that an idol is only a sham, yet we see men go (to the temple) crippled and return cured. How do you explain this? He replied to him: I will tell you a parable. To what can the matter be compared? To a trustworthy man in a city, in whose keeping all the citizens used to deposit (their valuables) without witnesses. One man, however, used to come and place his deposits with him in the presence of witnesses. On one occasion he forgot and left (his valuables) in his custody without witnesses. Said his wife to him, Come, let us deny it! He answered her: Because this fool acted improperly, shall we lose our reputation for honesty? It is so with the afflictions (of illness), too. When they are sent upon a man, they are adjured to come upon him only on a given day, and to leave him only on a given day, and through the medium of such-

and-such a person and such-and-such a remedy. When their time came to depart, (the sick person) happened to go to his idolatrous shrine. Thereupon the afflictions said: Rightly we should not leave, but because this fool acted improperly shall we renounce our oath?' (*T.B.* *ʿAvoda Zara* 55a). This narrative, which is of interest from many aspects, is entirely rationalistic, and the answer it contains could have been given by any Stoic. Contrariwise we find in a later work of the tenth century: 'It once happened that a certain lame Jew heard that there was an idol in a given place, to which all the sick in the world used to come and be healed. So he went to be cured. He entered the shrine with the sick people at midnight; a man came holding in his hand a small cruse filled with oil, and he anointed all the sick and they were cured. When he came to the Jew, he said: Are you not a Jew? He replied, Yes! Then what are you doing here? He replied, (I came) to be healed. Thereupon (his interlocutor) said to him: Know you not that (the idol) itself is a demon who does these things in order to entice people to idolatry, so that he can destroy them from the world? Verily you are guilty; tomorrow, actually, your time had arrived to be cured, but because you have come here, you will not be healed.'[26] The narrator used R. Akiba's answer, but made it apply only to Jews; the Gentiles are misled by the demons who are active in the idols. Although the idea of the deception of the Gentiles is expressly mentioned in the homily of Rav on Deuteronomy iv 19: ' "which the Lord thy God *ḥālaq* [correctly: 'hath allotted'] unto all the peoples" — this teaches *she-heḥĕlîqān* ['He caused them to slip'] with words in order to drive them from the world' (*T.B.* *ʿAvoda Zara*, *ibid.*), yet his statement contains no reference to demons who are active in the idols. Possibly this conception, which influenced also the readings of the Talmud,[27] percolated into popular belief already at an early period, but it was given a literary version only in a late source. The view of the Sages is expressed in the story concerning R. Akiba, to wit, that the idol has no reality. This view produced important Halakhic consequences. It led to lenient decisions by most of the Rabbis in the period between the second and fourth centuries in all that related to the use of the art of imagery and its production. But the painting of pictures in Synagogues, the making of mosaic floors, and the ornamentation of sarcophagi did not sanctify or deify the subject of the painting or the mosaic. Despite the consideration the Sages gave to the various reasons and factors that induced them to mitigate the prohibition 'Thou shalt not make unto thee a graven image', the motivation 'for ye saw no manner of form on the day that the Lord spoke unto you in Horeb out of the midst of the fire' (Deuteronomy iv 15) remained in full force. No *Ars Sacra* came into being, and even those who interpreted the law most leniently expounded the verse: 'Ye shall not make with Me [אתי] a god of silver — ye shall not make Me [אותי].'[28]

The belief in One God is the principle creed, and whoever negates it is called כופר בעיקר *kōfēr bā-ʿIqqār* ['one who denies the primary principle of the faith']. *Kāfar* in the sense of 'to deny' is found only in the Rabbinic idiom. *ʿIqqār* is an Aramaic loan-word and means 'root'. God is *ʿIqqār*, that is to say, He is the Root of all things (see the Targum to Job xix 28). The disavowal of the Lord does not connote denial of the existence of God in general. Athens always knew unbelievers. Plato states in his *Laws*[29] that there are some people who think that there are no gods at all, and there are others who hold that the gods do indeed exist, but they pay no heed to man. The term *kōfēr bā-ʿIqqār* refers to both types. At the end of the first century C.E. R. Ṭarfon declared that if the books of the Minim — which were almost certainly the writings of the early Christians — fell into his hands, he would burn them, including the Divine Names that they contain, 'for even if a pursuer were pursuing me, I would enter an idolatrous shrine, but not one of their temples, because idolaters disavow Him (כופרין אותו; *var. lect.*, כופרין בו) out of ignorance, whereas these know Him and yet deny Him.'[30] The idolaters disavow Him; they believe in their own gods and do not acknowledge the God of Israel. The Minim know Him, that is to say, they are familiar with the Jewish conception of One God, but they introduce other elements into it. If the Minim are Gnostics, the reference is to dualism; and if the Christians are meant, the allusion is to Jesus, the Son.[31] Thus both — the idolaters and the Minim — disavow Him, that is, the Root.

The *kōfēr-bāʿIqqār* is seen as the most extreme example of a man's estrangement from the world of the Torah and commandments, but this self-alienation is intrinsic testimony to the denial of God, without its being linked to any speculative declaration whatsoever. This conception is widely current among the Tannaim in the middle of the second century, and particular importance attaches to the following evidence: 'Once R. Reuben spent the Sabbath in Tiberias and a certain philosopher found him, and said to him: "Who is hated in the world?" (The Rabbi) replied: "This is the one who denies Him who created him [הכופר במי שבראו]." Said he to the Rabbi: "How so?" (The Sage) answered him: "Honour thy father and thy mother; thou shalt not murder; thou shalt not commit adultery; thou shalt not steal; thou shalt not bear false witness against thy neighbour; and thou shalt not covet. Thus a man does not deny anything until he disavows the Root, and a man does not go to commit a transgression unless he first denies Him who enjoined us (not to do) it." '[32] Here כופר בעיקר appears as a parallel expression to כופר במי שבראו. We do not know who the philosopher was, but R. Reuben stresses in his reply that the hated one is he who denies Him who created him — not just God in general, but the Creating God. This emphasis seeks to controvert the view that not the God of Israel, but the Demiurge, is the Creator of the World. The omission of the name of the Lord in the second part of the Decalogue teaches that no man commits a sin, unless he has first disavowed Him who enjoined us not to do it. 'He who denies the Root' is not therefore just one who denies God generally, but one who disavows God, the Creator of the universe, the God who gave the Torah and the commandments. It was necessary to stress this thought not only *vis-à-vis* a non-Jewish philosopher, but also, in the light of Tannaitic teaching in the second century, internally. Possibly this R. Reuben was none other than R. Reuben b. Strobilus of whom it is related that he went to make representations to have the imperial edict prohibiting the observance of the precepts revoked, the reference being to Hadrian's decrees (*T.B. Meʿila* 13a).

Of interest is the account of the religious position in Egypt ascribed to Hadrian himself. In a letter to the Consul Servianus, the Emperor writes: 'Hadrian Augustus sends greetings to Consul Servianus! Egypt, which you praised so highly to me, my dear Servianus, I have come to know as a frivolous land, which is quickly swayed to accept all nonsense. Here the worshippers of Serapis are Christians, and those who call themselves Christian bishops worship Serapis. Here you cannot find a head of a Jewish synagogue, a Samaritan, a Christian presbyter, who is not at the same time also an astrologer, a haruspex, and a magician all rolled in one... their One God is no God at all. He is worshipped by both Christians and Jews and all the other peoples.'[33]

In this situation of conceptual confusion and religious eclecticism it was necessary to emphasize that *kōfēr bā'-Iqqār* was one who does not believe in the Divine Creator of the universe and in Him who enjoined the observance of the Torah. He who transgresses precepts between man and man, he who deals falsely with his neighbour, and those who lend on interest,[34] are deemed to be 'deniers of the Root', because by their deeds they ignore the presence of God, who sees them.

The widespread use of the term *kōfēr bā-'Iqqār* in a hyperbolical sense in the middle of the second century shows that the term was known long before, apparently with the meaning of denying the very existence of God.

A special expression was employed to describe an affront to God's glory. He who blasphemed or cursed the Lord was called פושט יד בעיקר *pōšēṭ yād bā-'Iqqār* ['He who puts forth his hand against the Root'],[35] and the phrase also denotes an idolater.[36] On the other hand, with regard to the verse, Psalms xii 5 [4], 'Those who say, "With our tongue we will prevail, our lips are with us; who is our master?" ' it is stated: 'R. Joḥanan said in the name of R. Jose b. Zimra: If a man tells slanderous tales, it is as though he denied the Root.'[37] The *kōfēr bā-'Iqqār* is the one who says 'who is our master?' He does not say, 'there is no master'; he does not deny the existence of God, but disregards Him. He denies that God's providence watches over the actions of His creatures. R. Akiba annotated the verse Psalms x 13, 'Why does the wicked man renounce God, and say in his heart, "Thou wilt not call to account?" ', as follows: '(The wicked man says:) There is neither judgment nor Judge — but there is judgment and there is a Judge' (*Gen. Rab.* xxvi 6, p. 252). His disciple, R. Me'ir, said with respect to the generation of the Flood: 'That generation declared, "The Lord does not judge; there is no Judge in the world, the Omnipotent has forsaken the world" ' (*'Avot de-R. Nathan*, Recension I, xxxii). In this spirit, the Targum renders the verse Psalms xiv 1, 'The fool says in his heart, "There is no God" ': 'The fool says in his heart,

"There is no dominion of God upon earth." ' Similarly, the Amoraim expounded the verse as referring to the wicked 'who say, "We plot in our heart", as though to say: the Holy One blessed be He does not know what is in our heart (*Midrash Tehillim*, xiv 1), and concerning them Isaiah says (xxix 15): "Woe to those who hide deep from the Lord their counsel, whose deeds are in the dark, and who say, "Who sees us? Who knows us?" ' The Amoraim viewed the disregard shown for the All-seeing Eye — that is, the conduct of the man who seeks to evade Providence and is inclined to delude himself into believing that he is concealing his deeds successfully — as a matter of daily occurrence; hence, when they preached, their words were directed not against those who denied the Root in theory, but against those who denied Him in practice. 'R. Levi said: To what can the matter be compared? To an architect who built a city and made therein secret places, hide-outs and chambers, and eventually he became the ruler. He then sought to seize the bandits in the city, and they fled and hid themselves in those hiding-places. Said he to them: "Fools! are you seeking to hide from me? I, after all, am the craftsman who built the city, and I, therefore, know all the secret places, and the entrances and exits of the hide-outs, better than you." Even so the Holy One, blessed be He, said to the wicked: "Fools! wherefore do you conceal the wickedness in your hearts? It is I who have built man, and I know all the chambers and secret recesses within him." '[38] Although the dicta that regard one who negates Divine Providence as a *kōfēr ba-ʿIqqār* belong to the second century, yet it can easily be shown that they merely formulate a view and concept current in previous generations. In the light of this premise we can understand why the name of the Greek philosopher Epicurus became a widespread epithet for a sectarian and a heretic. According to the philosophical system of Epicurus, the gods are indifferent to all that happens in the world. They are not active, but abide in absolute tranquility. The Sages were not acquainted with Greek philosophy, and not one of its great representatives is mentioned anywhere in Rabbinic literature, except Epicurus. In the *Mishna Sanhedrin* x, 1, the Epicurean is counted among those who have no share in the world to come, but it is not explained wherein lay the Epicurean's disqualification. This we can learn, however, from the teaching of R. Eleazar b. ʿArakh (*M. 'Avot* ii, 14): 'Be alert to learn Torah, and know what answer to give to the Epicurean. And know before whom you labour, and faithful [*ne'ĕmān*] is the Master of your work to give you the wages of your toil.'[39] The knowledge of 'before whom you labour', that is to say, the relationship existing between man's acts and his God, is linked with the answer to the Epicurean, for this knowledge clearly posits God's interest in His creatures. In a later Midrash, indeed — but the dictum is anonymous — we are given a homiletical exposition of Proverbs xv 7, ' "The lips of the wise spread knowledge" — these are the Israelites who proclaim the Holy One, blessed be He, King every day continually, and declare the unity of His name every day continually, morning and evening. "Not so the hearts of fools" — these are the sectarians [*mīnīm*] who say: The world is self-moving (αὐτόματος).'[40] The disciples of Epicurus did in truth teach, τὸν κόσμον αὐτόματον εἶναι. Even Josephus, the contemporary of R. Eleazar b. ʿArakh, wages a polemic against this Epicurean view: '... and learn from these facts how mistaken are the Epicureans, who exclude Providence from human life and refuse to believe that God governs its affairs or that the universe is directed by a blessed and immortal Being to the end that the whole of it may endure, but say that the world runs by its own movement without knowing a guide or another's care.'[41]

He who does not believe that God governs the world is an 'Epicurean' or *kōfēr bā-ʿIqqār*. The proclamation of the Almighty's unity, evening and morning, serves not only to testify to the existence of One God, but also to the fact that the world is not automatous, but that God created it and He rules it. From our portrayal of the character of the *kōfēr bā-ʿIqqār*, it follows that belief in the One God included also the belief in a God who created and administers it.

The recognition of the Creator of Abraham, the first believer, is depicted in R. Isaac's parable: 'It is like one who was travelling from place to place and saw a castle in flames. "Is it to be supposed (he asked) that the castle has no governor?" Thereupon the owner of the castle looked out and said to him "I am the owner of the castle." So, too, because our father Abraham said "Is it to be supposed that the world has no Governor?" the Holy One blessed be He looked out and said to him "I am the Governor, the Lord of the whole world" '

(*Gen. Rabba* xxxix, 1, p. 365). In this case also R. Isaac is only reporting an ancient tradition. Josephus said of Abraham: 'He was thus the first boldly to declare that God, the Creator of the universe, is one, and that, if any other being contributed aught to man's welfare, each did so by His command and not in virtue of its own inherent power.'[42]

The antithesis to heresy is faith. But just as we find that heresy is not the negation of God's existence, but the denial of His providence, so the belief in God is not merely the recognition of His existence, but trust in Him. Israel are 'believers, children of believers' (*T.B. Shabbat* 97a), says the Amora Resh Laqish (end of the third century), and he finds support in the verse 'And the people believed' (Exodus iv 31) with regard to Israel, and in the verse 'And he believed the Lord; and He reckoned it to him as righteousness' (Gen. xv 6) with respect to Abraham. These two verses were already cited as an example of faith in the first century B.C.E. by Shemaʿya and Avṭalyon, the teachers of Hillel and Shammai. 'Shemaʿya said: (The Lord declared) "The faith in Me evinced by their father Abraham merits that I should divide the sea for them", as it is said "And he believed the Lord; and He reckoned it to him as righteousness." Avṭalyon said: (The Lord declared) "The faith that they showed in Me merits that I should divide the sea for them"' (*Mekhilta de-R. Ishmael*, Massekhta de-Wa-yĕhî, iii, p. 99). The dispute between them concerns the question whether the merit of the fathers or their own merit was responsible for the miracle, but both ascribe the parting of the Sea of Reeds to faith, that is, to trust in God. The succeeding Tannaim elaborated their words and interpreted them; for instance: 'Others say: Israel did a great thing. The faith they showed in Me merits that I should divide the sea for them. For they said not to Moses "How shall we go forth to the wilderness, when we have no provisions for the way?" But they believed and followed Moses' (*ibid.*). In this spirit the verse was rendered with reference to Abraham in the Targum Pseudo-Jonathan: 'And he had faith in the word of the Lord, and He accounted it to him as a merit that he did not speak rebelliously to Him.' Here emphasis is given to the meaning of Israel's faith as the Psalmist in Psalms cvi 12 already understood it, when he paraphrased the Torah verses 'And they believed in the Lord and in Moses his servant. Then Moses and the children of Israel sang', in the form 'Then they believed

His words and sang His praise.' In the Septuagint, too, faith means trust in a promise, and the signification of ἐπίστευσεν τῷ θεῷ is the same as the Hebrew *wĕ-he'ĕmîn ba-A'dōnay* ['and he believed in the Lord'], but the Greek πίστις implies more of the intellectual element of faith, as we learn already from Philo.[43] To the question whether Abraham was deserving of praise for believing in God — 'When it is God who speaks and promises, who would not pay heed, even though he were the most unjust and impious of mankind?' — Philo answers: 'If you should be willing to search more deeply and not confine yourself to the mere surface, you will clearly understand that to trust in God alone and join no other with Him is no easy matter, by reason of our kinship with our yokefellow, mortality, which works upon us to keep our trust placed in riches and repute and office and friends and health and strength and many other things. To purge away each of these, to distrust created being... to trust in God, and in Him alone... this is a task for a great and celestial understanding which has ceased to be ensnared by aught of the things that surround us.'

In the Rabbinic expositions of the verses in Genesis xv relating to Abraham's faith and of the passage in Exodus xv concerning Israel's faith, a given situation in which man finds himself is envisaged, and his behaviour in these circumstances is deemed 'faith in the Lord'. This is the conception that had been accepted from time immemorial. This is shown by the words addressed by Mattathias to his sons (*I Maccabees* ii 52): 'Was not Abraham found faithful when tested?'; thereafter he refers to the conduct of Joseph, Phinehas, etc. In Philo's statement the term expresses not an individual act, but the general attitude of a man to God. Although in his aforementioned statement faith still has the meaning of trust, yet this trust is the result of speculative thought and bears an intellectual character. Philo's observations on faith in other passages have a still more marked overtone of mystical knowledge and cognition. 'Faith', he states, 'is the knowledge of piety (γνῶσις εὐσεβείας), the heritage of happiness, the exaltation of the soul...' (*De Abr.* 268). Those who are endowed with the gift of contemplation, who strive to perceive the immaterial and ideal, and do not use their senses, but only their intellect and understanding, attain to faith in God. The first believer was Abraham.[44] The lacking in faith are the multitude. The believers are those who love wisdom (*De Somniis*, I, 151). The concept of faith in Philo's writings thus goes beyond trust in the Lord's word. It denotes man's relationship to his God as one that not every person can achieve. We may posit that in Hellenistic Judaism the word πίστις came to mean belief in One God (*IV Maccabees* xvi 22, and even more so, xvii 2). 'Those who feared the Lord', φοβούμενοι τὸν θεόν,[45] even when they were not converted, accepted the belief in One God, and joined the Jewish community by declaration. Paul, who addressed his words to these congregations, certainly did not give the word a new meaning, only a new orientation. While the verse 'And he believed the Lord; and He reckoned it to him as righteousness' (Genesis xv 6) is translated in the Septuagint καὶ ἐπίστευσεν Αβραμ τῷ θεῷ and πιστεύειν always occurs there with the dative, in Christian writings this verb is used with εἰς or is followed by the genitive.[46] The missionary character of the new religion found expression in a combination of declaration and faith (I Tim. iv 1, 6). πίστις became identified with Christianity (Tit. i 4). In Judaeo-Christian writings this concept is strongly opposed. In the Epistle of James we read:[47]

> What doth it profit, my brethren, though a man saith he has faith but have not works? Can faith save him?... Yea, a man may say, 'Thou hast faith and I have works.' Shew me thy faith without thy works, and I will shew thee my faith by my works. Thou believest that there is one God; thou doest well: the devils also believe, and tremble. But wilt thou know, O vain man, that faith without works is dead? Was not Abraham our father justified by works, when he had offered Isaac his son upon the altar? Seest thou how faith was wrought with his works and by works was faith made perfect? And the scripture was fulfilled which saith, Abraham believed God, and it was imputed unto him for righteousness; and he was called the Friend of God. Ye see then how that by works a man is justified, and not by faith only. Likewise also was not Rahab the harlot justified by works, when she had received the messengers, and had sent them out another way? For as the body without the spirit is dead, so faith without works is dead also (James ii 14–26).

the different positions of James and Paul on faith

Contrariwise, Paul speaks of 'obedience to the faith', ὑπακοὴν πίστεώς (Romans i 5). Faith recognizes no other obedience. 'The righteousness which is of faith' annuls 'the righteousness which is of the Law which a man doeth' (*ibid.* x 5–6). Faith ῥῆμα τῆς πίστεως means: 'That if thou shalt confess with thy mouth the Lord Jesus, and shalt believe in thine heart that God hath raised him from the dead, thou shalt be saved. For with the heart man believeth unto righteousness; and with the mouth confession is made unto salvation' (*ibid.* vv. 9–10). 'Faith' assumes a dogmatic character, and there is a parallelism between *faith* and *confession*. Faith no longer means trust, piety. It is only grace — grace that is independent of works, 'But if it be of works, then is it no more grace: otherwise grace is no more grace' (*ibid.* xi 6). Faith is by grace (*ibid.* iv 16), and is, in practice, identical with grace: 'For I say, through the grace given unto me, to every man that is among you, not to think of himself more highly than he ought to think; but to think soberly, according as God hath dealt to every man the measure of faith.'[48] Paul also bases himself on Abraham, but the meaning of Abraham's faith remained on a different conceptual plane from that of his own, which is altogether new. Although attempts to find support for Paul's view[49] were not lacking, yet they met with no success. In *IV Esdras* xiii 23 it is stated: 'He who shall bring the peril in that time, He Himself shall keep them who have fallen into the peril, even such as have *works* and *faith* towards the Almighty'; and *ibid.* ix 7 (vii 7): 'And everyone that shall be saved, and shall be able to escape *by his works*, or *by faith*, whereby he hath believed.' The question is whether we may not infer too much from the word 'or'. *IV Esdras (IV Ezra)* has been preserved in Latin translation, made from the Greek; its original language was Hebrew. The translators were Christians, and it appears likely that they understood the connotation of 'faith' according to their own conception. The original signification of this faith we may deduce from the context: this is belief in wonders, mighty deeds, and perils that had been foretold. In other passages, too, the sense is not different from the accepted meaning, not even in the Apocalypse of Barukh.[50]

In the Bible faith is man's reaction to the promise of God, or to His manifestation or action. This is the case in Genesis xv 6 and Exodus iv 31, which served us as our starting point, and so it is also in Exodus xiv 31: 'And Israel saw the great work... and the people feared the Lord; and they believed in the Lord and in His servant Moses'; and in Habakkuk ii 4: 'But the righteous shall live by his faith', which the Septuagint renders ἐκ πίστεώς μου. Paul cites the verse without the personal pronoun, that is ἐκ πίστεώς only: 'But that no man is justified by the law in the sight of God, it is evident: for the just shall live by faith' (Galat. iii 11). Faith stands over against the Torah, and in antithesis to it.

The saying of the Tanna R. Nehemiah, which belongs to the middle of the second century, appears to be directed against these views: 'R. Nehemiah said: Whoever accepts one precept in faith (*var. lect.*, 'Whoever fulfils one precept...') is worthy that the Holy Spirit should rest upon him, for so we find in the case of our fathers, that, in reward for the faith that our ancestors had in the Lord, they merited that the Holy Spirit should rest upon them, and they sang a song, as it is said: "and they believed in the Lord, and in His servant Moses" ' (*Mekhilta de-R. Ishmael*, Massekhta de-Wa-yĕhî, vi, p. 114). The Holy Spirit as the reward of faith is found also in Philo, but, as we have seen, the nature of the faith is different (see above p. 32 ff).

In the whole of this passage from the *Mekhilta*, *'ămānā* [literally, 'trust'] is used for 'faith', and also in the preceding excerpt the text in the MSS. is: 'Great is faith [*'ămānā*] before Him who spoke and the world came into being.' It appears that it is actually intended to identify *'ĕmūna* ['faith'] with *'ămānā*. In Nehemiah x 1 the Septuagint (*II Esdras* 20 1) renders διατιθέμεθα πίστιν, that is to say, entering into a covenant [*'ămānā*] to keep the commandments constitutes faith. Whoever accepts a precept fulfils the *'ămānā*; he is the believer, who trusts in the Lord, who enjoins and gives the Torah. In the Rabbinic idiom, the word *'ĕmūnā* retained its original sense of 'trust'; in *M. Bava Batra* x, 8 it is stated, 'for he had lent him the money through his trust in him [*'ĕmûnātô*]', that is, through the 'assurance' of the guarantor of the loan. In this very same sense the Tanna uses the word *'ĕmūnā* with respect to God. 'R. Joḥanan said in the name of R. Eleazar b. R. Simeon: The Holy One, blessed be He, said to Israel, "My sons, borrow on My account and celebrate the holiness of the day, and trust in Me, and I shall pay (the debt)." '[51] The term has the same connotation in the dictum of R. Eliezer the Great:

'Whoever has bread in his basket, yet says, "What shall I eat tomorrow?", is evidently of those who have little faith.' On this dictum R. Isaac based his interpretation of the expression *'anshê 'ămānā* ['men of faith'] in the Mishna: 'These are people who believe in the Holy One, blessed be He.'[52] Faith in the Holy One, blessed be He — that is, that He fulfils His word[53] — accompanies the believer in all that he does.[54]

A single thread, clearly manifest, runs from the time of the earliest Hasmoneans to the last of the Amoraim. The concept of faith in the Lord does not find exhaustive expression in the recognition of God's existence or in a declaration proclaiming this recognition, but includes the conviction that there is a permanent relationship between the Deity and the world and its creatures. Faith is trust in the existence of Divine Providence. The manifestations of man's faith are the love and fear of the Lord. But before we consider the ways of Providence and the expressions of faith, we must examine the signification attributed by the Sages to the Biblical names of God and to the epithets coined in their own days, for they reflect their views regarding the entire pattern of relationship between man and his God.

CHAPTER III

THE *SHEKHINA* — THE PRESENCE OF GOD IN THE WORLD

God's names bear testimony to His attributes and deeds and His relationship to man. A summary, as it were, of the connotations ascribed by the Sages to the Divine Names is found in the following statement of R. Abba bar Memel, who belonged to the first generation of the Palestinian Amoraim: 'The Holy One, blessed be He, said to Moses: "What dost thou seek to know? *I am called according to My acts.* Sometimes I am called *'Ēl Shadday* ['Almighty God'], or *Ṣĕvā'ôt* ['Hosts'], or *'Ĕlōhîm* ['God'], or *YHWH* ['Lord']. When I judge mankind I am called *'Ĕlohim*; when I make war against the wicked I am called *Ṣĕvā'ôt*; when I suspend man's sins I am called *'Ēl Shadday*, and when I have compassion on My world I am called *YHWH*," for the Tetragrammaton signifies none other than the quality of mercy, as it is said: "O *YHWH*, *YHWH*, God, merciful and gracious.' This is the meaning of the verse אהיה אשר אהיה, ['I am that I am'] — I am named according to my acts."[1] This interpretation of the Names, which implicitly nullifies all mythological exegesis, also holds good for the Names that were coined after the Biblical period.[2] From the Bible the Sages acquired their supramythological and supranatural conception of the Deity. He is spirit and not flesh. All possibility of representing God by means of any creature upon earth or the hosts of heaven is completely negated. 'To whom then will ye liken God? Or what likeness will ye compare unto Him?' (Isaiah xl 18). The war against the images was a war against the corporealization of the Godhead, against the belief that there is something divine in matter and its natural or magical-artistic forms. On the other hand, the idea of abstraction is wanting in the Bible.[3] God appears and reveals Himself to human vision in various likenesses — like a King sitting on His throne, or an Old Man full of compassion.[4] These literary images and other anthropomorphic expressions were able to convey the consciousness of God's nearness, but at the same time they could open the door to the infiltration of myth. On the other hand, complete and consistent abstraction of the concept of God was likely to lead to a deistic outlook, which removes God from the world and its affairs and leaves Him only a place as a passive observer. It has been rightly stated[5] that in the tension between the two aims — the insistence on the purity of the monotheistic idea on the one side, and on the vitality of faith on the other — is comprised the history of Israel's religion. The banishment of magic and myth demanded the creation of a gulf between God and man, but nevertheless the believer wishes to feel God's proximity, to recognize His character and to conceive to some extent His relationship to man and the world. This dualism is found in Scripture, where the two elements are found side by side. The Omnipotent God, the Creator of the universe, who governs it and cares for His creatures, is necessarily removed from the world, being above and beyond it; but in the same measure the concept of Providence incorporates God's nearness. The gulf is stressed in verses like 'It is He that sitteth above the circle of the earth, and the inhabitants thereof are as grasshoppers...' (Isaiah xl 22); 'For My thoughts are not your thoughts, neither are your ways My ways... For as the heavens are higher than the earth, so are My ways higher than your ways....' (*ibid.* lv 8–9). God is far from us; He is incomparable, and cannot be conceived; as Job puts it, 'Behold, God is great, and we know Him not' (xxxvi 26). Contrariwise, we find verses like 'Whither shall I go from Thy Spirit, Or whither shall I flee from Thy presence? If I ascend to heaven, Thou art there! If I make my bed in Sheol, Thou art there! If I take the wings of the morning and dwell in the uttermost parts of the sea, even there Thy hand shall lead me, and Thy right hand shall hold me' (Psalms cxxxix 7–10). His glory, therefore, fills the world, yet it is not, in consequence, a whit less sublime and wonderful. Thus the verses cited are preceded by 'Such knowledge is too wonderful for me, it is high I cannot attain it,' and they are followed (v. 14) by the words 'Wonderful are Thy works; and that my soul knoweth right well.'

The entire history of the patriarchs and the people is one multi-faceted testimony to the immanence of God, or in the words of the Torah: 'Because the Lord thy God walketh in the midst of thy camp' (Deuteronomy xxiii 15 [14]). In many passages, God appears as a Father who compassionates His children, the work of His hands (Psalms ciii 13; Isaiah lxiv 7). And the same prophet that gave expression to the vast distance between the thoughts of God and the thoughts of man, adds to the Divine glorification an expression that remains true to His nearness: 'For thus says the high and lofty One who inhabits eternity, whose name is Holy: "I dwell in the high and holy place, and also with him who is of a contrite and humble spirit, to revive the spirit of the humble, and to revive the heart of the contrite" (Isaiah lvii 15). The psalmists have immortalized their trust in and their consciousness of God's nearness in verses like: 'I keep the Lord always before me', 'O taste and see that the Lord is good!' God is thus both near and far. Recognizing the enormous interval between the transcendental God — a consciousness that exists in every religion that has passed the mythical stage — and himself, the believer also yearns to attain to the realization of his nearness, without reverting to dangerous identification. A great part of the history of religions, including the religion of Israel, consists of the quest for the solution of the problem of bridging the abyss that cannot be closed. It is just the extreme exclusion of all similitudes and anthropomorphic qualities from the concept of the Deity that leads to the filling, by means of intermediate beings, of the vacuum thus created. This is the way of Hellenistic Judaism in its various manifestations. The Jewish Hellenists, like the neo-Pythagorians and the later disciples of Plato, posited the existence of intermediate powers, through the medium of which God works in the world of phenomena. These forces are not God. They are an expression and reflection of God, but not God Himself, nor separate personalities. Already in the *Letter of Aristeas* (132; 195) a distinction is drawn between the ruling power of God, which is omnipresent, and God Himself, the greatest of all entities and the Lord of everything, who is not in need of anything, and dwells in heaven. But the world is governed by Divine power. This intermediary power appears most clearly in *The Wisdom of Solomon* — the estimated date of whose composition is in the eighties B.C.E. — in the form of Wisdom, which penetrates to all parts of the world as the force of life operating perpetually. Undoubtedly, there is to be observed here the influence of the doctrine of the *pneuma* — the Stoic reason (ἔννουν τὸ πνεῦμα), only the Jewish author of the *Book of the Wisdom of Solomon* holds that the *pneuma* is not immanent in the world and linked to its physical conception, but is the breath of life, which the Creator breathed into Adam.[6]

Philo, to whom God is just 'Existence' (ὁ ὤν), declares that He cannot be conceived by the intellect beyond the fact that He *is*.[7] He bridges the gulf between God and matter by means of the Logos.

The problem before us is not openly discussed in the Rabbinic sources, but it emerges from the manner in which many names and epithets of God are used. One of these is the title *Shĕkhînā* ['Divine Presence']. At this stage we may already enquire how close is the relationship between the concept of Wisdom (*Sophia*) and that of the Shekhina. The designation Shekhina connotes the personification and hypostasis of God's presence in the world, that is, of God's immanence. Gershom Scholem[8] has rightly stressed the importance of elucidating this term in all its ramifications and metamorphoses in the history of Israel's religion. Shekhina does not mean the place where the Deity is to be found, that is, the Dwelling Place, but His manifest and hidden Presence. Reference is made to 'the glory of the Shekhina', to 'the wings of the Shekhina'[9], or to 'pressing the feet of the Shekhina' [i.e. acting haughtily towards the Shekhina]. The question before us is whether the concept of the Shekhina and its use in the Talmuds and Midrashim evidences a view that separates the Shekhina from God. The scholars of the Middle Ages already differed on this issue. The philosophers among them — like R. Saadia Gaon, Maimonides, and even R. Judah ha-Levi — held the view that the Shekhina, which they identified with the Divine Glory, 'is a form superior to the angels, mighty in its creation, radiant with majesty and light, and it is called "the glory of the Lord" ... and the Sages refer to it as Shekhina'[10]; it is the creation of God — the first of His works, having preceded the formation of matter, and, in the language of Maimonides, is 'the created light, which God caused to dwell in a given place in order to show the distinction of that place'.[11] This view appeared less dangerous than the acceptance of the hypostasis of an uncreated being, which implies a complete contradiction of the principle of excluding all corporeality from the conception of God. The view of Maimonides, who wished to find support for his theory in Onkelos's method of translation, was already rejected by Naḥmanides in his commentary on Genesis xlvi 1. He raised the serious objection: 'If one should say that it is a created glory, in accordance with the view of the Master [Maimonides] in regard to the verse "and the glory of the Lord filled the tabernacle" and others, how can we apply thereto *bārûkh* ['Blessed be'] and *ha-mĕvōrākh* ['the blessed'] ? Moreover, one who prays to a created glory is, as it were, an idolater! However, many statements by our Sages point to the fact that the name Shekhina stands for God, be He blessed.' With this opinion a scholar like Moore finds himself in agreement; he observes that the concept of the Shekhina is 'a verbal smoke to conceal the difficulty presented by the anthropomorphic language'.[12] On the other hand, J. Abelson,[13] who devoted a complete monograph to the Shekhina, is inclined to find in the sources a conception of the Shekhina as light or some other material object, as well as the use of this concept in a personal sense. But it is doubtful if his interpretation of the sources that he cites is always correct, and if his apologetic purpose, which is to demonstrate the doctrine of 'immanence' in Rabbinic literature, did not overstep the mark. He also quotes dicta that can be related to the subject discussed by him only by forced exegesis. We must examine the relevant sources ourselves.

The term Shekhina is added in Onkelos's rendering of verses in which the verb *shākhan* ['to dwell'] is used in relation to God, or where reference is made to 'causing His name to dwell' or to 'putting His name', for example: 'And He shall dwell in the tents of Shem' — Onkelos: 'And He will cause His Shekhina to dwell in the dwelling-place of Shem' (Genesis ix 27); 'And let them make Me a sanctuary, that I may dwell among them' — Onkelos: 'And they shall make before Me a sanctuary and I shall cause My Shekhina to dwell among them' (Exodus xxv 8); 'But unto the place which the Lord your God shall choose out of all your tribes to put His name there, even unto His habitation shall ye seek, and thither thou shalt come' — Onkelos: 'But unto the place which the Lord your God shall choose out of all your tribes to cause His Shekhina to dwell there, even to the House of His Shekhina shall ye seek and thither shall ye come' (Deuteronomy xii 5). But the addition of the word Shekhina is also found in passages of another kind, where its purpose is to avoid the use of anthropomorphic expressions, such as 'And the Lord passed by before him' — Onkelos: 'And the Lord caused His Shekhina to pass before him' (Exodus xxxiv 6);[14] 'For I will not go up in the midst of thee' — Onkelos: 'For I will not remove My Shekhina from among thee' (*ibid.* xxxiii 3); 'For I lift up My hand to heaven' — Onkelos: 'For I shall establish the House of My Shekhina in heaven' (Deuteronomy xxxii 40); 'For what good is there in heaven?' — Onkelos: 'For Thou art the God whose Shekhina is in heaven above' (*ibid.* iv, 39); 'And the shouting for the king is among them' — Onkelos: 'And the Shekhina of their king is among them' (Numbers xxiii 21). The translator did not deviate from the wording of the text on his own initiative, but translated as he did because his generation considered that certain verses could not be rendered literally, as the Tanna R. Judah observed: 'He who translates a verse literally is a liar.'[15] The translator chose to add the epithet 'Shekhina', because in his time it was already used to indicate the presence of God in His sanctuary and among His congregation. In these contexts the designation appears in Tannaitic literature. It is noteworthy that in the Mishna the term occurs only twice — both references being in effect one — and belongs to the era of Bar Kokhba. R. Ḥanania b. Ṭeradion said: 'If two sit together and occupy themselves with words of the Torah, the Shekhina abides in their midst.'[16] About two generations later R. Ḥalafta of the village of Ḥanania said: 'If ten men sit together and occupy themselves with words of the Torah, the Shekhina is in their midst, as it is said, "God standeth in the congregation of the godly."'[17]

The use of Shekhina is more prevalent in the Tosefta, and especially in the Halakhic Midrashim. The Tabernacle [*Mishkan*, 'Dwelling-place'] is the sphere of the Sanctuary, which is the 'Camp of the Shekhina' (*Tosefta Kelim*, Bava Qamma, i, 12). 'From the entrance of the Temple Court inward is the Camp of the Shekhina' (*Sifre*, Nāśō, § 1, p. 4); the House in which the Lord dwells is 'the House of the Shekhina' — 'The land of Canaan is fit to contain the House of the Shekhina, but Transjordan is not fit for the House of the Shekhina' (*Sifre Zuṭa*, Nāśō, v. 2, p. 228). Whenever the manifestation of the Lord, His descent, ascent, or going forth, is spoken of, the term Shekhina is used.[18] 'The Shekhina went before Israel and prepared a place for them to dwell in.'[19] Whereas at first this epithet was used to denote a theophany at a given place, after the destruction of the Temple this designation was specifically chosen when reference was made to the Divine Presence not at a definite place but in the midst of the people. 'Wherever Israel went into exile, the Shekhina, as it were, was exiled with them; they were exiled to Egypt, the Shekhina was with them... they were exiled to Babylon, the Shekhina was with them... they were exiled to Elam, the Shekhina was with them, as it is said, "And I will set My throne in Elam" (Jeremiah xlix 38).'[20] The verse from Jeremiah provides clear evidence of the sense of 'presence' inherent in the designation Shekhina. The use of the epithet Shekhina, however, expresses not only 'presence' but also 'nearness', and has made possible expressions of intimacy. At times God speaks of the Shekhina as though it were separate from Himself: 'The Omnipresent said to Israel... the fact that I have put My Shekhina in your midst...'; 'therefore the Omnipresent detained for her [Miriam's] sake the Shekhina, the Ark, the priests and the Levites....'[21] Similarly, it is possible to speak of acts — bloodshed, incest,[22] perversion of justice, and falsification of measures[23] — that cause the Shekhina to depart. 'For whoever is humble will ultimately cause the Shekhina to dwell with man upon earth... but whoever is haughty brings about the defilement of the earth and the departure of the Shekhina....'[24] R. Eliezer said: 'Now if on one who cleaves to uncleanness the spirit of uncleanness rests, then it follows that on one who cleaves to the Shekhina, the Shekhina rests upon him.'[25]

We may sum up as follows: In Tannaitic literature the term Shekhina is used when the manifestation of the Lord and His nearness to man are spoken of.[26] It is in this sense that R. Akiba uses the epithet Shekhina in the following homily: 'When man and wife are worthy the Shekhina abides in their midst; if they are unworthy fire consumes them' (*T.B. Soṭa* 17a). The same applies to Rabban Gamaliel's answer to the Gentile who asked 'Why did the Holy One blessed be He reveal Himself to Moses in a thorn-bush?', 'It teaches us that there is no place upon earth void of the Shekhina.'[27] The mention of this Divine designation in the dicta of these Tannaim and in those of their contemporaries is no indication of the date of their origin; nor is the explanation probable that the use of this epithet became prevalent, as it were, only after the destruction of the Temple, in order to stress that God's Presence among Israel did not cease with the destruction of the sanctuary.[28] It is inconceivable that a new and unknown designation would have been used to emphasize the Divine Presence at a time of crisis. It is more probable that to give emphasis to the Lord's Presence it was actually an epithet expressing this concept in Temple times that was chosen. Moreover we found, in Targum Onkelos and in the works of the Tannaim, that the term Shekhina was used in respect of Biblical passages that appeared to them as anthropomorphic. It is not to be assumed that they would have done this unless the epithet had been widely current and well known for a long time. It is a fact that the use of this designation in Tannaitic literature is the most prevalent and always serves to denote certain phenomena. Exceptions that seem to occur in printed editions are not to be found in the MSS. In almost every instance where we should have expected the designation Shekhina to appear and it does not, the epithet occurs in MSS; and *vice versa*, when it is found in an unsuitable place, it is wanting in the MSS. This consistent usage shows that we have indeed before us a systematic tradition that continued for generations.

Abelson wished to prove that the Shekhina is light, that is to say, tangible matter, and he bases himself on various sources that speak of 'the splendour of the Shekhina', or 'the light of the Shekhina'. With reference to the verse 'The Lord make His face to shine upon thee' (Numbers vi 25) R. Nathan said: 'This means the brightness of the Shekhina' (*Sifre*, Nāśō, No. 41, p. 44); but this contains no more than the Targum of Onkelos, 'May the Lord cause His Shekhina to shine', which is interpreted in *Num. Rabba* xi 6 to mean 'that He will look upon thee with kindly [literally, 'shining'] and not angry mien'.[29] In the light of what we learnt concerning the origin of the concept 'Shekhina', we see that 'the brightness of the Shekhina' simply means the light of the Lord, and refers to the manifestation of the Lord, Shekhina being substituted for the Tetragrammaton in order to avoid anthropomorphism. Ezekiel's statement (xliii 2) 'and behold, the glory of the God of Israel came from the way of the east; and His voice was like the sound of many waters; and the earth did shine with His glory' is explained in *'Avot de-Rabbi Nathan* (Recension I, ii) thus: ' "And the earth did shine with His glory" — that is, the face of the Shekhina'. There is nothing more here than in the Targum 'And the earth shone with the splendour of his glory'; nor is it stated that the Shekhina is a definite, separate, or material entity; only transcendence and sublimity are expressed here. A number of the sources cited by Abelson even prove the reverse of what he wished to demonstrate. With reference to the verse 'that Moses knew not that the skin of his face sent forth beams' (Exodus xxxiv 29) it is stated in the *Tanḥuma* (Kî Tiśśa', xxxiii): 'Whence did Moses acquire the beams of glory? The Sages declare: From the cave, as it is said "And it shall come to pass, while My glory passeth by, that I will put thee in a cleft of the rock" — the Holy One, blessed be He, placed His hand over him and thence he acquired the beams of glory... Others say that at the time when the Holy One, blessed be He, taught him [Moses] Torah, he received the beams of glory from the sparks that issued from the Shekhina.' Here the Shekhina is none other than the Holy One, blessed be He, and neither of them is light.

Nor is the concept that the Shekhina is separated light to be found in the following Midrash, which describes Moses' eminence as compared with that of Isaac, who claims: ' "I am greater than thou, for I stretched forth my neck on the altar and saw the face of the Shekhina." Moses answered him: "I rose to higher heights than thou. Thou didst behold the face of the Shekhina and thine eyes grew dim, as it is said: 'And it came to pass, that when Isaac was old, and his eyes were dim, from seeing'; what is meant by 'from seeing'? — from seeing the Shekhina. But I spoke with the Shekhina face to face, yet my eyes were not dimmed...." '[30] The use also of the figure 'the splendour [*zîv*] of the Shekhina' lends no support to Abelson's interpretation.[31] In the Mishna *zîv* is mentioned only in the phrases 'the splendour [*zîv*] of the priesthood' and 'the splendour of wisdom' (*M. Soṭa* ix, 15). In the *Tosefta* the word does not occur at all. 'The splendour of the Shekhina' is found a number of times in the Halakhic Midrashim, and principally in the sayings of the Amoraim, such as 'Until their homes were filled with the splendour of the Shekhina' (*Mekhilta*, Ba-ḥōdesh, Jethro, ii, p. 220); 'They enjoy the splendour of the Shekhina' (*T.B. Berakhot* 13a); 'The Holy One, blessed be He sates them with the splendour of the Shekhina' (*T.B. Bava Batra* 10a); 'The splendour of the Shekhina from on high was bestowed upon them' (*Ecclesiastes Rabba*, viii, 3). *Zîv*, like *ma'or* ['light', 'brightness'], links the concept of Shekhina with a corporeal act, and the usage serves to make the incident comprehensible, but actually there is no difference whatsoever between 'the splendour of the Shekhina' and 'the Shekhina'. In truth we find that an expositor will use both of them alternately in a single homily, for example: ' "The inside thereof being inlaid with love": R. Judan said, This means the merit of the Torah... R. Azariah in the name of R. Juda in the name of R. Simon said, This refers to the Shekhina. One verse states, "So that the priests could not stand to minister by reason of the cloud; for the glory of the Lord filled the house of the Lord (I Kings viii 11)"; and another verse states, "And the court was full of the brightness of the Lord's glory" (Ezekiel x 4). How are the two verses to be reconciled? R. Joshua of Sikhnin in the name of R. Levi (said): To what could the Tent be likened? To a cave situated next to the sea. The sea was turbulent and flooded the cave; the cave was filled (with water), yet the sea was in no way diminished. So, too, was the Tent filled with the splendour of the Shekhina, yet the world lacked not a whit of the Shekhina' (Canticles iii 8). The splendour of the Shekhina is the same as the Shekhina, just as the water that flooded the cave is identical with the water of the sea.

Sometimes the sources speak of the 'light' ['*ôr*] of God, without using the term Shekhina. The verse 'In the light of the king's countenance is light' (Proverbs xvi 15) the Sages expounded as referring to 'the light of the Holy One, blessed be He', and to the 'fire from on high';[32] and when they declared that 'the Holy One, blessed be He, is all light', or spoke of 'this people whose God is light'[33] they did not mean to say that He was a substance of light, but that the light was His own, and that He had no need of any other light.[34] On the verse in Daniel (ii 22) 'and the light dwelleth with Him' the Rabbis comment: 'Thou dost find that he who is in darkness can see what is in the light, whereas he who is in the light cannot see what is in darkness; but the Holy One, blessed be He, can see both what is in the darkness and what is in the light. Said Daniel "He revealeth the deep and secret things; He knoweth what is in the darkness, and the light dwelleth with Him." ' (*Tanḥuma* ii Tĕṣawwe, § 6). God is the Source of light; hence here, too, the light does not denote the essence of God. The light is the δόξα that is linked to the Deity.[35]

Even the metaphor 'the wings of the Shekhina' is not a material figure of speech; again the Shekhina is none other than God, for thus we read in the *Mekhilta*:[36] 'R. Joshua said that when Amalek came to harm Israel beneath the wings of their Father in heaven, Moses said before the Holy One, blessed be He: "Sovereign of the universe, this wicked man comes to destroy Thy children beneath Thy wings. Who now shall read the Book of the Torah that Thou hast given them?" ' A similar dictum occurs there in the name of R. Eleazar of Modiʿim. God, or the Shekhina, spreads His wings over Israel 'As an eagle that stirreth up her nest, hovereth over her young' (Deuteronomy xxxii 11). He who joins Israel — the proselyte — enters beneath the wings of the Shekhina (*'Avot de-R. Nathan*, Recension I, xii). 'For Abraham, our father, used to convert them and bring them beneath the wings of the Shekhina' (*Sifre*, Wā-'etḥannan, § 32, p. 54; *'Avot de-R. Nathan*, Recension I, xii). Jethro said: 'Behold, I shall go to my land, and I shall convert all the people of my country, and I shall lead them to the study of the Torah, and I shall bring them under the wings of the Shekhina' (*Mekhilta de-R. Ishmael*, Massekhta da-ʿAmalek, Jethro, ii, p. 2). Abelson's interpretation that it is precisely the image of 'the wings of the Shekhina' that expresses the omnipresence[37] of God is a good example of his forced explanations. This presence is expressed by the term Shekhina alone. To be beneath the wings of the Shekhina signifies to be under the Lord's protection, as the Bible phrases it (Ruth ii 12): 'And be thy reward complete from the Lord, the God of Israel, under whose wings thou art come to take refuge';[38] and alongside 'wings of the Shekhina' we find 'wings of Heaven'.[39]

The omnipresence of God-Shekhina is one of the primary postulates. The dicta that speak of the Shekhina do not attempt to describe her, but to explain and reconcile her with the manifestations and presence of God at fixed places and times, whilst avoiding the solution of positing the existence of powers that are separate and emanate from the Lord. A question was asked by Gentiles and not by them alone: 'The Emperor said to Rabban Gamaliel: "You say that wherever there is a company of ten (Jews) the Shekhina abides in their midst. How many Shekhinas are there then?" '[40] In reply Rabban Gamaliel takes the sun as an example: It shines upon each individual and, at the same time, upon the world as a whole. Now the sun is but one of the thousand myriad attendants of the Holy One, blessed be He, 'how much more so (can) the Shekhina of the Holy One, blessed be He (do this)!' Here the Shekhina is not a separate entity, nor is it light. The fear that the Shekhina's presence in the world detracts, as it were, from her transcendentalism is popularly and naively expressed in a dialogue between the Holy One, blessed be He, and the angels: ' "And it came to pass [*wa-yĕhî*] on the day that Moses had made an end of setting up the tabernacle" — woe [*way*] was it to the ministering angels on the day that Moses made an end. They said: "Now He will take His Shekhina away from our midst and cause His glory to abide with His children." The Holy One, blessed be He, answered them: "Pay no heed to this, for My Shekhina is ever with you on high", as it is said, "whose majesty is rehearsed above the heavens". But it was vain comfort that He gave them, so to speak. On the contrary, primarily His Shekhina is below, as it is said "His glory is upon the earth" — first, and only afterwards — "(upon) the heavens." '[41] The reference is to Psalms cxlviii 13, 'His glory is upon [E.V. 'above'] the earth and the heavens.' The anonymous expositor stresses, from the human standpoint, the superiority of immanence. What is stated in this dialogue concerning the Shekhina is expressed in another discussion relative to the Almighty Himself. A certain Cuthean asked R. Me'ir: ' "Is it possible that He of whom it is written 'Do not I fill heaven and earth?' spoke with Moses from between the two staves of the Ark?" He replied: "Bring me magnifying mirrors!"; he did so. (R. Me'ir then) said to him: "Look at your reflection!" He saw it magnified. (He thereupon said:) "Bring me diminishing mirrors!" He did so. "Look at your reflection there!" He saw it diminished. (Whereupon R. Me'ir) said to him: "If you, who are but flesh and blood can alter yourself in whatever way you wish, how much more so (can) He who spoke and the world came into being!... When He wishes — 'Do not I fill heaven and earth?'; and when He wishes — He speaks with Moses from between the staves of the Ark" ' (*Genesis Rabba* iv 4, pp. 27–28). An entirely different view is voiced by R. Me'ir's colleague — R. Jose — which is found in the following Baraita: 'It is taught, R. Jose said: The Shekhina never descended to earth, nor did Moses and Elijah ever ascend to Heaven, as it is said "The heavens are the heavens of the Lord, but the earth hath He given to the sons of men."'[42] R. Jose's words astonished the Amoraim, since they are emphatically contradicted by many Biblical verses, and the Sages reconciled them by a compromise. In truth the Shekhina did descend, but not below ten handbreadths, and Moses and Elijah ascended heavenward, but not above ten (handbreadths). Ten handbreadths constitute another domain.[43] Despite the great proximity a certain distance was preserved. But this was not the original purport of R. Jose's statement. The extreme form of its wording is in keeping with his other dictum 'The Holy One, blessed be He, is the Place of the world, but the world is not His place',[44] and seeks to negate the view that the revelation of God is connected with ascent and descent; they are only figurative expressions. It may be assumed that R. Jose, who disputed with sectarians, sought to obviate arguments of the kind put by the Cuthean to R. Me'ir, and to contradict dangerous answers given in reply. Actually the question of the Cuthean implies an answer like this: He of whom it is written 'Do not I fill heaven and earth?' is not the same as He that spoke with Moses from between the staves of the Ark. The Cuthean-Samaritan, whose question hints at this answer, is a Gnostic, who distinguished between the Supreme Deity and the demiurge, who created the world. The early fathers of the Christian Church also used this doctrine in order to reconcile the aforementioned contradiction, for it opened the way for them to introduce a Christological interpretation. It will suffice to cite the words of Justin Martyr, who was born in Shechem and was the contemporary of R. Me'ir and R. Jose. He said: 'Let it not be thought that the uncreated God ascends or descends, for the Father and Master does not go to any place, does not walk about, does not sleep and does not wake; He remains in His place....' (*Dialogue*, 56, 60). So far we hear the words of R. Jose,[45] but not so in another passage. There Justin writes: 'How is it possible that He should speak to anyone, or appear to anyone, or that He should manifest Himself in a finite place, since the people cannot see the glory of Him who sent it?... Hence, neither

Abraham, nor Isaac, nor Jacob, nor any other human being saw the Father, the Lord of all things, who is ineffable; they only saw him who was deified by the will of the Father, namely, His son, being similar to His angel, who ministers before Him' (*ibid.* 127). R. Jose's teaching did not close the door to interpretations of the type advanced by Justin; indeed, it remained an individual opinion. The Amoraim, who sensed the contradiction between belief in God, whose glory fills the universe, and His speaking to Moses from between the staves of the Ark, followed the exegetical method of R. Me'ir. The example of the reflection in the mirror lessened the force of the question. The emphasis laid on the absolute will and omnipotence of God did not remove the actual contradiction, but made it a component of the Divine capacity and might, which in no way conform to the standards of human reason.

It is reported in the name of R. Joḥanan that when Moses heard from the Almighty the words 'And let them make Me a sanctuary' (Exodus xxv 8), he retreated in consternation, saying 'Sovereign of the universe, lo, the heavens and the heavens of the heavens cannot contain Thee, yet Thou sayest "And let them make Me a sanctuary"!' In reply the Holy One, blessed be He, said to him: 'Moses, it is not as thou dost think, but twenty boards to the north and twenty boards to the south, eight in the west, and I shall descend and confine My Shekhina among you upon earth.'[46] The term 'confinement of the Shekhina', which appears in a few other passages,[47] signifies special concentration of the Divine Presence in a given place,[48] and the more limited the space is the greater is His might. When He confines His Shekhina among five elders, who entered to intercalate the year, the Ministering Angels laud Him, saying: 'This is the Mighty One, this is the Mighty One, this is God, this is God. He of whom it is written "A God feared in the great council of the holy ones" leaves the assembly on high and descends and confines His Shekhina among those below.'[49] The confinement of the Shekhina in one place does not imply withdrawal from another place. We have already quoted in a different context the analogy of the sea and the cave, which seeks to illustrate the truth that 'although it is written "and the glory of the Lord filled the tabernacle", neither the beings on high nor those below lacked anything of the splendour of His glory.'[50]

The general opinion is that nothing is too low or too humble for the Shekhina to be manifested thereon. 'A Gentile once put the following question to Rabban Gamaliel: "Why did the Holy One blessed be He reveal Himself to Moses in a thorn-bush?" He replied: "Had He revealed Himself to him on a carob tree or a fig tree, what wouldst thou have said then? It serves only to teach that no place on earth is void of the Shekhina." '[51] In the middle of the third century, the Amoraim debated the manner chosen by God to dwell with the humble and contrite: ' "With him also that is of a contrite and humble spirit" (Isaiah lvii 15) — Rav Huna and Rav Ḥisda (discuss the verse): one says (it means) "the contrite is with Me"; the other says "I am with the contrite." ' The Talmud concludes: 'It appears that the one who holds "I am with the contrite" is right. For the Holy One, blessed be He, left all the (other) mountains and hills and caused His Shekhina to dwell on Mount Sinai, but Sinai did not rise up....' From this it is deduced that pride encroaches upon the Shekhina: 'Whoever is imbued with an overweening spirit, the Holy One, blessed be He, declares "I and he cannot abide together in the world" ', and hence the moral that a man 'should learn from the mind of his Maker'.[52]

These views are opposed to the concept of the immanence of the Deity in the world, which was widely accepted by the Greeks, and according to which the Divine immanence in nature is an immutable law. 'To say that God turns His face away from sinners is exactly like saying that the sun withdraws its face from the blind.'[53] The Rabbinic view is that God's presence in the world and the modes of His theophanies are linked to man's conduct and deeds.[54] Regarding the fact that God caused the Shekhina to dwell in the Tabernacle, there is a difference of opinion between R. Simeon b. Yoḥai and Rabbi. According to Rabbi,[55] this event was 'a new phenomenon'; R. Simeon b. Yoḥai, on the other hand, declared: 'It had once existed and then had ceased for a long period, and finally it reverted to the former position.' His words were elucidated by the Amoraim. R. Abba bar Kahana[56] explained: 'Primarily the Shekhina dwelt among the inhabitants of the earth', but since Adam sinned, it departed to the first heaven and in the subsequent generations it withdrew on account of the wicked from heaven to heaven as far as the seventh heaven, until Abraham, our father, arose and brought it down to the sixth heaven; his descendants up to Amram then brought it down from heaven to heaven as far as the first heaven. Only Moses succeeded in bringing it back again to earth, and erected the Tabernacle. The basic thought underlying the dramatic account of how the Shekhina came to dwell on earth is explained in the following homily of R. Isaac:[57] 'It is written "The righteous shall inherit the land, and dwell therein for ever" (Psalms xxxvii 29). Wherein shall the wicked dwell? In the air? This is the meaning: The wicked caused the Shekhina to leave the earth, but the righteous caused the Shekhina to dwell upon the earth.' The connection between the Shekhina's dwelling among the denizens of the earth and human merit is to be inferred also from Rabbi's view that the Shekhina did not abide among the terrestrial inhabitants when the world was created, but only when the Tabernacle was erected. Obviously, Rabbi did not deny all the manifestations of the Shekhina to people upon earth, which are expressly mentioned in the Torah and preceded the erection of the Tabernacle, but referred to the Shekhina's dwelling below permanently — in one place. This must be credited to the merit and high status of the generation that accepted the Torah. R. Judah bar Ilʿai already relates the following parable: 'It may be likened to the case of a king who had a daughter who was a minor. Until she grew up and came of age, he used to speak to her when he saw her in the street; he spoke to her in the alleyways. But when she grew up and came of age, he said: "It is not in keeping with my daughter's dignity that I should talk to her in public. Make her therefore a pavilion (παπυλιών), and I shall speak with her inside the pavilion." Thus at first it is written "When Israel was a child, then I loved him" (said God) — they saw Me in Egypt... they saw Me at the Red Sea... they saw Me at Sinai... But once they had accepted the Torah and become a complete nation unto Him, He said: "It is not in keeping with the dignity of My children that I should talk with them publicly, but let them make Me a Tabernacle and I shall speak (with them) from the midst of the Tabernacle." '[58] The first phase was deemed primitive, comparable to the age of childhood, when one does not insist on absolute propriety. But religious maturity cannot acquiesce in a state of anarchy.

The unique character of the Tabernacle, and subsequently of the

Temple, as the place of the Shekhina is related to the idea of election. The place 'where He shall choose to cause His name to dwell' (Deuteronomy xiv 23) is 'the Chosen House' [*Bêt ha-Bĕḥîrā*, i.e. the Temple].[59] The existence of the Shekhina in the Temple not only does not contradict its presence throughout the world, but, on the contrary, it is itself an essential condition of the maintenance of this presence, without which the latter would not be possible. Rabbi, who linked the descent of the Shekhina to the dwellers on earth with the erection of the Tabernacle, is also the author of the following homily: '...Thou dost say "and Mine eyes and My heart shall be there perpetually" (I Kings ix 3). Are they then there only? Behold, it has already been stated "the eyes of the Lord [that] run to and fro through the whole earth" (Zechariah iv 10) and it says "The eyes of the Lord are [in] every place, keeping watch upon the evil and the good" (Proverbs xv 3). What then is the significance of "and Mine eyes and My heart shall be there perpetually"? They are not, so to speak, only there, but since they are there, they are everywhere' (*Sifre Deuteronomy*, § 40). The perpetual, concentrated Presence in one place is essential to the recognition of the universality of the Divine Existence. When the Temple was built, the world was firmly established, as R. Samuel bar Naḥmani stated: 'Until the Temple was constructed the world stood on a throne of two legs; once the Temple was built the world was firmly established' (*Tanḥuma*, Tĕrūmā, § 9). The existence of the Deity in the world becomes firm, as it were, through His existence in one place.

It should be noted here that a distinction must be drawn between the existence of God, His presence and readiness to listen to those who pray unto Him, and the revelation of the Shekhina to individuals. This differentiation is required for the understanding of the following Tannaitic homily: '...It is to be inferred that the Shekhina does not reveal itself outside of Israel, for it is stated "But Jonah rose up to flee unto Tarshish from the presence of the Lord" (Jonah i 3). Was he then fleeing from the Lord's presence? Lo, it has already been said "Whither shall I go from Thy spirit?... If I ascend up into heaven, Thou art there..." (Psalms cxxxix 7–10), and it is written "the eyes of the Lord, that run to and fro through the whole earth" (Zechariah iv 10), and it is further written "The eyes of the Lord are in every place, keeping watch upon the evil and the good" (Proverbs xv 3)... The meaning is that Jonah said "I shall hie me beyond the borders of the Land of Israel, where the Shekhina does not reveal itself, for the Gentiles readily repent, lest (by comparison) I bring guilt upon Israel." '[60] Here the reference is to the manifestation of the Shekhina in the sense of Divine communication to the prophet, which takes place only in the Land; but the Shekhina's presence is, needless to say, throughout the world.[61]

The paradoxical concept that the specific presence of the Deity in a particular place not only does not contradict His presence throughout the world, but actually makes it possible, helped to solve a concrete, historical problem, namely the presence of God among His people and the singling out of this people as His dwelling place even after the destruction of the Temple and the nation's banishment from its land. Commenting on the verse '[in driving out] from before Thy people, whom Thou didst redeem to Thee out of Egypt, the nations and their gods?' (II Samuel vii 23; the *Mekhilta* reads 'nation', in the singular), R. Akiba stated: 'Were it not so written in Scripture, it would be impossible to voice such a thought. The Israelites said, as it were, to the Holy One, blessed be He: "Thou didst redeem Thyself." So, too, it is found that wherever Israel went into exile, the Shekhina, as it were, was exiled with them. When they were exiled to Egypt, the Shekhina was with them, as it is said "Did I reveal Myself unto the house of thy father, when they were in Egypt?" (I Samuel ii 27); when they were exiled to Babylon, the Shekhina was with them... and when they are destined to return, the Shekhina will return, so to speak, with them....'[62] However, there are dicta that speak of the departure of the Shekhina, when the Temple was destroyed. In a dramatic account, recalling that of the withdrawal of the Shekhina from the world after Adam had sinned, ten journeys[63] are mentioned, which preceded the departure of the Shekhina heavenward at the time of the destruction of the Temple. This account belongs to the Tannaitic period, for the early Amoraim base themselves upon it. 'R. Jonathan said[64]: Three and a half years the Shekhina abode on the Mountain of Olives and proclaimed thrice daily, saying "Return, ye backsliding children, I will heal your backslidings" (Jeremiah iii 22). Since they did not return, the Shekhina began to hover in the air, uttering the verse "I will go and return to My place, till they acknowledge their guilt and seek My face; in their trouble they will seek Me earnestly" (Hosea v 15).' According to another version, the Shekhina's station before returning to its place was the wilderness, and with reference to this 'R. Joḥanan[65] said: Six months the Shekhina waited for Israel in the wilderness, perchance they would return in penitence. Since they did not repent, the Shekhina said "Perish thy soul!"[66], as it is said "But the eyes of the wicked shall fail, and they shall have no way to flee, and their hope shall be the drooping [= perishing] of the soul" (Job xi 20).' This motif of the departure of the Shekhina, when the Temple was destroyed, recurs in the homilies of the Amoraim, for example: 'Zavdai b. Levi began his discourse thus: "God maketh the solitary to dwell in a house" (Psalms lxviii 7 [6]). You find that before the Israelites were redeemed from Egypt, they dwelt by themselves and the Shekhina by itself; but when they (the Israelites) were redeemed, they both (the Shekhina and Israel) formed an undivided whole (ὁμονοια). But when they were (again) exiled, the Shekhina once more dwelt by itself and the Israelites by themselves....'[67] Or, to take another example: 'When the Holy One, blessed be He, wished to destroy the Temple, He said: "So long as I am in it, the Gentile nations will not harm it. I shall, therefore, cease to regard it and I shall swear not to give it heed till the time of the End...." At that moment the enemy entered the Temple and burned it. When it was burnt, the Holy One, blessed be He, said "I no longer have a seat upon earth; I shall remove My Shekhina therefrom and ascend to My first habitation... At that moment the Holy One, blessed be He, wept and said: "Woe unto Me, what have I done! I caused My Shekhina to dwell below for Israel's sake, and now that they have sinned I have returned to My original place." '[68]

These homilies, expressing the shock and the sense of grief resulting from the destruction of the Temple, which disrupted the concord and created a division between the Shekhina and the people of Israel, conflict with the dicta of R. Akiba,[69] and of those who followed in his footsteps[70] which state that the Shekhina accompanied the people in exile. The difference between the two views is well reflected in two versions of Tannaitic homilies on the verses Deuteronomy xviii 11–12. In one Baraita it is reported: When R. Eliezer came to this verse, he used to say 'Alas for us! Now if on one who cleaves to uncleanness, the spirit of uncleanness rests, then it follows that on one who cleaves to the Shekhina, the Shekhina rests. And who caused it [i.e. that the Shekhina should not rest on us]? ' "But your iniquities have separated between you and your God." ' (Isaiah lix 2)[71] R. Eliezer attributes the withdrawal of the Shekhina from Israel to their sins. Just as repentance alone can bring, to his mind, redemption (see below, chapter XV), so only the removal of iniquities can restore the Shekhina to its place. On the other hand, it is reported in another Baraita: ' "Or that consulteth the dead" — this refers to one who starves himself and goes and spends the night in a cemetery, so that an unclean spirit may rest upon him. And when R. Akiba reached this verse, he wept, saying: 'If one who starves himself that the spirit of uncleanness should rest upon him (has his wish fulfilled), he who fasts that the spirit of purity should rest upon him how much more so! But what is one to do, seeing that his iniquities have brought this upon him, as it is said "But your iniquities have separated between you and your God"?'[72] Here the homily has changed and assumed an individual character: the spirit of purity — that is, of prophecy, the holy spirit — which does not rest upon a man who starves himself and is imbued with iniquity, is spoken of and not the Shekhina, which leaves Israel on account of their sins. R. Akiba's statement is connected with his Messianic outlook: 'All the time that Israel is in bondage, the Shekhina, so to speak, is in bondage with them.' The end of the homily explains its intent: 'And when they are destined to return, the Shekhina will return with them.' This is a homily of comfort, whereas the homily concerning the journeys of the Shekhina and its withdrawal is one of rebuke. The Shekhina is not with the people, but in heaven, and the conclusion of the homily, according to one of its versions, is: 'Behold, Israel seeks the Shekhina, but it will not return until the End comes.' But the continuation of the verse 'I will go and return to My place', which was expounded with reference to the departure of the Shekhina, is 'till they acknowledge their guilt, and seek My face; in their trouble they will seek Me earnestly'. Even when the Shekhina is in heaven, the possibility of offering supplications and prayers to heaven is not excluded, for God has not taken away His Providence from His people, in accordance with the words of R. Jannai: 'Although His Shekhina is in heaven, His eyes behold, His eyelids scrutinize, the children of men.'[73] However, at the end of the third century the Palestinian Amoraim still debated the question whether the Shekhina departed from the site of the Temple when the Temple was destroyed. While R. Samuel bar Naḥman held that 'Before the Temple was destroyed, the Shekhina rested in the Temple... but when the Temple was destroyed... He removed His Shekhina to heaven', his great contemporary, R. Eleazar b. Pedat, said 'Whether (the Temple) is destroyed or not, the Shekhina does not stir from its place.'[74] About a century later the Amora R. Aḥa gave the following exposition[75]: 'The Shekhina will never leave the Western Wall of the Temple, as it is said, "Behold, he standeth behind our wall" (Canticles ii 9)'; in an anonymous exposition of this verse a reason is added: 'Why? Because the Holy One, blessed be He, had sworn to it that it would never be destroyed.'[76] Since the Wall was not destroyed, there remains the part of the Sanctuary site from which the Shekhina has not departed. It is probable that this view underlies the testimony of R. Joshua: 'I have heard that sacrifices may be offered up although there is no Temple, and that the most holy offerings may be eaten although there are no curtains, the lesser holy offerings and the second tithe, although there is no wall, for the sanctity of the First Temple availed for its own time and for the future.'[77]

At all events, the view finds support in the Halakha relative to the orientation for praying, whose origin is old, but in whose various phases there is discernible the wrestling with the problem of the place of the Shekhina after the destruction of the Temple. It is true that prayer in the Bible[78] is not linked with any given site, and every place is deemed fit for prayer; nevertheless a certain uniqueness was attributed to the Temple even in respect of prayer. The worshipper is answered 'from His holy mountain' (Psalms iii 5 [4]), and Jonah's prayer from the bowels of the fish comes 'into Thy holy Temple' (Jonah ii 8).

In Solomon's prayer it is said of the captives in the land of the enemy: 'And they shall pray unto Thee toward their land, which Thou gavest unto their fathers, the city which Thou hast chosen, and the house which I have built for Thy name; then hear Thou this prayer

... in heaven Thy dwelling-place' (I Kings viii 48–49). Prayer from outside the Land of Israel reached His dwelling-place in heaven by way of the Land, the City and the Temple. Daniel prayed in his upper chamber, whose windows were open towards Jerusalem (Daniel vi 11). Accordingly, the Mishna teaches (*M. Berakhot* iv 5) that he who prays [i.e. recites the Eighteen Benedictions] must turn his face towards the Holy of Holies. A more detailed statement is found in a Baraita: 'Those who stand and pray [i.e. recite the Eighteen Benedictions] outside the Land of Israel should turn their faces towards the Land of Israel. What is the reason? (Because it is written:) "and they pray unto Thee toward [their land], which Thou gavest unto their fathers". Those who stand and pray in the Land of Israel should turn their faces towards Jerusalem. What is the reason? (Because it is written:) "and they pray unto the Land toward the city which Thou hast chosen". Those who stand up and pray in Jerusalem should turn their faces towards the Temple Mount, as it is said "and toward the house which I have built for Thy name". Those who stand and pray on the Temple Mount should turn their faces towards the Holy of Holies. What is the reason? (Because it is written:) "when they shall pray toward this place; yea, hear Thou in heaven Thy dwelling-place; and when Thou hearest, forgive". It is thus found that those who stand in the north face south, those who stand in the south face north, those who stand in the east face west, those in the west face east. In this way all Israel pray towards one place.'[79] The prayer-orientation, which is the same for the entire people, integrates them all around the place where God has chosen to cause His name to dwell. The turning of the face towards the Land, the City, and the Temple, is not merely an extraneous act but an expression of inner intent. Indeed, in the parallel sources to the text of the Baraita cited we find, instead of 'turn their faces', 'direct their hearts'[80], and this direction of the heart means two things: orientating the body and also one's thoughts. If one is so situated that he cannot orient his body, he can still direct his mind, his thoughts. Another significant variation, worthy of note, is this: while we are told in the Mishna that he who cannot determine the direction 'should turn his heart towards the Holy of Holies', it is stated in the Tosefta 'they direct their mind to the Omnipresent', and in the Baraita of the Palestinian

Talmud, 'they pray towards heaven'. These variant readings reflect the difference of opinion between the last Tannaitic Sages on the interpretation of the Mishna: 'To which Holy of Holies?' R. Ḥiyya Rabba said: Towards the heavenly Holy of Holies; R. Simeon b. Ḥalafta said: Towards the earthly Holy of Holies.' If it is not possible to orientate one's body to the earthly Holy of Holies, R. Ḥiyya holds that one's mind and thoughts should be directed straight to heaven. The Amora of Eretz-Israel, R. Phinehas bar Ḥama, reconciles the divergence of opinion by saying: 'They do not disagree: the earthly Holy of Holies faces the heavenly Holy of Holies.'[81] In orienting oneself towards the earthly Holy of Holies, one orients oneself at the same time to that in heaven. This ancient concept that the heavenly Temple faces the earthly one provides a special reason for directing the prayer of the Eighteen Benedictions towards the site of the Sanctuary even after the destruction of the Temple, that is, after the Shekhina had declared 'I will go and return to My place'. However, the orientation for the recitation of the prayer of the Eighteen Benedictions was not determined solely by the views concerning the place of the Shekhina.

The forms of cultic ritual and worship are not only decided by inner reasons of faith; frequently they are influenced by the rites of other religions either through adoption accompanied by the advancement of new reasons, or by negation and rejection. It happens at times that a new religion, or a nonconformist sect, by taking over a conventional religious custom and giving it a new interpretation, causes the custom to be changed or abandoned in its religious homeland, in whose soil it grew. The standing of the worshipper and his orientation were matters over which religions and sects were in conflict. Ezekiel (viii 16) sees in his vision an abomination perpetrated in the Temple: 'There were about five and twenty men, with their backs toward the Temple of the Lord, and their faces toward the east; and they worshipped the sun toward the east.' These people prostrated themselves to the sun and in this way linked sun-worship to the Temple. In the Mishnaic description of *simḥat bêt ha-Shô'ēvā* [the rejoicing in connection with the water-drawing ceremony on the second night of Succot],[82] it is related that when the procession of celebrants reached the gateway leading eastward, 'they turned their faces to the west and said: "Our ancestors who were in this place, their backs were toward the Temple of the Lord and their faces toward the east, and they prostrated themselves eastward to the sun; but as for us, our eyes are turned to the Lord"' (*M. Sukka* v, 4). Although the passage from Ezekiel is cited, it is not to be assumed that 'our ancestors who were in this place' refers to the men whom Ezekiel saw, and it is almost certain that the celebrants did not mean to say that their forefathers were sun-worshippers, but there is preserved here an allusion to a custom of praying towards the sun as an expression of reverence for the light. Josephus relates of the Essenes: 'Before the sun is up they utter no word on mundane matters, but offer to him certain prayers, which have been handed down from their forefathers, as though entreating him to rise' (*Wars* II, 8, 5). Philo reports a similar custom practised by the Therapeutae: 'Twice every day they pray, at dawn and at eventide; at sunrise they pray for a fine, bright day, fine and bright in the true sense of the heavenly daylight which they pray may fill their minds. At sunset they ask that the soul may be wholly relieved from the press of the senses and the objects of sense and, sitting where she is consistory and council chamber to herself, pursue the quest of truth.'[83] Even if we do not attribute mystical-philosophic thoughts of this kind to the ancestors of the participants in the Water-drawing Celebration, it is not impossible that the prostration to the sun contained an expression of reverence to the Creator of light. The worshipper came to the Sanctuary praying 'that I may walk before God in the light of the living' (Psalms lvi 14 [13]) and 'Many there are that say: "Oh that we could see some good!" Lord, lift Thou up the light of Thy countenance upon us' (*ibid.* iv 7 [6]). The joy at appearing in the Sanctuary of God, who is portrayed as 'The Lord is my light and my salvation' (Psalms xxvii 1),[84] found expression in the custom of prostration to the sun. It is not surprising that this custom aroused opposition on account of the part played by worship of the sun and the light both in the East — in the Persian religion — and in the Hellenistic-Roman world,[85] and also in view of our present knowledge concerning the dualistic *Weltanschauung* of the Qumran sectarians and the place that 'light' holds therein. 'The Sons of Light' — like the authors of *The Book of Jubilees*, The *Book of Enoch*, and *The Testaments of the Twelve*

Patriarchs — reckoned the annual calendar according to the course of the 'Great Luminary', the sun.[86] It appears that there has been preserved in the Mishna a tradition relating to a demonstration that caused an ancient custom to be abrogated in order to show the error of deviationists and sectarians. The worshipper faces only towards the west — 'as for us, our eyes are turned towards the Lord', and there is no need for him to face the sun in order to be vouchsafed 'the light of the Lord's countenance'. The light and the splendour are of the Shekhina.

However, the fixing of the praying-orientation towards Jerusalem also created a problem when Christianity came into being and was disseminated. The Church Father Epiphanius[87] relates that Elchasai, the founder and head of a Judeo-Christian sect,[88] who flourished *circa* 100 C.E., forbade his followers to turn in prayer towards the east, but enjoined them to face, from all the cardinal points, in the direction of Jerusalem: 'Those who live in the east — towards the west, facing Jerusalem; those who live in the west — towards the east, facing the same city; those who live in the north — towards the south; and those living in the south — towards the north. Thus from all directions they would turn towards Jerusalem.' The words of Elchasai seem exactly like a quotation from the Baraita on the prayer-orientation cited above. Other Judeo-Christian sects acted in the same way. Irenaeus relates[89] that the Ebionites revere Jerusalem as though it were the House of the Lord. It is obvious, however, that the reasons advanced for this attitude by these sectarians were not the same as those of the Sages. Epiphanius argues against Elchasai that on the one hand he negates the Temple services, and denies God's desire for sacrifices, and on the other he enjoins that one should pray towards Jerusalem. In truth, the Judeo-Christian traditions do not refer to praying towards the Sanctuary, but towards Jerusalem, and it may be presumed that their reason was not different from that found in the writings of the later Church Fathers,[90] who expounded the passages in Psalms cxxxii 7 'Let us go to His dwelling place; let us worship at His footstool!' and in Zechariah xiv 4 'On that day His feet shall stand on the Mount of Olives' as referring to the place where Jesus appeared. It appears that the tendency of a number of Sages to do away with a fixed prayer-orientation altogether, for the reason that 'the Shekhina is everywhere',[91] is a reaction to the arguments of the Judeo-Christians. This interpretation seems probable in so far as R. Ishmael is concerned, for he declared that 'The books of the sectarians create enmity, envy, and contention between Israel and their Father in Heaven... and should be burned together with their Divine names'.[92] Christianity in Egypt and in Western countries accepted in the second century a prayer-orientation to the east, taking into account the widespread practice in prayer among the Gentiles who had become Christians,[93] and in the third century it became universal in the Christian world even in Eastern countries. In the ordinances of the Syrian Church the rule was laid down that one had to face east in prayer, and, at the same time, a reason was given for it, namely that in time to come Jesus would appear from the east.[94] In the Land of Israel the Amoraim regarded the fixing of the orientation towards the Holy of Holies in the west as a barrier separating them completely from those who faced east. Particularly noteworthy is the dictum of R. Joshua b. Levi,[95] both from the viewpoint of style and of content. He said 'Come let us be grateful to our ancestors, who made known to us the place of prayer, as it is written "And the host of heaven worshippeth Thee". ' The words 'Let us be grateful to our ancestors' recall the words of the Mishna in the declaration made at the time of the Water-drawing Festival: 'Our ancestors who were in this place'. R. Joshua b. Levi invites us to be grateful to those ancestors who abrogated the practice of prostration towards the sun, and support for this action is to be found in the passage in Nehemiah (ix 6), which states that the host of heaven themselves, including the sun, prostrate themselves to the west. The view that 'the Shekhina is in the west'[96] is reflected in the Halakha that determined the form of the Synagogue structure: 'The entrances of the Synagogues are to be made only towards the east.'[97] Indeed, this ruling governed the construction of many synagogues that have been discovered in excavations both in Eretz-Israel and in the Diaspora, as, for example, in Dura-Europos.[98] In Babylonia there were Amoraim who continued to favour R. Ishmael's view that the Shekhina was everywhere. Rav Sheshet, who was blind, told his servant to position him for prayer facing whichever direction he pleased, but he excluded the east, 'because the sectarians teach this'. In the light of the observations that we have made above, there can be no doubt as to who the sectarians were that gave such instructions.[99]

The sources dealing with the orientation of prayer in relation to the place of the Shekhina corroborate that which we find also in other sources, namely that the epithet 'Shekhina' expresses the presence and proximity of God. But even in the epoch of the Tannaim it is not used to weaken the anthropomorphic character of Scriptural verses. On the contrary, we find that the designation Shekhina itself is accompanied by the expression *ki-vĕ-yākhôl* ['as it were', 'so to speak'][1] in passages that appear unduly daring.

A survey of all the passages referring to the Shekhina leaves no doubt that the Shekhina is no 'hypostasis' and has no separate existence alongside the Deity. This fact is stressed by Gershom Scholem,[2] even with respect to the literature of the *Hekhalot* ['Heavenly Halls'] and the surviving fragments of *Shiʿur Qoma* ['The Dimensions of God']. These do not regard the Shekhina as the embodiment of a separate entity. An exception to this rule, according to Scholem, is the dictum in *Midrash Proverbs*, xxii, 29: ' "Seest thou a man diligent in his business?" — When the Sanhedrin wished to count him [King Solomon] with the three kings and four commoners,[3] the Shekhina stood before the Holy One, blessed be He, and said unto Him: "Sovereign of the universe! Seest Thou a man diligent? — they wish to count him with 'mean men'." At that moment a Heavenly Voice went forth and said to them: "He shall stand before kings; he shall not stand before mean men." '[4] Scholem finds in this Midrash 'the beginning of a new development. For the first time a clear distinction is made between the Shekhina and the Holy One, blessed be He. They both appear in a dialogical relationship.' It seems that Scholem was influenced by the negative attitude of R. Moses b. R. Ḥasdai[5] to the aforementioned Midrash. The severe critic of both R. Saadia Gaon and Maimonides and the German Ḥasidim regarded the language of Midrash Proverbs as a source from which the philosophers could draw support for their conception of the Shekhina as 'a created form'.[6] R. Moses proceeded to deny them this source and declared: 'And now we need pay no heed to the reading in *Midrash Proverbs*, for our Talmud takes precedence.' But we are compelled to ask if we are permitted to ascribe a different intention to the expression 'the Shekhina stood before the Holy One, blessed be He' than to the phrase 'a Heavenly Voice went forth and said'. We have before us a Midrash that employs the well-known technique of interpreting a verse as a dialogue.[7] The verse (Proverbs xxii 29) is divided between two speakers. The first says: 'Seest thou a man diligent? — they wish to count him with mean men'; and the second answers: 'He shall stand before kings; he shall not stand before mean men.' There is no difference whatsoever between 'Shekhina' and 'Heavenly Voice'; they are both alternative expressions for 'the holy spirit' that speaks out of the language of Scripture. Indeed, we even find the holy spirit 'saying to the Holy One, blessed be He', and actually in an early Midrash[8] 'R. Aḥa said: This holy spirit is a counsel of defence — it defends both sides. It says to Israel: "Be not a witness against thy Friend without cause" (Proverbs xxiv 28); and it says to the Holy One, blessed be He: "Say not: 'I will do so to him as he hath done to Me.' " ' It will thus be seen that the concept of the Shekhina as a separate created being is not to be found in any Rabbinic source, not even in a late Midrash like *Pirqe de-R. Eliezer*. It is, in truth, stated there in chapter IV, with regard to the four companies of angels, 'The first company, of Michael, is on His right; the second company, of Gabriel, is on His left; the third company, of Uriel, is in front of Him; the fourth company, of Raphael, is behind Him; and the Shekhina of the Holy One, blessed be He, is in the middle; and He Himself sits on a throne, high and exalted.' But it seems that 'His Shekhina' and 'He' are one and the same. Even these Midrashim have not gone beyond what we found in the Halakhic Midrashim (above, p. 43). Only in the Midrash known as *Bereshit Rabbati*, which emanated from the circle of R. Moses ha-Darshan of Narbonne, in the eleventh century, which may have already been influenced by the philosophical exegesis of R. Saadia Gaon, is it stated: 'R. Akiba said: When the Holy One, blessed be He, scrutinized the action of the generation, and saw that they were corrupt and bad, *He withdrew Himself and His Shekhina from among them.*'[9] It is this very change in the conventional formula — 'the Holy One, blessed be He, withdrew His Shekhina'[10] — that points to a change of conception.

It is also necessary to emphasize that in the ideology of the Sages of the Talmud and the Midrash the term 'Shekhina' is not connected with 'Wisdom', and the two are not identified. In all the sayings and Haggadot in which reference is made to the Shekhina, figurative expressions like Princess, Matron (Lady), Queen or Bride, are absent. In brief, they contain no feminine element, an element that subsequently played a significant role in the Cabbala, under the influence of Gnostic doctrines,[11] and which, relative to Wisdom, is already found in Hellenistic literature. We must dwell on this for a moment in order to underline the difference, and thus we return to the starting point of this chapter. In *The Wisdom of Solomon*, Wisdom — whose gender is feminine in both Hebrew and Greek — is spoken of in one passage (viii 3) as the Bride and Spouse of God. The sublime source of Wisdom lies in its symbiosis with the Deity. The thought is even more clearly expressed by Philo. In his book *De Ebrietate*, 30, we read: 'Now "father and mother" is a phrase which can bear different meanings. For instance we should rightly say and without further questions that the Architect who made this universe was at the same time the father of what was thus born, whilst its mother was the knowledge (ἐπιστήμη) possessed by its Maker. With His knowledge God had union, not as men have it, and begat created being. And knowledge, having received the divine seed (τοῦ θεοῦ σπέρματα)... bore the only beloved son who is apprehended by the senses, the world which we see.' Such portrayals are found also in other passages of Philo. There is, of course, always a link between them and the verses that he expounds, as, for instance, in the example cited, the law of the stubborn and rebellious son (Deuteronomy xxi 20). But it is of consequence that in the Talmuds and the Midrashim such interpretations were never advanced, although the gender of Shekhina is feminine. We can observe here again the gulf between the way of thinking of the Talmudic and Midrashic Sages and speculative, philosophical thought. The concept of the Shekhina does not aim to solve the question of God's quiddity, but to give expression to His presence in the world and His nearness to man, without, at the same time, destroying the sense of distance.

CHAPTER IV

NEARNESS AND DISTANCE — OMNIPRESENT AND HEAVEN

The epithet 'Shekhina' expresses the presence of God, without any limitation whatsoever to this presence. There was no doubt in regard to the general meaning of the designation, and it could be used with a number of variations according to the degrees of proximity and distance in relation to God. It provides release from the tension of the polarity that marks the relationship between man and his God, and leaves the door wide open to a host of images that could not easily be linked to the classical Scriptural names of God, nor even to post-Biblical designations like 'Omnipresent' [*Māqôm*, literally: 'Place'] and 'Heaven', which we shall now discuss.

The use of the epithet 'Omnipresent' is very old. It occurs in a Baraita that tells of a Nazirite who came from the south to Simon the Just and told him the circumstances that had induced him to assume Naziriteship, and Simon the Just answered him 'My son, may those who do the Omnipresent's will like you multiply in Israel!' (*Tosefta Nezirut* iv, 7). There is no reason to doubt the authenticity of the expression, since it appears in all the parallel sources.[1] This epithet is employed even by the early Tannaim. Simon b. Sheṭaḥ sent word to Ḥoni ha-Me'aggel [Ḥoni the Circle-Drawer]: 'But what can I do to you? You act like a spoilt child before the Omnipresent' (*M. Ta'anit* iii, 8). Akavya b. Mahalal'el said: 'Rather would I be called a fool all my life than become, for a moment, wicked before the Omnipresent' (*M. 'Eduyot* v, 6). The term is found in the ancient formula used by the Great Sanhedrin of Israel, when it judged the priests and investigated their genealogy. Of a priest in whom no disqualification was found, they said: 'Blessed be the Omnipresent that no disqualification was found in the seed of Aaron' (*M. Middot* v, 4). Concerning the early Hasidim it is reported: 'They used to wait an hour and then pray, so that they might direct their hearts to the Omnipresent' (*M. Berakhot* v, 1); 'R. Judah said: He vowed to become a Nazirite, for the Hasidim of old used to assume Naziriteship as a free-will offering, for the Omnipresent did not permit any inadvertent error to be made by them' (*Tosefta Nedarim* i, 5). It is related of R. Joḥanan b. Zakkai that all his days he taught 'that Job served the Omnipresent only out of fear'.[2] Also in the Tannaitic sources in our possession — in the Midrash, Tosefta and the Halakhic Midrashim — the use of the epithet 'Omnipresent' is extremely common.[3] Although 'the Holy One, blessed be He' occurs in many passages in our printed editions, comparison with MSS., or parallel sources, nearly always produces witnesses, or at least one testimony, to the reading 'the Omnipresent'.[4] On the other hand, the number of passages where 'the Omnipresent' occurs in our texts, but there is evidence that the reading should be 'the Holy One, blessed be He', is negligible. In the majority of places where 'the Omnipresent' occurs, the reading is supported by all the textual evidence. It should also be noted that in many passages we find the abbreviation הב״ה in the MSS., and in the first editions, and that this has been interpreted as *Ha-Qādôsh bārûkh Hû* ['the Holy One, blessed be He'], but it could also stand for *Ha-Māqôm bārûkh Hû* ['the Omnipresent, blessed be He'].[5] Furthermore, the possibility of contamination can only explain the change of 'Omnipresent' to 'the Holy One, blessed be He', not *vice versa*. The scribes and copyists were accustomed to uttering and writing the latter designation and not the former, for 'the Holy One, blessed be He' is the one commonly found in the Amoraic sources, and even ousted the epithet 'Omnipresent'. In the Babylonian Talmud the use of 'the Omnipresent' remained restricted primarily to aphorisms and benediction formulas — for example, 'because there is no elevation before the Omnipresent' (*T.B. Berakhot* 10b), 'May the Omnipresent make good your loss!' (*ibid.* 16b), 'the Omnipresent visit thee in peace!' (*T.B. Shabbat* 12b) — and to passages containing stories or traditions about Tannaim. In *Genesis Rabba*, where 'the Holy One, blessed be He' occurs hundreds of times, 'the Omnipresent' appears only in three instances, but in two of them the MSS. — the best among them — read 'the Holy One, blessed be He'.[6] 'There is thus left in this great Amoraic Midrash only one instance of the use of 'the Omnipresent', namely in the saying of R. Ammi, cited below, which discusses the meaning of the epithet. It seems that in the light of this discovery we cannot doubt that a change took place in the use of the designation 'the Omnipresent' in the period of the Amoraim. No surprise should be felt at the passages where 'the Holy One, blessed be He' occurs in Tannaitic sources, but at their paucity; they evidence the great fidelity with which the teaching of the Tannaim was transmitted through the generations.

The signification and source of the epithet 'the Omnipresent' were no longer known to the Amoraim at the end of the third century. This is shown by R. Ammi's question:[7] 'Why is the Holy One, blessed be He, given an epithet and called Omnipresent?' His answer 'Because He is the Place of His world' is derived from the teaching of R. Jose b. Ḥalafta: 'We do not know whether the Holy One, blessed be He, is the Place of His world, or His world is His place. Since it is written "Behold, there is a place by Me" (Exodus xxxiii 21), it is to be inferred that the Holy One, blessed be He, is the Place of His world, and His world is not His place.' We have already dealt with the connection between this dictum of R. Jose and his statement that the Shekhina did not descend to the earth and that Moses did not ascend to heaven, and with the intent of these observations to stress the gulf between God and the world and to remove any semblance of corporeality from the Divine manifestations and revelations. R. Jose's saying seeks to repudiate the view that 'His world is the place' of God, and the question is: Does R. Ammi's explanation of the epithet 'the Omnipresent', which is based on this dictum, also come to exclude another — original-signification of the designation? In its concrete sense the word *māqôm* [literally, 'Place', rendered: 'Omnipresent'] is related to the world, and there is no place outside it. *Māqôm*, in connection with the manifestation of the Lord in the Bible, always refers to a concrete place, be it on earth or in heaven, for example, 'For, behold, the Lord cometh forth out of His place to visit upon the inhabitants of the earth their iniquity' (Isaiah xxvi 21), or 'I will go and return to My place, till they acknowledge their guilt, and seek My face'

(Hosea v 15; in Targum Pseudo-Jonathan *ad loc.*: 'I shall remove My Shekhina, I shall return to My holy dwelling place, which is in heaven'). The fact that the epithet *ha-Māqôm* is not to be found in the Targumim, rendered in Aramaic as *'Atar* or *'Atrā*, does not fit the premise that this designation had an abstract, speculative connotation, but, on the contrary, can only be understood if we suppose that the word had a concrete, corporeal meaning, and that in consequence the translators refrained from using this title, which was undoubtedly known to them.

This view also finds corroboration in the parallelism between *māqôm* and *shāmayim* ('heaven'). In the Bible God utters His voice from heaven ('Out of heaven He made thee to hear His voice' [Deut. iv 36]); the heavens are His holy habitation ('Look forth from Thy holy habitation, from heaven' [Deut. xxvi 15]) and His dwelling place (I Kings viii 30). The phrase 'the God of heaven' occurs in Jonah i 9 — 'and I fear the Lord, the God of heaven' — and is frequently found in Ezra and Nehemiah. In his proclamation Cyrus declares '... the Lord, the God of heaven, hath given me' (Ezra i 2). Nehemiah prays to the God of heaven (Nehemiah i 4–5; ii 4, 20). In all the authentic and official Aramaic documents in Ezra we find 'the God of heaven'; so, too, in Daniel we read, 'God of heaven' alongside 'King of heaven', 'Lord of heaven', and once even 'heaven' by itself — 'after that thou shalt have known that the heavens do rule' (iv 23). We thus have here metonymy of place, which is common in Semitic languages, that is, the use of the name of a place in the sense of the people of the place, as, for example, 'And the whole earth was of one language' (Genesis xi 1) instead of 'the inhabitants of the earth'; 'and to the land wherein thou hast sojourned' (*ibid.* xxi 23) = 'to the inhabitants of the land'; 'and the cry of the city went up to heaven' (I Samuel v 12) = 'the cry of the inhabitants of the city'.[8] This usage is common in the Apocryphal literature, and especially in the *Books of the Maccabees*, as in the famous speech of Judas 'and with Heaven (τοῦ οὐρανοῦ) it is all one, to deliver with a great multitude, or a small company'.[9]

In the Tannaitic literature, we find the epithet 'Heaven' in the same tradition as that which is linked with the name of Simon the Just, in which we first found the designation 'Omnipresent'. In the story about the one who came from the south — his eyes were beautiful, his appearance was handsome, and his locks were curly — the Nazirite recounts his vow in the words 'I shall cut thee off (O my hair) in the name of Heaven', and with reference thereto Simon the Just said to him 'May those who do the Omnipresent's will like you multiply in Israel!'[10] There is no reason to question the authenticity of this tradition, for we find it confirmed at the beginning of the period of the Hasmoneans, in the Book of Daniel and in the words of Judas Maccabeus. Antigonos of Sokho, who received the tradition from Simon, likewise speaks of 'the fear of Heaven'. Whence is the expression derived? Some have thought to discern extraneous influence in the usage;[11] and, indeed, it is correct that the Iranian religions regarded heaven as the highest deity, who is omniscient. Mithra is considered the god of heaven — particularly of the night — and so, too, Ahura Mazda, in the theology of Zarathustra. Herodotus (I, 131) informs us that the Persians designate the whole vault of the heavens 'Zeus', that is to say, god.[12] 'The god of heaven', or 'heaven', was a comprehensible expression to the Persians, and is almost natural in Cyrus's utterances in all those official documents. The concept 'heaven' (οὐρανός), in the sense of cosmos, was current in Greece before Pythagoras coined the term κόσμος, and it was also used subsequently.[13] Various Syrian gods were presented to the Roman world in the guise of Jupiter, the god of heaven, and, *vice versa*, Antiochus introduced Zeus as the god of heaven. In the *Books of the Maccabees* (II, vi, 2) Zeus is called in the Syriac rendering 'Baal ['Lord'] of heaven', and some have conjectured that *shiqqûṣ shōmēm* ['the detestable thing that causeth appalment'] in Daniel (xii 11) is a dysphemistic epithet for *baʿal shāmayim* ['baal of heaven'].[14] These facts help to explain the widespread use by Jews, in the early days of the Second Temple, of the expression 'the God of heaven' in their contacts with the outer world, without any fear that those who use this designation might be considered sky-worshippers.[15] A self-identification like that of Jonah, 'I fear the Lord, the God of heaven', implied a declaration attesting his faith in the God who is the God of the universe and not a deity of a given country or temple. However, the metonym 'Heaven' stems naturally from the language of the Bible and its figures of speech.[16] The use of the word 'Heaven' in the sense of 'the God of heaven' expressed primarily the attitude of reverence and homage of man towards his God, and stressed the difference between God and human beings. This is evidenced by the phrases 'fear of Heaven' (*M. 'Avot* i, 3; iv, 12), 'kingdom of Heaven' (*Mekhilta de-R. Ishmael*, Ba-ḥōdesh, v, p. 219), 'the yoke of the kingdom of Heaven' (*M. Berakhot* ii, 2), 'the yoke of Heaven' (*Tosefta Soṭa* xiv, 4; *Sifra*, Bĕ-har, v, 109c), 'the things dedicated to Heaven' (Baraita, *T.B. Pesaḥim* 57a), and the antitheses: 'the honour of Heaven' as opposed to 'the honour of man' (*Tosefta Yoma* ii, 8), 'the laws of Heaven' in contrast to the 'laws of man' (*M. Bava Qamma* vi, 4), 'a thing devoted to Heaven' as against 'a thing devoted to the priests' (*M. Nedarim* ii 4), and 'the Father in Heaven' in contradistinction to 'a father of flesh and blood' (*M. Yoma* viii, 9, etc.) or 'his father upon earth' (*Sifre Deuteronomy* § 48, p. 113). In the course of time, however, the specific character of the epithet 'Heaven' was blurred and came to be used in various other phrases. Thus, instead of 'the name of the Lord' we find 'the name of Heaven'.[17] But the note of reverence and awe (*tremendum*) is preserved in its use in votive formulas, oaths, and dedications.[18] But it should be pointed out that in respect of dedicated things the use of the epithet 'Most High' [*Gāvôah*] tended to oust that of 'Heaven', especially when the reference was to the domain, property, and ownership of the Temple in antithesis to the domain, money, property, and ownership of a person. Actually 'Most High' is not an epithet of God but a synonym for *heqdēsh* ['dedicated'] things,[19] in which the tone of reverence instinct in the designation 'Heaven' is not felt.

Bousset understood the meaning of the epithet 'Heaven', but the deductions he drew therefrom are unfounded. In his view, the use of this designation led to the strangulation of the living faith in God. 'When it becomes customary to speak of God in the abstract, religion becomes anaemic. How different is the way the New Testament speaks of God — a way full of life and light — from that of Judaism!'[20] This last sentence not only reveals the tendentiousness of Bousset's remarks, but also his basic failure to understand the tension between the sense of reverence and exaltation that fills the soul of the believer and the feeling of God's nearness and of being drawn to Him in love. The multiplicity of names and titles is not an indication of the absence of a sense of the strong and living reality that marks God's relation to man, but actually expresses a variegated and multifaceted reality. The tension that we have mentioned found its resolution in the pair of epithets *Shāmayim* ['Heaven'] and *Māqôm* ['Omnipresent']. The primary meaning of *Māqôm* is not space, and is not to be construed as 'the most abstract of all terms'.[21] Just as 'Heaven' is a metonym for 'the God of heaven', so is also *Māqôm* [literally, 'Place'] used metonymically and refers to the God who reveals Himself in whatever place He wishes; this epithet thus expresses God's nearness. The youth who was suddenly seized by his evil inclination, says to it: 'Wicked one, I vow to cut thee off in the name of Heaven...', but when Simon the Just wishes to say that his action found favour with God, he declares: 'May those who do the Omnipresent's will like you multiply in Israel.'[22] This difference remains firmly entrenched in the Tannaitic sources. Israel does the will of the Omnipresent,[23] and the Omnipresent is pleased;[24] and if 'will' [*rāṣôn*] and 'Heaven' are associated, it is only through the medium of 'Father' ['*Av*], as, for example, 'the will of his Father in Heaven', '[the public sacrifices] appease [*mĕraṣṣîn*, from the same stem as *rāṣôn*] and atone for Israel before their Father in Heaven'.[25] Moreover, in all the accounts of the reciprocal relations between Israel and God[26] and in the dialogues between God and individuals or the people of Israel,[27] the dominant epithet is 'Omnipresent', even as 'Heaven' expresses God's farness and withdrawal from man.[28] The few exceptions prove the rule.[29] Of special interest are the passages in which 'Omnipresent' and 'Heaven' occur together and preserve the distinction alluded to above; we shall give two examples. One is from the *Sifra* (Nĕdāvā, iv, 8, 5d), ' "and it shall be accepted for him": this teaches us that the Omnipresent accepts him [i.e. forgives him]. But for what does "the Omnipresent" forgive him? Should you say for offences for which one is liable to execution by the court, or death at the hands of Heaven, or extinction [*kārēt*, premature death] by Heaven... then for what does the Omnipresent forgive him?...' The second is from the *Sifre* (Numbers § 95, p. 95): 'If one drew a ballot on which "elder" was inscribed, Moses said to him "the Omnipresent has already sanctified you." But if one drew a ballot on which "elder" was not inscribed, Moses said to him "It is from Heaven...." '

In the light of what has been stated above, it is clear already that the views that ascribe a foreign origin to the epithet 'the Omnipresent' are to be disregarded; but, as we shall see, there is no real basis for these conjectures, whether it is a Persian or Greek source that is suggested, and they have nothing to support them. The theory of Persian influence[30] is based on the testimony of Eudemos of Rhodes, the disciple of Aristotle, 'that the Magi and the entire Aryan tribe gave the Totality possessed of reason, which is not subject to analysis, the designation "Time" or "Place", from which were separated a good god and an evil daemon, and, according to others, darkness and light before them'.[31] This is the Zarvanite myth, according to which the two principles — light and darkness, Ormuzd and Ahriman — have their origin in the Infinite Time-Space, and is based on the worship of Infinite Time and Space in the Iranian liturgy. It is difficult to find any connection between these notions and the epithet 'Omnipresent' and its usages; and, needless to say, there is no significance for our subject in Iranian texts that postdate the Sassanian epoch, and in which is discernible the influence of Greek speculation on time and space.[32] At first blush, it would seem that the view postulating Greek influence is better founded. Philo in his book *On Dreams*[33] interprets Jacob's dream, and when he comes to the words 'And he alighted upon the place' (Genesis xxviii 11), he states that the word 'place' [Hebrew, *Māqôm*], τόπος, has three meanings; first, space in the physical sense; secondly, 'the word of God', θεῖος λόγος, which God has imbued with immaterial powers. He finds this signification in the verse 'and they saw the God of Israel; and there was under His feet the like of a paved work of sapphire stone' (Exodus xxiv 10), citing the verse in the form 'and they saw the place (τὸν τόπον) where the God of Israel stood', in accordance with the Septuagint. 'There is also', he declares, 'a third signification, in keeping with which God Himself is called a place, by reason of His containing things, and being contained by nothing whatever, and being a place for all to flee into, and because He is Himself the space which holds Him... I, mark you, am not a place, but in a place; and each thing likewise that exists; for that which is contained is different from that which contains it, and the Deity, being contained by nothing, is of necessity Itself Its own place — ἀναγκαίως ἐστὶν αὐτὸ τόπος ἑαυτοῦ. In proof, Philo quotes the verse 'And he went unto the place of which

Philo

God had told him... and Abraham lifted up his eyes, and saw the place afar off' (Genesis xxii 3–4). Philo uses the Greek expression ὁ ἐλθὼν in the sense of 'and he came to the place' and he asks: How is it possible that a man who comes to the place should see it afar off? The explanation is that 'place' has two meanings here. First it signifies the Logos, and secondly — the God above it. He who attains to the Logos sees that the Deity is far removed from the whole of creation, and that the possibility of perceiving Him is very remote. The resemblance between the words of Philo and the dictum of R. Jose bar Ḥalafta led to the fact that for a century almost[34] scholars keep reiterating the view that the designation *Māqôm* is only a translation of the Greek term τόπος. Latterly Yitzhak Baer has dealt with the subject.[35] The basis of the epithet *Māqôm* is, in his view, to be found in Plato's teaching, and denotes the place beyond the perception of the senses, including all the entities of the world on high. The physical place on earth has no independent existence, but is subsidiary to the transcendental 'place'. Although the distinction made by Philo between 'the place' as Logos and 'the Place' as the Deity above it is not expressly mentioned in the Midrash, he holds that the Midrashic tradition preferred 'not to speak too openly about the primary power that was created and appointed to stand at the side of God.' The epithet *Māqôm* came into being, according to Baer, when our ancient Sages first encountered Greek wisdom, and it is one of the earliest signs of the meeting of Israel's religious intuition with Western abstract thinking.[36] Baer's conclusions are far-reaching, but do not accord with the sources. The designation *Māqôm*, as it is used in the Rabbinic sources, has no abstract, transcendental character, but, on the contrary, expresses the nearness of man to God, and contains not the slightest allusion to *Māqôm* as the Divine Logos, which was created and appointed to stand at the side of God. On the other hand, Abraham Geiger[37] already noted that among the men of Alexandria *Māqôm* was not in constant use as an epithet. Philo only interprets Pentateuchal verses allegorically, and the word 'place' occurring in them symbolizes the Logos. It is probable that R. Jose b. Ḥalafta, who lived in the middle of the second century, used the formulation of Philo's concept 'that He is the Place of His world but not His world His place' and brought Scriptural evidence in support of it. From the wording of his statement 'We do not know whether....' we recognize its novelty, and only about a century later did the Amoraim R. Isaac and R. Ammi, on the basis of his statement, explain the epithet *Māqôm*, which by that time had gone out of use. So long as the epithet was employed, it denoted the immanence of God, His nearness to man and to the place where he was.[38] The Amoraic interpretation sought to give also to this epithet a transcendental signification, but even their words are devoid of Philo's speculative thought and certainly of his concept of the Logos.[39] Unlike Philo, the Sages (even the Amoraim) refrained from identifying the word *Māqôm* in the Scriptures — apart from the passage on which R. Jose b. Ḥalafta based himself — as a Divine epithet. Even the verse 'and he saw the place afar off' (Genesis xxii 4), which plays such an important role in Philo's exposition, is interpreted in Midrash *Genesis Rabba* (lvi, 2, p. 595) in a different manner: 'What did he see? He saw a cloud attached to them. (Thereupon) he said: It appears that this is the place where the Holy One, blessed be He, told me to offer up my son.' Only in a late Midrash,[40] in *Pirqe de-R. Eliezer* (xxxi), do we find a version that identifies *Ha-Māqôm* in the verse as the Shekhina: 'On the third day they came to Scopos, and having reached Scopos, he saw the glory of the Shekhina standing upon the mountain, as it is said: 'On the third day Abraham lifted up his eyes and saw the place afar off.' The change in the interpretation of the epithet *Māqôm* has the same background as its elimination from use.

As stated above, 'Heaven' is also used *vis-à-vis* the outer world, while *Māqôm*, which is not found either in the Apocryphal literature, in Aramaic, or in the New Testament, is an epithet that came into being in the world of the early Sages out of a desire to emphasize the immanence of God, namely that the world is His place. 'Heaven' and *Māqôm* complemented each other. To the outer world only 'Heaven' remained — possibly to avoid creating the impression of dualism. But when Gnostic sects, which professed the concept of dualism, made their appearance within the Jewish camp as well, they refrained from using *Māqôm*, which was also open to the suspicion of identifying God with the world, and chose instead the name 'the Holy One, blessed be He', which puts the designation beyond the question of immanence or transcendentalism. The use of 'Heaven', in the course of time, also began to decline, and remained in the Midrashim only in the phrase 'the name of Heaven'. The controversial sting in the disuse of the designation *Māqôm* is evident in R. Ammi's observation, 'the world is not His place'.

Echoes of the polemic against Gnostic views, in which the use of the epithets 'Heaven' and '*Māqôm*' played a role, are to be heard in our sources. 'R. Ishmael asked R. Akiba a question, when they were going on a journey. He said to him: "You who have studied for twenty-two years under Nahum of Gimzo, who interpreted every את *'et* [sign of the accusative] in the Torah, (tell me) how did he interpret את השמים ואת הארץ *'et ha-shāmayim wĕ-'et ha-'āreṣ* ['the heaven and the earth'] ?" He replied: "Had it said *shāmayim wā-'āreṣ*, I might have thought, *shāmayim wā-'āreṣ* are names of the Holy One, blessed be He;[41] but now that it says *'et ha-shāmayim wĕ-'et hā-'āreṣ, shāmayim* means the actual heavens, *'āreṣ* means the actual earth." '[42] Clearly, 'Heaven' stands for a Divine epithet, but 'Earth' is only a synonym for '*Māqôm*'; thus we have proof here that the two epithets provided the Gnostic sects with the opportunity of pointing to a Scriptural source in support of the doctrine of dualism. Possibly, for this reason the Sages discontinued using 'Heaven' except in phrases like 'the name of Heaven', 'desecration of the name of Heaven', 'sanctification of the name of Heaven'.

Evidence in support of this interpretation of the aforementioned debate is to be found in a statement of the Church Father Irenaeus, who was born *ca.* 130 in the neighbourhood of Izmir, and was a younger contemporary of R. Akiba. He writes in his work *Contra Haereses*[43] that the Gnostics assert that Moses alluded at the beginning of his book to 'the mother of all',[44] when he declared 'In the beginning God created the heaven and the earth.' In naming the four of them — אלהים *'Ĕlōhîm* ['God'], ראשית *Rē'shît* ['beginning'], *Shāmayim* ['heaven'], and *'Ereṣ* ['earth'] — he expresses their fourfold relationship'.[45] Arguments of this kind played a great part in restricting the use of the epithets 'Heaven' and *Māqôm*. Indeed, these epithets retained their place in the ancient traditions, only the designation *Māqôm*, which commonly occurs in them, acquired a totally new meaning, which gave it a transcendental connotation and approximated it to the epithet 'Heaven'. From the third century onward, the designation 'the Holy One, blessed be He' gained increasing currency.

In our examination of the epithet *Māqôm* we found[46] a patent difference between the Tannaitic and Amoraic sources. While in the former *Māqôm* is usual, and in most cases where 'the Holy One, blessed be He' occurs there are variant readings in the MSS. or parallel sources, in the latter the position is reversed: the primary epithet is 'the Holy One, blessed be He' and variant readings testify against the few deviations. This discovery shows clearly that the designation 'the Holy One, blessed be He' belongs to a later period. Nehemiah Brüll[47] was the first to note the existence of the title הקדש *Ha-Qōdesh* ['Holiness'] and posited that this was the ancient form in the light of the Aramaic קודשא בריך הוא *Qudshā bĕrîkh Hû* ['the Holy One (literally, 'Holiness'), blessed be He']. He was followed by other scholars and latterly by Saul Esh,[48] who collected the passages in which the reading 'the Holiness' remained and came to the conclusion that 'the Holiness' parallels *Māqôm* in Tannaitic literature and can only be understood on the basis of the same metonymy, namely that Zion, the holy place, is used as an epithet for Him who dwells in the Sanctuary.[49] But we still do not know why 'the Holiness' ousted *Māqôm*, seeing that there is no difference in their signification, nor do we understand why the noun-form 'the Holiness' was preferred to the adjective 'the Holy (One)' [הקדוש *Ha-Qādôsh*], which is common in the Bible. But the main objection to this view lies in the fact that it ignores the religious connotation of the epithet, and it is precisely this that makes it impossible to regard it as a metonym. Not only is *qādôsh* linked to the names of God in the Bible as an adjective, but the word is also found as a substantive. It parallels אלוה *'Elôah* ['God'] in Habakkuk iii 3, 'God cometh from Teman, and the Holy One from mount Paran', and in Isaiah lvii 15 it is stated, 'the High and Lofty One, that inhabiteth eternity, whose name is Holy'. God is the source of holiness; He sanctified the Tent of Meeting (Exodus xxix 44) and He dedicated the Temple to His name (I Kings ix 7), and whatever is designated 'holy' is holy to the Lord. It cannot, therefore, be supposed at all that the epithet 'the Holiness' is used instead of 'the Sanctuary'. The designation denotes precisely what the word connotes — the entire religious content that it enshrines. It comprises a synthesis of the meanings and nuances of 'Heaven' and *Māqôm*. The attributive 'Holy' expresses the exaltation and sublimity of transcendentalism and also nearness. God is 'the Holy One of Israel', and with His sanctity He sanctified His people, His land, His city, and His Temple. On the one hand the prophet says 'For great is the Holy One of Israel in the midst of thee' (Isaiah xii 6), and on the other 'Yea, thou hast lifted up thine eyes on high, even against the Holy One of Israel!' (*ibid.* xxxvii 23).

It appears that it was actually the Greek-speaking Jewish dispersion that first used the epithet 'the Holy One.' In the Apocryphal and pseudepigraphical works ὅ ἅγιος[50] often occurs, and it undoubtedly renders 'the Holy' [*ha-Qādôsh*] and not 'the Holiness' [*ha-Qōdesh*]. If we find in one or two places in the Hebrew Sirach the expression 'the Holiness',[51] we must bear in mind that even those who assign an early date to the Hebrew text of the Genizah MSS. do not go further back than the second half of the second century,[52] that is, the close of the Tannaitic period, when we find 'the Holiness' in use. On the other hand we often find in the Greek version of Sirach ὅ ἅγιος, while the Hebrew has in these passages אדני *'Ādōnay* ['Lord'], אל *'Ēl* ['God'], or עליון *'Ēlyôn* ['Most High'].[53] We may presume that Ben Sira's grandson employed ὅ ἅγιος, because its use was current in the Egyptian exile some three hundred years before the epithet 'the Holiness' came into use in Eretz-Israel.[54] Semantically, there is no difference between *ha-qōdesh* and *ha-qādôsh*, and in not a few passages they are interchanged. *Qōdesh* is used as an adjective in the saying of R. Akiba 'For all the Scriptures are holy [*qōdesh*], but the Song of Songs is most holy [*qōdesh qodāshîm*]'[55] (*M. Yadayim*, iii, 5) and the term כתבי הקדש *kitvê ha-qōdesh* does not mean 'the writings of God' or 'the writings of the Temple'[56] but 'holy writings' [Hagiographa]. The expression לשון הקדש *lĕshôn ha-qōdesh* and רוח הקדש *rûaḥ ha-qōdesh* can be interpreted respectively both as 'holy tongue' and as 'the tongue of God', as 'the holy spirit' and as 'the spirit of God'. Why then was the form *ha-qōdesh* chosen? The probable explanation is that *ha-qādôsh* was used at the close of the Tannaitic period also as an attributive in connection with men,[57] and consequently an abstract and less common form was chosen; but not content with that the Sages added to the epithet the benediction ברוך הוא *bārûkh Hû* ['blessed be He'], in order to obviate any misunderstanding. However, when this distinguishing addendum was made, the abbreviation of it הקב״ה *HQBH* was interpreted as הקדוש ברוך הוא *Ha-Qādôsh bārûkh Hû* ['the Holy One, blessed be He'] and only Aramaic retained the formula [with the abstract noun, 'Holiness'] קודשא בריך הוא *Qudshā bĕrîkh Hû*. The epithets *Qōdesh* and קב״ה *QBH* express — like the designation קדוש ישראל *Qĕdôsh Yiśrā'ēl* ['the Holy One of Israel'], which occurs frequently in the Book of Isaiah (in the first and second parts) — both the sense of exaltation, sublimity, and reverence towards God, and the concept inclining to the ethical and rational aspect.[58]

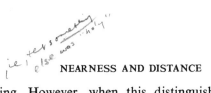

Among the appellations that have been ousted and changed is to be counted also עליון *'Elyôn* ['Most High']. The word occurs forty-four times in the Bible. In thirty-four of these it is an attributive of God (for example, 'God Most High') or serves as an epithet — 'the Most High' — in place of the Divine name. So, too, in Aramaic in the Book of Daniel: אלהא עליא *'Ĕlāhā 'Illā(y)'ā* ('God Most High' — iii 26, 32; v 18, 21) alongside *'Illā(y)'ā* ('the Most High' — iv 21, 29, 31). It has now also been established beyond doubt that the designation ὕψιστος, which occurs so frequently in the Greek Sirach, is only the translation of *'Elyôn* in the Hebrew original.[59] In the fragments discovered at Massada, *'Elyôn* appears even in passages where the Greek version renders κύριος. The widespread use of ὕψιστος in the pseudepigraphical literature, and in the Jewish diaspora, in papyri and in tombstone inscriptions, has already been noted by many scholars.[60] But no explanation has been given of the fact that *'Elyôn* does not occur either as an attributive of God, or as His by-name,[61] in the Midrash, or Tosefta,[62] or other Rabbinic sources. Incidentally, in the Dead Sea Scrolls,[63] too, the word is found only a few times, mostly in prayers, as in the Eighteen Benedictions or in rhetorical phrases borrowed from the Bible. The cause of this phenomenon lies, apparently, in the fact that *'elyôn* ['upper'] is very common in Rabbinic sources as an adjective applied to various objects and their parts in contrast to תחתון *taḥtôn* ['lower']. Whereas this usage is infrequent in the Bible, it is the rule in Rabbinic language and completely ousted the use of the word as a Divine epithet. In several sources *'elyôn* is replaced by מעלה *ma'ălā* ['on high'].[64] The occurrence of the Greek word ὕψιστος in the Midrash is rather doubtful.[65]

CHAPTER V

THE EPITHET *GĔVÛRĀ* AND THE MIGHT OF GOD

In our discussion thus far, one great fundamental was stressed — the omnipresence of God. With this Divine attribute is conjoined another, namely His 'omnipotence'. The idea of the power and ability of the Deity is deeply embedded in the foundation of every religion, beginning with the primitive cults. We know the Melanesian concept of *mana*, which expresses power, and the corresponding terms of other tribes including the names *'Ēl—'Ēlîm* [literally, 'power—powers'; rendered 'god—gods'].[1]

The power and might of God play an important role in many Rabbinic dicta, and it appears that the emphasis given to them had a practical significance in various periods. This significance is clearly evident in the homily of R. Abbahu in the name of R. Eleazar[2]: ' "Happy is he that hath the God of Jacob for his help..." What is written thereafter? — "who made heaven and earth..." But what is the connection between the one verse and the other? The answer is that if a human king has a patron, he rules over one province, but does not rule over any other; even if you take a cosmocrator, he rules over the land — does he also rule over the sea? But[3] the Holy One, blessed be He, rules over the sea and over the land, and He delivers on the sea from the water, and on land from fire; it was He who delivered Moses from the sword of Pharaoh, Jonah from the bowels of the fish, Hananiah, Mishael and Azariah from the fiery furnace, and Daniel from the pit of lions.' The images of the homily are borrowed from the *milieu* of the Roman Orient. The patron is the governor of a province, beneath whom are the *duces* and various kings. The cosmocrator is the Roman emperor, but above him is a Ruler of vaster and more embracing power and ability.

This omnipotence does not inspire dread, but, on the contrary, strengthens the feeling of nearness and man's trust in this proximity. The following story, which forms the sequel to the above exposition, expresses the thought with unique simplicity, showing how deeply the concept had penetrated the popular strata.

> R. Tanḥuma said: There is a story about a ship carrying Gentiles that was sailing from the Mediterranean [literally, 'the Great Sea'], and there was a Jewish youth [*tînôq*] on board. A great storm arose on the sea, and each passenger arose and began taking his god in his hand and calling (unto it), but to no avail. When they saw that (their prayers) did not avail, they said to the Jew: 'My son, arise, call unto thy God! For we have heard that He answers you when you cry unto him, and that He is mighty.' Forthwith, the youth arose and cried with all his heart, and the Holy One, blessed be He, accepted his prayer and the sea grew calm. When they reached land, they all disembarked to buy their requirements. Said they to the youth: 'Do you not want to sell anything?' Said he to them: 'What would you require from a poor stranger like me?' They replied: 'You are a poor stranger? It is they who are poor strangers! Some of them are here and their idols are in Babylon; others are here and their idols are in Rome; others again are here and their idols are with them, yet profit them nought. But you, wherever you go your God is with you', as it is written: 'as the Lord our God is whensoever we call upon him' (*T.P. Berakhot* ix, 1, p. 13b).

The narrative is noteworthy in that it puts these arguments in the mouth of non-Jews, and the representative of the absolute faith is a *tînôq* (literally, 'a child'; in Rabbinic literature and in the Middle Ages it denotes 'a young man'); and two truths are underlined here: first that God is mighty. The Deity must perforce have absolute power. The Gentiles on board ship mention Babylon and Rome. If their gods are active, they remain bound to a given place, whereas you, O Jew! — God is with you everywhere. The omnipotence of God — an omnipotence that brings into relief His greatness in the sense of sublimity, which in effect serves to underscore His farness — contains an assurance that this nearness is not a mere fantasy, lacking all value, and a figment of mythology. 'The Holy One, blessed be He, appears far away, yet is there none nearer than He', but 'the idol appears near, yet is actually far away' (*T.P. ibid.*, p. 13a). Here there is also an answer to the charges levelled by Gentiles against the Jewish faith, to wit, that they cannot accept a faith that is not represented by images and idols; such an abstract faith seemed to them a form of atheism, of denial of the Godhead. Hence came the reply: The Holy One, blessed be He, appears far away, yet none is nearer than He; and *vice versa* in the cases of the idol.

In order to elucidate the Rabbinic conception of God's all-embracing power and might, it is advisable to make a few preliminary observations about the problem inherent in this term and the manner of its solution in other religions. In the Greek religion, as it is reflected in the poems of Homer, the gods are clearly not omnipotent. There are bounds to the sphere of their dominion — not only to that of each invididual divinity, who is limited by another deity, but also to their collective power. The boundary is *death*. There is no god that can revive the dead. Even a goddess is unable to save her beloved from death, if the *Moira* — the decree of death — has decided it. We are familiar with the saying, found already in Herodotus, that the power of the gods cannot withstand fate and necessity. Fate is also intrinsically different from the gods. The latter help man, bestow good and light upon him. Fate is essentially negative. From it stems death, calamity, annihilation. The question, of course, arises: If calamities and misfortunes, and particularly death, are unalterable, what use or value is there in the help of the gods? Walter Otto answers[4] that, in truth, relative to a religion whose God transcends nature, the answer to such a question is necessarily negative. If the deity is outside Nature and is unable to obviate Fate, he is useless. But in the Greek religion, in which the divine is identical with the bliss of life, there is a gulf separating the divine from death. The gods differ from man only in knowing what the *Moira* determined. Now *Moira* is not a personality; it is the law that transcends everything and determines each one's fate,[5] that is, death and collapse. Death is outside the sphere of the dominion of the gods, which are a part of life. This conception implicitly raised the problem that was also formulated in the fifth century by Euripides, the author of the tragedies: If there exists something like Fate, the gods are superfluous; and if the gods are dominant, then Fate is of no consequence. In truth, the boundaries become blurred, and when the godhead, or a god, is spoken of in general terms, the reference is to Destiny or Fate — in effect to 'the course of events in the world', and the term 'god' is only 'an abstraction devoid of personality'.[6]

The religion of Israel included, *ab initio*, also death in the capacity and power of God. It thus excluded from its teaching any dualistic belief or magical concept, which necessarily posits the existence of forces that can affect the Deity and detract from His omnipotence. The God of the Bible contains all powers: He is the 'Almighty God' — He is the 'Lord of Hosts'. His might is expressed in His absolute dominion over nature, both in the normal course of its phenomena and in catastrophic occurrences. Of both categories the poet sang in Psalms civ 9, 'Thou didst set a bound which they should not pass, so that they might not again cover the earth' and also 'Who looketh on the earth, and it trembleth; He toucheth the mountains, and they smoke' (*ibid.* v. 32), and He is the God, who 'slayeth, and maketh alive; He bringeth down to the grave, and bringeth up' (I Samuel ii 6).

His might is manifested with special emphasis in the sphere of the history of the individual person and the nations. Of this the poet sang in Psalms cvi 2, 'Who can express the mighty acts of the Lord, or make all His praise to be heard?' He delivered Israel from Egypt 'that He might make His mighty power to be known'. His might also assures redemption, for God 'will punish the host of the high heaven on high, and the kings of the earth upon the earth' (Isaiah xxiv 21). This might is cited by the prophet of consolation as a reason, when he proceeds to describe the end of days and the universal goal of history. In Nebuchadnezzar's dream, according to Daniel's interpretation, God is the source of the kingdom, the power and the might, and He causes kingdoms to pass away and kings to rule (Daniel ii 31 ff). These two aspects of the Lord's might — His absolute dominion over nature and over history — are also emphasized in the teachings of the Sages, but their doctrine also has other aspects. They coined the epithet *Gĕvûrā* ['might'], which serves to stress the power and the omnipotence of God. In the Septuagint, *Ṣĕvā'ôt* ['Hosts'] is rendered παντοκράτωρ — the 'Omnipotent Ruler', and *YHWH Ṣeva'ôt* is Κύριος παντοκράτωρ. The pseudepigraphical literature also uses this expression, but does not call God *Gĕvûrā* ['Might'].[7]

In order to understand the specific character of this epithet, with all the ideas and intentions implicit in its use, we must carefully examine the passages in which it occurs. We find this designation as part of the phrase *mi-pî ha-Gĕvûrā* ['from the mouth of the Almighty'], but also apart from it already in the time of R. Eliezer and R. Joshua: ' "With the edge of the sword" ... R. Eliezer said ...from this we learn that this battle was fought specifically at the command of the Almighty [*ʿal pî ha-Gĕvûrā*']' (*Mekhilta de-R. Ishmael*, Massekhta da-ʿAmalek, Bĕ-shallaḥ, i, p. 181); 'R. Joshua said: Before they turned (to look towards the wilderness) the Almighty [*Ha-Gĕvûrā*] had revealed Himself' (*ibid.*, Massekhta de-Wa-yissaʿ, ii, pp. 162–163). ' "And Moses led": R. Joshua said: On this journey (the Israelites) went only at the bidding of Moses, but on all the other journeys they went at the injunction of the Almighty [*ʿal pî ha-Gĕvûrā*]... R. Eliezer said: They journeyed at the injunction of the Almighty...' (*ibid.*, Wa-yissaʿ, i, p. 152; in the *Mekhilta de-R. Simeon b. Yoḥai*, p. 101: 'R. Eleazar of Modiʿim'). ' "And the people murmured against Moses" ... R. Eleazar of Modiʿim said: The Israelites were accustomed to complain against Moses, and not against Moses only did they speak, but (even) against the Almighty [*Ha-Gĕvûrā*]' (*Mekhilta de-R. Ishmael, op. cit.*, p. 155; *Mekhilta de-R. Simeon b. Yoḥai*, p. 103). ' "I will give thee counsel, and God be with thee" — go and consult the Almighty [*Gĕvûrā*]' (*Mekhilta de-R. Ishmael*, Massekhta da-ʿAmalek, Jethro, ii, p. 197; *Mekhilta de-R. Simeon b. Yoḥai*, p. 133). The Tannaim, beginning with R. Ishmael, and likewise the Amoraim, use the epithet *Gĕvûrā* particularly in connection with the giving of the Torah and the revelation of God. On the verse 'Because he hath despised the word of the Lord, and hath broken His commandment' (Numbers xv 31) it is stated: 'Rabbi Ishmael said: Scripture speaks here of idolatry, for it is said, "Because he hath despised the word of the Lord" — he was contemptuous of the First Commandment uttered to Moses by the mouth of the *Gĕvûrā* "I am the Lord thy God... Thou shalt have no other gods before Me"' (*Sifre Numbers*, § 112, p. 121); and in the name of the same R. Ishmael it is reported: ' "I am" and "Thou shalt not have" we heard from the mouth of the *Gĕvûrā*' (*T.B. Horayot* 8a). In a Baraita it is further stated: 'The Rabbis have taught: What was the procedure of instruction in the Oral Law? Moses learnt from the mouth of the *Gĕvûrā*, then Aaron entered and Moses taught him his lesson...' (*T.B. ʿEruvin* 54b). In another Baraita that speaks of the giving of the Torah, R. Jose bar Judah says: '... And what did Moses answer the *Gĕvûrā*?'[8] ' "And all the people perceived the thunderings" ... R. Akiba said: They saw and heard that which was visible; they saw a word of fire issue from the mouth of the *Gĕvûrā* and become hewn out upon the Tables' (*Mekhilta de-R. Ishmael*, Massekhta de-Ba-ḥodesh, ix, p. 235). When R. Ishmael b. R. Jose was asked whether he was worthy of learning Torah from Rabbi, he replied: 'Was Moses then worthy to learn Torah from the mouth of the *Gĕvûrā*?' (*T.B. Yevamot* 105b). In the name of the Amora R. Joḥanan it is reported: 'What is the meaning of the Scripture, "The Lord giveth the word: They that publish tidings are a great host"? — Each word that issued from the mouth of the *Gĕvûrā* was divided into seventy tongues' (*T.B. Shabbat* 88b). 'No break is made in (the public reading of) the curses... Said Abbaye: This was taught only with regard to the curses in Leviticus, but in (the reading of) the curses in Deuteronomy a break may be made. What is the reason? The former are formulated in the plural, and Moses pronounced them in the name of the *Gĕvûrā*, but the latter are formulated in the singular and Moses pronounced them in his own name.'[9] 'The Holy One, blessed be He, said to him (Moses): By thy life, all the prophets prophesy each inspired by [literally, 'from the mouth of'] the other. Thus the spirit of Elijah rested upon Elisha, the spirit of Moses rested upon the seventy elders... but thou dost prophesy by the inspiration of the *Gĕvûrā*. "The spirit of the Lord God is upon me, because the Lord hath anointed me to bring tidings to the humble" ' (*Pesiqta de-Rav Kahana*, Naḥamu, Buber 125b–126a; ed. Mandelbaum, p. 270).

It seems that the expression occurs in this context also in the Gospels, only the translators and commentators have not understood its meaning. In Mark i, 22 it is stated: ὡς ἐξουσίαν ἔχων καὶ οὐχ ὡς οἱ γραμματεῖς. The accepted translations — 'as one who had authority' [English versions], Macht begabt, gewaltsam [German], Delitsch 'as a man of dominion' [Hebrew]—are incorrect.[10] The true interpretation is: not like the scribes who report the statements of others, but 'as one who speaks from the mouth of the *Gĕvûrā*'.[11] Thus we find that the epithet *Gĕvûrā* was used in connection with revelation already at the end of the first century. What is the significance of this use, and is it merely fortuitous that the epithet *Gĕvûrā* was widely used in the second and third centuries, particularly in this context? In order to answer this question, we should consider the conception of *Gĕvûrā* that obtained in the environment of the Sages. Without doubt, this epithet corresponds to the term δύναμις that occurs also in Matthew xxvi 64. Jesus declares: 'Hereafter shall ye see the son of man sitting on the right hand of the *Gĕvûrā* (ἐκ δεξιῶν τῆς δυνάμεως).[12]

The concept 'dynamis' played an important role in the moulding of religious views in the ancient world, beginning with the third century B.C.E. It derives from the sciences. Aristotle distinguished between 'dynamis', that is potential power, and 'energia', actual power. The doctrine of sympathy, which originated in the discovery of natural forces in objects, forces that could be used in medicine and in magic, was widely current in the first century B.C.E. It was adopted by astrologers, who made use of it in order to explain the influence of the heavenly bodies, and was given a central place in Stoic physics.[13] The force was depicted as a form of breathing. πνεῦμα, πνοή, and the concept of power, with all its obscurities, developed into the miraculous and the mysterious. About two hundred B.C.E. an occult literature began to burgeon in Egypt in the form of physical explanations, whose object was to reveal the miraculous powers of various objects in the organic and inorganic world, their hidden characteristics and the sympathies and antipathies attaching to them. This pseudo-science had a great influence on the conception of the term 'power' in religious literature, and also affected religious life at the end of the age of antiquity. At the close of the Hellenistic epoch the gods no longer appeared personally to perform miraculous deeds; the theophany was a manifestation of δυνάμεις or ἐνέργειαι. The deities were no longer revealed in natural phenomena but in their underlying powers.[14] At the close of the pagan era, those who had not abandoned their gods were reconciled to the monotheistic concept with the help of the doctrine of power. Thus, it was possible to describe the various gods as powers of the sungod. In *Poimandres*, the principal hermetic work, we find a description like this: When the soul ascends to the planetarian spheres and is stripped of its corporeal powers, it approaches the eighth sphere equipped with its own power, and it joins those who exist there in a song of praise to the Father. It hears the powers above the eighth sphere praising God. They ascend to the Father and deliver themselves to Him in order to be changed into powers, and when they become powers they are in God. That is the happy end of those who possess the highest illumination — the gnosis.

The worship of images received a new meaning (see above, p. 23). Even the philosopher Plotinus (the third century C.E.) was of the opinion that although the deities do not actually dwell in the idols, yet their powers reside in them. With the help of complicated rituals the worshippers sought to bring down the divine power to the image. In this notion is also to be found the explanation of the vast dissemination of acts of sorcery and magic arts, which is evidenced by the magical amulets, inscriptions, and papyri. Underlying them all was the concept of power.

Even the worship of the kings, as it was practised and accepted in Egypt with respect to the Ptolemies and in the Roman empire from the time that Octavian received the title *Divus*, was primarily a cult of force. The power found expression in the assurance of order and a secure régime for the social structure, particularly after periods of wars and disturbances, whether it was after the death of Alexander or the protracted civil wars of the first century B.C.E.[15] It is necessary to remember all these facts and to consider all the religious ideas bound up with the concept of power in the ancient world in the environment of the Talmudic and Midrashic Sages, in order to understand why this subject exercised them so much and why they devoted so much attention to it. Stories, conversations, and dicta, which at first appear to be devoid of value and meaning, assume significance and the reality underlying them becomes apparent, when they are read in the light of these facts.

The might of the Lord is underscored in contrast to that of a human king:

> 'I will sing unto the Lord, for He is highly exalted.' To what can this be compared? To a human king who entered a country,

and all praised him, saying that he was mighty, whereas he was weak; that he was rich, whereas he was poor; that he was wise, whereas he was foolish; that he was compassionate, whereas he was ruthless; that he was just and faithful, whereas he had none of these virtues, only everyone flattered him, but He who spoke and the world came into being is not so. However great the praise given Him, He transcends His praises. 'I will sing unto the Lord' that He is mighty, as it is said 'The great, the mighty, and the terrible God' (Deuteronomy x 17); and it says 'The Lord strong and mighty, the Lord mighty in battle' (Psalms xxxiv 8); and it says 'The Lord will go forth as a mighty man, He will stir up His fury like a man of war; He will cry, yea, He will shout aloud, He will prove Himself mighty against His enemies' (Isaiah xlii 13); and it says 'There is none like unto Thee, O Lord; Thou art great, and Thy name is great in might' (Jeremiah x 6). 'I will sing unto the Lord' that He is rich, as it is said 'Behold, unto the Lord thy God belongeth the heaven' etc. (Deuteronomy x 14); and it says 'The earth is the Lord's and the fulness thereof' etc. (Psalms xxiv 1); and it says 'The sea is His, for He made it' (*ibid.* xcv 5); and it says 'Mine is the silver, and Mine the gold' etc. (Haggai ii 8); and it says 'Behold, all souls are Mine; as the soul of the father, so also the soul of the son is Mine; the soul that sinneth, it shall die' (Ezekiel xviii 4)....' (*Mekhilta de-R. Ishmael*, Massekhta de-Shira, i, p. 119; see *Mekhilta de-R. Simeon b. Yoḥai*, p. 73).

In accordance with the practice of the Sages, their ideas are conveyed in a homiletical manner, and the concatenation of verses found here shows that we have before us a Tannaitic exposition, dating at least from the second century. Here is a new hymn on the Lord's might, which stands in absolute contrast to that of a human king, for the latter requires the eulogy. It signifies the recognition of his power, and those who laud him flatter him, his might not being according to their panegyrics. But the might of the Holy One, blessed be He, who is the One who spoke and the world came into being, is beyond all praise, it is absolute, and is not dependent on eulogy. This might connotes dominion over the whole world — over life and death. This is the meaning of the riches, wisdom, compassion, justice and splendour.

The second benediction of the *ʿAmida prayer* [the Eighteen Benedictions; literally 'Standing prayer'], which is called in the Mishna (*Rosh Ha-Shana* iv 5) *Gĕvûrôt* ['Mighty Deeds'], epitomizes Rabbinic teaching on *Gĕvûrā*. When the Sages saw the need to emphasize the belief in the resurrection of the dead (below, chapter xv), they gave it a central position in the blessing of *Gĕvûrôt* and made it begin and end with 'the resurrection of the dead', for death, too, is one of *the mighty deeds of the Lord*, but it is not the boundary — He rules over it, reviving the dead. With reference to the Mishna 'We make mention of the mighty deeds of rain in [the benediction of] The Resurrection of the Dead' (*M. Berakhot* v, 2), the Amoraim asked why rain is mentioned in this benediction, and they explained: 'Because it is equivalent to the resurrection of the dead' and 'just as the resurrection of the dead means life to the world, so rainfall means life to the world' (*T.B. Berakhot* 33a; *T.P. ibid.* v, 2, p. 9a). God is 'the Author of mighty deeds', and there is no power apart from His. 'Blessed be He with whose strength and might the world is filled' (*M. Berakhot* iv, 2). The anthropomorphic metaphors in the Bible that speak of God as a warrior, girded with a sword and wearing a coat of mail and helmet, provided an excuse for the deification of the warrior king, and, on the other hand, also paved the way for a dualistic interpretation, which saw in God the man of war, the intermediate deity, the demiurge. Answers to arguments of this kind are to be found in sources of the second century:

> 'The Lord is a man of war, the Lord is His name' — He wages war with His name, and needs none of these attributes... for He appeared at the sea like a Warrior who did battle, as it is said, 'The Lord is a man of war'; He appeared at Sinai as an Old Man full of compassion... so as not to give an excuse to the Gentile nations to say that *there are two divine powers*; hence (it is written) 'The Lord is a man of war, the Lord is His name' — it is He who was in Egypt, it is He who was at the sea... (above, p. 38).

To this polemic against the believers in two divine powers the redactor of the *Mekhilta* contributes a kind of hymn on the Lord's might, stressing the contrast between it and that of a national hero:

> There is sometimes a hero in a country, and he is equipped with

every weapon, but he has no strength and no power, no strategy and no ability for warfare; but the Holy One, blessed be He, is not so: He has strength and power and strategy and ability to make war... There is sometimes a hero in a country who has strength; but his strength at the age of forty is not like that which he has at fifty, nor is his strength at fifty like that at the age of sixty, nor is his strength at sixty like that of seventy, for the older he gets the more his strength diminishes; not so, however, is He who spoke and the world came into being, but 'For I the Lord change not'... There is sometimes a hero in a country, but once the arrow leaves his hand, he can no longer recall it; but the Holy One, blessed be He, is not so: for when Israel do not do His will, an edict, as it were, issues from Him... as soon, however, as they repent, He withdraws it... When a human king goes to war and provinces approach him and petition him for their needs, they are told: He is troubled, he is going to war; when he is victorious in battle and returns, then come with your petitions to him. But the Holy One, blessed be He, is not so: 'the Lord is a man of war', for He fights against Egypt; 'the Lord is his name', for He hears the cry of all mankind...[16]

His Power includes his ability to repent

Clearly, we have here a polemic directed against the conception of the hero emperor as a manifestation of power, the difference between this earthly phenomenon and the Divine revelation being brought into relief. The ending is actually based on historical realities: when a rebellion broke out in one of the provinces of the empire, or when the emperor went forth to war against the Persians and he passed through the various provinces, the representatives of the provinces would come to present their petitions. As a rule the answer was: When the emperor returns victorious from his wars, you can present to him your petitions.

The might and power of God are incomparable and illimitable. The contrast is emphasized in order to negate the worship of kings and of idols, both of which, as we have seen, are linked to a certain conception of power. In the light of these circumstances, the expositions of the Tannaim become comprehensible; for example, ' "Who is like unto thee, O Lord, among the gods?" — who is like unto Thee among those who call themselves divinities? Pharaoh called himself a god... Sennacherib called himself a god... Nebuchadnezzar called himself a god... the prince of Tyre called himself a god....' (*Mekhilta de-R. Ishmael*, Massekhta de-Wa-yĕhî, viii, pp. 142–143; *Mekhiltā de-R. Simeon b. Yoḥai*, p. 91). To this list of kings could be added 'the emperors of Rome who called themselves gods'. Every listener understood that this was the intention. The Sages were able to continue the polemic against the belief in the power of the idols — 'those which others called gods' — when they interpreted and carried forward the Biblical debate, like that in the last chapters of Isaiah. This disputation concerning the omnipotence of Israel's God assumed particular practical significance when the Temple was destroyed and Israel was deprived of its independence. We have testimony for it from both sides. That the teachers of the people whose independence had been taken away, whose land had been conquered, and whose Sanctuary laid in ruins should stand and proclaim that their God was all-powerful and 'the Lord of all creation' (*Mekhilta de-R. Ishmael*, Massekhta de-Wa-yissaʿ, vi, p. 175) could arouse only astonishment and derision among Gentiles. These are reflected in the words of Nebuchadnezzar, when he addressed Hananiah, Mishael, and Azariah: 'If your God has power and strength [dynamis], He will deliver you from my hand.'[17] The most drastic expression given to them is found in the famous Haggadah concerning Titus, who, upon entering the Temple, 'took a sword and cut down the curtain (of the Holy of Holies)... he dragged a harlot into the Holy of Holies and began to blaspheme, and revile, and insult, and spit at God on high, saying: "Is He the One of whom ye said that He slew Sisera and Sennacherib? Behold, I am in His house and in His domain; if He has power, let Him go forth and stand against me... he made a kind of enclosure and dismantled the lamps therein, and he collected the Temple vessels, and filled three ships with men, women, and children, that he might go and glorify himself overseas (i.e. in the triumphal procession in Rome)... he embarked, (thereupon) a billow arose (to drown him) in the sea; so he stood on (the) ship's deck and began to blaspheme, and revile, and insult, and spit at, (God on high). He said: "When I was in His house and in His domain, He had no strength to come and stand against me, yet now He confronts me here! Apparently (the) power of the God of the Jews resides in water: the generation of the Flood — it was only by water that He punished them; even as He did to Pharaoh so He seeks to do to me (that is to say, their God is only the God of the water and the sea). The Omnipresent then intimated to the sea and it ceased raging....' Thereafter it is related how a gnat caused the death of Titus (*'Avot de-R. Nathan*, Recension II, vii; it is also found in other sources). Here the doctrine of God's absolute power is expounded in contrast to the accepted polytheistic conception.

Titus's argument was not invented by the Sages. It was adduced by many. We shall cite it — on account of its clear foımulation — from the work of one of the church writers, Minucius Felix, who wrote at the beginning of the third century. A representative of the pagans, called Caecilius, argues: 'Who is the One God who is unknown to a free people, to a kingdom, or at least to a faith known in Rome? Only the hapless Jewish people also served One God, but they did so in public, in temples with altars, sacrifices and rituals. But the One is so lacking in strength and power (here we have the explicit argument: a God, but lacking power and might) that He as well as His people are captive in the hands of the Romans.'[18]

This is the argument that the Sages also put into the mouth of Titus, at the time when he destroyed the Temple,[19] and without doubt they heard this contention in public. It seems that the other legends, parables, and dialogues concerning power likewise had an actual significance.

Special interest attaches to the 'marginal' note added to the main narrative by the Tanna Abba Ḥanan, the disciple of R. Eliezer b. Hyrcanus: 'Abba Ḥanan said: "O Lord God of hosts, who is mighty as Thou art, O Lord?" (Psalms lxxxix 9 [8]) — Thou art mighty in that Thou dost hear the blasphemy and reviling and insults of that wicked man and dost remain silent.'[20] Obviously, Abba Ḥanan did not make his observation with reference to the narrative in the form in which we have quoted it, for in it Titus is punished; thus the Almighty was not silent. Possibly Abba Ḥanan is also the author of the following anonymous dictum in the *Mekhilta*:[21] ' "Who is like unto Thee among the *'ēlîm* [literally, 'gods'], O Lord?" — who is like unto Thee among the dumb [*'illĕmîm*], who, like Thee, hears the humiliation of His sons and remains silent?...' At any rate, the two dicta transcend the entire debate about power, since according to them God's might exists even when it is not demonstrated and visible. It was actually this view, as we shall see, that gained the acceptance of the Amoraim.[22]

But before we consider their teachings, let us revert to the epithet *Gĕvûrā*. We have found sources in which this designation appears specifically in connection with the revelation of God. The influence of this fact is discernible even in homilies in which the epithet *Gĕvûrā* is not expressly mentioned. The verse 'O Lord, my strength [ʿuzzî]' and my stronghold [*māʿuzzî*], and my refuge, in the day of affliction'[23] is expounded in the *Mekhilta* thus: ' "The Lord is my strength [ʿozzî] and song" — "my strength" means nothing else but Torah... Another explanation is, "my strength" is but another expression for sovereignty... "my strength" means only my power. Now all the nations of the world utter the praise of the Holy One, blessed be He, but mine is pleasanter and more beautiful before Him than theirs' (*Mekhilta de-R. Ishmael*, Massekhta de-Shira, iii, p. 126, and the parallels referred to there). ' "Thou hast guided them in Thy strength" — on account of the Torah, which they are destined to accept, "Thy strength" being but another designation for Torah...' (*ibid.*, ix, p. 146). 'But the Holy One, blessed be He, is giving His people and His loved ones the Torah, as it is said: "The Lord will give strength unto His people" ' (*ibid.*, Massekhta da-ʿAmalek, Jethro, i p. 188). In parallelism with the use of *Gĕvûrā* as a term for Divine revelation, the words 'strength' [*ʿoz*] and 'stronghold' [*māʿoz*] are expounded in the above-mentioned Tannaitic homilies in the sense of Torah, namely the revelation of God. Similar expositions are to be found also in the Amoraic homilies, for example: 'The Holy One, blessed be He, will have put on seven robes from the time that the world was created until He will punish wicked Edom... When He gave the Torah, He clothed Himself with strength, as it is said "The Lord hath girded Himself with strength" (Psalms xciii 1)...'[24]; ' "A wise man scaleth the city of the mighty": "the city of the mighty" — this means the heavens, which are the city of the angels. "A wise man scaleth" — this is Moses, who ascended to Heaven. "And bringeth down the stronghold wherein it trusteth" — this refers to the Torah. And how do we know that the ministering angels are called "mighty"? For it is said "Ye mighty in strength, that fulfil His word" (Psalms ciii 20). And how do we know that Moses ascended on high [to Heaven]? For it is said... And whence do we know that the Torah is called strength, for it is said "The Lord will give strength unto His people" (Psalms xxix 11)...' (*Midrash Tehillim* xxi 22).

The view that the Torah and its revelation are to be regarded as an expression of God's might and power finds parallels in *The Wisdom of Solomon* and in the writings of Philo. The author of *The Wisdom of Solomon* says of wisdom that it is 'the breath of the might of God' (τῆς τοῦ θεοῦ δυνάμεως). Thus God's might is expressed in wisdom, and wisdom is the product of this might. Philo, too, declares: 'Wisdom is the highest and chiefest of His powers'.[25] The powers are not visible in their essence, just as God, to whom they belong, cannot be thus perceived, but their work leaves an impress and effect, even as a wax seal leaves its impress without being in the least altered. Hence they are also called 'ideas'. We have here a complete identification of the powers with the ideas, with a play upon words: ἰδέας ἐπειδὴ ἕκαστα τῶν οὐτῶν εἰδοποιοῦσι (= give shape).[26] The whole universe exists by means of invisible powers, which the Creator has made to encompass existence from the ends of the earth to the ends of the heavens. These powers are unbreakable chains. What is the might of the Lord? His goodness and His lovingkindness.[27] Elsewhere he states: 'For He and His beneficent powers ever make it their business to transmute the faultiness of the worse wherever it exists and convert it to the better.'[28]

Both in *The Wisdom of Solomon* and in Philo's writings, the powers became something spiritual and immaterial, in contrast to the view prevailing in the non-Jewish Hellenistic world, which was unable — as one scholar put it — to think of power except in material terms. 'All power is material'[29]; hence even when they spoke of spirit, they depicted it as a celestial substance, as material of another kind. In *The Wisdom of Solomon* and in Philo these powers are presented as ideas, spiritual entities. In the light of this, we can also understand what the Sages did. The Divine power finds expression in Revelation, in the Revelation of the Torah. Thereby, the question of power and might is removed from the notions prevalent in the world with regard to power, and in this way we can understand the Rabbinic interpretations of the words עז *ʿōz* ['strength'] and מעוז *māʿōz* ['stronghold'], as well as the use of the term *Gĕvûrā* in the expression *mi-pî ha-Gĕvûrā* ['from the mouth of the Omnipotent'], when the revelation of the Lord is spoken of. These statements were not made in a vacuum. They form part of a complete system of thought, as reflected in the cited dicta.

But there is a difference between Philo's view and that of the Sages; for the latter could not be content with the theoretical interpretation only, which in the course of polemic and discussion led to exaggeration and the spiritualization of the concept of power — 'strength means Torah' — and to the paradoxical statement of Abba Ḥanan that God's silence is His might: 'Who is like unto Thee among the dumb?' God, who governs His world, also governs His people and congregation, protecting and preserving it. The question 'Is it fitting to give the name "Mighty" to One who sees the destruction of His House and remains silent... whose children are in chains — where is His might?'[30] never left them or ceased to trouble them. Hence they preached faith in the revelation of the Lord's strength in time to come, after the manner of the anonymous expositor of the verse 'Verily Thou art a God that hidest Thyself, O God of Israel, the Saviour' (Isaiah xlv 15): 'Isaiah said to the Holy One, blessed be He: Sovereign of the universe, verily [*'ākhēn*] Thou art a God that hidest Thyself. What is the meaning of *'ākhēn*? How canst Thou be a God that hidest thyself? Verily Thou hast power (δυνάμις in the original) and yet Thou dost hide thyself! He answered him: The God of Israel is a Saviour; I shall return and avenge' (*Canticles Rabba* iv, 8). The homilist asks here the same concrete question that had already been asked by Abba Ḥanan: How canst Thou stand and hear the blasphemy of that wicked one and remain silent? Only the preacher was not content with the Tanna's answer, to wit, that God's silence was His strength. The power and might of God exist absolutely, only their manifestation is a promise.

An eschatological orientation was given to the concept of power also by Paul, but he stresses the value of 'power' in contradistinction to the 'word'.[31] Its manifestation likewise became absolute and unconditional with the advent of 'the son of God with power according to the spirit of holiness...'; he is 'Christ the power of God, and the wisdom of God'.[32] In complete antithesis to this view, the Sages make the manifestation of the Divine power dependent on the conduct of the people and their attitude to the historic revelation of His strength, namely the Torah. We have already heard in one of the homilies that when the people repent, the Lord reveals His power. We have noted the analogy of the king, who cannot recall the arrow that has been shot, whereas God, even when He has decided to punish, withdraws His arrows, so to speak, if the people return in penitence. In one homily on the verse 'Of the Rock that begot thee thou wast unmindful, and didst forget God that bore thee' (Deuteronomy xxxii 18), the Rabbis do not argue 'Verily Thou art a God that hidest Thyself; Thou hast power and yet Thou dost hide Thyself', but they turn the argument against the people, who compel God, so to speak, to hide Himself and to withhold from them the manifestation of His might: ' "Of the Rock that begot thee thou wast unmindful" — whenever I wish to bestow good upon you, you weaken Heaven's power. You stood by the sea and said "This is my God, and I will glorify Him"; thereupon I wished to bestow good upon you, but you retracted, saying "Let us make a captain, and let us return into Egypt." You stood before Mount Sinai and said "All that the Lord hath spoken will we do, and obey"; I then wished to bestow good upon you, but you retracted and said of the calf "This is thy god, O Israel". Alas! whenever I wish to bestow good upon you, you weaken the power of Heaven' (*Sifre*, Ha'azinu, § 319, p. 365). This dictum is directed against oversimplified faith. The non-manifestation of God's power is not indicative of the absence of that power, and one must not come to God with the complaint 'where is Thy power?', but there is a nexus between the revelation of this power and the actions of human beings. Men's actions are able, as it were, to weaken His power and to prevent its being exercised; in the words of the Amora R. Judah b. R. Simon: 'So long as the righteous do the will of the Omnipresent they increase the strength of *Gĕvûrā*... but if not, then, so to speak, "they are gone without strength before the pursuer" (Lamentations i 6).'[33] We have already seen that evil deeds and transgressions can banish the Shekhina, as it were, from the world. In the view of the Sages, the ethical and religious conduct of man determines both the manifestation of God's presence in the world and the revelation of His power and might.

CHAPTER VI

MAGIC AND MIRACLE

The Rabbinic doctrine concerning God's all-embracing power has a bearing on other concepts. It excludes the possibility of the existence of magic power capable of influencing the laws of nature and the decrees of God. We have referred to the problem that confronted the Greeks in regard to the question of fate and the deity: if fate has independent and separate power, over which the gods have no control, what then is the nature of the divinities? If, on the contrary, the gods determine fate, what is the significance of fate as an independent force? The same reasoning applies to magic — it is impossible to reconcile it with the existence of an All-Powerful God. The Tanna R. Nathan, who flourished in the second half of the second century, said: 'If all the magicians of the world were to come together and seek to change morning to evening, they could not do so' (*Tanḥuma*, ed. Buber, Qoraḥ, § 6). Opposition to sorcerers is in keeping with the spirit of the Torah, only in Rabbinic literature it is much more detailed and is discussed with emphasis, indicating the actuality of the issue. Indeed R. Simeon b. Eleazar's appraisal of the matter in the Mishna is: 'fornication and sorceries have made an end of everything' (*M. Soṭa* ix, 13); and in the Tosefta (*Soṭa* xiv, 3): 'When the number of "whisperers" in court increased, wrath came upon the world and the Shekhina departed from Israel.' The Amoraim of the first generation, in the third century, held similar views: 'R. Joḥanan said: Why are they called *kashshāfîm* ['sorcerers']? Because they contradict the heavenly household [*KashshaFiM* is regarded as an abbreviation of *Kaḥash, Familia (shel) Maʿala*]' (*T.B. Sanhedrin* 67b). On the verse 'There is none else beside Him' (Deuteronomy iv 35) R. Ḥanina commented: 'Even in respect of sorceries' (*T.B. loc. cit.*). Rashi gives the explanation with precision: 'They are impotent before His decree, for there is no power besides Him.'

But this was not the accepted view among the broad masses of the people, and hence the prolonged debates and discussions on these questions. Magical practices and sorcery were widespread in the ancient world in the areas where the Sages lived, that is, throughout the Orient. The power manifested in sorcery and also the means employed in connection with it are called δύναμις.[1] The name of the God of Israel, as the God of power and might, is extensively used in magical papyri and invocations.[2]

In truth, there is a clear distinction regarding the concept of power between the prophetic-Biblical-Jewish ideology and the magical-mystic belief of the Hellenistic world. The might of God is revealed, in the Bible, in the act of creation, and in the historical Providence with which He watched over His people, which serves as a source of hope to those who love and revere Him. The power remains even when He manifests Himself — the power of an invisible God, who is immaterial. On the other hand, in the Hellenistic world the power was conceived as something impersonal, which was found in people and substances. It was a visible and material power. Magical acts were a concomitant of the nature of idolatry. Idolatry, in all its forms, believed in the existence of a source of power apart from the godhead, for it did not recognize a god who transcended the existential system that controlled everything and whose will was absolute. Magic flows from the desire to utilize these forces, and idolatry associates man with the deity in the need for magic.[3] Nor does the fact that there was also opposition to sorcery and sorcerers affect the position. Idolatry forbade injurious magic, especially in the case of a rejected and defeated religion.

To what extent the ancient world took the existence of magic for granted may also be deduced from the interesting story about R. Joḥanan b. Zakkai and the red heifer. The narrative is found, it is true, in a relatively late source, in an Amoraic account, but it may be assumed that it is older. 'A certain Gentile questioned Rabban Joḥanan b. Zakkai, saying to him: "These things that you do seem like magical practices. A heifer is brought and slaughtered and burnt and pounded and its ashes are collected, and when one of you is defiled by the dead, two or three drops are sprinkled upon him and you say to him: 'You are clean' ". He [Rabban Joḥanan b. Zakkai] answered him: "Has the spirit of *Tĕzāzît* [demon of madness or epilepsy] never entered you?" He replied: "No!" The (Sage) then said to him: "Have you not seen any one else into whom the spirit of *Tĕzāzît* has entered?" He replied: "Yes!" Thereupon (Rabban Joḥanan b. Zakkai) said to him: "And what do you do?" He replied: "We bring roots and fumigate under him and spray water upon it [the demon-spirit], and it flees." Said (the Rabbi) to him: "Do not your ears hear what your mouth speaks! Such, too, is this spirit—it is the spirit of uncleanness, as it is said: 'And also the prophets and the unclean spirit', etc. (Zechariah xiii 2)." When (the Gentile) had left, (Rabban Joḥanan b. Zakkai's) disciples said to him: "O Master, him you have thrust aside with a reed [i.e. dismissed with a paltry reply]; but what explanation will you offer us? Said he to them: "By your life! neither the dead person defiles nor does the water purify; only this is the decree of the Holy One, blessed be He. The Holy One, blessed He, hath said: I have ordained a statute, I have issued an edict, and thou hast no right to transgress mine edict." '[4] This narrative is instructive from many aspects. The enquiring Gentile wishes to show that in Israel's Torah, too, there are magical practices like those accepted in the ancient world round about. But the exorcism of the evil spirit is for him a fact not open to doubt; and when Rabban Joḥanan b. Zakkai explains to him that the sprinkling of the water mingled with the ashes is a form of exorcism, the explanation appeals to the Gentile. But to his own people, Rabban Joḥanan b. Zakkai reveals his true opinion, namely that this ritual of the sprinkling of the water of purification, which was prepared with the ashes of the heifer, has only a ceremonial significance. A corpse defiles, for this is the Halakhic rule, but this uncleanness is not an independent power, nor has the water any magical force; however, it is a precept, and by virtue of the precept, the corpse defiles and the water purifies.

We have here complete sublimation and demythologization of the heifer ritual, which served, of course, as an example of a statute [without stated reason], as it is said 'I have ordained a statute, I have issued an edict, and thou hast no right to transgress mine edict.' Whether the story was authentic — that is to say, belonged to the time of Rabban Joḥanan b. Zakkai — or not, it shows to what extent the problem was real and a subject for discussion.

But the Halakha, too, was compelled to take a stand with regard to the widespread magical practices. The Mishna defines who is a sorcerer. 'The sorcerer that performs an act is culpable,[5] but not he that (merely) creates an illusion. R. Akiba said in the name of R. Joshua: If two were gathering cucumbers (by sorcery), one may gather and not be culpable, and the other gather and be culpable: he who performs an act is culpable, (but) he who creates an illusion is not culpable (*M. Sanhedrin* vii, 11; *T.B. ibid.* 68a). According to this Halakha, which goes back to the generation of Rabban Joḥanan b. Zakkai's disciples, only one who performs a real act of magic is guilty; whereas one who creates an illusion — 'who merely pretends' — he is actually not held culpable.[6] A mere conjuror, who performs such conjuring tricks without being serious about the matter, is not guilty. The decisive condition is that the sorcerer who performs the magical act should treat his actions seriously, that is, that he should regard sorcery as something real.

Philo's approach was different from that of the Halakha; he distinguished between 'true magic', 'the visual science (ὀπτικὴ ἐπιστήμη) that examines the works of nature on the basis of clear concepts' — a most honoured science — and the delusive jugglery of itinerant magicians, who deceive and exploit the ignorant multitude. He is influenced by the Stoic definition of divination as 'the science of speculation (ἐπιστήμη θεωρητική) and of the interpretation of signs'. While the Mishna upholds the law of the sorcerer only with regard to one who performs a magical act, but not in respect of 'one who creates an illusion', Philo's entire opposition is directed principally against the latter.[7] This doctrinal attitude did not, of course, prevent the spread of magical practices — for which there is considerable evidence — especially among women. Simeon b. Sheṭaḥ ordered eighty women to be hanged in Ashkelon (*M. Sanhedrin* vi, 4). In the Palestinian Talmud (*Ḥagiga* ii, 2, 77d; *Sanhedrin* vi, 9, 23c) it is narrated at length that these women were witches. Referring to the verse 'Thou shalt not suffer a sorceress to live' (Exodus xxii 17), the

Baraita states: 'The Rabbis taught: (The law of the) sorceress applies to both man and woman. If so, why is "sorceress" specifically mentioned? Because mostly women engage in witchcraft' (*T.B. Sanhedrin*, 67a; cf. *T.B. Berakhot* 53a). R. Simeon b. Yoḥai testified: 'in the later generations when the daughters of Israel were addicted to magical practices' (*T.B. ʿEruvin* 64b); and in his name was reported the following dictum, phrased with the extremism characteristic of this Sage: 'The best of women is a sorceress' (*Tractate Soferim*, xv, end). But there is ample evidence of the widespread practice of sorcery, not only among women and simple folk, but also among the scholars in Eretz-Israel and even more so in Babylon.

In actuality, even the Sages of the Talmud and Midrash — despite their fundamental recognition that there is none besides God and that consequently witchcraft does not exist — could not ignore the facts, to wit, that broad masses of the people believed in and made use of these practices. They sought to find a compromise, in accordance with the teaching of R. Eliezer b. Jacob: ' "Neither shall ye practise divination nor soothsaying" — although there is no divination there are signs' (*T.P. Shabbat* vi, 10, p. 8c). Nor was any clear distinction drawn between science and magic, especially in the field of medicine. Among magical practices were included medicaments that originated in scientific experimentation. Hence the Sages, who prohibited an entire series of customary practices on account of 'the ways of the Amorite' [i.e. superstition],[8] were compelled to qualify their opposition. R. Samuel and R. Abbahu (said) in the name of R. Joḥanan: 'Anything that heals does not fall under the head of "ways of the Amorite" ' (*T.P. ibid.*, and *T.B. ibid.*, 67a in the name of Abbaye and Rava). We know that even Sages, especially in Babylon, used remedies that were obviously of a magical character.[9] Knowledge of witchcraft is attributed to R. Eliezer and R. Joshua (*T.B. Sanhedrin* vii, 4, 25d; *T.B. ibid.*, 68a). Rav recounted, as a fact, that 'a certain Arabian traveller' killed a camel and dismembered it [and that subsequently, it became alive again], while his uncle R. Ḥiyya told him that it was an illusion, and nothing more.[10] Of Rav himself it is said: 'He went up to a cemetery and performed certain acts', and Rashi explains what he did thus: 'He knew how to utter incantations over the graves and to comprehend, at each grave, by what kind of death (the occupant) had died, whether he had died at his proper time or through the evil eye.'[11] R. Ḥanina used to rely, in cases of inheritance, on the tradition that the spittle of the firstborn of a father heals.[12] R. Simeon b. Laqish did not refrain from allowing witchcraft to play a part in Halakhic argument.[13] There were Amoraim who endeavoured to make their curses against their enemies coincide with the moment of God's wrath, and even took steps to prevent the effects of sorcery.[14] Practices that were extremely widespread among the people were not always disallowed, but the attempt was sometimes made to give them a religious character consonant with the spirit of Israel's faith, although it was clear that the custom stemmed from a magic-mythological source. It is stated in a Baraita: 'If a tree casts its fruit, it should be painted with *siqra* [a red paint] and loaded with stones. Thereupon the Gemara asks: 'Granted that it should be loaded with stones so as to lessen its strength, but what remedy is effected by painting it with *siqra*?' The answer given is: 'So that people may see it and pray for it, as it is taught: "And he [the leper] shall cry, 'Unclean, unclean' " — he must make his grief known to the public, so that many may make supplication for him.'[15] Obviously, the original reason for the red paint derives from a popular belief in the power of the red colour. This is an example of the extrusion of magical aspects from widely current customs and their replacement by religio-ethical explanations.

A much more difficult problem than the spread of magical practices among the people was the question of legitimate miracles.

Undoubtedly, the religion of Israel, like every other religion and faith, postulates the possibility of miraculous acts. The problem is how to distinguish between miracles, which break nature's barrier and laws and accentuate the absolute power of God, and acts of magic, which likewise appear as wondrous deeds. This problem has confronted many religions, and it also challenged the Sages. Elijah's prayer on Mount Carmel, 'Hear me, O Lord, hear me' (I Kings xviii 37) was interpreted by the Amoraim of Eretz-Israel in the third century as follows: 'Hear me, that fire may come down from heaven; and hear me, that it should not be said these things are witchcraft.'[16]

Already in the Bible we find miraculous deeds — signs and portents — alongside acts of magic. The means are the same and common to both, but there is a clear, basic difference. God in the Bible does not employ, in contrast to the other gods, magical devices. Those who make use of them are only His messengers. The wonders of the Egyptian sorcerers emanate from their magical arts, which influence supradivine forces. Moses' wonders are a finger of God, who commanded him to perform them; they thus stem from His will. It is God who works miracles. The miracle serves in Scripture as a sign to the prophet-messenger, but the supreme criterion remains the same — whether it occurs by the command of the Lord. If a prophet comes and gives a sign or a portent, saying 'Let us go after other gods, which thou hast not known, and let us serve them; thou shalt not hearken unto the words of that prophet.'[17] Elisha, who seeks to heal Naaman by enjoining him to bathe seven times in the water of the Jordan, employs a means that has its parallel in Babylonian lore, but his object is to prove not only 'that there is a prophet in Israel', but also, and primarily, 'that there is no God in all the earth, but in Israel' (II Kings v 15).

The Sages of the Talmud and Midrash followed in this sphere, too, the Biblical lead, but, characteristically, they broadened and deepened their perception by viewing Biblical teaching as a whole, and by taking up an attitude towards manifestation of sorcery close to them, while controverting the beliefs and notions of their time. The common people were, of course, interested in one thing only — in the result of the action, without differentiating its source. On the other hand, the interest of the Sages was focused on emphasizing the fact that it was God who wrought the miracle[18] rather than on the miraculous act. Hence we find that their attitude to miracles, without which, as we have stated, religion cannot be envisaged, is ambivalent. The point is brought into relief in the well-known story about Ḥoni ha-Meʿaggel ['the Circle-Drawer'] and the attitude of Simeon b. Sheṭaḥ to his actions. Ḥoni ha-Meʿaggel worked a great miracle; he uttered a decree and the Holy One, blessed be He, fulfilled it and brought down rain when it was most needed. But Simeon b. Sheṭaḥ sent word to him: 'Were you not Ḥoni ha-Meʿaggel, I would pronounce a ban against you'.[19] One cannot fail to sense in Simeon b. Sheṭaḥ's words an expression of concern lest the language used by Ḥoni ('I swear by Thy great Name that I will not stir from here') and the act that he performed ('He drew a circle and stood inside it') should be misconstrued; only Ḥoni's personality and the veneration in which he was held by the people saved him from being banned. The same Simeon b. Yoḥai, who was opposed to the practice of witchcraft, was 'well-versed in miracles', and upon leaving the cave together with his son, he reduced men with a glance to heaps of bones,[20] and also exorcised an (evil) spirit from the emperor's daughter (*T.B. Meʿila* 17b). Both Talmuds and the Midrashim are full of miracles wrought by Ḥoni ha-Meʿaggel, Naqdimon b. Gorion, the Tannaim R. Ḥanina b. Dosa, R. Simeon b. Yoḥai, his son-in-law R. Phinehas b. Jair, and other wonder-workers down to the time of the last Amoraim.[21] However, Rav Papa enquired of Abbaye: 'Why is it that miracles happened to the former generations, but to us no miracle happens' (*T.B. Berakhot* 20a). This question testifies to a feeling of decline in miraculous deeds. But those who experienced miracles did not wholly come to an end; there are accounts of wonders that happened even to the last of the Amoraim (*ibid.* 54a).

In the interpretations that the Sages give to the Biblical miracles there is apparent the desire to emphasize the proof that they provide of God's strength and might. 'R. Simeon the Sidonite expounded:[22] When the wicked Nebuchadnezzar cast Hananiah, Mishael, and Azariah into the fiery furnace, Yurqamu,[23] the Prince of Hail, stood before the Holy One, blessed be He, and said to Him: "Sovereign of the Universe, let me go down and cool the furnace and deliver those righteous men from the fiery furnace." Said Gabriel to him: "The might of the Holy One, blessed be He, will not be (revealed) thereby, for thou art the Prince of Hail and all know that water extinguishes fire. But let me, the Prince of Fire, go down and cool it from within and heat it from without, and thus perform a miracle within a miracle." The Holy One, blessed be He, then said: "Go down!" At that moment Gabriel began (to praise God) and said: "And the truth of the Lord endureth for ever...." ' (*T.B. Pesaḥim* 118 a–b). Here emphasis is given to the greatness of the miracle with its inherent wonder, and *pari passu* the might that finds expression therein is demonstrated. In a parallel Midrash (*Canticles* vii 9) the practical outcome of the miracle is also mentioned: 'When the nations of the world saw the miracles and mighty deeds that the Holy One, blessed be He, had wrought for Hananiah and his companions, they took their false idols and broke them in pieces and made them into pairs of bells and hung them on their dogs and asses, and clappered them, saying: "Ye see now what we were worshipping." ' The miracle must lead to but one result, and therein lies its importance, namely the recognition of God's might and uniqueness, resulting in the breaking of the idols. Stories of this kind, which have a mythological aspect, preserve the essential principles held by the Sages. The importance of the miracle lies not in itself, but in the extent to which it accords with the faith in Him who performs the miracle. Thus R. Eleazar of Modiʿim expounded the verse 'And Moses built an altar, and called it Adonai-nissi [the Lord is my banner or miracle]': 'The Omnipresent called it "My miracle"... as long as Israel is in the miracle, so to speak, the miracle is before Him.'[24]

Most instructive is the following narrative, which has been preserved in a late Midrash, but its source is ancient. There the ethical aspect of miracles is made expressly clear to us:

> R. Phinehas said: It once happened in Damascus, where there was an idol-shrine, which had a priest called Abba Gulish, who ministered to the idol many years. Once trouble [*'ăninqê* (ἀνάγκη) *shel ṣaʿar*] came upon him. He cried to the idol many days, but to no avail. Thereafter he went out at night, and said: 'Sovereign of the universe, hearken unto my prayer and redeem me from my trouble.' Forthwith (God) hearkened to his prayer and he was healed; he then stole away and came to Tiberias and was converted to Judaism; he zealously kept the commandments and was appointed administrator of the poor. Now when money came into his custody, the hands that were accustomed to pilfer in the idol-house pilfered also the sacred funds; immediately one of his eyes began to hurt him and it went blind. Once again he misused the sacred funds, and his other eye began to pain and become blind. When compatriots of his came to Tiberias and saw that he was blind, they said to him: 'Abba Gulish, to what purpose did you mock the idol and forsake him?...' what did he do? He said to his wife: 'Arise, that we may go to Damascus. She took hold of his hand and they went. When they reached the hamlets in the vicinity of Damascus, people gathered about

him and said: 'Lo, it is Abba Gulish.' And they further said: 'The idol was right to blind your eyes'. Said he to them: 'I, too, have come only to entreat him and to make my peace with him; perchance he will restore my sight. Go and gather together all the people of the state.' They went and multitudes upon multitudes assembled in the idol-house and (even) went up on the roofs. When the place was full, he asked his wife to stand him upon a pillar that he knew there. He went and stood upon it and said to the assembly: 'My brethren, citizens of Damascus, when I was a priest and ministered to the idol, people used to leave deposits with me, and I subsequently denied receiving them, because the image has neither eyes to see nor ears to hear, so that he might punish me. Now I went to a God whose eyes roam the whole world, and no plot is hidden from Him, and my hands wished to pilfer and take as they were accustomed to do, but I scarcely managed to carry out my intention when he punished me; hence He blinded my eyes.' R. Phinehas ha-kohen bar Ḥama said, and R. Abbun also reported in the name of our teachers: Before ever he descended from the pillar the Holy One, blessed be He, gave him better sight than he had enjoyed before, so that His name might be sanctified in the world; and thousands and myriads of Gentiles were converted through him.[25]

R. Phinehas bar Ḥama belonged to the Amoraim of Eretz-Israel of the second half of the fourth century. This narrative, whose motif reminds us of the story of the conversion of Achior in the Book of Judith xiv 10, and whose language testifies that it was translated from Aramaic, makes it clear that the purpose of the miracle was to demonstrate the truth of Israel's faith and of his Torah, which forbids the misappropriation of charity or Temple funds. To the priest who was guilty of embezzlement while he was still ministering to the idol nothing happened, but once he was converted — and the conversion itself was the result of a miracle — then he was punished for his peculation. In Damascus he demonstrated this difference between idolatry and the worship of God, and the further miracle led to mass conversion.

Tales of this sort, which give expression to the purpose of the miracle in general terms, emphasizing at the same time the concept of power, are not many. More numerous are the dicta that use a miracle for the purpose of justifying the value of the commandments or of religious institutions. Of R. Akiba it is reported that he told Tineius Rufus that the River Sa(m)bation proved which was the Sabbath day.[26] Noteworthy for our subject is the story of the beast [cow] of a Jew that was sold to a non-Jew, and she refused to work on the Sabbath under the ownership of the Gentile, until her former owner came and whispered to her that she now belonged to a Gentile and is allowed to work on the Sabbath. The non-Jew said to the Jew: ' "I shall not let you go till you tell me what you did to her in her ear. I wearied myself with her and beat her, yet she would not get up." Thereupon the Jew began to console him, saying: "I performed no witchcraft nor sorcery; I merely told her thus and thus, and she stood up and ploughed." The Gentile was immediately seized with fear, saying: "Now if a cow, which has neither speech nor understanding, recognized her Creator, shall not I, who have been made by my Maker in His image and have been endowed by Him with understanding, go and acknowledge my Creator? Forthwith he went and was converted and studied and acquired knowledge of the Torah, and he was named Judah b. Torta, and to this day our teachers cite Halakha in his name.'[27] The non-Jew interpreted the whispering in the ear as an act of magic, but the Jew denied this. Undoubtedly we have a miracle here in the fact that the cow reacted to the whispered information that she had been transferred from the ownership of the Jew to that of the non-Jew, but this miracle is a consequence of the Halakha and confirms its truth; the Gentile was converted and merited the privilege that Halakha should be cited in his name. Miracles also serve to affirm the piety and virtue of the righteous in the past and in the present, as the Roman general said to Naqdimon b. Gorion 'I know that your God has brought this commotion upon the world only for your sake'.[28] Most of the miracles take place in order to deliver and save individuals or a community in times of trouble and distress, but the different motifs are frequently interlinked. The miracles and salvations that are wrought for the public are dependent upon their merit and deeds. The contradiction between the belief that God performs miracles and the difficult and depressed position of the nation served as a starting point for homilies of reproof; for example, on the verse 'Unto thee, O Lord, belongeth righteousness' (Daniel ix 7) the Midrash states:

> R. Eleazar asked, who said this verse? — Hananiah, Mishael, and Azariah uttered it. When they rose up from the furnace, all the nations of the world assembled, as it is stated, 'And the satraps, the prefects, and the governors, and the king's ministers, being gathered together,' (*ibid.* iii 27). And they stood up and spat in Israel's face, saying to them: 'You knew that your God performs such miracles and wonders, yet you brought it upon yourselves that He should destroy His house.' They spat into their faces, until they made all their bodies a mass of spittle, and Hananiah and his companions lifted their faces to heaven and justified the judgment, declaring: 'Unto Thee, O Lord, belongeth righteousness, but unto us confusion of face'.[29]

The argument put into the mouth of the Gentiles 'You knew that your God performs miracles and wonders' was derived from actual life. The belief of the Jews in miracles was well known. When Horace heard the story of the lamp that burnt without oil, he said: 'That the Jew Apella believes, not I.'[30] He was undoubtedly right in saying that Jews believed this, as the words of R. Ḥanina b. Dosa testify: 'He who commanded the oil to burn will likewise command the vinegar to burn' (*T.B. Taʿanit* 25a). But while Horace and other Greek and Roman writers regarded such tales as *Superstitio Judaica*, it was accepted in the time of R. Eleazar that the God of Israel wrought miracles and wonders, and the readiness to believe in miracles was exceedingly widespread. The problem was to reconcile this belief with the nation's destiny and with other elements of faith.

The religious value of the miracle is not absolute; it is controlled by and subject to other principles, and this is done, it appears, in various ways.

The former generations were vouchsafed miracles, because they gave their lives for the sanctification of God's Name. Precisely on account of the conception that a miracle served only to prove God's greatness and might — that is, the sanctity of his Name — the entire reason for the miracle is negatived if there is no willingness to sanctify God's Name on the part of those who perform miracles or wait for them. But whoever offers his life for the sanctification of the Divine

Name must not do so with a view that a miracle should be wrought for him. When Trajan was about to have Pappus and Lulianus executed in Laodicea, 'He said to them: "Are you not of the people of Hananiah, Mishael, and Azariah? Let your God come and deliver you from my hand." They replied: "Hananiah, Mishael, and Azariah were righteous men, and Nebuchadnezzar was worthy of having a miracle performed through him; but you are a wicked king and you are unworthy that a miracle should be wrought through you, and we are deserving of death unto Heaven...." '[31]

The best example of this standpoint, which regards the miracle as a means of sanctifying the Divine Name and makes it conditional on the other deeds of him who wishes to be vouchsafed the wonder, is to be found in the tales concerning R. Ḥanina b. Dosa, 'who was once praying when an *ʿarwād* [venomous lizard] bit him, but he did not interrupt his prayer. His disciples went and found the reptile dead at the mouth of its hole. Said they: Woe to the man whom an *ʿarwād* bites; but woe to the *ʿarwād* who bites Ben Dosa!' (*Tosefta Berakhot* iii, 20). In the Babylonian Talmud the story is recounted with differences of detail. There it is added: 'He put it on his shoulder and brought it to the House of Study, saying to them [the disciples]: "See, my sons, it is not the *ʿarwād* but sin that slays" ' (*T.B. Berakhot* 33a). Here the moral drawn from the miracle is expressly stated. The miracle points to an act sanctifying the Divine Name: by placing himself in danger and not interrupting his prayer, although the *ʿarwād* had bitten him, R. Ḥanina b. Dosa was vouchsafed a miracle. The miracle, which came in the wake of the act of self-sacrifice, still further enhanced the sanctification of the Divine Name by being instrumental also in others' regarding the miracle as a consequence of R. Ḥanina b. Dosa's devotion to prayer.

The connection between the miracle and the law of recompense is clearly brought out in another story about R. Ḥanina b. Dosa. 'The Rabbis taught: It once happened that the daughter of Neḥunia, the well-digger, fell into a large cistern and people came and informed R. Ḥanina b. Dosa. The first hour he said to them: "All is well." The second hour he (likewise) said: "All is well." The third hour he said to them: "She has come up..." So the people said to him: "Are you a prophet?" He replied: "I am neither a prophet nor the son of a prophet, but is it conceivable that in the work in which the righteous man is engaged his seed should come to grief?..." '[32] The miracle was necessary in order to prove God's righteousness.

The problem of the relationship between the laws of nature and miracles did not greatly exercise the minds of the Sages. Changes in the natural order are mentioned in Tannaitic sources in relation to the generation of the Flood — 'the Omnipresent changed for them the order of the universe, so that the sun rose in the west and set in the east'[33]; nevertheless they persisted in their rebellion. The changing of the order of the universe was not a miracle. Express differences of opinion in relation to change in the natural order is first found in the days of the Amoraim. 'The Rabbis taught: It once happened that a man's wife died and left a sucking son, and the father had not the means to pay for a wet-nurse; then a miracle happened to him and he developed breasts like the two breasts of a woman, and he suckled his son. Rav Joseph said: Come and see how great is this man that such a miracle was wrought for him! Said Abbaye to him: On the contrary, how inferior is this man, that the natural order was changed for him' (*T.B. Shabbat* 53b). Abbaye discerns an indication of inferiority in the change of the natural order that was wrought for the man, not only because 'he did not merit that the gates of remuneration should be opened to him' (Rashi), but primarily because we do not hear of any act of his warranting the miracle. The happening thus remained a breach of the order of nature[34] and was not a miracle.

Corresponding to Elihu's invitation to Job to stand and consider the wonders of God in natural phenomena (Job xxxvii 11), the view is current among the Sages that the order of creation — that is, the order of nature — bears greater testimony to the Lord's mighty deeds than the miracles that breach this law-bound system. When R. Akiba came to the verses in Leviticus xi, in which the names of beasts, birds, and crawling creatures are mentioned, 'he used to say: " 'How manifold are Thy works, O Lord!' etc. Thou hast creatures that live in the sea and that live on land. If those that live in the sea go on to the land, they die; and if those that live on dry land go into the sea, they die. There are creatures that live in fire and creatures that live in the air. If those that live in fire go into the air, they die; if those that live in the air go into the fire, they die. The place of life of the former spells death for the latter; and the place where the latter live spells death for the former. Thus Scripture declares: 'How manifold are Thy works, O Lord!' etc." '[35]

Similarly, Philo argues 'that these extraordinary and seemingly incredible events are but child's play to God' in comparison with the truly great things, namely the marvels of nature and existence.[36] At first blush it seems as though this view represents a return to primitive thinking, but it is precisely comparison with the latter that serves only to accentuate the difference. Primitive man lives in a world of miracles. Every event contains magical elements, and the sorcerer can perform miraculous deeds whenever he wishes,[37] but these miracles create no sense of wonder, nor do they serve as a sign or proof of God, who reveals His power through them and forms no part of nature. However, it is not only in nature but also in everyday life that the boundaries dividing the normal and natural from the miraculous are blurred. It once happened that 'two men went forth to do business, and a thorn got lodged in one of them; he thereupon began to blaspheme and revile (the Lord). After a time he heard that his companion's ship had sunk in the sea, whereupon he began to thank and praise (the Lord)... and this illustrates R. Eleazar's teaching: What is the meaning of the verse "Who doeth wondrous things alone; and blessed be His glorious name for ever"? — Even the one to whom the miracle happens is not conscious of the miracle vouchsafed him.' (*T.B. Nidda* 31a). R. Eleazar's statement, on the basis of which we say in the 'Prayer of Thanksgiving' [Singer's Prayer Book, p. 53] the words 'and for the miracles, which are daily with us', are explained in *Midrash Tehillim* (Psalms cvi, 1) thus:

> Many miracles and wonders dost Thou perform for us every day and no man knows. Then who does know? — Thou, O Lord. R. Eleazar b. Pedat said: See what is written: 'To Him who doeth great wonders alone' — He alone knows. And what is written thereafter? 'To Him who divided the Sea of Reeds in sunder' — the piece of bread [*pĕrûsā*, literally: 'the divided', i.e. livelihood][38] is equal in importance to the sea, which was divided in sunder. Just as the world cannot do without the piece of bread,[39] so it is not possible for the world to do without miracles and wonders. How are we to envisage this? A man is lying on a

bed, and a serpent is on the ground before him. When he seeks to rise, the serpent becomes aware of him. When he is about to put his feet on it, the serpent flees from him. And (the man) does not know what wonders the Holy One blessed be He performs for him...

Other Amoraim went even further than R. Eleazar and said that (the problem of) livelihood is greater than that of redemption and harder than the partition of the Sea of Reeds.[40] Although it is possible to argue that the miraculous construction put on earning one's livelihood is to be explained in the light of the difficult economic position obtaining in the third century in Eretz-Israel, yet this problem could have been solved by withdrawing the question of livelihood from the realm of miracles, in the spirit of Rav Naḥman bar Isaac's dictum[41]: 'Note that miracles are wrought ("by Heaven for the salvation of many human lives" — Rashi), yet food is not created' ('but that food should be created for the righteous in their homes, i.e. that they should find wheat growing in their houses, is not a common miracle' — Rashi). Hence it see msthat the sayings of the Amoraim of Eretz-Israel stem from their tendency to regard the natural order and normal occurrences as miracles. The bringing down of rain is accounted as equivalent to the resurrection, and according to R. Ḥiyya bar Abba and R. Abbahu 'The day of rain is greater than that of the resurrection of the dead.'[42]

The influence of this view is discernible also in the sphere of Halakha. With reference to the ruling in the Mishna (*M. Yevamot* xvi, 3) that evidence may be given of a man's death, in order to permit his wife to remarry, 'only after his soul has departed, even though he was seen amputated, or crucified, or being devoured by a wild beast', it is stated in the Palestinian Talmud (*ibid.* 5, p. 15c): ' "Even if he was seen amputated", for I presume that he was burnt with a heated blade and lived. "Crucified", in the case of a crucified person I presume that a Roman matron passed by and redeemed him. "Or being devoured by a wild beast", for I presume that Heaven had compassion on him. If he fell into a pit of lions, no testimony (concerning his death) is given, for I presume that he was vouchsafed miracles, as was Daniel. If he fell into a fiercy furnace, no evidence (of his death) is given, for I presume that miracles were wrought for him, as for Hananiah,

Mishael, and Azariah.' The explanations of the ruling of the Mishna are not essentially different from those given in regard to the statements of the Baraita:[43] 'If he fell into a pit of lions, if he fell into a fiery furnace.' Both sets of interpretations emanate from the presumption that we must take into account the possibility that 'Heaven would compassionate him', and that an unusual happening — in other words, a miracle — would occur to bring about the deliverance of the person in peril. The Mishna that we have cited — and also the additional Halakhot of the Baraita — is in accord with R. Meir's view, as we can infer from the next Mishna: 'If a man fell into the water, whether it has (a visible) end or not, his wife is forbidden (to remarry). R. Meir said: It once happened that a man fell into a large cistern and came up again after three days.' In the Baraita[44] the Sages dispute R. Meir's view and declare that (if a man fell) into water that has (a visible) end, his wife is permitted (to remarry), and concerning his story they said to R. Meir, 'miracles are not cited'. According to the interpretation of the Palestinian Talmud, we must conclude that they disagreed with R. Meir in regard to the other cases, too. They do not deny that the miracle occurred or the possibility of its recurring, only it may not be cited for the purpose of establishing the Halakha, because it does not belong to the permanent order. This view found its general formulation in the words of R. Jannai: 'A man should never stand in a place of danger, assuming that a miracle would be wrought for him, for perhaps it will not be wrought.'[45] R. Zera expressed himself in similar vein: 'A miracle does not happen every time'[46]; and after him Rava declared: 'We may not rely on miracles'.[47] Abbaye differed from him, saying that we may rely on a miracle. This is also related of Rav, at least when he was in the company of a scholar 'whose merit was great'. Those Sages who did not rely on miracles also did not wish to make use of their merits in order to effect a miracle. R. Jannai said: 'And if you should say that a miracle is wrought for him, his merits are reduced.' Rav Joseph also thought 'lest it be deducted from my merit in the world to come'.[48] Underlying the Sages' unwillingness to rely upon miracles is the tendency to restrict miracles. We also find a trend to limit the miracles of the past. The Mishna that informs us that the mouth of the earth that swallowed up Korah, the mouth of Balaam's ass, the rainbow, the rod, and the cloud were all created on Sabbath eve at twilight (*M. 'Avot*, v, 6) wishes to incorporate these miracles within the confines of nature. When the world was created, the universe was given the power to produce things that are outside the natural order. In the spirit of this Mishna is also the exposition of R. Jonathan, who belonged to the last of the Tannaim: 'The Holy One, blessed be He, stipulated with the sea that it should be rent asunder; this is the meaning of the verse "and the sea returned *lĕ-'ĕtānô* [E.V. 'to its strength']" (Exodus xiv 27) — that is, *li-tĕnāô* ['to its stipulation']' (*Gen. Rabba* v, 3, p. 35). R. Jonathan interprets the word *lĕ-'êtānô* in the sense of *li-tĕnāô* apparently with the intention to set the miracle within the bounds of the natural order. The passage continues there as follows: 'R. Jeremiah b. Eleazar said:[49] Not with the sea alone did the Holy One, blessed be He, make a condition, but with everything formed in the Six Days of Creation. This is the significance of the verse "I, even My hands, have stretched out the heavens, and all their host have I commanded" (Isaiah xlv 12) — I commanded the sea to be cleft, and the heavens to be silent before Moses, as it is said "Give ear, ye heavens", etc. (Deuteronomy xxxii 1); I commanded the sun and the moon to stand still before Joshua; I commanded the ravens to feed Elijah; I commanded the fire not to harm Hananiah, Mishael, and Azariah; I commanded the lions not to hurt Daniel, the heavens to open before Ezekiel, the fish to vomit out Jonah' — the entire gamut of Biblical miracles is included in the act of creation.

This view that the miracle was implanted in nature since the six days of creation is found also in Philo's writings. Although he holds that God fixed immutable laws of nature, to which powers (δυνάμεις) were given, yet, in opposition to Plato's teaching, which allows no room for miracles, Philo takes the view that these powers are not independent or autocratic. The qualities revealed in objects by miraculous acts — the sweetening of the water by means of the rod, the well in the rock — were inherent in their nature. The miracle consisted in the fact that God made them available to Moses at the requisite time. In a similar way the Stoics explained the existence of divination and astrology.[50]

It is difficult to say whether the Rabbinic dicta that we have cited on the subject resulted from extraneous influence, but it is clear that the incorporation of past miracles in the natural order is a form of rationalization that served the aim to restrict miraculous acts in the present. Just as the accentuation of God's might by means of analogies that compared Him with a human king, and by stories about miracles in the past and in the present, was explained by us against the background of religious life in the milieu of the Talmudic and Midrashic Sages, so, too, the restriction and limitation of miracles are to be understood against the background of the existing reality. Immanental tendencies and polemical aims in relation to other faiths are interlinked in this restriction. We have already stated that all faiths claim miracles in proof of their truth. That the miracle corroborates the truth and existence of God was an accepted principle in the ancient world. Stories about miracles close with the words 'Great is god so-and-so'. 'What is god? — That which is strong' is stated in a catechism preserved in a papyrus.[51] Every religion, especially one that raised the banner of proselytization, was confronted by the problem of what attitude to take towards miracles — the miracles of its own tradition and of those of other religions. Ancient Christianity adopted the principle that 'The mracle is legitimate magic, while magic is an illegitimate miracle.' On the one hand, the Apostles were opposed to magic and sorcery, and the Fathers of the Christian Church regarded the founders of sectarian groups as sorcerers, whilst the antagonism to Simon Magus (The Acts viii 9) is well known. But on the other hand, miracles occupied such an important place in the new faith that the Apostles and the Fathers of the Christian Church were caught up by the general prevailing trend and became integrated in it, while differentiating between permissible and forbidden magic. Without doubt miracles played a great role in the propagation of Christianity in the ancient world.[52] Instances of the exorcism of spirits, which occur very frequently in the Gospels, served as proof of the power of the new faith. Although it is easy to cite parallels to the miracles in the Gospels, both from the Bible and Rabbinic sources and from Graeco-Roman literature,[53] yet the importance ascribed to them by Christianity is to be explained against the background of the Messianic consciousness and the realization of the prophetic promises.[54] It is noteworthy that in the scant reports about Jesus and his disciples in Rabbinic literature they are primarily described as enchanters and

rabbinic refs to Jesus as a sorcerer

sorcerers. 'It once happened that R. Eleazar b. Dama was bitten by a snake, and Jacob of Kefar Samma came to heal him in the name of Jesus b. Panṭera, but R. Ishmael did not permit him. They said to him: "You are not permitted, Ben Dama." He answered him: "I shall bring you proof that he may heal me." But before he was able to bring such proof, he died. Said R. Ishmael: "Happy are you, Ben Dama, that you departed in peace, and did not breach the fence of the Sages, for whoever breaches the fence of the Sages suffers retribution in the end, as it is said: "He who breaketh through a fence, a serpent shall bite him." '[55] '... And a master said: Jesus practised magic, and enticed and led Israel astray.'[56] Needless to say, Christians denied this, but, on the other hand, they spoke of the power that inhered in the name 'Jesus' to exorcise evil spirits. Justin maintains (*Dial, c. Tr.*, 1, 2, 85) that the Jews cannot exorcise a single spirit by virtue of the names of their kings, saints, prophets, or patriarchs. In the light of this, we can understand the story about R. Eleazar b. Dama, which we cited above, and likewise the claim that the books of the Minim are diviners' books, that is, works on witchcraft.[57] Minim here denotes Christians or Gnostic sects. Past enemies of Israel — Pharaoh, Balaam, Amalek — appear as sorcerers. 'The Pharaoh who lived in the days of Moses was a Magus' (*T.B. Mo'ed Qaṭan* 18a). On the other hand, we find that Roman writers, including Pliny,[58] speak of Moses as a magician; his name also appears in magical papyri. It is noteworthy that, in the Midrash to the Scroll of Esther, Haman — he is the spokesman of all the revilers and blasphemers of Judaism, and sometimes the reference is not to the historical Haman — is made to say: 'There arose a sorcerer unto them called Moses the son of Amram, and he took his rod in his hand and muttered an incantation over the sea and it became dry, and he took them [the Israelites] across the seabed, but I do not know by what means he made it dry....'[59] Similarly, the victories of Joshua and David are there depicted as acts of magic. R. Jonathan and those who adopted his doctrine said, in reply to all this argumentation, that the miracles related in the Scriptures were not acts of Moses, Joshua and Elijah, but conditions made by the Holy One, blessed be He, with the work of creation.

An outstanding feature of the miracle stories in Rabbinic literature is the fact that the personality of the miracle-worker is not emphasized. The Sages were careful not to turn the person himself, who performed the miracle, into a wonder and marvel. The prayer 'He who answered Abraham' (*M. Taʿanit* ii, 4) is evidence of this. We do not pray to Abraham, our father, but to Him who answered Abraham. This point established a difference of principle between these stories and the tales about the miracles of Jesus, whose entire purpose is to accentuate his might and power. It will suffice to set side by side the following two narratives, which are similar in detail, but differ in their basic aim:

John iv 46–54

And there was an official, whose son was ill at Capernaum. When he heard that Jesus had come... he went and begged him to come down and heal his son... Jesus therefore said to him: 'Unless thou seest signs and wonders thou wilt not believe.' The man said to him... 'Sir, come down before my child dies.' Jesus said to him, 'Go, thy son will live.' The man believed the word that Jesus spoke to him and went his way. And as he was going down, his servants met him, and told him that his son was living. So he asked them the hour when he began to mend, and they said to him, 'Yesterday at the seventh hour the fever left him.' The father knew that was the hour when Jesus said to him 'Thy son will live'; and he himself believed, and all his household.

T.B. Berakhot 34b

Our Rabbis taught: Once the son of R. Gamaliel fell ill. He sent two scholars to R. Ḥanina b. Dosa to ask him to pray for him. Upon seeing them, he [R. Ḥanina b. Dosa] went up to an upper chamber and prayed for him. On coming down, he said to them, 'Go, for the fever has left him'. Said they to him: 'Are you a prophet?' He answered: 'I am neither a prophet nor the son of a prophet; but I have this tradition: if my prayer is fluent in my mouth, I know that he [the sick person] is accepted, and if not, I know that he is rejected. They sat down and wrote down the exact moment; and when they came to R. Gamaliel, he said to them: 'I swear by the Temple Service! you have stated the time neither too soon nor too late, but so it actually happened. At that moment the fever left him and he asked us for a drink of water.'

The Christian story seeks to confirm 'that this is indeed the Christ, the saviour of the world' (*ibid.*, v. 45), while the Jewish narrative puts into the mouth of R. Ḥanina b. Dosa — and also in the story that we cited above (p. 109) — the words 'I am no prophet, nor the son of a prophet'.

Even the line of demarcation drawn between the miracles of the pious and saints within the Jewish camp and the miracles of others, by proclaiming the latter witchcraft, did not satisfy everyone. There were those who preferred to regard the miraculous acts as due to the operation of God's edict, despite the fact that idolaters proclaim them to be miracles of their idols. This approach is clearly seen in the story that we cited in another connection,[60] according to which R. Akiba said to Zonin that 'when afflictions are sent upon a man, they are adjured to come upon him only on a given day and to leave him only on a given day, and through the medium of such-and-such a person[61] and such-and-such a medicine. When their time came to depart, (the sick person) happened to go to his idolatrous shrine. Thereupon the afflictions said: Rightly we should not leave. Then they added: But because[62] this fool acted improperly shall we break our oath?' R. Akiba's views in regard to Providence we shall discuss later on (ch. xi). At any rate, the reply he gave was acceptable to the questioner, who was apparently a follower of the popular Stoic philosophy, which taught that Fate decides the incidence and disappearance of suffering. This philosophy is also consonant with R. Akiba's inclination to regard God's miracles as forming part of the order of nature and creation (above, p. 110). The Sages were able to come to terms with miracles. Undoubtedly, personal leanings and experiences motivated each Sage either to emphasize or minimize miraculous happenings. There were always Sages who would not forgo miracles that transcended the bounds of nature, and did not refrain from relating and transmitting such occurrences even about Sages who themselves are seen to belong to those who reduced and limited all miraculous deeds. Even in regard to the role of transcendental forces and proofs, instead of logical reasoning, in the field of Halakha, there is no unified opinion. As against dicta and rules such as 'we pay no heed to a Heavenly Voice' (*T.B. Pesaḥim* 114a, and the parallels cited there), 'A prophet is not permitted from now on to introduce anything new' (*Sifra*, end of Leviticus; *T.B. Temura* 16a), 'Even if Elijah were to come and say... he would not be listened to' (*T.B. Yevamot* 102a), Talmudic tradition knows of the intervention of such forces in the Halakhic sphere, and R. Eliezer b. Hyrcanus was not alone in saying 'If the Halakha accords with my view, let this carob-tree prove it; thereupon the carob-tree was torn away a hundred cubits from its place... If the Halakha accords with my view, let the water-canal prove it; thereupon the water flowed backward... If the Halakha accords with my view, let the walls of the schoolhouse prove it; thereupon the walls of the schoolhouse inclined to fall... Again he said to them: If the Halakha agrees with me, let proof be given from heaven; thereupon a Heavenly Voice came forth and said: "Why do you dispute with R. Eliezer, for the Halakha accords with his view in all matters ....'[63]

Despite all the divergences of opinion, the essential premise that miracles are possible cannot be doubted; to believe in miracles is to believe in a Living, Omnipotent God. This omnipotence is beyond all doubt and is not subject to argument. Noteworthy from this standpoint is the criticism levelled by Galen against the Jewish concept of God's omnipotence: 'For Moses it sufficed to say that God willed the ordering of matter and forthwith it was set in order, for he believed that everything was possible to God, even if He should wish to form a horse or a bull out of dust. But we do not hold this view; we say that certain things are impossible by their nature, and God does not attempt to do them. He chooses the best of the creative possibilities.'[64] The Tannaim, who were contemporaries of Galen, strenuously rejected his viewpoint, for the actual belief in the unrestricted power of God was of primary importance in their estimation, and not the miracle. 'Like the case of R. Joḥanan, who sat and expounded: The Holy One, blessed be He, will bring precious stones and pearls, thirty (cubits) by thirty, and He will make an engraving within them ten (cubits broad) by twenty (cubits) high, and will set them up in the gateways of Jerusalem, as it is said: "And I will make thy windows of agates, and thy gates of carbuncle", etc. (Isaiah liv 12). A certain disciple derided him, saying: "Nowadays we do not find a gem the size of a dove's egg, shall we then find (precious stones) of such size?" After a time, he went on a sea-voyage and saw the Ministering Angels sawing precious stones and pearls. Said he to them: "What are these for?" They replied: "The Holy One, blessed be He, is due to set them up in the gateways of Jerusalem." Upon returning, he found R. Joḥanan sitting and expounding. Said he to him: "Master, teach, for it is fitting that you should teach; exactly as you have said, so have I seen." He (R. Joḥanan) replied: "Wretch!, *if you had not seen, you would not have believed!* You deride the words of the Sages!" He set his eyes upon him, and turned him into a heap of bones.'[65] The paradox in the story is that the disciple in question, called in one source 'a sectarian' [*Mîn*], believes in signs and wonders, but only if he sees them with his own eyes. Complete understanding of the mighty deeds and wonders of the Lord are in the end vouchsafed only to one who realizes his inability to conceive and depict these wonders, as the Amora R. Aḥa expressed it: 'We are unable to recount thy wonders and thoughts, which Thou dost execute; He is beyond praise. The case may be compared to two men, one of whom is strong and the other weak. Can the weakling relate the praise of the strong man? No! Why? Because he has no inkling of the strong man's prowess. But the strong man, who knows his own power, is able to tell the praise of (another) mighty one. This is the meaning of David's words: "Who can express the mighty acts of the Lord?" ' (*Midrash Tehillim* cvi 1). Here bounds are set to the praises of God's might.

We have before us a phenomenon similar to that which we observed when we spoke of the immanence of the Deity. In the feeling of God's nearness there is present religious explosive material; there lurks within it the danger of the identification of God with nature, just as in extreme transcendentalism there exists danger of removing God from the world. Praising God and stressing His might, that is, the fact that man is filled with wonder at His mighty deeds and miracles, contains much that is positive, but the attempt to express all His mighty acts and leaving this expression to human ability are liable to destroy our sense of distance and sublimity in regard to God, and thereby to detract from His greatness and majesty. Hence the Halakha proceeded to fix the praises of the Omnipotent. After they had been drawn up in proper order, 'it was forbidden, from then on, to relate the praise of the Holy One, blessed be He, for R. Eleazar said: 'What is the meaning of the verse "Who can express the mighty acts of the

Lord, or make all His praise to be heard (Psalms cvi 2)?" For whom is it fitting to express the mighty acts of the Lord? For one who can make all His praise to be heard. Rabba bar Ḥana said in the name of R. Joḥanan: Whoever eulogizes the Holy One, blessed be He, to excess is uprooted from the world.'[66] So, too, they acted in practice: 'R. Joḥanan and Jonathan went to establish order and harmony in certain cities of the South; on coming to one place, they found the superintendent saying "The great, mighty, and awe-inspiring, the eminent and the valiant God", and they silenced him. They said to him: "You are not permitted to add to the formula fixed by the Sages for the benedictions..." R. Jacob of Kefar Nibburaya interpreted in Tyre: "Praise is due to Thee, O God in Zion" (Psalms lxv 2 [1])... the case is comparable to a priceless pearl, the more one praises it one devalues it....'[67] The danger inherent in the free recitation of the Creator's praises is given its most original expression by the Amora R. Phinehas[68]: 'Moses formulated the wording of the prayer "The great, mighty and awe-inspiring God" (Deuteronomy x 17); Jeremiah said "The great, the mighty God" (Jeremiah xxxii 18), but he did not say "awe-inspiring". Why? He said: "the mighty" — it is fitting to call Him "mighty", because He sees the Temple in ruins and is silent. But why did He not say "awe-inspiring"? Because He inspires awe only in the Temple [*bĕ-ēt ha-miqdāsh*],[69] as it is said "Awe-inspiring is God out of the holy place". Daniel said: "The great and awe-inspiring God" (Daniel ix 4), but he did not say "the mighty". His children are held in chains — where then is His might? But why did he say "awe-inspiring"? It is fitting to call Him "awe-inspiring", because of the awe-inspiring things He did unto us in the fiery furnace. But when the men of the Great Assembly arose, they restored the greatness to its former estate, (saying): "The great, the mighty and the awe-inspiring God".' In this homily the question of giving expression to God's greatness is connected with that of theodicy. While the expositor ascribes to Jeremiah and Daniel a diminution of God's praise, corresponding to the reduced manifestation of Divine righteousness and power, the men of the Great Assembly restored the crown (of the Lord's attributes) to its former estate and fixed it for future generations out of absolute faith in God's unlimited power and in His righteousness, which transcends all human questions.

Like Job (xliii 1–3), who declares after the Lord's answer:[70] 'I know that Thou canst do all things... Therefore I have uttered what I did not understand, things too wonderful for me, which I did not know', the act attributed to the men of the Great Assembly ascribes an intrinsic value to the realization that God is inconceivable, a realization that is both calming and attractive to man, and, at the same time, a justification of the Godhead. However, this answer, which released the sovereign will of God from the ethical yardstick of man, and reaffirmed His mighty and awe-inspiring deeds in a world that appeared to deny them did not satisfy everyone, as can be seen from the explanation given for the action of the men of the Great Assembly in the Babylonian Talmud: 'They came and said: On the contrary, these are His mighty acts, these are His awe-inspiring deeds. Therein lies His might, that He suppresses His anger and is long-suffering towards the wicked. Therein lie His awe-inspiring deeds, for were it not for the awe-inspiring deeds of the Holy One, blessed be He, how could one nation maintain its existence among the (other) nations!'[71] According to this recension there is no difference in principle between the approach of the men of the Great Assembly and that ascribed to Jeremiah and Daniel. The latter formulated His praise according to the extent to which His power and might were felt, according to its actual manifestation, and they were not afraid 'to set a limit in these matters', for, as R. Isaac b. Eleazar expressed it, 'The prophets know that their God is truthful; hence they do not flatter Him'.[72]

The designation of a multiplicity of praises as flattery and the silencing of the superintendent who multiplied such eulogies in one of the towns of the South, seem to allude to mystic circles, which, like the literature of the *Hĕkhālôt* ['Heavenly Palaces'] in our possession, created hymns and prayers, basically composed of praise and glorification of God, by repeating and duplicating the honorific epithets, and the monotony of their rhythm was intended to induce in the worshipper a state of enthusiasm and ecstasy, and to arouse in him the *mysterium tremendum* towards the Holy King. In prayers of this kind the emphasis is primarily placed on the sublimity of the might and majesty of God, other aspects, such as the Lord's love and nearness to man, being set aside. Holiness transcends all ethical meaning, and is none other than the glory of His majesty.[73] Despite the opposition expressed in Halakhot, in the course of time the prayers formulated in these circles penetrated the established liturgy,[74] and it would appear that the prohibition was already relaxed in the days of the Amoraim. Thus R. Abbahu reports in the name of R. Lazar 'Wherever a worshipper has transgressed and said "glorious in majesty" [instead of "the Holy God"] he has not fulfilled his obligation, except if he substituted it for "the Holy God" in the New Year liturgy, and then only in Musaph ["Additional Prayer"].'[75] The use of this benedictory enuing 'glorious in majesty' instead of 'the Holy God' emanates apparently from these circles. Outside the house of prayer, praises of God free from all restrictions used to be composed at gatherings of joy or mourning. Resh Laqish once invited the Meturgeman Judah bar Naḥmani to say words of praise to the Holy One, blessed be He, and the latter 'began and said "The God who is great in the abundance of His greatness, majestic and strong in the abundance of His awe-inspiring deeds, who by His word revives the dead, does great things that are unsearchable and wonders that are numberless" ' (*T.B. Ketubbot* 8b).

CHAPTER VII

THE POWER OF THE DIVINE NAME

The psalms and hymns that lauded the gods at length went hand in hand, in the ancient world, with oaths and adjurations whose purpose was to exert influence and pressure upon the gods to fulfil the will and aspirations of human beings. The formula of the adjuration, the knowledge of which was in the possession of sorcerers, enchanters, and miracle-workers, was primarily based on knowledge of the Divine Name. The Name was endowed with power. The Name and the Power were synonyms.[1] The discovery of the secret name of the god, which implied control of the divinity, occupied an important place both in Egyptian mythology and in the magical practice of the diviners and sorcerers, whose magic arts consisted of the muttering of names.[2] Such concepts and practices were prevalent both in the Hellenistic and in the Roman periods not only in Egypt but also in Eretz-Israel.

It is true that in the Bible itself the magical element is excluded from the faith.[3] There is no adjuration by God's name, nor is use made of it. God's name is called, it is mentioned, when there is a desire for His blessing, for His response; but He that responds and blesses is God, not the priest by mentioning the Name.[4] But the Name itself, even if it is not an instrument or implement that works and achieves miracles and wonders, reflects the presence of the Deity and expresses His power and might; and it may be assumed that in the popular consciousness this distinction was not strictly maintained. Indeed we have many testimonies from the era of the Hasmoneans and after of the prevalence of the view that there was latent power in the Name and of its use in adjurations. In *I Enoch* (lxix 14), the Prince of Oaths tells Michael 'to show him the hidden name in order that he might enunciate it in the oath, so that those might quake before that name and oath'; and in the *Book of Jubilees* (xxxvi 7) Isaac adjures by 'a great oath... by the name glorious and honoured and great'. Ḥoni Ha-meʿaggel [the Circle-Drawer], who lived in the days of Simeon b. Sheṭaḥ and Alexander Jannaeus, 'drew a circle and stood within it and said... I swear by Thy great name that I will not stir hence until Thou have pity on Thy children' (*M. Taʿanit* iii, 8).

The Jewish Hellenistic writer Artapanus[5] narrates in the style of Egyptian stories that Pharaoh fell into a dead faint when Moses muttered the Name in answer to his question 'Who is the Lord?' Moses revived him, but the priest to whom Moses delivered the Name inscribed on a tablet died in great agony. Although Josephus does not cite the whole story of Artapanus, yet he also says 'Then God revealed to him (= Moses) His name, which ere then had not come to men's ears, and of which I am forbidden to speak.'[6] That the Name was used when Moses met Pharaoh is not mentioned in Josephus' writings nor in Rabbinic sources, but it is actually in the latter that there is a reference to Moses' use of the Name in other contexts. In one of the versions of the story about the raising of Joseph's coffin, which the Egyptians had sunk in the Nile, it is stated that 'Moses took a tablet of gold and engraved thereon the Ineffable Name and cast it therein [into the Nile].'[7] Güdemann already noted the resemblance between the legend about Joseph's coffin and the Egyptian legend of Osiris in Plutarch's account.[8] Possibly the Haggada about Joseph's coffin originated in Egypt, and it is not surprising that it mentions Moses' use of the Name. From there it reached Eretz-Israel and found a place in the Rabbinic homilies. On behalf of the Tanna R. Nehemiah it is reported that Moses pronounced the Name against the Egyptian and slew him. The same thought is expressed by R. Levi in other words: 'He slew him with Israel's mysteries'.[9] On the verse 'The sea saw it and fled' (Psalms cxiv 3) the Tanna R. Nehorai said: 'It saw the Ineffable Name engraved upon the rod and it was rent asunder'.[10] In the Apocryphal work designated *The Prayer of Manasses*, the author of which was apparently a Greek Jew, the worshipper says to God: 'Who hast bound the sea by the word of Thy command, who hast shut up the Deep and sealed it with Thy terrible and glorious Name.'[11] The first part of the verse recalls the Midrash that states that God sealed, with the Torah, 'the Okeanos that it should not issue forth and flood the world'.[12] Without doubt, in the second part the reference is to sealing with something on which the Name was written, resembling the legend transmitted by 'a certain Rabbi, who was arranging Haggadic material before R. Joḥanan',[13] concerning David, to wit, that when he dug the foundations of the Temple and the Deep threatened to flood the world, 'he wrote the Name on a sherd and threw it into the Deep'. The use of the Name, which is attributed here to David and to his counsellor Ahitophel, is also known from the Haggada about Solomon and Ashmedai (*T.B. Gittin* 68a). Unquestionably, the authors of the Haggadot regarding David and Solomon transmitted ancient legends that gained currency in circles that used the Name themselves. The Amora Rabba relates that certain seafarers smote the stormy sea with clubs on which was engraved the sentence 'I am that I am, Yah, the Lord of hosts', and it ceased its raging (*T.B. Bava Batra* 73a). When Josephus describes the great wisdom of Solomon — his knowledge, for example, of the way to wage war against the evil spirits — he adds that he left behind him formulas of exorcisms, and appends to this statement a story concerning one Eleazar, a fellow countryman and contemporary, who knew this wisdom and 'adjured the demon never to come back into him, speaking Solomon's name and reciting the incantations which he had composed' (*Ant.* viii, 2, 5). Circles that made use of names and adjurations fostered traditions and Haggadot about the acts of earlier generations in this sphere. In magical Greek papyri there are mentioned 'the holy secret book of Moses, which is called the Eighth or the Sanctified' and 'the secret book about the Great Name' by Moses.[14] In these papyri there occur Hebrew Names in Greek transcription, such as Αδωναῖε [*'Ădonay*, 'Lord'], Ιάω [*Yāhô* (part of the Tetragrammaton)], βασημμ, and also the phrase βεσεν βερειθεν βεριο, which represents *bĕshēm Bāryā*(*tha*)*n Bāryā*, 'In the name of our Creator, the Creator'.[15] These Names, most of which are only epithets, found their way into the Greek papyri after they had long been used in amulets and Hebrew invocations, and it appears that their use in lieu of the Tetragrammaton is the result of a lengthy process that led to the restriction of the writing of the Ineffable Name and to its substition by other sigla or various names and epithets[16], as well as to stringent limitations on its enunciation. The Name remained in its original spelling only in the Bible, but in the later books there are clear indications that it was pronounced *'Ădonay*,[17] just as it was rendered in the Septuagint by ὁ Κύριος;[18] and there are Greek MSS. in which the Tetragrammaton is written in ancient Hebrew letters, without being translated at all.[19] In this form the Name is written both in the Habakkuk Commentary and in the chapters of the Psalms recently discovered.[20] When Philo mentions the Name inscribed on the *ṣîṣ* [the golden plate in front of the high priest's turban], he adds that it 'shows a name which only those whose ears and tongues are purified may hear or speak in the holy place, and no other person, nor in any other place at all. That name has four letters, so says that master learned in divine verities [the *theologus*], who, it may be, gives them as symbols of the first numbers, one, two, three and four.'[21] Also in Synagogue worship the Name was not pronounced, and in blessing the people outside the Temple the priests used only a Divine epithet. In the Temple, however, they pronounced the Ineffable Name[22] in the benediction, and on the Day of Atonement the high priest used to mention the Name ten times: 'six times in connection with the bull, three times in connection with the he-goat, and once in connection with the lots' (*Tosefta Yoma* ii, 2). He likewise enunciated it in the confession in the version *'ānnā ha-shēm* ['O Lord'], and in the prayer in which he besought atonement: *'ānnā' ba-shēm kappēr nā'* ['I beseech Thee by Thy Name make Thou atonement'] — an oath that seems like an adjuration.[23] But we have clear evidence of the care that was taken in mentioning the Name even in the Sanctuary: 'At first he used to utter it aloud; when unruly men increased, he used to utter it softly. R. Ṭarfon said: I was standing among my brother priests in the line and I inclined my ear towards the high priest and I heard him muffle [literally, 'swallow'] it [the Name] in the melody of the priests. At first it was entrusted to all men; but when unruly men increased, it was confided only to those who were worthy.'[24] An example of the muffling of the Name is perhaps to be found in the testimony of R. Judah, that when they went in procession round the altar they used to say "*Ănî wā-Hô*, save us we pray!' (*M. Sukka* iv, 5). *'Ǎnî wā-Hô* is simply a mumbled version of *'Ǎnnā* and the Name.[25] It would appear that also in the sentence they uttered upon departing '*Yfy lĕkhā mizbēaḥ*', the word *yfy* is not an expression of eulogy ['beauty'] addressed to the altar but a Divine epithet, reminiscent of the enunciation of the Name (*yfy–ywy*),[26] and the meaning of the utterance is 'O Lord, the altar is Thine', as in R. Eliezer's phrase 'To *Yah*, yea to Thee is the altar!'[27] The testimonies to this caution that the high priest observed on the Day of Atonement, and which the priests certainly practised during the rest of the year when reciting the priestly benediction, belong to the close of the Temple area; there is reason, however, to suppose that it was not adopted instantaneously, but was undoubtedly the result of a long process. There is a tradition, it is true, that declares 'when Simeon the Just died, they ceased to use the Name in the benediction'[28] but in another version it is merely stated that 'after the festival he was ill for seven days and died, and his colleagues refrained from using the Name in the benediction'. The meaning may simply be that on account of their grief and mourning the priests refrained for some time after his death from using the Name in the priestly benediction.[29] At any rate, we must not regard this tradition as fundamental and infer from it, in contradiction of all other sources, that a law was promulgated forbidding the use of the Name in the priestly benediction in the Temple.[30] And undoubtedly this tradition did not antedate the enactment ordaining 'that a man should use the Name in greeting his fellow' (*M. Berakhot* ix 5). This Mishnaic text, which has been given various interpretations,[31] must not be deprived of its literal sense nor sundered from the preceding statement: 'At the close of every benediction in the Temple they used to say *min hā-ʿōlām* "From everlasting" [literally, "From the world", world in Hebrew meaning also "eternity"];[32] but when the sectarians corrupted their teaching, saying "there is but one world", the (Sages) enacted that one should say *min hā-ʿōlām wĕ-ʿad hā-ʿōlām* "from everlasting to everlasting [literally, 'from world to world']".' The expression *mē-ʿōlām wĕ-ʿad ʿōlām* 'from everlasting to everlasting' occurs several times in the Bible (Psalms xc 2; ciii 17) and also in benedictory formulas, as, for example, in the prayer attributed to David 'Blessed art Thou, O Lord, the God of Israel our father, for ever and ever' (I Chronicles xxix 10). At the close of the first section of the Book of Psalms we find 'Blessed be the Lord, the God of Israel, from everlasting to everlasting! [*mē-hā-ʿōlām wĕ-ʿad hā-ōlām*] Amen and Amen' (Psalms xli 14; and in analogous phrasing in Psalms cvi 48), and in Nehemiah ix 5 'Then the Levites... said, "Stand up and bless the Lord your God from everlasting to everlasting", etc.' This formula simply means 'through all generations', 'for ever' and the like, just as *mēʿattā wĕ-ʿad ʿōlām*, 'from now and for ever'.[33] The sectarians who corrupted their teaching and declared that there was only one world are apparently the Sadducees. Their corruption caused the Sages to insist that at the close of every benediction in the Temple one should say 'from everlasting to everlasting'. Before this reform this closing benedictory formula was not used at all.[34] Similarly, when the sectarians corrupted their teaching, the Sages enacted that a man should use the Name in greeting his fellow. Here it is not stated with regard to which corrupt teaching this enactment was made, but if the same sectarians are spoken of, we can infer from the remedial regulation that in this case, too, the reference is to Sadducees, who denied Divine Providence.[35] The reform, which renews an ancient benedictory formula of the Bible — 'The Lord be with you', 'The Lord bless thee' — was intended to instil the belief in Divine Providence, and is not at all concerned with the pronunciation of the Name. It is improbable that only at such periods as the priests employed an epithet exclusively in the priestly benediction when pronounced outside the Temple, the Name was not used in greetings but merely a Divine title; for we observed that in ancient times, going back to the early Hasmoneans, care was taken not to mention the Name, and other designations were substituted for it. If the exact date when caution began to be exercised in respect of the pronunciation of the Name in the Temple and it commenced to be muffled is unknown to us, the reason at least for the change is stated: 'when unruly men increased', and these unruly men are none other than people who used the Name irresponsibly; compare the expression 'be profuse in vows or levity' (*M. Demai* ii, 3).

The use of amulets was extremely widespread; this is attested both by the Halakhot that mention them incidentally, as for example, 'a man should not go out [on the Sabbath]... either with phylacteries or with an amulet' (*M. Shabbat* vi, 2), 'He that takes out [on the Sabbath] leather to make an amulet...' (*ibid.* viii, 2–3),[36] and by popular parables, such as: 'R. Ḥunya in the name of R. Benjamin b. Levi said: This is comparable to a king who said to his son "Go and do business". He replied "Father, I am afraid to journey on land because of bandits, and to travel by sea because of pirates. What did his father do? He took a rod and hollowed it out and placed an amulet in it and warned his son, saying to him: "Let this rod be in your hand and you shall not fear any creature".'[37] The very secrecy and fear that enveloped the Ineffable Name and its pronunciation strengthened the belief in its power and in the value of its use, and people did not refrain from employing it both in amulets and in enchantments. It is significant that to the statement of R. Akiba, who numbered one that uttered a charm over a wound among those who have no share in the world to come, Abba Saul added 'Also he that pronounces the Name with its proper letters' (*M. Sanhedrin* x, 1). It is probable that this pronunciation of the Name with its proper letters was connected with the utterance of charms. It was to this, apparently, that the Amora R. Mana referred in his comment on Abba Saul's ruling: 'like the Cutheans, when they take an oath' (*T.P. ibid.* x, 5, p. 28b), that is, like the Samaritans who swear by the Name when an oath is imposed.[38] Although we know that the earlier Samaritans, in contrast to the later Samaritans,[39] pronounced the Name with its proper letters, and made use of it for magical purposes, yet it is clear that Abba Saul, like R. Akiba, referred to Jews. Mention should be made in this connection of the teaching 'whoever makes use of the Ineffable Name has no share in the world to come', which is cited in *'Avot de-R. Nathan* (Recension I, xii, p. 56) as an explanation of Hillel's saying 'whoever uses the Crown perishes' (*M. 'Avot*, i, 13).[40]

The writing of the Names in amulets and for magical purposes was performed according to the usual practice in this art. The Name of twelve letters, mentioned in a Babylonian Baraita, and the Name of forty-two letters, of which Rav speaks (*T.B. Qiddushin* 71a), and the Name of seventy-two letters, with which, R. Avin tells us, the Holy One, blessed be He, redeemed the children of Israel from Egypt[41] — none of these is explained either in the Talmud or in the Amoraic Midrashim. On the other hand, there are numerous philosophical and mystical explanations.[42] But undoubtedly the discovery of the magical papyri has served to clarify the subject of these Names, as M. Gaster and L. Blau[43] have shown. In these papyri the sounds of the Greek alphabet are used for the combination of names ἑπτᾶγράμμᾶτον ὄνομα in various patterns. This combination of letters, which is called ἀναγραμματίζειν, was achieved by Jews by means of the Tetragrammaton. Writing it three times produced the Name of twelve letters. A triangular structure, whose base consists of twelve letters — that is, three times the Tetragrammaton — and the succeeding lines contain progressively one letter less, until at the apex the Tetragrammaton is attained, comprises a total of seventy-two letters. The first four rows form the Name of forty-two letters. Since these Names, which were called the 'Great Name', were based upon the Tetragrammaton, it is not surprising that the same rules of caution were applied to their transmission. In a Babylonian Baraita it is stated, in parallelism with what we learnt about the Tetragrammaton: 'The Rabbis taught: At first the twelve-lettered Name was entrusted to all men; but when unruly men increased, it was confined only to the pious members of the priesthood....' Even clearer restrictions are found in the statement of Rav Judah, who said in the name of Rav: 'The Name of forty-two letters is entrusted only to one who is pious and humble, is middle-aged, is not irascible, is not given to drunkenness, and is not insistent on his rights. And he who knows the Name, and uses it with due care, and keeps it in purity, is beloved in Heaven and cherished on earth, and his fellow creatures stand in awe of him, and he inherits two worlds — this world and the world to come' (*T.B. Qiddushin*, *ibid.*). All the conditions that those worthy to have the Name entrusted to them were required to fulfil have as their object that the one who knows the Name should be careful of it and keep it in purity, not using it for any unworthy purpose. The Halakha prescribes the penalty of flogging for whoever uses the Name in cursing his fellow. This is an ancient Halakha. It is taught in an anonymous Baraita (*Tosefta Makkot* v, 10, p. 444, and *T.P. Shevuʿot* iii, 12, p. 35a), which is transmitted in the name of R. Jose the Galilean.[44] It is noteworthy that in *The Manual of Discipline* it is stated with regard to one who curses, using the Name, 'that he may never return to the council [formal membership] of the Community' (*Serekh ha-yaḥad*, 7, 1, ed. Licht, p. 160).

As regards the use of the Name for cursing, it is related by the Amoraim: 'Samuel once heard, as he was passing, a Persian cursing his son by the Name and he died' (*T.P. Yoma* iii, 7, p. 40d). The effective power lies in the Name itself, and it does not matter whether the Divine designation is uttered by a Persian man or woman (*Eccles. Rabba* iii, 11). Whoever is not careful in using it may kill people; hence the condition not to entrust it to an irascible person. Another stipulation is that the Name may not be confided to one who is dependent on others, as we learn from the following story: 'A certain physician in Sepphoris said to R. Phinehas bar Ḥama: "Come! I will entrust it [the Name] to you." He replied: "I am unable to receive it." "Why?" (the physician) asked him. He replied: "Because I eat tithe, and one who is familiar with it [the Name] may partake of nothing given him by any man" ' (*T.P. loc. cit.*). The reason is more fully explained in the parallel source: 'Lest he ask something of a man, and if he does not give it to him, he will become angry with him and slay him.'[45] The inherent power in the Ineffable Name also serves to explain why it is concealed and unknown: 'Thus said the Holy One, blessed be He: Now if when I have concealed the Ineffable Name from them, they slay by using an epithet, how much more so would they do so, if I openly entrusted to them the Ineffable Name!' (*Eccles. Rabba, loc. cit.*). Those Sages who knew the secret of the Ineffable Name regarded its concealment from the general public as a punishment. Thus R. Joshua b. Levi in the name of R. Phinehas b. Jair replied to the question: Why are the Jews not answered when they pray? — 'Because they do not know the secret of the Ineffable Name'.[46] Knowledge of the Name is regarded as the privilege of certain generations. R. Abba bar Kahana said: 'Two generations used the Ineffable Name — the men of the Great Assembly[47] and the generation of the Hadrianic persecutions... and some say that also in the generation of Hezekiah and in that of Zedekiah the Ineffable Name was known, as it is said: (Therefore) "Thus saith the Lord [the God of Israel]: 'Behold, I will turn back the weapons of war that are in your hands' " (Jeremiah xxi 4). What are the weapons of war? The reference is to the Ineffable Name, for they used to go forth to war, but did not wage war, yet their enemies fell; when, however, their iniquities caused the Temple to be destroyed, they [the Israelites] fell into the hands of their enemies. R. Aibu and the Rabbis expressed different views. R. Aibu said: The angels scraped off the Name that was upon them [the soldiers]; while the Rabbis declared: It peeled off of its own accord' (*Midrash Tehillim* xxxvi 8). These Amoraim of the third century, who tell us that the soldiers of Zedekiah used the Ineffable Name by inscribing it on their bodies, limit the intrinsic power of the Name, since the sins caused it to be annulled. Similarly, it is stated that the Tanna R. Ḥanina b. Teradion, one of the heroes of the generation of the Hadrianic persecutions, who knew the secret of the Ineffable Name, was punished because he uttered the Name with its proper letters (*T.B. ʿAvoda Zara* 18a), apparently with a view to using it. Clearly, the view that R. Ḥanina b. Teradion was punished is that of the Amoraim. Noteworthy is the fact that in the narratives dealing with men who knew the secret of the Name there appear a 'physician' and an almost unknown Sage, while those to whom it is desired to reveal the secret — and in the end the knowledge is not imparted — are the leaders of the generation. On the one hand, knowledge of the Name was regarded as indicative of a high religious and spiritual degree, and on the other, the dangers involved in the revelation of the Name, and even more so in its use, were recognized. Hence, restraint, which implied a forgoing of privilege, was decided upon. R. Joḥanan ruled: 'the Tetragrammaton may be confided by the Sages to their disciples once in a septennate.' When Rava 'proposed to expound it at a public lecture, a certain old man [elder] said: it is spelt [Exodus iii 15] *lĕʿallēm*.'[48] He alluded thereby to the exposition transmitted by Rav Naḥman bar Isaac: ' "This is My name for ever [*lĕʿōlām*]"; but it is spelt *lĕʿallem* ["to conceal"]'.[49] A solution to the contradiction between this exposition and the continuation of the verse 'and this is My memorial unto all generations' can be found in another teaching of the same Amora: 'The world to come is not like this world; in this world (the Ineffable Name) is written with *Yôd Hēʾ* [the initial letters of the Tetragrammaton] and read *'Āleph Dālet* [the initial letters of *'Ădōnay*], but in the world to come it will all be one — (His name) will be read with *Yôd Hēʾ*, and written with *Yôd Hēʾ* '(*T.B. Pesaḥim* 50a). In this saying the Sage resigns himself to a religiously imperfect world: the knowledge of the Name and its pronunciation shall be complete only in the world to come, when

God's name will be one, and there will be no danger of its being contaminated by other names and used in a polytheistic-syncretistic sense, a practice that was widely current in the magical literature, in amulets, and in invocations. The sources that refer to the use by wicked people of the 'name of impurity' are few.[50] For such a concept opens the way to a dualistic outlook. Even Balaam is said to have used the Ineffable Name.[51]

It seems to me that the account we have given above suffices to refute the view of Christian theologians who sought to discover in the non-enunciation of the Name and the substitutic n of epithets for it a fundamental difference between Judaism and Biblical religion. Equally unacceptable is the view that the desistance from the pronunciation of the Name had its origin in the Babylonian Exile,[52] and that it resulted from fear of the Gentiles' mockery and blasphemies of the type mentioned in Ezekiel (xxxvi 20) and Psalms (xl 5 [4]; lxxiv 10). It appears that actually the discontinuance of the enunciation and mention of the Name was intended to prevent the blurring of the distance between God and man and the use of the Name for magical purposes. But this fact does not indicate a 'decline' in Israel's faith or the estrangement of Judaism from God, for it was precisely the sense of God's nearness that found expression, as we have seen, in the designations that are indicative of it; only in them and in their interpretations — as in relation to the Ineffable Name — there is also manifest that tension between the feeling of aloofness and nearness, which characterizes the attitude of the Sages to God.

CHAPTER VIII

THE CELESTIAL RETINUE

The epithets coined by the Sages for the designation of their Sovereign reflect the range of relationship between God, on the one hand, and the world and man on the other. They reveal His attributes and at the same time describe His actions. The question that emerges is: To what extent did the concepts and beliefs that we discovered in these epithets influence the attitude of the Sages to the angels that fill the space of the Biblical world? They include, to begin with, those simple messengers that are created, as it were, to carry out given assignments and to vanish from the world as soon as these have been completed, then the Temple ministers — the Seraphim and Cherubs — who appear in the visions of the seers, angels that multiply in their thousands and myriads, until we come to the Guardian Angels, who are permanently appointed over entire peoples, and finally the angels, with personal names, who have a fixed place in the Celestial Retinue and fulfil a permanent role in the world below.

Upon examining the Biblical verses, the Sages clearly realized that neither in the Pentateuch, nor in the Prophets, nor in the Hagiographa, is there a uniform and consistent angelology; on the contrary, we find there varied and dissimilar approaches. Thus the Rabbis felt that in many passages in which an angel is mentioned the reference is to the Lord Himself; but because of its disinclination to employ corporeal expressions, the Bible transferred the task to an angel. Hence there were Tannaim who did not hesitate to extrude the angels from verses whose purpose was actually to stress the nearness of the Lord to His people, or when they feared that the task assigned to the angel might raise him to the level of an independent power, a kind of demiurge. Because they possessed the epithet 'Shekhina', which expresses the presence of God, they had no difficulty in deducing from the verse 'And the angel of God, who went before the camp of Israel' (Exodus xiv 19): 'When they went down to the sea the Shekhina was with them'.[1] As a result of this outlook, the Sages often completely ignored in their homiletical expositions the word 'angel', as though it did not appear in the text at all. When R. Nathan asked R. Simeon b. Yoḥai: '(Why is it that) everywhere you find "the angel of the Lord": ["And the angel of the Lord found her"] (Gen. xvi 7), "And the angel of the Lord said unto her" (*ibid.*, v 9), whereas here it is said "And the angel of God ['*Ĕlōhîm*]... removed" (Exodus xiv 19)', R. Simeon b. Yoḥai answered in the spirit of the teaching of his teacher R. Akiba[2]: "*Ĕlōhîm* everywhere means nothing else but Judge. Scripture tells us that the Israelites were at that moment *sub judice* — whether to be succoured or to be destroyed with the Egyptians.'[3] In this exposition the word 'angel' in the text is voided of all meaning. Nay more, at times the concept 'angel' was introduced into the text, although the term does not appear there at all, in order to make it a peg on which to hang a homily on the relationship of the Shekhina to Israel, as, for example: ' "Even the selfsame day it came to pass, that all the hosts of the Lord went out" — these are the Ministering Angels. Thus you find that so long as the Israelites are in bondage, the Shekhina, so to speak, is in bondage with them, as it is said: "and they saw the God of Israel; and there was under His feet the like of brick work of sapphire stone" (Exodus xxiv 10). But when they were redeemed what does the text say? — "And like the very heaven for clearness". And it is further stated "In all these afflictions He was afflicted" (Isaiah lxiii 9).'[4] The tendency to take away the role of the angel from Biblical passages where the importance of Israel and its redemption are spoken of goes back to early times, and the very verse in Isaiah cited above, which the Sages interpreted according to the *Qrê*, is translated in the Septuagint according to the *Kĕtîv*: Οὐ πρέσβυς οὐδὲ ἄγγελος ἀλλ' αὐτὸς κύριος ἔσωσεν αὐτοὺς that is to say, the translators read: 'not an ambassador [*ṣir* for *ṣar*] nor angel, (but) His presence saved them'.[5] This interpretation corresponds to the Tannaitic exposition 'not by means of an angel, nor by means of an emissary', which is frequently found when there is a reference to God's vengeance on His people's foes and His salvation of Israel,[6] only the Sages went even further and associated the Shekhina directly with Israel's distress, servitude, and exile.

A special problem was engendered by the verses: 'Behold, I sent an angel before thee, to keep thee by the way, and to bring thee into the place which I have prepared. Take heed of him, and hearken unto his voice; be not rebellious against him; for he will not pardon your transgression; for My name is in him. But if thou shalt indeed hearken unto his voice, and do all that I speak; then I will be an enemy unto thine enemies, and an adversary unto thine adversaries' (Exodus xxiii 20–22). The Targumim have left the word 'angel', but have rendered 'for My name is in him' by 'for in My name is his word'.[7] No Tannaitic exposition of these verses have come down to us.

In the Amoraic interpretations there are to be found two lines of exegesis. The one moderates the words by establishing the rule: 'Wherever the angel appears the Shekhina appears';[8] other expositors connected these Scriptures with the verse 'behold, Mine angel shall go before thee', etc. (Exodus xxxii 34) and with Moses' challenging request 'If Thy presence go not with me, carry us not up hence' (*ibid.* xxxiii 15). The sending of the angel was construed as a punishment after the episode of the calf: 'The Holy One, blessed be He, said to Israel "If you had been worthy, I Myself would have become your Messenger, as I did in the wilderness (for it is said 'And the Lord went before them by day' [*ibid.* xiii 21]); but now that you have proved unworthy, I shall hand you over to a messenger (as it is stated 'Behold, I send an angel')." When were they put in charge of a messenger? When they worshipped idols. Whence do we learn this? For thus the Holy One, blessed be He, said to Moses: "Go, lead the people"; Moses replied: "If Thy presence go not with me, carry us not up hence." Moses further said: "Sovereign of the universe! What difference is there between us and the idolaters? We have prophets, and they have prophets; we have a Guardian Angel, and they have a Guardian Angel!' According to R. Levi, the Holy One, blessed be He, did indeed promise 'that the Israelites would not be put in the charge of a Guardian Angel in the lifetime of Moses', but when Moses died that Guardian Angel was restored to his place, for Joshua saw him, as it is said "And it came to pass, when Joshua was by Jericho... And he said: 'Nay, but I am captain of the host of the Lord; I am now come" (Joshua v 14). Therefore, it is said: "Behold, I send an angel before thee." '[9] Thus the verse tells of the punishment: 'Just as the Gentile nations are in the charge of Guardian Angels, so are you in the charge of Guardian Angels' (*Exod. Rabba, ibid.* § 7).

In Daniel the Sages encountered the Guardian Angels of the pagan nations, the Guardian Angel of Persia and of Greece among the heavenly host. Basing themselves on Isaiah xxiv 21 'And it shall come to pass in that day, that the Lord will punish the host of the high heaven on high, and the kings of the earth upon the earth', the Tannaim already expounded 'that the Holy One, blessed be He, will not punish the kingdoms in the time to come, until he has punished their Guardian Angels first'. Thus the Israelites actually saw, when standing by the sea, the Guardian Angel of Egypt fall[10]; only at the sea the Holy One, blessed be He, Himself punished the Guardian Angel of Egypt, and so it shall also be in the time to come.

The contrast between the Gentile peoples, who are ruled over by Guardian Angels, and Israel is reflected already in the Septuagint to Deuteronomy xxxii 8, where the words 'He set the borders of the peoples according to the number of the children of Israel' are rendered: κατὰ ἀριθμὸν ἀγγέλων θεοῦ, '...according to the number of the angels of God'. This is also the view of Ben Sira in the verse 'He appointed a ruler [i.e. Guardian Angel] for every nation, but Israel is the Lord's own portion'.[11] A similar notion is held by the author of *The Book of Jubilees* and is also expressed in *The War of the Sons of Light with the Sons of Darkness*,[12] and it was only Israel's sin that brought it about that they, too, were put in the charge of a Guardian Angel. This conception of the angel's task opened the way — but provided at the same time an opportunity of replying — to the arguments of the sectarians. A Sage called Idit or Rav Idi, of whom Rav Naḥman said 'He who knows how to answer the sectarians as Rav Idi let him do so, but if not let him not reply', was asked by a sectarian: 'It is written "And unto Moses He said: 'Come up unto the Lord' " (Exod. xxiv 1); it should have said "Come up unto Me"! He [R. Idi] replied: It is Meṭaṭron (who said this), and his name is the same as his Master's, as it is written "For My name is in him".

If so [said the sectarian], worship him! [R. Idi:] It is written "Be not rebellious [*tammēr*] against him", that is, exchange Me [*těmîrēnî*] not for him. — [The sectarian:] If so, why is it written "He will not pardon your transgression"? He [R. Idi] answered: We hold the belief that we did not accept him even as a messenger, for it is written: "If Thy presence go not, etc." '[13] Who was this sectarian who debated with Rav Idi, and what was the special reason for the praise accorded the latter? The sectarian's question clearly alludes to the belief in two divine powers, that is, in a demiurge or son of God, who fulfils an independent role beside the God Most High; it seems to me most likely that the reference is actually to a Christian sectarian. R. Idi's answer was that the angel referred to was the angel who was destined to be the guide — Meṭaṭron, who went before them[14] — in other words, that he was only a messenger, nothing more, and his power derived from the fact that the Lord's Name was in him. When the sectarian expressed the thought that he [Meṭaṭron] should be worshipped, R. Idi drew his attention to the admonition in the verse *'al tammēr bô*, which is interpreted to mean 'do not exchange Me for him'. By the question, Why did the Torah see fit to emphasize that 'He will not pardon your transgression', the *Min* revealed the identity of the angel; He that spoke to Moses was the one who had the power to forgive transgressions. To this came the sharp riposte of Rav Idi 'that even as a messenger' Moses did not wish to accept him; hence, we are to understand that the whole episode came as a punishment upon Israel. The words 'for My name is in him' are not an explanation of the name Meṭaṭron. It is doubtful if Rav Idi himself knew exactly the etymology or significance of this name. He was only interested to tell us that he who spoke to Moses was an honoured angel, who derived his power of action from the fact that his Master's name was upon him or within him. The name itself Rav Idi took from the onomasticon of angels current in his Babylonian environment.[15]

In the detailed acts of redemption wrought during the Exodus from Egypt and the parting of the Sea of Reeds tasks were assigned to angels, and at the same time corporeal expressions were thereby obviated. The Tannaim were able to do this by applying parallels to clearly-stated verses.

Moses' words 'Fear ye not, stand still, and see the salvation of the Lord' are explained in the *Mekhilta* (Massekhta de-Wa-yĕhi, ii, p. 94) in expanded dialogue form: 'They [the children of Israel] said to him: "When?" — He [Moses] answered them: "Tomorrow." They then said to him: "Moses, our teacher, we have not the strength to endure more." — Thereupon Moses prayed, and the Holy One, blessed be He, showed them legions upon legions of Ministering Angels standing by them, as it is stated in Scripture "...And his servant said unto him: 'Alas, my master! how shall we do?' And he answered: 'Fear not: for they that are with us are more than they that are with them!' And Elisha prayed, and said: 'Lord, I pray Thee, open his eyes, that he may see.' And the Lord opened the eyes of the young man; and he saw; and, behold, the mountain was full of horses and chariots of fire round about Elisha" (II Kings vi 15–17).' So, too, it is taught, on the basis of the verse in Ezekiel xxxviii 22, that the Ministering Angels threw arrows and hailstones, fire and brimstone upon the Egyptians. The verse 'And the Lord overthrew [*wa-yĕnaʿēr*] the Egyptians' the Sages explained thus: 'He delivered them, as it were, into the hands of youthful angels [*nĕʿārim*], as it were, into the hands of cruel angels, for it is said "And a cruel angel shall be sent against him" (Prov. xvii 11); and it says "Their soul shall perish at the hand of youth" etc. (Job xxxvi 14).'[16] In the stories about the miracles wrought for the Hebrew wives in the rearing of their children, it is stated: 'And the Holy One, blessed be He, used to send from the heavens on high one who cleaned and beautified them in the manner of a midwife, who makes the infant beautiful' (*T.B. Soṭa* 11b). However, a similar statement is transmitted in the name of R. Levi 'The Holy One, blessed be He, assigned to each of them two angels, one to wash him and the other to clothe him', but it appears that this Haggada is earlier than his time, for R. Ḥiyya the Great, already, reacted to it from the viewpoint that excludes angels from everything connected with Israel's redemption; it is he who said 'This was done not by angels but by the Holy One, blessed be He, Himself, as it is said "Then I washed thee" (Ezekiel xvi 9). Had the text said "Then I caused thee to be washed", I might have thought: Possibly by means of an angel; but it is written "Then I washed thee", and not by means of an angel. Praised be the name of the Holy One, blessed be He — He himself rendered them this service.'[17]

In the literature of the Tannaim — and the Amoraim followed their example — these angels remain anonymous and are not given names. R. Samuel bar Naḥman, the author of the saying that sustenance is greater than redemption — 'For redemption is (wrought) by an angel, whereas sustenance is (vouchsafed) by the Holy One, blessed be He, Himself; redemption is wrought by means of an angel (as it is said) "the angel who hath redeemed me" '[18] — did not specify the name of the angel. In this regard there is a great similarity between Rabbinic teaching and the *Books of the Maccabees*. Judas Maccabeus recalls in his prayers the salvations of the Lord in past wars (*I Maccabees* iii 18; iv 9, 30), and before the battle with Nicanor he supplicates 'when they that came from the king [i.e. Sennacherib] blasphemed, Thine angel went out and smote among them one hundred and eighty-five thousand. Even so crush this army before us today' (*ibid.* vii 41–42). It is obvious that the expression 'Thine angel went out' derives from the verse (II Kings xix 35) 'that the angel of the Lord went forth'; but in the continuation he forgot the angel as it were, and said 'Even so crush this army'. Yet even the author of *II Maccabees*, whose style is less restrained, is not immoderate, but phrases the prayer in parallel language 'So now... send a good angel before us' (xv 23). In another passage he prophesies, as it were, in language used by the Tannaim in relation to the Exodus from Egypt, when he describes how 'the enemy saw five resplendent men from heaven on horses... they also showered arrows and thunderbolts on the enemy...' (*ibid.* x 29–30).

Although the author of *I Maccabees* knew the story of Ḥananiah, Mishael and Azariah, who 'were saved out of the flame' and about Daniel, who was delivered from the mouth of the lions (ii 59), it is doubtful if he knew the visions concerning 'Michael, one of the chief princes, came to help me' (Daniel x 13), or those concerning 'Michael... the great prince who standeth for the children of Thy people' (*ibid.*, vii 1). In the case of the Tannaim there can be no doubt that they knew these verses; nevertheless they assigned no part to Michael in the past wars of Israel. Only in late Midrashim does Michael take his place as the Guardian Angel of Israel, who fights their battles, as in the apocalyptic works themselves.[19] Thus we find: 'From the day that the Holy One, Blessed be He, revealed Himself to Moses, He appeared to him only through an angel, as it is said "And the angel of the Lord appeared unto him in the flame of fire" etc. (Exodus iii 2) — that is Michael. At that moment he watched over Moses and Israel at the sea, for it is said ..."in Egypt"....'[20] Unlike the Books of Kings and the *Books of the Maccabees*, it is stated in the Midrash that Michael went forth to fight against Sennacherib. The apocryphal character of this Midrash, which attributes its dicta to Tannaim, will become clear in the continuation of our chapter. Also traces of the views opposed to this Midrashic statement, with which the author seeks to come to terms, are still quite evident:

> R. Nehemiah said: Come and see the love of the Holy One, blessed be He, towards Israel, for the Ministering Angels, who are the mighty of strength that do his bidding were appointed by the Holy One, blessed be He, as the guardians of Israel. And who are they? — Michael and Gabriel, for it is said 'I have set watchmen upon thy walls, O Jerusalem' (Isaiah lxii 6); and when Sennacherib came, Michael went forth and smote them, and Gabriel, by the command of the Holy One, saved Hananiah and his companions. Why was this? — The Holy One, blessed be He, made certain stipulations with them. When? — When He sought to go down to deliver Abraham from the fiery furnace, Michael and Gabriel said to Him: 'We shall go down to deliver them.' Said He to them: 'Had he [Abraham] gone down to the furnace for the sake of one of you, you would have delivered him; but since he has gone down for My sake, I shall go down and save him, for it is said "I am the Lord that brought thee out of the furnace ['*ûr*, in the sense of 'fire'] of the Chaldees" (Genesis xv 7). But I shall give you a time when you can go down, because you undertook to save him in honour of My name. You Michael (shall go) against the camp of Assyria, and you Gabriel against the camp of the Chaldees'... and Michael did as He told him, as it is said 'And it came to pass that night, that the angel of the Lord went forth' (II Kings xix 35). It has been taught: All the generals and commanders were drinking wine and they left their vessels lying about. The Holy One, blessed be He, said to Sennacherib: 'Thou hast done what thou didst wish, as it is said "By thy messengers [the same word as for angels] thou hast taunted"

(*ibid.* v. 23); I, too, shall act through My messenger.' What did He do to him? — 'And under his glory there shall be kindled a burning like the burning of fire' (Isaiah x 16)... the Holy One, blessed be He, said to Michael 'Leave their garments and burn their souls...' And just as the Holy One, blessed be He, wrought in this world by the hand of Michael and Gabriel, so He will act through them in the time to come, for it is said (Obadiah i 21): 'And saviours shall come up on mount Zion to judge the mount of Esau' — this refers to Michael and Gabriel. But our holy master [R. Judah ha-Nasi] said: This refers to Michael by himself, for it is said 'And at that time shall Michael stand up, the great prince who standeth for the children of thy people', for he pleads for Israel's needs and speaks concerning them, as it is said 'Then the angel of the Lord spoke and said: "O Lord of hosts, how long wilt Thou not have compassion on Jerusalem" (Zechariah i 12)'; and it is further said 'And there is none that holdeth with me against these, except Michael your prince' (Daniel x 21). R. Jose said: To what can Michael and Samma'el be compared? To a defending counsel and prosecutor standing in court; the one speaks and the other speaks. When the one finished speaking and the other finished speaking, the counsel for the defence knew that he had won the case. Thereupon he began to praise the judge, (asking him) to announce the verdict. Now the prosecutor wished to add a word; said the defending counsel to him: 'Hold thy peace and let us hear (the verdict) of the judge.' So Michael and Samma'el stood before the Shekhina, and the Satan was accusing and Michael was defending Israel. Then the Satan came to speak (again), and Michael silenced him. Wherefore? — As it is said (Psalms lxxxv 9 [8]): 'I will hear what God the Lord will speak; for He will speak peace unto His people.' This then is the meaning of the verse 'In the night I will call to remembrance my song' — for the miracle of Hezekiah (*Exodus Rabba* xviii 5).

Since the sources, out of which the expositor composed his exposition, are available to us, we can easily discern the interpolations and inventions of the author. With regard to the rescue of Abraham from the fiery furnace, a story that is first mentioned in the era of religious persecution by the disciples of R. Akiba,[21] the opinion was expressed by R. Eliezer b. Jacob: 'Michael went down and rescued Abraham from the furnace. The Rabbis declared: The Holy One, blessed be He, delivered him... And when did Michael go down? In the time of Hananiah, Mishael and Azariah.'[22] The succinct statement of the Sages was dramatized in the *Midrash Tanḥuma*: 'When our father Abraham was cast into the fiery furnace, the angels quarrelled among themselves. Michael said: "I shall go down and rescue him"; and Gabriel said: "I shall go down and rescue him." Thereupon the Holy One, blessed be He, said: "I Myself shall go down and rescue him", as it is said: "that brought thee out of Ur [i.e. the fiery furnace] of the Chaldees" (Genesis xv 7). He [God] said to them: "His [Abraham's] descendants you will deliver." When Hananiah, Mishael and Azariah went down into the fiery furnace, the angel came down and rescued them, as it is said "Nebuchadnezzar spoke and said: 'Blessed be the God of Shadrach, Meshach, and Abed-nego, who hath sent His angel, and delivered His servants...' "[23] In the rescue of Hananiah, Mishael and Azariah only one angel is mentioned, nor does the expositor explain who the angel was that rescued them. The argument between the two angels he composed, apparently, out of two sources: *Genesis Rabba*, according to which Michael was the rescuing angel, and a source in which Gabriel suggested that he should deliver Abraham, but the Holy One, blessed be He, rejected his suggestion and said to him: 'I am Unique in My world, and he is unique in his world; it is fitting that the Unique should deliver the unique.'[24] The author of the Midrash in *Exodus Rabba* harmonized the two expositions. Both Michael and Gabriel wished to save Abraham, only 'Had he [Abraham] gone down to the furnace for the sake of one of you, you would have delivered him; but since he has gone down for My sake, I shall go down and save him', but as compensation for this he added: 'You Michael (shall go) against the camp of Assyria, and you Gabriel against the camp of the Chaldees', that is, to save Hananiah, Mishael and Azariah.

However, the homilist did not refrain from citing a Baraita[25] — which is in fact a statement by R. Joshua b. Qorḥa — that justifies the use of angels in the war with Sennacherib, in contrast to the first action of the Lord against Pharaoh,[26] but he omitted the antithesis to Pharaoh, for actually he saw nothing objectionable in redemption by means of angels. On the contrary, to the words (which are not known from any other source) 'Come and see the love of the Holy One, blessed be He, towards Israel, for the Ministering Angels, who are the mighty of strength that do His bidding, were appointed by the Holy One, blessed be He, as the guardians of Israel', he added 'And who are they? — Michael and Gabriel', and in the continuation of the homily he assigned them a decisive role in the redemption of the time to come, and cited the divergent view of 'our holy master', who transfers the entire action to Michael, Israel's defending counsel, and he relies on the words of R. Jose, who describes the struggle between Michael and Samma'el. The very mention of Samma'el in a Tannaitic statement suffices to invalidate the trustworthiness of the entire tradition.[27] Whereas the later, anonymous homilist takes the angel mentioned in the story of Sennacherib and identifies him with Michael and raises him to the level of a redeeming angel in the past and in the future, we actually possess a contrary tradition! It reduces the stature of the angel and his role even in the war with Sennacherib, which it likens to the redemption from Egypt: 'R. Eliezer said: He smote them with His hand, as it is said "And Israel saw the great hand"; it was the same hand that was destined to punish Sennacherib. R. Joshua said: He smote them with His finger, for it is said "Then the magicians said unto Pharaoh: 'This is the finger of God' "; it was the same finger that was destined to punish Sennacherib. R. Eliezer, the son of R. Jose the Galilean, said: The Holy One, blessed be He, said to Gabriel: "Is thy scythe sharpened?" Said he to God: "Sovereign of the universe, it is sharpened and ready since the Six Days of Creation", as it is said: "For they fled away from the swords, from the sharpened sword..." (Isaiah xxi 15). R. Simeon b. Yoḥai said: It was the season when the fruits ripen; so the Holy One, blessed be He, said to Gabriel "When thou goest forth to ripen the fruits, deal with them", as it is said "As he passeth he shall take you; for morning by morning shall he pass by, by day and by night, and it shall be a sheer terror to understand the report" (*ibid.* xxviii 19)... And some say: He breathed into their nostrils....'[28] The starting point for the Tannaitic homily is the passage II Chronicles xxxii 21–22, and especially, apparently, the words 'Thus the Lord saved Hezekiah', which recall the verse (Exodus xiv 30) 'Thus the Lord saved Israel that day out of the hand of the Egyptians, and Israel saw....' In the dicta of R. Eliezer and R. Joshua, the angel disappears altogether.[29] Likewise in the homilies of R. Eliezer b. R. Jose the Galilean and R. Simeon b. Yoḥai the angel plays only a limited role; and the latter Sage identifies him particularly with Gabriel and not with Prince Michael! Many Amoraim, too, followed in the path of the Tannaitic homilies, and of special interest is the statement of R. Isaac Nappaḥa, who describes the end of Sennacherib's army thus: 'He opened their ears and they heard the song of the Living Creatures and died.'[30]

Whereas in the account of the Revelation on Mount Sinai in the Book of Exodus angels are not mentioned, they appear in their myriads in the allusions to the event in the other books of the Bible.[31] The Tannaim in their homilies wove, of course, the verses in Exodus into those of other passages. However, they also noted the difference, in this respect, between the theophany at the Sea of Reeds and that on Mount Sinai and said:

> The Holy One, blessed be He, does not act like a human being. When a human (king) goes forth to war, he issues forth with many men; and when he goes in peace he goes with but few retainers. But He who spoke and the world came into being is not so; when he goes out to war He goes alone, as it is said 'The Lord is a man of war, the Lord is His name' (Exodus xv 3), and when he returns in peace, he comes with thousands and myriads, as it is said 'The chariots of God are myriads, even thousands upon thousands' (Psalms lxviii 18).[32]

But the sayings and expositions of the Tannaim with reference to the Revelation on Mount Sinai are not essentially different from their utterances about His manifestation at the partition of the Sea of Reeds. They speak of direct revelation, without refraining from corporeal expressions, and of His appearing alone without retinue: 'Because He revealed Himself at the Sea as a Warrior doing battle, as it is said "the Lord is a man of war"; He revealed Himself at Sinai as an Elder full of compassion, for it is said "and they saw the God of Israel" (Exodus xxiv 10).'[33] R. Akiba rejected Pappus's attempt to interpret the verse 'To a steed in Pharaoh's chariot' (Canticles i 9) in a manner reminiscent of a chariot.[34] Also in the expositions, reported in R. Akiba's name, of the verses in Canticles that allude, in his view, to the Revelation on Mount Sinai,[35] there is no reference to angels or a chariot. Of primary importance in the estimation of the Sages was the fact of the direct manifestation in both theophanies: ' "In the sight of all the people" — this teaches that they saw at that moment what neither Isaiah nor Ezekiel saw.'[36] The verse 'And when the people saw it, they trembled, and stood afar off' (Exodus xx 15) they interwove with Psalms lxviii 13 [12] and expounded: 'This teaches us that the Israelites retreated twelve miles and then went forward again twelve miles, thus making twenty-four miles for each commandment; altogether, therefore, they walked that day two hundred and forty miles. At that time, the Holy One, blessed be He, said to the Ministering Angels: "Lead away and help your brethren", as it is said: "Kings of armies flee, they flee" (Psalms lxviii 13 [12]), they flee walking away and they flee coming back. Nor was it the Ministering Angels only, but also the Holy One, blessed be He, ...'[37] The participation of the angels in the Biblical passages is confined to the task of aiding and encouraging the Israelites.

A totally different attitude to the role of the angels at the Revelation on Mount Sinai is to be found in the Midrashim of the Amoraim. There, too, verses from Exodus are woven into those of Psalms lxviii, but it is the latter that are dominant:

> 'I am the Lord thy God' etc. — this is to be understood in the light of the verse 'The chariots of God are myriads, even thousands upon thousands; the Lord is among them, as in Sinai, in holiness.' R. Avdima of Haifa said: I learnt in my Mishna that there came down with the Holy One, blessed be He, to Sinai twenty-two thousand Ministering Angels... Another explanation is: 'The chariots of God are myriads, even thousands upon thousands' — He came down with twenty-two thousand chariots... chariots of God. In the name of the group that came up from Babylon they said that there came down with the Holy One, blessed be He, to Sinai twenty-two thousand chariots. So taught Elijah, may he be remembered unto good. 'The chariots of God are myriads, thousands upon thousands': R. Tanḥum b. Ḥanilai said: As far as the arithmetician (Sophist) can calculate — thousands upon thousands, myriads upon myriads.[38]

In another source, the words of R. Tanḥum b. Ḥanilai, who was the disciple of the celebrated Haggadist R. Joshua b. Levi,[39] are reported as follows: 'Thousands upon thousands, myriads upon myriads, up to the point where the arithmetician can no longer calculate'[40]; that is to say, in antithesis to R. Avdimi's view, R. Tanḥum said that the number of angels that came down was so great that even a σοφιστής could not count them. A similar exposition is given by R. Eleazar b. Pedat: 'When the Holy One, blessed be He, came, a thousand thousand and a myriad myriads (of angels) came down with Him.'[41] The Mishna in which R. Avdimi learnt the number of the angels, which amounted to twenty-two thousand, is reported in the name of 'the group that came up from Babylon' as a Mishṇa taught by Elijah, may his name be for blessing, in the following version: 'There came down with the Holy One, blessed be He, twenty-two thousand chariots; each chariot like the chariot seen by Ezekiel.'[42] The group that came up from Babylon were Amoraim, possessed of a mystic tradition, who went to Eretz-Israel, just as R. Eleazar b. Pedat also emigrated from Babylon, only he had a different version of the tradition, while R. Avdimi followed the Mishna of those 'Babylonian Rabbis' who were contemporaries of R. Eleazar b. Pedat.[43] At any rate, when the Tannaitic Midrashim speak of thousands and myriads being present at the manifestation of the Shekhina, the reference is not to angels but to the Children of Israel. 'R. Jose says: Had (only) two thousand and two myriads been present, they would have been worthy to receive (the Torah).'[44] Even when the exposition is centred on the verse Psalms lxviii 18, its intention and purport are different. It comes to teach 'that just as the Shekhina abides in heaven above only among thousands and myriads, so the Shekhina abides on earth below only among thousands and myriads'.[45] The number of the angels that descended on Mount Sinai is mentioned also in a homily of R. Joḥanan, but he linked this number with a given task to be fulfilled by the angels with respect to Israel — a motif that is found, without the number, in a Tannaitic homily:[46] '..."What shall I take to witness for thee?" (Lamentations ii 13) — with how many adornments did I adorn you! for R. Joḥanan said: On the day that the Holy One, blessed be He, came down to Sinai to give the Torah to Israel, sixty myriads of Ministering Angels came down with Him, and each one of them held a crown in his hand with which to crown the Israelites. R. Abba bar Kahana said in the name of R. Joḥanan: A hundred and twenty myriads, one (angel) to put a crown upon each Israelite, and one to gird him with weapons.'[47] In a late source R. Joḥanan's homily is reported in the name of the Tanna R. Eleazar b. Arakh.[48] However, the motif that the people of Israel were vouchsafed arms or special raiment or crowns, when they stood at Mount Sinai, is old. But in all the early sources in which the Haggada is reported in the name of Tannaim, it is not the angels who do the girding, clothing, and crowning, but the Holy One, blessed be He, Himself. This is how the verse 'And that is the sword of thy excellency' (Deuteronomy xxxiii 29) is expounded: 'The Holy One, blessed be He, said to him: "Moses, I shall in future give (back) to the Israelites the weapon that I took away from them at Horeb," as it is stated "And the children of Israel stripped themselves of their ornaments from mount Horeb onward" (Exodus xxxiii 6). "I have taken an oath that I shall return it to them," as it is said "As I live, saith the Lord, thou shalt surely clothe thee with them all as with an ornament, and gird thyself with them, like a bride" (Isaiah xlix 18).'[49] It seems that there is an allusion here to the following Baraita: 'R. Simeon b. Yoḥai taught: The weapon that God gave to the Israelites at Horeb had the Ineffable Name engraved upon it; and when they sinned in connection with the calf, He took it away from them. How did He take it from them? R. Aibu and the Rabbis disagree on the matter. R. Aibu said: (the Name) peeled off of its own accord; but the Rabbis declare: An angel came down and peeled it off.'[50]

In the source in which the motif ' "graven [*ḥārût*] upon the tables" — according to R. Neḥemiah — (means) freedom [*ḥērût*] from the angel of death' is connected with the raiment vouchsafed to the Israelites at Mount Sinai there is no mention of angels: 'R. Phinehas b. Ḥama in the name of R. Joḥanan, in the name of R. Eleazar the son of R. Jose the Galilean, stated: The Holy One, blessed be He, said: If the Angel of Death should come and ask "Why was I created?" I shall answer him "a *stationarius* have I created thee over the nations, but not over my children". For when they accepted the Torah, the Holy One, blessed be He, clothed them with the splendour of His majesty.'[51]

Apparently, the change that occurred in the homilies of the Amoraim was intended to avoid undue corporealization; hence the task of putting on and taking off, of dressing and stripping was assigned to the angels. But there were Amoraim who felt concern at the prominence given to the appearance of angels at the giving of the Torah in Biblical verses, and saw the need to stress even in this context the sovereignty of the Holy One, blessed be He, over them: ' "The Lord is among them" (Psalms lxviii 18). Said Resh Laqish: There is a tablet on the heart of each angel, and (on it) the name of the Holy One, blessed be He, is combined with the angel's name — Michael, Gabriel, Raphael. "The Lord is among them" — the text has *Adonay* [not the Tetragrammaton], (signifying that) My sovereignty is within them.'[52]

However, no fundamental differences are to be found among the Sages, when they come to consider the attitude of God to the angels on the one hand, and to Israel on the other. Both the Tannaim and the Amoraim have given expression in various ways to His preference for the people of Israel. Apparently, this preference serves to explain R. Akiba's exposition, which, however, R. Ishmael rejected as far-fetched and contradicting an express verse: 'The Rabbis taught: "Man did eat the bread of the mighty" (Psalms lxxviii 25) — bread eaten by the Ministering Angels; this is the view of R. Akiba. When the exposition was reported to R. Ishmael, he said to them: "Go, say to Akiba: Akiba, you are mistaken. Do angels eat bread? Has it not already been said 'I did neither eat bread nor drink water?' " (Deuteronomy ix 9). How then is (the verse) "Man did eat the bread of the mighty" to be explained? It was absorbed by the two hundred and forty limbs.'[53] R. Akiba did not reply to R. Ishmael's criticism, because he held that Moses' status transcended that of the angels, and he did not mind portraying them as eating manna.[54] In keeping with the teaching of R. Akiba, his disciple R. Me'ir stated in regard to the angels' eating at Abraham's house: 'The proverb has it: When you come to a city conform to its mores. In heaven where there is no eating, Moses, when he went up there, behaved like them (the angels), (as it is written) "Then I abode in the mount forty days and forty nights"; on earth where there is eating — (it is written) "And he stood by them under the tree, and they did eat." '[55]

R. Akiba's disciples continued to expound their master's teaching 'Beloved are Israel' (*M. 'Avot* iii, 14) and said: 'O Israel, you are more beloved of Me than the Ministering Angels... [O Israel] you are more honoured in My sight than the Ministering Angels... you are greater in My sight... holier in My sight... more praiseworthy than the Ministering Angels.'[56] The author of the homily 'The Israelites are more beloved than the Ministering Angels' is R. Me'ir. Actually, we find another homily in his name informed by similar sentiments: 'Who is greater, the guardian or the guarded? From the verse "For He will give His angels charge over thee, to keep thee" it is to be inferred that the guarded is greater than the guardian. R. Judah said: Who is greater, he that carries or he that is carried? From the verse "They shall carry thee upon their hands" (*ibid.* v. 12), we see that the one carried is greater than the carrier. R. Simeon said: Who is greater, the sender or the messenger? From the Scripture "Here am I: send me", we learn that the sender is greater than the messenger.'[57] An anonymous Baraita explains the dictum 'The Israelites are more beloved than the Ministering Angels' as follows: 'For the Israelites utter song (of praise to God) at all times, whereas the Ministering Angels utter song only once a day; others say, once a week; and others again, once a month... nor do the Ministering Angels utter song in heaven until the Israelites have said it upon earth' (*T. B. Ḥullin* 91 b). The passage appears to be directed against the apocalyptists, who transferred the main praise of God to the world of the angels.[58] The preference accorded to Israel is linked to the idea of election, although in R. Me'ir's view the Israelites are called 'sons' even when they do not behave as such.[59] But even he admits that there is a difference in their status when they perform God's will and when they do not. The concept of the absolute election is the outcome of the certainty that the chosen people will again choose to fulfil the Almighty's will. This view is reflected in the answer given to the arraignment of the angels at the time of the parting of the Sea of Reeds: 'When the children of Israel walked on dry land in the midst of the sea, the Ministering Angels expressed astonishment: People who worship idols (are allowed to) walk on dry land in the midst of the sea! And how do we know that the sea, too, was filled with wrath against them? For it is said "and the waters were a *ḥōmā* ['wall'] unto them"; read not *ḥōmā* but *ḥēmā* ['wrath']. And what caused Israel to be delivered on their right hand and on their left? "On their right hand" — by virtue of the

Torah, which they were destined to receive on their right hand, as it is said "At His right hand was a fiery law unto them" (Deuteronomy xxxiii 2); "and on their left" — this means prayer.'[60] The angels' arraignment of the creation of Adam found its answer when the Israelites uttered a song at the sea: 'And as for the angels who had said "What is man, that Thou art mindful of him?"... at that moment the Holy One, blessed be He, said to the Ministering Angels: "Come and behold the song that My children are hymning to Me." When they beheld, they, too, uttered song...'[61] When the people of Israel is spoken of, many of the Sages have almost no scruples in using anthropomorphic expressions to describe God's love for his people, or His distress and suffering at their calamities and troubles. In so far as love is concerned, it will suffice to point to the homilies that regarded Canticles as an allegorical portrayal of the pattern of relationship between the Shekhina and the Congregation of Israel from the time of the Exodus onward. R. Akiba, who proclaimed that Canticles was 'most holy'[62], did not hesitate to express part of the praise of the Holy One, blessed be He, in the language of the Song of Songs (v 10) 'My beloved is white and ruddy, pre-eminent above ten thousand'. The readiness that we found among some Amoraim, and especially in the case of R. Joḥanan, to transfer certain tasks to angels, in order to avoid corporeal expressions, also appears as a solution in the explanations of Canticles. Referring to the verse 'Let him kiss me with the kisses of his mouth', 'R. Joḥanan said: An angel brought forth the commandment from before the Holy One, blessed be He (in the case of each commandment), and presented it to every Israelite, saying: "Do you accept this commandment? It contains so-and-so many laws, and so-and-so many penalties..." And the Israelite answered, "Yea, yea!" Forthwith the angel kissed him on the mouth. This is the meaning of the verse: "Unto thee it was shown, that thou mightest know" — through a messenger.'[63]

However, the trend to avoid anthropomorphic interpretations by the introduction of angels did not stand the test of the polemic with Christian exegetes, who also expounded Canticles homiletically, only in their homilies the Church took the place of the Congregation of Israel. The Church Father Origen put an unfavourable interpretation on the mediation of angels and stressed the superiority of the Church, which was vouchsafed the kisses of Jesus.[64] It is not to be supposed that the Amoraim of the fourth century were less sensitive to anthropomorphic homilies, but the polemical need decided the issue; hence they did away with the role of the angels, and transferred it to the commandment itself, which visited every Israelite and said to him ' "Do you accept me? I contain so-and-so precepts..." and it taught him Torah.' Others adopted the view of R. Joshua b. Levi, who held that 'the Israelites heard two commandments from the mouth of the Holy One, blessed be He',[65] and on this basis the Sages interpreted the verse 'Let Him kiss me with the kisses [literally 'of the kisses'] of His mouth' to mean 'and not with all the kisses' but 'only with two commandments: "I am the Lord thy God..." and "Thou shalt have no other gods before Me..." '; thus there is no room left for 'a son of God' nor for 'the first-born of creation'. The Tannaitic dicta relating to the Almighty's participation in the troubles of His people — to the exile of the Shekhina together with them[66] — contain the most corporeal expressions among the Amoraic statements. R. Isaac b. Samuel said in the name of Rav: 'The night comprises three watches, and at every watch the Holy One, blessed be He, sits and roars like a lion, saying: "Alas for Me, that I have destroyed My house, and burnt My Temple and exiled My children among the nations of the world."[67] And even an Amora like Rav Qaṭṭina,[68] who himself was granted the vision of an angel, heard a voice that explained to him the meaning of the word זועות *zĕwāʿôt* ['earthquakes'] in the Mishna — which he rendered גוהא *gûhā*' [rumbling of the earth] — as follows: 'At the moment when the Holy One, blessed be He, remembers His children who abide in travail among the nations of the world, He sheds two tears into the Great Sea, and His voice is heard from one end of the world unto the other; and this is גוהא *gûhā*.' When he proceeds to add another explanation of his own, which is no less anthropomorphic, to wit, '[God] claps His hands', Qaṭṭina bases himself on the verse in Ezekiel xxi 22. In the name of other Amoraim we find similar expressions: '[God] heaves a sigh', 'He kicks at the heavens', 'He presses His feet beneath the Throne of Glory'.[69] The extent to which the Amoraim were undeterred by corporeal phrases, when their theme was the distress and salvation of their people, is brought home to us when we read the commentary of Rabbenu Ḥananel. He is, indeed, aware that all these things were said 'only with a view to showing Israel that the Holy One, blessed be He, had not forsaken them or forgotten them or abandoned them, but is destined to restore them; all this was intended to encourage them, so that they should not despair of redemption'. Yet at the same time he protects his Maker's honour by saying: 'Heaven forfend! that an (actual) tear welled from the eye; they were only drops that looked like tears... the Holy One, blessed be He, commands an angel and he claps his hands... He sighs — Heaven forfend! that the Almighty should sigh; it means only that the Holy One, blessed be He, enjoins an angel to utter a sigh... He orders an angel and he kicks at the heavens...'[70] Rav Qaṭṭina and other Amoraim, who were familiar with angels, nevertheless assigned them no place in the theme of Israel's troubles and redemption; in respect of this theme they were like Jonah and insisted on 'the honour of the son rather than that of the Father'.[71]

The attitude to the angels' place and status changes when the reference is not to the people of Israel but to individuals. Not only are the angels not ousted from the passages where they expressly appear in Holy Writ, and their actions not minimized, but they are given a role even when they are not mentioned in the Biblical stories and episodes; thus angels are added in order to avoid anthropomorphic expressions. In this regard there is a resemblance between the approach of the Septuagint and the Aramaic Targumim, on the one hand, and the Rabbinic homilies on the other. The verse Exodus iv 24 'that the Lord met him and sought to kill him' is translated by the Septuagint: συνήτησην αὐτῷ ἄγγελος κυρίου καὶ ἐζήτει αὐτὸν ἀποκτεῖναι — 'the angel of the Lord met him...'; also the Targum of Onkelos and the Targum Yerushalmi render in the same way. In similar vein R. Jose declared '...Because he (Moses) neglected his duty, securing his lodging before he performed the circumcision, therefore the angel sought to slay him.'[72] Likewise Rabban Gamaliel said 'The angel did not seek to kill Moses but the child.'[73] But both Sages were anticipated by R. Joshua in his exposition of the verse 'And the name of the other was Eliezer; for the God of my father was my help and delivered me from the sword of Pharaoh': 'At the moment when Dathan said to him "Who made thee a prince and a judge over us? ...Now when Pharaoh heard this thing" (R. Joshua) said: 'They seized Moses and brought him up to the scaffold and bound him and laid the sword upon his neck. At that moment an angel came down and appeared to them in the likeness of Moses; so they seized the angel and left Moses alone.'[74] The Tanna R. Eleazar b. R. Simeon enunciated the rule: 'We do not find that the Holy One, blessed be He, spoke with a woman save with Sarah alone.' The verses that contradict this rule the Amoraim reconciled by resorting to angels.[75] But the Sages did not see fit to appoint angels in all instances. When they deemed it necessary, they added details to the Pentateuchal narrative, and felt no concern that they had interpolated corporeal expressions. The story relating how Miriam 'was shut up seven days' was expounded in an anonymous Baraita as follows: 'Who shut Miriam up? Should you say Moses shut her up, but then Moses was not a priest, and a non-priest may not inspect symptoms of leprosy! And should you say Aaron shut her up — but Aaron was a relative, and a relative may not inspect symptoms of leprosy! The Holy One, blessed be He, however, accorded Miriam at that moment great honour. [He said:] "I am a priest, and I shall shut her up; I shall pronounce her definitely leprous and I shall free her." '[76] This account was apparently due to a desire to emphasize Miriam's righteousness despite her sin and the punishment inflicted upon her. It finds expression also in the following homily: 'Miriam waited a while for Moses, as it is said "And his sister stood afar off" (Exodus ii 4); therefore the Omnipresent delayed for her the Shekhina, the Ark, the priests, the Levites, and the Israelites.[77] The question whether the angels were higher than man was a matter of dispute, and we have already mentioned the views of those who placed man, as the élite of Creation, above the angels.[78] While the Septuagint translated the verse 'For Thou hast made him a little lower than *'Ĕlōhîm'* (Psalms viii 6), βραχύ τι παρ' ἀγγέλους, that is, 'less than the angels', the Tannaim and the Amoraim used this and the verses that follow as evidence of man's pre-eminence, whenever the angels argue against the Holy One, blessed be He. When man was created, He said to the angels that man's wisdom exceeded theirs, and Adam gave proof of this by giving names (to the animals).[79] Rav Judah reported in the name of Rav that the companies of angels who said 'What is man that Thou art mindful of him?' were punished by the Holy One, blessed be He, who 'put forth His little finger among them and burnt them' (*T.B. Sanhedrin* 38b). Rav and Samuel both stated 'Fifty gates of understanding were created in the world, and all were given to Moses except one', and they based their statement on the verse 'For Thou hast made him a little lower than '*Ĕlōhîm*.'[80] R. Joshua b. Levi taught that when Moses ascended to receive the Torah, the angels argued 'The hidden treasure that Thou didst keep concealed nine hundred and seventy-four generations[81] before the world was created, dost Thou wish to give to a human being?... Said the Holy One, blessed be He, to him [Moses] "Give them an answer." ' Thereupon Moses proceeded to show that it is not in the power of the angels to keep the Torah, and they 'retracted and acknowledged that the Holy One, blessed be He, was right, as it is said "O Lord, our Lord, how glorious is Thy name in all the earth!", whereas "(whose) majesty is rehearsed above the heavens" is omitted. Forthwith each one became his friend and transmitted something to him, for it is said "Thou hast ascended on high, thou hast led captivity captive; thou hast received gifts for man [באדם *bā'ādām*]" — in recompense for their having called thee man, thou has received gifts. Even the angel of death communicated a secret to him, as it is said "And he put on the incense and made atonement for the people", and it is further stated "And he stood between the dead and the living" etc. Had he [the angel of death] not told him [Moses], how would he have known?'[82] When the Holy One, blessed be He, wished to let His Shekhina dwell among men, the angels again objected, and David deduced from the phrasing of the verse 'O Lord, our Lord, how glorious is Thy name in all the earth! Whose majesty is rehearsed above the heavens' that the earth takes precedence over the heavens.[83] However, not only was 'the Shekhina primarily among the denizens of earth' (see above, p. 48), but the destruction of the Temple led to 'the diminution of the heavenly household' (*T.B. Ḥagiga* 13b). Nevertheless, man's high status and superiority over the angels is not immutable. The fulfilment and observance of the Torah, which he was privileged to receive on account of his virtues, are prerequisites of this eminence as of every other position of distinction. In an anonymous homily in the *Sifre* (Numbers § 119, p. 143), it is stated: 'Beloved are Israel, for when He calls them by a byname, He uses only the title "priests", as it is said "But ye shall be named the priests of the Lord..." (Isaiah lxi 6). Beloved are the priests, for when He calls them by a byname, He uses only the epithet of the Ministering Angels, for it is said "For the priest's lips should keep knowledge, and they should seek the law at his mouth; for he is the messenger [מלאך *mal'ākh*, rendered elsewhere angel] of the Lord of hosts" (Malachi ii 7). When the Torah issues from his mouth, he is like the Ministering Angels, but if not he is like the beasts or cattle, who know not their Creator.' This rule applied to all righteous men and even to Moses. The prophets were called angels. R. Joḥanan said 'They were called angels ['messengers'] from their father's house [origin], that is, by virtue of their essential task, for they are messengers of the Omnipresent. Verses that according to their simple sense referred to angels of the Most High, were interpreted by the Sages as relating to Moses and Phinehas.[84] But even so, R. Tanḥum b. R. Ḥanilai, the disciple of R. Joḥanan, expounded the verse 'Bless the Lord, ye angels of His, ye mighty in strength, that fulfil His word, hearkening unto the voice of His word' (Psalms ciii 20) as speaking of the earthly beings, whereas the continuation 'Bless the Lord, all ye His hosts' speaks of the celestial beings, for, since,the celestial beings are able to carry out the missions of the Holy One, blessed be He, it is said 'Bless the Lord, all ye His hosts', but in the case of the inhabitants of earth, seeing that they are unable to fulfil the tasks assigned to them by the Holy One, blessed be He, it is said 'Bless the Lord, ye angels ['messengers'] of His'.[85] Moses' triumph over the angels puts him in a unique position, which transcended even Jacob's struggle and victory. According to an anonymous Midrash, 'Jacob said to Moses "I am greater than you; I encountered an angel and conquered him." Said Moses to him "You encountered the angel in your domain, but I ascended to the Ministering Angels in their domain, and they were afraid of me, as it is said 'The angels [מלאכי *mal'ăkhê*; but the Masoretic text has מלכי *malĕkhê* ('kings')] of hosts flee, they flee' (Psalms lxviii 13 [12])" '.[86]

Moses' superiority over the angels stemmed from the fact that he was a righteous man who fulfilled the Lord's word[87], but since he was also an intermediary between Israel and their Father in heaven, 'he was affected by the sin' of the people, which lowered his standing *vis-à-vis* the angels. This was inferred from the same verse that testified in the preceding homily to the angels' fear of Moses: ' "Kings of hosts flee, they flee." R. Judan in the name of R. Aibu said: The text does not read "angels of hosts" but "kings of hosts", that is, the kings of the angels. Even Michael, even Gabriel, were unable to look at Moses' face. When Israel sinned, however, Moses could not even look at a *galearius* [subordinate angel], "For I was in dread of the anger and hot displeasure" (Deuteronomy ix 19).'[88]

The author of The Epistle to the Hebrews accepted the idea that the righteous were greater than the angels and transferred it to the 'Son', linking it up with his Christological doctrine. Of the 'Son' he says 'For unto which of the angels said He at any time, "Thou art my son, this day have I begotten thee" (Psalms ii 7)? And again, "I will be to him a Father, and he shall be to me a son"? And again, when He bringeth in the first-begotten into the world, He saith, "And let all the angels of God worship him..." But to which of the angels said He at any time "Sit on My right hand, until I make thine enemies thy footstool..."? For unto the angels hath He not put into subjection the world to come, whereof we speak. But one in a certain place testified, saying "What is man that Thou art mindful of him? or the son of man, that Thou visitest him? Thou madest him a little lower than the angels... Thou hast put all things in subjection under his feet." For in that He put all in subjection under him, He left nothing that is not put under him. But now we see not yet all things put under him. But we see Jesus, who was made a little lower than the angels for the suffering of death, crowned with glory and honour: that he by the grace of God should taste death for every man.'[89] The author of the epistle, who knew no Hebrew, cited Psalms viii 6 [5] according to the Septuagint,[90] and in agreement therewith he taught that Jesus in his lifetime was a little lower than an angel, for he came to save the children, who are flesh and blood, 'and he partook of flesh and blood like them, that through death he might destroy him that had the power of death, that is, the devil'. But when he died, he was exalted and became 'faithful to Him who appointed him, as also Moses was faithful in all His house. For this man was counted worthy of more glory than Moses... And Moses verily was faithful in all His house, as a servant... But Christ as a son over His house...'[91] The writer of the epistle argues against the view of those who wish to regard Jesus as a messenger, angel or archon, a view that was apparently widespread and against which Christian writers polemized even in the second century.[92] He made use of the motif 'The righteous are greater than angels', and especially of what was said concerning Moses, but in a Christological direction. It appears that it is against homilies of this type that the words of the Palestinian Amora of the fourth century, who knew Greek[93] and added to the dicta of his predecessors regarding the Ministering Angels and angels, were aimed: 'Rabbi Berechia said in the name of R. Abba bar Kahana: The Holy One, blessed be He, is destined to set the domain of the righteous in front of the domain of the Ministering Angels, and the Ministering Angels will ask them, saying "What hath God wrought?" "What hath the Holy One, blessed be He, taught them?" R. Levi bar Ḥayyuta said: Has He not already done so in this world? This is the meaning of the verse "Nebuchadnezzar answered and said: 'Lo, I see four men loose, walking in the midst of the fire, and they have no hurt' "... Scripture does not state "and the appearance of the first" but "and the appearance of the fourth". They were quenching the fire before him. "Like a son of God" — R. Reuben said: At that moment an angel descended and struck him on his mouth. He said to him: "Wicked man! amend thy words. Has He a son?" (Thereupon) he retracted and said "Blessed be the God of Shadrach, Meshach, and Abed-nego" — Scripture does not say here "who hath sent His son" but "who hath sent His angel, and delivered His servants that trusted in Him". '[94]

The views that we have thus far cited concerning the relationship between men and angels are based on the independence of the righteous man of angels. He casts his dread over all of them irrespective of whether they are good or bad angels. But alongside these dicta and homilies there are others that reflect a different outlook, which is to a large extent common also to the apocryphal literature and is likewise widely current in the Greek and Iranian worlds. Everywhere angels accompany man and guard him.[95] The problem, on the one hand, of the existence of evil in the world, and, on the other, the driving power that manifests itself in man to win through and do great things, called forth similar solutions in different places and periods. The Tanna, the Haggadist R. Eliezer the son of R. Jose the

accompanying angels

Galilean, adopted the concept of the accompanying angels, but distinguished between righteous and wicked men. He said 'If you see a righteous man about to set out on a journey and you wish to proceed on the same journey, start out three days earlier (than you intended) because of him, or three days later on account of him, so that you may journey with him. What is the reason? Because the Ministering Angels accompany him, as it is said "For He will give His angels charge over thee" (Psalms xci 11). And if you see a wicked man about to set out on a journey and you wish to proceed on the same journey, start out three days earlier (than you intended) because of him, or three days later on account of him, so that you may avoid journeying with him, since angels of Satan accompany him, as it is stated "Set Thou a wicked one over him; and let Satan stand at his right hand" (Psalms cix 6).'[96] The angels minister to the righteous and help them to fulfil their good intentions. Of R. Ḥanina b. Dosa it is related: 'He once saw the men of his town taking up votive and freewill offerings. Said he: They are all taking up votive and freewill offerings to Jerusalem, and I shall not bring anything? What did he do? He went to the city and saw there a stone, which he cleaned, chiselled and painted. (Then) he said: I vow to bring it up to Jerusalem. (Thereupon) five men appeared. Said he to them: Will ye bring up this stone for me to Jerusalem? They replied: Give us five *selas*, and we shall bring up your stone for you to Jerusalem; only you must lend us a finger. So he gave them a hand, and lo! they were standing in Jerusalem. When he wished to pay them the five *selas*, he did not find them. So he went into the Hewn Chamber. They [the Sages] said: Perhaps they were Ministering Angels? They then applied to him the following verse: "Seest thou a man diligent in his business? he shall stand before angels" [מלאכים *mal'ākhîm*, the Masoretic text has מלכים *mĕlākhîm* ("kings")].[97] The humble and natural task of the angels accords with the stylistic simplicity and freshness of the narrative, which belongs to the category of miracle tales, with which we have dealt earlier. (p. 118).

The concept of the angels who accompany a person penetrated deeply into the religious consciousness and left its mark on the Halakha: 'Upon entering a privy' — it is stated — 'a man pronounces two benedictions, one on entering and one on leaving.' While the blessing on leaving constitutes a thanksgiving for the creation of man and praise for the wisdom of the Creator, 'what does he say on entering? Honour to you, you honoured ones, who minister in the holy place; this is the way of nature. Make way; blessed be the honoured God.'[98]

It is true that alongside of the saving angel we find the destroying angel, and a cruel angel,[99] and among the host of heaven the enticing spirit[1] and the Satan ['Adversary']; but they are all engaged in the Lord's mission. In Rabbinic sources, too, both the ministering and destroying angels do the Lord's mission and belong to His household.[2] But the expression 'angels of Satan' in the dictum of R. Eliezer b. R. Jose the Galilean refers to the special 'familia' of Satan.[3] The statement of this Tanna on our subject has a distinct apocalyptic character.[4] However, the expression does not recur[5] even in the sayings of the Amoraim that accepted the motif of differentiation between the angels accompanying the righteous man and those escorting the wicked one. R. Eleazar said: 'When a righteous man passes from the world, three groups of Ministering Angels go forth to meet him... when a wicked man perishes from the world, three groups of Destroying Angels go forth to meet him...'[6] Contrariwise R. Zeriqa states 'The two Ministering Angels who escort him testify against him,'[7] and no distinction is drawn by this Sage between the wicked and the righteous. Although even in R. Eleazar's dictum it is not specifically stated that the angels of destruction are the same as the angels of Satan, yet his words are very similar to those of R. Eliezer b. R. Jose the Galilean. He also interpreted the events of the past as a conflict between Samma'el and Gabriel (*T.B. Soṭa* 10b), and it appears that the role he assigned to Samma'el and to the angels of destruction is connected with the concept that denies all evil to the Almighty, for he is the author of the dictum that 'the name of the Holy One, blessed be He, is not mentioned in relation to evil, only in relation to good.'[8] It is indeed also stated in the name of R. Joḥanan the teacher of R. Eleazar: 'Before the Holy One, blessed be He, there stand only angels of peace and mercy, but the angels of indignation are far from Him, as it is said "They come from a far country, from the end of heaven, even the Lord, and the weapons of His indignation, to destroy the whole earth" (Isaiah xiii 5).'[9] But the angels of indignation are not the angels of Satan; it is thus clear that R. Joḥanan did not go as far as R. Eliezer b. R. Jose the Galilean or R. Eleazar in removing evil from God. When he himself reports in the name of R. Eliezer the son of R. Jose the Galilean, he states: 'Even if nine hundred and ninety-nine angels arraign a man, and but one angel pleads in his favour, the Holy One, blessed be He, decides in his favour. Nor, in the end, need it be the whole of that angel, but even if nine hundred and ninety-nine facets of that angel indict him and but one facet of that angel pleads in his favour, the Holy One, blessed be He, decides in His favour.'[10] Although the accusers are only ordinary angels, yet R. Joḥanan kept them also far from the Holy One, blessed be He. As we shall see in our discussion regarding Creation,[11] the Sages included in that which was created by Him who spoke and the world came into being also darkness and evil, but despite their desire to avoid the slightest taint of dualistic belief they did not overlook the problem of the relationship between God — who is the God of good, lovingkindness and compassion — and evil. The existence of angels, including prosecutors and destroying angels, headed by Satan, the Angel of Death, sufficed to conjure up custodians of evil in the world; but bounds were always set to their independence and power of action. R. Joḥanan said in the name of R. Eliezer the son of R. Jose the Galilean: 'When the Israelites stood at Mount Sinai and said "All that the Lord hath spoken will we do, and obey" (Exodus xxiv 7), at that moment the Holy One, blessed be He, called the Angel of Death and said to him: "Although I have made you Cosmocrator (κοσμοκράτωρ) over My creatures, you must have nought to do with this nation. Why? Because they are My children." This is the meaning of the verse "Ye are children of the Lord your God" (Deuteronomy xiv 1). It further says "And it came to pass, when ye heard the voice out of the midst of the darkness" (*ibid.* v. 20). But is there darkness on high? Lo, it is written "And the light dwelleth with Him" (Daniel ii 22)! The meaning is that the Angel of Death, who is called Darkness...'[12] The significance of this homily now becomes perfectly clear against the background of the dualistic doctrine, according to the extreme formulation it receives in the Scroll of *The Manual of Discipline*, which states 'In the hand of the Prince of Lights is dominion over all the sons of righteousness; in the ways of light they walk. And in the hand of the Angel of

Darkness is dominion over the sons of wickedness; and in the ways of darkness they walk.'[13] Against views of this kind, R. Eliezer b. R. Jose the Galilean emphasizes that not only was the cosmocrator, the Angel of Death called Darkness, created by the Holy One, blessed He — this is admitted also by the author of *The Manual of Discipline* — but his very dominion is not a decree that cannot be changed, annulled, or restricted. On the contrary, the giving of the Torah served to annul his dominion over Israel, and only when they acted corruptly and made the calf were they again delivered into his power.[14]

However, not only the non-recurring episode of the receiving of the Torah, but the very possibility of the observance of the precepts diminishes the reality of the force of evil in the world — the danger and the menace connected with the angels of destruction and demons; nay more, it also lessens the need of protection by the good angels and intercessors. Not just two angels accompany man, but their number grows with the number of precepts; and sometimes it seems that the precepts themselves are the good angels. The Tanna R. Eliezer b. Jacob taught 'He who performs one precept acquires for himself one intercessor, and he who commits one transgression acquires for himself one accuser.'[15] This dictum was developed, through integration with other ideas and motifs, into the following homily:

> '...For He will give His angels charge over thee, to keep thee in all thy ways' (Psalms xci 11): If a man performed one precept, he is given one angel; if he performed two precepts, he is given two angels; if he did all the precepts, he is given many angels... And who are these angels? They who guard him against the demons, as it is said 'A thousand may fall at thy side, and ten thousand at thy right hand.' What is meant by 'fall'? They make peace with him... 'And ten thousand at thy right hand' — why a thousand at the left side and ten thousand at the right side? Because the left does not need many angels, for the name of the Holy One, blessed be He, is inscribed in the phylacteries and the phylacteries are placed on the left hand... Said R. Ḥanina to him: It is not written in Scripture 'may *be* at thy side' but 'may *fall*'. The left, which is not steeped in precepts, causes only a thousand demons to fall; but the right, which is steeped in precepts, causes ten thousand demons to fall. R. Joshua b. Levi

said: What is meant by 'A thousand may fall at thy side'? The Holy One, blessed be He, assigns to each Israelite a myriad and one thousand angels, to guard him and make a way for him, and one of them proclaims before him, saying: 'Grant honour to the image of the Holy One, blessed be He', for the entire world is full of spirits and demons. R. Judah bar Shalom said in the name of R. Levi: There is not a *bêt rōva'* [an area of ground capable of producing a quarter of a *qav* of seed] in the space of the world that does not contain nine *qav* of demons. What form do they take? R. Levi said: They have a mask (*forma*) over their faces, like the millers' asses, and when sins warrant it, the mask is removed, and the person becomes insane. So long as the angel utters the proclamation, a man is safe; but as soon as he is silent, the man is immediately injured, and the angel declares 'so-and-so's end has come', as it is said "Yea, his soul draweth near unto the pit, and his life to the destroyers" (Job xxxiii 22)'. Scripture does not say here 'to the dead' [*la-mēthîm*] but 'to the destroyers' [*la-měmîthîm*] — to those angels of destruction to whom he is delivered. And how do we know that the angel proclaims before him? For it is stated 'If there be for him an angel, an intercessor, one among a thousand' — if there is of those thousand (angels) one who proclaims before him 'to vouch for man's uprightness', then at that moment 'He is gracious unto him, and saith: "Deliver him from going down to the pit, I have found a ransom." ' From this we may infer that if a man is rich in precepts, a myriad and a thousand angels keep guard over him; but if he is flawless in Torah and good deeds, the Holy One, blessed be He, (Himself) guards him, as it is said 'The Lord is thy keeper, the Lord is thy shade upon thy right hand' (Psalms cxxi 7). And thus you find in the case of Jacob of whom it is written 'a perfect [*tam*] man, dwelling in tents' (Genesis xxv 26) — 'a perfect man' in good deeds; 'dwelling in tents', occupying himself with the Torah and growing rich in precepts — camps of angels were assigned to him to guard him, as it is said (*ibid.* xxxii 2): 'And Jacob went on his way, and the angels of God met him...' and it is further stated 'And, behold, the Lord stood beside him, and said... And, behold, I am with thee, and will keep thee whithersoever thou goest' (*ibid.* xxviii 13–15). R. Hoshaiah said: Happy is he that, born of woman, saw the King of kings and His household guarding him, and sending angels to perform his mission, as it is said (*ibid.* xxxii 4) 'And Jacob sent angels before him to Esau.'[16]

This homily has as its main object to exhort people to keep the commandments. The preacher accepted the prevailing view that the whole world was full of demons;[17] but the Torah had the power to confine the sphere and compass of their activity. On account of the merit of R. Ḥanina b. Dosa and his Torah-learning, the time when Igrat, the daughter of Mahalat, and her armies of destroyers have dominion was restricted to the nights of the Sabbaths and the nights of Wednesdays, and Abbaye even succeeded in banishing her from settled areas.[18] It is reported, however, in the name of Rava that he attributed dreams that have a prophetic character to an angel, whereas vain dreams he ascribed to demons. But Rava himself also said that 'a man is shown (in his dream) only the thoughts of his own mind.'[19]

It is not without interest to point to parallels in the sources of the Persian religion from the Sassanian era. The presence of Ahriman in the world is not an ontological fact; the created world is wholly the work of Ahura Mazda, only it serves as an easy sphere of activity for the destructive and negative groups of Ahriman. In the Sixth Book of the *Dēnkart*, which is an ethical treatise, the author wishes to persuade his readers that the struggle against the negation of the demons is not one against real creatures, but is primarily a conflict between man and himself, and every individual bears responsibility. For if they are not allowed to dwell in man, the demons cannot exist.[20] Similarly, but more profoundly, Plotinus developed his doctrine of the demon. In his opinion, we choose the demon for ourselves by the way of our lives, for by our conduct we select the supreme directing power.[21]

So far our discussion about the world of the angels was linked and subject to theological, historical, national, and ethical questions. The concepts concerning the relationship of God to man, whom He had created, and to His chosen people, the problem of the righteous and the wicked, the source of evil in the world — it was these that determined and regulated the acts and portrayal of the angels. But even within the restrained dicta and homilies there burgeoned motifs and expressions that did not grow out of the soil of reflective thought or religious-ethical preaching, but had its source in the imagination, motivated by the desire to penetrate into hidden worlds and the impulse to relate and convey what happens in them. The apocalyptic literature is characterized by descriptions of this kind, and even includes works that were actually dictated by angels. Undoubtedly these books and their like were popular in various circles. However, the Sages understood the difference between the visions of Daniel and those of the prophets. 'R. Simeon b. Laqish said: Also the names of the angels were brought by him from Babylon. At first (Scripture states) "Then flew unto me one of the seraphim" (Isaiah vi 6), "Above Him stood the seraphim" (*ibid.* vi 2), thereafter (we find) "the man Gabriel" (Daniel ix 21), "except Michael your prince" (*ibid.* x 21).'[22] But not only were the names of the angels in Daniel accepted; they were also augmented by the names of many other angels. They all constitute the Court of the Holy One, blessed be He, like the court of a king. In this Court there have occurred and there continue to take place acts and episodes that are revealed to those who are worthy; these are akin to mythological tales of various cultures. Stories of this nature are found not only in the apocryphal literature, but also in the Midrashic homilies and in the Talmuds. When these are anonymous, bearing the name of no Sage, they present us with a panoramic picture, emphasizing characteristics, names, attributes and conflicts. Although we find Tannaim and Amoraim who do not hesitate to mention 'the angels of Satan' or a struggle between 'Samma'el and Gabriel',[23] yet their remarks are always brief and colourless, lacking mythical characteristics. They serve to testify that ampler and more detailed accounts relating to the themes that have reached us through the apocryphal writings were also known to them, only they purposefully avoided transmitting them. But many of their colleagues did not proceed at all along the path of absorption and adaptation, but chose the way of interpretation, which led to eradication and nullification. Just as we have seen that there were Sages who, in consequence of their conception of the Torah and the precepts, eventually not only nullified the influence of the demons and angels upon earth, but, in effect, negated their reality, so there were scholars who turned the

Heavenly Court into a Heavenly Court of Law and Academy, which are a reflection of an earthly law court and academy, and thus they emptied the idea of its original content. The views and aim of the latter did not remain without influence on the sources that ostensibly appertain to the former category, and only by positing this influence are we able to understand their significance and intent. Also conversely, the trend towards eradication and reversal of the position likewise did not achieve perfection, and traces of early strata are still to be detected without difficulty.

To project clearly the phenomena that we have discussed, we shall cite conspicuous examples for each one of them. The story of the serpent in the Book of Genesis — on account of whom death came into the world — which left no further trace in the Biblical books, received extensive treatment in the apocryphal literature and in the Haggada. In the *Book of Adam and Eve* (xvi 1–7) Satan stands behind the serpent and says to him: 'Be only my instrument, and I shall speak by your mouth a word whereby you shall beguile him.' According to the Revelation to John (xii 9; xx 2) 'that ancient serpent' is called Devil and Satan, and Justin Martyr even found etymological proof for this identification. The word σατανάς is just a combination of סטה *sāṭā* ['deviate'] and נחש *naḥash* ['serpent'], i.e. 'a faithless, heretical serpent'.[24] In the early Midrashim there is no trace of such an identification, and Satan does not appear at all during the episode of the serpent; but the creation of the serpent itself is connected with that of Eve. On the verse 'And closed up the place with flesh instead thereof' (Genesis ii 21), R. Ḥanina the son of Rav Ada commented: 'From the beginning of the Book up to this point there is no *Samekh*; but as soon as she [Eve] was created, Satan was created with her.'[25] It is not to be supposed that this Amora was not thinking of Satan's rôle in the incident of Eve's sin. R. Jeremiah b. Eleazar, who called the serpent an 'Epicurian'[26], regarded him as a heretic. The angel standing behind the serpent is identified in *Pirqe de-R. Eliezer* as 'Samma'el', and his action is depicted as a sequel to the angels' denunciation of the creation of man, which we found in the early Midrashim. But whereas in them the angels become reconciled to man's creation and recognize his wisdom[27], in the Midrash that was edited later — but into which there infiltrated descriptions and stories current in apocalyptic liter-

the serpent (= satan = samma'el) = "he who made himself a god"

ature — the denunciation marks the beginning of man's downfall, and indirectly of the rebellion against God. After Adam had given names to all the creatures, the angels said: 'If we cannot devise a plan to make man sin before his Creator, we shall not prevail against him. Now there was Samma'el, the great prince of heaven, as well as the Living Creatures and the Seraphim, who have six wings, but Samma'el has twelve wings. He [Samma'el] took his company and went down and inspected all the creatures that the Holy One, blessed be He, had created, and he found none more cunning to do evil than the serpent... who had the appearance of a camel, and he [Samma'el] went up and rode on him, while the Torah cried aloud, saying: Samma'-el, the world was only just now created, is this a time to rebel against the Omnipresent, will you at this juncture stir up revolt on high?... As for the serpent, every act that he performed and every word that he spoke, he spoke and did only at the will of Samma'el.'[28] The resemblance to the account that we cited from the *Book of Adam and Eve* requires no stressing; only Satan's place is here taken by Samma'el. In addition to the penalty imposed in the Torah narrative on the serpent and on Adam and Eve — the *dramatis personae* of the Biblical drama — in the mythical story of *Pirqe de-R. Eliezer* Samma'el, too, is not exonerated and his punishment fits the crime. The Holy One, blessed be He, 'cast down Samma'el and his followers from their holy place in heaven'.[29] In the meantime 'Samma'el took hold of Michael's wing to force him down, but the Holy One, blessed be He, saved him [פלטו *pělāṭô*] from his hands'.[30] However, the matter did not end with the downfall of Samma'el's host. In the name of Rabbi the Midrash declares: 'The angels who fell from their holy place, from heaven, saw the daughters of Cain walking about with uncovered *pudenda* and with painted eyes like harlots, and they went astray after them, taking from among them wives, as it is said 'that the sons of God saw the daughters of men' (Genesis vi 1). Other sayings of the same *genre* are cited in the name of R. Joshua b. Qorḥa and R. Zadok.[31] Although the names of the Tannaim mentioned are apocryphal, the interpretation itself, that by 'the sons of God' angels are meant, is old, since R. Simeon b. Yoḥai already reacted to it. After his own explanation 'sons of judges' had been cited, it is stated 'R. Simeon b. Yoḥai used to curse all those who called them "sons of

God" '.[32] Samma'el's followers walked in the footsteps of their prince, for the author of *Pirqe de-R. Eliezer* relates of him, when he comes to the story of Cain's birth: 'A serpent-rider came to her [Eve] and made her pregnant; thereafter Adam came to her and made her conceive Abel, as it is said "And Adam knew Eve his wife". What is meant by "he knew"? — that she was pregnant and he saw, from its [the foetus's] likeness, that it belonged not to earth's creatures but to the celestial beings;[33] and she prophesied and said "I have gotten a man with the help of the Lord". '[34] Although the name of the 'serpent-rider' is not expressly mentioned, yet it is obvious that the reference is to Samma'el.[35] The erotic theme is old. The motif of jealousy is alluded to in *The Wisdom of Solomon* (ii 24) 'but through Satan's envy death entered the world', but the nature of the envy is not described.[36] In the Tosefta[37] it is stated: 'So, too, we find in the case of the serpent, who set his mind on killing Adam and taking Eve to wife.' In the name of R. Joshua b. Qorḥa it is reported: 'Because he saw them engaged in sexual intercourse and he lusted for her.'[38] According to the Amora R. Joḥanan, who was familiar with the apocalyptic sources, the desire and lust were implemented, and he says 'When the serpent went into Eve, he injected contaminating lust into her.'[39] However, the primary teaching of the dictum is found in the continuation, to wit, that 'The Israelites who stood at Mount Sinai lost their contaminating lust', and it seeks, as we shall see later, to refute the idea of original sin. But R. Joḥanan's statement and the dicta of the Tannaim testify that they knew the last-mentioned motif, which we have cited in a version similar to that of *Pirqe de-R. Eliezer* and Targum Pseudo-Jonathan; and it seems that R. Joshua b. Qorḥa and the anonymous Tanna of the Tosefta were also acquainted with it (only they tempered it), just as we find other testimonies to the Sages' familiarity with the myth of the Serpent-Satan-Samma'el, as it appears in the apocryphal literature. In the Slavonic *Enoch*[40] there stands at the head of the Watchers, who defected from the Lord, their 'chieftain' Satanail, and 'upon fleeing from heaven he became Satan'.[41]

But little is left of the original rebellious character of Satanail in Rabbinic literature. In a Baraita the role of Satan is defined thus: 'He goes down to earth and incites, he ascends to heaven and arraigns, and he has permission to speak. From this we learn that permission has been given to Satan to arraign.'[42] In addition to his task as inciter in the form of the serpent, he is also the accuser, as he appears in the prologue of the Book of Job. Influenced by the account in Job, R. Joḥanan makes the Almighty, so to speak, the object of the incitement and declares: 'Were it not written in Scripture, it would be inconceivable to say it — He was like a man who is incited and falls a prey to the incitement.' And even Resh Laqish, who identifies Satan with the evil inclination in man,[43] does not deprive him at the same time of the role of Satan-Accuser or that of the Angel of Death.[44] However, no distinction is drawn in the various sources between these functions; thus even Samma'el sometimes appears also as the inciting evil inclination.[45] But Samma'el's main influence is felt in the struggles against the supremacy of man, and therein he retains his rebellious character. Only the name Samma'el is not preserved in all the sources; at times his place is taken by Satan, without further qualification, or by another angel. The verse 'And there wrestled a man with him' (Genesis xxxii 25) was explained by R. Ḥama b. R. Ḥanina thus: 'It was the Guardian Angel of Esau; it was to him that he [Jacob] said "I have seen thy face, as one seeth the face of God, and thou wast pleased with me" (Genesis xxx 10). It is like the case of an athlete who was standing and wrestling with the king's son; on looking up and seeing the king standing over him, he allowed himself to be vanquished [literally 'trodden down'] by him [the son]' (*Genesis Rabba* lxxvii 3, p. 912). Nor is it surprising that Esau's Guardian Angel is identified in a later source with Samma'el;[46] especially as there were Midrashim that equated the man who wrestled with Jacob actually with Michael, the Guardian Angel of Israel,[47] and this identification also finds support in ancient sources.[48] But it seems that these, too, were preceded by a source that considered the man to be God Himself. Traces of this mythological Midrash are to be found in early and in late Midrashim. Thus it is stated in *Genesis Rabba* (lxxvii, 3, p. 921): ' "For thou hast striven with God and with men"... with celestial beings, that is, an angel. R. Ḥama b. R. Ḥanina said: It was the Guardian Angel of Esau... Another explanation is: "For thou hast striven with God" — thou art he whose image is engraven on high.' From the same source undoubtedly emanates also the daring homily on Genesis xxxiii 20: ' "And he erected there an altar, and called it

El-elohe-Israel." He said to Him: Thou art God among the celestial beings; I am god among the earthly inhabitants.' To this homily R. Simeon b. Laqish reacted sharply: 'Even the superintendent of the Synagogue does not assume authority unto himself, but you have taken authority unto yourself! Tomorrow your daughter will go out and be raped; this is the meaning of the verse "And Dinah... went out".'[49] Obviously the identification of the angel with Michael, the Guardian Angel of Israel, is an attempt to moderate this homily, while the exposition of R. Ḥama b. R. Ḥanina, like the comments of Resh Laqish, is an expression of opposition. The Guardian Angel of Edom — Samma'el — serves to oust here a grosser myth. We possess clear evidence that similar traditions were known in Jewish circles before the time of R. Ḥama b. R. Ḥanina and Resh Laqish. Origen cites from a work, current among the Jews under the title 'The Prayer of Joseph': 'Jacob, however, said: I am called Jacob by men, but my name is Israel, for by God I am called Israel, that is, a man that sees God (Yśr-'el), for I, behold I am the first-born of all the prophets who were created by God.' He adds: 'I came from across the River [Euphrates] in Syria, and behold the angel of the Lord Uriel appeared and said that I had come down and dwelt among the children of men, and therefore I was called Jacob. He was envious of me, and fought and wrestled with me, saying *that his name was above my name*, and above that of the angel appointed over all. And I told him his name and his place among the sons of God: Art thou not Uriel, the eighth after me, whereas I, behold I am Israel, the captain of the angels of the hosts of the Lord and the captain of the myriads of the sons of God? Am I not Israel, the first minister before the Lord (ὁ ἐν προσώπῳ θεοῦ λειτουργός πρώτος ἐν ὀνόματι ἀσβέστω), and I called my God by a name that is inerasable.'[50]

Against this myth is directed the homily attributed to R. Ḥiyya Rabba or to R. Yannai about the angels who found Jacob, whose image is engraven on high, asleep and they began to 'sport with him [*aliter*: 'dance round him'], to leap on him [or: 'round him'], to scoff at him [or: 'encompass him']' (*Genesis Rabba* lxviii, 12, p. 788). The angels who 'discovered the secret of the Holy One, blessed be He' were demoted in Jacob's dream by the Sages who expounded the subject. Bar Qappara, R. Joshua b. Levi and the Rabbis interpreted his dream as referring to the altar, to Mount Sinai, and to the Exiles (*ibid.*, pp. 781–785). R. Joḥanan completely nullified the dream and taught ' "And Jacob awaked out of his sleep [משנתו *mi-shěnātô*]", that is, from his study [ממשנתו *mi-mishnātô*]'.[51] R. Joḥanan's disciple, R. Abbahu, commented on the words ' "And he dreamed": dreams neither make nor mar' (*Genesis Rabba*, *ibid.*, p. 784). The Scripture 'And, behold, the Lord stood beside him' alone remains unaffected, and R. Abbahu himself drew attention to the difference between this verse and that which precedes it: ' "And, behold, the Lord stood beside him" (Genesis xxviii 13). What is stated earlier? — "And behold the angels of God ascending and descending on it" (*ibid.* v. 12). R. Abbahu said: This is like a prince who was sleeping in his cradle and flies were resting on him; but as soon as his nurse came, she bent over him and suckled him and the flies flew away from him. Even so (it was with Jacob): at first (we read) "And behold the angels of God ascending and descending on it", but as soon as the Holy One, blessed be He, appeared, they fled from him!' In the opinion of R. Joḥanan and R. Abbahu, the Almighty spoke with Jacob when he was awake, and this view also underlies apparently the homily of R. Ḥama bar Ḥanina: ' "Iron alone with [usually rendered 'sharpeneth'] iron; so a man is alone with the presence [literally, 'countenance'] of his friend" (Proverbs xxvii 17) ...as soon as our father Jacob arose, "a man alone with the presence of his Friend" — the Shekhina communed with him alone!'[52] It is also R. Ḥama b. R. Ḥanina who said that the angel who wrestled with Jacob 'was the Guardian Angel of Esau' (above, p. 170).

The introduction of Samma'el into the episode of Jacob bears a secondary character, and despite the struggle with the celestial beings, which is expressly mentioned in the Bible, we have seen that this story took the place of another ancient motif, and is in this respect different from the account of Satan-Samma'el in the episode of Adam.

Akin to it is the story of the passing of Moses. The primary motif, that it was not the Angel of Death who took his soul, is found in the Sifre:[53] 'At that moment, the Holy One, blessed be He, said to the Angel of Death: "Go, bring me Moses' soul." So he went and stood before him (Moses). Said Moses to him: "Where I dwell you are not allowed to stand, yet you say to me 'surrender your soul'!" Thereupon he (Moses) rebuked him (the Angel of Death) and he went forth reprimanded. The Angel of Death accordingly went and reported Moses' answer to the Almighty. The Omnipresent then said (again) to the Angel of Death: "Go and bring me his soul...".' The Angel of Death searched high and low for Moses but could not find him, until the mountains and hills[54] revealed to him 'that God had concealed him for life in the world to come.' The version given here, according to which the Angel of Death is deceived, appears to be an abridgement of a detailed narrative, and we actually possess such a narrative, although it is clear that it is not the source of the *Sifre*. To a certain extent it seems like the continuation of the angels' arraignment of the giving of the Torah to Moses, only the roles are changed. Whereas when Moses ascended to heaven, he struggled with angels and Seraphim who opposed him and sought to consume and destroy him, and the Holy One, blessed be He, shielded and sheltered him from them,[55] in the Midrash before us Moses himself is refractory, and Samma'el, as an angel, becomes a messenger. The version of the story that I cite well reflects the apocalyptic orientation in the description of the heavenly sphere, which, being powerful and concrete, also became popular. Hence I reproduce it in full; it will also serve as a frame of reference for pointing up the opposite trend, which is interpretative and speculative.

In this Midrash[56] it is stated:

> When Moses saw that his decree was sealed, he arose and drew a small circle and sat within it, saying: I shall not move from here until Thou dost abrogate that decree. What did Moses do at that time? He put on sackcloth and wrapped himself in sackcloth and rolled himself in the dust, and stood praying and supplicating before the Holy One, blessed be He, until heaven and earth and the natural order of the universe were in commotion, and they said 'Has the time come when the Holy One, blessed be He, wills (to destroy the world)?' Thereupon a Heavenly Voice went forth and declared: 'The time when the Holy One, blessed be He, wills the destruction of the world has not yet arrived,[57] only He holds in His hand the soul of every living thing, and the spirit of all the flesh of man [usually rendered: "the breath of all mankind"]', and 'man' refers to Moses, as it is said 'And the

man Moses was very meek'. What did the Holy One, blessed be He, do at that time? He proclaimed in every gate, and in every heaven, and in all the gates of every court of justice, that Moses' prayer should not be accepted, or brought before Him, because the Divine decree concerning him had been sealed. Now the angel appointed to make proclamations is called Akhraziel. At that moment the Holy One, blessed be He, called urgently and said to the Ministering Angels: Arise and lock the gate of every heaven. Until the voice of prayer prevailed and rose upward, seeking to ascend to heaven on account of Moses' prayer, which was like a sword, and rent and cut without cessation, for his prayer was like the Ineffable Name, which he had learnt from Zagza'el, his teacher, the scribe of all the heavenly beings.[58] Of this (moment) it is said 'and I heard behind me the voice of a great רעש *ra'ash*'; now *ra'ash* connotes commotion, and 'great' alludes to Moses, as it is said 'Moreover the man Moses was (very) great'. What is meant by 'Blessed be the glory of the Lord from His place'? When the Wheels of the Chariot and the flaming Seraphim[59] perceived that the Holy One, blessed be He, said 'Do not accept the prayer of Moses' and He showed no favouritism and did not grant him life and did not bring him into the Land, they cried 'Blessed be the glory of the Lord from His place', for He shows no favouritism either to small or great. And how do we know that Moses prayed 515 times? For it is stated 'And I besought [ואתחנן *wā-'etḥannān*] the Lord', and the numerical value of *wā-etḥannan* amounts to this. At that time Moses said before the Holy One, blessed be He: 'Sovereign of the universe, Thou knowest full well the toil and travail and distress that I endured on their [Israel's] account in connection with the precepts, until I established Torah and precepts among them. I thought that just as I had witnessed their distress so I should behold their prosperity. But now that the time of Israel's prosperity has come, Thou dost say to me "Thou shalt not go over this Jordan!" Thus, Thou dost falsify Thy Torah, for it is written "In the same day thou shalt give him his hire". Is this the recompense for the forty years that I toiled until they became a holy people? as it is said: "but Judah still ruled with God and was faithful to the

Holy One" (Hosea xii 1).' The angel Samma'el, the head of the demons [literally, 'satans'], was waiting every moment for Moses' death, saying: 'When will the moment come when Moses will die, when I shall go down and take Moses' soul from him?' Of him David said 'The wicked watcheth the righteous, and seeketh to slay him' (Psalms xxxvii 32). Among all the demons there is none so wicked as Samma'el, and among all the prophets there is none so righteous as Moses... Thus, the wicked Samma'el waited for the soul of Moses, saying: When shall Michael weep and I fill my mouth with laughter... At one time Moses said before God: 'Sovereign of the universe, if Thou wilt not permit me to enter the Land of Israel, let me be like the beasts of the field, which eat grass and drink water, but see the world; let me be even as one of them.' Said (God) to him: 'Enough unto you!' Then (Moses) said to Him: 'Sovereign of the universe, if not, let me be in this world like a bird, which flies in the air in all directions and daily gathers its food, and in the evening returns to its nest; let me be even as one of them.' Said (God) unto him: 'Enough unto you!' (Again Moses) said to Him [God]: 'Sovereign of the universe, leave one of my eyes beneath the door, and let the door be placed upon it three times a year, so that I may live and not die.' (God) answered him: 'Enough!'[60] When Moses saw that no creature could deliver him from death... What did Moses do? He took the scroll and wrote thereon the Ineffable Name, and before he had completed writing the Book of the Song the moment arrived for Moses to die. At that moment the Holy One, blessed be He, said to Gabriel: 'Go and fetch Moses' soul.' Said he before Him: 'Sovereign of the universe, he who is equal to the sixty myriads (of Israel) — how can I see him die? And he who possesses these things — how can I vent my anger upon him?' Then He said to Michael: 'Go and fetch Moses' soul.' Said he before God: 'I was the teacher and he was my disciple — how can I see him die?' Thereafter He said to Samma'el: 'Go and fetch Moses' soul'. Forthwith he donned his anger, and girded on his sword, and wrapped himself in ruthlessness, and went to meet Moses. When, however, Samma'el saw him sitting and writing the Ineffable Name, and the radiance of his countenance was like that of the sun, and he resembled an angel of the Lord of hosts, he was afraid of Moses. He thought: Verily, the angels are not able to take Moses' soul...[61] and Samma'el could not open his mouth to speak to Moses until Moses said to him: ' "There is no peace" saith the Lord "concerning the wicked"; what are you doing here?' He replied: 'I have come to take your soul.' Said (Moses) to him: 'Who sent you?' He replied: 'He that created the whole world.' Said (Moses) to him: 'you shall not take my soul...[62] Begone from me!...' Samma'el immediately returned and reported to the Almighty. Said the Holy One, blessed be He, to him: 'Go and fetch Moses' soul.' Forthwith he drew his sword from its scabbard and made ready to attack Moses. At once Moses became wroth with him and took in his hand the staff of God on which was engraved the Ineffable Name and smote Samma'el with it with all his might, until he fled before him, and (Moses) pursued him with the Ineffable Name and took a ray from between his eyes and blinded his eyes.[63] Thus far success attended Moses. A moment later a Heavenly Voice came forth and said: 'The moment of your death has at last arrived.' Said Moses before the Holy One, blessed be He: 'Sovereign of the universe, remember unto me the day when Thou didst reveal Thyself unto me in the thorn bush... I beg of Thee, deliver me not into the hand of the Angel of Death.' A Heavenly Voice went forth and declared unto him: 'Fear not, I Myself shall attend to you and to your burial.'[64] At that moment Moses arose and sanctified himself like the Seraphim, and the Holy One, blessed be He, descended from the highest heavens of the heavens to take away the soul of Moses, and the three Ministering Angels — Michael, Gabriel and Zagza'el — with him...' After they had attended to his body, 'the Holy One, blessed be He, called upon the soul to leave his body'. But she [the soul] still refused and countered with the question: 'Is there a purer body than that of Moses?' When the Holy One, blessed be He, said to the soul 'Go forth, tarry no more, and I shall raise you up to the highest heavens of the heavens, and cause you to dwell beneath the Throne of My Glory beside the Cherubim and Seraphim and Legions', she said before Him: 'Sovereign of the universe, from beside Thy Shekhina on high two angels, 'Azza and 'Azza'el, descended and lusted for the daughters of the earth, and they corrupted their way upon earth, until Thou didst suspend them between earth and heaven. But the son of Amram, from the day that Thou didst reveal Thyself to him in the thorn bush, did not visit his wife, as it is said "And Miriam and Aaron spoke against Moses". I beg of Thee, let me stay in Moses' body.' At that moment, the Holy One, blessed be He, sought out and took his soul with a kiss.

To the author of this Midrash the world of the angels was palpable and real, in whose lore and history he was well versed. There were even Tannaim and Amoraim with whom angels walked and in whose name they transmitted Halakhic and Haggadic dicta.[65] The last motif — that of the angels 'Azza and 'Azza'el — also reveals the nature of the sources with which the author of our Midrash was familiar.[66] He lived in the world of the apocalypse, but at the same time he exercised his imagination in the service of faith, holding that the world of the Torah conquers and subdues the world of the angels of the Most High. There is a difference between the two parts of the drama 'Moses and the Heavenly Retinue': While in the first part — 'Moses Ascends on High' — he does indeed defeat the angels, and according to one version brings about their surrender and subjugation, nevertheless he is in need of the help of the Holy One, blessed be He, in order to withstand the angels on high and to be protected from 'being harmed by them'. In the second part, on the other hand — 'The Death of Moses' — all the angels, including the Angel of Death, Samma'el, are afraid of him, and are unable to prevail against him, and only the Holy One, blessed be He, treasures his soul. Moses' power derives from the Torah, with which he occupied himself. The high status of this Torah is recognized even by those circles whose words are steeped in vision and fantasy, and here and there we also find an echo[67] of the activity of the Sages, who made the 'Heavenly Retinue' in the image, as it were, of the 'Earthly Retinue', transferring their academies and law courts to the celestial sphere.

The use of the word *familia* ['Retinue'] to denote the angels found in the entourage of God is peculiar to the Rabbis, and has no parallel in the Hellenistic or Christian literature.[68] The Tanna Abba Saul, the first who is known to have used this loan-word, likens Israel to the retinue of a king, and thus expounds the verse '"ye shall be holy."... the retinue of the King. And what must they do? Do as the King does.'[69] But already in the Midrash of the Tannaim the discrepancy between Job xxv 3 'Is there any number of His armies' and Daniel vii 10 'Thousand thousands ministered unto Him...' is resolved by the conjecture 'The Heavenly Retinue was, as it were, diminished'.[70] The fact that God is the Judge of the whole earth and passes judgement on His creatures easily led to His *familia* being pictured as a law-court. Although the Holy One, blessed be He, is called in Tannaitic literature 'Bet Din' ['Law-Court'],[71] yet the actual use of the term Bet Din in a context in which the Ministering Angels are to be found, whose existence no one doubted — either among the Sages or in the academies of the various schools of philosophers — opened the way to their being included in this Bet Din. R. Eleazar said 'Wherever there is no judgement there is judgement', and his words were interpreted to mean 'If justice is executed on earth, judgement is not executed in heaven; but if judgement is not carried out on earth, judgement is carried out in heaven.' There is also the following version: 'When the Bet Din execute judgement... and when the Bet Din do not execute judgement... There is judgement in heaven, and the Holy One, blessed be He, sits over them in judgement and exacts from them [i.e. punishes them].'[72] Although R. Ishmael b. R. Jose still emphasizes in his admonition 'Judge not alone, for none may judge alone save One' (*M. 'Avot* iv, 5), yet R. Akiba is already concerned to stress not the actual fact that God judges alone, but that His judgement is righteous and not arbitrary. When Pappos 'expounded the verse "But He is at one with Himself and who can turn Him? And what His soul desireth, even that He doeth" (Job xxiii 13) — He judges all mankind alone and there is none to reply to His words, R. Akiba said to him: "Enough, Pappos!" Rabbi Pappos countered: "And how do you explain the words 'But He is at one with Himself and who can turn Him'?" Said (R. Akiba) to him: "We do not argue against Him who spoke and the world came into being; but He judges all in truth and all with justice."'[73] R. Simeon b. Yoḥai, R. Akiba's disciple, did not refrain from associating the heavenly Bet Din with the making of man, in order to emphasize how perfect was the work of man's creation and to refute the arguments of the Gnostics. He did not hesitate to expound 'It is not written here "whom He has already made" but "whom they have already made". As it were, the King of the kings of kings, blessed be He, and his Bet Din voted for each part of you and set you up on your proper basis (as it is written) "Hath He not made thee and established thee?" (Deuteronomy xxxii 6).'[74] The earliest Amoraim — possibly also with the aim of discouraging even experts from judging alone[75] — also attributed to the Holy One, blessed be He, irreproachable judicial procedure. Thus we find 'R. Joḥanan said: The Holy One, blessed be He, never does aught in His world without first consulting the Bet Din on high. What is the reason? "And the word was true, even a great host" (Daniel x 1) — when is the seal of the Holy One, blessed be He, true? When He consults the Bet Din on high.'[76] In a parallel source we find in R. Joḥanan's dictum the expression 'the Heavenly Retinue [פמליה שלמעלא *pamalyā shĕlĕma'ălā*]'.[77] R. Eleazar, the colleague and disciple of R. Joḥanan, formulated the rule 'wherever it is stated "the Lord God", the reference is to Him and His Bet Din. The Scriptural determinant is: 'And the Lord hath spoken evil concerning thee' (I Kings xxii 23).[78] R. Eleazar apparently also used the fact of the heavenly Bet Din's existence in order to dissociate evil from the Holy One, blessed be He — a trend that we find clearly expressed in his teaching.[79] In this spirit, about two generations later, R. Judah b. Pazzi formulated the statement 'Even the Holy One, blessed be He, does not judge alone, as it is said "And all the host of heaven standing by Him on His right and on His left" — these arguing in favour and the others in condemnation. But although He does not judge alone, He seals alone ...'[80] The Amora R. Judan b. Polia gave the following interpretation to the words of Job (i 21): ' "The Lord gave and the Lord hath taken away..." — when He gave, He consulted no creature, but when He took away He consulted His Bet Din.'[81] The Heavenly Court (*familia*) operates only as God's agents, and R. Joḥanan indeed explained the word מכשפין *mĕkhashshĕfîn* ['sorcerers'] to mean 'they contradict [מכחישין *makhḥîshîn*] the Heavenly Court'.[82] But in the Heavenly Court, as in the earthly Bet Din, there are differences of opinion. The Palestinian Amora R. Alexandri, who was a contemporary of R. Joḥanan, and transmitted many dicta in the name of R. Joshua b.

Levi,[83] said: 'Whoever occupies himself with the Torah for its own sake makes peace in the Heavenly Court and in the Earthly Court, as it is said "Or else let him take hold of My strength, that he may make peace with Me; yea let him make peace with Me" (Isaiah xxvii 5).'[84] R. Safra said after his prayer: 'May it be Thy will, O Lord our God, to make peace in the heavenly *familia* and in the earthly *familia* and among the disciples who occupy themselves with Thy Torah, whether for its own sake or not; and may it be Thy will that all who occupy themselves (with the Torah) not for its own sake may eventually do so for its sake.'[85] R. Alexandri made peace in the heavenly *familia* depend on study of the Torah in the earthly *familia*, and he followed in the footsteps of his teacher R. Joshua b. Levi, who was able to report that, in respect of three matters, 'the earthly Bet Din retracted and the heavenly Bet Din concurred with them'.[86] Now while R. Joshua b. Levi spoke of past acts, the celestial concurrence in which was deduced from verses, his great contemporaries made similar observations about contemporary matters. In the name of R. Ḥama b. R. Ḥanina — or R. Hoshaiah — it is stated: 'In human procedure, when the governor announces that the court will sit today and the bandit says the court must sit tomorrow, who is obeyed? Is it not the governor? But in the case of the Holy One, blessed be He, it is not so. If the Bet Din declare that today is New Year, the Holy One, blessed be He, tells the Ministering Angels: "Set-up the platform [for holding court], let the prosecuting and defending counsel take their stand, for My children have announced that today is New Year." But if the Bet Din reconsidered the matter and decided to postpone it to the following day, the Holy One, blessed be He, says to the Ministering Angels: "Remove the platform, let the prosecuting and defending counsel leave, for My children have decided (upon reconsideration) to postpone it [the New Year] till tomorrow."'[87] A statement that appears to contradict this view is nevertheless explained in conformity with it. It is taught in the Mishna 'R. Eleazar b. R. Zadok said, if it [the new moon] was not seen at its proper time, it is not sanctified because it has already been sanctified by heaven.' In regard to this R. Ba b. R. Zavda said in the name of Rav: 'The reason for R. Eleazar b. R. Zadok's ruling is that since the Bet Din on high see that the Bet Din below are not sanctifying it [the new moon], they sanctify it.'[88] In place of 'Heaven'[89] we have here 'the Bet Din on high'. The Amora R. Abbahu introduces the motif of the envy of the angels,[90] when they see that the Holy One, blessed be He, prefers the Bet Din below. He explains the verse "Happy is the people that know the joyful shout; they walk, O Lord, in the light of Thy countenance" (Psalms lxxxix 16 [15]) with reference to the five elders, when they enter to intercalate the year. What does the Holy One, blessed be He, do? He leaves His counsellors (σύγκλητοι) and descends and causes His Shekhina to dwell below. The Ministering Angels declare: 'Behold, it is God, it is God! Behold, it is the Almighty, it is the Almighty! Behold, it is Truth, it is Truth! Should He of whom it is written "A God dreaded in the great council of the Holy ones, and feared of all of them that are round about Him" (Psalms *ibid.* v. 8 [7]) leave His counsellors and descend and cause His Shekhina to dwell with the inhabitants of the world below? Why then was all this done? — In case they erred, the Holy One, blessed be He, would illuminate the Halakha for them. This is the meaning of the verse "They walk, O Lord, in the light of Thy countenance.'[91] The role of the heavenly Bet Din is made subsidiary to that on earth, and the cultivation of the Halakha in the academy of heaven is like that in the earthly academy, but the final decision is in the hands of the latter.[92] The principle of the supremacy of the study of the Torah and the freedom the Rabbis took for themselves in its study made the heavenly *familia* subject thereto. Even one of the explicit and central tasks assigned by the Bible to the angels — namely, the uttering of song and praise — was greatly restricted by the increased importance given to the prayers and praises of Israel, to the point where the Sages said that 'The Ministering Angels on high utter no song until Israel do so below'.[93] Nay more, particularly in connection with this function there are to be found Baraitot and dicta of the last of the Tannaim and the first of the Amoraim which completely deny the angels' continued existence. R. Samuel bar Naḥman said in the name of R. Joḥanan: 'No company of angels utters praise more than once.' R. Ḥelbo explains his words to mean 'Every day the Holy One, blessed be He, creates new angels, who sing a new song and depart.'[94] Samuel transmitted to R. Ḥiyya, the son of Rav, the following saying of his father: 'Every day the Ministering Angels are created from the River of Fire [נהר דינור *Nĕhar Dînûr*] and they utter song and cease to exist.' R. Samuel bar Naḥman, on the other hand, said in the name of R. Jonathan: 'From every utterance that proceeds from the mouth of the Holy One, blessed be He, an angel is created.'[95] According to one account R. Joshua b. Hannaniah gave the Emperor Hadrian an answer similar to the view held by Rav.[96] Indeed, there is external evidence of the antiquity of this conception. Justin Martyr, the younger contemporary of R. Joshua, cites the view that 'the Father, if He so wills, causes a force to manifest itself, and, if He so wills, He brings about its extinction, and in this way — they teach — the angels, too, are created.' But he adds: 'There are angels who exist for ever, without returning to the source whence they came into existence.'[97] Likewise the Amora R. Ḥelbo excluded from the community of angels 'Michael and Gabriel; it is they who are the Princes of heaven. All of them [i.e. the angels] are replaced, but they are not replaced'. All these dicta and discussions are not different from the formulations of prayers, which have incorporated verses that speak of the praise and glory offered up by the angels, Serafim and Ofannim. It appears that in the sphere of the popular religion the worshippers were not content merely to mention the names of angels in hymns and praises, but did so also in prayers and supplications for the fulfilment of human needs, even of a very material nature. In condemnation of the worship of angels a Baraita teaches: 'If one slaughters... to Michael, the Prince of the Great Host... it is as flesh offered to idols.'[98] The following teaching of the Amora R. Judan is directed against prayers recited to angels: 'If a human being has a patron, then if he finds himself in trouble he does not enter his house suddenly, but he comes and stands at his patron's door and calls his slave or a member of his household, and he says: So-and-so is standing at the door of your court. Now he (the patron) may or may not invite him in. But the Holy One, blessed be He, is not so. If trouble comes upon a person, let him not cry either to Michael or to Gabriel, but let him cry unto Me, and I shall answer him forthwith. This is the meaning of the verse: "whoever shall call on the name of the Lord shall be delivered".'[99] Still stronger opposition than that evoked by prayer to, and worship of, the angels was aroused by the views that made the angels partners in the creation of the world; and, needless to say, the tradition that the whole world was created by angels, inculcated by various Gnostic doctrines,[1] appeared even to apocalyptic circles (which assigned a considerable role to Princes, and angels, and even to angels of destruction, and angels of Satan, Belial and *Masṭēmā* [hatred]) to be in conflict with Israel's Torah. But we shall discuss these problems in the chapters devoted to the creation of the world and of man.

CHAPTER IX

'HE WHO SPOKE AND THE WORLD CAME INTO BEING'

From the Bible the Sages received the belief in God as the Sole and Omnipotent Creator of the world. But the story of creation in the Book of Genesis, with its obscurities and discrepancies, presented them with problems and difficulties. There were still current among the people legends that resembled the remnants of the mythical epics that are to be found in the Scriptures themselves.[1] Ideas and motifs borrowed from the cosmogonic teachings of the Persians, Greeks and Gnostic sects infiltrated into the circles that came in contact with them. All these were sufficient to make the study of the 'Work of Creation' an esoteric doctrine, which can be transmitted only to individuals. Indeed, we learn in the Mishna (*M. Ḥagiga* ii, 1) that the 'Work of Creation' may not be expounded before two. Only the Palestinian Talmud states that this Mishna 'is by R. Akiba, but according to R. Ishmael we may expound (in the presence of two)'.[2] The significance of this dispute is to be explained in the light of another difference of opinion between these Sages regarding the interpretation of the first verse of Genesis: '[את השמים ואת הארץ *'et ha-shāmayim wĕ-'et hā-'areṣ* — 'the heaven and the earth'] — R. Ishmael asked R. Akiba a question: Seeing that you have studied twenty-two years under Nahum of Gimzo, (who taught that) אך *'akh* ['but'] and רק *raq* ['only'] are limitations of the text, and את *'et* and גם *gam*, are amplifications, how do you explain *'et* of this verse? He replied: Had Scripture written בראשית ברא אלהים שמים וארץ *bĕ-rēshît bārā' 'Ĕlōhîm shāmāyim wā-'āreṣ* ['In the beginning God heaven and earth created'], we might have thought that heaven and earth were also deities. Said [R. Ishmael] to him: "For it is no vain thing for you" (Deuteronomy xxxii 47), and if it be vain — it is due to you [literally 'from you', rendered above 'for you'], because you do not know how to expound the Scripture. This is the meaning: את השמים *'et ha-shāmayim* comes to include the sun and the moon, the stars and the planets; and ואת הארץ *wĕ-'et ha-'āreṣ* comes to include trees and herbage and the Garden of Eden.'[3] R. Ishmael asked R. Akiba the meaning of the verse according to the latter's method of exegesis, namely that of Nahum of Gimzo, who interpreted every את *'et*. But R. Akiba's reply sought to controvert a Gnostic explanation.[4] Thus, the particles את *'et* do not serve to amplify but to separate between God and heaven and earth, and to teach us that the last two are not creators but created things, and that the Holy One, blessed be He, had no partners in the work of creation. An exposition of this kind was of interest only to individuals that engaged in disputation with sectarians and were familiar with their views. It was out of place to give this exposition in public. R. Ishmael, who according to his exegetical method regarded את *'et* in the verse as part of its grammatical structure,[5] argues, contrary to the opinion of R. Akiba, that those who expound the particle את *'et* can find an amplification in this verse, too, namely that heaven and earth were created already on the first day together with all their host. This exposition could be given in public. Exegetical explanations of this kind were taught in the School of R. Ishmael, and possibly it was from this source that there emanated the dispute between the School of Shammai and the School of Hillel concerning the order in which heaven and earth were created: 'The School of Shammai said: The heavens were created first; the School of Hillel said: The earth was created first.' The School of Shammai and the School of Hillel seek to reconcile the contradiction between the verse 'In the beginning God created the heaven and the earth' and the verse 'in the day that the Lord God made earth and heaven.' The School of Shammai regard the verse 'The heaven is My throne, and the earth is My footstool' (Isaiah lxvi 1) as a third passage that harmonizes the first two, and they illustrate their viewpoint with an example: 'It is like the case of a king, who made a throne for himself and thereafter the footstool (ὑποπόδιον).' The School of Hillel, on the other hand, gave as an example 'The case of a king who built a palace — after building the lower floor, he builds the upper storey'[6] and their harmonizing verse was apparently 'Yea, My hand hath laid the foundation of the earth, and My right hand hath spread out the heavens' (Isaiah xlviii 13).[7] This dispute also falls within the category of explicatory expositions that reconcile conflicting verses by employing illustrations that are intended to make the matter comprehensible to simple folk. Another note is struck by R. Simeon b. Yoḥai, the disciple of R. Akiba. He reacts to this debate as follows: 'I am surprised that the Fathers of the world should differ on this subject; they were both created together like a pot and its lid, (as it is written) "when I call unto them, they stand up together" (Isaiah *ibid.*). He, too, uses an illustration and cites a verse as proof of his interpretation. But his illustrative example is not related to the Scriptural text, which is merely the conclusion of the passage in which the School of Hillel found support for their views. R. Simeon limits the duration of the work of creation: heaven and earth were not created one after the other but simultaneously — 'they are equal'.[8] Primacy is given not to the verses but to knowledge.[9]

R. Simeon b. Yoḥai reacts, with the same expression of surprise, to another dispute between the School of Shammai and the School of Hillel on the subject of creation. 'There is a difference of opinion between the School of Shammai and the School of Hillel. The School of Shammai say: The plan was formulated during the night, and the work was carried out by day. The School of Hillel said: Both the planning and the execution took place during the day. Said R. Simeon b. Yoḥai, I am surprised that the Fathers of the world, the School of Shammai and the School of Hillel, should differ about the creation of heaven and earth. The planning took place both by day and by night, and the execution was carried out at sunset.'[10] The dispute between the School of Shammai and the School of Hillel is not specially based on Scriptural exposition, but is linked to the verse 'These are the generations of the heaven and of the earth when they were created, in the day that the Lord God made earth and heaven' (Genesis ii 4). According to the School of Shammai the designing of creation took place at night, and the implementation during the day. According to the School of Hillel both of them occurred in the day time. It is obvious that in our case it was not the interpretation of the verse that led to the distinction between thought and act, since there is no basis for it in the Biblical text. On the contrary, it appears that the concept that the plan of creation preceded the execution was used to explain the verse: since the expression 'when they were created' comes before 'in the day', the School of Shammai posit that the planning was in the night, while the School of Hillel combine the two. R. Simeon b. Yoḥai accords primacy to the thought, declaring that it took place both by day and by night, while the act was restricted to sunset. In the Septuagint verses ii 4–5 are linked together. The words 'in the day that the Lord God made' are related also to 'no shrub of the field' and to 'no herb of the field'. On the basis of this translation, Philo asks 'What is the meaning of the words "God made every shrub of the field before it was upon the earth and every herb of the field before it had sprung up"? These words contain a reference to the Incorporeal Ideas, for the expression "before it was" alludes to the perfection of every shrub and herb, of the plants and trees. Since Scripture states that, before they had sprung upon the earth, He had made shrubs and herbs and other things, it is evident that He had formed Incorporeal Ideas.'[11] It might be argued that the dicta of the School of Shammai and the School of Hillel were intended to solve the same difficulty in the verses as that noted by Philo, but just as Philo's concept of the 'Ideas' was already to hand for him, so, too, the concept of the creation in thought was already in the possession of the School of Shammai and the School of Hillel, only the two are not to be identified, and there can be no question of attributing to the Schools of Shammai and Hillel knowledge of the doctrine of Ideas. The similes, by which they likened the creation of the world to the erection of a house and the making of a throne, brought in their train the premise of planning in thought. Philo also uses the illustration of a king who wishes to build a city and invites an architect who designs its buildings.[12] It is quite possible that such illustrations were employed by preachers both in the Land of Israel and in Alexandria even before the time of Philo and the disciples of the Schools of Shammai and Hillel; they actually have a basis in the metaphorical expressions of the Bible, only Philo introduces the simile to explain that the world of Ideas does not exist in a given 'place'. R. Simeon b. Yoḥai by his expression of surprise and his reply makes God's way of creating the world far different from man's method of construction, and he restricts the entire implementation to sunset alone. The dating of the exposition concerning the 'Work of Creation' to the time of the disciples of Hillel and Shammai accords well with the Haggada about Alexander the Great and the Sages of the South, according to which Alexander asked the Sages of the South ' "Were the heavens or the earth created first?" They answered: "The heavens were created first, as it is stated in Scripture 'In the beginning God created the heaven and the earth.' " He (then) asked them: "Was the light or the darkness created first?" They replied: "It is an insoluble question." '[13] To the first question the answer of the Sages of the South was in agreement with the view held by the School of Shammai, and in truth we know that 'There were Edomite disciples in the School of Shammai', Edomite signifying 'southerner'.[14] To the second question, the speculations in regard to which, as we shall see later, exercised the Sages of the subsequent generations to no small extent, they replied that there was no solution. Since nothing is stated in the story of Genesis concerning the creation of light, this question is connected with the problem of the existence of eternal matter and opened the way to the belief in two divine powers. The declaration that 'there was no solution' already failed to satisfy Rabban Gamaliel, who gave an unequivocal answer, when he was questioned on a similar subject. 'A certain philosopher once raised the following question before Rabban Gamaliel, saying to him: "Your God was a great Artist, but He had at His disposal fine ingredients to help Him." The (Patriarch) asked him: "What were they?" The philosopher replied: "*Tōhû* and *Bōhû* [usually rendered: 'without form and void'] and darkness and water and wind and deeps." Said Rabban Gamaliel to him: "Perish the thought! creation is stated in respect of all of them". '[15] In this reply there is a clear rejection of the conception of the creation of the world out of uncreated matter. We do not know who the philosopher was. However, he not only maintains the doctrine of eternal matter,[16] but even attempts to find support for it in the Bible; hence a Jewish sectarian is probably referred to.

Rabban Gamaliel's reply and likewise R. Akiba's homily on the meaning of את *'et* in the first verse of Genesis are clear evidence that these Tannaim were familiar with various doctrines on the subject of the 'Work of Creation'. Despite all the caution that the Rabbis exercised by transmitting their words to individuals and their avoidance of expounding these problems in public, it was impossible to prevent some traces of the views and concepts that they controverted from clinging to themselves, and there were some Sages who did not completely reject the alien views, but sought to harmonize what they absorbed with Biblical teaching. The following story about R. Joshua b. Ḥanania and Ben Zoma sheds light on our subject, if we correctly understand the meaning of its obscurities: 'Once Simeon b. Zoma was standing lost in wonderment. R. Joshua passed by and greeted him once and twice, but Ben Zoma did not answer him. At the third time he replied agitatedly. Said (R. Joshua) to him: "What is the matter Ben Zoma? What preoccupies you [מאיין הרגלים *mē'ayin hā-raglayim*, literally: 'Whence the feet', i.e. 'Whence do you come?']?" (Ben Zoma) replied: "לא מאיין *lō' mē 'ayin* [literally: 'Not from nothing', 'Not from where or whence'], Master." Said (R. Joshua) to him: "I call heaven and earth as my witnesses that I shall not stir from here until you tell me what the trend of your thoughts is." He replied: "I was contemplating the work of creation and (I found that) there is hardly two or three fingers' breadth between the upper and the lower waters. It is not written here 'And the spirit of God was blowing' but 'was hovering' — like a bird flying with fluttering wings, its wings all but touching." R. Joshua turned round and said to his disciples: "Ben Zoma is gone." Before many days were out Ben Zoma departed this world.'[17] An acute and interesting interpretation was recently advanced by S. Lieberman[18] for this obscure and difficult story. In his view, Ben Zoma's reply to R. Joshua's innocent question 'What preoccupies you?' hints that he was occupied with the questions that exercised the Gnostics. Ben Zoma's answer לא מאין *lō' mē'ayin* is explained by Lieberman to mean 'nought that comes from the "where?" '. The Gnostics used to ask 'From where do you come, and whither are you going?' However, they were accustomed to reply 'I have come from the place of light, from the place where the light was created,'[19] while Ben Zoma's answer is more reminiscent of the answers given by Israel's Sages,[20] namely that man originates in a place of darkness, a place of impurity, and proceeds to a place of darkness and impurity. Ben Zoma's reply was orthodox, only it showed that he was preoccupied with the question that constantly engrossed the attention of the sectarians. But according to this explanation we cannot understand R. Joshua's insistence or the transition to the subject of the Work of Creation. It therefore seems that the reply לא מאין *lō' mē'ayin* is already directed to the focal point of the narrative. When R. Joshua turned to Ben Zoma, who was so lost in thought that he did not return his greetings, with the question מאין לאן *mē'ayin lĕ'ān* ['whence — whither?'] or מאין הרגלים *mē'ayin hā-raglayim* [literally: 'Whence the feet'; rendered above: 'What preoccupies you?'], the surprised Ben Zoma understood that the question was directed to the subject of his thought, 'Whence, from what was the world created?' At first he denied that he was engaged in studying this question, and replied 'Not from whence', that is, I am not occupying myself with this question of 'whence?'. Needless to say, this formulation could be interpreted to mean that he wished to say that the world was not created out of nothing [*mē'ayin* may also mean 'ex nihilo'], and hence it is not to be wondered at that R. Joshua repeated his question in the form of an adjuration. Ben Zoma revealed to him the content of his contemplation of the Work of Creation[21], and R. Joshua found it to contain alien doctrine. It is difficult to identify Ben Zoma's account with one of the cosmologies current in the second century, and it is greatly to be doubted if Ben Zoma actually had in mind a definite Gnostic conception.[22] At most we can say that his words contain ingredients of a dualistic myth, which presupposes the existence of eternal matter.[23] The description of the spirit of God as 'all but touching' is in keeping with two other statements of Ben Zoma in which he limits the Divine work in the act of creation and preserves the distance between God and matter. With regard to the verse 'And God made the firmament' (Genesis i 7) it is stated: 'This is one of the Scriptures with which Ben Zoma set the world in commotion... "And He made" — how is this possible! Surely the world was created by a word, (as it is written) "By the word of the Lord were the heavens made; and all the host of them by the breath of His mouth!" (Psalms xxxiii 6).'[24] The commotion caused by Ben Zoma was due to the fact that in this verse 'And it was so' occurs after God's creative act, and not as in the account of the other days, where 'And it was so' appears after the Divine utterance. The wording 'This is one of the Scriptures with which Ben Zoma set the world in commotion' deserves attention. It indicates that many of Ben Zoma's homilies set the world of the Sages astir. At any rate Ben Zoma's portrayal sufficed to produce R. Joshua's reaction. Indeed R. Joshua rejected every interpretation and homily that contained the slightest hint of a dualistic conception, even though they were innocent in their formulation and content. R. Eliezer held that 'Everything existing in the heavens was created from the heavens; everything upon earth was created from the earth.' Contrariwise R. Joshua declared 'Everything in heaven and on earth was created from heaven only.'[25] This sensitivity on the part of R. Joshua is to be explained by the fact of his stay in Alexandria.[26] There he came to know the prevailing philosophical systems, and there too, it appears, he held those debates that are transmitted by the formula: 'Hadrian asked R. Joshua b. Ḥanania'. One of the questions was 'How did the Holy One, blessed be He, create His world?'[27] The answer has not been preserved in its original wording, but in the garb of an Amoraic dictum, which we shall discuss later. At all events it appears that the restrictions imposed upon occupying oneself with the 'Work of Creation' could not stand up to the pressure of questions, whether from within or without. The journeys of the Sages to Egypt, Syria, and Asia Minor, as well as the proliferation of sects in Eretz-Israel, intensified the need to know what answer to give. The circle of those who knew grew larger, and a Sage like Ben Zoma was not inclined to preserve this knowledge as purely esoteric teaching. But in most Tannaitic dicta there is no support to be found for overstepping the bounds of Scriptural expositions, although they considered it right to reply to questions that the earlier authorities refrained from even meditating upon. Whereas the Elders of the South proclaimed that the question 'What was created first, the light or the darkness?' cannot be resolved, we find the disciples of R. Akiba, R. Judah, and R. Nehemiah discussing it and offering solutions according to the method of R. Ishmael, by having recourse to Biblical texts and refraining from speculative and mythological thought. 'R. Judah said: The light was created first. The case may be compared to that of a king who wished to build a palace, but the site was in darkness. What did he do? He kindled lights and a lantern (φανός) in order to know where to lay the foundation (θεμέλιος).

Thus the light was created first. R. Nehemiah said: The world was created first. The case may be compared to a king who built a palace and adorned it with lights.'[28] R. Judah remains consistent in his view that 'The world was created in six days, for in the account of each day it is written "and it was so" '.[29] Hence he says that the light was created first, but — as we may infer from the simile, 'but the site was in darkness' — the darkness was not created, it was there already. In another version the point is more fully explained: '...but the site was in darkness... Even so was it when the Holy One, blessed be He, built the world — it was all in darkness.'[30] On the other hand, R. Nehemiah follows the view of R. Ishmael, who holds that 'The world was created on the first day'; thus there was a single act of creation, and hence the question of precedence does not arise. The creation of the light was only like decorating with lights. R. Judah draws no inference whatsoever from the existence of darkness, nor does he refer to the light as *materia prima*, from which the world was created; he presents it only as the first created entity.[31] To my mind, the Tannaitic dicta contain no trace of any discussion about primeval matter. The dispute of R. Eliezer and R. Joshua, which we cited above, is not concerned with the matter from which the heavenly bodies and the earth were created, but with the place from which they were formed. This is made clear by a parallel Baraita: 'R. Eliezer says: It was created from the middle... R. Joshua states: The world was created from the sides' (*T.B. Yoma* 54b). The world spoken of here is simply the earth. R. Eliezer, who holds that the offspring of the earth were created from the earth, sees this creation as taking place from the middle, from one central point. R. Joshua, on the other hand, in whose opinion even the progeny of the earth were created from heaven, declares: The earth was created from the sides, and not from a central point. Only this interpretation of their dispute enables us to understand the saying of the Sages 'Both were created from Zion', that is, both the issue of heaven and the issue of the earth were created from a central point in the earth — from Zion. According to one version[32] the author of the dictum is actually R. Judah, and the proof of the creation of the world from Zion is to be found in Psalms i 2 ' "Out of Zion, the perfection of beauty, God hath shined forth"... and "shined forth" refers to light.'[33] This means to say that the original creation of light was from Zion. At any rate, the Tannaim do not expressly deal with the question 'Whence was the light created?', just as there is no reference to be found in their teachings to *materia prima*. It is true that in the past century scholars[34] have endeavoured to find a reference to primeval matter in the warning given by R. Akiba upon entering Pardes ['Garden', 'Paradise']: 'When you come to the stones of pure marble, say not "Water, water"!' (*T. B. Ḥagiga* 14b). But this dictum has no connection with the Work of Creation[35]; it is only a warning — as has been shown — to those who speculate on the Chariot.

All that is stated in the name of the Tannaim with reference to the 'Work of Creation' contains nothing that may not 'be expounded'. They do not enquire what was 'before the world was created', nor 'What is above? What is beneath? What was beforetime? What will be hereafter?'[36], a formulation that bespeaks — like the warning of Ecclesiasticus (iii 21–22) 'Seek not (to understand) what is too wonderful for thee, and search not out that which is hid from thee' — the avoidance of mystic speculations. This opposition is not only directed to exposition in public or before disciples, but to any study of the subject, as is stated in the Mishna of *Ḥagiga* (ii, 1): 'Whoever meditates upon four things, it were better for him if he had not come into the world.'[37] This sentence emanates from a different source[38] from that of the first part of this Mishna, which permits exposition before one disciple.

A marked change took place in regard to speculation on the Work of Creation at the close of the Tannaitic period and the beginning of the Amoraic period. In the name of Rav, the foremost of the Babylonian Amoraim, there are transmitted, without any reservation, mythological teachings concerning the creation of the world. Basing himself on Job xxvi 12 'By His power He stilled the sea; by His understanding He smote Rahab', he elaborates the account and declares: 'When the Holy One, blessed be He, wished to create the world, He said to the Prince of the Sea: "Open your mouth and swallow all the waters of the world." He replied: "Sovereign of the universe, suffice it for me that I remain with my own." Thereupon, He struck him with His foot and slew him' (*T. B. Bava Batra* 74b]. In a late Midrash a parallel myth is found in the following form: 'Why did the Holy One, blessed be He, create His world in Nisan and did not create it in Iyyar? Because when the Holy One, blessed be He, created His world, He said to the Prince of Darkness: Depart from Me, because I wish the world to be created in light.'[39] The difference between the two narratives does not consist in the fact that Rav speaks of the Prince of the Sea, whom he identifies with the Scriptural Rahab, while the anonymous account refers to the Prince of Darkness. In point of fact, it may even be said that the world that contains Sea only is also a world of darkness. The fundamental distinction between them is that the Holy One, blessed be He, slays the Prince of the Sea, whereas the Prince of Darkness only departs from Him, but does not disappear altogether. The very independence of both the Prince of the Sea and the Prince of Darkness recalls the Iranian creation stories, like that of the first chapter of the *Bundahišn*,[40] but whereas in Rav's dictum the removal of the Prince of the Sea took place before the creation of the world and thereby the struggle came to an end and dualism was ousted from the world, the request of the Holy One, blessed be He, to the Prince of Darkness in the anonymous legend 'Depart from Me, for if you do not do so, I shall rebuke you...' brings to mind the Iranian legend according to which Ahriman, beholding the power and might of Ahura Mazda, 'runs back into the darkness', but the conflict continues there until the eschatological end arrives. It is not without reason that Rav introduced the remnants of the ancient Biblical myth about the rebellion of the sea and its helpers[41] and related them to the account of the creation of the world. His aim was to rebut other creation stories, such as that in the anonymous Midrash, which found currency in his area and absorbed new and contemporary mythical elements, although even in their case manifest dualistic myths were eschewed. When the Prince of Darkness asks God in the anonymous Midrash 'And what wilt Thou create after the light?', he receives the reply 'darkness'. Darkness is not formed by the Prince of Darkness but by the Creator of light.

Also in other teachings of Rav that deal with the Work of Creation there is found the theme of disobedience and rebellion on the part of the creatures. Rav Judah transmits in his name: 'When the Holy One, blessed be He, created the world, it continued to expand like two warp clews, until the Holy One, blessed be He, rebuked it and brought it to a halt, as it is said: "The pillars of heaven were trembling, but were astonished at His rebuke" (Job xxvi 11).'[42] What these two clews were we learn from another teaching of Rav: 'The Holy One, blessed be He, took fire and water and kneaded them into each other, and therefrom were the heavens made.'[43] R. Joḥanan combined, as it were, the two dicta and formulated them as follows: 'The Holy One, blessed be He, took two clews, one of fire and one of snow, and kneaded them into each other, and from them was the world made.'[44] But his statement lacks the motif of expansion, like the warp, and of rebuke; the fire is simply the light created on the first day. Rav Judah transmitted in the name of Rav:[45] 'Ten things were created on the first day, namely: heaven and earth, תהו *tōhû* [E.V. 'unformed'] and בהו *bōhû* [E.V. 'void'], light and darkness, wind, water, the nature of day and the nature of night.' All these created entities are mentioned in the first five verses of the Book of Genesis. But what is the meaning of the creation of תהו *tōhû* and בהו *bōhû*? In the verse it is stated 'Now the earth was תהו *tōhû* and בהו *bōhû*'! The explanation given by Rav[46] is: 'תהו *Tōhû* is a green line that surrounds the whole world, out of which darkness[47] proceeds, for it is said "He made darkness His hiding-place round about Him" (Psalms xviii 12 [11]). בהו *Bōhû*, this means slimy[48] stones that are sunk in the deep, whence issued the water, as it is said "And He shall stretch over it the line of תהו *tōhû* [E.V. 'confusion'] and the plummet of בהו *bōhû* [E.V. 'emptiness']" (Isaiah xxxiv 11).' The order of creation according to Rav is therefore as follows: the creation of תהו *tōhû* and בהו *bōhû*, from which, in turn, the darkness and water were formed; thereafter light was created — fire, and out of the fire and water the heavens were made. The creation of the land resulted from the withdrawal of the water, which was described in mythological terms. Rav's exposition seeks to remove the difficulty of the initial verses of the Torah, with reference to which Rav Huna said in the name of Bar Qappara: 'If Scripture had not stated it, it would not be possible to say it: "God created the heaven and the earth" — out of what? From "Now the earth was תהו *tōhû*" etc.'[49] These dicta of Rav differ from the simple and sharp answer given at the time by Rabban Gamaliel to the philosopher (above, p. 188). Rav not only declares that the term creation applies in Scripture to all of them, but he examines and expounds the order and development of creation. In the last dictum are to be found the beginning of the doctrine of the primordial elements and the emanations, as we find it in a later Midrash and as it appears in *Sefer Yeṣira* ['Book of Creation'].[50] Rav's teachings contain no Gnostic speculations. On the contrary, it seems that Rav's account of the 'Work of Creation' is expressly aimed against the doctrines of the 'Knowers' [Gnostics]. It appears that we possess the exordium of Rav's 'Work of Creation', which reads:[51] ' "Let the lying lips be dumb" (Psalms xxxi 19 [18]) — let them become deaf-mute, bound together, silenced...[52] "which speak *'ātāq* [E.V. 'arrogantly'] against the Righteous" (Psalms *ibid.*) — which tell, with pride and contempt, of the Righteous One of the world matters that He has hidden [העתיק *he'tîq*] from His creatures. This refers to one who exalts himself saying: I expound the Work of Creation. He thinks he is as one who exalts, but he is only as one who contemns... What is written thereafter? "Oh how abundant is Thy goodness, which Thou hast laid up for them that fear Thee!" (*ibid.* v. 20 [19]) — may he not have[53] "Oh how abundant is Thy goodness"! Normally[54] if a human king builds a palace on a site of sewers, and a dunghill and garbage, then if any one comes and says: This palace is built on a site of sewers, a dunghill and garbage, surely he will be guilty of disparagement! Even so if anyone comes and says: This world was created out of תהו *tōhû* and בהו *bōhû* and darkness, surely he is guilty of disparagement!' For a long time already scholars have noted the anti-Gnostic character of the analogy.[55] It is not ruled out that the exordium, which in effect is a curse, was initially intended against anyone who boasted of expounding the Work of Creation, but it was changed by Rav and directed towards those who expound with pride and contempt, that is the Gnostics, who used to begin their expositions with arrogant declarations, such as 'And the hidden way, the holy way called Gnosis, do I make known'.[56] They expounded with contempt, for their aim was to show the created world to be defective, and their knowledge to be arcane and esoteric wisdom. Not so is the account of the Creation in the Torah. To Rav is also attributed the saying 'By ten things was the world created: by wisdom, understanding, knowledge, strength, rebuke, might, righteousness and judgement, lovingkindness and compassion.'[57] Although all 'the things' are supported by verses in which they occur in connection with the creation of the world or its parts, yet not only is this nexus not always sufficiently clear, as, for example, in the case of 'Righteousness and judgement are the foundation of Thy throne' (Psalms lxxxix 15 [14]) or 'Remember, O Lord, Thy compassions and Thy mercies; for they have been of old' (*ibid.* xxv 6), but their very inclusion in the number of 'things by which the world was created' elevates them to the status of Divine attributes and forces.[58]

W. Bacher[59] wished to find in the ten things, by which the world was created, the Divine Name of forty-two letters, and connected this teaching of Rav with another dictum of his (*T.B. Berakhot* 55a): 'Bezalel knew how to combine the letters by which heaven and earth were created. It is written here "And He hath filled him with the spirit of God, in wisdom, in understanding, and in knowledge" (Exodus xxxv 31); and it is written elsewhere "The Lord by wisdom founded the earth; by understanding He established the heavens" (Proverbs iii 19); and it is further written "By His knowledge the depths were broken up (*ibid.* 2)".' We have already dealt above (p. 131) with the correct interpretation of the Name of forty-two letters and we have seen that it has no connection with the 'ten things'; and it seems that there is also no relationship between it and Rav's statement about the letters. The ten things, which are the forces and attributes that were active at the time of Creation, do not annul the ancient Mishna[60] 'By ten sayings the world was created' (*M. 'Avot* v, 1), but found their expression in them. These ten sayings are 'letters' in the sense that they are elements of speech and utterance, and not numbers or physical elements of the universe, and Rav states that Bezalel knew how to combine them, because he possessed three of the powers by which the world was created. Rav does not say that the world was created by a combination of letters, nor does his statement comprise the doctrine of Creation expounded by the *Sefer Yeṣira*, which is based on mutations and arrangements of the letters,[61] nor yet the numerical system of Pythagoras.[62] God created the universe only with an utterance. It appears that express opposition to the doctrine that attributes to God creation by the manipulation of letters is to be found in a dictum of R. Joḥanan, the younger contemporary of Rav in Eretz-Israel: '"when they were created" — R.

Abbahu said in the name of R. Joḥanan: He created them a *Hē*'. Just as the *Hē*' — unlike all the other letters, which require the use of the tongue — does not need the tongue (for its enunciation), even so the Holy One, blessed be He, created His world without toil or effort, but only "By the word of the Lord" (Psalms xxxiii 6), which was no sooner uttered than "the heavens were made".' In conformity with this teaching, R. Joḥanan's colleague and disciple, R. Eleazar, interpreted the verse כי ביה ה׳ צור עולמים *kî bĕ-Yah, YHWH, ṣûr ʿōlāmîm* [usually rendered: 'For the Lord [*YH*] is God, an everlasting Rock' (Isaiah xxvi 4)] as follows: 'With these two letters [*YH*] the Holy One, blessed be He, created [*ṣûr* = *ṣār*, 'formed'] ...this world was created with a *Hē*'..., and the next world was created with a *Yôd* [*ʿōlāmîm*, plural, indicates two worlds]'[63] — with two letters, which involve no toil and no effort, and not by combinations of letters or the use of the Divine Name.[64] At first blush, these dicta seem to contradict R. Akiba's teaching in the Mishna: 'Beloved are Israel for unto them was given the instrument by which the world was created; still greater was the love that it was made known to them that to them was given the instrument by which the world was created.'[65] The entire Torah, therefore, served as the instrument of Creation. Obviously, this idea posits the existence of the Torah before the creation of the world.

The notion of the pre-existence of the Torah is rooted in the mythological conception of the image of wisdom that prevailed in the ancient East and traces of which are discernible in the metaphors of the book of Proverbs[66], such as 'The Lord made me as the beginning of His way, the first of His works of old' (viii 22), 'Then I was beside Him, like a master markman ['*āmôn*]; and I was daily His delight' (*ibid.* v. 30). The identification of wisdom with the Torah[67] is old, and is alluded to in 'the praise of wisdom' of the Book of Sirach, where wisdom declares: 'Then the Creator of all things gave me a commandment... And He said, Make thy dwelling in Jacob, and in Israel receive thine inheritance' (xxix 8–9). Wisdom became Torah 'a possession for the assembly of Jacob', and in accordance with this concept the Amora R. Hoshaʿia expounded the verse in Proverbs thus: "ʿ*Āmôn* – '*Ûmān* [artisan, architect]; the Torah says: "I was the instrument of the Holy One, blessed be He." As a rule, when a human king builds a palace, he does not build it by himself, but calls in an architect, and the architect does not plan the building in his head, but he makes use of rolls and tablets, to know how to make the rooms and wickets. Even so the Holy One, blessed be He, looked in the Torah and created the world. And the Torah declares, "With *rē'shît* [E.V. 'In the beginning'] God created, and *rē'shît* means none other than Torah, as it is said "The Lord made me *rē'shît* [E.V. 'as the beginning'] of His way." '[68] In this homily the significance of the view that the Torah was the instrument of the Holy One, blessed be He, in the creation of the world is explained, to wit, 'He looked [מביט *mabbîṭ*] in the Torah and created the world.' Maimonides[69] wondered at the expression הסתכל *histakkēl* ['to look at', 'contemplate'], which corresponds to הביט *hibbîṭ*, and wrote: 'for Plato uses this very expression when he states that God contemplates the world of Ideas and thus produces the existing beings'. It is not surprising, therefore, that modern scholars[70] discovered the doctrine of Platonic Ideas in the saying of R. Hosha'ia, and found a parallel to the Amora's analogy in that employed by Philo[71] concerning the architect who was invited to build a city. But actually a careful comparison of the analogies and the points illustrated shows us the difference between Philo and the Sages and enables us to grasp the significance of their teaching. In Philo's analogy, the architect 'first sketches in his own mind well nigh all the parts of the city that is to be wrought out, temples, gymnasia, town-halls, market-places, harbours, docks, streets, walls to be built, dwelling-houses, as well as public buildings to be set up. Thus after having received in his own soul, as it were in wax, the figures of these objects severally, he carries about the image of a city which is the creation of his mind. Then by his innate power of memory, he recalls the images of the various parts of this city, and imprints their types yet more distinctly in it: and like a good craftsman (δημιουργὸς ἀγαθός) he begins to build the city of stones and timber, keeping his eye upon his pattern (παράδειγμα) and making the visible and tangible objects correspond in each case to the incorporeal ideas.' Similarly, Philo declares, God acted when He came to create the world. 'He conceived beforehand the models of its parts, and out of these He constituted and brought to completion a world discernible only by the mind, and then, with that for a pattern, the world which our senses can perceive.' Philo states in his introductory remarks that He adduces an illustration from our world in order to refute the erroneous view that the World of Ideas exists in a given place. In the analogy he emphasizes repeatedly that the forms are engraven on the soul of the Demiurge[72], and in accord with this he states, with reference to the point illustrated by the analogy, that 'the universe that consisted of Ideas would have no other location than the Divine Reason (θεῖον λόγον)'. On the other hand, R. Hoshaʿia's homily contains not the slightest reference to the world of Ideas or to the location of the Ideas. In the analogy, 'the architect does not plan the building in his head, but he makes use of rolls and tablets' — a fact that Philo carefully refrained from mentioning,[73] because it contradicted his purpose in adducing the analogy. Like the architect who looks at the rolls and tablets, so the Holy One, blessed be He, looked in the Torah, but it contains no forms and sketches of temples, gymnasia, markets and harbours, and this Torah is not a concept but the concrete Torah with its precepts and statutes, which are inscribed in letters. Out of those letters and not from numbers — their combinations and mutation — are the utterances with which the Almighty created the world constructed. It is precisely those who are of the opinion that the analogy in the Midrash reached the Palestinian Amoraim from Philo, directly or through intermediatory processes,[74] that must wonder at the absence of any substantial influence by Philonic thought. In truth, the analogy of the Midrash is only a literary embellishment, and in antithesis to Philo's analogy, whose purpose is to facilitate our understanding of the world of Ideas, which lacks a location of its own, the architect's study of his plans does not explain God's contemplation of the Torah. Indeed, in another — anonymous — Midrash the concept of R. Hoshaʿia's homily finds expression in a different form, which actually stresses the contrast between a human being and the Holy One, blessed be He: ' "My hand laid the foundations of the earth" (Isaiah xlviii 13) — said the Holy One, blessed be He: "For My thoughts are not your thoughts... For as the heavens are higher than the earth..." (*ibid.* lv 8–9) — a man sits and calculates, saying: This is how I shall build, this is how I shall make it; he thinks out in a little while what he does not accomplish in a decade. But the Holy One, blessed be He, is not so; for (what) He thinks out in a thousand years He builds in one day, as it is said: "Remember His covenant for ever, the word which He commanded to a thousand generations" (I Chronicles xvi 15). The heavens were created in one day, for it is said: "By the word of the Lord the heavens were made" (Psalms xxxiii 6). And when He created the world, the Torah, as it were, gave Him light, for the world was without form and void, as it is said: "For the commandment is a lamp, and the Torah is light." Said the Holy One, blessed be He, I seek workmen. The Torah answered Him: I shall put at your service twenty-two workmen, namely the twenty-two letters of the Torah....'[75] The whole Torah is written with twenty-two letters, including the account of Creation. However, the letters do not combine only to describe the work after the event, but it is they themselves that wrought at the time of Creation. The dicta concerning the part played by the Torah and its letters in the creation of the world are devoted more to the praise of the Torah than to the cosmogony and 'Work of Creation'. The homilies on the individual letters, their form and sound, serve paradoxically either to limit the study of the 'Work of Creation' in general, or to contradict the teachings of Gnostic sectarians. We have already cited the expositions of R. Joḥanan and R. Eleazar, whose aim was to emphasize that the world was not created with toil but by an utterance. Anonymous homilies came to explain why the story of creation begins with the letter *Bêt*[76]: 'Why was (the world) created with a *Bêt* [that of בראשית *Bĕ-rē'shît*]? Because it is an expression of blessing [ברכה *bĕrākhā*, 'blessing', begins with a *Bêt*]. And why not with an *'Ālef*? Because it belongs to an expression of cursing [ארור *'ārûr*, 'cursed', begins with an *'Ālef*]. Another explanation is... in order not to give the sectarians an excuse to say: How can the world stand, seeing it was created by a locution of cursing.' A different homily explains that the shape of the letter *Bêt*[77] implies that 'He that is above created us... and He... the Lord is His name.' The sectarians are Gnostics, who claimed that the created world was evil, for, according to Simon Magus,[78] it was not the work of the Good Most High God but of the Demiurge, who was originally sent by the Good God to create the world, but he rebelled against him and proclaimed himself the supreme god. Marcion[79] argued that the transcendental god of lovingkindness stands facing the god of judgement and righteousness, who is the god of the world and is evil, and hence the world is also evil. Clearly the second homily is likewise directed against such views, and stresses that the God of Israel, whose name is the Lord [the Tetragrammaton], is 'He that is above', and there is none superior to Him, and He is also the Creator of the world. The letters of the Torah, with which the world was created, were used by the Amoraim as symbols and intimations, in which they found support for the basic concepts, which were the heritage of generations, concerning the Creator and the created world, but they were forced to defend these ideas anew against sectarians and deviationists. The testimony of the verse 'And God saw everything that He had made, and behold, it was very good' (Genesis i 31) is reiterated in the Prophets and mentioned again in the Hagiographa. Although Philo[80] relies on Plato when he declares that the cause of Creation was the wish of God to vouchsafe of His goodness to the world and to make it more perfect, yet it is obvious that he could have based his words on the Holy Scriptures. It is not at all surprising, therefore, that the Sages reiterated this thought in various forms. The verse 'The Rock, His work is perfect' (Deuteronomy xxxii 4) is expounded in the Sifre[81]:

> His work is perfect in regard to all the inhabitants of the world, and there is not the slightest reason[82] for questioning his works. There is not one of them who would speculate and say: If I had three eyes, or three hands, or three legs, or if I walked on my head, or if my face were turned backwards, how it would befit me!

The homily appears to be directed against people who did, in truth, question 'the perfection of the work' in the creation of the world. Indeed, in a parallel source[83], where the dictum is attributed to R. Simeon b. Yoḥai, the polemical aim is underscored by 'An analogy to a human king who built a palace, and people entered it and said: If the pillars were taller it would have been more beautiful; if the walls were higher, it would have been more beautiful; if the ceiling were loftier, it would have been more beautiful.'

The question why insects and reptiles were created was put to the Sages just as to the Stoics.[84] Like Chrysippus, who lived 280 B.C.E., they also endeavoured to show the usefulness and purpose inherent in all creatures and beings, as Rav stated:[85] 'Of all that the Holy One, blessed be He, created in His world, He created nothing without a purpose. He created the snail (as a remedy) for a scab; He created the fly for the hornet's (sting); the mosquito for a serpent's (bite)...' This and similar sayings also contained an implicit answer to those who criticized the perfection and goodness of the world. There is also not wanting an isolated attempt to exclude certain creatures from the original creation. Thus it is stated in a Baraita in the name of R. Nathan:[86] 'Three were tried and four were declared guilty: Adam, Eve, and the Serpent (were tried), and the earth was punished together with them; (as it is said) "Cursed be the ground!" (Genesis iii 17) — that it should produce unto him cursed objects like gnats and fleas and flies....' Upon this the Amora R. Isaac Magdela'a remarked 'It, too, has its use'. This observation is in the spirit of the teaching of the Rabbis who differed from R. Nathaṇ and said: 'Even creatures that seem to you wholly superfluous in the creation of the world — such as fleas, gnats, and flies — are also an integral part of the creation of the world, and they all fulfil the mission of the Holy One, blessed be He....'[87] The anti-Gnostic trend is conspicuous in the sayings of the Amoraim of the end of the third century and of the fourth century. R. Isaac bar Marion, the contemporary of R. Eleazar, declared 'This is the story of the heavens and the earth' — their Creator praises them, who then shall condemn them? Their Creator lauds them, who then shall find fault with them? We must conclude, therefore, that they are beautiful and praiseworthy.'[88] R. Levi bar Ḥayeta, the author of the famous statement that the Jews recited the שמע *Shĕma*' at Caesarea in Greek (*T.P. Soṭa* vii, 1, p. 21b), who lived one generation after R. Isaac, applied an analogy to the subject that resembles the one that we have already encountered (above, p. 196) in another context, and whose anti-Gnostic character is manifest: 'If a human king builds a palace and puts a gutter at the entrance, it is not befitting. But the King of the kings of kings, blessed be He, created man, and placed his 'gutter' at his 'entrance', yet it constitutes his beauty and his excellence.'

The anti-Jewish and antinomian element found expression in the common and immutable principle, present in all Gnostic doctrines, that the world was created by angels.[89] Against this view are directed numerous polemical homilies of the Amoraim, which expressly negate all participation on the part of the angels in the act of Creation. This polemic manifested itself even in sayings dealing with the creation of the angels. Nothing is stated in the Pentateuch concerning the creation of the angels, but in the *Book of Jubilees* ii, 2, we find, 'For on the first day He created the heavens above and the earth and the waters and all the spirits which serve before Him — the angels of the presence and the angels of sanctification and the angels (of the spirit of fire)' etc. In the Slavonic *Enoch* xi, 8, the Creation begins with the statement: 'And I commanded the celestial beings that one that is visible should go forth from those who are invisible and Uriel, the exceeding mighty, went forth...' In the name of R. Joshua b. Qorḥa it is reported: 'When the Holy One, blessed be He, created the world on the first day, He created the Angel of Death.'[90] On the other hand, a different answer was given to the question 'When were the angels created?'[91] by the Palestinian Amoraim at the beginning of the third century. 'R. Joḥanan said: They were created on the second day... "who hast laid the beams of Thy chambers on the waters" (Psalms civ 3), and it is written "who makest the winds Thy messengers" (*ibid.* v. 4). R. Ḥanina said: They were created on the fifth day, for it is written, "And let birds fly above the earth" (Genesis i 20), and it is written "And with two he flew" (Isaiah vi 2).' The polemical purpose of these views was stressed by R. Joḥanan's disciple, R. Isaac, who said:

> Both according to R. Ḥanina and according to R. Joḥanan it is agreed that none [of the angels or active beings] was created on the first day, that you should not say[92] Michael was pulling in the south and Gabriel in the north, and the Holy One, blessed be He, was stretching in the middle, but 'I am the Lord, who made all things, who stretched out the heavens alone, who spread out the earth מאתי *mē'ittî* [*Qrê* (Masoretic reading): 'by Myself']' (*ibid.* xliv 24). The written text [*kĕtîv*] has מי אתי *mî 'ittî* ['who was with Me?'] — who was My partner in the creation of the world? In the ordinary course of events, when a human king is praised in a country, the great men of the country are praised with him. Why? Because they help him bear the burden (of state). But the Holy One, blessed be He, is not so — He alone created His world, He alone is glorified in His world.

Not only did the angels not create the world, but they did not even assist in its creation, for the created world is not evil and its Creator glories in it. The sectarians were given a handle by the plural in the Scripture 'Let us make man in our image' (Genesis i 26). The homilies of the Amoraim on this verse reflect various aims, and some of them are rooted, apparently, in an ancient exegetical tradition. The Baraitot that report the changes made by the Sages [in rendering the Pentateuch into Greek] for King Ptolemy[93] include also the emendation: 'I shall make man in an image and likeness.' Philo, who was puzzled by the wording of the passage, used it to find a solution to the problem of the existence of evil in the world. Although he expresses himself with great caution, stating that the true reason for creating man in cooperation with others is known only to the Creator, yet he advances the theory that God Himself created the plants and cattle, which have no intellect and hence are free from sin and iniquity. So, too, He created by Himself the celestial beings, which are living creatures possessed of intellect (ζῷα νοερά) but unaffected by evil. On the other hand man is subject to good and evil, righteousness and wrongdoing, beauty and ugliness; hence God was assisted by others in the creation of man. Only the good in man comes from God, whereas the evil in him emanates from others who are subservient to Him.[94] It was not only the debate in which the Sages were engaged with the sectarians that made it impossible for them to adopt Philo's explanation in its entirety and to make the angels partners in the creation of man; the very idea of making the angels responsible for the evil in man was unacceptable to them.[95] It is true that R. Ḥanina, who postponed the creation of the angels to the fifth day (of Creation), did not refrain from saying 'When (God) came to create the first man, he took counsel with the Ministering Angels.'[96] Thus while the Gnostics made the angels responsible for the creation of man in general, and Philo attributes to them the creation of the evil in man, the earliest Amoraim limited the association of the angels to consultation only. The nature of this consultation is described in the words of R. Simon as follows: 'When the Holy One, blessed be He, came to create the first man, the angels formed themselves into groups and factions; some said, "Let him be created", others said, "Let him not be created". This is the meaning of the verse "Lovingkindness and truth are met together; righteousness and peace have kissed each other" (Psalms lxxxv 11 [10]). Lovingkindness said, "Let him be created", for he performs acts of lovingkindness; Truth said, "Let him not be created", for he is wholly false...' However, the evil part of man was not created by the angels, but as R. Huna Rabba of Sepphoris stated: "While the Ministering Angels were arguing with one another, were wrangling with one another, the Holy One, blessed be He, created him, saying to them: "What can you do about it? Man has already been made." It was actually the angels who continued to argue 'Why was this trouble created?'[97] It was none other than the angels who were opposed to the creation of man on account of the evil in him, and it was God who created man, with all his evil, against the view of the angels. This was also the opinion of Rav, and it was transmitted by his pupil Rav Judah in drastic terms (*T.B. Sanhedrin* 38b):

> When the Holy One, blessed be He, sought to create man, He created a company of Ministering Angels and said to them: 'Is it your wish that we should create man in our image?' Said they before Him: 'Sovereign of the universe: What will his deeds be?' He replied: 'Of such and such a nature shall his deeds be.' Said they before Him: 'Sovereign of the universe, "What is man that Thou art mindful of him, and the son of man that Thou dost care for him?" (Psalms viii 5 [4]?' He thereupon put forth His little finger among them and burned them. The same happened with the second company. The third company said before Him: 'Sovereign of the universe, when the former angels spoke to Thee, what did they achieve? The whole world is Thine; whatever Thou dost will to do in Thy world, do!' When it came to the men of the generation of the Flood and the men of the generation of the Tower of Babel, who acted wickedly, they (the angels) said before Him: 'Sovereign of the universe, did not the former angels speak rightly before Thee?' He replied: 'Even to old age I am He, and even to grey hairs will I carry you' etc. (Isaiah xlvi 4).

These narratives are conspicuously antithetic to the Gnostic doctrines. But there were Amoraim who completely negated the consultation with the angels. R. Joshua b. Levi said: 'He consulted the work of heaven and earth... R. Ammi said: He took counsel with His heart....' R. Hilla[98] rejected the concept of consultation: 'There was no consultation here, but it was like a king who was strolling in front of his palace and saw a boulder (βωλάριον) lying on the ground. Said He: "What shall we do with it?..."' — that is to say, this is the way kings speak. R. Abbahu also ignored the difficulty presented by the plural 'Let us make' and from the verse (Isaiah xl 14) 'Whom did He consult for His enlightenment?', he proved, with the help of an analogy, the absurdity of the notion of consultation. In the spirit of his teaching the author of the following anonymous Midrash declared: 'It is a foolish error to say that He took counsel with another.'[99] At any rate it is doubtful if, in disputations with sectarians and Christians, they made use of the interpretation 'He took counsel with the Ministering Angels.' R. Joḥanan said generally 'Wherever the sectarians advanced heretical interpretations, their refutation is near at hand: "Let us make man in our image" — "So God created man in His own image"' (*T.B. Sanhedrin* 38b). When the sectarians asked R. Simlai concerning this verse, he replied 'Read what follows: "Scripture does not write, *wa-yivrĕ'u 'Ĕlōhîm* ['So God created' (*plural*)] the man", but "*wa-yivrā' 'Elōhîm* ['So God created' (*singular*)]."'[1] This occurrence is corroborated also by the exegesis of the Church Fathers, who found support for their doctrine in the verse in Genesis. Justin Martyr, who wrote the *Dialogue with Trypho* in the years 155–161 C.E., interprets the word 'Let us make' (ποιήσωμεν) as referring to 'Christ, the Logos, and Wisdom,' and rejects the interpretations of the Jewish Sages, who say that God spoke to Himself or that He addressed the elements (τὰ στοιχεῖα) of which man was formed. Regarding the interpretation that the plural alludes to the angels, he states that this is the explanation of 'what you call sectarianism (παρ' ὑμιν... αἵρεσις).'[2] We thus learn that the expositions of R. Joshua b. Levi and R. Ammi were already known in the middle of the second century C.E. as 'the interpretations of the Jewish Sages'; on the other hand the introduction of the angels into the verse was regarded as a sectarian-Gnostic interpretation. The Church Fathers, Theophilus of Antioch[3] and Irenaeus[4] disallowed the Gnostic idea of the association of the angels with the making of man and adopted the Jewish interpretations, namely that God addressed Himself, His heart, or in their terminology, His Sophia, Logos, or 'hands' — expressions that they identified with the 'son' or the 'holy ghost'. Tertullian[5] states expressly that those who argue that God consulted the angels do so from anti-Christian motives, in order to contradict the view that by the plural Scripture refers to the Trinity. In the light of these statements it is not surprising, therefore, if, in debates with Christians, Jewish homilists, who engaged in polemics with Christians and with Gnostics, did not refrain from using the specific form that they assigned to the Gnostic view, namely that God consulted the angels. The Church Father Basil[6], who lived in the fourth century, attributed truly to the Jews the opinion that God consulted the angels when He came to make man. None of the exegetical and polemical requirements changed in the least the basic concept of the Sages obtaining at all periods, which found expression in the words of the prophet 'I am the Lord, who made all things, who stretched out the heavens alone, who spread out the earth *mē'ittī*' (Isaiah xliv 24). This was interpreted by R. Ḥanina, as we have seen (above, p. 204), according to the *kĕtîv*: 'The written text was *mî'itti* ['Who was with Me?'] — Who was My partner in the creation of the world?', and he rejected, by virtue of his interpretation, all thought of the angels' taking part in the creation of the world.

The question of the creation of the light occupies a special place in the doctrine of the 'Work of Creation' of the Amoraim. We have already seen that the Tannaim wrestled with the question of the order of the creation of light and darkness (above, p. 191), but the Pentateuchal narrative also confronted them with the problem of the relationship between the light, which was created on the first day, and the luminaries, which were created on the fourth day. The Tanna R. Jacob, the teacher of the Patriarch R. Judah, distinguished between the two of them, saying 'By the light that the Holy One, blessed be He, created on the first day one could look and see from one end of the world to the other.' The Sages disagreed with him, declaring: 'They are the very same luminaries that were created on the first day, but they were not hung (in the sky) until the fourth day.' The Amora R. Eleazar accepted R. Jacob's opinion and added an explanation of the fate of the light of the first day: 'When the Holy One, blessed be He, observed the generation of the Flood and the generation of the Tower of Babel and saw that their deeds were corrupt, He arose and concealed it from them, as it is said "From the wicked their light is withheld" (Job xxxviii 15). And for whom did He hide it away? For the righteous in the time to come....'[7] While the dispute between the Tanna R. Jacob and the contemporary Sages is concerned with the removal of a Biblical difficulty, and only incidentally did R. Jacob reveal his view of the specific character of the light, we learn from the homilies of the Amoraim that the creation of light was bound up with esoteric teaching, only they made it — as in other instances — exoteric. R. Simeon b. R. Jehozadak asked R. Samuel b. R. Naḥman: 'Since I have heard that you are an authority on Haggada, (tell me): Whence was the light created? He replied: The Holy One, blessed be He, wrapped himself in it as in a garment and the splendour of His majesty shone from one end of the world to the other. He imparted this information in a whisper. Said (R. Simeon b. R. Jehozadak) to him: It is fully stated in the Bible, "who coverest Thyself with light as with a garment" etc. (Psalms civ 2), yet you speak in a whisper! The latter replied: Just as I heard it in a whisper so I transmitted it in a whisper.'[8] The whisper implies a mystic meaning,[9] other than the simple sense of the Scripture. This fact did not prevent R. Isaac, the younger contemporary of R. Samuel bar Naḥman,[10] from delivering this homily in public, and R. Berechiah, who lived about two generations later, observed: 'If R. Isaac had not expounded it,[11] would it be possible to say it?' He also transmitted the answer given before R. Samuel b. Naḥman and R. Isaac to the question: 'Whence was the light created?' — 'From the place of the Sanctuary was the light created....' In the early homilies of the Amoraim[12] the question, to which R. Samuel bar Naḥman gave an answer, is reported in the version that we have cited. However, in the homilies of the *Tanḥuma*[13] the text reads: 'How did the Holy One, blessed be He, create the world?' A number of scholars[14] have regarded this recension as the primary one, and have construed it as though the questions asked were 'Out of what did the Holy One, blessed be He, create the world?' Hence they have also interpreted the answer of R. Samuel bar Naḥman as if he meant to say that the primeval matter from which the world was created was the light. But the meaning of the question in the second version is simply 'In which way and in which order did the Holy One, blessed be He, create the world?'[15] and the answer puts the creation of the light first. But what in truth did R. Samuel bar Naḥman and those Sages who transmitted the teaching to him in a whisper have in mind? It seems that the scholars of the last century[16] were right in seeing a parallel to the Midrashic statement in the words of Philo[17]: 'The ruling faculty (τὸ ἡγεμοντκόν) is illumined by a brilliant light, so that it appears as though clothed in garments. The first being created by the True Being — the Logos (πρεσβύτατος τοῦ ὄντος λόγος) — wears the world as a garment.' In another passage he states:[18] 'Now that invisible light perceptible only by mind (ἀόρατον καὶ νοητὸν φῶς) has come into being as an image of the Divine Logos, which brought it within our ken: it is a supercelestial constellation, fount of the constellations obvious to sense. It would not be amiss to term it "all-brightness" (παναύγειαν), to signify that from which sun and moon, as well as fixed stars and planets draw, in proportion to their several capacity, the light befitting each of them.' The light that seems like a garment is only the emanation of the Logos. In similar vein R. Samuel bar Naḥman said that the first light issued forth when the Almighty wrapped Himself in light as with a garment. Indeed we find in one source[19] the wording of the question and answer in the following form: 'Whence did the light issue into the world? He replied: The Holy One, blessed be He, wrapped Himself in a white mantle[20] and the whole world shone from the radiance of His majesty.' Support for this interpretation of the dictum of R. Samuel bar Naḥman is to be found in another Midrashic exposition of this Amora: 'Because in this world people walk by the light of the sun by day and by the light of the moon by night, but in the time to come they will not walk by the light of the sun by day nor by the light of the moon by night... By whose light will they walk? By the light of the Holy One, blessed be He.'[21] The light in the time to come is the first emanation of light.

Among the ten things that were created on the first day, Rav included 'the nature of day' and 'the nature of night' (above, p. 195), that is, the creation of time. Contrary to this view, R. Judah b. R. Simon[22] said, with reference to the verse 'And there was evening and there was morning' (Genesis i 4): 'From this is to be inferred that there was an order of times before this.' It appears that R. Judah b. R. Simon, who lived three generations after Rav,[23] acquired the concept from his predecessors, for R. Abbahu, the contemporary of R. Simon, the father of R. Judah, stated with reference to the same

were there worlds before this world?

verse, 'From this is to be inferred that the Holy One, blessed be He, created worlds and destroyed them, until He created these, declaring, "These please Me, those did not please Me".'[24] This exegetical approach is followed by the author of the Midrashic exposition of Psalms iv 13: ' "Thou carriest them away as with a flood; they are as asleep" — these are the nine hundred and seventy-four generations that existed before the creation of the world, and were swept away in the twinkle of an eye because they were wicked.'[25] This is a variant version of the 'Baraita' that R. Simeon the Pious[26] taught relative to the verse 'Who were snatched away before their time, whose foundation was poured out as a stream' (Job xxii 16) — 'These are the nine hundred and seventy-four generations who pressed forward to be created before the world was created and were not created; the Holy One, blessed be He, arose and planted them in every generation, and they are the insolent ones of each generation.'[27] There is reason to believe that the anonymous homilist who asserted that the generations did exist and were swept away was a contemporary of R. Joḥanan and Resh Laqish,[28] and apparently R. Simeon the Pious already sought to contradict him.

The view that the existing world came after a series of worlds that had been created and destroyed is attributed by Philo to the majority of the Stoic philosophers. He rejects this view, for he states that no reason can be found for the destruction and creation of worlds. We cannot attribute to God either the desire to destroy or the wish to create new worlds. The former militates against His attribute of goodness, while the second can only be explained if the new world were more perfect than its predecessor, a supposition that is inconsistent with the perfection of the Creator's works.[29] Indeed Philo expressly states that 'Time there was not before there was a world.'[30] Whence did the aforementioned Sages derive the idea of a sequence of times prior to the world and of worlds that preceded our world?[31] It seems that the postulate that worlds and generations of inferior quality and degree existed before the creation of our world had as its purpose the enhancement of the value and perfection of the present world and its creatures and the contradiction of the views concerning the imperfection and defectiveness of the existing world, in accordance with the doctrine of Gnostics of the type of Valentinus[32] in the second century, who followed the teachings of Plato[33] regarding the relationship between eternal being (αἰὼν) and the Cosmos. The latter stated '...just as the model continues to subsist for ever. He wished to implant this quality, as far as possible, also in this our world. But the nature of that which lives is eternal and could not be vouchsafed in its entirety to something that came into being. Therefore He thought to make a kind of moving image of eternity. At the very time when He arranged the heavens, He made this eternity that abides in unity... it is this that we call "time".'[34] 'Eternity' is the world of ideas that stands in antithesis to time. Plato already identified the ideas with numbers. In the doctrine of the eternal beings of Valentinus, the aeons are the models of the times that are fixed by the stars. They unite to form 'a fullness' (πλήρομα), a spiritual world. The aspiration of the Gnostic was to be redeemed from the defective world and to attain to the world of the 'eternal beings'. In opposition to these views there was set up a series of worlds that preceded the more perfect one in the sequence of times.[35]

Our discussion of the concepts of the Sages concerning the creation of the world was based on dicta of the Tannaim and Amoraim, that is to say, on teachings that might be expounded. These homiletical expositions were partly derived from the section of Creation in the Pentateuch and from verses in the Prophets and the Hagiographa, in which the subject of Creation is mentioned. We have seen that in the days of the Amoraim the perspective was widened, and views that were at first regarded as esoteric and were transmitted only in a whisper percolated into the Midrashic expositions that were given in public and into the instruction of the academies. We find an unambiguous polemic against sectarian views and alien cosmogonies, but this polemic, too, did not remain without influence or consequences. Ideas that were prevalent in the Hellenistic world found lodgement in the world of the Sages, and it may apparently be assumed that not a few of the homiletical expositions of the Sages on the subject of the 'Work of Creation' are merely crumbs of cosmogonic and cosmological speculations that were cultivated in 'a whisper' in restricted circles of the Sages who 'knew' and mediated upon the 'Work of Creation'. It is also related of famous Babylonian Amoraim[36] of the fourth century that they combined study of the Halakhot of Creation with theurgical and magical practices. We do not know whether the esoteric teachings at the time of the Amoraim reached a stage of literary consolidation. At any rate, in so far as the Talmuds and Midrashim are concerned, even the dicta that bear a distinctly esoteric stamp are interwoven with the usual Midrashic expositions and are embellished with the customary analogies and images. Only in the circles of 'those who delve into the Chariot' and the authors of the *Hekhalot* [Books of Divine Palaces] literature was there an efflorescence of works of the type of *Sefer Yeṣira* [Book of Creation][37] and the 'Baraitot' of the 'Orders of Creation'.[38] It will suffice to compare the themes that are common to these works and to the Talmuds and Midrashim[39] in order to grasp the differences between them in both style and presentation and the atmosphere enveloping them. Whoever reads the various 'doctrines of creation', from that of Plato to those of the neo-Platonists, the cosmogonic 'dramas' of the Gnostics or the Pahlavi creation literature, and assumes that these theories were partly known to the Sages, will be surprised at the paucity of their influence, for despite the fact that the Sages broadened the canvas of the picture of creation in Genesis, adding to its details and explaining its obscurities, they still remained true to its fundamentals. God Himself and alone — without the help of Demiurge, angels or forces — created the world. Notwithstanding the emphasis they gave to the fact that the world was created by an utterance,[40] this utterance did not receive the connotation of 'Logos' in the Philonic sense.[41] It was not hypostatized and no independent existence was attributed to it, just as no such meaning can be assigned to the מימרא *Mēmrā*' of the Targumim.[42] The Rabbinic viewpoint in regard to the creation of the world found succinct expression in the epithet 'He who spoke and the world came into being', which according to one tradition was already used by Simeon b. Shetaḥ,[43] and in the use of the word בראשית *bĕ-rē'shît* ['In the beginning'] in the sense of 'world'.[44] The principle of faith that God created the world was incorporated in the wording of the *ʿAmida* prayer [Eighteen Benedictions] in the formula coined by the patriarch Abraham: 'God Most High, Maker of heaven and earth'.[45]

CHAPTER X

MAN

The ultimate purpose of the creation of the world was man. 'For one man is equal to the entire work of creation'[1], since it has been granted only to man to recognize Him who spoke and the world came into being. The interest of the Sages in man and his problems — in his person, his spirit, and his soul — is infinitely greater than in the order of nature and of the world. In a homily on the words of Jeremiah (ix 22) 'Let not the wise man glory in his wisdom', an anonymous homilist expressed this preference in the words: 'Human beings who have recognized the sun and the moon and the planets... they have the wisdom to instal this great device in order to know the work of God in the sky... they have the wisdom to improve others, but they lack the wisdom to improve themselves.'[2]

Before we begin discussing the views of the Sages concerning man, let us briefly summarize what there is to be learnt on the subject from the Bible.[3]

In the Bible a monistic view prevails. Man is not composed of two elements — body and soul, or flesh and spirit. In Genesis (ii 7) it is stated 'and man became a living soul [נפש *nefesh*]', but the term *nefesh* is not to be understood in the sense of *psyche*, *anima*. The whole of man is a living soul. The creation of man constitutes a single act. The *nefesh* is in actuality the living man, and hence *nefesh* is also used in place of the word אדם *'ādhām* ['man']. When the Lord says to Moses 'For all the men who were seeking thy life are dead' (Exodus iv 19), the reference is not to his *psyche* but to his whole being, and the same applies to the words of Elijah, when he states '...And they seek my life, to take it away' (I Kings xix 10). But on the other hand *nefesh* also expresses all the feelings and sentiments of a person. In the verse 'for ye know the heart [*nefesh*] of a stranger' (Exodus xxiii 9), and in similar verses, the word *nefesh* is used in the sense of 'existence', 'feeling', 'attitude' — in brief, what is called today the 'human condition'.

What is the essential nature of the *nefesh*? Although the Bible states 'for the blood is the *nefesh*' (Deuteronomy xii 23), yet the verse does not mean to say that the essence or material of the *nefesh* is blood. It merely informs us that when blood is shed human life grows weak and comes to an end. Blood is here only a manifestation of life like breathing, which is a symptom of life, or like flesh and spirit. In actuality the *nefesh* is constantly in man and is to be found in all his actions, and there is no difference between it and the flesh. 'O God... my *nefesh* thirsts for Thee; my flesh faints for Thee...' (Psalms lxiii 2), the poet sings. *Nefesh* is in parallelism here with 'flesh'. Hence it is possible to have an expression like 'he shall not go near a dead *nefesh*, that is, a dead person. Here *nefesh* stands in the place of *'ādhām*. Similarly רוח *rûaḥ* ['spirit', 'breath'] is only a manifestation of life. 'In whose hand is the soul [*nefesh*] of every living thing, and the breath [*rûaḥ*] of all mankind' (Job xii 10). The *rûaḥ* is not part of the components of man, but the form in which he finds expression; consequently it is possible to coin phrases like מורת רוח *môrat rûaḥ* ['bitterness of spirit'], רוח קנאה *rûaḥ qin'ā* ['spirit of jealousy'], רוח זנונים *rûaḥ zĕnûnîm* ['spirit of harlotry'], and others. Pedersen[4] rightly perceived that the *rûaḥ* is not the centre of the *nefesh* but the power that moves it, the force that acts on the centre and thrusts it forward in a given direction. Every organ of the body serves as a substitute for the entire body. Thus the heart stands for the whole body. *Nefesh*, גוף *gûf* ['body'], and *rûaḥ* form an indivisible entity, and it may be said that man is a psycho-physical organism. This unity finds expression in lack of differentiation between the word and the substance in the Hebrew tongue, and the relationship between the word and the substance is like that between *nefesh* and *gûf*. In order to denote the absence of existence, non-being, the Hebrew says: as 'naught' [לא דבר *lō' dābhār*] = non-existent. For the existent finds expression only in action and movement, and if there is no action

lit: no word

or movement, there is nothing [literally 'no word']. The *dābhār*, word, pertains only to that which exists; hence there is no difference between theory and practice, and there is no abstraction. Actuality is the fact of power and action, which are life. Life is conceived as power. Disease weakens this power. 'To heal' [רפא *rappē*'] means to revive, to restore to power, to bring life back. Hazael was sent by the king of Aram to ask Elisha 'Shall I live from this sickness?' (II Kings viii 8), that is to say, shall I recover [literally 'return to my strength']?

Sleep is the narcotization of this power, and even death is not the antithesis of life but its extreme enfeeblement; hence the dead are also called רפאים *rĕphā'îm*, that is, the weak. And to the king of Babylon, who descends to Sheol, the dead say: 'Thou, too, hast become weak as we!' (Isaiah xiv 10), as though life continued in Sheol, only in a weak form.

In the light of this interpretation, we may also understand the first story in Genesis concerning the tree of knowledge and the tree of life. Man may eat of the tree of life, which vitalizes him, whilst upon eating of the tree of knowledge, this power is taken away from him, and his life, as it were, grows weak. It is noteworthy that this narrative finds no further echoes in the Bible itself. Nor is it interpreted as an explanation of the nature of man or of the origin of evil, as in other doctrines. On the contrary, Scripture continues to speak of death as an integral part of life. Joshua declares 'And now I am about to go the way of all the earth' (Joshua xxiii 14) — as a fact. It is of interest to observe that Moses, too, does not argue against the actual decree of death. He knows that he must die, only he is unable to realize a portion of his life — to see the land. The dead person is gathered unto his fathers. The Bible's interest is in life upon earth, and this earth is the land of the living — the land that makes life possible, consequently there is no romantic nostalgia for the wilderness. If the prophet says 'O that I were in the wilderness' (Jeremiah ix 1 [2]), he does so only in a spirit of disappointment. On the contrary, the desert is an accursed place, and if the period of the wilderness is mentioned, it is only as a preparation for entrance into the Land.[5]

A man lives among his brethren, and isolation is an abnormal condition. The people is not merely an assemblage of a number of persons, but is a personality. The name of the people is the 'Children of Israel', and Israel is a personality. Hence it is sometimes difficult to decide whether the Bible refers to the individual or to the people.

The views of the Sages concerning man are linked to and hinge upon the Scriptures, and the spirit of the Bible informs them. But at the same time they result from the contemplation of human existence, with all the contradictions that manifest themselves in man's character and actions, and in particular they flow from a consideration of the paradox in man, in whom there is, on the one hand, existence and being, and, on the other, nothingness and void. Therefore they were very interested in probing into the creation and formation of man. The Sages found a basic principle in the verse 'In the image of God made He man'. In his dictum 'Still greater was the love in that it was made known to him that he was created in the image of God' (*M. 'Avot* iii, 14), R. Akiba declared that the election of man consists in the fact that it was made known to him that he was created in God's image. His disciple and colleague, Ben 'Azzai, pointed to the verse 'This is the book of the generations of Adam. In the day that God created man, in the likeness of God made He him'[6] as the great principle of the Torah. The function of man is to know the acts of God. The starting point is God, not man. In the way man was created and in the form that the Creator gave him, two principles find expression — that of human unity and that of the individual worth of each man. 'Hence man was created a single individual... and for the sake of peace among men, that one should not say to his fellow: My father was greater than yours... and to declare the greatness of the Holy One, blessed be He, for a man stamps many coins with one seal, and they are all identical, but the King of the kings of kings stamped every man with the seal of the first man, and none is identical with his fellow. Therefore it is the duty of every one to say: For my sake the world was created' (*M. Sanhedrin* iv, 5). This Mishna states, on the one hand, that no man is identical with his fellow, but is a separate personality, possessing his own worth and bearing responsibility for the existence of the world, but at the same time all men are stamped with the one seal, and no one can say to his fellow that he is unique. The Baraita[7], which elaborates the theme of the Mishna, also adds the question why 'man was born last'. The first answer, 'That the sectarians should not say that he was a partner with Him in His work', seeks to contradict dualistic conceptions (see above, p. 155). The second answer, 'Another explanation is: Why was he created last? So that if he becomes overweening, one can say to him: A gnat preceded you in the work of creation'[8], comes to emphasize the antithesis in man. On the one hand he is stamped with the seal of the Holy One, blessed be He, and on the other a gnat came before him. The awareness of man's greatness and nothingness, which the poet expressed in the verses 'What is man that Thou art mindful of him... Yet Thou hast made him little less than the angels' (Psalms viii, 5 [4]–6 [5]) the Tannaim discovered, even before Philo's time,[9] in the section of Creation in Genesis. The fact that death deprives man of the faculty of speech and of the ability to move, but leaves the body with all its organs, strengthened the sense of duality.

Man appeared to the Tannaim as composed of various parts. The first man was entirely created by God, but the making of a man that is born is shared by partners: 'The white is from the male, out of which brain and bones and sinews are formed; and the red is from the female, out of which the skin and the flesh and the blood are made; and the spirit and the life and the soul are from the Holy One, blessed be He. Thus all three have a share in him' (*T.P. Kil'ayim* viii, 4, p. 31c). In a Baraita in a parallel source (*T.B. Nidda* 31a) the division is more detailed: 'And the Holy One, blessed be He, endows him with spirit, soul [or, breath], beauty of features, eyesight, capacity to hear, speech, ability to walk, understanding, and discernment; and when his time arrives to leave the world, the Holy One, blessed be He, takes His share and leaves the portion of his father and mother before them. Said Rav Papa: This is the meaning of the folk saying 'Shake off the salt and throw the meat to the dog.' The popular adage quoted by Rav Papa, which declares in effect that 'Once you shake off the salt from the meat it is only fit for dogs', seeks to liken the soul to salt, which preserves the body. The superiority of God's share over those of the other partners is brought out clearly in a third source, in the analogy of R. Judah the Patriarch, which informs us incidentally that the idea of the threefold division was actually known before his time. It is stated there:

> And when his [man's] time to depart (from this world) arrives, the Holy One, blessed be He, takes His share and leaves that

> of his father and mother before them, and his father and mother weep. The Holy One, blessed be He, says to them: 'Why do you weep? Have I taken ought of yours? I have taken only that which is Mine.' They answer Him: 'Sovereign of the universe, so long as Thy portion was integrated with ours, our share was preserved from worms and maggots; but now that Thou hast taken away Thy share from ours, our portion is lying exposed to worms and maggots.' R. Judah the Patriarch illustrated this with the help of an analogy: To what can the matter be compared? To a king who had a vineyard, which he leased to a tenant farmer [for a share of the crop]. The king (one day) instructed his servants: 'Go, hold vintage in my vineyard, taking my share and leaving that of the tenant in its place. Forthwith they went and carried out the king's command, whereupon the tenant began to cry aloud and weep. Said the king to him: 'Have I taken anything of yours? Is it not my own that I have taken?' He replied: 'O my lord, the king! so long as your portion was with mine, my share was preserved from spoliation and theft. But now that you have taken your share, mine lies exposed to spoliation and theft.

The king (of the analogy) represents the King of the king of kings. The tenant symbolizes a man's father and mother. So long as the soul is in man, he is protected: but once he dies, he is subject to worms and maggots... (*Ecclesiastes Rabba* v, 10). The *nefesh* includes all the vital parts of man, all his senses; they are the portion of the Creator in man, without which the other parts cannot exist. Nevertheless the other parts of man are not disparaged. This truth finds expression in the special emphasis given to the precept to honour father and mother, which is equated with the honour to be shown to the Omnipresent. This equation is explained by the fact that all three are partners in man.[10] This idea which was already known to R. Simeon b. Yoḥai, has an analogue in Philo's writings.[11] The latter bases it on the Stoic view that parents have a human aspect, for they die, but also a Divine aspect, in that they bring to birth. Philo did not approve the worship of parents inculcated by the Stoics, and even opposed it[12]; and needless to say the honouring of parents, which the Sages preached and explained on the basis of the share of the father and mother in the birth of the child, was far removed from the Stoic conception. For it was they [the Sages] who taught ' "Ye shall fear every man his mother, and his father, and ye shall keep My sabbaths; I am the Lord" — you are all duty-bound to honour Me.'[13]

The concept of the three parts of which man is constituted and the explanation of the partnership of the three posit the existence of a schism between the parts. On the basis of this postulate the question was raised: When do body and soul become integrated. This question became a subject of discussion between the Sages and Gentiles. 'Antoninus asked Rabbi: "At which stage is the evil inclination [יצר הרע *yēṣer hā-rāʿ*] instilled in man?" He replied: "From the moment that he is formed." Thereupon (Antoninus) said to him: "If so, (the embryo) would dig its way through (the mother's) womb and go forth! The answer must therefore be when (the child) has gone forth." Rabbi admitted to him (Antoninus) that his view was in accord with that of the Bible: "For the imagination [יצר *yēṣer*] of man's heart is evil [רע *raʿ*] from his youth...". He further inquired: "At which stage is the soul instilled in man?" Said (Rabbi) to him (Antoninus): "As soon as he leaves his mother's womb." He replied: "Leave meat without salt for three days, will it not become putrid? The answer must be: From the moment that he (the child) is commanded (to come into existence)." And Rabbi admitted to him that Scripture also supports him: "[As long as my breath is in me] and the spirit of God is in my nostrils (Job xxvii 3), [and Thy command hath preserved my spirit]" (*ibid.* x 12) — when didst Thou give me the soul? From the moment that Thou didst command me.'[14] Rabbi accepts the answer of Antoninus that the soul is instilled the moment the embryo comes into being, and it is noteworthy that it is stated here explicitly that Rabbi received the idea from Antoninus, that is to say, the source itself testifies that the concept was of non-Jewish origin.[15] The emperor-philosopher,[16] the representative of Hellenistic culture, and the Jewish Patriarch both adhere to the view that draws a line of demarcation between the body and the soul. This was not merely the personal opinion of Judah the Patriarch, but a widely held notion. His contemporary, R. Simai, who belonged to the Ḥasidim ['Pietists'] and is designated 'the most holy'[17], said: 'All created beings that were created from heaven, their soul and body are from heaven; and all creatures that were created from the earth, their soul and body are from the earth, except man, whose soul is from heaven and his body from the earth. Therefore, if he observed the Torah and did the will of his Father in heaven, he is like the beings (of heaven) above, for Scripture states "I said: Ye are godlike beings, and all of you sons of the Most High" (Psalms lxxxii 6). But if he did not observe the Torah nor do the will of his Father in heaven, he is like the creatures of (earth) below, as it is said (*ibid.* v. 7): "Nevertheless ye shall die like man" ' (*Sifre*, Ha'azinu, § 306, pp. 340–341). Man accordingly holds a position between the higher beings (of heaven) and the lower creatures (of earth), but he is able wholly to exalt himself and be among the higher beings, if he deserves the Torah and does the will of his Heavenly Father. Contrariwise, if he does not observe the Torah, he becomes like the lower creatures. In another Baraita stress is laid on the difference between man's spiritual attributes and his bodily needs: 'Six things have been stated of human beings: in respect of three they are like the Ministering Angels, and in regard to three like beasts. In respect of three they are like the Ministering Angels: they have understanding like the Ministering Angels, and walk erect like the Ministering Angels, and speak the holy tongue like the Ministering Angels. In regard to three they are like beasts: They eat and drink like beasts, and they propagate like beasts, and they ease themselves like beasts' (*T.B. Ḥagiga* 16 a). The Palestinian Amoraim in the fourth century provided a Scriptural basis for these ideas: ' "So God created man in His own image, in the image of God He created him; male and female He created them" (Genesis i 27). R. Joshua bar Nehemiah in the name of R. Ḥanina bar Isaac, and the Rabbis in the name of R. Lazar said: He created in him [man] four features [literally, 'creations'] from (heaven) on high and four from (earth) below. He eats and drinks like a beast, he propagates like a beast, and relieves himself like a beast, and dies like a beast. From (heaven) on high: he stands (erect) like the Ministering Angels, he possesses understanding like the Ministering Angels, and he sees like the Ministering Angels' (*Genesis Rabba* viii, 11, p. 64). These concepts resemble those of Philo[18], only he, following Plato[19], distinguishes in man not two but three parts: the body that is fashioned from clay, the animal vitality that is linked to the body, and the mind that is instilled in the soul, this being the Divine mind. Man is a synthesis of earthly substance and the spirit of God (γεώδους οὐσίας καὶ πνεύματος θείου). Man has been created both mortal and immortal — mortal in respect of his body, immortal in regard to his mind.[20]

The mind is part of the blessed soul, something of that first mould, of the first man, who was wholly idea. A dualistic anthropology similar to Philo's in its extremism, but enunciated in rhetorical, homiletical fashion rather than in philosophical style, is presented by Josephus. In his speech in Galilee, in which he explains his refusal to put an end to his life, he declares 'All of us, it is true, have mortal bodies, composed of perishable matter, but the soul lives for ever, immortal: it is a portion of the Deity housed in our bodies' (*Wars* iii, 8, 5). This concept lies at the heart of the oration that Josephus puts into the mouth of the leader of the Zealots at Masada, but seeing that it seeks to serve the opposite purpose, namely to persuade the heroes of Masada to commit suicide, it is worded even more drastically:

> For from of old... we have been continually taught by those precepts, ancestral and divine — confirmed by the deeds and noble spirit of our fathers that life, not death, is man's misfortune. For it is death which gives liberty to the soul and permits it to depart to its own pure abode, there to be free from all calamity; but so long as it is imprisoned in a mortal body and tainted with all its miseries, it is, in sober truth, dead, for association with what is mortal ill befits that which is divine. True, the soul possesses great capacity, even while incarcerated in the body; for it makes the latter its organ of perfection, invisibly swaying it and directing it onward in its actions beyond the range of mortal nature. But it is not until, freed from the weight that drags it down to earth and clings about it, the soul is restored to its proper sphere, that it enjoys a blessed energy and a power untrammelled on every side, remaining, like God Himself, invisible to human eyes (*ibid.* vii, 8, 7).

The residence of the soul in the body is a downgrading, and its release from the chains of the body is freedom. The formulation here is more extreme than in the dicta of the Sages, for they assess this partnership positively, and man's ascent is achieved not by the liberation of the body from the soul, but by the performance of good deeds and precepts, whereas Josephus makes the severance of the bond between the body and soul the primary factor, a view that largely resembles that of Philo. Undoubtedly, the unusual circumstances[21] in which Eleazar uttered his speech help to explain the pungency and extremism of the wording, but at the same time Josephus' words testify to what extent the dualistic anthropological view was prevalent at the end of the Second-Temple epoch, before the time of R. Judah the Patriarch and R. Simai. The separation between body and soul gave rise to a problem in regard to the doctrine of requital: Who is responsible and to whom are reward and punishment due? If man is divisible and not a monolithic whole, what bearing has this position on the principle of reward and punishment, and how is it operated?

This question, too, is raised in the debate between Antoninus and Rabbi, which is reported in the *Mekhilta de-R. Ishmael* (Massekhta de-Shira, ii, p. 125): 'Antoninus asked our holy teacher [R. Judah the Patriarch]: When a man dies and the body disintegrates, does the Holy One, blessed be He, make him stand in judgement? He replied: Instead of asking me about the body, which is unclean, ask me about the soul which is pure. The case is analogous to that of a human king who had a beautiful orchard' etc. The question is more explicitly stated and the analogy is more complete in the Babylonian Talmud (*Sanhedrin* 91a–b): 'Antoninus said to Rabbi: The body and soul can free themselves from judgement. How? The body can say: It is the soul that sinned, for since the day that it left me, I lie still as a stone in the grave. And the soul can say: The body has sinned, for since the day that I left it, I fly in the air like a bird.[22] Said (Rabbi) to him: I shall give you an analogy. To what can the case be compared? To that of a human king who had a beautiful orchard that contained fine early fruit, and he posted two watchmen there, the one lame and the other blind... so the lame man was carried pick-a-back by the blind man, and they took them and ate them. After a time the owner of the orchard came. Said he to them: Where are the fine early fruits? Said the lame man to him: Have I then feet to walk with? Said the blind man to him: Have I then eyes to see? What did (the owner) do? He put the lame man astride the blind man and judged them as one. Even so the Holy One, blessed be He, takes the soul and casts it into the body and judges them as one....'[23]

Despite all the elements in dualistic anthropology that are common to the teachings of the Sages and the Stoic-Platonic views, which were prevalent in the Hellenistic world, the conception of dualism and the antithesis between flesh and spirit in Rabbinic dicta are less drastic. We do not find a distinction drawn by the Sages between souls that were never attached to a body and are the pure souls that serve the Creator and act as supervisors, on the one hand, and the souls that have an inclination towards matter and descend into the body, on the other, as Philo holds.[24] Concepts derived from foreign sources, and for which there is no Biblical authority, were bounded by the belief in reward and punishment and by the postulate of free will. Developments that occurred in these beliefs left their mark on the anthropological conception, just as the latter, in turn, influenced the former. Instructive in our context is the saying of the Tanna ʿAqavia b. Mahalal'el, who lived about the time of Hillel and Shammai, and possibly was still a contemporary of Philo: 'Reflect on three things, and you will not come within the power of sin: know whence you have come, and whither you are going, and before whom you are destined to give account and reckoning. Whence you have come: from a putrefying drop; whither you are going: to a place of dust, worms, and maggots; and before whom you are destined to give account and reckoning: before the Supreme King of kings, the Holy One, blessed be He.'[25] The Tanna does not mention body and soul, but addresses himself to the whole man, to whom he gives the answer: you come from a putrefying drop; and this whole man — as in the analogy that we have cited, but without stressing the dualism — will have to give account and reckoning. The words of the Tanna recall those of Job (x 9–22) 'Remember that Thou hast made me like clay; and wilt Thou turn me to dust again? Didst Thou not pour me out like milk and curdle me like cheese?...' But whilst Job is devoid of any unsavoury expression, and contains only the statement that man is like clay in the hand of the potter, the phrase 'putrefying drop' has an unpleasant significance. Job declares 'I should have been as though I had not been; I should have been carried from the womb to the grave'; but thereafter comes 'a land of gloom as darkness itself; a land of deep darkness without any order'. The question of reward and punishment appertains to life upon earth, which he regards with perplexity. In contrast to this, ʿAqavia b. Mahalal'el declared that after man has gone to the place of dust, worms, and maggots, he is destined to give account and reckoning. ʿAqavia does not seek to repeat the thought of Job (xxxiv 14–15) 'If He set His heart upon man, if He gather unto Himself his spirit and his breath... and man shall return unto dust', or that of Ecclesiastes (xii 7) 'And the dust returneth to the earth as it was, and the spirit returneth unto God who gave it'. Neither verse speaks of a sequel linked to human life. On the other hand ʿAqavia wishes to emphasize the responsibility and status of man, who is due to give account and reckoning before 'the King of the kings of kings', and he is the same man who emanates from a putrefying drop and goes to a place of dust, worms, and maggots, and the account and reckoning concern man's deeds when he was body and spirit. Only the outcome of this account and reckoning determines whether the soul shall return to Him that gave it. In this sense R. Samuel bar Naḥmani expounded in the name of R. Avdimi of Haifa the aforementioned verse of Ecclesiastes: 'Thus saith the Holy One, blessed be He, to man: Behold, I am pure, and My abode is pure, and My servants are pure, and the soul that I give you is pure. If you will give it (back) to me as I give it to you, well and good; but if not, I shall burn it before you.'[26] The purity of the soul is not something immutable but the outcome of the life of the whole man, both body and soul; hence the interest of the Sages in the human body.

The creation of man's body was discussed by the Tannaim, and their views were mostly transmitted by Amoraim. 'R. Ḥanina bar Pappa gave the following interpretation: What is the significance of the verse 'Thou measurest my going about and my lying down, and art acquainted with all my ways' (Psalms cxxxix 3)? It teaches that man is not formed from the whole (putrefying) drop, but from the purest part of it. The School of R. Ishmael taught: This may be compared to a man winnowing in the threshing floor: he takes that which is edible and leaves the refuse.'[27]

This conception of the formation of the child from the drop was known in antiquity since the days of Aristotle.[28] Philo[29] writes thus:

> Now in particular creatures the order we find is this, that they begin at what is lowest in its nature, and end in the best of all;

what this best of all is we must go on to show. Now seed is the original starting-point of living creatures. That this is a substance of a very low order, resembling foam, is evident to the eye. But when it has been deposited in the womb and become solid, it acquires movement, and at once enters upon natural growth. But growth is better than seed, since in created things movement is better than quiescence. But nature, or growth, like an artificer, or (to speak more properly) like a consummate art, forms living creatures, by distributing the moist substance to the limbs and different parts of the body, the substance of life-breath to the faculties of the soul, affording them nourishment and endowing them with perception. We must defer for the present the faculty of reasoning, out of consideration for those who maintain that it comes in from without, and is divine and eternal.

In estimating the drop of semen there is no difference between ʿAqavia and Philo. In regard to the formation of the various parts of the body there is a resemblance between the view of Philo and that of the Amoraim, only while Philo uses abstract concepts, the Amoraim, addressing themselves to simple people, employ images that are comprehensible to them. Philo, in speaking of the creation of man, uses the concept nature (φύσις), which he portrays as a craftsman (τεχνίτης), and does not speak, in the context of man's creation, about God, for man's body is earthly and transient, given to sin, and there is no connection between it and God, just as there is no nexus between the Deity and any form of evil, for evil does not emanate from the Godhead; from Him stems only good. Therefore He handed over the creation of the body to others, and consequently Scripture states with reference to the creation of man: 'Let us make man.'[30] All this applies to the first man, whereas relative to his descendants Philo's view is even more pessimistic, for Adam, the father of the whole human race, was more perfect both in body and in soul, and differed greatly from his offspring in his two constituent parts. In his scions a decline set in; in every generation there was further deterioration, and their powers and attributes of body as well as soul, became continually weaker.[31] It never entered the minds of the Sages, however, to say that the body was not created by God. The words 'In the image of God made He man' applies to man as a whole, as is apparent from the narrative about Hillel the Elder, which is the complete antithesis of Philo's view. ' "A man who is kind benefits himself" — this refers to Hillel the Elder. When Hillel the Elder took leave of his disciples, he continued to walk. Said his disciples to him: "Master, whither are you going?" He replied: "to perform a *miṣwa* ['precept', 'good deed']". Said they to him: "And what is the *miṣwa* that Hillel is going to perform?" He replied: "To bath in the bathhouse." Said they to him: "Is this a *miṣwa*?" He answered them: "Yea! If now in the case of the images of the kings, which are set up in their theatres and circuses, the superintendent in charge of them cleanses them and washes them and he is provided with sustenance [literally 'portions']... how much more so we, who have been created in the (Divine) image and likeness, as it is written "In the image of God made He man"!'[32] Hillel's view that the verse 'In the image of God made He man' refers to man as a whole was upheld by the Tannaim who came after him. R. Akiba did not hesitate to say 'Whoever sheds blood destroys the image', and his disciple Ben ʿAzzai even added 'Whoever does not engage in propagation of the species is deemed by Scripture to diminish, as it were, the likeness.'[33] In preserving the human race we preserve the 'image of God' in the world; and this is not achieved by the release of the soul from the body. This thought found expression in *Midrash Tannaim* in an analogy similar to that cited by Hillel: 'This may be likened to a human king who entered a country, and set up images of himself, and made statues of himself, and coins were struck with his likeness. Subsequently his images were overturned, his statues were broken and his coins were annulled; thus the likeness of the king was diminished. Even so, whoever sheds blood is deemed by Scripture to diminish, as it were, the likeness of the King.'[34]

We have seen that Philo distinguished between Pristine Man and the first historical man, and between him and his descendants.[35] Such a differentiation is not to be found in the teaching of the Tannaim. When Pappas interpreted the verse ' "Behold, the man is become as one of us" (Genesis iii 22) — as one of the Ministering Angels', R. Akiba said to him: 'Enough! Pappas.'[36] Although man was created from the ground, and Eve from Adam, and now 'It is impossible for man (to propagate) without woman, and for woman without man', yet even now 'It is not possible for both of them without the Shekhina.'[37] Dicta that describe the first man in a manner stressing the differences between him and other human beings, and representing him as a kind of 'macroanthropos', are enunciated by the Amoraim only from the beginning of the third century. Rav Judah said in the name of Rav[38]: 'The first man extended from one end of the world to the other... when he sinned, the Holy One, blessed be He, placed His hand upon him and diminished him.' R. Jeremiah b. Lazar said: 'When the Holy One, blessed be He, created the first man, He created him a hermaphrodite (ἀνδρόγυνος)...' And R. Samuel bar Naḥman said: 'When the Holy One, blessed be He, created the first man, He created him with two faces (διπρόσωπος); then He sawed him asunder and made him with a back on each side.'[39] Already a century ago and more scholars[40] pointed to the similarity between these descriptions and the story narrated in Plato's *Symposium*.[41] But it seems that actually this 'resemblance' does not shed light so much on itself as on the entire principle of comparisons and resemblances of this kind. In the *Symposium* we have a mythological tale, told by Aristophanes in order to explain the nature of Eros as a craving for the completeness of man, who is only a part of what he once was. In the Midrash no inference is drawn from the dictum. The notion of the hermaphrodite the Amora bases on the verse 'male and female created He them' (Genesis v 2), and R. Samuel bar Naḥman resolves the contradiction between his statement and the verse 'And He took one of his ribs', but no attempt is made there to invest the dictum with any implications whatsoever. We are confronted by a phenomenon similar to that which we found in the Amoraic exposition of the creation of the world.[42] Remnants of myths and legends, which had gained currency in various circles, were absorbed and Judaized and deprived of their hurtful mythological characteristics. We do not know if the myth became known to the Amoraim in its Platonic or another form, but what remains in their expositions is an altogether soulless myth. The hermaphrodite and the man with two faces are not represented as ideal or perfect forms; and when the Holy One, blessed be He, saws the man with two faces in half, this is not done in order to prevent an attempt on the part of the creatures to make war against the gods, and in the view of the Amora there is no difference between 'He sawed him in half' and 'He took one of his ribs'.

This man, who was a hermaphrodite, became a male and female, while Philo held that God first created 'man as a genus' (τὸν γενικὸν ἄνθρωπον), who was bisexual, and only subsequently did he form the special species known as 'Adam' (τὸ εἶδος... τὸν 'Αδάμ). [43] Even the homiletical expositions of the Amoraim that speak of the enormous proportions of the first man and thus resemble the statements of Philo lack the differentiation customary in the latter's writings between the heavenly man (οὐράνιος ἄνθρωπος), who was not fashioned but was 'stamped' with the likeness and image of God (οὐ πεπλάσθαι κατ' εἰκόνα δὲ τετυπῶσθαι θεοῦ),[44] and Adam who was formed out of the dust of the ground. On the contrary, it appears that they actually seek to contradict this conception.[45] Rav and R. Eleazar themselves not only declare that the stature of the succeeding generations was reduced, but they state of the first man that 'When he sinned the Holy One, blessed be He, placed His hand upon him and diminished him.'[46] A similar trend is to be found also in the Haggada that speaks of the beauty and radiance of Adam: 'R. Levi in the name of R. Simeon b. Menasia (said): The apple of the heel of the first man outshone the disk of the sun. And be not surprised at this; it is customary that a man makes two salvers (δισκάριον), one for himself and one for the son of his house. Whose does he make the more beautiful? Is it not his own? Even so was Adam created for the service of the Holy One, blessed be He, and the disk of the sun was created for the service of mankind. Does it not follow *a fortiori* that the apple of Adam's heel should outshine the disk of the sun?'[47] Despite all the radiant beauty of the first man he was only the servant of the Holy One, blessed be He. In the various Gnostic doctrines the gods, and in particular the supreme deity, bore the names 'the Complete Man' (ὁ τέλειος ἄνθρωπος), 'the First Man', 'the Man of Light', and also just 'Man' ('Ἄνθρωπος).[48] Apparently the Amoraim at the beginning of the third century knew of such doctrines. The dictum of R. Hoshaiah bears testimony to this: 'When the Holy One, blessed be He, created the first man, the Ministering Angels mistook him [for God] and wished to say before him, 'Holy!' To what can the matter be compared? To a king and a governor who were driving in a carriage (καρρούχα), and the citizens wished to cry 'domine!' to the king, and they did not know which was he. What did the king do? He pushed him [the governor] out of the carriage; then the people knew (who was) the king. So, too, when the Holy One, blessed be He, created the first man, the angels mistook him [for God]. What did the Holy One, blessed be He, do? He put him to sleep, and all knew that he was man. This is the meaning of the verse, 'Cease ye from man' etc. (Isaiah ii 22).'[49] In another Midrash the connection between Adam's size and his identification as a god is explained. ' "And God said: 'Let us make man in our image' " — He created him from one end of the world to the other. How do we know that this was so? It is written: "Since the day that God created man upon the earth, and from the one end of heaven unto the other" (Deuteronomy iv 32). When the angels beheld a new figure, they wished to prostrate themselves to it, but Michael, who is familiar with the Inner Sanctum, cried out to them: "It is man...." '[50] It seems that Rav himself, in his dictum 'The first man was a sectarian'[51], had in mind 'the first man' as envisaged by those sectarian groups. It is not impossible that in Rav's days the Jews in Babylon were also acquainted with the Iranian myths about the Pristine Man — the *gayōmard* — and about the first human pair — *mašyē* and *mašyānē* — 'who were joined to each other and were of the same stature. The splendour (*Xuarra*) came upon them. They were so like each other that it was not clear which of them was male and which female.'[52] It may well be that these speculations were linked to the Pentateuchal narrative and were integrated with it in Jewish circles, just as they left their impress on Christian Gnostic works.[53] Although the Iranian myth has reached us in sources of a late date, yet there is no reason to suppose that, having regard to all its complexities, it is merely the product of the influence of the isolated sentences of the Midrash.[54] On the contrary, the Amoraim absorbed remnants of the myths about the creation of man that were current in their neighbourhood, voided them of their mythological content, and superimposed upon them the principles of their faith. But in the process they were also influenced to no small extent. The very recognition that the First Man was different and unique reduced the importance attributed to the fact recorded in the section of Creation that he was the last of the created beings. Obviously, the Sages could not deny the express statement of the Bible, but a compromise was found. Adam was both the first man and the last.

R. Simeon b. Laqish, to whom too is attributed the view that Adam was created with two faces, explained the verse in Psalms (cxxxix 5) thus: אחור וקדם צרתני *'āḥôr wāqedem ṣartānî* [to be rendered according to the Sage: 'Last and first Thou didst form me']: *'āḥôr* ['last'] — of the work of the last day, *wāqedem* ['first'] — of the work of the first day... "And the spirit of God hovered over the face of the waters" — that was the spirit of the First Man, as Scripture states, "And the spirit of the Lord shall rest upon him" ' (Isaiah xi 2). The verse that was cited as proof could lead to an identification of the spirit of the First Man with that of the Messiah; and actually we find an eschatological exposition by Resh Laqish that is based on this verse. But the very possibility of the identification was sufficient for the exposition of Resh Laqish to be rejected. His colleague R. Eleazar negated the interpretation of the word *qedem* as referring to the first day, and gave instead the forced explanation to the verse 'Let the earth bring forth a living soul' (Genesis i 24) — 'this refers to the spirit of the First Man.'[55] In the fourth century R. Berechiah found another compromise solution: 'When the Holy One, blessed be He, wished to create the world, His first work of creation was none other than man, whom He made a lifeless body. When He came to instil a soul into him, He declared: If I set him up now, he will say that he was My partner in the work of Creation; I shall therefore leave him as a lifeless body until I create everything. When He had completed all things, the Ministering Angels said to Him: Art Thou not going to make man, as Thou didst say? He answered them: I have already made him, and he lacks nought but the infusion of a soul. So He set him up and completed with him the world — with him He began and with him He ended, as it is written: "Last and first Thou didst form me." '[56] The homilist used a mythological dictum concerning the creation of man: 'He [God] created him [man] as a lifeless body, which extended, as he was lying down, from one end of the world to the other,' and he linked the notion to the motif that we found in Tannaitic teaching — the fear of the sectarians — 'lest they say that he [man] was God's partner in His work [of Creation]' (above p. 217). The contemporary of R. Berechiah, the Amora R. Jeremiah b. R. Eleazar, who transmitted the dictum that man was created a hermaphrodite, did not refrain from giving the Tannaitic exposition of Proverbs ix 1–4, which begins with the analogy cited above (p. 218) and ends with the words: 'and thereafter: "She hath sent forth her maidens, and she calleth upon the highest places of the city: 'Whoso is thoughtless, let him turn in hither'; and to him who is without sense" — this refers to Adam and Eve. "Upon the highest places of the city" — (this connotes) that the Holy One, blessed be He, enabled them to fly and called them gods... this is the meaning of the Scripture, "and ye shall be as God". (Yet) after all this praise — "Whoso is thoughtless, let him turn in hither"; they forsook the will of the Holy One, blessed be He, and did the will of the serpent....'[57]

The primary interest of the Sages was focused on the offspring of the First Man — on living man. He was no less than Adam the work of God's hands. It is actually in the Midrashic expositions of the Tannaim[58] that emphasis was given to the miracle of the development of the child in its mother's womb as a work of the Creator that has no parallel: 'A human being is by nature incapable of forming a figure in darkness, but the Holy One, blessed be He, did form a figure in the dark[59], as it is said: "My frame was not hidden from Thee, when I was being made in secret, intricately wrought in the depths of the earth" (Psalms cxxxix 15). A human being, when he seeks to form a figure, naturally begins with its head or with one of the limbs, and then completes it; but the Holy One, blessed be He, forms the entire figure at once, as it is said, "for He forms everything at once" [E.V. "for He is the former of all things"], and it is further said "and there is no צור *Ṣûr* [E.V. "Rock"] like our God" (I Samuel ii 2) — there is no Artist [ציירי *Ṣayyār*] like our God. A human being goes to an image maker and says to him: "Make me the figure of my father", and he (the image maker) says to him: "Let your father come and stand before me", or "Bring me his portrait and I shall make his figure". But the Holy One, blessed be He, gives man a son from a drop of water [i.e. semen] and he resembles the form of his father.' Not all the Tannaim hold that the Holy One, blessed be He, formed the figure of the child at one stroke. In the name of R. Joḥanan b. Zakkai[60] it is stated that the form of the embryo is completed at the end of forty days; and while he does not differentiate in this regard between male and female, R. Ishmael was of the opinion that the male was completed in forty-one days and the female in eighty-one.[61] In the argumentation on this theme the Sages based themselves on a story about Cleopatra, the queen of Alexandria, whose maidservants were sentenced to death by royal decree, and they were examined.[62] This fact shows that these views were acquired from non-Jewish sources. Like Aristotle, Pliny, Galen, and others[63] the Sages also differed on the question as to which part of the embryo's body is formed first. Abba Saul held that the embryo developed from the navel, whilst others declared that the process began with the head.[64]

The view of man as 'a small world'[65], a microcosm, is likewise found already in Tannaitic teaching. R. Jose the Galilean said:[66] 'All that the Holy One, blessed be He, created upon earth He created in man... He created thickets in the world and He created thickets in man, that is, man's hair....' Thus the Sage continues to find parallels for all man's bodily parts among the created things of the world. Philo[67] also regarded man as a microcosm. He states that God is the supreme and most perfect Planter. His plant is the world, which is both soil and tree; even so is man, who is a miniature world. Taking as his basis the verse (Psalms xciv 9) 'He who planted the ear, does he not hear? He who formed the eye, does He not see?' he states: 'He (God) took our body, as though He were taking some deep-soiled plot of ground and made the organs of sense as tree-beds in it.' He then proceeds to describe the planting of the spiritual and intellectual powers. While the Tanna likens the parts of the body to the created things of the world, Philo is not interested in the body and its parts, but in the spiritual powers and the senses. The comparison of God to a planter, and the world and man to a tree, is not found in Rabbinic teaching. It is true that R. Jose the Galilean uses the analogy of sowing in his homily: 'What is the significance of the verse, "I will give thanks unto Thee, for I am fearfully and wonderfully made, wonderful are Thy works, and that my soul knoweth right well" (Psalms cxxxix 14)? Come and see that the ways of man are not like those of the Holy One, blessed be He. In the case of a human being, if a man puts (diverse) seeds in a garden bed, each one grows into its own kind (of produce); whereas the Holy One, blessed be He, forms the embryo in a woman's womb, and all of them grow into the same species' (*T.B. Nidda* 31a). But the analogy seeks to emphasize the difference between man the sower and the Holy One, blessed be He, who forms a figure. Nor did the Sages expound, in the manner indicated above, either the verse cited by Philo or the verse 'The branch of My planting, the work of My hands, wherein I glory' (Isaiah lx 21). Hence it is difficult to find in Philo's statement, mentioned earlier, 'a Hebrew mystic tradition'.[68] This tradition knows nothing of the 'Cosmic Tree',[69] and the images used by Jose the Galilean are not of a mystical character. Their purpose is solely to stress the wonder inherent in the formation of the embryo and its unfoldment in its mother's womb. The form given to it in forty days is that of the entire human being — both body and soul. Indeed there are sources that, in place of 'form' [צורה *ṣûrā*] or 'embryo' [ולד *wālād*], employ the terms 'soul' [נשמה *nĕshāmā*] and 'life' [נפש *nefesh*].[70] It is evident that the authors of these dicta, or their formulators, posited the separate existence of the soul before it entered the body. But there were scholars who stated categorically, on the basis of various Rabbinic sayings, that the concept of the pre-existence of the soul was also widespread in Judaism, both in that of the apocryphal writings and in that of Rabbinic literature itself. Plato's concept of the pre-existence of souls[71] — and as it was taught by Philo[72] under his influence — is part of the general dualistic doctrine, which counterposed matter and spirit, that is to say, the corporeal world, which we see, and the world of Ideas — the forms and forces that existed before they materialized, before they became visible entities. These Ideas are completely independent of the material phenomena of the world, for they preceded the latter. The evil in the world is connected with matter, and man's sin is linked to the body. Sin can be conquered only by fighting the body and by separating the soul from it. In the words of Plato: 'This is precisely the business of the philosophers — to pry the soul loose and isolate it from the body.'[73] Pre-existence implies immortality, whereas the existent and visible is not endowed with immortality, but is transient. Such an antithesis between matter and idea is not to be found in Rabbinic teaching. In the Greek conception the rational soul, which is pre-existent, forms the human personality. The distinction between the rational and irrational soul is unknown to the Sages. The soul is only a part of the man who was to be created — the spirit of life, which God breathed into man, who was formed from the ground. Greek thought found its most perfect expression in the dialogue *Phaedo*, which states that the task of philosophy is the liberation of the soul from the body. Unlike Greek thought, Rabbinic teaching does not speak of the immortality of the soul, but of the resurrection of the dead. Man dies, but he is destined to rise again to life. The term 'immortality' [אלמות *'almāwet*] is not to be found in the dicta of the Sages, and when they cite Aquila's translation of Psalms xlviii 15, על מות *'al māwet* — ἀθανασία', they interpreted it with reference to the future world, 'where there is no death'.[74] Philo also held the belief in metempsychosis; the soul is eternal and passes from man to man or from man to beast. On the other hand, the sayings of the Sages contain no reference to the transmigration of souls. The philosophers Pythagoras and Plato understood this concept of the soul's donning various bodies as a punishment, and the ideal was to be found in eternal separation, that is to say, in the cessation of this process of the soul's clothing itself in a body. Since in Plato's view the kingdom of eternal Ideas is of primary importance, man's ability to comprehend these Ideas is proof of that fact that the soul belongs to this realm. Moreover, since the Ideas cannot be grasped by the senses but only by memory, their pre-existence is thereby confirmed, for memory derives from the state wherein the soul itself existed as an Idea. The eternal soul undergoes metempsychosis until it attains its complete purification, and only absolute separation entitles it to the world of truth.

Let us now turn our attention to those sources in which it was supposed that the idea of the pre-existence of the soul could be discovered. But before we examine the teaching of the Sages, let us open the *Book of the Wisdom of Solomon*, whose author was influenced by Stoic philosophy, and possibly also by Plato, and in which it was thought that the concept of pre-existence[75] could be found. It states 'Because wisdom will not enter into a soul that deviseth evil, nor dwell in a body held in pledge by sin' (i 4), 'For a corruptible body weigheth down the soul, and the earthly frame lieth heavy on the mind that is full of cares.' (*ibid.* ix 15). Thus the author of *The Wisdom of Solomon* does indeed point to the antithesis between the corruptible body and the earthly frame, on the one hand, and the soul and mind, on the other, the former weighing down and lying heavy on the latter. There is a word-play here that recalls the σῆμα σῶμα (the body is the grave of the soul) of Plato. But actually the harmonizing verse (*ibid.* viii 19–20) 'Now I was a child good by nature and a good soul fell to my lot, nay rather, being good, I came into a body undefiled' speaks of 'a body undefiled', the personality being linked to the body. A pure soul fell to his lot, and no distinction is drawn between the body and the soul; it is an undivided personality — 'Now I was a child good by nature'. The writer speaks here equally of the pre-existence of the body as of the soul, as Yitzhak Heinemann[76] has noted. Thus even the author of *The Wisdom of Solomon* is still more of a Jew than a Platonist or Hellenist, and does not allude to the concept of pre-existence. The verse 'Because wisdom will not enter into a soul that deviseth evil' etc. does not express, according to Heinemann, flight from the body, but the conclusion that only a pure body and a pure soul can hope for wisdom. Scholars also sought to discover the concept of pre-existence in the exposition of R. Eleazar of Modiʿim: 'Why do you cry unto Me? Do I require a command where My children are concerned? "Concerning My sons, and concerning the work of My hands, command ye Me?" (Isaiah xlv 11). Lo, they have already been prepared before Me since the six days of Creation, as it is said "If these ordinances depart from before Me, saith the Lord, then the seed of Israel also shall cease from being a nation before Me for ever" (Jeremiah xxxi 36)'.[77] But in truth the Tanna only states that the election and eternal existence of the people of Israel were foreseen since the six days of Creation. The foreknowledge of God is referred to here, not the pre-existence of the soul.

Support for this concept is to be found only in the dicta of the Palestinian Amoraim of the second half of the third century: ' "But with him that standeth here". R. Abbahu said in the name of R. Samuel bar Naḥmani: Why is it written "But with him that standeth here... and also with him that is not here"? — Because the souls were there, but the body was not yet created; hence standing is not mentioned in connection with them.'[78] 'Scripture does not say "that standeth with us" but "with us this day" — this refers to the souls that were still to be born — with regard to whom standing is not mentioned — for they, too, were included.' The homilist asks: Why is it written in the first instance 'that standeth this day', whereas in the clause 'and also with him that is not here' the word 'standeth' does not occur? The answer is that all the souls destined to be born were there, only the Torah distinguishes between souls that were already clothed in bodies, with regard to which Scripture says 'standeth this day', and those that had not yet donned bodies. This dictum posits the pre-existence of the souls, but its primary concern is not with this concept *per se*; rather it seeks to stress the presence of all the souls of Israel throughout the generations at the time of the giving of the Torah. Rav Assi, a contemporary of R. Abbahu, said: 'The son of David will not come until all the souls in גוף *Gûf* have come to an end, for it is said, "For the spirit that enwrappeth itself from Me [and the souls which I have made]" (Isaiah lvii 16).'[79] The expression *Gûf* is explained by Rashi thus: 'There is a Treasure-house called *Gûf*, and at the time of Creation all the souls destined to be born were formed and placed there.'[80] However, Rav Assi's statement can be interpreted differently, in the light of the parallel dictum: 'R. Tanḥum bar Ḥiyya — others cite it in the name of the Rabbis — said: King Messiah will not come until all the souls that were originally planned (by God) to be born will be born, and these are the souls recorded in the Book of the First Man.'[81] It is not stated here that the souls exist in a given place. Accordingly it is possible that even the words 'all the souls in *Gûf* [literally 'body']' of Rav Assi's dictum refer to the souls that were predestined to be clothed in bodies. At any rate we also learn from R. Tanḥum's statement that the souls were fated for this since the days of Creation. Special significance, going beyond the subject of our discussion, attaches to R. Levi's homily on the Scripture 'Let us make man': 'R. Joshua of Sikhnin in the name of R. Levi said: He (the Almighty) took counsel with the righteous. This is the meaning of the verse "These were the 'creators' [usual rendering: 'potters'] and those that dwelt among plantations [i.e. Paradise] and hedges; there they dwelt occupied with the King's work" (I Chron. iv 23)... "They dwelt occupied with the King's work" — with the King of the kings of kings, the Holy One, blessed be He, dwelt the souls of the Righteous, with whom He took counsel and created the world' (*Gen. Rabba* viii, 7, p. 61). Here we have a reference to the existence of the souls before the creation of the world. We shall revert to the differentiation between the souls of the righteous and those of the wicked and discuss it in another context.

Several scholars imagined that they could find the theme of 'the Treasure-house of souls' that are due to be born in the dicta of the Tannaim who express, in their view, divergent opinions regarding the number of firmaments; but they achieved this only by not paying attention to the correct text, and in truth this source also corroborates our statement that the concept is not found before the third century, the reference being to the dispute in the Babylonian Talmud (*Ḥagiga* 12b): 'R. Judah said: There are two firmaments, as it is said... Resh Laqish stated: Seven... *ʿAravot*, in which there are right, judgement and righteousness, the treasures of life and the treasures of peace and the treasures of blessing, and the souls of the righteous and the spirits and the souls that are yet to be born, and dew wherewith the Holy One, blessed be He, will revive the dead. Right and judgement, for it is written... righteousness, for it is written... the treasures of life, for it is written... and the treasures of peace, for it is written... and the treasures of blessing... for it is written... the souls of the righteous, for it is written "Yet the soul of my lord shall be bound up in the bundle of life with the Lord thy God"; the spirits and souls that are yet to be born, for it is written "For the spirit that enwrappeth itself is from Me, and the souls which I have made".' Assuming that R. Judah is the Tanna R. Judah bar Ilʿai, Bacher[82] noted the difficulty that ר״ל 'R. L' [i.e. Resh Laqish] appears as his debating opponent; hence he conjectured that 'R. L' was a corruption of ר״מ 'R. M' [i.e. R. Me'ir], the chief disputant who engaged in controversy with R. Judah. The scholars[83] who dealt with this controversy relied on Bacher, but in the Munich MS. of the Babylonian Talmud[84] and in *Haggadot ha-Talmud* (Constantinople 1481) it is explicitly stated 'Rav Jehuda [יהוד׳] said in the name of Rav: There are two firmaments... Resh Laqish said: Seven...'; also in the first edition of *ʿEn Yaʿaqov* 'Rav Judah' is expressly named, and in the continuation 'Resh Laqish'. Likewise in the parallel sources[85] these dicta are attributed to Amoraim.

The 'Treasure-house of souls' is indeed mentioned already in the period of the Tannaim, but only in the sense of a place where the souls of the righteous are kept after their death. The Tannaim were not exercised by the question of the soul's source and the way it became attached to the body, but by the question of the fate of the souls of the righteous and the wicked. These Midrashic expositions are linked to verses from which, it would seem, we may infer that all the souls have one destiny, for example: ' "Who knoweth the spirit of man...?" (Ecclesiastes iii 21); it was taught: Both the souls of the righteous and the souls of the wicked ascend on high, only the souls of the righteous are placed in the Treasure-house, whereas the souls of the wicked are cast to the ground, for Abigail said to David under inspiration of the Holy Spirit (I Samuel xxv 29) "Yet the soul of my lord shall be bound in the bundle of life." Should I think that this applies also to the wicked? Therefore the Bible teaches "And the souls of thine enemies, them shall he sling out, as from the hollow of a sling." A Roman lady once asked R. Jose b. Ḥalafta, saying: "What is the meaning of the Scripture 'Who knoweth the spirit of man whether it goeth upward?' " He answered her: "These are the souls of the righteous, which are enshrined in the Treasure-house." She then asked him: "And what is the meaning of the verse 'And the spirit of the beast whether it goeth downward to the earth?' " He replied to her: "These are the souls of the wicked, which go downward, as it is said (Ezekiel xxxi 15), 'In the day when he went down to the netherworld I caused the deep to mourn and cover itself for him' " ' (*Ecclesiastes Rabba* iii, 21). R. Jose b. Ḥalafta reconciles the sceptical verse in Ecclesiastes with the doctrine of reward and punishment. This intent also underlies the homily of R. Eliezer b. R. Jose the Galilean: ' "Let the Lord, the God of the spirits of all flesh..." R. Eliezer b. R. Jose the Galilean said... that so long as a man is alive, his soul is in the charge of the Creator... when he dies, it is enshrined in the Treasure-house, as it is said "Yet the soul of my lord shall be bound in the bundle of life"... I might thus infer that this applies to both righteous and wicked; therefore the Scripture teaches "And the souls of thine enemies, them shall he sling out, as from the hollow of a sling." '[86] Also the Baraita that speaks of the introduction of the soul into the body and uses the analogy of the 'royal raiment' for the souls, mentions the word Treasure-house only with reference to the souls that have been separated from the bodies after death, and not before the birth of the child. 'The Rabbis taught: "And the spirit returneth unto God who gave it": Give it (back) to Him as He gave it to you — in purity; you, too, (return it) in purity. This is comparable to a human king who distributed royal raiment to his servants. The wise among them folded the garments and laid them in a chest; the fools among them went and did their work in them. After a time the king demanded (the return of) his garments. The wise among them returned them to him in immaculate condition; the fools among them returned them in a soiled state. The king was pleased with the wise, but was angry with the fools. Regarding the wise he said: "Let my apparel be deposited in the treasure-house, and they may go to their homes in peace"; with regard to the fools he said: "Let my garments be given to the fuller, and let them be detained in prison." So, too, the Holy One, blessed be He, declares concerning the bodies of the righteous: "He entereth into peace, they rest in their beds" (Isaiah lvii 2); and regarding their souls He says: "Yet the soul of my Lord shall be bound up in the bundle of life". But with regard to the bodies of the wicked He declares: "There is no peace, said the Lord, unto the wicked" (Isaiah xlviii 22), and of their souls He says: "And the souls of thine enemies, them shall he sling out, as from the hollow of a sling." '[87] An interesting parallel to the Baraita that we have cited is to be found in the *Book of Ezra* IV,[88] which was originally composed in Hebrew, and all scholars are agreed that its date is not later than the nineties of the first century C.E., that is, shortly after the destruction of the Temple:

> And concerning death [this] is the teaching: When the decisive decree has gone forth from the Most High that the man should die,
> as the soul from the body departs
> that it may return to Him who gave it,
> to adore the glory of the Most High, first of all: if one of those that have scorned,
> and have not kept the ways of the Most High,
> that have despised His law,
> and that hate those who fear God —
> Such souls shall not enter into habitations, but shall wander about henceforth in torture, ever grieving and sad, in seven ways...
> Of those, however, who have kept the ways of the Most High this is the order,
> when they shall be separated from the vessel of mortality...
> wherefore the matter as it relates to them is as follows... the fourth order (is):

they understand the rest which they now, being gathered in their habitations,
enjoy in profound quietness guarded by angels....

The 'Habitations' and the 'Treasure-house' are a location for the souls after man's death. At any rate, the dicta quoted earlier are far removed from the teaching of the Amora R. Levi, which we cited (above, p. 237), for they speak of the souls of the righteous, which come to the Treasure-house only after they have proved in their lifetime that they are righteous, whereas in the saying of R. Levi they have not yet been clothed in the body. R. Levi approaches the Platonic view, as we found it expressed in Philo's writings, but even he did not say that the ideal state of the souls is when they are unattached to the body; in his view, too, the function of all the souls is to be joined to bodies. The concept of pre-existence as it appears in the teaching of the Amoraim in the third century, and even in the form and formulation that it received at the end of the first century or the beginning of the second century C.E., in the Slavonic *Book of Enoch* and in the Syriac *Book of Baruch*[89], remained fundamentally different from the Greek philosophic view;[90] it does not stem from the conception of the basic antithesis between spirit and matter. The souls in *Gûf* are not actually lowered in status or changed by their attachment to the body. In Rabbinic lore the concept of pre-existence is integrated with that of the all-embracing knowledge of God, which includes the whole of man, his body and his soul, in the sense of 'Thine eyes did see mine unformed substance, and in Thy book they were all written' (Psalms cxxxix 16). At the same time, the speculations concerning the pre-existence of the soul led to a certain change in the appraisement of the relationship between the soul and the body and of the measure of their responsibility for human actions. While R. Ishmael uses the analogy of the lame man and the blind man in order to infer that the Holy One, blessed be He, 'restores the soul to the body and judges them together', at the beginning of the Amoraic epoch we find the analogy: 'It is like the case of a priest [Kohen] who had two wives, one was a priest's daughter and one was the daughter of an Israelite, and he handed to them dough of heave-offering and they defiled it; he thereupon blamed the priest's daughter, but left the Israelite's daughter alone. Said she [the priest's daughter] to him: "Our lord, priest, you gave (the dough) to both of us together; why then do you blame me and leave her alone?" He answered her: "You are a priest's daughter, and have been trained in your father's home; but she is an Israelite's daughter and was not trained in her father's home. Hence I blame you." In the same way the Holy One, blessed be He, will in the hereafter say to the soul: "Why did you sin before Me?" She will answer him: "Sovereign of the universe, the body and I have sinned together, why then dost Thou blame me and leave it alone?" He will reply to her: "You hail from the celestial beings on high, from a place where no sin is committed; whereas the body comes from among the earthly creatures below, from a place where sin is committed. Hence I blame you." '[91] The main responsibility rests on the soul, for it transcends all parts of the body.[92]

These views concerning the pre-existence of the soul and its status raised anew the question of the time when the soul becomes united with the body. It is true that in the Halakhot of the Tannaim opinions are to be found on the legal status of the embryo in its mother's womb, and similarly there exist Haggadic dicta based on the premise that the embryo possesses an active soul. But an explicit and elucidated discussion on this question comes down to us only from the time of R. Judah the Patriarch in a dialogue that he had with Emperor Antoninus, which we have cited earlier, and according to which Rabbi conceded that the soul was placed in man from the moment of conception. The ancient view of the Tannaim was that the embryo was not an independent being but a part of the mother's body, or, in Talmudic terminology, 'The embryo is the thigh [i.e. an integral part] of its mother'.[93] The Septuagint, followed by Philo, interpreted the verses Exodus xxi 22–23 as referring[94] to the embryo, and they distinguished between an embryo whose form is incomplete — in which case the person who caused its death pays a fine — and one whose form is complete, in regard to which Scripture prescribes 'But if any harm follow, then thou shalt give life for life'. On the other hand, the Tannaim explain that this verse speaks of 'harm' to the mother; only if she dies is the smiter liable to death, but there is no death penalty on account of the child.[95] In conformity with this view it is taught in the Mishna: 'If a woman is in hard travail, the child is cut up in her womb and brought out member by member, because her life has priority over that of the child. But if the greater part of it is already born, it is not to be touched, for one life may not be set aside on account of another.'[96] But before 'it goes forth into the atmosphere of the world, it is not a living being.'[97] Thus 'If a woman is due to be executed, we do not wait for her to give birth, but if she was (already) sitting on the birthstool, we wait for her to give birth.'[98] Only at the beginning of parturition is the embryo deemed a separate person.[99] Undoubtedly the Tannaim were acquainted with the view that considered the embryo a living creature, and, indeed, expressly sought to contradict it: 'I might have thought that if she was pregnant they would postpone (the execution) until she gave birth. Therefore, the Bible teaches "He that smote him shall surely be put to death." I might have thought that if she was three months pregnant, they should not postpone (the execution) until she gives birth; but if she was nine months pregnant, they should postpone (the execution) until she has given birth. Therefore Scripture teaches: "He shall surely be put to death." '[1] In the light of our knowledge that it was customary, where non-Jews were involved, to inflict the death penalty for the killing of an embryo, we can also understand the Halakha, transmitted in the name of R. Ishmael, that the Noachides are put to death even for killing embryos.[2] Among the Tannaim we do not find any one who upholds, in the field of Halakha, the view that the embryo, while still in its mother's womb, is a separate body, and regards it as a living being. The statement in the Babylonian Talmud concerning a Tanna who maintains that an embryo is not its mother's thigh is just a conjectural observation.[3] The attempts, too, of modern scholars[4] to discover this conception in Halakhot of the Tannaim have proved abortive.[5] It would appear that in the sphere of Halakha this opinion is not earlier than the time of the Amora R. Joḥanan,[6] although traces of it are already to be found in the Haggada of the Tannaim. In the name of R. Jose the Galilean the following interpretation is reported: ' "Out of the mouth of babes and sucklings hast Thou founded strength" (Psalms viii 3). "Out of the mouth of babes" — these are the embryos in their mothers' womb, as it is said "Or as a hidden untimely birth I had not been; [as babes that never saw light]" (Job iii 16).' So, too, R. Me'ir said,

'Even the embryos in their mothers' womb opened their mouth and uttered song unto the Omnipresent.' Rabbi, however, did not expound the verse thus, but declared ' "babes" means the infants that are out (of their mothers' body), as it is said "to cut off the children from without [usually rendered: 'from the street']" (Jeremiah ix 20); "sucklings" — these are the children at their mothers' breast... both the former and the latter opened their mouths and uttered song unto the Omnipresent....'[7] But the Haggada was not content until it had attributed the other view also to Rabbi. Whereas he ruled anonymously in the Mishna 'If a pregnant woman smelled (food and craved for it), she may be given food until she recovers herself' (*M. Yoma* viii, 5), and there is no indication that the 'will' of the embryo is taken into consideration, it is narrated in the Talmud that 'Once a pregnant woman smelled (food and craved for it); when people came to Rabbi (to ask for his ruling), he said: "Go, whisper to her that it is the Day of Atonement." They whispered to her, and she was dissuaded (from eating). (Rabbi) thereupon applied to her the verse, "Before I formed thee in the womb I knew thee" etc. R. Joḥanan was born of her.'[8] The Haggada comes, as it were, to stress the new teaching of R. Joḥanan, that while he was still in his mother's womb he observed the Halakha that 'The embryo is not its mother's thigh.' The extent to which the view that the embryo is 'alive' prevailed among R. Joḥanan's contemporaries is reflected in the dicta that express consternation at unethical phenomena by emphasizing the reaction of the embryos. For example, 'R. Eleazar said: A man in whom there is hypocrisy, even the embryos in their mothers' womb curse him' (*T.B. Soṭa* 41b). And 'Rav Ḥana bar Bizna said in the name of R. Simeon the Pious: Whoever withholds a Halakha from a disciple, even the embryos in their mothers' womb curse him' (*T.B. Sanhedrin* 91b). Both Sages refer, for support, to verses in which the word לאם *lĕ'ōm* [usually rendered, 'people'] occurs and they explained that '*lĕ'ōm* specifically connotes embryos, for it is said 'And the one embryo [*lĕ'ōm*] shall be stronger than the other.' This interpretation is based on the homiletical expositions of the Scripture 'And the children struggled together within her' (Genesis xxv 21), which portray the wars between Esau and Jacob and their political and religious conflicts as taking place while they were still in their mother's womb.[9] The movement of the embryo also served as proof that the embryo is a living creature.[10] The homilies on 'And they struggled together', which attribute conscious life to the embryo, are by R. Joḥanan, Resh Laqish and R. Levi. The diffusion of this conception, which became general, left its impress also in the sphere of Halakha. Characteristically it cleaves to the ancient principle long after it had been abandoned by the Haggada — that is, in reality — and the old Mishna remained unchanged. Since no explicit dispute is to be found among the Tannaim on the question of 'The embryo is its mother's thigh', we may explain various debates as centring on this subject and conclude that one Tanna or another is of the same opinion as R. Joḥanan, namely that 'The embryo is not its mother's thigh'[11]; nevertheless indications are to be discerned in the Talmudic discussions that a change of view had taken place.[12]

It would appear that the compilation of a whole tractate on "The Formation of the Child" is to be ascribed to the school of R. Joḥanan. Although the text of this tractate has reached us in late sources[13], yet almost all its ideas and motifs belong to the contemporaries of R. Joḥanan and his disciples. The Midrash begins with the words: 'R. Joḥanan said: What is the meaning of the verse "Who doeth great things past finding out; yea, marvellous things without number" (Job ix 10)? Know, that all the souls, those that existed since Adam and those that will still come into being until the end of the whole world, were created in the six days of Creation, and are all in the Garden of Eden, and were all present at the giving of the Torah.' Here the doctrine of the pre-existence of the souls is ascribed to R. Joḥanan in a form that seems to combine the sayings of R. Samuel bar Naḥman, R. Abbahu, R. Levi, and R. Tanḥum bar Ḥiyya, which we have cited above (p. 236). The motif of the angel who is in charge of conception belongs to R. Ḥanina bar Papa: 'The angel in charge of conception is called "Night". He takes a drop (of semen) and places it before the Holy One, blessed be He, saying to Him: Sovereign of the universe, what shall be the destiny of this drop? Shall (the person) be strong or weak, wise or foolish, rich or poor?'[14] The description of the state of the foetus and its behaviour in its mother's womb is derived from the homily of R. Simlai[15]: 'What does the foetus resemble in its mother's womb? A writing tablet lying folded: its hands rest on its two temples, its two elbows on its two legs, its two heels on its two buttocks, its head lies between its knees, its mouth is closed, its navel is open, it eats of that which its mother eats, it drinks of that which its mother drinks, it does not defecate lest it kill its mother... a lamp burns on its head, and it looks and sees from one end of the world to the other, as Scripture states "When His lamp shined above my head, and by His light I walked through darkness" (Job xxix 3)... and it is taught the whole of the Torah[16], for the Bible declares "And He taught me and said unto me: Let thy heart hold fast my words, keep my commandments and live" (Proverbs iv 4)... but as soon as it comes into the world, an angel arrives and slaps it on its mouth and causes it to forget the whole of the Torah... and it does not go forth until it is made to take an oath... and what kind of oath is imposed upon it? Be righteous and be not wicked; and even if the whole world says unto you "You are righteous", be wicked in your own estimation, for the Holy One, blessed be He, is pure and his ministers are pure, and the soul that He placed within you is pure. If you guard it in purity, well and good; but if not, I shall take it away from you.'

In the motif of the unborn child's knowledge of the Torah and his forgetting it upon being born, scholars, since Jellinek[17], have discerned the ἀνάμνησις of the Platonic myth.[18] In our time, too, Yitzḥak Baer[19] found in the dictum of R. Simlai a doctrine that is 'patently Platonic... and it becomes wholly comprehensible if we extrude the references to the child's stay in its mother's womb, a feature that was interpolated by peculiar and late copyists, for it is not possible to say of the child in its mother's womb that it "looks and sees from one end of the world to the other"; this ability can only be ascribed to the soul, when it abides above the arch of heaven as in the descriptions of Plato's *Phaedrus*, and it is understandable that in its pre-existent life in the celestial world the soul learnt the whole of the Torah.' The very need to declare, without giving any reason, that the basic subject-matter of the source was a feature 'that was interpolated by peculiar and late copyists' shows the weakness of the argument. What appeared to Baer as 'not possible' was considered by R. Simlai as highly feasible. R. Simlai aimed to describe the formation of the child in the mother's womb. The child with its temples, elbows, legs, and head is the one that looks from one end of the world to the other, and is also the one that learns Torah. This portrayal is far removed from the Platonic myth, whose theme is the doctrine of recompense, and its central motif is metempsychosis. The choosing soul is not *tabula rasa*, but it has behind it the experience of former incarnations and its choice is influenced by that experience. From this is to be inferred that the life of man is a preparation for the future existence of the soul in its new incarnation. Therefore man must strive to live a good life in order that his soul may choose well. There is no mention or indication of the doctrine of metempsychosis either in the discourse of R. Simlai, or in the long account of 'The Formation of the Child', although motifs that appear in the Platonic myth[20] have been added to it, but again with significant changes. In the Jewish Midrash the angel in charge of conception — לילה *Laylā* ['Night'] — takes the drop of semen and brings it before the Creator and 'forthwith the Holy One, blessed be He, decrees what shall happen to the drop in the end, whether it should be male or female, weak or strong, poor or rich, short or tall... and similarly He decrees its history. But whether the person is to be righteous or wicked, (God does) not (predetermine); this He leaves solely to man...' This choice is implemented after birth. In Plato's myth the souls choose, from among the various types of life, the way of life 'that will necessarily be the person's lot', and this choice is made 'according to what the soul was used to in its previous existence'. Those who err in their choice sometimes realize their error and lament their choice, but this plaint has nothing in common with the disinclination of the spirit to enter the 'drop', as portrayed in the Midrash: 'The spirit opens its mouth and declares before Him: "Sovereign of the universe, sufficient unto me is the world in which I have dwelt since I was created. Why is it Thy will to inject me into this foetid drop, for I am holy and pure, and I am hewn from the substance of Thy glory!" The Holy One, blessed be He, immediately answers the soul: "The world into which I bring you will be better for you than that in which you dwelt (hitherto); moreover, when I formed you I did so only for this drop." Forthwith the Holy One, blessed be He, compels it to enter therein.' The motif of the burning lamp above the head of the child, and likewise the theme of the angel who slaps the child on its mouth, which are featured in R. Simlai's exposition,[21] have no parallels in the Platonic myth. Furthermore, in the Talmudic account the forgetfulness is general and the same for all, whereas in Plato's myth 'Everyone is obliged to drink a certain measure of this water, but the one whose understanding fails to save him drinks more than the prescribed quantity, and in so doing he forgets everything.' It is unthinkable that R. Simlai or the anonymous author of the tractate on 'The Formation of the Child' knew the Platonic myth in the written form as we find it today in *The Republic.* The story, which originated according to Plato in Asia Minor, reached them from folk-sources voided of Plato's ideas and clothed in a Jewish garb. Its absorption into the world of the Sages occurred after the views regarding the pre-existence of the souls and the independent existence of the embryo in its mother's womb had become crystallized. However, this very combination of concepts and motifs attests the absence of an absolute dichotomy, 'body—soul', which is characteristic of Platonic thought.

Although there is a great gulf between the teaching of the Amoraim concerning man and the thought of the early Tannaim, and the amalgam of body and soul had disintegrated, yet the Amoraim never went so far as to negate the body altogether. In the dicta and homilies in which the soul and the body form an antithesis, this contraposition is not intended to underscore opposition, but to point to the division of functions, which, in combination, sustain man. Ten things in the human body serve the soul,[22] but the soul also serves the body. It pervades and nourishes the body,[23] and when a person is asleep, 'it ascends and draws life for him from on high.'[24] The soul also works for the body when it is asleep, and the bond between them is not severed. This teaching contradicts the statement about sleep that Josephus[25] puts into the mouth of Eleazar: 'Sleep, in which the soul, undistracted by the body, while enjoying in perfect independence the most delightful repose, holds converse with God by right of kinship, ranges the universe and foretells many things that are to come.' This description is intended to serve as 'convincing proof' of the rightness of the notion that upon death 'the soul is freed from the weight that drags it down to the earth.'

The fundamental difference between the Rabbinic view and the Hellenistic and Gnostic concepts is actually seen most clearly when the former and the latter are expressed apparently in identical images and phraseology, and yet do not convey the same idea. The comparison of the place and function of the soul in the human body with the relationship of God to the world is found in various formulations in the Midrashic expositions of the Amoraim and also in Philo's writings. But in the Midrashim the comparison leads to the conclusion: 'Let the soul, which permeates the body, come and praise the Holy One, blessed be He, who fills the universe... Let the soul, which bears the body, come and praise the Holy One, blessed be He, who bears His world... Let the soul, which is pure in the body, come and praise the Holy One, blessed be He, who is pure in His world... Let the soul, which sees but is not seen, come and praise the Holy One, blessed be He, who sees but is not seen....'[26] Contrariwise, Philo speaks in the style of Plato. The status of the human mind (ἀνθρώπινος νοῦς) in man is like that of the Great Ruler (ὁ μέγας ἡγεμὼν) in the Cosmos. It sees, but is not seen. The love for wisdom sweeps it beyond the entire palpable world; it is drawn to the loftiest height of all the concepts and it is comparable to one who goes to the Great King Himself.[27] This portrayal, which is nearer to that of Eros in Plato's *Phaedrus* than to the Midrash, is based *au fond* on the view of the body as a prison, a view that also pervades Philo's allegorical interpretations, like his commentary, for instance, on Exodus xxxii 27: 'Go to and fro from gate to gate throughout the camp, and slay every man his brother, and every man his companion, and every man his neighbour.' 'Brother' means the brother of the soul, that is, the body. 'Neighbour' [literally, 'near one'] denotes the senses that appertain to the soul, but are nevertheless its enemies; the Levites must remove from their soul all that is near to the flesh. Life constitutes a prison sentence for the soul.[28] Actually, Philo has no interest in this life, but in that which preceded it and in that which is to come after it. The whole course of history is a negative phenomenon, since it is only a product of decline and sin. The concepts of the Sages, even when they give expression to the anthropological dualism, and even when they stress the hereafter and the world to come, do not ignore 'this world'. God is the God of history and all that happens in it, and in the course of history the whole of man — both body and soul — is active. These principles were conducive to the fact that even those Sages who maintained the dualism 'body—soul' did not draw extremist inferences from it. Fundamentally, Talmudic Judaism retained, despite all influences and deviations, the concept of the unity of body and soul.

Like the Tannaim[29], the Amoraim also used the word 'body' to denote the whole of man. 'Body' was even substituted for 'soul'. The expression 'healing of soul' in the Mishna is interpreted by the Amoraim as healing of the body.[30] R. Judah b. R. Ḥiyya declares that the Torah is the elixir of life for the whole body of man.[31] Man is praised not only for his pure soul but also for his pure body. Thus even when Rabba bar Naḥmani died, a heavenly voice proclaimed 'Blessed are you, Rabba bar Naḥmani, that your body is pure and your soul went forth in purity.'[32] The Babylonian Talmud uses the same phraseology in reporting R. Ishmael's exclamation at the death of his sister's son, Ben Dama, while in the Tosefta he is quoted as saying 'Blessed are you Ben Dama, that you left the world in peace.'[33] But in Eretz-Israel, when the highest encomium was bestowed by the Sages upon a saintly Tanna, they also spoke of 'that holy body'.[34] The sinful man defiles both his body and his soul.[35]

A parallel to this conception of the relationship between the body and the soul is found in the teaching of Zarathustra, as it is reflected in the sources of this religion from the period of the Sassanids.[36] According to the Persian conception, which is common to all the sources, the body and soul, contrary to the teaching of Mani, form a unity, both fighting the power of falsehood. The body is the instrument, the garment of the soul. The soul works by means of the body, for without it no action is conceivable. The body was not created as the Manichaeans held, out of darkness, but is composed of material similar to that of the soul. The body is as necessary to the soul as a garment to the body, and if it is unseemly to walk about undressed, how much more so is it unbecoming to appear before the Creator naked; hence the soul must arise at resurrection clothed in a new and shining body. Falsehood fights against the body, defiles it, and thereby seeks to destroy the integrity of the human personality. The motif of the garment recalls the dictum, quoted earlier[37], that compares the body to clothes. Only the man who is privileged to have a healthy body is also granted a healthy soul; hence man must cultivate health of body and of soul at the same time. The soul is free and responsible to its Maker. Man, who has donned a garb of flesh, has free will, and he can impose his will on others. Ahura Mazda created the free will, which means man's control over his desires. The soul was created for the purpose of fighting against the powers of darkness, and the body serves as a weapon in this struggle; hence it is an act of folly not to guard its fitness and ability. The body is likened to a horse that carries one to battle, and no man goes to battle riding on a hungry steed. In this doctrine there is no room for the veneration of suffering and asceticism.[38] The views of the Sages on asceticism we shall discuss further on. For the time being we shall cite only an example that brings into sharp relief the nexus between the doctrine of asceticism and the conception of man and his essential nature, and shows to what extent it threatens our actual faith in the Creator and the created. In a sermon of an Ophite sect, as preserved in the writings of the Church Father Hippolytus,[39] it is stated that the secret of man was revealed only to a few individuals — the Gnostics. The beginning of perfection is gnosis. The gnosis of God is the goal of perfection. Primordial Man is actually the transcendental quintessence of man; and he is beyond sex differentiation — he is a hermaphrodite. When Primordial Man begot a human being, he begot himself. The essence of man is in the seed and in the Logos, but it also finds expression in the spirit and the will, and his essence as spirit is 'the word of the Lord' or 'the utterance of the Lord'. Man enshrines within himself the totality of the gods and the worlds and the ages. All nature yearns for the luminous spirit, in order to be incorporated in the life of light. Needless to say, this is only the inner man, but he exists within man, who descended into the abyss, a descent that finds expression in the fact that he — the outer man — was created by the Demiurge. And this abyss is the chaos and void. The true man, that primary will, exists in a chaotic world, namely the body, which comes from the dust, and the soul that gives it life is bound to it and does not break out of the body, but is incarcerated in it as in a grave. The whole of existence, with all its aspirations, including the vital and procreative power, is like the dream of a captive. The redemption of man is to be found only in ἀναγένησις, in rebirth, which means returning to oneself. The redeemer and the redeemed are identical;

man can attain selfhood by means of spiritual rebirth, that is extreme ascetism, which means the abolition of sexual life. Flight from the body implies escape from cosmic birth. The man who redeems himself opens the portals of spiritual existence by forgoing the mystery of birth. Man becomes a god, or, more correctly, the extreme abstraction of existence annuls both the man and the god. There is god only in so far as he is a form of man, and there is man only in so far as he is a form of god.[40] It is hardly necessary to say how far removed are speculations of this nature from the mode of Rabbinic thinking, which is wholly based on the distinction between God, the Creator, and man, the created,[41] and since man is a creature of God's making, he can regard his creation only as of positive value.

The following Baraita apparently contradicts what has been stated here: 'Our Rabbis taught: For two and a half years the School of Shammai and the School of Hillel engaged in debate, the former declaring that it had been better for man not to have been created than to have been created, and the latter maintaining that it was better for man that he was created rather than not created. They decided, upon voting, that it had been better for man not to have been created, but now that he has been created, let him examine his (past) deeds; others say, let him consider his (future) actions' (*T.B.* *ʿEruvin* 13b). This Baraita has been cited by many as the source of an entirely pessimistic outlook, and parallels to it from Graeco-Roman literature have been noted.[42] The very indication of the fact that the dispute lasted 'two and a half years'[43] and that it ended in a decision by vote calls for elucidation. We find nowhere else a Halakhic decision in respect of a dispute of this kind, and *a fortiori* there is no vote taken. The Baraita itself is known from no other source of Rabbinic teaching — only from the Babylonian Talmud; and even there its subject-matter is not discussed and there is no comment on its theme.[44] Strangely enough just that decision decided by majority vote leaves no traces, and there is not the slightest indication of its influence on Tannaitic doctrine. It does not accord with Hillel's attitude to the human body (above, p. 227), nor with the story told of Rabban Gamaliel the Elder, to wit, 'that he was once strolling on the Temple Mount, when he saw a non-Jewish woman and he pronounced a benediction regarding her' — the reference being to the blessing 'Blessed be He that He created such beatiful creatures in His world.'[45] And unquestionably it cannot be harmonized with the dictum of R. Akiba 'Beloved is man, for he was created in the image of God' (*M. 'Avot* iii, 14), or with his saying 'Whatever the Holy One, blessed be He, does is all for good' (*T.B. Berakhot* 60b), or with R. Jacob's aphorism 'Better is one hour of repentance and good deeds in this world than the whole life of the world to come' (*M. 'Avot* iv, 17). Nay more, it contradicts the Halakha jointly maintained by the School of Shammai and the School of Hillel: 'A man shall not abstain from procreation unless he already has children' (*M. Yevamot* vi, 6); and it was the School of Shammai that taught 'And was not the world created only for fruition and increase, as it is said (Isaiah xlv 18) "He created it not a waste; He formed it to be inhabited"?', and the School of Hillel retracted and taught according to the view of the School of Shammai, and both Schools regarded the propagation of the species as 'for the good of the social order' (*M. Giṭṭin* iv, 5). The formula 'It had been better for him not have been created' was applied by R. Ḥiyya[46] to one who studied (Torah) without the intent to observe it. Its concrete meaning is: It would be better for him not to exist, if only not to commit this sin. In similar vein it is reported in the name of R. Simeon b. Yoḥai — and, in the opinion of others, in the name of R. Simeon the Pious, or in the name of Rav: 'It were better for a man to cast himself into a fiery furnace rather than shame his fellow in public';[47] and they deduced this principle from Tamar, who was prepared to be burnt rather than put Judah to shame. Among the Amoraim who transmitted this dictum mention is made of R. Joḥanan; now R. Joḥanan is also the author of a parallel teaching to that of R. Ḥiyya: 'If a man studies (Torah) without the intent to observe, it had been better for him if his placenta had turned over on its face, and he had not emerged into the world.'[48] These dicta are a kind of curse upon those who commit transgressions or fall into sin, and was already used by Jesus when he said: 'But if a man is a cause of stumbling to one of these little ones who have faith in me, it would be better for him to have a millstone hung round his neck and be drowned in the depths of the sea.'[49] When the grandson of R. Joshua b. Levi had a choking fit, and there came a man and whispered an incantation for him in the name of Jesus b. Pandera and he recovered, R. Joshua b. Levi said: 'It would have been better for him if he had died.'[50] In a more general form it is stated in the Midrash:[51] 'It would have been better for the wicked to have been blind, for their eyes bring a curse upon the world'; and the preacher mentions in support of his view the case of 'the sons of God', of Ham, of the princes of Pharaoh, of Shechem, and of Balak, who were led into sin by what they saw. At any rate, the expression 'It were better for him not to have been created' in the aforementioned sources does not embody a pessimistic philosophy. Even if we wish to maintain the authenticity of the dispute, lasting two and a half years, between the School of Shammai and the School of Hillel, it is apparent that it was concerned not with the evaluation of human existence, but with the attitude to be adopted towards the wicked man, who studies but does not observe (of whom R. Ḥiyya speaks), or of one who neither studies nor observes. We may conjecture that the School of Hillel, who were 'gentle and submissive', undoubtedly maintained, in the spirit of their teacher, that even of such people it should not be said that 'it had been better for them not to have been born', and if they finally reached the conclusion — as R. Ḥiyya and R. Joḥanan held — that 'it had been better for them not to have been created', in the sense that 'The death of the wicked is beneficial to them and beneficial to the world' (*M. Sanhedrin* viii, 5), the edge of this assent was blunted by the addition 'But now that he has been created, let him examine his (past) deeds.' It certainly did not occur to them to assert that the very creation of man is a failure, for 'All that the Holy One, blessed be He, created in His world He created only for his glory, as it is said (Isaiah xliii 7): "Everything that is called by My name, it is for My glory I have created it, I have formed it, yea, I have made it."' Not only is man included in 'all that He created', but as R. Nehemiah declared 'One man equals in importance the whole work of creation.'[53] And this is the sense of the Mishna itself: 'Whoever saves alive a single soul, it is accounted to him as though he had saved a whole world.' It is in the saving alive of man that the relationship between the Creator and His world finds expression, and it is through him that His kingdom and providence are implemented.

CHAPTER XI

ON PROVIDENCE

The question of fate and choice was, according to the testimony of Josephus, one of the religious dogmas regarding which the sects in the time of the Second Temple differed. He declares that the Pharisees 'attribute everything to fate (εἱμαρμένη) and to God; they hold that to act rightly (i.e. do good) or otherwise (i.e. do evil) rests, indeed, for the most part with men, but that in each action fate cooperates'.[1] On the other hand the Essenes maintained that all human actions were predestined by providence, and that a man does naught of his own free will; while the Sadducees denied fate and the Creator's providential care for his creatures and argued that all acts lie within the power of human beings.[2] In *Antiquities* xviii, 1, 3, he adds the Pharisees' explanation of their doctrine: they state that 'It was God's good pleasure that there should be a fusion and that the will of man with his virtue and vice should be admitted to the council-chamber of fate.' In the past certain scholars cast doubt on Josephus, asserting that he equated, in his account, the concepts of the sects to those of the philosophical schools: the Pharisees were likened to the Stoics, the Essenes to the Pythagoreans.[3] But now, it seems, the modes of thought of the Qumran Sect and its doctrine of predestination have come to refute the sceptics, at least so far as the Essenes are concerned. The generally accepted identification of the Sect with the Essenes is borne out by Josephus, while Josephus' account finds corroboration in the teaching of the Sect.[4] But do his observations regarding the Pharisees truly cover all that the Sages taught on this subject? And does his general summary accord with the views of the Sages as a whole, or does it perchance represent only a single school of thought,[5] whereas actually there were divergences of view between different authorities at different periods?

The term *Hashgaḥa* ['Providence'] was, as we know, invented by the Tibbonides; the Sages did not coin a similar word, but found the theme of Providence mentioned in the Torah and iterated in the Prophets and mentioned yet again in the Hagiographa, and they devoted much time to studying its ways, to discerning its quiddity and to probing its significance. There are two aspects to Providence: one involves the government of the world, the control of nature, and the provision of the needs of all mankind.[6] This aspect of Providence comprises all human beings, including the wicked and the idolatrous nations.[7] The other aspect of Providence consists of scrutinizing the ways and deeds of mortals,[8] as stated by the prophet Jeremiah (xxxii 19): 'Great in counsel and mighty in deed; whose eyes are open to all the ways of men, rewarding every man according to his ways and according to the fruit of his doings.' God is a God who dispenses justice and does righteousness; hence He necessarily scrutinizes the actions of His creatures and takes cognizance of their deeds, and only an unbeliever would declare 'There is neither judgement nor Judge.'[9]

This belief in a twofold Providence gives rise to a number of questions. What is the relationship between the Divine concern to provide the needs of mankind and the supervision of their acts? Do these actions of theirs, which bring in their train punishment or reward, influence the processes of the government of the world, and does man, who is free to choose his ways, determine the ways of Providence, which reacts to his deeds? Or are human actions, too, perhaps only component details of the processes of the world, which is conducted by the will of the Creator, both the deeds of the righteous and those of the wicked being decided by Him, together with their reward and retribution, and is the twofold Providence only 'dual fate' — not, it is true, the edict of destiny or the law of nature, but the decree of the Creator? Let us now see if, and when, the Sages asked questions of this kind upon accepting the belief in Biblical Providence, and what answers they gave to them.

We shall begin with R. Akiba's teaching, not merely because his dictum is quoted by all who are concerned with our problem, but because his observations on the subject of Providence is on the one hand a summation of the view prevailing in the circle of the Sages up to his time, and on the other hand marks a new conception, which is linked, apparently, to a change in their understanding of other religious ideas. Since the days of Maimonides, R. Akiba's aphorism in *Mishna 'Avot* (iii, 15), 'Everything is seen and freedom of choice is given', has been interpreted as treating of the contradiction between God's omniscience and human free will. Maimonides himself also found therein the reconciliation of the contradiction, according to his method of interpretation. Others regarded it not as a solution of the difficulty but the postulation of two principles of faith and the duty of maintaining them together.[10] However, several of the earliest commentators of the Mishna already did not understand the phrase הכל צפוי *ha-kōl ṣāfûy* in the sense of 'Everything is revealed and known from the outset', but in the connotation 'All that a man does in the innermost chambers, the Holy One, blessed be He, watches and observes',[11] and as Rabbi said, 'Know what is above you — a seeing eye' (*M. 'Avot* ii, 1); this explanation accords with the use of the stem צפה *ṣāfā* in the idiom of the Tannaim. This verb does not signify knowledge of the future, but seeing that which exists and is present, like the Biblical usage 'The eyes of the Lord keep watch [צפות *ṣōfôt*] upon the evil and the good' (Proverbs xv 3). R. Akiba himself said: 'I was watching [צופה *ṣôfe*] Rabban Gamaliel and R. Joshua, (and I saw) that whereas all the people were waving their palm-branches, they waved them only at "We beseech Thee, O Lord" ' (*M. Sukka* iii, 9); Rabban Gamaliel also used the verb in a similar sense: 'I was watching [*ṣôfe*], and (I observed that) we were within the (Sabbath) limits before nightfall.'[12] The use of *ṣāfā* in the signification of 'to know beforehand', 'to see beforehand', as, for instance, 'He foresaw by the holy spirit [i.e. prophetic spirit] that they would...', The 'Holy One, blessed be He, foresaw that they would...' I found only in Amoraic sayings.[13] The content of the Mishna likewise shows that R. Akiba's intention was not to resolve the contradiction between [God's] foreknowledge and [man's] freewill, but to make man realize his responsibility for his actions.[14] This responsibility is grounded in two factors: in the permission given to man to choose his own way and in the realization that man is destined to account for his actions before Him who sees and examines his ways. It is on this responsibility that R. Akiba establishes his doctrine of recompense (*M. 'Avot* iii, 16).

R. Akiba walked in the footsteps of Hillel, who, on returning from a journey and hearing an outcry in the city, said 'I am confident that this does not come from my house' (*T.B. Berakhot* 60a). This attribute of confidence is linked to the clear realization of man's freedom of choice and his absolute responsibility for his deeds. And thus Hillel proclaimed at the rejoicing marking the ceremony of Water-Drawing: 'If I am here everything is here... to the place that I love there my feet lead me.'[15] In the spirit of these words the Sages also interpreted Hillel's dictum 'If I am not for myself, who is for me?' as aimed against the belief in the beneficent influence of ancestral merit: 'If I am not for myself, who shall be for me? If I have not acquired merit for myself in this world, who will endow me with the merit to enjoy life in the hereafter? I have no father, I have no mother, I have no brother; our father Abraham cannot redeem Ishmael, our father Isaac cannot redeem Esau....' (*'Avot de-R. Nathan* xii; *Sifre Deuteronomy* § 329). However, R. Akiba does not negate the value of the influence of ancestral merit; on the contrary, he is of opinion that the father dowers his son with wisdom, beauty, and wealth (see below, p. 265), and he declared 'Happy is he whom his forebears endowed with merit; happy is the man who has a peg to hang on!'[16] But even ancestral merit merely helps; it does not affect man's choice, nor diminish the extent of his responsibility. This responsibility is the great principle that R. Akiba inculcates in the Mishna in *'Avot* with which we are concerned. There is not to be found in it the belief in predestination nor foreknowledge (*Praescientia*). On the contrary, it is not inconceivable that it is actually directed against those who profess this belief.

A polemic of this nature contains no novelty. Sirach already argued against those who deny Divine reward and retribution because of a deterministic outlook: 'Say not: "From God is my transgression", for that which He hateth made He not...' (xv 11), 'He commanded no man to sin, nor gave strength to men of lies' (*ibid.* v. 20).[17] But R. Akiba's words are, in my opinion, directed against a conception akin to that which is represented in the doctrine of Paul. His theology of destiny teaches: 'For those whom he foreknew he also predestined... And those whom he predestined he also called; and those whom he called he also justified...' (Romans viii 29–30). He negates the value of deeds: 'In order that God's purpose of election might continue, *not because of works* but because of his call' (*ibid.* ix 11). Obviously there is no room for choice or permission, and therefore the matter 'depends not upon man's will or exertion, but upon God's mercy' (*ibid.* v. 16). Paul's doctrine of predestination is connected with his views on original sin, which cleaves to man, and on God's grace, which works through Jesus Christ upon those who believe in him, 'For sin will have no dominion over you, since you are not under law but under grace' (*ibid.* vi 14). It has already been shown that the ancient doctrine of predestination and of grace, which raises the elect above the sphere of flesh and sin, is also found — without the Christological elements — in the works of the Qumran Sect,[18] and that it is possible to restore many concepts of Paul's writings to the phraseology of the scrolls. Nevertheless there is an important difference. Despite all the emphasis laid on God's grace, the Covenanters scrupulously observed the precepts, though at the same time they regarded themselves alone as 'Israelites who walk blamelessly' (*Manual of Discipline* fol. 9, l. 11) and denied the election to Israel as a whole. For the Covenanters believed that the world, including the people of Israel, are divided into 'Children of Light', to whom has been granted the spirit of truth, and 'Children of Darkness', to whom has been given a spirit of wickedness.[19] From the doctrine of immutable predestination and election by grace Paul drew more far-reaching inferences, namely the annulment of the commandments and the separation of Christianity from the Congregation of Israel. It is not our task to determine in what ways Paul and the Qumran Sect were in touch with each other, but it is manifest, beyond any doubt, that the views that they held in common were prevalent in various circles at the end of the Temple period.

R. Akiba's teaching contradicts every single article of the aforementioned creed. The gulf between the two doctrines is also reflected in the phrasing and style. The Scrolls and Paul's writings are marked by prolixity and verbosity, charged with pathos and ecstasy; R. Akiba's Mishna is characterized by a succinct and lapidary style, which possibly indicates that we have here not an individual expression of opinion, but the final crystallization of a belief endorsed by generations of scholars. This doctrine is seen in its entirety, if we combine the Mishna of which we have been speaking hitherto with the preceding Mishna.[20] In complete contrast to the partition of the world into a realm of light and a realm of darkness, the unity of the human species is stressed in the saying 'Beloved is man, for he was created in the image of God.' In antithesis to individual election by Divine grace[21] stands the election of the whole people of Israel as a relationship of son to Father. The grace of election does not find complete expression in itself but in the giving of the Torah, the vessel whereby the world was created. Its observance is incumbent not only upon 'all the children of truth', who were vouchsafed an abundance of acts of grace (*Manual of Discipline* fol. 4, l. 5). Freedom of choice is given to all Israel. God looks upon the wicked and the good and judges the world by goodness, for He is the God of righteousness and justice as well as the God of grace and compassion, but it is not 'only through His goodness that a man shall be right' (*Psalms of Thanksgiving* fol. 13, l. 17: 'only through Thy goodness shall a man be right'), nor 'Those whom He called He also justified' (*Romans* viii 30), but 'all is according to the amount of work'. In fine, the dictum of R. Akiba under discussion does not seek to resolve, nor even to present, the problem of the contradiction between God's foreknowledge and man's freedom of choice, but to underscore the latter. A similar expression to 'Everything is seen and freedom of choice is given', in accordance with our interpretation, is also found in *The Psalms of Solomon* (ix 1–4): 'Where, then, can a man hide himself from Thy knowledge, O God? Our works are subject to our own choice and power (ἐν ἐκλογῇ καὶ ἐξουσίᾳ) to do right or wrong in the works of our hands; and in Thy righteousness Thou visitest the sons of men.'

However, the question is asked: If punishment and reward are dependent solely on the deeds of man, who is free to act according to his will, do they not influence God's providential care for the world and His governance? An answer to this question is apparently given in R. Akiba's observations about afflictions: 'When they are sent upon a man, they are adjured to come upon him only on a given day and to leave him only on a given day, and through the medium of such-and-such a remedy. When their time came to depart, (the sick person) happened to go to his idolatrous shrine. Thereupon the afflictions said: Rightly we should not leave, but because this fool acted improperly shall we renounce our oath?'[22] However, as we have seen, this story does not seek to give a ruling on the question of Providence and predestination, but contains a discussion concerning miraculous occurrences that are ascribed to the gods and which are used as evidence of their existence and power. Zonin,[23] the enquirer, who represents himself as an enlightened philosopher who does not believe in the reality of idols, nevertheless took cognizance, like most of the Stoics, of popular belief and its widespread experience of miracles that took place in the temples of the gods.[24] R. Akiba's reply accorded with the spirit and understanding of the Stoic enquirer, who conceded the nullity of idolatry,[25] but maintained the view that εἱμερμένη ['fate'] determined the time when the pains would come on and when they would cease, and likewise the remedy by which the cure would be effected. The conduct of the person concerned is unable to change anything in the chain of causation or in the natural order of the events. The future is necessarily predetermined. Also the personification of the afflictions, which remain under oath, conforms to the Stoic concept that the world is full of divine 'powers'. By means of this conception the Stoics attempted to draw closer to the world of popular polytheistic faith, while ignoring the difference between the gods, who possess personality and are closely related to human beings, and impersonal forces, which are related to the cosmos only. We may state that R. Akiba's reply belongs to the category of answers that are given to the disciples' question 'But what explanation will you give us?' (*Pesiqta de-Rav Kahana*, Para, p. 40b). The reply was able to satisfy Zonin, but was this the view of R. Akiba, namely that the afflictions that were due to go were compelled to do so, and that the sin committed by the ailing person could not change this 'compulsion'? However, in a later version of the narrative its character is wholly changed. The ailing or mutilated person who enters an idolatrous shrine is 'a worthy man who performs the precepts', and his cure is explained as follows: 'He was due to receive from the hand of the Holy One, blessed be He, the reward of the commandments standing to his account, and since he left his world (i.e. denied the fundamental principle of faith), the Holy One, blessed be He, said "Why should I retain this man's reward?" Forthwith the Holy One, blessed be He, paid him his reward by healing him, so that no recompense should be due to him from the Holy One, blessed be He, together with that of the righteous; hence he went forth cured.'[26] In this version *a man's deeds* are the determinant factors, and the surprising phenomenon of healing being effected in an idolatrous temple finds an explanation in the sphere of the law of requital and the ways of God in bestowing reward and inflicting punishment according to R. Akiba's doctrine: 'The Holy One, blessed be He, deals strictly both with the former and the latter: He is strict towards the righteous and punishes them for the few wrongful acts that they perpetrated in this world, so that He may send them an unreduced recompense in the world to come, and He bestows well-being upon the wicked and rewards them for the few good deeds that they have performed in this world.'[27]

The dictum that we cite next, which was transmitted by אחר *Aḥer* ['Other'] — that is, Elisha b. Avuyah — in the name of R. Akiba, teaches apparently, by its formulation, the doctrine of immutable fate, but an examination of its content shows that this is not the case. Aḥer asked R. Me'ir the meaning of the verse Ecclesiastes vii 14: 'God has made the one as well as the other.' Apparently Aḥer wished to find an allusion in this verse to fate, which determined the righteous and the wicked in the world. R. Me'ir diverted the verse to another homily, to which Aḥer reacted by saying: 'R. Akiba, your teacher, did not expound it thus, but (God) created righteous men (and) He created wicked men; He created the Garden of Eden (and) He created Gehenna. Every man has two portions, one in the Garden of Eden and one in Gehenna. The righteous man, having been found worthy [by the Heavenly Court], receives his own portion and that of his fellow in the Garden of Eden; the wicked man, having been found guilty, receives his portion and that of his fellow in Gehenna' (*T.B. Ḥagiga* 15a). To each one a portion is allocated both in the Garden of Eden and in Gehenna, and which of these falls to a man's lot depends purely on his actions. Were the righteous and the wicked predetermined, it would only be necessary to prepare for each one the place due to him. This view of R. Akiba regarding the unrestricted freedom of man's choice also underlies his controversy with R. Pappos concerning the interpretation of the verse 'Behold, the man hath become like one of us' (Genesis iii 22). R. Pappos explained it to mean 'like one of the Ministering Angels. Said R. Akiba: "Enough, Pappos!" Pappos retorted: "And how do you explain 'The man hath become like one of us'?" [Said R. Akiba to him]: "The Holy One, blessed be He, put two ways before him, one of death and one of life, and he chose the way of death." '[28] R. Pappos' exposition alludes to a concept that makes a fundamental distinction between man before and after he had sinned. The sphere of primordial man was interior to that of the Ministering Angels [i.e. nearer to God]. He was like the Only One (as it were) of the universe, and God thought to give him dominion over His world and to make him king over all His creatures. 'Said the Holy One, blessed be He: "I am King over the celestial beings, and man shall be king over the earthly creatures." ' These and similar dicta[29] are transmitted by Amoraim and are found in late sources, but they clearly recall the words of Philo about the First Man, who takes second place after God, as viceroy and ruler over all things;[30] he is the 'heavenly man' (οὐράνιος ἄνθρωπος) and the divine logos.[31] This First Man was, of course, perfect (τέλειος) and had no need of commandments and prohibitions. The first commandment was not given to this man, who was created in the image of God, but to the man who was taken from the ground.[32] It was not difficult to continue and say that man, after his fall, after he had erred in his choice, lost this potentiality and was placed under the dominion of sin. However, Philo did not draw this conclusion, which negates man's freedom of choice and repentance; but Paul came to that conclusion when he incorporated therein the Christological element: 'One man's trespass led to condemnation for all men' (Romans v 18), 'As was the one man of dust, so are all those who are of the dust' (I Corinthians xv 48). It is not possible to be redeemed save again by the help of the heavenly man: 'Just as we have borne the image of the man of dust, we shall also bear the image of the man of heaven' (*ibid.* v. 49).[33] R. Akiba rejected utterly the comparison of the first man to the Ministering Angels, and by implication all that flowed from this elevation. Man was placed from the outset beneath the yoke of the commandment, and he was given permission to choose between the way of life and the way of death. This right was not taken away from him after he had sinned and the penalty of death was imposed upon him. It remains within the power of every man to this day.

We have thus found so far in the teaching of R. Akiba a clear emphasis on the principle of the freedom of choice, but we have not discerned an antithesis between this principle and that of Providence presiding over the world and its natural order, which R. Akiba meditated and which aroused his wonderment (*Sifra*, Shemini, Sec. 5). Of his disciple, R. Simeon b. Yoḥai, it is related that he saw a fowler laying a snare with which to trap a bird, and behold, he heard a Heavenly Voice saying, 'Demos!' ['pardon!'], and the bird was saved. Thereupon the Tanna said: 'A bird, unless Heaven wills it, is not caught, how much more so a human being!'[34] Clearly neither R. Akiba nor his colleagues and disciples completely evaded the question of the relationship between the two principles, and if not explicit then implicit expression was given thereto. However, the belief in Providence is essentially different from that in fate, for it posits the free Will of God as a basic and fundamental verity, and thereby it also differs from both astrology and Stoic teaching. But this Will and its decisions perforce determine man's fate and the ways and circumstances of his life. On the other hand, they are also determined by the free choice of man.

It seems that neither the Tannaim in the first and second centuries, nor the Amoraim who followed them, produced a solution to the problem. Belief in the two principles — both in Providence and in freedom of choice — is common to them all, but they differ in fixing their boundaries and in the ways of reconciling them. The differences are to be understood in the light of their divergent experiences of life — for we are not dealing here with speculative thought but with pragmatic reflection — and also as due in no small measure to external influences, emanating from astrology and widely current popular beliefs on the one side, and from the solutions to the problem of predestination and freedom of choice, as advanced by the Stoics in the course of centuries, on the other. Both approaches came to the knowledge of the Sages, by diverse channels, at the end of the Tannaitic period only, and especially in the days of the Amoraim. The answers are reflected at times in the attitude they adopted towards other questions.

To R. Akiba is attributed the homiletical exposition of the verse ' "And righteousness delivereth from death" — not from violent death but from death itself' (*T.B. Shabbat* 156b). This is the reading in our printed editions, but in *Haggadot ha-Talmud* ['Talmudic Legends'] (Constantinople 1511) and in *ʿEn Yaʿaqov* ['Fountain of Jacob'], editio princeps (Salonica 1515), the text has: 'and not from death itself but from violent death.'[35] The importance and correctness of this reading becomes clear in the light of R. Akiba's express teaching in the Baraita on the predetermination of the number of years of a man's life. 'It is taught: "The number of thy days I will fulfil" — these are the years of the generations [i.e. the allotted span of life]. If a man is worthy, he is vouchsafed the full period; if he is unworthy, his years are reduced. This is the view of R. Akiba. But the Sages declare: If he is worthy the years of his life are increased, if he is unworthy they are reduced. They said to R. Akiba: Now Scripture states "And I will add unto your days fifteen years"! He answered them: The added years were of his own. Know now that this is so, for a prophet arose and prophesied "Behold, a son shall be born to the house of David, Josiah by name", although Manasseh had not yet been born....'[36] The length of the days of a man is predetermined, only his wicked deeds may lead to their reduction. 'If a man dies under the age of fifty, he dies by כרת *kārēt* ['cut off'] (*T.P. Bikkurim* ii, p. 1; *T.B. Moʿed Qaṭan* 28a). A man's good deeds bring about only the completion of his days and his delivery from violent death. Accordingly R. Akiba said (*M. ʿEduyot* ii, 9) that a father endows his son with years only in the framework of 'the number of the generations that have gone before him, and of them he [the son] is the end, as it is said: "Calling the generations from the beginning" (Isaiah xli 14).' In other words, the (ancestral) merit cannot prolong a man's years beyond the years of the generations that the Almighty allotted to him.[37] R. Akiba's doctrine is briefly summarized by Naḥmanides in his commentary on Exodus xxiii 26: 'As it is said "The number of thy days I will fulfil" — this means that he will not die in battle or through plague or change of weather, but only through old age, that is, that he will complete his days according to the number that forms the life of man in his generations.' Death is part of the order of the universe, and accordingly measured spans have been allotted to human life, and when the appointed time arrives it cannot be postponed, for new generations wait to take their place. When Moses wished to cross the Jordan, God said to him 'I created My world as a series of eras. Had Abraham then committed a sin that he died? The reason was that the age of Isaac was pressing to enter history, and Isaac passed away only because Jacob's epoch was pressing to begin; and now Joshua's term of office presses to commence.'[38] Although the Sages differ from R. Akiba and declare that good deeds are conducive to length of days, yet their teaching does not imply that 'There is no death without sin'. This doctrine appears only in the time of the Amoraim.[39]

Thus in the case under discussion a limit has been set to the influence of human free choice on the one hand, and on the other a certain segment has been removed from the area of fate's dominion. A similar compromise is found relative to other subjects in the answer given by R. Joshua b. Ḥananiah to the Alexandrians. They asked him: ' "What shall a man do to become wise?" He replied: "Let him devote more time to study and less to trade." Said they to him: "Many have done so without success!" — "Rather must they supplicate Him to whom wisdom belongs, as it is said 'For the Lord giveth wisdom, out of His mouth cometh knowledge and discernment' (Proverbs ii 6)..." "What shall a man do to become rich?" Said he to them: "Let a man engage in trade and deal honestly." They replied: "Many have acted thus without success!" — "Rather let a man supplicate Him to whom (all) wealth belongs, as it is said 'Mine is the silver and Mine is the gold' (Haggai ii 8)..." "What shall a man do that he may have male offspring?" He replied: "Let him take a woman meet for him and sanctify himself at the time of intercourse." They answered: "Many have done so without success!" — "Rather let him supplicate Him to whom children belong..." ' (*T.B. Nidda* 70b). The Gemara deduces from the remarks of R. Joshua that 'the one without the other was insufficient,' that is to say, that the deeds of man that are performed with understanding and in conformity with the laws of ethics and the precepts of religion can assure the desired results only if they accord with the designs of Providence, 'which knoweth what the future holds in store', in accordance with R. Joshua b. Ḥananiah's answer to the Romans (*T.B. Sanhedrin* 90b).

A kind of sequel to R. Joshua b. Ḥananiah's dicta is provided by the following dialogue: 'A Gentile (once) asked R. Joshua b. Qorḥa, saying: "Do you not aver that the Holy One, blessed be He, foresees that which will happen?" He replied: "Yea!" He then retorted: "But it is written 'And it grieved Him at His heart' (Genesis vi 6)." Said R. Joshua to him: "Has a male child ever been born to you?" He answered "Yea!" "And what did you do?" The Gentile replied: "I rejoiced and I gave a celebration for all to rejoice." Thereupon R. Joshua said to him: "But did you not realize that in the end he would die?" The Gentile answered: "In the hour of joy we must rejoice, in the time of mourning we must mourn" ' (*Genesis Rabba* xxvii, 4). Foreseeing an event is not conceived here as an arbitrary determination of the future event, just as in the analogy a man does not determine his son's ultimate death. On the contrary, it contains the possibility of choice, and in God's reaction there is an expression of grief at man's not having chosen the right path.

This integration of man's freedom of choice with the ways of Providence provides the rationale of numerous Halakhot of the School of R. Ishmael. The Torah enjoined: 'When thou buildest a new house, then thou shalt make a parapet for thy roof, that thou bring not blood upon thy house, when the faller falls from thence' (Deuteronomy xxi 8). In a Baraita the Sages stated: 'The School of R. Ishmael taught: "When the faller falls from thence" — this man was destined to fall since the time of Creation, for he had not (yet) fallen, yet Scripture calls him 'faller'; for good is brought about through the good and guilt [i.e. punishment] through the guilty' (*T.B. Shabbat* 32a; *Sifre Deuteronomy* Sect. 229). The fall had been decreed upon the falling man by Providence, but it was the house-owner's sin that caused him to fall through his neglect. A similar explanation was given of the verse 'And if a man lie not in wait, but God cause it to come to hand' (Exodus xxi 13): 'If one man killed a person accidentally, and another slew a person intentionally, the willful murderer — it comes about — falls by the hand of the innocent homicide' (*Mekhilta Mishpaṭim*, § 4; cf. *T.B. Makkot* 10b). This interpretation was already known to Philo, who concludes his annotation with the words: 'God uses as His ministers those whose sins are few and easily remedied, though He does not show approval of them but merely takes them as suitable instruments of vengeance. For He would not wish that anyone whose whole life is stainless and his lineage also should set his hand to homicide however justly deserved.'[40]

What we have finally shown corroborates to a certain extent Josephus' statement that the Pharisees, in asserting that everything is decided by fate, do not negate man's will to aspire after anything he desires. Since it is God's decree, He willed that there should be a synthesis and that the human will, which chooses between good and evil,[41] should also participate in the determination of fate. Nor is it surprising that this approach should bring to Josephus' mind the Stoic doctrine that teaches that the εἱμαρμένη does not nullify the intended and purposive action of man. Contrariwise, this is included in the εἱμαρμένη, and without it the outcome foreseen from the beginning would not be achieved. The wise man is distinguishable from the fool in that he discerns in fate προνοία ['foresight'], which seeks his good, and therefore he accepts it gladly and acts in conformity with it.[42] However, Josephus overlooked the fundamental difference between the Stoic εἱμαρμένη, which is only the law of nature and the chain of causation, and God, who has free will. But the factual account is correct at any rate in so far as a section of the Pharisaic Sages of his time is concerned.

Already in R. Akiba's generation there is discernible still another way of defining the relationship between Providence and free choice, namely the complete separation between man's religio-ethical conduct and his external life and its circumstances. Ben ʿAzzai said: 'Precept leads to precept and transgression to transgression. For the reward of a precept is a precept and the reward of a transgression is a transgression' (*M. 'Avot* iv, 2). This saying apparently refers to the view that in this world there is no reward except that which inheres in the actual observance of the precepts. Ben ʿAzzai does not state that a man is helped by Heaven to perform additional precepts, if he has fulfilled one. This idea, which we shall encounter soon, did not accord with his outlook. In *Mekhilta* (Wa-yassaʿ, Sec. i) we learn: 'Simeon b. ʿAzzai said: "שמוע *Shamoaʿ* ['Hearken']", why then does Scripture add "תשמע *tishmaʿ* ['thou shalt hearken']"? From this is to be inferred that if a man desires to hearken, he is given the opportunity to do so; to forget, he is (likewise) enabled to do so. But perhaps this means after a time? Hence Scripture teaches: "And it shall be if hearken thou shalt hearken" [usually rendered: 'And it shall come to pass, if thou shalt hearken diligently'] (Deuteronomy xxviii 1), "[and it shall be] if forget thou shalt forget" [usually rendered: 'And it shall be, if thou shalt forget'] (Deuteronomy viii 19). ["And it shall be"] — forthwith! How is this to be envisaged? If a man wishes to hearken, he is afforded the opportunity to hearken at once; to forget, he is enabled to forget at once. He (further) said: If a man wishes to hearken בטובתו *bĕṭôvātô* [literally, 'for his good'], he is granted to hearken שלא בטובתו *shellō' bĕṭôvatô* ['not for his good']; to forget *bĕṭôvātô*, he is enabled to forget not *bĕṭôvātô*. Freedom of choice is given, "If it concerneth the scorners, He scorneth them, but unto the humble He giveth grace" (Proverbs iii 34).' The earlier dicta stress that man is granted freedom of choice, and that Heaven does not stand in his way or hinder him, but his desire to hearken or to forget is immediately fulfilled. The commentators found it difficult, however, to explain the second dictum, and some emended the text. Saul Horovitz (*Mekhilta*, p. 158) gives this interpretation: 'That if a man learns voluntarily, the Holy One, blessed be He, brings it about that he should learn even where he himself had not intended to learn.' But this interpretation makes the word *bĕṭôvātô* redundant. Although we find the expression *shellō' bĕṭôvātô* used in the sense of 'perforce' (*T.B. Sanhedrin* 7b), yet in most Mishnayot and Baraitot the signification of *bĕṭôvā* and *shellō' bĕṭôvā* is 'for benefit' and 'and not for benefit'.[43] Here, too, it appears to me, this is the meaning to be given to the words: If a man wishes to hearken with a view to his benefit, that is to say, for the sake of the hoped-for reward, he is, indeed, vouchsafed to hearken but not for his benefit — without receipt of reward. On the other hand, if he wishes to forget for his benefit — out of a desire to gain thereby, he is allowed to forget, but the advantage is not granted him. A man's good is not dependent on his choice, nor is the welfare of the righteous.

A similar significance attaches also to his following dictum: 'When does the Holy One, blessed be He, show them (i.e. the righteous) the reward in store for them? Near their death' (*Genesis Rabba* lxii, 2, p. 672), and the dictum is akin to the view expressed in a subsequent generation by the Tanna R. Jacob: ' "That it may go well with thee" — this refers to the world that is wholly good; "And that thy days may be prolonged" — this refers to the world that is wholly long.' In other words: 'There is no reward for (the fulfilment of) precepts in this world'[44] — a doctrine that contradicts the ancient Mishna 'If a man

the case of Akiba suggests that
the just are not rewarded in this life

performs but a single precept, he is granted good and length of days.'45 As we have seen, R. Akiba disagreed with this Mishna, for he severed the connection between the length of a man's life and his actions. Although in regard to a man's livelihood he said: 'Whoever gives alms to the poor knows no dearth',46 yet without doubt both his teaching and the example that R. Akiba set in his life by his death led to the conclusion that precepts are not rewarded in this world. He expressed the view that 'suffering is precious', and when his flesh was combed with iron combs, he declared that all his days he had prayed for that moment. Clear expression is given to the effect of R. Akiba's death on the concept of reward and punishment and on that of Providence in the Haggada about Moses, attributed to Rav. After Moses had been shown R. Akiba's eminence in Torah-knowledge, he said: ' "Show me his reward"... he beheld his flesh being weighed at meat stands. So he said unto God: "Sovereign of the universe, such is Torah and such its reward!" The Lord replied: "Silence! Thus was it decreed by Me" ' (T.B. Menaḥot 29b). Rav made the death of R. Akiba the pivot of his Tannaitic predecessors' view that not only death but even 'violent death' does not depend on human actions alone. However, Ben ʿAzzai already placed all the other benefits of man in this world under the absolute control of Providence, human conduct having no effect thereon, and thus Ben ʿAzzai declared: 'Of that which belongs to you you will be given, and by your name you shall be called, and in your place you shall be seated, and there is no oblivion before the Omnipresent, and no man touches that which is prepared for his fellow.'47

Such a doctrine concerning the reward given for the fulfilment of the precepts could be held by a few individuals only. In instructing the general public, in preaching the observance of the commandments, even Ben ʿAzzai could not forgo the principle that 'The disciples of Abraham our father enjoy (their reward) in this world and inherit the world to come' (M. ʾAvot v, 19). And the same Ben ʿAzzai, when he warned the people to answer 'Amen' correctly — and this admonition was directed to the common folk, for whom this constituted their primary participation in congregational prayer — he said: 'Whoever answers an 'orphaned' Amen [i.e. in response to a benediction he himself has not heard], his children will be orphaned; a 'curtailed'

(Amen) [i.e. the *Nûn* not distinctly pronounced], his days will be curtailed; a 'prolonged' (Amen), his days and years will be prolonged.'[48]

The restriction of reward to the next world obviated the need to observe the ways of Providence in all that related to man's material life, but it did not solve the problem of the extent of his freedom in making religious and ethical decisions. Nay more, this very distinction between the holy and the profane enabled one to see the problem clearly. Was there then no connection between a man's piety and his wealth, or his beauty or ugliness? Indeed, we learn in a Baraita that if a poor man argues before the Heavenly Court 'I was a poor man and preoccupied with my livelihood', they say to him: 'Were you poorer than Hillel?' Similarly, R. Eleazar b. Ḥarsom condemned the rich, and Joseph condemned the wicked (*T.B. Yoma* 35b).[49] But perhaps these righteous men were vouchsafed attributes and virtues that were not granted to other people, and they were chosen to be righteous? In truth such a conclusion was actually reached at the close of the Tannaitic period: 'And there were three who were named by the Holy One, blessed be He: Isaac, and Solomon, and Josiah. What does Scripture say of Isaac? "Nay, but Sarah thy wife shall bear thee a son; and thou shalt call his name Isaac" (Genesis xvii 19). And what is stated with regard to Solomon? "Behold, a son shall be born to thee, who shall be a man of rest; and I will give him rest from all his enemies round about; for his name shall be Solomon, and I will give peace and quietness unto Israel in his days" (I Chronicles xxii 9). What is said of Josiah? "Behold, a son shall be born unto the house of David, Josiah by name" etc. (I Kings xiii 2). Some say: Also Ishmael among the Gentiles. We find the names and deeds of the righteous are revealed before the Omnipresent even before they are born, as it is said: "Before I formed thee in the belly I knew thee" (Jeremiah i 5). We thus find that the names of the righteous (are known to God beforehand); whence (do we know that this is also true of) the names of the wicked? Therefore Scripture teaches: "The wicked go astray from the womb" (Psalms lviii 4 [3]).' This exposition, which is found in the *Mekhilta* (Pisḥa § 16, ed. Horovitz, p. 60), resembles in meaning the observation in *The Manual of Discipline* (iv, 22) concerning the upright, 'For them God chose for an everlasting covenant', and the statement in *The Zadokite Document*[50] (ii, 12) regarding 'those who abominate the ordinance': 'For God disapproved of them from the beginning of the world, and ere their foundations were laid, He knew their deeds.' The first part of the passage in the *Mekhilta* occurs in *Genesis Rabba* in the name of R. Isaac, and he is, apparently, the Tanna from the School of R. Ishmael, who is often mentioned in the *Mekhilta* and in the *Sifre*. It seems that R. Isaac stated only of three righteous men that their names were designated before they were formed, but not of all the righteous. This differentiation finds support in another Midrashic exposition of R. Isaac. ' "The Lord bless thee..." — R. Nathan said: May He bless thee with property and keep thee in (health of) body. R. Isaac said: And keep thee from evil inclination' (*Sifre Numbers* § 40). Preservation from the evil inclination does not signify the foreordained election of the preserved, but it has at least the value of the active help of Providence in man's struggle against temptation. This view of the help afforded by Providence to man in making his choice was not the opinion of an individual but that of the entire School of Ishmael. Freedom of choice was limited to the initial decision. This is the meaning of the exposition in the *Mekhilta de-R. Ishmael* (Wa-yassaʿ i, p. 157): ' "And He said: 'If thou wilt diligently hearken' " [literally: 'If hearken thou wilt hearken'] — from this the Sages inferred: If a man hearkened to one precept, he is enabled to hearken to many precepts, as it is said, "If thou wilt diligently hearken". If a man forgot one precept, he is made to forget many precepts.' Not only does one precept lead to another, and if a man seeks to hearken, he is given the opportunity of doing so — as Ben ʿAzzai taught — but his desire and resolve are augmented. In another Baraita we find: 'The School of R. Ishmael taught: Transgression dulls the heart of man, as it is said: "Neither shall ye make yourselves unclean with them, that ye should be defiled thereby" (Leviticus xi 43). Read not ונטמאתם *wěniṭmē'tem* ['that ye should be defiled'] but ונטמטם *wěniṭṭamṭem* ['that ye should become dull-hearted']. The Rabbis taught: "Neither shall ye make yourselves unclean with them, that ye should be defiled thereby" — this means, if a man defiles himself a little, he is defiled much... The Rabbis taught: "Sanctify yourselves therefore, and be ye holy" (*ibid.* v. 44) — if a man sanctifies himself a little, he is sanctified much....'[51] This doctrine may be the result of meditation and experience; but it is difficult to consider it fortuitous that, both in the conception of free choice as in the explanation of Providence, there exists a certain similarity between the approach of R. Ishmael and his School, on the one hand, and the Stoics and Philo of Alexandria, on the other. From the first century B.C.E. onward the Stoics ascribe a decisive practical value to the recognition of man's freedom of decision and to the responsibility implicit in this decision.

The concepts of good and evil are inherent in man; decision means correct use of these ideas. For this purpose a *prior decision* (προαίρεσις) is necessary. Philo regarded freedom of choice as a gift from God, which was vouchsafed to man in order to nullify the laws of nature that rule him. Freedom of choice applies to both good and evil, but man is not left on his own in opting for good. After he has proved his power in subduing the evil inclination and preferring the good, and after he has realized that this power comes to him from God, God comes to his aid and helps him. This Divine grace is granted to all men, but there are some who are vouchsafed this even before they are born. On the other hand, the choice of evil is wholly in man's hands.[52] One cannot overlook the contradiction and difficulty of Philo's thesis. On the one hand, free will is a gift of God, and thereby man becomes most like Him,[53] but, on the other hand, it comes only to explain the choice of evil, which cannot emanate from God, from whom only good can issue.[54] Reasoning of this kind is completely absent in Tannaitic teaching. If Divine intervention is posited in the wake of man's choice, it is not restricted only to the option of those who choose good ('If a man hearkened to one precept, he is enabled to harken to many precepts'), but includes also the case of those who prefer evil ('If a man forgot one precept, he is made to forget many precepts'). But even when the issue is actually not man's choice of good or evil, but God's choice of man, we find that not only the names of the righteous and their deeds are revealed before the Omnipresent prior to their birth, but also the names and acts of the wicked. The wicked are not subject to the dominion of Belial, and the idea of the creation of the righteous and the wicked is not linked to a dualistic theology, as we know from the writings of the Qumran Sect. The view shared by the Tannaim is that all the creatures are subject in their lifetime to the rule of the Holy One, blessed be He. A Tanna of the

School of R. Ishmael expounded: ' "Let the Lord, the God of the spirits of all flesh, set..." — this teaches us that all the spirits go forth only from before Him.' R. Eliezer b. R. Jose the Galilean added: 'Grasp this verity, that so long as a man remains alive, his soul is in the keeping of his Maker, as it is said: "In whose hand is the soul of every living thing, and the breath of all mankind" (Job xii 10)'; the differentiation between the place of the righteous and that of the wicked obtains only after their death (*Sifre Numbers* § 139).

Even the Tanna R. Isaac only intended to say that certain righteous men were privileged to be chosen before their birth. However, a general deduction was drawn from this dictum, namely that all the righteous and all the wicked were named before they were formed, but it was not yet explained when the designation of the names took place, and it even seemed a probable inference from the verse in Jeremiah i 5, 'Before I formed thee in the belly I knew thee', that it refers to a recurring act. Finally, R. Yannai, one of the earliest Palestinian Amoraim came and gave the following interpretation: 'From the beginning of the creation of the world, the Holy One, blessed be He, saw the deeds of the righteous and the deeds of the wicked. "Now the earth was unformed and void" — this refers to the acts of the wicked; "And God said: 'Let there be light' " — this alludes to the acts of the righteous; "And God saw the light, that it was good" — this is a reference to the deeds of the righteous; "And God divided the light from the darkness" — (that is) the works of the righteous from those of the wicked. "And God called the light Day" — this connotes the deeds of the righteous; "and the darkness He called Night" — this is an allusion to the actions of the wicked.'[55] Thus the passage speaks of a determination that took place once only and of the division of humanity into two camps: the righteous who are 'children of light' and the wicked who are 'children of darkness'. But neither of these groups leaves the sphere of God's jurisdiction, as is stated at the end of this allegorical exposition: ' "One day" — this means that the Holy One, blessed be He, gave them a unique day. Which was that? — the Day of Judgement.'

R. Joḥanan, the contemporary and disciple of R. Yannai, went much farther in his formulation, saying: 'The name of the Holy One, blessed be He, is not mentioned relative to evil, but only in connection with good'[56]; he did not, however, state that evil was not created by the Holy One, blessed be He. Their aversion to the notion that evil does not emanate from God led the Amoraim to give an emphatic interpretation, in the reverse sense, to every Biblical verse in which any support or basis for this idea could be discerned. R. Eleazar,[57] the disciple of R. Joḥanan, who transmitted in his master's name the dictum that we have cited, expounded the verse 'Out of the mouth of the Most High proceedeth not evil and good' (Lamentations iii 38) thus: 'From the moment that the Holy One, blessed be He, said[58] "See, I have set before thee this day life and good, and death and evil" (Deuteronomy xxx 15), good has not gone forth to him who does evil nor evil to him who does good, but only good to the doer of good and evil to the doer of evil.' This exposition follows upon the interpretation of the verse 'Who is he that saith, and it cometh to pass, when the Lord commandeth it not?' as referring to the wicked men Pharaoh and Haman, who acted as they did not at the command of the Lord but on their own account, and it seeks to contradict the view that evil has its own domain; hence it emphasizes man's freedom of choice, and, in another version of R. Eleazar's dictum, even assumes an extreme form: ' "Behold, I set before you..." (Deuteronomy xi 26) — since the Holy One, blessed be He, proclaimed this at Sinai, from that moment evil and good do not issue (from God), but evil comes of its own accord upon those who do evil, and good comes to those who do good.'[59] But just as evil comes of its own accord as a result of human actions, so good also comes of its own accord, for the choice of good is not a necessity in the development of man, which flows from the very fact that he is endowed with a power that draws him near to God. This latter doctrine, which several of the Church Fathers adopted, restricts human freedom and limits it to a given period.[60]

The fear of the belief in dualism, which aims to solve the problem of the source of evil and militates against the ancient doctrine of predestination, thus led to the limitation of the area to which Providence applied and to the special emphasis laid on man's freedom of choice. This restriction served also to obstruct the influence of the belief in astrology, which was widely current in the epoch of the Amoraim. In the Roman era astrology was no longer a religion, although it originated in the late Babylonian cult, and it must be distinguished from the worship of the host of heaven, in the form, for example, of sun-worship, which was a kind of official religion of the Empire. Astrology posited a game involving a fixed number of abstract powers, that obeyed unchanging and enduring laws, and controlled all existence. The value of the sun and the heavenly host consisted not, as in natural religion, in their appearance and action, but in their role in the deterministic array of forces. Astrology was incorporated in various systems of thought — Pythagorianism, Stoicism, and Gnosticism — and for the very reason that it was not a religion, the various faiths felt the need and possibility of coming to terms with it.[61]

From the time of R. Me'ir and his contemporaries there has come down to us a discussion on the significance of eclipses: 'When the luminaries are eclipsed, it is an evil omen for the whole world... R. Me'ir said: When the luminaries are eclipsed, it is an evil omen for Israel's "enemies" [a euphemism, meaning: for the Israelites themselves], because they are accustomed to calamities... When the sun is eclipsed, it is an evil omen for the Gentiles; if the moon is eclipsed, it is an evil omen for the "enemies" of Israel, for the Gentiles regulate their calendar by the sun, but Israel by the moon[62]... R. Josiah said: When the planets are eclipsed in the east, it is an evil omen for the inhabitants of the east; in the west, it is an evil omen for the inhabitants of the west. R. Joḥanan said: Both sets of omens are intended for the Gentiles, as it is said: "Thus saith the Lord: Learn not the ways of the nations, and be not dismayed at the signs of heaven" (Jeremiah x 2).' Phenomena that are seen but infrequently among the heavenly bodies are interpreted here only as a sign and omen for evil to come; in another Baraita the phenomena are themselves regarded as a punishment for certain sins. But neither view ascribes the eclipses of the luminaries to independent forces; they are considered signs or messengers of Providence, and hence the aforementioned dicta are not to be regarded as astrology. But even in the sphere of this restricted meaning, a special place was assigned to Israel by almost all the Tannaim treating of the subject, and R. Jonathan even excludes the Jews completely by referring to the verse in Jeremiah. In a Baraita in the *Sifra* astrology is included in the prohibition 'Ye shall not practice divination.'[63] R. Jonathan's contemporary, R. Jose of Huṣal,[64] said: 'Whence do we know that we may not consult the Chaldeans, for it is stated "Thou shalt be whole-hearted with the Lord thy God" ' (*T.B. Pesaḥim* 113a).

This prohibition does not imply the denial of the actual value of astrology and its reality. This belief was shared by Tannaim and Amoraim alike.[65] The early Amoraim dispute over the question whether the planets and Chaldean lore affect the Jews. In R. Joshua b. Levi's notebook were recorded the indications of a man's character according to the day on which he was born, as, for example, 'He who is born on the second day of the week will be irascible'; R. Ḥanina, on the other hand, was of opinion that not the constellation of the day but that of the hour is the determining factor. Hence 'He who is born under the planet Venus will be rich and unchaste... he who is born under Jupiter (צדק *Ṣedeq*) will be a man who acts rightly...', in other words: 'The constellation makes wise, the constellation makes rich, and Israel is subject to planetary influence' (Rashi: 'This means that neither prayer nor alms-giving changes the planetary influence'). Contrariwise, Rav and Samuel held that the fulfilment of the precepts is able to nullify the influence of the planets, and R. Joḥanan deduced — as did R. Jonathan in his day — from Jeremiah x 2 that Israel does not stand under planetary influence.[66] He also stresses the question of freedom of choice. The verse '*I am that I am... I am* hath sent me unto you' (Exodus iii, 15) was thus expounded by R. Joḥanan: ' "I am that I am" applies to individuals, but in the case of the many [i.e. the people as a whole] I rule over them perforce, against their will, though their teeth be broken...'[67]; to the individual freedom of choice is granted. Thereon depends also the possibility of repentance, of which R. Joḥanan said 'Great is repentance, for it rends asunder the decree imposed upon a man' (*T.B. Rosh Hashana* 17b).

Astrology not only contradicted the freedom of human choice, but also impaired the concept of Providence, that is, the doctrine of the free will and unrestricted power of God. Apparently R. Ḥanina did not overlook this problem, but even the Amoraim who excluded Israel from the influence of the constellations and transferred them to the domain of Providence[68] stressed the ways of Providence in fullest detail and described them in expressions and images derived from the sphere of astrology. Rav Judah said in the name of Rav: 'Forty days before the formation of a child a heavenly voice goes forth and declares: The daughter of So-and-so is (to be married) to

So-and-so; such and such a house (shall belong) to So-and-so; such and such a field (shall belong) to So-and-so' (*T.B. Soṭa* 2a), and, on the other hand, he reports in the name of Samuel: '*Each day* a heavenly voice goes forth and declares: The daughter of So-and-so (is to be married) to So-and-so; such and such a field (shall belong) to So-and-so' (*T.B. Mo'ed Qaṭan* 18b). Rav, therefore, speaks of a decree that is determined before birth,[69] while Samuel is able to make the decision depend on human action, and R. Joḥanan and Resh Laqish agree with him, at any rate in so far as marriage is concerned (*T.B. Soṭa, loc. cit.*).

Belief in Providence makes man the focal point of the universe, and like Chrysippus[70], the most important representative of the ancient Stoics, Rav and the Amoraim who follow his view reach the conclusion that there is a benefit and purpose attaching to all beings and creatures: 'Said Rav Judah in the name of Rav: Of all that the Holy One, blessed be He, created in His world, there is naught that He created without purpose' (*T.B. Shabbat* 77b). And the Rabbis said: 'Even things that appear to you wholly superfluous in the creation of the world — like fleas, gnats and flies — also form an integral part of the world-creation, and the Holy One, blessed be He, uses them all in His service.'[71] The central position of man is not to be understood in the sense of 'Thou hast put all things under his feet' (Psalms viii 7 [6]). Everything is directed only towards him, but he himself directs nothing, not even his limbs. R. Joḥanan did not declare with Hillel 'To the place *that I love* thither my feet lead me', but he said 'A man's feet are responsible for him; they lead him to the place where *he is wanted*.'[72] Even a man's religious integrity is not entirely in his own hands. Following upon the ideas that we found expressed by the Tannaim, R. Joḥanan said: 'When the majority of a man's years have passed without his sinning, he will not sin thereafter, for it is said "He will keep the feet of His holy ones" ' (I Samuel ii 9).[73]

The last of the Amoraim, the Palestinian Haggadists, applied the inferences that they drew from this conception of Providence also to the question of reward and punishment and its relationship to human actions. In *Tanḥuma*[74] the following daring homily is cited: 'Come and see, when the Holy One, blessed be He, created the world, He created the angel of death already on the first day. Whence do we know this? Said R. Berechiah: Because Scripture states "And darkness was upon the face of the deep" (Genesis i 2) — this means the angel of death, who darkens the face of mankind; whereas man was created on the sixth day, yet he was blamed for having brought death into the world, as it is said "For in the day that thou eatest thereof thou shalt surely die" (*ibid.* ii 17). To what can the matter be compared? To a man who wished to divorce his wife. When he decided to go home, he wrote a bill of divorcement; then he entered his house, with the divorce in his possession, seeking a pretext for giving it to her. He said to her: "Mix me a cup (of wine) to drink." She mixed his cup. When he took the cup from her hand, he said to her: "Here is your divorce." Said she to him: "What sin have I committed?" He replied: "Go from my house, for you have mixed me a lukewarm cup (of wine)." She retorted: "You already knew beforehand that I should mix you a tepid cup (of wine), for you wrote the divorce and brought it with you!" Even so did Adam argue before the Holy One, blessed be He: "Sovereign of the universe, two thousand years before Thou didst create Thy world, the Torah was by Thee as an אמון *'āmôn* [variously rendered: 'nursling' or 'master-workman'] (Proverbs viii 30), and in it is written 'This is the law: when a man dieth in a tent' (Numbers xix 14); if Thou hadst not prepared death for mankind, wouldst Thou have written thus? Only Thou hast come to put the blame on me; this is the meaning of the verse 'He is terrible in His doing toward the children of men' (Psalms lxvi 5)." ' The passage merely states that man's sin did not cause death to come into the world; the decree of death would have existed even without him, and man's act served only as an instrument for implementing it. The homilist says the same with regard to Moses' death, and he cites in the name of R. Judan a similar explanation of Joseph's being brought down to Egypt, and finally R. Tanḥuma summarizes the thought with the analogy: 'To what can the matter be compared? To a cow on whose neck they (the owners) wish to put a yoke, but she prevents the yoke from (being placed on) her neck. What did they do? They took her son away from following her and drew him to the place that they wished to plough, and the calf lowed. When the cow heard her son lowing, she went reluctantly for her son's sake. So was it with the Holy One, blessed be He: He wished to fulfil the decree of

"Know of a surety", so He found a pretext for all those events, and they (Jacob's family) went down to Egypt and they "paid the debt"; hence Scripture declares "And Joseph was brought down to Egypt". This is the meaning of the verse: "He is terrible in His doing" etc.' Human deeds that appear to man as the decisions of his own will are in truth only links in a chain of events whose purpose is to realize what Providence has decreed. This concept is actually implicit in the aphorism 'A man's feet are responsible for him; they lead him to the place where he is wanted', and this is the position arrived at even by those Amoraim who excluded Israel from the rule of the planets. The gulf between them and the Amoraim who held that 'Israel is subject to the constellations' narrowed, especially when we take into consideration the fact that it was precisely the latter who felt it their duty to raise expressly the subject of human free will.

Even though he accepted the influence of the planets upon Israel. R. Ḥanina did not restrict the extent of the influence of Divine Providence. In opposition to the view of R. Joḥanan, who said that the sorcerers 'lessen (the power of) the Council [*Familia*] on High' (Rashi: 'For they slay those whom (Heaven) decreed to live'), R. Ḥanina proclaimed ' "There is none else besides Him" — even where sorcery is concerned' (Rashi: 'They [the sorcerers or sorceries] have not the power to *resist His edict*, for there is no power besides Him')[75]; sorcery and the planets are likewise subject to the Creator's Providence, 'For if it has not been decreed by Him, they cannot hurt the person.'[76] Hence R. Ḥanina said: 'A man does not bruise his finger below [upon earth] unless it be announced concerning him (Rashi: 'decreed concerning him') on high, for it is said: "A man's goings are of the Lord; how then can man look to his way?" (Proverbs xx 24).'[77] This emphasis placed on the all-embracing power of Providence does not nullify the value of man's deeds, nor does it exempt him from taking reasonable care in his conduct and actions. In the field of Halakha, too, the postulate that it lies within a man's power to act according to his decision forms the basis for rulings; thus 'All that is within a man's power (to do) is not regarded as though the act were lacking.'[78] It was none other than R. Ḥanina who said: 'All (ailments) are in the power of Heaven except cold and draughts, for it is said: "Cold and draughts [usually rendered: 'thorns and snares'] are in the way of the froward; he that doth keep his soul holdeth himself far from them" (Proverbs xxii 5).'[79] There are also everyday occurrences that happen to a person on account of his transgressions; undoubtedly R. Ḥanina did not mean only 'cold and draughts' and he mentioned them solely on account of the verse. Or in the words of the Palestinian Talmud:[80] 'Rav who lived where the evil eye was common, used to say: "Ninety-nine die of the (evil) eye, and (only) one by (the decree of) Heaven." R. Ḥanina, because he lived in Sepphoris where cold prevailed, used to say: "Ninety-nine die of cold, and (only) one by (the decree of) Heaven."' If this is the position with regard to everyday occurrences, a man must surely not rely on his constellation or on Providence alone in all that appertains to his conduct. Although R. Ḥanina said 'Everything is in the power of Heaven except the fear of Heaven, for it is said: "And now, Israel, what doth the Lord thy God require of thee, but to fear [the Lord thy God] (Deuteronomy x 12)', yet alongside this dictum stands the analogy used by R. Ḥanina: 'This is comparable to a man who is asked for a big article and he has it; (in which case) it seems to him but a small article. (If he is asked for) a small article and he does not possess it, it appears to him like a big article.'[81] Thus the attainment of the 'fear of Heaven' [i.e. piety] is not vouchsafed to every person in equal measure and as a result of the same effort. 'He who is like a man who has a big article' — that is to say, by nature and character he was born under the constellation of a righteous and pious man — the achievement of piety is a small matter for him, but for one born under another planet it is a difficult task.

The ultimate conclusion resulting from an exhaustive investigation of the various dicta of R. Ḥanina is not different from that which we reached from a study of the teachings of Rav and R. Joḥanan, despite the divergent starting point and postulates. Nor is it different from what their contemporary, the philosopher Plotinus, taught on this subject, notwithstanding the gulf between the former and the latter's thought and methods of thinking. According to Plotinus, the causes of our deeds lie within us and not in Providence; their consequences, however, are not in our power, but irresistibly follow the course designed by Providence. We may compare Providence and our relationship to it with the advice of a physician and our attitude to it. If we follow his advice, the action is in truth our own, but we act according to the understanding of the medical expert. If we act contrary to his advice, then, too, it is we who perform the deeds, but in opposition to the supervision [= providence] of the doctor. The fault is ours, and we must bear the consequences.[82] The experience of life and the compulsion of faith lead them to a complementary approach. A portion of the second principle combines with the first; the differences are of extent and degree of emphasis. This approach remains basically also the heritage of the later Amoraim, who never ceased meditating on the problem of Providence and to wonder about the significance of free choice. Rava proclaimed: 'Children, (length of) life, and sustenance do not depend on merit but on destiny [*mazzala*, 'planetary influence'].'[83] He based himself on the respective destiny of his teachers, Rav Ḥisda and Rabba. The former lived to the age of ninety-two and was wealthy, while the latter lived only forty years and his house lacked even barley bread. This realization did not prevent Rava from praying that he should be vouchsafed the wisdom of Rav Huna, the riches of Rav Ḥisda and the humility of Rabba bar Huna; and he adds that the first two requests were granted him, but not the third. Although it is possible to say that this prayer was not based on merit and righteous deeds, but was a supplication for the grace of Providence, which alone rules over fate, nevertheless Rava expressly attributed decisive importance to deeds, even though he did not overlook the contradiction between Providence and free choice, and even questioned the extent of man's responsibility for his actions. In the course of interpreting the words of Job (x 7), Rava said: 'Job sought to exempt the whole world from judgement; he said to Him [God]: "Sovereign of the universe, Thou hast created the ox with cloven hoofs and Thou hast created the ass with closed hoofs; Thou has created the Garden of Eden [Paradise] and Thou hast created *Gêhinnôm* [Gehenna]; Thou hast created righteous people and Thou hast created wicked people. Who hinders Thee?" But what did Job's companions answer him? "Yea, thou doest away with fear and restrainest devotion before God" (*ibid.* xv 4) — the Holy One, blessed be He, has created the evil inclination and He has created the Torah, its antidote.'[84] Thus, despite everything, he who has been created wicked can be made righteous by virtue of the Torah, which enables him to control his inclination,[85] and there is no argument capable of releasing man from judgement. The responsibility of man, who must account for his actions, set definite limits to the decrees of Providence; and as the feeling of responsibility and the frequency with which man is judged grew, so did the power of fate diminish, and man's mastery and his sense of freedom and the possibilities of his influence over his destiny increase. R. Simeon b. Yoḥai taught: 'If the Israelites were worthy on New Year, and abundant rains were decreed for them, and subsequently they sinned, then to reduce the rains is impossible, since the decree has already been issued. What does the Holy One, blessed be He, do? He scatters them over seas and deserts and rivers, so that the land does not benefit from them... If now they were not worthy on New Year, and scanty rains were decreed for them, and subsequently they repented, then to augment the rains is impossible, since the decree has already been issued. What does the Holy One, blessed be He, do for them? He sends the rains down for the needs of the land and causes dew drops to fall, and winds to blow with them, so that the land may benefit from them.'[86] Here the inference is drawn from the view, which is also held by most of the Tannaim, and forms the basis of our prayers on New Year and the Day of Atonement, namely that the sentence that receives the seal of finality on the Day of Atonement cannot be changed. Rava[87], indeed, asked why we pray the whole year round, and answered that we do so in accordance with the view of R. Jose that man is judged every day, 'for according to the Rabbis, who maintain that man is judged on New Year, once his judgement has been completed, (further) prayer is futile.'[88] If man is judged each day, he can influence his destiny by his prayer, and this is the view of Rava, who attributed, as we have observed, man's benefits to his constellation. The Torah, which, in Rava's opinion, the people of Israel accepted voluntarily,[89] set bounds to the rule of fate. By virtue of the Torah man became free and could pray to God and entreat His favour and grace. An anonymous Palestinian homilist expressly differentiated between two kinds of benefits: 'The Holy One, blessed be He, created three gifts in the world—wisdom, might, and wealth; if a man is vouchsafed one of them he takes all that is desirable in the whole world. This is true, however, (only) when the gifts come from the Holy One, blessed be He, and come through the power of the Torah. But the might and wealth of man are valueless, for thus said Solomon: "That the race is not to the swift, nor the battle to the strong, neither yet bread to the wise, nor yet riches to men of understanding" etc. (Ecclesiastes ix 11); and so, too, said Jeremiah (ix 22): "Thus saith the Lord: Let not the wise man glory in his wisdom neither let the mighty man glory in his might, let not the rich man glory in his riches"; and these gifts, since they do not come from the Holy One, blessed be He, are ultimately destined to leave him.'[90] But from whom derive 'the gifts that do not come from the Holy One, blessed be he'? It seems that this expositor was prepared to ascribe benefits to fate, as did Rava above, only he explicitly terms these benefits as imaginary and lacking value and durability in the estimation of one who believes in the power of the Torah, which bestows true benefits upon man.[91]

To sum up: We must state that we have found a multifaceted struggle extending over generations of Sages, which cannot be summarized in a dictum formulated by one or other scholar — not even in the formulation of Josephus, with which we commenced our discussion. We have seen that the Tannaim and Amoraim were divided in their views. The latter did not rely on the former, but renewed the discussion and study, at times even with greater daring and depth. We noted the influence of trends, from within and from without, on the extent of the emphasis placed both upon man's freedom of choice and upon his dependence on Providence. It seems to me that in the light of our account the views expressed in the scroll of the *Covenant of Damascus* [= Zadokite Document] and the Qumran Scrolls are less surprising than is generally supposed. One thing we did not find: the elevation of a single principle to the level of a systematic doctrine that imposed itself upon everything and endeavoured to reconcile the conflicting facts speculatively. Even those among the Sages — in particular the Amoraim — who were inclined to come to extreme conclusions in the direction of one principle, did not completely forsake the other. The bounds that the Sages set themselves were determined by other fundamentals in their religious thinking. They did not retreat from contradiction, for their aim was not to find a smooth philosophical solution, but to activate all man's powers

— both the potency inherent in the consciousness of freedom and the will to do good and that which flamed from the feeling of the nullity of man and his complete dependence on Divine Providence, for their religious thought was directed, in equal measure, towards God and towards the world and society.

CHAPTER XII

THE WRITTEN LAW AND THE ORAL LAW

In the two oldest traditions of the Oral Law the word 'Torah' is used in two different connotations. The Men of the Great Synagogue said three things: 'Be deliberate in judging, and raise up many disciples, and make a fence for the Torah' (*M. 'Avot* i, 1). The dictum is directed to the teachers and judges of the people, counselling them how to act in giving judgement and instruction. 'Torah' signifies here the teaching of precepts and Halakhot as in the ancient Mishna: 'They both came to the Great Court that was in the Chamber of Hewn Stone, whence *Torah* goes forth to all Israel' (*M. Sanhedrin* xi, 2). On the other hand, when Simon the Just declared: 'Upon three things the world is based: upon the *Torah*, upon Temple service, and upon deeds of loving-kindness' (*M. 'Avot* i, 2), he refered to Torah study[1], in which Temple service and deeds of loving-kindness are included. These three things are also enumerated in II Chronicles (xxxi, 21). It is stated of Hezekiah 'And in every work that he began in the service of the house of God, and in the Torah, and in the commandments....' In the saying of Simon the Just the Torah is placed first. Possibly this difference reflects a certain development. For the Chronicler 'the service of the house of God' was not yet implicitly included in the general term 'Torah'; it was the theme of תורת כהנים *Tôrat Kohănîm* ['the Torah of the priests'], as is evident also from the name of the third book of the Pentateuch, *Torat Kohanim*, which is undoubtedly early.[2] Contrariwise the term 'Torah', as used by Simon, includes both the law of the Temple service and the practice of loving-kindness. The study of the Torah is one of the pillars of the world. Torah alone is the covenant between God and His people, and the presence of the Shekhina among His people depends on the fulfilment and study of the Torah.[3] The study of the Torah implies also its expansion, and therefore the term 'Torah' in the mouth of Simon the Just is not confined to the Mosaic Torah. Whereas in Proverbs and in Job there is no mention of Torah and precepts on the basis of which a covenant has been made, and the term 'Torah' refers to the teaching of the father, the mother, the sage, and the teacher, or to the counsels of Wisdom itself, in Sirach the two concepts of Torah — that of Moses and that of Wisdom — are merged into a single idea. While in Jeremiah (ii 8) 'they that handle the Torah' correspond to the 'priests', in Sirach (xv 1) 'he that taketh hold of the Torah' is in parallelism with 'he that feareth the Lord'. The remnants of the Wisdom myth referring to Wisdom's pre-existence and its presence at the creation of the world, found in Proverbs (viii 22 ff)[4], were transferred to the Torah, and it was said that it existed before the creation of the world[5], while R. Eliezer b. R. Zadok and R. Akiba spoke of the Torah as 'an instrument wherewith the world was created'[6], although this myth militates against the doctrine of Revelation. It may be said that in the Hellenistic period, before the Maccabean Revolt, the word 'Torah' comprised the corpus of precepts, the teaching of the prophets, and the wisdom of the elders. But at the same time the term denotes particularly the Torah of Moses in all its parts and not just the section treating of the commandments and ordinances. Although it is stated in the Mishna in which the first classification of the precepts is found: '(The laws concerning) civil cases and Temple services, levitical cleanness and uncleanness, and the forbidden relations have what to rest on, and it is they that are the essentials of the Torah' (*M. Ḥagiga* i, 8), yet they are not the whole of the Torah. Echoes and traces of the twofold meaning of the term 'Torah' are still encountered in a later period, when the threefold division 'Torah, Prophets, and Hagiographa' had become a fact that also reflected the relative degree of holiness of each of them. Verses from the Prophets and the Hagiographa are cited in answer to the question 'Whence do we prove this from the Torah?' not only in Tannaitic but also in Amoraic dicta,[7] although the rule was already known that 'No inference may be drawn concerning Torah laws from statements in the post-Pentateuchal books of the Bible.'[8]

This fact shows to what extent the conception of the word 'Torah' in its broad and general connotation was perpetuated; it explains the fact that Paul and the author of the Gospel according to John refer to verses from the Prophets and from the Hagiographa as νόμος and is not to be regarded merely as a consequence of the use of νόμος as the translation of Torah.[9] They were only continuing an ancient tradition, as reflected in Daniel's words 'the Torah of Moses the servant of God' and 'His תורות *Tôrôt* ['laws'], which He set before us by His servants the prophets' (Daniel ix 10–13; see II Chronicles xxix 25; Ezra ix 10–14). The inclusion of prophecy and wisdom in the term Torah disproves the view that was current among theologians — and is still to be found today — which ascribes to Judaism, in the period following the destruction of the First Temple, a legalistic and unhistorical conception of 'Torah'.[10] But, on the other hand, it must be admitted that the replies given to the accounts of Weber, Bousset, and others are not altogether free from an apologetic undertone[11], and consequently helped somewhat to blur the distinctive connotation of the term 'Torah'. Principally they blamed the Septuagint, which rendered the word 'Torah' by νόμος and thus influenced the other Biblical translations. Even a scholar like C. H. Dodd, who well understood the meaning of 'Torah' in Hebrew in its various semantic nuances, writes:[12] 'It is clear that for the Jews of Egypt in the Hellenistic period the developed meaning of תורה as a code of religious observance, a "law" for a religious community, was the normal and regulative meaning, and they made this meaning cover the whole use of the word in the Old Testament. Thus the prophetic type of religion was obscured, and the Biblical revelation was conceived in a hard legalistic way. In thus rendering the term the translators are no doubt reflecting the sense in which their community read the Hebrew Bible, but their rendering helped to fix and stereotype that sense.' But the question is: Those communities were certainly not more legalistic than the local Jewry in Eretz-Israel, and if the latter continued to understand the word 'Torah' in a wider sense than that implied in the concept Halakha, why then did just Hellenistic Jewry deviate in comprehending it in its restricted sense? Dodd even attributes the very course taken by Hellenistic Judaism and Paulinian Christianity to the unfortunate translation of the word 'Torah':

'Where thinkers bred in Hellenistic Judaism sought to escape into a religion of greater spiritual freedom and spontaneity, it was not by any way of return to the prophetic idea of תורה, but by taking up a fresh attitude to religion conceived as Law. Philo accepted the Law as such and allegorized it: Paul declared that Judaism, being a legal religion, was superseded by the religion of the Spirit.'

This view actually characterizes Hellenistic Jewry as more legalistic than Palestinian Jewry, and overlooks Philo's testimony regarding the extreme allegorists in Alexandria, who maintained a Paulinian standpoint before Paul himself.[13]

Instead of decrying the Septuagint and charging it with distortions and misunderstandings belonging to later generations, it seems preferable to learn from it, and if we understand thoroughly the signification and development of the Hebrew term, we shall see that νόμος actually fits it. In the period with which we are concerned 'Torah' includes 'the commandment, and the statutes, and the ordinances' (αἱ ἐντολαὶ καὶ τὰ δικαιώματα καὶ τὰ κρίματα), whether they deal with a particular subject — such as 'the Torah ['law'] of the burnt-offering', 'the Torah of the sin-offering', 'This is the statute of the Torah', or 'This is the Torah: when a man dieth in a tent' — or whether they constitute a combination of heterogeneous statutes and ordinances that the Lord commanded by the hand of Moses, as in Deuteronomy (xvii 18). If now the concept of Torah was extended so as to include therein the admonitions regarding the observance of the precepts, the history of Israel, the biography of the Patriarchs and the story of Man,[14] this was all directed towards the making of the covenant and the acceptance of the commandments and statutes and ordinances and was centred on them. Without difficulty it was also possible to include in the definition of Torah the reprimands and promises of the prophecies and the ethics of the Wisdom books, while the enactments serving as a fence to the Torah themselves became Torah[15] viewed as δόγμα δ'ανθρώπων φρονίμων ('the instruction of wise men'). It would appear that for the Jews of Alexandria, too, the term 'Torah' was not a word but an 'institution', embodying the covenant between the people and its God, and reflecting a complex of precepts and statutes, customs and traditions linked to the history of the people and the acts of its rulers, kings, and prophets. If this was the connotation of 'Torah', it could not be translated διδαχή or διδασκαλία, but only νόμος, in the sense in which it was interpreted also by Pindar, Νόμος ὁ πάντων βασιλεύς, and as Plato understood it, namely as 'The constitution and living régime of a people, which is not comprised of a number of agreements and treaties, but is an institution of customs and traditions that are linked to one another by innumerable threads that tie them to the past of the people.'[16] In this sense the Greek translator of Isaiah i 10 understood the word Torah in the verse 'Give ear unto the Torah of our God, ye people of Gomorrah', when rendering it νόμος, since 'I cannot endure iniquity along with the solemn assembly' and 'Wash you, make you clean, put away the evil of your doings' are Torah. He also translated Isaiah xxiv 5 'Because they have transgressed the *Tôrôt*, violated the statute, broken the everlasting covenant' by διότι παρέβησαν τὸν νόμον and not by ἄγραφος νόμος[17], for νόμος is not φύσις, the law of nature[18], but Torah, which comes to master nature and the impulses.

The Greek word νόμος from the outset signified to the Jews of Alexandria neither more nor less than the word 'Torah', and there is no ground for assuming that it did not also comprehend the oral traditions, which were not written down. However, in the course of the constant contact with Greek culture, deviations occurred from the original conception of 'Oral Law', and at the same time a change took place in the actual attitude to the significance and meaning of Torah.

The term תורה שבעל פה *Tôrā she-bĕ-ʿal-pe* ['Oral Law'] first appears in the story about the proselyte who asked Shammai 'How many *Tôrôt* have you?' and the latter answered 'Two: the Written Torah and the Oral Torah'.[19] It is similarly related that Rabban Gamaliel gave the same reply to the general Agnitus.[20] This answer given to Gentiles who were candidates for conversion is evidence of the fact that they knew that alongside the Written Torah was to be found 'the tradition of the fathers' and apparently they also knew that this 'tradition of the fathers' was regarded as Torah. Otherwise the question 'How many *Tôrôt* have you?' is incomprehensible. The important point in the answer that was given is that the oral tradition is also Torah. The reply contains not the slightest indication that the two *Tôrôt* were differently evaluated. 'Just as you have accepted the one in faith so accept also the other in faith', said Hillel to the proselyte.[21] The tradition of the fathers is Torah. But at the same time it is clear that the term the 'Oral Torah' has not the signification of a Torah that preceded the Written Torah and transcends it in value, as is the case in the concept ἄγραφος νόμος — the Unwritten Law. For the unwritten law is in fact 'a law not given' by a divine or human lawgiver, but one that exists like nature, and it is of no consequence whether it was or was not written down, whereas the distinctive character of the 'Oral Torah' lies in the fact that it was not put in writing, yet it is also, like the written Torah, not a natural law, but one that was given, be its provisions fences made by the Men of the Great Synagogue and their successors, or interpretations given at Sinai, as R. Akiba held. Philo accepted the Greek view and identified himself with it. In his exposition of the verse 'Thou shalt not remove thy neighbour's landmark, which they of old have set' (Deuteronomy xix 14) he states: 'Now this law, we may consider, applies not merely to allotments and boundaries of land in order to eliminate covetousness but also to the safeguarding of ancient customs. For customs are unwritten laws (ἄγραφοι νόμοι), the decisions approved by men of old, not inscribed on monuments nor on leaves of paper, which the moth destroys, but on the souls of those who are partners in the same citizenship. For children ought to inherit from their parents, besides their property, ancestral customs which they were reared in and have lived with even from the cradle, and not despise them because they have been handed down without written record. Praise cannot be duly given to one who obeys the written laws, since he acts under the admonition of restraint and the fear of punishment. But he who faithfully observes the unwritten deserves commendation, *since the virtue which he displays is freely willed*' (*De spec. legibus*, iv, 149). Most important is the conclusion: the 'unwritten law' is kept voluntarily. As Yitzhak Heinemann has shown,[22] Philo's statement is derived from Aristotle's *Rhetoric*, despite its being based on a verse in Deuteronomy, and not withstanding that the exegetical tradition of the verse relative to the Torah was known in Palestine. The word ὅρος, 'boundary', whose signification also comprised, as we know, decision, rule, and canon[23], provided Philo with the opportunity for his exposition, just as the Hebrew 'Thou shalt not remove

(תסיג *tassîg*) thy neighbour's landmark' brought to mind the סיג *sĕyāg* ['fence'], and led to the teaching: 'Whence do we learn that one who interchanges the words of R. Eliezer for those of R. Joshua etc. transgresses a negative commandment? For Scripture teaches "Thou shalt not remove thy neighbour's boundary" ' (*Sifre Deuteronomy*, § 188, p. 227). But the very comparison of the two expositions underlines the difference between them. The Tannaitic Midrash does not speak of 'laws inscribed on the soul', but of the words of the Sages. The prohibition discovered by the Sages in this verse enjoins accuracy in giving the names of those who transmit the Halakhot and forbids us to change them, while Philo in his interpretation equates ἄγραφος παράδοσις with ἄγραφος νόμος and approximates it to the connotation it bore in his environment.[24]

The νόμος comes close to being φύσις. The higher law cannot be opposed to nature, as Aristotle taught. The author of the Hellenistic homily, called *IV Maccabees* (v 7), which represents a kind of synthesis of Judaism and Hellenism, not only attributed to Antiochus the argument 'For most excellent is the meat of this animal [the pig] which nature has graciously bestowed upon us, and why should you abominate it?', but Eleazar's answer was made in the same spirit: 'Therefore do we eat no unclean meat; for believing our Law to be given by God, we know also that the Creator of the world, as a Lawgiver, feels for us according to our nature' (*ibid.* v. 25). This conception of 'Torah' not only opened the way to allegorical exegesis, but also to the conclusion that the allegorical interpretation is the primary one, since it enables us to prove that *quod scriptum est* cannot be opposed to nature.[25] The dictum of R. Eleazar b. Azariah was against such a view: 'How do we know that a man should not say "I have no wish to wear mingled stuff [שעטנז *sha'aṭnēz*], I have no desire to eat the flesh of swine" ... but (he should say) "I do desire it, (but) what can I do, seeing that my Father in Heaven forbade it" ' (*Sifra*, Qedoshim, ch. xi). The Torah is not according to Nature, whereas Hellenistic Judaism transformed the Written Law into ἄγραφος νόμος, an unwritten law according to the inner meaning of the concept. At the same time the opposite development occurred in the understanding of the term 'Oral Law' in the Rabbinic world up to the time of the destruction of the Temple. The tradition of the fathers, the enactments, and the decrees became Torah alongside the Written Torah. It was not the exegetical dialectic nor the discussion that decided, but the authority of the institutions. The institutional character of the ancient Halakha is confirmed also by the two features that characterize it — the absence of controversy and anonymity. The expositions of the Scribes were recognized as Halakhot only in so far as they corroborated and validated traditions and enactments, testimonies and practices in the possession of the Sages.[26] But these, too, formed only a part of the Oral Law, which was indeed Torah, but contrary to the view of the Sadducees — who had 'a Book of Decrees written down and deposited' — it was forbidden to write it and to turn it into a Written Torah. The Written Law remained unchanged. Its interpretations and expositions formed the instruction of this Torah in all its parts. Its teaching embraced the law 'If an ox gored a cow' (*M. Bava Qamma* v, 1), the 'Work of the Chariot', the rules of defilement applying to the shield 'with which they sport in the arena' (*M. Kelim* xxiv 1), and those affecting the head-net 'of a harlot' (*ibid.* xvi), as well as the Halakhot relating to repentance and atonement.

Our account of the development of the conception of Torah, both that of the Tannaim and that of Hellenistic Judaism, may serve as a background to the understanding of the antithesis that Paul established between the letter (γράμμα) and the spirit (πνεῦμα), which aimed at the annulment of the Torah, 'For when the Gentiles, which have not the law, do by nature what the law requires, are a law unto themselves, even though they do not have the law. They show that what the law requires is written on their hearts...' (Romans ii 14). He addresses himself also to those who know the Torah, using the metaphor 'the law being dead', and hence 'We are discharged from the law, dead to that which held us captive, so that we serve not under the old written code but in the new life of the spirit' (*ibid.* vii 6). It is difficult to find in Tannaitic literature a dictum more opposed to Paul's teaching than that of Matthew[27] 'For truly, I say to you, till heaven and earth pass away, not an iota, not a dot, will pass from the law until all is accomplished. Whoever then relaxes one of the least of these commandments and teaches men so, shall be called least in the kingdom of heaven.'[28] It is not the observance of the precepts that is spoken of here, for in that case it is difficult to explain this wording even from a polemical aspect. At any rate the Tannaim were more moderate; R. Joshua said: 'If a man learnt two Halakhot in the morning and two in the evening, and the rest of the day he is engaged in his work, it is accounted unto him as though he had fulfilled the whole of the Torah.' R. Eleazar of Modiʿim said the same thing concerning 'Whoever transacts his business honestly and is popular with his fellow creatures' (*Mekhilta*, Wa-yissaʿ, i, p. 158, and *ibid.* ii, p. 161); and it is also reported in the name of R. Akiba that 'If a man fulfils one precept, it is as though he fulfilled them all' (*T.B. Sanhedrin* 81a; *Midrash Tehillim* xv, 3).[29] Hence it seems that Matthew's statement actually refers to the annulling in principle of the obligatory character of the Torah and precepts, including the instruction of others to do likewise, in the sense: 'If a man says, I accept upon me the whole Torah except this one thing', we apply to him the verse 'Because he hath despised the word of the Lord, and hath broken His commandments' (*Sifre Be-midbar*, § 112, p. 121).

Subsequently Jesus, too, makes statements in his sermon that go beyond the Written Torah. The formula is 'It was said... but I say to you'. 'It was said' refers to what is expressly stated in the Torah, 'but I say to you' marks his 'expansion', the outcome of the inner interpretation. The parallel text to that of Matthew is the Baraita of R. Ishmael: 'With respect to three passages the Halakha overrides the Scriptural instruction... *the Torah said* (the bill of divorcement should be written) on a "book" [i.e. parchment], *whereas the Halakha said* "on anything" (detached)', etc.[30] Sometimes the breaking of the law is in effect its observance, as R. Joḥanan and Resh Laqish taught when they expounded the verse ' "It is time to work for the Lord, they have made void Thy law" (Psalms cxiv 126), saying: Rather let a letter of the Torah be uprooted than the Torah should be forgotten in Israel'[31]; and their words are but another version of the interpretation contained in the dictum of Hillel the Elder: 'when you see that the Torah is forgotten in Israel and none pay attention to her, gather in [i.e. be withdrawn in your study], as it is said "It is time to work for the Lord, they have made void Thy law." '

There is not much point in citing parallels, be it from Rabbinic teaching or from other legal systems, that distinguish between 'the evidences of the Rabbis responses to the claims made by Paul (about annulling the effects of the law)

attribute of justice' and 'the attribute of mercy' or 'beyond the strict requirement of the law', or between λόγος and διάνοια, in order to explain Paul's standpoint. The question confronting him was not that of 'the spirit of the law', or of justice in antithesis to law. He went beyond the contrast between spirit and content, and when he declared 'For the letter kills, but the spirit gives life' (II Corinthians iii 6), he was not thinking of inner interpretation,[32] which reveals the letter, 'For the Lord is the Spirit, and where the Spirit of the Lord is, there is freedom' (*ibid.*, v. 17). Although he does not say that the Torah is sin, yet he declares that 'Apart from the law sin lies dead' (Romans vii 7–9). The time had arrived for the annulment of the Torah, 'For Christ is the end of the law, that every one who has faith may be justified' (*ibid.* x 4). It was the Messianic fulfilment that led Paul to arrive at the last conclusion: the annulment of the Torah. With the advent of the Messiah man is no longer in need of being liberated from sin and from thoughts of the flesh with the help of the spiritual-allegorical interpretation of the Torah. Freedom came to him from the power of faith in the Messiah. The function of the allegorical interpretation was only to provide corroboration and testimony to this fundamental fact.

Do we find any reactions in the Rabbinic world, be it to the extreme allegorization of the Torah and the reduction of its precepts to nullity, or to the eschatological reasons advanced for the abolition of the Torah? It seems that such reactions not only are to be found, but they also show that the alien, revolutionary approaches were not, despite the struggle against them, without influence, and that it behoves us to trace their effects. Our first information about the Sages' taking a stand against the Christians and about any contact with them dates from the time of Rabban Gamaliel of Jabneh. Indeed, we possess a dictum from this period that seems to be a reaction to Paul's teaching. The contemporary of Rabban Gamaliel, R. Eleazar of Modiʿim, said: 'If a man profanes the hallowed things, and despises the festivals, and gives (a wrong) interpretation of the Torah [Hebrew: מגלה פנים בתורה *mĕgalle pānîm ba-Tôrā*, literally: 'discloses a face (= aspect, meaning) in the Torah'], and makes void the covenant of Abraham our father, and puts his fellow to shame, even though he has good works to his credit, he has no share in the world to come.'[33] The expression *mĕgalle pānîm ba-Tôrā* is difficult and has received many interpretations,[34] because its simple meaning is 'one who discloses (= gives) an interpretation of (a passage of) the Torah, and this cannot be regarded as wrong. In order to overcome this difficulty there have been added in the Mishna the words 'which is not according to the Halakha'.[35] Although they are an addition, yet this interpretation alone shows us the correct way of understanding the expression, which is not to be dissociated from the other parts of the dictum: the interpreter of the Torah, referred to by the Mishna, is one who expounds the Torah in an allegorical sense, leading to the annulment of the festivals, the contemning of the hallowed things, and the abolition of the covenant of Abraham. Such an interpreter of the Torah has no portion in the world to come. Do not the words read like a riposte to Paul's teaching: 'Nor is true circumcision something external and physical. He is a Jew who is one inwardly, and real circumcision is a matter of the heart, spiritual and not literal' (Romans ii 28–29)? Although Philo polemizes against the extreme allegorists, who likewise explained circumcision symbolically and contented themselves with its inner significance (*De migratione*, 92), yet it appears from Philo's own statement that these were but few (*ibid.* 93), and certainly did not constitute a sect or a movement.[36] It is very doubtful if R. Eleazar of Modiʿim knew anything about them. On the other hand, it is probable that he, like Rabban Gamaliel, was acquainted with the Judeo-Christians against whom it was enacted that they should be expressly mentioned in one of the blessings of the Eighteen Benedictions, which includes an imprecation against those who withdraw from the Community[37]; it is to them that the expressions 'who makes void the covenant of Abraham our father and gives a (wrong) interpretation of the Torah' refer.[38] In the Baraita attached to the Mishna in Sanhedrin that enumerates those who have no share in the world to come, it is also stated: 'They added to them one who casts off the yoke [of Judaism], and one who makes void the covenant, and one who gives a (wrong) interpretation of the Torah.'[39] The verse 'Because he hath despised the word of the Lord, and hath broken His commandment' is expounded in the *Sifre* thus: ' "Because he hath despised the word of the Lord" — this refers to one who gives a (wrong) interpretation of the Torah; "and hath broken His commandment" — this means one who makes void the covenant of flesh' (*Sifre, Be-midbar*, § 112, p. 121). The contemptuous attitude adopted by the Christians towards the Temple and its hallowed things and towards the observance of the Sabbath and the festivals led to the association of offenders in these two respects with the 'one who makes the covenant void'. The expression 'He who puts his fellow to shame' is wanting in the recensions of the Mishna, and also in the parallel sources[40]; and even in the texts in which it occurs its position is not fixed,[41] and it is not impossible that the original dictum of R. Eleazar of Modiʿim also did not include 'one who profanes the hallowed things and despises the festivals'. The sting in the saying lies in the denial of a share in the world to come to 'one who gives a (wrong) interpretation of the Torah, and one who makes void the covenant', whereas Paul connects the beginning of the New Order specifically with (wrong) interpretation of the Torah and with the abolition of the covenant.

Is there to be found in Rabbinic teaching prior to Paul a basis for the view that the advent of the Messiah would lead to the annulment of the Torah, or to its exchange for a new Torah? This question is the subject of much discussion in the scholarly literature, both that dealing with Paul and that which treats of the problems of Jewish eschatology, and even special monographs have been devoted to the theme.[42] There are actually dicta that ostensibly do not belong to the subject and yet shed more light on it than sayings that speak expressly of 'the annulment of the precepts', and which are frequently cited, like the statement of Rabban Simeon b. Gamaliel 'When a man dies, he is exempt from (the observance of) the precepts.'[43] The Tanna does not come to inculcate a new teaching — namely that a dead man is exempt from keeping the commandments — but seeks to explain by this fact, which is well known — as Paul states — to all who have knowledge of the Law (Romans vii 1), the Halakha that we desecrate the Sabbath for the sake of a living person, but not for the dead. Rabban Simeon b. Gamaliel's statement is without any eschatological significance; on the other hand the words 'that the law is binding on a person only during his life' serve in Paul's mouth as the proem of his homily that with the death of Christ the authority of the Torah had ceased.

The oldest source pertaining to the subject of the Torah in the End of Days already clearly shows the difference in viewpoint between the close of the Temple era and that of Usha. 'R. Joshua said: I have received as a tradition from Rabban Joḥanan b. Zakkai, who heard it from his teacher, and his teacher from his teacher, as a Halakha given to Moses at Sinai, that Elijah will not come to pronounce unclean or clean, to remove (families) afar or to bring (them) nigh, but to remove afar those (families) that were brought nigh by violence and to bring nigh those (families) that were removed afar by violence... The like of these Elijah will come to pronounce unclean or clean, to remove afar or to bring nigh... R. Simeon said: To compose disputes, and the Sages said: Neither to remove afar nor to bring nigh, but to make peace in the world, as it is written "Behold I will send you Elijah the prophet... and he shall turn the heart of the fathers to the children and the heart of the children to their fathers." '[44] The starting point for Rabban Joḥanan b. Zakkai's statement was the passage at the end of Malachi concerning the mission of Elijah 'before the coming of the great and terrible day', and he regarded the purpose of the prophet's mission to be the imposition of his authority on the violent men who, in matters of family lineage, had been accustomed to remove afar and to bring nigh arbitrarily. This testimony of R. Joshua concerning Rabban Joḥanan b. Zakkai's exposition is linked to his other testimony that the widow of (a man belonging to) a family of doubtful purity — that is, a family of which a suspected *ḥālāl* [the male issue of a priest's illegitimate connection, who as such, is unfit for priesthood] was a member [and who might have been the widow's husband] — was eligible for marriage to a priest. To this Rabban Gamaliel reacted: 'We accept your evidence, but what shall we do, for Rabban Joḥanan b. Zakkai decreed that courts should not be set up for such cases? The priests would hearken to you if you ruled to remove afar, but not (if you ruled) to bring nigh.'[45] The words of the prophet 'And he shall turn the heart of the fathers to the children and the heart of the children to their fathers' are interpreted by the Tanna as referring to the settling of questions of family and peace. Modern commentators have also linked the verse to Malachi's rebuke (ii 11–15) to those who dealt treacherously with the wives of their youth and put them away.[46] The coming of Elijah is in no way connected with giving decisions and declaring doubtful cases permissible, but with imposing of authority to circumvent those who seek to undermine them. The reference, of course, is to the advent of Elijah before the coming of the Messiah, for in the world to come the question of family purity is not relevant. It is thus evident that R. Simeon's statement also has this period in view, but the task that he assigns to Elijah is different. In his opinion Elijah will come to decide which of the disputing Sages is right. At first there were no disagreements in Israel. One Torah went forth from the Chamber of Hewn Stone to all Israel, but when the Sanhedrin was abolished and the number of the disciples of Shammai and Hillel that did not wait sufficiently upon the scholars increased, the disputes in Israel multiplied (*Tosefta Sanhedrin* i, 1) 'and two Torahs were formed' (*Tosefta Soṭa* xiv, 9). This dictum is preceded there by a parallel saying 'When the proud [זהורי *zĕhûrê*] of heart increased, the disputes multiplied in Israel and became two Torahs.'[47] Although Rabban Joḥanan b. Zakkai attempted to organize anew the centre in Jabneh and Rabban Gamaliel aspired to invest the Patriarch and his court [*Bêt Dîn*] with decisive authority, yet these efforts did not suffice to renew the previous position and to restore 'the crown to its former estate'. R. Akiba drew the necessary inference from the changed circumstances and chose the way of his teachers, Nahum of Gimzo and Neḥunya b. Haqana, and weighed down the scales in favour of untrammeled freedom of exposition. On the one hand, Halakhot that originated in traditions, customs, acts, and testimonies found their validation in Scripture, and on the other, 'the niceties of Rabbinical exegesis and what the scribes are due to originate' had already been handed down — it was held — to Moses at Sinai and are only tradition. Even with regard to a certain formulation of a dispute between the School of Shammai and the School of Hillel, R. Eleazar b. ʿAzariah took an oath, which was worded as follows: 'I swear by the Torah! These are the things that were said to Moses at Sinai.'[48] R. Akiba incorporated the Oral Law in the Written Law, in its words, and in its letters. It is in this sense that his exposition in the *Sifra* is to be understood (Be-ḥuqqotay, viii, p. 112 c): ' "These are the statutes and ordinances and Torahs" — this teaches that two Torahs were given to Israel, one in writing and the other orally. Said R. Akiba: Did

Israel then have (only) two Torahs [literally: 'laws']? Behold many Torahs were given to Israel: "This is the Torah of the burnt-offering", "This is the Torah of the meal-offering", "This is the Torah of the guilt-offering", "This is the Torah of the sacrifice of peace-offerings", "This is the Torah: When a man dieth in a tent... in Mount Sinai by the hand of Moses" — this teaches us that the Torah with its Halakhot and details and interpretations were given by Moses at Sinai.' The giving of the Torah at Sinai is renewed, as it were, every day through the study of the Torah and its expositions. The verse 'And all the people perceived the thunderings' (Exodus xx 15) was interpreted by R. Akiba thus: 'They saw a word of fire issuing from the mouth of the Almighty and hewn out upon the tablets' (*Mekhilta de-R. Ishmael*, Ba-ḥodesh, ix, p. 235). R. Akiba's disciple, Ben ʿAzzai, stated concerning himself: 'I thread words of the Torah onto the prophets and words of the Prophets onto the Hagiographa, and the words of the Torah are as joyful as when they were given at Sinai.' The fact that fire flamed around him when he expounded words of Torah he explained as follows: 'Primarily when they [the words of the Torah] were given at Sinai they were given only in fire, (as it is written), "and the mountain burned with fire unto the heart of heaven." '[49] While Ben ʿAzzai transferred the experience of the Revelation at Mount Sinai to the study of the Torah in his days, Rabbi found that the verse ' "And all the people perceived the thunderings" came to tell us the praise of Israel, to wit, that when they all stood before Mount Sinai to receive the Torah, they heard the Divine word and expounded it' (*Mekhilta*, *ibid.*). The Revelation included not only the Torah and its interpretations, but also the bestowal of the authority to interpret. In accordance with this conception, Rav was able to sum up the view of R. Akiba and his disciples concerning the Oral Law with the following extraordinary story about Moses: When he ascended to Heaven and the Holy One, blessed be He, showed him R. Akiba sitting and expounding, Moses did not understand what he was saying, but nevertheless 'his mind was set at ease' when he heard that, in reply to a question of his disciples: 'Master, how do you know this?' R. Akiba answered: 'It is a Halakha of Moses given at Sinai' (*T.B. Menaḥot* 29b).

However, the freedom and multiplicity of the expositions cast doubt on the unity of the one Torah, for the disputes increased and the authority to decide declined. R. Simeon, the disciple of R. Akiba, insisted on laying down clear limits and fixed times [with reference to ploughing in the year preceding the Seventh Year], so that it could not be said: 'You give the law for each man into his own hand' (*M. Shevi'it* ii, 1). To his colleagues he said 'All the standard measures of the Torah are fixed' (*Tosefta Menaḥot* xiii, 8). Although he cited as examples of Torah standards forty *se'ah* for ritual immersion, and the size of an egg for uncleanness of food, that is to say, measures that are not explicitly stated in the Torah, but were accepted by the Sages as a whole, yet in regard to matters that were in dispute among the scholars themselves the fear remained 'that no regulation of the Torah would be like another' (*Tosefta 'Eduyot* i, 1, p. 454). Despite all efforts to achieve unity it was none other than R. Simeon who came to the conclusion that only Elijah would compose the differences of opinion and integrate the Torah again into a single whole. R. Simeon's statement is not to be equated with those passages in the Mishna and the Talmuds that declare 'Let it remain (undecided) until the coming of Elijah' or 'When Elijah comes he will say'; there Elijah is not depicted as deciding between different opinions, but as revealing the true position with regard to a certain set of facts of which human beings have no knowledge.[50] A similar instance is cited in the Book of Ezra (ii 62–63), where it is stated that the priests who were excluded as unclean from the priesthood had not found the record of their genealogy. 'And the governor said to them that they were not to partake of the most holy food, until a priest with Urim and Thummim should arise.'[51] R. Simeon's dictum, however, is to be understood in the light of the viewpoint of those Sages, like R. Eliezer b. Hyrcanus and others, who did not discount the possibility of the vouchsafement of a heavenly revelation, whether in the form of a *Bat Qôl* [Heavenly Voice] or a prophet, that would appear and decide in matters concerning which we could not, and never would, reach a conclusion by the force of our argumentation and reasoning; in the same way the Sages transmitted Halakhot that had been promulgated and enacted by the prophets through the power of their prophecy. Nay more, the prophets were invested with the authority to revoke temporarily a law of the Torah. The verse 'A prophet will the Lord thy God raise up unto thee, from the midst of thee, of thy brethren, like unto me; unto him ye shall hearken' (Deuteronomy xviii 15) was expounded thus: 'Even if he says to thee: Transgress temporarily one of the precepts ordained by the Torah, as did Elijah on Mount Carmel, hearken unto him' (*Sifre Deuteronomy*, § 175). On the other hand, R. Joshua and those who followed his views were opposed to the intervention of heavenly powers in deciding matters of Halakha. The Torah is not in Heaven, and we do not hearken to a *Bat Qôl*. In accordance with this standpoint the rule was formulated: ' "These are the commandments" — this implies that no prophet is permitted to originate any new ruling from now on',[52] and the Amora Rav inferred from this doctrine that in the hereafter, too, prophecy would not be able to intervene in Halakhic matters, and should Elijah come and decide against accepted custom, he would not be listened to. Matters of Halakha do not depend on the decision of the prophet who brings tidings (*T.B. Yevamot* 102a; *T.B. ʿAvoda Zara* 36a).

In the light of what has been stated above, it can clearly be seen that Paul found no existing view concerning the abolition of the Torah or its replacement by a new Torah in the Messianic era. At most a prophet could claim that by virtue of his prophecy he came to annul, as a temporary measure, a law of the Torah, or to promulgate an enactment, or to establish a custom that was prophetically revealed to him. But such was not the claim of Paul. In the person of Jesus as Messiah and redeemer Paul saw the fulfilment of prophecy and the realization of the Messianic promise: 'For Christ is the end of the law, and only he that believes in him shall be justified' (Romans x 4). Undoubtedly, Paul's remark about 'the end of the law' is bound up with his Messianic outlook. But this Messianic doctrine was moulded by his view that 'no human being will be justified in his sight by works of the law, since through the law comes knowledge of sin' (*ibid.* iii 20). His attitude to man and his concept of sin are the source of his antinomianism.[53]

Traces of Christian views on the place of the Torah in the new faith are to be found in the teaching of the Tannaim and Amoraim, but here, too, the difference between the reactions at the end of the first century and the beginning of the second and those of a later period is conspicuous. The first response in our possession also dates from the time of Rabban Gamaliel. In the neighbourhood of his sister,

Imma Shalom, the wife of R. Eliezer, there lived a philosopher, who also acted as a judge and had the reputation of not taking bribes. They wished to play a hoax on him and to put him to the test. Imma Shalom brought him a golden lamp and subsequently said to him: 'We wish to divide our (deceased) father's estate'; he replied 'Divide!' 'Said he (Rabban Gamaliel) to him: "It is written in the Torah that where there is a son, a daughter does not inherit." The latter replied: "Since the day that you were exiled from your land, the Law of Moses has been revoked and the Evangel has taken its place, wherein it is written: a son and a daughter inherit equally." ' The following day Rabban Gamaliel gave him a Libyan ass, and when he appeared before him, 'He said to them: "Look at the end of the Evangel, where it is written: 'I have come not to abstract from the Law of Moses, but I have come to add (thereto)'; and therein it is written: 'Where there is a son, a daughter shall not inherit.' " ' When Imma Shalom cried 'Let thy light shine forth like a lamp', Rabban Gamaliel said 'The ass has come and extinguished the lamp.'[54] Ninety years ago Güdemann showed[55] that we have here a sarcastic parody of one of the λόγια according to the Hebrews, which was used also by the author of Matthew (v 15–16): 'Nor do men light a lamp and put it under a bushel (τὸν μόδιον), but on a stand, and it gives light to all in the house. Let your light so shine before men.' This saying gave rise to the motif 'The ass has come and knocked the lamp over' by substituting חמור *ḥămôr* ['ass'] for חומר *ḥômer* ['bushel'].[56] But of greater interest to us is the ambivalent attitude to the Torah, which finds expression in the story that confirms the view that in the ancient Christian community they had not yet freed themselves from the yoke of the Torah, and seemingly they were afraid to draw inferences in the spirit of Paul's preaching; this is the background to the passage in Matthew (v 17–19).[57] The Jews saw no need to engage in a serious controversy with the New Testament and were content to underscore the hesitancy and inconsistency of those who professed it. Hence it is not surprising that we find no signs of struggle against Paulinian ideas, and certainly not of the influence of his views, before the end of the Tannaitic era and the beginning of the Amoraic period, that is to say, until the ideological crystallization of Christianity in the spirit of Paul's teaching and its popular expansion and diffusion. The following exposition of R. Joshua b. Levi is directed, apparently, against Paul's view that the Torah has been superseded by grace: 'To what do these twenty-six (verses of) "Give thanks" correspond? To the twenty-six generations that the Holy One, blessed be He, created in His world, and did not give them the Torah, but sustained them by His grace.'[58] There was need of grace so long as the Torah had not been given.

Development occurred in the conception of the Torah in two directions. On the one hand the Torah was completely removed from all dependence on supernatural forces — on prophecy inspired by the Holy Spirit, or on a *Bat-Qôl*. Not only was a Prophet not permitted to originate (laws), as several Tannaim stated, but R. Isaac and Resh Laqish said that all that the Prophets prophesied they received from Sinai. For the Voice that was heard on Mount Sinai already included the words of the Prophets throughout the generations, and only when the time arrived for proclaiming a given prophecy and the generation was fit for it to be made public, did there arise the Prophet assigned to the task, who had received the appropriate prophecy on Mount Sinai. Hence there is nothing really new in the utterances of the Prophets; the words existed from of old, and it is their publication that occurs at different times. But not only 'did all the Prophets receive their prophecy from Sinai, but also the Sages that have arisen in every generation received their respective teaching from Sinai.'[59] Similarly R. Joshua b. Levi taught: 'Bible, Mishna, Talmud, and Haggada, even what a senior disciple is due to teach in the presence of his master, was already stated to Moses at Sinai.'[60] The sole difference between the utterances of the Prophets and those of the Sages is that the former may be written down, whereas the latter must remain oral, and this distinction does not necessarily favour the former. Only Israel's sinfulness caused the Prophets to appear, as R. Ada b. R. Ḥanina taught: 'Had not Israel sinned, they would have been given only the Five Books of the Torah, and also the Book of Joshua, which describes the disposition of the Land of Israel (among the tribes). What would the reason for this be? "For in much wisdom is much vexation." '[61] If only they had listened to the words of the Holy One, blessed be He, they would not have needed the words of the Prophets. But the Oral Law is not so. The expositions of the Sages possess decisive authority and deserve at least the same place in the scale of religious values as the Written Torah, and in truth transcend it. According to R. Joḥanan the covenant was made at Mount Sinai only on account of the Oral Teaching (*T.B. Giṭṭin* 60b; *T.B. Shevuot* 39a). The dependence of the Written Law on the Oral Law is pungently expressed by R. Simeon b. Laqish: 'There are many verses that deserve to be burnt, yet they are basic parts of the Torah',[62] that is to say, there are verses that appeai to their readers to be unnecessary and need never have been written in the Torah, but the Sages are able to show that they are essential elements of the Torah, 'and important concepts derive from them.'

R. Samuel b. Naḥman, who was one of the leading Amoraim of Eretz-Israel in the middle of the third century, taught: 'Oral [בפה *bĕ-fe*, literally 'by mouth'] laws have been proclaimed, and written laws have been proclaimed and we cannot tell which of these is more precious; but since it is written, "For in accordance with [על פי *ʿal pî* literally 'by the mouth of'] these words I have made a covenant with thee and with Israel", we may infer that the oral precepts are more precious' (*T.P. Pe'a* ii, 4, p. 17a). This dictum intimates that primarily the covenant is based on the Oral Law. But the reason for the preference to be given to the Oral Torah was differently explained by one of the last of the Palestinian Amoraim. 'R. Judah bar Shalom stated: When the Holy One, blessed be He, said to Moses "Write down!", Moses asked for the Mishna to be in writing. But because the Holy One, blessed be He, foresaw that the Gentiles would translate the Torah and read it in Greek, and thereupon they would declare "We are Israel", and so far the scales would be even, so the Holy One, blessed be He, said to the nations: "You aver that you are My children? I cannot tell; only they who possess My arcana (מסטורין *misṭôrîn*) are My children." Which are these?—the Mishna.'[63] It is clear that this dictum explains the superiority of the Oral Torah as an answer to the claims of Christianity following upon Paul's statement concerning the Church as the true heir of Israel, since it is the son of the free woman, while Israel according to the flesh is at most the son of the bondwoman (Galatians iii 26, iv 21; Romans ii 28). The Fathers of the Christian Church, from Justin to Augustine, claimed that the Book of Books is no longer the property and heritage of the Jews.[64] The authors of the Apostolic writings and the Church Fathers based

MB

most of their teachings on passages from the Prophets, whom they regarded as their spiritual ancestors. Contrariwise, the Amoraim came and elevated the Sages of the Oral Torah to the level of the Prophets and even gave the former precedence over the latter. At the close of the third century R. Avdimi of Haifa declared: 'Since the destruction of the Temple, prophecy was taken away from the Prophets and given to the Sages' (*T.B. Bava Batra* 12a). The underlying reason for this view was transmitted at the beginning of the fourth century in the name of R. Tanḥum b. R. Ḥiyya: 'To what are a Prophet and Elder comparable? To a king who sent two of his agents σημαντήριον to a province. Concerning one he wrote: If he does not show you my seal and my signet, do not believe him! Concerning the other he wrote: Although he does not show you my seal and my signet, believe him! Thus, too, it is written of the Prophet: "and gives thee a sign or a wonder" (Deuteronomy xiii 2); but here (it is stated): "according to the instructions which they give thee" (*ibid.* xvii 11).'[65] As a result of this approach they denied the Prophets who were active in the past the possibility of initiating or amending anything in the conduct of life by Divine injunction, and if we find that innovations and enactments were ascribed to them, these were not only given at Mount Sinai together with all 'that a senior disciple was due to originate', but just as the disciple innovates by dint of his reasoning, so, too, the Prophets established what they did as a result of their argumentation (*T.B. Temura* 16a); and even Elijah offered up sacrifices on a high place only after he had expounded a given Scripture, but not by Divine injunction.[66] The teachings of prophecy are included in the Torah, and they, too, are Torah. Hence the Amoraim were able to polemize against sectarian groups that belittled the utterances of the Prophets. Evidence of such a polemic has survived in an anonymous homily: 'When Asaph came, he began to say: "Give ear, O my people, to my Torah" (Psalms lxxviii 1)... Said Israel to Asaph: "Is there then another Torah that you say 'Give ear, O my people, to my Torah'? We have already received it at Mount Sinai!" He answered them: "The transgressors of Israel say that the Prophets and the Hagiographa are not Torah and that they do not believe in them, as it is stated: 'Neither have we hearkened to the voice of the Lord our God, to walk in His laws, which he set before us by His servants the prophets' (Daniel ix 10) — thus we see that the Prophets and Hagiographa are Torah. Hence it is said 'Give ear, O my people, to my Torah.'" '[67] It seems that the homilist's polemic was directed against a Judeo-Christian sect that, although it was devoted to the 'New Testament', identified Jesus with Moses, but in its struggle against the antinomistic orientation of Paul refused to recognize the Prophets, who came after Moses and whose words were used by Paul and Barnabas and their followers to reject the Torah.[68] It is noteworthy that the author of the *Epistle of Barnabas* proceeds in the opposite direction. He endeavours to raise the teachings of the Torah to the plane of prophecy and to prove that the statutes upon which Paul vented his wrath are really words of prophecy, which allude to the life and work of Jesus.[69] Against both these views the homilist that we have cited argues that the Prophets and Hagiographa are Torah. The three of them form a threefold Torah. The compass and bounds of this Torah, as well as its significance, were determined by the Sages. It was already stated in an ancient Mishna that 'The laws concerning the Sabbath, Festal-offerings and acts of trespass are as mountains hanging by a hair, for they have scant Scriptural basis but many laws' (*M. Ḥagiga* i, 8), and the greatest of the last Babylonian Amoraim, Rav Ashi, following his predecessors, declared: 'Do not lightly regard a גזרה שוה *gĕzērā shāwā* [an analogy drawn between two laws based on verbal congruities in Scriptural verses], for the cases to which death by stoning applies are essential laws of the Torah, yet Scripture teaches (most of them) by *gĕzērā shāwā*' (*T.B. Keritot* 5a). Even Halakhot that were not based on verses were designated by the Amoraim 'Torah law'.[70] The realization of the difference between written and oral regulations finds expression in the appraisal that 'The Sages safeguarded their own enactments more than those of the Torah'[71] and in the hyperbolical statements concerning the supreme authority of the expositions and decisions of the Rabbis. The Almighty Himself is bound by them. God sits and occupies Himself with the section of the Red Heifer, and He cites a Halakha in the name of R. Eliezer, despite the astonishment of Moses, who cries: 'Sovereign of the universe, Thou dost hold in Thy power the creatures of heaven and earth, yet Thou dost sit and cite a Halakha in the name of a human being!' (*Pesiqta de-R. Kahana*, Para, ed. Mandelbaum, p. 73).

The Lord sits and recites the dispute between R. Abiathar and R. Jonathan, while Rabbah decides the controversy between God and the heavenly academy (*T.B. Giṭṭin* 6 b; *T.B. Bava Meṣiʿa* 86a). Nor is it surprising that to R. Akiba was attributed the dictum: 'Just as they debate Halakha on earth, so they debate Halakha in Heaven' (*Tanḥuma*, Exodus xviii).[72]

The Sages who professed these views allowed no possibility of change in the validity, compass, and nature of the Torah. The advent of the Messiah is incapable of altering anything therein, for 'It [the Torah] does not belong to [literally, 'is not in'] Heaven'. 'Moses warned them [i.e. Israel]: Say not another Moses will arise and bring us another Torah from Heaven. I declare to you now "It is not in Heaven" — nothing thereof was left in Heaven' (*Deuteronomy Rabba* viii, § 6). The expression 'another Moses' in this anonymous dictum is noteworthy, for its visualization of the Messiah as 'another Moses' was also likely to bring in its train the sequel that this 'other Moses' would bring another Torah. Actually Jesus was described as *Moses redivivus* or as *Moses novus*. However, these similitudes have their origin in Biblical similes and became a stereotyped motif in a considerable portion of the Messianic Haggadah.[73] It seems, therefore, that the homily that we have cited was directed against Messianic concepts that were current among the Rabbis, and to which the homilist was opposed. Underlying his exposition and those of the Amoraim that we have discussed so far is a Messianic conception not unlike that of the Sage Samuel, namely that 'the only difference between this world and the days of the Messiah will be (the termination of) the bondage of the kingdoms' (*T. B. Berakhot* 34b, and the parallel passages listed there). But there were Sages who envisaged the Messiah differently, and apparently their views concerning the Torah and the position occupied by prophecy were also different. Whereas Rav held that the world was created only for the sake of David, 'who would compose many hymns and praises (to God)' (Rashi), and Samuel was of the opinion that the creation was due to the merit of Moses 'who would receive the Torah' (*ibid.*), R. Joḥanan, on the other hand, considered that 'the world was created on account of the Messiah' (*T. B. Sanhedrin* 98b). Now R. Joḥanan testifies, concerning many a Halakha, that 'It was based on tradition deriving from Haggai,

Zechariah and Malachi', that is to say, that these laws were 'of the nature of prophecy and their plain reason is not known.'[74] It was he who said 'The rite of the willow-branch is an institution of the Prophets',[75] and the verse 'These words the Lord spoke unto all your assembly... with a great voice and it did not cease' (Deuteronomy v 19) he did not interpret like Resh Laqish 'that from it prophesied all the prophets that arose', but that 'One voice broke up into seven voices, and these were divided into seventy languages.'[76] On the other hand, he held: 'In all things if a prophet should say to you "Transgress the precepts of the Torah!" listen to him, except in the case of idolatry' (*T.B. Sanhedrin* 90a), and he left it to Elijah to come and elucidate passages of Scripture that we do not know how to interpret.[77] At the same time R. Joḥanan said 'The Prophets and the Hagiographa will be annulled, but the Five Books of the Torah will not be abolished' (*T.P. Megilla* i, 1, p. 70d). He did not disclose to us whether he meant the days of the Messiah or the world to come. At any rate it appears that he refers to a time when the prophetic promises will have been fulfilled and there will be no need for words of rebuke and comfort, in the spirit, as it were, of the dictum of one of the last of the Tannaim, R. Simeon b. Eleazar, whose exposition R. Joḥanan had heard in his youth (*T.P. Maʿasrot* i, 2, p. 48d): 'the days of the Messiah, when there will be neither merit nor guilt.'[78] R. Joḥanan was one of the transmitters of the dictum of the Tanna R. Menaḥem of Gallia [or Galatia], the contemporary of R. Simeon b. Eleazar: 'In the hereafter all the sacrifices will be abolished, but the thanksgiving offering will not be abolished; all prayers will be abolished, but thanksgiving will not be abolished.'[79] In a world where there is neither merit nor guilt there is no place for sacrifices, which are brought to make atonement for sins, nor for prayers for human needs. Nevertheless the Five Books of the Torah will not be annulled. R. Joḥanan's statement 'The generation in which the son of David will come the number of scholars will decrease...' is possibly based on the apocalyptic Baraita that contains an account of the septennium in which the son of David will come, and where it is said: '... In the third year there will be a great famine... and the Torah will be forgotten by Israel... in the fifth year there will be great abundance, and people will eat and drink and rejoice; the Torah will return to its pristine state and renew itself unto Israel.'[80] That means that the Torah, which will have been forgotten, will be restored to them. It is not stated here by whom this will be achieved, but in early Midrashim already the Messiah is allotted a role in the teaching of the Torah. A homily is transmitted in the name of the Rabbis on Genesis xlix 11: 'When he of whom it is written "Lowly, and riding upon an ass" etc. (Zechariah ix 9) comes, "he will wash his garments in wine", that is, he will compose for them Torah teachings; "and his vesture in the blood of grapes", that means, he will correct all their errors.' To this R. Ḥanin reacted by saying: 'Israel will have no need of king Messiah's teaching in the hereafter, for it is stated, "unto him shall the nations seek" (Isaiah xi 10) — but not Israel. In that case, why will king Messiah come, what will he come to do? — to gather the exiles of Israel and to give the Gentile Nations thirty commandments.'[81] The point about the thirty commandments is derived from Zechariah (ix 12), 'So they weighed for my hire thirty pieces of silver', which also serves as a basis for the thirty pieces of silver of Judas Iscariot (Matthew xxvii 9). Possibly the homilist wished to say that the Messiah will not come to remove the yoke of the commandments from Israel, but to impose their observance upon the Gentiles. The dictum of R. Ḥanin, who apparently held that God Himself would teach Torah to Israel in the world to come,[82] only serves to underscore the purpose of the Rabbis' homily. Concerning the Torah-instruction of the Messiah we are informed in another saying: 'The Torah that a man learns in this world is as nought compared with that of the Messiah' (*Ecclesiastes Rabba* xi, 8). The author of the dictum is mentioned in a parallel passage, which is, however, somewhat milder, and reads as follows: 'R. Hezekiah said in the name of R. Simon bar Zavdi: all the Torah that you learn in this world is as nought compared with that of the world to come, because in this world a man learns Torah and forgets, but in the hereafter lo, it is written (Jeremiah xxxi 33), "I will put My law in their inward parts" ' (*Ecclesiastes Rabba* ii, 1). It is difficult to regard the second part of the dictum, which begins with 'because', as an explanation of the first part; apparently it is another saying, which was attached here as an explanation,[83] while in truth its meaning is different. In asserting that the Torah of this world is as nought compared with the Torah of the world to come,

R. Simon was referring, as the commentators of the Midrash have also indicated,[84] to the quality of the Torah, in the sense of R. Avin's teaching 'The lowest form [נובלת *nôvelet*] of heavenly wisdom is Torah.'[85] The Torah that the Messiah would teach is heavenly wisdom, while the earlier Torah is like *nôvelet*, that is, fruit that drops from the tree before it has ripened. The Amoraim in the fourth century who created their vision of the Messianic era, and did not, like Samuel, regard it only as a time devoid of the bondage of the kingdoms, but gave it a Utopian and apocalyptic[86] character, came, as a result of these portrayals, to endow the Messiah also with authority to give decisions and expound Halakhot transcending the existing Torah. R. Simeon b. Judan describes a beast contest (κυνήγιον, literally: 'hunt') witnessed by the righteous in the hereafter, and in the course of it it is stated: 'Behemoth strikes Leviathan with his horns and slaughters him by piercing, and Leviathan hits Behemoth with his fins and tears him.' The Midrash makes the righteous ask in surprise 'Is this ritually correct slaughter?' and R. Abba bar Kahana attributes to God the answer: ' "For Torah shall go forth from Me" (Isaiah li, 4) — new Torah law [חידוש תורה *ḥiddush Tôrā*] shall come forth from Me.'[87] Although the 'hereafter' and Torah taught by the 'Holy One, blessed be He,' are spoken of here, yet in these Messianic legends the terms 'the days of the Messiah', 'the Garden of Eden', and 'the world to come' approximate to one another and the distinctions between them are blurred.[88]

Combined with the difference between the Torah that God and the Messiah will teach and the existing Torah, there is also a certain conception of the reasons underlying the precepts. Alongside commandments for which rational, historical, ethical, or utilitarian explanations can be adduced are to be found precepts for which no such reasons could be ascertained. The Tannaitic explanation, already ascribed to Rabban Joḥanan b. Zakkai, was that these commandments are (Divine) decrees, which may not be questioned, or argued against.[89] But there were Amoraim who were not satisfied with this answer and postulated the existence of esoteric reasons not only for the statutes and decrees, but also for precepts the grounds for which are apparently evident.[90] They held that the reasons for the law of the red heifer, which for others is a statute [i.e. a law for which there is no apparent explanation], the Lord had revealed to Moses. But if the motives underlying the Torah precepts remained hidden in this world, they were destined to be revealed in the world to come.[91] Not only are there concealed reasons for the commandments, but the letters of the Torah could also be combined differently from their present sequence. Rav said 'Bezalel knew how to combine the letters by which heaven and earth were created' (*T.B. Berakhot* 55a). The words of Job xxviii 13 'Man knoweth not the order thereof' were expounded by R. Eleazar thus: 'The sections of the Torah were not given in their proper order, for if they had been given in the correct order, any one reading them would be able to revive the dead and perform wonders; consequently the true arrangement of the Torah was concealed, but it is known to the Holy One, blessed be He, as it is said (Isaiah xliv 7) 'And who, as I, can proclaim and declare it and set it in order for Me' (*Midrash Psalms* iii, 2, p. 33). It follows from R. Eleazar's statement that the Torah in our possession cannot, in its present arrangement, be used for the working of miracles. The revelation of its original textual order is in the power of God and only He can divulge it. The Cabalists, however, attempted to decipher the esoteric structure of the Torah.[92] They did this by giving the words of the Sages a meaning that did not accord with their simple sense and original intent.[93] The reasons and intrinsic attributes of the Torah, which are not disclosed in this world, have been reserved for elucidation in the hereafter. The Torah, which the Almighty will teach the righteous Himself or through the medium of His Messiah, will be, from these aspects, 'a new Torah'. In the mystical Midrash *Otiyyot de-R. Akiba* ['The Letters of R. Akiba'] (*Bate Midrashot*, Pt. II, p. 367) it is stated: 'The Holy One, blessed be He, will sit in the hereafter in the Garden of Eden and expound the Torah, and all the righteous of the world will sit before Him, while the whole of the heavenly court will be upstanding. On the right of the Holy One, blessed be He, will be the sun and the planets, and on His left the moon and all the stars, and the Holy One, blessed be He, will expound before them the reasons of the new Torah that the Holy One, blessed be He, will give them through the Messiah.'

Those Sages who regarded the prophets of the past not only as reprovers and comforters, but also as teachers of Halakha under

Divine inspiration, and posited the possibility that the Mind of the Most High would continue to be revealed to human beings even in matters of jurisprudence and law, of ritual prohibition and permissibility, undoubtedly linked to their Messianic expectation the renewal of the Torah and the elucidation of its obscurities and inner reasons. Although this opened the way to an antinomistic spirit,[94] yet so long as the Messianic faith continued to be engrossed in its Utopian vision, there was no immediate danger. It in no way changed the attitude of the homilists and apocalyptists of the Messianic era to Torah and precept in the present, and they even occupied themselves with Halakhot whose observance was connected with the days of the Messiah in the spirit of 'Expound and receive reward!' (*T.B. Zevaḥim* 45a). Obviously the Amoraim who maintained that the Torah was completely free from the control of transcendental powers, and were extreme in their insistence on the independent existence of the Torah and the autonomy of its students, rejected out of hand the concept of change or mutation in Israel's attitude to the Torah in the Messianic epoch. It is entirely unnecessary to augment the existing Torah. In antithesis to the words of the Psalmist, who declared, without further interpretation, 'I have seen an end to every purpose; but Thy commandment is exceeding broad' (Psalms cxix 96), Rav Ḥisda transmitted, in the name of Mari bar Mar, a precise calculation of the size of the Torah in relation to the world. On the basis of Zechariah v 2 he calculated and found that 'The whole universe is one three-thousand-and-twentieth of the Torah.'[95] It is clear that the reference is to the Torah in our possession. In so far as the Torah was concerned, the days of the Messiah were in the eyes of the Sages an age when the Torah could be fulfilled in its entirety, and hence they continued to occupy themselves with the laws relating to the Temple and the holy things, and even decided Halakhot in respect of these subjects;[96] thus many enactments and Halakhot were explained in the light of the possibility that 'the Temple would soon be rebuilt.'[97] The two approaches existed side by side, and the express testimony for the annulment of the precepts in the hereafter has reached us with the addition of remarks by the other side: ' "The Lord permitteth forbidden things" [Psalms cxlvi 7, usually rendered: 'The Lord looseth the prisoners']. What is meant by "permitteth forbidden things"?

Some say: Every beast declared unclean in this world the Holy One, blessed be He, will declare clean in the hereafter... but others say: He will not permit them in the hereafter...' (*Midrash Psalms* cxlvi § 4, p. 535). So long as the Messianic expectation did not claim that it was in the process of being fulfilled, the two views — even if they were not integrated — could at least dwell in peace side by side. But when this claim was made, the clash came.

CHAPTER XIII

THE COMMANDMENTS

I. *Their Source and the Ways of Their Observance*

Despite all the expansion of meaning that the term 'Torah' underwent in Rabbinic literature, the precept remained its basic element; without commandments there could be no Torah. The spectrum of relationships between God and the individual Jew or the Jewish people, as it emerges from the Bible, is closely linked to the theme of the precept. God's first revelation to man is marked by the *commandment* 'And the Lord God commanded the man, saying: "Of every tree of the garden thou mayest freely eat; but of the tree of the knowledge of good and evil, thou shalt not eat of it; for in the day that thou eatest thereof thou shalt die" ' (Genesis ii 16–17). God reveals Himself to man as the *commanding* God, who permits and forbids. Man is allowed to choose whether he will observe the precept or not, but to transgress it spells death. The election of Abraham, the father of the people, was due to the fact that 'I have chosen him that he may command his children and his household after him to keep the way of the Lord by doing righteousness and justice' (*ibid.* xviii 19). The response of the people to the Divine Revelation was: 'All that the Lord hath spoken will we do, and obey' (Exodus xxiv 7). The word of the Lord must be made *deed* by man.[1] But the term 'commandment' includes also 'prohibitions' [literally, 'thou shalt not do'], as Scripture puts it 'And if any one of the common people sin through error, in doing any of the things which the Lord hath commanded not to be done [literally, 'one of the commandments which shall not be done'], and be guilty' (Leviticus iv 27). The commandment is indicative of the Commander's power to command. Indeed the Commanding Deity appeared on Mount Sinai accompanied by thunder and lightning. The people that received the precepts became a kingdom of priests and a holy nation of the God-King.[2] The commandments of the Lord constitute the content of the covenant made between Him and His people: 'And he wrote upon the tables the words of the covenant, the ten commandments' (Exodus xxxiv 28). Breaking the covenant means forsaking the precepts: 'And they rejected His statutes, and His covenant that He made with their fathers... and they forsook all the commandments of the Lord their God...' (II Kings xvii 15–16). The whole of Israel's history in the period of the First Temple, as it is described in the Former Prophets, and all the utterances of the Prophets of Israel centre on keeping or breaking the covenant. The covenant comprises all the commandments and, where any given transgression is referred to, there also occurs, as a parallel to the 'breaking of the covenant', the expression 'breaking of the precept'.[3] The pact made by Ezra with the people was 'with a curse and an oath, to walk in God's law, which was given by Moses the servant of God, and to observe and do all the commandments of the Lord our Lord, and His ordinances and His statutes' (Nehemiah x 30). To this general declaration is attached a series of detailed precepts, which are particularly stressed on account of their importance at the time when the pact was made. The place of prophetic rebuke and preaching, which warn against transgressing the Torah and the commandments in general, is taken by the exact definition of the commandments and the admonition to observe their details. Continuing the Biblical concept of the Kingdom of God,[4] the Sages portray the relations between God and His people in images taken from the actual circumstances of the Roman empire, and the analogies do not always come to emphasize the differences between the King of the kings of kings and a human sovereign. An anonymous dictum in the *Mekhilta*, which forms the exordium of the Rabbinic interpretation of the Decalogue, includes the following comparison: ' "I am the Lord thy God" — why were the Ten Commandments not cited at the beginning of the Torah? The Sages explained the matter with the help of a parable: To what can the matter be compared? To one who entered a country and said to the inhabitants "Let me reign over you". They replied: "Have you done anything for our welfare that you should reign over us?" What did he do? He built the (city) wall for them, introduced the water (supply) for them, and waged wars on their behalf. He (then) said (again): "Let me reign over you." They answered him: "Yea, yea!" In the same way the Omnipresent brought out the Israelites from Egypt, divided the sea for them, sent down for them manna, raised up for them the well, brought them a flight of quails, and waged for them the war with Amalek. (Then) He said unto them: "Let Me reign over you". They responded: "yea, yea!"' (*Mekhilta de-R. Ishmael*, Massekhta de-Ba-ḥodesh, v, p. 219).

The very question 'Why were the Ten Commandments not cited at the beginning of the Torah?' flows from the view that the whole concern of the Torah is the precept, and that the entire election of Israel took place only that the Torah might be accepted. All that preceded — the history of the Patriarchs, the bondage of Egypt and the Exodus — is not of primary importance. All these are to be understood as preparatory events leading to the Revelation. On the face of it, it appears from the homily cited above that the acceptance of the yoke of God's Kingdom is the result of the people's assent, but closer scrutiny reveals that this consent was not a matter of free choice, but a decision that was enforced and directed by God's will to impose the yoke of the Torah and commandments on the people chosen for this purpose. Undoubtedly this homily cannot serve as proof of the autonomous character of Jewish ethical teaching. Since the publication of Moritz Lazarus' work on 'The Ethics of Judaism',[5] there has been no halt to the attempts to point to various Rabbinic dicta as evidence of the correspondence between the fundamental principle of Kant's ethical system and the religious ethic of Judaism. However, Lazarus' hypothesis has been rejected in unambiguous terms by Hermann Cohen[6], who made it clear that an autonomous ethic means one that emanates from man and from him alone, that is to say, man is the source of the ethic and God is not its source but only its principle, whereas in all religions, and undoubtedly this is the case in the Jewish faith, God is the source of the ethical law. Hermann Cohen's criticism deals with the general conception. He did not enter into an analysis of the dicta of the Sages on which Lazarus relied[7], and which, as well as similar sayings, continued to form the basis for the arguments of scholars[8] whose main object was to prove the supremacy of the Jewish ethic, and in whose estimation there was no higher corroboration or imprimatur than approximation to the system of Kant. In the light of their contentions many scholars of standing have become accustomed to read and explain Rabbinic dicta and homilies not in consonance with their simple meaning, or according to the intent of their authors, by taking them out of their historical context.

One of the principal sources of the idea of the 'autonomy of ethics' was provided by the dicta concerning the recognition of God and the observance of the Torah by the Patriarch Abraham, such as those in the Mishna at the end of Tractate Qiddushin: 'We find that Abraham our father had kept the whole Law before it was given, for it is written "Because that Abraham obeyed My voice and kept My charge, My commandments, My statutes, and My laws".'[9] But this Mishna only states that Abraham observed the Torah before it was given to Israel. It does not state that he had arrived of his own accord at the recognition of the Torah. The very proof derived from the verse 'Because that Abraham obeyed My voice' precludes the possibility of such an interpretation. Indeed at the end of *Tosefta Qiddushin* it is stated: 'And the Omnipresent blessed him [Abraham] and magnified him in his old age more than in his youth, because he kept the Torah before it was promulgated, as it is said: "Because that Abraham obeyed My voice and kept My charge, My commandments, My statutes, and My laws" — this teaches us that the ordinances of the Torah and the enactments of the Scribes were disclosed [נגלו *niglû*][10] to him.' Thus it is expressly stated here that the ordinances of the Torah were disclosed to him, that is to say, that he was vouchsafed a prior revelation and not that he attained to the Torah of his own accord. In a figurative manner this concept is expressed in a saying attributed to R. Simeon b. Yoḥai: 'R. Simeon b. Yoḥai said: No father taught him; he had no teacher. Whence, then, did he learn the Torah? The Holy One, blessed be He, appointed unto him his two reins as two teachers, and they poured forth and taught him wisdom,[11] as it is written: "I will bless the Lord, who hath given me counsel; yea, in the night seasons my reins instruct me"...' (*Genesis Rabba* lxi, 1, pp. 457–658). It is true that R. Simeon b. Yohai's dictum is followed by the statement of the Amora R. Levi: 'He taught himself Torah, as it is said: "The dissembler in heart shall have his fill from his own ways; and a good man shall be satisfied from himself" (Proverbs xiv 14)...' (*Genesis Rabba* xcv, 3, p. 1189). But even this saying only avers that Abraham learnt Torah, but it may well be that this Torah was given and revealed to him. Even when Abraham proves the existence of One God to Nimrod empirically (*Genesis Rabba* xxxviii, 13, p. 363), it is not stated that Abraham came by himself in this way to recognize the Creator, but, on the contrary, 'R. Isaac said: The case could be compared to one who travelled from one place to another and saw a castle on fire. Said he: "Is it possible that the castle has no governor?" Thereupon the owner of the castle looked out and said to him: "I am the owner of the castle." Thus, because Abraham our father said: "Is it possible that the world has no governor, the Holy One, blessed be He, looked out and said to him: I am the Governor, the Sovereign of the whole world"' (*ibid.* xxxiv, 1, p. 345). Here, when the recognition of God is referred to, the matter is described as an actual act of revelation. 'The Holy One, blessed be He, looked out and said to him: I am the Governor, the Sovereign of the whole world.' Likewise in the apocryphal work 'The Apocalypse of Abraham',[12] Abraham's recognition of the One God comes as a result of revelation. Of his own accord he came to a negative conclusion only, namely the realization of the nullity of the idols.

Only in later Midrashim is the spontaneity of Abraham's recognition of God emphasized, as, for example, in the *Pesiqta Rabbati*: ' "...Thou hast loved righteousness" (Psalms xlv 8 [7]) — this refers to Abraham, for the Holy One, blessed be He, saw that while all those generations were idolaters, Abraham rose up and left them and was not like them. Whereas all of them were idolaters, Abraham arose and *gained wisdom by his own efforts* and served the Holy One, blessed be He...' (*Pesiqta Rabbati*, xxxiii, p. 150a). In one of the late Midrashim the group of men who learnt to recognize God of their own accord was even enlarged; thus we read: 'Another explanation is: "Who hath given Me anything beforehand, that I should repay him?" (Job xli 3 [11]): the verse speaks of Abraham, who of his own accord recognized the Holy One, blessed be He, as it is written: "The dissembler in heart shall have his fill from his own ways..." (Proverbs xiv 14;

this verse, as we have seen, was already expounded in *Genesis Rabba*). What is meant by "The dissembler [סוג *sûg*] in heart shall have his fill from his own ways"? R. Abba Kahana said: The heart that is full of dross [סיגים *sîgîm*] because of its ways is destined to have its fill. "And a good man shall be satisfied from himself" (*ibid.*) — this refers to Abraham, who of his own accord recognized the Holy One, blessed be He, for there was no one, but himself, to teach him how to know the Omnipresent. And he was one of the four human beings who spontaneously learnt to know the Holy One, blessed be He: Job of his own accord recognized the Holy One, blessed be He... Hezekiah, king of Judah, also recognized the Holy One, blessed be He, by himself... and King Messiah likewise recognized the Holy One, blessed be He, by intuition.'[13] In *Seder Eliyyahu Rabba* (ed. Friedmann, vii, p. 35) it is said with regard to Adam, Noah, Abraham, Isaac, Jacob, Judah, and Joseph: 'The Torah was not given to them, but they kept it of their own accord. Therefore the Holy One, blessed be He, loved them completely and he likened their name to His own great name.'[14] In all the ancient sources, however, in the statements of the Tannaim and early Amoraim, referring to the observance of the precepts by those enumerated above, it is not stated 'that they kept them of their own accord'.[15]

Before we suggest an explanation of the difference that we find between the early sources and the later Midrashim in regard to the Patriarchs' recognition of God and their observance of the commandments, let us deal with the other proofs derived from the statements of the Tannaim and early Amoraim respecting autonomous ethics. Repeated reference has been made to the anonymous dictum in the *Sifra*: ' "Mine ordinances shall ye do" — these are the laws written in the Torah that, if they had not been written, should by right have been written, such as the laws concerning robbery, forbidden relations, idolatry, cursing God, and bloodshed, for if they were not written (in Scripture) they should by right have been written.'[16] Are we in truth permitted to state on the basis of this dictum that the Talmudic Sages 'entertained the idea that the content of this ideal of holiness is uniform, and is to be found in the human consciousness in simple form and as something that is self-understood'?[17] Only tendentious reading that pays no attention to the continuation of the homily can lead to such a conclusion. Otherwise we cannot explain how one could attribute to a homilist of the second century the view that the laws of forbidden relations, idolatry, and cursing God constitute an ideal of holiness that is inherent in the consciousness of humanity Indeed, it is not this that the homilist had in mind. When he states that משפטים *mishpāṭîm* ['ordinances'] are laws 'that, if not written (in Scripture), should by right have been written,' he wishes to stress that the reasons underlying these precepts are known and can be explained, whereas חקים *ḥuqqîm* ['statutes'] are commandments 'against which the evil inclination argues, and the Gentile peoples argue, such as (the prohibition) to eat pig, and to wear a garment of two kinds of stuff; the law of removing the sandal of the brother of the deceased by the widow, of the purification of the leper, and of the he-goat that is to be sent away, against which the evil inclination argues, and the Gentile peoples argue. Therefore Scripture teaches "I am the Lord" — I have ordained these statutes, and you are not permitted to challenge them.' There is no other difference between the two categories of commandments. The observance of both of them is obligatory, because they are written in the Torah. Just as the latter are called 'My statutes', so the former are termed 'My ordinances'.

Lazarus thought that he had traced a very early source for the idea of the autonomy of ethics in the Targum of Onkelos to Genesis iii 22. The Scripture 'Behold, the man is become as one of us, to know good and evil' is translated there 'Behold, man has become alone in the world by himself to know good and evil.' Lazarus discovers in the Targum 'profound ethical understanding', for he finds it expressly stated therein that 'man recognizes good and evil of his own accord'.[18] But anyone conversant with the methods of the Targum knows that Onkelos seeks to remove here the anthropomorphic expression in the biblical phrase 'as one of us', and apparently in order to obviate the interpretation that he is referring to autonomous ethics, which is attributed to him, he rendered, after מניה *minnēh* ['by himself'], למידע טב וביש *lĕ-mîdaʿ ṭāv û-vîsh* ['to know good and evil'] and not (as *ibid.* iii 5: ותהון כרברבין חכמין בין טב לביש *û-tĕhôn kĕ-ravrĕvîn ḥakkîmîn bên ṭāv lĕ-vîsh* ['And ye would become like the great ones wise to distinguish between good and evil']) למיחכם בין טב לביש *lĕ-miḥkam bên ṭāv lĕ-vîsh* ['to be wise to distinguish between good and evil']. The reference is to the knowledge of the fact that good and evil exist, and not to discerning, by his own powers, between good and evil.[19]

As proof of the correctness of their view, Lazarus[20] and those who follow him have also cited the Baraita on wronging by means of words: 'The Rabbis taught: "Ye shall not therefore wrong one another" (Leviticus xxv 17) — Scripture speaks of verbal wrongs... How is this to be understood? If a man was a penitent, one must not say to him: "Remember your former deeds" ... If ass-drivers wanted (to buy) grain from him, he must not say to them: "Go to so-and-so, who sells grain", though he knows that he has never sold any. R. Judah said: A man should not feign interest in a purchase, when he has no money, for the matter is left to the heart [i.e. conscience], and of anything left to the heart it is stated "And thou shalt fear thy God" ' (*T.B. Bava Meṣia*ʿ 58b). 'Matters left to the heart' — they argue — are things that a man himself discovers; but clearly this is not the correct interpretation, and undoubtedly we must not deviate from Rashi's explanation that R. Judah seeks only 'to give the reason why the precept to fear God is mentioned in this connection... and this is what he means: For in all these cases the good or bad intent is known only to the heart of the person concerned — he alone knows whether he spoke sincerely or perversely, and he can say: I acted only for the best; I thought that you had grain to sell, or, I did wish to buy this commodity. And in regard to every matter that is left to a man's heart it is stated: Be afraid of Him who knows our thoughts, if they be for good or for deception' (Rashi, *ad loc.*, s.v. *Shĕhărê* ['For']; see *Sifra*, Be-har, iv, 2, p. 107d). The prohibition 'that one should not say "How much does this article cost?", when one does not wish to buy' does not emanate from a man's heart, but it is left to his heart 'that he should fear Him who commanded us concerning these things'; the same applies to the other commandments in regard to which it is written 'And thou shalt fear thy God'.[21] Only in the light of this interpretation can we understand the statement of R. Simeon b. Yoḥai, transmitted by R. Joḥanan: 'Verbal wrong is more reprehensible than financial wrong, because of the former it is said "And thou shalt fear thy God", but of the latter it is not said "And thou shalt fear thy God".'[22]

In the Tannaitic sources that we have cited so far, it is possible to discover the idea of moral autonomy at best by an exegetical method that, as we have seen, does not interpret them according to their natural sense, but imputes to them notions that the Sages never intended to convey. On the other hand, some scholars supposed that express statements about the sovereignty of the moral law and its independence of the Divine Commander could be found in the dicta of the early Amoraim, and they even injected into them the doctrinal dispute between the heteronomous and the autonomous conception. The latter is represented, in their view, by the saying of R. Joḥanan: 'Had the Torah not been given, we could have learnt modesty from the cat, (the prohibition of) robbery from the ant, and (the prohibition of) forbidden relations from the dove' (*T.B.* *ʿEruvin* 100b). Thus it is stated here explicitly, as it were, that even without revelation man can attain, by contemplating the life of nature, to moral conduct. The diametrically opposite view was found by scholars in the dictum of R. Ḥanina; 'Greater is he who is commanded and fulfils (the precept) than he who is not commanded yet fulfils it' (*T.B.* *Qiddushin* 31a), which expresses in the clearest terms the primacy of theonomy. Felix Perles[23] does not deal generally with 'the idea of the autonomy of the Jewish ethic';[24] following Hermann Cohen, he recognizes the theonomous basis of Judaism, but he seeks an explanation of those Rabbinic teachings that contradict this principle, and he proposes to solve the problem by positing Hellenistic influence wherever views in favour of autonomy are apparent. Primarily he had in mind Philo of Alexandria and his view concerning ἄγραφος νόμος, the unwritten law.

In another context[25] we have already pointed out that 'the unwritten law' is not the Oral Law. The classic example of the unwritten law is that upheld by Antigone against the law of Creon. Actually both were unwritten, but the difference was that one was a law promulgated by the king and the other was a law that had never been promulgated — it was a law of Nature — and as such it was also divine, and older than any written statute. Philo accepted these Greek views, and thus he was able to say: 'The Patriarchs went to no school; selftaught they loved to follow Nature, for they regarded Nature as the most venerable law' (De Abra. 6). This is the Stoic view concerning the place of law in nature, which is opposed to Jewish teaching regarding supernatural revelation.[26] Such concepts infiltrated also, according to Perles, into the world of the Sages, and because in their innocence they did not grasp the extreme conclusions implicit in the concept of autonomy, they adopted them as their own. But there is no proof that the Sages were indeed acquainted with the theory of 'the natural law', nor is there any need to recruit this idea in order to reconcile the antithesis between the teaching of R. Joḥanan and that of R. Ḥanina, if we comprehend their true meaning from their context. In the dictum preceding that of R. Joḥanan, R. Ḥiyya explains the words addressed by Elihu to Job (xxxv 11) 'Who teacheth us through the beasts of the earth, and maketh us wise through the fowls of heaven' as referring to certain attributes of living creatures from which man can learn. In conjunction with this verse he merely declares that God endowed the creatures with these qualities, 'that He instilled wisdom in them' (Rashi, *ibid.*), in order that man may learn from them.[27] R. Joḥanan limits R. Ḥiyya's teaching by stating 'Had the Torah not been given, we could have learnt...'; but since it was given, there is no need for this.[28] R. Joḥanan's saying is no more related to the subject of autonomy than to the verse in Job; in the same way R. Ḥanina, too, does not come to teach the doctrine of heteronomy, when he asserts that the one who is commanded and fulfils (the commandment) is superior to him who is not commanded, yet fulfils (the precept). For the latter also did not attain to fulfilment of the commandments as a result of intellectual cognition; he merely belongs to the category of people whom the Torah exempted from the observance of the precepts. This is made explicitly clear by the context in all the passages in which R. Ḥanina's dictum is cited. In *Tractate Qiddushin*, it follows upon the story of how a certain Gentile acted towards his father in Ashkelon. 'Rav Judah said in the name of Samuel: R. Eliezer was asked; To what extent is the honouring of parents (to be observed)? Said he to them: Go forth and see how a certain Gentile acted towards his father in Ashkelon; his name was Dama son of Nethina. The Sages wished to buy from him jewels for the ephod at a profit of 600,000 (gold denars) — Rav Kahana taught: 800,000 — but the key was lying beneath his father's pillow, and he would not disturb him. The following year the Holy One, blessed be He, gave him his reward: a red heifer was born to him in his herd. (Thereupon) the Sages of Israel came to him (to buy it). Said he to them: I know that if I were to ask all the money in the world, you would give it to me; but I ask of you only the money that I lost through honouring my father. Said R. Ḥanina: Now if one who is not commanded yet fulfils (the commandment) is so (rewarded), how much more so will he who is commanded and fulfils (the commandment be rewarded)! For R. Ḥanina said: Greater is he who is commanded and fulfils (the precept) than he who is not commanded yet fulfils (the precept).' If we examine the narrative and the dictum linked to it, we shall observe that it is not stated here that the deeds of one who is not commanded do not merit reward, nor is their value negated. Only their relative value is emphasized. The question whether the Gentile had come to observe the commandment of honouring one's father so meticulously as a result of his own thinking[29], or through having learnt it from his Jewish acquaintances, just as he derived from them his knowledge of the ephod and the red heifer, is irrelevant in the context of our story and likewise as regards the inference that R. Ḥanina drew from the incident. Furthermore, in the other passages where the saying of R. Ḥanina is cited the reference is to a Gentile who studies the Torah (*T.B. Bava Qamma* 38a; *T.B. ʿAvoda Zara* 3a), or to a Jew who is exempt from keeping the commandments, as in the statement of Rav Joseph: 'At first I thought: If one would tell me that the Halakha is according to R. Judah, who said "a blind man is exempt from (the observance of) the commandments", I would give a banquet for the Rabbis, for I am not enjoined yet I observe. But now that I have heard the teaching of R. Ḥanina "Greater is he who is commanded and fulfils (the commandment) than he who is not commanded yet fulfils (the commandment)", on the contrary, if one would tell me that the Halakha is not according to R. Judah, I would give a banquet for the Rabbis' (*T.B. Qiddushin*, *loc. cit.*; *T.B. Bava Qamma* 87a). When Rav Joseph regarded himself as one who is not commanded yet fulfils (the commandment) and consequently thought that he transcended one who kept (the commandments) because he was so enjoined, it never occurred to him to claim that he had discovered the precepts independently, but only that he was exempt from performing the precepts that had been ordained, yet kept them voluntarily. We must not, therefore, speak of autonomy but of free decision.

Even within the ambit of the theonomic conception and the observance of the commandments as one who keeps them because he is enjoined to do so, a man is enabled to make use of attributes and methods of observance that are related to his temperament, his will, and his nature. It is actually the fulfilment of the commandments as one who observes them because he is enjoined — with devotion and meticulous exactitude — that can give the religious observer the right, as it were, of regarding himself as joint-author of those precepts, and this is the significance of R. Joḥanan's dictum: 'Whoever performs one precept truly is accounted as though he had promulgated it from Mount Sinai, for it is said: "Thou shalt therefore observe and do" (Deuteronomy xxvi 16). What then is the meaning of the words "and (ye) shall do them"? It signifies that whoever observes the Torah and performs it truly is accounted as though he had enacted it and promulgated it from Mount Sinai. R. Joḥanan said further: Whoever keeps the Torah truly is accounted by Scripture as though he had made himself, for it is said: "And the Lord commanded me at that time to teach" etc. The text does not say "to do them" [לעשות אותם *laʿăśôt 'ôtam*] but "to make yourselves with them" [לעשתכם אתם *laʿăśōtkhem ôtām*] (Deuteronomy iv 14) — this implies that he is accounted as though he had made and created himself.'[30] The second dictum is not only intrinsically instructive, but also helps to elucidate the meaning of the preceding saying. Just as by the hyperbolical expression 'as though he had made and created himself' R. Joḥanan did not intend to detract in any way from the fact that man was God's creation, but sought to stress that in the proper fulfilment of the precepts there is, as it were — this qualifying phrase must be emphasized — an element of additional creation and fashioning of man, who becomes a partner of the Almighty in the work of creation,[31] so, too, when he declares that he who performs a precept truly is accounted as though he had promulgated it from Sinai, it did not enter R. Joḥanan's mind to detract from the source of the precept, which is in the Self-revealing and commanding God, but to emphasize that by keeping the Torah truly man is elevated to the status of becoming a revealer by his innate power.[32] The non-recurring Revelation on Mount Sinai is renewed by him, and he becomes a partner therein. In the manner of R. Joḥanan, and even in his very words, homilies are transmitted in the name of other Amoraim, both of Eretz-Israel and of Babylon, based on expositions of other verses[33], to the effect that one who fulfils the commandments willingly renews the Revelation at Mount Sinai. The Tanna R. Eliezer b. Jacob already taught: ' "And Moses and the priests the Levites spoke unto all Israel, saying: 'Keep silence, and hear, O Israel, this day thou art become a people" (Deuteronomy xxvii 9) — but did they receive the Torah this day? Surely they had received the Torah forty years ago, yet the verse says "this day"? This teaches us that when Moses taught them the Torah and they accepted it gladly, Scripture accounted it unto them as though they had received it this day from Sinai. Therefore it is said: "This day thou art become a people unto the Lord thy God" ' (*Canticles Rabba* ii, 5). But it is this very homily that brings into relief the specific significance of the Amoraic teachings that we have cited. R. Eliezer b. Jacob merely declares that when the Israelites accepted the Torah after the lapse of forty years, it was as though the Revelation at Mount Sinai had been renewed; he does not say that it was as though they themselves had promulgated the Torah from Sinai, as R. Joḥanan and R. Ḥama b. R. Ḥanina had stated. They express in their dicta the paradox that the reward of theonomy is the feeling of autonomy, and is the privilege only of one who accepted the Torah and its commandments as they were revealed, and fulfils them in truth. This acceptance is the result of the choice and free decision of each individual, and indeed R. Joḥanan received and transmitted the Haggadah that was current in the academies of the Tannaim[34] to the effect that God had offered the Torah in turn 'to every nation and tongue, but they did not accept it until He came to Israel and they accepted it' (*T.B. ʿAvoda Zara* 2b). But he was not content with the willing acceptance of the people as a whole; he emphasized: 'An angel brought forth the commandment from before the Holy One, blessed be He [in the case of each commandment] and presented it to every Israelite, saying: "Do you accept this commandment? It contains so-and-so many laws..." And the Israelite answered: "Yea!...." '[35]

A view that is diametrically opposite to the concept of choice is to be found in the dictum of R. Avdimi bar Ḥasa, apparently a Babylonian Amora of the second generation,[36] who expounded ' "And they stood at the nether part of the mount"... This teaches that the Holy One, blessed be He, tilted the mountain over them like a cask and said unto them: "If you accept the Torah, well and good; and if not, there shall be your burial." ' This homily of R. Avdimi is an individual view, which has no parallel. The image, however, of the Israelites' actually standing beneath the mountain is already to be found in the *Mekhilta*, but it is precisely there that the phrasing emphasizes that they did this voluntarily: 'This teaches us that the mountain was plucked up from its place and they [the Israelites] drew near and stood under the mountain, as it is stated: "And ye came near and stood under the mountain" (Deuteronomy iv 11). Concerning them it is stated in post-Mosaic Scriptures (*Canticles Rabba* ii, 14): "O my dove, that art in the clefts of the rock... for sweet is thy voice, and thy countenance is comely." '[37] In an anonymous Talmudic passage (*T.B.* *'Avoda Zara* 2b) it is already pointed out that R. Avdimi's homily not only contradicts that of the Mekhilta, which states that the Gentile peoples were given an opportunity to accept the Torah, but also deprives it of its underlying reason: 'Hence the Gentile peoples were called upon to accept the Torah, so that they should not be able to argue before the *Shekhina* ['Divine Presence'], saying: Had we been asked, we should certainly have accepted the obligation (of the Torah)' — and the Talmud offers the explanation it thinks fit. Some of the Geonim and *Risho'nim* [the post-Geonic authorities] attempted to reconcile R. Avdimi's dictum with the Scripture 'We will do, and obey'.[38] But the Amoraim of his generation and the next did not accept his view. R. Aḥa bar Jacob's reaction, 'This provides a powerful protest against the Torah', expresses opposition, declaring, in effect, that the view that the Torah was accepted under coercion nullifies the demand for its observance.[39] Apparently in an attempt to justify the attitude of the people to the Torah in the period of the First Temple, Rava is inclined to leave R. Avdimi's homily in its place, only he adds to it: 'Even so the generation in the days of Ahasuerus accepted it (anew).' 'The voluntary acceptance of the Torah' is a fundamental principle in the estimation of Rava.[40] Indeed, we find him maintaining the view of those Amoraim who hold that the free decision of man does not find complete expression in the acceptance of the yoke of the Torah and commandments alone, but continues in the course of their observance, and it not only has the power to elevate man 'as though he had made himself',[41] but also to give him a share in the ownership of the Torah and the moulding of its nature. Thus said Rava: 'A man should always study that part of the Torah that his heart desires, as it is said "But whose desire is in the Law of the Lord". Rava further said: At first (the Torah) is named [i.e. in the verse] after the Holy One, blessed be He, but in the end it is called after him [i.e. the student], as it is said "Whose desire is in the Law of the Lord and in his [i.e. his own] Law doth he meditate day and night." '[42] It is noteworthy that Rava's dictum in the Talmudic discussion is preceded by another exposition of the same verse, namely: 'R. Avdimi bar Ḥama said: The Holy One, blessed be He, fulfils the desires of everyone who occupies himself with the Torah, as it is said "If he (occupies himself) with the Law of the Lord, his desire (is granted)." ' In the view of R. Avdimi, the revelation of a man's desire to study the Torah is not a decisive factor, for the study is incumbent upon him. In his exposition he detaches the words 'his desire' from 'the Law of the Lord'. To this Rava reacts, when he declares that a man's desire (to occupy himself) with the Torah transforms it from the Lord's Torah into the Torah of the one who studies it. It seems that this doctrinal difference between the two Amoraim also lies at the root of their different homilies on Deuteronomy xxx 11–13: 'For this commandment which I command thee this day... It is not in heaven... Neither is it beyond the sea....' R. Avdimi bar Ḥama bar Dosa expounded: ' "It is not in heaven", for if it were in heaven, it would be incumbent upon you to go up after it; and if it were "beyond the sea", it would be incumbent upon you to cross (the sea) after it.' On the other hand, Rava, like R. Joḥanan, declares: ' "It is not in heaven" — it is not to be found in one who, on account of it, allows his conceit to soar to the heavens; nor is it to be found in one who, on account of it, allows his arrogance to grow vast as the sea.'[43] While R. Avdimi deduces from the verse the duty to keep the Torah and to study it in all circumstances, Rava predicates this upon a man's attributes and qualities.

Our analysis has, we believe, made it amply clear that Rava's view summarizes the prevailing opinion in the academies of the Amoraim. Nor is this surprising, since it is consonant with the history of the Halakha, which is based on the authority of the Sages to extend and restrict the application and ambit of the precepts. It is true that R. Akiba and his disciples held that 'The Torah with its laws and subtle distinctions and interpretations was promulgated through Moses at Sinai'[44], and we have already seen (above, p. 300) that this theory of a general and comprehensive Revelation nullifies in fact the difference between the two Torahs; but in this very extremism emphasis is given to the freedom of the Sage to interpret the words of the Torah, to expound, to enact, and to decree (prohibitions), secure in the knowledge that he is realizing the Revelation, transforming the potential into actuality, and revealing to his generation that which it needs.[45]

But there also remained a sphere, transcending the law and Halakha of the Oral Torah, in which man could introduce innovations and additions by his own initiative; this sphere is called 'beyond the strict letter of the law'. R. Eleazar of Modiʿim expounded the verse 'And thou shalt show them the way wherein they must walk, and the work that they must do' (Exodus xviii 20) as follows: ' "and the work" — that means the strict letter of the Law; "that they must do" — that connotes beyond the strict letter of the Law' (*Mekhilta de-R. Ishmael*, Massekhta da-ʿAmalek, Yitro, ii, p. 198). He thus learnt from the Scripture the duty to act beyond the strict requirements of the Law. R. Joḥanan even said 'Jerusalem was destroyed only because they judged therein (strictly) according to Torah law'; and the meaning, as the Talmud explains there, is 'that they based their judgements (strictly) on Torah law and did not act beyond the requirements of the Law'.[46] The requirement of the law is actually the Halakha, according to which the judge must give his decision, but sometimes the Halakha itself ordains that the judge is not obliged to act according to 'the letter of the Law', and they are the cases in which the strict requirement of the Law is not consonant with, and even runs counter to, 'the public weal'.[47] But the detailed nature of that which is 'beyond the requirement of the Law' has not been determined and is left to the human heart, and this is also borne out by the stories in the Talmuds about acts that were 'beyond the requirement of the Law',[48] from which it is clearly to be seen that what is defined as 'beyond the requirement of the Law' is not prescribed by law. This needs to be emphasized in the light of what has been said on this subject on the basis of the following narrative in the Babylonian Talmud (*T.B. Bava Meṣiʿa* 83a): 'Certain porters broke a barrel of wine belonging to Rabbah bar bar Ḥanan; so he seized their cloaks. Thereupon they went and told Rav. Said he (to Rabbah bar bar Ḥanan): 'Give them their cloaks." "Is this the law?" the latter inquired. (Rav) replied: "Yea, (as it is written) 'That thou mayest walk in the way of good men' " (Proverbs ii 20). So he returned to them their cloaks. (The porters) then said (to Rav): "We are poor, and we have toiled all day and we are hungry, and we have nothing. Said (Rav) to (Rabbah bar bar Ḥanan): "Go, pay them." The latter rejoined: "Is this the law?" (Rav) replied: "Yea, (as it is written:) 'and keep the paths of the righteous' (Proverbs *ibid.*)." ' The word 'Yea' fired the imagination of the homilists and scholars and led them to proclaim that 'beyond the requirement of the Law' became law.[49] But unfortunately the word 'Yea' is missing in the MSS. and the works of the *Risho'nim*[50], just as it is wanting in the version of this story cited in the Palestinian Talmud: 'Once a potter delivered his pots to a man, who broke them; so the potter seized his cloak. Thereupon the man went (and complained) to R. Jose bar Ḥanina. The latter said to him: "Go, tell him: 'That thou mayest walk in the way of good men.' " He went and told the potter, and he returned his cloak. Subsequently (R. Jose bar Ḥanina) asked the complainant: "Did he pay you?" The man replied "No". So he said to him: "Go, tell him: 'And keep the paths of the righteous.' " So he went and told the potter, and the latter gave the man his pay.'[51] R. Jose bar Ḥanina and the Amora in the Babylonian Talmud advised the potter, or the owner of the wine casks, to act beyond the requirement of the Law, and they based themselves on the verse in Proverbs ii 20 and not on the verse in Exodus xviii, because they did not accept the exposition of R. Eleazar of Modiʿim, but agreed with R. Joshua (*Mekhilta loc. cit.*): ' "That they must do" — that means the good deed', i.e., the good deeds that are the Torah precepts, and which R. Eleazar of Modiʿim deduced from the beginning of the verse. On the other hand, the Scriptures 'the way of good men' and 'the paths of the righteous' implied acts to which the good men and the righteous attained of their own accord.

If a Sage instructed someone else to act according to this standard, he felt the need to inform him that his instruction was not based on law. Although in the story that we have cited, Rav explained the position only in reply to Rabbah bar bar Ḥanan's question 'Is this the Law?', it is possible that he supposed that Rabbah would understand of his own accord that he was referring to the way of good and righteous men and not to strict law. When R. Eleazar wished to give a practical decision and to rule that daughters be given alimentation from moveable property (of their deceased father's estate), 'R. Simeon b. Eliakim said to him: "Master, I know full well that you are not acting according to the strict requirement of the Law but in accordance with the principle of compassion; but (there is the danger) that the disciples may note (your ruling) and fix it as a Halakha for the future" ' (*T.B. Ketubbot* 50b). Not only are these good deeds not identifiable with the Law, but not even with what is accepted as right and good in the estimation of most people. The Sages of Nehardea had this last point in mind when they ruled with regard to 'a person who takes possession (of an estate situated) between brothers or partners... He is removed even on account of the right of pre-emption, for it is said "And thou shalt do that which is right and good in the sight of the Lord" (Deuteronomy vi 18).'[52] Apparently they expounded the verse in the same way as R. Akiba: ' "That which is good" — in the sight of Heaven, and "That which is right" — in the sight of man.'[53] And man must fulfil his duty in both directions; hence matters that fall within the category of 'And thou shalt do that which is right and good' may also be Halakha[54]; whereas the things that are beyond the requirement of the Law[55] are not Halakha[56], but acts of piety.[57] The pious man forgoes his rights (*M. 'Avot*, v, 10), and acts beyond the requirement of the law, and this is the attribute of piety.[58] Similarly the Palestinian Talmud explains the contradiction between the decision Rav gave to 'a certain man' and his own conduct by the antithesis: 'There (in the case of the man, he ruled) according to strict law, but in his own case Rav acted according to the quality of piety' (*T.P. Shevi'it* [end], p. 39d). The Mishna does, indeed, teach (*Shevi'it* [end]): 'All moveable goods are acquired (only) by the act of drawing (the article towards oneself); but whoever keeps his word (alone), the spirit of the Sages finds pleasure in him', and accordingly one who does not keep his word, 'the spirit of the Sages does not find pleasure in him'. But from the context and from the *Mishna Bava Meṣiʿa* iv, 2, we see that the reference is to one who received money, without the act of drawing having taken place, and retracted, or, at least according to Rava (*T.B. Bava Meṣiʿa* 48a), to a case of 'words unaccompanied by money', that is to say, where one had agreed to sell, but had not received any money, and in such circumstances 'the Sages find no satisfaction in this man's conduct' (Rashi, *ibid.*).[59] Rav, however, said: 'When I tell my household to give a gift to a person, I do not retract' (*T.P. Sheviʿit* [end]). Rav did not say anything to the recipient of the gift but to his household[60], yet even so he did not wish to retract, and this constitutes 'pious conduct'. Of a Sage of the calibre of R. Joshua b. Levi it is expected that he would act beyond legal requirements; hence his argument 'But did I not fulfil the ruling of a Mishna?' is countered by Elijah with the remark, 'But is this a Mishna-ruling followed by the pious?' (*T.P. Terumot* viii, 5, p. 44b; see also *T.B. Bava Batra* 7b).

While the opinions of the Tannaim were divided, in the case of man's duties to God, as to whether every man has a right to act with special stringency where he himself is concerned, and R. Simeon b. Gamaliel declared 'Not every one that wishes to assume the name (of a pious personage) may proceed to do so' (*M. Berakhot* ii, 8), for 'if he has not the reputation of a Sage and a pious man in the public estimation, this is only a form of arrogance' (Rashi, *T.B. Berakhot* 17b), and people react with displeasure;[61] yet in all that appertains to the precepts to be observed by a man towards his fellow, such a restriction cannot, of course, apply. Without doubt, when the Sages urged people to go beyond the letter of the law, they also employed the argument that a man prays to God to act towards him in accordance with the attribute of compassion. In the name of Rav it is reported that the Almighty Himself prays: 'May it be My will that My compassion may conquer My anger, and that My compassion may prevail over My (other) attributes, so that I may deal with My children mercifully and act towards them with charity that goes beyond the requirement of the law' (*T.B. Berakhot* 7a). On the other hand a man is not truly pious unless he observes the 'laws of damages' [i.e. of *Neziqin*], that is to say, the practice of the Early Pious Men in this sphere.[62]

The dicta that we have cited relative to 'beyond the requirement of the law' and 'pious conduct' indicate how wide is the range of matters, even for the person who keeps the precepts because he is enjoined, that remain subject to his desire and will, to his temperament and attributes. There is no autonomy. In contrast to Kant's ethical system, in which God is no more than an Idea that serves to complete the science of ethics, in the doctrine of the Sages God ever remains the Source and Giver of the commandments. But even the man who does good, because he regards it as a precept and law, is allowed to determine his own ways of fulfilling the observance, so that he may achieve perfection through them and also introduce innovations and augment them. For freedom of decision, which marked the acceptance of the Torah, whether at Sinai, or at a later period — in the sense of 'the generation accepted it' — was not taken away from those who keep the Torah and fulfil its commandments. The Amora Rava, who, we found, maintained the merit of the voluntary acceptance of the Torah, likewise praised Israel's uttering 'we will do' before 'we will hear' (*T.B. Shabbat* 88a–b), and he regarded the linking of 'the enactments of the Scribes', which are 'new regulations ordained in each generation to provide a hedge and a fence', to the old laws of the Torah as a corollary to them both. In the same spirit he expounded the verse ' "New and old, which I have laid for thee, O my beloved" (Canticles vii 14) — the Congregation of Israel declared before the Holy One, blessed be He: "Sovereign of the universe, I have imposed more restrictive edicts upon myself than Thou hast, and I have fulfilled them" ' (*T.B. ʿEruvin* 21b and Rashi *ad loc.*). Rav ʿAwira, a contemporary of Rava, attributes, in the name of his teachers — R. Ammi and R. Assi — a similar appraisement to God. To the contention of the angels that He shows favouritism towards Israel, 'He answered: Why should I not favour Israel? For I enjoined them in the Torah "And thou shalt eat and be satisfied and bless the Lord thy God" (Deuteronomy viii 10), yet they are so meticulous as (to say grace) for food the size of an olive or of an egg' (*T.B. Berakhot* 20b). When the Amoraim contemplated the image of the precepts in their generation after they had become studded with the minutest detailed regulations introduced by the 'fence'-makers and ordinance-ordainers and the acts of the pious, and when they considered, again, the image of the observers of the precepts, they could — with complete conviction — declare that whoever fulfils a commandment correctly 'it is as though he had promulgated it from Sinai' and 'as though he had created himself' (see above, p. 326).

These and similar dicta, which serve as an appraisal of the role of the human personality in the fulfilment of the precepts, explain the change that had taken place in the consciousness of the past, that is to say, in the evaluation of the observance of the commandments by the Patriarchs, with which we dealt above (p. 320). We are confronted by a phenomenon that may be termed 'the acts of the scions are a sign to their sires'. The tradition is common to the ancient sources — both to the apocryphal literature, like the *Book of Jubilees* and the *Testaments of the Twelve Patriarchs*, and to the Haggadot of the Tannaim and early Amoraim — that the Patriarchs kept the Torah and the commandments, be it that they were directly enjoined concerning them by God, or that they received the laws as an oral or written tradition from their predecessors. The other way (to account for the patriarchal observance of the Torah), which is preferred by the pseudepigraphic literature, in which Enoch fulfils the central role in the transmission of the Torah and commandments,[63] is also not altogether wanting in the homilies of the Sages.[64] The function of Enoch, who is not mentioned in Tannaitic literature at all — and even in the Amoraic homilies the attitude to him is not positive[65] — is, however, fulfilled by Shem and Eber. In their academy Jacob studied fourteen years, and they transmitted to him Halakhot, which he in turn handed down to Joseph[66]; but primarily the observance of the precepts by the Patriarchs is conceived, as in the case of the Torah itself, as the outcome of direct revelation.[67] There were also Tannaim who were disinclined to attribute to the Patriarchs the observance of more commandments than those expressly mentioned in the Torah. This emerges from the following Mishna that treats of the law of the sinew of the hip: 'It applies to clean but not to unclean beasts. R. Judah said: (It applies) also to unclean beasts. R. Judah argued: Was not the sinew of the hip forbidden from the time of the sons of Jacob, when unclean beasts were still permitted to them? They replied: It was enjoined at Sinai, but it was recorded in its (due) place.'[68] Neither the Sages nor R. Judah, however, solve the question by positing that the Patriarchs observed the prohibition not to eat unclean beasts.

While we found neither in the apocryphal literature nor in the dicta of the Tannaim and the Amoraim the view that the Patriarchs came to observe the commandments of their own accord,[69] this is expressly stated in later Midrashim. However, it is not, as some scholars have thought[70], the result of Philo's influence,[71] but flows from the internal development in the evaluation of man's part in the performance and moulding of the precepts. If the Sons were allowed to act 'as though they had created the commandments' and as though 'they had promulgated them from Sinai', how much more so was this permitted the Fathers![72] The role assumed by the observers of the precepts and the glory with which they had been crowned were linked to a qualitative change that had taken place in the actual connotation of the term 'precept', and hence they also conduced to a new appraisal of the range and number of the commandments. The Rabbinic use of the term 'precept' became greatly extended. It not only comprises the positive and negative precepts explicitly mentioned in the Torah,[73] which are also called עשה *ʿăśē* [literally 'do'] and לא תעשה *lōʾ taʿăśe* [literally 'do not'], but every verse of the Torah is called a precept. R. Joḥanan said 'in the name of R. Simeon b. Yoḥai: Moses wrote for us three sections in the Torah, and each one contains sixty precepts; these are: the Section of the Passover Sacrifice, the Section of Damages, and the Section of *Qĕdôshîm* ['Be ye holy']'.[74] Whoever examines these sections will readily see that they do not contain sixty commandments each, but that each comprises sixty verses. We learn from the statements of the Tannaim that they scrutinized the compass and content of the precepts from many aspects. The very multiplicity of the commandments in the Torah leads them to the view that man is obliged to perform a precept with everything given him by God. 'There is not a thing in the world that is not subject to precepts to be performed in the name of the Omnipresent. Produce entails many commandments: the heave-offerings, the tithes, the dough-offering, the first-fruits, the gleanings, the forgotten sheaf, and the corner of the field. To the gates of houses and cities pertains a precept dedicated to the Omnipresent, as it is said: "And thou shalt write them upon the door-posts..." (Deuteronomy vi 9). To the cloak and garments belongs a precept ordained by the Omnipresent, as it is said: "Thou shalt not wear a mingled stuff... Thou shalt make the twisted cord..." (*ibid.* xxii 11–12). Clean beasts embrace a precept enjoined by the Omnipresent, as it is said: "All the firstling males that are born of thy herd and of thy flock thou shalt sanctify unto the Lord thy God; thou shalt do no work with the firstling of thine ox, nor shear the firstling of thy flock" (*ibid.* xv 19). Unclean beasts are affected by a precept of the Omnipresent, as it is said: "And the firstling of an ass thou shalt redeem with a lamb; and if thou wilt not redeem it, then thou shalt break its neck" (Exodus xxxiv 20). With regard to beasts that grow up wild and birds that fly in the air, Scripture ordained that when they come into your possession they should not lack a precept, as it is said: "that taketh in hunting any beast or fowl that may be eaten..." (Leviticus xvii 13); and other kinds of cattle and beasts that Scripture does not specify by name are combined together so that they should not be devoid of a precept, as it is stated: "Notwithstanding, no devoted thing, that a man may devote unto the Lord of all that he hath, whether of man or beast..." (*ibid.* xxvii 28). The holy things of the Sanctuary, though they are all holy, are classified in numerous degrees.'[75] 'A man performs ten precepts before ever he eats a piece of bread' (*T.P. Ḥalla* i [end], p. 58a).

In the light of what has been stated about matters that belong to the heart, about acting beyond the requirements of the law, and about the way the commandments are to be fulfilled, it is not surprising that in the term מצוה *miṣwā* ('precept', 'religious act', 'meritorious deed') were included even things that are not obligatory. Not only acts of charity are called *miṣwā*.[76] While R. Ile'a reports in the name of R. Eleazar b. R. Simeon that 'A man may deviate from the truth for the sake of peace, as it is said "Thy father did command... so shall ye say unto Joseph: Forgive, I pray thee now..." (Genesis l 16–17)', R. Nathan disagrees with him and maintains that it is a *miṣwā* [a religious act] to do so in the interests of peace;[77] that which is a matter of free choice has thus become a *miṣwā*. In a similar manner R. Joḥanan explained the dispute between the first quoted authority and R. Judah in the Mishna in *Soṭa* (viii, 7): 'To what does the foregoing refer? To an optional war [רשות *rĕshût*], but in a war waged in a religious cause [*miṣwā*] all go forth, even the bridegroom from his chamber and the bride from her bridal chamber. R. Judah said:

To what does the foregoing refer? To a war waged in a religious cause, but in an obligatory [חובה *ḥôvā*] war all go forth, even the bridegroom from his chamber and the bride from her bridal chamber.' While Rav Ḥisda differentiates between an optional war and a war waged in a religious cause and an obligatory war, 'R. Joḥanan said: There is a semantic difference between them; R. Judah called an 'optional war' a 'war waged in a religious cause', but in an obligatory war every one goes forth....'[78] The enlargement of the sphere to which *miṣwā* applied and the upgrading of optional matters to the status of *miṣwā* reduced the original obligatory character of the term and it bifurcated into a precept that is optional and one that is obligatory. When Samuel formulates the point of dispute in regard to the evening service, he states that 'Rabban Gamaliel says: It is obligatory; R. Joshua says: It is optional.'[79] For the term *miṣwā* could be interpreted as 'an optional precept', which was what R. Joshua actually had in mind, for it is clear that he, too, considers that one who recites the evening prayers performs a *miṣwā*[80], only this precept is not of an obligatory nature, so that a person would be liable to punishment for failing to observe it. Since an optional religious act was also called just *miṣwā*, it became necessary to designate an entirely obligatory religious act *ḥôvā* ('duty'). Thus R. Abba is not satisfied with the formulation of 'R. Ile'a in the name of R. Eleazar b. R. Simeon: Just as it is a meritorious act [*miṣwā*] for a man to say that which will be listened to, so is it meritorious for a man not to say that which will not be listened to,' and he declares 'It is a duty [*ḥôvā*], for it is said: "Reprove not a scorner, lest he hate thee; reprove a wise man and he will love thee" (Proverbs ix 8)' (*T.B. Yevamot* 65b). The meaning is: Just as one who reproves a wise man fulfils a precept, so one who rebukes a scorner and says something that is not listened to commits a transgression. The use of the term *miṣwā* in two senses sometimes caused misunderstanding. When Abbaye declares that 'It is a *miṣwā* for orphans to pay their father's debt', he meant to say, as Rashi states, 'On account of their father's honour, only the court must not compel them to do this, because it is not an express positive commandment like that of the "Tabernacle" and "palm branch", but merely a meritorious act [*miṣwā*] prescribed by the Rabbis.'[81] Hence, when Rav Papa, using the same expression, said 'Payment of the debt due to a creditor is a *miṣwā*', Rav Kahana raised an objection: 'In view of your statement that payment of the debt due to a creditor is a *miṣwā*, what is the position if he says "I have no desire to perform a meritorious deed [*miṣwā*]?" ' Thereupon Rav Papa replied that he had in mind a positive commandment, that is, one whose observance is obligatory and concerning which it has been taught in a Baraita: '...But in the case of a positive commandment, for instance, if he is told "Make a tabernacle!" and he does not do so, (or carry) a "pa'm branch" and he does not do so, he may be beaten till he expires. [82] From our previous remarks, it is clear that Rav Papa's statement and Rav Kahana's objection do not involve a disagreement in principle on the question whether payment of a creditor is a religious duty or an obligation under civil law.[83] Such a distinction was far from the mind of the Amoraim. Undoubtedly even Rav Kahana did not recognize an obligation under civil law that did not fall within the category of the commandments. That which is not a commandment (*miṣwā*) is certainly not obligatory but optional; yet within this option it was possible, as we have seen, to upgrade and approximate certain acts to the status of commandment, even acts not included in the concept of 'an obligation under civil law'.

The idea that even human actions that are related only to man's bodily needs are to be regarded as having religious merit [*miṣwā*] is attributed to Hillel the Elder. The dictum of R. Jose in the Mishna (*'Avot* ii, 12) 'And let all your deeds be for the sake of Heaven' is glossed in *'Avot de-R. Nathan* (Version II, xxx, p. 66): 'Like Hillel, for when Hillel went anywhere (and) he was asked: "Whither are you going?" (he would answer): "I go to perform a precept." — "What precept, Hillel?" — "I am going to perform my needs." — "Is this then a religious act?" He replied: "Yea, so that the body be not impaired." (Or on another occasion they might say to him:) "Whither are you going, Hillel?" — "I go to perform a precept." — "What precept, Hillel?" — "I am going to the bathhouse." — "Is this then a precept?" — He replied: "Yea, in order to cleanse the body. Here is proof that this is so: If now in the case of the statues (εἰκόνιον) that stand in the royal plazas, the officer appointed to cleanse and polish them is given an annual state salary, and furthermore is raised to the status of the nobility of the kingdom, how much more so we, who have been created in the Divine image and likeness, as it is said 'For in the image of God made He man!'" (Genesis ix 6). Shammai expressed a different view: 'Let us fulfil our obligations with this body.'[84] Shammai also recognized a man's duty to care for his body, so that it should not become impaired and should be clean. Man must maintain his body in the sense of 'perforce you live', and he does not require the verse 'For in the image of God made He man.' A man's duty towards his body is to be differentiated from the precepts between man and God and between man and man, and is not included among the acts to be performed for the sake of Heaven. In the light of the foregoing we can explain another dispute between Shammai and Hillel, which scholars have found difficult to understand:[85] 'It is taught, It was said of Shammai the Elder: All his days he used to eat in honour of the Sabbath. If he found a fine beast, he would say: This is for the Sabbath. If he (subsequently) found another that was still better, he would set aside the second (for the Sabbath) and eat the first. But Hillel the Elder had another attitude, for all his works were for the sake of Heaven, as it is said "Blessed be the Lord day by day." '[86] It appears that the words 'all his works were for the sake of Heaven' have the same meaning as in *M. 'Avot* and in the story in *'Avot de-R. Nathan*, namely that Hillel regarded even eating on week days as an act to be dedicated to Heaven, and in this sense he interpreted the verse 'Blessed be the Lord day by day.'[87] Shammai said otherwise; concerning eating during the week-days, which he considered necessary, he declared: 'Let us fulfil our obligations with this body.' He considered that the direction of thought to Heaven found fulfilment in the observance of commandments not necessary to the body: 'It was said of Shammai the Elder that he never ceased speaking of the Sabbath; if he bought anything good, he would say: This is for the Sabbath; a new vessel, he would say: This is for the Sabbath' (*Mekhilta de-R. Simeon b. Yoḥai*, p. 148). We are confronted by a doctrinal dispute. In Hillel's view a man is able — and consequently he is so enjoined — to dedicate all his acts, even where natural functions are concerned, to Heaven; whereas Shammai posits such a possibility only in the case of acts that are precepts. In the spirit of Hillel's approach it was taught in a Baraita 'A man should wash his face, hands and feet every day for the sake of his Maker, for it is said "The Lord hath made everything for His own purpose" (Proverbs xvi 4).'[88] Similarly Bar Qappara expounded: 'Which is the short Scriptural passage on which the fundamentals of the Torah are dependent? — "In all thy ways acknowledge him" (Proverbs iii 6)'; and Rava further inferred from his words: 'even where a transgression is involved'.[89] At first blush Rava's remark recalls the dictum of R. Naḥman bar Isaac 'More meritorious is a transgression performed with good intent [i.e. for the sake of Heaven] than a precept fulfilled with an ulterior motive',[90] but, as we shall see below (p. 398), it is doubtful if the thought is the same. At all events committing a transgression for the sake of Heaven only means doing it in order to fulfil a precept, as is to be inferred from the statement of ʿUlla: 'Tamar was guilty of adultery (and) Zimri was guilty of adultery. Tamar committed adultery and kings and prophets were descended from her; Zimri committed adultery, and myriads of Israelites fell on his account.'[91]

One cannot overlook the danger to the observance of the precepts from the standpoint of Hillel, for if every act can be done in the name of Heaven, then something is abstracted from the absolute value of the precept and a way is opened for the nullification of the worth of the ritual laws whose connection with the knowledge of the Lord is not clear or simple. In truth, Jesus reached such extreme conclusions in his polemic against the Halakha, as is reported in the Gospels.[92] The danger was evident to Hillel himself, and in the light of it we must understand the Baráita: 'Hillel the Elder said: When (the scholars) draw in, scatter, when they disseminate, draw in. When you see that the Torah is beloved of all Israel, and all rejoice in it, scatter it abroad, as it is said "There is that scattereth and yet increaseth" (Proverbs xi 24). When you see that the Torah is being forgotten by Israel, and not all take heed of it, draw it in, as it is said: "When it is time to work for the Lord" (Psalms cxix 126).'[93] The scattering that finds expression in the demand that all one's actions should be in the name of Heaven, and regards the washing of the body as a religious act, is suited to a time when the Torah is beloved of all Israel, and all rejoice therein; but when all do not take heed of the Torah, it is a 'time to work for the Lord'. I have deviated from the interpretation of the commentators who have explained Hillel's statement to refer to 'Torah study', and I have interpreted it to relate to the observance of the precepts. It would seem that R. Me'ir already interpreted in this way the saying of Hillel 'They have made void Thy law — it is time to work for the Lord'[94], referring it to times when the observance of the precepts was prohibited, and many indeed did not stand up to the test. Thus 'R. Me'ir used to say: There is not a man in Israel who does not perform a hundred precepts each day... there is not a man in Israel who is not encompassed by precepts....' Noteworthy is the addition to the Baraita that parallels the dictum of R. Me'ir: 'The Rabbis taught: Beloved are Israel, for the Holy One, blessed be He, encompassed them with precepts — phylacteries on their head, and phylacteries on their arms, and fringes on their garments, and *mĕzûzôt* on their portals, and concerning them David said: "Seven times a day do I praise Thee, because of Thy righteous ordinances" (Psalms cxix 164); and when David entered the bathhouse and saw himself naked, he said: "Woe is me, for I am naked, without precepts"; but when he remembered the circumcision in his flesh, his mind was set at rest' (*T.B. Menaḥot* 43b). At a time when the observance of the commandments was forbidden, including circumcision, it was inappropriate to say that the very entry into the bathhouse was in itself a religious act, but primarily it was necessary to emphasize the value and importance of the precepts, in accordance with the teaching of R. Me'ir's contemporary R. Simeon b. Yoḥai: 'If you see that people have grown very lax in matters of the Torah, arise and be strong therein.'[95] On the other hand it seems that the dicta of Bar Qappara, Rava, and Rav Naḥman bar Isaac are to be understood against the background of the feeling of generations in which 'the Torah was beloved of all Israel and all rejoiced therein', a feeling that found expression in the words that Rava attributed to the Congregation of Israel.[96]

II. *The Number, Classification, and Evaluation of the Precepts*

The consciousness that Israelites were encompassed every moment by precepts, and that the Lord 'Left nothing in the world unendowed by a precept',[97] serves as a background to the homily of R. Simlai: 'Six hundred and thirteen precepts were given to Moses — three hundred and sixty-five of them are negative commandments, like the number of the days of the solar year, and two hundred and forty-eight are positive commandments, corresponding to the parts of the human body' (*T.B. Makkot* 23b). It is the idea that there is a precept for every day of the year and every part of man's body[98] — 'each part says to man: pray, perform this precept through me... each day says to man: pray, do not commit this transgression on me'[99] — that led to the fixing of the exact number six hundred and thirteen. In the Tannaitic sources this number is unknown, and in the passages where it appears in the printed editions it is only an interpolation that is wanting in the MSS; for instance: '...Now it is surely an argument from minor to major: If they (the Gentiles) failed to observe the seven precepts enjoined upon the Children of Noah, how much less (would they be able to keep) the six hundred and thirteen commandments!' But in the MSS the reading is: '...how much less all the commandments of the Torah!'[1] The other Amoraim that speak about the number of the precepts, including those who find support for the number 613 in the numerical value of the word Torah [תורה TWRH, which adds up in Hebrew to 611] plus the first two commandments of the Decalogue, which were uttered by the Almighty,[2] based themselves on the homily of R. Simlai. We know of no attempt to count the precepts in the Talmudic era, but the enumerators of the commandments from the time of the compiler of the *Halakhot Gedolot* onward encountered many difficulties. Maimonides severely criticized the enumerators of the precepts who preceded him, he shows lack of method and system in their ways of enumeration. However, even the principles and rules that he set forth as the basis of his Book of Precepts[3] aroused much criticism; it is worthwhile citing the summary remarks of R. Simeon b. Ṣemaḥ Duran at the end of his work *Zohar ha-Raqiaʿ* ['Splendour of the Heaven'][4]: 'And now, O reader, note carefully what I have written: both in the case of the positive and negative precepts there are many differences of opinion and much confusion in respect of the number of the commandments... and if all the leading authorities could not find their way in this regard, how can the least of them hope to work out the calculation where one builds and the other demolishes, one fences in and the other breaches the fence, one raises an objection and the other resolves it...

and perhaps the consensus of opinion that the number of the precepts is 613 — 345 and 248 — conforms to the view of R. Simlai and his interpretation of the precepts, but we do not rely on his interpretation in deciding the Halakha, but on the Talmudic study of the subject. The reason why this number is mentioned everywhere is that we find no other Sage who counted them, and so we have taken his enumeration, and even if the number is too low or too high, it is approximately correct, and as the Sages often say (*T.B. Sukka* 8a; *T.B. Bava Batra* 27a): "It is a small amount, and a small amount is disregarded." ' This epitome supports our observations about the beginning of R. Simlai's homily and its purpose.[5] The matter becomes clear if we consider the continuation of the exposition: 'David came and reduced them to eleven, as it is written: "A Psalm of David. Lord who shall sojourn in Thy tabernacle..." (Psalms xv 1–5); Isaiah came and reduced them to six, as it is written: "He that walketh righteously, and speaketh uprightly..." (Isaiah xxxiii 15); Micah came and reduced them to three, as it is written: "It hath been told thee, O man" (Micah vi 8); Isaiah further reduced them to two, as it is said: "Thus saith the Lord, keep ye justice and do righteousness" (Isaiah lvi 1); Amos came and brought them down to one, as it is said: "Thus saith the Lord unto the house of Israel, Seek ye Me and live" (Amos v 4).'[6] Although an Israelite has been given precepts corresponding to each day of the year and every part of his body, yet the prophets already came and reduced them to a few commandments, even to one. Only these precepts are really principles, which, if you wish to fulfil them, you must particularize and interpret them, and consequently you observe many commandments.[7] R. Simlai's homily is cited in the Talmudic discussion on the teaching of the Tanna R. Hananiah b. Gamaliel in the Mishna: 'If now he that commits a single transgression forfeits his soul thereby, how much more so shall he that fulfils a precept be granted his soul!'[8] It is possible that R. Hananiah derived his teaching from the reply given by R. Akiba to Rabban Gamaliel, the father of R. Hananiah: ' "He is just, he shall surely live" (Ezekiel xviii 9) — when Rabban Gamaliel reached this verse, he wept and said: Only he that does all these things shall live; but not if he does one of them! R. Akiba answered him: If so, when Scripture enjoins "Defile not yourselves in all these things" (Leviticus xviii 24), does it also mean only in all of them, but not in one of them? Surely it means in one of these things! Likewise here the sense is that by (doing) one of these things (he shall live).'[9] R. Simlai's statement is thus in the nature of a comment that dissociates itself from both R. Ḥananiah's saying and R. Akiba's reply. It is true that a man may become meritorious by virtue of a single precept, but only if this precept has special and all-embracing significance.

The question of the relative value of the commandments found expression in many varied forms in the teaching of the Sages. On the one hand we find dicta that proclaim the absolute equality of all the precepts, and on the other we encounter clear distinctions drawn between more important and less important commandments, and methods of classifying precepts and transgressions according to various criteria. An exhaustive study of the sources shows us that they do not indicate so much disagreement between the Sages over principles as they reflect the result of reciprocal influence between doctrinal approaches and the experiences of the Rabbis regarding the realities of observing the precepts. The formulation and style of the evaluative dicta were largely determined by the desire to influence these realities and the possibility of directing them. The Mishna (*Shevuot* i, 6) 'And for all other transgressions specified by the Torah, light or grave... involving positive or negative commandments, the penalty of "extinction" [Divine punishment through premature or sudden death], or of death by sentence of the court, the scapegoat makes atonement' is interpreted by the Amora Rav Judah thus: 'This is the meaning... the light (transgressions) are those involving positive or negative commandments; and the grave (transgressions) are those punished by "extinction" or death by sentence of the court.'[10] The differentiation between light and stringent precepts is based, therefore, on the severity of the penalty that the transgressions entail.[11]

The distinction between stringent and light commandments was differently understood by Ben ʿAzzai. On the verse ' "Only be steadfast in not eating the blood..." R. Simeon b. ʿAzzai remarked: Now there are three hundred similar positive precepts in the Torah! It comes to teach us, therefore, that if in regard to blood, than which there is no lighter precept among all the commandments, Scripture admonished you thus, how much more so in the case of the other precepts.'[12] The eating of blood is something repulsive; consequently it is easy to abstain from it. Lightness and stringency are not measured by the extent of the reward or punishment involved in doing the precept or transgression, but according to the effort required to fulfil the commandments or to refrain from the transgressions. So, too, a precept not entailing expenditure of money, or involving danger to life, is called 'a light commandment'. The criterion of reward and punishment is disregarded and does not determine the issue. Indeed, Ben ʿAzzai maintained the principle of 'The reward of a precept is a precept, and the reward of a transgression is a transgression.'[13] In a similar manner R. Simeon b. Yoḥai explained the stringency of the commandment to honour parents. The effort required to keep it elevates this precept to an especially high plane: 'For it is taught, R. Simeon b. Yoḥai said: Great is (the precept of) honouring father and mother, for the Holy One, blessed be He, put it above the honour due to Him. It is stated "Honour thy father and thy mother", and it is said "Honour the Lord with thy substance" (Proverbs iii 9). With what should you honour Him? With the substance that He graciously bestows upon you — setting aside the gleanings, the forgotten sheaf, the corners of the field; separating the heave-offering, the first tithe, the second tithe, the poorman's tithe, and the dough-offering; preparing a booth, a palm-branch, a ram's horn, phylacteries, and fringes; feeding the poor and the hungry, giving drink to the thirsty. If you have, you are obliged to do all these things; but if you have not, you are not obliged to do any of these things. But when we come to the commandment of honouring parents, whether you have substance or not, you must "honour thy father and thy mother", even if you have to go begging.'[14] The duty is absolute, and the effort required is great. It is noteworthy that R. Simeon b. Yoḥai's homily is cited in relation to a Mishna that particularly specifies a series of precepts in the light of reward: 'These are things whose fruits a man enjoys in this world, while the capital is laid for him in the world to come: honouring father and mother, the practice of loving kindness, and making peace between a man and his fellow; but the study of the Torah is equal to them all' (*M. Pe'ah* i, 1). The Mishna groups all these precepts together on the basis of reward. R. Simeon's statement in the Baraita lacks the criterion of reward; in its place he makes the measure of personal sacrifice required for the fulfilment of the commandments the yardstick of their importance.

Alongside the formal scale used to determine the relative significance of the precepts, there are not wanting sources that employ an individual measuring-rod that discovers in this or that commandment characteristics that raise the importance of the precept; for example, ' "the Lord will pass over the door, and will not suffer... (Exodus xii 23)" — a conclusion *a minori* may be drawn from this: If now in the case of the blood of the passover sacrifice offered up in Egypt, which was a light precept, and was of a temporary character, and was not to be observed day and night, and was not enjoined for all times, Scripture declares "and He will not suffer the destroyer", then in the case of the *mĕzûzā*, which is a weighty commandment, containing the Tetragrammaton ten times, and is to be kept day and night, and is enjoined for all times, how much more so that He will not suffer the destroyer!...' (*Mĕkhilta de-R. Ishmael*, Massekhta de-Pisḥa, xi, p. 39). It appears that the Tannaim adopted this method with a view to endearing certain precepts to the people, and for this purpose they did not refrain from hyperbole, particularly in respect of commandments that were lightly esteemed by the public. In one Baraita it is stated that the precept of fringes is 'a light commandment'[15], whereas in another Baraita the opposite is asserted: 'This precept is equal to all the precepts put together, for it is written: "that ye may look upon it, and remember all the commandments of the Lord" ' (*T.B. Menaḥot* 43b). R. Simeon b. Yoḥai expounded: 'Whoever is meticulous in the observance of this commandment is privileged to receive the Divine Presence; for here it is written "that ye may look upon it ['*ōtô*]" (Numbers xv 39), and elsewhere it is stated "Thou shalt fear the Lord thy God, and Him ['*ōtô*] shalt thou serve" (Deuteronomy vi 13)' (*T.B. Menaḥot*, *loc. cit.*). R. Me'ir found an internal proof of the importance of the precept based on its nature: 'It is not said here "that ye may look upon them" but "that ye may look upon Him" — thus Scripture teaches that whoever observes the commandment of fringes is deemed as though he had received the Divine Presence, for תכלת *tĕkhēlet* ['blue' of the cord inserted in the fringes] resembles the (colour of the) sea, and the sea resembles the sky and the sky resembles the Throne of Glory.'[16] Concrete evidence of the punctiliousness with which the precept of fringes was observed is in our possession from the time of Bar Kokhba. In the caves of Bar Kokhba there have been found bundles of fringes and even a woollen fleece dyed blue [*tĕkhēlet*][17]; this shows that even the remaining fighters living in the caves scrupulously observed the commandment of fringes. Possibly this strict observance actually developed after the destruction of the Temple as a remedy for the crisis emanating from Israel's inability to receive the Divine Presence in the Temple. The precept of the fringes served as a surrogate: whoever kept this easy commandment 'received, as it were, the Divine Presence'. The edicts prohibiting the observance of the precepts, which followed the rebellion, made it particularly hard to keep the commandment of fringes, for it was difficult to conceal them. The sayings of R. Simeon b. Yoḥai and R. Me'ir were intended to encourage and stimulate the observance.

We also find a similar evaluation of the precept of the Sabbath and of that of circumcision. 'Rabbi said: This (is) the commandment of the Sabbath, which is equal to all the commandments of the Torah. R. Eleazar bar Avina said: It is written, (Nehemiah ix 14) "And madest known unto them Thy holy Sabbath, and commandments and statutes". [Why is מצוות *miṣwôt* ('commandments') written *plene*?] To teach you that it [the Sabbath] is equal to (all) the precepts of the Torah.'[18] Similarly it is taught 'In the Pentateuch and the Prophets and the Hagiographa we find that the Sabbath is equal to all the commandments of the Torah....' Concerning the precept of circumcision it is stated that since this commandment supersedes the Sabbath, it is necessarily of greater importance: 'It is like the case of two noble ladies who proceed side by side, so that you cannot tell which is the greater of the two. But when one steps down on account of the other, you know that the other is the greater of the two' (*T.P. Nedarim* xiii, 14, p. 38b).

The extent to which the evaluations of the ordinances by the Sages were liable to changes due to social and political circumstances is particularly manifest in their dicta concerning the precept of charity. On the one hand we have sayings and homilies, in uninterrupted succession, from the time of R. Joḥanan b. Zakkai and his disciples to that of the Amoraim R. Eleazar and R. Jose, that extol charity and elevate it to the level of the Temple service and the reception of the

Divine Presence; and on the other, there are enactments against dissipation of all one's wealth in giving charity and dicta that encourage a person to spare his possessions. Both the former and the latter are to be understood against the background of political, religious, and social conditions: the destruction of the Temple, taxes, and forced labour. The charitable deeds of the Christian communities influenced, separately or jointly, the dicta evaluating charity and the practice of loving kindness.[19] The saying 'Dwelling in Eretz-Israel is equal to all the commandments of the Torah' is found incorporated in a narrative about a journey of Sages abroad after the revolt of Bar Kokhba, at the time of the Ḥadrianic persecution (*Sifre Deuteronomy* § 80).

The emphasis given to the inner worth of the precepts restricted, in no small measure, the concept of reward as the criterion of the appraisal of the precepts, but it did not entirely nullify the need to stress the idea of reward for the precepts — not only in the world to come, but also in this world — in exhortations to observe the commandments. Not all accepted the view of Ben ʿAzzai (above, 249), nor was everyone prepared to be content with 'The reward of a precept is another precept', or to agree with the opinion of R. Jacob that 'There is no reward for precepts in this world.'[20] R. Nathan taught: 'There is not a single precept, even a light one, enjoined in the Torah whose reward is not given in this world; as to the world to come, I have no conception how great the reward is there.'[21] But even R. Nathan equated the commandments from the viewpoint of their reward, much as Rabbi taught in the Mishna (*'Avot* ii, 1): 'And be heedful of a light precept as of a weighty one, for you know not the reward given for the precepts.' The precepts are conceived in their entirety as a single body, and the individual commandments are, as it were, organs of equal value that sustain this body. In one analogy we are told: 'R. Ḥiyya taught: To what can the case (of the precepts) be compared? To a king who had an orchard, into which he brought workers, but he did not disclose to them the (respective) recompense for the saplings to be planted in the vineyard. For had he revealed to them the (respective) reward for his plantings, they would see which sapling carried a high recompense and plant that; thus the work of the orchard would be partly left undone and would (only) partly be accomplished.'[22] The Torah is compared here to an orchard containing various plants, and it is necessary to maintain all the plants without distinction.[23] This view that the commandments are of equal importance has a bearing also upon the Halakha, for the law is that 'He that is occupied with a precept is exempt from (performing another) precept' (*T.B. Sukka* 25a), and irrespective of the precept with which he is occupied, he is not obliged to interrupt its observance in order to fulfil another.

From the homily of R. Simeon b. Yoḥai on the stringency of the commandment to honour father and mother, and from the fact that the reward of longevity mentioned in connection therewith is the reward promised in the Torah also for fulfilling the command to let the mother-bird go (before taking the young), the Amora R. Abba bar Kahana inferred that 'Scripture equated... the lightest of precepts, namely that of letting the mother-bird go, and the weightiest of precepts, to wit, that of honouring father and mother' (*T.P. Pe'a* i, 1, p. 15d; *T.P. Qiddushin* p. 61b [end]). Not only the promise of equal reward for these two precepts, but also the absence of any mention of reward in respect of other precepts, makes the evaluation of the commandments by the measure of their reward nugatory. Thus the same Abba bar Kahana expounded: 'It is written: "Lest תפלס *tĕfallēs* the path of life, her ways wander so that thou shouldst not know" (Proverbs v 6) — the Holy One, blessed be He, made the bestowal of reward to those who fulfil the precepts irregular, so that they should perform them באמונה *be-'ĕmûnā*.'[24] He interprets the Scripture 'Lest *tĕfallēs* the path of life': Lest thou come to weigh (connecting the verb with *peles*, 'a balance' [literally, 'make level']) the commandments, which are the path of life. In order to obviate this — i.e. that you should not choose which precept to keep and which not — 'her ways wander so that thou shouldst not know', the Torah concealed their reward, and 'so that they should perform them *be-'ĕmûnā*' — that is, 'in faith'. A similar exposition (of another verse) is given by 'R. Aḥa in the name of R. Isaac: It is written "Of every charge keep thy heart; for out of it are the issues of life" (Proverbs iv 23) — of all that you are told in the Torah take heed; for you do not know from which of the precepts life will issue forth unto you.'[25]

However, it was just this comparison of the precepts from the aspect of their reward that did not prevent the Amoraim from promising the reward of longevity for commandments whose observance was lax, like phylacteries, for example: 'Resh Laqish said, He who puts on phylacteries lives long.'[26]

What we have stated so far related to positive precepts. The question now arises whether negative precepts, where the penalties, in the case of transgression, were disclosed by the Torah — e.g. flogging, 'extinction', death by order of the court — were also subjected to changes in the criteria of evaluation. Are there indications here, too, that the appraisal of a transgression is independent of the punishment inflicted for it? In truth we find in this respect as well that the gravity of certain offences was emphasized without regard to the penalty. The need for differentiation crystallized at times of oppressive religious decrees and ordeals, when the Sages had to decide for which offences a man was required to give his life rather than transgress, and a concrete Halakha emerged that specified, out of the entire corpus of precepts, three things — idolatry, incest, and murder — for which alone a man should prefer death to sin. Although each of these three iniquities carries the penalty of death, yet the form of execution is not alike. Forbidden relations include transgressions that are punished by extinction, and others that involve execution by order of the court. But the penalty of death is to be found for other wrongful acts, regarding which it was not ordained 'Let him be slain and not transgress'. Thus these three offences were singled out not on account of the punishment they involve, but because they rest on fundamental principles the abolition of which could undermine the entire existence of Judaism. The source treating of this is the teaching of R. Joḥanan: 'In the name of R. Simeon b. Jehozadak it was reported that it was decided by vote in the upper chamber of the house of Nitza in Lydda: In respect of any law of the Torah, if a man is ordered "Transgress and be not slain!", let him transgress rather than be slain, except in the case of idolatry, incest and murder.'[27] But where the Sabbath is concerned, for example, a man should desecrate it rather than be put to death, even though the Sabbath, too, involves death by order of the court. The Amoraim extended the obligation of the maxim 'Let a man be slain and not transgress' to particular circumstances: 'When Rav Dimi came back (from Eretz-Israel) he said in the name of R. Joḥanan:

This was taught only in regard to a time when there is no religious persecution, but at a time of persecution a man should suffer death rather than violate even a minor law.[28] When Rabin came back he reported in the name of R. Joḥanan: Even when there is no religious persecution, the law that we have stated [limiting the obligation of martyrdom to three precepts] applies only (when the transgressions are committed) in privacy, but publicly a man should face death and not infringe even a minor commandment[29].' Thus the dicta of these Amoraim add considerably to the stringency of the principle, in that one should suffer martyrdom and not transgress even a minor precept in public; and what is meant by a minor precept is explained in the name of Rav as 'Even to change one's shoe strap'.[30] At first glance it might seem that the explanation represents a later interpretation in the direction of greater severity, but we have evidence that it is precisely this interpretation that reflects the actual position. In *IV Maccabees* (v 19–22), which was composed near the time of the destruction of the Temple, Eleazar declares: 'Think it not, then, a small sin for us to eat the unclean thing, for the transgression of the Law, be it in small things or in great, is equally heinous; for in either case equally the Law is despised.' On the Scripture 'of them that love Me and keep My commandments' (Exodus xx 6) we find the comment: 'R. Nathan said: "Of them that love Me and keep my commandments" — these are the Israelites who dwell in the Land of Israel and give their lives for the precepts. Why are you going forth to be executed? Because I circumcised my son. Why are you going to be crucified? Because I ate unleavened bread. Why are you being scourged? Because I performed the palm-branch ritual.'[31] Here we have practical corroboration of the Halakha transmitted by the Amoraim, to wit, that in times of persecution Jews gave their lives not only for the three laws on which a vote was taken at the house of Nitza in Lydda, but for every precept, if transgression in public was involved. Indirect evidence for this is to be found also in the following story related by R. Me'ir: 'We were once sitting before R. Akiba and we were reading the *Shĕma*ʿ, but we did so inaudibly on account of a quaestor who was standing at the entrance.' R. Me'ir wished to infer from this that the *Shĕma*ʿ need not be recited audibly, but the Sages 'said to him: A time of peril is no proof' (*Tosefta Berakhot* ii, 13, p. 4), that is to say, they acted thus in privacy at a time of danger. But even in public Jews did not give their lives for all the commandments, as we learn from the following Baraita: 'R. Simeon b. Eleazar said: Every precept for which Israel submitted themselves to death at the time of the Roman persecution — for example, idolatry and circumcision — is still scrupulously observed by them; but every precept for which they did not give their lives at the time of the Roman persecution — like phylacteries, for instance — is still laxly observed.'[32] In the parallel passages to this Baraita the examples of the precepts, both those for which the Jews gave their lives and those for which they did not submit to death, vary. Thus it is stated that 'the Sabbath, circumcision, study of the Torah, and ritual ablution, for which they laid down their lives, are retained by them'; and that, on the other hand, such institutions as 'the Temple, the civil courts, the Sabbatical year, and the Jubilee, for which the Jews did not submit to death, have not been preserved by them.'[33] These differences are not to be regarded as just *variae lectiones*; they appear to reflect differences of fact, for not all the actual — or proximate — periods of persecution were alike, nor were all places treated equally, as R. Isaac noted: 'There was a city in Eretz-Israel... for the wicked kingdom once promulgated an edict (prohibiting Jewish religious observances) against the Jewish people, but against that city it did not promulgate the decree.'[34] Although it was stated that the people did not give their lives for the precepts of the year of Release, and hence they remained lax in observing them, yet it is stated: 'In the district of R. Judah the Sabbatical year was strictly observed.'[35] Even when there was no religious persecution, the avoidance of given transgressions did not correspond to their gravity or to the punishment incurred by the transgressors. There were times and places in which greater heed was taken not to commit minor sins than graver ones; and contrariwise there were those who treated minor transgressions and Rabbinic prohibitions lightly.[36]

The attitude to prevailing transgressions affected also the adoption of preventive measures and safeguards in Halakhic matters,[37] but primarily it influenced the homilies and preaching of the Sages. For example, 'Rava expounded: What is the meaning of the verse "And furthermore, my son, take heed: of making many books..." (Ecclesiastes xii 12)? My son, pay greater heed to the words of the Scribes than to those of the Torah. For the injunctions of the Torah contain positive and negative commandments; but as regards the enactments of the Scribes whoever transgresses them is worthy of death. Should you argue: If they (the Rabbinic laws) have real substance, why were they not written down? Therefore Scripture declares: "Of making many books there is no end; and much study is a weariness of the flesh" (*ibid.*).'[38] The concluding remarks of Rava imply that in his initial statement, too, he had in mind one who transgresses the enactments of the Sages by denying the principle of the Oral Law, holding that it is valueless. It appears that this is also the purport of the following Baraita, which may have been the source of Rava's exposition: 'R. Ishmael taught: In the case of Torah ordinances, there are things that are prohibited and things that are permitted, there are light and weighty precepts; but all the injunctions of the Scribes are stringent.'[39] R. Ishmael declares that in contrast to the precepts of the Torah, which contain light and weighty commandments, the enactments of the Scribes are all equally strict, for transgressing them implies denial of the authority of the Oral Law. With regard to this R. Eleazar, or R. Samuel bar Naḥmani, said that the case resembles 'a heap of stones—if one of them is disturbed, they are all disturbed.' This analogy and those like it seek to explain the consequences of the disrespect shown to the Sages by those who say 'that scribe' or 'those Rabbis'; these detractors exemplified, in the opinion of R. Joḥanan and R. Eleazar, the 'Epicurean' who, the Mishna[40] declares, has no share in the world to come.[41] The enactments of the Rabbis are of equal stringency, for in implementing them one fulfils, according to Abbaye, the principle 'It is a precept to hearken to the injunctions of the Sages'[42], and in transgressing them one transgresses, in the view of Rav Ivya — the younger contemporary of Rava — the prohibition 'Thou shalt not turn aside from the sentence which they shall declare unto thee, to the right hand, nor to the left' (Deuteronomy xvii 11)[43], while Rav Kahana declares: 'All Rabbinic enactments are based on the prohibition "Thou shalt not turn aside".'[44] The homilies of the Palestinian Amoraim on the endearing character of the Rabbinical ordinances and Rava's remarks about their stringency[45] have as their purpose the reinforcement of the Oral Law as against those who assail it and its foundations. However, these expositions did not aim to abolish the difference in principle between Torah and Rabbinical legislation, which found expression in the rule 'A doubtful case involving Torah-law must be decided stringently; a doubtful case involving Rabbinical law is decided leniently.'[46] The differentiation in principle between prohibitions carrying the penalty of death by order of the court and those bearing the penalty of 'extinction', as well as ordinary negative commandments, also remained unchanged. The transgressions that were subject to the rule 'Let a man submit to death rather than transgress' were regarded, of course, as transgressions that could wholly undermine the Torah and precepts; as the Tanna R. Simeon b. Eleazar expressed it: 'He who blasphemes and worships idols has no precept left (to keep).'[47] But the recognition of basic differences and distinctions did not prevent the Sages from conjoining light and weighty precepts, when the times called for this. In antithetic parallelism to the first Mishna of *Tractate Pe'a,* which enumerates 'things whose fruits a man enjoys in this world while the capital is laid up for him in the world to come', the Tosefta states: 'For which things is a man punished in this world, while the fundamental retribution is kept in store for him in the world to come? For idolatry, incest, murder, and also for slander, which is accounted equal to all of them put together.'[48] To the three transgressions that come under the rule 'Let a man submit to death rather than transgress', and for which one is punished in both worlds, the Sages not only added slander, but said that it is as grave as all of them put together. The extreme gravity ascribed to slander and the retribution attached to it[49] simply testify that this sin was very widespread at all times. In similar vein to the statement in the Tosefta concerning slander, R. Joḥanan expounded the subject of larceny: '...R. Yudan said in the name of R. Joḥanan: It may be compared to a basket full of iniquities — who lays the charge against them all? Larceny! R. Phinehas in the name of R. Joḥanan said: It is comparable to a number of people that included idolaters, murderers, and the incestuous; yet it is the larceny inherent in them all that is as grave an iniquity as all of them put together.'[50] It is clear that from the aspect of punishment larceny is less heinous than the other crimes enumerated with it in the same homily. But R. Joḥanan's statement concerning the gravity of the sin of larceny is to be understood in the light of his comments on another verse: ' "...He that killeth an ox is as if he slew a man" (Isaiah lxvi 3)... R. Joḥanan said: Whoever robs his fellow to the value of a *peruṭa* is deemed to have killed him. And there are many verses (that prove this): "He that killeth an ox is as if he slew a man" (Isaiah *ibid.*); "And he learned to catch the prey, he devoured men" (Ezekiel xix 6); "So are the ways of every one that is greedy of gain; it taketh away the life of the owners thereof" (Proverbs i 19); "For the violence against the children of Judah, because they have shed innocent blood" (Joel iv 19); "And they said unto the king: 'The man that consumed us' " (II Samuel xxi 5). But did he slay them or plan to destroy them? Rather the meaning is that because he destroyed Nob, the city of priests, which provided them with food, it is accounted to him by Scripture as if he had slain them.' Another reason for the gravity of the sin of robbery is given in the homily of R. Joḥanan's contemporaries following the preceding exposition: 'R. Lazar asked R. Ḥanina... saying to him: What is the meaning of the verse "Two things have I asked... falsehood and lies... lest I be full, and deny" (Proverbs xxx 7–9) — which is the worse, the first or the second? He replied: The second, adding: We find that the Holy One, blessed be He, overlooked idolatry, but not חילול השם *Ḥillûl ha-Shēm*, "Desecration of the Divine Name" [i.e. disgracing the Jewish religion].'[51] To explain the homily it is necessary to cite the verses in full: 'Two things have I asked of Thee; deny me them not before I die: remove far from me falsehood and lies; give me neither poverty nor riches; feed me with mine allotted bread; lest I be full, and deny, and say: "Who is the Lord?" Or lest I be poor and steal, and profane the name of my God.' Riches are apt to lead to heresy, and poverty to theft, and the last to desecration of the Divine Name.[52] The greater gravity of the sin of robbery is thus to be understood as due to *Ḥillûl ha-Shēm*, which is liable to result therefrom.

The motive of profanation of the Divine Name can transform a light transgression into the gravest, just as קידוש השם *Qiddûsh ha-Shēm*, 'Sanctification of the Divine Name' [an act that redounds to the glory of Heaven and the Jewish religion] is able to elevate an act of but slight import to a religious deed of the highest significance. That *Ḥillûl ha-Shēm* is a graver transgression, from the punitive aspect, than offences involving 'extinction' and death by order of the court was already taught by R. Ishmael in the Baraita stating that 'There are four categories of persons with respect to atonement... if a man committed a transgression entailing 'extinction' or death by order of the court and repented, (penitence) and the Day of Atonement suspend (the punishment), and suffering makes atonement... But if one profaned the name of Heaven, and repented, penitence has not the power to suspend (the retribution), nor the Day of Atonement to expiate (completely); but repentance and the Day of Atonement atone one third, and suffering throughout the other days of the year atones a third, while the day of death purges it, for it is said: "surely this iniquity shall not be expiated by you till ye die" (Isaiah xxii 14); this teaches us that the day of death cleanses it away.'[53] The exposition of this Tanna implies that *Ḥillûl ha-Shēm* is a graver sin than idolatry, and so the Palestinian Amoraim actually taught: 'We find that the Holy One, blessed be He, overlooked idolatry but not *Ḥillûl ha-Shēm*'; and they based their exposition on the verse in Ezekiel (xx 39) 'As for you, O house of Israel... Go ye, serve every one his idols, even because ye will not hearken unto Me; but My holy name shall ye no more profane.'[54] The desecration of Heaven's name occurs in public acts, and thus R. Abbahu stated in the name of R. Ḥanina the Babylonian: 'Rather let a man transgress in secret than profane Heaven's name in public.'[55] R. Ḥanina's teaching is in accord with that of the following Baraita: 'For it is taught, R. Ile'ai the Elder said: If a man sees that his evil inclination is getting the better of him, let him go to a place where he is unknown, and put on sordid clothes and wrap himself in a sordid cloak, and do what his heart listeth, but let him not desecrate the name of Heaven in public.'[56] This view of R. Ile'ai is disputed by the Tanna R. Joḥanan b. Beroqa, the disciple of R. Joshua, who says: 'He that profanes the name of Heaven secretly shall be requited openly; in profaning the Name it is all one whether it be done inadvertently or wantonly.'[57] The purport of this Mishna is that if a man 'committed a transgression in secret', which, if known to the world, would have constituted desecration of the Divine Name, then 'the Holy One, blessed be He, punishes him openly by doing something to him that discloses to all that he committed the wrong and thus makes his shame public'[58], as is stated in a Baraita: 'Hypocrites are exposed on account of the Name.'[59] In keeping with the view of R. Joḥanan b. Beroqa concerning *Ḥillûl ha-Shēm* perpetrated in secret, R. Isaac declared: 'When one commits a transgression in secret, it is as though he thrust aside the feet of the Divine Presence'; and Rav Joseph said that the dictum in the Mishna (*Ḥagiga* ii, 1) 'Whosoever takes no thought for the honour of his Maker, it were a mercy if he had not come into the world' referred to 'one who commits transgression in secret'.[60] Even harsher words were uttered by R. Benjamin. He interpreted the verse 'But I returned and considered all the oppressions that are done under the sun; and behold the tears of such as were oppressed, and they had no comforter' (Ecclesiastes iv 1) as alluding to 'the hypocrites of the Torah: all the people think that he is a Bible scholar, but he is not; (that he is) a Mishna authority, but he is not; he is wrapped in his cloak and wears phylacteries on his head, "and behold the tears of such as were oppressed, and they had no comforter." Said the Holy One, blessed be He: I must bring them to account, as it is said (Jeremiah xlviii 10) "Cursed be he that doeth the work of the Lord deceitfully." '[61] In a certain sense the statement of R. Joḥanan b. Beroqa and the dicta of the Amoraim mentioned above may be regarded as a reaction to the overemphasis on *Ḥillûl ha-Shēm* in public, which implied the diminution of the gravity of sins and iniquities performed in secret, a view that in truth found expression in the teaching of R. Ileʿai the Elder.

It is manifest, however, that the primary and decisive factor in *Ḥillûl ha-Shēm* is the public performance of the acts; hence the matter does not depend on the gravity of the offences alone, but on the circumstances of the time and place, such as a period of harsh decrees and persecution directed against religious observance.[62] Consequently the factor of *Ḥillûl ha-Shēm* exerted considerable influence on the framing of laws relative to non-Jews. Rabban Gamaliel decreed that an object robbed from a Gentile should be forbidden because it involves desecration of the Divine Name;[63] R. Akiba said that Jewish judges, before whom a Gentile and Jew came for judgement, 'may not circumvent him [the Gentile], on account of *Ḥillûl ha-Shēm*'[64]. Some Sages regarded it as a profanation of the Name to refrain from a public act of *Qiddûsh ha-Shēm* in the presence of Gentiles, even if the deed itself was lawful and was not generally known, nor liable to cause *Ḥillûl ha-Shēm*. A case in point is the story told about Simeon b. Sheṭaḥ, that he returned the lost property of a Gentile, and when his disciples expressed surprise and questioned his action, seeing that the lost property of a Gentile may be kept, he replied: 'What do you think, that Simeon b. Sheṭaḥ is a barbarian? Simeon b. Sheṭaḥ prefers to hear "Blessed be the God of the Jews!" to receiving the reward of this whole world.' This is an anonymous account of the Palestinian Talmud, but stories similar to that about Simeon b. Sheṭaḥ are also cited about Amoraim who acted in a given way in order that Gentiles might bless the God of the Jews.[65] R. Abba bar Zemina used to work as a tailor for a Gentile in Rome. The latter wished to compel him to eat the flesh of נבלה *nĕvēlā* [an animal not slaughtered according to Jewish ritual law], and threatened to kill him, if he did not do so. Said R. Abba to him 'If you wish to kill, kill; for I shall not eat the flesh of *nĕvēlā*.' Subsequently the Gentile said to him: 'Now I can tell you that if you had eaten, I should have killed you. If one is a Jew, let one be a Jew; or if one is an Aramean [= Gentile], let one be an Aramean.'[66] R. Mana remarked on this story that if R. Abba bar Zemina had known of the Rabbinic teaching that when a man is compelled to infringe any of the precepts of the Torah in private, he should transgress rather than be killed, he would not have refrained from eating. But R. Abba bar Zemina was faithful to the principle that he transmitted in the name of R. Hoshaiah: 'Greater is *Qiddûsh ha-Shēm* than *Ḥillûl ha-Shēm*',[67] and the words of the Gentile constituted *Qiddûsh ha-Shēm*.

Notwithstanding the great store that the Amoraim set by the outward aspect of their conduct, they nevertheless regarded their duty in its inward aspect as of primary importance, and the stringency of their demands was linked to the personality of those concerned and to the position that they occupied in the social order. To the question 'What constitutes *Ḥillûl ha-Shēm*?' Rav answered 'In my case, if I took meat from the butcher and did not pay at once.' Rashi annotates: 'When I am late in paying, he (the butcher) thinks that I am a robber, and he learns from me to view robbery lightly.'[68] Instead of adducing an example of an act of *Ḥillûl ha-Shēm*, Abbaye cites the following Baraita: ' "And thou shalt love the Lord thy God" — this means that Heaven's name should become beloved through you; that a man should study Scripture and Mishna and attend upon the scholars, and conduct his business courteously with people in the market-place. What will people then say of him? Happy is this person who has learnt Torah, happy is his father who taught him Torah, happy is his teacher who instructed him in Torah. Woe to the people who have not learnt Torah! This man who has learnt Torah — see how noble are his ways, how perfect his actions! With respect to him Scripture declares: "And He said unto Me: Thou art My servant, Israel, in whom I will be glorified" (Isaiah xliii 3). But if one studies Scripture and Mishna, and attends on the scholars, and does not know how to conduct his business (properly) in the market-place, and does not speak courteously to people, what do people say of him? Woe to this man who learnt Torah, woe to his father who taught him Torah, woe to his teacher who instructed him in Torah! This man who learnt Torah — have you seen how bad are his ways, how ugly his deeds? Of him Scripture says: "In that men said of them: These are the people of the Lord, and are gone forth out of His land" (Ezekiel xxxvi 20).'[69] The Tanna R. Simeon b. Eleazar said: 'When Israel do the will of the Omnipresent, then His name is magnified in the world... and whenever they do not do His will, His name is profaned in the world.'[70] He is called 'one that does the will of his Father in Heaven' who fulfils the Torah and studies it.[71]

Despite all the distinctions that we find in their relative assessment of the precepts and the emphasis given to one or other commandment, the Sages never attained to a permanent classification of the precepts, either according to their inner character, or on the basis of the source of their revelation and the ways of their promulgation. This is particularly noticeable in their attitude to the Decalogue and in the difference between their conception of the Ten Commandments and that of Philo of Alexandria. In Philo's view all the precepts of the Torah are the detailed regulations of the Ten Commandments, which he calls roots, principles, or sources. He treats of the matter in his works *De Decalago* and *De Specialibus Legibus*,[71a] and arranges the individual precepts in groups according to the 'roots', i.e. classifies them according to the Ten Commandments.

Wolfson, in his big work on Philo of Alexandria,[72] observes simply that in Rabbinic literature, just as in Philo, it is stated that the Decalogue includes all the commandments. He bases himself on the dictum in *Canticles Rabba* (v, 14): 'Hananiah the son of R. Joshua's brother said: Between each commandment (of the Decalogue) the sections and detailed interpretations of the Torah were indited. When R. Joḥanan expounded the Scriptures and reached the verse "set with Tarshish" (Canticles v 14. Tarshish is apparently taken here to be the Sea of Tarshish; cf. Jonah i 3) he said: The son of the brother of R. Joshua gave me a beautiful interpretation of this: "Just as in the case of waves, between one big billow and another there are small waves, so between one commandment and another (of the Decalogue) the sections and detailed interpretations of the Torah were indited." ' The source of this dictum is in the Palestinian Talmud: 'Hananiah the son of the brother of R. Joshua said: Just as in the case of the sea there are small waves between one big billow and another, so between one commandment and another came the detailed interpretations and signs of the Torah' (*T.P. Sheqalim* vi, 1, p. 49d [end]). But these expositions merely intend to state that between one commandment and another the interpretations and detailed regulations of the commandment in question were written down, as R. Joḥanan observed in the passage quoted (above, p. 336). In these homilies it is not asserted that the Ten Commandments incorporate all the precepts of the Torah; only that every commandment forms the basis of interpretations and subtle inferences, detailed laws and general rules, and deductions by argument from minor to major and by analogy, in other words, all that the Halakha originated in the Oral Law was, as it were, written beside each commandment.[73] It seems that for very definite reasons the Sages refrained from introducing the concept that all the precepts were enshrined in the Decalogue. With reference to the Mishna[74] that states that in the Temple it was customary to read the Ten Commandments every day, the Palestinian Talmud declares: 'Rightly the Ten Commandments should be read every day. Why then are they not read? On account of the contention of the Minim; that it should not be said: These alone were given to Moses at Sinai.'[75] Obviously the Sages were concerned not to give prominence to the Ten Commandments and not to accord them a special status, in order not to provide sectarians with the opportunity to assert that only these commandments were promulgated at Sinai, but not the other precepts. In reply it was stated that alongside the Ten Commandments were written their interpretations. The 'sectarians' mentioned in the Palestinian Talmud are undoubtedly members of sects close to Christianity, who, in their antinomian approach, repudiated the observance of the precepts, and confined themselves to keeping the moral commandments only.[76]

The concept of the special status of the Ten Commandments, in its Philonian form, first appears only in late Midrashim, beginning with the eleventh century. The clear language employed by these Sages also demonstrates the difference between Philo and these works on the one hand, and the views of the Tannaim and Amoraim on the other. In *Bereshit Rabbati*,[77] which emanated from the circle of R. Moses ha-Darshan, it is stated: '...corresponding to the Decalogue, which the Holy One, blessed be He, uttered at Sinai, in which the whole Torah is comprised, the 613 precepts....' Here it is explicitly asserted that all the commandments are included in the Decalogue, and this concept occurs also in other Midrashim that belong to this circle.

It seems that the idea reached these works from R. Saadia Gaon. In his *'Azhārôt* he declares at the beginning of the First Commandment: '...And His word is like fire, whose sparks are many precepts shining in each Commandment / In His wisdom, which incorporated in the Ten Commandments six hundred and thirteen precepts to teach....' At the end of the first commandment he sums up thus: 'The wisdom of the first commandment is that I have included therein eighty honoured precepts....' In the case of the other commandments, too, the number of implicit precepts and a summary are given. Finally it is stated: '...I have laid up in the Ten Commandments the six hundred and thirteen precepts of the Law of Thine adherents... corresponding to the six hundred and thirteen letters from אנכי *'ānōkhî* ["I"] to אשר לרעך *'ăsher lĕ-rē'ekhā* ["that is thy neighbour's"] ....'[78]

This is the basis on which the *'Azhārôt*, the liturgical poems composed on the theme of the 613 precepts, are constructed, including those in R. Saadia Gaon's Prayer Book, and thence the concepts reached R. Judah Albarceloni in Spain, and apparently also the circle of R. Moses ha-Darshan and other writers. It is noteworthy that R. Saadia Gaon does not base himself on any internal source. Rashi, again, in his commentary on the Pentateuch (Exodus xxiv 12) simply relies on R. Saadia Gaon, stating: ' "The tables of stone, and the law and the commandment, which I have written that thou mayest teach them" means that all six hundred and thirteen precepts are implied in the Ten Commandments, and R. Saadia explained, in the *'Azhārôt* that he composed for each of the commandments, the precepts connected therewith.' Needless to say the sources that we first cited from the Palestinian Talmud and the Midrashim were known to Rashi, but he did not base himself on them, because apparently he, too, interpreted them in the way that I have explained, and did not regard them as a source for R. Saadia's doctrine. Precisely the verse to which Rashi attached the interpretation of R. Saadia Gaon is expounded by Resh Laqish in a form that entirely precludes the opinion that the whole Torah was implied in the Decalogue: 'R. Levi bar Ḥama said in the name of R. Simeon b. Laqish: What is the meaning of the verse: "And I will give thee the tables of stone, and the law and the commandment, which I have written, that thou mayest teach them"? "Tables" signifies the Decalogue, "law" the Pentateuch; "and the commandment" the Mishna; "which I have written" the Prophets and Hagiographa; "that thou mayest teach them" the Talmud. This teaches us that they were all given to Moses at Sinai.'[79] Rashi himself refrained from introducing R. Saadia Gaon's view into the Talmudic sources, even when their formulation was anachronistic. It is stated that Moses broke the tables because he argued from minor to major as follows: 'If now in the case of the passover offering, which is but one of the 613 commandments, the Torah enjoined: "there shall no alien eat thereof", how much more so when the entire Torah is involved and the Israelites have apostatized.'[80] The expression 'one of the 613 commandments' put into the mouth of Moses is anachronistic; but 'the entire Torah' means only the 'whole Torah' existing at the time, namely the Decalogue. Rashi, too, glossed 'the entire Torah is dependent upon these tablets', and not that the whole Torah is comprised in the Decalogue.[81]

The difference between the two conceptions is to be seen in two commentaries on *Tractate Sheqalim*. In a commentary composed by a native of Ashkenaz it is stated: ' "With Tarshish"... and my teacher told me in the name of his uncle R. Samuel Ḥasid ["the Pious"] "set with תרשיש — Tarshish", that is, with 600 [ת״ר] and 6 [שש] precepts, plus the seven Noahide laws, which make 613.'[82] He thus found an allusion to the fact that all the precepts are dependent on the Ten Commandments. On the other hand it is stated in another commentary, attributed to a disciple of R. Samuel b. R. Shneor:[83] 'Between one commandment and another of the Decalogue were its details, reasons, and signs; the explanation of *scriptio defectiva* and *plena*...' (*ibid.*), that is to say, that the explanations and details of the precepts that were linked to each commandment were inscribed on the tables.[84]

The early Midrashim do not distinguish between the importance of the Decalogue and of the other commandments, although they, too, endeavour to concentrate the Divine revelation throughout the generations into that of Mount Sinai. But they do this in a different way: 'R. Isaac said: That which the prophets were destined to prophesy in each generation they received at Mount Sinai. For thus Moses said to Israel: "But with him that standeth here with us this day before the Lord our God, and also with him that is not here with us this day" — (the end of) the verse does not read "that standeth here with us this day", but "with us this day"; this refers to the souls that were still to be born... for, although they were not in existence at the time, each one received his due. So, too, Scripture says "The burden of the word of the Lord of Israel by the hand of Malachi" (Malachi i 1) — the text does not state "in the days of Malachi", but "by the hand of Malachi", because the prophecy was already in his hand since Sinai, but he was not given permission to prophesy till that moment. Similarly Isaiah... nor was it only the prophets who were vouchsafed their prophecy at Sinai, but also each of the Sages, as they arose in their respective generations, received that which was due to him from Sinai...' (*Exodus Rabba* xxviii, 6). These matters were not incorporated in the Decalogue, but were revealed at the moment in the One Revelation. The concentration of the revelation was due to two motives, which have polemical overtones. The first arose from the fact that the Oral Law was held in light esteem; the amalgamation aimed to give it equal importance with the Written Law. The second reason was to obviate the claim of an additional revelation, for all was revealed at that time. But there is no attempt here to elevate the value and distinctive character of the Ten Commandments; on the contrary all the precepts are equated here with the Decalogue.

III. *The Reasons of the Precepts*

When the question of heteronomy and autonomy and the term 'precept' were discussed, it was seen that the Sages did not adopt a one-sided stand on these problems. Although the precepts are heteronomous, yet there remained ample opportunity for man to exercise his creative power, which is, as it were, autonomous, in the sphere of the observance of the commandments. The precept is obligatory, but it extends also to the domain of will. The Sages regard the commandments as of equal importance, but do not refrain from magnifying or emphasizing the value of one or other precept, either for educational reasons or for motives connected with prevailing circumstances. It is obvious that if the commandments are decrees that are not to be questioned, and there is no difference between them, the question of the reasons of the individual precepts has no basis whatsoever. Also to the question as it concerns the entire body of precepts the heteronomous view has apparently only one answer: the will of the commanding God.[85] But the picture that emerges from the sources is not simple or unambiguous, either in regard to the reason of the commandments as a whole or in respect of the purpose of the individual precept. One reason of the precepts is the reward. 'R. Hananiah b. ʿAqashya said: The Holy One, blessed be He, wished to grant merit to Israel, therefore he multiplied for them Law and commandments, as it is written: "The Lord was pleased, for His righteousness' " sake, to make the teaching great and glorious" (Isaiah xlii 21).'[86] If we read the dictum in its present context, the purport appears to be that the Holy One, blessed be He, vouchsafed precepts to Israel in order to grant them reward, for in the preceding Mishna in *Tractate Makkot* it is stated: '...R. Simeon b. Rabbi said: (Scripture enjoins) "Only be steadfast in not eating the blood; for the blood is the life" etc. (Deuteronomy xii 23). If now a man that abstains from blood, which fills one with a sense of loathing, is rewarded, how much more so shall a man who refrains from robbery and incest, which a person lusts after and craves, gain merit for himself and his generations and the generations of his generations to the end of all generations!' But R. Ḥananiah b. ʿAqashya expresses the view (incidentally this is the only saying by this Sage known to us)[87] that all the precepts were given with a view to granting Israel reward.[88] But if this dictum is a later addition to the Mishna, and is to be read by itself, its intent may be that the multiplicity of Torah and precepts brings merit to those who observe them, for the Divine Commander has no need of the commandment, but the commandment subserves only the benefit of man. The sole purpose of the precept is to endow man with righteousness. Indeed R. Hananiah b. ʿAqashya's teaching was thus interpreted by the Amora R. Aḥa: ' "The Lord was pleased for his righteousness' sake" — "for his righteousness' sake", that means, for your righteousness' sake; in order to grant you merit did I enjoin it upon you.'[89]

The concept that the commandments were given for the sake of man was expressed by Rav in his interpretation of the verse 'As for God, His way is perfect; the word of the Lord is tried...' (Psalms xviii 31). 'Rav said: The precepts were given only for the purpose of trying [i.e. refining, disciplining] people thereby. For what difference does it make to the Holy One, blessed be He, whether one slaughters at the neck or at the nape? This proves that the purpose is to try mankind.'[90] Rav formulated his principle on the basis of what Tannaim before him had said concerning individual precepts, namely that their observance preserves a man from sin. Thus R. Eleazar b. Jacob said: 'Whoever has phylacteries on his head, phylacteries on his arm, fringes on his garment, and a *mĕzûzā* on his door (post) is entirely secured against sinning, as it is said "And a threefold cord is not quickly broken", and it is further said "The angel of the Lord encampeth round about them that fear Him, and delivereth them" (Psalms xxxiv 8)' (*T.B. Menaḥot* 43b).

The two explanations of the reason for the precepts — that of reward and that of the refining of mankind — are to be found in two interpretations of the term חוקים *ḥuqqîm* ['statutes']. 'R. Levi said in the name of R. Ḥama b. R. Ḥanina: *ḥuqqîm* (are so called) because they are engraven חקוקים (*ḥăqûqîm*) upon the evil inclination... R. Abba b. Eliashiv said: *ḥuqqîm* (are so called) because they bring man to life in the world to come...' (*Leviticus Rabba* xxxv, 5–6, pp. 822–823). The first dictum states that the precepts strengthen man in his fight against temptation — 'in order to refine mankind thereby'; while the second saying stresses the thought of reward.

The precepts constantly test man. The very testing constitutes the refining process and suffices to save a person from making mistakes, and there is no need for him to add thereto other tests. Rav, who said that the precepts were given 'in order to refine mankind thereby', is also the author of the dictum 'A man should never offer himself to be tested, for David king of Israel offered himself for testing and failed. He said unto God: "Sovereign of the universe! why do we say (in the *Amida* prayer) 'the God of Abraham, the God of Isaac, and the God of Jacob', but not 'the God of David?' He answered: "They were tried by Me, but you were not." Thereupon he (David) said to Him: "Sovereign of the universe! examine and try me", as it is said: "Examine me, O Lord and try me" etc. (Psalms xxvi 2). Said He "I shall try you and yet vouchsafe you a privilege, for whereas I did not apprise the Patriarchs (beforehand how they would be tested), I tell you (now) that I shall put you to a test of chastity...." ' When David had failed to stand up to the test, he declared: "...Thou hast proved mine heart; Thou hast visited me in the night; Thou hast tried me, and shalt find nothing; I am purposed (זמותי) that my mouth shall not transgress." He said (in effect): "Would that a bridle had fallen in mine enemy's [i.e. my] mouth, and he [i.e. I] had not spoken thus"[91], that is to say: Would that my mouth had been bridled, so that my word could have been restrained and this request "Examine me" obviated.'

The precepts are intended to augment man's strength, so that he can stand up to the test; and if he succeeds then the observance of the precepts also gives him added holiness. This concept, that the observance of the commandments brings greater sanctity, is already to be found in Tannaitic literature. Of the Sabbath it is said ' "for it is holy unto you" — this teaches us that the Sabbath enhances Israel's holiness.'[92] R. Judah the Prince said with regard to the precept of fringes: '...What is the meaning of the Scripture "and be holy unto your God"? This refers to the holiness of fringes. It teaches us that the fringes add to Israel's sanctity.'[93] Similarly all the commandments serve to heighten Israel's sanctity, as is stated by the Babylonian Tanna: 'Issi b. Judah said: When the Omnipresent enjoins a new precept upon Israel, He endows them with new holiness.'[94] Holiness means abstinence, as is stated in the Sifra: ' "Ye shall be holy" means: Ye shall be abstinent.'[95] The Amora R. Levi did not refrain from explaining in this way the precept of offering sacrifices in the Tent of Meeting: 'Because the Israelites were avid idolaters in Egypt, and offered their sacrifices to demons... and the Israelites used to transgress the prohibition of high places in offering up their sacrifices... (therefore) the Holy One, blessed be He, said: Let them offer their sacrifices to Me at all times in the Tent of Meeting, and so they will abstain from idolatry....'[96] The general applicability of this reason for the commandments is borne out by the formulation of the benediction 'who sanctified us by His commandments and commanded us....'[97] The sanctity is, as it were, withdrawn from the precept itself and transferred to the act of the precept and to him that performs it. The commandment is thus voided not only of any magical-mythical quality, but also of its very ritual-cultic basis.

In the Torah, too, the Sabbath day is not intrinsically holy; it is God who blessed and sanctifies it.[98] The Tannaim, however, gave special emphasis to the verse 'Ye shall keep the sabbath therefore, for it is holy unto you' (Exodus xxxi 14), as does R. Simeon b. Menasya in the following exposition: 'The Sabbath is delivered to you, but you are not delivered to the Sabbath.' The Sages regarded the Sabbath as given over to them not only to decide the nature of its rest, the way to honour it, how to fill it with delight and hallow it, but even how to annul it. Thus we find that 'Once R. Ishmael and R. Eleazar b. Azariah and R. Akiba were going on a journey, and Levi ha-Saddar ['systematizer'; or, reading סרד *sārād*, 'net-maker'] and R. Ishmael the son of R. Eleazar b. Azariah were walking behind them, when the following question was put to them: Whence do we learn that the saving of life supersedes the Sabbath?' and each one endeavoured to find a Scriptural basis for this principle, which had undoubtedly already been accepted before their time.[99] When Rabbi expounded the verse ' "And be holy unto your God", (saying:) This refers to the sanctity of the fringes', or when the Sages interpreted the same Scripture with respect to 'the sanctity of all the precepts', these expositions have no mythical-magical connotation, as in the Cabbala[1], nor do they allude to holiness emanating from the substance of the ritual observance that is linked to the object of the precept. When Samuel heard Rav Assi declare 'It is forbidden to assort coins in front of the Ḥanukka lamp', he asked in surprise 'Has a lamp sanctity then?' Rav Joseph explained that the reason of Rav Assi's Halakha was 'that the precepts should not appear contemptible.'[2] However, not only the Ḥanukka lamp, but also the sanctity of the Torah scroll and phylacteries is linked to the observance of the commandments connected with them, and it is thus taught in a Baraita: 'A Torah scroll, phylacteries and *mĕzûzôt* that were written by a sectarian, an informer, a Gentile idolater, a slave, a woman, a minor, a Samaritan, or an apostate Jew are invalid, for it is said "And thou shalt bind them", "and thou shalt write them" — this implies that those enjoined to bind might write, but those not thus enjoined might not write.'[3] In other words, a Torah scroll and phylacteries, although written and prepared according to law, are devoid of sanctity, if they were written by one who does not observe the relevant precept or by one who is not obliged to do so. Furthermore, their sancity depends also on their having been written with proper intent.[4] The commandments enhance Israel's sanctity, but this sanctity has its source only in the observance of the precepts themselves, not beyond it. Hence even if the original reason for the precept's promulgation no longer obtains, the motive for its observance and the sanctity belonging to its performance are not abolished. Consequently it was possible for R. Levi to continue to extol the sacrifices and even to find[5] grounds for their detailed regulations, although the original reason had ceased to apply.

Insofar as symbolic reasons are given, they refer to details in the observance of rituals that are not mentioned in the Torah. Thus 'Rav Judah said: The knot of the phylacteries must be placed high and not low, so that Israel may be high and not low, and it must face frontwards, so that Israel may be in front and not behind' (*T.B. Menaḥot* 35b). Similar reasons are transmitted in the name of R. Joḥanan and in the name of R. Jose b. Ḥanina for the waving of the meal-offering, as it is described in the Mishna: 'He swings them forward and backward and upward and downward.'[6] Following on R. Me'ir's teaching concerning the importance of the commandment of the fringes (above, p. 347), the number of the windings in the segments of the fringes was explained symbolically :'One should not make less than seven [segments; *aliter*, windings], corresponding to the seven heavens', and if one makes more, he should not exceed thirteen, corresponding to the seven heavens and the six intervening spaces.[7]

The Sages noted the fact that apart from the general reasons there are precepts whose grounds are explained in the Torah itself, such as love of the proselyte and the prohibition of wronging him, the reason for which is immediately stated: 'For ye were strangers in the land of Egypt' (Exodus xxii 20). In regard to the Sabbath Scripture declares: 'For in six days the Lord made heaven and earth' etc. (Exodus xx 11), and 'That thy man-servant and thy maid-servant may rest as well as thou. And thou shalt remember that thou wast a servant in the land of Egypt' (Deuteronomy v 14–15). With respect to the restoration of a pledge that is a night covering, it is said 'And it shall come to pass, when he crieth unto Me, that I will hear; for I am gracious' (Exodus xxii 24). For the prohibition that no Ammonite or Moabite shall marry into the community of Israel the explanation given is: 'Because they met you not with bread and with water... and because they hired against thee Balaam the son of Beor...' (Deuteronomy xxiii 5). The educational motive is also not wanting: 'to fear the Lord our God' (Deuteronomy vi 24; xiv 23), especially where punishments are concerned: 'And all the people shall hear, and fear' (*ibid.* xvii 13) and similar expressions. Both Tannaim and Amoraim continued this approach, when they asked with regard to various laws and precepts 'For what reason did the Torah say', 'Why did the Torah say?', or 'Why is this matter different?' The tradition of questions of this kind bears, to begin with, the name of Rabban Joḥanan b. Zakkai. In his replies he advances an ethical educational idea, which goes beyond the explicit law; his interpretation, however, is not allegorical, but is based on a close examination of the language of Scripture, or on deep analysis of the nature of the deeds and the doers. For example, ' "For if thou lift up thy tool upon it" etc. — Rabban Joḥanan b. Zakkai comments: Scripture enjoins: "Thou shalt build... of unhewn stones" (Deuteronomy xxvii 6), that means stones that bring peace. Now we may argue from minor to major: If in the case of the stones of the altar, which neither see, nor hear, nor speak, the Holy One, blessed be He, commanded "Thou shalt lift up no iron tool upon them", because they make peace between Israel and their Father in heaven, how much more so shall no retribution be visited upon one who makes peace between one man and another, between a man and his wife, between city and city, between nation and nation, between government and government, or between family and family!'[8] To the question why the Torah saw fit to be more stringent in the case of a thief, who has to pay twofold, whereas a robber has only to restore the value of the robbed article, R. Joḥanan b. Zakkai replied: 'The robber put the honour of the servant on the same level as that of his master; the thief apportioned greater honour to the servant than to his master. The thief acted, as it were, as if the Eye on high does not see, and as if the Ear does not hear, as it is said "Woe unto them that seek deep to hide their counsel from the Lord, and their works are in the dark..." (Isaiah xxix 15), "And they say: 'The Lord will not see, neither will the God of Jacob give heed' " (Psalms xciv 7).'[9] In the law of the thief and the robber, R. Joḥanan b. Zakkai discovers a reason that amounts to a principle: The punishment of hypocrites, who act secretly, is severer than that of those who commit transgressions openly.'[10] The principle that the Holy One, blessed be He, has consideration for people's dignity R. Joḥanan b. Zakkai learnt from the law that the thief who slaughters an ox pays fivefold, 'because (the ox) walks by himself; for a sheep, however, since he [the thief] has to carry it on his shoulder, he pays (only) fourfold', if he slaughtered or sold it.[11] Similarly R. Joḥanan b. Zakkai's disciples down the generations explained the reasons of the laws and precepts. R. Akiba said that a thief who slaughtered or sold (a stolen animal) has to pay fourfold or fivefold 'because he has become rooted in sin'.[12] R. Me'ir differed from R. Joḥanan b. Zakkai in the inference he drew from the disparity in the penalties to be paid for stealing an ox and a sheep. 'Come and see — he said — how highly labour is esteemed by Him who spoke and the world came into being: for an ox who has work to do, he must pay fivefold; for a sheep, who has no work to do, he pays (only) fourfold!'

The principle of 'measure for measure', whose influence is discernible in very many spheres of Rabbinic thought, also played an important role in the elucidation of the reasons of the precepts and their details.[13] In this instance, too, the inaugurator was R. Joḥanan b. Zakkai, who said with regard to the ear-piercing of a Hebrew slave who refused to be freed: 'His ear had heard "Thou shalt not steal", yet he went and stole, therefore let it [his ear] of all his organs be pierced.'[14] By means of the principle of 'measure for measure' an entire series of details — down to the minutest particulars — of the laws of *soṭa* [a woman suspected of infidelity] has been explained, apparently by R. Me'ir.[15] Concerning the heifer whose neck is broken, R. Joḥanan b. Saul said: Why did the Torah ordain that a calf should be brought into a ravine? The Holy One, blessed be He, said: Let that which has produced no fruit come and have its neck broken in a place that yields no fruit, and atone for one who was not granted to produce fruit.'[16] A calf one year old has not yet calved, and its neck is broken in a rough ravine, which does not produce fruit, in order to atone for the murder of a man, who has been prevented from raising up seed. The answer given to the question 'Why is the leper different that the Torah enjoined "He shall dwell alone; without the camp shall his dwelling be"?' does not explain the isolation on hygienic grounds, but declares 'He caused a division between husband and wife, between a man and his fellow; therefore the Torah ordained "He shall dwell alone" etc.' (*T.B. ʿArakhin* 16b). This reason is based on the belief that leprosy serves only as retribution for slander[17], which causes disunity; hence part of the leper's punishment consists of isolation. In the course of a certain Talmudic explanation of the purpose of offering the incense in the innermost sanctuary on the Day of Atonement, expiation is also found for slander on the principle of 'measure for measure': 'The School of R. Ishmael taught: For what does incense atone? For slander; let the ritual performed in secret come and atone for the act committed in secret.'[18] This Baraita was unknown to R. Jonathan of Bet Guvrin, since R. Simeon reports in his name another form of atonement for slander, and this, too, conforms to the principle 'measure for measure', only the measure is different: 'For him that speaks slander there was no atonement, but the Torah appointed as his atonement the bells of the (high priest's) robe: "And it shall be upon Aaron to minister; and the sound thereof shall be heard" — let sound come and atone for sound.' R. Simeon himself found iniquities for which other priestly vestments served to atone.[19] The sin of the golden calf also provided an opportunity for discovering in details of the precepts an atonement for this misdeed. For example, 'R. Josa b. Ḥanina taught the following Baraita: "And thou shalt make an ark-cover of pure gold" — let the gold of the ark-cover come and atone for the gold of the calf.'[20] Although the law of the red heifer is considered a divine decree, which has no reason,[21] R. Levi explained one of the details of its laws as an expiation for the making of the calf: 'Why are (all) the congregational sacrifices males, and this one (the red heifer) alone is a female? R. Levi said: The case may be compared to the son of a female slave who dirtied the royal palace. Said the king: "Let his mother come and clean up the dirt." Even so the Holy One, blessed be He, said: "Let the heifer come and atone for the misdeed of the calf." '[22]

The attention paid to the reasons of the precepts emanated also from a practical need. Additions and adjustments were made to the laws and precepts in the course of their daily observance in ever-changing circumstances. Often it was explained that it was precisely these innovations and amendments that fulfilled the basic reason of the commandment, whereas its literal observance nullified its original intent. An instructive example is the enactment of *prosbol* [Jastrow: 'A declaration made in court, before the execution of a loan, to the effect that the law of limitation by the entrance of the Sabbatical year shall not apply to the loan to be transacted'] by Hillel the Elder: 'When he saw that the people refrained from giving loans to one another and transgressed the Scripture "Beware that there be not a base thought in thy heart, saying: 'The seventh year, the year of release, is at hand'; and thine eye be evil against thy needy brother, and thou give him naught" (Deuteronomy xv 9), Hillel enacted the *prosbol*' (*M. Shevi'it* x, 3). The Mishna rules: 'Compensation for damages must be assessed on the best land, a creditor (is paid) out of medium land, and a wife's marriage contract out of the poorest land' (*M. Giṭṭin* v, 1). The first Halakha was based on the Torah law concerning one who lets his beast loose and it feeds in another man's field: 'Of the best of his own field and of the best of his own vineyard, shall he make restitution' (Exodus xxii 4). 'R. Akiba said: The verse comes only to tell you that compensation damages must be assessed on the best land.'[23] R. Simeon, of whom it is said 'that he expounded the reasons of Scripture' gave the following explanation: 'Why did the Sages ordain that "Compensation must be assessed on damages of the best land?" On account of robbers and men of violence [i.e. those who take by force, though they pay], so that a man may say to himself: Why do I rob, and why do I take by violence? Tomorrow the court of justice will seize my possessions and take my finest field, basing themselves on the verse "Of the best of his own field, and of the best of his own vineyard, shall he make restitution." Therefore they ordained: "Compensation for damages must be assessed on the best land"' (*T.B. Giṭṭin* 49b). The purpose of this stringent enactment[24] is prevention and deterrence — to discourage the greed of robbers and men of violence. While the law of payment for damages is expressly stated in the Torah — 'Of the best of his own field' etc. — the collection of a debt from land is only a Rabbinic law, which is based, however, on the underlying motive inherent in the precept to lend to the needy, on which Hillel grounded his enactment. In the continuation of the above Baraita R. Simeon says: 'Why did the Sages rule that "A creditor (is paid) out of medium land"? In order that a man, on seeing that his fellow has a fine field or dwelling, should not say to himself: "I shall hasten to give him a loan, so that I may take it [the field etc.] in repayment for my loan." Therefore the Sages said: "A creditor (is paid) out of medium land." But if so, why should he not collect his debt out of the poorest land? In that case you would lock the door before borrowers.' The Amora 'Ulla, following R. Ishmael's view, said[25]: 'Under Torah law a creditor should be paid out of the poorest land, for it is said: "Thou shalt stand without, and the man to whom thou dost lend shalt bring forth the pledge without unto thee" (Deuteronomy xxiv 11). What does a man as a rule bring forth without? The least valuable articles. For what reason then did the Sages say "A creditor (is paid) out of medium land"? In order not to lock the door before borrowers.' R. Simeon's view that the reasons of Scripture may be expounded is disputed in several passages by R. Judah. In the Mishna it is stated: 'A pledge may not be exacted from a widow whether she is poor or rich, as it is said "Thou shalt not take the widow's raiment in pledge" (Deuteronomy xxiv 17).' But in the Baraita there is a difference of opinion: 'A pledge may not be exacted from a widow whether she is poor or rich, as it is said "Thou shalt not take the widow's raiment in pledge" — this is the view of R. Judah. R. Simeon says: If she is rich she is subject to distraint, but not if she is poor, for you are required to restore (the pledge) to her, and you give her (thereby) a bad reputation among her neighbours. What does he mean? This is what he means: Since you exact a pledge from her, you are obliged to return it to her; and as a result of having to return it to her, you give her a bad reputation among her neighbours.'[26] According to the law of the Torah, if a lender has possession of a poor borrower's pledge and the latter needs the pledged article every day or every night, he is obliged to return the pledge each day: if it is a garment worn by day, he must return it every morning and may take it away (only) in the evening; and the reverse procedure applies if it is a night covering. R. Simeon is of the opinion that the reason of the prohibition 'Thou shalt not take the widow's raiment to pledge' is that to a poor widow the lender who has taken a pledge will have to return the pledge each day and will thereby bring her into disrepute; therefore the Torah referred in this verse only to a poor widow, but from a rich widow a pledge may be taken. In the discussion of the subject in the Babylonian Talmud the question is raised: 'Are we to infer that R. Judah does not expound the reasons of Scripture, whereas R. Simeon does? But we have learnt the reverse. For it is taught: "Neither shall he multiply wives to himself" — not more than eighteen. R. Judah says: He may multiply (wives) to himself, provided that they do not turn his heart away. R. Simeon said: Even if one is liable to turn his heart away he may not marry her. Thus we see that R. Judah expounds the reasons of Scripture, but R. Simeon does not.' The Sages answer: 'Generally R. Judah does not expound the reasons of Holy Writ, but this case is different, since its reason is stated: Why must he not multiply (wives) to himself? So "that (his heart) turn not away".' This means to say, here the reason is explicitly given in Scripture, and hence if there is no cause to fear that they will turn his heart away, the king is permitted to multiply wives to himself. 'But R. Simeon holds that generally we interpret the reasons of Scripture, but the present case is different, for the Bible could have stated "Neither shall he multiply wives", without having recourse (to the explanation) "that (his heart) turn not away", and I would have known that the reason underlying (the injunction) "Neither shall he multiply" was "that (his heart) turn not away". Why then did Scripture write "that (his heart) turn not away"? So that even if there be one who may turn his heart away, he may not marry her. If so, why does the Bible ordain "Neither shall he multiply wives to him"? Even such as Abigail.'[27] R. Simeon's view is, therefore, that the Torah did not reveal the reasons of its precepts, but left this matter to the Sages. If a reason is specifically stated, it becomes an additional commandment, and itself requires a reason. In the instance just cited R. Simeon says: I should, of my own accord, have concluded that the reason of the prohibition 'Neither shall he multiply wives to himself' is that they should not turn away his heart. Now that the Torah has added 'that his heart turn not away', we have here another law: 'Neither shall he multiply wives' in any circumstances, even if they be like Abigail, because many wives are liable to turn away his heart. 'That his heart turn not away' forbids him to take even a single wife who may turn away his heart. On the other hand R. Judah, understanding the stated motivation literally, makes it the primary factor, and consequently he limits the prohibition only to cases where the given reason applied.

R. Simeon employs the expository method of 'the reason of Scripture' even where only Rabbinic enactments are involved. In this way he raises them to Torah status and creates thereby new Halakhot. In the Mishna (*Yevamot* viii, 3) it is taught: 'An Ammonite or a Moabite is forbidden and forbidden for all time [to marry an Israelite], but their females are permitted forthwith.' R. Simeon adds the comment: Since the Torah explains that their sin lay in their not having met the children of Israel with bread and water, we may infer that the Torah intended to prohibit only the males, for it is not the way of women to meet guests with bread and water.

Undoubtedly this enactment based on the differentiation 'An Ammonite but not an Ammonitess' etc. is an ancient Halakha, dating, apparently, from as early as the Hasmonean period, from the time of the conquests, when the Jewish population spread to Transjordan. At any rate the ruling 'An Ammonite, but not an Ammonitess, a Moabite, but not a Moabitess' is not to be regarded as an exegetical inference, for if so we could also by the same token conclude 'an Egyptian man but not an Egyptian woman', 'a male bastard but not a female bastard', an argument, in truth, that is advanced in the Talmuds.[28] Now R. Simeon proceeds to expound the reason stated in the Torah 'because they met you not with bread and with water': 'It is the way of a man to meet (wayfarers), but it is not the way of women to do so.'[29] Thus the Torah itself excluded an Ammonitess and a Moabitess from the prohibition, and even explained the reason for the prohibition of the Ammonite and Moabite, for it made it possible thereby to deduce that Egyptian and Edomite women were also permitted: 'R. Simeon said: It is an inference from minor to major: if where the males are forbidden for ever, the females are permitted forthwith, how much more so, where the males are forbidden for but three generations, should the females be permitted forthwith!'[30] For the stringent prohibition of the Ammonites and Moabites [to marry an Israelite] — in contrast to the Egyptians and Edomites — R. Simeon also found a reason: 'R. Simeon said: The Egyptians drowned the Israelites in the sea, and the Edomites met the Israelites with the sword, yet Scripture forbade them for only three generations. The Ammonites and Moabites, because they took counsel to ensnare Israel in sin, were forbidden by Scripture for all time. This teaches you that he that causes a man to sin commits a graver crime than he who kills him; for he that slays him does not put him out of this world and the world to come, whereas he who makes him sin puts him out of both this world and the world to come' (*Sifre Deuteronomy*, § 252).

Not for all the precepts could there be found particular reasons of the kind that we have mentioned. Certain cultic ceremonies even astonished the Sages by their resemblance to cultic ceremonies current among Gentile idolaters. It is actually of Rabban Joḥanan b. Zakkai, who revealed the motivation of many precepts, that we are told that he preferred not to search for allegorical interpretations and occult reasons for the red heifer. He left the Gentile who asked him the meaning of the rite in the realm of belief prevailing in his environment, but to his disciples he said: 'By your life! the corpse does not defile nor does the water purify; it is simply a decree of the Holy One, blessed be He. The Holy One, blessed be He, declared: I have ordained a statute, I have decreed a decree, and you may not transgress my decree — "This is the statute of the law".'[31] There are pointers to the fact that the story was related about R. Joḥanan b. Zakkai, because he witnessed the preparation of the ashes of a red heifer in his day,[32] and his disciples asked him questions concerning the laws of the heifer.[33] We do not, indeed, find reasons for the rite of the heifer in the dicta of the Tannaim — either for its general laws or its particular regulations — but neither did they interpret the word חוקה *ḥuqqā* ['statute'], which is used by Scripture in connection with the heifer, as exceptional; they regarded it as signifying a rule in the same way as 'This is the ordinance of the passover' (Exodus xii 43). R. Eliezer formed an analogy between the word statute here and the verse 'And this shall be an everlasting statute unto you', which refers to the Day of Atonement (Leviticus xvi 34), and taught that the rites of the heifer must be performed in white vestments.[34] Not all the Tannaim held that חוקים *ḥuqqîm* ['statutes'] are גזרות *gĕzērôt* ['decrees'], and even those who adopted this interpretation did not consider גזרה *gĕzērā* ['decree'] to signify an injunction that has no rationale. R. Joshua expounded: ' "The statutes" mean decrees, and "the laws" [תורות *tôrôt*] mean injunctions'; but R. Eleazar of Modi'im said: ' "The statutes" refer to incestuous relations... and "the laws" signify decrees.'[35] Irrespective of whether the dictum attributed to R. Joḥanan b. Zakkai was actually uttered by him in the version transmitted, or is merely ascribed to him, there is nothing to be found in Tannaitic teaching to indicate that they know more about the reasons of the rites of the heifer than they disclosed. It is true that in the preparation of the heifer, as in other sacrificial rites, we are confronted by ancient ritual ceremonies, for which it is not difficult to find parallels in temple practices and sacrificial laws that were current in antiquity.[36] Even if the Sages were aware that these rituals were shared by other cults,[37] they certainly did not know and did not think about the original significance of these customs in non-Jewish worship. Hence, if they compared the laws of the red heifer to those of the Day of Atonement, they did so only because they had already found a basis for this in the Pentateuchal sections, and because both rituals are distinctly ceremonies of purification, but they undoubtedly did not have in mind the well-known Greek antithesis between the Chthonian and Olympian gods.[38] The Amoraim are divided in their views regarding the underlying reason of the red

the reason-less precept.

heifer and the reasons of similar precepts. There were some who regarded these commandments as void of any rationale and found difficulty in understanding their details, but the word 'statute' determined their decretal character, even though the evil inclination criticizes them, as 'R. Joshua of Sikhnin said in the name of R. Levi: The evil inclination criticizes four laws, and in each case Scripture writes "statute". These concern: the wife of a brother, diverse kinds of stuff, the scapegoat, and the (red) heifer. Whence do we learn (that one is forbidden to marry) the wife of a brother? (The Bible enjoins) "Thou shalt not uncover the nakedness of thy brother's wife" (Leviticus xviii 16), yet it is written "her husband's brother shall go in unto her" etc. (Deuteronomy xxv 5). While the husband is alive, she [i.e. his wife] is forbidden (to his brother); but if the husband dies childless, she is permitted to the brother; and Scripture terms it a "statute": "Ye shall therefore keep My statutes, and Mine ordinances, which if a man do" (Leviticus xviii 5). Whence do we learn (the prohibition) of diverse kinds of stuff? "Thou shalt not wear mingled stuff" etc. (Deuteronomy xxii 11), yet a linen garment with (woollen) fringes is permissible; and Scripture terms it a "statute": "Ye shall keep My statutes" etc. (Leviticus xix 19). Whence do we learn (the law of) the scapegoat? "And he that letteth go the goat for Azazel (shall wash his clothes) (Leviticus xvi 26), although it itself makes atonement for others; and Scripture terms it a "statute": "And it shall be a statute for ever unto you" (*ibid.*, v. 29). Whence do we learn (the law of) the (red) heifer? We have learnt there (in the Mishna): "All who engage in the (rite of the red) heifer, from the beginning to the end, defile their garments" (*M. Para* iv 4); yet the heifer itself purifies the unclean; and Scripture terms it a "statute": "This is the statute of the law" (Numbers xix 2).'[39] R. Levi, therefore, regarded the word 'statute' as referring to a decree concerning the observance of precepts that arouse astonishment, not from the aspect of the Scriptural ordinance — the general reason discussed above (p. 368) sufficed him to explain this — but actually from the viewpoint of the Rabbinic interpretation, as, for instance, a linen garment with (woollen) fringes.[40] The law of mingled stuff *per se*, and likewise the precepts of the scapegoat and the red heifer as such, require no explanation, except for enigmatic particulars of their detailed regulations. R. Joḥanan and R. Eleazar, like R. Levi, drew attention to laws and Halakhot that contain an inner contradiction and have no manifest reason, applying to them the verses: 'Who can bring a clean thing out of an unclean? Not one' (Job xiv 4) and (Ecclesiastes vii 23) 'I said: "I will get wisdom"; but it was far from me' (*T.B. Nidda* 9a). A similar note is struck by an anonymous homily, not unlike a poem in its language and form, in which the motif of the reasonless precept and decree constitutes a refrain:

' "Who can bring a clean thing out of an unclean? Not one" — like Abraham from Terah, Hezekiah from Aḥaz, and Mordecai from Shimei; Israel from among the nations, (and) the world to come out of this world.

Who did so? Who commanded so? Who decreed so? Is it not the One? Is it not the Only One of the universe?

There we have learnt (*M. Nega'im* viii, 2): A bright spot the size of a split bean (makes a man) unclean; (but) if it spread throughout his skin, he is clean.

Who did so? Who commanded so? Who decreed so? Is it not the Only One of the universe?

We have learnt there (*M. Ḥullin* iv, 3): If a woman's child died within her womb and the midwife put forth her hand and touched it, the midwife becomes unclean for seven days, but the woman remains clean until the child comes forth. So long as the dead (child) is within (his mother's womb) he is clean; (but) as soon as he goes forth, he is unclean.

Who did so? Who commanded so? Who decreed so? Is it not the One? Is it not the Holy One of the universe?

And we have learnt there (*M. Para* iv, 4): All who are engaged in the rite of the (red) heifer, from beginning to end, defile their garments, yet the heifer itself purifies the unclean.

The Holy One, blessed be He, however, said: I have framed a statute and issued a decree, and you may not transgress My decree.'[41]

Evidently the attempt to discover the reason of the precepts is completely relinquished here, and instead there is a sense of joy at their observance as decrees of the Only One of the universe. This was also the view of R. Jose b. R. Ḥanina. R. Aḥa says in his name: 'When Moses ascended to heaven, he heard the voice of the Holy

One, blessed be He, as He was sitting and studying the section of the red heifer, and citing a Halakha in the name of the one who said it: "R. Eliezer said: The calf (whose neck is broken) must be a year old, and the (red) heifer two years old." Said Moses to the Holy One, blessed be He: "Sovereign of the universe, the beings of heaven and earth belong to Thee, yet Thou dost sit and say Halakha in the name of a mortal!" Said the Holy One, blessed be He, to him: "Moses, a certain righteous man is due to arise in My world and he will commence his exposition with the section of the (red) heifer: 'R. Eliezer says: The calf (whose neck is broken) must be a year old, the (red) heifer must be two years old.' " Said Moses to God: "Sovereign of the universe, may it be Thy will that he come forth from my loins." (The Almighty) replied: "By your life, he shall issue from your loins...." '[42] The Lord does not reveal to Moses the hidden reason underlying the section of the (red) heifer, but 'teaches a Halakha' in the name of him who said it. In accord with this view, R. Jose b. R. Ḥanina explained the word 'thee' in the Scripture 'that they bring thee a red heifer' to mean 'He intimated to him: All the heifers will come to an end, but yours will remain'; He did not, however, reveal any secret to him. It is possible that this exposition is already directed against the homily that found in the word 'thee' a basis for the view that to Moses were revealed things that were not disclosed to others. In our sources, indeed, the following homily is transmitted in the name of R. Isaac: 'Moses, to you I reveal the reasons of the (red) heifer, but for others it is a "statute".'[43] But we find dicta, even by early Amoraim, concerning Torah reasons that were revealed to individuals. In the name of Rav a homiletical interpretation is transmitted of the verse 'And the prophet Ahijah the Shilonite found him in the way; now Ahijah had clad himself with a new garment; and they two were alone in the field' (I Kings xi 29), namely 'that all the reasons of the Torah were open to them like a field' (*T.B. Sanhedrin* 102a). R. Eleazar expounded the verse 'For her gain shall be for them that dwell before the Lord, to eat their fill ולמכסה עתיק *wĕ-li-mĕkhasse ʿatîq* [E.V. 'and for fine clothing'] (Isaiah xxiii 18): 'What is meant by *li-mĕkhasse ʿātîq*? This denotes one who reveals the things concealed [*mĕkhasse*] by the Ancient [*ʿattîq*] of days. What are these things? The reasons of the precepts.'[44] The reasons of the Torah are regarded as concealed, but they were revealed to individuals. R. Ṭarfon said to R. Akiba: 'Akiba, of you Scripture declares "He bindeth the streams that they trickle not; and the thing that is hid bringeth he forth to light" (Job xxviii 11)', and he explained the verse to mean: 'Things hidden from men R. Akiba hath brought forth into the light.'[45] R. Ṭarfon's interpretation undoubtedly refers to the Halakhot and homilies of R. Akiba, who 'expounded (Scripture) so that it accorded with the Halakha' (*Tosefta Zevaḥim* i, 8); but the Amoraim R. Ḥuna and R. Aḥa, echoing the words of R. Ṭarfon, said that the reasons of the Torah laws that were not revealed to Moses were disclosed to R. Akiba and his colleagues.[46]

The Amoraim who were opposed to the study and revelation of the reasons of the commandments could not ignore the fact that the reasons of many precepts are stated alongside of them in the Torah itself. Indeed R. Isaac, who depicted God as saying 'Moses, to you I reveal the reasons of (the rites of) the (red) heifer, but for others it is a statute', did not refrain from explaining the concealment of the rationale of the Torah laws to be due to the misjudgement caused by the revelation of expressly stated reasons. 'R. Isaac further said: Why were the reasons of the Torah precepts not revealed? Because the reasons of two Scriptures were made known and the greatest man in the world stumbled on account of them. It is written "He shall not multiply wives to himself". Said Solomon: I shall multiply and my heart shall not be turned away. Yet it is written: "When Solomon was old, his wives turned away his heart." It is further written "He shall not multiply to himself horses", but Solomon said: I shall multiply and not cause (the people) to return (to Egypt). Yet it is written: "And a chariot came up and went out of Egypt for six" etc.'[47] R. Isaac disagrees both with R. Simeon, who expounded the rationale of Scripture, and with R. Judah (see above p. 375), and it appears that his extreme statements were inspired by the fear that the quest for the reasons of the commandments was liable to undermine not only the observance of the precepts whose motives were not known, but also, in particular, the fulfillment of those for which reasons were found. The very question regarding the purpose of a thing attributes, to a certain extent, more importance to the reason than to the thing itself, and there is the danger that the reason will become the primary consideration and the actual matter subsidiary. Especially when the enquirer succeeds in finding a profound reason for a precept that appears to be of little significance, or of a strange and dubious nature, there is the danger that the observance of the precept will fall into desuetude and the reason itself will be regarded as sufficient. Actuated by an approach similar to that of R. Isaac, there were some Palestinian Amoraim who strongly objected to the motivation of commandments by God's attributes of compassion. In the Torah itself 'for I am gracious' (Exodus xxii 26) is expressly given as the reason for the law of the pledge, and the Tanna Abba Saul defined the imitation of God and the copying of His ways in the following terms: 'Just as He is compassionate and gracious, so you be compassionate and gracious.'[48] But the Amora R. Josa be R. Bun said 'They do not do right to interpret the attributes of the Holy One, blessed be He, as compassion, namely those who expound "My people, the children of Israel" to mean: Just as I am compassionate in heaven, so be you compassionate upon earth; whether it be a cow or a ewe you shall not slaughter it with its young in one day. They do not do right to evaluate the decrees of the Holy One, blessed be He, as compassion.'[49] This view, which does not accept Abba Saul's teaching as a reason for observing the commandments, follows upon the attempts of the Amoraim to interpret the Mishna: 'If a man says (in his prayer) "Unto [על *'al*] a bird's nest doth Thy compassion extend", or "May Thy name be remembered for well-doing", or "We give thanks, we give thanks", he is silenced.'[50] Whereas the formulas 'We give thanks, we give thanks' and 'May Thy name be remembered for well-doing' were regarded as allusions to a belief in dualism, opinion was divided as to why exception was taken to saying 'Unto a bird's nest doth Thy compassion extend',[51] nor was its wording certain.[52] Some read 'Up to [עד *'ad*] a bird's nest' etc., and according to this text R. Jose, in the name of R. Simon, explained that the defect of this prayer was that it set a limit to the attributes of God: 'Up to a bird's nest Thy compassion extends, but no further.' But even the first version was interpreted by R. Phinehas in the name of R. Simon as follows: 'He is as one who finds fault with the attributes of the Holy One, blessed be He. To a bird's nest Thy compassion extends, but to this man [i.e. himself] they do not extend.' The flaw in the prayer is not therefore, according to R. Simon, that it represents the attributes of the Lord as compassion, but, on the contrary, that this attribute is not sufficiently emphasized, or that the slightest doubt is cast upon its action. However, from the Mishna itself it is evident that this formula, like the others, was used by sectarians.[53] From this point of view it certainly appears that the citation of the reproachful dictum of R. Josa b. R. Bun was directed against the translators — to whom belonged the author of the existing Palestinian Targum (Leviticus xxii 28) — who assess 'the decrees of the Holy One, blessed be He, as compassion'[54] by making the reason of the precept '(ye shall not slaughter) it and its young' the basis for teaching the virtue of compassion. In quoting the observations of R. Josa b. R. Bun, the Sages intimated that one who said in his prayer 'Unto a bird's nest doth Thy compassion extend' likewise belonged to this category of translators, for they too give a similar reason for the commandment to let the dam go from the nest. In Babylon, where translators of the type we have mentioned did not exist, they did not object to additions being made to the text of the *Tefilla* ['Prayer', i.e. Eighteen Benedictions]. Thus it is related of Rabba, the contemporary of R. Josa b. R. Bun: 'A certain (reader) went down (before the Ark) in the presence of Rabba and said: "Thou hast taken pity upon the bird's nest, have Thou pity and compassion upon us; Thou hast taken pity on 'it and its young' [see Leviticus xxii 28], have Thou pity and compassion upon us." Said Rabba, How well this scholar knows how to placate his Master with praise!'[55] But in truth even in Eretz-Israel there were Amoraim who considered the Divine attribute of compassion to be the underlying reason of the commandments to send the dam away from the nest and not to slaughter on the same day both 'it and its young'. In the name of R. Levi, who, as we have seen, said with regard to only four laws 'that the evil inclination criticizes them, and in each case Scripture writes "statute" ', R. Berechia transmitted the following homily: 'It is written "The Righteous One regardeth the life of His beast" (Proverbs xii 10): "The Righteous One regardeth" denotes the Holy One, blessed be He, in whose Torah it is written "Thou shalt not take the dam with the young" (Deuteronomy xxii 6); "but the tender mercies of the wicked are cruel" (Proverbs *loc. cit.*) alludes to the wicked Sennacherib, to whom Scripture refers in the verse "The mother was dashed in pieces with her children" (Hosea x 14). Another interpretation: "The Righteous One regardeth the life of His beast" — this is the Holy One, blessed be He, in whose Torah it is written "And whether it be cow or ewe, ye shall not kill it and its young both in one day"; "but the tender mercies of the wicked are cruel" signifies the wicked Haman....'[56] R. Levi's homily is not far removed from the rendition of 'Those who translate'.

The story of the exodus from Egypt is mentioned in the Torah not only in connection with precepts of which it is expressly said that they are a reminder of this event, but also in association with commandments like 'Just balances, just weights, a just ephah, and a just hin shall ye have: I am the Lord your God, who brought you out of the land of Egypt' (Leviticus xix 36). In *Torat Kohanim* the verse is expounded by the Tannaim thus: 'On this condition have I brought you forth from the land of Egypt, namely that you accept the precept of measures; for whoever acknowledges the commandment of measures acknowledges the exodus from Egypt, and whoever denies the commandment of measures denies the exodus from Egypt.'[57] A similar exposition is given of the reference to the exodus from Egypt in connection with the prohibition of usury: '(I brought you forth from the land of Egypt) on condition that you accept the precept of usury, for whoever acknowledges the precept of usury acknowledges the exodus from Egypt, and whoever denies the commandment concerning usury denies the exodus from Egypt.'[58] This condition attaching to the exodus from Egypt is certainly not to be restricted only to weights and usury. Actually, in a third passage it is stated: 'On condition that you accept the yoke of the precepts, for whoever acknowledges the yoke of the precepts acknowledges the exodus from Egypt....'[59] However, this all-embracing version makes the mention of the exodus from Egypt specifically in relation to these and not to other commandments meaningless. Apparently the Sage who used the general formula 'Whoever acknowledges the yoke of the precepts acknowledges the exodus from Egypt...' in the context of the section dealing with reptiles does not follow the view that explains, in a similar way, the mention of the exodus from Egypt in connection with weights and measures and in relation to the prohibition of usury. The difference is made clear in Tannaitic expositions that elucidate the reference to the

Exodus in the Section of Fringes: 'What has the exodus from Egypt to do with (our subject) here? Its significance is this: that a man should not say: I shall put (threads of) coloured stuff or of *qĕlā' 'îlān* [wool treated with dye made of wood ash] (in the fringes), since they resemble *tĕkhēlet* ['blue', 'violet']; for who will inform against me publicly? "I am the Lord your God"—remember what I did to the Egyptians, whose deeds were wrought in secret and I made them known publicly.' Here a special reason is given for the mention of the Exodus in connection with fringes: it contains an admonition to those who perform the precept improperly, yet pretend to have observed it. But in the continuation of this homily it is stated: 'Another interpretation: Why is the exodus from Egypt mentioned in relation to every commandment? The matter may be compared to a king whose friend's son was taken captive, and when he redeemed him, he did so not to make him a free man but a bondman; so that if he issued a command and he (the former captive) should refuse to obey, he would say to him: "You are my bondman." Upon entering the country, he said to him: "Tie my sandals, and carry my belongings before me and bring them to the bathhouse." When the young man began to object, he produced a bond against him and said: "You are my bondman." So, too, when the Holy One, blessed be He, redeemed the descendants of Abraham, His friend, He did not redeem them to be His sons but His bondmen; so that if He issued a decree and they refused to obey, He could say to them: "You are My bondmen." When they had gone forth to the wilderness, He began to impose upon them some light precepts and some stringent commandments, like those pertaining to the Sabbath, incest, fringes and phylacteries. Thereupon they became recalcitrant; then said He to them: "You are My bondmen; it is to this end that I redeemed you, namely that I should decree and you should fulfil." '[60] Here it is explained that the condition laid down at the Exodus was that all the commandments should be observed as decrees, that Israel should carry them out as servants, and that there is no difference in practice between precepts in conjunction with which the Exodus is expressly mentioned and those unrelated to this event. The former come to teach us concerning the latter.[61] The acknowledgement of the exodus from Egypt means the acceptance of the yoke of the kingdom of Heaven;

the denial of the Exodus signifies the refusal to accept that yoke.

The difference between this conception and that of the first interpretation, which explained the reference to the Exodus in connection with the law of fringes by a particular feature of this precept, thus becomes perfectly clear. The Amora Rava, who, it was noted, adopted a voluntaristic view — namely that the yoke of the commandments is to be accepted willingly and that the proper fulfilment of the precepts implies their remaking — accepted the first interpretation of the mention of the Exodus in the Section of Fringes; he was not, however, content with this, but transferred it and adapted it also to other commandments. 'Said Rava: Why did Scripture mention the exodus from Egypt in connection with interest, fringes, and weights? The Holy One, blessed be He, declared: It is I who distinguished in Egypt between the seed that became a first-born and the seed that did not; it is I, too, who will exact retribution from one who nominally transfers his money to a Gentile and lends it to an Israelite on interest, and from one who steeps his weights in salt, and from one who inserts a thread dyed with *qĕlā' 'īlān* (in his fringes) and asserts that it is *tĕkhēlet*.'[62] The reference to the exodus from Egypt in connection with these precepts serves not only to remind us that the Israelites went forth from Pharaoh's bondage on condition that they should be the Lord's servants and accept the yoke of the commandments, but it points to the way that the precepts should be kept and to the duty to observe them truly. This homily of Rava fits in with his entire outlook regarding the precepts and accords with his view on acting for the sake of Heaven (see above, p. 329). The effect of his views can also be seen in his Halakhic decisions. We shall illustrate our observations by reference to one of the laws of interest: 'Our Rabbis taught: If an Israelite borrowed money on interest from a Gentile, who settled the sum [i.e. the principal and interest] on him as a loan and became converted, then if this settlement as a loan preceded the conversion, he [the proselyte] may collect both the principal and the interest. But if this settlement took place after the conversion, he [the convert] may collect the principal but not the interest. R. Jose said: If a Gentile borrowed money from an Israelite, the latter may in either case collect both the principal and the interest. Rava said in the name of Rav Seḥora in the name of Rav Huna: The Halakha is according to R. Jose. Said Rava: What is R. Jose's reason? So that it should not be said: This (Gentile) became converted because of his money.'[63] At first blush it seems that R. Jose's ruling is unfair to the proselyte, because if he settled the debt on the Israelite after his conversion, he does not receive the interest from him, but in the reverse instance, if the convert was the borrower, the Israelite can exact the interest from him. Furthermore, the decision of Rav Huna and Rav Seḥora is a halakhic pronouncement without a reason. Now Rava came and revealed the rationale of R. Jose's ruling and of the Halakha: 'So that it should not be said: This (Gentile) became converted because of his money', and the conversion will be discredited as not having been genuine.

Notwithstanding all the divergences that we have found between the Tannaim and Amoraim in their attitude to the motivation of the precepts, one view is common to all, namely that the reasons are not a condition of the fulfilment of the precepts.[64] Even those who sought to discover reasons do not consider the motive to have absolute value, but maintain the primacy of the precept and the observance. This is also the focal point of difference between them and the Hellenistic Jews, and not necessarily the extremists among them, who gave an allegorical interpretation to the commandments. Thus even Philo, who insisted on the practical observance of the precepts, maintained their fundamental thesis that the simple meaning of Scripture is analogous to the body and the esoteric reasons are comparable to the soul. Although he requires us to concern ourselves with the needs of the body in order that we may attain to the soul, to the hidden truth, yet it is (in his view) only the deep thinker who can achieve spiritual perfection.[65] It is inconceivable that Philo would have answered the question regarding the reason of the red heifer or of any other commandment with the words: 'I have ordained a statute, I have decreed a decree' etc. He could not have given this answer, because he did not recognize the yoke of the commandments, since he shared the view of the Greek autonomous ethical doctrine[66]; hence he has to find ethical and social reasons for every precept. Should those who discover the reasons of the precepts think for a moment that there is no need to fulfil the commandments practically, Philo has one answer: Even a person who attains to recognition of the truth, must take care of his good name, and this he cannot achieve unless he respects the statutes and customs that are generally accepted.[67] There is no need to stress how far this motivation is from the view of the Sages. To them the very observance of the commandments is of primary importance and the goal, and if the reason of a particular precept is not known, there still remains the motivation of the entire order of commandments, and this is valid for all sections of the nation. 'Beloved are Israel, for Scripture encompassed them with precepts — phylacteries on their heads and phylacteries on their arms, a *mĕzûzā* on their doors, fringes on their garments... The Holy One, blessed be He, said to Israel thus: "My children, be distinguished by your observance of the precepts, so that you may be pleasing to Me." '[68] The observance of the precepts is the link between God and the Israelite; and there is no difference between the Sages, who know the reasons of the precepts, and simple folk, or between precepts whose reasons have been disclosed and those whose rationale is concealed. It was actually Rava who formulated the rule 'The precepts were not given for enjoyment', that is to say, they were not given to Israel to afford them pleasure by their fulfilment, but to be a yoke upon their neck, for 'their observance is the King's decree imposed upon them'.[69] Even when the Sages interpret Scriptural passages allegorically, they give emphasis to the intrinsic importance of the precept and not to its motive. We shall illustrate the point by reference to a Midrashic exposition of the verse 'Behold, thou art fair, my love' (Canticles i 15), which was interpreted as a duologue between the Holy One, blessed be He, and the Congregation of Israel: ' "Behold, thou art fair, my love, thou art fair" — you are fair in (the observance of the) precepts; in acts of lovingkindness; in (keeping) positive precepts; in (keeping) negative precepts; in (the fulfilment of) domestic precepts, to wit, the dough-offering, the heave-offerings, and tithes; in (honouring) precepts of the field, namely gleanings, the forgotten sheaf, the corners of the field, the poor man's tithe, and ownerless property, in respect of the sowing of diverse kinds of seed....'[70] The motif of this homily is the same as that which we found already in the Tannaitic dicta[71] relating to the commandments that encompass man. Similar to it is the motif that the Lord left nothing in the world for which He did not ordain a precept: 'This is the meaning of Scripture "Light is sown for the righteous, and gladness for the upright in heart" (Psalms xcvii 11); and it further says "The Lord was pleased, for His righteousness' sake, to make the teaching great and glorious" (Isaiah xlii 21). The Holy One, blessed be He, sowed the Torah and the precepts for Israel so that He might enable them to inherit the life of the world to come. He left nothing in the world for which He did not ordain a precept unto Israel. When he [the Israelite] goes forth to plough (he is enjoined) "Thou shalt not plough with an ox and an ass together"; to sow — "Thou shalt not sow thy vineyard with two kinds of seed"; to reap — "When thou reapest thy harvest in thy field [etc.]"; if he kneeds — "Of the first of your dough ye shall set apart a cake for a gift"....'[72] Such homilies are, as it were, hymns to the precepts. Furthermore, the allegorical interpretations of certain verses form, so to speak, an addition to the precepts. 'Rav Aḥa bar Ḥanina expounded: What is the meaning of the verse "He hath not eaten upon the mountains, neither hath lifted up his eyes to the idols of the house of Israel, neither hath defiled his neighbour's wife, neither hath come near to a woman in her impurity" (Ezekiel xviii 6)? "He hath not eaten upon the mountains" (means) that he did not eat on account of his ancestors' merit; "neither hath lifted up his eyes to the idols of the house of Israel" (signifies) that he did not walk with haughty mien; "neither hath defiled his neighbour's wife" (denotes) that he did not harm (by unfair competition) his neighbour's trade; "neither hath come near to a woman in her impurity" (implies) that he did not benefit from the charity fund.'[73] Undoubtedly, the homilist did not intend to negate the simple sense of the verse, but since the prophet repeats, in different words, the prohibition expressly stated in the Torah, he set out to find in them an additional connotation, and added prohibitions that are not stated in the Torah.[74]

Although the precepts were not given for enjoyment, yet the discovery of their reasons and the very observance of the commandment can afford the one who fulfils it a feeling of gratification and joy. The Sages created the concept 'the joy of the precept'. Testimony to joy of this kind is to be found as far back as Temple times. It is stated in the Tosefta (*Pe'a* iii, 8): 'Once a certain *ḥasid* ['pietist'] forgot a sheaf in his field and he said to his son: "Go and offer up a bull as a burnt offering and a bull as a peace-offering." He (the son) asked:

"Father, why do you rejoice over this precept more than over any of the other precepts ordained in the Torah?" He answered: "All the other commandments of the Torah the Omnipresent gave us to perform consciously, but this one we perform unconsciously. For if we did it wittingly before the Omnipresent, we should not be fulfilling this commandment..." Now we can argue from minor to major: If in the case of one who did not intend to act meritoriously but did so, it is accounted to him as if he had earned merit, how much more does this apply to one who has the intention to act meritoriously and does so!' The joy of the pious farmer lay in the fact that a precept had been performed without his knowledge, and this is possible only in the case of the forgotten sheaf, which 'automatically becomes the property of the poor, and is acquired by the poor before it becomes known to the owner that he had forgotten it, and thus the entire precept is fulfilled without his knowledge', for if this were done intentionally, it is no longer the precept of the forgotten sheaf but ordinary charity.[75] It is possible that this story was already known to R. Eleazar b. Azariah, who said: 'Whence do we know that if a man dropped a *sela*ʿ from his hand and a poor man found it and supported himself with it, Scripture accounts it to him as if he had performed a meritorious act? Because the Torah teaches: "It shall be for the stranger, for the fatherless, and for the widow, that the Lord (thy God) may bless thee." Now we may argue from minor to major', etc.[76] The syllogism in the *Tosefta* and in the *Sifre* is a note of the redactors, who hold, of course, that he who intends to perform a meritorious deed and does so, will certainly be vouchsafed blessing, and he has every right to rejoice at the fulfilment of the precept.

It is praiseworthy of a man to fulfil the commandments from a spirit of joy, and Rabbi already said: 'To make known the praise of Israel, that when they all stood on Mount Sinai to receive the Torah, they were all of one mind to accept the kingdom of Heaven with joy.'[77] On 'And Moses did as the Lord commanded him' or 'as Thou didst command me' the Halakhic Midrashim comment: 'He went and did (God's command) with joy.'[78] On 'And Aaron and his sons did' the Sages add 'They were as glad and joyful when they received instructions from the mouth of Moses, as if they had received them from the mouth of the Holy One, blessed be He....'[79]

The ascription to former worthies of joy in the observance of the precepts of the Lord is indicative of the high esteem in which this joy was held by the Tannaitic homilists themselves. This clearly emerges from the express statements of the Palestinian and Babylonian Amoraim. R. Isaac bar Marion said: 'The Torah teaches you proper conduct: when a man performs a commandment, he should do it with a joyful heart.'[80] R. Ile'a said to 'Ulla that when he goes up to Eretz-Israel he should give his greetings to his brother Berona 'in the presence of the whole college, for he is a great Torah scholar and rejoices in the observance of the precepts'.[81] The contradiction in Ecclesiastes, which states 'Then I commended joy' (Ecclesiastes viii 15) and also 'And of joy: "What doth it accomplish?" ' (*ibid.*, ii 2), is harmonized thus: ' "Then I commended joy" — this refers to the joy of (observing) the precept; "And of joy: 'What doth it accomplish?' " — this alludes to joy that does not emanate from (the fulfilment of) a precept. Thus Scripture teaches you that the Divine presence does not rest (upon a person) either when he is in a melancholy, or indolent, or frivolous mood... but only when he is inspired by a joyful cause [דבר שמחה].'[82] Regarding the addition to the precepts[82a] made by one who is enjoined to observe them, it is stated in an anonymous homily on Leviticus xii 2: ' "And in the eighth day the flesh of his foreskin shall be circumcised": the Torah does not ordain here that one should incur expenses (on the matter). See, however, how much the Israelites cherish the precepts, how great is their outlay in order to observe them! Said the Holy One, blessed be He, "Since you augment the commandments, I shall also enhance your joy, as it is said (Isaiah xxix 19) 'The humble also shall increase their joy in the Lord.' " '[83] On the other hand the very observance in joy is regarded as an act of righteousness.[84]

But the Sages were not unaware that not every person is capable of achieving joy when performing a precept, and that not every one is able to fulfil the commandments at all times in a spirit of joy. Thus 'R. Samuel bar Naḥmani said R. Jonathan pointed out a contradiction: It is written "The precepts of the Lord are right, rejoicing the heart" (Psalms xix 9), and it is also stated "The word of the Lord tries [literally, 'is tried']" (*ibid.* xviii 31).' He replied: 'If he is worthy, it gives him joy; if he is unworthy, it tries him.'[85]

The whole subject of the joy of the precept is linked to the observance of the commandments for their own sake, that is to say, a man should observe the commandments not with a view to gaining thereby honour, status, and recognition, but because he was enjoined to do so and as an expression of his love of the Lord. The verse 'to love the Lord your God' (Deuteronomy xi 22) is thus expounded in the *Sifre*: ' "To love" — lest you say: I shall study the Torah that I may be called Rabbi, that I may sit in council, that I may enjoy length of days in the world to come, Scripture enjoins us "to love": study without thought of gain, and the honour will come in the end.'[86] 'R. Eleazar b. R. Zadok taught: Do things for the sake of doing them, speak of them for their own sake';[87] that is to say, do things for the sake of observing them. The reference here is to study of the Torah, for the verse also deals with that subject, but the principle applies equally to the keeping of the precepts themselves. If a man thinks of the reward of the precept when performing it, this is not considered observing the commandment for its own sake, and he certainly does not rejoice over the commandment itself but over the reward attaching to it. There were Tannaim who found manifestations in nature itself inculcating the observance of precepts for their own sake. Thus R. Dostai b. R. Jannai said: 'Why did the Omnipresent not create hot springs in Jerusalem like those of Tiberias? In order that a man should not say to his fellows: "Let us go up to Jerusalem, for if we go up for but a single dip, it is worth it." The pilgrimage in that case is not for its own sake.'[88]

As we have already indicated in another connection[89], the Sages realized that not every man was capable of attaining to this level of studying the Torah and observing the precepts for their own sake, and held that 'all were equal relative to the Torah' (*Sifre Deuteronomy* 48), which had not been given to the elders and prophets alone, but to the whole community of Israel. It is indeed stated in the name of R. Joḥanan: 'What is the meaning of the verse "For the ways of the Lord are right, and the just do walk in them; but transgressors do stumble therein" (Hosea xiv 10)? It is analogous to the case of two men who roasted their paschal lambs; one of them ate it for the sake of the precept, and the other for the sake of eating a full meal. To the one who ate it in order to fulfil the commandment (applies) "and the just do walk therein", while to him who ate it to enjoy a good meal (applies) "but the transgressors do stumble therein" ' (*T.B. Nazir* 23a). R. Joḥanan differentiates between those who consume the paschal lamb out of gluttony and those who eat it in order to fulfil a religious duty. To the former he applies the Scripture 'but the transgressors do stumble therein', but to the latter (the words) 'and the just do walk in them'. Resh Laqish, however, disagreed with him and countered: 'You call this man "wicked"? Granted that he has not fulfilled the commandment ideally, he has at least prepared the paschal lamb!' In other words, the precept was performed, even if the intent was invalid. R. Eleazar agreed with Resh Laqish. Torah studied for its own sake he designated 'Torah of lovingkindness', whereas Torah that is studied with an ulterior motive he called 'Torah that is not of lovingkindness' (*T.B. Sukka* 49b [end]), although he is also the author of the dictum ' "That delighteth greatly in His commandments" (Psalms cxii 1) — "in His commandments", but not in the reward of His commandments' (*T.B. ʿAvoda Zara* 19a). A favourite saying of Rava was: 'The goal of wisdom is penitence and good deeds. A man should not study much Scripture and much Mishna, and then kick at his father and mother and teacher, or at one who is superior to him in wisdom and authority, as it is said "The reverence of the Lord is the beginning of wisdom, a good understanding have all they that practise it" (Psalms cxi 10). The Bible does not say "all they that study it" but "all they that practise it", (that is,) practise it for the sake of the ideal, and not from other motives. All who practise it for other reasons, it were better that they had not been created.'[90] This drastic teaching is not directed against those who perform the precepts from ulterior motives, but against those who study Torah without the intention to observe and practise it, making the Torah a spade to dig with or a crown wherewith to magnify themselves, to use the expressions of R. Zadok and Hillel.[91] Indeed Rava employed strong language against scholars who studied Torah from other than religious motives. After the saying of R. Samuel bar Naḥmani in the name of R. Jonathan 'Woe betide the enemies of the scholars [a euphemism for the scholars themselves] who occupy themselves with the Torah, but have no reverence for Heaven' and the proclamation of R. Jannai 'Alas for him who has no courtyard, yet makes a gate for his court!', Rava's dictum is cited: 'He said... to the Rabbis: I beseech you, do not inherit a two-fold Gehenna!'[92] It seems, therefore, that, as Rashi explains, it was only with reference to those who do not study the Torah for its own sake that Rava said 'it were better that they had not been created', using the phraseology of R. Ḥiyya, who also taught 'that he who studies (the Torah) without the intention to practise it, it were better that he had not been created.'[93] On the other hand Rava adopted a more lenient attitude towards the observance of precepts from ulterior motives. The contradiction between the verse 'For Thy lovingkindness is great *unto* the heavens and Thy truth *unto* the skies' (Psalms lvii 11 [10]) and the verse 'For Thy lovingkindness is great *above* the heavens' (*ibid.* cviii 5 [4]; the Biblical text lacks the definite article, though inserted in the Talmud) is explained by Rava as follows: 'The latter verse refers to those who perform (the precepts) for their own sake, the former verse refers to those who perform them from other motives.' The Talmudic redactor states that Rava was of the same opinion as Rav Judah, who said in the name of Rav: 'Let a man ever occupy himself with (the study of the) Torah and (the observance of the) precepts, even though it is not for their own sake, for from doing these things from ulterior motives he will eventually come to do them for their own sake.'[94]

However, as we have seen, Rava agreed with him only as far as the precepts were concerned, but as regards Torah-study, he held the same view as R. Ḥiyya and R. Joḥanan. At any rate even to those who perform the commandments for ulterior reasons Rava applied the verse 'For Thy lovingkindness is great unto the heavens', and not 'it were better that they had not been created'. It appears that with regard to the observance of the precepts, he accepted the reasoning of Rav: 'for from doing these things from ulterior motives he will eventually come to do them for their own sake'.

The attitude to be taken in respect of precepts not performed for their own sake was not a theoretical issue only, but also had practical Halakhic bearings, for the question was raised whether a man who observed a commandment without the intention of fulfilling his religious duty actually discharged his obligation or not. However, the question of the principle whether the observance of precepts requires intention or not appears only in discussions of the Babylonian Talmud. Rava, who holds that one who blows the Shofar [ram's horn] to make music fulfils his religious duty, clearly represents the view that the fulfilment of the precepts does not require intent.[95] But the Amoraim and the redactors of the Talmud were also able to base themselves on Mishnayot and Baraitot, where the rule, though not explicitly stated, was at any rate implied, only it is not always possible to decide if the Tanna had in mind a general principle or a detailed regulation. In the Babylonian Talmud the following Baraita is cited on the subject of blowing the Shofar: 'The listener hears for himself, and the Shofar-blower does so with no one specifically in mind. Said R. Jose: This applies only to a congregational precentor, but a private individual does not discharge his obligations until both he that listens and he that blows the Shofar intended (the religious duty to be duly performed thereby, the former by hearing, the latter by causing him to hear the Shofar-blowing).'[96] From this it was inferred that R. Jose holds that the performance of the precepts requires intent; but the question arises whether such an inference is really justified, for possibly R. Jose's ruling applies only to the Shofar, in which case the precept consists primarily of hearing. Indeed, in another Baraita we find 'It is taught: An Israelite may circumcise a Cuthean [= Samaritan], but a Cuthean may not circumcise an Israelite, because the former is circumcised in the name of Mount Gerizim, this is the view of R. Juda. Said R. Jose to him: But where do we find it (ordained) in the Torah that circumcision needs intention? On the contrary, let him go on circumcising in the name of Mount Gerizim, till he perish!'[97] Nor is the Tanna's reason always clear; sometimes it is possible to find another explanation for his ruling, unconnected with the question of intention. In the Babylonian Talmud (*Pesaḥim* 114b) the Sages wished to infer from a Baraita that R. Jose was of the opinion that 'the precepts require intent', but subsequently they rejected the inference, arguing: 'Perhaps R. Jose holds that the precepts do not require intent.'[98] Often even the formulation of the statements is not unambiguous, and sometimes the dictum of an Amora, to whom the Babylonian Talmud ascribes the view that the precepts require intent, is reported in the Palestinian Talmud in a version that does not corroborate this conclusion.[99] But even the

Sages who took the view that precepts do not require intent, made an exception in the case of prayer, which is the 'service of the heart.'[1] Not only the pious men of old used to wait an hour before they said the תפלה *Tĕfillā* ['Prayer', i.e. Eighteen Benedictions], 'that they might direct their heart toward the Omnipresent' (*M. Berakhot* v, 1), but even artisans were forbidden to say the *Tĕfillā* 'on top of a tree or on top of a course of stones' (*ibid.* ii, 4), and a porter might not say the *Tĕfillā* until he had laid down his burden,[2] for 'he who says the *Tĕfillā* must concentrate his mind'.[3] Obviously a distinction must be drawn between כונה *kawwānā* ['devotion', 'concentration', 'intention'] in regard to *Tĕfillā* and *kawwānā* applied to the precepts, for in the former case it does not mean to fulfil one's obligation in respect of the precept of *Tĕfillā*, but concentration of the mind on the subject and content of the *Tĕfillā*. In view of this distinction it is possible to understand the differences of opinion concerning *kawwānā* during the recitation of the *Shĕmaʿ*. In the name of R. Akiba and in the name of R. Judah it was transmitted that if a man concentrated his mind in the first paragraph, he fulfilled his duty. According to R. Eliezer and Bar Qappara only the first three verses of the first paragraph require *kawwānā*, while R. Me'ir and R. Judah the Patriarch held that only the first verse requires concentration of the mind.[4] The matter was still the subject of dispute in the days of the Amoraim. Thus R. Mana, one of the last of the Palestinian Amoraim, said: 'Even if you say that the recitation of the *Shĕmaʿ* does not require *kawwānā*, the *Tĕfillā* does require *kawwānā*.'[5] Some Amoraim insisted on *kawwānā* also in the case of other commandments, if they involved hearing. In the Mishna (*Megilla* ii, 1) it is stated that if a man read the *Mĕgillā* [the Scroll of Esther] drowsily, he has discharged his obligation. But in the Palestinian Talmud it is related: 'Menasseh was sitting before R. Zeʿira and dozing (while reciting the *Mĕgillā*); said he [R. Zeʿira] to him [Menasseh]: 'Repeat the passage, because you were not concentrating.'[6] This was also R. Zera's attitude in respect of the blowing of the Shofar: 'R. Zera said to his attendant: "Put your mind to it and blow for me." '[7]

The problem confronting the Sages is known in every religion and in every system of ethics. What significance can a man's conduct have, if he observes the laws of ethics and religion as stereotyped, conventional acts without giving them an inner meaning? Some people declare: These are 'precepts learned by rote', and actions that are merely external and unaccompanied by inner feeling — inward devotion — only do harm, and it is better to dispense with them. On the other hand it is realized that not everyone is capable of being constantly in that high state of tension requisite to action intentionally and consciously performed for its own sake. Religions and sects professing strict ideals and demands — which set out with the clear intention to preserve the consciousness of their ideals in daily life, and did not accept the observance of acts that lacked inner faith — eventually suffered not only from apathy, but, in most cases, even from licentiousness. In the light of such experiences the question arises whether the absolute demand that, where people are unable to keep observances ideally, it is better for them not to keep them at all does not actually contain from the outset an encouragement and invitation, as it were, to those who seek a dispensation from the yoke of the commandments. Apparently such considerations presented themselves to the Sages and they enable us to explain the dictum of one of the later Amoraim — Rav Naḥman bar Isaac — which is sharply worded: 'A transgression committed with good intent is better than a precept performed from ulterior motives' (*T.B. Nazir* 23b). The saying occasioned surprise already in the Talmud, which emends it: 'Rather say "as good as a precept performed from ulterior motives", that is to say, a transgression committed with good intent is not better than a precept performed from ulterior motives, but is equal to it. From the context of the Talmudic discussion it is evident that 'a transgression with good intent' [literally 'a transgression for its own sake'] is taken to mean one that is committed for the sake of a religious principle [מצוה *miṣwā*: 'precept', 'religious duty', religious principle', 'good deed'].[8] Thus a good deed [*miṣwā*] 'resulting from a transgression is, as it were, a precept that is performed through a transgression committed with good intent.[9] It is surprising therefore that this should be termed עברה לשמה *'ăvērā li-shĕmāh* [literally 'a transgression for its own sake']! Hence it seems that originally *'ăvērā li-shĕmāh* signified a transgression committed with intent to transgress, just as מצוה לשמה *miṣwā li-shĕmāh* means a precept performed for the sake of the precept. Undoubtedly Rav Naḥman bar Isaac is not speaking in praise of transgression, but in dispraise of the observance of a precept from ulterior motives; and just as Rava worded his dictum strongly, saying 'it were better that they had not been born', so Rav Naḥman bar Isaac formulated his remarks in similar fashion. He who commits a transgression from a sense of religious idealism is better than one who fulfils a precept insincerely. In other words, the aphorism seeks to emphasize the importance of the spirit in which a deed is performed, and that intention and devotion transcend the action itself. This is an individual view, and it was not shared by Rav, Resh Laqish, R. Eleazar, or Rava. The observance of the precepts for their own sake was not less important in their estimation, but the inherent difficulty of the matter, which already found expression in the words of the Tanna R. Nehemiah, 'Whoever accepts one commandment in faith is worthy that the Holy Spirit should rest upon him',[10] made them realize that by keeping and performing many precepts a man may eventually attain the capability of fulfilling at least part of them for their own sake, in faith and with perfection.[11] A man may not, however, postpone the observance of a precept until such time as he can perform it perfectly, as is stated by the Tanna R. Josiah: 'Just as we may not allow מצה *maṣṣā* ['unleavened bread'] to become leavened (through delay), so we must not allow a *miṣwā* ['precept'] to become "leavened" [i.e. to delay its observance]; but if you have the opportunity to perform a precept do so forthwith.'[12] The reason is explained in an Amoraic homily on the verse 'Whatsoever thy hand attaineth to do by thy strength, that do' (Ecclesiastes, ix 10) — 'whatsoever precept you can perform whilst you still have the strength, do. Why? When a man is no more in the world, his intention is likewise no more. Grasp whatever precept you can, while you are still alive.'[13] The observance of a precept brings in its train love of the precepts, and 'He who loves the commandments is never sated with them.'[14]

CHAPTER XIV

ACCEPTANCE OF THE YOKE OF THE KINGDOM OF HEAVEN

Love and Reverence

The purpose of the Torah and the precepts is the acceptance of the yoke of the kingdom of heaven, which finds expression in the fear [i.e. reverence] and love of the Lord. But even when explaining the order of the Ten Commandments on Mount Sinai, and likewise the order of the sections of the *Shĕma*ʿ, the Tannaim ruled that the intended and desired procedure for a Jew is first to assume the yoke of the kingdom of heaven and then the yoke of the commandments. ' "Thou shalt have no other gods before Me": Why is this stated? Because Scripture said "I am the Lord thy God". The matter may be compared to a human king who entered a province. Said his servants to him: "Impose decrees upon the people." He answered them: "No; when they accept my sovereignty, I shall impose decrees upon them; for if they do not accept my sovereignty, they will not accept my decrees either..." '[1] To the question 'Why does the paragraph "Hear, O Israel..." precede the paragraph "And it shall come to pass, if ye shall hearken..."?' R. Joshua b. Qorḥa replied: 'So that a man should first take upon himself the yoke of the kingdom of heaven and thereafter the yoke of the commandments' (*M. Berakhot* ii, 2). The acceptance of the yoke of the kingdom of heaven means to acknowledge the God who is One and Unique, and to bear witness that there is no other god. Thus the section 'Hear, O Israel' is characterized in Tannaitic exegesis as 'a section containing the acceptance of the kingdom of heaven, while idolatry is diminished therein'.[2] The thought is elaborated in the Amoraic homily on the words of the Psalmist (lxxiii 25): 'Whom have I in heaven? And with Thee I desire none upon earth' [this is a literal rendering of the verse] — 'Israel said to the Holy One, blessed be He: Sovereign of the universe, whom have I in heaven? We recognize no other god, only the God of heaven. "And with Thee" — nor do we associate with Thee any god upon earth; but we declare Thy unity and proclaim "Hear, O Israel, the Lord, our God, the Lord is One". '[3] The assumption of the yoke of the kingdom of heaven by the recitation of the verse 'Hear, O Israel' finds expression in the response that follows it, 'Blessed be the name of the glory of His kingdom for ever and ever',[3a] which was the response recited in the Temple after the benediction[4] and after the utterance of the Divine Name by the High Priest on the Day of Atonement.[5] Undoubtedly this response also originated in the reading of the *Shĕmaʿ* in the Temple[6], only the usage spread beyond its precincts. However, when the recital of the *Shĕmaʿ* became an individual obligation, some Sages abolished completely the saying of 'Blessed be the name of the glory of His kingdom for ever and ever', because they were concerned not to make an unnecessary breach between two verses of the Torah[7]; but the majority continued to pronounce the response in a low voice.[8] This emerges from the tradition reported by R. Abbahu: 'In Usha they instituted that it (the response) should be said aloud on account of the heresies of the sectarians.'[9] This enactment was due to the fear that saying the response in a low voice would make it easy for people with Christian heretical tendencies to interpolate their credal professions. The enactment of Usha is therefore to be regarded as a kind of sequel to that of 'the benediction concerning sectarians' in the *Tĕfillā*, whose aim was to exclude those suspected of sectarian heresy.[10] Just as the Sages abolished the daily recitation of the Decalogue, which was customary in the Temple, 'because of the assertion [טענת *ṭaʿănat*] of the sectarians — that they should not say: These precepts only were given to Moses at Sinai'[11], so they maintained the saying of 'Blessed be the name of the glory of His kingdom for ever and ever' in a loud voice for a similar reason. Both the abolition of the one custom and the preservation of the other aimed to deny the views of the sectarians any purchase in the customs of Israel and to prevent the spread of their influence. But while attempts to restore the recitation of the Decalogue are known to us only in places where sectarians were not to be found[12], the enactment of Usha was disregarded and the response 'Blessed be the name of the glory of His kingdom for ever and ever' was said in an undertone not only in Nehardea, where no sectarians existed[13], but also in various parts of Eretz-Israel.[14] At all events the response 'Blessed be the name of the glory of His kingdom for ever and ever' lent emphasis to the acceptance of the yoke of the kingdom of heaven implicit in the utterance of 'Hear, O Israel'[15], only this utterance did not give it exhaustive expression. The Sages regarded it as merely a beginning or preamble, which was expressly continued in the second verse of the passage of the *Shĕmaʿ*, ' "And thou shalt love the Lord thy God" — act from love.' Although acting out of love is deemed in this homily the highest stage in man's relationship to God, yet it must be linked to fear [reverence], 'for love where there is fear and fear where there is love are only found in relation to the Omnipresent.'[16] The explanation of this nexus is given in another homily: 'Act from love and act from fear. Act out of love, for should you wish to hate, know that you love, and he that loves does not hate. Act out of fear, for should you wish to rebel, know that you fear, and he that fears does not rebel.'[17] Actually, we are presented here with an explanation of the fact that love and fear are found in close association in the Bible, especially in Deuteronomy[18] and Psalms — thus corresponding to the attribute of God, who is 'a jealous God' and at the same time 'shows lovingkindness'[19] — and in the prayer of Nehemiah (i 5), which begins 'I beseech Thee, O Lord, the God of heaven, the great and awe-inspiring God, that keepeth covenant and steadfast love *with those who love* Him and keep His commandments' and concludes (*ibid.* 11) '...let Thine ear be attentive... and to the prayer of Thy servants who delight *to fear* Thy name'.[20]

However, we still have to consider whether this appraisement of love and fear in relation to the Lord and the suggested reconciliation between them was a generally accepted view, and if so when it acquired this formulation. The expression מורא שמים *môraʾ shāmayim* ['fear of heaven'] first occurs in the saying of Antigonus of Sokho 'Be not like servants that minister to the master for the sake of receiving a reward (פרס *pĕrās*), but be like servants that minister to the master not for the sake of receiving a reward; and let the fear of Heaven be upon you' (*M. 'Avot* i, 3). Irrespective of whether 'not for the sake of receiving פרס'[21] refers to wages, or the maintenance [פרוסה *pĕrûsā*, literally 'piece of bread'] of the slave[22], or whether it means a gratuity as a token of the benefactor's appreciation[23], a servant who does not await a reward undoubtedly serves his master out of love, or at least out of gratitude. Antigonus, not yet satisfied with this attitude, adds 'and let the fear of Heaven be upon you'. In commenting on this Mishna, *'Avot de-R. Nathan* states: 'It is like a man who does the will of his master, but is presumptuous in regard to his master's will, (or like a man who does the will of his father) but is presumptuous in regard to his father's will. One that acts out of love cannot be compared with one who acts out of awe and fear... for we find that the Early Fathers served (God) in awe and fear... Of Abraham it is said "for now I know that thou art a God-fearing man" (Genesis xxii 12); of Joseph it is stated "I fear God" (*ibid.*, xlii 18); of Jonah it is written "and I fear the Lord, the God of heaven I fear" (Jonah i 9).'[24] Clearly this Baraita understood Antigonus' dictum to mean that the service of God which is inspired by awe and fear transcends that which is motivated by love alone, because a servant who serves his master without expectation of reward may possibly be presumptuous in regard to his master's will. This opinion is opposed to the view that we have indicated as generally accepted, but its strangeness is not sufficient ground for assigning to it a late date.[25] If, however, we re-examine the teaching of Antigonus, we shall see that actually it does not contain the differentiation between 'fear' and 'love' found in the Baraita, nor the preference given to the former over the latter, but the 'fear of heaven' of which it speaks enshrines as a precondition service of God out of love, for only by serving Him without expectation of reward can a man prove that the fear of Heaven rests upon him. Thus the author of the Baraita was justified in drawing his conclusions from the Sages' words. The new approach in Antigonus' teaching becomes evident when his dictum is compared with the words of Ben Sira:[26] 'With all thy heart fear God, and hallow His priests, With all thy strength love thy Maker, and His ministers do not forsake.' 'Fear' and 'love' are also used as synonymous verbs when he speaks of 'They that fear the Lord... and they that love Him'. There is no difference whatsoever to be found between the two categories;[27] on the other hand the motive of reward is prominent in the verses

'Ye that fear the Lord wait for His mercy; and turn not aside, lest ye fail. Ye that fear the Lord, put your trust in Him, and your reward shall not fail. Ye that fear the Lord hope for His benefits and for eternal gladness and mercy.'[28]

The impact of the personality of Abraham and his ordeal in the episode of the עקדה *ʿĀqēdā* [the Binding of Isaac] had a decisive influence on the conception of the terms 'fear' and 'love'. The ancients pointed to Abraham's ordeal. Nehemiah referred to him in the words 'and foundest his heart faithful before Thee' (ix 8). Ben Sira wrote 'He established the covenant in his flesh, and when he was tested he was found faithful' (xliv 20). So, too, it is stated in *I Maccabees* (ii 52): 'Was not Abraham found faithful when tested?' But only the Tannaim proceeded to draw definite conclusions regarding man's relationship to his God. Antigonus defined the relationship of man to God as 'fear of Heaven', and this term included the love that was exemplified by the servant who served his Master not for the sake of receiving reward. His saying is unrelated to reward and punishment, and contains no allusion to God's attributes in His dealings with man. Philo of Alexandria also employed the analogy of a servant in his discussions about love and fear in man's relations with the Deity. However, comparison with Antigonus' dictum points up the difference between the doctrine of the Sage and that of Philo. The latter's[29] starting point is the Torah's teaching on God's jealousy, anger, and wrath. In speaking thus Moses does not address himself to those who do not overlay their conception of God with attributes of created beings; the lawgiver is also bound to take into account the multitude. Whether they are unintelligent or failed to receive a proper education, they are unable to see clearly, and consequently they are in need of physicians in the form of mentors who will provide them with treatment suited to their condition: 'Thus ill-disciplined and foolish slaves receive profit from a master who frightens them, for they fear his threats and menaces and thus involuntarily are schooled by fear. All such may well learn the untruth, which will benefit them, if they cannot be brought to wisdom by truth.' In this homily[30] Philo grasps the fear peculiar to untutored slaves, who need a master that strikes awe. Fear has a pedagogical justification merely for people who think of God in terms of the verse 'that, as a man chasteneth his son, so the Lord thy God chasteneth thee.'[31] Love of the Lord, on the other hand, is the heritage only of those 'into whose conception of the Existent no thought of human parts or passion enters, who pay Him the honour meet for God for His own sake only.'[32] Philo does not recognize 'fear of Heaven' as a true value, and certainly not as a supreme value. Love is linked to a correct understanding of the nature of God, and is not the portion of 'servants that minister to the master not for the sake of receiving a reward'. Philo's statement concerning the servants recalls the verses of the Odyssey: 'Servants, when their masters are no longer there to order them about, have little will to do their duties as they should' [translation by E. V. Rieu].[33] On the other hand, it is actually Seneca's view[34] that appears far removed from the course of Philo's thought. Seneca teaches that the master should implant in the hearts of his servants not a feeling of dread but of reverence, giving as his reason: 'For that which suffices for a god must necessarily suffice also for a human master.' Seneca does not transfer a concept belonging to the ethics governing human relations to the sphere of theology, but, conversely, he deduces from man's relationship to the deity what a servant's attitude to his master should be. In his view 'he that is revered is also loved; but love cannot be harmonized with fear.'[35] Seneca comes close to Antigonus' dictum. Possibly there is actually to be discerned in the observations of Seneca, who was almost a contemporary of Rabban Joḥanan b. Zakkai, the influence of the teaching of the Jewish Sages.[36] Undoubtedly Philo's arguments and Seneca's approach are completely congruent.[37] Philo does not distinguish between 'fear resulting from terror' and the fear which is reverence, and Seneca, again, does not connect his statement concerning fear and love with the attributes of Deity. Only where Philo freed himself, in the course of his discussion, from the nexus between the attributes of God and the two ways of serving Him, was he capable of grasping the concept of the fear of God more positively. A contributing factor, apparently, was also the transmission of Palestinian traditions, although he did not always cite them in their correct context.[38]

The words of the Lord to Abraham, following upon the incident of the *'Ăqēdā*, 'For now I know that thou art a God-fearing man, seeing thou hast not withheld thy son, thine only son, from Me', show clearly that after the unconditional act of sacrifice and devotion Abraham was granted the designation of 'a God-fearing man'. Yet there is no more perfect expression of love of the Lord than the act of the *'Ăqēdā*; moreover Abraham was the friend of the Lord, as was stated by the prophet Isaiah (xli 8): 'the seed of Abraham My friend'. Indeed, it appears that R. Me'ir's observation '(the term) "a God-fearing man" applied to Abraham (means that he was so) out of love'[39] was a generally accepted view. Thus we are told in *The Book of Jubilees* (xvii 18): 'And in everything wherein He had tried him, he was found faithful, and his soul was not impatient, and he was not slow to act; for he was faithful and a lover of the Lord.' In conformity with this view the disciples of R. Akiba attributed the observance of their teacher's exposition ' "With all thy soul" — even if He takes your soul'[40] to the Patriarch Abraham himself. R. Simeon b. Yoḥai taught that the Lord said to Abraham: 'By your life, I account it unto you as if, had I bidden you to slaughter yourself, you would not have resisted for My sake, but would have obeyed and allowed yourself to be slaughtered on My account.'[41] Another disciple of R. Akiba, R. Eliezer b. Jacob, even went so far as to represent Abraham as offering his life in the fiery furnace for the principle of God's Unity.[42] In accordance with this view the Sages expounded the verse 'of them that love Me and keep My commandments' as follows: ' "Of them that love Me" — this refers to the Patriarch Abraham and his like...', that is, those who sanctify the Divine Name through religious martyrdom.[43] It is even reported in the name of R. Judah, R. Akiba's disciple, that all the glory vouchsafed Abraham was only on account of the ordeal in the fiery furnace: '...Abraham's deeds were not known until he was cast into the fiery furnace; and just as anyone who gathers myrrh gets his hands gummed with the bitter myrrh, so Abraham embittered his life and afflicted himself with sufferings.'[44]

Although none could doubt that Abraham's fear of God was inspired by love, the Sages were nevertheless conscious of the existence of a type of fear that stemmed only from dread of punishment and the possibility of losing one's reward. This kind of fear is unable to stand up to the test of suffering and tribulation. Thus R. Joshua reported that his teacher Rabban Johanan b. Zakkai used to expound all his days: 'That Job served the Omnipresent only out of fear, as it is stated (Job i 8): "a whole-hearted and an upright man, one that feareth God, and shunneth evil" '.[45] Rabban Joḥanan b. Zakkai could not regard Job as 'a God-fearing man' in the same sense as Abraham, since, in contrast to the Patriarch, Job did not stand the test of suffering without uttering harsh reproaches against Heaven.[46] Hence he said that Job did not serve God out of fear flowing from love, but out of fear resulting 'from anxiety lest retribution be visited upon him'. Possibly the Scriptural proof is based on the fact that the words 'a God-fearing man' are followed by the phrase 'and shunneth evil'.[47] The subjoined homily of Rabbi Akiba reads like a commentary on Rabban Joḥanan b. Zakkai's dictum, but reflects a more extreme viewpoint:[48] 'A certain king had four sons: One remained silent when punished; another protested when punished; another pleaded for mercy when punished; and another, when punished, said to his father "Punish me (still more)". Abraham was silent when punished, as it is said: "Take now thy son, thine only son, whom thou lovest, even Isaac... and offer him there for a burnt-offering" (Genesis xxii 2). He could have answered: "Yesterday Thou didst tell me 'For in Isaac shall seed be called to thee' " (*ibid.* xxi 12). Yet it is stated "And Abraham rose early in the morning" etc. (*ibid.* xxii 3). Job remonstrated when punished, as it is said "I will say unto God: Do not condemn me; make me know wherefore Thou contendest with me" (Job x 2). Hezekiah begged for mercy when punished, as it is stated "and he prayed unto the Lord" (II Kings xx 2)... David said to his Father "Punish me (even more)", as it is said "Wash me thoroughly from mine iniquity, and cleanse me from my sin" (Psalms li 4).'[49] In accordance with this view of Job as a rebel, Akiba grouped him with the generation of the Flood, Egypt, Gog and Magog, and the wicked who are punished in Gehenna for twelve months.[50]

While Antigonus of Sokho included love in the term 'fear of Heaven', which is in consequence man's religious ideal as portrayed in the utterances of the Prophets and the Psalmist,[51] Rabban Joḥanan b. Zakkai's statement that we have elucidated demonstrates that the fear of Heaven was understood by others as a concept devoid of love; this was apparently an outcome of the undue emphasis placed on the principle of reward and retribution.[52] But the formulation of

Rabban Joḥanan b. Zakkai's dictum does not yet contain the antithesis 'fear-love'; underlying it is rather the contrast between fear out of love and fear from dread of punishment. This interpretation is also confirmed by another source. Before his death R. Joḥanan said to his disciples: ' "May it be the Divine will that the fear of Heaven be upon you like that of mortals." Said his disciples to him: "Is that all?" He answered: "Would that it were so! Observe when a man commits a transgression, he hopes: May no one see me!" '[53] The surprise of the disciples at the comparison of the fear of Heaven to that of human beings is to be understood on the basis of the identification of the 'fear of Heaven' with fear of Heaven's retribution, which is not present in the fear of men. In this reply Rabban Joḥanan b. Zakkai emphasizes that the fear of Heaven implies the consciousness of the awe-inspiring character of God at all times and in the performance of every human act. Just as the proximity of an honoured and beloved man will hold a man back from perpetrating a transgression out of a sense of shame, so the feeling of God's nearness, glory, and love should prevent a man from sinning, and not primarily the fear of punishment. Only after the meaning of the concept 'fear' had become restricted and was applied to one aspect — fear on account of reward and retribution — did the clear contrast 'love-fear' come into being. It first appears about two generations after Rabban Joḥanan b. Zakkai. R. Joshua b. Hyrcanus expounded: 'Job served the Omnipresent only out of love, as it is said 'Though He slay me yet will I wait for Him" (Job xiii 15). The matter, however, is still undecided (for the *Kĕthîv* here is לא איחל *lō' 'ăyaḥēl*, whereas the *Qĕrê* is לו איחל *lô 'ăyaḥēl*): Is the sense "I wait for Him", or "I do not wait for him"? Therefore Scripture declares: "Till I die I will not put away my integrity from me" (*ibid.* xxvii 5) — this teaches that he acted from love.' R. Joshua b. Ḥananiah accepted his view and said: 'Who will take away the dust from your eyes, O Rabban Joḥanan b. Zakkai!... and has not Joshua, the disciple of your disciple, now taught that he acted from love?'[54] Two things must be noted in the homily of R. Joshua b. Hyrcanus. First, that he does not deny the fact that Job's words contain reproaches against Heaven, and there is no attempt here to expound all his utterances favourably. Even in regard to xiii 15 he observed that it was a moot matter, for one could also read 'Though

another view of Job

He slay me I will not wait for Him'. Secondly, the decisive proof that Job acted out of love is derived from the last chapter of Job containing a charge against God (*ibid.* xxvii 2): 'As God liveth, who hath taken away my right; and the Almighty who hath dealt bitterly with me.' He did not, however, interpret even this verse contrary to its plain meaning, but only noted that it is followed by Job's declaration 'Till I die I will not put away my integrity from me',[55] that is to say, despite his complaints Job preserved his integrity. Integrity connotes submission out of a sense of devotion and love.[56] Round about the time of R. Joshua b. Hyrcanus, a Sage called Ben Peṭuri also expounded the verse 'As God liveth, who hath taken away my right; and the Almighty, who hath dealt bitterly with me' in Job's favour. He argued that 'No one vows by the life of the king unless he loves him.'[57]

In the homilies of R. Joshua b. Hyrcanus — which were approved by R. Joshua b. Ḥananiah and by Ben Peṭuri — wherein Job is depicted as serving God from love, there is a change in the very conception of the term love. It is no longer just fear emanating from love, which accepts suffering with complete devotion without question or protest, but also love stemming from chastisement and even from reproach of Heaven. This view is summed up in R. Me'ir's homily: 'For the term "a God-fearing man" is applied to Job and it is also applied to Abraham. Just as the expression "a God-fearing man" when applied to Abraham means out of love, so, too, when applied to Job it signifies from love.' As for 'all the charges made in the Book, they were uttered only relative to the occasion'.[58] But not all the Tannaim and Amoraim agreed that Job was to be adjudged one who served God from love. On the contrary, there were some who criticized his 'fear of God', and even the Sages who defended him did so only by interpreting his reproaches in a manner that took the sting out of the complaint and indictment. The issue came to the fore already in the dispute between R. Eliezer and R. Joshua: ' "The earth is given into the hand of the wicked" (Job ix 24). R. Eliezer said: Job sought to overturn the Divine order. Said R. Joshua to him: Job was only referring to Satan.'[59]

The problem of the harsh words and reproaches of Job assumes special importance in the *Targumim* [translations of Scripture] of the Book. The question already troubled the Sages in ancient times.

R. Jose relates: 'Once R. Ḥalafta visited Rabban Gamaliel at Tiberias. He found him sitting at the desk of Joḥanan b. Nazif and in his hand was a *Targum* of the Book of Job, which he was reading. Said R. Ḥalafta to him: I remember that Rabban Gamaliel the Elder, your grandfather, was sitting on a step on the Temple Mount, when a *Targum* of the Book of Job was brought to him, and he ordered the builder to build it into the wall. At that time Rabban Gamaliel (II) sent instructions to withdraw it from circulation.'[60]

We do not know what translation was brought to Rabban Gamaliel the Elder — whether Greek or Aramaic; certainly not that which we have today.[61] But whether this was the Septuagint,[62] or a translation that rendered the Book quite literally,[63] the reason for its suppression is to be found in the very fact of translation — on the same principle as 'The incident of Reuben is read (in Hebrew), but is not translated' (*M. Megilla* iv, 9) — or at most in the manner of the rendition, which did not find favour with Rabban Gamaliel. But the blame is not to be put on the differences of opinion between the Pharisees and the Sadducees.[64] If in truth Rabban Gamaliel was afraid that the Sadducees could find support for their views in the Book of Job, his fears would have applied not only to the translation but to the original. But we do not find that the Sages sought to withdraw Job from circulation. On the contrary, according to the Mishnaic tradition (*M. Yoma* i, 6) it was customary to read before the High Priest, on the evening of the Day of Atonement, from the Book of Job, and this tradition probably dates back to the time of Rabban Gamaliel the Elder. Furthermore, it is hard to imagine that the Sadducees, who denied the doctrine of determinism, could have approved the rebellious conduct and charges of Job. It appears that until the time of Rabban Gamaliel the Elder a translation of Job was not current at all,[65] and that when a translation was brought to him, he found that it deserved only to be suppressed. But the withdrawal did not prevent a *Targum* from appearing in the days of his grandson Rabban Gamaliel of Jabneh, when he visited Tiberias. We do not know the nature of this translation, which apparently *per se*, without the story told by R. Ḥalafta about the action of his grandfather, would not have been suppressed by Rabban Gamaliel. At any rate it seems that the renderings that were not withdrawn were oriented towards the exegesis that explained away the harsh charges of Job and were therefore motivated by the desire to put his personality in a favourable light, after the manner of R. Joshua. This is also the attitude adopted, in many passages, by the translator of the Septuagint. His Job is much more long-suffering and humble than the Hebrew Job. In not a few passages the Greek Job speaks almost with composure, and his words lack that quality of self-assurance and protest found in the Hebrew original. He mitigates the indictments by means of interpretations, omissions, and interpolations.[66] To the verse at the end of the Book, 'So Job said, being old and full of days', the translator adds 'And it is written that he will rise to life again with those whom God will raise up'. This addition accords with the spirit of the translation of several verses that, in contrast to the original, express the hope in life after death.[67] The renditions that toned down Job's rebelliousness and contention facilitated the creation of a story about Job totally different from that of the Biblical book. In the Greek pseudepigraphical work called *The Testament of Job*, or *The Words of Job*,[68] not only are all Job's arguments and charges thrust aside, but he himself is depicted there in the image and character of the Patriarch Abraham; he is not merely a liberal host but an iconoclast who purges his area of idolatry, casts down the idols, and closes their temples. His struggle is entirely directed against Satan. The roles of Job and his friends are interchanged. It is they who lament and complain about his bitter fate, but he stands up to the trial and cries 'Shall I sin with my lips against the Lord? It shall surely not come to pass!' (xxxviii 2), even as he had undertaken at the beginning (v 1) 'to stand the ordeal, and not to weaken till the day of his death'.[69] Here the position is completely reversed. Needless to say, not a little must be attributed to the 'artistic' character of the composition. Imaginative, legendary works of this kind are accustomed to glorify the image of their hero to the point of overlooking other personalities. Hence it is interesting to note that in a book that strongly resembles in form *The Testament of Job*, namely the *Testament of Abraham*[70], the angel Michael says to God: 'There is none like him (Abraham) in the land, not even Job, that excellent man.'[71] The viewpoint of *The Testament of Job* is prevalent also in ancient Christian literature. 'The patience of Job and the end of the "Lord" ' are presented together as an example to sufferers in the Epistle of James (v 11), and this line of interpretation was followed by Tertullian and other church fathers in the Christian church.[72] But this approach was not accepted by the Sages, not even by those who argued in Job's favour.[73]

While R. Joshua saves Job by diverting his harsh words to Satan, R. Eliezer declares that he was a blasphemer. R. Ishmael, too, was far from comparing Job to Abraham, but said 'Job was one of Pharaoh's servants, one of his leading courtiers, as it is written "He that feared the word of the Lord" etc. (Exodus xi 2); and Scripture says of him "a wholehearted and an upright man, one that feareth God, and shunneth evil'.[74] Job was therefore only one that feared the Lord from fear of punishment. A similar statement is made by R. Ḥiyya concerning Job: 'I had but one righteous Gentile in My world, and I gave him his reward and dismissed him from My world.'[75]

This appraisal is still more evident in the wording of an anonymous Baraita: 'There was once a pious man among the Gentile nations called Job, and he came into the world only with the object of receiving his recompense. When the Holy One, blessed be He, brought upon him afflictions, he began to revile and blaspheme. So the Holy One, blessed be He, doubled his reward in this world, in order to exclude him from the world to come' (*T.B. Bava Batra* 15b). A Baraita that enumerates the various types of Pharisees and distinguishes between a 'God-fearing Pharisee' and a 'God-loving Pharisee' illustrates the two by observing: 'A God-fearing Pharisee is (exemplified) by Job, a God-loving Pharisee is Abraham; the noblest of them all is the God-loving Pharisee like Abraham.'[76]

In all these sources Job appears as one who fears God only on account of reward and punishment. The Amora R. Levi explains the difference between Abraham and Job actually on the basis of their reactions, which ostensibly appear alike: 'R. Levi said: Two men — Abraham and Job — said the same thing. Abraham said "far be it from Thee to do such a thing, to slay the righteous with the wicked" (Genesis xviii 25); Job said "It is all one — therefore I say: He destroyeth the innocent and the wicked" (Job ix 22). Abraham was rewarded for this, Job was punished for it. Abraham said it with due deliberation; Job spoke intemperately — "It is all one" ' (*Genesis*

Rabba xlix, §9, p. 509). Abraham made his statement with calm deliberation; he could not imagine that God would slay the righteous with the wicked, whereas Job made a definite and unqualified charge — 'It is all one'![77]

R. Levi enlarged the scope of Abraham's doubts. To the question 'Why did the Holy One, blessed be He, make the revelation to Abraham?' he replied: 'Because he questioned in his heart (the justice of destroying) the generation of the Flood, and thought: It is inconceivable that there were no righteous men among them.'[78]

It should also be noted that a similar conception of a confrontation between Abraham and God is to be found in Philo's work *Quis Rerum Divinarum Heres?* On the verse Genesis xv 2 he comments: 'When, then, is it that the servant speaks frankly to his master? Surely it is when his heart tells him that he has not wronged his owner, but that his words and deeds are all for that owner's benefit. And so when else should the slave of God open his mouth to Him who is the ruler and master both of himself and of the All, save when he is pure from sin and the judgements of his conscience are loyal to his master, when he feels more joy at being the servant of God than if he had been king of all the human race...'[79] 'For to whom should a man speak with frankness, but to his friend?.... But observe on the other hand that confidence is blended with caution. For while the words "What wilt Thou give me" (Genesis xv 2) show confidence, "Master" shows caution... He who says "Master, what wilt Thou give me?" virtually says no less than this, "I am not ignorant of Thy transcendent sovereignty; I know the terrors of Thy power; I come before Thee in fear and trembling, and yet again I am confident... Thou hast given me a tongue of instruction that I should know when I should speak... Why then shall I not take courage to say what I feel? Why shall I not inquire of Thee and claim to learn something more? Yet I, who proclaim my confidence, confess in turn my fear and consternation, and still the fear and the confidence are not at war within me in separate camps, as one might suppose, but are blended in a harmony.'[80] Undoubtedly these remarks of Philo contain a totally different appraisal of the fear of God from that which characterizes his other homilies. This indicates that Philo also absorbed something of the ancient Rabbinic conception of the fear of God that flows from love, and that echoes of their homilies on Abraham's confrontation with his God had reached him too. But the fact that Philo bases his homily specifically on the verse 'What wilt Thou give me?' and not on the daring verses uttered by Abraham when he came to pray for the men of Sodom is puzzling. Yet it is actually his exposition of these verses in other treatises[81] that enables us to understand his viewpoint; for he removes from these passages the daring characteristics that mark Abraham's questions, which, although asked unprovocatively, are nevertheless prompted by a sense of bewilderment that an entire city, which possibly also contains some righteous people along with the wicked, should be overturned. According to Philo, Abraham's concern was also extended to those people in whom elements of 'the righteous and the wicked' were intermingled. On the other hand, even the question 'What wilt Thou give me?' gave Philo the opportunity to interpret it as a request for added knowledge.[82]

Even those Sages who were most emphatic in their praise of Job and his virtues, irrespective of whether they considered him a Jew or a pious Gentile, confined their praise to the first period of his life, which preceded his ordeal. When R. Joḥanan said 'Greater tribute is paid by Scripture to Job than to Abraham' (*T. B. Bava Batra* 15b), he had in mind Job's earlier years, and it is he also who stated 'There was no more righteous Gentile than Job, yet he came only with reproaches... There were no greater prophets than Moses and Isaiah, yet both of them came only with entreaties' (*Deuteronomy Rabba* ii, 4). This assessment is not far removed from the differentiation between Job and Abraham reported in the name of R. Levi, who expressed his criticism of the comparison drawn between Job and Abraham in an original manner. He declared that Satan acted from pious motives, for when he saw that the Holy One, blessed be He, was inclined to favour Job, he said: 'Heaven forbid that He should forget Abraham's love.'[83] In the generation following R. Joḥanan, R. Ḥanina bar Papa said of Job: 'Had he [Job] not reproached (God) then just as we now say "The God of Abraham, the God of Isaac, and the God of Jacob", so we should have said "and the God of Job" ' (*Pesiqta Rabbati* 190a). God's name was not linked to Job's because of the charges he hurled against Him; hence we do not include his name when we mention the God of the Patriarchs in the

Tĕfillā. Rava, who applied to many of Job's utterances the words 'Dust to Job's mouth!', because he reviled, blasphemed, and denied God[84], found no other argument in Job's favour than 'a man is not to be held responsible for what he says in his distress', and Job spoke by reason of his distress and suffering.

The different evaluations of Job's religious personality are connected with the views of the Sages relative to the ways of fearing and loving God, and not with their attitude to the Gentile world and its pious men; and it would certainly be out of the question to represent the polarity between the views of Rabban Joḥanan b. Zakkai, R. Eliezer, and R. Ḥiyya, on the one hand, and of R. Joshua b. Hyrcanus, Ben Peṭuri, and R. Joshua, on the other, as based on the antithesis between the particularistic notion that a Gentile saint like Job could not attain to the spiritual plane of Abraham, and the universalistic conception that a Gentile could likewise reach such heights.[85]

The opinion of R. Joshua b. Hyrcanus, with which R. Joshua b. Ḥananiah agreed, that Job — despite his complaints and protests — served God out of love was not acceptable to the majority of Tannaim and Amoraim. The discussion on Job's personality and utterances indicates the way in which the concepts of 'fear of God' and 'love of God' had crystallized. Fear emanating from love is no longer fear but love; but love that induces a man to be presumptuous towards his master, to complain of his ways, and to be insolent to him, is not love, and fear due to dread of punishment is to be preferred to it. When Rabban Joḥanan b. Zakkai expressed to his disciples the wish that their fear of Heaven might be like their fear of human beings[86], he sought to convey to them two teachings on the subject. He had in mind, firstly, the abolition of the fear of men and the acceptance of the yoke of the kingdom of heaven in its place. Rabban Joḥanan b. Zakkai's answer to another question of his disciples supports our interpretation. When his disciples asked him 'Why should a slave have his ear bored rather than any of his other organs?' he answered them: '(The ear) had removed from itself the yoke of the kingdom of heaven and accepted the sovereignty of the yoke of a human being; therefore Scripture said 'Let the ear come and be pierced, because it did not keep what it had heard.'[87] The second thing that R. Joḥanan b. Zakkai wished to teach them was that the practical significance of this fear of Heaven, of the sense of the presence of God, to whom everything is revealed and known, was fear of sin. It meant primarily withdrawing from transgression. But clearly the compass of the term's meaning in Temple times was very wide. The name of the 'Chamber of Secrets', which was situated in the Temple, is explained in the Mishna (*M. Sheqalim*, v, 6) as follows: 'The God-fearing used to put (their gifts) there secretly, and the poor of good families received their support from it secretly.' Thus these God-fearing people scrupulously observed the precept to give charity in secret. In the story about the families that outwitted the guards stationed by Jeroboam the son of Nebat along the roads to prevent pilgrims from going up to Jerusalem reference is made to 'whoever was worthy and sin-fearing in that generation' and they were the people 'who risked their lives for the Torah and the precepts'.[88] It may also be assumed that the tribute paid to ʿAqavya b. Mahalalel, that the Temple court, when full and locked, did not hold anyone to compare with him in wisdom or the fear of sin, did not refer to the fear of transgressions only.

It seems that the sources we have cited suffice to show that before the Destruction, about the time of Rabban Joḥanan b. Zakkai, the designation 'sin-fearing' was specifically applied to men who in the same measure as they were careful to avoid transgressions were scrupulous in the observance of the commandments with devotion and love, just as the expression 'fear of Heaven', when used by Rabban Joḥanan b. Zakkai, denoted fear out of love and piety and not from dread of punishment or hope of reward. As we have seen, already in the days of the Tannaim 'love' was differentiated from 'fear' (*Sifre Deuteronomy* § 32), a distinction being drawn between a 'Pharisee from love' and a 'Pharisee from fear'.[89] But an extreme connotation, which is quite distinctive, is given to the term 'love' in R. Akiba's teaching. Love assumes both a martyrological and mystical character. The ideal son among the King's four sons is, according to R. Akiba, David, who is punished yet says to his Father 'Punish me still more!'[90] His watchword is 'suffering is precious',[91] completely severing the nexus between 'suffering' and the doctrine of retribution in this world or in the world to come, and regarding it as a supreme good for the servant of the Lord. This constitutes, according to Ben ʿAzzai (*Sifre Deuteronomy* § 32), love 'until the draining of life', and this R. Akiba observed at the moment of his death, when he declared: 'All my life I was troubled about the verse "with all thy soul", (which means) even if He takes your soul. I said: When will it be granted me to fulfil it?'[92] At that moment he did not think of suffering as conducive to repentance, as an indication of atonement, or even as a sign of the Lord's love for His righteous ones, ideas that find expression in Psalms (xciv 12), Proverbs (iii 11–12) and Job (v 17–20). Likewise the author of *The Psalms of Solomon* approximates[93] more closely to the concepts of the Biblical verses referred to than to R. Akiba's approach.[94] The portrayal of the overpowering love of man's soul in its yearning for God's fellowship, for entry into *Pardes*, and for knowledge of the 'Work of the Chariot', R. Akiba found in the Song of Songs, which he proclaimed to be 'most holy' (*M. Yadayim* iii, 5). To him is likewise attributed the saying 'If the Torah had not been given to us, the Song of Songs would have sufficed to guide the world.'[95] When R. Akiba entered *Pardes* in peace and left it in peace, the Sages applied to him the verse from the Song of Songs 'Draw me, we will run after Thee'; and when he died sanctifying God's name as a martyr, his disciple Joshua b. Jehonathan applied to him the verse from the Song of Songs מישרים אהבוך *mĕshārîm 'ăhēvûkhā* [usually rendered: 'rightly do they love Thee'], which he interpreted to mean: 'They loved Thee far more than the righteous of old' [reading מִישִׁירִים *mîshārîm* for מֵישָׁרִים *mĕshārîm*].[96] This mystical-martyrological conception of love could only be adopted by a few, and just as in explaining the dictum 'suffering is precious' the Sages already in the generation following R. Akiba began to resort again to reasons, both old and new, linked to the principle of reward and punishment[97], so too they explained the difference between love and fear as one reflected in the measure of the reward. The Tanna R. Simeon b. Eleazar said: 'Greater is he that acts from love than he that acts from fear, for the merit of the latter remains for a thousand generations, whereas that of the former endures for two thousand generations.'[98] The early Amoraim — R. Ḥama b. R. Ḥanina, Rav Judah, and R. Joḥanan — explained away contradictions between the assurances and promises in various verses by stating that 'in the one case (the penitence) was from love, in the other from fear'.[99] Even for the ten ordeals with which Abraham was tested an explanation is offered that declares:

'And why so many? In order that when our forefather comes to receive his reward, the nations of the world may say: "More than all of us, more than any one, is Abraham worthy of receiving his reward." '[1]

Even those Tannaim and Amoraim who appraised the love of God[2] most highly, nevertheless regarded the fear of Heaven as an indispensable condition for attaining to love.[3] With reference to the verse 'And now, Israel, what doth the Lord thy God require of thee but to fear the Lord thy God' (Deuteronomy x 12) the Babylonian Talmud raises the following objection: 'Is the fear of Heaven such a small thing? Did not R. Ḥanina say in the name of R. Simeon b. Yoḥai: The Holy One, blessed be He, has naught in His treasury save a store of the fear of Heaven, as it is said: "The fear of the Lord is His store" (Isaiah xxxiii 6)?' The answer given is to the effect that in Moses' eyes the fear of God was but a small thing: 'It is like the case of a man, who is asked for a big article, and he has it, then it appears to him like a small article; (but if he is asked for) a small article, and he does not possess it, it seems to him like a big article.'[4] Apparently experience showed that there were many to whom the fear of heaven was 'a small article that they did not possess'. There were even scholars 'who occupied themselves with the Torah, but had no fear of Heaven', and in regard to them R. Jannai proclaimed 'Woe to him who has no court, but makes a gateway to his court!' (*T.B. Yoma* 72b). About two generations later, this type of scholar was compared by Rabba bar Rav Huna in Babylon 'to a treasurer, to whom the inner keys were entrusted but not the outer keys' (*T.B. Shabbat* 31b). In urging that the attribute of the fear of God should be regarded as fundamental, the Amoraim were nevertheless not led to overlook the attribute of love. Abbaye was accustomed to say: 'A man should always be subtle in the fear of Heaven, (remembering that) "A soft answer turneth away wrath"; he should be on the friendliest terms with his brethren and relatives and, indeed, with all men, even with the Gentile in the street, so that he may be beloved in Heaven and well-liked upon earth, and be acceptable to his fellow men.'[5] The dictum serves to reduce the tension between the two concepts by giving a moderate interpretation to them both. The verse 'And thou shalt love the Lord thy God' was already expounded even by the

Tannaim in the sense of 'Make Him beloved of all men', but they add 'like our father Abraham, as it is said "and the souls that they had gotten [literally 'made'] in Haran" (Genesis xii 5)... for our father Abraham used to convert them and bring them under the wings of the Divine Presence.'[6] The ways suggested by Abbaye for instilling the love of God among men do not demand proselytization; deeds that make a man acceptable to his fellow creatures are considered sufficient. Such deeds are not far removed from those characterizing 'him who is subtle in the fear of Heaven'. If Abbaye did not explicitly abolish the distinction between love and fear of God, this was done by his colleague Rava, as is clearly to be seen from the following story: 'Two disciples were once with Rava. One said to him: "In my dream they read to me 'O how great is Thy goodness which Thou hast laid up for them that fear Thee' (Psalms xxxi 20)." The other said to him: "In my dream they read to me 'But let all those that put their trust in Thee rejoice, let them even shout for joy... let them also that love Thy name exult in Thee' (*ibid.* v 12)." Said he [Rava] to them: "Ye are both wholly righteous Rabbis, one being actuated by love and one by fear." '[7] Clearly Rava's words are opposed to the teaching of R. Simeon b. Eleazar, that one who acts from love is greater than one who acts from fear, and to the concept that the reward of him who acts from love is immeasurably greater.[8] The Amora who related to Rava that they read out to him the verse wherein he was included among the lovers of God undoubtedly regarded this love as taking the form not only of devotion to the observance of the commandments, but also, without doubt, of abstention from transgression.[9] So, too, we may be sure that his colleague, who was counted among the God-fearing, observed the precepts in accord with the ruling of a disciple of Rava, namely 'He that fears Heaven will seek to satisfy both views.'[10]

CHAPTER XV

MAN'S ACCOUNTING AND THE WORLD'S ACCOUNTING

I. Sin and Death

The problem of requital — reward and punishment — and the question of the existence of suffering and evil in the world arose incidentally in the course of our discussion of some of the subjects dealt with in the previous chapters.[1] Now we shall proceed to examine these questions *per se*, but in this investigation, too, we shall need to treat once again of topics whose connection with the problems under review is not always apparent, but emerges in the course of the exposition and clarification.

In the Bible itself the Sages found a variegated tapestry of the 'doctrine of requital', embroidered and interwined with threads from the skein of myth, closely linked to the feeling of belonging to the family-tribe, refined and purified in the crucible of the suffering and afflictions of prophets and poets. The daring of their protest and the heroism of their surrender in accepting and justifying the Divine judgement found expression in the words of Jeremiah and Ezekiel, in the Psalms and in the Book of Job.[2]

The Tannaim and Amoraim did not overlook the great disparities and variegation of this tapestry. They discovered contradictions between the Scriptural passages. Some were content just to note them, but others attempted to reconcile them by introducing views and concepts of which hardly a hint can be found in the verses themselves. They aimed not only at enlarging and deepening the ideas and motifs of Holy Writ, but also at raising new questions and finding new solutions to old problems. This was the outcome of their renewed examination of past events, or of their personal wrestling with the problems of their existence, or the result of the absorption of views that were current in the world in whose environment they lived and worked.

The story of Adam and his transgression against the prohibition of eating of the fruit of the 'tree of the knowledge of good and evil' establishes unequivocably the causal nexus between sin and punishment. The first sin brought into the world death,[3] birth pangs, toil, and fatigue. The story of Adam's sin does not purport in the Bible to explain men's sins and weaknesses. Furthermore, the entire episode is nowhere alluded to subsequently.[4] Ben Sira does, indeed, declare (xxv 28 [24]) 'From a woman did sin originate, and because of her we all must die.' However. these words occur in a chapter that treats of the woman in general, the first verse of the passage (*v*. 16 [13]) being 'Any wound, but not a heart-wound! Any wickedness, only not the wickedness of a woman!', and includes warnings against a wicked woman, though it ends on an optimistic note: 'A good wife (is) a good gift; she shall be given to him that feareth God, for his portion' (xxvi 3).

Ben Sira states only that iniquity began on account of woman and because of her, death came into being, but the concept of 'original sin' and predestination never entered his mind in the least. On the contrary, elsewhere (xv 14–15) he expressly states: 'God created man from the beginning, and placed him in the hand of his *yeṣer*. If thou (so) desirest, thou canst keep the commandment, and (it is) wisdom to do His good pleasure. And if thou trust in Him, of a truth thou shalt live.' Death is a natural law: 'All flesh withereth like a garment; and the eternal decree is: "Thou shalt surely die!" ' (xiv 17).

The episode of Adam and Eve only marks the time when death came into being. A similar interpretation is to be given to the following sayings ascribed to R. Joshua regarding the precepts specifically devolving upon women: 'Because they brought death into the world, they are the first to go to a dead person... because she [the woman] quenched the soul of the first man, therefore she was given the precept of (kindling) the Sabbath light.'[5] Only death came with Adam's sin, but not the necessity to sin. In regard to the possibility of transgressing and the freedom of choice between the way of life and the way of death, Ben Sira made no distinction between Adam and his offspring.

As we have seen (above, p. 264), this was the opinion of R. Akiba. It is true that there were Sages who did not subscribe to his view regarding the complete separation between a man's deeds and the duration of his life in this world (above p. 265), but then did they also dispute the very concept that death was an inescapable decree? It was not possible to ignore the difficulty of attributing the actual existence of death in the world — and needless to say of other afflictions — to Adam's sin. If free will was given to men, and it is in their power to be wholly righteous, why should they be punished 'on account of the serpent'? Why does death, or the angel of death, continue to have dominion? Even the postulate that there is no righteous man who does not sin raises a grave problem. If predestination is not involved, what prevents a man from preserving his integrity? Or is man evil from birth, and this evil cannot be wholly cured? If so, who and what brought about this evil? Within the framework of monotheistic faith there is no place for a solution that puts the blame for corruption and sin on any power beyond the control of God; this fact underlies the story of Adam's transgression. The serpent, who was the cause of death, is one of God's creatures and was punished for its deed. This punishment implies a change in its original nature and qualities.[6] We have already observed (above, p. 229) that Adam was regarded, prior to his sin, as one endowed with special qualities, and there were also Sages who went to extravagant lengths in portraying his attributes. Adam's punishment consisted not only in the decree of death, but in losing his former virtues, and one might almost say that just as he brought 'death to his descendants', so he caused deterioration in their very nature and made them incline ineluctably towards sin.[7]

Was this concept known in Rabbinical circles, and, if so, what was their attitude towards it? To answer this question we shall first have recourse to an extraneous source, where this idea is formulated with great extremism, and without any qualifications. The reference is to Paul's statement (Romans v 12–21): 'Therefore as sin came into the world through one man and death through sin, and so death spread to all men because all men sinned — sin indeed was in the world before the law was given, but sin is not counted where there is no law. Yet death reigned from Adam to Moses, even over those whose sins were not like the transgression of Adam... Then as one man's trespass led to condemnation for all men, so one man's act of righteousness leads to acquittal and life for all men. For as by one man's disobedience many were made sinners, so by one man's obedience many will be made righteous.'

Paul's statements and their precise meaning gave rise to dogmatic theological discussions within Christianity,[8] and have been variously interpreted by its modern expositors.[9] But no one disputes that Paul held that the first sin affected all mankind, and that Adam bequeathed to his descendants, by his trespass, a body infected by lust and desires, and consequently they were predestined to sin. The question whether he thought this tendency already existed in the flesh to begin with and Adam's downfall was a transformation of the potential into the actual, or that it came into being with his sin, is of no importance here. The main consideration, in Paul's view, is that sin is inherent in man, and hence death, too, which comes to every human being, is a punishment for his own sin, and at the same time also the consequence of the first sin. The problem that interests us is whether this doctrine originated with Paul, who wished to serve thereby his Christological purpose, or whether he derived its basic idea from his Jewish environment and only added that, through the giving of the Torah, sin, which was already in existence, but did not yet count, became sin that does count, and from which a man can only free himself by the enthronement of grace through belief in Jesus.

The doctrine built upon the first sin and its consequences was known to the author of the *Syriac Apocalypse of Baruch* (liv 15–19), but he firmly rejected it. He states 'For though Adam first sinned and brought untimely death upon all, yet of those who were born from him each one of them has prepared for his own soul torment to come, and again each one of them has chosen for himself glories to come... Adam is therefore not the cause, save only of his own soul, but each of us has been the Adam of his own soul....' The polemical tone of his words is obvious, and the purpose is to emphasize man's personal responsibility for his deeds.

The author of *IV Ezra* comes nearer to Paul's view of the consequences of Adam's sin than to that of the author of the *Syriac Apocalypse of Baruch*; his statement is particularly significant, because he also deals with the problem of sin in relation to the giving of the Torah. In reviewing the history of mankind and that of the people of Israel, he declares: 'And to him Thou commandest only one observance of thine, but he transgressed it. Forthwith Thou appointedst death for him and for his generations, and from him were born nations and tribes... And every nation walked after their own will... And it came to pass that when Thou leddest forth his seed out of Egypt, and didst bring them to the Mount Sinai... to give Law to Jacob's seed and Commandment to the generation of Israel. And yet Thou didst not take away from them the evil heart, that Thy Law might bring forth fruit in them. For the first Adam, clothing himself with the evil heart, transgressed and was overcome; and likewise also all who were born of him. Thus the infirmity became inveterate; the Law indeed was in the heart of the people, but (in conjunction) with the evil germ; so what was good departed, and the evil remained' (iii [i] 7–23). The difference between the view of this anonymous author and that of Paul is clear.

Although the giving of the Law did not of itself uproot the evil in man, yet he was given a means of choosing the good. The author did not refrain from saying to the angel who spoke to him: 'Better had it been that the earth had not produced Adam, or else, having once produced him, (for them) to have restrained him from sinning. For how does it profit us all that in the present we must live in grief and after death look for punishment? O thou Adam, what hast thou done! For though it was thou that sinned, the fall was not thine alone, but ours also who are thy descendants!...' And the angel answered him: 'This is the condition of the contest which (every) man who is born upon earth must wage; that, if he be overcome, he shall suffer as thou hast said: but if he be victorious, he shall receive what I have said. For this is the way of which Moses, while he was alive, spoke unto the people, saying: Choose thee life, that thou mayst live!' (*ibid.* vii [v] 116–129). In the light of these words it can be seen that the primary difference between Paul and his predecessors and his circle does not lie in the evaluation of Adam's sin and its consequences, but in Paul's complete negation of the Torah. He speaks of the inability of the Torah (ἀδύνατον τοῦ νομοῦ) to give man life (Romans viii 3) and to bring about a change in his nature and character. Paul's views on sin served him as a basis on which to erect the structure of his concept of redemption.

In the dicta of R. Joshua and R. Akiba (above, p. 422) we only found that Adam's sin was blamed for the death of all the generations, but not for the sins of his offspring. Accordingly R. Akiba's disciples discussed the influence exerted by the acceptance of the Torah not on man's inclination to sin, but on the decree of death.

The word of the Lord after the giving of the Torah, 'Oh that they had such a heart as this always, to fear Me' etc. (Deuteronomy v 26), is expounded by an anonymous Tanna as follows: 'Had it been possible to remove the angel of death, I should have removed him, but the decree has already been promulgated.' R. Jose disagreed with him and said: 'On this condition the Israelites took their stand at Mount Sinai — on condition that the angel of death should not have dominion over them, as it is said "I said: Ye are godlike beings, and all of you sons of the Most High" (Psalms lxxxii 6); (but) ye corrupted your deeds, (therefore) it is written "Nevertheless ye shall die like men, and fall like one of the princes".'[10] An exposition similar to that of R. Jose was given by his colleague R. Judah, or Nehemiah, on the verse 'And the writing was the writing of God, graven [חָרוּת *ḥārût*] upon the tables' (Exodus xxxii 16): this means 'freedom חֵרוּת [*ḥērût*] from the angel of death'.[11]

In one of the sources in which this dictum is cited the homilist proceeds to interpret it by drawing a parallel between the action of Israel and that of Adam, and he concludes with the teaching of R. Jose mentioned above: 'When Israel declared "All that the Lord hath spoken will we do, and obey", the Holy One, blessed be He, said: "I gave Adam one commandment to fulfil and I compared him to the Ministering Angels, as it is said 'Behold, the man is become as one of us' (Genesis iii 22); these [the Israelites] who perform and observe 613 commandments — apart from the general rules, the detailed regulation, and the minutiae — are *a fortiori* entitled to everlasting life"... but when they said "This is thy god, O Israel", death came upon them. Said the Holy One, blessed be He, "Ye have walked in the footsteps of Adam... I said 'Ye are godlike beings', but ye followed the ways of Adam, (therefore it is written) 'Nevertheless ye shall die like men'."'[12] The view of R. Jose and his colleague

R. Nehemiah, or R. Judah, is that it was the sin of the calf that was the cause of death. The giving of the Law provided an opportunity to choose life once again and to banish death from the world. But after the Children of Israel had sinned, and the decree of death was renewed, the people of Israel re-enacted the story of Adam, who first sinned and only thereafter was death imposed upon him.

Just as there was no Tanna among R. Akiba's disciples that attributed the existence of sin to Adam's transgression, so none among them, or among their disciples, attributed the actual existence of death to human sins. However, a Baraita is cited in the Babylonian Talmud to corroborate the opinion of an Amora that 'There is no death without sin.' It reads as follows: 'R. Simeon b. Eleazar said: Even Moses and Aaron died on account of their sin, as it is said "Because ye believed not in Me" (Numbers xx 12) — (otherwise) your time to depart from this world had not yet come.'[13] The conclusion of the Baraita shows that it was not the Tanna's intention to say that if Moses and Aaron had not sinned, they would have lived for ever. He only stated that they would not have passed away before their time and it would have been granted them, as the rest of the verse implies (*ibid.*), to bring 'this assembly into the land which I have given them'. The following explanation is given in a parallel Baraita: 'R. Simeon b. Eleazar said: Moses and Aaron, too, died prematurely [literally, 'by being cut off'], as it is said "because ye sanctified Me not" (Deuteronomy xxxii 51); hence, if you had sanctified Me, your time would not yet have come to depart (this world).'[14] Another Baraita dissociates even Moses' death from his sin: 'The Ministering Angels said to the Holy One, blessed be He: "Sovereign of the universe, why did Adam die?" He replied: "Because he did not fulfil My commandment." Said they to Him: "But Moses did fulfil Thy commandments!" He answered them: "It is My decree, the same for all men, as Scripture states 'This is the law: when a man dieth' " (Numbers xix 14).'[15] The punishment for his sin was limited to the fact that he was not privileged to enter the land either in his lifetime or after his death.[16] The conception of death as a decree — whether it came into the world with Adam's sin and was never annulled, or whether it was abolished and renewed when the calf was made — puts an end to the connection between the sin of Adam and the sins of his descendants. By the same token there is no necessity to search for sins in the life of the righteous; hence sayings like that attributed to R. Eliezer Ha-Gadol 'If the Holy One, blessed be He, were to bring Abraham, Isaac, and Jacob to judgement, they could not stand before the indictment'[17] and similar dicta are not to be linked with the view that 'There is no death without sin'.[18] Exceptional is the Baraita that was considered to uphold the idea of original sin:[19] 'Four died because of the serpent, namely Benjamin the son of Jacob, Amram the father of Moses, Jesse the father of David, and Chileab the son of David.'[20] The meaning of this Baraita is unambiguous: All men die on account of their sins; and there is no death without sin.[21] There were only four exceptions to the rule, and these were not Jacob, the father of the nation, who was a man of perfect integrity, nor our teacher Moses, who delivered Israel and gave them the Torah, nor King David, the elect of the Lord, but the fathers or sons of these great men,[22] men of whose sins, it is true, nothing is known, but neither are we informed of their meritorious deeds. Only they died 'because of the serpent'. The polemical — almost paradoxical — character of this dictum, which is directed against the idea that finds expression in the Paulinian theology, is obvious, and only when thus understood does the saying become meaningful. The restriction of the effect of the first sin to the fate of four not very important persons annuls the significance of the episode, and hence takes away the basis of Paul's doctrine of redemption. A similar polemical attitude was adopted by R. Joḥanan in a passage that is cited in three places in the Babylonian Talmud, but in order to understand it, it is important to quote it as it appears in its original context. There it is related that R. Ḥiyya bar Abba and Rav Assi were sitting before R. Joḥanan, and while their teacher was dosing, R. Ḥiyya bar Abba asked his colleague physiological and physiognomical questions about animals and human beings. To the last question 'Why are the Gentiles contaminated with lust?' he replied: 'Because they eat the flesh of abominable and creeping things.' Thereupon R. Joḥanan awoke and rebuked his disciples, calling them 'infants', and in place of the naive answers, he gave them other explanations, which were deeper and more symbolical. In reply to the last question he said: 'Why are the Gentiles contaminated with lust? Because they did not stand at Mount Sinai.

For when the serpent came upon Eve he instilled contaminating lust into her; when, however, Israel stood at Mount Sinai, their lust ceased. But since the Gentiles did not stand at Mount Sinai, their contamination did not disappear.'[23] R. Joḥanan used the erotic motif of the serpent myth (see above, p. 169), and attributed to the serpent the lust of human beings, but it was taken away — contrary to Paul's teaching — precisely from those who stood at Mount Sinai and continued to infest the Gentiles. The concept of contaminating lust, dirt, and filth, became as it were — like the notion of defilement — synonymous with sin,[24] and indeed R. Joḥanan himself employs the word זיהום *zihûm* ['contamination'] in the sense of 'unfitness' and 'disqualification', in regard to the religious admissibility of a woman to be married to a priest.[25] The Amora R. Abba bar Kahana declared the contamination from the children of Jacob to have been removed even before the revelation at Sinai: 'Up to three generations — he asserts — the contaminating strain did not disappear from our ancestors: Abraham begot Ishmael, Isaac begot Esau, but Jacob begot the twelve tribes who were untainted.'[26]

The Baraita concerning the four who died on account of the serpent and the statements of R. Joḥanan and R. Abba bar Kahana regarding the contamination that was injected, likewise because of the serpent, into the human species, seem at first blush to accept the doctrine of original sin, but in actual fact they void it of all meaning in all that pertains to the question of sin and its punishment relative to the people of Israel. This very fact serves to corroborate the statement regarding the polemical character of these dicta. A polemical undercurrent, it seems to me, is also discernible in the discussion of R. Joḥanan's contemporaries, R. Ḥama b. R. Ḥanina and R. Jonathan, on the cause of the penalty of death. R. Ḥama b. R. Ḥanina said: 'Adam did not deserve to know the taste of death. Wherefore, then, was death imposed upon him? Because the Holy One, blessed be He, foresaw that Nebuchadnezzar and Hiram would declare themselves gods, therefore was death imposed upon him... Said R. Jonathan: If so, He should have decreed death on the wicked, but not on the righteous! (The reason, however, was) to prevent the wicked from presenting a hypocritical appearance of repentance — that they should not say: Do not the righteous live only because they lay up precepts and good deeds? Let us, too, lay up precepts and good deeds! Their action will thus be insincere.'[27] It was not Adam's sin that brought death to the generations that succeeded him, but, on the contrary, because of those generations that would proclaim themselves gods was the penalty of death inflicted on Adam. If there remained the slightest doubt that not just Nebuchadnezzar and Hiram alone were meant, R. Jonathan proceeds to explain not the death of the wicked generally, but that of the wicked who know how to store up precepts and good deeds insincerely. In this homily the position is completely reversed. Not through 'the obedience of one' shall the many be redeemed from sin and death, caused by the first man; on the contrary, death was decreed upon Adam for fear of the faith preached by Paul.

This polemical homily, like all the dicta and various expositions cited so far, is based on the premise that death — and certainly untimely death — is a punishment,[28] and consequently a negative phenomenon. The view of R. Me'ir is an exception. The very style of its transmission by one of the great Haggadists among the Palestinian Amoraim testifies to its unusual character. 'R. Samuel bar Naḥman said: I was riding on my grandfather's shoulder and going up from my town to Kefar Ḥanna by way of Bet Shean, when I heard R. Simeon b. R. Eleazar, as he was sitting and expounding in the name of R. Me'ir, say: ' "And, behold, it was very [מאד *mĕ'ōd*] good" — and, behold, death [מות *môt*] is good.'[29] Death is not an evil decree nor a punishment, but forms part of the order of the universe from the beginning. We do not know how R. Me'ir interpreted the story in Genesis iii, but it is not improbable that he regarded this episode as an account of the origin of death rather than an explanation of its cause. R. Me'ir's teaching influenced several Amoraim, and as we have seen (above, p. 279), they applied it to the question of Providence, developing for themselves a doctrine that removed the explanation of the existence of death from the act of the serpent and the sin of Adam. This separation in itself liberated them from the need to engage in a polemic with the adherents of the doctrine of original sin. But even an Amora like R. Joḥanan, who answered this contention in his own way (above, p. 427), independently explained the decree of death as follows: 'R. Joḥanan said: Why was death imposed upon the wicked? The reason is that as long as the wicked live, they vex the Holy One, blessed be He, as it is written "Ye have wearied the Lord with your words" (Malachi ii 17); but when they die they no longer vex the Holy One, blessed be He, as Scripture states "There the wicked cease from troubling" (Job iii 17) — there the wicked cease vexing the Holy One, blessed be He. Why was death inflicted upon the righteous? The reason is that as long as the righteous live, they wage war with their inclination; but when they die, they are at rest, as it is written "And there the weary are at rest" (*ibid.*) — (as if to say:) we have wearied ourselves enough!'[30]

Death is thus not the consequence of sin, but is linked to the doctrine of reward and punishment. R. Joḥanan, who posited free will for the individual, regarded the death of the righteous as a form of reward, since it brought to an end their exhausting struggle against their evil inclination. The death of the wicked causes them, in his view, to cease vexing God, but actually it implies punishment, since they derive satisfaction from their provocative actions. Resh Laqish, R. Joḥanan's colleague, related the subject of death to reward and punishment, only he holds that death comes to give twofold reward to the righteous and to inflict on the wicked twofold punishment: 'To give reward to the righteous, who did not deserve to know the taste of death, yet accepted it, hence (they are) promised "Therefore in their land they shall possess double" (Isaiah lxi 7); and to impose retribution on the wicked, for the righteous did not deserve to know the taste of death, yet because of them they accepted death, therefore (it is written) "and destroy them with double destruction" (Jeremiah xvii 18).'[31]

Death *per se* is not a punishment for sin. Although there was no need for the righteous to experience death, and they deserved to continue living, yet the implementation of the principle of reward and punishment — according to R. Akiba's[32] conception of the relationship between predestination and free will — necessitated imposing death on the righteous, too. The Amoraim R. Joḥanan and Resh Laqish, and likewise R. Samuel bar Naḥmani, differentiated between the death of the righteous and the death of others, following the view of R. Ḥiyya that the righteous are called living even in their death.[33]

All the sources that we cited, whether of the Tannaim or of the Amoraim, dealt with the explanation of the existence of death as a universal phenomenon either in confrontation with the story in Genesis, which they interpret and adapt, or by ignoring it. Only the Baraita concerning the 'Four who died because of the serpent', whose polemical and tendentious character we have discussed above (p. 427), postulated that each man's death is the result of his own sin. Allowing foı no exception, and motivated by a totally different purpose and ideological nexus, the Amora Rav Ammi, the disciple of R. Joḥanan and Resh Laqish, formulated the following principle: 'There is no death without sin, nor suffering without iniquity. There is no death without sin, for it is written "The soul that sinneth it shall die; the son shall not suffer for the iniquity of the father nor shall the father suffer for the iniquity of the son; the righteousness of the righteous shall be upon himself, and the wickedness of the wicked shall be upon himself" etc. (Ezekiel xviii 20). There is no suffering without iniquity, for it is stated "Then I will visit their transgression with the rod, and their iniquity with strokes" (Psalms lxxxix 33).'[34] The very linking of death and suffering to verses that are cited as proofs shows that Rav Ammi did not intend to explain the general phenomenon of death, its source and origin, but rather its place and function in the life of each individual person. It is connected with the question of the ways of expiating iniquities and the teaching of the Tannaim on this subject. An anonymous Mishna states: 'Death and the Day of Atonement effect atonement, if combined with repentance' (*M. Yoma* viii, 8). From R. Ishmael, who taught that 'There are four categories of persons with reference to atonement'[35] we learn: 'If a man committed transgressions involving premature death (*kārēt*) or execution by the court, and he repented, then repentance and the Day of Atonement suspend (the guilt), while suffering endured during the rest of the year purge it, for it is said "Then will I punish their transgression with the rod" (Psalms lxxxiv 33 [32]). If anyone desecrated the name of Heaven and repented, repentance has not the power to suspend (the iniquity), nor the Day of Atonement to atone (for it); but repentance and the Day of Atonement atone for a third (of the transgression), and sufferings atone for a third, while death, together with suffering, purges, and in relation to this it is stated "Surely this iniquity will not be forgiven you" (Isaiah xxii 14), which teaches that the day of death purges.' The Tanna R. Judah said that the day of death is like repentance, and the latter atones, like death, for (the non-fulfilment of) positive precepts.[36] R. Judah the Patriarch said: 'I might have thought that the day of death does not effect atonement. Since, however, Scripture declares "when I open your graves" (Ezekiel xxxvii 13), behold you learn that the day of death does effect atonement.'[37] The various categories of transgression for which also death atones, and the broad interpretation given to the concept of 'the desecration of the Divine Name' on the basis of a man's standing, function, and piety,[38] were able to lead Rav Ammi to the conclusion that 'There is no death without sin'. The following Midrash supports the interpretation that we have given to his statement:[39] 'R. Ḥiyya taught: Hypocrites are exposed on account of the desecration of the Divine Name, as it is said "Again, when a righteous man doth turn from righteousness and commit iniquity" (Ezekiel xviii 24). And why does the Holy One, blessed be He, set an evil path before him? In order to expose his deeds to the world, for (otherwise) if[40] anything should befall him because of his transgressions, people would complain against God's justice. Therefore the Holy One, blessed be He, exposes his deeds.' In expounding the Baraita, the Midrash based itself on the verse in Ezekiel, from which Rav Ammi learned that there is no death without sin, just as it sought support in the verse in Psalms, from which R. Ishmael deduced that suffering purges, in order to prove that 'There is no suffering without iniquity'. The connection between Rav Ammi's dictum and the view that attributed the power of atonement to death and to suffering is clear, but when did this view gain currency?

The doctrine of R. Ishmael, R. Judah, and Rabbi that death — even death without repentance — has the power to atone originated only after the Destruction, for with regard to the Temple period it is stated: 'And for all other prohibitions ordained in the Torah, be they light or grave... premature death and execution by the court, the scapegoat makes atonement' (*M. Shevuʿot* i, 6). In truth on the subject of 'the four categories of persons with reference to atonement', including the teaching 'that death purges', R. Joḥanan said: 'This is the view of R. Eleazar b. Azariah, R. Ishmael, and R. Akiba, but the Sages maintain that the scapegoat effects atonement.'[41]

We do not know who these Sages were, but since the Baraita on the categories of atonement was taught after the Destruction, for it contains no reference to the scapegoat, they must have held that even after the Destruction death does not replace the scapegoat as an atonement.

At the time when the Temple still stood, it was certainly unnecessary and inappropriate to regard death as an atonement. The scapegoat of the Day of Atonement apart, a man could bring sacrifices for his unwitting transgressions, and 'R. Eliezer said: A man may offer of his own free will a suspensive guilt-offering on any day and at any time that he pleases, and this is called "the guilt-offering of the pious". It was said of Bava b. Buṭi that he offered of his own free will a suspensive guilt-offering every day except on the day after the Day of Atonement. He said: "By the Temple! if only they permitted me I should bring one (even then), but they say to me: Wait until you can be in doubt"' (*M. Keritot* vi, 3). Of Hillel it is told that 'Never in all his life did anyone commit trespass in connection with his burnt-offering. For he brought it unconsecrated to the Temple Court, consecrated it, laid his hand upon it, and slaughtered it.'[42] His disciple Rabban Joḥanan b. Zakkai said: 'Happy is the generation whose leader brings a sin-offering for his unwitting transgression.'[43] The offering of sacrifices was conjoined to the duty of confession;[44] and it was implied that the sacrificer was ready to repent, for the confession was the sign of penitence. With regard to the early Ḥasidim ['pious men'] R. Judah said: 'Seeing that the Holy One, blessed be He, does not allow an offence to be perpetrated by them, what did they do? They arose and made a free-will vow of naziriteship to the Omnipresent, so that they should be liable to bring a sin-offering to the Omnipresent.'[45] R. Nathan testified that R. Ishmael had written in his account book: 'Ishmael b. Elisha tilted the lamp on the Sabbath. When the Temple will be rebuilt, he will be liable to bring a sin-offering.'[46] The sacrifices only expiated iniquities between man and God, for which it was not in the power of an earthly court to impose punishment. Transgressions that were liable to punishment by a court were not atoned for by sacrifices, and only the penalty brought with it atonement for the sin. Those who were sentenced to death were told to make confession, 'For such is the way of those condemned to death to make confession, because every one that makes confession has a share in the world to come... and if he does not know to make confession, he is told: "Say, May my death be an atonement for all my iniquities" ' (*M. Sanhedrin* vi, 2). Similarly, it is stated regarding the penalty of lashes: 'Lashes are precious, for they atone for sins, as it is said: "according to [כדי *kĕdê*] the measure of his wickedness" — the lashes suffice [כדאי *kĕda'y*] to atone for his wickedness.'[47] The Sages even said 'For all who are liable to extinction, if they have received lashes, are exempted from their penalty of extinction.'[48]

When the court's right to impose the death-penalty was abrogated and the Temple was destroyed, involving the abolition of the sacrifices, a sense of despair and the feeling that Israel had been deprived of the possibility of atonement prevailed. 'It once happened that Rabban Joḥanan b. Zakkai was leaving Jerusalem and R. Joshua was walking behind him, when the latter saw the Temple in ruins. Said R. Joshua: "Woe to us that this is in ruins — the place where the sins of Israel were expiated!" Rabban Joḥanan b. Zakkai replied: "My son, be not grieved, we have a means of atonement that is commensurate with it. Which is this? It is the performance of acts of lovingkindness, as it is said 'For I desire loving kindness and not sacrifice' " (Hosea vi 6).'[49]

In the spirit of this teaching of Rabban Joḥanan b. Zakkai, the Tanna R. Eliezer b. Jacob said: 'Whoever entertains a scholar in his house and lets him enjoy his possessions it is accounted to him by Scripture as if he had offered up the daily burnt-offerings' (*T.B. Berakhot* 10b). The atonement of sins depends on the sacrifice of the daily burnt-offerings, and the Scripture 'he-lambs [כבשים *kĕvāśîm*] of the first year' (Numbers xxviii 3) was expounded by the School of Shammai thus: '*Kĕvāśîm* (are so called) because they suppress [כובשים *kôvĕshîm*] the sins of Israel.' The School of Hillel said: '*Kĕvāśîm* (are so called) because they cleanse [כובסין *kôvĕsîn*] the sins of Israel.'[50] The fasts that multiplied after the Destruction also assumed the character of a surrogate and replacement for the atonement effected by the sacrifices. This fact found concrete expression in the prayer attributed to Rav Sheshet: 'Sovereign of the universe, it is known to Thee that when the Temple was in existence, if a man sinned he would bring a sacrifice, of which only the fat and the blood were offered up, and he would be granted atonement. Now I have observed a fast and my own fat and blood have been diminished.

May it be Thy will that my diminished fat and blood be accounted as though I had offered them up before Thee on the altar, and do Thou show me favour.'[51]

In the light of the preceding dicta it is not surprising that after the abrogation of the death-penalty at the hands of the court, the power of atonement and purging was attributed also to death from natural causes. Just as execution by court decree is preceded by confession, so, R. Nathan also said, 'All who are dying require confession.'[52] But Rabbi and R. Judah were of the opinion that death, even without repentance, atones for sins that the burnt-offering expiated and for people who are endowed with knowledge of the Torah and good deeds.[53]

The Tannaim who ascribed to death and suffering the power to purge and expiate did not necessarily say that there was no death without sin. For we have seen that there were 'the early Ḥasidim', who offered up sin-offerings and brought each day a suspensive guilt-offering. In his dictum 'There is no death without sin, and no suffering without iniquity' R. Ammi took up a very extreme position, and indeed in our treatment of the subject of Divine providence and the reasons of the precepts[54] we noted that many Sages were not in agreement with his apodictic statement. Moreover, the Talmudic discussion in which his saying is cited concludes with the words: 'This proves that there is death without sin and suffering without iniquity, and Rav Ammi stands refuted.'[55] Nevertheless his saying is not an isolated view. Another, anonymous, Talmudic passage propounds the question whether '(the purpose of) burial is to save (the dead) from disgrace (so that he should not be made contemptible in the sight of those who see him dead and putrefying and disintegrating — Rashi) or to effect atonement (so that he should win atonement by the interment, for he is lowered and humbled in the recesses of the earth)', and the answer is — for atonement. To the query 'Do the righteous need atonement?' the Sages reply 'Yea! for it is written "There is not a righteous man upon earth, that doeth good, and sinneth not" (Ecclesiastes vii 20).'[56] This pessimistic view of Ecclesiastes, which was also shared by Job's friends, was approved by Rav Ammi, by the author of the interpretation of the Baraita of R. Ḥiyya (above, p. 432), and by the Talmudic passage that we have just cited. Death and suffering prove that the man who was deemed to be righteous was not really so. The aim of this approach is to demonstrate clearly and unequivocally that the world is ruled according to righteousness and justice. Obviously this view excludes any idea of inherited sin, such as might have been inferred from the story of Adam.

II. Reward and Punishment

Although it was seen that the Sages did not refrain from discussing the subject of sin and death and the teachings flowing therefrom, such opinions did not determine their views and their main dicta on the theme of sin and its punishment. The fundamental reward for the observance of the commandments and the punishment for transgressions in a man's lifetime are stated again and again in the Torah and reiterated in the Prophets and Hagiographa. If a Jew but heard the Decalogue, there would be imprinted on his memory the verses 'visiting the iniquity of the fathers upon the children of the third and fourth generation of those who hate Me, but showing steadfast love to thousands of those who love Me and keep My commandments'. If he recited the *Shĕma*ʿ, he learned to link the blessing of the land and its produce, his own length of days and that of his children, with the keeping of the Lord's precepts, and the curse of dearth and destruction with transgressing His words. Long historical experience, with all its catastrophes and calamities, taught the Jew to evaluate the passages of rebuke in Leviticus and Deuteronomy, not as a mere threat, but as warnings that were translated into reality, and to realize that not merely the threnodies of Lamentations bore testimony thereto.

The objections and questions bound up with the problems of the relationship between the actions of the individual and collective retribution, or between the sins of the fathers and the punishment of the children, did not disappear when the belief in the judgement of the souls after death[57] and the doctrine of requital connected therewith took root, for this belief did not eradicate or nullify the view that a man is brought to judgement for the things he does in this world even in his lifetime. Thus it was taught: 'If a man says give this *sela*ʿ to charity in order that my children may live, or in order that I may merit thereby life in the world to come, he is a wholly righteous man.'[58] This Baraita reflects a widespread belief among the people, which the Sages continued to strengthen and even to utilize in urging the observance of the commandments and in denouncing transgressors (see above, p. 349). When he stated 'And faithful is the Master of your work, who will pay you the wages of your toil; and know that the giving of the reward to the righteous is in the time to come', R. Ṭarfon made the reward in this world precede that in the world to come,[59] only the account is not concluded upon death. This thought R. Akiba expressed figuratively: 'The ledger lies open, and the hand writes, and whosoever wishes to borrow may come and borrow, but the collectors regularly make their daily rounds, and exact payment from a man whether with or without his knowledge, and they have that whereon they can rely in their demand, and the judgement is a judgement of truth, and everything is prepared for the feast.'

The collectors are the tribulations and sufferings. Sometimes a man knows why they come upon him, that is to say, he realizes that they are a punishment for his actions; but at times they befall him without his being able to justify them, and then he remembers that everything is prepared for reward in the world to come.[60] The statements were made not only in a generalized form, but even the calamities that occur to people as punishments for given transgressions were expressly specified. For instance it is taught in the Mishna: 'For three transgressions women die in childbirth: for negligence in observing the laws of menstruation, the dough-offering, and the kindling of the (Sabbath) lamp.'[61] The Tanna R. Nathan added: 'Also on account of (their) vows women die in childbirth.'[62] To this sin R. Eleazar the son of R. Simeon b. Yoḥai — followed also by R. Judah the Patriarch[63] — ascribed another tribulation, no less common than the death of women in childbirth, namely the death of young children. R. Nehemiah said: 'For the sin of causeless hatred there is great contention in a man's house and his wife miscarries, and a man's sons and daughters die when they are young.' In an anonymous Baraita causeless hatred is considered to produce disease of the bowels. 'It is taught there are four signs: the sign of transgression is dropsy; the sign of causeless hatred is jaundice; the sign of conceit is poverty; the sign of slander is cramp [or, diphtheria].'[64] Within the framework of the collective retribution mentioned in the reproofs of the Torah and the Prophets are also specified the sins that bring upon the people punishments like war, exile, plagues, and famine. The Tannaim widened the scope, classified and adapted the punishments to the sins, and taught in the Mishna 'Seven kinds of penalties come to the world for seven chief transgressions.'[65] The prevailing rule, both in personal and collective retribution in the existing world, is that of 'measure for measure'. The Mishna teaches: 'With what measure a man metes it shall be meted out to him again: she prinked herself for transgression — the Omnipresent disgraced her; she laid herself bare for transgression — the Omnipresent likewise laid her bare...; Samson went after (the desire of) his eyes — therefore the Philistines put out his eyes...; Absalom gloried [ניתנווה *nitnawwā*] in his hair — consequently he was hanged by his hair... So, too, in the case of good deeds: Miriam waited for Moses one hour... therefore Israel tarried for her seven days in the wilderness...; Joseph was privileged to bury his father, and none of his brothers was greater than he... Whom have we greater than Moses? Thus only the Omnipresent occupied Himself with him...'[66] This principle the Sages even introduced into their interpretation of sections of the Torah where actually both the sin and the punishment are expressly stated, such as the story of the generation of the Flood and that of the people of Sodom, and thus they expounded in a Baraita:[67] 'The men of the Flood waxed haughty only on account of the good (they enjoyed), as it is said "Their houses are safe from fear, neither is the rod of God upon them. Their bull gendereth, and faileth not... They send forth their little ones like a flock... They take the timbrel and the harp... They spend their days in prosperity, and their years in pleasures." It is this that brought it about that "They said to God: 'Depart from us... What is the Almighty that we should serve Him? And what profit should we have, if we pray unto Him?' " (Job xxi 9–15). They said "Do we need Him for aught but rain? Lo, we have rivers from which we supply our needs, and we do not require Him", as it is said "But there went up a mist from the earth, and watered the whole face of the ground" (Genesis ii 6)... Said the Holy One, blessed be He, to them: "Because of the very good that I vouchsafed you, you wax proud before Me? I shall punish you", as it is said "For in seven days I will send rain upon the earth" etc. (*ibid.* vii 4).

The men of Sodom waxed proud only on account of the good (they enjoyed). What does Scripture state of Sodom? "As for the earth, out of it cometh bread; and under it it is burned up as it were with fire. The stones of it are the place of sapphires... That path no bird of prey knoweth, and the falcon's eye hath not seen it" (Job xxviii 5–6). They argued: "Since silver and gold come forth from our lands, we do not require people to come to us, for they come only to deprive us of our possessions." Said the Omnipresent to them: "On account of the good that I lavished upon you, do you cause the foot (of the traveller) to be forgotten from among you? I shall, therefore, cause you to be forgotten from the world", as it is said "They are forgotten by travellers, they hang afar from men, they swing to and fro" (*ibid.* *v.* 4); "In the thought of one who is at ease there is contempt for misfortune; it is ready for those whose feet slip. The tents of robbers are at peace, and those who provoke God are secure..." (*ibid.* xii 5–6); it is this that brought it upon them: "in that which God brought into their [literally 'his'] hand" (*ibid.*) ....' The homilist cites the words of Job, wherein he argues and shows that the wicked are at ease and spend their days in prosperity, and it is just these verses that the expositor expounds with reference to the men of the generation of the Flood and the men of Sodom and Gomorrah, in order to refute the argument that 'the wicked man prospers'.

Numerous dicta, aphorisms, stories, and parables were added by the Sages to those already found in the Bible in order to prove that the principle of 'measure for measure' was not abolished.[68] Indeed the weighing and measuring of details, down to the minutest particulars, of actions and their consequences became an unfailing source of expository-poetic enjoyment. But just as the Halakha, which ordained that 'an eye for an eye connotes monetary damages', did not diminish the sense of justice informing the earthly court's ruling, so the Sages were not concerned with the extent to which human actions and Heaven's punishment truly correspond, but with the actual presence of 'reward and punishment' in the Divine administration of the world.

We shall later revert to the problems and difficulties aroused by the belief in reward and punishment in this world, when the Sages came to compare it with other cardinal doctrines and principles. But undoubtedly this belief was so widespread and had so many adherents that it could not be ignored even by those Sages who personally were inclined to transfer the entire subject of reward and punishment to the hereafter, or had reached the conclusion that the precept was its own reward and transgression its own punishment (see above, p. 346). How deeply rooted was the belief in reward and punishment in this world may be learnt from certain tales of a distinctly folk character, although the date of their origin is difficult to determine. But their very occurrence in ancient Midrashic collections and their numerous versions show that they were known to wide circles. We shall cite, as an example, a story taken from *Leviticus Rabba*:[69] ' "For according to the work of a man He will requite him, and according to his ways He will make it befall him" (Job xxxiv 11): There was once a man who had two sons. One of them made many contributions to charity, but the other gave no alms at all. The son who was very charitable sold his house and all that he possessed in order to give to charity. Once on the Day of הושענא *Hôsha'nā'* [Seventh day of Tabernacles, now called הושענא רבא *Hôsha'nā' Rabbā'*] his wife gave him ten fallera [small coins] and said to him "Go, buy something in the market for your children." As soon as he went to the market place, the charity collectors met him. Said they: "Behold, the philanthropist is coming." They then requested him: "Give your share in this good deed [*miṣwā*], for we wish to buy a garment for the orphan girl so-and-so." Thereupon he took the money (his wife had given him) and gave it to them. But he felt ashamed to go (back) to his wife. What did he do? He went to the Synagogue, where he saw some of the citrons carried by the children on the Day of *Hôsha'nā*... He took some of them and filled his sack and sailed away on the Great Sea [the Mediterranean], until he reached a distant land [literally 'a country overseas']. When he arrived there, it was found that the king was suffering from a bowel complaint. His physicians said to him: "If you had one of the citrons that the Jews carry on the Day of *Hôsha'nā'*, you could eat it and be cured." Messengers forthwith went and searched throughout the country and in all the ships, but found none. They went, however, and found the (charitable) man lying on his sack. Thereupon they said to him: "Have you aught to sell?" He replied: "I am a poor man, and possess nothing." They then opened his sack and found it full of citrons. They asked him: "Whence are these?" He answered: "They are citrons that Jews use during Divine service on the Day of *Hôshaʿnāʾ*." So they brought him before the king... who ate of the citrons and was cured. He [the king] then ordered: "Empty his sack and fill it with denars"... Then the king said to him: "Make any request, and I shall fulfil it." He replied: "I request that my possessions be restored to me and that all the people come forth to meet me." His request was fulfilled. When he reached the harbour, the herald went before him and all the people went forth to meet him, and his brother and his sons also went out to meet him. When they crossed the river, the current swept them away and carried them off. It thus came about that when he entered his home, he took possession of his own property and inherited that of his brother, in fulfilment of the Scripture "For according to the work of a man He will requite him" etc.' Stories of this kind and many parables about the relationship between a master and his workmen and hired labourers[70] were of help to preachers and teachers in encouraging and inspiring their listeners to observe the commandments and eschew sin and transgression. However, as against such stories the homilists easily found, without doubt, examples and episodes testifying to the success of the wicked and transgressors and to the sufferings and afflictions of those who kept the precepts and feared the Lord. Nor did the Sages confine their questioning to the two commandments whose reward is expressly mentioned in the Torah; thus it is argued in the Talmud 'Now if his father said to him "Go up to the loft and fetch me some pigeons", and he ascended to the loft and let the dam go and took the young, and on his return he fell and died, where is his happy life and where his length of days?'[71] Although they conjoined with the reward in this world the reward of the world that is wholly good, and with the punishments of this world also the punishments of the hereafter, yet they did not intend to minimize the former on account of the latter. At any rate this was not the intention of those scholars who taught in the Mishna: 'These are the things whose fruits [מפירותיהן *mi-pêrôtêhen*] a man enjoys in this world, while the capital is laid up [מתקיימת *mitqayyemet*] for him in the world to come',[72] and it was certainly not in the mind of those who urged the observance of the precepts on the basis of the promised reward. Especially difficult was their explanation of the afflictions and sufferings that befell righteous men for no particular reason. The argument that these righteous people were due to receive compensation after death was treated with derision in various quarters, as may be seen from the remarks put into the mouth of the Sadducees, who said: 'The Pharisees have a tradition that they afflict themselves in this world, and have nought in the world to come.'[73]

The conventional 'doctrine of reward and punishment' underwent a grave crisis in the period of Hadrian's religious persecution, which led to a change in Rabbinic thinking on theodicy. It was not the tribulation that came upon the righteous from a higher power that called for an explanation, nor the bitter outcry against the troubles that were equally the lot of the wicked and the righteous that demanded an answer, but the fact that the resolve to observe the commandments was itself the cause of death and suffering!

However, there is not wanting the stereotyped explanation that views the tortures and sufferings of the (ten) martyrs as punishment for miniscule transgressions: 'When R. Ishmael and R. Simeon went forth to execution, R. Simeon said to R. Ishmael: "Master, my heart is ill at ease, because I know not the cause of my execution." Said R. Ishmael to R. Simeon "Did it never happen that a man came to you for judgement, or to ask you a law, and you kept him waiting until you finished sipping your drink, or you tied your sandal, or put on your cloak? But the Torah declared 'If thou delay [usually rendered 'afflict'] in any wise', and the principle applies irrespective of whether the delay is long or short." Thereupon he replied "Master, you have comforted me." '[74] Clearly this source was influenced by the Mishna cited earlier (p. 438) 'The sword comes to the world on account of the delay of justice.' In a later source[75] the Rabbis did not wish to attribute so grave a sin to Rabban Simeon b. Gamaliel, and reacting to this explanation, R. Simeon said: 'The attendant was instructed that whether I was sleeping or dining, no one should be prevented from entering.' R. Ishmael then raised another possibility: ' "Perhaps when you were sitting and expounding on the Temple Mount and all the multitudes of Israel were sitting before you, you grew arrogant?" He replied: "Ishmael, my brother, a man must be prepared to accept his affliction." '

It seems, however, that these explanations do not emanate from the generation that suffered the persecution; at all events they did not satisfy R. Akiba.[76] He and his colleagues were not required to commit transgressions that made them liable to the death penalty, and concerning which it was ordained that 'a man should let himself be killed rather than transgress'. With regard to persecutive decrees of this nature it could be said that the people on whom they were imposed 'were liable to death at the hands of heaven',[77] and thus they attained their punishment and atonement and share in the world to come. But R. Akiba and those of his colleagues — but not all of them[78] — who adopted his attitude observed the commandments[79] demonstratively and in defiance of the ruling power. 'Once when R. Akiba was being tried before the wicked Tineius Rufus, the time arrived for reading the *Shĕma*ʿ and he began to recite it joyfully. Said he [T. Rufus]: "Old man, old man, either you are a magician or you bear pain with contumacy." R. Akiba answered him: "Woe to that man! I am neither a magician nor do I bear pain with contumacy; but all my life I have read this verse: 'And thou shalt love the Lord thy God with all thy heart and with all thy soul [i.e. life] and with all thy might [i.e. wealth].' (Truly) I loved Him with all my heart, and I loved Him with all my wealth, but I was never called upon to face the ordeal of 'with all my soul'. Now that I experience (the test of) 'with all my soul', and the time for reading the *Shĕma*ʿ has arrived, and I have not thrust it aside, therefore I am reciting the *Shĕma*ʿ with joy." '[80] This acceptance of suffering is voided of its reason and significance, if it is explained as a punishment for any sin. Indeed it is told that 'When R. Akiba was killed at Caesarea, the news reached R. Judah b. Bava and R. Ḥananiah b. Teradion. They arose and girded their loins with sackloth and rent their garments and cried: "Oh, our brethren, hearken unto us! R. Akiba was not slain for robbery, or for not toiling in the Torah with all his strength. R. Akiba was slain only as a sign, as it is said 'Thus shall Ezekiel be to you for a sign; according to all that... then ye will know that I am the Lord God' (Ezekiel xxiv 24)".'[81] This doctrine of R. Akiba, which regards the acceptance of suffering with love as the highest goal of him that serves the Lord, performing the commandments in the spirit of 'with all thy soul — even though He takes thy soul', has no parallel[82] except in the conduct and words of Socrates before his death[83]; but the difference in the manner of their execution should be noted. R. Akiba, and his disciples who followed in his footsteps,[84] not only saved, by their acts, Israel's Torah and the observance of its precepts, but also radically transformed the evaluation of the relationship between the troubles and tribulations that befall the individual or the community, and sin and iniquity.

III. The Reason for Suffering

The change that occurred in R. Akiba's own outlook is reflected in a twofold tradition concerning R. Akiba's visit to the house of his teacher R. Eliezer, who was on his death bed. In one tradition it is stated: 'When R. Eliezer fell ill, his disciples came to visit him. Said he to them: "There is fierce wrath in the world." They burst into tears, but R. Akiba began to laugh. Said they to him: "Why do you laugh?" He countered: "And why do you weep?" They answered: "Shall we not weep when a 'scroll of the law' lies in distress?" R. Akiba rejoined: "For this very reason I am laughing. So long as I saw that my master's wine did not go sour, nor was his flax smitten, nor did his oil become rancid, nor did his honey ferment, I thought: Perchance my master has received his reward in this world. But now that I see my master in distress, I rejoice." Thereupon R. Eliezer asked him: "Akiba, have I omitted aught of the whole Torah?" He answered: "You have taught us, O our master, 'For there is not a righteous man upon earth that doeth good and sinneth not.' " '[85] Here R. Akiba still cleaves to the view accepted by himself and his teachers that we must not rebel against suffering, for no man is without sin. In the parallel account[86] R. Akiba's colleagues say 'whereas my master is for this world and the world to come'. But R. Akiba observed 'Suffering is precious'. The author of the story describes the surprise of R. Eliezer, who said: 'Support me that I may hear the words of my disciple R. Akiba, who has declared "Suffering is precious". He then asked him "Akiba, how do you know this...?" '[87] Although the period of evil decrees and religious persecution came to a close, yet the example set by R. Akiba, demonstrating that we are enjoined to die for the sanctification of the Name, remained in the Halakha for generations, and his watchword 'Suffering is precious' was examined again and again by his disciples,

R. Eliezer b. Jacob, R. Me'ir, R. Nehemiah, and R. Simeon b. Yoḥai, in order to find therein a justification and explanation for the normal sufferings that come to a person even in times free of evil decrees and religious persecution. 'R. Eliezer b. Jacob said: Scripture declares: "My son, do not despise the Lord's discipline" etc. Why? "For the Lord reproveth him whom He loveth" (Proverbs iii 11–12). You say so? Come and see, what was it that enabled the son to obtain his father's forgiveness? You must say, suffering... R. Simeon b. Yoḥai said: "Suffering is precious, for three good gifts were given to Israel... and they were granted only through suffering, to wit, the Torah, the Land of Israel, and the world to come... Which then is the way that leads a man to life in the world to come? You must say "It is suffering." '[88] Also in the School of Ishmael it was taught: 'Anyone who for forty days has known no suffering has received his reward in this world.'[89] Just as R. Akiba's martyrdom exerted a historic influence, and his disciple R. Eliezer b. Jacob was the first of the Sages to mention that Abraham was thrown into the fiery furnace,[90] so, too, an anonymous Tanna adorned the first believer with the merit of suffering as a sign of love: 'Before the advent of our father Abraham (so to speak), the Omnipresent judged the world ruthlessly: When the men of the generation of the Flood sinned, He drowned them with storm winds upon the face of the waters; when the men of the Tower (of Babel) sinned, He scattered them from one end of the world to the other; when the men of Sodom sinned, He swept them away with fire and brimstone. But when Abraham our father came into the world, he was vouchsafed suffering, which gradually began to manifest itself, as it is said: "Now there was a famine in the land, and Abram went down to Egypt" (Genesis xii 10). Should you ask: Why does suffering come? On account of (God's) love for Israel, (as it is said): "He fixed the bounds of the peoples according to the number of the sons of Israel (Deuteronomy xxxii 8)." '[91]

Even the view that corporate suffering was a sign of the love of God for His people and its righteous men, which found expression in the teaching of R. Eliezer b. R. Zadok — 'The Holy One, blessed be He, inflicts suffering upon the righteous in this world in order that they may have an inheritance in the world to come'[92] — did not reduce the tension and self-scrutiny and search for sins. At a time when the means of livelihood were scarce and the Sages earned a living with difficulty, R. Simeon b. Eleazar said:[93] 'Have you ever seen a wild beast or a bird practising a craft? Yet they sustain themselves without distress. Now they were created only to serve me, and I was created to serve my Maker; how much more ought not I to sustain myself without worry? But I have done wrong and have (thus) forfeited my sustenance.'[94] However, this searching and delving is a matter for the individual who suffers and is being chastised, not for anyone else. Another person transgresses the prohibition 'Ye shall not wrong one another; but thou shalt fear thy God', if, seeing that his fellow is subjected to disease and pain and buries his children, he says to him 'As Job's companions said to him: "Is not thy fear of God thy confidence, and thy hope the integrity of the ways? Remember, I pray thee, who ever perished, being innocent? Or where were the upright cut off?" (Job iv 6–7).'[95]

From the close of the Tannaitic period we find stories about Sages who invited suffering to come upon them for fear lest they were guilty of any transgression. But there were some who were accustomed to do this, even when they had no such fear,[96] like the pious men of old who wished to offer a guilt-offering even when it was obvious to them that they had committed no transgression (above, p. 433). The earliest Amoraim distinguished between two kinds of suffering: suffering that is not due to iniquity is suffering of love, but visitations due to sin are not chastenings of love. Signs indicative of the suffering of love were transmitted in the name of R. Joḥanan, namely afflictions that do not involve interruption of Torah study or of prayer.[97] On the other hand the same Amora said: 'If anyone is able to occupy himself with the (study of the) Torah and fails to do so, the Holy One, blessed be He, inflicts ugly sufferings upon him.' Similar sayings were transmitted in the name of the Babylonian Amoraim Rav Huna,[98] Rav Ḥisda, and Rava. In the name of the last two it is reported: 'If a man becomes subject to suffering, let him search his deeds, as it is said "Let us search and try our ways, and return to the Lord!" (Lamentations iii 40). If he searched and found no fault, let him attribute it to neglect of the study of the Torah, as it is said "Blessed is the man whom Thou dost chasten, O Lord, and whom thou dost teach out of Thy law" (Psalms xciv 12). If he did so and (still) found no fault, it is assuredly suffering of love, as it is said "For the Lord reproveth him whom He loveth" (Proverbs iii 12).' Those who accept suffering lovingly and consciously bring salvation to the world.[99] There were also Sages who did not wait for the coming of suffering, but performed acts of self-affliction and mortification. In conformity with the teaching of R. Akiba that 'vows are a fence for abstinence'[1] they made vows to restrain themselves and withdraw from the pleasures of the world, and to spur themselves to observe the precepts. Thus R. Joḥanan said: 'I vow to fast until I finish my chapter, (or) until I complete my Scriptural section.'[2] But most fasts were linked to the fear of sin. R. Ḥiyya bar Ashi, the disciple of Rav, who practised extreme abstinence and fought against his inclination, was given to fasting all his life until he died thereof.[3] Even the fasts attributed in Amoraic sources to Tannaim on account of slight transgressions, which are alluded to in Tannaitic texts, point to the tendency that prevailed in the time of the Amoraim. Once R. Joshua said: 'I am ashamed of your words, O School of Shammai'; but when their reason was explained to him by one of the Shammaite disciples, 'R. Joshua retracted and taught according to the explanation of the disciple. He said: "I crave your forgiveness, O bones of the School of Shammai." ' But the Babylonian Amoraim were not content with this; they were not satisfied until they had asserted that R. Joshua prostrated himself[4] upon the graves of the School of Shammai, adding that 'all his days his teeth were blackened on account of his fasts'. The same thing was told of R. Simeon, because it was considered that when he said 'And until the day of his death R. Akiba used to declare it unclean, but whether he retracted after his death, I do not know' he was disrespectful to his teacher.[5] Similarly the Amora R. Hananiah said of R. Eleazar b. Azariah 'His teeth became black on account of the fasts', which he observed because he had acted in a certain matter contrary to the will of the Sages.[6]

Alongside this tradition concerning the last of the Tannaim and the Amoraim, who invited suffering and fasted much, there existed a parallel tradition voicing opposition to the practice of mortification and self-affliction, irrespective of its motives.[7] The reasons for this opposition were many and varied[8]; we shall mention only those that give expression to the antithesis between the Halakha and asceticism.

In the name of Resh Laqish it is stated: 'A scholar may not practise fasting, because he diminishes the work of heaven'[9], and Rav Dimi said in the name of R. Isaac with reference, in general, to those who make vows: 'You are not content with what the Torah has forbidden you, but you seek to augment the things prohibited to you.'[10] The opponents of asceticism also adopted a different attitude to suffering. In a Baraita it is taught[11] that if a man's body is racked with pain, his life is no life. So that it should not be said that they had received their reward in this world, these scholars were prepared to fulfil the duty of suffering at a minimum. According to Rava 'Even if a man put his hand in his pocket to take out three (coins) and he took out only two' (this is accounted suffering).'[12] As a means, too, of purging sins Rava saw no need for suffering; instead he prayed: 'And the sins that I have committed wipe out in Thine abundant mercies, but not through suffering and evil diseases.'[13] By appealing to the Lord's mercies to purge his sins, Rava actually implied that strictly he deserved to be subjected to suffering and evil diseases, and his view is thus not different from that of other Amoraim who said 'Is then the Holy One, blessed be He, suspect of dispensing justice unjustly?'[14]

IV. The Attribute of Justice and the Attribute of Mercy

Whence and when did the idea originate that it was possible to request, as did Rava, for iniquities to be purged by the Lord's mercies? Moses, it is true, proclaimed 'The Lord, the Lord, a God merciful and gracious, slow to anger... forgiving iniquity and transgression and sin', but he continued 'but who will by no means clear the guilty, visiting the iniquity of the fathers upon the children and the children's children, to the third and the fourth generation' (Exodus xxxiv 5–6). The psalmist (ciii 7–13) explained Moses' words as follows: 'He made known His ways to Moses... The Lord is merciful and gracious... He does not deal with us according to our sins... For as the heavens are high above the earth, so great is His steadfast love toward those who fear Him... As a father pities his children, so the Lord pities those who fear Him.' Not the complete purging of iniquities without any punishment is promised here, but the diminution of the sin, so that the retribution should not be according to the full measure of the sin; furthermore, both the steadfast love and the mercies are promised only to those who fear Him but have stumbled. Even he who prays 'But He, being full of compassion, forgiveth iniquity'... concludes by saying 'and doth not stir up all His wrath' (Psalms lxxviii 38). The Lord's compassion only diminishes the severity of the sentence, but does not annul it or replace it.

It seems that in the Book of Jonah, too, the outlook is not different. The people of Nineveh repented after Jonah's proclamation, nevertheless they expressed themselves with doubt; they said in their prayer 'Who knoweth, God may yet repent and turn from His fierce anger, so that we perish not.' Indeed it is then stated 'When God saw... how they turned from their evil way, God repented of the evil.' Regarding this episode Jonah declares 'For I knew that Thou art a gracious God, and compassionate, long-suffering, and abundant in mercy, and repentest Thee of the evil' (Jonah iii 9; iv 2), that is to say, he cites the words of Moses in the sense that the nullification of the punishment on account of the penitence of the sinner is an act of grace and compassion on the part of God. Also in the seventh benediction in the order of service for fast days — 'May He that answered David and his son Solomon in Jerusalem answer you and hearken to the voice of your crying this day. Blessed art Thou, O Lord, that hast compassion on the land'[15] — compassion follows only after repentance and acts of atonement, as is shown by the reference to David's act after the famine that visited the land (II Samuel xxi) and to Solomon's prayer (I Kings viii 36–39). The fulfilment of God's promise is also considered to reveal His mercy, and when R. Eliezer was asked when prayers should be offered up for the rains to cease, he replied: 'When a man should stand on the top of Ophel and dabble his feet in the brook of Kidron; but we are sure that the All-Merciful will not bring a flood upon the world. What is the reason? "For this is as the waters of Noah unto Me; for as I have sworn that the waters of Noah should no more go over the earth." '[16] The fact that God refrains, as he has sworn, from bringing another flood upon the world makes Him 'All-Merciful'. This very oath, like the readiness to take back the penitent, are examples of His mercies.

Another approach, it might seem, finds expression in the prayer of Onias the Circle-maker, who 'drew a circle and stood within it and said... "I swear by Thy great name that I will not stir hence until

Thou hast compassion on Thy children" ' (*M. Ta'anit* iii, 8). Onias asks for compassion irrespective of whether those whom he represents deserve it, according to law and justice, or not. He gives the following reason for his request: 'Thy children have turned their faces to me, for that I am like a son of the house before Thee.' Thus Onias, too, does not request compassion without any justification; his right as a 'son of the house' gives him the courage to ask for the exercise of mercy. Before, however, we elucidate the meaning of the term 'attribute of mercy', we must consider the pair of concepts, the 'attribute of retribution' and the 'attribute of good', which are current in Tannaitic literature. The actual expression 'attribute' [מידה *middā*, literally 'measure'] is linked, as we have seen (above, p. 439), to justice and law. The judge metes out the measure of punishment or the measure of good entirely in accordance with the acts of the person judged.[17] Although it is stated that the attribute of good exceeds that of retribution, yet the proof adduced for this fact shows that this surplus is also comprised within the confines of justice. 'The attribute of good exceeds that of retribution five hundred times. In the case of the attribute of retribution Scripture declares "visiting the iniquity of the fathers upon the children..."; in the case of the attribute of good it is stated "and showing mercy unto the thousandth generation". It is thus seen that the attribute of good exceeds that of retribution.'[18] But this 'mercy unto the thousandth generation' is promised in the verse only to 'them that love Me and keep my commandments'. This homily is old, for its motif was already used by R. Eleazar of Modi'im in the exposition he delivered before R. Ṭarfon and the elders.[19] Indeed there are numerous Midrashic interpretations that seek to prove that the Lord is wont to enlarge the measure of good due to a person.[20] Among these homilies there is one that confirms the construction we put on Onias' prayer.

On the verse 'If thou afflict them in any wise, and they cry out to Me, I will surely hear their cry' (Exodus xxii 22) the Sages comment 'Now if in the case of the attribute of retribution, which is scant, this is what happens when an individual cries out against the many, how much more so does it apply to the attribute of good, which is abundant, when many pray for an individual!'[21] This argument from minor to major also applies where 'an individual prays for many'.

The use of the correlatives 'attribute of retribution — attribute of good' points to the extrusion of 'compassion' [or 'mercy'] from the sphere of justice, although we found it still included therein in Scriptural passages and even in ancient translations and Rabbinic sources.[22] The attribute of justice — including the elements of beneficence and punishment inherent in it — was completely separated from that of compassion in heavenly as in human judgements.[23] Also the word *middā* changed its signification. The Sages no longer speak of 'a measure' meted out by the judge or ruler; it becomes an epithet of God, which may be used as a Divine designation in place of His name.[24] The attribute of justice and the attribute of compassion are found alongside each other, and apparently are transformed into self-subsistent powers, into hypostases, in the imagery of the homilies and dicta of the Amoraim.[25] They are careful, however, not to provide any semblance of support to those who believe in dual deities. The following homily was directed against this doctrine: ' "The Lord is a man of war" — why is this stated? Because He revealed Himself at the sea as a mighty man who wages war, as it is said "The Lord is a man of war", (and) He revealed Himself at Sinai as an old man full of compassion, as it is said "And they saw the God of Israel" (Exodus xxiv 10)... so as not to provide an excuse for the nations of the world to claim that there are two divine powers. But "The Lord is a man of war; the Lord is His name..." '[26] Whence would the nations of the world have derived this pretext? What compelled the homilist to declare that the Lord manifested himself in various forms? Apparently the homilist already bases himself on the rule that 'Where יהוה YHWH ['Lord'] occurs it refers to the attribute of compassion, as it is said "The Lord, a God compassionate and gracious"; (but) wherever אלהים *'Ĕlōhîm* ['God'] is mentioned, the reference is to the attribute of justice, as it is stated "The case of both parties shall come before God", and Scripture further enjoins "Thou shall not revile God" (*ibid.* xxii 27–28).'[27] This postulate that each Name refers to one of the attributes seeks to refute the view that the two Names allude to more than one God.[28] But even the transformation of the Names to attributes did not altogether close the door to those who were searching for indications of the belief in dualism. Now the Tanna who delivered the exposition found in the sentence 'The Lord is a man of war; the Lord is His name' an allusion to the fact that even when the Egyptians were being punished and drowned in the sea, He was still the merciful Lord, and in the expression 'the God of [אלהי *'Elōhê*] Israel', used in connection with the giving of the Torah, he discerned a reference to compassion. The use of a Name that denotes one attribute does not annul the existence of the other. Both attributes are of equal importance. The same source that seeks to refute the claim that there are two divine principles also contains the following exposition of the verse ' "This is my God [אלי *'Ĕlî*], and I will praise him, [my father's God (*'Ĕlōhê*), and I will exalt Him]": this means that He dealt with me according to the attribute of compassion, and with my fathers He dealt according to the attribute of justice. And how do we know that *'Ĕlî* signifies none other than the attribute of compassion? As it is said "My God, my God [*'Ĕlî*, *'Ĕlî*], why hast Thou forsaken me?" (Psalms xxii 2); and it is written "Heal her, O God [אל *'Ĕl*], I beseech thee" (Numbers xii 13); and Scripture further declares "The Lord is God [*'Ĕl*] and He has given us light" (Psalms cxviii 27).'[29] It is obvious that the fathers, with whom God dealt according to the attribute of justice, were not inferior in any respect to the scions, towards whom He acted in conformity with the attribute of compassion.

Many scholars have noted that Philo, too, identified the names of God with His powers, but in his view κύριος — which is the Septuagint translation of the Tetragrammaton — is the power that judges, rules and punishes, whereas θεός — the Septuagint rendering of *'Ĕlōhîm*[30] — is the power that is good and beneficent. While Zacharias Frankel was inclined to ascribe this deviation of Philo from Palestinian Midrashic exegesis to his ignorance of Hebrew[31], more recent scholars[32] have suggested that Philo's interpretation is indicative of an ancient Midrashic exposition, traces of which can be found also in Rabbinic teaching, only for polemical reasons the ancient rule was changed and reversed. However, the suggested explanation that the thesis of the sectarians — to wit, that the Jewish God, the God who judges, is jealous, and vengeful, is only the demiurgos, while the Most High God is the good and compassionate Deity — brought about a drastic change, namely the declaration that *Y.* represents the attribute of compassion and *'Ĕlōhîm* the attribute of justice, was insufficient to refute the dualistic claim, and it would, in the circumstances, have been preferable to abolish this entire distinction. Moreover, the very conjecture that *Y.* once signified 'the attribute of justice' and *'Ĕlōhîm* 'the attribute of compassion', has no foundation whatsoever in the sources,[33] nor any basis in Biblical language, whereas it is possible to find verses (Exodus xxi 6; I Samuel ii 25) in which *'Ĕlōhîm* feasibly has the connotation of judge. It is the Greek translation that caused Philo to reverse the Palestinian tradition. The rendering of *Y.* by κύριος, whether due to the reading of the Tetragrammaton as אדני *'Ădōnay*,[34] or whether it was independently chosen as a substitute for a Divine Name that was not to be pronounced, gave this word the meaning of lordship and dominion. Whilst in the original text the readers saw the Specific Name as it was spelt, and even when they did not read it according to its spelling, they knew that the spelling was of primary importance, the Hellenistic reader was confronted by the word κύριος in its accepted sense. If Philo wished to find the idea taught by Jewish tradition, namely that the God of Israel was both the God of justice and righteousness and a compassionate and gracious God — in Philo's terminology: the One who possesses 'the powers', in the dual sense of attributes and of created entities[35] — he had to adapt it to the version before him. Without doubt Philo came across verses that contradicted the principle of his differentiation — that is to say, where κύριος is used when compassion is spoken of[36] and vice versa — just as the Amoraim encountered passages that were in conflict with the rule laid down by the Tannaim. Further on we shall deal with the solutions that were suggested.

The important thing in the view of the Tannaim was to preserve both attributes. The Mishna that declares 'If a man said "To a bird's nest do Thy mercies extend"... he is silenced'[37] is not opposed to stressing God's attribute of compassion, but to giving emphasis to this attribute alone. When the Amora R. Jose bar Bun said[38] 'They do not well (to) interpret the attributes of the Holy One, blessed be He, as compassion (only)', he expressed opposition to predicating the reason for the precept of driving away the mother-bird from the nest (Deuteronomy xxii 7) on the Lord's compassion.

We have already dwelt on the anti-Gnostic character of the aforementioned Mishna, and quite possibly the dictum of R. Jose b. R.

Bun — who apparently possessed an interpretative tradition[39] — also had an anti-Christian motive directed against the exclusive doctrine of love.

The first Sage reported to have used the Divine designation 'All-Merciful' [רחמנא *Raḥmānā*] is R. Akiba: 'Rav Huna said in the name of R. Me'ir and so, too, it was taught in the name of R. Akiba: A man should ever be accustomed to say "All that the All-Merciful does is for good." '[40] This Baraita is cited in explanation of the Mishna 'A man must bless (God) for the bad even as he blesses (Him) for the good', and this anonymous Mishna conforms to the view of R. Akiba, who expounded ' "Ye shall not make with Me (gods of silver)" — (this means), that you shall not treat Me as others treat their divinities, to wit, when good comes to them, they honour their gods, as it is said "Therefore they sacrifice unto their net" (Ḥabakkuk i 16), but when tribulation befalls them, they curse their gods, as it is said "And it shall come to pass that, when they shall be hungry, they shall be enraged, and curse their king and their god" (Isaiah viii 21). But you, if I bring you good, give thanks, or if I inflict suffering upon you, give thanks... both for the bestowal of good and for that of retribution.'[41] Even he who transmitted this teaching in the name of R. Me'ir, did so in the spirit of the latter's teacher R. Akiba. Only he who held that 'suffering is precious'[42], and did not interpret it as an act of justice, for in his opinion 'compassion does not enter into judgement',[43] could bless for calamity and affliction and designate God in his benediction as 'All-Merciful', since the suffering did not come as a consequence of justice, but as a token of the Lord's love.

The saying 'All that the All-Merciful does is for good' was not interpreted according to its original meaning, but was understood as a promise of 'a happy ending'. Following upon the Baraita just cited, the version in the Babylonian Talmud contains a story intended to portray the occasion on which R. Akiba made his statement: 'R. Akiba was once going on a journey and came to a town, and he sought lodgings but was refused. Thereupon he said: "All that the All-Merciful does is for good." So he went and spent the night in the open field. Now he had with him a cock (Rashi: "to wake him from his sleep"), and an ass, and a lamp. A gust of wind came and extinguished the lamp; a cat came and devoured the cock, and a lion came and devoured the ass. He (still) said: "All that the All-Merciful does is for good." That same night a band of marauders came and captured the town. Said (R. Akiba) to them [to his disciples, or, subsequently to the townsmen]: "Did I not tell you 'All that the Holy One, blessed be He, does is entirely for good'?" The aetiological, popular character of the story is self-evident, and the late date of the attribution of the episode to R. Akiba does not require much proof. It will suffice to point to the motif, which is common to this narrative and to those concerning Nahum of Gimzo.[44]

R. Akiba's heroic conception that suffering is inherently precious, and that God in inflicting it upon a man does this for the person's benefit, and is even at that very moment the All-Merciful, is far removed from the simple, folk notion that 'every untoward happening is destined to have a happy ending'. Between these two extreme views there exist quite a number of intermediate positions. We have already referred above to the homily delivered by R. Eliezer of Modiʿim before R. Ṭarfon to the effect that the bestowal of good exceeds that of retribution, and we explained that this surplus is promised only to those worthy of it, namely, the righteous. Now the same Tanna expounded the verse 'Because ye rebelled against My commandment... in the wilderness of Sin' as follows: 'Come and see how much the righteous are beloved of the Holy One, blessed be He, for wherever He mentions their death he also mentions their transgression. What is the reason for all this? So that people may have no excuse for saying: "They must have been guilty of evil deeds in secret; hence they died." Thus (we find that Scripture) mentions the death of Aaron's sons, and wherever it refers to their death it also refers to their sin, to let you know that this was their sole offence. Now an argument from minor to major may be applied: If in the hour of wrath the Omnipresent gives such consideration to the righteous, how much more so (will He be gracious to them) at the time of favour....'[45] The syllogism at the end of this homily is reported in another source in the name of R. Ṭarfon thus: 'Now it is an argument from minor to major: seeing that when the righteous are subject to (God's) wrath they are compassionated, how much more so at the time of (God's) mercy.'[46] 'The time of mercy' corresponds to 'the time of favour', but mercy at the time of wrath is vouchsafed only to the righteous.

In accordance with this conception the verse 'In wrath remember mercy' (Habakkuk iii 2) is translated in the Targum 'And the righteous, who do Thy will, remember in mercy.'[47] The application of the attribute of mercy to the righteous is paralleled by that of the attribute of justice to the wicked. R. Simeon b. Yoḥai said: 'When is the name of the Holy One, blessed be He, magnified in His world? At the time when He executes justice upon the wicked.'[48]

A different approach was adopted by Rabban Gamaliel. He incorporated the attribute of justice into that of compassion; the Lord's compassion came as a reward for man's compassion. 'R. Judah said in the name of Rabban Gamaliel: Behold, Scripture declares "And show thee mercy, and have compassion upon thee, and multiply thee" — take hold of this principle: so long as you are compassionate, the All-Merciful will have compassion on you.'[49] Preceding this teaching of Rabban Gamaliel there is a Baraita that illustrates man's compassionate deeds and their reward: 'If a man injures his fellow, the injured must make supplication for him, even though not requested by the assailant, as it is said "And Abraham prayed unto God, and God healed (Abimelech etc.)" (Genesis xx 17). So, too, you find in the case of Job's friends, as it is said "Now, therefore, take unto you seven bullocks... and My servant Job shall pray for you" etc. And what does Scripture state (thereafter)? "And the Lord restored the fortunes of Job when he prayed for his friends...." (Job xlii 8–10)'! While Abba Saul demands that a man should imitate his Maker — 'Just as He is compassionate and gracious, so you be compassionate and gracious'[50] — Rabban Gamaliel assures the compassionate man that his Maker will have mercy on him. It is in man's power, therefore, to influence and to change the attribute of justice to that of compassion, and vice versa. This concept also made it possible to explain the deviation in the use of the Biblical Names from the rule that *Y.* signifies the attribute of compassion, and *'Ĕlōhîm* the attribute of justice. The words of Isaiah (xxvi 21) 'For, behold, the Lord cometh forth out of His place to visit upon the inhabitants of the earth their iniquity' were interpreted as meaning 'He comes forth from the attribute of justice and enters the attribute of compassion upon Israel.' The passage in Hosea 'Return, O Israel, unto [עד *'ad*] the Lord thy God' was expounded thus: 'While [*'ad*] He is still to be found in the attribute of compassion; and if not — "thy God"; ere the defence becomes indictment.'[51] This idea, that the compassion of man, and not necessarily of a righteous person, but even of a wicked man, can awaken the compassion of Heaven, was accepted to such an extent that the Amora R. Aḥa relates that the blood of Zechariah, the priest and prophet, continued to seethe after Nebuzaradan had brought eighty thousand young priests and slaughtered them: 'At that moment he (Nebuzaradan) rebuked him, saying to him: "What do you wish, that we should destroy the whole of your people because of you?" Forthwith the Holy One, blessed be He, was filled with compassion and said: "If this man, who is but flesh and blood and ruthless, was filled with compassion for my children, how much more so shall I, of whom it is written (Deuteronomy iv 31) "For the Lord thy God is a compassionate God; He will not fail thee or destroy thee or forget the covenant with thy fathers", (have mercy upon them).'[52]

The transformation of the Lord's compassion into a reward for human compassion deprived it to a certain extent of its absolute character and made this attribute subject to man's conduct. In the last story paradoxical expression was given to the idea: The Almighty requires, as it were, an *aide mémoire*, containing the verse 'For the Lord thy God is a compassionate God'. R. Aḥa, who relates this story, followed the view of R. Joḥanan, in whose name he transmitted: ' "Slow to anger [אפים *'appayim*, a dual form]" — He is long-suffering before He collects [i.e. punishes]; when He begins to collect, He does so patiently.'[53] Without doubt, it was in conformity with this doctrine that R. Ḥanina, the younger contemporary of R. Aḥa, declared 'Whoever says the All-Merciful is lax (in executing justice), may his bowels be relaxed! He is merely long-suffering, but (ultimately) He collects His debt.'[54] These Amoraim were not only opposed to making the attribute of compassion the one, absolute attribute of the Lord (see above, p. 453), but they maintained the view that the attribute of justice was of primary importance, and that the function of the attribute of compassion was to delay and slow down the collection of the debt.

In contrast to these opinions the Amora R. Samuel bar Naḥman reverts to the concept of the Tannaim that the two attributes are to begin with equal (above, p. 451), but adds that it lies within the power of the righteous and the wicked to make one of them dominant. He gave the following exposition: 'Woe unto the wicked, who transform the attribute of compassion into that of justice! Wherever *Y.* is mentioned the attribute of compassion is referred to, (thus Scripture states) "The Lord, the Lord, God compassionate and gracious" (Exodus xxxiv 6), yet it is written "And the Lord saw that the wickedness of man was great... and it repented the Lord that He had made... And the Lord said: 'I will blot out man' " (Genesis vi 5–7). Blessed are the righteous who convert the attribute of justice to that of compassion. Wherever *'Ĕlōhîm* occurs, the attribute of justice is alluded to: "Thou shalt not curse *'Ĕlōhîm*" (Exodus xxii 27), "The cause of both parties shall come before *'Ĕlōhîm*" (*ibid.* *v.* 8); yet it is written "And *'Ĕlōhîm* heard their groaning, and *'Ĕlōhîm* remembered His covenant" (*ibid.* ii 24), "And *'Ĕlōhîm* remembered Rachel" (Genesis xxx 22), "And *'Ĕlōhîm* remembered Noah" (*ibid.* viii 1).'[55] In the same way he also explained the verses that appear to contradict the rule concerning the Names that allude to the Divine attributes. The Amora Rava solved this problem with dialectical acuity. He did not represent the Lord as lax in the execution of justice. On the contrary, he retained for the attribute of justice its original sense of 'meting out measure for measure' and declared: 'He who forbears to retaliate — in that he does not insist on fully requiting those who hurt him, but lets his rights go unclaimed — all his iniquities are (likewise) passed over', that is to say, 'the attribute of justice is not meticulous in searching out the misdemeanours of such people, but leaves them unpunished'.[56]

One of the Amoraim of the fourth century, who transmitted many of the dicta of R. Samuel b. R. Naḥman, explained, in accordance with the latter's doctrine, the creation of man and the phrasing of the verse 'And *'Ĕlōhîm* said: "Let us make man..." ' (Genesis i 26) as follows: 'R. Berechiah said:[57] When the Holy One, blessed be He, came to create the first man, He foresaw that righteous and wicked persons would descend from him. He said (to Himself): "If I create him, wicked people will descend from him; if I do not create him, how shall righteous people issue from him?" What did the Holy One, blessed be He, do? He removed the way of the wicked from before Him, made the attribute of compassion a partner in His action, and created man....' A Scriptural basis for the idea of this partnership is to be found in the wording of the verse 'In the day that *Y. 'Ĕlōhîm* made heaven and earth'. The juxtaposition of the two Names was expounded by an anonymous homilist, under the influence of R. Samuel bar Naḥmani, as follows: 'It is like the case of a king who had empty cups. The king thought: If I put hot water in them, they will crack; cold water, they will become warped. What did the king do? He mixed hot with cold water and put it in them, and they remained undamaged. Even so the Holy One, blessed be He, argued: "If I create the world with the attribute of compassion, there will be many sinners; if I do so with the attribute of justice, the world will not endure. Therefore, I shall create it with both the attribute of justice and the attribute of compassion, and may it endure! — (this is the meaning of) "*Y. 'Ĕlōhîm*". '[58] Although the creation of the world is spoken of, yet the reference is to the heart of the world — man. In keeping with this conception, the Amora R. Eleazar interpreted the verse in Psalms (lxii 13) 'Also unto Thee, O Lord, belongeth lovingkindness; for Thou renderest to every man according to his work': 'At first "Thou renderest to every man according to his work", but in the end "Unto Thee, O Lord, belongeth lovingkindness" ' — that is to say, when He sees that the world cannot endure on the basis of justice alone.[59] R. Eleazar changed the order of the verse, but others expounded it as it stands, in conformity with the view of his teacher, R. Joḥanan (above, p. 457): 'Unto the Lord belongeth lovingkindness' — this implies that He delays the punishment, but thereafter He collects His debt. Whoever wished to temper the attribute of justice itself, made the deduction that God requites a man 'according to his work', but not 'his (actual) work', that is to say, He does not deal strictly with him.[60] If one held, however, that the attribute of justice was of primary importance, it was difficult for him to agree to the full partnership of the attribute of compassion in the creation of man. Indeed, following upon the homily of R. Berechiah, cited above, it is stated: 'R. Ḥanina gave a different exposition: When (the Almighty) thought of creating the first man, He consulted the Ministering Angels. He said to them: "Let us make man." They asked him in reply: "What is his nature?" He answered them: "Righteous men shall descend from him"... He revealed to them that righteous men would spring from him; for had He disclosed to them that the wicked (too) would issue from him, the Attribute of Justice would not have permitted him to be created.'

In the last homily we encounter a phenomenon to which we have already alluded, namely, that the attribute assumes the character of an independent and separate power: 'For had He disclosed to them that the wicked (too) would descend from him, the attribute of justice would not have permitted him to be created' — the Attribute of Justice becomes a prosecuting angel. Thus we find[61] the Attribute of Justice standing before the Lord and saying: 'In what way are these different from those? He answered: "These are wholly righteous, and those are wholly wicked." Justice countered: "Sovereign of the universe! It was within their power [i.e. of the righteous] to protest, but they did not do so." The Lord replied: "I know full well that if they had protested to them, they would not have accepted their protest." Said Justice before God: "Sovereign of the universe! If it was known to Thee, was it also known to them?" '

This dialogue, built up by R. Aḥa b. R. Ḥanina on the basis of Ezekiel ix 4, ended, he informs us, in an exceptional manner: for 'never was the attribute of good, once it had issued from the mouth of the Holy One, blessed be He, changed to evil — save in this one case'.

In the Haggada that we have cited, and in similar stories,[62] the Attribute of Justice strives to maintain its position unimpaired. Its aim is to prevent the scales from being unjustly inclined towards mercy, and the Lord answers its arguments. But in the course of the debate the struggle changes its aspects. From being a contest between two attributes it becomes a struggle between the Attribute of Justice and the Almighty, who becomes identified with the Attribute of Compassion. In this way R. Samuel bar Naḥmani — who, we have seen, is inclined to give precedence to the Attribute of Compassion — understood the words of Isaiah (xxx 18) 'And therefore will the Lord wait, that He may be gracious unto you, and therefore will He be exalted, that He may have compassion upon you.' Without paying attention to the continuation of the verse 'For the Lord is a God of justice' he asks: 'Seeing now that we wait and He waits, who causes the delay?' and answers 'It is the Attribute of Justice that is responsible for the delay.'[63] The Attribute of Justice assumes, as we have stated, the image of a heavenly prince or angel acting for the prosecution; it ceases to act according to its allotted function and invades a sphere that does not belong to it. This transformation also brought in its wake a qualitative change in the connotation of the Attribute of Compassion, particularly in the dicta of the Amoraim who were opposed to the preference given to the Attribute of Compassion and to the undue reliance placed upon it. The Attribute of Justice does not complain against those who say that 'the Holy One, blessed be He, is lenient', but against the readiness of God to receive back the penitent.

Resh Laqish reports in the name of R. Judah Nesi'a: 'What is the meaning of the verse "And the hands of [ידי *yĕdê*] a man under their wings" (Ezekiel i 8)? The *Kĕthîv* is *yādô* ['His hand']. This means the hand of the Holy One, blessed be He, which is stretched out beneath the wings of the living creatures to receive the penitent on account of (the opposition of) the Attribute of Justice.'[64] In similar terms R. Joḥanan said in the name of R. Simeon bar Yoḥai concerning King Manasseh: 'What is meant by the verse "And he prayed unto Him, and an opening was made [reading ויחתר *wa-yēḥātēr* instead of ויעתר *wa-yēʿātēr*, "and He was entreated of him"] for him"?... It teaches us that the Holy One, blessed be He, made a kind of opening in the sky in order to receive him in penitence on account of (the opposition of) the Attribute of Justice.'[65] In parallel sources the Attribute of Justice is not mentioned, but it is stated 'that the Ministering Angels closed up the windows so that Manasseh's prayer might not ascend to the Holy One, blessed be He'.[66]

The possibility of such an interchange in the sources — the Attribute of Justice transmuted into angels — provides proof of the growing power of the Attribute of Justice, but, paradoxically, its potential activity became at the same time contracted and a limit was set to it. When it clashes with the cardinal belief in the power of repentance, the Lord conceals His actions from it and its significance is consequently annulled.[67]

V. The Power of Repentance

The scholars who attributed primary importance to the 'attribute of compassion' did, not as we have seen, uproot justice and law, or transform the attribute of compassion into a 'law of grace', unrelated to human action and conduct (see above, p. 457). Similarly the Sages who regarded the attribute of justice as central, in that it symbolized the justice and law inherent in the ways of the Lord, proceeded to set bounds to its dominion, when it might threaten to deprive man of the ability to repent and consequently of the possibility of escaping the jurisdiction of the attribute of justice. The subjection of the attribute of justice to the power of repentance, which we observed in the last dicta quoted, raises the question of the antithesis between the principles of reward and punishment and that of repentance. We have seen how great was the interest of the Sages not only in the doctrinal existence of 'reward and punishment', but also in demonstrating their application and realization in this world (above, p. 440). Yet how could these be reconciled with the possibility of repentance at any and every moment?

Before we proceed to answer this question, let us thoroughly examine the idea of repentance as it was understood by the Tannaim and Amoraim and the transmutations that it underwent. The term תשובה *Tĕshûvā* ['repentance'] was coined by the Sages[68], but the concept it signifies is a cardinal principle of the Biblical legacy — a legacy that is intrinsically full of problems and contradictions in respect of this central theme. On the one hand repentance finds no place at all in the stories about the Flood, the Tower of Babel, and the people of Sodom. They were, it is true, all wicked and sinners, but they were not called upon to repent. Likewise in the entire account of the provocations, complaints, and rebellions of the Israelites in the wilderness there are admonitions against sin and warnings of the infliction of punishment, but no call to repentance; and even Moses in his prayers does not rely upon the regret or repentance of the people, but on the promise given by the Lord to the Patriarchs. He appeals to God 'Turn [שוב *shûv*] from Thy fierce wrath' and presents his request as a plea for the Father's honour: 'Wherefore should the Egyptians speak' etc. (Exodus xxxii 12–17). In the expiation ceremony of the Day of Atonement, as it is depicted in Leviticus xvi, reference is made to atonement, confession, and purification from defilement, but the verb *shûv* ['return', 'turn', the stem of *tĕshûvā*] does not occur in any of its various forms. On the other hand, Moses' entreaty was of no avail, and the penalty imposed upon him not to cross over to the Promised Land is not rescinded (Deuteronomy iii 23–26). Sometimes repentance removes the sin, but not the punishment, as in the case of David (II Samuel xii 7–17; xxiv 10–17), or merely suspends it, as in the case of Ahab (I Kings xxi 27–29). It also happens that God grants the prayer of a wicked person like Manasseh (II Chronicles xxxiii 10–17). God not only hardened the heart of Pharaoh, but He even said to Isaiah (vi 10), when he charged him with the mission of prophecy, 'Make the heart of this people fat, and their ears heavy, and shut their eyes; lest they see with their eyes, and hear with their ears, and understand with their hearts, and turn and be healed.' On the other hand, Jonah goes to Nineveh and proclaims 'yet forty days, and Nineveh shall be overthrown!' (iii 4), and in the end 'when God saw what they did, how they turned from their evil way, God repented of the evil which He had said He would do to them; and He did not do it' (*ibid.* v. 10). All the prophets of Israel called the people to repent, but the relationship between these appeals and the prophecies of reproof, warning, and imprecation, on the one hand, and the prophecies of consolation and salvation, on the other, is not at all equal, just as there is not a single style for calling to repentance.

Although the Sages did not consider it their function to portray the idea of repentance, its ways, and development in the Bible[69], yet they were not unaware of — nor did they overlook — the various divergent approaches. The Palestinian Amora, R. Phinehas, expounded: 'It is written "Good and upright is the Lord; therefore doth He instruct sinners in the way" (Psalms xxv 8). Why is He good? Because He is upright. The Torah was asked: "What is the sinner's punishment?" It replied: "Let him bring a sacrifice and he shall win atonement." Prophecy was asked: "What is the sinner's punishment?" It replied: "The soul that sinneth, it shall die" (Ezekiel xviii 4). David was asked: "What is the sinner's punishment?" He replied: "Let sinners cease out of the earth" etc. (Psalms civ 25). Wisdom was asked: "What is the sinner's punishment?" It replied: "Evil pursueth

NB

sinners" etc. (Proverbs xiii 21). The Holy One, blessed be He, was asked: "What is the sinner's punishment?" He answered them: "Let Him repent and I shall accept him", for it is written "Good and upright is the Lord".'[70] Obviously the homilist intended to ascribe to God the view that the power of repentance was absolute, transcending that of atonement through sacrifices and the importance of the law of retribution. Without doubt he knew that in the same chapter of Ezekiel (xviii 32) on which he based 'the view of prophecy', it is stated 'For I have no pleasure in the death of him that dieth, saith the Lord God; wherefore turn yourselves, and live'. Indeed, he did not refrain from expounding this verse as proof that God does not close the portals of penitence, even before the utterly wicked: 'Said R. Phinehas bar Ḥama, the priest: The Holy One, blessed be He, does not wish to condemn any person, as it is said "For I have no pleasure in the death of him that dieth"... And in what does He find pleasure? — in justifying His creatures... Know that this is so, for when people sin and vex him, and He is angry with them, what does the Holy One, blessed be He, do? He goes about seeking an advocate to defend them, and He opens a way before counsel for the defence....'[71] The elimination, or at least, the unqualified rejection of the law of requital, accords with what we have learnt concerning the ousting and disregard of the attribute of justice by providing an opportunity for repentance, but the view of R. Phinehas himself is only the end-result of a long development.

Primarily repentance calls for the abandonment of the way of sin and the inner resolve never to return to it, and not the outward acts that accompany it, such as fasting and prayer. On the fast day the elder spoke words of admonition: 'O brethren! it is not said of the men of Nineveh that "God saw their sackcloth and their fasting", but "And God saw their works that they turned from their evil way" (Jonah iii 10), and in the Prophets it is enjoined "Rend your heart and not your garments" (Joel ii 13).' This is the version of the admonition given in the Mishna (*Taʿanit* ii, 1). According to the Tosefta[72] the elder recited the verses Isaiah lviii 3–8, adding: 'If a man had a reptile in his hand, then even though he immersed himself in the Shiloah [Siloam] and in all the waters ever created, he can never be clean. If, however, he has cast away the reptile, immersion in forty *sĕ'ā* suffices.' Thus, too, the Bible teaches 'But whoso confesseth and forsaketh them shall obtain mercy' (Proverbs xxviii 13); and it is further stated 'Let us lift up our heart with our hands unto God in the heavens' (Lamentations iii 41). The analogy of the reptile is also old, and Ben Sira (xxxiv 25–26) uses a similar argument: 'He who washeth after (contact with) a dead body and toucheth it again, what hath he gained by his bathing? So a man fasting for his sins and again doing the same — who will listen to his prayer? And what hath he gained by his fasting?'

Despite the clear emphasis laid on the nature of repentance and the high esteem in which it is held, we have already seen (above, p. 432) that in the Tannaitic teaching on the categories of atonement repentance by itself atones only for light transgressions, whereas in respect of other iniquities it is required that repentance should be augmented by additional methods of expiation. There were also Tannaim who held that there were ways of atonement — like the Day of Atonement and the day of death — that expiated even without repentance (above, p. 435). Furthermore, specific cases are recorded where the repentance of individuals was of no avail. The Sages represent Moses as arguing: 'See what transgression I committed and how many supplications I offered up, but I was not forgiven; and see how many transgressions you committed, yet the Omnipresent said to you "Repent, and I shall receive you." '[73] The Tanna who counted Manasseh among the kings who have no share in the world to come[74] was of the opinion that his repentance, mentioned in Chronicles, was of no avail in his case. Elisha b. Avuya despaired of penitence, 'For once — he said — I passed by the Holy of Holies riding on my horse on the Day of Atonement, which fell on a Sabbath, and I heard a heavenly voice go forth from the Holy of Holies and declare: "Return ye backsliding children, except Elisha b. Avuya, who knew My power and yet rebelled against Me....'[75] His reference to the heavenly voice that he had heard reflects a view that had gained currency. Elisha b. Avuya belonged to the category of men of whom the Mishna says (*M. 'Avot* v, 18) 'Anyone who makes the many sin is not given opportunity to repent'. The Tosefta gives the following reason for this view: 'That his disciples may not descend to Sheol, whilst he inherits the world, as it is said "If a man is burdened with the blood of another, let him be a fugitive unto death; let no one help him" (Proverbs xxviii 17).'[76] However, his disciple R. Me'ir had no fears on this score, but we know nothing of the extent of Elisha's influence. At all events the negation of his repentance may also be justified on the ground that he was guilty, of 'the desecration of the Divine Name', which was implicit in his conduct, a sin that the Lord does not pardon, but exacts for it 'immediate retribution'.[77] Nevertheless, despite all the reasons that can be found to justify the heavenly voice, the abandonment of the hope of repentance, proclaimed by Elisha himself, was tainted by heresy. Indeed in the continuation of that narrative it is stated: 'After a time Elisha fell ill. People came and said to R. Me'ir: "Behold, your teacher is sick." He went to visit him and found that he was ill. Said he [R. Me'ir] to him: "Do you not repent?" He replied: "And if a man repents is he accepted?" Said [R. Me'ir] to him: "Is it not thus stated in Scripture 'Thou turnest man back to דכה *dakkā*'? — that means, he is received until life is crushed [דכדוך *dikhdukh*]." At that moment Elisha wept and passed away. And R. Me'ir rejoiced in his heart, saying: "Methinks that my teacher died in a state of penitence." '[78] The authenticity of this story is self-evident. Elisha's doubt never left him. Even after R. Me'ir had expounded (Psalms xc 3) 'he is received until life is crushed', it is not stated that Elisha repented, only that he died; and R. Me'ir only used the expression 'Methinks that my teacher died in a state of penitence'. The authenticity is also apparent in the light of the legend that follows, which tells of the fire that arose from Elisha's grave.[79] R. Me'ir did not wish to give the sectarians an opportunity to claim that man was not allowed to repent. In truth, also in other dicta transmitted in his name the importance of repentance is stressed: 'It is taught: R. Me'ir used to say, Great is repentance, for on account of one person who has repented, the whole world is forgiven, as it is said "I will heal their backsliding; I will love them freely, for Mine anger is turned away from him" (Hosea xiv 5 [4]); the verse does not say "From them", but "from him".'[80] The universal character of repentance is emphasized in the teachings of a number of Tannaim who were contemporaries of R. Me'ir: The right hand of the Lord is outstretched to all mankind[81] since time immemorial; the Lord gave a period of grace to the generation of the Flood in order that they might repent; and likewise to the men of the Tower of Babel and the people of Sodom and Gomorrah.

The dictum of R. Eliezer b. Hyrcanus 'And repent one day before your death'[82] was apparently interpreted already by himself as meaning 'that a man should say every day: Today I shall repent lest I die tomorrow'. The saying resembles the admonitions of Ben Sira:[83] '...And in the time of (committing) sins, show forth repentance... And wait not till death to be justified.' But in R. Me'ir's day, whenever doubt was expressed about the actual power of repentance, greater emphasis was laid on the possibility of repenting up to the very last moment of one's life: 'R. Judah b. Bava said: It is like the case of a man who is charged by the state: though he give ever so much money he cannot extricate himself. But thou (O Lord) sayest: "Repent and I shall accept (you)", for it is written "I have blotted out, as a thick cloud, thy transgression, and, as a cloud, thy sins" (Isaiah xliv 22).'[84] R. Simeon deduced from Ezekiel xxxiii 12–14: 'If a man was wholly wicked all his days, and repented in the end, the Omnipresent receives him, for it is stated "And as for the wickedness of the wicked, he shall not stumble thereby".'[85]

The Amoraim followed the doctrine of the Tannaim, and even enlarged the sphere and power of repentance, to the point of extravagance, yet they did not overlook the problems raised in consequence. Resh Laqish gave a cosmic character to repentance by incorporating it in the list of things that were created before the creation of the world.[86]

The Amora Ḥanana bar Isaac gave an early date to the manifestation of repentance, ascribing it to Cain. Unlike the Amoraim who interpreted the verse 'And Cain went out' (Genesis iv 16) pejoratively, he gave it an ameliorative sense: 'He went out rejoicing, as it is said "He goeth out to meet thee; and when he seeth thee, he will be glad in his heart" (Exodus iv 14). Adàm met him [Cain], (and) said to him: "What sentence was pronounced upon you?" He replied: "I repented and became reconciled." (Thereupon) Adam began to slap his (own) face (saying), "Such is the power of repentance, but I did not know it." Forthwith he arose and said "A Psalm, a Song. For the sabbath day. It is a good thing to give thanks unto the Lord" (Psalms xcii 1–2 [1]).'[87] This Amora, whose date is not certain, is apparently transmitting a homily whose source is earlier than the dispute between R. Joshua b. Levi, who holds that 'Repentance accomplishes all and prayer only half', and R. Judah b. R. Ḥiyya, who maintains that prayer accomplishes everything 'and repentance only half. From whom do you deduce this? From Cain, on whom a severe penalty was imposed, as it is written "A fugitive [נע *nāʿ*] and a wanderer [נד *nād*] shalt thou be in the earth", yet when he repented half the sentence was remitted, as it is stated "And Cain went out from the presence of the Lord, and dwelt in the land of Nod" — the text does not say here "in the land of *Nāʿ* and *Nād*", but "in the land of Nod, on the east of Eden". '[88] To this exposition R. Joshua b. Levi doubtless replied that Cain only stood and prayed, and the Lord said to him: 'Cain, had you repented, I should have released you from "*Nāʿ* and *Nād*", but now that you have left repentance and taken hold of prayer, I shall relieve you of one (only).'[89]

Even the Sage that held that Cain's repentance was not wholehearted but merely 'repentance of deception'[90] could have continued to read 'I accepted the repentance of Cain, shall I not then accept your repentance?' In the same way R. Joḥanan and Resh Laqish, who for anti-Christian polemical reasons minimized the merit of the repentance of the people of Nineveh and declared it to be 'repentance of deception', [92] could not deny the fact that it won acceptance, but were only able to argue with greater force: 'I accepted the repentance of Cain, shall I not then accept your repentance?'[91] R. Joḥanan combined prayer and repentance and explained, by their joint power, the Lord's attribute of compassion: ' "And the Lord passed by before him, and proclaimed" — R. Joḥanan said: If it were not stated by Scripture, it would not be possible to say it. The verse teaches us that the Holy One, blessed be He, drew His robe round Him like a reader and showed Moses the order of prayer. He said to him: Whenever Israel sin, let them conduct their prayers before Me according to this order and I shall pardon them. "The Lord [YHWH], the Lord" — I am He [i.e. YHWH] before a man sins and I am the same after a man sins and repents. "A God merciful and gracious".' The mercies of the Lord are assured to sinners who have repented, even as to those who have not sinned, in accordance with R. Joḥanan's own statement: 'Great is repentance, for it rescinds a man's sentence.'

Repentance finds expression in the recitation of the thirteen attributes according to the underlying intent ascribed to them by R. Joḥanan. This is the covenant made with the thirteen attributes, that they do not fail of their purpose, as Rav Judah stated.[94] R. Samuel bar Naḥman found in the verse, Psalms lxv 6, an allusion to the fact that repentance is comparable to the sea: 'Just as the sea is ever open, so are the gates of repentance ever open.'[95] R. Yuda b. R. Simon expounded: ' "Return, O Israel, unto the Lord thy God" (Hosea xiv 2) — even if you have denied the primary principle of the faith.'[96] Thereby he wished to say that there is no sin for which repentance does not atone. Continuing the teaching of the Tannaim and Amoraim concerning the help vouchsafed by Heaven to those who come to sanctify and purify themselves,[97] R. Yossa said: 'It is written "Open to Me" (Canticles v 2). The Holy One, blessed be He, said "Open unto Me an entrance no bigger than the eye of a needle, and I shall open unto you an entrance through which (entire) camps and fortifications can pass.'[98]

Although it was fully recognized that the duty of repentance devolved on man at all times, and despite the liberal view taken of the opportunity afforded man to repent, both because the demands of repentance were so small and the time allowed for it so long — until his last day — it was yet felt necessary to stress the special penitential character of certain days, namely the Ten Days of Penitence, extending from New Year to the Day of Atonement. How and when did these days acquire this specific character? The Torah appointed the tenth of the seventh month as a fast day and as the Day of Atonement — 'to make atonement for the children of Israel because of all their sins once in the year' (Leviticus xvi 1–34). The first of the seventh month is designated in the Torah only as 'a day of blowing the horn' (Numbers xxix 1), or as 'a solemn rest unto you, a memorial proclaimed with the blast of horns' (Leviticus xxiii 24). In the Book of Nehemiah it is related that Ezra the Scribe read in the Book of the Law before the congregation on the first of the seventh month, and when he had brought the people to tears, Nehemiah and Ezra said to the people-'Mourn not nor weep... Go your way, eat the fat and drink sweet wine and send portions to him for whom nothing is prepared; for this day is holy to our Lord; and do not be grieved, for the joy of the Lord is your strength' (Nehemiah viii 2–10). The verse in Psalms, 'Blow the horn at the new moon, at the full moon for our feast-day. For it is a statute for Israel, an ordinance of the God of Jacob' (Psalms lxxxi 4–5 [3–4]), comes to link, if not according to its actual meaning at least according to its Midrashic interpretation, the theme of the blowing of the horn to that of judgement. In all these sources the first of the seventh month is not designated as **ראש השנה** Rōsh ha-Shānā ['the beginning of the year', 'New Year'];[99] and even when we refer to the Mishnaic tractate bearing this name, we find that it ennumerates four New Years, the last being the first of Tishri, which is 'The New Year for (the reckoning of) the years (of foreign kings), of the Years of Release and Jubilee years, for the planting (of trees) and for vegetables' (*M. Rosh ha-Shana* i, 1), that is to say, the numbering of the years commences on the first of Tishri.[1] In the next Mishna it is stated: 'At four seasons in the year the world is judged: on Passover in respect of produce, on Pentecost in respect of the fruit of trees, on New Year all that come into the world pass before Him כבנומרון'[2] (νούμερον — like a troop of soldiers). 'All that come into the world' means all mankind, and without doubt this judgement may also be considered to include the things comprised in the other seasons. Furthermore, the Mishna overlooks the Day of Atonement, which is connected with the expiation of sins. But it is surely not possible that a man's sentence should be passed before his sins are forgiven! The solution of these difficulties already forms a subject of dispute among the Tannaim: 'Everything is judged on the New Year, and their sentence is sealed on the Day of Atonement — this is the view of R. Me'ir. R. Judah says: Everything is judged on the New Year, but the sentence of each is sealed in its due season: at Passover (sentence is passed) on the produce, at Pentecost on the fruit of trees, at the Festival (of Tabernacles) on water, while man's sentence is sealed on the Day of Atonement.'[3] The Mishna is formulated according to the view of R. Judah, but there was also a view that each thing is judged in its due season and that its sentence is (likewise) sealed in its due season, a view that is akin to the opinion of R. Jose, who holds that man is judged each day.[4] Yet a fourth view maintains: 'All of them are judged on New Year and the sentence of each one is (likewise) sealed on New Year.' In accordance with this opinion 'It was stated in the New Year Prayers (interspersed with the blowing of the Shofar) of Rav: This day is (the anniversary of) the beginning of Thy work [i.e. creation], a memorial to the first day, yea it is a statute unto Israel, an ordinance of the God of Jacob. Thereon it is decreed which countries are destined for the sword and which for peace, which for famine and which for plenty, and thereon the fate of every mortal is decided, whether to be recorded for life or for death.'[5] This prayer was accepted, but a way was found to reconcile it with the view that the Day of Atonement is the day on which judgement is sealed.

In the name of R. Joḥanan it is stated: 'There are three account books, one of the wholly righteous, and one of the wholly wicked, and one of intermediate persons. As regards the one of the wholly righteous — they have already received their sentence [איפופסי = ἀπόφασις] of life on New Year; as for that of the wholly wicked — they have already received their sentence on New Year; regarding the intermediate — they have already been given the Ten Days of Penitence between the New Year and the Day of Atonement: if they repent, they are inscribed with the righteous; and if not they are inscribed with the wicked.'[6] In this way specific days of repentance came into being. To those who are acquitted during these days the Lord declares 'I account it to you as though you were re-created'.[7] But, needless to say, they do not exempt a man from the duty of repentance during the rest of the year. Indeed, in the prayer of the Eighteen Benedictions recited throughout the year a special benediction was composed for repentance, which in its ancient version was composed of a Scriptural text and the closing formula of the blessing: 'Turn Thou us unto Thee, O Lord, and we shall be turned, renew our days as of old; blessed art Thou who takest pleasure in repentance.'[8]

VI. The Two Inclinations

To the question why the blessing for penitence was placed after that for knowledge the Sages replied in the words of the prophet Isaiah: 'Make the heart of this people fat, and their ears heavy, and shut their eyes... and lest they understand with their hearts, and turn.' Despite the extravagant advocacy with which they stressed how easy the way of repentance was, the Sages did not overlook the fact that it not only calls for will, but also for knowledge and understanding in man's fight against his passions.

The stereotyped phrase 'the evil inclination' [יצר הרע *yēṣer hā-rāʿ*] to express the antithesis of 'the good inclination' [יצר הטוב *yēṣer ha-ṭôv*] was coined by the Sages. This dualism in no way corresponds to the dualism of body and soul. The Sages do not maintain that the evil inclination resides in the body and the good inclination in the soul. This widespread view current in the Hellenistic world, and also in Jewish Hellenism (*IV Maccabees*), found its sharpest and most popular expression in the words of Paul (Romans vii 22–24) 'For I delight in the law of God after the inward man; but I see another law in my members... and bringing me into captivity to the law of sin which is in my members.' There is no need to emphasize that the Sages rejected this conception in the light of what we have stated above (p. 223) regarding their views on the relationship between the body and the soul. In Sirach, as in the Bible, the *yēṣer* is the natural inclination of man[9], and also in the teaching of the Tannaim and Amoraim it sometimes denotes the power of thought, or serves as a synonym for the heart as the source of human desires.[10] However, Rabbinic teaching did to some extent personify 'the Evil Inclination', to whom were ascribed attributes, aims, and forms of activity that direct man, even before he was explicitly identified, as by the Amora Resh Laqish, with Satan and the Angel of Death.[11] Just as all the angels, including Satan, are God's creatures, so, too, was the Evil Inclination created by God, only at the same time God gave man the power to rule over the Evil Inclination: 'Thus the Holy One, blessed be He, said to Israel: "My children, I have created for you the Evil Inclination, (but I have at the same time) created for you the Torah as an antidote. As long as you occupy yourselves with the Torah, he shall not have dominion over you...." '[12] In the School of R. Ishmael[13] it was taught: 'My son, if this hideous (wretch) encounters you, drag him along to the schoolhouse; if he is of stone, he will dissolve, and if of iron, he will be shattered....' Similar analogies are cited in the name of other Tannaim.[14] Despite their great faith in the power of the Torah to be of help in the struggle against the *Yēṣer*, the Sages did not think that the Torah was able, so long as it was in the possession of man, to uproot the Evil Inclination completely. The Tanna R. Nehemiah expresses, in an interesting form, the view that any distance or partition introduced between man and his God creates a domain for the activity of the Evil Inclination. He declares: 'When Israel heard (the words) "Thou shalt have no (other gods)", the Evil Inclination was eradicated from their hearts. (Then) they came to Moses (and) said to him: "Moses, our teacher, be a πρέσβεις — an emissary — between us, as it is said "Speak thou with us, and we will hear — Now therefore why should we die?" What benefit will there be if we perish? Forthwith the Evil Inclination returned to his place. (Thereupon) they went back to Moses and said to him: "Moses, our teacher, would that He revealed Himself to us a second time, would that "He would kiss me with the kisses of His mouth". He answered them: "This will not happen now, but in the time to come, as it is written: "And I will take away the stony heart out of your flesh" (Ezekiel xxxvi 26)'[15] The very fact that 'other gods' are identified with the Evil Inclination is evidence of the power attributed to him, and the consoling thought that he would be eradicated in the future was insufficient to put their minds at rest, and many, indeed, investigated his devices and methods. To R. Akiba, the teacher of R. Nehemiah, already was ascribed the simile 'At first he is like a thread of spiderweb, but in the end he becomes like a ship's hawser, as it is written "Woe unto them who draw iniquity with cords of falsehood, and sin, as it were, with cart ropes" '[16]; and continuing his thought, the Amora R. Isaac said 'At first he is like a transient lodger, then a guest, and after that the host.'[17] R. Reuben expounded ' "And the Lord will take away from thee all sickness" (Deuteronomy vii 15): this refers to the evil inclination, which is sweet at the beginning and bitter at the end.'[18] The ready response given by man to the evil inclination found expression in a widely current simile: 'And the evil inclination is (like) a king over two hundred and forty-eight parts of the body. When a person goes to perform a precept, all his bodily parts become indolent, because the evil inclination in his bowels is king over the two hundred and forty-eight parts of man's body; but the good inclination is only like one confined in prison, as it is said "For out of prison he came forth to be king" (Ecclesiastes iv 14) — this refers to the good inclination.'[19]

He who conquers the evil inclination establishes his sovereignty over his bodily members, and of him the Tanna Ben Zoma said 'Who is mighty? He who subdues his *yeṣer* ['inclination'], as it is said "He that is slow to anger is better than the mighty, and he that ruleth over his spirit than he that taketh a city" ' (Proverbs xvi 32).[20] The verse cited by Ben Zoma shows that he identifies the *yeṣer* — without the adjective רע *ra'* ['evil'] — with the tendency to anger and impatience. But in the name of the Tanna R. Joḥanan b. Nuri it is taught that they are actually the devices of the evil inclination: 'If a man pulls out his hair, rends his garments, breaks his vessels, or scatters his money in his wrath, regard him as no better than an idolater. For if his *yeṣer* had said to him "Go and worship idols", he would have done so, for such is the work of the evil inclination.' It is clear that the Tanna merely intends to say that a man who loses control of himself and does, in the moment of his anger, the things just described is liable also to go so far as to perpetrate the gravest of sins, namely idolatry.[21] Actually his dictum is no more than a commentary on R. Akiba's simile cited earlier. Other Tannaim illustrated the transition from a light transgression to other iniquities of a grave nature[22] but not necessarily idolatry. We have already referred to the widespread view that the desire for idol-worship was wholly eradicated from Israel already at the beginning of the Second Temple period.[23] But in a homily attributed to the Amora Rav or R. Joḥanan[24] it is narrated that after the prayer for the elimination of the craving for idolatry had been granted, 'the Sages said: Since this is a time of grace, let us make supplication concerning the Tempter who incites to (sexual) sin. (Accordingly) they prayed and he was delivered into their hands. Said (a prophet) to them: Beware, you will slay the whole world, if you slay him. So they imprisoned him for three days. (Then) when they sought throughout Eretz-Israel a new-laid egg for a sick person, it was not to be found... Thereupon they blinded him ['with stibium' — Rashi] and let him go; and it availed, for he no longer entices men to commit incest.' A similar exposition is quoted in the name of R. Samuel bar Naḥman:[25] ' "And, behold, it was very good" — this refers to the evil inclination. But is the evil inclination very good? Surely not! The fact is that but for the evil inclination, a man would not build a house, nor take a wife, nor beget children.' The destruction of the evil inclination also implies the annihilation of this world, for as long as a man is alive — and he lives perforce — he has a duty to perpetuate the human species. The struggle against the *yeṣer* does not therefore mean withdrawal from the world and from activity therein, but the conquest of the *yeṣer* while working in the world. The evil inclination ceases to be evil — it even becomes very good — when it is the 'inclination of life'; hence it is possible for a man to love the Lord 'with both his inclinations — with the good inclination and the bad'.[26] He who knows — as did our father Abraham — how to transform the evil into the good inclination,[27] and likewise he who fights and refuses to surrender to his evil inclination — they both love the Lord.

In the name of the Tanna R. Jose the Galilean it is reported that the righteous, the wicked, and average people are to be differentiated as follows: 'The righteous are ruled [literally 'judged'] by the good inclination... the wicked are ruled by the evil inclination... average people are ruled by both.'[28] Apparently the Tanna meant to convey a similar thought to that contained in the anonymous dictum 'The wicked are controlled by their heart... but the righteous control their heart.'[29] That is to say, the righteous man is one who makes the good inclination his ruler, and even his heart — whose inclination is evil — is under his control. Not so the wicked: the evil inclination rules them, and they are controlled by their heart. These dicta do not purport to indicate a permanent relationship between the righteous and their inclination or between the wicked and theirs. They do not seek to deny the freedom of choice granted to man,[30] who can at best expect only minimal help in his struggle, but to explain the nature both of the righteous and of the wicked, and by implication to point to the severity of the conflict.

There are differences of opinion about the methods to be employed in this struggle, and countermeasures were suggested against the wiles of the evil inclination. The School of R. Ishmael recommended the study of Torah (above, p. 472). The Tanna R. Josiah said that one's evil inclination must be adjured, for we find that all the righteous men adjured their evil inclination.[31] R. Simeon b. Laqish drew up a plan of campaign, so to speak: 'A man should always incite the Good Inclination against the Evil Impulse (Rashi: 'he should wage war against the evil inclination')... If he conquers him, well and good, if not, let him study the Torah...; if he conquers him, well and good... but if not, let him recite the *Shema'*...; if he conquers him, well and good, but if not, let him bring to mind the day of death.'[32] But this same Resh Laqish also realized that there were times when no strategy availed a man without the help of the Almighty: 'R. Simeon b. Laqish said: A man's (Evil) Inclination gathers strength against him each day and seeks to slay him, as it is said "The wicked watcheth the righteous, and seeketh to slay him" (Psalms xxxvii 32), and were it not that the Holy One, blessed be He, comes to man's aid, he would not overcome him, as it is said "The Lord will not leave him in his hand, nor suffer him to be condemned when he is judged" (Psalms *ibid.*, *v.* 33).'[33] When the Babylonian Amora Rabbah heard the definition of R. Jose the Galilean as to what constitutes righteous, wicked, and average people, he commented: 'Such as we are average people.'[34] His disciple Abbaye reacted to this by saying 'The master lets no man live' (Rashi: 'If you are of the average people, there is not a truly righteous person in the world'). But in the course of time, it seems, Abbaye became convinced that his teacher was right, and from personal experience he learned that the Evil Inclination incites scholars 'more than anyone else', and because of his distress 'A certain old man came to him (and) taught him: The greater the man the greater is his (Evil) Inclination.'[35] When R. Ze'ira was meticulously careful and abstained from the slightest prohibition, he wished to avoid self-gratification and the praise of others by saying: 'Not that (Rabbi) Ze'ira is so virtuous, but we do the things to which the (Evil) Inclination assents'[36], that is to say, the deed does not pertain to the things wherein lies temptation.

Neither wisdom nor age intrinsically enable a man to withstand his Inclination. R. Joshua b. Levi said that the Evil Inclination grows with man 'from his youth until his old age, and if he finds (an opportunity) at the age of seventy, he brings about his downfall; (and even) at the age of eighty, he overthrows him.'[37] Hillel's saying 'Trust not yourself until the day of your death' (*M. 'Avot* ii, 4) served as a source for this view, and corroboration was also found for it in actual occurrences, for example: 'Once a pious man was sitting and learning: Trust not yourself until the day of your old age — like me. Thereupon a certain (female) spirit came and tempted him, and he began to bethink himself (in remorse). Said she to him: Be not distressed, I am (only) a spirit; go, be now like your colleagues.'[38] With respect to such an incident the Sages said 'If we have escaped (actual) transgression, we have not escaped sinful thoughts.'[39]

Even recalling the day of death, which appeared to Resh Laqish as the last resort in his list of expedients to be employed in the struggle against the Evil Inclination, did not, it seems, stand the test. Not all the Sages were of the opinion 'that the Evil Inclination was not to be found in the cemetery'.[40] R. Isaac expounded: ' "Wherefore doth a living man mourn [יתאונן *yit'ōnēn*], a strong man because of his sins?" (Lamentations iii 39) — even in a man's state of אנינות *'ănînût* [the period of mourning between the time of a relative's death and his burial] his (Evil) Inclination overcomes him';[41] and the Rabbis were able to tell stories that justified his words. Notwithstanding the emphasis they placed on the difficulties and severity of the struggle against the Evil Inclination and the relative value they ascribed to the resources available to man, it never entered the thoughts of the Sages to regard surrender to what they considered enticement to sin and transgression as of the least remedial worth. Certainly the Tanna R. Simeon b. R. Eleazar did not have this in mind when he said 'The *yeṣer*, a child, and a woman should be repelled by the left hand, but encouraged by the right.'[42] The phrase 'repelled by the left, but encouraged by the right' does not tell us what kind of *yeṣer* is referred to. But the juxtaposed words 'child and woman' show that it is not an evil inclination to begin with. Rashi's interpretation, therefore, seems correct: 'If a man alienated his desire completely, he would reduce the propagation of the species; and if he encouraged it completely, he would eventually do that which is forbidden, for he would not be able to restrain his passion from committing sin.' This approach was also voiced by R. Joḥanan in his saying: 'Man has a small organ — starve it and it is sated, sate it and it remains hungry.'[43] However, there were Amoraim who were indeed implacable in rejecting any compromise with the Evil Inclination, and demanded extreme resistance to his devices, yet within the area of permissibility they were prepared to concede even more than with the 'right hand'. The story transmitted in the name of Rav as a decided Halakha of the

Sages may serve as an example of the uncompromising attitude:[44] 'Once a man set his heart on a certain woman and he fell a prey to impure desires. When the doctors were consulted, they said "There is no other remedy for him but that she should submit to him." The Sages, however, said "Let him die rather than she should yield." (Said the doctors) "Then let her stand before him naked." (The Sages replied) "Let him die, but she must not stand before him nude." (The doctors then suggested that) "She should converse with him from behind a fence." (But the Sages insisted) "Let him die rather than she should converse with him from behind a fence."' Rav also demanded that a man should repent 'while he is (still) a man',[45] that is to say, while he is a young man in full vigour, but at the same time he did not call for drastic abstinence and asceticism in legitimate sexual life as a means of suppressing the evil inclination. This is attested by both his instructions to others[46] and the testimonies to his own behaviour[47] in this sphere. In order to explain these there is no need to dive into the deep waters of apologetics;[48] it will suffice to remember that Rav did not negate licit pleasure and joy,[49] and possibly he regarded them as a bulwark against the breaching of forbidden fences and barriers. His views were shared by other Amoraim in Eretz-Israel and Babylon. R. Joshua b. Levi said: 'A man should visit his wife when about to go on a journey' ('because he desires her most [at such a time]' — Rashi), and Rav Joseph glossed his ruling.[50] R. Tanḥum said in the name of R. Ḥanilai: 'A Jew who has no wife abides without joy, blessing, (or) good.'[51] And the maxim 'He that has bread in his basket is not to be compared with one who has no bread in his basket', which originally referred to food,[52] became a proverbial saying, denoting the difference between a married man and one without a wife. This approach does not imply any underestimation of the dangers threatening man, or a lessening of tension in the struggle that he must wage.

There were Sages who did not overlook the very fact that the observance of the precept of procreation involves the satisfaction of a man's desire, nor the difficulty of distinguishing between the two. The Amora R. Aḥa gave the following exposition: ' "Behold, I was brought forth in iniquity, and in sin did my mother conceive me"... in complete iniquity; even the most pious person cannot possibly be without an element [of desire]. David said before the Holy One, blessed be He "Sovereign of the universe, did my father Jesse really intend to bring me into existence? Actually he was thinking only of his own needs." You can tell that this is so from the fact that when they perform their needs, each one turns his head in a different direction and Thou dost introduce every drop that a man has. This is the meaning of David's words "For though my father and my mother have forsaken me, the Lord will take me up" (Psalms xxvii 10)'.[53] The conclusion of the homily clearly shows that R. Aḥa did not infer extreme abstinence from the drastic language that he ascribed to David, language that recalls the arguments of the Cynics.[54]

It is precisely man's weakness that serves as a reason for intensifying the demand for the suppression of human passions. A man must force himself to subjugate his inclination.[55] Hence it is taught in a Baraita that if one has the option of either unloading the burden of a friend's beast that is lying under its burden, or of helping an enemy to load, he must help his enemy, in order to subdue his impulse.'[56] R. Ḥanina and R. Jonathan acted thus even in matters that were not obligatory. When they had a choice of two roads, one leading to an idolatrous shrine and the other to the entrance of a brothel, they did not take the first path, because the craving for idolatry had already been destroyed (above, p. 22) and there was no need to overcome it, but chose the second route in order to master their inclination.[57] The dispute about the desirability of submitting to temptation in secret rather than profaning the Divine Name in public, with which we dealt already above (p. 357), is also bound up with the fear lest a man's capacity for controlling his inclination become weakened. In the name of Rav Huna, the disciple of Rav, it is reported: 'when a man commits a transgression more than once... he comes to regard it as something permitted.'[58] Wrongful acts of this kind, which people treated lightly, were enumerated by two other disciples of Rav. Rav Judah said 'Most people (are guilty) of robbery,[58a] a minority of unchastity, and all of slander.' Rav Amram regarded 'Sinful thoughts, עיון תפלה *ʿiyyûn tĕfillā* ['calculating on prayer'; *aliter*: '(lack of) devotion in prayer'], and slander' as sins to which a man succumbs daily.[59] In the School of Rav[60] the verse 'In that day, saith the Lord, will I assemble her that halteth... and her that I have afflicted' (Micah iv 6) was expounded as expressing God's regret at having created the Evil Inclination; and this homily R. Joshua b. Levi transmitted in the name of R. Phinehas b. Jair.[61] The same verse was used by R. Joḥanan as a basis for justifying a man who fell into sin.[62] The Lord admits, so to speak, that by creating the Evil Inclination, who incites man to sin, He was the cause of all the troubles. An anonymous preacher integrated the homilies of R. Phinehas b. Jair and R. Joḥanan and elaborated them thus: 'Israel said: "Sovereign of the universe, Thou hast caused to be written concerning us 'Behold, as the clay in the potter's hand, so are ye in My hand, O house of Israel' (Jeremiah xviii 6). Therefore, although we sin and anger Thee, do not leave us. Why? For we are the clay, and Thou art our Potter. Come and consider the potter! If he makes a jug and leaves a pebble in it, then when the vessel is taken out of the kiln and liquid is put in it, it leaks where the pebble is embedded and loses its liquid. Who caused the jug to leak and lose its contents? (Surely) the potter, who left the pebble in it!" Even so Israel argued before the Holy One, blessed be He: "Sovereign of the universe, Thou hast created within us the Evil Inclination from our youth, as it is said 'For the imagination of man's heart is evil from his youth' (Genesis viii 21). Now he is the cause of our sinning before Thee, yet Thou dost put the blame on us! We entreat Thee, therefore, remove the Evil Inclination from us, that we may do Thy will and not sin." He answered them: "Thus shall I do, as it is said 'In that day, saith the Lord, will I assemble her that halteth, and I will gather her that is driven away' ".'[63] Indeed, help is given to the righteous in this world to subdue the Evil Inclination. It is related that both R. Akiba and R. Me'ir scoffed at transgressors; so Satan once disguised himself as a woman and would not let them in peace until he heard the proclamations in heaven 'Take heed of R. Akiba and his Torah-learning', 'Take heed of R. Me'ir and his Torah-learning.'[64]

The Amoraim who told such stories about the great Tannaim did not take it for granted that they would be vouchsafed the same grace as their predecessors;[65] hence they were accustomed to add in the special prayers that they said upon waking from sleep, or in supplements to the statutory prayer, supplications for the conquest and suppression of the Evil Inclination. The School of R. Jannai said 'And I have sinned unto Thee; may it be Thy will... that Thou give me a good heart, a good portion, a good inclination....' R. Ḥiyya bar Va (= Abba) used to pray 'May it be Thy will, O Lord our God... that Thou incline our hearts to repent wholeheartedly before Thee....' R. Tanḥum (son of) Scholasticus (Σκολαστικός) composed a prayer that is wholly concerned with breaking the power of the (Evil) Inclination. It is worded 'May it be Thy will, O Lord our God... that Thou break and remove the yoke of the Evil Inclination from our heart, since Thou hast created us to do Thy will, and we are duty-bound to do Thy will. Thou dost wish it and we wish it; who then prevents it? The leaven in the dough [i.e. the incitement of the Evil Inclination]. It is well known that we have not the strength to withstand him. May it, therefore, be Thy will, O Lord my God... to remove him from us and subdue him, so that we may do Thy will as our own with a perfect heart.'[66] From this prayer we clearly learn that there is no intention to exempt man from the obligation of fighting against his inclination, nor to cast his burden on the Lord. The worshipper wishes to do the will of God with a perfect heart, and he is asking for the help promised to those who come to sanctify and purify themselves.[67] This response implies the exercise of the attribute of compassion before the commencement of judgement. It is a corollary of God's goodness. From the Almighty's answer 'I will make all My goodness pass before thee' to Moses' request 'Show me, I pray Thee, Thy glory' the Tanna R. Nehemiah concluded 'When he [Moses] approached Him wholeheartedly, the Holy One, blessed be He, responded accordingly.'[68] In this spirit the verse 'The Lord is good to all; and His tender mercies are over all His works' (Psalms cxlv 9) is expounded by the Amora R. Levi: 'The Lord is good to all and He bestows of His compassion upon His creatures.' This dictum is followed by an illuminating story: 'In the days of R. Tanḥuma, Israel needed to fast. When the people came and said to him: "O Master, proclaim a fast!" he decreed a fast — the first day, the second, and the third, but no rain fell. He then entered and preached to them, saying "My children, feel compassion towards each other, and the Holy One, blessed be He, will be filled with compassion for you".'[69]

Man's compassion derives from God's compassion, but a man must first show compassion in order that the Lord should compassionate him. In the Pentateuchal section 'on which most of the essential parts of the Torah are dependent'[70] the Lord said to Moses: 'Go say to the Children of Israel: My children, just as I am abstinent, so must you abstain (from sin); just as I am holy, so must you be holy.'[71] Holiness and abstinence are attributes of God and it is His will that His creatures should (also) cleave to them, and He even helps them, if they begin to walk in His ways. A similar exposition was given to the verse ' "May He send forth thy help from the sanctuary [*qōdesh*, literally 'holiness']" — on account of the hallowed deeds you have performed; "and support thee out of Zion" (Psalms xx 3 [2]) — on account of the distinguished acts you have done.'[72] The idea that the good God helps to bring about good, led the Sages to emphasize it and to develop it into the doctrine that the Evil Inclination was not created by the Lord.[73] He put 'the evil leaven in the dough'[74], but for the fermentation of the leaven man alone is responsible; and he may bring himself by his actions to such a stage that the help promised to one who wishes to do good will be denied him, for by sinking into uncleanness and by doing evil he may become obtuse and regard the forbidden as permitted and even deprive himself of the possibility of repenting. He may consider the Evil Inclination itself as his god, as R. Jannai put it: 'Whoever listens to his (Evil) Inclination is, as it were, an idolater. What is the reason? "There shall no strange god be in thee; neither shalt thou worship any foreign god" — make not the stranger within you your sovereign.'[75] The enthronement of the Evil Inclination is idolatry; and the prayer, customarily recited in the School of R. Jannai, 'that Thou mayest give me... a good inclination', and similarly formulated supplications (see above, p. 480), implied the acceptance of the yoke of the kingdom of heaven, and was an expression of readiness to fight against the Evil Inclination.

In the teaching of the Sages on sin and the Evil Inclination the influence of the personal experience of the man who struggles with and lives by his faith plays a prominent role. Without doubt the Tannaim and Amoraim, whose dicta and definitions we have cited above, were capable of advancing sharp-witted arguments against the views of their predecessors, against the sayings of their colleagues, and even against their own statements, just as they demonstrated these qualities in the thrust and parry of Halakhic discussion, where they spared no effort to pursue the merest shadow of a contradiction, lack of consistency or exactitude, whether the question was one of civil law or the rules governing holy things and levitical purity. Against the Stoics, whose central interest was the problem of theodicy, which they endeavoured to solve and put on a firm basis, the Academic thinkers[76] put forward a dialectic argument, such as undoubtedly could have been heard in the schoolhouses of the Sages. According to the Stoic doctrine a man is obliged to acquire good for himself; it is not given to him by the deity. This concept is a necessary corollary to the principle of free will. But if the gods are able to bestow good upon man, but do not do so, they are not good. Should you argue that they are incapable of doing this, then again they are of no benefit at all. Such a contention had no place in the world of our Sages, for their entire approach in discussing this theme was fundamentally different from that of the Stoics. They did not occupy themselves with philosophical dialectics, but with the variegated experiences of the man who believed in the good God and was tested by his ability to endure the trial of faith and trust.

VII. The Righteous and Wicked

Our exposition is further illumined by the description of the ideal of the righteous man found in Rabbinic teaching. We have learned that the struggle against and defeat of the Evil Inclination make a man righteous. The term צדיק *ṣaddîq* 'righteous' denotes in this context that a man remains pure, uncontaminated by sin. Indeed we find that the word נקי *nāqî* ['pure', 'innocent'] is translated four times in the Septuagint by δίκαιος, i.e. 'righteous';[77] so, too, Onkelos renders the verse 'and the innocent [*nāqî*] and righteous [*ṣaddîq*] slay thou not' (Exodus xxiii 7) — ודיזכי ודי נפק דכי מן דינא לא תקטול ['Him who is innocent and goes forth guiltless from judgement shalt thou not slay'].[78] Man is righteous so long as his guilt has not been proved. In this manner the Tannaim explained the verse just cited, which they exemplified as follows: 'If one witness testified that he worshipped the sun, and another that he worshipped the moon, I might have thought that their evidence should be combined and the man should be declared guilty; therefore Scripture teaches us "and the innocent and righteous slay thou not". If Reuben was pursuing his fellow to kill him, holding a sword in his hand, and (witnesses) said to him: "Take cognizance that he [the one pursued] is of our covenant and the Torah has ordained 'Whoso sheddeth man's blood, by man shall his blood be shed' " (Genesis ix 6); and he answered them: "I know, but even so." And (for a time) the witnesses lost sight of them and subsequently they found (the fugitive) in his death throes and the slayer holding a sword dripping blood, then I might have thought that he (the pursuer) should be held guilty. Therefore Scripture teaches us "and the innocent and righteous slay thou not". '[79] Alongside the use of *ṣaddîq* for a man who is declared not guilty at his trial, the term also serves as a designation for those who do God's will,[80] and for those who have accepted the Torah,[81] which fits a man to be a *ṣaddîq*.[82] The name *ṣaddîq* is also given to one who gives charity [*ṣĕdāqā*], which is simply termed 'precept',[83] and in fulfilling it a man imitates the deeds of his Creator and merits to be called by His name: ' "Whosoever shall be called [reading *Niphʿal* instead of *Qal*] by the name of the Lord shall be delivered" (Joel iii 5). But how is it possible for a man to be called by the name of the Holy One, blessed be He? The answer is that just as the Omnipresent is gracious and compassionate, so you, too, must be gracious and compassionate and donate free gifts; (just as) the Omnipresent is called *Ṣaddîq*, as it is stated "For the Lord is righteous (*ṣaddîq*), [He loveth righteousness]" (Psalms xi 7), so you, too, must be righteous....'[84] The designation of the Lord as 'the Righteous One, who lives for ever' is based on the verse 'The Lord is righteous in all His ways' (Psalms cxlv 17).[85] The Tannaim and Amoraim indulged in many hyperboles in describing the importance, weighty character, and greatness of charity [צדקה *ṣĕdāqā*, literally: 'righteousness']. It has the power to atone for iniquities, even for the sin of idolatry.[86] Thus R. Nathan taught: 'From Gareb to Shiloh is a distance of three *mil* [= 6,000 cubits], and the odour of the smoke of the (Temple) altar and the smoke of Micah's image intermingled. The Ministering Angels wished to thrust him aside. Said the Holy One, blessed be He, to them: "Let him be, because his bread is available to wayfarers." ' For this reason Micah was not counted among the commoners who have no share in the world to come.[87] But acts of charity do not always atone for iniquities or deliver a man from punishment for his transgressions; sin even has the power to extinguish the merit of precepts.[88] Furthermore, if one commits transgressions with the intention of atoning for them by the performance of precepts, he remains wicked, even if he has fulfilled them. If, now, 'one who says I shall transgress and repent' does not attain to true penitence (see above, p. 464), it is obvious that if a man gives liberally to charity, but at the same time sins, he is not to be designated a *ṣaddîq*. This was the accepted view.[89] The exaggerated story set in homilies by the expiatory value of acts of charity and lovingkindness gave rise to the need for express expositions opposing the attitude of shallow levity towards the gravity of sin. With people of such mentality in mind R. Joḥanan commented on the verse 'Hand to hand, (but) he shall not go unpunished for the evil' [see Rashi *ad loc.*] as follows: 'It may be compared to the case of a man who went and committed a sin and gave the harlot her hire, but he had hardly gone out of the door of her house when a poor man met him (and) said to him "Give me alms." The man gave him and went on his way, thinking to himself: Had not the Holy One, blessed be He, wished to grant me atonement for my sins, He would not have sent that beggar so that I might give him alms and gain atonement for what I had done. Thereupon the Holy One, blessed be He, said to him: "Wicked wretch! do not suppose such a thing; but go and learn from the wisdom of Solomon, who explained, saying "Hand to hand, (but) he shall not go unpunished for the evil".'[90] Such homilies are to be found not only relative to ordinary people, and not only with regard to transgressions of the kind mentioned, but also with reference to one who 'acquired Torah like Moses our Teacher', but is filled with overweening conceit.[91]

A special term 'a book-keeping Pharisee' denotes the man who performs 'one sin and one precept, and balances one against the other.'[92] In discussing the Evil Inclination, we encountered a differentiation between those whose heart and inclination are under their control and those who are controlled by their inclination and heart.[93] The former are righteous, but if they rule their impulse and refrain from sin without doing any acts of charity, they are not deemed completely righteous. Rava reports the explanation that he heard from the Palestinian Amora, Rav Idi, of the verse 'Praise the righteous [*ṣaddîq*] when he is good, for they shall eat the fruit of their doings'

(Isaiah iii 10): 'But is there a *ṣaddîq* that is good and one that is not good? The meaning is: He that is good to Heaven and to men is a good *ṣaddîq*; he that is good to Heaven and bad to men — is a *ṣaddîq* that is not good. Similarly Scripture states "Woe unto the wicked man [רשע *rāshāʿ*] that is bad!" But is there a *rāshāʿ* that is bad and a *rāshāʿ* that is not bad? The meaning is: He that is evil to Heaven and evil to men is a bad *rāshāʿ* he that is evil to Heaven, but not to men is a *rāshāʿ* that is not bad.'[94] The homily belongs to an Amora, but the idea that it is not possible to be a *ṣaddîq* without outstanding acts of charity is old. The Sages had already decided by vote in the upper chamber of R. Ṭarfon and declared: 'Who are they that "do righteousness at all times" (Psalms cvi 3)? Should you say: They are those who teach children Bible and Mishna — but do they not eat and drink and sleep? Alternatively (should you suppose that) they are the writers of Tefillin and Mezuzot — but do they not (likewise) eat and drink and sleep? Who then are they that "do righteousness at all times"? You must conclude that this alludes to one who brings up an orphan in his home. But can you claim that he [the orphan] does not uncover himself at night? Said (the Sages): We still need the Sage of Modiʿim. R. Eleazar of Modiʿim came and taught: Scripture refers only to the piece of bread that he eats in his house.'[95]

We have already seen that even in the case of a man who is wholly righteous there is no absolute assurance that he will always remain so, 'and will not in the end rebel, and regret his former conduct'.[96] R. Joḥanan does indeed state in the name of R. Jose that the Lord acceded to Moses' request and let him know His ways, explaining to him why it may go ill with the righteous and well with the wicked. However, not only did R. Me'ir disagree with him and say that this knowledge was not vouchsafed to Moses, expounding ' "And I will be gracious to whom I will be gracious" — even though he is unworthy'; "And I will show mercy on whom I will show mercy" — even though he is unworthy; but even according to R. Jose's view the Gemara finds it difficult to discover the explanation given to Moses, and only after the rejection of one conjecture is the opinion put forward: 'A righteous man with whom it is well is wholly righteous; a righteous man with whom it is ill is not wholly righteous; a wicked man with whom it goes well is not wholly wicked.'[97] This answer does not accord with the widely current view that 'a righteous man with whom it is well' is a rare phenomenon, as Rava stated: 'The world was created only (for the following): This world for Ahab the son of Omri, and the world to come for Ḥanina b. Dosa.'[98] Although a man 'with whom it is well' may be 'a wholly righteous person'[99], yet this fact certainly does not *per se* constitute a criterion. Doubts with regard to a man's complete righteousness remain unchanged until his last day.

However, this rule, which recurs in various forms, did not prevent the creation of 'a legend of the righteous', which contains popular motifs alongside literary themes known to us from the folk-tales concerning 'men of God', saints and righteous men from outside the world of the Sages. These were integrated both with the histories of the Patriarchs, the Prophets, and other Biblical figures deemed worthy, and with the stories of men of piety and miracle workers of the time of the Second Temple and of the period of the Tannaim and Amoraim itself.

In our discussion of Providence we have already pointed out that the views of the Tannaim and Amoraim regarding the righteous and the wicked that were named before birth did not result from any compromise with a dualistic outlook. In truth it appears that primarily they emanate from the deeply rooted belief that the existence of the righteous is a condition of the survival of the world. From the verse 'But the righteous is the foundation of the world' (Proverbs x 25) the Tannaim[1] already inferred that 'One righteous man is equivalent to the entire world', and R. Eleazar b. Shammuaʿ explained the Scripture figuratively, declaring that 'the world rests on a single pillar, called "Righteous".'[2]

To a student who spoke up and said 'Master, who is greater, the world or the righteous?' the Patriarch R. Judah, the distinguished disciple of R. Eleazar b. R. Shammuaʿ replied: ' "The righteous." "Why?" (asked the scholar). (The Patriarch answered): "When Jochebed gave birth to Moses he was equivalent to the entire world." And where do we find that Moses was equal to all the people? For it is said "As the Lord commanded Moses and the children of Israel"; and it is also said "Then sang Moses and the children of Israel"; and it is further said "And there hath not arisen a prophet since in

Israel like unto Moses (Deuteronomy xxxiv 10).'' '[3] Rabbi's homily referred in its source to Moses[4], but the inference drawn relative to the relationship between the righteous and the world is of general application. R. Ḥiyya bar Abba transmitted in the name of R. Joḥanan: 'No righteous man departs from this world until another righteous man like him is created, as it is said "The sun also ariseth, and the sun goeth down" — ere the sun of Eli set, the sun of Samuel the Ramathite had arisen.'[5] In this teaching the criterion of 'a righteous man like him' is laid down, but in the name of the same Amora two other dicta are reported, which indicate a progressive decline: 'R. Ḥiyya bar Abba also said in the name of R. Joḥanan: The Holy One, blessed be He, seeing that the righteous were few, proceeded to plant them in each generation, as it is said "For the pillars of the earth are the Lord's, and He hath set the world upon them" (I Samuel ii 8). And R. Ḥiyya bar Abba further said in the name of R. Joḥanan: The world exists even for the sake of one righteous person, as it is said "And the righteous is the foundation of the world." '[6]

However, R. Joḥanan reported a homily in the name of R. Simeon b. Jehozadak which states that the world exists on account of the merit of a given number of righteous men. The expositor links the words of Hosea (iii 2–3) 'So I bought her to me for fifteen pieces of silver and a homer of barley, and a half-homer of barley; and I said unto her: "Thou shalt sit solitary for me..." ' with the verse in Zechariah (xi 12) 'And I said unto them: "If ye think good, give me my hire; and if not, forbear." So they weighed for my hire thirty pieces of silver', giving the following exposition: ' "A homer of barley and a half-homer of barley" — these are the forty-five righteous men on account of whom the world exists. Still I do not know whether thirty are here and fifteen in Eretz-Israel, or thirty in Eretz-Israel and fifteen here. When, however, Scripture states "And I took the thirty pieces of silver, and cast them into the treasury, in the house of the Lord", you must infer that thirty are in Eretz-Israel and fifteen here. Abbaye said: And the majority of them are to be found in the Synagogue called "Under the Balcony".'[7] It is clear that the words 'Still I do not know' etc. belong to the redactor of the Babylonian Talmud, and 'here' means Babylon in antithesis to Eretz-Israel. It also appears that Abbaye's statement should come earlier, for it refers directly to the dictum of R. Simeon b. Jehozadak, and this is what Rashi had in mind in his annotation 'And the majority: of the righteous of Eretz-Israel'.[8]

But the homily of R. Simeon b. Jehozadak was not acceptable to R. Joḥanan. The latter did not expound the verse in Hosea at all allegorically, and on the verse in Zechariah there is reported an authentic dispute between him and Rav: ' "So they weighed for my hire thirty pieces of silver" — Rav said: These are the thirty righteous. Said R. Joḥanan to him: Has not Rav heard that the verse refers only to the Gentile nations? According to Rav "And I said unto them" means to Is[rael]; according to R. Joḥanan "And I said unto them" means to the Gentile nations. In Rav's opinion, when Israel are worthy the majority of them are in Eretz-Israel and the minority in Babylon; but when Israel are unworthy the majority of them are in Babylon and the min[ority] in Eretz-Israel.'[9] According to this tradition the verse in Zechariah, too, was not expounded by R. Joḥanan with reference to the thirty righteous men of Israel, but with regard to the Gentile nations and the thirty commandments that they will accept in the days of the Messiah.

The source of both the view of R. Joḥanan concerning one righteous man as the foundation of the world and of the opinion attributed to Rav, which the former rejects, regarding the thirty righteous men, is to be found in the dictum of R. Simeon b. Yoḥai, whose formulation is paradoxical: 'R. Hezekiah in the name of R. Jeremiah said as follows: R. Simeon b. Yoḥai declared: The world does not lack thirty righteous like Abraham. If there are thirty, my son and I are two of them; if there are twenty, my son and I are two of them; if they are ten, my son and I are two of them; if they are five, my son and I are two of them; if they are two, they are my son and I; if there is (but) one, it is I.'[10]

The conclusion of the dictum, which, like similar sayings, expresses this extraordinary Tanna's consciousness of his own worth, testifies that, although he knows the tradition of the thirty righteous by whose merit the world exists, he does not regard this number as a *sine qua non*. The world can exist even by the merit of one righteous person. However, the concept that a certain number of righteous men was needed became the accepted view of the Palestinian Amoraim in the second half of the fourth century. They found support for the theory in the Pentateuchal story about Abraham, who terminated his prayer for Sodom, when ten righteous men could not be found there (Genesis xviii 13). Furthermore, in the opening verse of the section ואברהם היו יהיה 'Seeing that Abraham shall surely become' the Sages found an allusion to the fact 'that the world does not lack thirty righteous like Abraham'[11], that is, the tradition known to R. Simeon b. Yoḥai.

The Babylonian Amora Abbaye, whom we found reacting to the tradition of R. Simeon b. Jehozadak (above, p. 488) also adopts another fixed number of righteous; however, it is not only the number, but also the definition of the function of these righteous men that is different. 'Abbaye said: The world never lacks thirty-six righteous, who greet the presence of the Shekhina in each generation, as it is said "Happy are they that wait *lô* ['for Him']" (Isaiah xxx 18) — and the numerical value of *lô* is thirty-six.'[12]

It has already been pointed out[13] that the quoted verse can hardly be interpreted to allude to Abbaye's dictum, and that apparently the choice of the number thirty-six righteous, who are vouchsafed to greet the Shekhina, was influenced by the concept prevailing in ancient Egypt[14] with reference to the dominion of the thirty-six *decani*, that is, the thirty-six gods of the sky, who appear in the course of the nights of the year in the vault of heaven. In the astrology of the late Hellenistic system a complete system was evolved that traced the influence of the thirty-six *decani* and their demons on the various organs and parts of man's body. We also know of prayers and supplications offered to the *decani* — many of them still bearing Egyptian names — as demons who protect certain organs.[15]

The Judeo-Hellenistic apocryphal work *The Testament of Solomon*[16] also enumerates thirty-six πνεύματα, which are divided according to the twelve signs of the zodiac and produce diseases in various sections of the human body. It is not to be supposed that Abbaye was the only one among the Amoraim who was acquainted with these beliefs;[17] and apparently even the numbers forty-five and thirty righteous, mentioned by the early Sages, also had the aim of establishing specifically — against the prevailing views of the influence of the thirty-six *decani*-god-demons on man — the power and influence of man. The existence of the entire world depends on a given number of righteous. Possibly the Sages purposely adopted numbers other than thirty-six, when referring to the righteous who live in the world and sustain it.

We have seen that even Abbaye left the number forty-five unchanged and only added his comment on the place where the majority of the righteous of Eretz-Israel are to be found (see above, p. 488). The number thirty-six is mentioned by Abbaye only when those who behold the presence of the Shekhina are spoken of. In relation to this dictum the Talmud cites also the teaching of R. Simeon b. Yoḥai, but there, too, the reference is not to the righteous who sustain this world, but to the group who welcome the presence of the Shekhina[18], of whom R. Simeon b. Yoḥai said: 'I have seen the men of high standing [Heaven-destined] and they are but few: if they number a thousand, my son and I are among them... if they be two, they are my son and I.' These 'Righteous who are destined to welcome the presence of the Shekhina' were compared by R. Simeon b. Yoḥai himself to the stars, and he applied to them[19] the verse 'And they that are wise shall shine as the brightness of the firmament; and they that turn the many to righteousness as the stars for ever and ever' (Daniel xii 3). While the Tanna did not fix the number of these righteous either in heaven or on earth[20] — for the essential point in this dictum, as in the parallel saying, is the emphasis given to the consciousness of his own worth — the Amora Abbaye proceeded to equate the number of the righteous who greet the presence of the Shekhina and resemble the stars with the number of *decani*.

The idea of the dependence of the existence of the world on that of the righteous led to the attempt to solve the problem of theodicy, in so far as the matter relates to the premature death of the righteous and the longevity of the wicked. 'Samuel ha-Qaṭan [the Younger] was asked: What is the meaning of the verse "There is a righteous man that perisheth in his righteousness" (Ecclesiastes vii 15)? He replied: It is fully revealed to Him who spoke and the world came into being that the righteous man would eventually degenerate. Said the Holy One, blessed be He: While he is still righteous, I shall take him away....' With regard to the wicked R. Josaiah said that the Lord shows them forbearance, 'for perchance righteous children may issue from them, for thus we find that He was forbearing with Ahaz and he sired Hezekiah; with Amon, and he begot Josiah; (with) Shimei and Mordecai was descended from him.'[21] The principle also holds good for Gentiles, since from them, too, proselytes and righteous men may come forth.[22]

The nature of the righteous man, who is the foundation of the world, is not expressly defined. The one man who is specifically given the title 'righteous' in the Bible is Noah: 'Noah was a righteous man, blameless in his generation' (Genesis vi 9); 'For I have seen that thou art righteous before me in this generation' (*ibid.* vii 1). Around his personality has been woven a widely ramified Haggada linked to the verses 'This one shall bring us relief from our work and from the toil of our hands...' (*ibid.* v 28), 'But Noah found favour in the eyes of the Lord' (*ibid.* vi 8); but its motifs — like many of those found in the legends of other righteous men of the Bible — are shared by Θεῖος ἀνήρ, the Greek man of God. He is a man beloved of the gods, mediates between them and mortals, and his life has typical features. His birth is announced beforehand and mostly takes place in unusual circumstances and conditions. The man of God matures rapidly in body, spirit, and moral understanding, and he arouses, as an infant or child, the wonder of all who see him. His knowledge comes direct from God. He has wonderful powers at his disposal: he hears and sees hidden things; he knows the secrets of the future; he is able to control both animate and inanimate nature. In his youth people persecute him, but subsequently he appears as a saviour, counsellor, and pleader, and uses his powers for the benefit of mankind, saving people from the wrath of God, warding off natural disasters, and helping the poor and suffering in everyday life. He dies an unnatural death, either as a martyr or a death accompanied by marvels, and miracles are wrought on his body. His death does not mean the cessation of existence but entering into a higher sphere.[23] In *The Book of Enoch* (cvi 1–12) we find a description of the extraordinary nature of the child Noah: 'And his body was white as snow and red as the blooming of a rose, and the hair of his head and his long locks were white as wool, and his eyes beautiful. And when he opened his eyes, he lighted up the whole house like the sun, and the whole house was very bright. And thereupon he arose in the hands of the midwife, opened his mouth, and conversed with the Lord of righteousness.' Lamech, the father of Noah, was frightened and went to his father Methuselah to ask him to find out the meaning of the matter from Enoch. A parallel to the portrayal in the *Book of Enoch* occurs in a Qumran scroll.[24] In the homiletical expositions of the Sages the child Noah is not accorded such an enthusiastic description; possibly the link with the personality of Enoch, whom the Amoraim did not regard as completely righteous,[25] sufficed to oust the legend of Noah's extraordinary birth. On the other hand the Rabbis, cleaving to the Scriptural expression 'This one shall bring us relief', emphasized the idea expounded by R. Joḥanan: 'When the Holy One, blessed be He, created man, He gave him dominion over everything: the cow obeyed the ploughman, the door obeyed the carpenter. When, however, man sinned, God caused them to rebel against him: the cow no longer obeyed the ploughman, nor the door the carpenter. But when Noah arose, they became submissive again.'[26] This motif, that upon the birth of a righteous man good comes to the world, occurs often.[27] Of Isaac we are told: 'When he was born all rejoiced — heaven and earth, sun and moon, and the planets. And why were they glad? For if Isaac had not been created, the world could not have existed!'[28] But the motifs of the apocryphal Haggada of Noah recur in the homilies of the Amoraim on the birth of Isaac and Moses. R. Ḥanina b. Levi said: 'On the day that Isaac was born the Holy One, blessed be He, made the light of the sun's orb forty-eight times as great.'[29] In the name of Rav it is reported that 'When Moses was born, the whole house was filled with light.'[30] In the Midrash that describes Moses' struggle with the angel of death, Moses testifies regarding himself: 'On the day that I was born, I was able to speak and to walk, and I spoke with my father and my mother, and I did not even suck milk. And when I was three months old, I prophesied, declaring that I would receive the Torah from the midst of flaming fire.'[31]

The signs that foretell the birth of the righteous man, his external characteristics, his beauty, his might, even his odour[32] do not yet give assurance that a righteous man is indicated. The decisive proof is to be found in his deeds, as was stated by 'R. Jeremiah in the name of R. Samuel bar R. Isaac: Each day a Heavenly Voice went forth, pealing throughout the world and proclaiming: "A righteous man will arise called Samuel." Thereupon every woman who gave birth to a son named him Samuel, but when they saw his deeds, people would say: "Is this Samuel? This cannot be that Samuel!" But when he [the true Samuel] was born, and people saw his deeds, they said: "It seems that this is he." '[33]

The righteous, by their deeds, bring blessing and prosperity to the world. R. Eleazar b. R. Simeon said: 'I approve the words of R. Jose: So long as the righteous are in the world, there is blessing in the world, but when the righteous depart from the world, blessing too departs from the world.'[34] The reference is to normal material benefits like 'plenty and ease',[35] as well as marvellous happenings and miracles:[36] 'The righteous see from one end of the world to the other.'[37] And not only the Patriarchs ruled over nature and prevailed over its laws, but the sages, righteous, and pious of every generation did so too.[38] Elsewhere we have treated of the nature of these miraculous deeds.[39] We wish to emphasize, however, that many of them are indicative of the heavy demands made on the ideal of the righteous man. The following example will suffice here: 'R. Phinehas b. Jair was once going to the schoolhouse when the river Ginnai was in flood. Said he to it: "Ginnai, why do you prevent me from going to the schoolhouse?" Thereupon it parted before him and he crossed. His disciples then said to him: "Can we cross?" He replied: "Whoever is quite sure that he never acted irresponsibly towards any Jew may cross and will not be harmed." '[40] The righteous man not only controls the laws of nature but also God's decrees, which he has the power to annul.[41] In the spiritual accountancy of the world the righteous man has a special task. With respect to every person R. Simeon b. Eleazar said: 'Because the individual is judged by the majority of his (deeds) and the world is judged by the majority of its (deeds), a man should always regard himself as half innocent and half guilty. If he performs one precept, he is blessed, for he weighed down the scales for himself and the world on the side of merit; if he commits one transgression, woe betide him! for he has weighed down the scales for himself and the world on the side of guilt.'[42]

But the righteous have an additional task: their very existence serves to influence people, for those who draw near to them, even though they do not attain to their level, yet acquire something of their fragrance, and 'it is well with the righteous (and) well with his neighbour.'[43]

However, they must not be content with this. As men of righteousness they must protest against the actions of the wicked, even though their rebuke is of no avail.[44] On the other hand the duty also rests upon them to stand before their creator as defending counsel and advocates for their fellow creatures, for they have it in their power to transform the attribute of justice into the *attribute of compassion*.[45] This power is given them only by virtue of their deeds and loyalty to the Torah and precepts. The righteous person does not become a law and precept unto himself.[46]

We find, however, that the Sages spoke in defence of the sins of the great men of the past, just as they added to the charges against certain prophets and righteous men, accusing them of misdeeds beyond what is expressly attributed to them in Scripture.[47] But we do not find, even among the most zealous defenders, anyone who is prepared to justify the transgressions of the righteous on the ground that they are not really sins, but are misjudged as such by other people who lack understanding.[48] Many attempts were made to extenuate David's crime in the affair of Bathsheba, the most extreme being the contention that 'whoever says David sinned undoubtedly errs... for he intended to do (wrong), but did not', for 'whoever went to battle in the wars of the House of David wrote a bill of divorcement for his wife... and Uriah the Hittite... was guilty of rebellion against the king's orders' (*T.B. Shabbat* 56a). But even R. Samuel bar Naḥmani and R. Jonathan and R. Judah the Patriarch, in whose name this advocacy is reported, never thought for a moment of presenting the transgression as a good deed. They merely discovered extenuating circumstances, and even this approach was rejected by Rav, who observed caustically 'Rabbi who is descended from David tries to whitewash him' (*ibid.*). Rav reduced David's sin by portraying it as a challenge to the Evil Inclination, since the king submitted himself to an ordeal and failed. But primarily he based David's vindication on the suffering and penitence that he accepted,[49] and this is also the traditional method of exoneration: 'The School of R. Ishmael taught: If you have seen a scholar commit a transgression at night, do not think ill of him by day; perhaps he repented.' This is the wording of the Baraita, but the Talmud adds anonymously ' "Perhaps"? Can there be any doubt! Unquestionably he has repented' (*T.B. Berakhot* 19a). We find here confidence that there was repentance; but there is no annulment or minimization of the sin.

However there is not lacking the feeling that there is a decline in the generations, which impairs even the power of the righteous. This feeling is accurately expressed in the following story: 'Invading troops once came to Levi bar Sisi's town. Thereupon he took a scroll of the Torah and went up to the roof-top and said: "Sovereign of the universe, if I left one word of this Book of the Torah unfulfilled let them enter; but if not, let them go!" Forthwith they were sought, but not found. His disciple acted likewise; his hand withered, but they (the invaders) went away. His disciple's disciple did the same; his hand did not wither, nor did they (the troops) leave.'[50]

Together with the stories about the diminution of the power of the revealed and well-known righteous there arose tales about 'covert men of righteousness', simple folk who by one deed won eternity for themselves and brought relief and prosperity to the world. It was disclosed to illustrious Sages in a dream that the prayer of a certain ass-driver, or of a certain theatre decorator and attendant of the dancing girls, would bring down rain. Only subsequently are the good deeds of these righteous men made known.[51]

The activity of the righteous and the influence of their merit do not cease with their death.[52] The covenant that God made with Noah and with the Patriarchs, and which He swore to remember and to fulfil, is due to the merit of the good deeds of the Patriarchs. Their descendants, it is true, are required to keep this covenant, and breaking it brings punishments in its train, as it is written: 'And if ye shall reject My statutes... but break My covenant; I also will do this unto you...' (Leviticus xxvi 15). But the punishment will not go so far as the annulment of the covenant itself on the part of God (*ibid.*, *v.* 44). To the merit of the early Patriarchs are added those of the righteous in every generation. On the respective share to be accredited to the deeds of the living generations and to the merits of former generations in preventing the abolition of the covenant, and likewise in the acts of salvation and redemption, there are differences of opinion between the Sages since the time of Shemaʿya and Avṭalyon. 'Shemaʿya said: The trust that their father Abraham reposed in Me suffices that I should divide the sea for them, as it is said "And he believed in the

Lord; and He counted it to him for righteousness" (Genesis xv 6). Avṭalyon said: sufficient is the trust that they reposed in Me that I should divide the sea for them, as it is said "And the people believed and when they heard..." (Exodus iv 31).'[53] There is a similar dispute between R. Joshua and R. Eleazar of Modiʿim, when they came to interpret the section of the manna. ' "Then said the Lord unto Moses: 'Behold, I will [הנני *hinnĕnî*] cause to rain... for you.' " R. Joshua said: The Holy One, blessed be He, said to Moses: "Behold, I shall reveal Myself forthwith and shall not delay." R. Eleazar of Modiʿim said: The text says *hinnĕnî* — only on account of the merit of Abraham, Isaac, and Jacob. "For you." R. Joshua said: It is assuredly due only to you. R. Eleazar of Modiʿim said: Scripture says "for you" — only because of the merit of Abraham, Isaac, and Jacob.'[54] There is a similar difference of opinion between the two Tannaim in connection with the section of Amalek.

Avṭalyon, R. Joshua, and the long series of Tannaim who ascribed the miracles and salvations to the merit of Israel's deeds[55], and not to that of the Patriarchs, were afraid of too much reliance on this merit and the consequent weakening of the sense of duty and of the need to fulfil the commandments. The subject is explained in the Midrashic exposition that was taught in the School of R. Ishmael: 'Should you ask: Why do the Gentiles, who ser[ve] strange gods, worship idols, and prostrate themselves to images, continue to live? (The answer is:) On account of the merit of Noah, as [it is said] "While the earth remaineth" etc. (Genesis viii 22). When will this covenant be annulled? When day and night will cease, as [it is said]: "While the earth remaineth", "And there shall be one day, it is known to the Lord" etc. (Zechariah xiv 7). Now we might argue from minor to major: If the Gentiles, who are idolaters, live because of the merit of Noah, shall not we live on account of the merit of Abraham, Isaac, and Jacob? Therefore Scr[ipture] tea[ches] us "If thou shalt keep all this commandment" — it is the reward of the commandment that gives you life, not the merit of the Patriarchs.'[56] However, no difference in principle is to be inferred here between the School of R. Ishmael and the School of R. Akiba, for we find Tannaim from both schools who stress the value of the merit of the Patriarchs,[57] and also Sages who base everything on the fulfilment of the commandment, while others conjoin the merit of the Patriarchs with that of observing the precepts.[58] In this spirit the Amora R. Avin also expounded the prayer of Moses after the episode of the golden calf: ' "Remember Abraham". Why did Moses mention here the three Patriarchs?... The Holy One, blessed be He, said to Moses: "I require of you ten, just as I did of Sodom. Point to ten righteous men among them, and I shall not destroy them." He replied: "Sovereign of the universe, I shall do so. There is myself, Aaron, Eleazar, Ithamar, Phinehas, Joshua, and Caleb." Said God to him: "These make seven; where are the (other) three?" (Moses) did not know what to do. (Then) he said to God: "Sovereign of the universe, are the dead alive?" He replied: "They are." (Thereupon) he [Moses] said: "If the dead live, remember Abraham, Isaac, and Jacob." These make ten. Hence he [Moses] mentioned the three Patriarchs.'[59] Here the merit of the Patriarchs serves only to complete the minimum number of righteous requisite for the deliverance of Israel from annihilation. In an anonymous homily God promises Abraham: 'From your seed I shall raise up shields of righteous men; furthermore, when your children will come to commit transgressions and evil deeds, I shall see one righteous man among them, who can say "Enough!" to the attribute of justice, (and) I shall take him and grant them atonement (on account of him).'[60]

Alongside the views that attribute the salvations of the past either to the deeds of those who possessed their own merits, or to the merit of the Patriarchs, or to the merit of both, we find yet another opinion, which ascribes them to the merit of the promises and the great deeds of the future. R. Ishmael himself declared: ' "Wherefore criest thou unto Me?" On account of [בזכות, *bizĕkhût*] Jerusalem I shall divide the sea for them....'[61] An anonymous preacher expounded the verse: ' "And the waters were a wall unto them on their right hand, and on their left" — Who caused Israel to be delivered? "On their right hand, and on their left"; "on their right hand", on account of the Torah, which they were destined to receive on their right, as it is said "At His right hand was a fiery law unto them"; "and on their left" — this refers to the phylactery [תפלה *tĕfillā*, sing.]. Another interpretation is: "On their right hand, and on their left" — "on their right hand" refers to the *mĕzûzā* that the Israelites would affix, "and on their left" refers to the phylacteries [תפילין *tĕfillîn*, plural].'[62] The underlying thought in these and similar dicta[63] is that historical happenings, like the redemption from Egypt or the parting of the Sea of Reeds, are not dependent on a tally of reward and punishment of the nation at the time concerned, but serve to bring near the ultimate goal that the Lord appointed for His people. The idea is repeated in the following form: 'And the Sages say: For the sake of His name did He act thus towards them, as it is said "For Mine own sake, for Mine own sake, will I do it" (Isaiah xlviii 11), and it is (also) written "That divided the water before them" (*ibid.* lxiii 12). For what reason? "To make Himself an everlasting name."'[64] From a later Midrash we learn that R. Nehemiah was the Tanna who said that the Israelites went forth from Egypt 'on account of the Torah that they were due to receive.'[65] From the concept that on account of future happenings previous generations were vouchsafed Divine grace, some Amoraim drew the conclusion that the righteous of later generations are also able to help their ancestors by their merit. They transformed the merit of the sires into that of the scions, and they said that the Israelites went forth from Egypt because of the merit of the generation of Isaiah or on account of Hananiah, Mishael, and Azariah.[66]

The dispute among the Tannaim regarding the place and importance of the merit of the fathers was not confined to the history of the nation as a whole, but also had a bearing on the nature and destiny of the individual.

In keeping with his view concerning Providence R. Akiba taught: 'The father endows the son with beauty, strength, wealth, wisdom, and (length of) years....'[67] In agreement with R. Akiba's doctrine, Rabban Gamaliel, the son of R. Judah the Patriarch, taught in the Mishnah: 'And let all who labour with the community labour with them for the sake of Heaven, for the merit of their fathers helps them and their righteousness endures for ever....'[68] In the spirit of these teachings it was related of R. Akiba himself in connection with the appointment of R. Eleazar b. Azariah as Patriarch: 'And R. Akiba sat grieving and said: Not that he is more learned in the Torah than I, but his family tree is nobler than mine. Blessed is the man who has ancestral merit; blessed is the man who has a peg to hang on.' And the narrator explains: 'What now was R. Eleazar b. Azariah's peg? He was the tenth generation in descent from Ezra.'[69] This dictum explains why it was said at the beginning of the age of the Amoraim that the Patriarchs are 'three great pegs in the world',[70] that is to say, that the world rests upon them, and this was the purport of R. Simeon b. Laqish's words, when he said that the Patriarchs are 'a throne with three pegs', and of his dictum that 'It is the Patriarchs who constitute the Chariot.'[71]

Just as we find Shemaʿya disagreeing with the opinion of Avṭalyon that the redemption from Egypt came on account of Abraham's faith, so we have ancient testimonies to a point of view that disputes R. Akiba's opinion, at least in the period close to his own time. The polemical character of the following Tannaitic homily is quite evident: ' "And there is none that can deliver out of My hand" — fathers cannot deliver their sons: Abraham cannot deliver Ishmael, and Isaac cannot deliver Esau. We have thus learned only that fathers cannot deliver sons. How do we know that brothers cannot save brothers? Scripture teaches us "No man can by any means redeem his brother" (Psalms xlix 8) — Isaac cannot deliver Ishmael, and Jacob cannot deliver Esau. And though he be given all the money in the world, he is not granted his atonement [כפרו *kofrô*, literally 'ransom'], as it is said "No man can by any means redeem his brother, nor give to God a ransom for himself [כפרו *kofrô*], for too precious is the redemption of their soul, and must be let alone for ever" (*ibid. vv.* 8–9) — too precious is the soul, for when a man sins he cannot compensate for it.'[72] We apparently encounter unmitigated opposition to the concept of ancestral merit in *IV Ezra*. To the question 'Whether in the Day of Judgement the righteous shall be able to intercede for the ungodly, or to entreat the Most High in their behalf' the angel that spoke to him answered him: '...Even as now a father may not send a son, or a son his father, or a master his slave... that in his stead he may be ill, or sleep, or be healed; so shall none then pray for another on the Day, neither shall one lay a burden on another; for then every one shall bear his own righteousness or unrighteousness.'[73]

However, the very manner in which the opposition is expressed shows how deeply the belief in the merit of the fathers was rooted. Characteristic is the story in *Liber Antiquitatum Biblicarum* ascribed to Philo. Before Deborah's death the people cry: 'Mother, you are dying and forsaking your children!... Pray for us, and after your death let your soul remember us forever.' Deborah answers the people: 'So long as a person lives, he can pray for himself and for his sons, but after his death he cannot pray for others, nor can he remember them. Put not your trust in your ancestors, they will not profit you, if you be not like them.'[74] Here a chink of compromise is opened, for it is possible to infer that if they will be like them (their ancestors) they will profit them, in the sense of 'Blessed is the man who has a peg to hang on'. However, the objections raised to reliance on the merit of the fathers did not succeed in diminishing its significance or centrality. It even found support in other principles and the difficulties they entailed. The righteous, who were not vouchsafed their reward in this world, not only stored up for themselves treasures of reward in the world to come, but, in the view of Amoraim like R. Simon and R. Phinehas, also accumulated merits for the benefit of future generations. Of a man who gives alms or performs a precept and asks for the reward thereof at once, R. Simon said that is 'like a man who says: Here is a sack, and a *sela*ʿ, and a *se'a*, proceed to measure out! You can see that this is so, for if the fathers of the world had sought to receive the reward of the precepts that they performed in this world, how could there have existed merit for their children after them? This is the meaning of Moses' words to Israel "Then will I remember My covenant, with Jacob" etc.'[75] R. Phinehas expounded the verse ' "Hand to hand, the evil man shall not be unpunished" (Proverbs xi 21): If a man performs a precept in this world and seeks to receive his reward for it at once... he is wicked, and leaves nothing for his children.'[76] These Amoraim obligate the righteous man not to settle the account of his reward, but to see to it that those who succeed them have merit.

Without doubt these views are connected with the evaluation of acts of martyrdom since the time of the religious persecution under Hadrian, which led as we have shown elsewhere[77], to past events being interpreted retrospectively. Some of those who endowed the generations with merit were also appraised by their act of martyrdom. Not only were Hananiah, Mishael, and Azariah[78] placed on the same plane as the three Patriarchs, but the attitude to the Patriarchs themselves likewise changed.

The Tanna R. Jose the Galilean does not ascribe the parting of the Sea of Reeds to Abraham's faith in general, but to the act of the *ʿĂqēdā* ['the binding of Isaac', i.e. his attempted sacrifice], and he depicts the scene dramatically: 'When the Israelites went into the sea, Mount Moriah had already moved from its place, with Isaac's altar built upon it, and the faggots arranged on it, and Isaac as it were bound and lying on the altar, and Abraham as it were stretching out his hand and holding the knife to slaughter his son.'[79]

While in the Pentateuchal story the hero of the *ʿĂqēdā* is Abraham, and even in the benediction in the ancient order of service for fast days recorded in the Mishna (*M. Taʿanit* ii, 4) it is still stated 'May He that answers Abraham on Mount Moriah answer you...', in the tradition of the age of the Hadrianic persecutions, and especially in that of the succeeding period, Abraham is more and more ousted in favour of Isaac, the victim himself.[80] The latter is not only made a full partner in the test — ' "So they went both of them together": the one to bind and the other to be bound, the one to slaughter and the other to be slaughtered'[81] but, furthermore, the ordeal is accounted an act. Consequently Isaac became the real hero of the epic. In one of the earliest sources that testify to this change the motif is linked to a dispute that bears upon the very subject of merit: ' "And when I see the blood" — R. Ishmael said: But is not everything fully revealed to Him... wherefore, then, does Scripture say "And when I see the blood"? The meaning is that on account of the precepts that they perform He reveals Himself unto them and takes pity on them... Another explanation is: "And when I see the blood" — I see the blood of Isaac's *ʿĂqēdā*, as it is said "And Abraham called the name of that place *Adonay-yir'e* ['the Lord seeth']" etc. (Genesis xxii 14); and subsequently it is stated "The Lord beheld, and He repented Him of the evil" (I Chronicles xxi 15) — what did He see? The blood of Isaac's *ʿĂqēdā*.'[82] While R. Ishmael ascribes the deliverance of the first-born of Israel to the merit of the precepts that they fulfilled, an anonymous expositor — his contemporary or a scholar of the succeeding generation — attributes the salvation not to the merits of the fathers in general, but to the merit of Isaac and that of 'the blood of his *ʿĂqēdā*', as though it had actually been shed. Similarly another Tannaitic homily speaks of the ashes of Isaac. With respect to the verse 'Then will I remember My covenant with Jacob, and also My covenant with Isaac, and also My covenant with Abraham will I remember' (Leviticus xxvi 42) the expositor asks: 'Why is remembering mentioned relative to Abraham and Jacob, but not with regard to Isaac? The reason is that his ashes are regarded as lying heaped up on the altar.'[83] While in the Mishna proper we find no allusion to Isaac in the order of service for fast-days, there were Amoraim who introduced it into the Mishna by their interpretation: 'The ark is brought forth into the open place of the city and wood ashes are placed on the ark. R. Judan the son of R. Manasseh and R. Samuel bar Naḥman (differ with regard to the reason): one said in order to recall the merit of Abraham, and the other said in order to recall the merit of Isaac. The one who said in order to recall the merit of Abraham (permits the use of) either dust or ashes, in accordance with (the verse) "I who am but dust and ashes" (Genesis xviii 27); the one who said in order to recall the merit[84] of Isaac (allows the use of) ashes only, Isaac's ashes being regarded as heaped upon the altar.'

The verse in Chronicles (i Chronicles xxi 15), which served in Tannaitic Midrash as proof that the Lord beheld on the night of the plague of the first-born 'the blood of the *ʿĂqēdā* of Isaac', is differently interpreted by Rav and Samuel: ' "And as He was about to destroy, the Lord beheld, and He repented Him of the evil." What did He see? Rav said: He beheld our father Jacob... and Samuel said: It was the ashes of Isaac that He saw....'[85] Thus the Tannaim and early Amoraim used the expression 'the blood of the *ʿĂqēdā* of Isaac' and 'the ashes of Isaac' as synonyms for 'the merit of Isaac'.

It is true that R. Isaac Nappaḥa ['the smith'], R. Joḥanan's disciple, did not employ the phrase 'as though', and in answer to the question how did those who returned from Babylonia know the site of the altar, he answered 'They beheld the ashes of Isaac lying on that site'.[86] Nevertheless it was undoubtedly not his intention to imply that Isaac was actually burned at the time of the *ʿĂqēdā*, but that 'the ashes of the ram' took his place. R. Isaac's teaching is thus explained in a homily based on an exposition of R. Banna'a, one of the last of the Tannaim[87]: 'Since Scripture tells us that Abraham "took the ram, and offered him up for a burnt-offering" (Genesis xxii 13), is not the verse quite complete? What then is the meaning (of the words) "in the stead of his son"? Abraham said: "Sovereign of the universe, I am slaughtering the ram, look upon it as if my son were slain before Thee." When he took its blood, he said "Look upon it as if Isaac's blood were sprinkled before Thee." When he took the ram and flayed it, he said to Him: "Look upon it as if Isaac's skin had been flayed before Thee upon the altar." When he burned it, he said to Him: "Look upon it as if his ashes were heaped before Thee on the altar." '[88] Isaac's willingness to be bound and slaughtered and burned was accounted an act, and the acts performed to his substitute — the ram — were deemed as though they had been done to him; thus the Sages spoke of the blood of his *ʿĂqēdā*, and the ashes of the ram were regarded as his ashes.

From being a story about Abraham's ordeal, the episode of the *ʿĂqēdā* evolved, in the dicta of the Tannaim and Amoraim, into an account of Isaac's atonement. R. Banna'a's disciple, the great Amora R. Joḥanan himself, put in Abraham's mouth an explanation of the story of the *ʿĂqēdā*, whose sole purpose was to provide a defence for Israel: 'R. Bevai the Great stated in the name of R. Joḥanan: Abraham said to the Holy One, blessed be He: Sovereign of the universe, it is well known to Thee that when Thou didst enjoin me to offer up my son Isaac, I could have countered and replied: But yesterday Thou didst tell me "For in Isaac shall seed be called to Thee", yet now Thou dost command me "Offer him there for a burnt offering!" Did I — Heaven forfend! — disobey Thee? No! I suppressed my inclination and did Thy will. So be it Thy will, O Lord my God, that when the descendants of Isaac, my son, find themselves in trouble, and have no one to plead their cause, do Thou defend them. "The Lord seeth": Remember unto them the *ʿĂqēdā* of their father Isaac and be filled with compassion for them.'[89]

In the light of what has been stated it is not surprising that the Tannaitic pronouncements against dependence upon ancestral merit[90] did not meet with much success. As we have already indicated, the idea of the merit of the fathers became permanently entrenched in the prayers of the fast days and of the Day of Judgement, that is, New Year. R. Levi in the name of R. Ḥama Ḥanina used the following analogy: 'It is like the son of a king who had a lawsuit before his father. Said his father to him: "If you wish to win the suit before me, appoint so-and-so as your advocate (νικολόγους — successful pleader), and you will win the case before me." Even so did the Holy One, blessed be He, say to Israel: "My children, if you will cite the merit of your fathers, you will win the suit before Me." '[91] The verse Leviticus xxiii 24 is expounded allegorically: ' "One [usually rendered 'First']" — this refers to our father Abraham, "Abraham was one" (Ezekiel xxxiii 24). "A memorial proclaimed with the blast of horns" — this refers to our father Isaac, "And he looked, and behold behind him a ram caught in the thicket by his horns" (Genesis xxii 13). "A holy convocation" (Leviticus, *loc. cit.*) — this refers to our father Jacob, "Hearken unto Me, O Jacob, and Israel My called" (Isaiah xlviii 12). When shall you cite the merit of the fathers and succeed in your plea before Me? "In the seventh month" (Leviticus, *loc. cit.*).'[92]

There were indeed Amoraim who attempted to fix a date: 'How long did the merit of the fathers avail?' Some ascribed to R. Ḥiyya the view[93] that (the benefits of) ancestral merit ceased in the days of Joahaz; Samuel said that it continued till the time of Hosea. R. Joshua b. Levi said 'until the time of Elijah', and R. Judah said 'until the age of Hezekiah'. Actually the view of R. Aḥa was accepted, namely that 'The merit of the fathers endures for ever; "for the Lord thy God is a merciful God... and will not forget the covenant of thy fathers" (Deuteronomy iv 31)'[94], only the demand for Torah study and the observance of the precepts was added thereto.

Paradoxically, those who bestowed merit on the community were themselves sent, after their great deeds of martyrdom, to study Torah in the schools of their contemporaries. From the time that Hananiah, Mishael, and Azariah arose from the fiery furnace, they are no longer mentioned. To the question 'Whither did they go?' R. Joshua b. Levi replied: 'They changed their abode and went to Joshua b. Jehozadak to study Torah.' In a similar manner R. Berechiah expounded in the name of the Rabbis of Babylonia: ' "So Abraham returned unto his young men": Where now was Isaac?... (Abraham) sent him to Shem to study Torah.'[95]

The early Amoraim were not unconscious of the problem that both ways — both that which depends on ancestral merit and that which derives from the power of precepts fulfilled and good deeds performed — lack completeness and may even be dubious from the viewpoint of the integrity of faith and devotion. R. Joḥanan said in the name of R. Jose b. Zimra:[96] 'Whoever makes (his prayer) depend on his own merit, (his salvation) is attributed to the merit of others; and whoever makes (his prayer) depend on the merit of tohers, (his salvation) is attributed to his own merit. Moses made (his prayer) depend on others, as it is said "Remember Abraham, Isaac, and Israel thy servants" (Exodus xxxii 13), (hence the salvation) was attributed to his own merit, as it is said "Therefore He said that He would destroy them, had not Moses His chosen stood before Him in the breach to turn back His wrath, lest He destroy them" (Psalms cvi 23). Hezekiah made (his prayer) depend on his own merit, as it is written "Remember now, I beseech Thee, how I have walked before Thee" (II Kings xx 3), (therefore the salvation) was ascribed to the merit of others, as it is written "For I will defend this city to save it, for Mine own sake and for My servant David's sake" (*ibid.* xix 34).' Here R. Joḥanan expresses opposition to reliance on one's own merit. On the other hand Resh Laqish terms those who rely on ancestral merit as 'those who come with power', or 'those who come with a (mighty) arm'.[97]

R. Abbahu states, in connection with the interpretation of the verse, ' "Hearken unto Me, ye stout-hearted, that are far from charity": R. Joḥanan and Resh Laqish differ. One said: The whole world come [to ask Heaven for sustenance] as an act of charity, whereas these come with power [with good deeds and precepts]; the other said: All the benefits and consolations that are vouchsafed to the world are bestowed on account of their merit, but they themselves derive no benefit from them; for example, Mar Zuṭra, who, when praying for others, was answered, but for himself he was not answered.'[98] The first view is apparently that of Resh Laqish. He holds that 'the stout-hearted' is an epithet for the righteous, who come on the strength of their good deeds, and do not have to rely on the Lord's grace and charity, which are vouchsafed on account of ancestral merit. The second view is that of R. Joḥanan. 'The stout-hearted' are those who keep far from their own righteousness and do not benefit from it, but bestow the merit upon their generation. A similar opinion was also held by Rav, in whose name Rav Judah transmits the dictum: 'Every day a Heavenly Voice goes forth and declares: The whole world is sustained on account of My son Ḥanina, yet My son Ḥanina is content with a *kab* of carobs from one Sabbath eve to the other.'[99] The merit of the righteous avails others but not themselves. The righteous, by their deeds, arouse the Lord's charity, which is His attribute of compassion, or — in the phraseology of the Midrash that we have cited above — they are able to say 'to the attribute of justice — "Enough!" '.[1] This power and right were given to them by the covenant made with the Patriarchs. The merit of the fathers consists in the direction of the later generations towards their Father in heaven. The prophet (Isaiah lxiii 16) declares: 'For Thou art our Father; for Abraham knoweth us not, and Israel doth not acknowledge us; Thou, O Lord, art our Father, our Redeemer from everlasting is Thy name.' According to their simple sense, these words represent a rejection of the concept of the merit of the fathers and its power. The homily of R. Samuel bar Naḥman in the name of R. Jonathan does not divest the verse of this meaning, but in a dramatic manner, which is not devoid of humour, actually makes Isaac, the outstanding exemplar of the idea of ancestral merit, as its hero, although he is nowhere mentioned in the passage. And this is how he expounded the Scripture: (In the time to come the following dialogue will take place): 'The Holy One, blessed be He, says to Abraham: "Your children have sinned against Me." He answers Him: "Sovereign of the universe, let them be blotted out for the sanctification of Thy name."[2] God then says: I shall speak to Jacob, who knew the tribulation of parenthood; perhaps he will entreat for them. The Lord tells him: "Your children have sinned." He answered Him: "Sovereign of the universe, let them be blotted out for the sanctification of Thy name." To this God replies: "There is no reason in old men and no counsel in children." He then says to Isaac: "Your children have sinned against Me." Isaac thereupon answers God: "Sovereign of the universe, my children and not Thy children? ... If Thou wilt bear them all, well and good; but if not, let half be upon me and half upon Thee. And shouldst Thou say they are all my responsibility, behold, I have offered up my life unto Thee." (Thereupon) they (the children of Israel) begin to say "For thou art our father...." But Isaac says to them "Instead of praising me, praise the Holy One, blessed be He." Forthwith they all begin to proclaim "Thou, O Lord, art our Father; our Redeemer from everlasting is Thy name." '[3]

Taking account of the merit of the Patriarchs represents the grace and righteousness of God. But these again are vouchsafed only to those who are willing to cleave to good deeds. This thought finds expression in the dictum transmitted in the name of the Palestinian Haggadist of the fourth century, R. Berechiah: 'R. Judan bar Ḥanan in the name of R. Berechiah stated: The Holy One, blessed be He, said to Israel: "My children, if you see the merit of the Patriarchs declining and the merit of the Matriarchs tottering, go and cleave to lovingkindness. What is the reason for this? 'For the mountains may depart' (Isaiah liv 10). — this refers to the merit of the Patriarchs; 'and the hills totter' — this refers to the Matriarchs. From now on 'But My kindness shall not depart from thee, neither shall My covenant of peace decline [E.V. 'be removed'], saith the Lord that hath compassion on thee". '[4] When men on their part forsake lovingkindness, this causes the merit of the fathers to decline, whereas the renewal of devotion to lovingkindness can bring about the renewal of the merit. R. Berechiah sums up the compromise approach that we have found in the teaching of many of his predecessors (above, p. 497). On the other hand, Rava expounded the verse 'Come, now, and let us reason together' (Isaiah i 18) in a manner that stresses the disinclination of Israel to rely on the merits of the fathers. This attitude vouchsafes them the Lord's answer: 'Since you have relied upon Me, "Though your sins be as scarlet, they shall be as white as snow".'[5]

Above (p. 499) we have dwelt on the view that sought to explain the acts of redemption in the past as due to the merit of the righteous who were due to be born; in other words: the living endowed the dead with merit. This concept is not far removed from the notion that the living are able to atone for the sins of the dead. Indeed, this question also formed a subject of discussion in the schools of the Amoraim in both Eretz-Israel and Babylon in the wake of the expositions of the Tannaim. With reference to the prayer of the priests, when the heifer's neck was broken (Deuteronomy xxi 1 ff), 'Forgive, O Lord, Thy people Israel, whom Thou hast redeemed', the Sages said: '(The words) "whom Thou hast redeemed" teach us that this act of expiation atones for those who went forth from Egypt. "Forgive Thy people" — this refers to the living; "whom Thou hast redeemed" — this refers to the dead. Scripture teaches us that the dead need atonement, and we learn at the same time that he that sheds blood sins as far back as those who went forth from Egypt.'[6] The sin of shedding blood rests also on the fathers and on the fathers' fathers of the murderer, and the atonement for the living is likewise an expiation for the dead. The Tanna R. Judah declared with reference to the verse Ezra viii 35: ' "The children of the captivity, that were to come out of exile, offered burnt-offerings unto the God of Israel" — they brought them for (the sin of) idolatry.' Rav Judah explained his statement in the name of Samuel thus: 'for the idolatry that obtained in the days of Zedekiah'. In answer to the objection 'But those who sinned are dead!' Rav Papa explained: 'The tradition that a sin-offering whose owner has died must be left to die applies only to the offering of an individual but not to that of a community, because a community does not die.' The Talmud seeks to trace the source of the distinction drawn by Rav Papa and eventually suggests the homily in the passage of the *Sifre*, quoted above in regard to the calf whose neck was broken, but this conjecture is rejected, because the calf whose neck was broken comes primarily to atone for the living 'and since it atones for the living, it also atones for the dead'.[7] The conclusion of the Talmudic discussion is that the act in the days of Ezra was based on 'a temporary ruling'. However, despite the conclusion of the Gemara that there is no expiation even for a community of dead, this belief was not entirely ousted, and it emerges in various sources even with reference to individuals.

The early Amoraim already sought the reason for the fact that the Mishna did not include Ahaz among the kings who have no portion in the world to come. In the Palestinian Talmud[8] it is stated: 'R. Hoshaiah the Great said: Because his father was righteous. But was not Manasseh's father righteous? In the case of Manasseh, his father was righteous, but his son was wicked... in the case of Ahaz, both his father and his son were righteous; this is the meaning of the verse "My hand upon it! the evil man shall not be unpunished, but the seed of righteous men shall escape" — Scripture does not state here that "the seed of the righteous man shall escape", but that "the seed of righteous men shall escape", that is, seed placed between two righteous men shall escape.' This explanation, namely, that the merit of the father and the merit of the son combine to endow him that is between them with merit, is cited also in the discussion of the Babylonian Talmud[9] on this subject in the name of R. Jeremiah bar Abba, but there the text continues: 'Why did the Sages not include Amon? In deference to Josiah. Let Manasseh, then, also not be included in deference to Hezekiah? A son's merit can protect his father, but a father's merit cannot protect a son, as it is written "And there is none that can deliver out of My hand" — Abraham cannot deliver Ishmael....' Thus the Sages accept the view of the Baraita cited above (p. 500), which rejects the idea of ancestral merit, but affirm the view that sons protect their fathers with their merit after the latters' death. This concept already found expression in the laws of honouring parents, as they are taught in the following Baraita: 'The Sages taught: (the son) honours him (the father) in his lifetime and honours him in death... How does he do so in death? When he states a tradition in his name, he must not say "Thus my father said", but "Thus said my father, my teacher. May I be an atonement for his resting place!" '[10]

Atonement for the dead by the living was not restricted to sons only. Thus the Sages in the Babylonian Talmud declared that David's prayer availed to endow his son Absalom with merit and bring him to life in the world to come.[11] In a late Midrash it is stated generally: 'Should you say that having descended into Gehenna, one can no longer ascend, (this is not so). When intercession is made for him, he is cast out from Gehenna.'[12] In the spirit of this concept, there was added to the homily on the calf whose neck was broken: ' "Whom Thou hast redeemed" — this refers to those who are atoned for by the alms of the living', but already in the Middle Ages they noted that this is an interpolation[13] intended to justify the prevailing custom.

We shall conclude our exposition of the idea of the sons' endowing their fathers with merit by examining a notion that seemingly accords with the essence of our concept, but actually gives it a meaning at variance with its accepted signification. 'R. Simeon b. Yoḥai said: If one has a son that toils in the Torah, it is as though he never died....'[14] It is not said that he enables him by his merit to attain to life in the world to come, or that he delivers him from retribution,[15] but that he continues his life, so to speak. Here we return to the old conception that a man's reward is to be found in his life in this world.

This concept lies at the base of the ancient laws of inheritance, and Ben-Sira gave expression to it in the words 'When his father dieth he dieth not altogether, for he hath left one behind him like himself. In his life he saw and rejoiced, and in death he hath not been grieved. Against enemies he hath left behind an avenger, and to friends one that requiteth favour.'[16] But, while former generations regarded the surviving heir and the inheritance as constituting a name and memorial to the dead, the Tanna mentioned above found this only in the son who toiled in the Torah. This very toil of the sons, without any special acts or prayers designed to expiate the sins of the deceased or to bestow merit upon them, was a continuation of the life of the fathers. The dictum of R. Simeon b. Yoḥai, whose meaning we have just attempted to understand, may be taken as a logical sequel to this Sage's daring statement about the ability of himself and his son not only to reinstate and exempt from judgement the generations to come, but also the preceding generations.[17] Generations, like that of Simeon b. Yoḥai, who accepted the yoke of the Torah and precepts, justify the existence of the previous generations.

We have already observed (above, p. 498) that the Tannaim R. Ishmael and R. Nehemiah professed the doctrine that attributes the redemptions and salvations that were wrought for the nation in the past to the merit of the later generations. R. Simeon b. Yoḥai gave this concept an individual character; following in his footsteps certain Amoraim reversed the merit of the fathers. R. Samuel bar Naḥman[18] declared that Abraham 'was delivered from the fiery furnace only on account of the merit of our father Jacob... that is the meaning of the verse "Therefore thus saith the Lord concerning the house of Jacob, who redeemed Abraham" (Isaiah xxix 22) — Jacob redeemed Abraham.' In Babylon a similar exposition was transmitted in the name of Rav.[19]

VIII. Interpretations of Theodicy

The themes included in this chapter are the constituent elements of the spiritual stocktaking of the world and of the individual Jew. But even when the individual does this accounting from his own point of view, he is unable to overlook the fact that he is the son of the Lord's people, which was chosen from the family of nations, and that a covenant was made with him to keep the Torah. On each of the subjects treated in this chapter we found differences of opinion. Nor is there lacking parallelism between the conclusions reached by the Sages regarding one subject and those concerning another, and they certainly sought to reconcile contradictions between verses. But their explanations are not to be appraised as merely apologetic interpretations.[20] It is true that the views and conclusions arrived at by the Tannaim and Amoraim as a result of their own experiences helped them to explain Biblical passages. The actual existence of 'three successive generations of wicked men'[21] served to exemplify the truth of the verse 'visiting the iniquity of the fathers upon the children' (Exodus xx 5), but it ceased to be a binding postulate after they observed that there were also sons of the wicked who were righteous. R. Jose bar Ḥanina said: 'Four decrees did Moses, our teacher, impose upon Israel, but four prophets came and abrogated them... Moses said "visiting the iniquity of the fathers upon the children"; came Ezekiel and revoked it: "The soul that sinneth, it shall die" (Ezekiel xviii 4).'[22] But even Ezekiel's declaration, which, according to the Amora, invalidated the unfavourable decree contained in Moses' statement, was not accepted as a rule that applied at all times and in all circumstances, for, as we have seen, the martyrs who prayed for the moment when they could fulfil the precept 'and with all thy soul', testified against it. And as against the view that 'There is no death without sin', many held the doctrine that 'There is death without sin, and there is suffering without iniquity.'[23] R. Jose b. R. Ḥanina, or another Amora, could have continued in the style of the above homily and said: The prophet Ezekiel decreed that every man should die for his own sin, but R. Akiba came and repealed the decree....

The truth 'that there is no family containing a publican that may not be deemed to consist wholly of publicans, or one that contains robbers that may not be considered to consist wholly of robbers, because they protect him'[24] R. Simeon b. Yoḥai was able to learn from his personal experience, for his father Yoḥai held a position in the Roman police administration;[25] and indeed there were in his days, as in all ages, families that protected transgressors in their midst. But it is clear that even R. Simeon b. Yohai did not regard this experience as a rule, but it sufficed to interpret the verses 'And if the people of the land do at all hide their eyes from that man, when he giveth of his seed unto Molech, and put him not to death; then I will set My face against that man, and against his family, and will cut him off...' (Leviticus xx 4–5). The realities of life justify the punishment of the family, for there are families that cover up for their members; yet our sense of justice demands that the punishment meted out to the family should not be as severe as that of the transgressor. In truth the Tanna continues his exposition as follows: 'I might have thought that his family should also be liable to *kārēt* [death by Divine visitation, premature death]. Therefore Scripture states "him" — he (the offender) is to be punished by *kārēt*, but not his family, upon whom only pains are inflicted.'[26] In this part the exposition is tied to the Scriptural text, to wit, that the sinner who did not receive his due punishment at the hands of the earthly court will receive it at the hands of Heaven, either in the form of the death of *kārēt* or — according to the Sages who mitigated the punishment of the family — through suffering. But in the first part of this exposition[27] we find the concept that sin carries within itself the factor that operates the punishment. Needless to say, the deductions have but a flimsy basis in the verse: ' "And if hide they will hide" [this is the literal meaning of the words rendered above 'do at all hide']: How do we know that if they connive at one thing, they will in the end connive at many things? Therefore Scripture declares "if hide they will hide". And how do we know that if one court connived, in the end many courts will connive? Therefore Scripture states "if hide they will hide". And how do we know that if the tribal high courts [Sanhedrins][28] connived, in the end the Great Sanhedrin of Israel will connive, and they will be deprived of the right to judge capital cases? Hence it is written "And if hide they will hide".'

Weakness on the part of the court and its connivance at one offence brings in its train the collapse of the entire judiciary and the system of justice among the people. However, not only dereliction of duty by the custodians of law and justice involves penalties affecting the public as a whole, but, as we have seen, even the sin of an individual leads to the infliction of retribution upon the entire community. Numerous examples may be given, but for the present we shall only indicate that this idea is also represented in the homily dealing with the sin of Molech, from which we have quoted the preceding expositions. This concept was also read into the verse: ' "Because he hath given of his seed unto Molech, to defile My sanctuary, and to profane My holy name" — this teaches us that he defiles the Sanctuary, desecrates the Divine Name, causes the Shekhina to depart, makes Israel fall by the sword, and exiles them from their land.'[29] We have cited expositions relating to a single section, all of which are Tannaitic — if they are not ascribed to R. Simeon b. Yoḥai himself, they belong at least to his contemporaries — in order to demonstrate again the variegated spectrum of the dicta of the Sages on the doctrine of retribution comprised in just one small segment of Scriptural homilies.

It seems that there is hardly a view, which modern scholars have propounded in order to formulate the Biblical doctrine of retribution, that is not to be found in the dicta of the Sages. Only the Sages, in contrast to these savants, did not claim, even when they based their opinions on Biblical verses, that they were revealing the actual meaning of the texts. In their groping attempts to find answers to the problems of the doctrine of retribution and of cognate subjects the Rabbis did not unravel this Gordian knot, but in their tackling of it and their constant occupation with this doctrine there stand out certain beliefs that form a firm foundation common to them all. These beliefs revert again to the plain meaning of the Biblical texts, that is, to citing them without interpretation. Irrespective of the answer given to the question of 'the righteous man who fares ill and the wicked man who fares well', or of the meanings ascribed to the terms 'reward and punishment' — be it in this world or in the world to come — or of the explanation of the concept 'the reward of a precept is (another) precept', the actual existence of reward and punishment is not in doubt. It is implicit in the very idea of God, who is Judge (above, p. 28), and in the Torah that He gave to His people, in whose observance and fulfilment judgement is involved, as the anonymous homilist put it: 'It is written "O Lord, Thou hast enticed me, and I was enticed" (Jeremiah xx 7) — the Congregation of Israel said to the Holy One: "Sovereign of the universe, Thou didst entice me until Thou didst give me the Torah, and I placed upon my neck the yoke of the kingdom of the commandments, and I was punished on account of them. Had I not accepted the Torah, I should have been like one of the other nations, (receiving) neither reward nor punishment....'[30]

We have seen that the elements of which a man's sentence is composed are many, and the relative portion therein of a man's actions — the precepts fulfilled and the transgressions committed — the merit of the past and present righteous men, the attribute of the compassion of the Holy One, blessed be He, and its place within and alongside the attribute of justice — all these are moot questions and may only be evaluated conjecturally. But the demand for the justification of the Divine judgement is obligatory, and in this respect deed and theory go hand in hand: 'When they [the Romans] seized R. Ḥanina b. Teradion, it was decreed to burn his scroll upon him. They told him "It is decreed to burn your scroll upon you." He (thereupon) recited this verse: "The Rock, His work is perfect." They (then) said to his wife: "It has been decreed to burn your husband's scroll upon him and to execute you." She recited (in response) this verse: "He is a God of faithfulness and without iniquity." They (then) said to his daughter: 'It has been decreed to burn your father's scroll upon him, to execute your mother, and to put you to forced labour." She (thereupon) recited this verse: "(Thou art) great in counsel, and mighty in work — whose eyes are open... to give every one according to his ways, according to the fruit of his doings" (Jeremiah xxxii 19). Rabbi said: Great are these acts, for in the hour of their trouble they caused three verses that vindicate the Divine judgement to burgeon....'[31] The acts yielded the verses not merely because the passages occurred to righteous people in the hour of their ordeal, but because in the mouths of these martyrs they acquired significance of unmitigated and absolute justification of God's judgement. This is illustrated by the next homily: ' "The Rock, His work is perfect" — when Moses came down from Mount Sinai, all Israel came to him. They said: "Moses, our teacher, tell us, what was the nature of the attribute of justice on high." He replied: "I do not only say when the righteous are cleared and the guilty are condemned, but even when the reverse takes place, '(He is) a God of faithfulness and without iniquity'." '[32] This means to say that even if the Lord appears to convict the innocent, He remains a God of faithfulness. This absolute justification of the Divine judgement is connected with the change that occurred in the conception of the suffering that befalls man, as we have explained (above, p. 443).

When a child died in the house of R. Abbahu, R. Jonah and R. Yassa came to comfort him and they asked him to tell them a Torah teaching. On the basis of the Mishna ruling that after the burial of those who were executed by the court 'The relatives come to greet the witnesses and the judges, as though to say: Know that we bear you no grudge for you have delivered a true judgement', R. Abbahu said to them: 'If now in the case of the earthly judiciary, in which are to be found falsehood, lying, deception, partiality, and bribery, and they are here today and gone tomorrow, it is ordained: The relatives come and greet the judges and the witnesses, as though to say: We bear you no grudge, for you have delivered a true judgement, then how much more, in the case of the Heavenly Judiciary, where there is to be found neither falsehood, nor lying, nor deception, nor partiality, nor bribery, and He lives unto all eternity, are we duty-bound to accept the judgement meted out....'[33] This absolute theodicy was also adopted by the Amoraim towards drastic Biblical episodes, and it was even attributed to the heroes of the remote past, although they attempted at the same time to invest the express statements with added meaning in order to justify them. The incident recorded in II Samuel xxi concerning the delivery of seven members of the family of Saul into the hands of the Gibeonites and their hanging was regarded by the Sages as perplexing from the viewpoint of the law of retribution. Actually it is explicitly stated that the Lord said that the famine lasting three years came on account of Saul's sin, 'because he put to death the Gibeonites', and so it is to be understood, for Scripture already blames the Gibeonites for what happened, since it was they who said to David 'It is no matter of silver or gold between us and Saul, or his house... The man that consumed us, and that devised against us, so that we have been destroyed from remaining in any of the borders of Israel, let seven men of his sons be delivered unto us, and we will hang them up unto the Lord' (*ibid. vv.* 4–6); and as if the narrator was anxious from the first to whitewash the act, he added the information 'Now the Gibeonites were not of the children of Israel, but of the remnant of the Amorites; and the children of Israel had sworn unto them...' (*ibid. v.* 2). An anonymous homilist continued the defence along the lines of Scripture and even added thereto[34]; but not all the Sages were content to solve the difficulty in this way and argued: 'It is written in the Torah "The fathers shall not be put to death for the children...", whereas these died for the sin of their fathers!' Two types of solution to this problem are reported in the name of R. Hoshaʿya. One explanation follows the road of absolute theodicy: ' "And Rizpah the daughter of Aiah took sackcloth, and spread it for her upon the rock..." — what is meant by "upon the rock"? R. Hoshaʿya declared: She said "The Rock, His work is perfect".' The second explanation extends the existing story and introduces therein a new element that gives it a general application, which deviates considerably from the framework of the event in the Bible, and the injustice in it is reduced and ousted in the light of the purpose achieved by the act: 'R. Abba bar Zemina in the name of R. Hoshaʿya said: The sanctification of the Divine Name is greater than the desecration thereof. In the case of the desecration of God's name it is written "His body shall not remain all night upon the tree" (Deuteronomy xxi 23); but in the case of the sanctification of God's name it is written "From the beginning of harvest until water was poured upon them from heaven" (II Samuel, *loc. cit.*, *v.* 10).[35] This teaches us that they remained hanging from the sixteenth of Nisan to the seventeenth of Marḥeshvan, and the passers-by said: What sin did these commit that the law was changed in their case? And they were told: They stretched forth their hands against self-made proselytes. They (the Gentiles) then said: Now if these who were not converted for the sake of Heaven, the Holy One, blessed be He, avenged their blood thus, how much more so (will He avenge) him who is converted for the sake of Heaven! There is no God like your God, and there is no people like your people, and we must join you alone. At that time many became converted.'

This explanation serves to convey the Halakhic teaching that the measure of justice to be shown towards proselytes — even to those who were not converted for the sake of Heaven — may be achieved by injustice towards Jews themselves. What is the relationship between this explanation and the first? Apparently there is no contradiction between them, and in truth it is possible that both were enunciated by the same Amora, only the first was given in the original situation, without any argumentation beyond the complete justification of the judgement for which no reasons or grounds are offered, while the second explanation regards the episode from the viewpoint of passers-by and the Gentile nations, who contemplate with amazement the act of justice done for the sake of the self-made proselytes, the Gibeonites. The words 'Now the Gibeonites were not of the children of Israel' acquired a new significance. However, this explanation does not diminish the intrinsic difficulty of the problem inherent in the incident *per se*, and it still needs vindication of the Divine judgement, such as R. Hoshaʿya put into the mouth of Rizpah the daughter of Aiah, but the elucidation opened the way to instruction and moral teaching that appeared to the homilist no less important than finding a reason for justifying the retribution.

However, harsh Scriptural occurrences did not always provide an opportunity for elaboration, which, even if it did not offer a direct answer, nevertheless contained a surrogate. Nevertheless, the Amoraim did not refrain from enlarging upon them, although they thereby primarily gave added weight to the problem. In the generation after R. Hoshaʿya, Amoraim discussed the incident of Saul and Amalek: ' "And Saul came to the city of Amalek, etc." (I Samuel xv 5) — R. Ḥuna and R. Benaiah declared: He began to argue against His Creator, saying: Thus said the Holy One, blessed be He, "Go and smite Amalek" (*ibid.* v. 3). If the men sinned, what sin did the women commit, what sin did the children commit, what sin did the herd and the oxen and asses commit? (Thereupon) a Heavenly Voice went forth and said to him: "Be not righteous overmuch" (Ecclesiastes vii 16) — more than your Creator.'[36]

Another Amora expounded in similar fashion the continuation of the verse: ' "And he strove for the valley" [E.V. "And he lay in wait in the valley"] — R. Mani said: Over the affairs of the valley. When the Holy One, blessed be He, said to Saul "Go and smite Amalek", he argued: If now in respect of one soul the Torah enjoined that a heifer whose neck was to be broken should be brought, how much more so in the case of all these souls! And if man has sinned, what sin have the cattle committed? And if the adults have sinned, what sin have the minors committed? A Heavenly Voice (thereupon) went forth and said to him: "Be not righteous overmuch." '[37] These

Amoraim by their exposition enlarged and deepened the gravity of the problem. It is clear that the questions that they put in the mouth of Saul troubled the Amoraim themselves, and they had no answer except the justification of the Divine judgement both in regard to the annihilation of Amalek and in respect of the punishment imposed upon Saul. Resh Laqish, indeed, did attempt to find fault with Saul and said 'Whoever is merciful when he should be ruthless in the end is ruthless when he should be merciful. And whence do we learn that he (Saul) became ruthless when he should be merciful? For it is said "And Nob, the city of the priests, smote he with the sword" (I Samuel xxii 19).'[38] But the incident at Nob came as a result of the punishment inflicted on Saul; however, the Rabbis so formulated the dictum of Resh Laqish that it contains no explanation but only a justification of the Divine judgement: 'Whoever is merciful when he should be ruthless is in the end stricken by justice.' Rav Huna, who ascribed to Saul the argument against the injunction to destroy Amalek, also said that Saul 'never knew the taste of sin',[39] and when he compared his fate with that of David, he declared: 'How little does he whom the Lord helps need to grieve or trouble himself! Saul sinned but once and he suffered disaster, whereas David sinned twice and he did not suffer calamity!' Rav Huna employed the saying[40] in the sense that David who committed two transgressions was vouchsafed this help, whereas Saul transgressed only once and yet he was not granted this aid. The fact is recorded without any reason being sought, but possibly the reason is implied in the interpretation put by Rav Huna on Saul's sin. It was no ordinary sin but outright rebellion against the Lord's commandment and an impugnment of its justice; hence Divine help was denied him, although he subsequently confessed his sin.[41] His forfeiture of the kingdom is also given an explanation that deviates from the Biblical account. Rav Judah, the colleague of Rav Huna, stated in the name of his teacher Samuel: 'Why did the dynasty of the House of Saul not endure? Because he was free from any family stigma... for an administrator is not appointed over a community unless he has a basket of reptiles hanging over his back, so that if he becomes arrogant, he is told: Look back!' In the name of his teacher Rav he states: 'And why was Saul punished? Because he forwent the honour due to him....'

Rav and Samuel undoubtedly did not overlook the Scriptural statement 'For thou hast rejected the word of the Lord, and the Lord hath rejected thee from being king over Israel' (I Samuel xv 26 and xvi 1), only they found additional reasons for the nature of the punishment, but not for the sentence itself. They and all those Amoraim who agreed with them concerning Saul's righteousness merely justified the Divine judgement.

However, the judgement and fate of the heroes of the past have a historical explanation in the light of the subsequent development of events, and in this way there is also found a reason for justifying the Divine judgement that appeared to them preferable to that given in the Bible. The explanation offered in Chronicles (I Chronicles xxii 4–8) for the fact that the Temple was not built by David, the anointed of the Lord, but by his son Solomon, is that David shed much blood and waged great wars. But did he act on his own accord and not by the command of the Lord? This explanation did not satisfy the Tanna R. Judah b. R. Il'ai. He declares on the basis of another verse in Chronicles (*ibid.* v. 8) that the prophet Nathan said to David 'Thou shalt not build a house unto My name, because thou hast shed much blood', and the Tanna continues 'When David heard this, he was afraid and said: Lo, I have been disqualified from building the Temple... The Holy One, blessed be He, thereupon said to him "Fear not David. By your life! all the blood that you have shed (is in My sight) as that of the hart and gazelle..." Said (David) to Him "If so, why may I not build it [the Temple]?" The Holy One, blessed be He, answered him "If you should build it, it will stand enduringly and never be destroyed." He [David] countered "But surely that is a good thing!" The Holy One, blessed be He, replied "It is revealed before Me that Israel is destined to sin, and I shall assuage My wrath by venting it upon the Sanctuary and destroying it, but the Israelites will be saved."'[42] Thus it was not David's actions that prevented him from building the Temple, but the fate of his people in the distant future. The spiritual balance sheet of individuals — their reward and punishment — is not a personal one only, but part of the audit of the Congregation of Israel. Both the wicked and the righteous must pay their portion of this account, for it is not confined to their generation alone, but belongs both to the future and past generations. However, these computations are invariably made long after the actual deeds and events.

Among the Tannaim who witnessed the martyrdom of their teachers and colleagues in the days of persecution under the Emperor Hadrian, or lived close to their time, there were such as sought to fasten the blame for what occurred onto certain individual sins of the heroes. There were those who insisted on absolute justification of the Divine judgement without entering into specific calculations, or they accepted the doctrine of R. Akiba 'Precious is suffering', and regarded the hallowing of God's name by submission to martyrdom as an example to future generations. However, in the course of time, when the stories concerning the martyred Sages were combined and a kind of martyrological literature developed, in which a total of 'Ten Martyrs'[43] was reached, the theme as a whole was incorporated into the course of history and a common factor was found for all the episodes, namely the atonement of a single iniquity perpetrated in the national past, which had so far not been expiated, and this was none other than the sin of the sale of Joseph. The concept that this sin was never atoned for and that it rests on all the generations, is old, although it was rejected by the Tannaim and Amoraim. They found no stigma or disqualification in the sons of Jacob (below, p. 530). The author of *The Book of Jubilees* states that Joseph was sold on the tenth of the seventh month, and gives the event as the reason for the incidence of the Fast of Atonement on that date. This is how he expresses it: 'For this reason it is ordained for the children of Israel that they should afflict themselves on the tenth of the seventh month — on the day that the news which made him weep for Joseph came to Jacob his father — that they should make atonement for themselves thereon with a young goat on the tenth of the seventh month, once a year for their sins...' (xxxiv 18–19). When the Temple was destroyed, the sin remained without an atonement, and it appears that the burden of expiation was imposed on the righteous in each generation. And thus it is stated in the late Midrash on the Book of Proverbs in the name of the Amora R. Avin: 'In each generation ten have been punished, but the sin is still unexpiated.'[44] The influence of the literature of the *Hekhalot*, which developed the tradition of the ten martyrs, on Midrash Mishle is not in doubt,[45] and indeed before the dictum of

R. Avin we find one in the name of R. Joshua b. Levi: 'The ten martyrs were dragged to execution [נמשכו] only on account of the sin of the sale of Joseph.'[46] In the Midrash emanating from the circle of R. Moses ha-Darshan,[47] who accepted this tradition, the question is raised: 'And should you say: But the Torah ordained "neither shall the children be put to death for the fathers" (Deuteronomy xxiv 16), why then did these die for the iniquity of their fathers? This is no contradiction. (The Sages) said: This was the point of contention between the Attribute of Justice and Michael the guardian angel of Israel. The Attribute of Justice said: It is written in the Torah "For it is no vain thing for you" (Deuteronomy xxxii 47). Now the tribal eponyms sold Joseph and transgressed (the law of) "And he that stealeth a man..."; they were therefore liable to death, but neither they nor their children have yet paid the penalty for the wrong done to Joseph. Michael answered: It is, however, written in the Torah "neither shall the children be put to death for the fathers", and so the children are not liable to death on account of their fathers. Said the Attribute of Justice to the Holy One, blessed be He: Dost Thou then show respect of persons? If Thou dost give a good reward to the children because of the merit of the fathers, wilt Thou not (also) exact retribution from the children on account of the iniquity of their fathers? ... Either make the children pay the penalty or annul the oath! By this argument the Attribute of Justice defeated Michael, for there was no answer, and so he agreed that their children should pay the penalty. And their sentence was that righteous men should die rather than that the Holy One, blessed be He, should annul the oath concerning their merit.' The execution and torture of the Sages during the Hadrianic persecutions received a significance in the course of the nation's history that transcended the confines of their time and age. By atoning for the sin of Jacob's sons in selling Joseph, they saved the merit of the fathers for the benefit of future generations. From the aspect of the latter the element of the merit of the fathers outweighed in the scales of the world's moral reckoning the rule that 'neither shall the children be put to death for the fathers', which underlies the doctrine of retribution. The Attribute of Justice triumphed at the time of the religious persecutions in order that the Attribute of Mercy might prevail for the generations to come.

However, such an evaluation of the various elements composing the world's moral balance sheet is possible and permissible only in respect of the remote past. But no man may have the presumption to imagine that he may act in the present contrary to the duties and precepts imposed upon him, because he foresees the outcome. When King Hezekiah fell ill, Isaiah came to visit him and told him: 'Set thy house in order; for thou shalt die, and not live.' This visit and harsh announcement were expounded, it seems, already in the first generation of the Amoraim as follows:[48] ' "Thou shalt die" in this world, "and not live" in the world to come. Said (Hezekiah) to him: "Why all this?" He replied: "Because you did not engage in the propagation of children", (Hezekiah) answered: "The reason is that I saw by means of the Holy Spirit that unvirtuous children would issue from me." Said (Isaiah) to him: "What have you to do with the mysteries of the All-Merciful?[49] You must do what you are bidden, and that which pleases Him will come to pass." ' Hezekiah exchanged the world's reckoning for its secret. He sought to penetrate into the arcana of the future by ignoring his obligations towards his generation and his society. Actually the spiritual accounting of the individual Israelite is intimately linked to that of the Congregation of Israel. The concepts and beliefs of the Sages concerning the nature, place, and function of the latter will be treated in the next chapter.

CHAPTER XVI

THE PEOPLE OF ISRAEL AND ITS SAGES

We shall begin our portrayal of כנסת ישראל *Kĕneset Yiśrāʾēl*, 'the Congregation of Israel' — this designation does not differ in signification from עם ישראל *ʿam Yiśraʾel*, 'the people of Israel', or just ישראל *Yiśrāʾēl*, 'Israel' (see below, p. 645) — with two extraneous testimonies: the first belongs almost to the commencement of the period of which we are treating, and the second pertains wellnigh to the end of it. Hecataeus of Abdera, a writer who reached middle age in the time of Alexander the Great and was active in Egypt at the beginning of the reign of Ptolemy I (323 B.C.E.)[1], related that the work of the priests at Jerusalem was not confined to the sacrificial service and Temple duties, but also included the supervision of the observance of the Torah laws and judicial functions. The High Priest is called by him ἄγγελος τῶν τοῦ θεοῦ προσταγμάτων, 'emissary of God's precepts', that is, the supreme authority in Torah matters. Hecataeus states that at the assemblies of the people 'the High Priest brings forth the commandments of the Torah (in the sight of the people) and the people are, of their own volition, so obedient to the Torah that they forthwith fall upon their faces to the ground and prostrate themselves to the High Priest, who reads and explains (the Scriptures) to them'.[2] More than seven hundred years later the church father Augustine wrote: 'It is in truth a surprising fact that the Jewish people never gave up its laws, either under the rule of pagan kings or under the dominion of Christians. In this respect it is different from other tribes and nations; no emperor or king who found them in his land was able to prevent Jews from being differentiated, by their observance of their Law, from the rest of the family of nations.'[3] In the eyes of strangers, who lived in such widely separated periods in which the conditions of Jewish life were fundamentally different, Israel's Torah remained the decisive factor in moulding the character of this people. But just as the situation described by Hecataeus was the result of struggles against intrigue and antagonism,[4] as they are known to us from the Books of Ezra and Nehemiah, so the astonishing phenomenon referred to by Augustine was the product of the activity of generations of Sages. By their Halakhot, which embraced every sphere of life, by their religious and rational thinking, and by their struggle against trends and views of which they did not approve, they determined the image of the nation. Nevertheless, in doing this, the Sages did not cease studying the history of the Jewish people and its destiny during the vicissitudes that time had brought; they did not refrain from inquiring into the individual's position in the community, or from examining the questions relating to the nation's social and economic stratification and its political and spiritual leadership, or from investigating the significance of its survival and its place in the family of nations in the existing world with all its faults and imperfections, as well as in the world that would be wholly good at the end of days.

I. Election and Reality

The concept of Israel's election, as it is explained in the Bible, served, of course, as a basis for the homilies of the Tannaim and Amoraim on the verses of the Torah and the Prophets touching on the subject. It is not our intention to thread together a string of these homilies,[5] which elaborate the Pentateuchal and Prophetic teachings concerning the fact that the election is founded on the covenant made with the fathers at the revelation on Mount Sinai, that it is essentially dependent on the observance of the covenant by the Jewish people, and that it finds expression in the Lord's love for his people and in His acts of grace.[6] We have already discussed in another context (above, p. 138) the significance of the election in placing the people of Israel under the guidance and direct rule of God in contrast to other peoples who came under the dominion of 'Princes' and angels. Now we propose to deal primarily with specific problems with which the Sages were confronted by the belief in the election of their people, in view of the changes and vicissitudes wrought by time.

The words of the prophet Amos (iii 2) 'You only have I known of all the families of the earth; therefore I will punish you for all your iniquities' served to explain Israel's tribulation and sufferings as an educational and reformative factor, but the explanation was not identical in all ages. The author of *II Maccabees*, who described the treachery of the Hellenizers, the religious persecutions instituted by Antiochus, and the experiences of the martyrs who made the supreme sacrifice, already knew the results of the rebellion, namely the conquest of the city and the Temple. In the light of these events he explains to his readers: 'That our people were being punished by way of chastening and not for their destruction. For indeed it is a mark of great kindness when the impious are not let alone for a long time, but punished at once. In the case of other nations, the Sovereign Lord in his forbearance refrains from punishing them till they have filled up their sins to the full, but in our case he has determined otherwise, that His vengeance may not fall on us in after-days when our sins have reached their height. Wherefore He never withdraweth His mercy from us; and though He chasteneth His own people with calamity, He forsaketh them not' (vi 12–16).

The prayer that the author put in the mouth of Judah Maccabaeus and his men on the day of the purification of the Temple was: 'That they might never again incur such disasters, but that, if ever they should sin, He would chasten them with forbearance, instead of handing them over to blasphemous and barbarous pagans'. In the third century C.E., when the Jewish people had been under the rule of foreign nations for over two centuries, there were found vilifiers who made use of the verse in Amos (cited above) in order to challenge the claim of the Jews to be the Chosen People. The long duration of the exile and oppression made it impossible to give an answer like that of the author of *II Maccabees*. To the sectarians who asked 'Does a friend vent all his wrath upon those whom he loves?', R. Abbahu replied: 'The case may be compared to a man who has two debtors, one his friend and the other his enemy. From his friend he accepts payment a little (at a time); from his enemy he exacts (the whole amount) at once.'[7] The sectary who asked the meaning of the verse in Amos was undoubtedly a Christian. If the conversation took place at the end of the third century, then he himself was used to hearing the derisive remarks of the pagans against the doctrine of election held alike by the Jews and the Christians. Origen, who, like R. Abbahu, lived in Caesarea but at an earlier period, reports the argument put forward by Celsus against him: 'But, see pray, how much (God) helped them and you! Instead of being the lords of the earth, they have remained without a land and without a Temple of their own. And in regard to you, if one of you wanders secretly, he is discovered and sentenced to death.'[8] Origen's answer is not for the moment our concern, but it is evident that long before Celsus, at least from after the destruction of the Temple and even more so after the failure of the revolt in the time of Hadrian, the Jews were subjected to the derision of Gentiles who scoffed at their inferior political position and their degraded status, which were in glaring contrast to their claim to be the Chosen People and close to God.[9]

These arguments influenced the Jewish sectarians, whether they were Christians or belonged to other sects; but what certainly seemed even more dangerous to the Tannaim was the threat they posed to the faith of the members of their own community. It was to the strengthening of the latter that they devoted their attention. The replies they gave the sectaries were of a paltry nature and even the accounts of the debates themselves bear a grotesque and derisive character.[10] More weighty are the answers they gave their own people on the question of the relationship between Israel and the Gentile nations and regarding the significance of the election. Many passages that have been interpreted by scholars as polemical, as answers to pagans and sectarians, are in truth wrestlings with problems that exercised the Sages themselves and were solved by them in various ways. Some Tannaim regarded Israel's election as a cosmic act. The verse Exodus xiv 15 was expounded by the Tanna R. Eleazar of Modiʿim thus: ' "Wherefore criest thou unto Me?" — do I require an instruction where My sons are concerned? "Concerning My sons, and concerning the work of My hands, command ye Me?" (Isaiah xlv 11). Have they not already been designated to be before Me since the six days of creation? For it is said "If these ordinances depart from before Me, saith the Lord, then the seed of Israel shall also cease from being a nation before Me for ever" [Jeremiah xxxi 35].'[11]

R. Eleazar of Modiʿim merely reverts in his exposition to the concept that had been widely accepted long before the destruction of the Temple, as is also attested by extraneous sources.[12] The view that the election of Israel had been planned by God when the world was created makes the election, of course, absolute and independent of any circumstances. This was the doctrine of R. Akiba, who said 'Beloved are Israel in that they are called children of the Omnipresent. Still greater is the love in that it was made known to them that they were called children of the Omnipresent, for it is said "Ye are children of the Lord your God" (Deuteronomy xiv 1).' The great Tanna himself explained the expression and connotation of the love: 'Beloved are Israel in that He gave them the instrument with which the world was created. Still greater is the love in that it was made known to them that He gave them the instrument with which the world was created, as it is said "For I give you good doctrine; forsake ye not My Law" (Proverbs iv 2).'[13] Israel were chosen to be children of the Almighty, and to these children He gave the instrument — that is, the Torah — with which He created the world. The still greater love consists in the fact that the Lord has made known to them that they are His children and that He has given them a good doctrine. R. Me'ir, in the spirit of the teaching of his master, R. Akiba, said: 'Although they are full of blemishes, they are called children, as it is said "Is corruption His? No, His children's is the blemish" (Deuteronomy xxxii 5).'[14] On the basis of these Tannaitic expositions the Amoraim placed the Torah and Israel at the head of the things that preceded the creation of the world, and it is stated in the name of R. Samuel b. R. Isaac: 'The thought of (creating) Israel preceded everything... Had not the Holy One, blessed be He, foreseen that after twenty-six generations Israel would accept the Torah, he would surely not have written in it "Command the children of Israel"!'[15] The consciousness that their election had a cosmic and eternal character accompanied the feeling of tension that emanated from the discrepancy between this consciousness and the reality, as is attested by the words of the visionary, the author of *IV Ezra*: '...Thou hast said that for our sakes Thou hast created the world in the beginning. But as for the other nations, which are descended from Adam, Thou hast said that they are nothing, and that they are like unto spittle; and Thou hast likened the abundance of them to a drop of a bucket.

And now, O Lord, behold these nations which are reputed as nothing lord it over us and consume us. But we, Thy people whom Thou hast called Thy first-born, Thy only-begotten, Thy beloved [most dear], are given up into their hands. If the world has indeed been created for our sakes, why do we not enter into possession of our world? How long shall this endure?'[16] This feeling of tension between the reality and the spiritual consciousness found release in the belief in redemption in its various senses, which we shall discuss later (p. 649).

But not all the Tannaim and Amoraim accepted the doctrine of cosmic-eternal election. Against it can clearly be discerned other views, which may be termed a historical-relativist approach. It is related to conditions and circumstances, and in it the Chosen People plays an active role, being at times even the chooser. Thus R. Eleazar b. Azariah expounded: ' "Thou hast avouched the Lord this day... and the Lord has avouched thee this day" (Deuteronomy xxvi 17–18). The Holy One, blessed be He, said to Israel: You have made Me a unique object of your love in the world, and I shall make you a unique object of My love in the world. You have made Me a unique object of your love in the world, as it is written "Hear, O Israel, the Lord our God, the Lord is One" (*ibid.* vi 4); and I shall make you a unique object of My love in the world, as it is said "Who is like unto Thy people Israel, a nation one in the earth" (I Chronicles xvii 21).'[17] The Lord was chosen by Israel before Israel was chosen by God; R. Ishmael expressed a similar thought in his exposition: ' "And ye shall be holy men unto Me..." (Exodus xxii 30) — when you are holy you are Mine.'[18] First Israel must sanctify themselves and only thereafter do they merit to be called a holy people.

Although the view that Israel chose the Lord first is rejected in an anonymous Tannaitic Midrash, yet the process of election portrayed in it falls within the ambit of history and is not an act that preceded Creation: ' "For the portion of the Lord is his people" (Deuteronomy xxxii 9): The case is comparable to that of a king who had a field, which he leased to tenant farmers. The tenants began to steal from it; so he took it away from them and gave it to their sons. They soon proved themselves worse than the first. He thereupon took it away from their sons and gave it to their grandsons, but they showed themselves to be still worse. When, however, a son was born to him, he said to the tenants: "Go forth from my (land); you cannot remain there. Give me (back) my portion so that I may declare it to be mine." Even so when our father Abraham came into the world, there issued from him the refuse of Ishmael and all the sons of Keturah; when Isaac came into the world there issued from him the refuse of Esau and all the chiefs of Edom, and they were even worse than the first. When Jacob, however, arrived, no refuse issued from him, but all the sons born to him were worthy, as it is said "And Jacob was a perfect [תם *tām*; EVV 'quiet'] man, dwelling in tents" (Genesis xxv 27). Who is the first to be claimed by the Omnipotent as His portion? Jacob, as it is said "For the portion of the Lord is His people, Jacob the lot of His inheritance", and it is further said "For the Lord hath chosen Jacob" (Psalms cxxxv 4). But the matter still remains ambiguous and we cannot tell whether the Holy One, blessed be He, chose Jacob or whether Jacob chose the Holy One, blessed be He, therefore Scripture teaches us "Israel for His own treasure" (*ibid.*). However, the matter is still undecided, and we do not know if the Holy One, blessed be He, chose Israel for His own treasure, or if Israel chose the Holy One, blessed be He, therefore Scripture teaches "And the Lord thy God hath chosen thee to be His own treasured people" (Deuteronomy xiv 2). And how do we know that Jacob also chose the Lord?; for it is said "Not like these is the portion of Jacob" (Jeremiah x 16).'[19] The homily as we have it is composed of two homilies, and the point of their juncture is still discernible. The first emphasizes the idea of choice and clearly establishes that it was God who chose His portion, as is also to be inferred from the verse in Deuteronomy, which serves as the starting point. The second homily finds the verse Psalms cxxxv 4 ambivalent and accordingly 'we cannot tell whether the Holy One, blessed be He, chose Jacob or whether Jacob chose the Holy One, blessed be He'.[20] The expositor's solution is, as it were, a twofold concept of election. From the verse in Deuteronomy he deduces that the Lord chose Israel, and from the verse in Jeremiah, where it is stated, after the prophet had spoken about people who had elected to serve idols, 'Not like these is the portion of Jacob', he infers that Jacob chose the Lord.[21] The Lord's choice was answered by Jacob's choice, and, indeed, also the Tanna R. Judah made the latter a condition of the maintenance of the first. He disagreed with his colleague R. Me'ir and expounded ' "Ye are the children of the Lord your God"... If you act like children you are (deemed) children, but if not you are not (accounted as) children.'[22] The selective process of the election, which, continuing for generations, is enshrined in verses of the Prophets and of the Hagiographa[23], and is depicted, in a manner similar to the exposition of the Tannaim, also in the pseudepigraphical literature[24], removes the arbitrary aspect from the question of the election. The chosen people becomes the choosing people. 'A certain noblewoman put an objection to R. Jose, saying: "Your God brings near [i.e. favours] whom He wishes!" He thereupon brought before her a basket of figs from which she selected well, eating what she selected. He then said to her: "You know how to choose; (can you imagine that) the Holy One, blessed be He, does not know how to choose! When He sees one whose deeds are good, He elects him and brings him near." '[25] The Amora R. Judah b. R. Simon took the old belief that the world was created on account of the Torah and combined it with the motif of free choice, and in his hands both ideas, woven into a beautiful homily, transform the people of Israel from the Chosen to the Choosing People. ' "As a lily among thorns" (Canticles ii 2): It is like the case of a king who had an orchard. He planted in it rows upon rows of figs, a row of vines, and a row of pomegranates. After a time when the king went down to see his vineyard, he found it full of thorns and thistles. So he appointed for it mowers to mow it down. But he found in it one rose blossom; he took it and smelt it and felt refreshed. Thereupon he said: This blossom deserves that the entire orchard should be saved for its sake. Even so the whole world was created only on account of the Torah. After twenty-six generations the Holy One, blessed be He, glanced at His world and found it full of thorns and thistles, such as the generation of Enosh, and that of the Flood, and the men of Sodom. He thereupon wished to destroy it utterly, as it is said "The Lord sat enthroned at the Flood" (Psalms xxix 10). But He found there a single rose blossom — to wit, Israel — and He took it and breathed its fragrance at the time when He gave them the Ten Commandments, and His soul was refreshed when they said "We will do, and obey." '[26]

It was Israel's positive response and their acceptance of the Torah that made the election of Israel a reality, and when the Torah was accepted the world was firmly established. It was still possible, of course, to contend that the Lord had not offered His Torah to other peoples, and this very fact, even if the Israelites accepted the Law voluntarily and not under compulsion, makes the election an arbitrary act, and indeed it seems that some did argue thus. In order to answer this objection the Tannaim already completed the Pentateuchal story by declaring:

'Therefore the Gentile nations were asked to receive the Torah, in order not to afford them an opportunity to say to the Shekhina: "Had we been asked we should certainly have accepted it." Thus they were asked, but did not accept it, as it is said "And he said: 'The Lord came from Sinai' etc." (Deuteronomy xxxiii 2) — He revealed Himself to the children of the wicked Esau, and said to them: "Will you accept the Torah?" Said they to Him: "What is written therein?" He answered them: "Thou shalt not murder." They replied: "This is the heritage that our father has bequeathed to us, as it is said 'And by thy sword shalt thou live' (Genesis xxvii 40)." He next revealed Himself to the children of Ammon and Moab, saying to them: "Will you accept the Torah?" Said they to Him: "What is written therein?" He answered them "Thou shalt not commit adultery". They then said: "We are all the offspring of adultery, for it is written 'Thus were both the daughters of Lot with child by their father' " (*ibid.* xix 36). He then revealed Himself to the children of Ishmael, saying to them: "Will you accept the Torah?" Said they to Him: "What is written therein?" He answered them: "Thou shalt not steal." They replied: "This is the benison bestowed upon our father. for it is written 'And he shall be as a wild ass of a man' (*ibid.* xvi 12) and it is further written 'For, indeed, I was stolen away' (*ibid.* xl 12)." But when He came to Israel and "At His right hand was a fiery law unto them" (Deuteronomy xxxiii 2), they all cried aloud and said "All that the Lord hath spoken will we do, and obey" (Exodus xxiv 7).'[27]

By the Gentile nations [literally 'nations of the world'], to whom the expositor did not wish to give an excuse, he doubtless meant the pagans. The Emperor Julian asked the Christians: If the Deity is not only the God of the Jews but also the God of the Gentiles, why did

He send them so much grace of prophecy, and Moses, and anointing, and the prophets and the Torah... whereas we have no prophet, no anointing, no teacher, no herald, to make known to us the grace of His love, which is in store for us... Nay more, He even hid Himself from us for myriads — or, if you will, for thousands — of years, and He let all those who dwell from the rising of the sun to the setting thereof, and from the north pole to the recesses of the south, serve idols, as you call them, out of such ignorance, except for one small people that settled in a part of Palestine less than two thousand years ago....'[28]

The apostate emperor's argument was directed specifically against the doctrine of Paul and his followers, who maintained that the Gentiles who believed in Jesus had inherited Israel's place; but from the Tannaitic expositions we learn that in point of fact he repeated arguments adduced by the pagans against the Jews some two centuries earlier. The answer given by the Sages did not aim at the placation of the non-Jews, but constitutes a counterattack. It establishes a fact, as it were: The Gentiles were given an opportunity to accept the Torah, but did not do so. The precepts that prompted their refusal — 'Thou shalt not murder', 'Thou shalt not commit adultery', and 'Thou shalt not steal' — are not exclusive ordinances of the people of Israel; they are counted among the Noachide laws,[29] whose observance is incumbent upon the whole human race. Indeed in another version of the answer it is stated: 'There was not one among the nations to whom He did not come and speak and upon whose door He did not knock, (asking) whether they wished to accept the Torah... Should you think that they hearkened and accepted, Scripture teaches us "But do them not" (Ezekiel xxxiii 31), and it further says "And in anger and wrath I will execute vengeance upon the nations that did not obey" (Micah v 14). Nay, even the seven commandments that the children of Noah accepted they failed to keep, till in the end they set them aside and gave them to Israel.'[30] Undoubtedly we have here evidence of the Sages' evaluation of the ethical standard of the Gentiles with whom they came in contact[31], although it was exacerbated by the polemical trend of the source; but the effect of this homily, too, was primarily internal. It was transmitted in the course of generations and served to justify the giving of the Torah to Israel and thus to consolidate the sense of election, specifically in its active signification. On Lamentations iii 1, 'I am the man' we find the following homily:[32]

'R. Joshua b. Levi said: The Congregation of Israel said before the Holy One, blessed be He: "Sovereign of the whole universe, I am the one that is inured (to affliction); all that Thou wishest comes upon me."[33] It is like the case of a noblewoman with whom the king was wroth and she was expelled from the palace. What did she do? She hid herself, standing behind a pillar. When the king passed, he said to her "You were insolent". She answered him: "My lord, the king, so it is fitting, and so it is comely, and so it is proper for me, for no woman accepted you but me." Said the king to her: "Nay! It is I who disqualified all the women on account of you." She replied: "Nay! It is they who did not accept you." Even so the Congregation of Israel said to the Holy One, blessed be He: "Sovereign of the whole universe, thus it is proper for me (to act), for no nation received Thy law, only I." The Holy One, blessed be He, answered: "Nay! It is I who disqualified all the nations on account of you." Said she to Him: "Nay! It is they who did not accept it. Wherefore didst Thou go to Mount Seir? Was it not to give the Torah to the children of Esau, but they did not accept it? So, too, (Thou didst go) to the wilderness of Paran — was it not to give the Torah to the children of Ishmael, but they did not accept it? Wherefore didst Thou go to the Ammonites and Moabites? Was it not to give the Torah to the children of Lot, but they did not accept it?.... How many kindnesses have I not done Thee? I sanctified Thy name at the sea; I uttered song unto Thee; with joy I accepted the Torah, which the Gentile peoples did not accept. Yet after all this glorification 'I am the man that hath seen affliction'!" '[34]

The answer given in the Tannaitic homily to the charge of the Gentile nations against the arbitrary character of Israel's election is used by the Congregation of Israel in the homily of R. Joshua b. Levi as proof that the Israelites accepted the Torah of their own volition, and it opens the way again for their complaint at their cruel fate, which contradicts the fact that they are the Chosen People. This remonstrance on the part of the Congregation echoes to some extent the arguments advanced by non-Jews, which were cited above (p. 526); but it called forth varied reactions, especially from those

Sages who did not regard the election of Israel as an arbitrary cosmic act, and likewise did not wish to give up the idea that the Congregation of Israel voluntarily accepted the Torah and adopt instead the view that the Holy One, blessed be He, 'tilted the mountain over them like a cask' (above, p. 324).

It is possible to distinguish three kinds of reaction to this reproach: the first emanates from a consideration of the history of the nation and its relationship to its God since receiving the Torah; the second is based on the contemporary view of the people as a community of individuals who are responsible for one another; and the third cut the Gordian knot by opening the way to a universal conception of Israel's election.

Following close upon the acceptance of the Torah is the story of the golden calf. Some Tannaim emphasized the gravity of the sin into which the whole people fell, so that a shadow was cast upon the revelation at Mount Sinai and it lost its positive significance: 'Thus we find that our ancestors, when standing at Mount Sinai, sought to deceive the Most High, as it is said "All that the Lord hath spoken will we do, and obey" (Exodus xxiv 7) — and, so to speak, the (Heavenly) Court was deceived, as it is said "O that they had such a heart as this always" (Deuteronomy v 36). Should you suppose that not all things are revealed and known to Him, Scripture teaches us "But they beguiled Him... For their heart was not steadfast with Him". Nevertheless "He, being full of compassion, forgiveth iniquity" (Psalms lxxviii 36–38).'[35] Uttering 'We will do' before '(We will) obey,' contained an element of deception, which was manifest to the Holy One, blessed be He, only He, as it were, overlooked it, just as He was ready to grant atonement for the sin of the calf. The diminution of Israel's prestige at the revelation on Mount Sinai weakens the impression of treachery produced by the episode of the calf, and reduces the tension that finds expression in the complaint. But reference to the story of the calf sufficed even for the Sages who in no way impugned the integrity of the act of receiving the Torah to moderate the complaint. By the incident of the calf the Israelites lowered the status that they had attained at the revelation on Mount Sinai. The Tanna R. Simeon b. Yoḥai accepted the words of the prophet Amos (v 25) 'Did ye bring unto Me sacrifices and offerings in the wilderness?' etc. as a fact and interpreted it as a punishment upon Israel. 'The Israelites — he said — did not offer sacrifices. To whom then did the tribe of Levi sacrifice, for it is said "They put incense before Thee, and whole burnt-offering upon Thine altar" (Deuteronomy xxxiii 10)... The Israelites served idols, but the tribe of Levi did not worship idols, as it is said "For they have observed Thy word" (*ibid. v.* 9)'.[36] But the punishment was temporary, for the sin of the calf was neither the first nor the last transgression. Some Sages adopted the historical assessment of Ezekiel in chapter xx, which states that Israel's rebellion began when they were still in Egypt, and said that the Israelites did not hearken to Moses (Exodus vi 9) when he came to announce to them the news of the redemption, 'for it was hard for them to give up idolatry'.[37] Notwithstanding, God brought them out from Egypt and gave them the Torah and the precepts 'that they might know that I am the Lord that sanctifies them' (Ezekiel xx 12). The Amora R. Samuel bar Naḥman combined the words of Ezekiel with the verse in Proverbs (x 12) 'Hatred stirreth up strifes; but love covereth all transgressions', and gave the following exposition: 'For nearly nine hundred years Israel felt pent-up hatred for their Father in Heaven, from the time they left Egypt until Ezekiel arose and said to them "Cast ye away every man the detestable things of his eyes" etc. (Ezekiel xx 7)..." "but love covereth all transgressions" — the love with which the Holy One loved Israel, as it is said "I have loved you, saith the Lord" (Malachi, i 2).'[38] Only the 'Hatred that Israel felt for their Father in Heaven' induced the prophet Ezekiel to reveal the sin that they committed in Egypt and which in His love the Holy One, blessed be He, covered up for nine hundred years. This love finds expression in the fact that the evil deeds tend to be forgotten but not the covenant. Thus Resh Laqish said:

'The Congregation of Israel declared before the Holy One, blessed be He: "It is the way of the world that even when a human king takes an additional wife, he remembers the acts of the first; but Thou hast forsaken me and forgotten me." Said the Holy One, blessed be He, to the prophet: "Go tell the Congregation of Israel: My daughter, I have created twelve constellations in the firmament, and for each constellation I have created... and all of them have I created only for your sake, yet you say: Thou hast forsaken me and forgotten me. 'Can a woman forsake her sucking child, that she should not have compassion on the son of her womb?' (Isaiah xlix 16)...." Thereupon the Congregation of Israel spoke before Him: "Sovereign of the universe, since there is no forgetfulness before the Throne of Thy Glory, perhaps Thou wilt not forget unto me the incident of the calf." God answered her: " 'Yea, these will be forgotten (*ibid.*).' " The Congregation of Israel then rejoined: "Sovereign of the universe, since there is forgetfulness before the Throne of Thy Glory, perhaps Thou wilt forget unto me what happened at Sinai." The Lord assured her: "Yet I [the initial word of the Decalogue] will not forget thee." This, too, is what R. Eleazar said in the name of R. Oshaʿya: What is the meaning of the verse "Yea, these will be forgotten"? This refers to the episode of the calf; and "Yet I will not forget thee" — this refers to Sinai.'[39]

This conviction of Resh Laqish that Israel's response at Sinai would not be forgotten is only an expression of his trust in the eternity of the election of Israel. But it did not make him oblivious of the absence of manifestations attesting the election of Israel by the Lord and of their nearness to Him, and he explained this by the conduct of the people at crucial junctures of their history. Concerning the period of the Second Temple the Sages declared that it lacked five things possessed by the First Temple, among which they included the Holy Spirit.[40] Resh Laqish did not attribute the absence of the Shekhina from the Second Temple — as did R. Joḥanan — to the fact that the Temple was built by Cyrus, who was a descendant of Japhet, but to the exiles of his day who did not respond to his call 'Whosoever there is among you of all His people — his God be with him — let him go up [to Jerusalem]' (Ezra i 3), 'For thus said the Holy One, blessed be He, if all Israel go up the Shekhina shall rest upon them, but if not, they would have to avail themselves only of a *Bat Qol*' ('Heavenly Voice').[41]

In the generation following Resh Laqish the Sages in Eretz-Israel gave the following exposition: ' "If she be a wall" (Canticles viii 9): Had the Israelites gone up from exile like a wall [i.e. undivided, in their entirety], the Temple would not have been destroyed a second time.'[42] Thus they found the cause of the destruction of the Second

Temple to have existed already at the beginning of the era. These homilies had topical significance, for they were expounded by Amoraim in Eretz-Israel, who did not love their Babylonian colleagues.[43] More perhaps than by expressions of explicit unsympathy or dislike this is attested by the sarcastic explanation of the delay that occurred in Ezra's immigration: '...Ezra and his disciples and his colleagues did not go up at the time. Now why did Ezra not go up at that time? Because he needed to clarify his learning before Baruch the son of Neriah. Then Baruch the son of Neriah should have gone up! But (the Sages) said: Baruch the son of Neriah was a great man and old and even in a sedan-chair (*lectica*) he could not have been carried.'[44]

Even if we attribute no small part of the evaluation of the Second Temple period and its beginning, in particular, to the contemporary polemical aim of these Amoraims, we cannot overlook the element in their dicta that makes the realization of the election — its merits and its characteristics — dependent on the numerical state of the people. These views were expressed by the Amoraim in accordance with the doctrine of R. Simeon b. Yoḥai. It was actually this Tanna, who held extravagant individualistic opinions (above, p. 489), that said: 'Whence is it to be inferred that even if Israel lacked one person the Shekhina would not have appeared to them? Because it is written: "For the third day the Lord will come down in the sight of *all* the people upon Mount Sinai" (Exodus xix 11)'[45]; that is to say, the giving of the Torah, which is the quintessence of Israel's election, was conditional on the total presence of the people — not a soul was absent. With this view also R. Judah, the Patriarch, agreed.[46] But unity, and not only numerical wholeness, was required, and it was Rabbi, too, who emphasized this fact and explained its significance:

'Rabbi said: This tells us the merit of Israel. When they all stood at Mount Sinai to receive the Torah, they all resolved, with like mind, to accept the kingdom of God with joy. Nay more, they pledged themselves for one another. Nor was it for the overt acts alone that the Holy One, blessed be He, intended to reveal Himself to them in order to make a covenant with them, but also for the secret deeds. However, they said to Him: For the overt acts we shall make a covenant with Thee, but not for the secret deeds, lest one of us sin in secret and the whole community be held liable, as it is said 'The secret things belong unto the Lord our God; but the things that are revealed belong unto us and to our children" (Deuteronomy xxix 28).'[47]

The election was of one entire people and the covenant was made on condition that all 'Israel be sureties for one another (ישראל ערבין זה לזה)'.[48] R. Simeon b. Yoḥai, who stressed the importance of the wholeness of the nation at the time of their election, also explained the significance of the mutual guaranties: 'R. Simeon b. Yoḥai taught: This may be compared to people who were in a boat, and one of them took a drill and began to drill a hole beneath himself. Said his companions to him: "Why are you doing this?" He retorted: "What concern is it of yours? Am I not drilling under myself?" They replied: "Because you will flood the boat for us all!" Even so Job argued "And be it indeed that I have erred, mine error remaineth with myself" (Job xix 4). Said his companions to him: " 'When he addeth to his sin, he attacheth rebellion to us' [EVV: 'For he addeth rebellion to his sin, he clappeth his hands among us'] (*ibid.* xxxiv 37) — you attach your iniquities to us." '[49]

Only the punishment of the sinners frees the community from the responsibility resting upon it. The homily ' "And that soul shall be cut off from among his people" — then his people will be at peace' recurs in all[50] the Tannaitic Midrashim, a fact that attests its antiquity.

From the verse 'And who is like Thy people, Israel, a nation one in the earth' (II Samuel vii 23), which the Sages regarded as expressing the election of Israel (above p. 529), as 'a holy nation' in the sense of 'separated from the nations of the world and their abominations'[51], they also inferred that Israel was 'as one body, as one soul... if one of them sinned all were punished, as it is said "Did not Achan the son of Zerah commit a trespass concerning the devoted thing, and wrath fell upon all the congregation of Israel? and that man perished not alone in his iniquity" (Joshua xxii 20). If one of them is smitten they all feel pain; therefore it says "Israel is a scattered sheep" (Jeremiah l 17) — just as when a ewe is afflicted in one of its limbs, all the limbs are affected, even so is Israel, when one of them is afflicted they all suffer. But the Gentiles all rejoice at one another's downfall.'[52] Israel has become one nation by virtue of the covenant and cannot rejoice when part of it is punished or suffers as do other peoples; for even if they are members of one faith, they are divided into nationalities and fight one another. Already the Tanna R. Joḥanan b. Torta, who lived at the time of the Revolt of Bar Kochba, cited as a cause of the destruction of the Second Temple the fact that 'they hated one another without cause'[53]; and an Amora who gave a dramatic description of Abraham's intervention on behalf of his children on the night of the Ninth of Av makes the Holy One, blessed be He, give as the final reason for the Destruction '...Moreover, they rejoiced at one another's downfall.'[54] The punishment of the whole people of Israel is a consequence of their mutual responsibility and is inherent in the act of election, which made Israel one nation upon earth. The very concept of the election implies mutual responsibility and consequently also collective punishment; there is no room, therefore, for complaint, for this reciprocal suretyship makes it possible to gain atonement and to preserve the special relationship between Israel and his God. With reference to the story of Achan, in which the Sages found testimony to the fact that 'Israel are sureties for one another', R. Abba bar Zavda states in the name of Rav ' "Israel hath sinned" — this implies that although they have sinned they are still "Israel" '[55], and, as Rashi explains: 'Since Scripture does not say "the people hath sinned", their holy name still belonged to them.'

The mutual suretyship, which brings punishment upon the whole people bearing the responsibility, implies also a guarantee that Israel would return to the path of rectitude, and by the same token is an assurance of the nation's eternal existence. The verse in Jeremiah (xi 16) 'The Lord called thy name a leafy olive-tree, fair with goodly fruit' was expounded by R. Joshua b. Levi and by R. Joḥanan. The former said: 'Why are the people of Israel likened to an olive-tree? To tell you that just as an olive-tree does not shed its leaves either in summer or in winter, so Israel shall not come to an end either in this world or in the world to come.' R. Joḥanan said: 'Why are the people of Israel compared to an olive-tree? To tell you that just as the olive produces its oil only through pounding, so do Israel return to the path of righteousness only after suffering.'[56] The two homilies complement each other. The Israelites are not easily reformed, but the attribute of obduracy also assures their survival. R. Joḥanan's colleague, Resh Laqish, declared that the people of Israel were the

עזין *ʿazzîn* ['fierce, impetuous ones'][57] of the nations. The meaning of his dictum is made clear by the Baraitot cited in the same context. 'It was taught in the name of R. Me'ir: Why was the Torah given to Israel? Because they are impetuous [*ʿazzîn*]; the School of R. Ishmael taught: "At His right hand was a fiery law unto them" — the Holy One, blessed be He, said: These deserve to be given a fiery law. Some say: The laws of these are sheer fire, for had not the Torah been given to Israel, no nation or tongue could have withstood them.'[58] From the exposition of 'Some say' — that only the Torah transforms the attribute of impetuosity [עזות *ʿazzût*] into a virtue and that otherwise it might have been a source of harm to the world — we learn that the School of Ishmael regarded impetuosity as the quality that made Israel worthy of receiving the fiery law. This last dictum, which to begin with portrayed Israel's character and concluded — through its metaphor — with the thought that the giving of the Torah to Israel was also of benefit to the Gentile world, enables us to make the transition to the third group of dicta and homilies that bridges the gulf between Israel's election and its present position of subjection, as well as its history, which is replete with hard and bitter ordeals. This is achieved actually by emphasizing the universal element in Israel's election.

II. Election and Proselytization

In the Midrash, which was likewise taught in 'the School of Ishmael', it is stated:

' "Before the Lord God, the God of Israel" (Exodus xxxiv 23). Why is this [the last part] stated? Has it not already been said "Before the Lord God"? Why then does Scripture add, "the God of Israel"? The explanation is that He conferred His name particularly on Israel. Similarly, "Hear, O Israel, the Lord our God, the Lord is One" (Deuteronomy vi 4). Why is this [the last part] stated? Has it not already been said "the Lord our God"? What then is the significance of "the Lord is one"? The meaning is that He conferred His name particularly on us. Similarly, "Therefore, thus saith the Lord, the God of Israel" (II Kings xxi 12). Why is this stated? Has it not already been written "Behold, I am the Lord, the God of all flesh" (Jeremiah xxxii 27)? What then are we taught by the words "The God of Israel"? The fact that He conferred His name particularly on Israel. Similarly, "Hear, O My people, and I will speak; O Israel, and I will testify against thee: God, thy God, am I..." (Psalms l 7). I am the God of all people; nevertheless I have conferred My name specifically on Israel.'[59]

Apparently the practical significance attaching to this emphasis on the particular conferment upon Israel of the name of God, who is the God of all flesh, is that it is Israel's function to bring the recognition of the God of Israel to the knowledge of the world. The fact of the dissemination of Israel's faith among the Gentiles in the Jewish Diaspora and of the resultant large number of proselytes and 'fearers of the Lord' in the countries of the Roman Empire and in the area of Hellenistic civilization is well known; we shall not, therefore, discuss it in detail.[60] Our primary interest here is the reflection of these circumstances in the views expressed concerning the place of the Congregation of Israel in the family of nations and its distinctive character and mission.

Our concern will be to trace to what extent and in which way events like the destruction of the Temple, the loss of the residual political independence of Judea, the spread of Christianity, and its missionary activity influenced these views and in what measure they remained fundamental beliefs that were unaffected either by these events or by the cessation of Jewish proselytization. We shall begin particularly with dicta of the second half of the third century C.E.: 'R. Eleazar also said: The Holy One, blessed be He, exiled Israel among the nations only to the end that proselytes might join them, as it is said "And I will sow her unto Me in the land" (Hosea ii 25). Surely one sows a *se'a* in order to reap a number of *kor*[61]... R. Osha'ya said: What is the meaning of the verse "Even the righteous acts of פרזונו *pirzono* [understood as equivalent by metathesis to *pizrono*, 'His scattering'] to Israel" (Judges v 11) — an act of charity [literally: 'righteousness'] did the Holy One, blessed be He, to Israel in that He scattered them among the nations. And this is what a Min once said to R. Judah Nesi'a:[62] "We are better than you. Of you it is written 'For Jacob and all Israel remained there six months, until he had cut off every male in Edom' (I Kings xi 16), whereas you have been with us many years, yet we do you no harm." Said (R. Judah Ne'sia) to him: "If you wish, one of the disciples will take up the argument with you." R. Hoshaʿya debated with him, saying: "Because you do not know how to act. Should you think of destroying them all, they are not among you. (Should you consider destroying only) those in your midst, you would be called a barbarous kingdom."[63] Replied (the Min): "I swear by the גפא *gappā* of Rome![64] With this (thought) we rise up and with this (thought) we lie down (Rashi: 'We are constantly preoccupied with this thought')." ' The two dicta cited together reflect totally different explanations of the dispersion of the Jewish people among the nations, but it is actually the view of the younger scholar, R. Eleazar, who declared that the Lord exiled Israel among the nations only that proselytes might join them, that was the legacy of preceding generations, who gloried in the influence exerted by Israel's Torah on their non-Jewish environment[65], and was acceptable to all and remained the belief of the majority even after the decline of proselytization.[66] R. Hoshaʿya's reply was given in a specific situation and originated not as an explanation of the existence of the Dispersion, but as a polemical argument between a Min and the Sage. The Min referred to was a Gentile and a pagan,[67] only he was apparently interested in the sacred Scripture of the Jews. There were pagans who in this manner found their way either to conversion to Judaism and admission to the Congregation of Israel,[68] or to Christianity.[69] But there were also others whose antipathy and antagonism towards Judaism, ingrained in them from the first, were further strengthened by such reading. For we must not forget that even in the period when the Jewish diaspora and Israel's Torah had an appeal for the Gentile world and attracted converts, they also aroused hatred and sharp criticism,[70] which advanced arguments that laid the foundations of theoretical anti-Semitism.

The type of Gentile that they encountered and their experiences with the pagans who were drawn towards Judaism and read the Bible also determined the reactions of the Sages. Against the view of R. Eliezer that 'No Gentile has a share in the world to come', R. Joshua argued: 'But there are righteous men among the nations who have a share in the world to come' (*Tosefta Sanhedrin* xiii, 2, p. 434). Probably the dictum 'Even a Gentile who studies the Torah is like the High Priest' is only the outcome of a positive experience. In some sources it is ascribed to the Tanna R. Jeremiah, who belonged to the *entourage* of R. Judah the Patriarch and knew the relationship between 'Rabbi and Antoninus'.[71] In other sources the author of the saying is given as R. Me'ir,[72] who actually lived and worked in troubled days of religious persecution, but even in such times the Rabbis encountered exceptional individuals who stood by the Jews in their hour of adversity, and it is not surprising that they attributed the acts of these people to the merit of their study of the Torah and precepts. It was the disciple of R. Me'ir, Judah b. Shammuaʿ, who was given advice, at the time of religious oppression, by 'a certain noblewoman, who entertained all the leading Romans. She counselled them (the delegation): "Go and cry out at night." So they went and cried out at night, saying: "Oh, in heaven's name, are we not your brethren, are we not the children of one father? Why are we different from all other nations and tongues that you impose harsh decrees upon us?" The decrees were thereupon annulled.'[73] On the other hand, at times when the government was better disposed towards the Jews, many Gentiles continued to favour the policy of Hadrian. To them belonged the Min who met R. Judah Nesi'a. He made use of the knowledge he had acquired from the Book of Kings regarding the acts of Joab in Edom in order to establish his pagan charge concerning the ἀπανθρωπία of the Jews in contrast to the Graeco-Roman φῖλανθρωπία.

R. Hoshaʿya, to whom R. Judah Nesi'a assigned the task of replying to the Min, did not choose the apologetic approach in order to defend Joab's actions, but proceeded to counterattack. This φῖλανθρωπία not only does not exist where Jews are concerned, but the Roman government has given thought to the possibility of annihilating the Jewish people from off the face of the earth — the memory of Hadrian's edicts had not yet dimmed — and if the intention was not implemented, it was because of the kindness that the Lord had done to His people in that they were only partly subject to the rule of the wicked empire, and hence it did not have the power to destroy them. The Min admits, at the end of his speech, and even swears to reinforce his words that the question of ridding the world of Jews does not cease troubling him and his associates.

This story proves that even in the period of the spread of Christianity it is not possible to speak of a rapprochement between Gentiles and Jews for the reason that 'Jews and Gentiles had to fight against the common dangerous enemy',[74] just as, on the other hand, the Jews and Christians were not allies in the common struggle against the heathen Roman Empire.[75] Although Celsus — followed by Porphyry, the emperor Julian, and others like them — was prepared to recognize and even to praise the loyalty of the Jews to the tradition of their ancestors and their laws,[76] yet at the same time they were most emphatically opposed to the claim of the Jews that their God is 'One and there is none beside Him', that they are His chosen people, and certainly to the contention that the Jews cannot give up their belief that the idols shall utterly pass away and that they are enjoined to encourage idolaters to enter the fold of Judaism. The struggle of the Christians against idolatry did not make them partners of the Jews, since this struggle was waged by the Christians while cleaving to the postulate that the election of Israel had been completely annulled and with it the age of the Torah and precepts had likewise passed away, and that the Church, 'which had been gathered from among the Gentile peoples'[77] had replaced the Congregation of Israel. In their endeavour to condition the minds of the pagans to accept their Gospel, the Christians were at the same time fanning the flames of hatred towards 'Israel in the flesh', and preparing the background for the anti-Jewish legislation and persecutions of the Jews in the fourth century,[78] after 'the entire kingdom [i.e. Roman Empire] had gone over to the Christian heresy'.[79] From that time on the Sages regarded it as 'The wicked kingdom, which seduces the world and leads it astray with its falsehoods'.[80]

For about a hundred and fifty years, from after the Revolt of Bar Kokhba until Christianity became dominant in the Roman Empire, the Sages of Israel stood embattled on two fronts — one facing them and the other at the rear. They joined issue with the pagans, who proceeded to negate Israel's election with politico-territorial arguments: a subjugated people, which had neither independence nor temple, could not be regarded by them as a chosen but as an inferior people; and they polemized against the Christians, who boasted that they had inherited the election-birthright of the Jewish people and its covenant with its God, as well as the accompanying spiritual attributes, precisely because they were 'not a people' but 'a church of the peoples'.[81] Although the polemic — as we noted even in the case of the pagans — was conducted on the basis of Scriptural verses, their interpretation and exposition, yet it was also nourished by actual relations and deeds which determined, in no small measure, its form and its intensity. The reply given by R. Ḥoshaʿya to the pagan Min, at the injunction of the Patriarch, was not delivered in a vacuum but as a result of definite knowledge of the heathen's thoughts and his attitude towards the Jews. This attitude was not peculiar to this Min alone, but it is likewise clear that he and his congeners did not represent the whole of pagan society.[82] Just as his point of view justified the answer that the dispersion of Israel was a means of protecting them from annihilation, so does the existence of pagans who come to be converted form the background of R. Eleazar's explanation that the dispersion of the nation was due to the desire of Providence to augment the number of proselytes. Undoubtedly this fact was also known to Rav Hoshaʿya, but it would have been out of place to emphasize it in the debate with his interlocutor. On the other hand Origen tells of a disputation that he had, with one who was accounted a scholar among the Jews, on the passage in Isaiah lii 13–liii 8. When Origen gave it a Christological interpretation, the Jew said to him: 'That these prophecies refer to the whole people as though they were a single individual, for they are scattered in exile and are afflicted, so that as a result of the Jews' being dispersed among other peoples, many of the latter may be converted'. In this way the Jew interpreted the verses: 'So marred was his visage unlike that of a man', 'For that which had not been told them shall they see'.[83] R. Eleazar's dictum is given here verbatim, only while the Amora based his teaching on Hosea ii 25, Origen states that the Jewish Sage with whom he debated expounded the verses in Isaiah lii–liii. But it seems that the Church father abridged his opponent's argument, for to begin with he reported in his name 'that the Jews are in exile and afflicted', but in the continuation he explains only the fact of the dispersion. Needless to say, Origen is concerned in his work not with the Jew but with his antagonist Celsus, and it is him that he wishes to convince of the correctness of the Christian claim that the verses in Isaiah, mentioned above, referred to Jesus, and thus prevent him from using the Jewish interpretation that it is the people of Israel which is spoken of. But what is important to us is the fact that, even in disputations with churchmen of the type of Origen, a Jewish Sage would make use of the proselytizing mission as a justification of the exile. It is inconceivable that a Jew would have advanced this argument, if it could have been easily refuted by an actual situation at variance with it. The importance of the continuing fact of proselytization in Judaism's struggle with Christianity is attested by Origen himself in another passage: 'Although Celsus, or the Jew whom he represents, may deride what I have to say, let it nevertheless be stated that many have turned to Christianity as though by compulsion: some spirit — through a vision by day or by night — suddenly changed their mind from hatred of the Gospel to readiness to die for it.'[84] Against such successes and their dialectical exposition it was possible to retaliate only by counteraction. This background enables us to understand the homily — apparently of the Amora R. Phinehas of the end of the fourth century — ' "If he do not declare it, then he shall bear his iniquity" (Leviticus v 1): the Holy One, blessed be He, said to Israel: If you will not declare my Godhood among the nations of the world, I shall exact retribution from you....'[85] At the same time the Sages did not deny the actual fact of degradation inherent in subjection and the imposition of an alien yoke, nor did they hide it from would-be proselytes. The procedure governing the reception of converts as taught in the Baraita undoubtedly reflects the condition prevailing after the promulgation of Hadrian's edicts: 'When an intending proselyte comes to be converted[86] at the present time, we say to him: "What reason have you for seeking conversion? Do you not know that Israel today are in travail, persecuted, swept (from place to place), harassed, and full of suffering?" If he answers: "I know and I am unworthy", he is immediately accepted....' This version appears to be a more general formulation of the text that was composed actually at the time of the persecution, namely: 'But do you not see that this people are the most debased and afflicted of all the peoples and are full of suffering... and they are slain for circumcision, ritual immersion, and all the other precepts, and cannot conduct themselves in public like all other people....'[87] These very statements are reported as the argument of Hadrian. When his relative Aquila came to inform him of his wish to be converted to Judaism, he said to him: 'You wish (to join) this people? How much have I degraded them, how much have I massacred them! You wish to attach yourself to the most despised of the nations...?'[88] In the second recension of the procedure of conversion it is prescribed that after the proselyte has come up from his ritual immersion, 'We speak (to him) kindly and comfortingly: "Happy are you! To whom do you cleave? To Him who spoke and the world came into being, blessed be He; for the world was created only for Israel's sake, and only Israel have been called children unto the Omnipresent, and we said all those things only for the purpose of increasing your reward." '[89] In another version of the story of Aquila's conversion he bases himself on the advice given by Hadrian in matters of business: 'Whatever merchandise you see debased and fallen to the ground trade in it, for eventually it will rise (in value) and you will make a profit.' He [Aquila] argued thus: 'I went the rounds of all the nations, and I did not find a nation so lowly and prostrate as Israel, but in the end it will rise, for so said Isaiah (xlix 7): "Thus saith the Lord, the Redeemer of Israel, his Holy One, to him who is despised of men, to him who is abhorred of nations, to a servant of rulers: kings shall see and rise, princes and they shall prostrate themselves, because of the Lord that is faithful, even the Holy One of Israel, who hath chosen thee." '[90] Presumably Aquila heard these words of comfort at the time of his conversion. Words of consolation were said to the proselytes, but the actual existence of candidates for conversion was a source of solace to the converters, for it served to bridge the gulf between the reality of the situation in which they found themselves and the consciousness of election, which we discussed above (p. 526). We may reasonably conjecture that such were not the sentiments expressed at the induction of proselytes before the promulgation of Hadrian's edicts, and even less so when the Temple existed; however, we are not dependent in this matter on mere supposition, but have express testimony as it has survived in the Tannaitic homily[91] on Deuteronomy xxxiii 19: ' "They shall call peoples unto the mountain": From this you may infer that the nations and kings foregathering to do business in Eretz-Israel would say: "Since we have gone to the trouble of coming here, let us go up and see what Jerusalem is like." Thus they go up to Jerusalem and see the Israelites serving one God and eating one kind of food — for in the case of the Gentiles the god of the one is not that of the other, nor is the food of one person like that of another — and they declare: "This is the best people to join." How do you know that they do not stir from there until they become converted and go and offer up sacrifices and burnt offerings? Therefore Scripture declares "There shall they offer sacrifices of righteousness" (Deuteronomy, *ibid.*). The people of Israel is not compared here to poor merchandise, but even when it appears in this guise, it does not cease being a chosen people and the nexus between election and proselytization remains. The homiletical discourses of the Sages in the synagogues and the colleges, at the time of assemblies, on occasions of rejoicing, or of mourning, attracted non-Jewish listeners, and in the name of Rabbi it was stated: 'There is a kind of pigeon that is fed and its companions smell her and come to her cote. So, too, when the elder sits and delivers his exposition, many proselytes are converted.'[92]

It is not feasible to attempt to classify the Sages according to their dicta relative to proselytes and to distinguish between those who had a liberal-universalistic outlook and spoke in favour of converts and conversion, and those who, holding a particularistic-exclusive view, were opposed to proselytization and spoke disparagingly of proselytes.[93] Such a division is an oversimplification, as is evidenced by the Tanna R. Simeon b. Yoḥai. He was the strongest opponent of the Roman Empire, and completely refused to give it credit for its philanthropic and civilizing acts. In his opinion 'All the improvements that they have made are for their own benefit. They established market-places in order to instal harlots there; baths for their own pleasure; bridges with a view to levying tolls.'[94] Despite this attitude and his bitter, disillusioning experience with proselytes and 'fearers of the Lord',[95] which induced him to say 'The best of the heathens slay', it was just this Tanna who taught: 'Behold Scripture says "But they that love Him shall be as the sun when he goeth forth in his might" (Judges v 31). Now who is greater, he who loves the king or he whom the king loves? You must say: He whom the king loves. And it is written "And loveth the stronger" (Deuteronomy x 18).'[96] This exposition and the homiletical hymn 'Beloved are proselytes, for they are everywhere given the same designations as Israel' were intended to encourage both the converts and the converters, 'so as not to close the door before future proselytes'.[97] His hope for proselytization led Simeon to rule that even outside Eretz-Israel, if one sees an idol, one must say the benediction for its eradication, 'because (the idolaters) are destined to be converted, as it is said "Then will I turn to the peoples a pure language, that they may all call upon the name of the Lord, to serve Him with one consent" (Zephaniah iii 9).'[98]

R. Simeon b. Yoḥai's attitude tends to show that the harsh expressions employed by other Sages, too, regarding Gentiles and proselytes do not necessarily attest opposition in principle to conversion or even to action in this respect, just as contrariwise kindly remarks about non-Jews do not of necessity imply enthusiasm for drawing them near to Judaism. R. Joḥanan[98a] is the author of the following dicta: 'Whoever says a wise thing among the nations of the world is called a sage' (*T.B. Megilla* 16a); 'Gentiles outside Eretz-Israel are not idolaters; they are merely keeping to their ancestral customs' (*T. B. Ḥullin* 13b). But at the same time he held, in opposition to the view of Tannaim (above, p. 543): 'A Gentile who studies the Torah is deserving of death, as it is said "Moses commanded us Torah (for) an inheritance" (Deuteronomy xxxiii 4) — it is an inheritance for us, but not for them' (*T. B. Sanhedrin* 59a). The exposition of the verse supports the assumption that the claim of the Christians, who sought to make the Torah their heritage, led to this sharp repudiation; but experiences of the kind that befell R. Judah Nesi'a (above, p. 542) suffice to explain such reactions. However, in actual practice it seems that R. Joḥanan held that even with regard to Minim 'one should thrust them aside with the left hand and bring them near with the right', and he even encouraged 'the bringing of people beneath the wings of the Shekhina.'[99]

R. Ḥelbo's saying, which has received wide publicity[1] as testimony against proselytization, that 'Proselytes are as difficult for Israel (to endure) as a scab [ספחת *sappaḥat*], as it is said "And they shall cleave [ונספחו *wĕ-nispĕḥû*] to the house of Jacob" (Isaiah xiv 1)' is not clear and unambiguous evidence, for other things are described as difficult[2]; nevertheless a man is not obliged, nor is he even able, to refrain from them. Incidentally, it is R. Ḥelbo who maintained the view that the Lord adjured Israel not to rebel against the non-Jewish governments.[3]

Nor does there appear to be any development from a more lenient to a stricter attitude, or evidence that later Amoraim are more inclined to close the door before proselytes. Actually the most unequivocal dictum against those who accept proselytes was uttered by a Sage who lived in the generation before R. Ḥelbo, namely R. Isaac Nappaḥa, who said 'Evil after evil shall come upon those who accept proselytes'.[4] He was not content to state that converts were hard to endure, but curses those who receive them. Possibly this clear opposition originated in unpleasant experiences with גרים גרורים *gērîm gĕrûrîm* ['dragged-in' proselytes, who converted out of fear][5], and in the desire to prevent blurring of the distinction between proselytes who joined the Jewish people and those of the Gentiles who turned to the new church. Against their usurpative claims R. Isaac fought a hard and bitter fight,[6] and many of his dicta against the Gentile peoples can be clearly understood only if we regard them as directed against the church from among the peoples.[7] His saying was therefore an ephemeral expression of opinion emanating from his policy towards the new trouble that had befallen the Congregation of Israel. But it was actually a Sage that lived about two generations after R. Isaac, namely R. Berechiah, who did not agree with this approach, and did not even interpret the verse, Isaiah xiv 1, according to R. Ḥelbo, although as a rule he transmitted his expositions.[8] R. Berechiah's teaching is linked to an anonymous homily, which was also, it seems, enunciated close to his own time. We shall cite the exposition fully: '...Job said "The stranger will not lodge in the street", for the Holy One, blessed be He, disqualifies no one, but accepts everyone; the gates are open at all times and all who wish to enter may do so. Therefore the text says "The stranger will not lodge in the street"... the reference is to the Holy One, blessed be He, who bears with His creatures. R. Berechiah said: With respect to whom is it said "The stranger will not lodge in the street"? The meaning is that proselytes [the same as that rendered 'stranger'] will in time to come be priests ministering in the Temple, as it is said "And the stranger shall join himself with them, and they shall cleave to the house of Jacob" (Isaiah xiv 1), and "cleaving" means none other than priesthood, as it is said "Put me, I pray thee, into one of the priests' offices" (I Samuel ii 36).'[9] It may well be that R. Berechiah was reacting to the homily of R. Ḥelbo. Although proselytes are difficult to endure, nevertheless people generally are also difficult, yet the Lord bears with them. The anonymous homilist disagreed with R. Isaac's view, and maintained that proselytes should be accepted, for the Almighty does not disqualify any creature, but accepts everyone.

The hope for conversion did not cease so long as the belief in Israel's election and in the power of the Torah was a living and dynamic faith that deemed its purpose to be the perfection and renewal of the world. This faith was shared by both the first and the last of the Amoraim, both in Babylonia and in Eretz-Israel. R. Joḥanan said 'Just as a thorn-bush is used to make a hedge for a garden, even so is Israel a hedge for the world.'[10] In keeping with this thought 'R. Joḥanan declared: I am to whom I am (cf. Exodus iii 14) applies to individuals, but where the multitude is concerned, I shall reign over them perforce, against their will, though their teeth be shattered, as it is said "As I live, saith the Lord God, surely with a mighty hand, and with an outstretched arm, and with fury poured out, will I be king over you" (Ezekiel xx 33).'[11] The eternity of Israel for the sake of the world is linked in another dictum — which in a number of versions is transmitted in the name of R. Joshua b. Levi — with the nation's dispersion: 'For I have spread you abroad as the four winds of heaven, said the Lord...' 'This is the meaning: Just as the world cannot be without winds, so the world cannot be without Israel.'[12] Their great contemporary in Babylonia, Rav, found satisfaction in the fact that there were many Gentiles who, though they had not become converted, yet esteemed Israel and his God. He is the author of the dictum: 'From Tyre to קרטיגיני (Carduene) Israel and their Heavenly Father are recognized, but from Tyre westwards and from קרטיגיני (Carduene) eastwards neither Israel nor their Father in Heaven are recognized.'[13] In the name of R. Joḥanan's disciple, R. Abbahu, it is reported by R. Berechiah that the very election of Israel posits the continued election of proselytes: '...But had it been stated "And I set the nations of the world apart from you" the nations of the world would not have survived. But (it says) "And I have set you apart from the peoples, that ye should be Mine" (Leviticus xx 26), (signifying) that He chooses the good from the bad, choosing again and again; but when He selects the bad from the good, he does so once but not again.'[14] However, the attraction of proselytes was dependent on Israel's conduct. R. Berechiah describes an analogy, the moral of which is: 'So long as they [Israel] do the will of the Holy One, blessed be He, then whenever He sees a righteous person among the nations of the world — like Jethro, Rahab, and Ruth, and like Antonius — He makes him come and join Israel....'[15] Rav Ashi, the greatest of the last Amoraim in Babylonia, said that the guiding star (מזל *mazzal*) of the proselytes was present at the Revelation on Mount Sinai and that the contaminating lust injected by the Serpent into man left them just as it left the Israelites.[16] He was dissatisfied with the paucity of proselytes in his day and he declared that the inhabitants of his city were stubborn 'for they see the glory of the Torah twice a year and not one of them is converted'.[17]

The intensity of the consciousness of election found its true expression in the orders of the prayers and benedictions among the Jews. On the Day of Atonement the High Priest pronounced, during the service, eight benedictions, including 'who choosest the Sanctuary', 'Who choosest Israel', 'Who choosest the priests'.[18] R. Eleazar b. R. Zadok reports that his father, who still lived in the Temple period, used to pray on Sabbath evening as follows: 'And out of Thy love, O Lord our God, that Thou didst love Israel, Thy people, and out of Thy pity, O our King, that Thou didst feel for the children of Thy covenant, Thou didst give us, O Lord our God, this great and holy seventh day in love.'[19] The blessing for the Torah, which was originally a separate blessing formulated like 'Who choosest the Torah', 'Who hast given the Torah unto Israel',[20] was also prefaced by thanksgiving for the election of Israel. The Babylonian Amora, Rav Hamnuna, gives us the wording of the blessing that he regards as 'the best of the benedictions': 'Who hast chosen us from all the peoples and hast given us Thy Torah, blessed art Thou, O Lord, who hast given the Torah.'[21] In the Palestinian version of the liturgy we find: 'Blessed art Thou, O Lord, King of the universe, who hast chosen the flocks of Thy sheep and hast made known to them the ways of Thy will.'[22]

The closing benedictory formulas for Israel's election occur in the recensions of the second benediction preceding the *Shema*ʿ (which is also a kind of blessing for the Torah), namely in אהבה רבה *'ahăvā* *rabbā* ['With abounding love'], the version recommended by Samuel and R. Eleazar, and in the formulation of the 'Rabbanan' [Rabbis], אהבת עולם *'ahăvat ʿōlām* ['With everlasting love'].[23] It would be superfluous to add examples from the liturgical formulas of the festivals, in which the idea of election is central; but we would point out that with reference to the נעילה *Nĕʿîlā* ['Closing of the Gates'] prayer of the Day of Atonement — at one time it used to be recited also on fast-days and at the מעמדות *Maʿămādôt*[24] — which was essentially a confession, it is likewise related that ' ʿUlla bar Rav (once) descended (to the reader's desk) — in the presence[25] of Rava (and) commenced "Thou hast chosen us" and concluded "What are we, what is our life?" and he praised him.' The combination of the confession according to Samuel's formulation — which expresses, not in the singular but in the plural, the insignificance of man standing before his Maker, a fact that won the approval of the great Amora Rava — with the prayer 'Thou hast chosen us from all the peoples' sheds light on the meaning of Israel's election.

The active conception of the election, which postulates that Israel chose his God (above, p. 529), at least in the sense of proclaiming the uniqueness of His name and power in the world, was censured as a source of self-gratification: a homily, whose date it is difficult to fix[26], declares: ' "I said unto the Lord, Thou art my Lord; My gratefulness is not with thee" (Psalms xvi 2): The Congregation of Israel said before the Holy One, blessed be He: "Sovereign of the universe, be grateful to me that I made Thee known in the world." He answered "My gratefulness is not with thee" — I am grateful only to Abraham, Isaac, and Jacob, who were the first to make Me known in the world, as it is said "With the holy that are in the earth; they are the mighty ones in whom is all My delight" (*ibid.* v. 3).'[27]

III. Indictment and Defence of the Congregation of Israel

The consciousness of election did not blind the Sages from seeing the weaknesses of the Congregation of Israel, and they had no need of the accusations of extraneous traducers — idolaters and all kinds of sectarians. It was just these charges that led to counter-attacks, but at times also to a manner of defence that could only be described as 'brushing aside with a reed'. But neither type of rejoinder was able to put a good complexion on negative facts; it will suffice to underline what occurred in the episode of the golden calf. Needless to say this incident was seen by the Tannaim in all its gravity and characteristically they gave added emphasis to the matter. They not only justified the twofold punishment that the people suffered at the hands of Moses and of God,[28] and even augmented it,[29] but they allowed the shadow of the sin of the calf to fall upon the revelation at Mount Sinai and even impugned the sincerity of the people's response at the time;[30] similarly they called in question the liberality of their offerings for the erection of the Tabernacle. R. Simeon b. Yoḥai said: 'To what may the matter be compared? To a man who welcomed Sages and disciples and everyone praised him. Then Gentiles came and he welcomed them (too) and people said: "It is his nature to welcome everybody." Even so Moses said: "And 'Di-zahab' (Deuteronomy i 1) [interpreted as 'much gold'] — (they gave) to the Tabernacle and 'Di-zahab' (they gave) to the calf." '[31] The lesson drawn from the parable is not analogous to the parable, for the episode of the calf preceded the work of the Tabernacle; this is a clear indication that the parable was of primary importance to the Tanna. He wished to rebuke men of wealth who befriended Sages and disciples and at the same time also sought the intimacy of Gentiles from among government circles. Whether he referred to the period before the Revolt and to people like his father, who were state officials, or whether he had in mind burghers in Galilee after the Revolt, his words were directed to his own people, and the story of the calf merely served as a peg for his criticism, but was not his primary concern. But when the Gentiles began to vex Israel 'and said to them: "you made the calf" ', and consequently even God had, as it were, exchanged them for others, the Amoraim adopted polemical and apologetic measures. The Haggadist R. Samuel bar Naḥmani took an extreme line of defence, saying 'The Israelites are exonerated from that episode, for had the Israelites made the calf they would have said "These are our gods, O Israel". It was the proselytes who went up with Israel from Egypt and also the mixed multitude that went up with them (Exodus xii 38) who made the calf and vexed them, saying to them "These are thy gods, O Israel" (*ibid.* xxxii 4).'[32] In conformity with the rule enunciated by R. Samuel b. Naḥmani that when the Lord sees the nations of the world gleeful at the thought that He is about to chastise Israel, He transmutes the chastisement into benefit,[33] R. Levi came and found confirmation of the view that God Himself 'investigated the charges and found no substance in them', and therefore He enjoined that the ox should head all the sacrifices.[34] It was actually R. Isaac, opposed though he was to accepting proselytes (above, p. 551), who did not blame them for the sin of the calf. To the Gentile nations who say 'This people has changed its Glory', Israel answered, he states, as follows: 'If now in one moment I have become so guilty, how much more so are you (blameworthy)! Furthermore, the Israelites say to the nations of the world: We shall tell you what we are like: we are comparable to a prince who went forth to the pasture-land adjoining the city and the sun beat down on his head and his face was tanned. But on entering the city (again), with the help of a little water and a little bathing in one of the bath-houses, his body became white again and his beauty was restored as at first. Even so is it with us, if the sun of idolatry scorched us. But you are scorched from your mother's womb. While you were still in your mother's womb you worshipped idols. How? When a woman is pregnant, she enters her pagan temple and kneels and prostrates herself to the idol — both she and her son.'[35] The conclusion accords with R. Isaac's opposition to the acceptance of converts and for a good reason: people who have already served idols in their mother's womb are not likely to be weaned from it. But this fact in no way diminishes the sin of the calf. When they were not engaged in controversy, other Amoraim also regarded this incident as a reminder of iniquity. Thus R. Abbahu gave the following exposition: ' "And with twain he covered his feet" (Isaiah vi 2) — so that they should not behold the presence of the Shekhina, as it is written "and the sole of their feet was like the sole of a calf's foot" (Ezekiel i 7), and it is further written "They have made them a molten calf" (Exodus xxxii 8), for Scripture declares "And it shall be no more the confidence of the house of Israel, bringing iniquity to remembrance" (Ezekiel xxix 16).' In this way, too, R. Abbahu explained the reason underlying the Halakha taught in the Mishna of *Rosh-ha-Shana*: 'All *shofars* are valid save that of a cow' (*M. Rosh ha-Shana* iii, 2), 'because it is the horn of a calf, and it is written "They have made them a molten calf", for Scripture declares "And it shall be no more the confidence of the house of Israel, bringing iniquity to remembrance." '[36]

Like R. Simeon b. Yoḥai (above, p. 555), one of the early Amoraim, R. Ba bar Aḥa[37], proceeded to compare Israel's conduct when the calf was made and when the Tabernacle was erected, and he came to the general conclusion: 'One cannot understand the nature of this people: if appealed to for the calf they give, and if appealed to for the Tabernacle they give.'[38] This dictum expresses the fickleness and polarity that marked Israel's behaviour and hence it is difficult for this Amora 'to understand the nature of this people'. This evaluation recalls the homily of the Tanna R. Judah on the destiny of the nation, which also fluctuates from one extreme to the other: 'R. Judah b. R. Ileʿai expounded ...this people are likened to the dust and to the stars; when they decline, they go down to the dust, and when they rise, they ascend to the stars.'[39] The Amora R. Judah bar Pazzi reached a far more pessimistic conclusion than that of R. Ba b. R. Aha.[40] He also compared the story of the calf with that of the Tabernacle, but he added comparisons with the account of the giving of the Torah, of the exodus from Egypt, and of the spies, and he sums up as follows: 'Shall we read and not feel abashed? For a good cause (we find) "as many as were willing-hearted" (Exodus xxxv 22), but for evil "And all the people broke off the golden rings which were in their ears" (*ibid.* xxxii 3); for good "And Moses brought forth the people" (Exodus xix 17), for evil "And ye came near unto me every one of you" (Deuteronomy i 22); for good "Then sang Moses and the children of Israel" (Exodus xv 1), for evil "And all the congregation lifted up their voice, and cried" (Number xiv 1).' The homilist stresses that the tendency of the Israelites towards evil, during their stay in the wilderness, was stronger than their inclination to do good, and in this respect he associated himself with similar appraisals found in the Prophets (above, p. 216); but as in their case the focal interest in this evaluation and similar pronouncements lay in their bearing on the present and on the attitude of the Sages to the Jewish people in their own times. However, it is precisely in this sphere that the fundamental difference between the Sages and the Prophets is clearly to be seen. The Rabbis contemplated the prophetic work and reproof as well as their outcome, and they studied and eval-ated the reciprocal relationship between the Prophets and Israel.

R. Akiba said that only for Israel's sake did the Lord speak with Moses, 'for during the entire period of thirty-eight years that He was wroth with Israel He did not speak with him.' His disciple, R. Simeon b. Azzai, added to his teaching, saying that 'God spoke with all the Prophets only for Israel's sake.'[41] The Prophets were called upon to offer their lives for Israel; they were God's messengers and transmitted His word, but they were also the representatives of the people. Although it was likewise the Prophet's task to demand that the honour of the Father be respected, yet it was forbidden him to ignore the honour due to the son. Jeremiah was a prophet who sought to assure both the Father's and the son's honour. Elijah, on the other hand, claimed only the honour due to the Father, and therefore the Lord said to him ' "And Elisha the son of Shaphat... shalt thou anoint to be prophet in thy room" (I Kings xix 16) — now there was no need to say "prophet in thy room"; the purport is: I do not desire your prophecy.' Jonah insisted on the honour of the son but not on that of the Father; therefore it is said ' "And the word of the Lord came unto Jonah the second time, saying" (Jonah iii 1) — He spoke to him a second but not a third time.'[42] The reference in this homily is to Jonah's flight and refusal to go and prophesy to Nineveh. However, the use made already by the Gospels of the story of Jonah brought in its train another interpretation of Jonah's flight. The authors of the Gospels argued: 'The men of Nineveh will arise at the judgement with this generation and condemn it; for they repented at the preaching of Jonah, and behold something greater than Jonah is here.'[43] The words of the Midrash read as a reply to this, namely that Jonah's flight was not due to the fact that he did not wish to rebuke the men of Nineveh, but 'Jonah said to himself as follows: "I shall go outside the borders of Israel, where the Shekhina does not reveal Itself, for the Gentiles soon repent, and I shall thus avoid condemning Israel." '[44] But the Lord rejected Jonah's argument; Israel had no reason to fear the repentance of the people of Nineveh. Only the exacerbation of the Judeo-Christian conflict led to the negation of the value of this penitence.[45]

Just as the Sages regarded the prophet's function as that of one who demanded both the honour due to the son and to the Father, so they considered themselves to hold a brief for both the honour of the prophets and of the people. In the wake of the testimonies of the Bible regarding the bad relationship between Israel and its prophets, legendary tales were current in various circles that supplemented what was missing in Scripture. Verses like 'Shall the priest and the prophet be slain in the sanctuary of the Lord' (Lamentations ii 20), or 'Nevertheless they were disobedient, and rebelled against Thee, and cast Thy law behind their back, and slew Thy prophets that did forewarn them to turn them back unto Thee...' (Nehemiah ix 26), opened the way for visionaries to embroider the story of the prophets' lives and to relate their end and death and even to indicate their burial place. Such tales were preserved in their entirety in apocryphal works, which the Fathers of the Christian church adopted and even made interpolations in them: but their Jewish and Hebrew origin is not to be doubted.[46] Fragments of them have been preserved in the Talmuds and Midrashim. Simeon b. ʿAzzai said that he had found 'a scroll of genealogical records in which was written... Manasseh killed Isaiah'[47], and Amoraim in Eretz-Israel and in Babylonia even transmitted details of the story of how Isaiah was sawn asunder at the command of King Manasseh[48], a legend that is also known to us from the pseudepigraphical work *The Ascension of Isaiah*.[49] Around the verse in Lamentations concerning the priest and prophet who were slain in the Temple, a cluster of tales has been woven about the murder of the prophet Zechariah.[50] It is not surprising that the authors of the Synoptic Gospels seized upon this legendary tradition, in which they found support for their charges against 'Jerusalem, which killest the prophets and stonest them that are sent unto thee.'[51] The Fathers of the Church discovered in these stories parallels to the behaviour of the Jews towards Jesus and his apostles and already in the middle of the second century Justin argues against Trypho: 'Had your teachers and sages known and understood (the passages in the Bible alluding to Jesus), they would assuredly have taken care to expunge them, just as they suppressed the story about the death of Isaiah.'[52]

However, the truth is, as we have seen, that they did not suppress the story of Isaiah's martyrdom, either in the time of the Tannaim or in that of the Amoraim. Even more, in a Tannaitic Midrash it is stated generally 'In the end you will do violence to the prophets',[53] and in the name of R. Me'ir it is transmitted that 'The men of Jerusalem were smitten because they contemned the Prophets.'[54] The Amora R. Judah b. R. Simeon described Isaiah's appointment as a prophet dramatically, making his readiness to accept suffering the central feature of his account: 'Isaiah said: I was walking about in my schoolhouse, when I heard the voice of the Holy One, blessed be He: "Whom shall I send, and who will go for us?" (Isaiah vi 8); I sent Micah and they smote him on the cheek, as it is written "They smite the judge of Israel with a rod upon the cheek" (Micah iv 14); I sent Amos and they called him ψελλός... that inarticulate fellow... whom then shall I send and who will go for us? Forthwith I said "Here am I: send me" (Isaiah *loc. cit.*). Said God to him: Isaiah, My children are sinners and troublesome, if you will agree to be abused and beaten by My children, you can go on My mission; but if not, do not go. Isaiah replied: Even so, "I gave my back to the smiters, and my cheeks to them that plucked off the hair" (*ibid.* l 6).'[55] From the same verse it is deduced, in another homily, that the righteous have a duty to restrain their people, 'to suffer abuse for the sanctification of the Name, and to accept and suffer blows from Israelites as the prophets suffered at the hands of Israel, for Jeremiah endured much trouble from Israel, and so did Isaiah....'[56] This willingness to suffer is indicative of the Prophets' readiness to assert the honour due to the Father, but we have already seen that Tannaim criticized Elijah for not fulfilling his mission properly, in that he did not insist on the honour due to the son. Just as the travail and sufferings of the Prophets were generalized and Jonah did not remain the only one to 'demand the honour of the Father', so, too, the Amoraim transferred the character of Elijah to other Prophets. Let us begin with the homily of R. Simon, the father of R. Judah, to which were juxtaposed the dicta of Amoraim who preceded him and served him as a source:[57] ' "Look not upon me that I am swarthy" (Canticles i 6) — R. Simon began his exposition thus: "Slander not a servant unto his master" (Proverbs xxx 10), the Israelites are called servants, as it is said "For unto Me the children of Israel are servants" (Leviticus xxv 55) and the Prophets are called servants, as it is said "For the Lord God will do nothing,[58] [but He revealeth His counsel unto

His servants the prophets]" (Amos iii 7). Thus we learn that a servant should not slander a (fellow) servant. The Congregation of Israel says to the Prophets: you have denigrated me before Him who spoke and the world came into being. None loved me more than Moses, yet because he said "Hear now, ye rebels" (Numbers xx 10) it was decreed that he should not enter Eretz-Israel. Nor was there anyone that loved me more than Isaiah, but because he sa[id] "Woe is me! for I am defiled [נטמאתי]..."[59] (Isaiah vi 5), the Holy One said: You may proceed, of yourself you are perm[i]tted (to speak thus). "And I dwell in the midst of a people of unclean lips" — why? You see what is written there "Then flew unto me one of the seraphim, with a רצפה *riṣpa* ['glowing stone'] in his hand" (*ibid. v.* 6). What does it mean? [R.] Samuel bar Naḥman said *riṣpa* (connotes that) the mouth of him who speaks evil of Israel is to be crushed [רוצצים *rôṣĕṣîm*]. It is likewise written of Elijah (I Kings xix 10) "I have been very jealous for the Lord, the God of hosts; for the children of Israel have forsaken Thy covenant..." Said God: It is My covenant; is it then yours? "And thrown down Thine altars" — Said God to him: It is My altars; are they then your altars? — "And slain Thy prophets with the sword"—Said God (to him:) They are My prophets; what concern are they of yours? Said (Elijah) to God[60] "And I, even I only, am left" — what is written there? "And he looked, and, behold, there was at his head a cake baked on the hot stones [*rĕṣāfîm*]" (*ibid. v.* 6); R. Samuel bar Naḥman said: The mouth of him who speaks ill of Israel is to be crushed.' R. Simon transmitted R. Samuel bar Naḥman's exposition, and made it the basis of his own homily in answer to the accusations levelled by the Prophets against Israel, and it seems that also R. Joḥanan's dictum on this theme was reported by R. Simon as follows: 'R. Joḥanan heard it [the homily] in connection with the following verse: "The burden of Damascus. Behold Damascus... The cities of Aroer are forsaken" (Isaiah xvii 1–2) — he stands in Damascus and makes a proclamation concerning Aroer, but Aroer is surely within the borders of Moab! The meaning, however, is that there were six hundred and sixty-five idol shrines in Damascus and they used to worship each one on a particular day, but there was one day when they worshipped all of them on that day.[61] Said the Holy One to him: Elijah, instead of denouncing these, go and denounce these; "Go, return on thy way to the wilderness of Damascus...." ' Although a polemical note is to be discerned in R. Johanan's words, which is attested by the expression 'instead of denouncing these, go and denounce these', yet they were not said for polemical reasons only. The verse from Proverbs cited above R. Johanan interpreted in the name of R. Simeon b. Yohai as follows: 'Even a generation that curse their father and do not bless their mother, slander not a servant unto his master', and he learnt this from Hosea: 'R. Johanan said ...The Holy One, blessed be He, said to Hosea "Thy children have sinned"; he should have answered "They are Thy children, the children of Thy favoured ones, the children of Abraham, Isaac, and Jacob; be compassionate to them." Not enough that he did not speak thus, but he said before Him: "Sovereign of the universe, the whole world is Thine — exchange them for another people." Said the Holy One, blessed be He: "What shall I do with this old man? I shall tell him: Go and take a harlot and beget children of harlotry, and thereafter I shall say to him: Send her away. If he will be able to send her away, then I, too, will send Israel away."'[62] Doubt about the actual effectiveness of a general indictment is expressed in another dictum of R. Johanan: 'Pharaoh's removal of his ring to validate the oppression of Israel in Egypt was more beneficent than the forty years of prophesying against them by Moses, for the former resulted in redemption but the latter did not bring redemption.'[63] R. Abba bar Kahana, who mostly transmits dicta in the name of R. Johanan, formulated the idea in more general terms: 'Of greater avail was the removal of the ring (by Ahasuerus) than the forty-eight prophets and seven prophetesses that prophesied to Israel, for none of them restored the Israelites to the path of rectitude, whereas the removal of the ring did bring them back to the way of righteousness.'[64] His homily is formulated this time after the pattern of Resh Laqish's dictum: 'The removal of Ahasuerus' ring had a greater effect upon Israel than sixty myriads of prophets in the day of Elijah....'[65] The criticism of these Amoraim was directed against the all-embracing denunciation and the arraignment of the Congregation of Israel, which they regarded as an act of denigration on the part of the prophets in view of its ineffectiveness. However, it is clear that their purpose was not to criticize the prophets, but to point the moral for their own conduct. The following story is linked with the name of Resh Laqish: 'R. Abbahu and Resh Laqish were entering Caesarea, when R. Abbahu said to Resh Laqish: Why are we going into the city of blasphemers and revilers! Thereupon Resh Laqish alighted from his ass and took sand and put it into his mouth. Said (R. Abbahu) to him: What is the meaning of this? Resh Laqish replied: Does the Holy One then take pleasure in one who speaks ill of Israel?'[66]

Whilst in the homilies treating of the prophets the Amoraim criticize them for not fulfilling their function in demanding the honour due to the son — that is to say, they did not crave to justify the children of the Holy One, blessed be He, nor were they averse to condemning them[67] — in the story just cited opposition is expressed to the use of derogatory expressions regarding the Congregation of Israel, or concerning an entire city in Israel, even if no 'tale-bearing' is involved. Undoubtedly, Resh Laqish does not intend to deny the Sages the right and the duty to rebuke. This duty is ordained in the Torah, and the Sages regarded it as incumbent upon every individual Jew and even determined its proper measure: 'Whence do we know that when one observes something reprehensible in his fellow that he must rebuke him? For Scripture declares הוכח תוכיח *hôkhēaḥ tôkhîaḥ* "Thou shalt surely rebuke" (Leviticus xix 17). If he rebuked him, but he did not accept it, whence do we know that he must rebuke him again? Because the verse states תוכיח *tôhîaḥ*, "Thou shalt rebuke" [i.e. the expression of rebuking is repeated: *hôkhēaḥ tôkhîaḥ*, literally, 'Rebuke thou shalt rebuke'], in any circumstances. One might have assumed (that this is to be done) even if his face changed colour; hence the Torah teaches "Thou shalt incur no guilt because of him." '[68] With regard to the extent of the rebuke, even Amoraim differed: Rav said: To the point of smiting — that is, until the offender smites the rebuker; and Samuel said: until he curses; and R. Joḥanan said: until he loses his temper. The same dispute is transmitted in the name of the Tannaim R. Eliezer, R. Joshua, and Ben Azzai.[69] But other Tannaim, who were contemporaries of theirs, wondered if it was at all possible to rebuke: 'R. Ṭarfon said: Upon my faith! There is no one in this generation capable of reproving; R. Eleazar b. Azariah said: Upon my faith! There is no one in this generation able to receive reproof. R. Akiba said: Upon my faith! There is no one in this generation who knows how to reprove.'[70]

IV. The Status of the Sages in the Days of the Hasmoneans

The phrase 'There is no one in this generation' shows that, although the statements were made in connection with the precept to rebuke, which devolves on each individual, they actually refer to the leaders of the generation, who regard themselves as responsible for shaping its image. The responsibility is necessarily linked to a feeling of authority. This section will be devoted to the elucidation of the nature of this authority, its sources, and its manifestations in the position of the Sages within the Jewish community. Some of the facts may be gleaned from the sources we have cited with reference to the evaluation of the work of the prophets in relation to the people of Israel, but we have to enlarge the canvas in two directions. On the one hand, we shall consider the general appraisement of the phenomenon of prophecy by the Sages and, by implication, their self-evaluation through confrontation with it. On the other hand, we shall carefully observe the social situation at the different periods and places in which the Sages have expressed their views about themselves and their people.

The prevailing feeling in the Books of the Maccabees, as in all the Rabbinic sources, is that prophecy was absent in the era of the Second Temple, either throughout the period or, at least, from the beginning of Greek rule in the days of Alexander.[71] Prophecy is a highly complex phenomenon and when its disappearance is spoken of the question arises: Which of its elements are being referred to? The prophets appear in the Bible as ecstatics, as folk miracle-workers, who were unusual in their attire and customs and left the impression of 'madmen', as apostles who uttered words of rebuke and brought tidings of consolation.[72] Which of all these aspects ceased to exist? What remained of all these qualities, and how was the prophetic image conceived? It is clear that the Baraita which states 'When the last prophets, Haggai, Zechariah, and Malachi died, the Holy Spirit departed from Israel'[73] refers to the ending of prophecy as a part of the Holy Scriptures. Josephus, who tells us much about prophets in his time and in the preceding generations as miraculous men, who foretold future events and reprimanded, declares at the same time that 'From Artaxerxes to our own time the complete history has been written, but has not been deemed worthy of equal credit with the earlier records, because of the failure of the exact succession of the prophets... For, although such long ages have now passed, no one has ventured to add, or to remove, or to alter a syllable.'[74] However, the cessation of prophecy was not understood merely as the exclusion of the words of the prophets that had appeared, or were destined to appear, from the canon of the Biblical Prophets. From this aspect, there were not only a hundred and twenty myriads of prophets, or sixty myriads of prophets, mentioned by the Amoraim Rav Samuel bar Isaac and R. Joḥanan[75], but also 'one prophet in the morning and another at twilight', to whom Rabbi refers, and twice the number transmitted in the name of R. Nathan,[76] and even the prophets that are expressly cited in the Bible and are enumerated in the Baraita among the 'forty-eight prophets and seven prophetesses who prophesied to Israel,'[77] yet none of these had their utterances published. The explanation given of this phenomenon is: 'Every prophecy that was required at the time and was (also) needed for future generations was published, but the prophecy that was required at the time, but was not needed for future generations was not published.'[78]

From the postulate concerning prophecies that were needed at the time is to be inferred that their authors had the authority to demand that their generation should listen to them. The non-incorporation of prophetic utterances from the Holy Scripture is not yet sufficient, therefore, to negate their authority or that of their authors. This, however, is precisely the implication of the Baraita that links the cessation of prophecy with the beginning of Greek rule: 'This is Alexander the Macedonian [i.e. Alexander the Great], who reigned 12 years. Till now the prophets prophesied through the medium of the Holy Spirit; from now on incline your ear and hearken to the words of the Sages.'[79] Here the most characteristic feature of prophecy is negated, namely the express and manifest mission of the prophet, who claimed for himself direct authority in the name of the Lord, who speaks with him.

There may be visionaries and seers, men who foretell future events and work miracles and wonders — and, in truth, we have seen that there were many such in the days of the Second Temple and also in the period of the Tannaim and Amoraim, even in their very own circles — but they do not appear as prophets and messengers of God.[80]

Elsewhere we have noted the process that led to the divestment of prophecy of all authority in relation to the Torah and precepts and to the liberation of the latter from all dependence on supernatural forces. We have seen that, indeed, not all easily forwent supernal revelations even in these spheres; but the development that took place in the Oral Law and the struggles of its banner-bearers against sects and doctrines that launched attacks against it and its sources weighed down the scales in favour of the authority of the Sages, their expositions, and decisions. The enactments, practices, and innovations introduced by the prophets, of which information has come down to us, derived not from the power of their prophecy, but was the product of their explanations and argumentation, or the traditionary lore that they had received — in other words, the prophets were also Sages.[81] It would be superfluous to prolong this discussion in order to disprove the theory that connects the termination of prophecy with the dominance accorded the Torah in the days of Ezra. This hypothesis — whether it interprets the causal nexus unfavourably by supposing that prophecy could not survive in a framework of a fixed and crystallized Law of worship and precepts[82], or whether it interprets the link favourably by suggesting that the Torah, which grew to be the practical rule of life in the time of the Second Temple, made the reproofs of the prophets unnecessary[83] — overlooks two factors in the reality that emerges from the sources of the Oral Law, namely the attitude of the Torah exponents, the Sages, to prophecy and the prophets, on the one hand, and the function of these Sages as mentors, on the other.

The Baraita that makes the age of Alexander the Great the close of the era of 'those who prophesied by the Holy Spirit', and transfers their preaching and reproof to the Sages, was undoubtedly formulated at the conclusion of the process, and it merely retrojects the end-results to the initial stage. However, the various stages leading to the creation of the unique class of the Sages in actual history, and to its emergence as an elite of leadership unfold, *pari passu* with the crystallization of a given concept of prophecy and the prophets.

The prophets, whose teachings were conjoined with those of the Torah and who were portrayed as a link in the chain of tradition preceding the Men of the Great Synagogue, were not connected through their work with any particular social class, and were not affiliated to any state or cultic institution. Nor did they constitute a class of their own after the manner of their predecessors in the days of Samuel and in the days of Elijah and Elisha.

The Divine word that they uttered, their prophetic visions, their symbolic and ecstatic acts, their personal experiences — these were all directed to the improvement of the social order in all its aspects — in the spheres of worship, ethics, and justice — and to educating people to see the connection between their way of life and their attitude to the precepts of the Lord, on the one hand, and their destiny in the past, present, and future, on the other. However, their appearance as prophets and the consciousness of the direct mission that inspired them all, despite the individual differences between them, gave the prophetic teachers the image of a special and separate class.

We know neither the nature nor the date of 'the Great Synagogue', to whose members the prophets handed down the Torah (*M. 'Avot* i, 1).[84] But it is clear that these men — at least the majority of them — were not prophets, and we shall not err if we call them 'Sages'.[85] At any rate the earliest dictum attributed to them 'Be deliberate in judgement, raise up many disciples, and make a fence around the Law' shows that they were interested in the dispensation of justice and its methods, in making enactments and decrees, and in increasing the number of disciples[86] from whom Sages would arise. It seems that this was the highest legislative institution, which met whenever necessary.[87]

The statement that Simeon the Just was one of the last of the Great Synagogue implies that it was dissolved near his time. It is possible that the Greek conquest, which led to the establishment of Macedonian colonies, brought about administrative changes[88] that rendered the 'Great Synagogue', as an institution representative of all the people of the land, an impossibility or a fiction, and it was replaced by the 'Gerousia', the council that functioned in conjunction with the High Priest and represented Jerusalem and the adjacent region. At any rate it is only after the liberation of Judea in the days of Simon the Hasmonean that 'the Great Synagogue' reappears (below, p. 570).

Ben-Sira, who wrote in the years 190–170 B.C.E., shortly after Eretz-Israel passed from the rule of the Ptolemies to that of the Seleucids, describes the situation in his time as one marked by a great gulf between those engaged in work and those who wielded power and dominion. It is true that without the farmer, the smith, the refiner, and the potter 'a city cannot be inhabited, and wherever they dwell they hunger not. But they shall not be inquired of for public counsel, and in the assembly they enjoy no precedence. On the seat of the judge they do not sit, and law and justice they understand not' (xxxviii 32–33). On the other hand, the sage has no occupation; he sits upon the judge's seat 'and sets his mind upon the Law of the Most High; who searcheth out the wisdom of all the ancients, and is occupied with the prophets of old... who serveth among great men, and appeareth before princes' (*ibid.* xxxix 1–4). The Sages, as Ben-Sira portrays them, were wealthy and saw in their function election and mission. They were members of the Court of Justice and members of the Supreme Council, which is the γερουσία mentioned in the letter of Antiochus III, of the year 190 B.C.E., together with the 'priests and the scribes of the Temple'.[89] These members of the Gerousia, like the men of 'the Great Synagogue' who preceded them, or the members of the Sanhedrin who came after them, took no pay whatsoever for their public and judicial work. The scribes of the Temple were, it appears, custodians of the Holy Scriptures, called 'the books'. At first their work consisted only of writing and of copying the Holy Scriptures, and of taking meticulous care in transmitting them correctly. The explanation of their name given in a later period, namely 'Therefore the early Sages were called *Soferim* [understood here as 'Counters'; usually rendered 'Scribes'], because they counted all the letters of the Torah' (*T.B. Qiddushin* 30a) is not to be regarded as an etymology but is correct in substance. The revisers of the Temple scrolls, who were considered to have special authority, received their salary from the Temple fund,[90] and in all probability were priest-scribes. At any rate they did not belong to the highest hierarchy, and neither they nor the scroll-writers outside the Temple were rich. Ben-Sira also regarded the wisdom of the scribe as a form of art, which did, in truth, increase wisdom, but did not advance one to a position of power.

There was a difference between the scribes and the Sages similar to that which subsisted, as we know from the history of the earliest period of Roman jurisprudence, between the jurists, who decided and fixed the law, and the ancient interpreters of the legal prescriptions.[91] However, the Sages, too, were not merely legalists, but, as Ben-Sira states (xxxix 1–4), they set their minds upon the Law of the Most High, meditated upon prophecies, searched out the wisdom of all the ancients, the discourses of men of renown, the deep things and hidden meanings and parables. To meditation and knowledge they added also piety, which found expression in prayer, in thanksgiving, and in deducing wise instruction. Undoubtedly the Sage of Sirach, like that of the Book of Proverbs, was required to be constant in his fear of the Lord and the performance of the precepts (i 23; xix 20; xxv 14–15), to keep far from violent and presumptuous men and to associate with saintly men. But the wise man is not found as a sociable type. Although the public spoke in praise of him, and many lauded his understanding, yet he was not close to them, nor do we hear of his activity in their midst and on their behalf. The saying of Jose b. Jo'ezer, who lived in the generation preceding the Maccabean Revolt, 'Let your house be a meeting-place for the Sages, and sit amid the dust of their feet, and drink in their words with thirst' (*M. 'Avot* i, 4), fits the exclusive character of the class of the Sages in the Hellenistic period prior to the Maccabean Revolt. However, next to this dictum there is a demand of an entirely different kind expressed by his contemporary Jose b. Joḥanan of Jerusalem, who declares 'Let your house be opened wide and let the needy be members of your household' (*ibid.* i, 5). But although this saying emphasizes charitable and welfare work, and not wisdom, it does not diminish the aristocratic and philanthropic character of the request addressed by both of them to the householder. The restrictive edicts of King Antiochus Epiphanes directed against the Jewish religion in 167, the acts of martyrdom that followed in their wake, the raising of the standard of rebellion, at the head of which stood the priestly family of the Hasmoneans of Modi'im, who were joined by 'those who were seeking righteousness and justice' and 'a company of Hasideans... every one who offered himself willingly for the Law', the military victories of the Maccabees and the growing strength of Judea — all these factors led to the establishment of a new leadership. The solemn decision in 140 B.C.E., 'in a great congregation (ἐπὶ συναγωγῆς μεγάλης) of priests, and people, and chiefs of the nation, and elders of the country',[92] to appoint Simon as High Priest and Ethnarch opened the era of the Hasmonean monarchy with all the hopes and disillusionments, as well as the political and spiritual struggles, it involved. The changes that occurred in the institutional and governmental sphere are less apparent. Indubitably the rise to power of the House of the Hasmoneans resulted in the deposition of families of noble lineage who belonged to the extreme Hellenizers, while elevating, together with the new rulers, the families of the loyal fighters to governatorial and administrative positions. The replacement of the family of High Priests descended from Zadok by the priestly families of the Hasmoneans had political significance, but did not express the primary transformation. Typologically, Simons son John (Joḥanan) Hyrcanus approximates the figure of the 'Judge', the leader-deliverer. He was High Priest and also *'Av Bet Din* [Head of the Court of Justice]; he introduced reforms in the order of the Temple service[93] and made politico-religious enactments in regard to the collection and distribution of the tithes.[94]

Josephus, moreover, not content with this, attributed to him the power of prophecy: 'He was the only man to unite in his person three of the highest privileges: the supreme command of the nation, the high priesthood, and the gift of prophecy. For so closely was he in touch with the Deity, that he was never ignorant of the future; thus he foresaw and predicted that his two elder sons would not remain at the head of affairs.'[95] Although the Sages do not mention prophecy, for in their view the Holy Spirit ceased in Israel 'when the last prophets, Haggai, Zechariah, and Malachi died', yet they, too, related in a Baraita: 'Joḥanan the High Priest heard (a voice) from the Holy of Holies (saying) "The youths that went to do battle at Antioch were victorious" '; and the teacher of the Baraita added: 'And they determined the exact moment and found that it was precisely at that time that they triumphed.'[96] John Hyrcanus, however, was a unique phenomenon. It is certain that in his days men who belonged to the 'company of Hasideans' and those who offered themselves for the Law came to fulfil functions in the Temple and in institutions of the judiciary and Halakhic decisions, and it was the period of the activity of the 'Bet Din [Court, Sanhedrin] of the Hasmoneans'.[97] Although the priests continued to be scribes and judges in civil cases, yet the Sages penetrated all these classes, and from now on there were Sages who were priests, Sages who were judges, and Sages who were Ḥasidim ['Pietists'].

The earliest Sages about whom we have any tradition of real significance appear to us like the early prophets — Nathan, Gad, Ahijah, and Elijah — as reprovers of kings and despots. Only their reproof did not emanate from prophecy and their influence was not due to charisma, but to their wisdom; and this wisdom implies knowledge of the Torah and Halakha and absolute faithfulness to their injunctions and principles.

Let us piece together the tradition in our possession concerning the first Sage, who belongs to the Hasmonean period, namely Simeon b. Sheṭaḥ. We meet him sitting in the Bet Din to judge the slave of King Jannaeus, who had killed a person. In accordance with the Halakha that the owner of the slave must appear before the Bet Din, Simeon b. Sheṭaḥ summoned Jannaeus, 'And when he came, he said to him: "King Jannaeus, stand up and let them [the witnesses] testify against you..." Said he [the king] to him: "It is not as you say, but as your colleagues will say." When (Simeon) turned to the right, they [his colleagues] looked down at the ground, and when he turned to the left, they looked down at the ground. Whereupon Simeon b. Sheṭaḥ said to them: "Are you full of thoughts (of expediency)? Let the Master of thoughts [i.e. God] come and call you to account...." '[98] Simeon's colleagues may have shared in his function (as judges), but they did not share his views.

Simeon's activities were directed to the improvement of judicial procedures. This is attested by his rulings in regard to the examination of witnesses, so as to prevent punishment on the basis of estimated testimony, that is, on the basis of circumstantial evidence; so, too, with respect to the punishment of זוממים *zômĕmîm* witnesses [i.e. false witnesses against whom other witnesses testify that the former

Simeon b Sheṭaḥ

were with them elsewhere at the time of the crime].[99] His general instruction to judges was: 'Examine the witnesses diligently and be cautious in your words lest from them they learn to tell falsehood' (*M. 'Avot* i, 9). His enactment that the husband should write in his wife's *ketubba* ['marriage contract'] that all his property is pledged to her, was intended to make hasty divorce difficult and to secure the economic position of the woman on being divorced.[1] According to one source Simeon b. Sheṭaḥ enacted 'that children should go to school'.[2] The exact nature of the enactment and how it fits into other traditions concerning the establishment of a school system are not clear, but for our purpose this very statement regarding his activity in the field of popular education is of importance. We find Simeon b. Sheṭaḥ rendering assistance to poor nazirites and helping them to free themselves from their nazirite vows and to bring the sacrifices incumbent upon them.[3] As in the case of Elijah, so it was also related of Simeon b. Sheṭaḥ that he performed an act of zealotry, ordering, as an emergency measure, that eighty women be hanged in Ashkelon for engaging in witchcraft and illicit love.[4] The narrative tradition also portrays Simeon b. Sheṭaḥ as on friendly terms with King Jannaeus.[5] He dines with him at a banquet in honour of the emissaries of the King of Persia, who recall his words of wisdom on previous visits. But even in these narratives the extent of the Sage's individualism and independence is stressed. In his conversation a reproachful tone blends with friendliness. Undoubtedly this period of concord was the time to which many of his acts and enactments, mentioned above, belonged. However, he attributed his honour and status entirely to his Torah-knowledge. For his livelihood he engaged in flax work, and his principle in commercial transactions was so to conduct himself as to inspire people to glorify the name of his God, to declare 'Blessed be the God of the Jews'.[6]

In these fragmentary notices concerning this ancient Sage are enshrined a number of fundamental attributes that were to characterize the Sages throughout their generations, and served as ideals that they were brought up to honour and which, in turn, they inculcated in others. The work of the Sage and the administration of his community were not necessarily dependent on the fulfilment of any official function. Whether he held office or not, he was duty-bound to guide

"Re Sage" contrasted with the miracle-worker Onias (e.g. Simeon)

and to lead the community. The power of his leadership he drew first and foremost from his knowledge of the Torah. His attitude to the government and to wealth was determined only by the conduct of the officers of the government and the owners of the wealth. He did not seek their intimacy, but he did not shun them either. He preserved his independence and freedom and earned his livelihood by working. The dictum of Shemaʿya, the disciple of Simeon, 'Love labour and hate mastery and seek not acquaintance with the ruling power' (*M. 'Avot* i, 9), is a kind of briefing, emanating from the life-story of his master, that defines the ideal to be followed by the Sage in his relationship to work, the exercise of power, and the government. The activity of the Sage aimed to ameliorate the life of the community in the sphere of justice and righteousness, and in that of family relations and the education of the people in Torah and piety. Even the attributes and virtues that are absent from Simeon b. Sheṭaḥ's limited spectrum of activity are instructive. It contains no contemplative-mystical, or miraculous-supernatural, element. One may certainly not infer from this that Simeon b. Sheṭaḥ adopted a negative attitude to these aspects; but they are not to be regarded as dominant characteristics. Miracle-workers lived in close proximity to Simeon. Onias, the Circle-maker — like Elijah before him — delivered his people by his prayer from severe drought. Onias's importunate pleading before the Lord, expressed in the terms 'I swear by Thy great name that I shall not stir from here until Thou shalt take pity on Thy children', and the prominence he gave to himself by saying 'Thy children have turned their faces to me' were not pleasing to Simeon b. Sheṭah. Although Onias's prayer was answered, yet Simeon did not refrain from sending him a message in which rebuke and recognition were, so to speak, intermingled: 'Were it not that you are Onias, I would decree a ban against you. But what can I do with you? For you importune the Omnipresent and he fulfils your will, like a son who importunes his father.'[7] Although this pronouncement does, to some extent, find fault with Onias's method of working, yet it contains, at the same time, an acknowledgement of his standing with his Creator, and also, apparently, of the esteem in which he was held by wide sections of the people.

If we find that Simeon b. Sheṭaḥ assumed one facet of the early prophets' activity, namely to intervene in political life, to reprove rulers and men of power openly, and to wage war against corrupt conduct, Onias, on the other hand, the first of the line of pietists and miracle-workers who are known to us by name, inherited the ability to perform miracles and wonders. In the case of the early prophets the two aspects were integrated; and although they are separated here, they existed in juxtaposition. Undoubtedly the simple folk looked upon Onias as a type of Elijah and the bringing down of rain even enhanced his popularity. Simeon, however, was content to put his own interpretation on the episode. God fulfilled Onias's wish as a father fulfils that of his son. Simeon b. Sheṭaḥ's attitude to Onias is characteristic of that of the Sages towards concepts and beliefs, trends and tendencies, that were not wholly to their liking. Their approach was to set their seal upon them by penetrating the affected circles and adopting them as their own. On account of this attitude they did not hasten to ban or eliminate phenomena or groups of which they did not approve, even when they had the power to do so. This is attested by the history of the relations between the Sages and the Sadducees. Whereas the latter, when they held office and were in power, sought to turn their opponents into a group of secessionists — and hence they also designated them 'Pharisees' [פרושים *Pĕrûshîm*, literally 'Separated', i.e. seceders][8] — yet when the Sages prevailed and their influence was decisive, they did not oust the Sadducees. At any rate the tone of the discussions between them and the testimonies concerning them[9] do not bear out such an aim. Although the attitude towards sectarians became greatly exacerbated, yet this exacerbation came as a reaction to the secession of individuals or sects, like the Christians in the second century[10], who on the one hand argued that the Congregation of Israel should cease to exist as a separate entity, and on the other wished to be regarded as its inheritors.

The Sages' desire and intent to live amidst the broad strata of the people, to lead them and guide them, was prompted to no small extent by the fact that they themselves came from all classes and strata. There were among them priests of noble lineage, men of wealth, sons of big landowners, poor artisans, metayers and farmers, hired labourers, and sons of proselytes. This entire variegated community, without exception, the Sages wished to mould and to guide. Undoubtedly Hillel's teachers, Shemaʿyah and Avṭalion, also acted in accordance with his maxim 'Keep not aloof from the community' (*M. 'Avot* ii, 4). But this principle did not exhaust the communal policy of these Sages. They refused to swear an oath of allegiance to Herod, but Shemaʿyah's dictum 'Seek not acquaintance with the ruling power' was complemented by the teaching of his colleague Avṭalion 'Oh Sages, give heed to your words, lest you incur the penalty of exile' (*M. 'Avot* i, 11). A tyrannical ruler like Herod might sentence those who spoke incautiously to be banished from the country, or to work in the mines. He must not easily be provided with a pretext for ridding himself by this method of the leaders, who knew his nature, and so deprive the broad masses of their leadership.

The popularity of these Sages and their relationship to the contemporary High Priest — the reference may be to Aristobulus the Hasmonean, or to a High Priest appointed by Herod — is indicated by the following story: 'It once happened that a certain High Priest went forth from the Temple and all the people escorted him; but when they saw Shemaʿyah and Avṭalion they left the High Priest and followed them. Finally Shemaʿyah and Avṭalion came to take their leave of the High Priest and said to him: "May the son of Aaron go in peace!" He replied: "May the descendants of the Gentiles come in peace!" They riposted: "May the descendants of the Gentiles, who act like Aaron, come in peace, but may not the son of Aaron, who does not act like Aaron, come in peace!" '[11] The two Sages paid due honour to the High Priest. But when he, incensed by the preference shown by the people for the Sages, expressed himself contemptuously by alluding to their non-Jewish origin, they replied that what mattered was not genealogy — belonging to the sons of Aaron — but acting like Aaron. In the spirit of this answer their disciple Hillel enjoined: 'Be of the disciples of Aaron, loving peace and pursuing peace, loving mankind and bringing them nigh to the Torah' (*M. 'Avot* i, 12). All who possess these attributes are deemed disciples of Aaron, and they are to be preferred to the sons of Aaron who do not walk in his ways.

The families of the High Priests, who occupied the important posts of treasurers and trustees (*Amarkalim*), made the Temple the pivot

MB

of their activities. Dynasties were created in which appointments were concentrated for generations, and they also had knowledge of certain cultic services, whose secrets they guarded from generation to generation. One Sage, Abba Saul b. Botnit, who owned a store in Jerusalem shortly before the destruction of the Temple, criticised the priestly dynasties and the concentration of functions in their hands as well as the violence of the office-bearers. He declared: 'Woe is me because of the House of Elisha, woe is me because of their fist, woe is me because of the House of Ishmael b. Phiabi, who are High Priests and their sons are treasurers and their sons-in-law are trustees, and their servants come and beat us with sticks!'[12] Indeed we also hear in another source of 'the leading priests', who came and took by force the skins of the holy offerings in the Temple and prevented their just division among the priestly watches.[13] The houses of the experts, who refused to teach their craft to others, the Sages mentioned unfavourably and said that they intended to enhance their own glory and to diminish that of Heaven.[14] Nor did the Sages refrain from protesting against the exaggerated scrupulousness of the priests in regard to the laws of purity and impurity, 'so that the uncleanness of the knife was considered by them a graver matter than the shedding of blood'.[15] But the Sages were not content merely to voice their criticism; they also endeavoured to permeate the sphere of the Temple and its service with their influence and views, and to weigh down the scales in favour of the traditions and the customs, or the interpretations of the details of the service arrangements that they approved.

V. Hillel's Character and Work

Hillel, who immigrated from Babylonia, influenced the Sons of Bathyra — also apparently a Babylonian family — who had been appointed to one of the important Temple offices, after Herod had deposed the Hasmoneans from the High Priesthood. In his debate with the Sons of Bathyra he made use of the seven exegetical rules by which the Torah is expounded in order to prove that the offering of the Passover sacrifice overrides the Sabbath, if the fourteenth of Nisan falls on the Sabbath, and this accorded with the tradition he had received from his teachers Shemaʿyah and Avṭalion. This Halakha was forgotten and differences of opinion arose on the subject, not necessarily because it but rarely happens that Passover eve falls on the Sabbath. Not only was his teachers' tradition on Hillel's side, but it seems that the masses of the people who went on pilgrimage were of the same opinion. When the Sons of Bathyra said to him 'If so, what will be the position with regard to the people who have not brought their knives and their Passover offerings to the Temple?' he replied: 'Leave it to them; the holy spirit rests on them. If they are not prophets, they are sons of prophets.'[16] Indeed the people found a way of bringing their Passover lambs and knives to the Sanctuary, and they undoubtedly acted as did their fathers.

The way in which Hillel expressed himself — 'The holy spirit rests on them. If they are not prophets, they are sons of prophets' — is of great significance. While, on the one hand, he himself went to the trouble of applying the principle of 'the standard rule' and the argument *a fortiori* in his exposition and even made use of the tradition he had received from his teachers, Shemaʿyah and Avṭalion, in order to prove that the Passover sacrifice overrides the Sabbath, on the other hand, he evaluated the popular usage as a reflection of prophecy, as a kind of Heavenly Voice. The holy spirit had departed from individuals, but it rested on the community as a whole. The aphorism uttered by Hillel at the Water-Drawing Celebration 'If you will come to My home, I shall come to your home; but if you will not come to My home, I shall not come to yours'[17] contains an allusion to the etymological exposition of R. Joshua b. Levi: 'Why is it called בית השואבה *Bêt ha-Shô'ēvā* [literally 'House of Drawing'; rendered above 'Water-Drawing']? Because the holy spirit is drawn from there.'[18] The holy spirit as a permanent factor ceased to exist in the days of the Second Temple, but certain situations of exaltation and joy deriving from the performance of a Divine precept bring about its reappearance; more than this, however, the generation does not merit. This explanation is confirmed by another story concerning Hillel: 'It once happened that when the Sages entered the house of Guryo in Jericho, they heard a Heavenly Voice say "There is a man here who is worthy of the holy spirit, but his generation is not worthy of it and they all looked at Hillel...."[19]

The very expressions 'a generation worthy', 'a man worthy', in relation to the holy spirit and prophecy point to a fundamental change that had occurred in the conception of this phenomenon. In the Bible we find no description whatsoever of the prophetic attributes considered essential qualifications for the gift of prophecy. The prophet is called and responds or is sent and runs away; a mighty hand takes hold of him, and the prophecy is like a fire shut up in his bones; while according to the Sages a man is vouchsafed the holy spirit by virtue of his fitness and the qualities of character and virtues that he has acquired[20], and even these are insufficient and he requires certain external, objective conditions.[21] Prophecy evolved into a mystic experience.[22] It is told of Hillel 'that he had eighty disciples, thirty of whom were worthy that the Divine Presence should rest upon them... the most junior of them all was Rabban Joḥanan b. Zakkai'[23] and with his name, in truth, are linked the earliest traditions and accounts of the experiences of those among the Sages who occupied themselves with the 'Work of the Chariot'. But this mystic encounter remained an esoteric doctrine, the tradition relating to it being restrained and reserved.[24] Even if it raised the status of its heroes in the estimation of their friends, it was not the factor that gave them authority and standing, just as these were not acquired by the performance of miracles, although they may have brought those who wrought them fame in the eyes of the masses.[25] The 'Work of the Chariot' became a theme of Torah study, a part of the wisdom of those Sages who continued to learn and expound it. It was the Amora R. Avdimi of Haifa, who himself belonged to this type of Sage[26], that stated: 'Since the destruction of the Temple prophecy was taken away from the prophets and given to the Sages'[27]; and, apparently, by 'prophecy' he meant a mystic experience, which could be acquired only by one who was also a Sage. The Sage could also be a prophet, but one who professes to be only a prophet, is not even a prophet. This is what Amemar had in mind when he said 'a Sage transcends a prophet.' One aspect of prophecy — namely foretelling future events — also continued to be found among the Sages. In this sense Amoraim said that certain Tannaim 'foresaw' or 'divined' by the holy spirit, and actually the stories show that this 'holy spirit' was their understanding and wisdom or a miraculous act.[28] R. Joḥanan referred to foretelling and divining the future in his dictum 'Since the day that the Temple was destroyed, prophecy was taken away from the prophets and was given to idiots and children.'[29] He not only interpreted the verse 'And thine ears shall hear a word behind thee' (Isaiah xxx 21) to mean that 'one may make use of a Heavenly Voice [literally 'the Daughter of a Voice']'[30], in the sense of divining the future and drawing inferences from a voice heard by chance, but he acted in accordance with this rule. The voice of a lad, who read in his school the verse 'And Samuel died', led him and Resh Laqish to the conclusion that the Amora Samuel in Babylonia had died, and caused them to put off their intended journey to Babylonia in order to visit him.[31] The voice may be of a child or of a woman, but it is used for instruction. A different connotation attaches to the expression 'a Heavenly Voice went forth', which refers not only to that which went forth from the Holy of Holies, or was heard at the time when the voice of prophecy had not yet become silent; the phrase 'a Heavenly Voice went forth and said' serves at times as a substitute for 'the holy spirit said'.[32] Tannaim and Amoraim also heard 'a Heavenly Voice' of this kind.[33]

It is, nevertheless, clear that neither the manifestations of prophecy in its later aspects, nor the working of miracles, nor the demonstration of superhuman power in bestowing good upon the meritorious and in punishing the wicked, nor ardent words of revelation (which, however, were delivered as interpretations of verses) are characteristic of the Sages in the context of their status among the people and their leadership of the Congregation of Israel. The stories about R. Simeon b. Yoḥai and R. Joḥanan, who cast their eyes on people and turned them into 'a heap of bones',[34] are not different from many other stories regarding righteous and saintly men. The homilies of Sages and others that contain hyperbolical descriptions of the world to come recall the visions of the apocalyptists.[35] What stamps them as Sages is the fact that, like their colleagues who were not known as miracle-workers, they lived in the midst of their people, and that all their actions, expositions, and Halakhot served to guide and perfect the Congregation of Israel. This aim unites the Sages from first to last, despite the differences of type and many divergences of view.

Let us revert to Hillel. The fact that he was found worthy of the inspiration of the holy spirit highlights his personal attributes and virtues as they are revealed in his deeds and activities, which endowed him with influence and status. Even if his appointment as Nasi [Patriarch, Chief] by the Sons of Bathyra had only limited significance — that is to say, he was accepted as Nasi over them[36], as a teacher of Halakhot in the sphere of the Sanctuary — his influence is nevertheless also proved by his enactments. One concerned the Temple treasury, which likewise served as a depository in the charge of trustees and treasurers. In order to circumvent the law of the Torah, which gives the seller of a house in a walled city the right to redeem it during the entire period of twelve months, the buyers used to hide themselves on the last day of the year, so that the seller should not find them and the house should become theirs permanently. 'Hillel, however, ordained that he [the seller] should deposit his money in the (Temple) Chamber.'[37] This enactment obliged the trustees and the treasurers in charge of the Temple treasury to carry out certain banking operations — to register the name of the depositor and the name of the buyer to whose credit the money was deposited. The one who sold his house was certainly a person in distress, and Hillel's enactment was prompted by concern lest he be deprived of his right to return to his house, just as the enactment of *Prosbol*, which Hillel introduced, sought to secure the interests of artisans, shopkeepers, and small businessmen who were in need of credit — 'so as not to close the door to borrowers'.[38] This enactment, which in practice annulled the law of the cancellation of debts in the Sabbatical year, preserved its purpose and its spirit.

As we have seen, the Sages were not always pleased with the ways of the kings and princes, with the members of the Sanhedrin, with the actions of priests and with the practices obtaining in the Temple. But their criticism did not lead them to negate these institutions or to secede from them. On the contrary, they held to the principle: to protest against wrongdoing by members of the administration and government, whilst maintaining an attitude of esteem and respect for the hallowed institutions of the people, namely the Temple, the Sanhedrin, and the priesthood. Furthermore, neither the earthly kingdom of the Hasmoneans[39], nor even that of the House of Herod, was completely and absolutely invalidated.

The merit of Herod himself, 'a slave of the House of the Hasmoneans'[40], was not impaired as a builder of the Temple; and a saintly Sage, Bava b. Buṭa, one of the elders of the House of Shammai[41], was his counsellor in this undertaking.

King Agrippa, the validity of whose lineage was in doubt, won the praise of the Sages when he publicly demonstrated his faithfulness to the Torah.[42] The verse 'The sceptre shall not depart from Judah' was rendered by Onkelos 'Rulership shall not depart from the House of Judah',[43] and in this version it appeared at the end of the High Priest's prayer in the Temple[44], when kings who were not of the House of Judah reigned.

As for the age of Hillel, to it also is applicable the statement in the Mishna that the elders of the Beth Din used to adjure the High Priest not to change anything of all that they had instructed him regarding the order of the service.[45] It appears that due to Hillel's endeavours there were to be found High Priests who were themselves Sages, or at least disciples of the Sages.[46] If we come to evaluate the influence of the Sages in Temple matters and in the ordering of the service, we must not forget that the cultic arrangements, the offering of the sacrifices and cereal oblations, the laws of sacred dedications and vows of evaluation, the Sanctuary structures, its chambers and Temple equipment, were in practice for centuries in the hands of the priests. Needless to say, the priestly families, the officers, and the trustees were well versed in these laws, and they also determined what was to be preserved and what had to be changed.[47] Not a few of the cultic forms and temple ceremonies of the Gentile peoples of antiquity were taken over by the Temple of Jerusalem, which, at the same time, came under their architectural influence,[48] and imported gates as well as craftsmen from Alexandria.[49] On the other hand, specific details of many laws were directed against practices that had wide currency among non-Jews. In certain matters differences of opinion arose between the families of the High Priesthood, and when they were in power, they imposed their own procedures.[50] The Sages ceased to regard the Temple and the sacrificial laws as a priestly code and made them an order of their Mishna. The Sages decided between the various traditions; such a decision was made by Hillel in regard to the offering of the Passover sacrifice on the Sabbath. In this matter — of a sacrifice that every individual Jew was obliged to bring — he also took into account the usage prevailing among the people (above, p. 577). The Sages gave particular attention to the glorification of ceremonies and the observance of precepts in the Temple in which all the people participated. Apart from the laws connected with the Passover offering they strove to consolidate customs and precepts about the details of which there were divergent opinions — for instance, the offering of 'the sheaf' — or such as were entirely disputed, like the libation of water and the ceremonial use of willows on the seventh day of the Festival of Tabernacles. In rituals of this type, in processions and festivities, in offering the First Fruits, in the Water-Drawing Ceremony, or on the occasion of the Assembly [הקהל *Haqhēl*, Deuteronomy xxxi 10–13] at the termination of the Year of Release, the participation of the masses of the people was ever of primary importance.[51] Reference has already been made to the meticulous care with which the priests observed the laws of levitical purity and impurity (above, p. 576), and there are copious testimonies, both internal and extraneous, regarding this scrupulousness in all that concerns the Temple and its environment,[52] and about the multiplicity of preventive measures to safeguard the hallowed things and the priests from being defiled.[53] The restrictive decrees and enactments of the early Sages, like Jose b. Jo'ezer, Jose b. Joḥanan, and Simeon b. Sheṭaḥ, dealt with matters of levitical purity and impurity. Ancient regulations in this sphere that had been forgotten were renewed in later courts,[54] and the Tanna R. Simeon b. Eleazar said of the earlier generations: 'Come and see, how far the observance of the laws of purity had spread among Israel!'[55]

However, the desire to make it easier for the pilgrims who went up to Jerusalem for the festivals and enable the multitudes to participate to a greater extent in the experiences of staying in the Temple, and to show them its glory and greatness, led to the introduction of many alleviating practices and rules, and it appears that these not only had the consent of the Sages, but were even due to their initiative. The roads by which the Babylonian pilgrims were accustomed to go up to Eretz-Israel were pronounced clean, although they formed part of the land of the Gentiles which had been declared unclean.[56] It was the duty of every Jew to purify himself for the festival,[57] and no one entered the Temple Court — even if he was clean — until he had undergone ritual immersion.[58] Hence even the ignorant people [עמי הארץ *'ammē hā-'areṣ*, 'peoples of the land', who were not scrupulous in the observance of the laws of purity and in separating the tithes] were trusted in Jerusalem at festival times even in respect of the heave-offering.[59] They [the Temple officials] used to bring forth and show the table to the pilgrim, 'and they entered the chamber of vessels and brought forth from there ninety-three utensils of silver and gold'.[60] After the festival they 'entered upon the cleansing of the Temple Court' and immersed the vessels in the Temple;[61] once it happened that 'they immersed the candelabrum on a festival and the Sadducees said: "Come and see, the Pharisees are immersing the light of the moon".'[62] The reason for these lenient rulings was explained by R. Joshua b. Levi in the following homily: ' "Jerusalem that art builded as a city that is compact [*ḥubběrā*] together" (Psalms cxxii 3) — a city that makes all Israel חברים *ḥăvērîm* ['Associates'; scholars who observe the laws of levitical purity].'[63] Similarly it is taught in a Baraita that the reason for accepting sacrifices from 'people who are like cattle (Rashi: 'wicked')' and from 'Israelite transgressors' is 'that they might repent'.[64]

The ideal of the Sages was to make all Israel 'associates', and not merely at the time when the people went up to Jerusalem. Hence we must consider the social consequences of the insistence on the meticulous observance of the laws of purity and impurity in everyday life. The prevailing view in the Halakha is apparently that all the laws of purity and impurity — followed also by the Rabbinical rules of impurity — really affected only priests and Nazirites, and they concerned the Israelites as a whole only when they came into contact with Temple matters and hallowed objects. Even the verse 'Of their flesh ye shall not eat, and their carcasses ye shall not touch; they are unclean unto you' (Leviticus xi 8), which applies to all Israel, is explained as referring only to the time of the festivals.[65] However, not only individuals — priests, Levites, Israelites, and proselytes — were accustomed to eat unconsecrated food in various degrees of purity[66], but from early sources, Mishnayot and Baraitot, there emerges what appears to be an Order of *Ḥăvērîm* (חברים), who share the ideal of observing 'the principles of associateship' in matters of purity and impurity, the separation of heave-offerings and tithes, and the avoidance of certain forms of contact with those who do not belong to their associateship, namely those called *ʿam ha-ʾareṣ*. Separate societies organized for the observance of the laws of purity and holiness, sects who remained apart from the other members of their community, city, or people, are known in the framework of other religions.[67] To the enrolment procedure of the *Ḥăvûrā* of Pharisees there are parallels in the order of initiation into the group of Essenes, as described by Josephus, and especially in the system of initiation of the sect of 'the Men of the *Yaḥad*' [the Qumran Covenanters] not only in respect of its regulations and their ceremonial details, but also in regard to the phrasing and expressions of the ritual.[68]

However, despite all the similarities in details and major aspects, there is a fundamental difference between the Pharisaic groups and the Essenes and the Qumran Sect. The object of the Pharisaic groups was to facilitate the observance of the laws of purity in all their stringency. Joining a group meant separation from those who were not Associates — from the *ʿam hāʾāreṣ* — and this not only gave rise to problems in everyday life, but was a problem in itself, and could create class and sectarian polarity. Although we are unable to determine the exact time when the groups first appeared, it seems that initially they limited the separation to necessary spheres and maintained unity in the matters that they shared with non-Associates. After all it appears that the Pharisee Associates were closer to the *ʿammê hā-ʾāreṣ* than sects of the type of the Essenes or the Men of the *Yaḥad*. In the view of the latter the laws of membership held no problem or difficulty, but on the contrary, served to fortify a society that was separated from 'the habitation of men of wickedness'; it was essentially an order of brethren, living in community and sharing their property, an order that created for itself substitutes for all the institutions that were sacred to the nation as a whole. The Men of the *Yaḥad*, who called themselves 'holy men', 'men of truth', 'men of the destiny of God', regarded those who did not belong to them 'as men of violence', 'men of wickedness', 'men of corruption', and 'men of the destiny of Belial',[69] but not as *ʿam hā-ʾāreṣ*. On the other hand, in the world of the Sages the connotation of the term *ʿam ha-ʾāreṣ* underwent a change. It does not only mean one who does not eat unconsecrated food in purity, or is suspected of not setting aside the tithes,[70] but also one who is not learned in the Torah and does not study it. In this sense apparently Hillel already used the term *ʿam hā-ʾāreṣ*; and from the context it seems possible that he even employed it vis-à-vis people of the type of the Men of the *Yaḥad*. His dictum 'A brutish [בור *bûr*] man dreads not sin, and an *ʿam hā-ʾāreṣ* cannot be saintly' consists of two parallel members.[71] *ʿAm hā-ʾāreṣ* corresponds to *bûr* in the sense of brutish and empty of Torah.[72] The antithesis between *bûr* and 'Sage' in the following Baraita is particularly instructive for our subject: 'He who begins (a benediction) with YH [יה, part of the Tetragrammaton] and concludes with YH is wise [a Sage]; (begins) with YH and concludes with *'Alef Lamed* [אל, 'God'] is brutish [*bûr*]; (begins) with *'Alef Lamed* and concludes with YH is intermediate; (begins) with *'Alef Lamed* and concludes with *'Alef Lamed* — this is another [i.e. heretical] way.'[73] In another version of this Baraita 'brutish' is applied to one who begins with 'El and ends with 'El, and 'another way' is referred to one who is only careful to end with 'El.[74] Indifference in regard to the benedictory formulas was characteristic of the members of the Qumran sect, who used the name 'El in the conclusions of benedictions.[75] This method was termed 'another way' or the act of a brutish man, although those who followed this practice intended to demonstrate 'fear of sin', for a 'brutish' person is not sin-fearing. And as 'a brutish man' is the antithesis of 'a Sage', so does *ʿam hā-ʾāreṣ*, which is a parallel term, denote one devoid of Torah knowledge, who, even if he observes abstinence and purity, cannot be deemed saintly. It is not accidental that the Mishna which speaks of the attitude to property designates the one who says 'Mine is yours and yours is mine' — that is the one who believes in community of wealth and property — an *ʿam hā-ʾāreṣ*.[76] It is obvious that ordinary *ʿammē hā-ʾāreṣ* were not wont to speak thus; apparently the reference is to an *ʿam hā-ʾāreṣ* who is to be identified with the members of a sect similar to that of the Qumran Order.[77] It is possible that the Men of the *Yaḥad* adopted for their purpose earlier procedures of 'Associateship' (חברות *ḥăvērût*), just as these methods of adaptation are evident in the Halakhot of the Sages. Thus it is stated: 'Even a disciple has to accept (Associateship), but a Sage who sits in the academy need not accept (Associateship) for he already accepted it when he took his seat (in the academy). Abba Saul said: Even a disciple need not accept (Associateship). Furthermore, even others may accept (Associateship) before him.'[78] The compiler of this Baraita had in mind the Mishna of Abba Saul in which he taught that a disciple — and not only a Sage — need not accept (Associateship).[79] Abba Saul was a contemporary of R. Ṭarfon, and like the latter testified to matters that occurred in the Temple,[80] as well as to the rules applicable to 'Associates' and *ʿammê hā-'āreṣ* in regard to partaking of sacrifices of the lower grade and second tithe in certain parts of the city of Jerusalem.[81] The Mishna that he taught represents, therefore, the state of affairs shortly before the destruction of the Temple. It also appears that in the version of the Baraita cited above there are discernible two stricter views, which represent two earlier stages, namely the opinion that even a Sage must accept (Associateship), and the view that an appointed Sage (= one who sits in the academy) does not need to so, but a disciple must. Of the stringent ruling R. Joḥanan said: 'This Mishna was taught in the days of the son of R. Ḥanina b. Antigonus.'[82] He, too, was a Tanna who lived in Temple times. The aim reflected in these rulings is to assure preferential standing for a Sage ànd a disciple even in the framework of the *Ḥăvûrā* of the Pharisees. The Associations of the Pharisees were not all of the same character, and certainly did not observe the same stringencies at all times and in all matters. The divergences are still reflected in the statements of the later Tannaim in which the Halakhot of the earlier generations are embedded. It seems that in the ancient period, when the associates were not numerous, their laws were stricter, but when the ways of the *Ḥăvûrā* became popular practice, the tendency towards leniency developed. Sometimes this difference is expressly stated: '*At first* they used to say: An associate who became a tax-collector is expelled from his society. *Subsequently they declared*: So long as he is a tax-collector he is not deemed trustworthy; but once he gives up his work as tax-collector he is (again) trusted.'[83] Apparently even laws that have not been formulated in this way, but as a dispute between Tannaim, are, in truth, Halakhic traditions belonging to different periods; for example: 'And none of them, if they retracted, are ever accepted again — this is the view of R. Me'ir. R. Judah said: If they retracted openly (παρρησία) they may be accepted (again); if they did so covertly, they may not (again) be accepted [i.e. if they reverted to their former evil practices secretly, but outwardly acted like associates, they may not be accepted on account of their hypocrisy]. R. Simeon and R. Joshua b. Qorḥa [said]: In either case they are accepted.'[84]

It is difficult to regard R. Me'ir's statement as his personal opinion, because it is a complete contradiction of his teaching concerning the power of repentance (above, p. 466); hence it is to be viewed only as a relic of stringent regulations of a society, which has a parallel in the *Scroll of the Rule of the Yaḥad* [Manual of Discipline] vii, 1: 'If a man utter a curse... then he is to be excluded and never allowed to return to the Council of the Community.' Although the extant laws of associates were taught in the period of Usha, yet it is clear that this fact does not indicate the date when the laws[85] came into being, but merely that at that time, or approximately so, they were resuscitated with a view to making regulations that had once pertained to small societies the Halakhot of corporate Israel. This is implied by R. Me'ir's dictum 'Whoever lives permanently in Eretz-Israel and eats unconsecrated food in purity and speaks the holy tongue and reads the *Shĕma*ʿ morning and evening is assured of life in the world to come.'[86] R. Me'ir wished to introduce greater stringency, whereas the Tannaim who disagreed with him preferred to proceed along the path of leniency. The renewal of these laws after the Revolt of Bar Kokhba is also to be explained, perhaps, by the general ascetic trend prevailing at the time.[87] However, it appears that in practice these stringencies were chiefly confined to the Sages and their disciples. Possibly this tendency is reflected in the dispute between Rabban Simeon b. Gamaliel and Rabbi, which was epitomized in the Talmudic dictum: 'Rabbi holds that an Associate prefers to transgress a minor prohibition so that an *ʿam hā-'āreṣ* should not transgress a major prohibition; and Rabban Simeon b. Gamaliel maintains that an Associate prefers an *ʿam hā-'āreṣ* to transgress a major prohibition rather than that he himself should transgress even a minor prohibition.'[88] It is probable that Rabbi had in mind an Associate who was primarily a Sage, just as in enunciating the rule 'An Associate does not require admonition, because admonition serves only to distinguish between one who commits a transgression unwittingly and one who does so wittingly.'[89] Rabbi's colleague, R. Jose b. R. Judah, was thinking primarily of a Sage and not necessarily of a *Ḥāvēr* in the earlier connotation of the term. In the Amoraic period the designation *Ḥāvēr* became a synonym for a scholar [literally, 'disciple of the Sages'], so that it was possible to say '*Ḥăvērîm* are none other than scholars'.[90]

Now we must examine how the development that we have described in the meaning of the terms *Ḥāvēr* and *ʿam hā-ʾāreṣ* affected the mutual relationship of the two types. Was not the combination of wisdom and Torah-knowledge with the observance of the laws of purity and impurity and scrupulous care in regard to the laws of tithes liable to exacerbate further the rift between the Sages-Associates and the *ʿam hā-ʾāreṣ*? Ostensibly we have already answered this question in the negative; but actually we have considered only the measures taken to prevent sectarian secession and preserve unity within the framework of the sacred institutions common to all. But this does not provide a complete answer. At any rate an additional examination of the question of the relationship between the Sages and the broad masses is necessary. Let us revert to the image of Hillel. At his funeral eulogy no mention was made of the fact that he was worthy that the Shekhina should rest upon him, but it was said 'Alas, the humble man, alas the saint, the disciple of Ezra!' The reference to Ezra is to be explained by the dictum of Resh Laqish: 'When the Torah was forgotten in Israel, Ezra came up from Babylon and re-established it; when it was again forgotten, Hillel the Babylonian came up and re-established it.'[91]

Hillel founded the Torah anew by virtue of the fact that he was both saintly and humble. His saintliness found expression in the testimonies to his acts, which were all for the sake of Heaven (above, p. 340), and to his absolute faith in God, which left no room for misgivings or fears.[92]

The attributes of humility, patience, love of one's fellows, and the pursuit of peace, which Hillel displayed, did not diminish the stringency of his ethical and religious demands, or prevent him from placing full responsibility on man, whom he required to act for his own perfection and for the public weal. Man is obliged to make endeavours, for 'If I am not for myself, who will be for me?' But he cannot achieve much through seclusion and separation, and he must remember 'And being for my own self, what am I?' Nor may he forget that his time is limited and he dare not procrastinate — 'And if not now, when?' (*M. 'Avot* i, 14). Man's relations with his fellow man were defined by Hillel not only in the rule attributed to him as a reply to a proselyte who asked to be taught the whole Torah while standing on one foot — 'What is hateful to you do not do to your fellow'[93] — the like of which the would-be proselyte might also have heard from others, but in the demand that one must not pass hasty judgement on the actions of another person, just as one is forbidden to be confident of one's own righteousness. The principle is: 'Be not sure of yourself until the day of your death, and judge not your fellow until you come into his place' (*M. 'Avot* ii, 4). However, a man's humility and self-criticism are no excuse for keeping aloof from the community. Hillel even instructs the Sage who has acquired the qualities of saintliness and humility: 'Sever not yourself from the community... and where there are no men strive to be a man' (*ibid.* ii, 5).

In the cycle of stories about Hillel's humility and patience the strictness of Shammai is also portrayed.[94] One may ask if the tales about Shammai do not act merely as a background and literary device that serve to highlight the attributes of the real hero, whose virtues are presented as an example for future generations. This question is undoubtedly justified in regard to details of the stories even in the light of Shammai's dictum 'and receive all men with a cheerful countenance' (*ibid.* i, 15). But the actual tradition regarding Shammai's severity is not to be denied. This is evidenced not necessarily by lack of politeness and impatience, but by his insistence on the scrupulous observance of commandments without considering the consequences, to the point of endangering the life of a child; and this is true not solely of the individual and personal sphere, but also of the laws and precepts that appertain to the entire community.[95] Only four disputes between Hillel and Shammai,[96] it is true, have come down to us, and one of these was a subject of controversy in earlier generations, namely that of סמיכה *sĕmîkhā* (see below). But it is clear, on the one hand, that there were other matters on which they differed, but they still adhered to the old Halakhic traditional method of citing only 'a decided Halakha without controversy'.[97] On the other hand, it appears that even the three controversial matters referred to were transmitted in this form only because no decision had been arrived at, and afterwards the issues were decided in accordance with neither view.

Hillel's attributes and his conduct were responsible for the fact that not only his enactments but also his views were accepted, even when others differed from him. Thus 'When the Alexandrians married, one would go and snatch the bride from the street, and a case of this kind came before the Sages. They wished to declare their children bastards; but Hillel the Elder said to the Alexandrians: "Bring me your mothers' *kĕtubbā* [marriage contract]." They brought them and it was found written therein: "When thou shalt enter my house, thou shalt be my wife according to the Law of Moses and Israel." '[98] We do not know who were the Sages who wished to declare the Alexandrians bastards, but it is clear — as in the case of the Passover sacrifice — that Hillel considered the public custom authoritative. As Naḥmanides explains:[99] 'And although it was an ignorant custom, he ruled in accordance with it, as if they had acted on the instruction of the Sages. And although they had become used to writing thus without Rabbinic mandate, he made this practice a (court) condition... since it was a simple custom and every one acted in this way...' R. Solomon b. Abraham Aderet (Rashba) went further[1] in explaining the broad-minded understanding of Hillel: 'In the matter brought up before Hillel, it was not the *kĕtubbôt* of the mothers of those who were being stigmatized as bastards that were produced, but the meaning is that he was shown the *kĕtubbôt* of other people of that place. From these he learned that the local people were accustomed to write thus, and on the basis of these documents he also validated all the others that were not drawn up in precisely the same manner, but in general terms....' This decision, like his enactments, gave Hillel such standing and authority among the people, that they deemed the time opportune to come to a decision also in respect of the one disputed issue that had not been decided in the course of the generations, namely the question of *sĕmîkhā* [putting hands on the head of a sacrifice]. Despite the many strange conjectures advanced concerning this controversy, the reason for its continuance for generations and its background has not been elucidated; only one thing is clear, that the point involved was whether or not *sĕmîkhā* could be performed on a festival.[2] Hillel not only stated theoretically that one was allowed 'to put on hands', but he acted accordingly in practice, and thus brought about a decision with the help of the people who supported him: 'It once happened that Hillel the Elder performed *sĕmîkhā* on a burnt-offering in the Temple court, and the disciples of Shammai gathered about him in protest against his action... (however,) he put them off with words and they went away.'[3]

The abolition of the laying on of hands on a festival resulted in the diminution of those who brought offerings. This is how it is explained in a story of later origin: 'After a time the School of Shammai prevailed and they wished to decide the Halakha according to their ruling; now Bava b. Buṭa, one of the disciples of the School of Shammai, was present and he knew that the Halakha was in accord with the view of the School of Hillel. Once, on entering the Temple court, he found it deserted. Thereupon he said: May the homes of those who have made the House of our God desolate become desolate! What did he do? He ordered three thousand lamb[15] of the sheep of Kedar to be brought and he examined them for blemishes and placed them on the Temple Mount and proclaimed: "Hearken unto me, O my brethren of the House of Israel! whoever so wishes let him bring burnt offerings, (let him bring) and lay on hands; let him bring peace offerings and lay on hands." At that moment the Halakha was determined according to the School of Hillel, and no one said a word to the contrary.'[4] This episode, which occurred at the time when the Shammaites prevailed — we shall still revert to this incident — teaches us that Hillel, in acting as he did, decided in favour of *sĕmîkhā*[5] for a similar reason — that is to say, that the Temple court should not be desolate on a festival — but he gained the decision by virtue of the persuasive power of his arguments. As in the case of the decision taken in regard to the offering up of the Passover sacrifice on the fourteenth of Nisan that fell on a Sabbath, when account was also taken of the current trend and attitude of the people, Hillel's own dictum was exemplified in himself: 'My humiliation is my elevation, and my elevation is my humiliation.'[6] His personality became an educational exemplar, and when later generations highly eulogized a departed Sage they said: 'Ah, humble man, ah saint, disciple of Hillel!'[7]

In the dispute between the School of Hillel and the School of Shammai regarding the interpretation of the dictum of the Men of the Great Assembly 'And raise up many disciples', the view expressed by the Hillelites reflects the outcome of Hillel's activity. His maxim 'Be of the disciples of Aaron, loving peace and pursuing peace, loving your fellow creatures and drawing them near to the Torah' (*M. 'Avot* i, 12) means 'the disciples of Aaron', but not necessarily 'the descendants of Aaron'. 'Fellow creatures' in general — even if they are not Sages and meek, of good family and worthy — should be drawn near. Accordingly the School of Hillel said: 'One should teach everyone'; and they based their teaching on the result of this approach, 'for there were many transgressors in Israel, but when they began to study Torah, there came forth from among them righteous men, saints, and worthy men.'[8] Hillel was responsible for the fact that the Sanhedrin, which consisted of 'priests, Levites, and Israelites who could give their daughters in marriage to priests',[9] became a Sanhedrin of 'all Israel', as it is designated in Mishnayot and Baraitot that refer to the period after Hillel, as for instance in the Mishna 'The Chamber of Hewn Stone — there the Great Sanhedrin of Israel used to sit and judge the priesthood.'[10] Confirmation of the general character of the Sanhedrin is contained in the following statement of R. Joshua, who, like the redactor of the Mishna cited above, lived when the Temple was still in existence: 'Did proselytes then enter the *Hêkhal* [the Holy]? Lo, no Israelite entered the *Hêkhal*! The meaning is that they sat in the Sanhedrin and taught the words of the Torah.'[11]

Hillel and his disciples pursued the path of gradual penetration into the institutions of the Temple and the Sanhedrin and endeavoured to influence their methods and actions, but at the same time they did not regard themselves as an élite that aspired to power and leadership, but as an élite that served as an example.

Love of one's fellow creatures, which was Hillel's guiding principle, his open policy, and his readiness to receive into the circle and association of the Sages all who came to learn, served to reduce the tension and to limit the gulf between the sections of the people, dangers that were inherent in the laws of fellowship governing levitically clean foodstuffs, heave-offerings, and tithes, and in the emergence of an intellectual stratum that had also gained influence in the institutions of government and authority. But we may state that at least until the destruction of the Temple, and even till the period of Jabneh, the principal task of the Sage still remained in the field of teaching and Halachic ruling, in works of charity and acts of lovingkindness. He lived among the multitude of the people. He sought to influence the sacred institutions of the people — the Temple, the Sanhedrin, and the priesthood — and to decide Halachic matters. But the power of his influence was derived solely from his wisdom, and the source of his authority lay in his deeds and qualities of character. This is the testimony of Josephus at the end of his work *Antiquities of the Jews*, concerning a period close to that of Hillel: 'For our people do not favour those persons who have mastered the speech of many nations, or who adorn their style with smoothness of diction... But they give credit for wisdom to those alone who have an exact knowledge of the law and who are capable of interpreting the meaning of the Holy Scriptures.' Concerning these Sages he observes elsewhere 'that even when they speak against a king or high priest, they immediately gain credence'.[12]

VI. The Regime of the Sages after the Destruction of the Temple

In the world of the Sages in the days of the Second Temple until the time of Hillel we find no bureaucratic organization, no system whatsoever of appointments, no promotion, no remuneration, and in truth no training arrangements or definition of functions. But it was just the success and achievements of Hillel's acts that led to a far-reaching change in the status of the Sages. It is a fact that for the first time we encounter *Bêt Hillēl* (the 'House of Hillel') as denoting a dynasty, although the son and grandson of Hillel — Rabban Gamaliel and his son Rabban Simeon — were not נשיאים *Nĕśî'îm* ('Princes') in the sense that Simeon the Hasmonean was a נשיא *Nāśî'*, nor in the connotation given to the function of the *Nĕśî'îm* of the House of Hillel in the period following the Destruction.[13] But undoubtedly they had a special status in the Sanhedrin, and enactments made in certain spheres bore their name. Rabban Simeon b. Gamaliel decided the Halakha in a matter concerning the Temple in a manner resembling that of his grandfather Hillel: 'It once happened that a pair of doves in Jerusalem cost a golden denar. Said Rabban Simeon b. Gamaliel: "By this Temple! before the night is over they will cost but a (silver) denar." He entered the *Bet Din* ('court') and taught: If a woman suffered five miscarriages that were not in doubt... she need bring (only) one sacrifice and she may then partake of the animal offerings, and she is not under obligation to bring the other offerings. That same day the price of a pair of doves went down to a quarter of a denar each.'[14] On the other hand it must be pointed out that the intervention of the Sages in the affairs of the Temple and their influence over the priests did not prevent antagonism between them and 'the Bet Din of the priests',[15] whose views differed from those of the Sages, and the latter did not always have the power to oppose the priests and to effect a decision contrary to their opinion.

Until the beginning of the Revolt the differences of opinion, which grew with the increase of the number of disciples, did not lead to sharp schisms between the two schools — the School of Shammai and the School of Hillel. On the contrary, 'Joezer of the Bira [Temple structure] was one of the disciples of the School of Shammai and he said: 'I asked Rabban Gamaliel the Elder, when he was standing in the Eastern Gate'.[16] Joḥanan the Ḥoronite, although a disciple of Shammai, always acted in accordance with the views of the School of Hillel.[17] On the other hand we find that 'the more scrupulous of the Hillelites used to act according to the School of Shammai',[18] 'And once the elders of the School of Shammai and the elders of the School of Hillel went into the upper chamber of Jonathan b. Bathyra and ruled that there was no prescribed length for fringes [see Numbers xv 37 ff]; so, too, they decided that there is no prescribed length for the palm-branch [used on the Festival of Tabernacles].'[19] The position changed with the start of the Great Revolt; whereas previously the Sages were able to adopt a positive attitude in principle to the actual institutions of the state and government, without refraining from protesting against acts of injustice and without seeking unduly close relations with the ruling power, once the Revolt broke out, which seemed to many an obligatory war, and to others a hopeless struggle that endangered the existence of the people, the relationship between the two Schools became severely strained, and it may well be that the dividing line did not correspond precisely to the academic division. It is clearer to us today than ever before that the Zealots — the freedom-fighters in the years of the Great Revolt — not only were not a sect motivated by a given philosophy, but were more divided and diversified in respect of their views and their ideological affiliation than in regard to their politico-strategical and social outlook.[20] The discovery of a scroll at Massada[21], the like of which is to be found only among the Qumran writings, proves, beyond any shadow of doubt, that there were also members of this sect among the Zealots and fighters, and that the case of John, the Essene, who is mentioned in Josephus[22] as one of the commanders, was not exceptional. Undoubtedly there were, on the other hand, Essenes and Qumran covenanters who were opposed to the zealotry of their colleagues. Political zealotry both united and divided. Rabban Simeon b. Gamaliel supported the preparations for the Revolt and cooperated with John of Gischala.[23] Zechariah b. Eucolus is regarded in the Talmudic stories about the destruction of the Temple as responsible for stopping the offering of sacrifices for the welfare of the state.[24] Josephus, who puts the blame for this incident on Eleazar b. Ananias, the High Priest, an official of the Temple, mentions Zechariah b. Eucolus as one of the extremist Zealots, who, jointly with Eleazar b. Simeon, invited the Idumeans to Jerusalem.[25] In the Talmudic sources we are told that the disciples of the School of Shammai stood with swords and spears 'and slew disciples of the School of Hillel'[26], forcing them to accept their restrictive decrees, that is 'the decrees of the eighteen measures'. These decrees were not promulgated in the Temple, nor on the ascent of the Temple Mount, but in the upper chamber of Eleazar b. Ḥananiah b. Hezekiah b. Garon, one of the Shammaite disciples, who had previously filled the office of general of the army in Idumea.[27] In a late Midrash[28] there is preserved an ancient source portraying fragmentary incidents that took place in the war against the Romans, and it is stated there: 'And Eleazar went up accompanied by disciples, and they smote Elhanan and cut him up into pieces.' The reference, apparently, is to the murder of Ḥanan b. Ḥanan [Ananus], the High Priest, by the Idumeans;[29] and it is not surprising that the Idumeans are called 'disciples', for the Sages declared, with reference to the time when the School of Shammai prevailed, that 'there were Idumean disciples in the School of Shammai'[30], and we have already seen (above, p. 591) that an attempt was even made to change a Halakha, once decided by Hillel, regarding *sĕmîkhā* on a festival. The appraisement of the younger generation, who, if they did not themselves witness the episode that occurred that day, could have heard about it from those who did, is reflected in the words of R. Eliezer and R. Joshua: 'That day they overfilled the measure', or 'struck the measure'; and some said that that day 'was as grievous for Israel as the day on which they made the calf.'[31] The politico-military struggle was exploited for the purpose of securing decisions by force.

It is almost certain that this event had political consequences, for it led the disciples of the School of Hillel to adopt a negative attitude towards the groups of freedom-fighters. The internal dissensions, which became aggravated, caused R. Ḥanina, the prefect of the priests, to say in those hard times: 'Pray for the welfare of the state, for were it not for the fear of it, we should have swallowed [בלענו *bālaʿnû*] each other up alive.'[32]

It appears that Rabban Joḥanan b. Zakkai's attitude to the Revolt was from the outset more reserved than that of Rabban Simeon b. Gamaliel, who cooperated with him in Halakhic decisions.[33] Although it is not known that Rabban Joḥanan held any official position when he was in Jerusalem,[34] he acted like his master Hillel and strove to infiltrate the views of the Sages into the Temple service and into the sacrificial regulations[35], and without doubt he had access to both the circles of the High Priesthood and the leaders of the group of rebels. His moderate attitude at the time of the victories at the beginning of the Revolt after the defeat of Cestius Gallus found expression in his admonition: 'Be not in haste to pull down the high places of the Gentiles, lest you have to rebuild (them) with your own hand; lest you pull down those made of bricks and they order you: "Rebuild them of stone!", or those made of stone and they enjoin you: "Rebuild them of wood!" '[36] It is not to be inferred from these words 'that R. Joḥanan b. Zakkai advised the acceptance anew of the Roman yoke'.[37] It seems, however, that when internal schisms became intensified, that is to say, 'when the murderers multiplied',[38] he saw danger threatening the very existence of the people and resolved to work for peace. Possibly the following homily of his contains an apologia for his attitude: 'It is stated "Thou shalt build... of unhewn [שלמות *shĕlēmôt*] stones' (Deuteronomy xxvii 6) — stones that bring peace [שלום *shālôm*]." It is an argument from minor to major: If now the stones of the altar, which neither see nor speak, yet, because they make peace between Israel and their Father in heaven, the Holy One, blessed be He, said "Thou shalt lift up no iron tool upon them"; how much more so shall one who makes peace between man and man, between a man and his wife, between city and city, between nation and nation, between government and government, or between family and family, not suffer tribulation.'[39]

According to one version of the story about the attempts of Rabban Joḥanan b. Zakkai to come in touch with the emperor Vespasian, who had laid siege to Jerusalem, the Sage was aided by his sister's son, Abba Siqra, chief of the outlaws.[40] At any rate Rabban Joḥanan b. Zakkai left Jerusalem, after he was convinced that the fate of the City and the Temple was sealed, and he received permission to go to Jabneh, the seat of a Bet Din, which was apparently administered by the Sons of Bathyra, who were also *personae gratae* with the Roman authorities.[41] The destruction of the Temple he regarded as a punishment and he reacted to it as did Eli when Shiloh was destroyed[42], but primarily his thoughts and deeds were devoted to his reconstructive activity, and in this respect he was able to rely only upon the power of his influence. Whether he served from the beginning as head of the Bet Din, or whether he left this office to the Sons of Bathyra, it is clear that their Bet Din was based on the authority of the members collectively. This trend is also reflected in the designation 'the place of assembly' and in Rabban Joḥanan b. Zakkai's enactment 'that wheresoever the head of the Bet Din might be, the witnesses should go only to the place of assembly'.[43] It is possible that on account of this Rabban Joḥanan b. Zakkai preferred to dwell in Beror Ḥayil, in order to remove from himself any suspicion that he was seeking his own honour. His main aim was to restore unity to the association of the Sages and to heal the breaches. Testimony to this activity of Rabban Joḥanan b. Zakkai in the House of the Assembly at Jabneh is to be found, to my mind, in the old and original portion of the at Jabneh

Mishna and Tosefta of *'Eduyot*: 'When the Sages entered the Vineyard of Jabneh, they said: A time will come when a man will seek a Torah teaching and not find it, a ruling of the Scribes and not find it... so that one precept of the Torah would not be like another. (Hence) they declared: Let us begin with Hillel and Shammai.'[44] The Sages who assembled came to rectify the position that one precept of the Torah was not like another. The purpose of the convention was not therefore literary — it was not to systematize the Halakhot — but to arrive at decisions regarding disputed Halakhot. They began to discuss differences of view between Shammai and Hillel themselves, and 'decided neither according to the one or the other'; they collected Halakhot in respect of which 'the School of Hillel retracted and ruled in accordance with the view of the School of Shammai', and the Halakhot on which the two Schools agreed. In these decisions they were aided by the testimonies of the elder Sages of the generation, like R. Hananiah, the prefect of the priests; R. Dosa b. Harkinas, whose younger brother Jonathan was a disciple of Shammai but he himself decided according to the School of Hillel;[45] R. Joḥanan b. Gudgada; R. Zadok; and apparently also 'Aqaviah b. Mahalalel, who, however, held firmly to his views and did not give way to the opinion of the majority. It appears to me that the story related about this last Sage is significant for determining the status of Rabban Joḥanan b. Zakkai; we shall therefore cite it verbatim and explain it: 'Aqaviah b. Mahalalel testified to four matters... a woman proselyte and a freed bondwoman are not made to drink of the waters of bitterness... They said to him: It happened in the case of Karkemit, a freed bondwoman who was in Jerusalem, and Shema'yah and Avṭalion gave her to drink. He replied: It only appeared that they made her drink.'[46] The reliance on an incident that took place in Jerusalem, expressed in this wording, shows that the testimony of "'Aqaviah was not given in Jerusalem but in Jabneh.[47] The Sages disagreed with him in three other matters and said to him: "'Aqaviah, retract the four opinions that you expressed and we shall make you Av (Father of the) Bet Din of Israel. He replied: It is better that I be called a fool all my days than become for a while a wicked man before God; lest people say that he retracted for the sake of attaining to high office.' At what particular time was this suggestion made to

ʿAqaviah b. Mahalalel? I am inclined to conjecture that the incident occurred near the time of Rabban Joḥanan b. Zakkai's death, and just as Rabban Joḥanan b. Zakkai himself was not appointed and did not succeed anyone, so, too, he did not transfer his status and did not appoint a successor. The position was offered to a Sage of whom it was said 'that the Temple court was not closed to any man in Israel so wise and sin-fearing as ʿAqaviah b. Mahalalel'; but the condition was that he should yield to the majority opinion.

The problem of appointments and the exercise of authority in the world of the Sages is discernible here in its initial stages. It is a fact that shortly after Rabban Joḥanan b. Zakkai we find in Jabneh not an Av Bet Din, but a Nasi [Prince, Patriarch] who was descended from Hillel, namely Rabban Gamaliel, and his position was authorized by the governor in Syria.[48] This circumstance is indicative of the status of his rule externally, and internally, too, he appears as a leader of the nation, whose authority is derived not only from his being Av Bet Din and a Sage, but also from the prestige of his lineage.

Indeed the dynasty of the Patriarchs of the House of Hillel — which at a later period discovered a geneological table showing that 'Hillel was descended from David'[49] — stood at the head of the nation for over three hundred years, until the last Rabban Gamaliel died — the fifth or sixth — without an heir — in the reign of Theodosius II, *circa* 425 C.E.[50] The very fact that the office remained in one family for so long a period, marked by numerous changes, fluctuations, and vicissitudes, bears testimony to the high standing and esteem that it had achieved.

Clearly much depended on the personality, scholarship, and the administrative capacity of the Patriarch, and to no small extent also on the relations between him and extraneous factors, namely the Roman authorities. But it is precisely the fact that not all the Patriarchs were alike in stature and ability, and that the government's attitude towards the Jews of Eretz-Israel and their institutions was not the same at all times, which also serves to demonstrate the stability of the Patriarchal institution. Although this durability is primarily noticeable when measured in terms of centuries, yet when we scrutinize it closely, in so far as we have evidence, the crises in the institutions' history are many. Just as its strength derived from a general desire to regard it as a remnant of national freedom and independence — a kind of shadow monarchy — so, too, the crises and difficulties arose chiefly from its character as such. Since the existing leadership emanated from the body of Sages, there was the danger that the people would look upon all the Sages as the ruling class, and would also blame them for all the faults and perversions connected with government. This danger was largely averted owing to the fact that in all periods there were to be found among the Sages outstanding men who undertook to continue the struggle of former generations against governmental authorities, High Priests, kings and despots, only this struggle was presently directed against a ruling power and authority that stemmed from their own midst and now sought to dominate them. Political circumstances imposed upon the Patriarchs duties that had formerly belonged to other institutions. The supervision of Halakhic decisions in civil and religious law found expression in the centralization of appointments and in the strict selection of disciples. Rabban Gamaliel II of Jabneh considered it a function of the Patriarchate to organize a judicial system in the towns and settlements and to establish a link between them and the central authority, as well as to maintain relations with the Diaspora communities, which involved not only journeys to Rome, where the Patriarch himself had travelled accompanied by elders, but the sending of emissaries to distant parts — to Arabia, Cilicia, Africa, Galatia, Cappadocia, and Gazaka in Media.[51] All these activities necessitated the appointment of office-bearers and the installation of public administrators.[52] The supervision of the Halakhic decisions, introduced by Rabban Gamaliel, led him not only to denounce severely the Sages who continued to stand for freedom in Halakhic rulings, but even to punish them,[53] and this resulted in a revolt against Rabban Gamaliel and in his deposition from the Patriarchate. Although the revolt ended in a compromise that created a kind of oligarchic administration,[54] yet there were several Sages who would not submit even to this control and insisted on complete freedom in Halakhic decisions. R. Eliezer b. Hyrcanus (the great Tanna that was placed under the ban), who dwelt in Lydda,[55] eulogized the understanding vouchsafed to Nethanel, the Nasi of Issachar,[56] the tribe that had maintained law courts in Egypt, saying 'that he brought his offering immediately after the king, because he was learned in the Torah, and it was he who had advised the tribes to bring wagons.'[57] Possibly these homilies were intended to emphasize the difference between a Nasi that is learned in the Torah and advises the tribes and one who is a king. R. Eliezer did not agree to submit even to the majority view and adhered to his tradition and opinion against the view of the Sages, and it was this attitude that led to his being banned.[58] However, Eliezer was exceptional. In this first crisis, as in crises that were to take place subsequently, the majority were not inclined to undermine the actual existence of the patriarchal institution linked to the House of Hillel, and were content to protest with extreme vehemence against this or that Patriarch, or to condemn his actions and practices.

A most serious phenomenon that changed the economic and social position of many Sages, and even endangered their moral image, was connected with the maintenance of the Sages who fulfilled public functions. The acceptance of remuneration from the public was forbidden. If they were not wealthy with means of their own, the leader of the generation, the Patriarch, was charged with their maintenance. However, the support of the Patriarch, as the common benefactor who provided many Sages with their livelihood, served as a decisive factor in underscoring the class and social distinctiveness of the Sages. A confrontation was created between scholars who made the Torah their profession and those who followed other vocations. The conception of 'Torah' as a vocation also opened the way to its being passed on from fathers to sons like other skills. Dicta that emphasize the thought that the Torah cannot be transferred as a legacy are directed against the trend to bequeath Torah-knowledge and its ranks, including the privileges attached thereto, to the Sages' own families. The very formation of a spiritual and national leadership, which combined with instruction in the Torah and elucidation of the Halakha also the administration of the community by means of institutions and modes of government, establishing a hierarchical system and ceremonial honours — all this constituted a change. It created the image of a Sage that is not only a teacher and guide, and as such draws people nearer to the Torah and engages in beneficent works, but is, at the same time, an administrator, appointed over the community, who transmits his office to his sons. These developments were factors contributing, at the close of the Tannaitic age and during the Amoraic period, to the distinctive character of the Sages, who became a class of men that were differentiated 'by their manner of walking, of speaking, and by the cloak they wore in the street.'[59]

Strangely it is the time of R. Judah ha-Nasi (Rabbi), who not only knew how to conduct his patriarchate on a high level and to consolidate anew the position of the nation and to heal its disaster, but also won recognition as a Sage, so that none challenged his religious-Halakhic eminence — it is just the period of this Patriarch to which critical testimonies are found. The criticism was levelled not only against his 'honouring the rich' and against the style of living, the exercise of authority, and the royal pomp that obtained in Rabbi's court, but against the very institution of the Patriarchate in Eretz-Israel and the office of Exilarch in Babylonia.[60] Rabbi himself was not oblivious of the problem of conflicting aims in the attempt to combine the custodianship of the ideals of the world of the Sages, whose base was the Torah and precepts and its apex the Kingdom of Heaven and the world to come, with the ways of hegemony, whose outward expression was wealth and lordship. Indeed in his will the great Patriarch enjoined the separation of the two domains: the Patriarchate by itself and the headship of the Bet Din by itself.[61] This severance of the Patriarchate, as the supreme politico-national administrative institution of the people, from the headship of the colleges prevailed in practice, even when the Patriarch himself was a great scholar, throughout the existence of the Patriarchate after Rabbi. The dichotomy characterizes the Jewish leadership in Babylonia from its inception as, on the one hand, the institution of 'the Exilarch'[62] — which appears definitely for the first time at the end of the reign of R. Judah ha-Nasi — and, on the other, as the headship of the academies.

With the increase of the evidence about the Babylonian centre our information about the tension and clashes between the Exilarchs and the heads of the academies likewise grows. The disputes were concerned both with the problems of the relative authority of the institutions and with questions regarding the proper mode of life and the methods of government. The duality of authority did not prevent schisms in the circle of the Sages itself, for there were not a few among them who maintained close family ties with the House of the Nasi in Eretz-

Israel or with the House of the Exilarch in Babylonia, and many of them carried out functions on behalf, and in the vicinity, of the central administrative institutions. It was natural that such Sages should tend to restrict their criticism and to give greater recognition to the authority and status of the administration. In this way they, too, came into conflict with scholars who adopted an extreme attitude in their criticism and refused to compromise with aspects that appeared negative to them, to the point of forgoing all contact with the authorities. Tannaim like R. Phinehas b. Jair and R. Jonathan b. Amram avoided even the semblance of benefiting from honour shown to their Torah erudition, and the Amora R. Eleazar not only refused to receive gifts from the House of the Patriarch, but did not even accept the Patriarch's invitations, whereas R. Zera permitted himself such benefits, declaring 'They are honoured by my presence' ('They are honoured by the fact that I dine with them; hence it is not a gift' — Rashi).[63] The very rivalry between the authorities, and likewise the mutual criticism, prevented the relaxation of the moral tension among the Sages and preserved the distinctive character of their leadership, whose strength lay not in the exercise of power and in institutions, but in their personalities and devotion to their main function, which was to study the Torah, to teach disciples, and to direct the life of the nation throughout its strata and classes.

VII. The Struggle Between Learning and Practice in the Creation of the Image of the Sage

Our last remarks here, expressed in general and summary terms, require methodical elucidation, which may also provide a substantive explanation. The nature of our sources — to which we have repeatedly referred in various contexts — makes it particularly difficult to appraise personalities and their relationship to their colleagues and to members of other classes. In one respect the character of a given Sage may be emphasized with particular and extreme sharpness, but in another respect there may be found contradictory testimonies, which are sometimes given no less prominence. There are certainly stories and legends whose aim is harmonistic, that is to say, they seek to make the attributes congruent and this congruence is in the form that appeals to the narrators and transmitters. We must not, however, overlook the possibility that diverse and conflicting testimonies do not necessarily cancel one another, but may be explained on the basis of different experiences, separated from one another by long intervals of time, occurring in the life of the same Sage. Caustic expressions and harsh words of denunciation are not infrequently clear indications of temporary reactions and not of fundamental attitudes. Undoubtedly there are many sources whose principal aim is to speak in praise of certain Sages and their virtues, but on the other hand there are by no means lacking narratives and testimonies that are very far from the literary category of 'eulogies'; intentionally or unintentionally they underline occurrences, qualities of character, and deeds that are negative. A correct assessment of the sources is particularly important and difficult in regard to the subject that we shall soon be summing up, namely: the Sages of Israel and the Congregation of Israel. Therefore, before we commence this summation, we shall consolidate our general remarks on other aspects of social relations. We shall augment our previous remarks about the attitude of the Sages to the exercise of authority and rulership, and we shall devote some attention to the question of the relations between the Sages in the sphere of the academy. I believe that observation of the relationships in internal areas will make it easier to give a more balanced evaluation of the attitudes towards other classes.

We have seen (above, p. 600) how R. Akiba fought for freedom of Halakhic decision, but at the same time supported Rabban Gamaliel in organizing the centre at Jabneh. We do not know the date of Rabban Gamaliel's death, but it is certain that his son did not succeed him. Scholars are divided on the question of who stood at the head of the Sages in the period prior to the Bar Kokhba Revolt. But it is certain that there was no Patriarch at their head.[64] The dynastic principle was annulled and the way was prepared for the recognition of Bar Kokhba as Patriarch, which administratively meant the separation of the national-political rule of the Patriarch from the spiritual-religious leadership of the Sages and their contemporaries. It is not surprising, therefore, that R. Akiba enjoined his son R. Joshua: 'Do not dwell in a city whose heads are scholars!'[65] The renewal of the centre in Usha was connected with the restoration of the crown of leadership to the Hillelite dynasty of Patriarchs, but the leadership remained in the Patriarch's hands only in so far as he recognized the authority of the Sages and cited decided Halakhot agreed to by his Bet Din.[66] R. Judah b. R. Ile'ai, who is designated 'the first of the speakers on every occasion'[67], was 'the teacher of the House of the Nasi'.[68] On the other hand, R. Me'ir was not reconciled with the Patriarchate of R. Simeon b. Gamaliel, and even after the surrender of R. Nathan, his comrade in rebellion, he did not yield and refused to appease the Patriarch.[69] Also R. Simeon b. Yoḥai remained faithful to the charge of his teacher R. Akiba, and prided himself on not being a judge.[70] Clashes of this type recurred repeatedly in subsequent generations in varying degrees of bitterness. From personal experience Rabban Simeon b. Gamaliel came to the conclusion that 'There is not a single scholars' session without complaints being heard as to why so-and-so participated and so-and-so did not';[71] and indeed his words were fulfilled in the case of his descendants.[72] However, the centuries that the Patriarchate existed created a hierarchy and protocol not only in respect of the Patriarch. The following Baraita belongs to the time of R. Simeon b. Gamaliel: 'When the Patriarch entered, all the people stood up and did not sit down until he told them: "Be seated!" When the Av Bet Din entered, two rows were formed, one on each side, until he came in and was seated in his place; when a Sage entered, one stood up and one sat down, until he came in and sat in his place; the sons of Sages and the disciples of Sages, when needed by the public, may even leap over the heads of the people....'[73] About five generations later, the Galileans asked who was to be called to the Torah after the Kohen and the Levite, and R. Isaac Nappaḥa replied: 'After them are called up scholars who have been appointed public administrators, and after them the sons of scholars whose fathers have been appointed public administrators, and after them the heads of synagogues and the general public.'[74] The special status granted to scholars who were appointed public administrators, and even to their sons, testifies to a trend that regards this synthesis of Torah with communal work as a blessing.[75] Indeed R. Joḥanan, the teacher of R. Isaac Nappaḥa, considered it a duty and a privilege for scholars to shoulder the burden of administration. This, in his estimation, was the way to obviate the appointment of unworthy persons. Indeed he also said 'If you see a hypocritical and wicked man leading the generation, it were better for the generation to fly in the air, and not to make use of him.'[76] However, he was not content with protest, but demanded that the scholars should be 'builders', that is, 'should occupy themselves with the building of the world',[77] and he even defined 'Who is a scholar that may be appointed a public administrator?' 'Who is a scholar whose lost property may be returned to him on the basis of his general impression [without his specifying any particular identifying marks]?' and 'Who is a scholar whose fellow townsmen are enjoined to do his work?' and insisted that the scholar's outward appearance should be immaculate. In his view it is not only 'a disgrace for a scholar to go out to the market place with patched shoes', but 'any scholar on whose garment a grease spot is to be found is deserving of death.'[78] Undoubtedly there were Sages who conformed to R. Joḥanan's definition that a scholar is 'One who is able to answer a Halakhic question on any subject', nevertheless they avoided accepting the yoke of public administration,[79] because they regarded all occupation, with the exception of Torah-study, as worthless. They thus expounded the verse ' "Surely oppression [העשק *hā-ʿōsheq*] makes the wise man foolish" (Ecclesiastes vii 7): whoever occupies himself [המתעסק *ha-mitʿassēq*] with communal affairs forgets his learning.'[80]

R. Simeon b. Yoḥai's extremism does not necessarily find expression in his demand that scholars should devote themselves entirely to the study of the Torah, without giving a thought to questions of livelihood. His colleagues, too, shared this approach, with differences of emphasis, not only in their dicta,[81] but also in their way of life.[82] Of greater significance, however, for our subject is the following story: 'It once happened that R. Simeon b. Yoḥai was visiting the sick, when he came across a man who was languishing and lying prostrate with a bowel ailment and was reviling the Holy One, blessed be He. Said he to him: "Wretch, you should be making supplication for yourself; instead you are reviling!" The other replied: "May the Holy One, blessed be He, remove the sickness from me and give it to you." He (R. Simeon b. Yoḥai) said: "The Holy One, blessed be He, acted rightly towards you, for I left the study of the Torah and occupied myself with worthless matters." '[83] Possibly R. Simeon b. Yoḥai's reaction was due to the sick man's curse, but the actual formulation of the statement testifies that R. Simeon b. Yoḥai understood the words 'The study of the Torah is equal to them all'[84] literally. Undoubtedly he went far beyond the view of his teacher Akiba. Although it was R. Akiba who gained the decision in the house of Nitza in Lydda on the question 'Which is greater? Is study greater or is practice greater?' when he said 'Study is greater', yet those who answered after him 'Study is greater, for study leads to practice' understood his reason, a fact that is demonstrated by the following episode: 'It once happened that one of his pupils became ill, and the Sages did not come to visit him. But R. Akiba did visit him, and because he [R. Akiba] swept and sprinkled (the floor) before him, he [the sick man] said to him: "Master, you have given me new life!" (Thereupon) R. Akiba went forth and taught: "If one fails to visit the sick, it is as though he shed blood." '[85] We do not know which incident occurred first, and whether R. Akiba wished perhaps to teach the disciples who made light of the precept of visiting the sick a lesson. Without doubt it is possible to argue that R. Simeon's conduct accords with the characteristics of his personality as we know it (above, p. 491), namely that of an absolute individualist, who esteems the person who acquires perfection by the hard way of suffering and tribulation. Unlike his teacher R. Akiba, who knew how to use his laughter as a means of dissipating pain and despair (*T.B. Makkot* 4b), R. Simeon b. Yoḥai held that it was forbidden 'for a man to fill his mouth with laughter';[86] no wonder, therefore, that he was disinclined to reconcile himself to human weaknesses. However, in the case under discussion it is possible to argue *per contra* that opposition to those in authority and to despots does not necessarily go hand in hand with the attitude of forgiveness and indulgence towards the frailty of ordinary folk. R. Simeon b. Yoḥai was different from both his colleagues — from R. Judah, 'the teacher of the Patriarch' and from R. Me'ir, the opponent of the Patriarch. When a man said to his wife 'קונם *Qônām* [a form of vow] that you shall not benefit from me until you make R. Judah and R. Simeon taste of your cooking, R. Judah tasted, saying: It stands to reason: If now in order to make peace between a man and his wife the Torah enjoined: Let My name, written in sanctity, be blotted out by "the waters that curse" in a matter of doubt; how much more so I! R. Simeon did not taste, saying: Let all the widow's children die rather than Simeon should move from his position.'[87] Like R. Judah acted also his Halakhic opponent, R. Me'ir, the bitter adversary of the Patriarch Rabban Simeon b. Gamaliel. In order to enable a woman — who had been forbidden by her husband to come home, unless she first spat in R. Me'ir's face — to fulfil her husband's vow, he pretended to suffer pain in his eyes and had it proclaimed that any woman who knew how to cure a (sore) eye by charm should come and perform the charm on his eye. The woman who had been expelled from her home by her husband's vow came and spat seven times in R. Me'ir's eye.[88] When his disciples said to him 'Is the Torah to be thus abused?', he replied to them: 'Should Me'ir's honour exceed that of his Maker?' And he continued: 'If now with regard to the Holy Name, which was written in sanctity, Scripture enjoined that 'it should be blotted out by the water in order to make peace between a man and his wife, how much more so in the case of R. Me'ir's honour!'[89] R. Akiba's disciple, R. Judah b. R. Ile'ai, acted in his master's spirit. It was told of him 'that he used to interrupt his study of the Torah to attend a funeral or a wedding ceremony... and he used to take a twig of myrtle and dance before the bride....'[90] Undoubtedly the author of the following Baraita was right, when he summed up the situation of the Bar Kokhba Revolt thus: 'And the world was desolate until R. Akiba came to our masters in the south and taught it [the Torah] to them, namely R. Me'ir, R. Judah, R. Jose, R. Simeon, and R. Eleazar b. Shammua', and it was they who revived Torah learning at that time.'[91] R. Judah's portion was not less than that of R. Simeon. The generation of which it was said that six disciples covered themselves with a single garment and studied the Torah was called 'the generation of R. Judah b. Ile'ai.'[92]

Just as the problem of the livelihood of the Sages in the framework of the question of studying Torah and practising a craft did not cease troubling, complicating, and confusing the circles of the Sages,[93] so, too, no unambiguous solution was found to the question of the relationship between learning Torah, on the one hand, and performing good works and occupying oneself with communal needs, 'both religious and mundane', on the other. With reference to the Baraita, 'The pious men of old used to wait an hour, and pray for an hour, and again wait an hour', the question was raised 'Since they spend nine hours a day in prayer, how is their Torah-knowledge preserved and how is their work done?' The answer given was: 'Because they are men of piety, their Torah-learning is preserved and their work is blessed.'[94] At least in all that appertained to the study of the Torah even Pietist-Sages were not inclined to rely on this explanation. The extravagant praise bestowed upon students of the Torah was undoubtedly on occasion prompted by prevailing circumstances at periods and places that witnessed a falling-off in Torah-study,[95] but chiefly it attests the complete identification of Torah-students with their Torah-study, and it served to weaken their allegiance to other values and at times even to exchange and substitute them. The establishment of a scale of relationships and the discovery of a ratio between Torah-study and occupation with worldly affairs, work and marital connection, and between studying Torah and observing the precepts, were themselves difficult topics in the teaching of the Sages, who wrestled and struggled with them throughout the generations. On the one hand, we find the injunction of the Men of the Great Synagogue 'Raise up many disciples' (*M. 'Avot* i, 1); in the same spirit Hillel declared 'And he that does not study is deserving of death'[96], and the School of Shammai enjoined 'Fix a period for the study of the Torah' (*ibid.* xvi), and R. Neḥemiah b. Ha-Qana stated 'Whoever accepts the yoke of the Torah, from him the yoke of the kingdom and the yoke of worldly care are removed' (*ibid.* iii, 5), and R. Me'ir urged 'Lessen your occupation with business and busy yourself with the Torah' (*ibid.* iv, 8); and this, too, is the burden of all those extreme statements of the Amoraim that we shall cite subsequently. But on the other hand, there is the dictum of Shemaʿyah 'Love work and hate lordship' (*ibid.* i, 9); that of R. Zadok 'Make not of the words of the Torah a crown wherewith to aggrandize yourself, nor a spàde wherewith to dig... whoever makes profit out of the words of the Torah destroys his own life' (*ibid.* iv, 5); and that of Rabban Gamaliel, the son of R. Judah the Patriarch, 'An excellent thing is study of the Torah together with worldly occupation, for the toil in them both puts sin out of mind; but all study of the Torah without work comes to naught in the end and brings sin in its train [גוררת עוון].[97] Let all who labour with the community do so for the sake of Heaven....' (*ibid.* ii, 2).

This dictum of the Patriarch can easily be credited to his experience, and that of his family, in dealing with the problem of the livelihood of the Sages and with the difficulties encountered in appointing Sages to public posts. But this explanation, as in similar instances, does not exhaust the nature of the problem nor the facts. Rav Huna, who worked his own fields and picked his fruit himself, and, when people came before him for judgement, asked that someone be appointed to irrigate his field,[98] taught that 'Whoever occupies himself with Torah only is like one who has no God.' In the spirit of this homily it is related in a Baraita in the Babylonian Talmud that R. Ḥanina b. Teradion said to R. Eleazar b. Peraṭa: 'Happy are you that you have been seized on five charges, but will be saved. Woe unto me who have been seized on one charge and will not be delivered! For you have occupied yourself with Torah-study and deeds of benevolence, whereas I engaged in Torah-study only.'[99] R. Abbahu was a wealthy man and close to the government and was called 'leader of his people'.[1] He himself knew Greek and wished to teach this language to his daughter[2], and without doubt he also occupied himself, in addition to his Torah-study, with 'both secular and religious matters'. Nevertheless, when he learned that his son R. Ḥanina, whom he had sent to Tiberias to study Torah, occupied himself with charitable works, he sent him this message: 'Is it because there are no graves in Caesarea that I sent you to Tiberias?'[3] But we shall certainly be wrong if we attempt to explain the dicta that speak in praise of Torah-study and give it precedence over everything else as though they were directed solely to students. R. Samuel bar Naḥmani said in the name of R. Jonathan: 'Scholars who engage in the study of the Torah anywhere in the world are regarded by Me as though they burned and offered oblations unto My name.' Two sayings are reported in the name of R. Joḥanan: one — 'Scholars who occupy themselves with the study of the Torah at night are accounted by Scripture as though they were engaged in the Temple service'[3a]; the other — 'When scholars occupy themselves with the laws of the Temple service, it is accounted to them by Scripture as though the Temple were built in their days.' While Resh Laqish expounded the verse ' "This is the law for the burnt-offering, for the meal-offering, for the sin-offering and for the guilt-offering" (to mean that) whoever occupies himself with the study of the Torah is deemed as though he had offered up a burnt-offering, a meal-offering, a sin-offering, and a guilt-offering', and R. Isaac taught 'Whoever occupies himself with the law of the sin-offering is regarded as if he offered up a sin-offering, and whoever occupies himself with the law of the guilt-offering is regarded as though he offered up a guilt-offering.' Rava came and said 'Whoever occupies himself with the study of the Torah needs no burnt-offering nor sin-offering, no meal-offering nor guilt-offering.'[4] The wording of Rava's dictum 'needs no' etc. is more extreme than the dicta of his predecessors and their like, such as 'A Sage who sits and expounds (Torah) in public is accounted by Scripture as though he offered up fat and blood upon the altar',[5] for all these sayings contain the expression 'as though (if)'. Even in the anonymous homily that states 'When the Temple is not in existence, how shall you find atonement? Occupy yourselves with the words of the Torah, which are comparable to the sacrifices and they shall make atonement for you...',[6] the study of the Torah serves only as a surrogate and replacement for atonement by the sacrifices. Even this concept is already the result of a late development, for when the Temple was destroyed, Rabban Joḥanan b. Zakkai declared that acts of charity and benevolence were Israel's atonement,[7] while others again looked upon fasts as substituting for and replacing sacrifices.[8] The supersession of fasting and the practice of benevolence as a means of expiation by the study of Torah accords with the views of various Sages who chose the way of R. Simeon b. Yoḥai, rather than that of R. Judah b. Ileʿai.

Rav Joseph cited a Baraita[9] to the effect that when Mordecai became viceroy, he found favour only with the majority of his brethren, not with all of them; some of the Sanhedrin left him, 'because he ceased to study Torah and entered upon rulership'. The Sage drew the moral 'Greater is the study of the Torah than the saving of lives.' Indeed Rav Joseph also said that the Torah protects and saves both when one is studying it and when one is not studying it, whereas the precept saves only when one is performing it. This, too, is an inference, which he derived from the teaching of R. Menaḥem b. R. Jose: 'Scripture equates the commandment with a lamp... just as a lamp protects only temporarily, so the commandment also protects only temporarily; but the Torah is equated with light to tell you that just as light protects permanently, so the Torah protects for ever... another explanation is: Sin quenches the commandment, but it does not extinguish the Torah.'[10] The dictum of the Babylonian Amora 'Study of the Torah transcends the building of the Temple, for as long as Baruch the son of Neriah was alive, Ezra did not leave him to go up (to Eretz-Israel)' may possibly be regarded as an apologia for the continued residence of the Sages in Babylonia;[11] but this certainly does not apply to the saying of the same Amora 'Study of the Torah transcends honouring father and mother.' Rava followed the view of Rav Joseph, and his statement that he who occupies himself with study of the Torah has no need of burnt-offering or sin-offering emanates from the absolute conviction of these Rabbis that the expiatory power of Torah-study is greater than that of sacrifices. This is further indicated by the following dispute between Rava and Abbaye, which is linked to the homily of R. Samuel bar Naḥmani in the name of R. Jonathan: 'Whence do we know that a Divine decree accompanied by an oath is not abrogated? For it is said "Therefore I have sworn unto the house of Eli that the iniquity of Eli's house shall not be expiated with sacrifice nor offering" (I Samuel iii 14).' On this Rava commented 'It is not expiated with sacrifice or offering, but it is atoned for with study of the Torah'; as against this Abbaye said 'It is not expiated with sacrifice or offering, but it is atoned for by Torah-study and the practice of benevolence.' The anonymous view of the Talmud expresses agreement with the opinion of Abbaye by stating: 'Abbaye and Rava were descended from the House of Eli. Rava who engaged in Torah-study only lived forty years; Abbaye[12] who occupied himself with the study of the Torah and with the works of benevolence lived sixty years.' Rava prepared in anticipation, as it were, an answer to this proof by his dictum 'The length of one's life, children, and sustenance are not dependent on merit but on fate.'[13]

Rava's appraisement of Torah-study as the supreme value also found expression in his attitude to prayer. With reference to the Baraita wherein it is taught 'Associates who are engaged in the study of the Torah interrupt their study for the reading of the *Shĕma*ʿ, but not for the Prayer [Eighteen Benedictions]', the view of R. Joḥanan was cited in Babylonia: 'This was taught only with respect to scholars like R. Simeon b. Yoḥai and his colleagues, in whose case Torah-study was their sole occupation, but such as we must interrupt our study for the reading of the *Shĕmaʿ* and for the Prayer.'[14] It is hard to imagine that Rava, who engaged in wine trade, possessed fields and ships, métayers and slaves[15], acted as a judge and even imposed floggings, and had contacts with royalty and with princes[16], considered himself — unlike R. Joḥanan — as one 'whose Torah-study was his sole occupation'. Nevertheless, when he saw Rav Hamnuna prolonging his prayers, he said 'They forsake eternal life and occupy themselves with ephemeral existence.'[17] Also in relation to prayer the study of the Torah is exalted to an absolute value, irrespective of the amount of time that a man devotes to such study, and without any demand, as a result of this conception, for one's complete withdrawal from all other interests of the world. However, despite the absolute character of Rava's appraisement, it is certain that we may not attribute to him any lack of reverence for all those matters of which he held Torah-study took precedence. It will suffice to note the number of times that Rava's name appears in discussions relative to the Halakhot of prayer and the Halakhot of the Temple and its sacrifices. These subjects, just like the laws of Shabbat and the festivals, of damages and levitical purity, constitute that very Torah that he praises and extols; and undoubtedly he did not forget the fact that 'the Torah begins with an act of benevolence and ends with an act of benevolence'.[18] We find, moreover, express dicta of his that serve to balance the element of hyperbole that characterize his sayings in praise of the Torah. Needless to say, he did not regard the study of the Torah as an offset to transgressions. Against such an opinion Rava declared: 'Whoever has intercourse with a married woman, even if he has studied Torah — of which it is written "It is more precious than rubies [מפנינים *mi-pĕnînîm*]", that is, than the High Priest who enters the innermost part [לפני ולפנים *lifĕnay we-lifĕnîm*] of the Temple — will be hunted down by her to the judgement of Gehenna.'[19] It is actually of Rava that it is related that he was accustomed to say 'The goal of wisdom is penitence and good deeds; a man should not study Bible and Mishna and rebel against his father and his mother and his teacher, or one who is superior to him in wisdom, as it is said "The reverence of the Lord is the beginning of wisdom, a good understanding have all they that do thereafter" (Psalms cxi 10) — Scripture does not say "to all those who study them [לומדיהם]" but "to all those who do thereafter [עושיהם]" ....'[20] It is he, also, who added each day after his prayer 'My God, before I was formed I was unworthy, and now that I have been formed I am as though I had not been formed; I am dust in my lifetime, how much more so in my death. I am before Thee as a vessel full of shame and confusion. May it be Thy will, O Lord my God, that I sin no more, and the sins that I have committed before Thee purge away by Thy great compassion, but not by suffering and evil diseases.'[21] A man who sees suffering coming upon him he advised first to examine his deeds, and only 'If he finds no reason, should he attribute it to neglect of the study of the Torah.'[22] Right practice is harder to achieve and less commonly found than the fulfilment of the duty of Torah-study, and Rava himself declared 'Is there any virtue in propounding problems... the Holy One, blessed be He, requires the heart, for it is written "But the Lord looketh on the heart" (I Samuel xvi 7).'[23] In the spirit of his teacher, Rav Pappa explained the obscure Baraita of R. Jose, 'Whoever says he has no (interest in the study of) the Torah, has no (reward for the study of the) Torah' in the sense of 'Whoever says that he is only concerned with the study of the Torah, receives no (reward) even for (the study of) the Torah... "that ye may learn them and observe to do them" — whosoever observes is also regarded as studying, but he who does not observe is not regarded as studying.'[24]

Rav Pappa adopted the view of Rav Huna and almost repeated his words verbatim despite the changes that had occurred in the intervening years and despite the differences in the circumstances of the lives and character of the two Sages. It is important to note that the views and dicta that we have cited on the themes under discussion not only reflect divergent opinions between different Sages and diverse trends, but also contradictions in the teachings of a single Sage, which are the outcome of inner questing and struggles. We have encountered them in the sayings of the Amora Rava,[25] and we shall come across them again, if we revert to that personage of ostensibly unequivocal approach and character, namely R. Simeon b. Yoḥai.

We have seen him as one who rejects any synthesis of Torah-study with another occupation and as one who prefers occupation with the Torah to any deed of benevolence, leadership, or position of authority. However, not only does an Haggadic tradition represent him as effecting an improvement for the benefit of Tiberias[26], and as going on a mission of intercession in order to get an edict rescinded in Rome[27], but a homily is cited in his name praising the existence of juridical institutions: 'R. Simeon b. Yoḥai: Why do the civil laws precede all other precepts of the Torah? Because when there is a lawsuit between a man and his fellow, there is strife between them. But once the case has been decided, peace reigns between them.'[28] However, it was actually as judges that Sages came to know difficult litigants and realized that peace did not always follow the verdict. Nevertheless they agreed in principle with the dictum of Rabban Simeon b. Gamaliel that the world 'rests on judgement, truth, and peace' (*M. 'Avot*, i, 18). But, taking the view that 'Where there is judgement there is no peace, and where there is peace there is no judgement', R. Joshua b. Qorḥa came to the conclusion that arbitration should be preferred to law, and that it was 'meritorious to arbitrate', But R. Eliezer the son of R. Jose the Galilean said: 'It is forbidden to arbitrate, and he who arbitrates commits a sin, and whoever blesses an arbitrator actually contemns ... but let the law pierce through the mountain.'[29] This dispute was not decided, and one could say in this matter that 'not all men, or places, or times are alike'. However, even those Sages who undertook to establish the land by justice and to make litigants obey the court by imposing the fear of 'the judges' instruments'[30], which they had at their disposal, observed the counsel of R. Jonathan: 'A judge should always imagine himself as having a sword hanging over his head [literally 'lying between his thighs'], and Gehenna gaping beneath him.'[31] The verse 'The king by justice establisheth the land; but the man of *terumot* [literally 'heave-offerings'; the usual rendering is 'he that exacteth gifts'] overthroweth it' (Proverbs xxix 4) is interpreted as referring to a man 'who makes himself like a heave-offering, which is cast in a corner of the house and declares: Why should I bother with the affairs of the community, why should I concern myself with their lawsuits, why should I have to hear their noise? Peace be upon you, O my soul! — such a person destroys the world.'[32] But from the same verse the

Sages also learned at that time: 'If a judge is like a king, who is in need of naught, he establishes the land; but if he is like a priest, who makes the rounds of the threshing floors, he overthrows it.'[33] R. Simlai, who was a member of the household of the Patriarch, found in the verses 'And I charged your judges at that time' (Deuteronomy i, 16), 'And I commanded you at that time' (*ibid. v.* 18), 'an admonition to the community that they should show the judge due deference, and an admonition to the judge to be forbearing towards the community.'[34] Those Sages who, on account of the awe with which the act of judging filled them, refrained from accepting the burden of judgeship were also not free from pangs of conscience, as the following story testifies: 'When R. Assi was about to depart from the world, his sister's son came to visit him, and found him weeping. Said he to him (to R. Assi): "Master, why are you weeping? Is there a part of the Torah that you did not learn or teach? Behold, your disciples sit before you. Is there an act of benevolence that you did not perform? Yet despite all your attributes you eschewed giving judgement, and never allowed yourself to be appointed as administrator of communal affairs." He answered him: "My son, it is for this very reason that I weep, lest I am held culpable for having been able to dispense justice to Israel (but not having done so)." '[35] The disciple considered the avoidance of exercising authority a virtue, but when R. Assi 'drew near to the shadow of death'[36] he began to doubt the rightness of his attitude.

The retreat from giving decisions and sitting in judgement is also to be explained against the background of the ramification of Torah-study, of the proliferation of expositions and interpretations, and of the harmonization of conflicting Mishnayot, Baraitot, and traditions. R. Akiba's maxim 'Why should we concern ourselves with the practice? I am not concerned with the act but with the express Scriptural statement'[37] opened wide the way to freedom of Halakhic decision that was no longer subjected to institutions and testimonies regarding acts of the Bet Din. Nor was he disturbed by the question 'Shall we impose on this woman (the severer penalty of) death by burning because you expound the *Waw* of the word ובת *û-bat* ['and the daughter']?'[38], but interpreted the text and harmonized it with the traditional law.[39] In truth the expositions conquered the Halakha,[40] but the signification of the term 'Halakha' underwent a change. At the beginning of the Amoraic period it no longer connotes 'A practice that continues from earlier times to the end, or the path in which Israel walks',[41] or a firmly fixed decision, but denotes the result of argument and study, not a practical ruling, so that it became necessary to coin a special term 'a practical Halakha' in order to restore its original sense. Samuel said 'The whole of the Halakha at the beginning of the last chapter of Nidda obtains in theory but not in practice.'[42] Of R. Joḥanan it is related that he expounded the law to the men of Tiberias 'according to the view of R. Simeon b. Eleazar; he taught it to them theoretically, but they thought it was to be observed thus in practice....'[43] According to another tradition: 'R. Assi said to R. Joḥanan "When the master tells us that the Halakha is so and so, may we act accordingly?" He replied: "Do not act accordingly, unless I declare it to be the law for practical purposes." '[44] R. Joḥanan even went so far as to say that an expressly stated Mishna was taught only with a view to sharpening the minds of the disciples.[45] R. Bun and the Rabbis put several questions to R. Ze'ira concerning the laws of the 'booth', to which he replied; commenting on his answers R. Abbahu said: 'All these statements serve the purpose of argumentation, but it is forbidden to rule thus.'[46] Possibly this caution was actually the result of R. Joḥanan's aim 'to make the teaching agree with the Halakha' and to lay down rules for deciding in matters that were disputed by Tannaim; but this procedure did not put an end to the disputes. Indeed we find that his disciples disagree as to whether a 'Halakha' derived by rules of this kind is a real Halakha, or merely a case where we 'incline towards', or 'favour' the view in question. The Amora Rav Mesharshia said, again in the form of a rule, 'The Halakha is not according to these rules.'[47] It was the realization that underlying these rules was the desire to obtain a substantive decision in a given matter in conformity with a given view[48] that engendered the attitude of scepticism towards them, even if — or, perhaps, just because — they were formulated by Sages who were well known for their power to decide. Rav Naḥman said of a series of Baraitot containing conflicting views of Tannaim on matters of civil law, in which he was considered a leading expert: 'The Halakha is according to R. Judah, and according to R. Jose b. Judah, and according to Rabban Simeon b. Gamaliel.' When, however, Rav Kahana reported his statement to Rav Zevid, he said: 'It was not the Halakha that was stated but the principle (which all three follow).'[49] When Rav Naḥman said in the name of Rav 'The Halakha in the entire chapter (is in accordance with the Mishna) except where there is a difference of opinion, Rav Sheshet remarked: I should say that Rav was half asleep and going to bed when he stated this tradition.'[50] The Sages not only pointed out the errors in the decisions of other scholars, but Rav Naḥman himself, and subsequently Rava — several times — announced in public 'I erred in the statement I made to you.'[51] An additional difficulty in fixing the Halakha was to be found in what appeared to be a contradiction between the prevailing practice and local customs[52], between the conclusions derived from the discussion in the schoolhouse and the sources or traditions in the possession of the Sages.[53] On the one hand there was the desire to reach as far as possible a unified decision, and on the other, unity could only be attained by concessions to local customs and by leaving questions open to various possible decisions. The Tannaitic homily ' "לא תתגדדו *Lō' titgōdĕdû* [usually rendered 'ye shall not cut yourselves']" — you shall not form factions [אגודות *'aggûdôt*], but you shall all be a single band [אגודה *'aggûdā*]'[54] was already considered in the period of the Tannaim a desideratum to be prayed for and corresponded to the reality only in a very general way.

The sharply worded statement in the Baraita 'When the disciples of Shammai and Hillel who had not waited upon their teachers sufficiently grew in number, the disputes in Israel increased and two Torahs were formed'[55] may perhaps be linked to the schisms that took place before the Destruction. But actually the Baraita describing the state of reconciliation provides even stronger evidence: 'Although the School of Shammai differed from the School of Hillel in regard to associate wives, sisters, a woman whose marriage is in doubt, an old bill of divorce, one who marries a woman with something worth a *peruṭa*, and a man who divorces his wife, but she spends the night with him at the (same) inn, nevertheless the Shammaites did not refrain from marrying women from Hillelite families, nor the Hillelites women from Shammaite families, but truth and peace prevailed between them as it is said "Therefore love ye truth and peace" (Zechariah viii 19). Although these prohibited and the others permitted, they did not refrain from preparing levitically pure food with one another [i.e. using one another's utensils], fulfilling the Scripture "Every way of a man is right in his own eyes; but the Lord weigheth the hearts" (Proverbs xxi 2). R. Simeon said: They did not refrain from doubtful matters, but did refrain from that which was certain.'[56] Not only the statement of this R. Simeon as well as the restrained wording in the Mishna,[57] but even the idyllic phrasing of the Baraita does not indicate a diminution of the disunity. This is attested by the Baraita which already knows that 'the Halakha is always according to the School of Hillel'; nevertheless it finds fault only with one who acts according to the stringent rulings of both or according to the lenient decisions of both, but not with one who acts in agreement with the opinion of the School of Shammai, 'in accordance with both their lenient and stringent rulings'[58]; moreover, the Sages continued to mention 'the view of an individual among the majority'.[59]

The Amoraim Abbaye and Rava drew the requisite inference from the existing situation. Abbaye said: 'We apply the rule of *lō' titgōdĕdû* only where there are two courts in one town, and the one decides according to the School of Shammai and the other according to the School of Hillel; but there is no objection to two courts in two towns (ruling differently).'

Rava went further and said: 'We apply the principle of *lō' titgōdĕdû* only in the case of a court in one town half of which decide according to the School of Shammai and half according to the School of Hillel; but there is no objection to two courts in one town (ruling differently).'[60] For 'the battle of the Torah is Torah'; and this included also what was defined as 'Messianic laws' (see above, p. 313, n. 96), and as 'what happened happened' (above, p. 305, n. 62). With regard to them R. Eliezer the son of R. Jose the Galilean already expounded the verse in Proverbs (xxiii 27): ' "Prepare thy work without" — this refers to Scripture, Mishna, and Talmud; "and make it ready for thee in the field" — this refers to good deeds; "and afterwards build thine house" — this means: Research and receive reward.'[61] Between 'Scripture, Mishna, and Talmud' and 'Research and receive reward' the Tanna inserts the demand for 'good deeds'. Likewise Rava said 'The goal of wisdom is penitence and good deeds' (above, p. 613);

by 'wisdom' he referred to the wisdom of the Torah. An anonymous homilist broadened the canvas and expounded the words of the prophet (Jeremiah ix 22) as follows: ' "Thus saith the Lord: Let not the wise man glory in his wisdom": If he does not know who created him, how can he be wise? Even among the wicked there are those who are wise in their own eyes, men who recognize the sun and the moon and the planets... and determine the months according to the solar cycle... they are wise to know the work of God in the sky, but they are unable to recognize Him who created them, even the whole world. They are also wise to build up provinces and districts and houses, to make weapons... they are wise to put things right for others, but lack the sagacity to set their own soul in order. They are wise in all respects, but in one matter they are foolish; thus through one thing they lose their wisdom, in that they have failed to recognize God....'[62] By undertaking not only to learn Torah but to teach it[63] and to engage in the thrust and parry of its 'warfare'[64], the Sages created in the world of the Torah — despite all the antitheses and dichotomies to be found in it — an educative and reformative instrument for themselves and their people.

VIII. The Internal Relations in the Academies of the Sages

The concomitant phenomena that are familiar in every academic society that values intellectual achievements of erudition, acuity of reasoning, and dialectical ability[65], did not pass by the academies of the Tannaim and Amoraim. Debates on principles and objective disputes were not free from personal overtones and the desire to annoy one's opponent: 'After R. Me'ir's death R. Judah said to his disciples: Let not R. Me'ir's disciples enter here, because they are disputatious and would come not to learn but to overwhelm me with Halakhot...'[66] There exist dicta of the Palestinian Sages, R. Oshaʿya and R. Isaac, that speak in praise of their compatriots, who are gracious and pleasant to one another in Halakhic discussion, and in dispraise of the Babylonian Sages, who are hurtful and bitter towards one another in Halakhic debate.[67] However, it is quite clear that in reality this distinction did not depend on territorial boundaries.[68] In the course of the sharp debates it also happened at times that a colleague was offended, and that harsh expressions and abusive words were exchanged in the moment of anger, and not necessarily by Sages who did not value good manners. Collegiates did not always view with favour the addition of disciples to their ranks. Rabbi himself complained: 'When I went to study Torah under Rabbi Eleazar b. Shammua', his disciples converged upon me like the cocks of Bet Buqya ('experienced and fierce, and they did not allow a strange cock among them' — Rashi), and did not permit me to learn more than this one thing in our Mishna.'[69] 'When R. Eleazar b. R. Simeon entered the college — it is related — Rabbi's face fell.'[70] Rabbi is the author of the dictum 'I learned much from my teachers, and even more from my colleagues, but most from my disciples.'[71] But he himself said of his disciple Levi 'It appears to me that he has no brains in his skull';[72] and he enjoined his son Rabban Gamaliel: 'Conduct your Patriarchate with men of high standing, and throw bile among the disciples [i.e. insist on strict discipline].'[73]

Resh Laqish, who expressed strong opposition to anyone speaking ill of Israel (above, p. 563), is also the author of the dictum 'When two scholars are gracious to each other in Halakhic discussion, the Holy One, blessed be He, hearkens to them.'[74] However, when R. Ḥiyya bar Joseph cited, upon immigrating to Eretz-Israel, a ruling by Rav, Resh Laqish did not refrain from observing contemptuously: 'Who is this Rav, who is this Rav? I don't know him....' Even when R. Joḥanan reminded him, he still asked 'What was his forte?' In this instance he yielded;[75] but he called two Sages, who were considered worthy of intercalating the year, 'cowherds' and they regarded him as 'a troublesome fellow'.[76] Indeed he was very strict with his colleague R. Eleazar.[77] The same R. Eleazar, when asked R. Me'ir's reason for a certain ruling, replied crossly: 'You ask me in the schoolhouse about a matter for which the earlier scholars gave no reason in order to put me to shame!'[78] Rav replied to Rav Huna's question 'It seems that this Rabbi thinks that people cannot explain a tradition'; in similar style Rav Assi reacted to R. Ze'ira's question, and 'Ulla to R. Abba's question.[79]

The practice of recounting the praise of disciples is already ascribed to Rabban Joḥanan b. Zakkai (*M. 'Avot* ii, 8). At times the discussion would begin with censure and end with praise. When R. Akiba taught that the priests who blew the trumpets had to be perfect, without blemish, R. Ṭarfon strongly opposed him, saying: 'How long will Akiba keep piling upon us (groundless teachings): I cannot tolerate it any longer'; but when he was convinced of the correctness of his disciple's teaching, he said to him: 'By the Temple Service! you did not invent this. Be happy, O Abraham our father, that Akiba went forth from your loins. Ṭarfon saw and forgot; Akiba gives his own exposition and is in agreement with the Halakha. Lo, whoever departs from you is as one who departs from his life!'[80] Some looked upon this eulogizing as redress for the harsh language employed. Isi b. Judah said: 'Why do scholars die prematurely? Not because they commit adultery, nor because they commit robbery, but because they abuse one another.'[81] Indeed, he recounted the praise of Sages and gave them epithets. So long as the observations were confined to an assessment of the qualities and the method of study of former Sages, even if they contained no particular tribute, they aroused no response, but not so if they referred to Sages who were still alive. Isi b. Judah himself learnt that even encomiums could lead to an unexpected reaction.[82] He said of R. Simeon 'He learns much and forgets little.' However, when R. Simeon met him, he said to him: 'Why do you babble about me to the scholars?' Isi answered R. Simeon's complaint with surprise, but at the same time amended his previous remarks, saying: 'What then did I say about you, except that you learn much and forget little; and what you forget is merely the bran of your study?'[83] R. Simeon had no need of the esteem of others, and he himself said to his disciples: 'My sons, learn my rules, for my rules are *crème de la crème* of those of R. Akiba.'[84] And if he took objection to praise that did not appeal to him, it is certain that Sages of lesser standing and self-assurance were not pleased with praise that in the end turned out to be censure, and needless to say they took umbrage at express dispraise, for it was a common phenomenon that those Sages who were accustomed to be lavish of their praises were also not sparing of censorious and disparaging remarks. The Sage that praised had to give heed not only to the reaction of the person praised, but also to that of his colleagues. Rabbi, who was skilled at appraising Sages and their character, once eulogized R. Ḥiyya extravagantly, when he entered the schoolhouse, saying: 'Let R. Ḥiyya the Great enter further in front than I. Said R. Ishmael b. R. Jose: Even in front of me?' Then Rabbi replied: 'Heaven forfend! I mean: Let R. Ḥiyya the Great enter into the interior [i.e. front benches] and R. Ishmael bar Jose into the innermost part [i.e. the very first bench].'[85] We should also bear in mind that in appraisements figurative phrases were transmitted as stereotyped formulas and *façons de parler*, to which no particular weight should be attached. When Rabban Simeon b. Gamaliel wished to give expression to the importance of R. Simeon b. Yoḥai, he said to his son that, compared with R. Eleazar the son of R. Simeon, he was like 'a lion the son of a fox *vis-à-vis* a lion the son of a lion'.[86] A similar figure of speech was used many generations later by Rav Naḥman bar Isaac. When Rav Naḥman bar Rav Ḥisda invited Rav Naḥman bar Isaac to come to him, he said to him 'We have learned in a Baraita: R. Jose said: It is not a man's place that honours him, but he that honours his place....' But when Rav Naḥman bar Ḥisda expressed his readiness to come to him, he said to him: 'Rather let a "mina" the son of "half a mina" [i.e. an eminent person the son of a less eminent person] come to a "mina" the son of a "mina" than that a "mina" the son of a "mina" should come to the son of "half a mina".'[87] This story also shows how swift was the transition from standing on one's dignity to submission. Rav Naḥman bar Isaac himself had an eloquent tongue, and he was full of witty sallies, in both praise and dispraise.[88] This attribute also characterized his great colleague Rava. On the one hand we find him saying of Rav Judah and Rabba bar Abbuha: 'Why did I interfere with the interpretation of the elders!'[89] ('Why did I have to dispute the ruling of these elders' — Rashi), and he calls his colleagues 'the lion of the company', 'a great man', 'an eminent person'.[90] Of Rav Sheshet he said: 'The question was raised by a hard man, who is as hard as iron.'[91] On the other hand, he rebuked his disciples and said to them: 'Have I not told you not to ascribe "empty bottles" [i.e. valueless opinions] to Rav Naḥman....'[92]; and he called his colleagues 'black pot' ('earthen vessel' — Rashi), 'untrained [literally 'arbitration'] judges'.[93] Of the stubborn and disputatious R. Jeremiah, who called Rav Sheshet, Abbaye, and even Rava 'foolish Babylonians',[94] Rava said: 'When one of us goes up there [to Eretz-Israel], he is worth two of them. For R. Jeremiah, who did not know what the Rabbis were talking about, when he went up there called us foolish Babylonians.'[95] But even with regard to Rav Sheshet, when Rami bar Ḥama praised his question in the words 'Here is a man and here is a question!' Rava replied 'I see the man, but I do not see [the point of] the question.'[96] Friction was also caused by competition for distinguished disciples, who wandered from the school of one Rabbi to that of another.[96a] The attempts of disciples to evaluate their teachers, even if they were careful not to offend them but only to praise that which seemed to them worthy of praise, aroused objection and tension. Rav Ḥisda said to the Sages: 'I should like to tell you something, but I am afraid that you will leave me and go away: Whoever studies Torah under one master, never makes real progress. So they left him and went to study with Rava. He explained to them, however, that this is true of logical deduction ('to acquire sharpness and subtlety of mind' — Rashi), but oral tradition it is preferable to learn from one master.'[97] The rule stated by Rav Ḥisda was brought from Eretz-Israel — from the school of R. Jannai — to Babylonia, but in Eretz-Israel Tannaim already held this view before R. Jannai.[98] It was accepted by scholars without their giving due attention to Rav Ḥisda's qualification. Thus it is related that Rav Isaac bar Rav Judah, who was accustomed to attend the discourses of Rami bar Ḥama, left him one day and went to Rav Sheshet. When Rami bar Ḥama met him and charged him with pride and presumptuousness, he replied that he acted as he did because he preferred the erudition of Rav Sheshet to the argumentations of Rami bar Ḥama.[99] Rav Ada bar Abba used to say to the disciples: Instead of going to gnaw bones (i.e. to acquire paltry knowledge) with Abbaye, come and eat fat meat with Rava.[1]

The debates at the colleges of the Tannaim and Amoraim were conducted in a free spirit. There were scholars who made their teachers wise[2], and the decision did not depend on age or status, but on reasons and arguments.[3] Many dicta are to be found against undue strictness on the part of the teacher[4], just as, on the other hand, the disciple's conduct and duties toward his teacher are defined with the greatest particularity.[5] There were scholars who said: 'Never should a man speak in praise of his fellow, because through praising him he will come to speak ill of him.'[6] But the reality was different. Sometimes praise served only as a preamble to dispraise.[7] In the light of all that we have stated above, there is no need to cite many additional examples in order to show that in practice many could not resist the great temptation of belittling their fellows. In everyday relations even the gentlest of the Sages were not always — as R. Joḥanan demanded[8] — like an angel of the Lord; nevertheless students also sought Torah from the Sages who were exacting and abusive.[9] Disciples who did not give due heed to their teachers' honour in all respects[10] disputed their views, and were not concerned if they put them to shame publicly;[11] while the relationship between colleagues — both Sages and disciples — sometimes led to *nidduy* [lighter ban] and *ḥerem* [severer ban].[12] Despite all the eulogies showered on earlier scholars and expressions of self-abasement before them, R. Oshaʿya did not refrain from saying: 'Rabban Gamaliel gave that general a fallacious answer'; and Resh Laqish reported in his name 'R. Akiba gave a fallacious answer to that disciple';[13] and Rava said: 'May the Lord forgive R. Ṭarfon!'[14] The story that 'R. Neḥunya b. Haqana was asked by his disciples "What is the cause of your longevity?" and he replied "I have never sought honour through the degradation of my colleague" ' and the parallel account about R. Zera, who replied to this question 'I have never rejoiced at my colleague's downfall' prove that the narrators of these stories did not regard these qualities as very common.[15]

We have described the internal relationship at the academies of the Sages in their various aspects, but it is clear that all the antitheses, clashes, and sharp words in no way detract from the integrated character of the class of the Sages. Verses like 'As arrows in the hand of a mighty man, so are the children of one's youth. Happy is the man that hath his quiver full of them; they shall not be put to shame, when they speak with their enemies in the gate' (Psalms cxxvii 4–5) were applied to students of the Torah, but undoubtedly the true position is also portrayed by the statement of R. Ḥiyya bar Abba: 'Even a father and son, a master and disciple, who study Torah at the same gate [the same academy, or subject], become hostile to each other, but they do not depart thence until they become friends again.'[16]

The bitterness of debate and the acerbity of the verbal exchanges at the academies did not prevent the creation of class consciousness, which found expression, as we saw, in many of the sources that we cited, either expressly or implicitly, and we shall augment them with dicta that speak in favour of the feeling of solidarity and fellowship, and emphasize and justify the right of scholars to preference and privileges. We shall now cite principally dicta of the greatest of the last of the Babylonian Amoraim. Although they designate the Sages צורבא מרבנן *ṣôrĕvā mē-rabbānān* ['a student of Rabbinical lore'] — a term found only in the Babylonian Talmud[17] — the sayings do not reflect, in their content, merely the personal opinions of those who utter them, but epitomize the views of many generations in a clear and trenchant formulation. In truth parallels can be cited for most of them from early sources.[17a] Rava permitted a *ṣôrĕvā mē-rabbānān* to make known, in a place where he was unknown, that he was a Rabbinical scholar, so that he might benefit from the privileges due to him such as the right to have his case decided before that of others, to take precedence in all things like a priest, and to receive exemption from paying the poll-tax.[18] In Eretz-Israel the dictum 'a scholar must make himself known' was transmitted in the name of Abbaye, but it was interpreted there thus: 'When a man knows one tractate and goes to a (new) place, and they honour him as though he knew two, he must declare: "I know (only) one tractate." '[19] This interpretation restricts the scholar's right to make himself known by imposing the duty of exactitude. In the style of 'Remember unto me, O my God, for good' Rava said: 'May I be rewarded for this, that if a scholar came before me for judgement, I did not lay my head on the pillow until I had sought out (arguments) in his favour.'[20] The consideration shown to litigants who were scholars[21] in the sense that their case was dealt with before that of others, and that they were exempted from the duty of standing when adducing their arguments — for their sake their opponents also enjoyed this privilege[22] — is attributed to Rabba bar Rav Ḥuna, to Rav Naḥman, to Rav Joseph[23], and to Rav Papa (in this instance 'the court messenger' made the *'am hā-'āreṣ* stand, and Rav Papa did not object). When Rav Yemar came to testify on behalf of Mar Zuṭra, Amemar made even the witnesses sit, and when Rav Ashi observed to him: 'All agree that witnesses must stand — since it is written "then both the men... shall stand"

(Deuteronomy xix 17)' — he answered him: 'The one is a positive commandment and the other is a positive commandment; the positive commandment of honouring the Torah takes precedence.'[24] However, even Sages who acted according to this rule had doubts as to whether they were not neglecting the principle of justice and inviting disaster. When Rav Ashi said that legally the plaintiff may demand an oath from the defendant 'but if he is *ṣôrĕvā mē-rabbānān*, we do not impose an oath upon him', Rav Yemar said to him: 'May a *ṣôrĕvā mē-rabbānān* strip people of their cloaks? But we do not attend to his case' (he is not compelled to swear, so that he should not appear to be under suspicion, but neither do we collect for him, if his opponent demands: 'Swear to me!').[25] Mar bar Rav Ashi recused himself from trying the case of a scholar and gave his reason: 'He is as dear to me as myself, and a man does not find arguments to his own detriment.'[26] Many of the concessions granted to the Sages appear to be due to the difficulty experienced in solving the problem of providing the Sages with a livelihood.[27] But frequently none of the remissions helped, and the Sages were unsuccessful in their business: 'Simon bar Wa (Abba) was an expert in pearls and in all things, but he had no bread to eat, and R. Joḥanan applied to him the verse "neither yet bread to the wise" (Ecclesiastes iv 11).' It appears that this Sage, too — who was for a time in Damascus, and in the meantime his juniors received appointments, but he was not appointed to any office[28] — had no alternative but to ask R. Judah Nesi'a for a testimonial letter, which contained a recommendation, in order that he might find a livelihood.[29] But even the appointments to offices did not solve the problem, since Sages who received appointments, but were not wealthy or the owners of prosperous businesses[30], were dependent for their maintenance on the support of the local people.

Numerous dicta accord high praise and promise great reward to those who support and maintain Sages and their disciples.[31] To the support given to Torah-scholars by 'precept-performers' (i.e. generous donors to charity) the Rabbis devoted a whole series of homilies that symbolized the recipients and donors under the figure of the two tribes Issachar and Zebulun: 'Issachar occupies himself with the study of the Torah, while Zebulun sails the seas and, on his return, supports him [Issachar], and thus is the Torah promoted in Israel.'[32] The evidence of the homilies and hortatory dicta is transcended by the stories that tell of the honour that great Sages showed to householders who helped to maintain Sages.[33]

It is clear that even those Sages who exhorted the people to support scholars were not unaware of the danger that threatened the status of the Sages in the estimation of those householders who had means and from whose possessions the scholars benefited. On the one hand R. Eleazar said: 'Whoever does not benefit a scholar with his possessions, never sees a sign of blessing'[34], and 'whoever marries his daughter to a scholar, and does business on behalf of scholars, and benefits scholars with his possessions, is regarded by Scripture as though he cleaved to the Shekhina [Divine Presence]'; and it was only on account of such deeds that he found it possible to assure the ignorant [*ʿammē ha-'ărāṣôt*] of resurrection.[35] On the other hand he could not overlook the fact that the honour of the Sages was lowered in the eyes of their supporters, and he declared: 'What is a scholar like in the eyes of an ignorant person? At the outset he appears to him like a golden ladle... once he has benefited from him he seems to him like an earthen ladle ...'[36] At the same time it must be stressed that the mutual attachment between scholars and ignorant folk, or between *ṣôrĕvā dĕ-rabbānān* and 'the ordinary person', left its mark even when no family relationship was formed. The hosts who gave of their bounty to their guests received bounty in return. In Eretz-Israel they said of scholars who entered the homes of the ignorant: 'That they feed them with words of the Torah... that they teach Israel to distinguish between the clean and the unclean, and instruct them to do the will of their Father in heaven.'[37] Rava also had this in mind, when he said: 'He who loves the Rabbis will have sons that are Rabbis; he who honours the Rabbis will have sons-in-law who are Rabbis; he who is in awe of the Rabbis will himself become *ṣôrĕvā mē-rabbānān*; and if he has not the capacity for this, his words will be heeded as those of a *ṣôrĕvā mē-rabbānān*.'[38]

Rava's dictum, which begins by praising those who honour and love the Rabbis, ends by stating the purpose for which this homily is preached, namely that the words of the Sages should be accepted by their congregation. This dictum holds a warning for the researcher who proceeds to collect Rabbinic sayings that treat of such questions as the maintenance of Sages, their social standing, their relationship to other classes, and the like. The stringing together of these dicta so that they ostensibly form combinedly an account of a complete subject gives no assurance of the reliability of the account, even if one succeeds in fitting it into moulds that are eminently suited to sociological terminology. The criterion adopted is easily capable of causing 'visual distortion' and one-sidedness, not merely because great store is set by sayings and homilies whose forceful wording is intended to persuade and exhort, but because in dealing with them one is inclined to overlook homilies and dicta that are formulated at times with no less extremism by the same Sages in other fields. The sources serve less as testimony to the existing social structure than to the painful struggles between loyalty to ideals and the hard reality, as well as to inner conflicts regarding the determination of priorities in the scale of various values. When we deal with the subject of the maintenance of the Sages in its various aspects, we must not forget the homilies and Halakhot and acts of the Sages, from the first to the last, in matters of charity and benevolence, which affected every poor and needy person in Israel.[39]

The test of the Sage was whether, and in what measure, his deeds and conduct conduced to the sanctification or the desecration of the Divine Name. The principle, attributed already to Simeon b. Sheṭaḥ (above, p. 572), remained valid and was given a superabundance of detailed annotation. A kind of epitome may be found in a Baraita transmitted by Abbaye: ' "And thou shalt love the Lord thy God" (Deuteronomy vi 5): This means that the Name of Heaven may become beloved through you — that a man should study the Scriptures and the Mishna and attend upon scholars, and his dealings with people should be courteous. What will people say of him? Happy is the father who taught him Torah, happy is his teacher who taught him Torah, woe to the people who have not learned Torah! This man who has learned Torah — see how gracious are his ways, how faultless his deeds! Of him Scripture declares "And He said unto me: Thou art My servant, Israel, in whom I will be glorified." If, however, one studies the Scriptures and attends upon scholars, but his business is not done honestly and his conversation with people is not courteous, what do people say of him? Woe to this man who studied Torah — see how corrupt are his deeds and how ugly his words...!'[40]

All questions of honour and status fell away, perforce, wherever there was any danger of desecrating the Divine Name. The rule 'Wherever desecration of the Divine Name is involved no deference is shown to a Rabbi' is reported in the name of Rav and Samuel, and in the name of Rav Ashi, and as an anonymous statement of the Gemara.[41] The strict insistence on the upright conduct of the individual Sage served to prevent any decline of the honour in which the class of the Sages and their institutions, and in the final analysis of the Torah in general, was held: 'If an Associate is caught committing a transgression, he is disgraced, because he mingles pure with impure things. He contemns the very Torah that was so precious to him.'[42]

However, the Sage was not permitted to be satisfied with his personal perfection. Since he was required to lead, instruct, and guide his community, he was guarantor to the whole Congregation of Israel. Although this feeling of being surety was required of every Jew (above, p. 539), yet it had a special significance where the Sage was concerned. The Tanna R. Nehemiah interpreted the verse 'My son, if thou art become surety for thy neighbour, if thou hast struck thy hands for a stranger' (Proverbs vi 1) thus: 'It speaks of *Ḥăvērîm*. So long as a man is an Associate, he need not be concerned with the community and he is not punished on account of it. But once a man has been placed at the head and has donned the *Ṭallît* [cloak of office], he may not say: I have to look after my welfare, I am not concerned with the community; but the whole burden of communal affairs rests on him. If he sees a man doing violence (βία, violence, wrong) to his fellow, or committing a transgression, and does not seek to prevent him, he is punished on account of him, and the Holy Spirit cries out: "My son, if thou art become surety for thy neighbour" — thou art responsible for him. "If thou hast struck thy hands for a stranger [*zār*]" — you have entered the arena [*zîrā*]; he who enters the arena is either conquered or conquers....'[43]

IX. The Sages Among Their People

When they entered the arena as reprovers, guides, and teachers of the people the Sages found themselves most of the time in a dilemma regarding their relations with their community and congregation. On the one hand they wanted to maintain intimacy with the public and enjoy its support; they longed to show it good will and to be accepted by it. But on the other hand they were enjoined to refrain from realizing this aspiration at the cost of principles. The Babylonian Amora Abbaye gave extreme expression to this danger. He said that when a scholar is beloved of his fellow townsmen, it is not a sign of his exceeding virtue, but of the fact that he fails to rebuke them properly.[44] However, it was not reproof alone that caused tension between the Sages and different sections of the community. Indeed a distinct trend is discernible to emphasize equality and to demolish social barriers not only in respect of everything that bears on Halakhic questions, but also in matters of usage and etiquette. In the name of R. Ishmael and R. Akiba it was taught 'All Israel are worthy of that robe'[45], and R. Simeon declared: 'All Israel are princes.'[46] At the same time R. Akiba demanded an attitude of reverence towards scholars, and he gave a most daring expression to his demand in his exposition: ' "Thou shalt fear (את *'et*) the Lord thy God" — this comes to include scholars.'[47] Yet he also admonishes his colleagues, with similar forcefulness, against the vice of haughtiness and pride. From his personal experience before he became a Sage he knew that arrogance caused the *ʿammê ha-'āreṣ* to hate the Sages.[48] Hence he said: 'Whoever exalts himself on account of his knowledge of the Torah, to what is he to be compared? To a carcass lying in the road; everyone that passes by puts his hand to his nose and proceeds to get far away from it.'[49]

The attempt to find a middle way between preserving the attitude of deference towards the Sage, which was regarded as also implying respect for the Torah, and the avoidance of hauteur — concerning which R. Akiba[50] declared 'What caused you to become a base fellow through Torah-learning? The fact that you exalted yourself thereby' — followed a chequered course. The possibility of reconciling, on the one hand, the demand for faithfulness to principles, and even for a measure of stubbornness and self-sacrifice where they were concerned, with the requirement, on the other hand, to complement this, at the same time, with love of one's fellow-man was epitomized, as it were, by sayings of the last of the Babylonian Amoraim. Rav Ashi said: 'A scholar who is not as hard as iron is not a true scholar, for it is said "And like a hammer that breaketh the rock in pieces" (Jeremiah xxiii 29)... Ravina said: Even so, a man must train himself to be gentle, for it is said "Therefore remove vexation from thy heart, and put away evil from thy flesh" (Ecclesiastes xi 10).'[51]

Our conclusions regarding the evaluation of the specific and factual significance of Rabbinic dicta, homilies, and stories concerning the internal relationship between the Sages themselves, and between them and their disciples, hold good also for understanding those sources that give clear expression to the complex of relations between the Sages and the *'am ha-'āreṣ*. As we have seen (above, p. 588) there can be no doubt about the actual fact of the separation and schism between *Ḥăvērîm* and Sages, on the one hand, and the *'ammĕ ha-'āreṣ* and uncultured, on the other. This situation, which continued for centuries, is reflected in sharp verbal exchanges between the two sides. The vehemence of expression does not necessarily testify to a great gulf dividing the classes. It is likely that even at times when a rapprochement took place between the ignorant folk and the Sages and their disciples, the scholars continued to employ the same stereotyped phrases that were commonly applied to the *'ammê ha-'āreṣ* in earlier generations and even added some of their own, when they denounced those that had little knowledge of the Torah, behaved coarsely, and lacked culture and refinement. The Sages of Usha, who sought to re-establish the study of the Torah, are cited as the authors of many of these dicta, which reveal their own orientation and also that of the Tannaim and Amoraim who came after them and expressed similar ideas. The struggle to attract the masses to the study of the Torah and the observance of the precepts was accompanied by denunciation of the contemptuous attitude shown towards the performance of the commandments and the negative manifestations and practices that were current among various strata of the people, and not necessarily among the poor classes. In Galilee there were to be found powerful burghers who lent money on interest, removed the yoke of imposts from their own necks and placed 'the yoke of taxation on the poor and needy and unfortunate', offered sums of charity in public but failed to pay them,[52] hated scholars,[53] and prevented the local children from receiving a Torah education.[54] The extent to which the designation *'am hā-'āreṣ* came to be used loosely and had deviated from its original signification is shown by the following discussion in the Babylonian Talmud. In the Mishna (*M. Berakhot* vii, 1) we learn 'and a Cuthean may be included in the three required for common grace', and an objection is raised to this in the Talmud:[55] 'Why should he not be regarded simply as an *ʿam hā-ārеṣ*? For the master has taught: An *ʿam hā-'āreṣ* is not included in the company for the purpose of saying common grace. Abbaye said: The reference is to a Cuthean who is a *Ḥāvēr*. Rava said: You may even refer the ruling to a Cuthean who is an *ʿam hā-'āreṣ*, but here the term *ʿam hā-'āreṣ* is used according to the definition of the Rabbis. For it is taught (in a Baraita): Who is an *ʿam ha-'āreṣ*? Whoever does not eat non-sacred food in levitical purity — this is the view of R. Me'ir. But the Sages say: Whoever does not tithe his produce properly. Now the Cutheans are meticulous in observing what is enjoined in the Torah. The Rabbis taught: Who is an *ʿam hā-'āreṣ*? Whoever does not recite the *Shĕmaʿ* morning and evening — this is the view of R. Eliezer.[56] R. Joshua says: Whoever does not put on *Tĕfillīn*. Ben ʿAzzai declares: Whoever has no *mĕzûzā* on his door or fringes on his garment. R. Jonathan bar Joseph[57] is of the opinion: Whoever has sons and does not bring them up to study the Torah. Others hold: Even if one studied the Scriptures and the Mishna, but did not attend on scholars, he is deemed an *ʿam hā-'āreṣ*.' In the continuation it is narrated that Rami bar Ḥama did not wish to include Rav Menashia bar Taḥlifa in the quorum for common grace because he had not attended on scholars.

From the possibility of a 'Samaritan *Ḥāvēr*' to Rav Menashia bar Taḥlifa, whom Rami bar Ḥama judged to fall within the category of *ʿam hā-'āreṣ*, is a very far cry, and the various definitions given by the Tannaim of the nature of the *ʿam hā-'āreṣ* show that the term had gradually ceased to be a defined designation and had become a pejorative epithet for those who were neglectful of the observance of the precepts, and it is now manifest that he who observes these commandments does not deserve this epithet, and even if he is not an Associate in the ancient connotation, he can be an 'Associate' in the sense of a 'Sage'. Resh Laqish warned the wives of 'the scholars of the School of Jannai' that 'I am an *ʿam hā-'āreṣ* in respect of levitical purity'.[58] All the laws that were connected with 'acceptance as an Associate', so as to remove one from the category of *ʿam hā-'āreṣ*, have no relevance to the definitions of an *ʿam hā-'āreṣ* given by R. Eliezer and R.

Joshua, Ben ʿAzzai and R. Jonathan bar Joseph, which are cited in the second Baraita. Furthermore, a *Ḥāvēr* and a trustworthy man [נאמן *ne'ĕmān*, epithet for one who is scrupulous in giving tithes and heave-offerings] and even a pietist [חסיד *ḥāsîd*] could be included in the definition of *ʿam hā-'āreṣ*, of whom R. Simeon b. Yoḥai said: 'An *ʿam hā-'āreṣ*, even if he is upright, even if he is a holy and trustworthy man, is cursed unto the God of Israel.'[59] The expression 'trustworthy man' is derived from the laws governing Associates.[60] A complete Talmudic discussion[61] has been preserved in which there is a collection of Tannaitic and Amoraic dicta that speak in similar vein about the *ʿammê hā-'āreṣ* and which also mention harsh expressions of animosity uttered by the ignorant against scholars. 'R. Eleazar said: An *ʿam ha-'āreṣ* may may be stabbed (even) on the Day of Atonement that falls on a Sabbath. Said his disciples to him: Say "to slaughter him [i.e. ritually]". He replied to them: The one requires a benediction, whereas the other [i.e. stabbing] does not require a benediction. R. Eleazar further said: It is forbidden to join company with an *ʿam hā-'āreṣ* on the road. R. Samuel bar Naḥman said in the name of R. Jonathan: An *ʿam hā-'āreṣ* may be torn asunder like a fish. Said R. Samuel bar Isaac: Even along the back.[62] It is taught [in a Baraita], R. Akiba said: "When I was an *ʿām hā-'āreṣ*, I used to say: Would that I had a scholar (in my power) and I would bite him like an ass." Said his disciples to him: "Master, say like 'a dog'."[63] He replied to them: "The one [the ass] bites and breaks a bone, while the other bites without breaking a bone." It is taught: R. Me'ir used to say: If a man gives his daughter in marriage to an *ʿam hā-'āreṣ*, it is as though he bound her and put her in front of a lion. Just as a lion rends and eats (his prey), and feels no shame, even so an *ʿam hā-'āreṣ* beats (his wife) and has sexual intercourse, and has no sense of shame. It is taught: R. Eliezer said: Were it not that we are necessary to them for trade, they would kill us. It is taught: R. Ḥiyya said: If one studies Torah before an *ʿam hā-'āreṣ*, it is as though he raped his betrothed before him... The animosity felt by *ʿammê hā-'āreṣ* towards the scholar exceeds the hatred felt by the Gentiles towards Israel, and their wives are even more hostile. It is taught: One who studied the Torah and then abandoned it (nurses) the greatest (enmity) of them all. The Rabbis taught: Six things have been said with regard to the *ʿammê hā-ʾāreṣ*: We do not commit testimony to them, nor do we accept any from them; we reveal no secret to them; we do not appoint them guardians of orphans; we do not appoint them administrators of the charity fund; and we do not join company with them on the road. And some say: We also do not proclaim their lost property.' In the Talmud the question is raised: 'And the first Tanna?' — that is to say: Why did he not also include the proclamation of lost property? The answer given is: 'Sometimes they have worthy descendants.' This very conclusion shows that even the redactors of the Talmud did not understand R. Ḥiyya's statement about one who studies the Torah before an *ʿam hā-ʾāreṣ* in an absolute sense. R. Ḥiyya's great efforts to spread knowledge of the Torah in the towns where there were no 'primary teachers'[64] also show that he did not mean to oppose the teaching of Torah to *ʿammê hā-ʾāreṣ* generally, but only to one kind of them, namely those who hated the scholars, and apparently the reference is to *ʿammê hā-ʾāreṣ* who were close to the *Mînîm* [Sectarians]! This is indicated by the additional passage introduced by the word תנא *tĕnāʾ* ['It is taught'], which includes in the term *ʿam hā-ʾāreṣ* 'One who studied the Torah and then abandoned it', and possibly there is an allusion to the matter — though it constitutes no actual proof — in the figure 'it is as though he raped his betrothed'[65] and in the phrase 'exceeds the hatred felt by the Gentiles towards Israel'.[66] The Geonim have already pointed out that in this Talmudic discussion the reference is not to one type of *ʿam hā-ʾāreṣ*, for 'the *ʿam hā-ʾāreṣ* has many aspects.'[67] 'When R. Eliezer says that an *ʿam hā-ʾāreṣ* may be stabbed even on the Day of Atonement that falls on a Sabbath, would anyone with any sense suppose that this may be done to any *ʿam hā-ʾāreṣ*? For even the execution of those who are put to death by the Bet Din for idolatry, and cursing God, and the penalty imposed on (the inhabitants of) a condemned city [see Deuteronomy xiii 13–18] does not override the Sabbath....'[68] Although Rav Sherira sought to refer this dictum to 'an *ʿam hā-ʾāreṣ* who pursues his fellow with the intent to slay him on the Day of Atonement that fell on a Sabbath',[69] he did not refrain from remarking that the earlier Baraitot are 'like the laws of right conduct, or like stories in condemnation of *ʿammê hā-ʾāreṣ*, or like rhetorical hyperbole'. Indeed the undertone of mockery is palpable in the dialogue between R. Eliezer and his disciples, and even the Baraita concerning 'the six things (that) have been said with regard to the *ʿam hā-'āreṣ*', which 'are all Halakhot', does not allude to a single type. Only one who has no knowledge of Scripture, or Mishna, or right conduct, that is, 'one who is uncivilized'[70] did R. Joḥanan disqualify as a witness;[71] while Rav Papa said that nowadays we accept the testimony of an ordinary *ʿam hā-'āreṣ*, and he relied for this ruling on the statment of R. Jose in the Baraita: 'Why are all trusted throughout the year in regard to the levitical purity of the wine and oil (that they bring for use in the Temple)? Lest each one go and build a high place for himself and burn a red heifer for himself.'[72] Obviously an *ʿam hā-'āreṣ* to whom a secret is not revealed because he is suspected of being an informer[73] does not belong to the type of person of whom it is necessary to state that they may not be appointed administrators of charity funds. Indeed, this distinction between ordinary ignorant people and sectarians and informers is explained in the interpretation of R. Joshua's teaching: 'The evil eye, the evil inclination, and hatred of his fellow-creatures put a man out of the world. How is this to be understood? It teaches us that a man should not have it in his mind to say: Love the Sages and hate the disciples, love the disciples and hate the *ʿammê hā-'āreṣ*; but (he should say:) Love all of them and (only) hate the sectarians, the apostates, and the informers. So, too, David said: "Do not I hate them, O Lord, that hate Thee? And do not I strive with those that rise up against Thee? I hate them with utmost hatred; I count them mine enemies" (Psalms cxxxix 21–22).'[74] Also the persons to whom the words were addressed largely determined their tone, and at times even their content. R. Me'ir's severe words concerning 'one who gives his daughter in marriage to an *ʿam hā-'āreṣ*' (see above, p. 634) were not necessarily directed to scholars; likewise the *ʿam hā-'āreṣ* spoken of was of a special type, and there is even evidence for this. In a Baraita that does not deal with an *ʿam hā-'āreṣ* that did not study Bible or Mishna, but treats of the laws of Associateship, we learn: 'We may buy male and female slaves from an *ʿam hā-'āreṣ*... and we may take their daughters who are minors in marriage, but not those who are of age; so R. Me'ir. But the Sages say: (Even) a daughter who is of age, provided she undertakes (to observe the laws of Associateship). We do not, however, give them in marriage either daughters who are of age or minors; so R. Me'ir. But the Sages say: A daughter who is of age may be given to an *ʿam hā-'āreṣ* in marriage, provided it is stipulated that she should not prepare levitically pure food in his home.'[75] As in another passage, so also here R. Me'ir taught ancient and stringent laws of Associateship (above, p. 588), but they contain no revilement or aspersions. On the other hand the reason underlying the dictum 'One who gives his daughter in marriage to an *ʿam hā-'āreṣ*' is ethical; it does not refer only to an *ʿam hā-'āreṣ* who is not observant of the laws of levitical cleanness and uncleanness. While R. Me'ir denounced one who married his daughter to an *ʿam hā-'āreṣ*, the same Talmudic section[76] contains several Baraitot that require every Jew to marry a scholar's daughter: 'The Rabbis taught: A man should always sell all that he has and marry a scholar's daughter. If he does not find a scholar's daughter, let him marry the daughter of (one of) the great men of the generation. If he did not find the daughter of (one of) the great men of the generation, let him marry the daughter of (one of) the Synagogue-heads. If he did not find the daughter of (one of) the Synagogue-heads, let him marry the daughter of (one of) the charity treasurers. If he did not find the daughter of a charity treasurer, let him marry the daughter of a primary schoolteacher. But he should not marry the daughter of *ʿammê hā-'āreṣ*, because they are detestable and their wives are reptiles, and of their daughters it is said "Cursed be he that lieth with any manner of beast".'[77]

This Baraita is addressed to 'a man' in general, encouraging him to marry the daughter of a scholar and admonishing him, in forceful language, not to marry the daughter of an *ʿam hā-'āreṣ*. Clearly 'a man in general' in this and similar Baraitot, which exhort one to marry the daughter of a scholar and to give his daughter in marriage to a scholar, and which promise that by virtue of this meritorious action he would have sons that are scholars, are not addressed to scholars only, but it is equally certain that they are not directed to *ʿammē hā-'āreṣ*, 'who are detestable and their wives are reptiles' etc. — that is to say, to clear transgressors, and it need hardly be said that such were to be found at all times and at all places.[78] As we have seen (above, p. 628) R. Eleazar found a remedy for the *ʿam hā-'āreṣ* who is ignorant even of Torah law, namely that he should marry his daughter to a scholar, for he hoped, like the authors of the Baraitot cited above, that out of this union there would issue sons dedicated to the Torah. The same R. Samuel bar Naḥmani, who said in the name of R. Jonathan that an *ʿam hā-ʾāreṣ* may be torn asunder like a fish, also reported in the latter's name 'Whoever teaches the son of an *ʿam hā-ʾāreṣ* Torah, even if the Holy One, blessed be He, pronounces a decree, He annuls it for his sake.'[79] R. Zera's dictum, which he cited in the name of Rav Judah, 'Take heed of the sons of *ʿammê hā-ʾāreṣ* for knowledge of the Torah shall issue from them'[80] was prompted by the realization that many of the Tannaim and Amoraim — if they were not originally like R. Akiba, who was himself an *ʿam hā-ʾāreṣ* — were the sons of *ʿammê hā-ʾāreṣ*, or of fathers who were not scholars. It is indeed reported in the name of R. Joḥanan 'If one is a scholar, and his son is a scholar, and his grandson is a scholar, knowledge of the Torah will never cease from his descendants'[81]; and basing himself on the same verse in Isaiah lix, R. Jeremiah said 'Henceforth Torah learning is hereditary in the family [literally: 'goes round to its lodging place'].' But not only did the Tanna, R. Jose the priest, say 'Fit yourself to study the Torah, for it is not an inheritance of yours' (*M. 'Avot* ii, 12), as an admonition to scholars not to rely on their lineage, but it was taught in Tannaitic Midrashim: 'Lest you say: There are the sons of the elders, the sons of the great... Scripture teaches us that all are alike in regard to the study of the Torah'; ' "A heritage" but not "an inheritance", so that the son of an *ʿam hā-ʾāreṣ* should not say, "Since I am not a scholar, what benefit shall I gain by studying the Torah?" — but "Water shall flow from his buckets [דליו *dolyaw*]" (Numbers xxiv 7), from the lowly ones [דלים *dullim*] among them.'[82] The Amoraim, from Rav Joseph to Rav Ashi and Ravina — that is for a century and more — occupied themselves with seeking an answer to the question 'Why do we find that the sons of scholars are not scholars?' While the answer of Rav Joseph — 'That it should not be said that the Torah is your inheritance' — and that of Rav Shisha son of Rav Idi — 'In order that they should not dominate the community' — explain the phenomenon and even discover a positive aspect to it, Rav Ashi, on the other hand, regarded it as a punishment and said 'Because they call people asses'.[83] He referred not just to the contemptuous attitude adopted towards the simple folk, but also to the abusive epithets that the scholars were accustomed to use in the academies.[84]

At all events the pedigree of a Sage was not a determining factor. When R. Perida was told: 'Rabbi Ezra, the grandson of R. Avṭilos, who is the tenth generation from R. Eleazar b. Azariah, who (in turn) is the tenth generation from Ezra, is standing at the gate, he replied: Why all this? If he is a scholar, it is very fine; if he is a scholar and of noble ancestry, fine; but if he is of noble ancestry but not a scholar, may fire consume him!'[85] The very fact that the academy was open to all and the free competition therein prevented the rise of a genealogical aristocracy in the sphere of the Torah and assured a stream of fresh, creative forces. The contact of the Sages, in all generations, with broad strata of the people of all classes not only led to the discovery of manifestations of estrangement from Judaism, of disrespect for the Torah and precepts, of abuse of the Sages and the like, but also to the revelation of good qualities, of simple faith, of piety and outstanding acts of charity and benevolence on the part of the common people. With the same honesty and candour with which the sources preserved the negative views of the Sages about the *ʿammê hā-'āreṣ* and the evidence of the mutual tension between them, they also reported the positive phenomena among the fringe classes of Jewish society, and even cultivated a tradition of stories in which the *ʿammê hā-'āreṣ* appear as the teachers of the Sages in virtues, and the reproved become reprovers. These narratives[85a] are better evidence of the self-criticism of the Sages in respect of their relationship to other classes than direct statements that speak in praise of the *ʿammê hā-'āreṣ*, of their merits, and the duties towards them. Let us begin with a story about the Tanna R. Simeon b. Eleazar of the generation of Usha: 'The Rabbis taught: Once R. Simeon b. Eleazar[86] was coming from the house of his teacher at Migdal-Geder and he was riding on an ass in leisurely fashion along the lake-shore, feeling greatly elated at having learned much Torah. On the way he chanced to meet a man who was exceedingly ugly. Said he to him: "Wretch, are all the people of your city as ugly as you?" The man replied: "Go and tell the Craftsman who made me 'How ugly is this vessel that Thou hast made!' " Realizing that he had done wrong, he [the Sage] dismounted from the ass and, prostrating himself before the man, said to him: "I crave your pardon, forgive me!" But he answered: "I shall not forgive you until you go to the Craftsman who made me and say to Him: 'How ugly is this vessel that you have made!' " He followed him until he reached his city. When he came to his city, the men of his city came to meet him [the Sage], saying: "Peace be unto you, O master!" Said (the man) to them: "Whom do you address as 'Master' (Rabbi)?" They replied: "Him that is following you." Said (the man) to them: "If he is a Rabbi, may his type not increase in Israel." Said they to him: "Heaven forfend! What did he do to you?" He told them: Such and such a thing he did to me. They (then) said to him: "Even so, forgive him, for he is a great Torah scholar." He replied: "I forgive him, only let him not make a habit of behaving thus." (Thereupon) R. Simeon b. Eleazar entered the schoolhouse and expounded: Let a man ever be pliant as a reed, and not hard as a cedar.' This maxim, the like of which is found among non-Jewish proverbs[87], was possibly cited in praise of the ugly man, and it served as a reason for quoting the story as a sequel of the theme, which dealt with the reed and the cedar. But clearly it is not the focal point of the story, which comes to show what even a great Sage may do when he becomes overweening through the joy of having learned much Torah.

About two generations after R. Simeon b. R. Eleazar it is related: 'Once R. Jannai[88] was walking along the way, when he met a man who was handsomely attired. Said he [R. Jannai] to him: "Would the master mind being my guest?" He replied: "As you please." He then took him home and questioned him on Bible, but he knew nothing; on Mishna, but he knew nothing; on Talmud, but he knew nothing; on Haggada, but he knew nothing. (Finally) he asked him to say grace. He replied, however, "Let Jannai say grace in his house." He then asked him: "Can you repeat what I tell you?" He answered "Yes." He then exclaimed: "Say 'A dog has eaten Jannai's bread.' " (Thereupon the guest) rose and seized him, demanding of him: "What of my inheritance with you, that you are cheating me?" Said (R. Jannai) to him: "What inheritance of yours have I?" He replied: "The children recite 'Moses commanded us the Torah, an inheritance of the congregation of Jacob' (Deuteronomy xxxiii 5). It is not written here 'congregation of Jannai' but 'congregation of Jacob'." When they became reconciled, (R. Jannai) asked him: "Because of what merit was it granted to you to eat at my table?" He replied: "Never have I heard slander about anyone and repeated it to him; nor did I ever see two people quarrelling without making peace between them." He (R. Jannai) then said: "You conduct yourself so well, yet I called you 'dog'!" Thereupon he applied to him the verse "And to him that שם [pointed שָׂם *śām*, with a *Sîn*, and usually rendered 'ordereth aright'] his way will I show the salvation of God" (Psalms l 23): it is written with a *Shîn*, signifying "He that appraises his way is to be highly appraised".' R. Jannai brought home a rich man whose external appearance deceived him, so that he thought him to be, if not a scholar, at least one who moved among the Sages; but when he realized his mistake, he reviled him. He discovered, however, that this man knew how to direct and appraise his ways in matters in which even Sages failed to make the grade. At times the Sages came to realize — no doubt with pleasure — that even simple folk, who were unknown to them, not only possessed noble qualities of character and fine manners, but also had knowledge of Torah and could debate successfully.

It is related of R. Jonathan[89], the younger colleague of R. Jannai: 'R. Jonathan was going up to pray at Jerusalem, when he passed by a certain terebinth (πλάτανος) and a Samaritan saw him. Said the Samaritan to him: "Whither are you going?" He replied: "To pray at Jerusalem." The Samaritan retorted: "Is it not better for you to pray on this blessed mountain than on that dunghill?" The Sage then asked him: "Why (do you think that) it is blessed?" The Samaritan answered: "Because it was not inundated by the waters of the Flood." R. Jonathan could not for a moment think of a rejoinder. (Thereupon) his ass-driver said to him: "Master, permit me to answer him." R. Jonathan answered 'yes'. Said the ass-driver to the Samaritan: "If it is one of the high mountains, then it is written 'And all the high mountains... were covered' (Genesis vii 19); and if it is one of the lower hills, the Bible ignored it." Forthwith R. Jonathan dismounted from the ass and made the ass-driver ride on it three miles, and he applied to him the following three verses: "There shall not be male or female barren among you, or among your cattle" (Deuteronomy vii 14) — even among your cattle-drivers; "Thy temples (*raqqātēkh*) are like a pomegranate split open" (Canticles vi 7) — even the ignorant (*rêqānîn*) among you are as full of counterarguments as a pomegranate (is full of seeds). This is the meaning of the verse "No weapon that is formed against thee shall prosper" (Isaiah liv 17).'[90]

Although there were *'ammê hā-'āreṣ* of the type of this ass-driver, yet it is obvious that there were also others of a different sort.[91] Hence there is undoubtedly an element of exaggeration in the eulogy no less than in the disparaging remarks that we have cited above, but after allowances have been made for hyperbole in each case, there remains a grain of truth in both groups of sources. It is not possible to fix boundaries of development and to differentiate between the beginning of the Usha era and the subsequent age, ascribing to the former all the harsh statements against the *'ammê hā-'āreṣ*, and to the latter the kindly and pleasant dicta and friendly acts. Such a theory is refuted by all the sources that we have cited above, belonging as they do to periods before and after Usha,[92] and other passages to this effect can also be quoted. We shall content ourselves, however, with citing only the words of R. Judah the Patriarch 'Tribulation comes upon the world only on account of the *'ammê hā-'āreṣ*'[93], and the saying of Resh Laqish, the Sage who was careful not to speak ill of Israel (above, p. 563), 'Though a scholar be vengeful and unforgiving like a serpent, yet gird him upon your loins; but even if an *'am hā-'āreṣ* is pious, do not dwell in his vicinity.'[94] A scholar who does not behave like a pious man is preferable to an *'ām hā-'āreṣ*, who is liable to act like a foolish pietist, whom R. Joshua numbered among 'the destroyers of the world'.[95] In the Palestinian Talmud the explanation is given: 'Who is a foolish pietist? One, for example, who saw a child struggling in the river and said: "When I have taken off my phylacteries I shall rescue him." While he takes off his phylacteries, the child breathes his last!' In the Babylonian Talmud a different example is cited: 'If a woman, for example, was drowning in a river, and he said: It is improper for me to gaze upon her and (this precludes my) saving her.'[96] It is manifest, however, that the Amoraim were not always pleased even with the scholarly pietists who preceded them.[97]

The last observation is not intended to minimize the demand to keep away from the *ʿam hā-ʾāreṣ* expressed in Resh Laqish's dictum. Although R. Akiba enjoined his son not to live in a city whose leaders were scholars (above, p. 604), yet Resh Laqish is only repeating, in point of fact, the admonishment of the Tannaim in different words, for example, the dictum of R. Dosa b. Harkinas (*M. ʾAvot* iii, 10), who counted 'sitting in the meeting-houses of the *ʿammê hā-ʾāreṣ*' among the things that put a man out of the world; or the Baraita that counted sitting down to a meal 'in the company of *ʿammê hā-ʾāreṣ*'[98] among the things unfitting for a scholar. The meeting-houses of the *ʿammê hā-ʾāreṣ* and their companies were considered places without holiness or Torah. This, too, is how R. Simeon b. Eleazar's saying 'On account of two sins do the *ʿammê hā-ʾāreṣ* die: because they call the holy ark 'chest' and because they call a בית כנסת *Bêt Kĕneset* [synagogue, meeting-house] בית העם *Bêt hā-ʿĀm* [the people's house]'[99] is to be understood, for it is as though they took away the sanctity and uniqueness of the synagogue. Statements of this kind concerning the *ʿammê hā-ʾāreṣ* and their institutions — the scathing criticism and acrimonious expressions — are to be regarded in the same light as the parallel phenomena that we have encountered in the internal problems of the world of the Sages. They reflect an authentic reality — not infrequently expressed in a particularly extreme and vehement form — from a circumscribed viewpoint. But it is clear that the authors of these dicta did not intend to reconcile themselves to the situation that they defined or denounced, since the Sages never made concessions at the expense of the integrity of the Congregation of Israel in all its sections and factions. Undoubtedly the Sages were far from overlooking faults, but the acceptance of the yoke of the Torah, in the sense of the duty of elucidating and inculcating it to the masses, strengthened their faith in the power of repentance, whose gates were never closed to the individual Jew and *a fortiori* not to Jewish groups and associations. R. Judah b. R. Ileʿai, in whose name there are also recorded disparaging remarks about the *ʿammê hā-ʾāreṣ* — although not to the same extent as those ascribed to his colleague R. Me'ir — gave the following exposition: '"Hear the word of the Lord, ye that tremble at His word" (Isaiah lxvi 5) — this refers to scholars; "your brethren have said" (*ibid.*) — this refers to Bible students; "that hate you" (*ibid.*) — this refers to Mishna students;

"that cast you out" — this refers to the *ʿammê hā-ʾāreṣ*. Should you think that their hope is completely cut off, Scripture teaches — "That we may gaze upon your joy; but it is they who shall be put to shame" — and not "Israel shall be put to shame." '[1] This Tanna was lenient in his demands where the *ʿammê hā-ʾāreṣ* were concerned, and stringent in regard to scholars. He expounded: ' "And declare unto My people their transgression and to the house of Jacob their sins" (Isaiah lviii 1): "Declare unto My people their transgression" — this refers to scholars, whose unwitting mistakes are likewise accounted intentional sins; "and to the house of Jacob their sins" — this refers to the *ʿammê hā-ʾāreṣ*, in whose case even the intentional sins are deemed unwitting errors.' R. Me'ir went even further: he not only did not give up the hope of reclaiming deviationists and sinners, even if they belonged to the category of 'one who studied (Torah) and abandoned (it)', like Elisha b. Abuya,[2] but he regarded Israel's election as absolute, and, in opposition to R. Judah, he declared that, whether they acted as sons or not, the Jewish people were children of the Omnipresent.[3] This sentiment arose from the conviction that it was within the capacity of his colleagues to strive, if not for the complete removal of sin, and hence of sinners, from the world,[4] at least for the ideal of drawing their fellow men nearer to the Torah by their willingness not merely to reprove others, but to prefer in their own case reproof above all eulogy. Thus he stated: 'If you have companions, some of whom rebuke you while others praise you, love him that rebukes you and dislike him that praises you; because he that reproves you brings you to life in the world to come, whereas he that lauds you puts you out of the world.'[5] There is hardly any need to add that in the light of their experience, R. Me'ir and the other Sages, both those who came before him and after him, realized that the formulation of a dictum of this kind was easier than its practical observance. However, the Sages, who knew the weakness of human beings generally as well as their own but engaged all their life in an unceasing struggle against the evil impulse and its temptations, motivated by a desire to attain to love of their fellow men, felt in their very being a compulsion to preserve the existence of the Congregation of Israel and to transform it from a chosen to a choosing people.

The Sages endeavoured to fulfil, towards the Congregation of Israel as a whole, R. Me'ir's teaching concerning the attitude a person should adopt towards his reprovers and his praisers. R. Simeon b. Laqish said: 'This people is like a vine: its branches are the burghers, its clusters are the scholars, its leaves are the *ʿammê hā-'āreṣ*, its twigs are the worthless in Israel.' Anonymously the Babylonian Talmud adds: 'This is the meaning of the message sent from there [Eretz-Israel]: "Let the clusters pray for the leaves, for were it not for the leaves the clusters would not exist." '[6] Needless to say the dictum refers not only to intercession, but also to action leading to the sinners' repentance through the scholars' willingness to 'be sureties for their fellows' (above, p. 539). Like Resh Laqish others, too, thought that only the preservation of unity could bridge the differences between the various sections of the nation in respect of their religious-ethical level and at the same time assure the improvement of those who were backward and those who were weak. An anonymous preacher stressed the thought in the form of an allegorical interpretation of the Torah precepts relative to the 'four species' (Leviticus xxiii 40): ' "The fruit of goodly trees" refers to Israel; just as the *'etrôg* (citron) has flavour and fragrance, so does Israel contain people that possess knowledge of the Torah and good deeds. "Branches of palm-trees" refer to Israel; just as the date has flavour but no fragrance, so are the Israelites; they contain people that have Torah-learning but no good deeds. "And boughs of thick trees" refer to Israel; just as the myrtle has fragrance but no flavour, so do the Israelites contain people that possess good deeds but no Torah-learning. "And willows of the brook" refer to Israel; just as the willow has neither flavour nor fragrance, so are the Israelites — they comprise people that possess neither knowledge of the Torah nor good deeds. What now does the Holy One, blessed be He, do with them? To destroy them is not possible. Hence the Holy One, blessed be He, declares that they should all be bound together as a single bunch, so that they may atone for one another.'[7] These and similar homilies are very significant, particularly in the light of their portrayal of the many problems with which the Sages contended in daily life. These included both the internal attitudes of their alma mater — the evaluation of the scholars' functions and the determination of the correct relationship between the study of the Torah and the responsibilities of leadership and administration, between withdrawal and the acceptance of life's realities, on the one hand, and activity and struggle, on the other — and all that concerned the complex of relations with other classes and the Sages' place as leaders and teachers of the people. In their actions and ways the Sages were guided by the consciousness that they were teachers and educators and that it was their duty to teach and train the entire people of Israel, in accordance with the Midrashic exposition: ' "And Moses and the priests the Levites spoke" (Deuteronomy xxvii 9): What words were spoken there? The verse teaches you that the Israelites came and said to Moses: "You have taken the Torah and given it to the priests", as it is said "And Moses wrote this law, and delivered it unto the priests" (*ibid.* xxxi 9). Said Moses to them: "Is it your wish that they should make a covenant with you that whoever desires to study Torah should not be prevented?" They replied "Yes". So they stood up and swore that no one should be prevented from reading the Torah, as it is written "unto all Israel saying"[8] (*ibid.* xxvii 9). Moses then declared to them "This day thou art become a people" (*ibid.*).' Our account has raised the question of the conflicting aims inherent in the combination of the principle of preserving high ideals with that of carrying out administrative and tutorial duties. The Sages realized that in the existing order of the world there was no possibility of achieving the fulfilment of social and hegemonic ideals in their purity. Nevertheless they undertook to work within the Congregation of Israel as it was with all its defects, knowing full well their own weaknesses and the difficulties involved in their labours.

This 'Congregation of Israel', despite its dispersion and despite the absence of all those hallowed institutions that characterized its existence in the past, did not cease to be, in the estimation of the Sages, identical with the people of Israel — separate, sanctified and elect. There is no ground whatsoever for the conjectures that the term 'Congregation of Israel' [*Kĕneset Yisrā'ēl*] was accepted in the early centuries of Christianity owing to the fact that the Christian community was designated ἐκκλησία[9], or because the 'Congregation of Israel' meant the 'Jewish Church' in the sense of Catholic Judaism, but, in contrast to Catholic Christianity, it was inclusive and not exclusive, and also incorporated within itself seceders and deviationists.[10] These explanations not only do not fit the content of the statements made about the 'Congregation of Israel', but they also disregard the nature of the sources in which the expression occurs. It does not appear at all in Tannaitic literature,[11] even when the relationship of the Holy One, blessed be He, to His people is compared to that between a bride and bridegroom,[12] nor does it occur in the MSS. of the ancient Haggadic Midrashim.[13] It is chiefly found in homilies on verses of the Prophets that liken Israel to a woman, a mother, or a daughter,[14] or on passages of Canticles that were interpreted allegorically as referring to Israel,[15] but even in homilies of this type 'Congregation of Israel' and 'Israel' are used indiscriminately.[16] The phrase 'Congregation of Israel' did not enter into the formulations of the prayers and benedictions either. These speak only of 'His people Israel', 'Thy people Israel', or of 'Israel'.[17]

In the Amora R. Berechia's exposition of verses in Canticles the Congregation of Israel declares 'Before the Holy One, blessed be He... My Beloved is unto me...';[18] but the same Amora, who delivered ardent homilies in favour of proselytization (see above, p. 553) interpreted 'Behold (הן *hēn*), ye are nothing (מאין *mē-'ayin*), and your work is a thing of naught' (Isaiah xli 24) as follows: '*Hen* is a Greek word (ἕν — one)... The Holy One, blessed be He, said: You are one nation unto Me from among the nations of the world; *mē-'ayin*, from among those of whom it is written "All the nations are as nothing (אין *'ayin*) before him".'[19]

In Christianity the annulment of nationalism became an actual problem, since it espoused the idea that the Messianic era had already begun and the dominion of the princes of the nations had come to an end. The cosmopolitan conception of Alexander the Great's kingdom — the abolition of antagonism between peoples — and likewise the Hellenistic doctrine that regarded the national gods as satraps of the Most High God, who formed a kind of administrative hierarchy,[20] could be integrated into the new religion. There were, however, Christian teachers who did not ignore the difficulties and perceived that although the σφραγίς [seal] gives the same colour to all the sealed objects, yet after a time their appearance changes again and acquires different tints. But Eusebius found the solution in the Roman Empire[21], which overcame, in his opinion, the problem of peoples and nationality. Since the angel had brought the tidings of peace at Jesus' birth, peace came in the days of Augustus. The national states disappeared from the world, and with the triumph of the new religion the national religions followed suit. He saw the earthly kingdom — the Empire — as corresponding to the Heavenly Kingdom.[22] In the estimation of the Sages the antithesis 'Israel — nations of the world [Gentiles]' remained unchanged, whether the reference was to pagan or Christian nations. Paul had expounded ' "But in Isaac shall thy seed be called" (Genesis xxi 12). That is, They which are the children of the flesh, these are not the children of God; but the children of the promise are counted for the seed' (Romans ix 7–18), as though it was his intention to oppose the teaching of the Mishna (*Nedarim* iii, 11) '[If he said, "*Qônām*!] if I have any benefit from the seed of Abraham!" he is forbidden to have benefit from Israelites, but not from other nations.' In order to counter Paul's homily and the claims of those who followed in his footsteps, the Amoraim added to the Mishnaic statement their exposition of the aforementioned verse: 'And Ishmael is not included among the seed of Abraham; "But in Isaac shall thy seed be called", and Esau is not included among the seed of Isaac.'[23] In order to avoid any possibility of mistaking who is meant — whether Esau or Jacob — the Sages cited the exposition of R. Gershom in the name of R. Aḥa: ' "A star hath stepped forth from Jacob" (Numbers xxiv 17): From whom did a star step forth and is destined to rise in the future? From Jacob';[24] and they added the homily of R. Aḥa in the name of R. Huna: 'The wicked Esau will wrap himself in a Ṭallit and take his seat among the righteous in the Garden of Eden in the time to come, but the Holy One, blessed be He, will drag him out from there.' Esau, who wraps himself in a Ṭallit, is the kingdom that has gone over to 'sectarianism'.

The Sages regarded the kingdom that conquered their country, destroyed their Temple, and exiled their people as a wicked kingdom, and the alliance made between the religion that issued from its bosom and this empire increased their opposition to both. The words of Zephaniah (iii 9) 'that they may all call upon the name of the Lord, to serve Him with one consent' remained linked to the act of future redemption and 'to the abolition of Israel's subjection to the world.'[25]

The Sages' views of the nature and significance of this redemption we shall discuss in the coming chapter.

CHAPTER XVII

ON REDEMPTION

The teaching of the Sages concerning the Redemption are closely linked to verses in the Pentateuch, to the promises of the Prophets, and to the visions recorded in the Book of Daniel. However, their interpretations and homilies were not aimed at elucidating the original meaning of the Scriptural passages; possibly in this sphere, more than in regard to any other theme, there is evident the independent approach of the Sages, which finds expression in a variety of views and conceptions. At times this diversity exceeds the standards of normal differences of opinion and reaches down to fundaments. It is not confined to divergences within the framework of the generally accepted system of concepts, but reaches antitheses that imply the complete negation of one doctrine by the other. Needless to say there are also not wanting intermediate and harmonizing attitudes.

The polarity and variegation are the result of numerous factors: the great divergences marking the use of the verb גאל *gā'al* ['to redeem'] and the noun גאולה *gĕ'ûlā* ['redemption'] in all their different forms, even in the Bible itself;[1] the integration of the concept into a terminology that is only in part derived from the Scriptures, and in part from a later source. The terms referred to are: 'end of days', 'End', 'days of the Messiah', 'resurrection of the dead', 'the world to come', 'the future to come', 'the new world'. Ostensibly all these concepts appear to be close to the idea of redemption, but they are not necessarily identical with it. The growth and consolidation of some of them are connected with entirely different questions and phenomena. The notions of 'the world to come' and 'the resurrection of the dead' are bound up with the problem of reward and punishment, and the doctrine of the soul and retribution. The portrayals of the 'End' and 'the days of the Messiah' are drawn from the vision of 'the end of days' conceived by the prophets of Israel.[2] This vision already has two aspects: The one regards the future as the time when the existing world would be perfected, when it would be freed from its faults, from wickedness and injustice, from wars and catastrophe, and the world would be full of knowledge, and the spirit of the Lord would be poured upon all flesh (Isaiah iv 2–6; xi 6–9; Joel iii 1–4). The other aspect conceives 'the day of the Lord' as a day of ruin and destruction of the present world. That day will be 'a day of darkness and gloom' (Zephaniah i 15). The earth will again be without form and void, and the Carmel a wilderness (Jeremiah iv 23).

The transition to redemption is conditioned by revolutionary upheaval, by catastrophe.[3] In prophetic teaching the idea of the world's 'end of days', in both its aspects, is linked to the new revelation of God as the universal God and to the realization of the kingdom of the Almighty, to the redemption of the people of Israel and to its liberation from the servitude to the (Gentile) kingdoms. The integrity of the world is dependent on the integrity of Israel.

To the array of terms connected with the idea of redemption and the various ways of understanding them, to which we have alluded, is also linked the evaluation of the redeemer's image, and here, too, there are many possibilities. One is that God Himself will redeem the people, and the redeemed people will be His servant, in the sense of 'I, even I, am the Lord; and beside Me there is no saviour... therefore ye are My witnesses, saith the Lord, and I am God' (Isaiah xliii 11–12); or he might be a human king who would appear — like the judges and kings of old — as a saviour who conquers foes, in fulfilment of Balaam's prophecy 'There shall step forth a star out of Jacob, and a sceptre shall rise out of Israel, and shall smite through the corners of Moab, and break down all the sons of Seth' (Numbers xxiv 17). Although he will be a shoot out of the stock of Jesse, yet he will not strike with the sword, but 'He shall smite the land with the rod of his mouth, and with the breath of his lips shall he slay the wicked. And righteousness shall be the girdle of his loins, and faithfulness the girdle of his reins... unto him shall the nations seek; and his resting-place shall be glorious' (Isaiah xi 1–10). In addition there is the description of the servant of the Lord who 'shall prosper, he shall be exalted and lifted up, and shall be very high', but before this 'He had no form nor comeliness... But he was wounded because of our transgressions, he was crushed because of our iniquities... and the Lord hath made to light on him the iniquity of us all' (Isaiah lii 13; liii 2–6). Each one of the prophetic concepts could be restricted or expounded.

In the days of the Second Temple, in the period preceding the Hasmoneans, there were circles that assumed, primarily, one of the functions of the prophets, namely to foretell coming events. The vision of the future became central in apocalyptic literature. One of these works, the vision of Daniel, found a place in the Bible — not, it is true, among the Prophets but in the Hagiographa — and hence became an authoritative source to which interpretations and homilies were attached.[4] However, it is clear that the Sages were familiar with apocalyptic writings, both of those that have come down to us and of similar compositions that have been lost. In this type of literature, too, called apocryphal or pseudepigraphical, no uniform picture emerges of the theme of redemption, but the features that these books have in common far exceed the differences, a fact that finds expression not only in their indubitable eschatological trend, but also in their style and formulation. Some of the Sages not only knew compositions of this kind, but were actually close, in their spiritual leanings and turbulent imagination, to the circles from which they emanated, and were very susceptible to their ideas and visions. When we seek to explain the doctrines of the Sages concerning redemption and to distinguish between the different elements of which they were composed, we are compelled to have recourse to the apocryphal-apocalyptic literature, to the writings of the early Christians, and now also to the Qumran Scrolls. They are all important both for determining the dates of very many ideas in the Rabbinic doctrine of redemption, and for differentiating between concepts that are a heritage from ancient generations and views that represent reactions to certain events and actions, or are due to opposition to notions that appeared alien and even dangerous to them.[5] They are also of value for ascertaining clearly the meaning of eschatological terms that are often used in different senses[6], like 'world to come', which 'is neither the Messianic era nor that of the resurrection of the dead, but refers to the celestial world in which the souls of the righteous abide.'[7] The existence, on the one hand, of separate terms, and their fusion, on the other hand, into a single term through semantic blurring, show that the different trends did not come into being interrelated and linked together.[8]

While the idea of reward and punishment after death already appears about a century before the destruction of the Temple[9], we do not find any explicit statements in Rabbinic sources about redemption and the days of the Messiah before the generation of the disciples of Rabban Joḥanan b. Zakkai. However, the absence of express dicta about redemption dating from the days of the Second Temple is no proof that there was no concern with the subject in the long, tempestuous period from the time of the dominion of the High Priests, under the auspices of the Persian kingdom, to the destruction of the Temple. It may well be that belief in redemption actually found expression and a permanent formulation, which remained unchanged, while the Temple was still standing. That this was indeed the position can be definitely proved in the case of 'resurrection'.[10] There can be no doubt that in various passages of the Bible — in almost all its parts — there are to be found figures of speech and similitudes that recognize the possibility of the resurrection of the dead and the power of God — and even of the prophets — to revive the dead. But we are referring to the belief in the *general* resurrection of the dead at the end of days. The subject is mentioned in the Mishna: 'And these are they that have no share in the world to come: he who says that there is no resurrection of the dead, and (he who says that) the Torah is not from Heaven, and an Epicurean.'[11]

The very fact that R. Akiba adds to this Mishna the words 'Also he who reads apocryphal books and he who utters an incantation over a wound' shows that the first part of the Mishna preceded his time, but the belief in the resurrection of the dead is regarded as traditional already in *II Maccabees*. The author of the book makes the martyrs, at the time of Antiochus' religious persecution, say: ' 'Tis meet for those who perish at men's hands to cherish hope divine that they shall be raised up by God again; but thou — thou shalt have no resurrection to life' (vii 14). The Mishna commentators already found it difficult to explain the threat that one who denies the resurrection will have no share in the world to come. But it is clear that the entire Mishna — including R. Akiba's supplement — is directed against sectarians who held certain views.[12]

Here there is a difference between the world to come and resurrection. The latter refers to the return of the soul to the body, which becomes resuscitated, and the belief is based on the notion of the unity of body and soul, and is in no way connected with the Hellenistic concepts regarding the immortality of the soul. Underlying the latter ideas is actually the absolute antithesis between the soul and the body, which is only a prison from which the soul longs to be freed. This concept is the basis of the Platonic myth of the transmigration of souls. Josephus attributed the belief in the resurrection of the dead to the Pharisaic sect, while the belief in the survival of the soul, which, escaping to freedom after a long servitude, is uplifted 'with joy on high', he ascribed to the Essenes and related to the Greek view.[13] The Essenes held that the world to come, as the sequel to this world, is the sphere of the redeemed souls. The Mishna, however, denies those who do not believe in resurrection even a share in the world to come. The verses in Daniel — 'And many of them that sleep in the dust of the earth shall awake, some to everlasting life, and some to reproaches and everlasting abhorrence' (xii 2), 'But go thou thy way till the end be; and thou shalt rest, and shalt stand up to thy lot, at the end of the days' (*ibid.* v. 13) — place the resurrection before reward and punishment in the world to come in the form of the three groups referred to in the dicta of the School of Shammai and the School of Hillel.[14] The very resurrection to everlasting life is the reward, and the author of *II Maccabees* has in mind the pious martyrs who offered up their lives for the sanctification of His name, and was not content with 'the good name', which constituted human survival according to Ben-Sira. The mention of 'the resurrection of the dead' in the Mishna in *Tractate Sanhedrin* does not attest the commencement of this belief, but the struggle for its acceptance against its opponents.

Let us now see whether we can determine the nature of the beliefs in the redemption of the nation and country in the period preceding the Destruction. In the order of service for fast days given in the

Mishna twenty-four benedictions are mentioned, 'the daily eighteen, to which six are added'. The additional blessings begin with the benediction for redemption, and in the Tosefta and in the Baraitot we find the version used in the Temple, namely 'Blessed be the Lord, the God of Israel, from everlasting to everlasting; blessed be the Redeemer of Israel.'[15] Clearly the benediction and prayers that were added on public fasts were introduced, like the fasts themselves, for current troubles, like drought. But what of the actual benediction for redemption in the Eighteen Benedictions? Is it a Messianic prayer for the political redemption of the Jewish people, for its liberation from subjection? The formulation of the prayer, in its Palestinian form, 'Behold our affliction and champion our cause and redeem us speedily for Thy name's sake; blessed art Thou, O Lord, the Redeemer of Israel'[16], and likewise other recensions, remain undecisive. The Amoraim tried hard to show that, as R. Aḥa had stated in the name of R. Joshua b. Levi, 'Also he that composed this Prayer [Eighteen Benedictions] did so according to a fixed order', and to the question 'and what was their reason for juxtaposing... the benediction for forgiveness to that for redemption' R. Jeremiah replied by referring to the passage in Psalms ciii 3–4 'Who forgiveth all thine iniquity; who healeth all thy diseases; who redeemeth thy life from the pit.'[17]

This explanation is based on the conception that the prayer for redemption speaks not of national redemption, but of the redemption of individuals from their affliction, trouble, and distress, just as the term 'redeem' is used in many verses[18] for the deliverance of an individual. Actually this conception is already expressed in *Midrash Tannaim.* With reference to Moses' blessing the Tannaitic homilist declares: 'Scripture teaches us that when Moses began (to bless Israel), he did not commence with Israel's needs, but with the praise of the Omnipresent... and likewise the Eighteen Benedictions, which the early Sages had ordained that Israel should recite as prayer, do not begin with Israel's wants, but with the praise of the Omnipresent — in the words of the Prayer: 'the great, mighty, and revered God... holy art Thou and revered is Thy name', and then 'loosest the bound', followed by 'healest the sick', and thereafter 'We give thanks unto Thee'.[19]

Undoubtedly by 'loosest the bound' the expositor had in mind the Benediction of Redemption, and mentioned its theme but not its closing formula, just as he did in 'We give thanks unto Thee'. Alongside the reason we have cited for the position of the Benediction of Redemption in the Eighteen Benedictions another reason is given by the Amora R. Aḥa: 'Why was "who redeemest Israel" made the seventh benediction? To teach you that Israel will be redeemed only in the seventh year (of the Messiah's advent).'[20] This explanation is given in the Babylonian Talmud in the name of Rava.[21]

In the Talmud a difficulty is pointed out by reference to a distinctly eschatological Baraita[22], which describes the events of the septennium preceding the advent of the son of David, and in which it is stated 'in the *sixth* year (Heavenly) sounds; in the seventh, wars; and at the termination of the septennium the son of David will come', and the Gemara answers 'War is also the beginning of redemption.' It is obvious that these Amoraim regarded the benediction of redemption as referring to the redemption of the Jewish people by their Messiah. Rashi who realized the difference between Rava's dictum and what preceded — where the statements are cited in the form of a Baraita — found it necessary to note 'And although this redemption does not refer to redemption from exile, but is a request that (God) should redeem us from the troubles that constantly come upon us, for as regards the prayers for the gathering of the exiles and the rebuilding of Jerusalem and the branch of David, each one constitutes a separate benediction apart from this prayer for redemption, yet since it bears the name redemption, it has been inserted in the seventh benediction.'[23]

Rashi's remarks certainly hold good for the period of the Second Temple. So long as the Temple stood and self-rule in one form or another obtained in Judea, the national-Messianic hopes were not expressed in general terms of redemption, but in particular forms with concrete meanings. Indeed a Mishna dating from Temple times sheds light on them. In the order of the service of the Day of Atonement we are told that the High Priest read from the Torah, and thereafter it is stated: 'And he pronounced thereon eight benedictions: for the Torah, for the Temple-Service, for the Thanksgiving, for the Forgiveness of Sin, for the Temple, for Israel, for the Priests, and for the rest a (general) prayer.'[24] In the Palestinian Talmud the portion of the Mishna pertaining to our subject is explained thus: 'For the Temple, "who choosest the Temple" — but Rav 'Idi said: "who dwellest in Zion";[25] for Israel, "who choosest Israel"; for the Priests "who choosest the priests". 'Clearly the reference here is to the closing formulas of the prayers, of which the general theme only was known. Maimonides writes as follows:[26] 'And he said a separate benediction for the Temple, whose theme was that the Temple should (continue to) stand and the Divine Presence (dwell) therein, concluding it "Blessed art Thou, O Lord, who dwellest in Zion". And he pronounced a separate benediction upon Israel, which was a petition that the Lord should deliver Israel and that a sovereign should not depart from them, and concluded it "Blessed art Thou, O Lord, who choosest Israel". And he uttered a separate benediction for the priests, requesting the Omnipresent to accept their acts and service with favour and bless them, and concluded it "Blessed art Thou, O Lord, who sanctifiest the priests".' Other commentators cited different versions, for example: 'May it be Thy will, O Lord our God and God of our fathers, that Thou shouldst let Thy Temple stand before Thee for ever, and that Thou shouldst be pleased with it and cause Thy Divine Presence to dwell therein constantly. Blessed art Thou, O Lord, who choosest the Temple.'[27] Undoubtedly even at the outset the formulations of the High Priest's prayers were not uniform, and it was common practice to make innovations in them and to variegate them according to circumstances; similarly the Tosefta explains the phrase 'and for the rest a (general) prayer' not by citing a text, but by defining the content thus: 'And for the rest a prayer, petition, and supplication that Thy people Israel need to be delivered before Thee, concluding "who hearest prayer".' We possess an ancient prayer of this kind for the salvation of Israel in the *Book of Sirach*.[28] The worshipper appeals to God to show the Gentiles anew his mighty deeds, entreating 'Subdue the foe and expel the enemy'. In clear allusion to Habakkuk ii 3 he adds 'Hasten the end and ordain the appointed time.' Without doubt the reference is to actual events that were connected with the Ptolemaic and Seleucid kingdoms. The phrases in which he expressed the hopes and expectations inherent in salvation are: 'Gather all the tribes of Jacob, that they may receive their inheritance as in the days of old' — an expression that corresponds to 'who gatherest the banished ones of Thy people Israel'; 'Compassionate the people that is called by Thy name' corresponds to 'who choosest Israel'; 'Compassionate Thy holy city' parallels 'who choosest the Temple'. The nexus with the Eighteen Benedictions and the prayers of the High Priest is clear. The verse 'Fill Zion with Thy majesty, and Thy Temple with Thy glory' may indicate the content of the High Priest's benediction, whose closing formula 'Who dwellest in Zion' is cited by Rav 'Idi, and the theme of the prayer for Jerusalem that was recited in place of our text.

We gain further clarification of the Messianic hopes and expectations in the pre-Hasmonean period in chapter li of *Sirach*[29], which is patterned after the Great Hallel of Psalms cxxxvi, and from the viewpoint of its content and language has much in common with the prayer of the *'Ămîdā* [Eighteen Benedictions]. We shall quote the lines that appertain to our subject: 'Give thanks unto the Keeper of Israel... Give thanks unto the Redeemer of Israel... Give thanks unto Him that gathereth the banished ones of Israel... Give thanks unto Him that buildeth His city and His Sanctuary... Give thanks unto Him that maketh a horn to sprout for the house of David... Give thanks unto Him that chooseth the sons of Zadok to be priests... Give thanks unto Him that hath chosen Zion.' This psalm has been omitted in the Greek translation, and apparently it has not been wholly preserved in its original recension. But its general authenticity cannot be doubted.

In the light of what we have shown above, both by reference to chapter xxxv of the *Book of Sirach* and with regard to the prayer of the High Priest and the prayer of the *'Ămîdā*, the psalm is a synthesis of thanksgiving for hopes and expectations that had been realized and supplication for assurances and promises that were still being hoped for. 'The Redeemer of Israel', like 'the Keeper of Israel', is the Lord, who rises up to help His people and redeems them from troubles and misfortunes; the Sanctuary is built, the elect sons of Zadok the (High) Priest minister in it, but the gathering of the banished ones of Israel has not been completed, and 'the sprouting of a horn unto the house of David' is still hidden in the womb of time; all the hopes bear a realistic and sober character, and contain no catastrophic-eschatological elements. Of all the eschatological images found in the utterances of the Prophets Ben-Sira mentions only the words of Malachi concerning the mission of Elijah 'before the coming of the great and terrible day'; but while the words of the last prophet 'And he shall turn the heart of the fathers to the children, and the heart of the children to their fathers' (Malachi iii 23–24) may be interpreted as the hope of the realization of a social ideal that would put an end to family strife and to tension between the generations,[30] Ben-Sira retains the first half of the verse, 'To turn the heart of the fathers to the children', but continues 'and to restore the tribes of Israel',[31] that is to say, Elijah will play a role in the restoration of the diaspora — in his own words, cited above, 'that they may receive their inheritance as in the days of old'. It would seem that also the ancient version of the fourth blessing of the grace after meals contained at first a prayer for the deliverance of Israel and the restoration of the kingdom of the House of David and the ingathering of the dispersed sons of Israel. In the name of R. Eliezer it was taught 'Whoever has not mentioned... the kingdom of the House of David in the benediction "who buildest Jerusalem" has not fulfilled his obligation', but R. Jose b. R. Judah said that the conclusion of the benediction should be 'Who savest Israel'.[32] In the Genizah fragments of the Palestinian version the blessing includes the verse 'The Lord doth build up Jerusalem, He gathereth together the dispersed of Israel', and there is ancient, extraneous testimony for this recension.[33]

The conception of redemption in *Sirach* and also in sources close to it in time is realistic, and is primarily concerned with the supplementation of the deficiencies of Israel's sovereignty, well-being, and prosperity. The belief in the resurrection of the dead is not found there, and the notion of reward and punishment in the world to come is also wanting. Indirectly this confirms our thesis that the belief in resurrection dates from the beginning of the Hasmonean era.

This period intensified the sense of revival and redemption, and this is attested by the coins of the epoch, which carried the inscription 'To the redemption of Zion'.[34] The reference, however, is not to the redemption of 'the time of the end', but to redemption from national trouble, for which it was ordained that Hallel be recited; in the words of the Sages: 'The prophets among them instituted that the Israelites should say it [the Hallel] at every turning point and every trouble — Heaven forfend! — and when they are redeemed they should recite it (as a thanksgiving) for their redemption' (*T.B. Pesaḥim* 117a).

Nevertheless, for the present there stood at the head of the people a family of priests that was not of the House of Zadok, and a shoot of the House of David had not appeared. The pietist rebels and the Hasmoneans themselves were not influenced by the idea of 'the end of days'. The author of *I Maccabees* put into the mouth of Mattathias before his death the sentence 'David, for being merciful, inherited the throne of a kingdom for ever and ever' (*I Maccabees* ii 56). After Judah the Maccabean had entered Jerusalem and the desecrated altar had been pulled down, its stones were hidden in a special place 'until a prophet should come and decide concerning them' (*ibid.* iv 46; see *M. Middot* i, 46). The decisive step in the appointment of Simon is described thus: 'And the Jews and the priests were well pleased that Simon should be their leader and high-priest for ever, until a faithful prophet should arise' (*I Maccabees* xiv 41). The belief in the appearance of Elijah continued, nor did the belief in the kingdom of the House of David cease, but it is not characterized by a sense of urgency and actuality. This feeling found expression in a Baraita: 'When the First Temple was destroyed the (Levitical) cities with pasture land [cf. Numbers xxxv 2] were abolished, the Urim and Thummim ceased, and there was no longer a king from the House of David, and should anyone insinuate a doubt, quoting "And the governor said unto them that they should not eat of the most holy things till there stood up a priest with Urim and Thummim" (Ezra ii 63), (say to him: The verse speaks of the remote future), as one who says to his fellow "Until the resurrection of the dead and the advent of the Messiah son of David." '[35] The true prophet Elijah will come to announce the Messiah's advent and will resolve matters in doubt, but the expansion of the borders of the land and the settlement of the Jews in their inheritance were carried out by the Hasmoneans. Furthermore, after they had proclaimed themselves kings, the Sages recognized them as kings of Israel. The Mishna ruling 'The king neither judges nor is judged' was interpreted as applying to Israelite kings, but not to kings of the House of David, and tradition regards this Halakha, which implies that the monarch is deprived of the right to give judgement and is not subject to the authority of the Sanhedrin, as a compromise reached after the clash between Simeon b. Sheṭah and King Jannai.[36]

In principle the Sages recognized the kingship of the House of the Hasmoneans. The enactments of the Hasmoneans[37] were accepted, and we find Simeon b. Sheṭaḥ also on good terms with King Jannai.[38] The clashes and expressions of opposition do not go beyond what we know of the attitude of the prophets to the kings of the House of David and even to David himself. It was the open rebuke of strong-willed and dominating men. In the collision between the Pharisees and Jannai, Judah b. Gedidiah did not argue against Jannai's right to be king. On the contrary, he said 'Be content with the crown of sovereignty; leave the crown of priesthood to the seed of Aaron',[39] and even here the reason was not one of opposition in principle to the unification of two domains, but the fact 'that it was said: His mother was taken captive at Modiʿim.' Shemaʿyah and Avṭalion went to greet the High Priest and paid him due honour, and it was only when the latter insulted them publicly by alluding to their low origin or to their being proselytes that they reacted sharply. Despite all the criticism that they levelled against the conduct and leadership of the last of the Hasmoneans and of the kings of the House of Herod,[40] the Sages never went so far as to negate the existing institutions of the monarchy, the priesthood, and the Temple. Nor did they withhold appreciative recognition from Herod for his work of rebuilding the Temple, or words of praise and comfort from Agrippa.[41] There were some Sages who held office in administrative and governmental institutions. They infused their spirit and ideals into the affairs of government and administration[42], but they considered their primary function to be the teaching of Torah, the clarification of Halakha, the interpretation of the Holy Scriptures, and the devoted instruction of the people in the principles of faith in Divine Providence, in reward and punishment, and in the resurrection of the dead. But very little is said on 'esoteric subjects'[43] or about attempts to penetrate the arcana of the future. Apart from the dispute between the School of Shammai and the School of Hillel in regard to the three companies[44] we find only one tradition, and again it relates to Elijah:

'R. Joshua said: I have received a tradition from Rabban Joḥanan

b. Zakkai, who heard it from his teacher, and his teacher from his teacher, as a Halakha given to Moses at Sinai, that Elijah will not come to declare clean or unclean, to put away or to bring nigh, but to put away those that were brought nigh by violence and to bring nigh those that were put away by violence. The family of Bet Ṣerefa was in Transjordan and Ben Zion put it away by force. And yet another (family) was there, and Ben Zion brought it nigh by force. The like of these Elijah will come to declare clean or unclean, to put away or to bring nigh.'[45]

For the elucidation of the matters *per se* — such as family purity and trustworthiness — Elijah was not required. These things fall within the jurisdiction of the Sages, but the authorized institutions were too weak to right wrongs that were perpetrated by force, and therefore they left them to Elijah.

Another function was thus assigned to Elijah. But the fundamental aspects that characterized the conception of redemption in the preceding era remained unchanged, and apparently were also shared by Jewry in the Diaspora, at any rate to the extent that they found expression in Philo's writings.[46] There were other circles, however, whose interest was centred essentially on these themes and all that they involved. The authors of works like the *Book of Enoch*, the *Testaments of the Twelve Patriarchs*, the *Sibylline Oracles*, the *Apocalypse of Baruch*, *II Esdras* [Apocalypse of Ezra], *et al.* took over a single aspect of the ancient prophecy — the vision of the future. They made use of motifs derived from prophetic utterances and visions, but since their works were pseudepigraphical,[47] ascribed to great men of the past, they were completely unrestrained in their depiction of the scenes in the upper worlds. Despite feelings of awe and trepidation they continue to walk about in them and to stand in close contact with Guardian Princes and angels, drawing nigh to the Chariot and to Him who sits upon the Throne of Glory, and they are easily able to acquire information and receive revelations concerning the changes and upheavals that are about to take place in the history of the Gentile nations and kingdoms, and regarding the role that the people of Israel and their Messiah are destined to play in this drama (see Daniel vii 13–19). They are able to describe the Day of the Lord as a day of world judgement in all its detailed terrors; the fulfilment of the Messianic promises, determining their dates and portents; and likewise the figure of the Messiah (Book III of the *Sibylline Oracles* and *Enoch*); the dominion of death until the end of the corrupt world; the resurrection of the dead, their judgement, and the rise of a new world in which human beings will resemble angels (*Apocalypse of Baruch*). It is not to be denied that the belief of apocalyptic circles was nourished by their disillusionment with the existing reality, both with the Maccabean War, and with the Temple, in which priests who were not of the sons of Zadok ministered, and with the dominion of wickedness holding sway in Israel and in the world. They saw no possibility of improving the present world, and hence the urgent need for salvation and redemption. Since the exact date of some of these works is not known, it is difficult to determine certain events, depicted as though forming the background of the vision. The attempts made in this direction have led at times to various extraordinary conjectures, but the principle underlying them remains valid. In the work known as the *Testaments of the Twelve Patriarchs* two Messiahs are referred to — a Messiah who is a priest and one who is an Israelite. In the 'Testament of Reuben' it is stated 'For to Levi God gave the sovereignty... because he shall know the law of the Lord, and shall give ordinances for judgement and shall sacrifice for all Israel until the consummation of the times, as the *anointed* [Messiah] High Priest....' In the continuation, again, concerning Judah we find: 'because him hath the Lord chosen to be king over all the nation. And bow down before his seed... and will be among you an eternal king' (vi 7–12). Similar statements, with different nuances and additional motifs, are to be found also in other testaments. Scholars were amazed by the idea of the two Messiahs, and various theories were advanced in order to resolve the difficulty, but from the Qumran scrolls it is clear that this belief in two Messiahs was accepted by the *Yaḥad* [Qumran] sect.[48]

Because of the opposition of these sectarians to the transfer of the High Priesthood to the Hasmoneans, who pursued the path of warriors and conquerors and adopted a Hellenistic style of life, they departed to the wilderness under the leadership of a Priestly Teacher of Righteousness.

Influenced by the prophecies of Zechariah, who refers to 'the two anointed ones' (iv 1–2, 14), they developed this eschatological conception of the Messiah descended from Aaron and out of faithfulness to the promises given to the House of David in the Scriptures — including Zechariah (xi 4) — they juxtaposed to him the Israelite Messiah. The Messianic idea in *The Rule of the Community* [*Yaḥad*] bears a distinctly restitutive character, and in *The Rule of the Congregation* [*Hā-ʿEdā*] the Messiah does not even appear as the one who brings the redemption.[49]

It appears that consequent upon the internecine strife within the House of the Hasmoneans, the wars between the brothers Aristobulus and Hyrcanus, and the capture of Jerusalem by Pompey, which came in their wake in 63 B.C.E., the Messianic consciousness acquired greater strength and actuality. We possess the work called *The Psalms of Solomon*[50], which has been preserved in Greek translation only, but was originally written in Hebrew at Jerusalem; it treats of the events in the years 70–45 B.C.E. The author is vehemently opposed to the monarchy of the House of the Hasmoneans and to the ruling circles in Jerusalem; he attributes to them every kind of criminal and abominable act; and he describes the capture of Jerusalem by Pompey, at the invitation of Aristobulus, in anguished language mixed with irony:

> The princes of the land went to meet him with joy: they said unto him:
> Blessd be thy way! Come ye, enter ye in with peace. They made the rough ways even, before his entering in;
> They opened the gates to Jerusalem, they crowned its walls.
> As a father (entereth) the house of his sons, (so) he entered (Jerusalem) in peace;
> He established his feet (there) in great safety.
> He captured her fortress and the wall of Jerusalem;
> For God Himself led him in safety, while they wandered.
> He destroyed their princes and every one wise in counsel;
> He poured out the blood of the inhabitants of Jerusalem, like the waters of uncleanness.
>
> (viii 18 [16]–23 [20]).

In truth the struggle against the Roman conquerors did not cease, and for two decades (57–37) the revolts of Aristobulus and his sons

the Psalms of Solomon
anticipates Messiah, King David

living in the shadow of Hasmonean King

continued, but the author placed no real hope either in what was done or in the doers, although he was granted to hear of Pompey's death in the year 48 and to portray his bitter end as Divine retribution on the wicked (ii 26–37). The anonymous poet sees hope of salvation only in the coming of the Messiah of the House of David and in the perfection of the world in the kingdom of the Almighty. Psalm xvii — the Messianic psalm, which commences with the words 'O Lord, Thou art our King for ever and ever, for in Thee, O God, doth our soul glory' — rejects, in unambiguous terms, the monarchy of the Hasmoneans:

> Thou, O Lord, didst choose David (to be) king over Israel,
> And sworest to him touching his seed that never should his kingdom fail before Thee.
> But, for our sins, sinners rose up against us...
> They set a (worldly) monarchy in place of (that which was) their excellency...
> But Thou, O God, didst cast them down, and remove their seed from the earth,
> In that there rose up against them a man that was alien to our race...

The Hasmoneans are usurpers who introduced an alien form of government into the country. The poet does not distinguish between Aristobulus and Hyrcanus; he has but one prayer:

> Behold, O Lord, and raise up unto them their king, the son of David,
> At the time in which Thou seest, O God, that he may reign over Israel Thy servant.
> And gird him with strength, that he may shatter unrighteous rulers...
> At his rebuke nations shall flee before him...
> And he shall gather together a holy people...
> And he shall divide them according to their tribes upon the land.
> And neither sojourner nor alien shall sojourn with them any more...
> And he shall purge Jerusalem, making it holy as of old;
> So that nations shall come from the ends of the earth to see his glory...
> And he (shall be) a righteous king, taught of God, over them,
> And there shall be no unrighteousness in his days in their midst.
> For all shall be holy and their king the anointed of the Lord.

For he shall not put his trust in horse and rider and bow,
Nor shall he multiply for himself gold and silver for war,
Nor shall he gather confidence from(?) a multitude for the day of battle.
The Lord Himself is his king, the hope of him that is mighty through (his) hope in God.
All nations (shall be) in fear before him,
For he will smite the earth with the word of his mouth for ever...
And he himself (will be) pure from sin, so that he may rule a great people.
He will rebuke rulers, and remove sinners by the might of his word...
His words (shall be) like the words of the holy ones in the midst of sanctified peoples.[51]
Blessed be they that shall be in those days...
May the Lord hasten His mercy on Israel! ...
The Lord Himself is our king for ever and ever
(xvii 23 (21)–51 (46)).

I have quoted many verses from this Messianic document, and although its elements appear to be no more than an amalgam of prophetic promises and the utterances of visionaries like Daniel, yet its distinctiveness lies not in the combination of the themes, but in the centrality of the figure of the Messiah son of David, who although manifestly a redeemer of the land and nation, is at the same time a cosmic redeemer, who promises the kingdom of the Lord upon earth. This document is also unique in respect of what it omits. It does not mention either reward or punishment in the world to come, or the resurrection of the dead, nor does it describe catastrophic scenes. Although the document contains no indications of a sectarian orientation, yet at the same time it clearly represents only a faction within Pharisaic Judaism about a century before the Destruction, for despite all the frictions the majority of the Sages continued, as we have already emphasized, to adopt a positive attitude even to the last representatives of independent rule in Judea. Both those who subsequently supported the revolt against the Romans and those who endeavoured to come to terms with the foreign rule, so long as the Temple stood in its place and some measure of independence was allowed them in internal affairs, did not consider the Messianic expectation a matter of immediate and practical significance. Both sections understood the concept of redemption realistically, as implying the enlargement of Jewish independence, whether by force of rebellion and war, or by virtue of patience and reconciliation. The belief that the Messiah, who was due to come, must necessarily be of the House of David, was primarily used to reject the claimants to the crown of the Messiah.[52]

With the destruction of the Temple and all that it involved the question of redemption and its entire conception underwent a great change. From the aspect of the sources in our possession, the apocalyptic literature is now augmented by such books as the *Apocalypse of Baruch* and *IV Ezra*. But alongside of them there exists an abundance of Rabbinic dicta and homilies dealing with the problems of redemption, in which are to be found the variegation and polaric contrasts that we discussed at the outset. Comparison with the apocryphal works enables us to distinguish between such views as form the ancient heritage of the Sages and concepts that were absorbed through the closer mutual understanding between the Sages and certain apocalyptic circles, and also to discern, in no small measure, the realities behind the words.

Rabban Joḥanan b. Zakkai, who sensed the approaching Destruction, began to prepare the people to live without Temple and sacrifices. In a Haggadic Baraita, which might be called 'an apocalypse in reverse', it is related:

Forty years before the destruction of the Temple the lot did not come up in the right hand, nor did the crimson strap become white, nor did the westernmost light burn; and the doors of the היכל *Hêkhāl* [the *Holy* of the Temple] opened of their own accord (Rashi: 'A sign to the enemies to enter'), until Rabban Joḥanan b. Zakkai rebuked them. He said to it [the Temple]: '*O Hekhal*, *Hekhal*, why do you alarm yourself? I know full well that you are destined to be destroyed, for Zechariah the son of Ido has already prophesied concerning you "Open thy doors, O Lebanon, that the fire may devour the cedars" (Zechariah xi 1).'[53]

We know from Josephus[54] that years before the Destruction there walked about Jerusalem prophets and presagers who spoke about the Temple in ruins, and visionaries and sectarians who, in their enthusiasm, already saw a glorious new Temple descending from

Heaven. The destruction of the Temple was a shattering blow to the Jews of that generation. For the Temple service was one of the three things on which the world rested, and the effect of the disaster on Rabban Joḥanan himself is depicted thus: 'Rabban Joḥanan was sitting and looking towards the wall of Jerusalem to see what would happen to it, as it is narrated of Eli "Lo, Eli sat upon his seat by the wayside watching" (I Samuel iv 13). When Rabban Joḥanan b. Zakkai saw that the Temple was destroyed, and the *Hekhal* was burnt, he rose and rent his garments, and took off his phylacteries, and sat and wept and his disciples with him.'[55] But already then he started the work of reconstructing the life of Torah and precept, and although he did this in the hope that the Sanctuary would be rebuilt and the people redeemed, he realized that these things could not happen in the near future. 'Once Rabban Joḥanan b. Zakkai was going forth from Jerusalem, followed by R. Joshua, when he saw the Sanctuary in ruins. Said R. Joshua: "Woe unto us that this place, where the iniquities of Israel were expiated, lies in ruins!" Said (Rabban Joḥanan) to him: "My son, be not grieved! We have a means of atonement that is its equal, namely the practice of benevolence, as it is said: 'For I desire lovingkindness, and not sacrifice' (Hosea vi 6)." '[56] It may be that this answer was also intended to contradict R. Joshua's view: 'I have heard that sacrifices may be offered although there is no Temple; and that the most holy sacrifices may be eaten although there are no curtains; and the lesser holy sacrifices and the second tithe although there is no wall; because the first sanctification availed for its own time and for the time to come.'[57] The immediate urge to attempt to rebuild the Sanctuary and to proclaim that the Messiah would come soon did not cease. It is against them, apparently that the dicta of Rabban Joḥanan b. Zakkai are directed; possibly they were not uttered at one time, although they are aimed against similar trends: 'If the young people say to you "Let us go and build the Temple", do not listen to them. But if the old people say to you "Come, let us pull down the Temple", listen to them, because the construction of youths is destruction, and the destruction of the aged is construction. Proof of this is Rehoboam the son of Solomon.' Another dictum is: 'If there was a plant in your hand, and you are told: "Behold, the Messiah is here", go and plant the plant, and then go forth to welcome him.'[58] All his life Rabban Joḥanan b. Zakkai occupied himself with making enactments, with laying foundations for the national institutions, and with inculcating Torah and precepts and ideals that would improve the life of the individual and the community, and also with the acceptance of the yoke of the kingdom of Heaven. Thus he expounded: 'Why was it seen fit to bore the ear...? Because it heard on Sinai "For unto Me the children of Israel are servants, they are My servants", yet he removed the yoke of Heaven and caused the yoke of flesh and blood to reign over him....'[59] Undoubtedly Rabban Joḥanan b. Zakkai held to the actual belief in the advent of a redeeming Messiah, but since the early accounts of the study of mystic doctrines and the Work of the Chariot, which are linked with the name of Rabban Joḥanan b. Zakkai and the circle of his disciples, are distinguished by their unpretentious and restrained character,[60] he saw no reason for detailed discussions about the Messiah and his times and acts.

Only near to his death, he revealed a little of his Messianic ideal, corroborating what we have stated thus far: 'R. Jacob bar Idi said in the name of R. Joshua b. Levi: Rabban Joḥanan b. Zakkai sensing the approach of death, said: "Clear the house on account of defilement, and set a throne for Hezekiah king of Judah." '[61]

King Hezekiah, to whom a number of Isaiah's Messianic prophecies are applied,[62] is the monarch concerning whom Scripture testifies: 'And he wrought that which was good and right and faithful before the Lord his God. And in every work that he began in the service of the house of God, and in the law, and in the commandments, to seek his God, he did it with all his heart, and prospered' (II Chronicles xxxi 20–21). Him R. Joḥanan b. Zakkai sees at the time of his death as coming to greet him, and it is only fitting to prepare a throne for such a Messianic king and to welcome him.

Dicta have been transmitted in the names of R. Joḥanan b. Zakkai's disciples relating to the study and discussion of the principles and details of the future redemption. The Tannaim R. Eliezer b. Hyrcanus and R. Joshua differ on the relationship between penitence and redemption. The dispute has come down to us in two versions. According to one of them: 'R. Eliezer said: If Israel repent they will be redeemed, but if not, they will not be redeemed. Said R. Joshua to him: If they do not repent, they will not be redeemed? Nay, the Holy One, blessed be He, will raise up for them a king whose decrees will be as brutal as those of Haman, and (in consequence) Israel will repent, and he will thus bring them back to the right path.'[63] In this short text the type of redemption is not defined, but we may assume that both Tannaim had in mind religious-national redemption, which would restore the former position, that is to say, liberation from servitude, renewal of national freedom, rebuilding of the Temple as a condition requisite to perfecting the world under the sovereignty of the Almighty and to the fulfilment of the prophetic promises concerning the end of days and all that this entails. R. Eliezer makes redemption dependent on repentance: 'If they do not repent, they will not be redeemed.' Repentance comes first. Redemption is not, therefore, an eschatological act, having an independent existence, and it has no fixed time. R. Joshua, too, does not sever the nexus between repentance and redemption, only he incorporates this in the eschatological act, for it is inconceivable that Israel will not be redeemed, even if they do not repent. Hence the Lord will raise up a king, whose decrees are as brutal as those of Haman, and Israel will ineluctably repent. Upon examination it becomes clear that the dispute, which is ostensibly centred on the question of redemption, is actually concerned with the predetermined End. According to R. Eliezer there is no 'time of the end' or absolute 'end of the wonders', and consequently there is no point in all the attempts to discover this End and the signs connected with its coming. R. Joshua's view makes room for 'the calculators of the End', for those who envision catastrophic events and 'the throes of the Messiah', which precede the redemption; but there is one condition, namely that the act of repentance must be fitted into all these.

That the basis of this dispute is related to the apocalyptic visions is clearer still in the parallel tradition in which each one of the Tannaim brings Scriptural proof for his viewpoint. Against R. Eliezer's verse 'Return, ye backsliding children, I will heal your backslidings' (Jeremiah iii 22), R. Joshua adduces the verse 'Ye have sold yourselves for naught; and ye shall be redeemed without money' (Isaiah lii 3), and so they continue to counter one prophetic passage with another, until R. Joshua says: 'But it has already been stated "And I heard the man clothed in linen, who was upon the waters of the river, when he lifted up his right hand and his left hand unto heaven, and swore by Him that liveth for ever that it shall be for a time, times, and a half; and when they have made an end of breaking in pieces the power of the holy people, all these things shall be finished" (Daniel xii 7).' The transmitters of this tradition conclude the debate with the words 'Rabbi Eliezer went away', or 'And R. Eliezer was silent.' When R. Joshua sought support in the words of an apocalyptic vision of the type of Daniel, R. Eliezer saw no further possibility for continuing the argument, for it was precisely this view that he opposed in his dictum 'If they do not repent, they will not be redeemed.' However, R. Joshua also did not accept the vision of the End without a certain compromise. He placed repentance before redemption by relying on the power of a wicked king like Haman to force Israel back to the right path. It should be noted that in the battle of verses R. Eliezer did not seek support in Isaiah lix 20 'And a redeemer will come to Zion, and unto them that turn [ולשבי *û-lĕ-shāvê*] from transgression in Jacob'. Possibly both R. Eliezer and R. Joshua already knew an interpretation of this verse which they rejected. Whereas the Masoretic version supports the view of R. Eliezer, and Aquila, Symmachus and Theodotian rendered it accordingly, the Septuagint translates: καὶ ἀποστρέψει ἀσεβείας ἀπὸ 'Ιακούβ ('and He shall turn away [ישיב *yāshîv*] ungodliness from Jacob'.[64] Paul, too, cites the verse in this version (Romans xi 26). According to the interpretation inherent in this translation repentance does not actually precede redemption, but it is the redeemer who puts transgression away. This translation accords with the antinomian doctrine of Paul, which taught that 'Therefore by the deeds of the law there shall no flesh be justified in his sight: for by the law is the knowledge of sin' (*ibid.* iii 20). Hence there is no possibility of repentance, in his view, before the advent of the Messiah, 'For Christ is the end of the law, that every one who has faith may be justified.' Paul himself indicates the apocalyptic character of his words by declaring (*ibid.* xi 25) that he came to reveal by his words μυστήριον, which is the tidings of the redemption unto the Gentiles, who are 'all Israel' (*ibid. v.* 26), and He made a covenant with them after He had removed their sins. According to this view Paul also changed the first part of the verse from the Septuagint, and instead of ἕνεκεν Σιὼν he read ἐκ Σιὼν, that is to say, the redeemer will not come to Zion, but from Zion to the Gentiles.[65] Obviously this was not R. Joshua's conception. At any rate it is reported in the name of R. Jose the Galilean 'Great is repentance, for it brings redemption near, as it is said "And a redeemer will come to Zion", because of "them that turn from transgression in Jacob".'[66] This homily accords with the view of R. Joshua and contradicts the translation cited above. Hence, despite the absolute value R. Jose attributed to redemption, he could not but make repentance precede it. R. Eliezer did not wish to rely even on catastrophic events as reliable incentives to repentance. Repentance was an absolute value in itself. However, he, too, was acquainted with apocalyptic portrayals and visions — and undoubtedly not only with those in the Book of Daniel — but he endeavoured to limit their absolute value. The following homily is transmitted in his name: 'If you will succeed in keeping the Sabbath you will be delivered from three visitations: from the Day of Gog and Magog, from the throes of the Messiah's advent and from the Day of the Great Judgement.'[67] When his disciples asked him 'What shall a man do to save himself from the throes of the Messiah's coming?', he replied 'Let him occupy himself with the study of the Torah and with the practice of benevolence.'[68] If repentance alone makes redemption possible and brings it near, then there is no need for the Messianic sufferings.

Another dispute between R. Eliezer and R. Joshua is concerned with the month in which the Israelites are destined to be redeemed. According to R. Eliezer 'In Nisan they were redeemed (from Egypt), and in Tishri they will be redeemed in time to come', and according to R. Joshua 'They were redeemed in Nisan, and in Nisan they will be redeemed in time to come.'[69] Undoubtedly they based themselves on expositions of verses[70]; yet it appears that this dispute is related to the first dispute, and is likewise grounded in a principle. R. Joshua likens the last redemption to the first even from the aspect of time, and just as the redemption from Egypt was given a fixed date at the 'Covenant between the Pieces' — and according to one view the Israelites were devoid of all religious observance, and were even idolaters, and it was only to endow them with some merit that they were given just before the hour of redemption two commandments, the blood of circumcision and the blood of the passover offering[71], in order that they might be worthy of redemption — so also would it be in the coming redemption. On the other hand, in the opinion of R. Eliezer the future redemption would occur only in the month of Tishri, the first day of which was the anniversary of Creation, the Day of Judgement, and the Day of Repentance. R. Joshua's compromise in considering redemption to have a predetermined time combined with repentance makes it easier for him to accept literally the catastrophic events before the advent of the Messiah. One must not overlook the fact that the element of compromise is not wholly wanting in the apocalyptic literature itself. The author of *IV Ezra*, who was a contemporary of R. Eliezer and R. Joshua, and whose visions are full of portents of the End, declares that he heard from the archangel that the world to be would not come into existence until the number of the righteous is complete, 'For he has weighed the age in the balance, and with measure has measured the times... neither will he move nor stir things, till the measure appointed be fulfilled' (iv 36–37).

In the tradition relating to the dispute between R. Eliezer and R. Joshua 'Redemption' is spoken of generally, but there is no reference to the days of the Messiah, or the coming of Messiah the son of David, and certainly the concept of redemption is not defined as including the End, 'the resurrection', 'the time to come', 'the new world' — all those terms, in fact, that are closely linked to the idea of redemption. We shall now seek to discern to what extent and in what way the various views have affected the relationship between repentance and redemption, the conception of the nature of redemption itself and its component elements, and the conception of the redeemer's image.

The attitude to practical movements of redemption was determined to no inconsiderable extent by the two views cited above. When indications of redemption appeared — troubles and cruel suffering, or a lenient attitude on the part of the (Roman) government, or a political constellation that appeared to signalize its fall could all be reckoned as signs of redemption — it was possible to entertain hopes that indeed 'the voice of the turtle was heard in our land and the time had arrived for Israel to be redeemed' (*Canticles Rabba* ii, 13). R. Joshua b. Hananiah himself knew such an experience. In his days 'the (Roman) government decreed that the Temple should be rebuilt'. The story attributes the failure of the project to the calumniations of the Samaritans (Cutheans). Thereupon the Jews wished to revolt, but R. Joshua b. Hananiah dissuaded them from doing this by citing the fable of the Egyptian heron that put its beak into the lion's throat and left unhurt. Even so, said R. Joshua, 'Let it suffice us that we came among this nation in peace and left in peace'.[72] R. Joshua strove to convince his people that the time had not yet arrived to rebel against the government.

The criterion of repentance that R. Joshua conjoined to the belief in the End always made it possible, after the failure of attempts at redemption and of the Messiah to appear, to put the blame on the fact that the generation was not yet worthy. It may be assumed that R. Akiba adopted his teacher's doctrine. He did not abandon the idea of the End, but he saw the possibility of hastening it in a generation that merited it.[73]

In the light of the information now available to us about the period of Bar Kokhba from the letters and finds in the caves of the Judean desert[74], that generation may be largely considered as one of penitent and observant Jews. Nay more, R. Akiba held, like the author of *IV Ezra*, that a generation could even be saved by the virtue of its righteous men alone, and of the redemption from Egypt he declared that by 'the merit of the pious women in that generation were they [the Israelites] redeemed.'[75]

This approach made it easier for R. Akiba to adopt a positive attitude to Bar Kokhba; he saw the question of the redemption of the nation and the land as an internal, practical process in the world of history. From Bar Kokhba and his triumph he expected only the realization of Haggai ii 7, and, according to another source, the fulfilment of Zechariah's prophecy (viii 4) 'There shall yet old men and old women sit in the broad places of Jerusalem, every man with his staff in his hand for very age.'[76] He did not connect the restoration of the Ten Tribes and their resettlement in the land with this redemption,[77] nor did he find therein a role for Elijah, or the realization of the visions concerning 'the day of the Lord' or 'that day', and he certainly did not await new revelations or hope to penetrate into the Work of Creation, or the upper worlds, or the mystery of the Godhead.

R. Akiba did, however, occupy himself with the Work of Creation and the Work of the Chariot, and he was the only one of whom it is stated that 'he went up in peace and came down in peace', and apparently the reference is to 'seeing the Chariot'.[78]

The catastrophic events he transferred to 'the time to come', and in his Mishna he taught 'The judgement of Gog and Magog (Ezekiel xxxviii–xxxix) in the time to come will endure twelve months, the judgement of the wicked in Gehenna will endure twelve months'.[79] The Sages, who disapproved of R. Akiba's attitude to Bar Kokhba, also disagreed with his principles. When R. Akiba applied to Bar Kokhba[80] the verse 'There shall step forth a star out of Jacob, and a sceptre shall rise out of Israel' — a verse that had already been translated and expounded in an early period with reference to Messiah the son of David[81] — R. Joḥanan b. Torta reacted sharply and said 'Akiba, grass will grow out of your jaws, and the Son of David shall not yet have come.' This Tanna's opposition emanated apparently from his view that the Messiah must necessarily be descended from the House of David.[82] In addition to proof of his descent, evidence was also required of the fulfilment of the signs postulated by the prophet Isaiah with regard to the shoot of the stock of Jesse. In an anonymous Haggada it is narrated in the Babylonian Talmud: 'Bar Koziba reigned two and a half years. He then said to the Rabbis: "I am the Messiah." They answered him: "Of the Messiah it is written that he can judge by the scent. Let us see: If he can judge by the scent, well and good; if, however, he cannot, let us kill him." When they saw that he could not judge by the scent, they slew him.'[83] The Tanna R. Eleazar of Modiʿim, who according to one account was killed by Bar Kokhba,[84] taught that in reward for the observance of the Sabbath 'The Holy One, blessed be He, will give you six good portions: the Land of Israel, the world to come, the new world, the sovereignty of the House of David, the priesthood and the Levites' offices.'[85] The observance of the Sabbath does indeed assure redemption, but the Sage visualized it in the form of the monarchy of the House of David, and connected it with the world to come and the new world.

It is against the background of such opinions that the sharp rejoinder of R. Joḥanan b. Torta is to be understood, and it may be assumed that the attitude to Bar Kokhba caused a schism not only in Rabbinic circles. The same R. Joḥanan b. Torta said: 'But in the time of the Latter Temple we observe that they toiled in the study of the Torah and were meticulous in giving the tithes. Why then were they exiled? Because they loved money and hated one another. This teaches you that hatred between people is grievous in the sight of the Omnipresent.[86]

The failure of Bar Kokhba's revolt and the religious persecutions that followed brought in their wake various reactions to the hopes of the early advent of the Messiah. The Sages of the time devoted their attention to the survival and consolidation of the Jewish settlement in Eretz-Israel. Thus we learn in a Baraita: 'Let a man dwell in the Land of Israel, even in a town inhabited mainly by Gentiles, rather than outside the Land, even in a town that is entirely inhabited by Israelites. This teaches us that dwelling in the Land of Israel is as meritorious as the observance of all the precepts of the Torah....'[87] R. Simeon was strict in forbidding departure from Eretz-Israel, applying the prohibition even in periods of dearth and distress, and he apparently was also the one who said '... So long as they [the Israelites] are on it, it is as though the Land were not conquered; if they are not on it, it is as though the Land were conquered... whoever leaves the Land in peacetime and goes abroad, he is accounted an idolater ...', and R. Simeon b. Eleazar said 'Israelites living outside the Land of Israel are idolaters....'[88] The Tanna R. Nathan expounded ' "Of them that love Me and keep My commandments" — this refers to the Israelites who dwell in the Land of Israel and give their lives for the commandments. "Why are you going forth to be decapitated?" "Because I circumcised my son." "Why are you going forth to be burnt?" "Because I read the Torah." "Why are you going forth to be crucified?" "Because I ate the unleavened bread." "Why are you being lashed?" "Because I performed the ceremony of the Lulav [palm-branch and the other three species]." And it says: "Those with which I was wounded in the house of my friends" (Zechariah xiii 6): these wounds caused me to be beloved of my Father in heaven.'[89] The same R. Nathan declared with reference to the Scripture (Habakkuk ii 3) 'For the vision is yet for an appointed time, but at the end it shall speak, and not lie: though he tarry, wait for him; because it will surely come, it will not tarry' — 'This verse penetrates down to the very deep.'[90] The meaning of his words is as Rashi explains: 'Just as the deep has no end or limit, even so man cannot understand the ultimate significance of this verse, for there is no final date for the Messiah, but "though he tarry, wait for him", for he is under no limitation of time.' He who cited this Baraita of R. Nathan added: 'Nor according to R. Akiba, who expounded ' "Yet once, it is a little while, and I will shake the heavens, and the earth", but... and the kingdom of Ben Koziba (shall last) two and a half years.' It is obvious that R. Akiba also applied the continuation of the passage — Haggai ii 7 — 'And I will shake all nations, and the choicest things of all nations shall come, and I will fill this house with glory, saith the Lord of hosts' to Bar Kokhba. Whoever interpolated in the Gemara the words 'but' etc. took the passage from *Seder ʿOlam Rabba*, or from its source, that is, from the Baraita of R. Jose b. Ḥalafta, according to which the reign of Bar Kokhba lasted two and a half years.[91]

The failure of the redemption of the country on the stage of history and its separation from the Utopian-apocalyptic events also led to a totally different reaction from that of R. Nathan, namely complete abandonment of the realistic elements surrounding the redemption and its absolute integration into supernatural processes built on the ruins of existing history and actualities. The passage in *T.B. Sanhedrin*, chapter *Ḥēleq* ['Portion'] (XI), from which we cited the statement of R. Nathan, consists chiefly of Baraitot and homilies that read like actual parallels to the apocalyptic literature. It will suffice to compare the Baraita about the septennium at the end of which the son of David will come — in part we have already encountered it as a dictum of Rava — with the Syriac *Apocalypse of Baruch:*

Baraita

The Rabbis taught: The septennium at the end of which the son of David will come — in the first year the following verse will be fulfilled 'And I will cause it to rain upon one city and cause it not to rain upon another city'; in the second, the arrows of famine will be sent forth; in the third, there will be a great famine and men, women, and children, men of piety, and miracle

> workers will die, and the Torah will be forgotten by its students; in the fourth, there will be partial plenty; in the fifth, there will be great plenty, and people will eat and drink and rejoice, and the Torah will be restored to its students; in the sixth, there will be (heavenly) voices; in the seventh, wars; at the end of the septennium the son of David will come.[92]

Apocalypse of Baruch

> And I answered and said: 'Will that tribulation which is to be continue a long time, and will that necessity embrace many years?'
>
> And He answered and said unto me: 'Into twelve parts is that time divided, and each one of them is reserved for that which is appointed for it. In the first part there shall be the beginning of commotions. And in the second part (there shall be) slayings of the great ones. And in the third part the fall of many by death. And in the fourth part the sending of the sword. And in the fifth part famine and the withholding of rain. And in the sixth part earthquakes and terrors... For these parts of that time are reserved, and shall be mingled one with the other... so that those may not understand who are upon the earth in those days that this is the consummation of the times.
>
> Nevertheless, whosoever understandeth shall then be wise... And it shall come to pass when all is accomplished that was to come to pass in those parts, that the Messiah shall then begin to be revealed....[93]

There is a difference of style. The visionary sees the heavens open, and a voice from on high makes the proclamation to him. In the Baraita, which begins with a verse, the words are transmitted as though they were a tradition. But there are also revelations of Elijah. To this category belongs the famous Baraita: 'A Tanna of the School of Elijah taught: The world will exist six thousand years: for two thousand years there was desolation; for two thousand, Torah; and for two thousand years there will be the Days of the Messiah.'[94] Clearly this Baraita was taught before the end of the fourth millenium, that is to say, in the middle or the end of the second century C.E.

Since it is known only in the Babylonian Talmud, but not in the Palestinian Talmud or the ancient Midrashim of Eretz-Israel,[95] it probably reflects the influence of the Iranian apocalyptic chronology.[96] The expectation that the Messiah would come suddenly found expression in the Baraita that enunciates the Halakhic rule that one who vows ' "I shall be a Nazirite on the day when the son of David comes may drink wine on Sabbaths and festival days (Rashi: 'For the Messiah will certainly not come then'), but is forbidden to drink wine on any weekday' (Rashi: 'in case he comes').[97] It is possible that those who vowed this type of Naziriteship intended to bring nearer the day of the coming of the son of David. At the close of the Tannaitic era we find evidence again, for a short period, of a practical conception linking the hopes of redemption to an actual historical event. It is associated with the particular personality of R. Judah the Patriarch. R. Ḥiyya the Great and R. Simeon b. Ḥalafta said 'This is the way of Israel's redemption: to begin with it comes little by little, but as it progresses it grows greater and greater.'[98] To Rabbi was applied the verse 'The breath of our nostrils, the anointed of the Lord.'[99] The watchword 'David, king of Israel continues to live' was chosen as a signal for the sanctification of the new moon.[1] Rabbi wished to abolish the fast of the Ninth of Av[2], and to him is attributed a question put to R. Ḥiyya 'Has one like me to bring a he-goat?' [see Leviticus iv 23][3] — that is to say, was his law like that of a king? Possibly there is a connection between the discovery of the genealogical scroll in which it is stated 'Hillel is descended from David',[3a] the Sages' going up to Jerusalem and the renewal of 'the holy congregation in Jerusalem'[4], on the one hand, and the realistic Messianic hopes on the other. But if there were such hopes, they were quickly dissipated, and already in the period of the first Amoraim a Utopian trend prevailed in the vision of redemption. This was undoubtedly due to the decline of the Roman empire, the wars it waged against the Persians[5], the degeneration in the economic position, and also the criticism levelled against the administrative institutions, the Patriarchate, and the courts. There actually exists a kind of competition in depicting anarchy and upheaval as indications of the advent of the son of David. The two sons of R. Ḥiyya — Judah and Hezekiah — declared, when they were dining with Rabbi and had become intoxicated: 'The son of David will not come until the two dynasties in Israel come to an end, namely the Exilarchate in Babylonia and the Patriarchate in Israel.'[6] It may be presumed that they did not think up this criticism on the spur of the moment, but repeated a saying that was bandied about just as R. Simlai stated in the name of R. Eleazar b. R. Simeon 'The son of David will not come until all the judges and officers come to an end in Israel'.[7] R. Joḥanan, the leading Amora of Israel, said 'If you see a generation continually declining, wait for him [the Messiah]'; he was also the author of the dictum 'The son of David will come only in a generation that is wholly wicked.'[8] The magnitude of the degeneration, anarchy, and sufferings heralding the Messiah will be matched by the brilliance and glory of the Days of the Messiah; and indeed the sons of R. Ḥiyya, mentioned above, and R. Joḥanan pictured Jerusalem in the time to come in a manner recalling the accounts that the apocalyptists transmitted in the names of angels, only the Amoraim based their descriptions on verses.[9] R. Ḥiyya bar Abba reports in the name of R. Joḥanan 'All the prophets prophesied (in speaking of redemption) only of the Messianic era, but as for the world to come, "the eye hath not seen, O Lord, beside Thee" '[10], an interpretation that completely contradicts the view of R. Akiba and those who followed his opinion. Hence the Gemara adds, with reference to R. Joḥanan, 'Now he disagrees with Samuel, for Samuel said: the present world differs from the Messianic era only in respect of the servitude of the kingdoms.' R. Jose b. R. Ḥanina, the disciple and colleague of R. Joḥanan, drew a practical inference from the Utopian conception of redemption, and basing it on the verse 'I adjure you, O daughters of Jerusalem' (Canticles ii 7), he expounded: 'There are two oaths here, one for Israel and one for the nations of the world. He adjured Israel that they should not rebel against the kingdoms, and He adjured the kingdoms that they should not make Israel's yoke oppressive, for if they were to make Israel's yoke oppressive, they would cause the End to come prematurely.' 'The End at its due time' is something different from liberation from the servitude of the kingdoms, and cannot be attained by rebellions.[11]

R. Joḥanan also conceived the figure of the Messiah as transcending all previous conceptions of him. While Rav said 'The world was created only for David', and Samuel said 'for Moses', R. Johanan said 'for the Messiah'.[12] R. Joḥanan also did not refrain from depicting the work of redemption in anthropomorphic language that has erotic overtones. Balaam's words 'Alas, who shall live after God hath appointed him?' R. Joḥanan expounded as follows: 'Alas for the nation that will be found (obstructing), when the Holy One, blessed be He, is engaged in the redemption of His children. Who would (dare) cast his garment between a lion and a lioness at the moment of copulation?'[13] The actual image has its roots in the allegorical interpretations of Canticles, but it appears to be directed against the 'nation' that intervenes and desires to separate the Congregation of Israel from its God, in order to inherit its place. Corroboration of this interpretation can be found in Rash Laqish's exposition of this verse: 'Alas for him who restores himself to life by the name of God' [*mi-śûmô 'ēl* is interpreted as *mi-shĕmô 'ēl*].

Even among the Amoraim there were not wanting 'calculators of the End', who were vouchsafed revelations of Elijah and added meanwhile the years that had passed since the previous revelations. Thus it is related: 'Elijah said to Rav Judah, the brother of Rav Salla the Pious: The world shall endure not less than eighty-five jubilees, and the son of David shall come in the last jubilee. Said Rav Judah to him: "At the beginning (of the jubilee) or at the end?" He replied: "I know not." "Shall it be completed or not?" He answered: "I know not".'[14] Actually less importance is to be assigned to the fact that the calculation is in jubilees than to the end of the story regarding its uncertainty. The explanation is to be found in another story concerning the revelation of Elijah to the same Sage. Elijah said to Rav Judah, the brother of Rav Salla the Pious: 'You say: Why does not the Messiah come? Now today is the Day of Atonement, yet were many virgins violated in Nehardea.'[15] Against the calculators of the End R. Samuel b. R. Naḥmani declared in the name of R. Jonathan: 'Blasted be the bones of those who calculate the End, for they used to say: "Since the (time of the) End has arrived, but he has not come, he will never come.'[16] The disillusionment after the passing of the dates fixed for the End was profound, and it was precisely those who waited and hoped that feared the disappointment of the weak in faith. The extreme view against any figure of a human Messiah was represented by the Amora R. Hillel, who said 'Israel will have no Messiah, for he has already been vouchsafed to them in the days of Hezekiah.'[17] The Babylonian Amora Rav Joseph reacted sharply to this: 'May his Master forgive R. Hillel! When did Hezekiah live? In the period of the First Temple. Yet Zechariah, prophesying during the era of the Second Temple, said: "Rejoice greatly, O Daughter of Zion; shout, O daughter of Jerusalem; behold, thy king cometh unto thee! he is just, and having salvation; lowly and riding upon an ass, and upon a colt the foal of an ass".'[18] When Rabba exclaimed, on hearing an account of the throes of the Messianic era, 'Let him come, but may I not see him!', Rav Joseph retorted 'Let him come, and may I be privileged to sit in the shadow of the dung of his ass!'[19] The Messianic fervour of this Amora was tremendous, and apparently he also took the trouble to obtain apocalyptic writings, without investigating their origin and source. Thus it is narrated: 'Rav Hanan bar Taḥlifa sent (word) to Rav Joseph: "I met a certain man, who had in his possession a scroll written in Assyrian [i.e. square] characters and in the holy tongue. So I asked him: 'Where did you get this?' He replied: 'I hired myself as a mercenary to the Persian forces, and I found it among the Persian archives. It is stated therein: After four thousand two hundred and ninety-one years after the creation of the world, the world will be orphaned. (Of the subsequent years) some will be marked by wars of the sea monsters, some by the wars of Gog and Magog, and the remainder will constitute the Days of the Messiah, and the Holy One, blessed be He, will renew His world only after seven thousand years.' " '[20] This scroll, which a soldier found in the archives of Persia, is on the face of it suspect, lest it was written by an Iranian eschatologist. The name of R. Hanan bar Taḥlifa, who is not known from any other passage of the Talmud, could add another element of strangeness to this story. But the truth is that the word *Pāras* ['Persia'] was introduced here by Marcus Marinus Brixianus, the censor of the Basel printing press (1578–1581), who erased the name *Rômî* [Rome] wherever it occurs and sometimes changed it to 'Babylonia' or 'Aramaea'. In this particular case, it seems, he chose 'Persia' in order to confuse scholars, and indeed he succeeded in no small measure.[21] At all events, in all the MSS. and the early editions the text reads 'I hired myself to the Roman forces, and I found it in the Roman archives.'

In some of these recensions the name of the Sage who sent the information to Rav Joseph is given as Rav ʿAnan bar Taḥlifa, one of the disciples of Samuel.[22] From the aspect of structure and motifs this scroll adds nothing to what we know from other apocalyptic writings.[23] The date 291 is a corruption of 231[24], and this date appears also in another apocalyptic Baraita: 'It is taught in a Baraita: After four thousand two hundred and thirty-one years *anno mundi*, if one should say to you "Buy a field worth a thousand denars for one denar", do not buy.'[25] The date was determined on the basis of an exposition, being equivalent to four hundred years after the destruction of the Second Temple, and just as the first redemption came after four hundred years of servitude in Egypt, so shall it also be in the case of the last redemption. About a century after Rav ʿAnan had sent the information about the contents of this scroll to Rav Joseph, Jerome wrote[26] that the Jews of his time used to say that just as Pharaoh, king of Egypt, and all his host were drowned in the Red Sea after holding the people of Israel in captivity for four hundred and thirty years,[27] so, too, the Romans would be destroyed by the vengeance of the Lord when they would have ruled over the Jews that number of years. The discovery of the scroll in the archives of Rome in the days of Rav Joseph served to give this exposition the aspect of an ancient vision; in the words of R. Me'ir ha-Levi Abulafia in his book *Yad Rama* on Sanhedrin: 'And the reason for informing us that it [the scroll] was written in square characters and in the holy tongue was to show that the Romans had not written it, but that it was brought from the exiles of Jerusalem.'[28]

Needless to say, it was just the apocalyptic stories and dicta of the Sages that were not always handed down in their original form; sometimes the narrators presented them in a sharp dialectical form that appeared to nullify their original intention. It is related, for instance, that R. Joshua b. Levi met Elijah at the entrance of R. Simeon b. Yoḥai's burial-cave and asked him: "When will the Messiah come?" He answered him: "Go and ask him himself." "Where does he abide?" — "At the entrance of Rome" — "How is he to be recognized?" — "He sits among the sick; now all of them untie and tie up (all their bandages) at one and the same time, while he unties and reties (his bandages) one at a time, saying (to himself): In case

I am needed, I shall not be delayed." So he [R. Joshua b. Levi] went to him (and) said to him "Peace be upon you, O my master and teacher!" He replied: "Peace be upon you, O son of Levi!" He then said to him: "When will the master come?" His reply was "Today". He [R. Joshua b. Levi] then returned to Elijah, who asked him "What did he tell you?" He answered him "Peace be upon thee, O son of Levi!" Said (Elijah) to him "He assured you and your father of (a share in) the world to come." (R. Joshua b. Levi) rejoined "But he lied to me; for he told me 'I shall come today', yet he did not come." Said (Elijah) to him "This is what he meant: 'Today, if ye will hearken to His voice'." '[29] In this story, which does not lack overtones of humour and irony,[30] R. Joshua b. Levi is told, after he had troubled Elijah and the Messiah himself, that which his contemporary, Rav, had said in more prosaic form: 'All the (calculated) dates of redemption have passed, and the matter now depends upon repentance and good deeds.' Now he himself disagreed with Rav and said 'It suffices the mourner to keep his mourning'[31], implying that even without repentance Israel will be redeemed. The narrator undoubtedly held similar views to those of the hero of his narrative, that is to say, he belonged to the circles of the Sages that cultivated the Messianic vision in the apocalyptic spirit. These were the Sages who, projecting the present into the past, said of the Israelites in Egypt: 'This teaches us that they possessed scrolls, in which they took delight on Sabbaths, and these held out the promise that the Holy One, blessed be He, would redeem them.'[32] The Haggadist's witness is, therefore, reliable, namely that precisely in these circles, despite all their attachment to the fantastic conception of redemption, they again accepted the doctrine of R. Eliezer that 'If they do not repent, they will not be redeemed.'

Confirmation of our view is to be found in another dictum, transmitted in the name of R. Joshua b. Levi, in which he explicitly makes the figure of the Messiah — whether his place is among the clouds of heaven, or whether he is a poor man riding on an ass — depend on the merits, that is, the deeds of Israel.[33]

The synthesis of repentance with the apocalyptic Messianic system enabled the Sages who cultivated it to adopt ideas that ostensibly should have been rejected on polemical and apologetic grounds. In truth the fact that certain modern scholars ignored the role played by the integration of the idea of repentance led them to account for matters that appeared surprising to them by discovering signs of polemics in expressions that were perfectly innocent in themselves.

We shall discuss two motifs to both of which references were already found in the sources that we have cited. One concerns the 'pre-existence' of the Messiah. In several sources[34], which enumerate six or four things that preceded the creation of the world, 'the name of the Messiah' occurs. Louis Ginzberg[35] regards the reference to 'the name of the Messiah' instead of the 'Messiah' as an intentional change for anti-Christian polemical reasons, just as he discovered a distinction between real pre-existence and ideal pre-existence in the source that includes the Messiah's name among the things that were planned to be created and not among the things that were actually created. However, among the latter are counted only the Throne of Glory and the Torah, which may be said to have actually preceded Creation, whereas 'the name of the Messiah' is mentioned together with the Patriarchs and with Israel, which preceded it in thought. As for 'the name of the Messiah, it is clearly linked to the verse on which its pre-existence is based, namely 'His name burgeoned before ever the sun was' (Psalms lxxii 17, which is rendered in JPS 'May his name be continued as long as the sun'). In one source, which I published from a MS.,[36] the author of the list of pre-existent things is given as R. Simeon b. Laqish. This same Resh Laqish gave an allegorical, apocalyptic interpretation to the second verse in Genesis: 'R. Simeon b. Laqish interpreted the verse with reference to the kingdoms: "Now the earth was waste and void" — this is Babylonia (as it is written): "I beheld the earth, and, lo, it was waste and void" (Jeremiah iv 23); "and void" — this means Media... "and darkness" — this refers to Greece... "over the face of the deep" — this alludes to the present wicked kingdom, just as the deep is unfathomable, so the wicked kingdom is unfathomable; "and the spirit of God hovered" — this connotes the spirit of the Messiah, as it is said "And the spirit of the Lord shall rest upon him" (Isaiah xi 2). By what merit does its ministration begin? — "hovered over the face of the waters", through the merit of repentance, which is likened to water, (as it is said:) "Pour out thy heart like water" (Lamentations ii 19).'[37] Here 'the spirit of the Messiah' is mentioned; there are no grounds, therefore, for the distinction between the 'pre-existence' of his name and the 'pre-existence' of his personality.[38] It is the pre-existence of repentance that also prepared the way for the 'pre-existence' of the Messiah. It is noteworthy, however, that in seven sources out of nine[39] the 'Torah and repentance' invariably head the list and 'the name of the Messiah' concludes it, in conformity with the homily of Resh Laqish.

Circles that, like R. Joshua b. Levi, lived the Messianic hope very intensely and deemed it important to know where the Messiah, who dwelt in secret, was to be found, endeavoured also to discover his name, especially since the Christians called the Messiah by a personal name. The conjectured names, their sources, and explanations are highly variegated. Most of them — such as David, Ṣemaḥ, and Menaḥem — are based on Messianic verses.[40] Some of the passages mention not only the supporting verse but also the names of the homilists themselves,[41] their attributes, or their views about the nature of the redemption and the image of the redeemer.[42] Among the names suggested on the basis of various verses is also found the name חוליא *Ḥûlyā* ['the ailing one'],[43] based on the verse 'Surely he has borne our sicknesses and carried our pains; yet we esteemed him stricken, smitten by God and afflicted' (Isaiah liii 4). We have already met, in the story about R. Joshua b. Levi, the poor and afflicted Messiah, who sits in the gateway of Rome.

His disciple, R. Alexandri, did not refrain from expounding the verse 'And הריחו *hăriḥô* [usually rendered 'his delight shall be'] in the fear of the Lord...' thus: 'This teaches us that He loaded him with precepts and suffering as with a millstone [ריחים *rêḥayîm*].'[44] The verse Ruth ii 14 is expounded by R. Joḥanan allegorically of the King Messiah, and the expositor accordingly declares: ' "And eat of the bread" — this means the bread of sovereignty; "and dip thy morsel in the vinegar" — this refers to the suffering, as it is said "But he was wounded because of our transgressions". "And she sat beside the reapers" — this connotes that his kingdom would temporarily be taken away from him...; "and they reached her parched corn" — this signifies that it is destined to return to him... R. Berechiah in the name of R. Levi said: The last redeemer would be like the first: just as the first redeemer was revealed and then hidden again from them (Israel) ... and how long would he be hidden from them?... forty-five days....'[45]

The second part of the homily is derived from Daniel xii 11–12 and is found in parallel passages[46] without any connection with the verse in Ruth. But the interpretation of the dipping into vinegar as referring to the sufferings of the Messiah is reminiscent of John xix 28–29: 'That the scripture might be fulfilled, saith, I thirst. Now there was set a vessel full of vinegar; and they filled a sponge with vinegar and put it upon hyssop, and put it to his mouth'; the intent was to fulfil the verse in Psalms (lxix 22) 'and in my thirst they gave me vinegar to drink'.[47] The manifestation of the Messiah and his disappearance for forty-five days are alluded to in Daniel, but they become days in which the faith of the people is tested, for the Messiah leads them into the wilderness, where they eat salt-plants and brooms. One receives the undoubted impression that in these Messianic Midrashim there exists a trend similar to that in the Gospels, namely to find the fulfilment of all the Scriptures and visions containing Messianic descriptions. Only while in the Christian sources these are referred to the lifetime of a Messiah who had already lived and died, in the homilies of the Sages the allusions are to the Messiah who has still to come. When the Christians themselves began in the second century[48] to speak of the delay in δευτέρα παρουσία, the signs and portents that were interpreted with respect to the Messiah's first appearance inevitably lost their significance. The Rabbis felt no misgivings, therefore, in applying to the Messiah even a verse like Zechariah xii 10 'And they shall look unto Me because they have thrust him through; and they shall mourn for him, as one mourneth for his only son.'[49] Thus it is stated in a Babylonian Baraita:[50] 'The Holy One, blessed be He, will say to Messiah the son of David — may he be destined to reveal himself speedily in our days! — "Ask Me for anything and I will give it to you", for it is said "I will tell of the decree... this day have I begotten thee, ask of Me and I will give the nations for thy inheritance." But when he will see that Messiah the son of Joseph has been slain, he will say to Him "Sovereign of the universe, only life do I ask of Thee." Then He will say to him: "Life? Before ever you spoke, your father David already prophesied concerning you, as it is said "He asked life of Thee; Thou gavest it him" ' (Psalms xxi 5). This source, which is termed a 'Baraita', is apparently connected with the preceding debate in the Babylonian Talmud regarding the interpretation of the verse in Zechariah: 'R. Dosa and the Rabbis differed on the point: one held that it [the mourning] was on account of Messiah, son of Joseph, who had been slain; while the other maintained that it was on account of the Evil Inclination, which had been slain.' This dispute is identical with that of the 'two Amoraim' in the Palestinian Talmud:[51] 'One said: This refers to the mourning for the Messiah; and the other said: This refers to the mourning for the Evil Inclination.' Thus according to the Amora who interpreted the verse in Zechariah as alluding to the Messiah, there is no difficulty in assuming a nexus between this motif and the Haggada that declares that the Messiah 'would be revealed and then hidden again'. Apparently apocalyptic circles no longer had misgivings about interpreting the verse with regard to a suffering and afflicted Messiah. Such views were put by Justin Martyr in the mouth of Tryphon. He accepts the view that the Messiah will suffer after his first advent, but he rejects Justin's belief that this Messiah was Jesus.[52] Be the source that gave rise to the figure of Messiah the son of Joseph[53] what it may, it was not the motif of the suffering and afflicted Messiah that produced it. The truth is that cautious and hesitant homilists used this motif in order to liberate the image of the Messiah the son of David from suffering, afflictions, and death.

In the speculations about the figure of the suffering Messiah there is naught left apparently of the idea of repentance as a factor in the process of redemption, but deeper examination of the problem leads us to a different conclusion.

The afflicted and suffering Messiah, who 'is wounded because of our transgressions', who is slain or is compelled to disappear, actually contains a paradox, since it diminishes his power as a redeemer, and in fact deprives his function, as the one that fulfils the redemption, of its absolute character. It is not the redemptive act *per se* that liberates the world from sin and transgression, but there is need of the purging sufferings and afflictions of the Messiah, which are preconditions of the work of redemption. Actually it is nowhere stated in the ancient Amoraic sources that the afflictions and suffering of the Messiah constitute in themselves an atonement and redemption, as Paul had stressed (Romans iii 23). Even in *IV Ezra* the apocalyptist negates the possibility of 'vicarious' repentance. His opinion is unambiguous: 'For then every one shall bear his own righteousness or unrighteousness' (vii 105). R. Simlai expounded the verse in Isaiah liii 12 with reference to the first redeemer, Moses, as follows: ' "Because he poured out his soul unto death" — for he delivered himself unto death...; "Yet he bore the sin of many" — because he made atonement for the making of the golden calf; "And made intercession for the transgressors" — for he entreated that the transgressors of Israel might repent' (*T.B. Soṭa* 14a). Even the late apocalyptic homilist, living at the end of the period of Byzantine rule in Palestine, who reunited the figures of Messiah the son of Joseph and Messiah the son of David into one Messiah, 'Ephraim our righteous Messiah', and made the subject of his afflictions and suffering a central theme in his 'Messianic Tractate', which is incorporated in *Pesiqta Rabbati*[54], concluded his exposition of the verse, Isaiah lxi 10, as follows: ' "As a bridegroom decketh himself with a garland" — this teaches us that the Holy One, blessed be He, will clothe Ephraim, our righteous Messiah, with a garment whose splendour will span the world from end to end...; "And as a bride adorneth herself with her jewels"... just as a bride is not accepted without her adornments, even so the Congregation of Israel does not put her adversaries to shame except by merit...'[55] It is this merit that gives assurance that the Congregation of Israel will never return to her servitude. Just as the Amora's interpretation of the mourning in Zechariah xii as lamentation for the Messiah — an exposition that marks a climax in straining the apocalyptic aspect of redemption — still requires its measure of repentance, so, too, the homily of the Amora who takes a different view and explains the words of the prophet as a lament for the slain 'Evil Inclination', reveals its apocalyptic-eschatological ingredients, which combined with the idea of repentance as a decisive factor in the process of redemption. Ostensibly it is repentance that must bring about the destruction of the Evil Impulse, but rightly the Talmud raises an objection to this interpretation: 'Should there be mourning for such an event? (On the contrary) there should be rejoicing! Why then should they weep?' The answer is: 'As R. Judah b. R. Ileʿai expounded: In the time to come the Holy One, blessed be He, will bring the Evil

Inclination and slaughter him in the presence of the righteous and the wicked. To the righteous he will appear as a towering mountain, while to the wicked he will seem like a (mere) strand of hair. Both groups will weep. The righteous will weep and say: How were we able to conquer this towering mountain! And the wicked will weep, saying: How was it possible for us not to vanquish this strand of hair!'[56]

Notwithstanding all their hyperbolical estimates of the power of repentance (see above, p. 462), even those Tannaim and Amoraim who expounded its merit and ability to hasten the coming of redemption, Sages of the type that taught that 'If Israel were to repent but a single day, the son of David would come forthwith'[57] — even they learnt from their long historical experience how hard was the road of repentence for individuals, and still more so for an entire nation. Nor were all of them sure of the power of afflictions and misfortunes to hasten the process. Regarding the people of Sodom R. Jeremiah b. Eleazar said: 'Twenty-five years the Holy One, blessed be He, brought upon them volcanic eruptions and earthquakes, so that they might turn to repentance, but they did not.'[58]

The conduct of Pharaoh, concerning whom Scripture testifies 'for I have hardened his heart', drew the attention of two scholars whose interest in the subject of redemption and repentance we have already pointed out.

R. Joḥanan did not hesitate to say 'This provides an opportunity for the sectarians to say: It was not in his power to repent.' In the light of what we have stated earlier, it will not be difficult to identify the sectarians who could cite this verse to confirm the negation of the power of repentance. Although R. Simeon b. Laqish said 'May the mouth of the sectarians be closed!' yet he continued: 'For the Holy One, blessed be He, warns a man once, twice, and thrice, and if he does not retract, then He closes his heart to repentance in order to punish him for his sins. So was it with the wicked Pharaoh... The Holy One, blessed be He, said to him: "You have made yourself stiff-necked and hard of heart; therefore I shall add defilement to your defilement" ' (*Exodus Rabba* xiii, 2). It is true that repentance, according to Resh Laqish, preceded the creation of the world, but he, too, recognized that there are situations in which the way of penitence is hidden from mortals. To prevent the Evil Impulse from returning in the time to come, and to enable man to be redeemed from the tendency to sin, it seemed to Rav Judah — an Amora who had no special interest in redemption in the national sense — that the surest course was for God Himself to come and slaughter the Evil Impulse in the presence of the righteous.

A parallel manifestation of the removal of the work of redemption from human control is also to be found in the other aspect — in the conception of redemption in the national-political connotation. The fear that there might be renewed servitude after the coming redemption continued to cling to the Tannaim and Amoraim, and they gave expression to it in various ways.[59] The Amora R. Aḥa, who possibly witnessed the Emperor Julian's attempt to rebuild the Temple, expounded, out of a sense of disillusionment, ' "The cords of Death compassed me"... I turned hither and thither, but I have no redeemer but Thee.'[60] In an anonymous homily the expositor attributed the following argument to the people of Israel: 'Israel said to the Holy One, blessed be He: "Hast Thou not already redeemed us by the hands of Moses and of Joshua and of judges and kings? And now we are again enslaved and put to shame, as though we had never been redeemed!" Said the Holy One, blessed be He, to them: "Because your redemption was by human agency, and your leaders were mortals who are here one day and in the grave the next, therefore your redemption was of a temporary nature. But in the future I, who live for ever, shall redeem you Myself; I shall redeem you with an everlasting redemption." '[61]

The homilist in effect negates the figure of the personal Messiah. The Holy One, blessed be He, will Himself be the ultimate Redeemer, and only His redemption will be everlasting. This homilist expresses in his own way the view of Hillel 'Israel has no Messiah.'[62]

The abolition of the figure of the personal Messiah is thus to be found in both conceptions of redemption — in that which regards it as the time of the End, and also in that which integrates it with preliminary repentance. Furthermore, dicta of Tannaim who held different conceptions of the actual nature of redemption lend support to this view. If we have regarded R. Akiba, who separated the national redemption from all other events of the end of days, as the outstanding representative of restitutory pattern, it must be borne in mind that it was nevertheless he who remarked with reference to the verse 'Before Thy people, whom Thou didst redeem Thee out of Egypt, the nations and their gods' (II Samuel vii 23): 'Were not the verse written, it would be impossible to say it. So to speak, Israel said to the Holy One, blessed be He, "Thou hast redeemed Thyself"...'[63] The God who redeems Himself together with His people from exile does not need even a deliverer like Moses; He can also make use of Bar Kokhba, or choose any other way. Redemption was, of course, subject to the condition that the people would wish to be redeemed; but the Sages were not always sure of this desire. The Amora R. Berechiah gave expression to the scant enthusiasm for redemption in his exposition of the verse 'Egypt was glad when they departed' (Psalms cv 38) with the help of the following analogy: 'It is like a stout man riding on an ass; the ass waits for the moment when the man will get down from him, and he waits for the moment when he will get down from the ass. When he does so, the man is glad and the ass is glad. But I do not yet know who rejoices more; you must conclude that the ass rejoices more. Even so was it with Israel in Egypt: The plagues were coming upon the Egyptians and they were awaiting the moment when the Israelites would depart, and the Israelites were waiting for the moment when the Holy One, blessed be He, would redeem them. When the Exodus took place and they were redeemed, both sides were glad. But we do not know who rejoiced more, until David came and said "Egypt was glad when they departed"; thus we know that the Egyptians rejoiced more.'[64]

However, also in the name of the Sage who opposed R. Akiba's attitude to Bar Kokhba, namely R. Eleazar of Modiʿim — he held a different doctrine, which identified the national redemption with the transformation of the nature of the world — a homily is transmitted that abolishes the role of the personal Messiah in the eschatological task and bases everything upon the absolute belief in redemption:

'As R. Eleazar of Modiʿim said: The Guardian Angels of the heathen nations are destined in the time to come to denounce Israel before the Holy One, blessed be He, saying: "Sovereign of the universe, these [i.e. the Gentiles] were idolaters and these [the Israelites] were idolaters, these committed incest and these committed incest, these were guilty of bloodshed and these were guilty of bloodshed. Why then do these [the heathens] go down to Gehenna, but not the others?"[65] The Holy One, blessed be He, will answer them, saying: "If so, let all the peoples descend with their gods to Gehenna." This is the meaning of the verse "For let all the peoples walk each one in the name of its god" (Micah iv 5). R. Reuben said: If Scripture had not written it, it would be impossible to say it. So to speak, "For by fire will the Lord be judged [the literal meaning of נשפט *nishpāṭ*]" (Isaiah lxvi 16). It is not written here "The Lord will judge" [שופט *shôfēṭ*], but "will be judged" [*nishpāṭ*]. This is implied in what David said through the holy spirit: "Yea, though I walk through the valley of the shadow of death, I will fear no evil for Thou art with me" (Psalms xxiii 4).'[66]

NOTES

CHAPTER I

THE STUDY OF THE HISTORY OF THE BELIEFS AND CONCEPTS OF THE SAGES

1. It appeared in German under the title *Die Philosophie des Judentums*, München 1933. A Hebrew translation, with amendments and supplements by the author, was published by Mosad Bialik, Jerusalem 1951. The English version, called *Philosophies of Judaism*, was issued by the Jewish Publication Society of America, Philadelphia 1964. The critical survey of works dealing with our subject is limited to those of a general and comprehensive nature. Books, monographs, studies and essays treating of particular problems will be evaluated in their respective places. I must mention, however, two scholars whose contribution to our subject is most important, although their books have a different character and aim. I refer to Wilhelm Bacher and Louis Ginzberg. Bacher in his works on the Haggada of the Tannaim and Amoraim — *Die Agada der babylonischen Amoräer*, Strassburg 1878 (it was published in the same year also in Budapest in *Jahresbericht der Landes-Rabbinerschule*), supplements and amendments to this work, Frankfort 1913; *Die Agada der Tannaiten*, Strassburg, Pt. I, second edition, 1903, Pt. II 1890; *Die Agada der palästinensischen Amoräer*, Strassburg Pt. I 1892, Pt. II 1896, Pt. III 1899; (the last two works were rendered into Hebrew by A. Z. Rabinowitz and appeared in the years 1920–1938) — arranged the dicta of the Tannaim and Amoraim according to subject-matter, an arrangement that makes it possible to examine the world of their ideas. His numerous notes include not a few explanations and elucidations, which are important for the understanding of Rabbinic dicta. In the two volumes of notes to L. Ginzberg's large work *The Legends of the Jews*, Philadelphia, Vol. V, 1925 and Vol. VI, 1928, are incorporated entire studies not only on the ideas and views of the Haggada concerning Biblical events, acts, and personalities, but also on the principles of the Jewish faith as they are reflected in the Haggadic sources.
2. Pt. I, ch. XXIII, pp. 216–232.
3. Several chapters of the book appeared earlier in the *JQR*, beginning with the year 1894.
4. *Ibid.*, p. 3.

5. H. Strack and P. Billerbeck, *Kommentar zum Neuen Testament aus Talmud und Midrasch*, Munich 1922–1928. This monumental work, which contains a complete collection in German translation of Rabbinic dicta that have any bearing on the New Testament, was compiled by Billerbeck; Strack only arranged and edited the material; see the introduction to Pt. I, Vol. IV. All that has been written in the course of the last forty years by Christian authors — and also by not a few Jews — on themes relating to Judaism in antiquity is based on Billerbeck's compilation, only most of these writers did not take the trouble to check and compare the sources, and made the mistake of taking statements out of their context and attributing to them unintended meanings. For a critique of the book, see J. Krengel, *MGWJ*, 1924, LXVIII, pp. 68–82.
6. *Op. cit.*, p. 50. Schechter already argued against this book in his aforementioned work, p. 27.
7. Bousset's *Religion des Judentums kritisch untersucht*, 1903. M. Güdemann, 'Das Judentum in Neutestamentlichen Zeitalter', *MGWJ*, 1903, pp. 38 ff, was less stringent in his criticism. He acknowledged Bousset's achievements and admitted that he found many instances where the latter evinced an earnest desire to be objective. J. Wohlgemuth, *Das jüdische Religionsgesetz in jüd. Beleuchtung*, II, Berlin 1919, pp. 94 ff does not mention Güdemann's views, but repeats the remarks of his predecessors with an added measure of apologetics.
8. *Im Namen Gottes*, Berlin 1903, pp. 64–65.
9. F. C. Burkitt, *The Gospel History and its Transmission*, Edinburgh 1906, pp. 169–174.
10. In his critique of Moore's book, Frank C. Porter, 'Judaism in N. T. Times', *Journal of Rel.*, 1928, VIII, pp. 30–62, argues that Moore's work should properly have been called 'The Judaism of the Tannaim', and even this aspect has not been completely portrayed. This contention is correct, but Porter (p. 53) accuses Moore of refraining from dealing with the Halakhic details of the Mishna for fear that such a discussion would prevent him from creating the impression of esteem and sympathy for Judaism, in which he was interested. It appears that this attitude offended the critic, and characteristically he condemned his own fault in someone else. J. Bonsirven, *Le Judaisme palestinien au temps de Jésus-Christ*, Paris 1934, already used Foot Moore's book and a number of the observations that we have made apply to him, too; only he wrote his book in the spirit of Catholic Christianity, and did not even refrain from intruding Christian ideas into the Rabbinic sources.
11. In a series of articles in *Zion*, XVII, 1952, pp. 1–55, 173; XVIII, 1953, pp. 91–108; XXVII, 1962, pp. 117–155; in his book *Yisrā'ēl bā-'Ammîm* [Israel among the Nations], Jerusalem 1955, and in a compendious article 'Ha-Mishnā wĕ-ha-Histôryā [The Mishna and History]', *Molad*, 1964, pp. 308–323.
12. Consequent upon this premise, he proceeded to give a late date to the compo-

sition of the Qumran Scrolls, assigning them to the second century C.E., and to argue that they were written under the influence of the New Testament; see *Zion*, XXIX, 1964, pp. 1–60. J. Efron, 'Mizmôrê Shĕlōmō, ha-Shĕqî'ā ha-Ḥashmônā'ît wĕ-ha-Naṣrût' [The Psalms of Solomon, the Hasmonean Decline, and Christianity], *Zion*, 1965, pp. 1 ff follows Baer, who takes the view that the Apocryphal books, which were preserved by the Church, are Christian compositions.

13. It was first published in 1938, and has now appeared in a third edition, 1962, with the addition of an Introductory Note, pp. 47–137, and a Supplement in Vol. II, pp. 627–780.
14. *Op. cit.*, p. IX.
15. *Ibid.*, p. XIV.
16. *Ibid.*, p. 634, despite the express statement 'At first there were no controversies in Israel'.
17. p. CXXXIV and p. 797.
18. 'Ha-Mishnā wĕ-ha-Historyā', *Molad*, 1964, p. 323.
19. See Isaac Heinemann, *Darkhê hā-'Aggādā* [Haggadic Methodology], Jerusalem 1950, and in my article in *Kirjath Sepher*, XXVI, 1950, pp. 223–228; cf. also S. Lieberman, *Hellenism in Jewish Palestine*, pp. 47–82.
20. Numerous examples of the neglect of these principles are furnished by A. J. Heschel's *Theology of Ancient Judaism*. (The English title of his Hebrew book *Torah min hashāmayin*, London and New York, Vol. I 1962 Vol II 1965). In truth the author attempts to adumbrate in it a theology of his own, in the same way as in his book *God in Search of Man*, 1955. On Heschel's own pragmatic-existential approach, see J. M. Chinitz, *Judaism — The Elusive Revelation*, 1965, pp. 198 ff; and on modern Jewish theology as a whole, see S. Sandmehl, 'Reflection on the Problem of Theology for Jews', *The Journal of Bible and Religion*, 1965, pp. 101 ff.

CHAPTER II

THE BELIEF IN ONE GOD

1. *M. Berakhot* I, 1–2. It is true that when the Talmud raises the question 'On what does the Tanna base himself when he asks "From what time?"' the answer given is 'The Tanna bases himself on Scripture, for it is written, "when thou liest down and when thou risest up"' (*T.B. Berakhot* 2a). But there were other Amoraim who held that the recitation of the Shĕmaʿ is a Rabbinic regulation, and they interpreted the verse according to its simple meaning: 'And thou shalt talk of them when thou sittest in thy house, and when thou walkest by the way, and when thou liest down, and when thou risest up'; they said 'Scripture refers here to Torah study' (*ibid.*, 21a).
2. *M. Tamid*, v, 1.
3. *T.P. Berakhot* i, p. 3c.
4. Herodotus, I, 131–132; see Nyberg, *Die Rel. des alten Iran*, Leipzig 1938, pp. 369 ff.
5. Nyberg, p. 105. See G. Widengren, *Die Religionen Irans*, 1965, pp. 76 ff, and cf. the critique of S. Shaked, *BSOAS*, XXXII, No. 1, 1969, pp. 160–162.
6. See M. H. Segal, 'Ha-Gōme' shel Nash [The Nash Papyrus]', *Lĕšonénu*, XV, 1947, pp. 27–36. The argument of J. Guttmann, *Ha-Sifrût ha-Yĕhûdît ha-Helenîstît* [Jewish Hellenistic Literature], I, Jerusalem 1954, p. 126, n. 16, is unconvincing.
7. *Sifre Deuteronomy*, § 31, p. 54; cf. *Midrash Tannaim*, p. 25. In *Sifre Numbers*, § 134, p. 180: 'Thou art Lord [אדון] of all mankind'; in *Sifra*, Ṣaw, 'Millu'im', i 15, p. 41d: 'When the Lord [אדון] of the universe commanded', and in the homily of Eleazar b. Azariah, *T.B. Ḥagiga* 3b: 'From the mouth of the Lord [אדון] of all works' (= *'Avot de-R. Nathan*, Version I, xviii, p. 68: 'Sovereign [רבון] of all works'). Sirach also uses the epithets 'the God of all [אלהי הכל]' (xxxvi 1), and 'God of all [אלה כל]' (xlv 42 [= 23], Segal, *Sēfer Ben-Sîrā ha-Shālēm* [The Complete Ben-Sira]). On the designation 'the Lord of all [אדון הכל]' in the psalm 151 of Qumran, see A. Hurvitz, *Tarbiz*, XXIV, 1965, pp. 224 ff.
8. I have quoted the *Mekhilta* according to the recension of *Yalquṭ Shimʿoni*,

Kings, § 229. In *Mekhilta*, Jethro, Amalek, i, pp. 194–195, it is stated, 'Naaman acknowledged one thing more than he did... and so, too, Rahab the harlot said', see the v.l. *ibid.*; there is no difference here between Naaman and Rahab. It appears that in a number of MSS. the reference to Rahab is omitted at this point, but is added at the end. In the *Midrash ha-Gadol*, Exodus, ed. Margulies, p. 360, and thence in *Mekhilta de-R. Simeon b. Yoḥai*, ed. Epstein-Melamed, p. 131, we read 'And so, too, Rahab the harlot left something over.' In *Yalquṭ*, Joshua, § 10, the dictum from *Deuteronomy Rabba*, ii, 27, is cited. Although the reference given there is to the *Mekhilta*, yet this pertains only to the beginning of the quotation, to the saying of R. Simeon b. Eleazar, which is taken from *Mekhilta*, Shira, iii, p. 128, whereas the rest emanates from *Deuteronomy Rabba*, only instead of 'And Naaman acknowledged a part of it', i.e. a part of idolatry, the text was changed to 'And Naaman acknowledged one thing more', and in place of 'Rahab set Him in heaven and earth' we have 'And Rahab acknowledged one thing more than they did'. The fact that Naaman is mentioned before Rahab is understandable in *Deut. Rab.*, because of the addition by Moses, who cited the same verse with the addendum 'and none else'.

9. *Deut. Rab.*, *ibid.*; on the quest for the true God and the correct form of worship in the ancient world, in the first and second century, see A. D. Nock, *Conversion*, Oxford 1933, pp. 108 ff.
10. This is the wording of the dictum as it is cited in *Sifre Deuteronomy*, § 28, ed. Finkelstein, p. 123. See also *Sifre Numbers*, § 111, p. 116: 'Whoever acknowledges idolatry disavows the Ten Commandments, and that which was enjoined upon Moses and the prophets and the patriarchs; but whoever disavows idolatry acknowledges the whole Torah.'
11. The expression מודה ב... ['acknowledges'] like כופר ב... ['disavows'] derives from the language of negotiation: טענו חטין והודה לו בשעורין ['If a man claimed wheat from another and the latter admitted a debt of barley'], *M. Shevuot* vi, 3.
12. *T.B. Yoma* 69b, and the other passages listed in my essay 'The Rabbinic Laws of Idolatry in the Second and Third Centuries in the Light of Archaeological and Historical Facts', I–II, in *IEJ*, 1959–1960, No. 3, pp. 149 ff; No. 4, pp. 229 ff; and see S. Lieberman, 'Rabbinic Polemics against Idolatry', in *Hellenism in Jewish Palestine*, New York 1950, pp. 115–127.
13. viii 18.
14. τὸ μὴ ἀνθρωπόμορφον εἶναι τὸν θεόν; see Joshua Guttmann, *Ha-Sifrut ha-Yehudit ha-Helenistit*, I, p. 60.
15. Josephus, *Against Apion*, I, p. 192.
16. *II Maccabees*, xii 39–40.
17. *Legatio ad Gaium*, 203.
18. *Midrash Tannaim*, ed. Hoffmann, p. 58; *'Avot de-R. Nathan*, Version II, xxxi, p. 66. See S. Lieberman, 'Palestine in the Third and Fourth Centuries', *JQR*, N.S., XXXVI (1946).

CHAPTER II

19. *M. Berakhot* ix, 1.
20. *Tosefta Berakhot* vi, 2, p. 33; see S. Lieberman, *Tosefta ki-Fshuṭah* [A Comprehensive Commentary on the Tosefta], p. 104.
21. *Tosefta, ibid.*; see *T.P., ibid.* i, 2, p. 12b: 'If it [idolatry] was uprooted in one place and established at another'.
22. *T.B. 'Avoda Zara* 55a.
23. See, on the other hand, S. Lieberman, *Hellenism in Jewish Palestine*, p. 126.
24. See *Pirqê de-R. Eliezer* xlv: 'R. Judah said Satan entered it (i.e. the calf) and lowed in order to mislead the Israelites'; this dictum contradicts *Tanḥuma*, Ki Tiśśa', § 19.
25. P. Wendland, *Die Hellenistisch-Römische Kultur in ihren Beziehungen zu Judentum und Christentum*, Tübingen 1912, p. 218.
26. *Midrash 'Áśeret ha-Dibberot* [Midrash of the Decalogue], Jellinek's *Bet Ha-Midrash*, Pt. I, p. 71.
27. *T.B. 'Avoda Zara* 55a: 'Rava b. R. Isaac said to R. Judah: Behold there is an idol-house in our locality, where, when the world needs rain, (the idol) appears (to the priests) in a dream, saying "Slay a man unto him [קטולו ליה גבריה, so in Munich MS.; in printed edd.: ואמר להו שחטו לי ('and he said unto them "Slaughter unto me" ')] and he will send rain." They slaughter a man unto him and he brings rain.' This recension was before R. Ḥanan'el and R. Isaac b. Samuel the Elder (Ri) [see Tosafot, *ibid.* 27b, s.v. *Shā'nê*], and the latter explained it thus: 'For sometimes the demons have the power to mislead in order to drive them (from the world).' But in the Spanish MS., ed. Abramson, p. 51a, the words מתחזי בחלמא קטולי לי גברא are missing; they are likewise wanting in the *Haggadot ha-Talmud*, in the *'En Ya'aqov* and in the *Yalquṭ*; see *Diqduqe Soferim*, p. 119 n. 9.
28. See my article 'Hilkhot 'Avoda Zara' (cited above), pp. 198 ff. Cf. now Morton Smith, 'Goodenough's Symbols in Retrospect', *JBL*, LXXXVI, 1967, pp. 53–68.
29. *De Leg.*, X, 885c; see M. P. Nilsson, *Gesch. der Griechischen Rel.*, I, Munich 1941, p. 770; cf. *ibid.*, II, p. 538, and more fully above p. 28.
30. *Tosefta Shabbat* xiii 5; ed. Lieberman, p. 58; see *Tosefta ki-Fshuṭah, loc. cit.*, p. 206.
31. See *Sifre Zuṭa*, p. 286: והנפש ['and the soul'], this means one who says, There is no Authority in heaven; נפש ונפש ['soul and soul'], this refers to one who declares that there are two Authorities in heaven'; on the polemic against the Christian dualism in the dicta of the Amoraim, see A. Marmorstein, 'The Unity of God in Rabbinic Literature', *HUCA*, I, pp. 467–499. See also my article 'Dĕrāshôt Ḥazal 'al Nĕvî'ê 'Ûmmôt hā-'Ôlām wĕ-al Pārāshat Bil'am' [Rabbinic Homilies on the Gentile Prophets and on the Pericope of Balaam], *Tarbiz*, XXV, 1956, pp. 286–287.
32. *Tosefta Shevu'ot* iii 7, ed. Zuckermandel, pp. 449–450; on the interpretation of this Baraita, see *'Arugat ha-Bośem*, Pt. I, p. 232.
33. Flavius Vopiscus, *Vita Saturnini*, viii. Regarding the authenticity of the letter,

see W. Bauer, *Rechtgläubigkeit und Ketzerei im ältesten Christentum*, Tübingen 1934, p. 51; Th. Mommsen, *Röm. Gesch.*, 1885, V, p. 485, has already pointed out: 'Not from Hadrian, but clearly from someone conversant with the facts.'

34. *Tosefta Shevu'ot* iii, 6, p. 449; *ibid.*, *Bava Meṣi'a* vi, 17, p. 385; *T.B. ibid.*, p. 71b.
35. *Sifre Deuteronomy* § 221; *T.P. Sanhedrin* vi, 9, p. 23c; in *T.B. ibid.*, p. 45b the difference has been blurred, and *kôfēr bā-Iqqār* is spoken of.
36. *Ibid.*, see Rashi, Genesis xi 9 on 'the Generation of Division' [i.e. the Tower of Babel]. 'These put forth their hand against the Root to make war against Him.' But Rashi's source is not known to me; at any rate in Rabbinic literature (*T.B. Sanhedrin* 109a; *Tanḥuma*, Noah, § 18) I have not found this expression., see however Genesis Rabba xxxviii, 7, p. 356.
37. *T.B. 'Arakhin* 15b; so, too, the Targum, *loc. cit.* With regard to the text of the Targum, see Jacob Levy, *Neuhebräisches und Chaldäisches Wörterbuch.*
38. *Midrash Tehillim*, xiv, 1, p. 112; see *Genesis Rabba* xxiv, 1, p. 229; *Yalquṭ ha-Makhiri* on Psalms, p. 79.
39. In *'Avot de-R. Nathan*, Version I, ed. Schechter, p. 66: ודע לפני מי אתה עמל ומי הוא בעל מלאכתך ['And know before whom you labour and who is the master of your work'].
40. *Midrash Tehillim*, i, 21; see ed. Buber, p. 22, and the notes *ibid.*
41. *Antiquities*, x, 278: ἄμοιρον δὲ ἡνιόχου καὶ ἀφρόντιστον τὸν κόσμον αὐτομάτως φέρεσθαι λέγουσιν. See M. Stein, *Dat wa-Da'at* [Religion and Science], 1938, p. 46; S. Lieberman, 'How Much Greek in Jewish Palestine?', *Philip W. Lown Institute of Advanced Judaic Studies*, Brandeis University, I, p. 130.
42. *Antiquities*, i, 156; we have already observed Josephus' use of ἡνίοχος, 'one who governs'.
43. *Quis Rer. Div. Heres*, 91–94; see C. H. Dodd, *The Bible and the Greeks*, London 1935, p. 67.
44. *De Praemiis* 26–27. Cf. *De Migr. Abrah.*, 43–54; C. Siegfried, *Philo von Alexandria*, Jena 1875, p. 307; Dodd, *op. cit.*, p. 199.
45. See Schürer, *Geschichte des jüd. Volkes im Zeitalter Jesu*, 1901, Pt. III, p. 174.
46. καὶ ἡμεῖς εἰς χριστὸν Ἰησοῦν ἐπιστεύσαμεν. 'Even we have believed in Jesus Christ' (Galat. ii 16); cf. R. Bultmann, *Theologie des N.T.*, 1953, pp. 89–90.
47. The date of its composition is not certain. See A. Harnack, *Die Chronologie der altchristlichen literature*, I, pp. 485 ff; Eduard Meyer, *Ursprung u. Anfänge des Christentums*, 1923, III, p. 227, n. 2.
48. Romans xii 3; the μέτρον πίστευς corresponds to *middat ha-ḥesed* ['attribute of grace']. See Bultmann, *op. cit.*, pp. 310–326.
49. Bousset, *op. cit.*, p. 195.
50. xlii 2; this work, too, has been preserved only in a Syriac translation made from the Greek.
51. *T.B. Beṣa* 15b. See also R. J. Z. Werblowsky, 'Faith, Hope and Trust, A Study in the Concept of Bittahon', *Papers of the Institute of Jewish Studies*, London 1964, pp. 104–118.

52. *T.B. Soṭa* 48b; in the *Mekhilta de-R. Ishmael*, Wa-yissaʿ, xii, p. 161, the dictum is cited in the name of R. Eleazar of Modiʿin, but, in a number of recensions, it is reported in the name of R. Eliezer; see the vv.ll. *ibid.*

53. See *T.B. Taʿanit* 8a: 'R. Ammi said: Come and see how great are the men of faith. Whence (is this to be inferred)? From the weasel and the well. Now if this is the case in respect of one who trusts in the weasel and well, how much more so does this apply to one who has faith in the Holy One, blessed be He!' Here the expression is used in the sense of 'making Him a Witness between himself and his neighbour'; see Rashi, *ibid.* Cf. *T.B. Tamid* 28a: 'Let him practise scrupulous faithfulness', which is explained by the Commentary *ad loc.*: 'Let him transact his business with people honestly and not cheat his fellow men.'

54. ' "The testimony of the Lord is faithful" — this refers to the Order Zeraʿim, for he believes in the Life of the world and sows' — *Yalquṭ Shimʿoni*, Psalms, § 675; Tosafot, *T.B. Shabbat* 31a, s.v. *'Emūnat*, in the name of the Palestinian Talmud, which is not, however, found in our text, but may have been known to the Early Authorities; see Ratner, *'Ahăvat Ṣiyyôn wî-Yerûshalayim* [Love of Zion and Jerusalem], Berakhot, p. 131. Cf. p. 484, note 85.

CHAPTER III

THE SHEKHINA — THE PRESENCE OF GOD IN THE WORLD

1. In *Exodus Rabba* iii 6, before the dictum of R. Abba, it is stated: 'At that moment Moses asked the Holy One, blessed be He, to reveal to him the Great Name'; see also *Tanḥuma*, Shemot, §20. On the divine name concealed in Egyptian mythology, see E. A. T. Wallis Budge, *Egyptian Magic*, London 1899, pp. 157–181; reprinted edition: University Books, Evanston [Ill.], [1958]; Erman-Ranke, *Ägypten*, 1923, pp. 301 ff. Additional examples are to be found in B. Jacob, *op. cit.*, pp. 87–89; and cf. above, p. 124.
2. Seventy names of God are mentioned in *Aggadat Shir ha-Shirim*, p. 9, and in *Deuteronomy Rabba* xiv, §12; most of them, however, are not names but epithets, and just those designations with which we are concerned are omitted! A. Geiger's view (*Jüd. Zeitschrift f. Wissen. u. Leben*, Pt. xi, p. 228) that these Names were used only as a substitute in order to avoid mentioning the Tetragrammaton cannot be accepted. See *T.B. Soṭa* 42b 'for the Name and all His epithets lie in the ark'; in *T.B. Bava Batra* 14b, the dictum is quoted in the name of 'R. Joḥanan in the name of R. Simeon b. Yoḥai'.
3. See Yeḥezkel Kaufmann, *Tôlĕdôt hā-'Emūnā ha-Yisrā'ēlît* [History of the Religion of Israel], I, Book ii, pp. 226 ff.
4. *Mekhilta de-R. Ishmael*, Ba-ḥodesh, V, p. 219 and references *ibid.*
5. See G. Scholem, *Zur Kabbala und ihrer Symbolik*, Zürich 1960, p. 119.
6. On the development of the *pneuma* in the various stages of the Stoic system, see M. Pohlenz, *Die Stoa*, Göttingen 1948, p. 368 *et al.*, according to the Index.
7. *Quod Deus Immutabilis Sit*, 62.
8. In his essay 'Kabbalistische Konzeption der Schechinah', *Eranos-Jahrbuch*, 1953.
9. This expression corresponds in certain sources to 'beneath the wings of Heaven' — *Tosefta Horayot* ii, 7; *Mekhilta de-R. Simeon b. Yoḥai*, Be-shallaḥ, p. 126.
10. *'Ĕmûnôt wĕ-Dē'ôt* [Beliefs and Opinions], II, p. 51, ed. Slucki, Leipzig 1864.
11. *Môre Nĕvûkhîm* [Guide of the Perplexed], Pt. I, ch. LXIV; see *ibid.*, LXVI.

CHAPTER III

12. See 'Intermediaries in Jewish Theology — Memra, Shekinah, Metatron', *HTR*, 1922, pp. 41–85; cf. idem, *Judaism*, I, p. 432.
13. *The Immanence of God in Rabbinical Literature*, London 1912.
14. In the Palestinian Targum, *ad loc.*, 'and the glory of the Shekhina of the Lord passed by'; see *ibid.*, xxxiii 23.
15. *T.B. Qiddushin* 49a; see also Tosafot, *ibid.*, s.v. *Ha-mĕtargēm* [He who translates], and *Otzar ha-Geonim* [Thesaurus of the Gaonic Responsa and Commentaries], 'Liqqûṭê Pērush R. Ḥananel', p. 34: 'R. Ḥananel explained "He who translates a verse literally" to mean that if, for example, one translated "And they saw the God of Israel" verbatim one is a liar, because they did not actually see the Shekhina (in Albarceloni's commentary on the *Sēfer Yĕṣîrā* [Book of Creation] the text reads: "for the Creator is invisible"), for it is written "for man shall not see Me and live"; and he who adds thereto, saying "and they saw the angel of God", is a blasphemer, for he accords to an angel the praise due to the Omnipresent. But this is how the verse should be rendered: "And they saw the glory of the God of Israel".' But in a late Midrash, *Midrash ha-Gadol* to Exodus, p. 555, it is stated: 'If he translated, "And they saw the glory of the Shekhina of the God of Israel", he is a blasphemer and libeller, for he names three deities here — Glory and Shekhina and God.' This rendering was regarded as pointing to the Trinity. See A. M. Goldberg, 'Die spezifische Verwendung des Terminus Schekhina in Targum Onkelos als Kriterium einer relativen Datierung', *Judaica*, XIX, 1963, pp. 43–61.
16. *M. 'Avot* iii, 2; this is the reading in the Kaufmann MS. See also *Māgēn 'Āvôt* of Simeon b. Ṣemah Duran, p. 41a; *Tôsĕfôt Yôm Ṭôv* and *Mĕle'khet Shĕlōmō* on this Mishna, and C. Taylor, *Sayings of the Jewish Fathers*, Cambridge 1877, p. 14.
17. *Ibid.* iii, 6; cf. the references given in the preceding note. R. Ḥalafta's thought is transmitted in *T.B. Sanhedrin* 39b in the name of R. Gamaliel; see above, p. 47. In *M. Sanhedrin* vi, 5, where the printed editions read 'When a man is suffering, how does the Shekhina express herself?...', the word Shekhina is missing in the old recensions; see J. N. Epstein, *Māvô' lĕ-nōsaḥ ha-Mishnā*, p. 87. In keeping with this dictum, the Targum translates Psalms lxxxii 1: 'God's Shekhina abides in the assembly of the righteous who are strong in the Law'; see also *T.B. Berakhot* 6a, and *Diqdûqê Sôfĕrîm, ibid.* 40a.
18. *Mekhilta de-R. Ishmael*, Massekhta da-Amalek, Jethro, i, p. 193: 'The Shekhina went forth with them'; *ibid.*, Ba-ḥodesh, iii, p. 213: 'The Shekhina departed'; see also *Tosefta Yoma* i, 12. *Sifra*, Mekhilta de-Millu'im, Shemini, p. 44c: 'And the Shekhina rested... the Shekhina descended'; *Tosefta Menaḥot* vii, p. 522; *Sifre Numbers* §143, p. 110.
19. *Sifre Numbers*, § 80, p. 78; *ibid.* § 84, p. 80.
20. *Mekhilta de-R. Ishmael*, Massekhta de-Pisḥa, xiv, pp. 51–52; see also *ibid.*, Massekhta de-Shira, iii, pp. 127–128; *Mekhilta de-R. Simeon b. Yoḥai*, p. 79.
21. *Sifre Numbers*, § 94, p. 94; § 106, p. 105; *Sifre Zuṭa*, p. 278; and *ibid.* p. 289: 'Just as it is impossible for any created being to hurt My Shekhina, so is it

impossible, when you are holy, for any created being to hurt you.'

22. *Sifre Numbers*, § 161, pp. 221–222; *Sifre Deuteronomy*, § 148, p. 203; § 254, p. 280; § 258, p. 282.
23. *Sifra*, Qedoshim, iv, 89a; *ibid.* viii, 91a; *T.B. Sanhedrin* 7a.
24. *Mekhilta de-R. Ishmael*, Massekhta de-Ba-ḥodesh, vi, p. 238; see also Massekhta di-Neziqin, x, p. 282.
25. This is the MS. reading; see the vv.ll. in *Sifre Deuteronomy*, § 173, p. 220. Cf. *T.B. Sanhedrin* 65b, and above p. 56.
26. See the Baraita, *T.B. Shabbat* 12b and *T.B. Nedarim* 40a, 'For the Shekhina rests above the bed of a sick person'; but the Amoraim phrase the passage: 'Whence do we know that the Holy One, blessed be He, nourishes the sick?...'; cf. *Diqdûqê Sôfĕrîm* on *Tractate Shabbat*, p. 19, n. 8.
27. *Pesiqta de-Rav Kahana, Wa-yĕhî bĕ-yôm kallōt Mōshe*, ed. Mandelbaum, p. 4; but in *Canticles Rab.* iii, 9, the dictum is reported in the name of R. Joshua b. Qorḥa.
28. See A. Landau, *Die dem Raume entnommenen Synonima für Gott in der neuhebräischen Literatur*, Zürich 1888, p. 47 ff; A. Marmorstein, *The Old Rabbinic Doctrine of God*, London 1927, p. 103.
29. See Abelson, *op. cit.*, p. 83. In *Sifre Zuṭa*, p. 247, it is stated: 'And how do we know that the Shekhina, too, will be in their midst? Therefore, the text teaches us, "The Lord make His face to shine upon thee" — also the Shekhina shall be in their midst.' With regard to the continuation of the exposition, ' "The Lord make His face to shine" — He will shield thee from the brightness of the Shekhina', see the next note.
30. *Deuteronomy Rabba* xi, 3, and *Leviticus Rabba* xxxi, 9, p. 729: 'Rav said: When the disk of the sun and of the moon enter to receive permission from the Holy One, blessed be He, their eyes grow dim from the brightness of the Shekhina, and when they seek to go forth to illumine the world, they cannot see anything....'
31. *Op. cit.*, pp. 85 ff. He does not differentiate between the sources and includes among them the views of Naḥmanides.
32. *Numbers Rabba* xv, 6; *Leviticus Rabba* xxxi, 8, p. 727.
33. *Tanḥuma*, II, Bĕ-ha'ălōtĕkhā, § 7; *Midrash Tehillim* xxii, 11.
34. The Temple Lamp was only 'a witness to all the world that the Shekhina abode in Israel', *T.B. Menaḥot* 86b; see also Philo, *Quaest. in Ex.*, II, § 47; cf. F. N. Klein, *Die Licht-Terminologie bei Philon von Alex. und die Hermet. Schriften*, 1962, p. 67.
35. See Sverre Aalen, *Die Begriffe Licht und Finsternis im A.T. und im Spätjudentum im Rabbinismus*, Oslo 1951, p. 195 and p. 314. On the question of the creation of light, see p. 192.
36. Massekhta Amalek, Be-shallaḥ, ii, pp. 185–186; *Mekhilta de-R. Simeon b. Yoḥai*, ed. Epstein-Melamed, p. 126, 'beneath the wings of Heaven'.
37. *Op. cit.*, pp. 90–91.
38. And Targum *ibid.* 'beneath the shadow of the Shekhina of His glory'.

39. *Tosefta Horayot*, ii, 7: 'Whoever introduces a single person beneath the wings of Heaven is deemed to have created him', etc. A similar v.l. to that mentioned in note 36 is found in *Pesiqta Rabbati*; while in ed. M. Friedmann 14a, it is stated: 'Since he came to Mount Carmel to bring Israel beneath the wings of the Shekhina'. The reading of the Parma MS. 1240 is: 'under the wings of Heaven'.
40. *T.B. Sanhedrin* 39a.
41. *Tanḥuma*, Nāśo', 12: 'Primarily the Shekhina dwells among the inhabitants of the earth'; *Pesiqta de-Rav Kahana* i, 1a; ed. Mandelbaum, p. 2; see also *Tanḥuma*, Têrûmā, 9.
42. *T.B. Sukka* 5a, and *Mekhilta de-R. Ishmael*, Ba-ḥodesh, iv, p. 217: 'R. Jose said: Scripture declares "The heavens are the heavens of the Lord; but the earth hath He given to the children of men" — Moses and Elijah never ascended to heaven, nor did the Glory descend to earth; the verse only teaches us that the Omnipresent said to Moses "Lo, I shall call you from the top of the mountain and you shall ascend...." '
43. *T.B. Sukka, ibid.* and *T.P., ibid.* i, p. 51d: 'Whence do we know that above ten (handbreadths) there is another domain? R. Abbahu said in the name of R. Simeon b. Laqish: "And there I will meet with thee, and I will speak with thee from above the ark-cover", and it is written, "Ye yourselves have seen that I have talked with you from heaven" — just as the subsequent utterance came from a different domain, so the utterance mentioned here came from a different domain.' See also 'Ha-Kotev' in *'En Ya'aqov*: 'The descent is not actually to our domain, but to one higher than ours, which is, however, near to our own.' An allusion to a solution of this nature apparently occurs in the passage from the *Mekhilta* cited above, in the dictum preceding that of R. Jose: '...this teaches us that the Holy One, blessed be He, bent the lower heavens and the upper heavens of heavens over the top of the mountain, and the Divine Glory descended and was spread on the summit of Mount Sinai, like a man who spreads the mattress on top of the bed and like a man who speaks from above the mattress.'
44. *Gen. Rabba*, lxviii, 8, p. 777; on the epithet 'Omnipresent' [*Māqôm*], see above p. 68; the connection between R. Jose's two sayings have been pointed out by W. Bacher, *Die Agada der Tannaiten*, Pt. II, p. 185.
45. It is noteworthy that about two centuries later, Jerome cited, in his commentary on Isaiah lvii 9, the dictum of R. Jose as 'the view of the Jews'.
46. *Pesiqta de-Rav Kahana*, Ki tiśśā', ed. Mandelbaum, p. 73; see also *Exod. Rabba* xxxiv, 1.
47. *Lev. Rabba* xxix, 4, p. 673, where parallels are given; cf. the vv.ll. *ibid.*, note 2 and note 5. *Midrash Shir ha-Shirim*, ed. Grünhut, p. 15b, *Num. Rabba* xii, 8.
48. The term *ṣimṣûm ha-Shĕkhînā* ['confinement of the Shekhina'], as used by the Sages has nothing in common with the doctrine of *ṣimṣûm* expounded by R. Isaac b. Solomon Ashkenazi Luria (ARI); and G. Scholem, *Major Trends in Jewish Mysticism*, Jerusalem 1941, p. 257.

49. *Lev. Rabba, loc. cit.*; see *ibid.* S. Lieberman's note, p. 879, and *Pesiqta de-Rav Kahana*, ed. Mandelbaum, p. 337.
50. See above, p. 35; cf. also *Pesiqta Rabbati*, p. 19a.
51. *Pesiqta de-Rav Kahana*, Wa-yehi be-yom kallot Moshe, ed. Mandelbaum, p. 4, where parallel passages are cited; *Exod. Rabba* ii, 5, in the name of Joshua b. Qorḥa, with the addition 'not even a thornbush'; cf. also *Midrash ha-Gadol* to Exodus, ed. Margulies, p. 45.
52. *T.B. Soṭa* 5a. These are the words of Rav Joseph, which are based on the dicta of R. Eleazar and of 'Rav Ḥisda, and some say, Mar ʿUqba', *ibid.*
53. The observation was made by Sallustius, the friend of Julian the Apostate, in his work *Concerning the Gods and the Universe*, edited with Prolegomena and Translation by A. D. Nock, Cambridge 1926, XV, p. 28; see also G. Murray, *Five Stages of Greek Religion*, The Thinker's Library, London 1935, p. 218; on the author see *ibid.*, pp. 179 ff.
54. See above, p. 34, and *Seder Eliahu Rabba* xviii, p. 104.
55. In *Tanḥuma*, Naśo', § 16 and in *Pesiqta Rabbati*, p. 18b; *Num. Rabba* xii, 5, the reading is 'Rav'; but in the MS. of the *Tanḥuma* it is 'Rabbi'. See *Tanḥuma*, ed. Buber, Naśo', § 24 and *ibid.* note 121. This point escaped the attention of A. Marmorstein, *The Old Rabbinic Doctrine of God*, II, 1927, p. 84, note 219.
56. *Gen. Rabba* xix, 7, p. 176; see *ibid.* the vv.ll. and note 4.
57. *Ibid.*; I have cited the full text found in *Num. Rabba* xiii, 2.
58. *Pesiqta de-Rav Kahana* § i, ed. Mandelbaum, p. 3. In MS. ק the reading is: 'R. Eleazar b. R. Judah', who is identical with R. Eleazar b. Judah of Bartota; but in *Num. Rabba* xii, 4, we have 'R. Judah bar Il'ai'. In *Tanḥuma*, Be-midbar, § 3 and in *Num. Rabba* i, 3, we find a somewhat similar, anonymous homily concerning Moses: 'When the Tabernacle was erected, He (God) said: Modesty is a good thing, as it is said "and walk modestly with Thy God"; He thereupon began to speak with him in the Tent of Meeting.'
59. The expression is not very common. In the Mishna it occurs only once, *Maʿaser Sheni* v, 12; in the Tosefta twice — *Sanhedrin* iv, 5, *Menaḥot* vii, 8; in the *Mekhilta*, four times. See Benjamin Kosovsky, *Oṣar Leshon ha-Tanna'im* [Concordantiae Verborum quae in Sifra aut Torat Kohanim reperiuntur], I, Jerusalem 1965, p. 302; cf. also *Sifre Deuteronomy*, §§ 62, 70, 352. It likewise appears a few times in the Babylonian Talmud; see Rabbi H. J. Kosovsky, *Oṣar Leshon ha-Talmud* [Thesaurus Talmudis], vii, p. 385.
60. *Mekhilta de-R. Ishmael*, Massekhta de-Pisḥa, i, p. 3.
61. See *ibid.*, p. 2: 'Until Eretz Israel was chosen, all lands were fit for Divine communications. When Eretz Israel was chosen, all the (other) countries were excluded.' Abelson, *op. cit.* differentiates, without justifiable grounds, between God and the Shekhina in this saying.
62. *Mekhilta de-R. Ishmael*, Massekhta de-Pisḥa, xii, pp. 51–52; *Sifre Numbers*, § 84, p. 82; *ibid.*, p. 83, note 7; in *T.B. Megilla* 29a in the name of R. Simeon b. Yoḥai; in *Sifre Numbers*, § 161, p. 222, *Num. Rabba* vii, in the name of R. Nathan; *ibid.* there is added 'when they are dispersed, the Shekhina is

with them'; 'He hinted to them that, wherever they would be exiled, the Shekhina would be with them'.

63. *'Avot de-R. Nathan*, Version 1, xxxiv, p. 102; *Pesiqta de-Rav Kahana*, Divrê Yirmĕyāhû, ed. Mandelbaum, p. 234; *T.B. Rosh ha-Shana* 31a; *Aggadat Shir ha-Shirim* v, 6, ed. Schechter, p. 39. See also *Yalquṭ Makhiri*, Psalms, ed. Buber, p. 200; according to the corrected text there, the withdrawal of the Shekhina began in the time of Isaiah: 'When Menasseh set up the image in the Temple, the Shekhina departed from the first cherub to the second.'
64. *Pesiqta de-Rav Kahana*, *loc. cit.*; so, too, *Lam. Rabba*, proem § 25, ed. Buber 15b.
65. *T.B. Rosh ha-Shana*, *loc. cit.*, and also *Aggadat Shir ha-Shirim*, *loc. cit.*: 'From the Mountain of Olives to the wilderness... from the wilderness to heaven'. The conclusion there is: 'Behold, Israel seeks the Shekhina, but it will not return until the End arrives.'
66. See *Diqduqe Soferim*, Rosh ha-Shana, 31a.
67. *Lam. Rabba*, proem § 29, ed. Buber, p. 16a.
68. *Ibid.*, proem § 24, p. 13a; see also *ibid.*, proem § 25, p. 15b.
69. See above, note 62.
70. Baraita, *T.B. Yoma* 56b: 'Who dwells with them in the midst of their defilements; even when they are unclean the Shekhina is with them'; *ibid.* 57a, R. Ḥanina gives this answer to a sectarian. *Exod. Rabba* xv, 5: 'R. Simeon (see the *Novellae of R. David Luria* (RaDaL) § 8, who cites the reading of R. Beḥai [Baḥya]: 'R. Simeon b. Laqish') said: 'Great is the love in which Israel is held [by God], for the Holy One, blessed be He, revealed Himself in a place of idolatry, of impurity, and of defilement, in order to redeem them.'
71. See above, p. 43, note 25.
72. *T.B. Sanhedrin* 65b.
73. *Exod. Rabba* ii, 2, and the continuation there: 'So, too, is the Holy One, blessed be He; although He appears to have withdrawn His Shekhina from the Temple, His eyes behold, his eyelids scrutinize, the children of men'.
74. *Tanḥuma*, ed. Buber, Shemot, and *Midrash Tehillim* xi, 3. On the relationship between R. Samuel b. Naḥman and R. Eleazar b. Pedat, see Isaak Halevy, *Dorot Harischonim*, Pt. II, p. 340; W. Bacher, *Die Agada der Pal. Amoräer*, vol. I, p. 479, note 1.
75. *Tanḥuma*, *loc. cit.*; *Exod. Rabba*, *loc. cit.*; *Midrash Tehillim*, *loc. cit.*
76. *Cant. Rabba* ii, 9; see also *Pesiqta de-Rav Kahana*, Ha-ḥodesh, ed. Mandelbaum, p. 92.
77. *M. 'Eduyot* viii, 6; see *T.B. Megilla* 10a, and *ibid. Tosafot* s.v. *Dĕ-khullê 'ālmā* [All agree]; *T.B. Shevuot* 16a; *T.B. Zevaḥim* 107b; cf. also Maimonides, *Code*, 'Laws concerning the Temple', vi, 16, who adds the reason: 'And why do I say that in the case of the Temple and Jerusalem the first sanctity availed also for the future, whereas the sanctity of the rest of the Land of Israel, in regard to the Sabbatical Year, the tithes, and the like did not

apply to the future? Because the sanctity of the Temple and Jerusalem is due to the Shekhina, and the Shekhina has never been nullified.'

78. See Y. Kaufmann, *Tôlĕdôt ha-'Ĕmûnā ha-Yisrĕ'ēlît*, II, p. 500.
79. *T.P. Berakhot* iv, 5, p. 8b–c; see also L. Ginzberg, *Pērûshîm wĕ-Ḥiddûshîm bi-Yĕrûshalmî* [Comments and Novellae on the Palestinian Talmud], Pt. III, p. 378; the expression 'turn their faces' occurs also in *Sifre Deuteronomy* § 29.
80. *Tosefta Berakhot* iii, 15; *T.B. ibid.*, 30a; *Pesiqta Rabbati* 149b; see also S. Lieberman, *Tosefta ki-Fshuṭah*, Pt. I, p. 44.
81. *T.P. loc. cit.* above, note 79; on the heavenly Temple, see A. Aptowitzer, *Tarbiz*, II (1931), pp. 137–153; pp. 257–287. See also p. 146, note 1, and on p. 260 the citation, from *Midrash Shoḥer Ṭov* (MS.), *Bātê Midrāshôt*, Pt. IV, p. 32, of the dictum of the same R. Phinehas in the name of R. Simeon b. Laqish: 'Phinehas is identical with Elijah, may he be remembered for good and for blessing, for were it not for him we could not have lived in wicked Edom. That is the meaning of the saying of our teachers: "From the time when the Temple was destroyed, he offers up two perpetual offerings each day to make atonement for Israel."' Cf. *ibid.* note 6.
82. On the vv.ll. *'ha-shĕ-'ûvā, ha-shûvā, shĕ'ûvă, ḥāshûvā'*, see J. N. Epstein, *Mavo' le-Nosaḥ ha-Mishna*, pp. 320 ff; *ibid.*, p. 322, note 4, he rejects the conjectures of Geiger, Schorr, and Krochmal (see also S. Lieberman, *Kirjath Sepher*, XII, p. 56) regarding the connection with the Syriac 'שובתא' (the meaning 'torch' ascribed to it is, incidentally, doubtful).
83. *De Vita Contemplativa*, 3, 27. About a thousand years after Ezekiel and hundreds of years after the Mishna and Philo, Pope Leo preached against Christians who, before entering the church of St. Peter in Rome, were accustomed to turn round and bow their heads to the rising sun. He declared that undoubtedly some of them thought more about the Creator of the light, whom it was their wish to honour, than about the light itself. But he that would take heed of his soul should avoid the slightest suspicion of such worship. See Migne, *In Nativitate Domine*, PL 54, pp. 218–219; cf. F. J. Dölger, *Sol Salutis*, Münster, 1925, pp. 3 ff.
84. On the relationship between *rā'ā 'ôr* and *ra'a pĕnê* in the Bible, see J. L. Seeligmann, ΔΕΙΞΑΙ ΑΥΤΩΙ ΦΩΣ, *Tarbiz*, XXVIi, 1958, p. 130.
85. See Dölger, *op. cit.*, pp. 20 ff and pp. 38 ff.
86. See S. Talmon, *Ḥeshbôn ha-Lûaḥ shel Kat Midbar Yĕhûdā — Meḥqārîm bi-Mĕgillôt ha-Gĕnûzôt* [The Calendar Reckoning of the Qumran Sect], Jerusalem 1961, pp. 77 ff.
87. 'Haer.', XIX, 3, 5, ed. I. K. Holl, p. 200, in *Die Griechischen Christlichen Schriftsteller der ersten drei Jahrhunderte*, Leipzig 1915. Dölger, *op. cit.*, p. 197, wished to infer from Elchasai's statement that in his time already there were Christians who claimed the east to be the sole direction for prayer, but this seems unlikely. See also E. Peterson, *Frühkirche, Judentum und Gnosis*, Freiburg 1959, p. 6, note 28. Peterson, who criticizes Dölger for not knowing how to distinguish between Mishna and Tosefta, is himself unaware of the

difference in date between the Baraitot and that of the compilation of the Tosefta, and there is clearly no basis for his observations *ibid.*, p. 4, note 22. Peterson, who attempts to find an allusion to Christian 'Cabbala' in the words of the Gemara, *T.B. Sanhedrin* 107b (see *Diqduqe Soferim*, p. 339), 'He went and set up a brick and prostrated him to the Lord', writes, *op. cit.*, p. 14, note 63: 'It should be noted that the date given in the *Talmud Sanhedrin* for the origin of the Christian tradition (R. Joshua b. Peraḥiah lived a century after Jesus!) excellently fits the date discovered by us (130–150).' On the preceding page he refers to H. L. Strack's *Einleitung in Talmud und Midrasch*, Munich 1921, p. 117, but there it is stated that the story is anachronistic, because Jesus lived a hundred years after Joshua b. Peraḥiah. On the passage in the Gemara cited above from *T.B. Sanhedrin*, see H. J. Zimmels, 'Jesus and "putting up a brick"', *JQR*, NS, XLIII, 1953, pp. 225 ff.

88. See G. Alon, *Tôlĕdôt ha-Yĕhûdîm bĕ-'Ereṣ Yisrā'ēl bi-Tĕqûfat ha-Mishnā wĕ-ha-Talmûd* [History of the Jews in Eretz-Israel in the period of the Mishna and Talmud], I, p. 189.
89. *Adversus Haer.*, I, 22.
90. Clemens Alex., *Paedagog*, II, 8, 61, 62–63. Ed. Stählin, I, p. 194 in the series *GCS*. In the work ascribed to Athanasius (see O. Bardenhewer, *Patrologia*, Freiburg 1894, p. 236), Migne, *Quaestiones ad Antiochum ducem*, PG, 28, p. 617, the question is asked: 'Why do we Christians pray towards the east and why do the Jews (pray) towards the west?' An answer based on the exposition cited above is given in respect to the Jews; other answers are advanced in regard to the pagans and the Christians.
91. *T.B. Bava Batra* 25a; needless to say, no inference is to be drawn from the Gemara's explanation 'It is the constant abode of the Shekhina' with regard to R. Akiba's view.
92. *Tosefta Shabbat*, xiii (xiv), 5; on the text, see *Tosefta ki-Fshuṭah*, *ibid.*
93. Tertullian, *Ad Nationes*, I, 13; *Apologeticum*, 16, 9–11; see Dölger, *op. cit.*, pp. 136 ff.
94. F. Funk, *Didascalia et Constitutiones Apostolorum*, Paderborn 1905 (Torino 1962), I, pp. 160–162; *ibid.*, p. 165; see Dölger, *op. cit.*, p. 172. Peterson, *op. cit.*, p. 7, is right in stating that the Messianic argumentation underlying Christian mysticism comprised a dialogue with the Jews, since the Jewish prayer-orientation towards the Sanctuary in Jerusalem was accompanied, after the destruction of the Temple, by Messianic hopes. See above, p. 57.
95. *T.B. Bava Batra, loc. cit.*; Rav Hosha'ya, on the other hand, holds the view of R. Ishmael.
96. R. Abbahu, *ibid.*, and he adds an intimation: 'What does *'ûryā* mean? — *'ăwîr Yāh* ['the air of God'].' See Rashi's commentary *ibid.*, and the interpretation that he heard 'So is the west called in Persian'; cf. also the commentary of R. Zechariah Aghmati to the three *Bavot*, ed. J. Leveen, London 1961: 'R. Sherira Gaon explained that it was so in Persian... and the western side (is called) *'ôdît*, and therefore, he says to you: It is stated here *'ôdît hôdāyā*,

i.e., in the west, there I shall give thanks to the Lord ['*ôde Yāh*]'; and in the name of R. Ḥananel: 'He explained that in Persian the west is named '*ôrît*'. B. Geiger, in *Additamenta ad librum Aruch Completum*, p. 13, questions all the interpretations based on Persian.

97. *Tosefta Megilla* iv (iii), 22; see S. Lieberman, *Tosefta ki-Fshuṭah*, p. 1200.

98. See S. Krauss, *Synagogale Altertümer*, Vienna 1922, pp. 327 ff, but his view is entirely ill-founded; cf. Elbogen, *Der Jüdische Gottesdienst*², Frankfort-on-Main 1924, p. 460 and p. 573; also E. L. Sukenik, *Ancient Synagogues in Palestine and Greece*, London 1934; idem, *Bêt ha-Kĕnesset shel Dura-Europos wĕ-Ṣiyyûrāw* [The Synagogue of Dura-Europos and its paintings], Jerusalem 1947, p. 46.

99. In Rashi, according to the current recension, 'Minim, i.e. the disciples of idolaters'; but the Venice ed. reads 'disciples of Jesus'; this is also the reading in '*Aggadot ha-Talmud* and in '*En Ya'aqov*. In Soncino-Pisaro ed., however, the reading is: 'The Minim taught this, i.e. they ruled that one should pray to the east.' Ginzberg's argument, in *Perushim we-Ḥiddushim bi-Yerushalmi*, Pt. III, p. 375, that the number of Christians in Babylonia was small, is invalid. The number does not affect the issue in this case. Rav Sheshet wished to avoid the impression that the Jews and the Minim have a common orientation in prayer; on the clashes between Rav Sheshet and the Minim, see *T.B. Berakhot* 58a. W. Bacher, *Die Agada der bab. Amoräer*², Frankfort-on-Main 1913, p. 78, n. 12, wishes to identify the Minim with the Manichaeans, but the sect of Mani did not have a fixed orientation towards the east; they faced, when praying, towards the sun, according to its position at the time of day. See Dölger, *op. cit.*, p. 28.

1. In the vv.ll. of the *M. Sanhedrin* vi, 5, in which the word Shekhina is missing, the word *ki-vĕ-yākhōl* is also wanting. See above, p. 42, n. 16; cf. above, the saying of R. Akiba, p. 54, and p. 705 note 62. W. Bacher already noted in *Die exegetische Terminologie der jüd. Traditionsliteratur*, I, 1899, p. 72, n. 5, against Brüll, in Kobak's *Jeshurun*, vii, pp. 1–5, that it was not R. Akiba who originated the expression, but that it was already ascribed to R. Joḥanan b. Zakkai. Marmorstein, *op. cit.*, p. 127, repeats this statement without mentioning Bacher, although all the material was cited by the latter, *op. cit.*, II, 1905, p. 78. Marmorstein's explanation, *loc. cit.*, p. 131, that *ki-vĕ-yākhōl* is an abbreviation of *Kĕ-yōṣē' Ba-dāvār Yēsh Kōaḥ Wĕ-'efshār Lômar* ['similarly, it is feasible and possible to say'] is not better than that of the author of *Hălikhôt 'Ōlām* [Ways of the World], who is laughed at by Elijah Baḥur; see Marmorstein, *ibid.*, p. 126. The correct interpretation is that given by W. Bacher (*Die exegetische Terminologie der jüd. Traditionaliteratur, I, Tannaiten*, 1899), following Rashi, *T.B. Yoma* 3b, s.v. *Ki-vĕ-yākhōl*: 'as though it were of one of whom you could say this'.

2. In the article cited above, pp. 58–59.

3. Who have no share in the world to come, *T.B. Sanhedrin* 90a.

4. This reading is confirmed by *Yalquṭ Makhiri*, ed. Grünhut 34b; in all the

parallel sources of this Haggada the word 'Shekhina' is wanting. In *T.B. Sanhedrin* 104b the reading is: 'An apparition of his father came... a fire issued from heaven and licked their benches, but they disregarded (it); (then) a Heavenly Voice called out to them, "Seest thou..."' Cf. *Cant. Rabba* i, 1; *Tanḥuma,* Mĕṣōrā', i; *Pesiqta Rabbati* 23b.

5. In his work 'Kĕtāv Tāmîm', '*Oṣar Neḥmād*, Pt. III, p. 63. The quotation from *Pesiqta ha-Gedola* differs from the present text of *Pesiqta Rabbati*; see above, note 102, which accords with the recension of *Canticles Rabba.*
6. '*Emunot we-De'ot*, 42, ed. Slucki, p. 51.
7. See Yitzḥak Heinemann, *Darkhe ha-Aggada*[2], Jerusalem 1954, pp. 131 ff.
8. *Lev. Rabba* vi, 1, p. 127. See also *Deut. Rabba* iv, 2: 'The Holy One, blessed be He, said: I have written of My glory "I will be with him in trouble"'; here 'My glory' means 'Myself'.
9. *Bereshit Rabbati*, ed. H. Albeck, p. 27.
10. See above, pp. 32–34; Scholem, *op. cit.*, p. 62, note 32, has already pointed out that even in R. Moses ha-Darshan's source in Midrash '*Otiyyôt de-R. Akiba* [Midrash of the Letters of R. Akiba] (*Bate Midrashot*, New Edition, II, 1949, p. 351) it is only stated 'I removed My Shekhina from among them'.
11. See Scholem, *op. cit.*, p. 48 and pp. 68 ff.

CHAPTER IV

NEARNESS AND DISTANCE — OMNIPRESENT AND HEAVEN

1. *Sifre Numbers* § 22, p. 20; *T.P. Nedarim*, i, 1, p. 36d; *T.P. Nazir* i, 6, p. 51c. Only in *T.B. Nedarim* 9b and *T.B. Nazir* 4b the reading is 'May those who assume Naziriteship like you multiply in Israel'; see below, note 21.
2. *M. Soṭa* v, 5; see A. Marmorstein, *The Old Rabbinic Doctrine of God*, I, London 1927, p. 92, and cf. *ibid.* note 36; but *ibid.* p. 109 we find only, 'Simon b. Sheṭaḥ'. The statement of Bousset-Gressmann, *op. cit.*, p. 316, that no trace of the epithet 'Omnipresent' is to be found until the first century C.E. is without foundation.
3. This has already been discussed by A. Spanier in his article 'Die Gottesbezeichnungen *Ha-Māqôm* und *Ha-Qādôsh Bārûkh Hû* in der frühtalmudischen Literatur', *MGWJ*, 1922, p. 309, and more fully by Marmorstein, *op. cit.*, pp. 108 ff. Because of his desire to multiply the testimonies to the fundamental difference between the period of the Tannaim and that of the Amoraim in regard to the use of the names 'Omnipresent' and 'the Holy One, blessed be He', Marmorstein was inclined to force the meaning of the texts by assuming interpolations, additions, and the like. Saul Esh in his dissertation *Der Heilige* (הק(ב״ה, Leiden 1957, is right in his arguments, in this respect, against Marmorstein — see *ibid.*, p. 14, note 2; p. 19, note 10 — but from this criticism to Esh's conclusion — *ibid.*, p. 9 and p. 39 — that in the Tannaitic epoch 'Omnipresent' and 'the Holy One, blessed be He', were used indiscriminately, is still a far cry. Our findings, as we have adumbrated them in this chapter, contradict this view, and the material cited by Esh likewise testifies in most instances against his contention.
4. Out of seventy examples of Tannaitic dicta cited by Esh, pp. 8–38, which contain the epithet 'the Holy One, blessed be He', there are only fourteen that have no variant reading giving 'Omnipresent' or omitting 'the Holy One, blessed be He'. Six of these belong to the time of Rabbi and his contemporaries! It is noteworthy that with every additional manuscript the number of passages without different recensions grows smaller. On p. 23, No. 36, Esh refers to *Tosefta Yom ha-Kippurim*, ii, 7, where R. Akiba states 'He

said to me, in the end the Holy One, blessed be He, is destined to rejoice His children', and he (Esh) adds 'there is no other version in the *Tosefta* tradition'. But S. Lieberman has now also indicated in his edition of the *Tosefta* the vv.ll. of the London MS., which Zuckermandel did not have, and there the reading is: 'In the end the Omnipresent...'! On p. 50 Esh enumerates 14 passages in the *Sifra* in which the designation 'the Holy One, blessed be He', occurs, but now that we have the edition based on the Rome MS., No. 66, published by Louis Finkelstein, New York 1957, it emerges that in four of them the designation 'Omnipresent' appears, in four other places there is no epithet in the MS. text at all, and in one passage the text has ה׳ ב״ה, which could also stand for המקום ברוך הוא ['the Omnipresent, blessed be He']. Incidentally, also in the Baraita of R. Ishmael at the beginning of the *Sifra*, a MS. reads 'This teaches us that the Omnipresent, blessed be He, bent' instead of 'the Holy One, blessed be He', etc. found in the printed editions.

5. See the end of the preceding note, and the dictum of R. Joḥanan b. Zakkai, *Mekhilta de-R. Ishmael*, Ba-ḥodesh, xi, p. 244. In the later printed editions of the *Yalquṭ Shimʿoni* the reading is, 'the Holy One, blessed be He [הקב״ה] said', but the *editio princeps* has 'הב״ה said'.
6. The references are listed by Marmorstein, *op. cit.*, p. 143, but he did not yet have the complete edition of Theodor-Albeck. *Ibid.* lxvii, 2, p. 752, we read 'Who was it that became the intermediary between him and the Omnipresent?' but the best MS., that of the Vatican, has 'the Holy One, blessed be He'. In lxxxiv, 14, p. 1017, and also in the London MS., which forms the basis of the Theodor-Albeck edition, the text has 'which are the attributes of the Holy One, blessed be He'; only in the printed editions do we find 'Omnipresent'. MS. ת, mentioned in the vv.ll. as having this reading, is merely a copy of the Venice edition. See Albeck, Introduction to *Genesis Rabba*, p. 116.
7. *Gen. Rabba* lxviii, p. 777, and the note *ibid.*, see the fragment from *T.P. Makkot*, published by S. Wieder, *Tarbiz*, xvi, 1946, p. 135, and S. Lieberman, *Hilkhot Yerushalmi le-ha-Ramban z.l.*, New York 1948, p. 67. Cf. idem, *Tarbiz*, xxvii (1958), p. 186, and the fragments of *Tanḥuma-Yelammedenu*, which I published in *Qoveṣ ʿal Yad*, Book VI (XVI), 1966, p. 22. In *Midrash Tehillim* xc, ed. Buber, 196a, there is added in one MS.: 'Abraham called Him Omnipresent... Jacob called Him Omnipresent... Moses called Him Omnipresent...'; this addition is missing in the printed edition, and in the other MSS.; see *ibid.* note 59.
8. For further examples see E. Landau, *Die dem Raume entnommenen Synonyma für Gott in der neu-hebräischen Literatur*, Zurich 1888.
9. *I Maccabees* iii, 18; see also Bousset, *op. cit.*, p. 314, n. 1. But his entire remarks on the subject are incorrect.
10. *Sifre*, Naśo', § 22, p. 26; *Tosefta Nazir* iv, 7; see above, p. 66.
11. See Nyberg, *Die Rel. des alten Iran*, Leipzig 1938, pp. 59 ff; pp. 100 ff.
12. οἱ δὲ τὸν κύκλον πάντα τοῦ οὐρανοῦ Δία καλέοντες.

13. See J. Guttmann, *Ha-Sifrut ha-Yehudit ha-Helenistit*, I, p. 23.
14. See A. Kahana on *I Maccabees* i, 54 [Hebrew]; Nestle, *ZAW*, 1884, p. 248; Moore, *op. cit.*, I, p. 367; also W. W. Baudissin, *Kyrios als Gottesname im Judentum*, III, 1927, pp. 36–37; and *ibid.* IV, p. 22.
15. This was actually maintained by Petronius and Juvenal; see Th. Reinach, *Textes d'auteurs grecs et romains relatifs au Judaisme*, Paris 1895, p. 266 and p. 292. Celsus also charges that the Jews worship the heavens, but refuse to serve the sun, moon, and stars — Origines, c. *Cels.*, v, 6.
16. It will suffice to point to I Kings viii 32, 'then hear Thou in heaven' in comparison with v. 30 *ibid.* 'yea, hear Thou in heaven Thy dwelling-place'. Noteworthy are the words of *Sēfer ha-Bāhîr* [Book of Bahir (Brightness)], § 43, ed. Margulies, p. 44, 'And how do we know that "Heaven" means the Holy One, blessed be He? For it is written, "then hear Thou in heaven". Did Solomon pray to the heavens that they should hear their prayer? He meant, of course, Him whose name is called upon the heavens.' The author introduced the epithet [Heaven] into the verse, and interpreted the Scripture in the sense of 'and Thou, O Heaven, hear'.
17. See *M. Sanhedrin* vi, 4; *M. 'Avot* i, 11, *et al.*
18. R. Jose (*Sifre Deuteronomy*, § 354) and R. Nehorai (*ibid.* § 306 and the same subject in *T.B. Berakhot* 53b and also in *T.B. Nazir* 66b) used the term *Ha-Shamayim* ['Heaven'] when taking an oath. In *M. Shevu'ot* iv, 13, it is taught: '[If a man said,] "I adjure you... by heaven and by earth", they are exempt'. In *T.B. ibid.* 35b Rava explains that one who swears by heaven and earth is open to the suspicion that he is not swearing by Him to whom heaven and earth belong, but the actual heavens and earth. It appears that the reference in the Mishnah is not to the Divine epithet 'Heaven'. Philo mentions swearing by heaven and earth (*De Specialibus Legibus* ii, 5, referred to by Albeck in his 'Supplements', p. 471); see the *Slavonic Enoch* II, 13, 76, and the Epistle of James v, 12.
19. See below, p. 720, note 65.
20. Bousset-Gressmann, *op. cit.* p. 316; naturally, the phrase βασιλεία τῶν οὐρανῶν in Matthew embarrasses him, and he is forced to save Jesus' honour by doubting whether he actually used this phrase. See *ibid.* p. 314, note 3.
21. Bousset-Gressmann, *op. cit.* p. 316; see also Spanier, *op. cit.*, p. 314.
22. This change of epithet is firmly fixed in all the Palestinian sources: in *Tosefta Nazir* iv, 7; *Sifre Numbers* § 22, p. 26; *T.P. Nedarim* i, 1, p. 36d; *Num. Rabba* x, 7. Only in *T.B. Nazir* 4b and *T.B. Nedarim* 9b is the reading: 'May Nazirites like you multiply in Israel!' On the unusual and ancient phrasing of this narrative about Simon the Just and the Nazirite, see Spiegel, '*Mi-Lĕshôn Payyeṭanim*' [Of the Language of Paytanim], *Ha-Doar*, 1963, XXIII, p. 398.
23. *Tosefta Pe'a* iii, 8; *Tosefta Menaḥot* vii, 9; *Mekhilta de-R. Ishmael*, Kaspa, xx, p. 329; *ibid.*, Shabbeta, i, p. 342; *Sifre Numbers* § 42, p. 45; § 72, p. 67; *Sifre Deuteronomy* § 38, p. 76; § 40, p. 83; § 42, p. 90; § 47, p. 106; § 114, p. 174; § 190, p. 232; § 305, p. 325; § 346, p. 403. Regarding the short prayer

of R. Eliezer 'Do Thy will in heaven above, and vouchsafe gratification to those who fear Thee here below', see Rashi *T.B. Berakhot* 29b, s.v. *'Ăśā.* On the relationship of this prayer to that of Jesus 'Thy will be done, on earth as it is in heaven' (Matthew vi 10), see Joseph Heinemann, *Ha-Tĕfillā bi-Tĕqûfat ha-Tannā'îm wĕ-hā-'Ămôrā'îm* [Prayer in the Period of the Tannaim and the Amoraim], Jerusalem 1964, p. 116.

24. *Sifra,* Mekhilta de-Millu'im, 43d.
25. *Tosefta Demai* ii, 9; *Tosefta Sheqalim* i, 6; *Sifra,* Qedoshim, x, 92c; *Sifre Deuteronomy* § 306, p. 341; *ibid.* § 352, p. 409; But v.l. has: *Ha-Māqôm.*
26. The relationship of the Omnipresent to man: 'The Omnipresent had consideration' — *Sifra,* Millu'im, 45a; *Sifre Zuṭa,* Bĕ-ha-'ălōtĕkhā, p. 273; *Sifre Deuteronomy* § 192, p. 233; § 203, p. 239. 'The Omnipresent brought her near' — *Sifre Numbers* § 78, p. 74. 'Which the Omnipresent has given us' — *Mekhilta de-R. Ishmael,* Massekhta Amalek, i, p. 194. 'The Omnipresent delivered him', *ibid.,* p. 192. The Omnipresent performs miracles — *Sifre Numbers* § 131, p. 172. 'With whose words the Omnipresent agrees', *ibid.* § 134, p. 177. 'The Omnipresent receives him' — *Sifra,* Millu'im, i, 43b. 'For the Omnipresent desires Israel to toil in (the study of) the Torah' — *Sifra,* the beginning of pericope Bĕ-ḥuqqōtāy. 'The Omnipresent promised' — *ibid.* viii, 112b. 'The Omnipresent gave him out of love' — *Sifre Zuṭa,* Bemidbar, p. 263; 'For the Omnipresent is grieved on account of one elder', *ibid.,* p. 271. Relationship to the Omnipresent: 'the praise of the Omnipresent' — *Sifra,* Be-ḥuqqotay, ii, 111a; *Sifre Deuteronomy,* § 343, p. 394. 'Cleave to the Omnipresent' — *Sifre Deuteronomy* § 85, p. 150. 'They seek their reward from the Omnipresent' — *Sifra,* Be-ḥuqqotay, ii, 111a. 'To minister before the Omnipresent' — *ibid.,* Shĕmînî, 43d.
27. *Mekhilta de-R. Ishmael,* Massekhet Amalek, i, p. 191; *ibid.,* Ba-ḥodesh, iii, p. 210; *ibid.* iv, p. 217; *Sifre Numbers* § 94, p. 94; and many other passages.
28. Extinction (*Kārēt*) at the hands of Heaven — *M. Yevamot* iv, 13; 'Would you rob Heaven so that they send down neither dew nor rain, for it is written "Will a man rob God?..." ' (*M. Yadayim* iv, 3) — the verse makes it clear that 'Heaven' not only denotes the actual heavens, but is also a Divine epithet. Death by a heavenly agency — *Mekhilta de-R. Ishmael,* Neziqin, x, p. 285; *ibid.* xvi, p. 303. This is paralleled by the use of the epithet 'on high' [*Ma'ălā*] cf. 'to steal [i.e. deceive] the Mind Most High' — *ibid.* xiii, p. 294. 'He acted as though the Eye of the One on high does not see', *ibid.* xv, p. 299. While it is reported in the name of R. Simeon b. Yoḥai (*T.P. Shevi'it* ix, 1, p. 38d), 'a bird, if it be not Heaven's will, is not snared', R. Ḥanina expressed it thus: 'No one bruises his finger (on earth) below unless it is decreed (in heaven) above (*lĕ-ma'ălā*)' — *T.B. Ḥullin* 7b; see below, p. 719, note 62.
29. 'Reverence of the Omnipresent' — *Mekhilta de-R. Ishmael,* Ba-ḥodesh, viii, p. 231; 'who cast off the yoke of the Omnipresent' — *Sifre Deuteronomy* § 93, p. 154; but in the corresponding Baraita, *T.B. Sanhedrin* 111b the reading is: 'who cast off the yoke of Heaven from their necks'. 'They rebelled

against the Omnipresent' — *Sifre Deuteronomy* § 43, p. 92, but in the context of 'The Omnipresent said to them "On account of the bounty that I have given you, you have become haughty" ', 'enemy of the Omnipresent' — *ibid.* § 171, p. 218 is merely an addition there, see the note *ibid.* 'They acted sinfully against the Omnipresent' — *ibid.* § 306, p. 330. Rabban Gamaliel be-Rabbi uses the expression 'You will be compassionated by Heaven' — *Sifre Deuteronomy* § 96, p. 157; so, too, 'mercy will be shown by Heaven' — *T.B. ʿAvoda Zara* 18a, but in the formula of blessings used by R. Judah and R. Jose, the wording is 'the Omnipresent will show mercy' — *T.B. Shabbat* 12b.

30. See E. Landau, *op. cit.*, pp. 42 ff, and H. H. Schäder and R. Reitzenstein, *Studien zum antiken Synkretismus aus Iran und Griechenland*, Leipzig 1926, p. 81.
31. Damascius, περὶ ἀρχῶν, I, p. 322.
32. See R. Zaehner, *The Dawn and Twilight of Zoroastrianism*, London 1961, pp. 64, 92; pp. 195 ff, and pp. 218 ff.
33. *De Somniis*, I, 62–66, 72; see *ibid.* 118.
34. See J. Freudenthal, 'I Hellenistische Studien' (in *Jahresbericht* of the Jüdisch-Theologisches Seminar, Breslau), 1874, pp. 73 ff; see I. N. Weinstein, *Zur Genesis der Agada*, Frankfort-on-Main 1901, pp. 88 ff.
35. *For the elucidation of the doctrine of the End of Days*, *Zion*, XXIII–XXIV, 1958–1959, pp. 25 ff. The sources of Philo are fully discussed by H. A. Wolfson, *Philo*, Cambridge (Mass.), I, 1947, pp. 227 ff, and pp. 246 ff; see *ibid.*, p. 248, note 44. Mention must also be made of the conjecture of Menaḥem Stein, *Dat wa-Daʿat*, Cracow 1938, pp. 7 ff, that it was the Jews of Alexandria who began to use the expression *Maqom* in place of Lord, since they relied on the Septuagint rendering of Exodus xxiv 10, 'And they saw the place (τὸν τόπον) on which the God of Israel stood'. But as we have already stated in the text, the epithet *Maqom* was not known among Hellenistic Jewry. The word τόπος is not used as a Divine designation either in the apocryphal literature, or in the Hellenistic literature, nor yet in the Evangelical writings. It is obvious that the introduction of the word 'place' into the Septuagint is intended to give remoteness to the concept of seeing God, and not to identify Him with the place, very much in the spirit of the exposition that we find in the *Midrash ha-Gadol* to Exodus, ed. M. Margulies, p. 555: 'Here it is stated "and they saw" and elsewhere it is said "and he saw the place afar off"; just as there it was "afar off" so, too, here it was "afar off".' The expositor explains by analogy that the word 'saw' signifies seeing from a distance without making 'place' an epithet for the Lord. S. Belkin, 'Ha-Midrāsh ha-simlî 'ēṣel' Fîlôn [Symbolic Exposition in Philo], the *H. A. Wolfson Jubilee Volume*, Hebrew Section, 1965, pp. 66–67, does not distinguish between the sources and writes as though no one had ever written on the subject before.
36. *Op. cit.*, pp. 33–34.

37. *Jüdische Zeitschrift*, Pt. II, p. 224 = *Nachgelassene Schriften*, 1885, Vol. IV, p. 324.
38. *Pirqe de-R. Eliezer* xxxv, 82a: 'And why is His name called *Maqom*? Because in any place where the righteous stand He is to be found.' See the comment of R. David Luria (RaDaL), note 33.
39. Y. Baer, *op. cit.*, p. 34, and *ibid.* note 34, wishes to find continuity of thought from the Midrashic statements regarding the epithet *Maqom* to the verses of 'The Hymns of Unity' for the third day of the week (*Shîrê ha-Yiḥûd*, ed. A. M. Habermann, Jerusalem 1948, pp. 25 ff): 'They are all in Thee and Thou art in them all... Thou encompassest all and fillest all, and since Thou art the All Thou art in all....' These verses, which aroused at the time the sharp opposition of R. Moses Taku (see A. Berliner, 'Der Einheitsgesang', in the Proceedings of the Rabbinical Seminary, Berlin 1910; and now A. Berliner, *Kĕtāvîm Nivḥārîm* [Selected Writings], I, Jerusalem 1945, pp. 147 ff), have a clear parallel in Paul's statement, Romans xi 36: ὅτι ἐξ αὐτοῦ καὶ δι' αὐτοῦ καὶ εἰς αὐτὸν τὰ πάντα 'For of him, and through him, and to him, are all things'. E. Norden, *Agnostos Theos*, Leipzig 1913, pp. 240 ff, has already shown that this is a Stoic doxology, as is evident from the dictum of Emperor Marcus Aurelius, ἐκ σοῦ πάντα, ἐν σοὶ πάντα, εἰς σὲ πάντα 'From thee is all, to thee is all, in thee is all'. This formula is, in Norden's view, an ancient Stoic legacy, which passed over to the syncretistic religions, including Christianity, and became a kind of κοινὴ ἔννοια; see *ibid.*, p. 250. R. Moses Taku already perceived the dependence of this Hymn of Unity on R. Saadia Gaon's book *'Emunot we-De'ot* in a translation that differs from that of Ibn Tibbon. Now that this translation, which is merely a paraphrase, has been discovered in manuscript, scholars can confirm his view and add to his arguments. But we must not forget that 'The Hymns of Unity' are religious songs, which express with great fervour the thought of God's universal presence (see the studies mentioned by Berliner *op. cit.*, and especially P. Bloch, *MGWJ*, XIX, 1870, pp. 451–454; cf. also G. Scholem, *Major Trends*, p. 108, who suggests the influence of Scotus Erigena). I should like to refer here to the affinity between 'The Hymns of Unity' and the hymns in the *Scroll of the Thanksgiving Psalms* from Qumran; cf. *Hôdāyôt* fol. I, lines 7–8 (ed. J. Licht, Jerusalem 1957, p. 58) and *Shire ha-Yiḥud*, ed. Habermann, p. 24; *Hôdāyôt* I, 16 (p. 59) — *Shire ha-Yiḥud, loc. cit.*, l. 33; *Hôdāyôt, loc. cit.*, l. 20 — *Shire ha-Yiḥud, loc. cit.*, l. 24; *Hôdāyôt*, X, 6 (p. 151) — *Shire ha-Yiḥud*, p. 26; *Hôdāyôt*, X, 20 (p. 156) — *Shire ha-Yiḥud*, p. 19; *Hôdāyôt*, XIII, 7 (p. 181) — *Shire ha-Yiḥud*, p. 23. But despite this similarity in style and pathos, no pantheistic expressions are to be found in the *Thanksgiving Psalms*. Apparently, their absence is connected with the dualistic principle that prevails in them.
40. We cannot accept Bacher's statement, *Die Agada der Tannaiten*, Pt. I, p. 200, that R. Eleazar of Modi'in in the *Mekhilta de-R. Ishmael*, Wa-yassa', vi, p. 175, '...nimmt das Wort מקום in seiner damals schon lang üblichen Bedeutung also Bezeichnung Gottes als Subjekt'. The author of *'Êphat Ṣedeq* emended

the text there to read 'From this we learn that God is called *Maqom*', but this emendation has no basis; see Horovitz's notes *ad. loc.* R. Joshua and R. Eleazar of Modiʿin disagree as to who called the name of the place Massah and Meribah. According to R. Joshua it was Moses, of whom it is said earlier 'And Moses did so...'; but according to R. Eleazar of Modiʿin, the Lord named it so, for the words 'And Moses did so...' is a parenthetic statement, and 'And the Lord called unto Moses' is the continuation of the verse 'And the Lord said unto Moses'. This, it seems, is the exegetical explanation of the dispute. At any rate, the reason for R. Eleazar of Modiʿin's opinion is not to be sought in the words 'For it is said "and he called the name of the place Massah and Meribah" ', for precisely the same words are cited in support of R. Joshua's view, for which they also provide no explanation. The continuation of the Midrashic passage 'From this we learn that the High Court is called *Maqom*' is not part of R. Eleazar's dictum, but is an anonymous statement of the *Mekhilta*, and is an inference that can also be drawn from the words of R. Joshua, and from the verse 'Massah and Meribah' itself — it means the court of justice, and it is called here *Maqom*, as it is written 'and get thee up to the place'. Nor is there any reason to suppose that the reference is to the Heavenly High Court. Israel Lewy, 'Ein Wort über die Mechilta des R. Simon', *Jahresbericht des jüd. Theol. Seminars zu Breslau* 1904, p. 9, note 3, accepted Bacher's view (in the second edition of his book, *ibid.*, n. 2, Bacher refers to Lewy), although he observed there that the Scriptural proof is wanting, according to four textual witnesses, in the dictum of R. Eleazar of Modiʿin, and in two other texts it is also missing in the statement of R. Joshua. Undoubtedly, there is no need to interpret 'the High Court' in *Tosefta 'Ahilot*, *ad fin.*, in the sense of 'the Holy One, blessed be He'; while in *Deuteronomy Rabba* xi, 10, 'until the High Court revealed themselves to him' means 'He and His Court'; see *Yĕdê Môshe* [The Hands of Moses] *ad loc.*; Strack-Billerbeck, II, p. 310, are also of opinion that R. Eleazar of Modiʿin wished to provide Scriptural proof that God was called *Maqom*, and they also explain the epithet *Maqom* itself as denoting God's place in Heaven, regarding it as a substitute for the title 'Heaven', which the Sages refrained from using when it assumed the character of a Divine Name. All these observations, however, have no foundation in the light of what we have shown above.

41. According to the reading of *ʿEn Yaʿaqov*; see *Diqduqe Soferim* to *Tractate Ḥagiga*, p. 36.
42. *T.B. Ḥagiga*, 12a; see *Gen. Rabba* i, 14, ed. Theodor, p. 12.
43. *Contra Haereses*, I, 18, Migne, *PG*, Paris 1882, VII, p. 642.
44. εὐθὺς ἐν ἀρχῇ τὴν μητέρα τῶν ὅλων ἐπέδειξεν.
45. See above, p. 184; see Marmorstein, *op. cit.*, II, 1937, p. 12.
46. See above, p. 67.
47. *Jahrbücher für jüdische Geschichte u. Literatur*, VII, 1885, p. 85.
48. *Op. cit.*, pp. 51 ff; to the bibliography listed *ibid.* should be added S. Lieberman,

Hilkhot Yerushalmi le-Rambam, p. 67, note 12. He states there: 'Although God was undoubtedly called "Holy"... it nevertheless appears that in the period of the Amoraim He was called "Holiness".... 'But he gives no explanation of this epithet; see now also *Tosefta ki-Fshuṭah* on Moʿed, p. 1094.

49. See Esh, *op. cit.*, pp. 79 ff.
50. The passages are noted in Bousset-Gressmann, *op. cit.*, p. 312, note 4, and in Strack-Billerbeck, *op. cit.*, Pt. III, p. 762.
51. One passage is *Sirach* iv 14, ed. M. H. Segal, p. 24, 'ministers of Holiness are her ministers'. The expression 'ministers of Holiness' occurs in the wording of a prayer in *T.P. Berakhot* ix, (6) p. 14b; even the conclusion of the benediction 'Blessed be the Glorious (*kāvôd*) God' arouses doubt as to whether this prayer originated in the circles of the Sages. The second passage, *û-vārĕkhû 'et shēm ha-qā*[*dôsh*] ['and bless you the name of the Holy One'], *Sirach* xxxix 47, p. 262, reads in the margin *shēm qodshô* ['the name of His Holiness'], and in the Greek version actually: τὸ ὄνομα κυρίου.
52. Segal in his Introduction, p. 68, 'One or two generations before Rav', but subsequently 'perhaps', 'apparently', before the fall of Bethar!
53. This fact is brought out more forcibly by the fragments found at Masada; see Y. Yadin, *Mĕgillat ben Sira she-nitgallĕtā bi-Meṣādā* [The Ben Sira Scroll from Masada], Jerusalem 1965, p. 31. While the Greek version has ἐν λόγοις ἁγίου, we find in MS. B of the Genizah *mi-dĕvar 'Ēl...* ['by the word of God...'] and in the Masada Scroll *bi-dĕvar 'Ădōnay* ['by the word of the Lord'].
54. It should be noted that in the New Testament *Ha-Qādôsh* [The Holy] appears once — in the Second Epistle of Peter i 21.
55. *Qādōsh* [קָדֹשׁ] is frequently written defectively [without *Wāw*] and could also be read *qōdesh* [קֹדֶשׁ]; see Leviticus xxi 7, Numbers vi 8, Ezekiel xlii 13, etc. Cf. also Y. Kutscher, *Ha-Lāshôn wĕ-hā-Reqaʿ ha-lĕshōnî shel Mĕgillat Yĕshaʿyāhû ha-Shĕlēmā mi-Mĕgillôt Yam ha-Melaḥ*, Jerusalem 1959, p. 291.
56. Compare 'And ye shall be holy [*qodesh*] men unto Me' (Exodus xxii 30), which is translated in the Septuagint ἄνδρες ἅγιοι, and in Targum Onkelos 'and holy men'. The same usage is to be observed in *'anshê qôdesh* ['holy men'] in the Manual of Discipline viii, 18, ed. J. Licht, Jerusalem 1965, p. 185; so, too, *'îsh ha-qodesh* ['holy man'], *ibid.* v, 17; *ʿădat ha-qodesh*, *ibid.* v, 21, p. 134, which is only another way of saying *ʿēdā qĕdôshā* ['holy congregation']. In the *Damascus Document* v, 22–vi, 1, we read 'For they spoke evil of the commandment of God by the hand of Moses and also against *mĕshîaḥ ha-qodesh...*', the last term being the same as *māshîaḥ ha-qādôsh* ['the holy Messiah'], as L. Ginzberg has already noted in *Eine unbekannte Jüdische Sekte*, New York 1922, p. 318, note 3. See also Ch. Rabin, *The Zadokite Documents*², Oxford 1958, p. 21.
57. See my article 'The Rabbinical Laws of Idolatry in the Second and Third Centuries in the Light of Archaeological and Historical Facts', *IEJ*, IX, 1959, p. 153. Out of 36 occurrences of the word הקדש in Tannaitic sources

21 contain the phrase מפי הקדש ['from the mouth of the Holy'], and it is found another 4 times in connection with speaking and saying. The expression מפי הקדש [which could refer to God or man], used alone, was open to misunderstanding; see *T.B. Sanhedrin* 23a, where Resh Laqish says of R. Me'ir: 'Would the holy mouth [*pe qadôsh*] say such a thing?'

58. See R. Otto, *Das Heilige*[6], Breslau 1921, p. 92.
59. See Y. Yadin, *Megillat ben Sira mi-Meṣada*, Jerusalem 1965, pp. 19, 20, 27 and 35; see *ibid.* note 7, which clears up the doubt expressed by Bousset-Gressmann, p. 311, note 2.
60. See *ibid.*, 310–311; W. Bauer, *Wörterbuch zum N.T.*, p. 1682; cf. J. B. Frey *CIJ*, II, 1952, 769.
61. A. Marmorstein, *op. cit.*, p. 94, states: 'In our period, the epithet was already an archaism, but it was still used occasionally.' But he cites only two examples. One is the dictum of R. Aibu, *Gen. Rabba* xxii, 13, p. 220, *kĕgônēv daʿat ha-ʿelyônā*, 'as one who deceives the Most High' [literally, 'as one who steals the Most High Mind'], only this is merely the well-known rhetorical phrase of Rabban Joḥanan b. Zakkai 'to deceive the Most High' — *Tosefta Bava Qamma* viii, 2, p. 358; *Mekhilta de-R. Ishmael* xiii, p. 294 (in the *Tosefta, loc. cit.*, viii, p. 358 we also find *gônēv 'et ʿayin hā-ʿelyônā*, 'deceives the eye of the Most High' [literally, 'to steal the Most High Eye']). The very use of the expression *daʿat hā-ʿelyônā*, 'the Most High Mind' in antithesis to *daʿat ha-bĕriyyôt*, 'the mind of people', and not in the form of the Scriptural phrase *daʿat ʿElyôn* ['the mind (*aliter*: knowledge) of the Most High'] (Numbers xxiv 16) shows that the epithet *ʿElyon* had gone out of use (in *Gen. Rabba* we find in several recensions *daʿat ha-ʿElyonim* ['mind (or, knowledge) of the angels'], and only in the MS. of the commentary attributed to Rashi does the reading *daʿat ʿElyon* occur). The second example quoted by Marmorstein from *Midrash Tehillim* xlii 2, p. 267, 'that the right hand of the Most High [*ʿElyon*] changed' proves the contrary, for the expositor merely repeats the text that he is expounding 'This is my sickness, that the right hand of the Most High [*ʿElyon*] has changed' (Psalms lxxvii 11 [10]; see also the Midrash *ibid.*, p. 340). But when the expositor uses his own words, he says, *wĕ-khî yēsh ḥōlî lĕ-maʿălā* ['Is there any sickness on high?']; this is added proof for our own contention above. Only in a late interpretation of the saying of R. Simeon b. Yoḥai 'Even a bird is not captured without Heaven's consent', which occurs in *Midrash Tehillim* xvii 13, p. 134, and is wanting in all the early parallel passages, do we find 'Just as birds are not caught except by the will of the Most High [*daʿat ʿElyon*]'; see above, p. 714, note 29.
62. It is true that in *'Ôṣar Lĕshôn ha-Tosefta* [Thesaurus Thosephthae, Concordantiae Verborum] xxv, p. 343, one passage is cited, *Menaḥot* vii 9, 'and thou shalt pay to the Most High [*ʿElyon*] thy vows', but Psalms i 13 is being expounded there.
63. See A. M. Habermann, *Megillot Midbar Yehuda* [The Scrolls from the Judaean Desert], 1959, Concordance, p. 113. Even in the few passages in which *ʿelyon*

occurs as an adjective, the reference is to poetic phrases borrowed from the Bible; see J. Licht, *Megillat Hodayot* [The Thanksgiving Scrolls], p. 96; idem, *Megillat ha-Serakhim* [The Manual of Discipline], p. 233; cf. also *ibid.*, p. 216.

64. See B. Kosovsky, *'Oṣar Leshon ha-Mekhilta* [Concordantiae Verborum quae in Mechilta D'Rabbi Ismael reperiuntur], III, p. 994; cf. A. Marmorstein, *op. cit.*, p. 91, but not necessarily in the restricted sense mentioned by him; see also *T.P. Sanhedrin* vi, 12, p. 24a.

65. *Canticles Rabba* i, 9, 'The horse says to its rider *rāmā ba-yām* — look at the sea, אפתוסים *'ptwsys* has been manifested [literally, 'was made'] unto you in the sea'. In a note to S. Krauss, *Lehnwörter*, p. 117, Immanuel Löw observes that the author of *'Ôt 'Emet* referred to *Exodus Rabba* xxiii 14, 'and the horse said to him *rāmā ba-yām*, see what is in the sea, the Height [*rûmô*] of the world I behold in the sea'; the expression 'the Height of the world' is simply the translation of ὕψιστος. The homilist did not choose the term *'Elyon* ['Most High'] or *Ma'ala* ['On High'], because he was interpreting the words *rāmā ba-yām*. Marmorstein overlooked the Midrash in *Canticles Rabba*, and *op. cit.*, p. 100 he listed *Rûmô shel 'ōlām* ['The Height of the world'] as an epithet of God on the basis of *Exod. Rabba*; see *Targum Onkelos* to Numbers xxiii 22; xxiv 8. It is true that in Habakkuk iii 10 *rôm* ['on high'] is found instead of *mārôm* (in Targum Pseudo-Jonathan: *mĕrômā*) in antithesis to the 'deep'; also in *Sifre Deuteronomy* § 199, we read 'that those who dwell on high [*rôm*] need peace, for it is said "He who maketh peace in His high places" ' (but in the parallel passage *Sifre Numbers* § 42, p. 47, the text reads *she-dārê 'elyonim* ['that those who dwell in high places' i.e. heaven] and a variant reading has, *she-dārê ma'alyā* ['that those who dwell on high']). The phrase *rôm 'ālmā* ['Height of the world'] in Targum Pseudo-Jonathan to Jeremiah xxxi 14 is only a Targum-Midrash [i.e. a homiletical rendering of the Targum]; 'a voice is heard in Ramah' is translated by the Targum 'a voice is heard in the height [*rôm*] of the world', i.e. 'a voice is heard in heaven'. In this sense the expression is found in the *Scroll of the Thanksgiving Psalms*, fol. iii, 20, 'And from Sheol of destruction Thou hast raised us up to the height (*rôm*) of the world'. The contrast Sheol–Height reminds us of the antithesis 'deep–on high [*rôm*]' in Habakkuk. J. Licht, in his edition of the *Scroll of the Thanksgiving Psalms*, p. 84, does not refer in his commentary to the parallel in Habakkuk, but he is right in stating that the expression has no eschatological signification in the Thanksgiving Psalm. The lengthy remarks of H. W. Kuhn, *Enderwartung und Gegenwärtiges Heil*, Göttingen 1966, pp. 52–58, can in no way change our conclusions on the subject under discussion. The phrase '*be-rûmô shel 'ôlām*' ['on the height of the world'] in the dictum of R. Joḥanan (*T.B. Pesaḥim* 118a), and in that of Rav Ashi (*T.B. Menaḥot* 59a), stands for 'in heaven', and *rûm 'ôlām* is similarly used in the prayers *titbārakh* ['Be Thou blessed' — Singer's Prayer Book, p. 39] and *'ezrat* ['The help of' — *ibid.* p. 44], although the expression is not found in the

Palestinian recension or in the Prayer Book of R. Saadia Gaon; see Elbogen, *Geschichte d. Jüd. Gottesdienstes*, 1924, p. 16 and p. 23. Ben Yehuda, *A Complete Dictionary of Ancient and Modern Hebrew*, vol. XIII, p. 6505, cited *rûmô shel ʿolam* only from *T.B. Berakhot* 6b 'the things that stand on the height of the world [*bĕ-rûmô shel ʿōlām*], and *T.B. Megilla* 14a 'from men that stood on the height of the world [i.e. very high]'. The word *gāvôah* ['high'] is used as an adjective in connection with sacred (Temple) property in contradistinction to *hedyoṭ* ['ordinary, common'] and not as an epithet of God; this usage is not restricted to early sources, as is stated by Marmorstein, *op. cit.*, p. 81. On its frequent occurrence in the Babylonian Talmud, see H. Y. Kosovsky, *'Oṣar Leshon ha-Talmud*, VIII, pp. 37–39; it is also very common in the Palestinian Talmud (see above, p. 71). The phrase *govhô shel ʿōlām* ['the height of the world'] in *Ecclesiastes Rabba* xii 5 is only an exposition of the verse 'Also when thy shall be afraid of that which is high [mi-gāvôah]' and is similar to the case of *rûmô shel ʿōlam*. See also E. S. Rosenthal, *Tarbiz*, XL, 1971, p. 178, and *ibid.*, p. 180, note 18. But cf. *T.B. Soṭa* 40a 'Through me and him the All-Highest is glorified.'

CHAPTER V

THE EPITHET GEVÛRĀ ['MIGHT'] AND THE POWER OF GOD

1. G. van der Leeuw, *Phänomenologie der Religion*², Tübingen 1956, pp. 4 ff.
2. In *T.P. Berakhot* ix, 1 (12) p. 13b: 'R. Zeʿira the son of R. Abbahu, R. Abbahu in the name of R. Eleazar...', but in *Yalquṭ Shim oni,* Tehillim, § 588, the text agrees with ours. In *T.P. ʿAvoda Zara* iii, 1, p. 43c: 'R. Zeʿira the son of R. Abbahu expounded *in the presence of* R. Laʿzar'. In *Yalquṭ ha-Makhiri* to Psalms cxlvi: 'R. Zeʿira the son of R. Abbahu in the name of R. Eliezer expounded'.
3. In the Leiden MS., *Tractate ʿAvoda Zara*: 'But the Holy One [HQ - הק̇] is not so; He has dominion over the sea and over the land'.
4. *Die Götter Griechenlands,* Frankfort 1947, pp. 259–281, where the origin of the word 'moira' in the earlier strata of the Greek religion is discussed.
5. See also E. R. Dodds, *The Greeks and the Irrational,* University of California Press, 1964, pp. 6 ff.
6. See M. P. Nilsson, *Greek Piety*, Oxford 1948, p. 64.
7. Moore, *op. cit.*, Pt. I, p. 374, does not note the difference, and incorrectly identifies the two.
8. *T.B. Shabbat* 87a; see *Sifra Leviticus*, ii, 4b.
9. *T.B. Megilla* 31b. In a number of passages, apparently, the use of *mi-pi ha-qodesh* ['from the mouth of the Holiness'] ousted the epithet *Gevura* — *Sifre Deuteronomy*, § 5, ed. Finkelstein, p. 13, but the reading *mi-pi ha-Gevura* is also found here; see *ibid.* § 19, p. 31, and the vv.ll. Cf. also *Sifre Numbers* § 45, p. 51 'until it was said to him by the Holy One [literally 'from the mouth of the Holiness']'; but *ibid.* § 46 the text has *mi-pi ha-Gevura*; see *ibid.* § 52, p. 53, and above, p. 78.
10. The conjecture of H. P. Chajes, *Markus-Studien*, Berlin 1899, p. 11, that the original text read 'for he taught by *mashal* ['parable'] and not like the scribes', and that *mashal* was changed to *moshel* ['ruler', 'person in authority'], is ingenious, but certainly incorrect, for the scribes, too, taught by means of parables.
11. See Strack-Billerbeck, *Commentar*, Pt. I, p. 470; cf. I. Bergmann, *Jüdische Apologetik*, Berlin 1909, p. 33, n. 3.

12. Only once is it stated in a Baraita that the tribe of Benjamin became the host of the *Gevura*, as it is said, 'and He dwelleth between his shoulders' — *'Avot de-R. Nathan*, Version I, xxxv; *T.B. Yoma* 12a; *T.B. Soṭa* 37a. It is true that in *T.B. Zevaḥim* 54a we find 'the host of the Holy One, blessed be He' (see *Diqduqe Soferim, ibid.*), but all the other vv.ll. should not be rejected. See A. M. Goldberg, 'Sitzend zur Rechten der Kraft', *Biblische Zeitschrift*, 1964, pp. 284–293.
13. See Karl Reinhardt, *Kosmos und Sympathie*, Munich 1926, p. 108; R. M. Grant, *Miracle and Natural Law in Graeco-Roman and Early Christian Thought*, Amsterdam 1952, pp. 9 ff.
14. M. P. Nilsson, *Geschichte der griech. Religion*, II, Munich 1950, pp. 511 ff; idem, *Greek Piety*, pp. 102–103.
15. H. J. Bell, *Cults and Creeds in Graeco-Roman Egypt*, Liverpool 1953, pp. 22–25. See Th. Mommsen, *Röm. Geschichte*, 1885, pp. 318 ff; *ibid.*, pp. 516 ff; G. Wissowa, *Religion und Kultus der Römer*, Munich 1912, pp. 73–76.
16. *Mekhilta de-R. Ishmael*, Massekhta de-Shira, iv, pp. 129–131; see vv.ll. *ibid.* and in *Mekhilta de-R. Simeon b. Yoḥai*, pp. 81–82.
17. Targum to the Decalogue, *Maḥzor Vitry*, p. 337. The reading there is *wĕ-dînamîṭ*; see *ibid.*, p. 321; the annotator read *namîṭ*, and the passage from the Palestine Talmud cited there, which is wanting in our text, also, apparently, read, *lêt dînamîs*; cf. *Esther Rabba* vii, 13.
18. *Unde autem vel quis ille aut ubi deus unicus, solitarius, destitutus, quem non gens libera, non regna, non saltem Romana superstitio noverunt. Judaeorum sola et misera gentilitas unum et ipsi deum, sed palam, sed templis, aris, victimis caerimoniisque coluerunt, cuius adeo nulla vis nec potestas est, ut sit Romanis hominibus cum sua sibi natione captivus.* Minucius Felix, *Octavius*, X, 3–4. On the date of the work and its sources, see Carl Becker, *Der Octavius des Minucius Felix*, Munich 1967, pp. 49, 97, 102–103. For similar arguments see below, the chapter on 'The Congregation of Israel and its Sages'.
19. Mommsen, too, wondered at the significance of the triumphal arches that were built in honour of Titus on the Capitol and in the Circus, and which bear no relationship to his military achievements in the war against a little people that had long lost its political independence. His explanation is identical with the view of the Sages. Titus and his contemporaries regarded the burning of the Temple as a politico-religious triumph, namely the liquidation of the Jewish cult; see idem, *op. cit.*, pp. 538–539, and cf. my article "Ishiyyûtô shel Yosephus Flavius lĕ-'ôr Sippûrô 'al Sĕrēfat ha-Bayit' [The Personality of Josephus in the Light of his account of the burning of the Temple], *Mo'znayim*, 1942, pp. 290–295.
20. *'Avot de-R. Nathan*, Version II, vii; the sentence 'Tomorrow when his measure is filled, Thou wilt bring retribution upon him' appears to me to be an addition by the editor, who wished to bridge the difference between Abba Ḥanan's comment and the narrative.
21. *Mekhilta de-R. Ishmael*, Massekhta de-Shira, viii, p. 142. Abba Ḥanan is

mentioned eight times in the *Mekhilta de-R. Ishmael*; see B. Kosovsky, *'Oṣar ha-Shemot shel Mekhilta de-R. Ishmael.* [Thesaurus of the Names of the Mekhilta], Jerusalem 1965, p. 1.

22. See above, p. 94.
23. Jeremiah xvi 19 is translated by the Targum 'The Lord is my strength and my support'; similarly *'ozzî wĕ-zimrāt YH* is rendered by Onkelos 'my strength and my praise'. The Septuagint has βοηθὸς καὶ σκεπαστὴς — 'saviour and shield'. They must therefore have read *'ezri* ['my help', instead of *'ozzî*]; but in Jeremiah xvi 19, the Septuagint also renders κύριε σὺ ἰσχὺς μου καὶ βοήθεια μου.
24. *Pesiqta de-Rav Kahana*, ed. Mandelbaum, p. 469; Buber, 148a. See *Midrash Tehillim* xciii, § 1, 2.
25. ἡ σοφία τοῦ θεοῦ... ἣν ἄκραν καὶ πρωτίστην ἔτεμεν ἀπὸ ἑαυτοῦ δυνάμεων, *Legum Allegoriae*, II, 86.
26. *De Specialibus Legibus*, I, 46–48.
27. *De Migratione Abrahami*, 179–183.
28. *De Specialibus Legibus*, IV, 187.
29. See Diogenes Laert., VII, 38, 56; cf. Eduard Schweizer, *The Spirit of Power*, *Interpretation*, 1952, pp. 259–278.
30. *T.P. Berakhot*, vii, p. 11c; see *T.B. Yoma* 69b.
31. 'For our gospel came not unto you in word only, but also in power and in the holy spirit....' (I Thessalonians i 5). 'For the kingdom of God is not in word, but in power' (I Corinthians iv 20).
32. Romans i 3–4; I Corinthians i 24; see Otto Schmitz, 'Der Begriff δύναμις bei Paulus', *Festgabe für Adolf Deissmann*, Tübingen 1927, pp. 139–167.
33. *Pesiqta de-Rav Kahana*, ed. Mandelbaum, p. 380; see *ibid.*, p. 379, that Moses 'reinforces the power of *Gevura*'; cf. *'Arugat ha-Bośem*, Pt. II, p. 116.

CHAPTER VI

MAGIC AND MIRACLE

1. Julius Röhr, 'Der Okkulte Kraftbegriff im Altertum', *Supplement-Philologus*, vol. I, XVIII (1923), pp. 1–33.
2. A. D. Nock, *Conversion*, pp. 62–63.
3. On the relationship 'Idolatry — Myth and Magic', see Yeḥezkel Kaufmann, *Toledot ha-'Emuna ha-Yisra'elit*, Bk. II, pp. 286 ff.
4. *Pesiqta de-Rav Kahana*, Pārā, ed. Mandelbaum, p. 44. Buber supplemented and emended on the basis of parallel sources.
5. *Ḥayyāv* ['culpable'] is wanting in the texts of the Munich MS., Kaufmann MS., Lowe, Maimonides, and Mishna according to the Palestinian Talmud. *Mele'khet Shelomo* states 'Another opinion is that it means one who performs an act, not one who creates an illusion; and this appears to me correct....' Cf. *Diqduqe Soferim*, p. 190, n. *Pē'*, and p. 191, n. *Shîn*.
6. Although not an offence, it is nevertheless forbidden; see Maimonides' *Commentary on the Mishna*, and *Mishna Torah*, Hilkhot ʿAvoda Zara, xi, 15.
7. *De Specialibus Legibus*, III, 100–103; see Leopold Cohn's German edition of Philo, Breslau, Pt. II, 1910, p. 214, n. 1; Heinemann, *Philons griechische und jüdische Bildung*, Breslau 1932, pp. 388–389. Colson in his notes to the English edition of Philo, p. 636, questions the connection with the Stoic view.
8. *Tosefta Shabbat*, vi–vii; see S. Lieberman, *Tosefta ki-Fshuṭah*, Moʿed, pp. 74 ff; also S. Ch. Kook, *ʿIyyûnîm û-Meḥqārîm* [Studies], Jerusalem 1959, Pt. I, p. 103. The dictum גד גדי וסנוק לא אושכי ובושכי (*T.B.* *Shabbat* 67b; in the Oxford MS., וכושכי; cf. *Diqduqe Soferim*, p. 146, n. *Shîn*), which scholars found difficult to understand (L. Blau, *op. cit.*, p. 67; *Addendum to Aruch Completum*, p. 69) is none other than the Greek 'Εφεσια γράμματα; ˇΑσκιον Κατάσκιον, cf. Th. Hopfner, *Griechisch Agyptischer Offenbarungszauber*, I, Leipzig 1921, p. 192.
9. See Ludwig Blau, 'Das altjüdische Zauberwesen', in *Jahrbuch* of the Rabbinical Seminary, Budapest 1898, pp. 65 ff. On the struggle against witchcraft and the compromise with it after Christianity had become dominant in the Roman Empire, see the excellent article of A. A. Barb, 'The Survival of Magic Arts'

in *The Conflict between Paganism and Christianity in the Fourth Century*, Oxford 1963, pp. 101–126.

10. *T.B. Sanhedrin* 67b; see also *T.B. Ḥullin* 7b.
11. *T.B. Bava Meṣi'a* 107b, s.v. *'ăvad*, but R. Ḥananel cites in the name of a Gaon — i.e. Rav Hai Gaon — the following explanation: 'We do not read *'ăvad ma da'ăvad* ['performed certain acts'], [as for] the statement that "he went up to a cemetery", it means, for instance, that he inquired through a dream, and in his dream he was told that ninety-nine die on account of the evil eye and (only) one naturally' (*Or Zarua'* on *T.B. Bava Meṣi'a*, § 347; see also *Shîṭā Mĕqubbeṣet, ibid.*). R. Ḥananel himself read *'avad ma da'avad*; cf. *'Arukh ha-Shalem*, s.v. *'ăvad*², p. 157. On Rav Hai Gaon's attitude to the beliefs in enchantments, see S. Asaf, *Tĕqûfat ha-Gĕônîm wĕ-Sifrûtāh* [Period of the Geonim and its Literature], 1956, p. 267.
12. *T.B. Bava Batra* 126b; on healing with spittle, see J. Preuss, *Biblisch-talmudische Medizin*, 1923, pp. 321–322; Cf. *T.P. Terumot* viii, 5, p. 45d: 'R. Ammi said, we should take care to avoid anything that people consider dangerous.'
13. *T.P. Nazir* viii, 1, p. 57a. One may claim 'I was forced by the spell she cast over me.' See S. Lieberman, *Greek in Jewish Palestine*, p. 83, and M. Margulies, *Sefer hā-Rāzîm* [Book of Secrets], Tel-Aviv 1967, p. 75.
14. *T.B. Sanhedrin* 67b: 'Jannai came to a certain inn....'; Rashi, *ad loc.*, s.v. *Yanna'y*, says: 'We do not read "R. Jannai", for a man of standing would not have practised witchcraft', but in the *Yalquṭ* MS., in *'En Ya'aqov*, and in *Yad Rama*, the text has 'R. Jannai'; see *Diqduqe Soferim, ibid.*, p. 192, n. 10, and also the narrative, *ibid.*, 'Ze'iri came to Alexandria of Egypt....' Cf. *T.B. Pesaḥim* 110a–111a; *T.B. Yoma* 84a. For the belief in sorcery of an historian of the calibre of Ammianus Marcellinus, and of an orator like Libanius, see Barb, *op. cit.*, pp. 114–116; and *ibid.*, p. 118, on the part played by the Jews of Alexandria in the dissemination of books on magic.
15. *T.B. Shabbat* 67a; see Blau, *op. cit.*, p. 165, and S. Lieberman, *Greek in Jewish Palestine*, pp. 103 ff. Cf. *T.B. Nidda* 66a: 'A certain woman once came before R. Joḥanan....'
16. *T.B. Berakhot* 6b in the name of 'R. Ḥelbo, who said in the name of Rav Huna'; but *ibid.* 9b the text reads 'R. Abbahu said', and the Munich MS. has 'R. Ammi'; see *Diqduqe Soferim, ibid.*, 19a, n. *Samekh.*
17. Deuteronomy xiii 3–4; Kaufmann, *Toledot ha-'Emuna ha-Yisre'elit*, I, pp. 474 ff, does not pay sufficient attention to this verse, which states that it is possible for a sign and portent to take place, but nevertheless they signify nothing, if they are excluded from the sphere of the Worker of miracles, for that is the meaning of 'Let us go after other gods'.
18. See *T.B. Berakhot* 50a 'There the meaning is obvious: Who performs miracles? — the Holy One, blessed be He!'
19. *M. Ta'anit* iii, 8, and the parallel passages; see Gad Ben-Ammi Zarfati, '*Ḥăsîdîm wĕ-'Anshê ma'ăsê wĕ-ha-Nĕvî'îm hā-Ri'shônîm*' [The Pietists and Miracle Workers and the Early Prophets], *Tarbiz*, XXVI, 1957, pp. 126–130.

20. *T.B. Shabbat* 33b; *Pesiqta de-Rav Kahana*, ed. Mandelbaum, p. 193; ed. Buber 90b.

21. See Yitzḥak Heinemann, 'Die Kontroverse über das Wunder im Judentum der hellenistischen Zeit', in the *Bernhard Heller Jubilee Volume*, Budapest 1941, pp. 170–191. Cf. Alexander Gutman, 'The Significance of Miracles for Talmudic Judaism', *HUCA*, XX, 1947, pp. 263–406. S. Lieberman, *op. cit.*, New York 1941, pp. 97–114; Max Ḳaduschin, *The Rabbinic Mind*, New York 1952, pp. 152–167.

22. This is the reading in the MSS. and not 'ha-Shiloni', as in the printed editions.

23. The etymology is obscure; perhaps it stands for יורק־מי [spitting water].

24. *Mekhilta de-R. Ishmael*, Massekhta da-Amalek, ii, p. 186; see *Gen. Rabba* lix, 5, p. 634: 'Moses was the wonder-worker [*nes*] of Israel... Who, now, was the wonder-worker of Moses? — The Holy One, blessed be He....'

25. *Midrash ha-Gadol* to Exodus, ed. Hoffmann, p. 17; ed. Margulies, p. 32. See *ibid.* n. 10; possibly, we should read: לשון צער (ἀνάγκη) אנקי [אנקי, an expression of grief].

26. *T.B. Sanhedrin* 65b; see *Gen. Rabba* xi, 5, p. 93, and *ibid.*, n. 3, where reference is made to the observations of Pliny and Josephus regarding the Sabbatic river. Note should also be taken of the other proofs: 'the familiar spirit proves it' (Rashi: 'in that it does not rise up on the Sabbath'); 'the grave of his father proves it, in that it causes no smoke to rise up on the Sabbath'.

27. *Pesiqta Rabbati* xiv, ed. Friedmann [Meir Ish-Shalom] 57a. The reading there is 'Joḥanan b. Torta', but Friedmann, in a note *ibid.*, has already drawn attention to *Tosafot Yeshanim*, *T.B. Yoma* 9a, where the text has 'Judah', and this, in fact, is the reading in the MS. of *Pesiqta Rabbati*, Parma 1240, and also in the MS. of *Yiḥûsê Tanna'im wa-'Amora'im* [The Genealogy of the Tannaim and Amoraim].

28. *T.B. Ta'anit* 20a. According to the printed edition, Naqdimon said in his second prayer 'Make known that Thou hast loved ones in Thy world', but in the MS. we find instead 'As Thou didst perform a miracle for me in the beginning, even so perform a miracle for me at the end'. See *Diqduqe Soferim ibid.*, p. 110, n. *Samekh*; ed. H. Malter, p. 78.

29. *Tanḥuma*, Ki Tiśśa', xiv; *ibid.* Rĕ'ē, xvi, ed. Buber *ibid.* xv; see *Pesiqta de-Rav Kahana*, ed. Mandelbaum, p. 170. In all these passages, the author of the homily is given as R. Eleazar, and only in *T.B. Sanhedrin* 93a is the name R. Tanḥum b. R. Ḥanilai found.

30. *Sat.*, I, 5, *credat Judaeus Apella, non ego...*

31. *Sifra*, 'Emor, ix, 99d; *T.B. Ta'anit* 18b; *Ecclesiastes Rabba* iii, 6; *Semaḥot* viii.

32. *T.B. Yevamot* 121b; *T.B. Bava Qamma* 50a; in the continuation there it is stated: 'R. Aḥa said: Even so his son died of thirst, as it is written "And round about Him it stormeth mightily" — this teaches us that the Holy One, blessed be He, deals strictly with those round about Him, to a hair's breadth' (In *Yevamot* edd., the reading is 'R. Abba'; but in the Munich MS. it is 'R. Aḥa'). In *T.P. Demai* i, 3, p. 22a and *Sheqalim* v, 1, p. 48d,

it is related: 'R. Haggai said in the name of R. Samuel bar Naḥman: It is told of a certain pious man that he used to dig cisterns, ditches, and caves for the benefit of wayfarers. Once his daughter was on her way to be married, and a river swept her away... R. Phinehas b. Jair came to him, wishing to comfort him, but he did not accept his consolation. Said R. Phinehas b. Jair to the people: "Is this your man of piety?" So they said to him: "Master, this is what he used to do, and this is what happened to him." He replied: "Is it possible that he honoured his Creator with water and He brought disaster upon him through water?" Immediately it was bruited about in the town that the man's daughter had arrived....' In *T.P. Sheqalim*, R. Aḥa's statement is found at the beginning of the discourse, after the story concerning Neḥunia, the ditch-digger. It is almost certain that R. Aḥa's remarks were originally made with reference to the Baraita cited in the Babylonian Talmud as a reaction to the superficial faith it expresses, but after the tradition in the Palestinian Talmud has quoted this story with reference to R. Phinehas b. Jair (in tractate *Demai* it forms part of a cycle of stories linked to his name) the original connection was severed. On the question of recompense in this discourse, see below, chapter xvi.

33. *Tosefta Soṭa* x, 4, p. 314. *'Avot de-R. Nathan*, Version I, xxxii, 47a, reads: 'The Holy One, blessed be He, changed for them the order of the universe [*siddûrô shel ʿōlām*]... in the hope that they would understand and fear and repent, but they did not'; and *T.B. Sanhedrin* 108b has: 'The Holy One, blessed be He, changed for them the order of Creation [sēder bĕ-rē'shît]....'
34. Not all shared this view. The Palestinian Amoraim said that when Mordecai did not find a wet-nurse for Esther, 'he developed milk and suckled her'. When R. Abbahu expounded this in public and the assembly laughed, he said to them: 'But is not this taught in a Mishna? R. Simeon b. Eleazar said: The milk of a male is levitically pure' (*Gen. Rabba* xxxviii, p. 275). R. Abbahu cited evidence from the Mishna in *Makhshirim* vi, 7, that milk in a man is possible. For the subject proper, see Preuss, *Biblisch Talmudische Medizin*, Berlin 1923, p. 477.
35. *Sifra*, Shĕmînî, Sec. 5, 52b, according to the Rome MS., ed. Finkelstein, p. 218. See *T.B. Ḥullin* 127a, and in conformity with this rule of his, R. Akiba taught (*M. Kelim* xvii, 13) 'All that lives in the sea is pure except the sea-dog, because he seeks refuge on land'; see the *Commentary to the Mishna* by Maimonides *ad loc.* Cf. *Tosefta Maʿasrot* iii, 14, p. 85: 'And Rabban Simeon b. Gamaliel said: Since the six days of Creation [i.e. in the natural order] there is no quadrangular creature'; *T.P. ibid.* v, 7, p. 52a: 'And it is taught: There are quadrangular forms among food stuff, but not among creatures.'
36. *De Vita Mosis*, I, 212–213; see E. Bréhier, *Les Idées philosophiques et religieuses de Philon d'Alexandrie*[3], 1950, pp. 136–151.
37. See G. van der Leeuw, *Phänomenologie*, pp. 643 ff.
38. This [*pĕrûsā*] is the reading in the Parma MS. 1232 (on which Buber based his edition of *Midrash Tehillim*) and also in the Vatican MS. 76 and Vatican

MS. 81. Only in the Paris MS. 152, which Buber (introduction 44a) described as full of errors, and in the Cambridge MS. do we find *parnāsā* ['livelihood'], yet it is the latter reading that Buber (227a) published, without referring to the texts of the other MSS.

39. This is the reading in the Vatican MS. 76 and MS. 81, and in *Yalquṭ ha-Makhiri*; but in ed. Buber the passage is omitted on account of the similarity of wording.
40. *Gen. Rabba* xx, 9, pp. 192–193, in the name of R. Samuel bar Naḥman and R. Joshua b. Levi; see *T.B. Pesaḥim* 108a, and cf. *Pesiqta Rabbati*, ed. Friedmann 152a.
41. *T.B. Shabbat* 53b, according to the text of the Munich MS. and the *Haggadot ha-Talmud*; see *Diqduqe Soferim, ibid.*
42. *T.P. Berakhot*, v, 2, p. 9a; *Gen. Rabba* xiii, 6, p. 116; *T.B. Berakhot*, 33a; *T.B. Ta'anit*, 7a.
43. In *Tosefta Yevamot* xiv, 4, p. 258 and in *T.B. ibid.* 121a–b, but in the latter reference the reading is: '[If a man fell] into a fiery furnace, evidence may be given concerning his death.' (See S. Lieberman, *Tosefta ki-Fshuṭah*, Pt. vi, 1967, p. 173).
44. *Tosefta, loc. cit.*, 5–6; *T.P. loc. cit.* d; *T.B. loc. cit.*; see Tosafot *ad loc.* s.v. *'Ĕn* [Miracles *cannot* be mentioned]: 'According to this, the rabbis disagree with the Baraita cited above', following the reading of the Maharshal [R. Solomon Luria]; cf. Maimonides, 'Hilkhot Gerushin' [Laws of Divorce], xiii, 17, who cites the *Halakha* 'If he was seen to fall into a lion's den... no evidence may be given of his death', adding the explanation 'possibly they will not devour him.'
45. *T.B. Shabbat* 32a; *T.B. Ta'anit* 20b; see *T.P. ibid.* iii, 13, p. 67a. Cf. also *T.P. Berakhot* iv, 4, p. 8b: 'Whenever R. Jannai left for another place he entrusted his will to his household.'
46. *T.B. Megilla* 7b; *T.B. Pesaḥim* 50b, an anonymous Gemara statement.
47. *T.B. Pesaḥim* 64b. See J. Engel, *Gilyônê ha-Shas*, to *Pesaḥim, ibid.*; he refers to the Earlier [*Rî'shônîm*] and Later [*Aḥărônîm*] Authorities, who discuss this question.
48. *Shabbat* and *Ta'anit ibid.*; on Rav Joseph, see *T.B. Shabbat* 140a.
49. He, too, is a Tanna. In *Exod. Rabba* xxi, 6, the same dictum is given in the name of R. Eleazar ha-Qappar, and in *Lev. Rabba* xx, 8, p. 461, it is cited by Bar Qappara in the name of R. Jeremiah b. Eleazar.
50. See H. A. Wolfson, *Philo*, Pt. I, 1947, pp. 347 ff.; *ibid.*, p. 351, n. 24; cf. R. M. Grant, *Miracle and Natural Law*, Amsterdam 1952, pp. 218 ff on Augustine and his doctrine concerning the *Semina* (*De Trinitate*, III, *De Genesi ad Litteram* 5–10) that were sown in the world at the time of Creation and which beget the miracles.
51. See A. D. Nock, *Conversion*, pp. 89–91.
52. See A. Harnack, *Die Mission und Ausbreitung des Christentums*[4], I, Leipzig 1924, pp. 136 ff.

53. See Paul Fiebig, *Rabbinische Wundergeschichten des neutestamentlichen Zeitalters*, Bonn 1911; A. von Schlatter, *Das Wunder in der Synagogue*, 1912; R. M. Grant, *Miracle and Natural Law*, pp. 165–181.
54. This nexus is also clearly evident in the stories of Josephus about the miracles performed by rebels against the government and by those who tried to force the advent of the Messianic Era — *Wars*, II, 259–262.
55. *Tosefta Ḥullin* xxii, 23; *T.P. ʿAvoda Zara* ii, 2, p. 40d *ad fin.*; *T.B. ibid.*, 27b. Eusebius (*Dem. Ev.*, II, 6, 35) boasts of exorcizing demons by the mention of Jesus' name, while Augustine *De Civ. Dei*, XVIII, 53, engages in a polemic with those who maintain that Peter's acts of magic helped to preserve Christianity for 365 years.
56. *T.B. Sanhedrin* 107b; *T.B. Soṭa* 47b; this is the wording of the printed editions preceding that of Basel, and also in *Haggadot ha-Talmud.*
57. See the story about R. Joshua and his colleagues in *T.P. Sanhedrin* vii, 19, p. 25d; also the second story there and the episode of the calf.
58. So, too, Celsus — Origines, *c. Cels.* V, 41.
59. *Qoveṣ Midrashim Qeṭannim* [Collection of Small Midrashim], published by H. M. Horovitz, Berlin 1881, p. 69; see *Esther Rabba* vii, 13. Cf. *T.B. Menaḥot* 85a, and Rashi, *ibid.*, s.v. *Yoḥana u-Mamrē.* See also Schürer, III, pp. 403–405; L. Ginzberg, *Legends*, V, p. 425.
60. *T.B. ʿAvoda Zara* 55a; see above, p. 23.
61. In R. Ḥananel's commentary the words 'through the medium of such-and-such a person' are missing. This omission removes a difficulty, for if it was decreed that the afflictions should depart through the medium of such-and-such a person, and the individual concerned went instead to the idol-house, there is in that case no breach of oath. For this reason, R. Jacob Emden offered this explanation in his notes: 'This seems to me to be the meaning: and also through the medium of so-and-so and such-and-such a medicine you shall leave at the end of the appointed day, even though strict justice demanded that, since he (the sick man) did not have faith in the Lord and put his trust in man and medicine, they should not leave'; needless to say, this is a forced interpretation. Such-and-such a person is undoubtedly the doctor who gives the medicine to the sick person, but the patient, who goes to the pagan shrine, ascribes his cure to this temple.
62. The words *wĕ-ḥôzĕrîn wĕ-'ômĕrîn wĕ-khî* [translated above: 'Then they added: But because'] are omitted in the Spanish MS., ed. S. Abramson.
63. *T.B. Bava Meṣiʿa* 59b; I dealt with this problem, which goes beyond our subject and touches upon other topics, in my article 'Halakha û-Nĕvû'ā' [Halacha and Prophecy], *Tarbiz*, 1947, pp. 1 ff.
64. See R. Walzer, *Galen on Jews and Christians*, Oxford 1949, p. 27.
65. *T.B. Sanhedrin* 100a; *T.B. Bava Batra* 75a; see *Pesiqta de-Rav Kahana*, ʿAniyyā Sôʿărā, ed. Buber 136b; ed. Mandelbaum, 297–298; *ʿArugat ha-Bośem*, Pt. I, p. 254; S. Lieberman, *Tosefta ki-Fshuṭah*, Zeraʿim, p. 54, n. 84; *Pesiqta Rabbati*, 149b. See Tosafot, *T.B. Ḥullin* 57b, s.v. *'Ĕzêl.*

66. *T.B. Megilla* 18a; there is a similar dictum there in the name of R. Eleazar. On the other hand, in *T.B. Makkot* 10a it occurs in a secondary application to the study of the Torah, and in this application the saying is cited in the name of R. Me'ir in *T.B. Horayot* 13b, while *Pirqê de-R. Eliezer*, ch. iii reads: 'R. Eliezer b. Hyrcanus opened (his homily with the words) "Who can express the mighty acts of the Lord, or make all His praise to be heard?" etc.' In the Paris MS. 710, the text has only 'R. Eliezer'! It is clear that the original source is the teaching of R. Eleazar in *T.B. Megilla, ibid.*
67. *T.P. Berakhot* ix, 1, p. 12d; *Shoḥer Ṭov* 19b; see S. Lieberman, 'Ḥazzanut Yannai', *Sinai*, 1939, p. 224.
68. *T.P. ibid.* vii, 3, p. 11c; *T.P. Megilla*, iii, *ad fin.* p. 74c; *Shoḥer Ṭov*, which reads: 'Phinehas ha-Kohen bar Ḥama'. In the Palestinian Talmud our dictum is preceded by 'R. Simon said in the name of R. Joshua b. Levi: Why were they called Men of the Great Synagogue, because they restored the greatness to its former estate'. In *T.B. Yoma* 69b the continuation of the saying is also attributed to R. Joshua b. Levi.
69. This is the reading [with prepositional *Bêt*, which is omitted in the printed editions], in *Yerushalmi Fragments*, ed. L. Ginzberg, p. 27.
70. See the apt remarks on the significance of the answer in Rudolf, *Das Heilige*[6], Breslau 1921, pp. 97–98; cf. J. Guttmann, *Philosophies of Judaism*, pp. 16–17; M. Tsevat, 'The Meaning of the Book of Job', *HUCA*, XXXVII, 1966, pp. 99 ff.
71. *T.B. Yoma* 69b, according to the reading of the Munich MS.; see *Diqduqe Soferim, ibid.*
72. In *T.P., loc. cit.*, the statement of R. Isaac b. Eleazar comes as an answer to the question 'Has a human being the power to set a limit to such things?' In *T.B., loc. cit.*, the question is formulated thus: 'How could the Rabbis act thus, uprooting an enactment made by Moses?' (The prophets are here designated 'Rabbis'!) and the answer is: [R. Isaac b.] Eleazar (this is the reading in the MS.; in the *'En Ya'aqov* and the *Yalquṭ* MS.; see *Diqduqe Soferim, loc. cit.*, 102a) said: Because they know that the Holy One, Blessed be He, is truthful, therefore they did not lie to Him (this is the text in the Munich MS., and the *Yalquṭ* MS.; see *Diqduqe Soferim, loc. cit.*).
73. On the nature of this movement, see G. Scholem, *Major Trends*, the chapter on 'Merkabah Mysticism and Jewish Gnosticism', pp. 40 ff, especially pp. 56 ff.
74. On the celebrated hymn 'Hā-'Adderet wĕ-hā-'Emûnā lĕ-Ḥay hā-'Ōlāmîm' ['Majesty and faithfulness are His, the Life of world'], which emanates from *Sefer Hekhalot* [Book of the Palaces], see P. Bloch in *Monatsschrift*, 1893, p. 259.
75. *T.P. Rosh Hashana* iv, 6, p. 59c; see *Pĕnê Mōshe* and *Qorban hā-'Ĕdā ad loc.*; Ramban [Naḥmanides], *Milḥămôt 'Ădônay* [Wars of the Lord]; Rif [Alfasi], *Rosh ha-Shana*, iv *ad fin.*, referred to in *Ṣiyyûn Yĕrûshālayim.* In the liturgical fragments from the Genizah published by J. Elbogen, *Monatsschrift*, LV, 1911, p. 595, there is found the benedictory ending 'Blessed art Thou, O Lord,

glorious in majesty and the Holy God'; and in the fragments published by Jacob Mann, *HUCA*, II, 1925, p. 329, there occurs: 'Glorious in majesty and the holy King'; these are apparently conflated formulas. The blessing 'Blessed art Thou, O Lord, glorious in majesty' is also found as the conclusion to the 'Song of the Sea' in a formulary of benedictions; see A. J. Schechter, *Studies in Jewish Liturgy*, Philadelphia 1930, p. 84, and Joseph Heinemann, *Ha-Tefilla bi-Tequfat ha-Tanna'im we-ha-'Amora'im*, Jerusalem 1964, p. 103, both of whom overlooked the passage from the Palestinian Talmud that we cited.

CHAPTER VII

THE POWER OF THE DIVINE NAME

By what power, or by what name, have you done this?

1. See The Acts of the Apostles IV 7. Onkelos rendered the Scripture 'and that My name be declared' — 'and that they may relate the mighty acts of My name'.
2. See above, p. 701, n. 1.
3. See Kaufmann, *Toledot ha-'Emuna ha-Yisre'elit*, I, p. 481, n. 17. Despite Kaufmann's strictures, Buber, in *Königtum Gottes*, Berlin 1932, pp. 83–85, appears to be right in his interpretation of Exodus iii 13 ff, according to which these verses express the annulment of the magic character of the Name. Kaufmann's argument that it is nowhere stated in the Torah 'Do not practise magic with the name of the Lord' is not valid, for it is obvious that the general prohibition of witchcraft includes also sorcery of this kind.
4. See L. Löw, *Gesammelte Schriften*, I, Szegedin 1889, pp. 187 ff; B. Jacob, *Im Namen Gottes*, 1903, pp. 1 ff.
5. Fragments of his work 'On the Jews' have been preserved in that of Eusebius, *Praep. Ev.*, IX, 27. See J. Freudenthal, *Hellenistische Studien*, pp. 160 ff and p. 235; A. Dietrich, *Abraxas*, 1891, pp. 70 ff; cf. B. Jacob, *op. cit.*, p. 109, and Julius Guttmann, *Ha-Sifrut ha-Helenistit*, II, p. 130.
6. *Ant.*, II, 275; on his attitude to Artapanus, see Freudenthal and Guttmann, *loc. cit.* On the various interpretations of the expression *Shēm ha-Mĕfôrāsh* [literally 'the Tetragrammaton pronounced'; rendered in the text: 'the Ineffable Name'], see Max Grünbaum, *Gesammelte Aufsätze zur Sprach- und Sagenkunde*, Berlin 1911, pp. 238–258; it is clear that from the practical aspect, the Name, which only few knew how to pronounce and to interpret, was a 'Hidden Name' set apart and holy.
7. *Mekhilta de-R. Ishmael*, Massekhta de-Wa-yehi, Petiḥta, p. 78, according to the Munich MS.; the parallel passages are indicated in the notes *ibid.* It seems to me that this reading (similarly, in *Midrash Aggada*, ed. S. Buber, Vienna 1894, p. 143 we find: 'and Moses wrote the Ineffable Name and cast it into the Nile') is old and not a later addition. In other recensions of the *Mekhilta* the text has: 'He took a pebble and cast it therein', which is, appar-

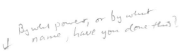

ently, an abridgement of the recension of the *Tanḥuma*, Be-shallaḥ, § 2: 'He took a pebble and engraved on it "Arise, O ox!".' In the *Mekhilta de-R. Ishmael, loc. cit.*, and in the parallel passages dependent on it, it is stated only that Moses said 'Joseph, Joseph! (the time) has arrived (for the fulfilment of) the oath that the Holy One, blessed be He, swore to Abraham', etc.

8. M. Güdemann, *Religionsgeschichtliche Studien*, Leipzig 1876, pp. 26 ff; see J. Guttmann, *op. cit.*, pp. 111 ff.
9. *Leviticus Rabba* xxxii, 4, p. 745; *Tanḥuma*, Exodus ix. On the different interpretations *ad loc.*, see M. Kasher, *Torah Shlemah* [Talmudic-Midrashic Encyclopedia on the Pentateuch], Exodus, p. 80, n. 102.
10. *Deut. Rabba* iii, 8; in ed. Lieberman, p. 87, the dictum is in the name of R. Judah; in *Pesiqta de-Rav Kahana*, p. 308, the reading is: 'R. Nehemiah said, The Ineffable Name was engraven on it — "The Lord of hosts is His name"'; but in the Carmoly MS. the text has 'R. Judah' (see the vv.ll. *ibid.*). In *Yalquṭ Shimʿoni*, Pt. I, § 181, there is cited in the name of a 'Midrash': 'When Moses and Aaron came, they stood before Pharaoh... and in their hand was the rod of God on which was engraved the Ineffable Name'; and *ibid.* § 168, excerpted from the annals of Moses, 'Behold, there was engraved on it the name of the Lord God of hosts, written in full on the rod'. The version of the Haggada given in *Pirqê de-R. Eliezer* xl implies that the letters were inscribed on the rod, as is also stated in *Tanḥuma*, Wa-'era' 8, ed. Buber; see *Śekhel Ṭov* to Exodus, ed. Buber, Berlin 1901, p. 27. All this contradicts the *Mekhilta de-R. Ishmael*, Wa-yehi, iv, p. 102, where it is stated that the sea did not flee on account of the Holy Name (see vv.ll. *ibid.*), nor at the sight of the rod, but only when 'the Holy One, blessed be He, revealed Himself'; see above, p. 136.
11. The interpretation given by E.S. Hartom, *Ha-Sĕfārîm ha-Ḥîsônîm* [Apocrypha], ed. A. Kahana, I, p. 332, to this verse is improbable.
12. *Tanḥuma*, Bereshit i. See *Pirqê de-R. Eliezer*, iii, 'Until the world was created, there was only the Holy One, blessed be He, and His Name'; this is the reading in the first printed edition, Constantinople 1514, and in the Venice edition, 1544.
13. *T.B. Sukka* 53a; this is also the reading in the Munich MS. and in the Berlin MS. According to Rashi's interpretation — '*He said to him*: since you have reminded me of the matter, this is what was said' — the speaker was Rav Ḥisda; but according to the text of the MSS. we must read before this 'If so, fifteen' etc. 'He answered him, Fifteen', in which case the speaker was 'a certain Rabbi'. See *Diqduqe Soferim*, Sukka, p. 174, nn. 4 and 8. The story is related in answer to Rav Ḥisda's question 'With reference to what did David utter these fifteen Songs of Ascent?'
14. Preisendanz, *Papyri Graecae Magicae*, Pt. II, Berlin 1931, pp. 105, 120, and also p. 28; see G. Alon, *Tarbiz*, XXI, 1950, p. 33 (= *Meḥqarim be-Toledot Yisra'el*, 1957, Pt. I, p. 196).
15. So correctly interpreted by S. Lieberman, *Tarbiz* XXVII, 1958, p. 184; see *Mekhilta de-R. Ishmael*, Mishpaṭim, XVII, p. 310: 'R. Simeon b. Yoḥai

said... whoever associates the name of the Holy One, blessed be He, with idols deserves annihilation'; possibly his statement was made with reference to the use of the Divine Names and the letters of the Torah in amulets and invocations alongside the names of idols.

16. See J. Z. Lauterbach, 'Substitutes for the Tetragrammaton', *Proceedings of the AAJR*, XXII, 1930–1931, pp. 39–67.

17. Compare II Sam. vii 28: *wĕ-ʿattā 'Ădōnay YHWH 'attā hû hā-'Ĕlōhîm* ['And now, O Lord God, Thou alone art God'] with I Chron. xvii 26: *wĕ-ʿattā YHWH 'attā hû hā-'Ĕlōhîm* ['And now, O Lord, Thou alone art God']. In Ezekiel we find *kō 'āmar 'Ădōnay YHWH* ['Thus saith the Lord God'] 122 times and *nĕ'ûm 'Ădōnay YHWH* ['Saith the Lord God'] 81 times, but in Haggai, Zechariah, and Malachi there is not a single instance. The Masoretic vocalization of the Tetragrammaton in all the above-mentioned passages is that of *'Ĕlōhîm*; cf. the annotation of R. Elijah Gaon of Vilna to *'Oraḥ Ḥayyîm* § 5 '...and therefore when two Names are in juxtaposition, its vocalization is sometimes that of *'Ĕlōhîm*, but the pointing of the Name itself [i.e. the Tetragrammaton] is unknown like all the cases of *Kĕtîv* in the Torah, and its vocalization is the secret of the Ineffable Name; see B. Jacob, *op. cit.*, pp. 165 ff.

18. Lev. xxiv 16 is translated ὀνομάζων δὲ τὸ ὄνομα κυρίου θανάτῳ θανατούσθω; see A. Geiger, *Urschrift*², Frankfort-on-Main 1928, pp. 262 ff, and the Addenda *ibid.* pp. 11 ff; F. Perles, *Annalekten zur Textkritik des Alten Testaments*, Munich 1895, pp. 12–20; I. L. Seeligmann, *The Septuagint Version of Isaiah*, Leiden 1948, p. 66.

19. As in the Genizah fragment containing Psalms translated by Aquila; see C. Taylor, *Cairo Genizah Palimpsests*, Cambridge 1900, pp. 54–65. So, too, in all five columns of the palimpsest of the Hexapla of the *Codex Ambrosianus*, the Tetragrammaton is written in Hebrew letters. See P. Kahle, 'Die von Origenes verwendeten griech. Bibelhandschriften', *Studia Patristica*, IV, 1961, p. 107. Kahle's conclusion is that the translation of the Name by κύριος does not pertain to the original Septuagint text. Nor is κύριος found in the sense of the Divine Name in the Hellenistic literature of the third and second centuries B.C.E.; see *ibid.* p. 116. But compare above p. 718, n. 51, and also W. Baudissin, *Kyrios*, I, p. 5; II, pp. 236 ff.

20. See A. M. Habermann, *Megillot Midbar Yehuda*, 1959, p. 31. In view of the fact that this feature is not found in the Scroll of Isaiah, it seems that the practice was restricted to annotations and to the Psalms that were used for instruction. See *Discoveries in the Judaean Desert of Jordan*, Oxford 1962, Vol. III, pp. 55 and 95; cf. also *ibid.* Vol. IV, 1965. See further Y. Yadin, 'Another Fragment of the Psalms Scroll from Qumran 11', *Textus*, V, 1966, pp. 6–7.

21. *De Vita Mosis*, II, 114; the Septuagint, Exodus XXVIII 36, already translates: καὶ ἐκτυπώσεις ἐν αὐτῷ ἐκτύπωμα σφραγῖδος, Ἁγίασμα Κυρίου. See the *Letter of Aristeas* 98; Josephus, *Wars*, v, 5, 7 (235); *Ant.* iii, 7, 6 (178); *T.P. Yoma* iv, 1, p. 41c; *T.B. Shabbat* 63b; I. Heinemann, *Philons griechische*

und jüdische Bildung, Breslau 1932, pp. 19–21; S. Belkin, *Philo and the Oral Law*, Cambridge Mass. 1940, p. 41.

22. *M. Soṭa* vii, 6; *Sifre*, Naśo', § 39, p. 43; see *ibid.* note to line 9; H. Albeck, *Seder Nashim*, Supplements, p. 387.
23. See S. Lieberman, *op. cit.*, p. 184; *Tosefta ki-Fshuṭah*, Mo'ed, p. 755.
24. *T.P. Yoma* iii, 7, p. 40d. In *Sifre Zuṭa*, Be-midbar VI, 27, p. 250, the tradition regarding R. Ṭarfon is transferred to the 'priestly benediction', in which case the expression 'and I inclined my ear towards the high priest' is strange. In *T.B. Qiddushin* 71a, the beginning of the Baraita is also different. Instead of 'Once I was standing among my brother priests in the line', we find there 'Once I went up after my mother's brother to the priests' platform....' The Baraita concerning R. Ṭarfon is taught there immediately after the Baraita regarding the Twelve-Lettered Name. S. Ch. Kook, 'Bĕ-'inyānê Shēmôt ha-Qĕdôshîm' [On the Sacred Names], in his volume of essays, *'Iyyûnîm û-Meḥqārîm*, Pt. I, Jerusalem 1959, pp. 164 ff, suggests that also the last sentence in the Palestinian Talmud 'At first it was made known...' refers to the Twelve-Lettered Name, but this is without foundation. There is no reference to this Name either in the Palestinian Talmud or in *Sifre Zuṭa*, and even in the Babylonian Talmud there is no need to regard the Baraita about R. Ṭarfon as referring to the Name spoken of in the preceding Baraita. In the current editions it is stated 'And I heard him swallow the Name in the melody of his brother priests', and in the MS. Munich the reading is '...for they swallowed the Name in the chanting...'; and the reference is undoubtedly to the Tetragrammaton.
25. See A. Geiger, *Qĕvûṣat Ma'ămārîm* [Nachgelassene Schriften], Berlin 1877, p. 102; Ben Yehuda, *Millon* [Complete Dictionary of Ancient and Modern Hebrew], III, p. 1264, n. 3, deals with the subject at great length, but does not mention Geiger's views. Other explanations are given by L. Blau, *op. cit.*, p. 134, n. 2; G. Alon, *Meḥqarim*, Pt. I, p. 200. H. Yalon, *Kirjath Sepher*, XXVIII, 1952, p. 71 already dealt with *HW'H*, *HW'H'* in *Serekh ha-Yaḥad* ['Manual of Discipline'] (See ed. Licht, Jerusalem 1965, pp. 160, 181) and *'Ănî wā-Hû'*; possibly these forms simply reflect what was indistinctly heard [as a result of the muffling ('swallowing') of the Name by the high priest].
26. See Blau, *op. cit.*, p. 131, where he refers to the names in the papyri ιωφη, ιωπη; the whole subject is an addition to the Mishna from the Baraita. Cf. J. N. Epstein, *Māvô' lĕ-Nōsaḥ ha-Mishnā*, pp. 928, 952; S. Lieberman, *Tosefta ki-Fshuṭah*, Mo'ed, p. 871. Similar to יופי is the epithet יוסי, *M. Sanhedrin* VII, 10, spelt in MSS. יוסה (*Diqduqe Soferim* 80a) and vocalized, in the Kaufmann MS., *Yôsēh*; possibly the other epithet was pronounced *Yôfēh*.
27. In the light of this interpretation it is also possible to understand the objection raised by the Babylonian Talmud, *loc. cit.*, p. 46b, that the expression *Lĕ-Yāh û-lĕkhā* appears to imply that *lĕ-Yāh* ['to the Lord'] and *lĕkhā* ['to Thee'] do not refer to the same Being; see S. Lieberman, ''Alê 'Ayin', the *S.Z. Schocken Jubilee Volume*, Jerusalem 1948–1952, p. 81.

28. *Tosefta Soṭa* xiii, 8, p. 319; the first version is that of the printed edd. and the Vienna MS., and the second is that of the Erfurt MS.
29. This is also the explanation of B. Jacob, *op. cit.*, p. 175, n. 3.
30. This is the approach of A. Marmorstein, *The Old Rabbinic Doctrine of God*, Pt. I, p. 29; he freely emends the text of the Mishna and the Tosefta of Berakhot, but his whole historic structure is unsound. It is based on the dictum of R. Joshua b. Levi (*T.P. Berakhot* ix, p. 14c; *T.B. Makkot* 23b): 'Three things were enacted by the earthly court, to which the Heavenly Court gave assent. These are: the reading of the Scroll (of Esther), greeting with the Divine Name, and the bringing of the (Levite's) tithe (to the Temple chamber)' (In the Palestinian Talmud 'the banned property of Jericho' is counted but not 'the bringing of the tithe'). Marmorstein links all the things together and attributes them to adjacent periods, and in this way he comes to the enactment made against the priests who succeeded Simon. The aforementioned dictum is supported by verses pertaining to periods far removed from one another, and the number is only intended to indicate enactments made by the earthly court to which assent was given by the Heavenly Court. Marmorstein's interpretation of Psalms cxxix 8, according to which 'they that go by' are the Hellenists, who did not accept the enactment of the Sages to use the Ineffable Name in their greetings, is purely imaginary; and undoubtedly Sirach xli 20 has no bearing on our subject. See M. H. Segal, pp. 281–282.
31. See H. Albeck, *Seder Zeraʿim*, Supplements, p. 339.
32. In the Kaufmann MS., Lowe, and the MS. of Maimonides, the reading is: 'At the close [*ḥôtam* sing. instead of *ḥôtĕmê*] of every benediction recited in the Temple was the formula "from everlasting"....'
33. See A. Krochmal, *ʿIyyun Tefilla* [Prayer Study], 1885, p. 22; S. A. Lowenstamm, *Tarbiz*, XXXII, 1963, pp. 313–316.
34. The Mishna enumerates Temple usages, including the formula used at the close of the benedictions. The sentence beginning 'When the sectarians corrupted their teaching' does not mark the beginning of a new subject, but states when this closing formula was introduced. The *Tosefta Berakhot*, vi, 21, adds the reason for the enactment: 'thus making known that this world....' The Mishna gives us the beginning of the concluding phrase, 'from everlasting', the Tosefta cites the end of the phrase 'to everlasting' (but there is evidence of the opposite version, both in the Mishna and in the Tosefta), and there is no disagreement between them; both refer to the same formula 'from everlasting to everlasting'. This explanation removes the difficulties that both the earlier and later expositors struggled to solve: see S. Lieberman, *Tosefta ki-Fshuṭah*, Zeraʿim, pp. 122–123. According to our interpretation, therefore, the ending was never 'from everlasting' or 'to everlasting' alone, but when the concluding formula was instituted, it took the familiar form 'from everlasting to everlasting'.
35. This explanation of the enactment concerning salutations was also given by Mann, *Text and Studies*, Pt. I, Cincinnati 1931, pp. 581–582; only, following

the opinion of A. Büchler (*Priester und Cultus*, Vienna 1895, p. 176) regarding the first enactment, he dated it to the close of the Temple era, but there is no proof of this. On the views relating to Divine Providence, see below, chapter xi.

36. See *T.B. Shabbat* 115b: 'Benedictions and amulets, although they contain letters of the Name and many Torah passages, may not be rescued from a fire [on the Sabbath]. See *ibid.* 61b; *Tosefta ibid.* xiii, 14; *Tosefta ki-Fshuṭah ibid.*, p. 205; cf. L. Blau, *op. cit.*, pp. 44–95.
37. *Lev. Rabba*, XXV, p. 567. On the great care that they took in writing the Name, see *Tosefta Berakhot* iii, 22; cf. *Tosefta ki-Fshuṭah*, Pt. I, p. 47. For one who enquires of his staff, see *Tosefta Shabbat* vii (viii), 4; *Tosefta ki-Fshuṭah ibid.*, p. 93; cf. also *T.P. Nedarim* x, 1 p. 41a (= *Mo'ed Qaṭan* iii, 2, p. 82a): 'R. Me'ir's staff was in my hand and it instructed me'.
38. See Israel Lévi, 'Ueber einige Fragmente aus der Mischna des Abba Saul', *Bericht über die Hochschule für die Wissenschaft des Judenthums in Berlin*, 1876, pp. 33–34. Epiphanius, *Contra Haer.*, 24, 14, states that Peter ascribed his power to the knowledge of barbaric names — καὶ ὀνόματα βαρβαρικά. In *Tanḥuma*, Wa-yeshev, § 2, in the account of the War of the Samaritans at the beginning of the period of the Second Temple, it is stated: 'What did Ezra and Zerubbabel and Joshua do? They assembled the entire Congregation in the Temple of the Lord... and the Levites sang and played and they banned, anathematized, and excommunicated the Cutheans by the mystery of the Ineffable Name.'
39. See Z. Ben Ḥayyim, '*Ha-Hôgîm ha-Shômĕrônîm 'et ha-Shēm bĕ-'Otiyôtāw*? [Do the Samaritans pronounce the Name as it is spelt?]' *Sefer Eretz-Israel*, iii, 1954, p. 147; cf. *ibid.*, p. 150, n. 48.
40. See the commentary of R. Beḥai to *M. 'Avot*, ed. J. L. Deutsch, Jerusalem (undated), p. 17; cf. G. Scholem, *Jewish Gnosticism* etc., p. 54.
41. *Gen. Rabba*, xliv, 19, p. 442.
42. See *More Nevukhim* [Guide of the Perplexed], Pt. I, lxii; cf. *'Oṣar ha-Ge'onim* to *Qiddushin*, p. 176, and the note of B. Lewin *ad loc.* The arithmetical combination of W. Bacher, *Die Agada des bab. Amoräer*, Strassburg 1878, pp. 17 ff, who thought he could find the Name of forty-two letters in the dictum of Rav concerning the ten things with which the Holy One, blessed be He, created the world, *T.B. Ḥagiga* 12a, was already rightly rejected by L. Blau; see also above, p. 197.
43. M. Gaster, 'The Sword of Moses', *Journal of the Royal Asiatic Society*, London 1896, pp. 156 ff (= *Studies and Texts in Folklore*, *Magic* etc., vol. I, London 1925, pp. 295 ff); Blau, *op. cit.*, pp. 141–145.
44. *T.B. Shevu'ot* 21a: 'R. Judah said in the name of R. Jose the Galilean', and so, too, *T.B. Makkot* 16a; in *T.B. Temura* 3a the text has only 'in the name of R. Jose the Galilean', but the Munich MS. reads: 'R. Judah said in the name of R. Jose the Galilean'. In Tractates *Makkot* and *Temurah*, Rashi explains 'by the Name' to mean 'by the Name of the Holy One, blessed be He', but in *Shevu'ot* he glosses, 'by the Specific Name'.

45. *Eccles. Rabba, loc. cit.* There the order is reversed: it is R. Phinehas bar Ḥama who asks the physician to reveal to him the secret of the Ineffable Name, and the physician refused for the reason mentioned, but the version of the Palestinian Talmud appears to be the more original. In the *Qundres 'Aḥaron* [Addendum] of the *Yalquṭ Shim'oni* (see L. Ginzberg, *Yerushalmi Fragments*, p. 311) the reading is: 'R. Jose in Sepphoris said to R. Phinehas bar Ḥama...', but this appears to be a corrupt version. A similar divergence is found also in the story about R. 'Onyani bar Susai and R. Ḥanina of Sepphoris. According to the Palestinian Talmud, R. 'Onyani offers to reveal the Name to R. Ḥanina; but in *Eccles. Rabba* the reverse is stated. R. 'Onyana bar Susai, unlike R. Ḥanina, is not a well-known Sage, and is cited in the Palestinian Talmud only four times; see my remarks in *IEJ*, IX (1959), p. 152. Cf. also *Pesiqta Rabbati* § 21, p. 104a: 'Just as I create and destroy worlds, so does My Name create and destroy worlds.'
46. *Pesiqta Rabbati* § 22, p. 114b; cf. S. Lieberman, *Tosefta ki-Fshuṭah*, Mo'ed, p. 755, n. 14.
47. Lieberman, *ibid.*, refers to *T.B. Yoma* 69b, where Rav declares that Ezra magnified God by pronouncing the Ineffable Name; see also *T.P. Berakhot* vii, p. 11c.
48. *T.B. Qiddushin* 71a, where the passage is preceded by a Baraita that explains the *Mishna 'Eduyot* viii, 7: 'It is taught: There was another (family) there, and the Sages did not wish to disclose it, but they confided the information to their sons and disciples once in a septennate', etc. With regard to this statement, too, Rav Naḥman the son of Isaac said 'Reason supports' etc. Now it may be argued that the dictum of R. Joḥanan regarding the Name is only an interpretation transferred from elsewhere, especially since in *T.P. Qiddushin* iv, 5, p. 65c only the first topic is cited, and with reference to it R. Joḥanan observes: 'By the Temple! I recognize them, but what can be done seeing that the leaders of the generation have become mixed up with them!' Nevertheless, it seems that the authenticity of the saying is not to be doubted, since it begins a complete discussion on the subject of the pronunciation of the Name and the teaching of the secret thereof. Apparently it was transferred here on account of the similarity between the Baraita and the dictum of R. Joḥanan.
49. So, too, is Ecclesiastes iii 22 expounded in the homilies of *Ecc. Rabba, ibid.*; see also the Targum, *ibid.*
50. On the verse, Gen. xxv 6, 'But unto the sons of the concubines, that Abraham had, Abraham gave gifts', R. Jeremiah bar Abba said: '(It means) that he confided to them the name of impurity' (*T.B. Sanhedrin* 91a). Rashi in his commentary to Genesis, *loc. cit.*, cites the saying, and the commentators go to great trouble in their endeavour to explain away the difficulty of the dictum. Some have emended the text to read 'the Name in impurity'; see M. Kasher, *Torah Shelemah*, Ḥayyê Sārā, p. 596. Compare also L. Ginzberg, *Legends*, V, p. 265, and p. 301. The attempt by H. J. Schoeps, *Aus frühchristli-*

chen Zeit, Tübingen 1950, pp. 252 ff, to identify Balaam with Simon Magus, who is also alleged to have flown, is no more probable than the identification with Jesus; see my observations in *Tarbiz*, XXV (1956), pp. 281 ff. In the description of the teraphim of Laban in *Pirqê de-R. Eliezer* xxxvi (omitted in the ed. containing the commentary of R. David Luria) it is also stated 'On the golden plate [*ṣîṣ*] (of the high priest) is inscribed the name of the spirit of impurity' (in the Ginzburg MS. 111, 'on the golden *ṭas* [= 'plate', like ṣîṣ above]'); while on our verse Targum Pseudo-Jonathan declares 'and they inscribed magical formulas on a golden plate'; see above, p. 734, n. 10.

51. In the *Yelammedenu*, cited in *Yalquṭ Shimʿoni*, Be-midbar, § 785, it is stated that Balaam 'flew and ascended by using the Ineffable Name'. In Targum Pseudo-Jonathan to Numbers xxxi 8 it is already stated 'He performed an act of magic and flew in the air of the sky'. See H. M. Horowitz, *Aggadat Aggadot*, Berlin 1881, pp. 78–79, and *ibid.* n. 26; he did not see the *Yalquṭ Shimʿoni*, hence he wrote that the author of the Haggadah derived it from the statement of Targum Pseudo-Jonathan; cf. *Tanḥuma* Maṭṭot, § 4; *Num. Rabba*, xx, 20.
52. See B. Jacob, *op. cit.*

CHAPTER VIII

THE HEAVENLY HOUSEHOLD

1. *Mekhilta de-R. Ishmael*, Massekhta de-Shira, iii, p. 128. The parable belongs to the Rabbinic exposition of the verse 'This is my God, and I will glorify Him': 'And the Sages said (that God declared) "I will accompany him until I come with him to his Temple". The case is comparable to that of a king...' and it is the continuation of R. Akiba's exposition *ibid.*, p. 127. See also *ibid.*, Massekhta de-Pisḥa, xiv, p. 51: 'R. Akiba said: Were it not that it is written in Scripture, it would not be possible to say it. Israel, so to speak, said to the Holy One, blessed be He, "Thou hast redeemed Thyself". Similarly, you find that wherever the Israelites were exiled, the Shekhina went into exile with them'. Cf. *Mekhilta de-R. Simeon b. Yoḥai*, pp. 79 and 232.
2. See above, p. 178.
3. *Mekhilta de-R. Ishmael*, Wa-yehi, iv, p. 101, but in Genesis xxi 17 it is stated 'and the angel of God [*Elohim*] called'; but there, too, R. Simon expounded 'The Ministering Angels sprang forward to indict him' etc. — *Gen. Rabba*, liii, 14, p. 572; see the parallel passages indicated *ibid.*, n. 8.
4. *Mekhilta de-R. Ishmael*, Massekhta de-Pisḥa, xiv, p. 51. In the *Yalquṭ*, however, the words 'these are the Ministering Angels' are missing; but see *Mekhilta*, *loc. cit.*, ix, p. 33; cf. also *Mekhilta de-R. Simeon b. Yoḥai*, p. 34 (*ad fin.*).
5. See I. L. Seeligmann, *The Septuagint Version of Isaiah*, 1948, p. 62; and cf. my observations in *Tarbiz*, 1961, p. 153; *Kirjat Sepherh*, xxxvi (1961), p. 146, n. 17. In the Septuagint, Ἄγγελος is still used in the sense of a human messenger, like *mal'ākh* in the Bible, but in the Rabbinic idiom *mal'ākh* has only its special connotation. 'The Holy One, blessed be He, carries out His mission through every medium' (*Gen. Rabba* x, 7, p. 80) but 'one angel does not perform two missions, nor do two angels perform one mission' (*ibid.* l, 2, p. 516). R. Ḥanina said: 'Before they have performed their mission, they are human beings; once they have performed their mission, they have assumed the character of angels' (*ibid.*, p. 518); see Max Grünbaum, *Gesammelte Aufsätze zur Sprach- und Sagenkunde*, 1901, p. 287.
6. See *Mekhilta de-R. Ishmael*, Massekhta de-Pisḥa, vii, p. 23; xiii, p. 43; *Sifre*

Deuteronomy § 42 and § 325; *Haggada shel Pesaḥ*, ed. D. Goldschmidt, Jerusalem 1960, p. 44, n. 60; cf. below, p. 734, n. 10 [See now J. Goldin, 'Not by means of an Angel and not by means of a Messenger', *Studies in the History of Religions*, 1968, pp. 412 ff; but he did not take note of the aforementioned rendering of the Septuagint — see above, n. 5.].

7. So in Targum Onkelos and in Targum Pseudo-Jonathan. In the Septuagint: τὸ γὰρ ὄνομα μοῦ ἐστιν ἐπ' αὐτῷ 'for My name is upon him'.
8. *Exod. Rabba* xxxii 9; the author of the saying is apparently R. Joshua b. R. Neḥemiah; see *Gen. Rabba* xcvii, 3, p. 1246 and note *ibid.*
9. *Exod. Rabba* xxxii 2–3; *Tanḥuma*, Mishpaṭim, § 17; see also *ibid.* § 18; *Gen. Rabba* xcvii, 3, p. 1246, and *ibid.* n. 4.
10. *Mekhilta de-R. Ishmael*, Shira, ii, pp. 124–125. It is actually in the homilies of the Amoraim that the phrasing is sometimes changed and the Guardian Angel becomes a 'god'. See *Exod. Rabba* ix, 9: 'Said the Holy One, blessed be He: "I first smite the god and afterwards his people." ' As the popular proverb puts it: "Smite the gods and the priests tremble." ' On the smiting of the deities see M. P. Nilson, *Geschichte der griechischen Religion*, I, p. 781; *ibid.*, II, p. 181. See also L. Friedländer, *Sittengeschichte Roms*, III, p. 546. On the names of the Guardian Angels see *Exod. Rabba* xxi, 5, where the Midrashic expositions are reported fully in the name of R. Eleazar b. Pedat; *Midrash Samuel* xviii, p. 98, in the name of R. Ḥanina — see *ibid.* Buber's note; *Cant. Rabba* viii (*ad fin.*); *Deut. Rabba* i, 22 in the name of R. Tanḥuma; this passage was undoubtedly taken from his Midrash, cf. *Tanḥuma*, Be-shallaḥ, xiii.
11. xvii 17; see ed. Segal, p. 106, and the version he cites there from *Pirqe de-R. Eliezer* XXIV, Constantinople ed., 1502 and Venice ed. 1544: 'And He appointed an angel over every nation, but Israel fell to His own portion and share, and with regard to this it is said....' In the edition containing the commentary of David Luria [RaDal] we find only 'and He appointed an angel over every tongue. And whence do we know that the Holy One, blessed be He, descended?'; the omission is due to the censor. But the Casanatense MS., from which Higger published extracts, *Horeb*, p. 158, lacks the whole sentence 'and He confused their tongue (giving it) to seventy nations and (in) seventy languages. And whence do we know that the Holy One, blessed be He, descended?' I found the same also in the Warsaw MS. 240/5, but in the Paris MS. 710 the text is identical with that of the first edition and the Venice edition. The connection with the generation of the Tower of Babel is to be found in the *Testament of Naphtali* in the Hebrew version; see *Bet ha-Midrash*, I, p. 196.
12. See *Jubilees* xv, 32; the *Scroll of the War of the Sons of Light with the Sons of Darkness*, ed. Y. Yadin, Jerusalem 1955, p. 338; cf. the Introduction *ibid.*, p. 213. See also Origines, *c. Cels*, V, 25–30.
13. *T.B. Sanhedrin* 38b; see *Diqduqe Soferim ibid.*, 55a, where all who read *'Îdî* are listed. But even so it is difficult to determine which R. Idi is intended.

14. R. Ḥananel, Rashi, and Me'ir ha-Levi Abulafia (RaMaH) all explain that it was Meṭaṭron who said 'Come up unto the Lord'; Naḥmanides (Ramban) in his commentary on Exod. xxiv 1 states that it was the Lord who said to Moses 'Come up to Meṭaṭron, who is called by My name, the Lord'; but it is clear that he introduced his own doctrine here, and he also admits 'that the words of the Sages in this Haggadah have an esoteric meaning'; see also his annotation *ibid.* xxiii 20, where he distinguishes between the 'way of truth' and between what 'our Sages said that he was Meṭaṭron, which is a term for a guide.'
15. On the various attempts to explain the name Meṭaṭron, see H. Odeberg, *Enoch*, 1928, pp. 125–142. G. Scholem (*Major Trends*, p. 68) rightly stated that they are all guesswork. But his own conjecture, that the name comes to replace the original name *Yĕhô'ēl* as a *vox mystica*, also does not appeal to me, for it is likewise based — like the cryptograph (gematria) *šdy* [Shaddai] = *mṭṭrwn* [Meṭaṭron] — on the view that 'for My name is in him' is an explanation of the name. The fact that *Yĕhô'ēl* appears at the head of the list of the seventy names of Meṭaṭron in the *Book of Enoch*, ed. Odeberg, xlviii, does not prove anything; nor does the statement of Qirqisani, *HUCA*, vii, p. 317, 'and they say Meṭaṭron is the Little Lord, and his name is the same as his master's' etc., attest the fact that such words were to be found in *T.B. Sanhedrin ibid.*, as G. Scholem conjectures, *op. cit.*, p. 366, n. 107. S. Lieberman, *Shĕqîʿîn* [Shekiʿin], 1939, p. 15, has already pointed out that there is no sign of this in any of the Talmud MSS., nor in the recension used by Raymond Martini; the statement is found in *'Otiyyot de-R. Akiba*, in the *Book of Enoch* and in the *Books of Hekhalot*, and, as we have shown above in this chapter, it is also out of place in the context of the story of R. Idi. The far-reaching conclusions drawn by G. Scholem in *Jewish Gnosticism* etc., p. 41, from the fact that there is not a trace left in the entire magical literature of the transcription of *Yeho'el* as *Meṭaṭron*, while the name *Yeho'el* appears in various forms, do not appear to me correct. On the contrary, this fact calls for further investigation. A feature common to all the commentators is the fact that they completely overlook the context in which the words occur, and wrench the piquant expression from it. Rav Naḥman praises Rav Idi for his answer. It is not to be supposed that it was just in this case that there was an accumulation of points that made it difficult for him to reply and weakened his argument; hence, I suggest the following interpretation of the passage: Rav Idi chose the name of an angel that signifies only 'a guide' (see *ʿAvoda Zara* 3b — *Meṭaṭron* as a teacher of children; and cf. *Sifre Deut.* § 338, p. 388: 'R. Eliezer said: The finger of the Holy One, blessed be He, was the Meṭaṭron of Moses', etc.). His task was to teach Moses how to ascend. Since he identified him with the angel of whom it is said 'for My name is in him', in the sense given the statement in the Targumim (see above), it was easy for the circles interested in angelology to introduce here the exegetical interpolation 'whose name is the same as his Master's', and

possibly to add also 'the Little Lord'. Just as some of the redactors of the Talmuds and the Midrashim — and not only the redactors but also the transmitting scholars — removed passages from their sources to avoid anthropomorphism, or for fear of allusions to dualistic belief, so there were also Amoraim and editors who, because of their affinity and identification with mystic circles, augmented the stories and homilies with additional matter and expressions in keeping with their concepts. The context enables us to determine whether we have an omission or addition before us, and in our case the character of the narrative obliges us not to regard 'the Little Lord' mentioned by Qirqisani as an omission, but, on the contrary, to consider the words 'whose name is as the name of his Master' an addition. For the whole tenor of the narrative is opposed to any conception of an independent angel or power. This assertion does not detract from the evidence, based on non-Jewish Gnostic literature, concerning the antiquity of the name *Yeho'el* and of the epithet 'the Little Lord', which were undoubtedly derived from Jewish circles, only they find no support in Rabbinic sources, and particularly not in sources of the character of the story about Rav Idi. Michael, the great Prince, who offers up sacrifices on the altar built in heaven, according to the dictum of Rav in *T.B. Menaḥot* 100a, is replaced in *Num. Rabba* xii 12 by 'the youth whose name is Meṭaṭron', who offers up, in the Tabernacle on high, 'the souls of the righteous'.

16. *Mekhilta de-R. Ishmael*, Massekhta de-Wa-yehi, vi, p. 111.
17. *Deut. Rabba*, ed. S. Lieberman, 1940, p. 14; *Exod. Rabba* i, 12; in *Seder Eliyahu Rabba*, vii, p. 43, as in tractate *Soṭa*, angels are mentioned. Only in *Pirqê de-R. Eliezer*, xlii, 'The Holy One, blessed be He, put a stone in the mouth of each one'.
18. *Gen. Rabba*, xciii, 3, p. 1245.
19. See *Enoch* i, 20, 5; the *Apocalypse of Baruch* ii, 11, 2; cf. *Mĕgillat Milḥemet Bnĕ 'Ôr bi-Bĕnê Ḥoshekh* [The Scroll of the War of the Sons of Light against the Sons of Darkness], xxvii, 6, ed. Yadin, p. 354, and the Introduction *ibid.*, p. 215.
20. *Aggadat Bereshit*, xxxii, p. 64. On the identity of the angel who revealed himself to Moses we find a difference of opinion: 'R. Joḥanan said: This is Michael; R. Ḥanina said: This is Gabriel.' (*Exod. Rabba* i, 5). But even R. Joḥanan did not identify him with the angel that went before Israel. This dispute is mentioned in *Tanḥuma*, ed. Buber, Genesis xxiii in connection with the verse Daniel viii 13.
21. See my essay "Askezis wĕ-Yissûrîm bĕ-Tôrat Ḥazal' [Asceticism and Suffering in Rabbinic Teaching], in the *Yitzḥaq Baer Jubilee Volume*, 1961, p. 59.
22. *Gen. Rabba* xliv, 13, p. 435. It is difficult to determine whether the ending 'and when did Michael descend?' etc. is part of the statement of the Sages or the words of the redactor of the Midrash. A complete parallel to *Gen. Rabba* is to be found in *Cant. Rabba* i 12, only in the latter passage Michael is given his full title 'the Great Prince'; see above, n. 15. On the question

of the identity of 'the Prince of the world — Meṭaṭron', see *T.B. Yevamot* 16b, Tosafot s.v. *Pāsûq*; *T.B. Ḥullin* 60a, Tosafot s.v. *Pāsûq*; *'Arugat ha-Bośem*, Pt. I, p. 240.

23. *Tanḥuma*, ed. Buber, Teṣawwe, § 8; I restored the verse from *Tanḥuma*, cur. ed., *ibid.*, § 12, for it is clear that the homily is based on the difference between the two verses.

24. *T.B. Pesaḥim* 118a; current editions read: 'And some say: "And the truth of the Lord endureth for ever" — Gabriel said it when....', but in the Munich MS. the reading is: 'R. Joḥanan said: Gabriel', etc.; see *Diqduqe Soferim*, p. 374, n. *Samekh.* It seems that the continuation of the passage there 'And because the Holy One, blessed be He, does not deprive any being of its due reward, He said "You shall be vouchsafed the opportunity to deliver three of his descendants", etc.' belongs to the anonymous text of the Gemara and is derived from the homily of R. Simeon ha-Shiloni (and according to another reading 'R. Simeon ha-Ṣidoni', neither Sage being known from any other source), where Yurqamu, the Prince of Hail, proposed to cool the fire, and Gabriel said to him that 'the might of the Holy One, blessed be He, will not be demonstrated, if you, the Prince of Hail... but I, the Prince of Fire, will go down and cool....' R. Simeon does not explain the choice of Gabriel, as is done above, by the Lord's desire not to deprive him of his reward.

25. Also in the two MSS. of *Exodus Rabba*, the Oxford MS. 147 and the Paris MS. 187/15 we find: *ta'nē' kullān* ['It is taught (in a Baraita): All of them'].

26. See above, p. 136. Clearly the homilist utilized *T.B. Sanhedrin* 94a: 'A Tanna taught in the name of R. Joshua b. Qorḥa: Pharaoh who himself blasphemed was punished by the Holy One, blessed be He (Himself); Sennacherib who blasphemed through a messenger was punished by the Holy One, blessed be He, through a messenger', and thence he derived the exposition of the verse 'and beneath his glory', and he decided in accordance with the view of R. Joḥanan 'that the whole body was burnt beneath the garments'; see the commentary attributed to Rashi *ibid.*, s.v. *Hākhê Garsînān*; and cf. *T.B. Shabbat* 113b and Rashi *ad loc.* In our text of the Midrash the reading is: 'Leave their garments and burn their soul', which the commentators found difficult; see *Mattenot kehunna* and the *Novellae of Samuel Strashun* [RaShaSh]. But the above-mentioned Oxford MS. reads: 'Leave their garments and burn them'. A statement similar to that of R. Joḥanan already appears in the *Apocalypse of Baruch* lxiii, 8; the note of A. Kahana, *Ha-Sefarim ha-Ḥiṣonim*, p. 396, requires correction.

27. However, in the MS. of the Midrash we find 'R. 'Aḥa'' instead of 'R. Jose'; in the Oxford MS. the reading is 'Aḥa'; and in the Paris MS. — 'Aḥay or 'Aḥ'.

28. *T.B. Sanhedrin* 95b; see *Diqduqe Soferim*, p. 277.

29. See also *Mekhilta de-R. Ishmael*, Massekhta de-Shira, vi, p. 136; 'Thou hast greatly exalted Thyself against those who rose up against Thee', and the

text compares Pharaoh, Sisera, and Sennacherib; the last verse is from the passage in Chronicles cited above.

30. *T.B. Sanhedrin ibid.*; see also the homily of R. Isaac in *Deuteronomy Rabba* ii, 30.
31. Deuteronomy xxxiii 1–3, Psalms lxviii 9–18.
32. *Sifre Numbers* § 102, p. 100; see *Sifre Zuṭa*, p. 249; cf. *Pesiqta Rabbati* 104a and notes *ibid.*
33. *Mekhilta de-R. Ishmael*, Massekhta de-Shira, iv, p. 129.
34. *Ibid.* Massekhta de-Wa-yehi, vi, p. 112, and the parallel passages indicated there, n. 13.
35. *Mekhilta de-R. Simeon b. Yoḥai*, p. 143; see *Mekhilta de-R. Ishmael*, Massekhta de-Ba-ḥodesh, iii, p. 214; *ibid.* ix, p. 238.
36. *Mekhilta de-R. Ishmael, ibid.*, iii, p. 218; see *ibid.*, Massekhta de-Shira, iii, p. 126.
37. *Mekhilta de-R. Ishmael*, Massekhta de-Ba-ḥodesh, ix, p. 236; apparently the homilist read 'Angels of armies' [*mal'ăkhê* instead of *malĕkhê*], a reading that is also found in MSS. of the *Mekhilta* and in Biblical MSS.; see the vv.ll. to line 16. In *T.B. Shabbat* 88b, in the dictum of R. Joshua b. Levi, the text is 'Angels of armies'; so, too, in the Munich MSS., but this is not indicated by Rabbinovicz in *Diqduqe Soferim*, p. 188; see *ibid.* note *Shîn*. The Targum renders 'The kings with their hosts'; so, too, Rashi, Abraham ibn Ezra, and cf. the sources listed in *Mekhilta ibid.*, n. 13, and *apud* Aptowitzer, 'Dĕrāshā bĕ-Shevaḥ ha-Tôrā' [A Homily in Praise of the Torah], *Sinai*, iv (1940), p. 197, notes 170–172.
38. *Pesiqta de-Rav Kahana* § 12, ed. Mandelbaum, p. 219; see *ibid.* 220, n. 7. The explanation there is based on Levy's *Wörterbuch*, Pt. II, p. 319; see the next note. The English rendering of the passage in the text above is based on the corrected reading; see n. 40.
39. See W. Bacher, *Die Agada des Palästinischen Amoräer*, Vol. I, p. 131, n. 1.
40. *Pesiqta Rabbati* xxi, ed. Me'ir Ish Shalom [Friedmann], p. 103b, according to the Parma MSS. 1240. The correct reading כיליאי כיליאדס מריאי מיריאדס represents the Greek χίλιαι χιλιάδες μύριαι μυριάδες, which is the Septuagint translation of Daniel vii 10: 'Thousand thousands ministered unto Him, and ten thousand times ten thousand stood before Him'; and thus R. Azariah and R. Judah b. R. Simon transmit, in the continuation *ibid.*, in the name of R. Joshua b. Levi: '*Ribbôtayîm*, which are innumerable; '*alĕfê*, which are countless.'
41. Both he and R. Tanḥuma expounded the word *Shin'ān* from the root *shānā'* — *shānā* in the sense of 'doubled and redoubled' [manifold]. But in R. Eleazar's name three expositions are also reported: one makes the word signify 'with sharpened (swords) [*shĕnûnîm*] to destroy Israel's enemies [a euphemism for Israel], for if they had not accepted the Torah, they would have destroyed them'; the second connects the word with the root *na'a* ['beautiful']: 'the finest and noblest among them [i.e. the angels], yet, even so, the Lord was

among them — distinguished among them'; the third relates the expression to the verse 'Moab hath been at ease [*sha'ănan*] from his youth' (Jeremiah xlviii 11): 'Wherever there are large numbers there is crowding, but at Sinai... there was nevertheless ample room.'

42. This is apparently the correct reading [instead of 'and upon each chariot that Ezekiel saw'], as in *Tanḥuma*, ed. Buber, p. 76. See also *Seder Eliyahu Rabba*, p. 119, and *ibid.* n. 5; it is clear that the reference is not to the current editions of *Seder Eliyahu Rabba* and *Seder Eliyahu Zuṭa*, as is also pointed out *ibid.* p. 179. S. Lieberman, however, in the Hebrew Appendix to G. Scholem's book, *Gnosticism*, etc., p. 122, n. 23, notes that the Geonim also called the Haggada Midrashim 'Mishnayot', 'but in our case (he states) the reference is to Mishnayot proper, to Tannaitic Baraitot....' With reference to *Canticles Rabba* i, 12,the word מסטתא in the *editio princeps* is undoubtedly a corruption of מסכתא ['tractate']; we likewise find in the Parma MSS. of *Pesiqta Rabbati* 'in the tractate that they brought with them'; and R. Azariah and R. Judah b. R. Simon in the name of R. Joshua b. Levi also report in the continuation there: '*Ribbôtayim*, which are innumerable, *'alĕfê*, which are countless'.

43. See *Midrash Tehillim* civ 22, p. 446: 'These are the *Mishnayot* of Bar Qappara and of Rav Ḥiyya and of Rav and of the Babylonian Rabbis'; see J. N. Epstein, *Mavo' le-Nosaḥ ha-Mishna*, p. 171.

44. *Mekhilta de-R. Ishmael*, Massekhta de-Ba-ḥodesh, iii, p. 212. The first view cited there is that of R. Simeon b. Yoḥai in *Deuteronomy Rabba* vii, 8.

45. *Sifre Numbers* § 84, p. 84. At the first blush it would appear that there is a tradition contradicting our statement; I refer to the following dispute: 'R. Eleazar b. Azariah and R. Eliezer of Modiʿim (expounded the verse as follows:) One of them declared: But could the mountain contain them? Only the Holy One, blessed be He said to it: Grow longer and wider and receive the children of thy Lord. And the other said: And when the Holy One, blessed be He, will return to Jerusalem, He will restore the exiles to her, as it is said "These shall come from afar; and, lo, these from the north and from the west" (Isaiah xlix 12)' (*Pesiqta de-Rav Kahana*, *ibid.*, p. 221). But this tradition is mutilated and has no connection with what precedes; it is also difficult to understand the expression 'One of them declared... And the other said' when both of them speak of different subjects. However, a correct recension is found in a later source, which is dependent on that which we have cited. In *Pesiqta Rabbati*, p. 103b, in the Parma MSS. 1240, the text reads: 'Once R. Eleazar b. Azariah and R. Eliezer of Modiʿim were sitting discussing this verse: "The chariots of God are myriads, even thousands". R. Eleazar b. Azariah put a question to R. Eliezer of Modiʿim: But could Mount Sinai contain them all? The latter replied: Behold it is written "At that time they shall call Jerusalem The Throne of the Lord; and all the nations shall be gathered unto it" (Jeremiah iii 17). Is it to be supposed that Jerusalem will contain them all? Only the Holy One, blessed be He, will say to her: Grow longer, grow wider'. But the homily concerning Jerusalem is found,

without any connection with the Revelation at Mount Sinai, in early Amoraic Midrashim: 'And also in Jerusalem they were pressed together when standing, but when they prostrated themselves there was ample room... and so, too, it shall be in the time to come (as it so said) "At that time they shall call Jerusalem" (Jeremiah iii 17). R. Joḥanan once went up to pay his respects to R. Ḥanina. He found him sitting and expounding this verse: "At that time they shall call Jerusalem The Throne of the Lord", etc. So he said to him: My master, but will she (Jerusalem) contain (them all)? Surely not! He replied: The Holy One, blessed be He, will say to her "Grow longer, grow wider"...' (*Genesis Rabba* v, 7, p. 37; *Leviticus Rabba* xix, 9, p. 218). Even in *Midrash Tanḥuma*, where the comparison was created between Sinai and Jerusalem, this is not transmitted as a Tannaitic tradition: 'But could it contain them? Only a miracle occurred. The Holy One, Blessed be He, said: "Grow wider... and so you will find in the time to come that the Holy One, blessed be He, will extend Jerusalem...' (*Tanḥuma*, ed. Buber, xcvi, 16; *Tanḥuma ibid.*, 12; *Tanḥuma*, ed. Buber, Jethro xiv, is only an excerpt from *Pesiqta de-Rav Kahana*). We must not, therefore, regard the tradition pointing to a Tannaitic difference of opinion on the subject as authentic.

46. See above, p. 147.
47. *Pesiqta de-Rav Kahana*, Naḥămû, p. 266, and the parallel passages indicated there; see A. Aptowitzer, 'Derasha be-Shevaḥ ha-Tora', n. 166, who refers also to *T.B. Shabbat* 88a. There a similar homily is transmitted in the name of R. Simai [סימאי]: 'When the Israelites said "we will do" before "we will hear", sixty myriad Ministering Angels came to each Israelite and crowned him with two crowns, one for "we will do" and one for "we will hear". But when the Israelites sinned, one hundred and twenty myriad destroying angels came down and removed the crowns, as it is said: "And the children of Israel were stripped of their ornaments from Mount Horeb onward."' Here the homily is linked to the utterance of 'we will do and we will hear', and not to the Revelation on Mount Sinai. However, we find R. Joḥanan reporting in the name of R. Simai [סימיי] (*T.P. Ma'asrot* i, 5, p. 48d; see W. Bacher, *Tradition und Tradenten*, p. 98; A. Hyman, *Toledot Tanna'im wa-'Amora'im* [History of the Tannaim and Amoraim], p. 961), but R. Joḥanan's statement in *T.B. Shabbat*, *loc. cit.*, 'and it was Moses' privilege to take them all' (see Rashi's commentary *ad loc.* and Pseudo-Jonathan to Exodus xxxiii 7), which refers to the dictum of Rav Ḥama bar Ḥanina preceding it, clearly shows that R. Simai's exposition was unknown to him. Furthermore, doubt also arises regarding the very attribution of the homily to R. Simai; see below, n. 51.
48. *Pirqe de-R. Eliezer* xlvii; so, too, in Cincinnati MS. 75, Paris 710, and Ginzberg MS. 111_2. But the Warsaw MS. 240/5 reads: 'R. Eliezer said'.
49. *Sifre Deuteronomy* § 356; see *Midrash Tannaim*, p. 223.
50. *Canticles Rabba* i, 3; iv, 12; viii, 5; *Lamentations Rabba*, proem, 24 ed. Buber, p. 24. In *Pirqe de-R. Eliezer*, the author of the aforementioned Haggada

transposed the order: first he cites R. Joḥanan's homily concerning the angels, then he adds to it the motif of the angel of death, and 'states anonymously', of course, the view of the Rabbis, 'not one angel, however, but sixty myriads took off their ornaments'. But he also disclosed his source by adding: 'and some say: It peeled off of its own accord'; see below, n. 52.

51. *Exodus Rabba* li, 8, according to the Venice edition, 1545; it is clear that the continuation 'And what was the garment...?' is not the dictum of R. Eliezer the son of R. Jose the Galilean but of the redactor; and the opening passage there 'R. Joḥanan said: he clothed them with crowns' is certainly corrupt, and we should read as in *Exodus Rabba* xlv, 2: 'What is the meaning of the earlier verse "And the children of Israel stripped themselves of their ornaments"? R. Ḥanin of Sepphoris (said): The crown that He had placed on their heads, as it is said "and a beautiful crown upon thy head" (Ezekiel xvi 12), the girdles with which he had girded them. And R. Simi said: Purple robes, as it is said "I decked thee also with garments" (*ibid.*, v. 11).' See the *Novellae of David Luria* (*RaDaL*) § 3. Perhaps the dictum of R. Joḥanan on the crowns, as we find it in the *Pesiqta*, dropped out; see *Tanḥuma* ed. Buber, addendum to pericope, Shĕlaḥ, p. 76; cf. *Midrash Tehillim* ciii, 8, and *Midrash ha-Gadol* to Exodus, ed. M. Margulies, p. 696. In all the sources the text reads: 'R. Simai says: He clothed them in purple'; see also *Numbers Rabba* xvi, 24, which is in antithesis to the homily in his name in the Babylonian Talmud; cf. above, n. 47.

52. *Pesiqta de-Rav Kahana*, Ba-ḥodesh, p. 221; see also *Tanḥuma*, ed. Buber, Jethro, § 14, in the name of Resh Laqish. In *Pesiqta Rabbati*, p. 104b: 'R. Levi said: His טבלרין engraven upon their heart'. In the above-mentioned Parma MS.: '... טבולרין ... like a [literally, 'this'] טראטיגה'. It is obvious that the expression in our text 'in this Sinai in holiness' and the interpretation of R. Meir Ish Shalom *ibid.*, n. 73, are improbable; the difficulty is due to the fact that the word טראטיגה has dropped out. The correct reading appears to be 'like an איסטרטגוס ['general']', as in *Midrash Tehillim* xvii, 3, p. 125. This explanation was also given by E. Z. Margolioth in his commentary *Zeraʿ 'Ephrayim*, Lemberg 1853; similarly we find in *Exodus Rabba*, Venice edition, xxix, 2: 'R. Levi said: A tablet containing the Ineffable Name was written on their heart'; so, too, in the Paris MS. 187; and in the Ox. MS. 147: 'Said R.: A tablet was there containing the Ineffable Name....' This was omitted in later editions, and in Romm's edition the text was restored in accordance with Buber's note in his edition of the *Pesiqta de-Rav Kahana*; see the 'Masoret ha-Midrash' *ibid* § 3. The ending in *Pesiqta de-Rav Kahana* 'and do not say that His sovereignty' etc. is not found in the parallel passages; in *Exodus Rabba* there is a different conclusion. On the emendation אסטריסגוס – ἀστερίσκος, which was accepted by Scholem, *Jewish Gnosticism*, etc. p. 71, n. 21, see the comment of Immanuel Löw *apud* S. Krauss, *Lehnwoerter*, p. 84.

53. *T.B. Yoma* 75b; in *Mekhilta*, Wa-yissaʿ, iii, p. 167 and *Sifre Numbers* § 88, p. 84, only R. Ishmael's view is given. In *Midrash Tehillim* lxxviii, 4, p. 345,

there is a change of wording in R. Akiba's homily: 'They became mighty like angels'.

54. R. Akiba's interpretation is also in keeping with the Septuagint rendering of Psalms lxxviii 25 — ἄρτον ἀγγέλων.

55. *Gen. Rabba* xlviii, 14, p. 491; the continuation 'Did they actually eat? They only appeared to be eating' is not R. Me'ir's dictum but, as appears from the Oxford and Munich MSS., the statement of R. Judan; similarly, in *Exodus Rabba*. See L. Ginzberg, *Legends*, V, p. 236.

56. *'Avot de-R. Nathan*, Version II, xliv, p. 124; it is apparently the continuation of the dicta of R. Eliezer the son of R. Jose the Galilean, who had also previously annotated R. Akiba's saying in *M. 'Avot*. See *Midrash Tannaim*, p. 71, in the name of R. Me'ir; *T.B. Ḥullin* 91b, an anonymous Baraita; and the homilies on it in *Gen. Rabba* lxv, 21, p. 737 in the name of R. Levi, R. Simon, and R. Samuel bar Naḥmani.

57. *Gen. Rabba* lxxviii, 1, p. 918; only in a later Midrash, in *Exodus Rabba* xv, 7, do we find a homily worded 'for the Holy One, blessed be He, compared Israel to the angels', the assumption being that the status of the latter was higher. This is what is stated there: 'The angels say each day "Holy, Holy, Holy", and the Israelites say "God of Abraham, God of Isaac, and God of Jacob" '; this provides no evidence, of course, that in the homilist's day it was not customary to say the *Qedushsha* every day, as A. Marmorstein wished to infer in 'Anges et hommes dans l'Agada', *REJ*, LXXXIV (1927), p. 41, n. 1. See *Tosefta Berakhot* i, 9 and *T.P. ibid.*, v, 4, p. 9c. Only it appears that the expositor thought that the Israelites learnt the recitation of the *Qedushsha* from the angels, whereas the mention of the Patriarchs is, as it were, a parallel doxology.

58. See the Revelation to John iv 8 'the four living creatures... and day and night they never cease to sing, "Holy, Holy, Holy...." ' This chapter belongs to the Jewish portion of the apocalypse. See my observations in my article 'Yĕrûshālayim she-lĕ-maʿălā vi-Yerushalayim she-le-maṭṭā [The Heavenly and Earthly Jerusalem]' in *Sefer Yĕrûshālayim lĕ-Dôrôtehā*, The Twenty-Fifth Archaeological Convention, Jerusalem 1969, pp. 164 ff. Hence the remarks of E. Peterson, 'Von den Engeln', *Theologische Traktate*, 1921, p. 333 and *ibid.*, p. 385, n. 8, have no foundation.

59. *Sifre Deuteronomy* §§ 96 and 308; *Midrash Tannaim*, *loc. cit.*; *T.P. Berakhot* ix, 1, p. 13a; *T.B. Qiddushin* 36a; *T.B. Bava Batra* 10a; *'Avot de-R. Nathan*, Version I, xxxix (59b) and Version II, iv (62b).

60. *Mekhilta de-R. Ishmael*, Massekhta de-Wa-yehi, vi, p. 112; on the opposition of the sea, see *ibid.*, iv, p. 102. Cf. *Mekhilta de-R. Simeon b. Yoḥai*, pp. 67–68.

61. *Tosefta Soṭa* vi, 5, p. 304; see *ibid.* the vv.ll., and *Yalquṭ Makhiri* on Psalms viii 8, p. 49.

62. *M. Yadayim* iii, 5; see my article 'Dĕrāshôt Ḥazal u-Pērûshê Origines lĕ-Shîr ha-Shîrîm we-ha-Wikkuaḥ ha-Yĕhûdî-Noṣrî', *Tarbiz*, XXX (1961), pp. 148 ff [= 'The Homiletical Interpretations of the Sages and the Expositions of

Origen on Canticles and the Jewish Disputation', *Scripta Hierosolymitana*, XXII, 1971, p. 247 ff].

63. *Canticles Rabba* i, 2, 2. The words that I have enclosed in brackets appear to me superfluous; in the Parma MS. 1240 the text reads: 'R. Joḥanan said: An angel went forth before each commandment and went up to every Israelite and said to him....'

64. See my article (cited above) pp. 153–154.

65. See *Canticles Rabba ibid.*, and my aforementioned article, p. 154, n. 24; in *T.B. Horayot* 8a the dictum is cited in the form 'R. Ishmael taught'. Cf. *T.B. Makkot* 24a and Rashi *ad loc.*, s.v. *mi-pî ha-Gĕvûrā* ['from the mouth of the Almighty'].

66. See above, p. 43. Cf. *Mekhilta de-R. Ishmael,* Masskehta de-Shira vi, p. 134; *Sifre Numbers* § 84, p. 81; *Midrash Tannaim*, p. 195.

67. *T.B. Berakhot* 3a. See *Diqduqe Soferim ibid.*, p. 4; S. Lieberman, *Sheqiʿin*, p. 70; cf. *ʿArugat ha-Bośem*, Pt. iv, p. 78, n. 41*. A Marmorstein, *The Old Rabbinic Doctrine of God*, 1937, p. 64, considers that Rav elaborated the statement of R. Eliezer b. Hyrcanus, previously quoted in the Baraita: 'R. Eliezer said, The night is divided into three watches, and at each watch the Holy One, blessed be He, sits and roars like a lion, as it is said "'The Lord doth roar from on high, and utter His voice from His holy habitation; He doth mightily roar because of His fold" '. But it is clear that this is a Babylonian Baraita, for in *Tosefta Berakhot* i, 1 and in *T.P. ibid.* i, 1, p. 2d, Rabbi and R. Nathan disagree with regard to R. Eliezer's statement. According to Rabbi the night comprises four watches, while R. Nathan holds that the night has three watches, and the Babylonian Baraita accords with R. Nathan's view. See L. Ginzberg, *Perushim we-Ḥiddushim bi-Yerushalmi*, Pt. I, p. 57. The Baraita that relates there that R. Jose heard a Heavenly Voice in the cave, which cooed like a dove and spoke precisely the words used by Rav 'Alas for Me!...', is also apparently Babylonian and its continuation is worthy of note: 'Nor is this all; whenever Israelites enter Synagogues and Houses of Study and answer "May His great name be blessed!", the Holy One, blessed be He, nods His head and says "Happy is the King who is thus praised in His house; (but) alas for the Father who has banished His children, and alas for the children who have been banished from their Father's table!" ' See *Diqduqe Soferim ibid.*, p. 5.

68. *T.B. Menaḥot* 41a. The angel rebuked Rav Qaṭṭina for not performing correctly the precept of 'fringes', and in the anonymous Talmudic passage it is stated that Rabba bar Rav Huna 'disagreed with the view of the angel'. See Rashi *ibid.*, s.v. *û-Pĕlîgā*.

69. *T.B. Berakhot* 59a; see *Diqduqe Soferim ibid.*, p. 333.

70. See B. M. Lewin, Appendices to *Oṣar ha-Geonim*, Berakhot, Commentary of R. Ḥananel, pp. 62–63; cf. *ʿArugat ha-Bośem*, Pt. III, p. 108.

71. *Mekhilta de-R. Ishmael*, Massekhta de-Pisḥa, i, p. 4.

72. *Mekhilta de-R. Ishmael*, Massekhta da-Amalek, Jethro, i, p. 192; this is the

reading of the Oxford MS. and the Munich MS. See vv.ll. *ibid.* In the printed editions we find *ha-Maqom*; in *Midrash Ḥakhamim* it is missing. Also in the *Midrash ha-Gadol* to Exodus iv 24, p. 77 the reading is 'the angel sought'.

73. *Mekhilta, loc. cit.*, so, too, in *T.P. Nedarim* iii, 14, p. 38b. But in the Talmud Bavli *ibid.*, 32a, the text has 'Satan sought to slay him'; the same version is found in the Munich MS. and in the *Haggadot ha-Talmud*, and it is thus cited in *'Arugat ha-Bośem*, Pt. III, p. 200. This recension accords with the rendering of Targum Yerushalmi to vv. 25–6, 'destroying angel'. The 'other recension', given in the margin of the Babylonian Talmud, which reads 'that angel', is merely an emendation based on the Midrashim in the spirit of *Exodus Rabba* v, 8, 'You find that he was an angel of mercy, but nevertheless he sought to slay him.' In later sources the name of the angel is also mentioned; see M. Kasher, *Torah Shelemah*, VIII, p. 198, § 141.
74. *Mekhilta de-R. Ishmael, ibid.*; see the parallel passages listed there, n. 11. According to *T.P. Berakhot* ix, 1, p. 13a, Bar Qappara and R. Joshua b. Levi differed on the subject. Cf. also *Mekhilta de-R. Simeon b. Yoḥai*, p. 129, where the statement of R. Joshua is transmitted in the name of R. Eliezer of Modi'im.
75. See *T.P. Soṭa* vii, 1, p. 21b; *Gen. Rabba* xlviii, 20, p. 495; *ibid.* xlv, 10, p. 437, and cf. the notes there.
76. *T.B. Zevaḥim* 101b–102a; see *ibid.* Tosafot s.v. *'Ahărōn qārôv*; in *Sifre Numbers* § 106, p. 105, we find a shortened version 'The Holy One, blessed be He, shut her up; and the Holy One, blessed be He, declared her unclean; and the Holy One, blessed be He, pronounced her clean', and so, too, in *Sifre Zuṭa*, p. 278.
77. *Sifre Numbers* ibid; see vv.ll. line 6, and cf. above, p. 43.
78. Above, p. 150; see *Sifre* § 103, p. 101, and the parallel passages indicated there in n. 17.
79. *Gen. Rabba* xvii, 4, p. 155. The author of the teaching is R. Aḥa, but in *Midrash Tehillim* viii, 2, p. 73 it is Rav, who says 'We find three instances in which the angels argued against the Holy One, blessed be He'. In the continuation *ibid.* there is a dictum in the name of R. Aḥa, which appears earlier in *Gen. Rabba* in the name of R. Joḥanan b. Zakkai. In *Pesiqta de-R. Kahana*, Para, p. 60, and in *Pesiqta Rabbati* 59b, the statement is anonymous and only at the end is it stated 'R. Aḥa said' etc.; see also *Canticles Rabba* viii, 11. R. Aḥa attributes to the Holy One, blessed be He, the admonition: 'Take heed that you do not hate one another, and are not envious of one another... lest the Ministering Angels say before the Master of the universe "The Torah that Thou didst give to Israel they do not keep...." '
80. *T.B. Nedarim* 38a; see *T.B. Rosh ha-Shana* 21b; cf. *Diqduqe Soferim* p. 47, n. *Lāmed.* The matter of the 49 gates of understanding was derived from the verse Psalms xii 7; see *T.P. Sanhedrin* iv, 2, p. 22a; *Midrash Tehillim* xii, 4, p. 107.
81. The source is the statement by R. Eliezer b. R. Jose the Galilean in ***Gen.***

Rabba xxviii, 4, p. 263. Particularly noteworthy is the wording in *'Avot de-R. Nathan*, Version I, xxxi, 46a: 'Nine hundred and seventy-four generations before the creation of the world the Torah was written and lying in the bosom of the Holy One, blessed be He, uttering song with the Ministering Angels [to God].' The figure recalls the words of *Enoch* xlii, 2: 'Wisdom went forth to make her dwelling among the children of men, and found no dwelling-place: Wisdom returned to her place, and took her seat among the angels.' The Torah replaced Wisdom, but we nowhere find in the dicta of the Sages that the Torah returned to her place after she had been given to the children of men; see above, the chapter on the Torah, p. 297.

82. *T.B. Shabbat* 88b–89a; see *'Avot de-R. Nathan*, Version I, iv, p. 10; *Exodus Rabba* xxviii, 1. Cf. also the continuation of the homily on man in *Midrash Tehillim ibid.*, but it is the Holy One, blessed be He, who answers there, and, as Buber remarks, *ibid.*, p. 75, n. 20, the continuation is derived from *Pesiqta Rabbati*, ʿaśśer tĕʿaśśēr, 128a, where the text reads: 'What did the Holy One, blessed be He, do? He merely removed them and gave the Torah to Israel. But they rejected "Thou shalt not have [other gods before Me]" (Exodus xx 3) at the end of forty days. [Thereupon] the angels said before the Holy One, blessed be He, "Sovereign of the universe! did we not say to Thee that Thou shouldst not give the Torah to them?" Hence when the Holy One, blessed be He, wished to write it for them a second time, the angels did not let Him. The Holy One, blessed be He, then said to them: "Is it you who keep the Torah? A weaned child of Israel observes it more than you do. On leaving the school, if he has meat and milk to eat, he does not eat until he has washed his hands from the meat; but you, when you came to Abraham, you ate meat and milk together, as it is said "And he took curd, and milk, and the calf... and they did eat" (Genesis xviii 8), and having silenced them with this reply, the Holy One, blessed be He, said to Moses ' "While the time is still free, write down these words...." ' This homily is cited in *Sefer ha-ʿIṭṭur*, Pt. II, First Gate, ed. R. Meir Jonah, p. 26, as 'the Haggadah of ʿaśśēr tĕʿaśśēr', and I have corrected the text according to the version quoted there; so, too, in Tosafot Ḥîṣoniyyôt in *Shiṭṭā Mĕqubbeṣet* to *T.B. Bekhorot* 6b, § 2, in the name of the Palestinian Talmud, but it is not to be found in the extant Palestinian Talmud.

83. See *Midrash Tehillim, loc. cit.*, and *Tanḥuma*, Tĕrûmā, xlii 8; but in *Cant. Rabba* viii, 11, it is God who answers the angels respecting their protest at the giving of the Torah to mortals. He persuaded them to agree to the giving of the Torah to Israel after assuring them that only 'My Torah do I give the inhabitants of the earth, but I shall dwell with you on high'. For the opposition of the Ministering Angels to the acceptance of King Manasseh's repentance, see *T.P. Sanhedrin* x, 2, p. 28c; *Lev. Rabba* xxx, 3, p. 697. On the indictment of Jotham, cf. cf. *Gen. Rabba* lxiii, 1, p. 678.

84. *Lev. Rabba* i, 1, pp. 2–3, where the text reads: ' "and He sent an angel, and brought us forth out of Egypt" (Numbers xx 16). But was he an angel? Lo,

it was Moses! Then why is he called an angel? This teaches us that the prophets are called angels.' See *ibid.* n. 5.

85. *Lev. Rabba ibid.* p. 1; see there n. 2. But there is no proof that the proem is based on the words of the Amora mentioned at the end of the section. In his statement there angels are not spoken of, but Moses is compared to Israel, and only in *Midrash Tehillim* ciii, 18, p. 438, did the homilist proceed to weave the homily: ' "And He called unto Moses" — but no harm befell him, thus teaching us that the righteous are greater than the Ministering Angels. For the Ministering Angels cannot hear His voice, as it is said "And the Lord uttereth His voice before His army; for His camp is very great" (Joel ii 11) — these are the Ministering Angels... and who can hear His voice?... that is the righteous man who fulfils His word, for he is greater than the Ministering Angels. And who is he? — Moses.' The exposition of R. Tanḥum b. Ḥanilai is neither in the printed editions nor in the MS. of *Shoḥer Tov*; see Buber *ibid.*, n. 70. Nor is it found in the *Yalquṭ ha-Makhiri* to Psalms, *ibid.* p. 134; Buber added it on the basis of *Lev. Rabba.*
86. *Deuteronomy Rabba* xi, 3; *Yalquṭ Shimʿoni*, Deuteronomy, § 951, in the name of *Deut. Zuṭṭa*, *Yalquṭ Makhiri* to Psalms lxviii 55, p. 330; *Yalquṭ Makhiri* to Proverbs xxxi 29, in the name of *Tanḥuma*, but *Deut. Rabba* is intended. See Zunz-Albeck, *Ha-Dĕrāshôt bĕ-Yisrāʾel* [*Die Gottesdienstliche Vorträge der Juden Historisch entwickelt*], p. 123, and my observations in the Introduction to *ʿArugat ha-Bośem*, Pt. IV, p. 171. The expression *nitpaggesh* ['encountered'], which I have cited in the text, is taken from *Yalkuṭ Makhiri*, and is characteristic. See *Sĕrîdê Tanḥuma-Yĕlammĕdēnû*, *Qoveṣ*, *ʿal Yad*, Book VI, p. 49, and *ibid.* n. 11, and cf. below, p. 761, n. 46.
87. See above, p. 753, n. 82.
88. *Pesiqta de-Rav Kahana*, Ha-ḥodesh, p. 84; see the vv.ll., and for the reading 'Kings of armies, angels of armies', cf. above, p. 746, n. 37.
89. Hebrews i 4–13; ii 5–9.
90. See above, p. 155.
91. *Ibid.*, ii 12–15; iii 2–6.
92. *Ep. ad. Diognetam* 2, 7, and the *Apocalypse of Zephaniah*; see A. Harnack, *Lehrbuch der Dogmengeschichte*, I, 1931, p. 204, n. 4.
93. See *Lam. Rabba*, proem § 31, p. 33.
94. *T.P. Shabbat* vi, 9, p. 8d, which I amended according to the text of *ʿEn Yaʿaqov*; see S. Lieberman, *Ha-Yerushalmi Kiphshuto*, p. 117. On the anti-Christian trend of the dictum, Z. Frankel, *Mĕvôʾ ha-Yĕrûshalmî* [Introductio in Talmud Hierosolymitanum], p. 122b, already commented. In *Deut. Rabba* i, 12, the statements of R. Abba and R. Levi are cited, but not that of R. Reuben. In *Pesiqta Rabbati* 160b the text reads: 'And the appearance of the fourth is like a son of God... this was Gạbriel, who walked after them like a disciple before (in the Parma MS.: 'after', which is correct) his master; this teaches us that the righteous are greater than the Ministering Angels.' This is also cited in *Yalquṭ Shimʿoni* to Daniel § 663; cf. *T.B. Sanhedrin* 93a; for

the expression 'this teaches us that the righteous...' see above, n. 82.

95. *The Book of Adam and Eve* vii, 4; *The Book of Jubilees* iv, 25; *Testaments of the Twelve Patriarchs*, Asher, vi, 5–6; Benjamin, vi, 2. The concept was known in the Greek world since the days of Homer and was connected with the word δαίμων. Plato already reports it as a well-known fact 'that it is related that the "genius" to whom a man appertains in his lifetime stands ready to conduct the deceased to a given place where the dead are assembled and undergo judgment' (*Phaedon*, 1070; in the *Republic*, 617E, the motif of the 'daemon' is integrated with the doctrine of reincarnation). Against the prevailing view regarding the two daemons that accompany a man, Menander polemized already at the end of the fourth century, maintaining that evil is not caused by the daemon who accompanies a man from his birth, but calamity results only from his character and conduct; P. Nilsson, *Geschichte der griech. Religion*, II, 1950, pp. 199–202. On the Stoics and Neoplatonists, see Th. Hopfner, *Griechischer Ägyptischer Offenbarungszauber*, 1921, pp. 27 ff. Regarding those who accompany the soul in the Iranian religions, see F. Böklen, *Die Verwandschaft der Jüdisch-Christlichen mit der Persischen Eschatologie*, Göttingen 1902, pp. 40 ff; cf. G. Widengren, *Die Religionen Irans*, Stuttgart 1965, pp. 32 ff, pp. 102 ff, and p. 166.

96. *Tosefta ʿAvoda Zara* i, 17–18, p. 461, whence *Tosefta Shabbat* xviii (18), 2, p. 136 is derived. See S. Lieberman, *Tosefta ki-Fshuṭah*, Moʿed, p. 283.

97. *Cant. Rabba* i, 4; I have cited the version found in the Parma MS. 1240. In the printed editions — beginning with the Pesaro edition of 1519 — the narrative has been augmented by additions that dilute it; see also *Ecclesiastes Rabba* i, 1. On the angels that appear in Ashkelon in the guise of pilgrims and guard their homes on account of their Gentile neighbours, see *T.P. Pe'a* iii, 8, p. 17d; and regarding the angel that appeared in the form of R. Phinehas b. Jair, cf. *T.P. Demai* i, 3, p. 22a.

98. *T.P. Berakhot* ix, 2, p. 14b; in *T.B. Berakhot* 60b the text reads: 'Be honoured, you holy honoured beings, ministers of the Most High. Give honour to the God of Israel. Leave me, while I enter and perform my needs and come back to you.' Clearly this is a valediction said on parting from the accompanying angels, and it appears that its author was well versed in angel lore, and it may even be doubted if he belonged to the circle of the Sages. This is attested by its dictum; the expression 'who minister in the holy place' is found in *Sirach* iv 14. In any case the conclusion of the blessing 'Blessed be the honoured God' pertains to a version described as 'another way'. (In *Tosefta Berakhot* vi, 20, ed. Lieberman, p. 39 'If he begins... with *'Alef Lāmed* [*'Ēl*] and concludes with *'Alef Lāmed*, this is another way'; but in *T.P. ibid.* ix, 1, we read 'If he begins... with *Yôd Hē'* and concludes with *'Ālef Lāmed*, this is another way'. See *Tosefta ki-Fshuṭah*, *ibid.*, p. 122.) Indeed, it was the way of the men of the Qumran sect to commence with 'Blessed art Thou my God', 'Blessed art Thou, the God of compassion and grace', or 'Blessed is the God of Israel' (*Megillat ha-Serakhim*, ed. Licht, 1965, p. 235; *Megillat*

ha-Hodayot, ed. idem, Jerusalem 1957, p. 168; *Milḥamot Bene 'Or bi-Bene Ḥoshekh*, ed. Yadin, p. 334), but I have found no instance of a benedictory conclusion such as ours, nor have I seen any comments on it. It is noteworthy that it is omitted in the Babylonian Talmud, and it seems that Abbaye, who disapproved of the formula 'Leave me...' for fear 'lest they should forsake him altogether', cited a parallel formula 'Guard me, guard me; help me, help me; support me, support me; wait for me till I have entered and come forth, for such is the way of the children of men'; it is this version that Maimonides quotes in 'Hilkhot Tefilla' [Laws of Prayer], vii, 5.

99. Proverbs xvii 11; see *Mekhilta de-R. Ishmael*, Wa-yehi, vi, p. 111.
1. I Kings xxii 21.
2. See *T.P. Ta'anit* ii, 1, p. 65b; *T.B. Shabbat* 88a; *T.B. Nedarim* 32a. As regards the good angel and bad angel see the dictum of R. Jose b. R. Judah, *T.B. Shabbat* 119b.
3. Known to us from the *Testaments of the Twelve Patriarchs*, Asher, vi, 4 γνωρίζοντες τοῦς ἀγγέλους κυρίου καὶ τοῦ Σατανᾶ; see also Dan, vi, 1, and *The Book of Jubilees* (x, 7–11), which declares that God left a tenth part of the spirits to Mastêmā. The idea is linked with the myth of 'the fallen angels'. Paul in II Corinthians xii 7 speaks of 'the angel of Satan', but earlier, *ibid.* xi 14, he states that Satan disguises himself as an angel of light, and his attendants disguise themselves as ministers of righteousness. See R. M. Grant, 'Les Êtres Intermédiaires dans le Judaisme Tardif', *Studi e Materiali di Storia delle Religioni*, 1967 (38), pp. 244 ff; but he, too, failed to note that Philo, in a manner similar to that of Paul, interpreted the existence of evil angels: οὑτοί εἰσιν οἱ πονηροὶ τὸ ἀγγέλων ὄνομα ὑποδυόμενοι, *De Gigantibus*, § 17; cf. H. Wolfson, *Philo*, I, p. 383.
4. See above, p. 752, n. 81, and below, p. 757, n. 10.
5. Also in the Christian work, the *Shepherd of Hermas*, Mandata, VI, 2, 1, it is only stated 'Two are the angels that abide with men, the one of righteousness (εἷς τῆς δικαιοσύνης) and the other of wickedness (εἷς τῆς πονηρίας).
6. *T.B. Ketubbot* 104a. The Münich MS. has R. Eliezer, but the recension of *Haggadot ha-Talmud* accords with our reading. In *Sifre Zuṭa*, pp. 248–249, which is based on *Midrash ha-Gadol*, the text has 'R. Simeon used to say', but *Yalquṭ Shim'oni, editio princeps*, reads 'Zuṭi. Great is peace...' without giving the author's name; *Num. Rabba* xi 7: 'R. Me'ir used to say...'; *Pesiqta Rabbati* 5b and *Midrash Tehillim* xxx 3, p. 234, cites the passage in the name of H. Ḥiyya ha-Gadol. In *Visio Pauli* there is a detailed description of the angels of destruction, who greet the wicked, and of the angels who receive the souls of the righteous. See M. R. James, *The Apocryphal New Testament*, Oxford 1924, pp. 529–530, and cf. *ibid.*, n. 1, where a parallel from the *Apocalypse of Zephaniah* is cited. See also A. D. Nock, *H.T.R.*, xxxiv (1941), pp. 101–109; H. Wolfson, *Philo*, I, pp. 370 ff.
7. *T.B. Ḥagiga* 16a (*T.B. Ta'anit* 11a in the name of R. Shila; see vv.ll. in ed. H. Malter, p. 38). I would point out that we find R. Zeriqa reporting in the

name of R. Joḥanan in the name of R. Eliezer b. R. Jose the Galilean, *T.P. Berakhot* v, 1, p. 8d, and it is not impossible that his dictum was known in our version.

8. *Gen. Rabba* iii, 6, p. 23, only in the name of R. Eleazar, and so it is given in all the MSS. But in *Tanḥuma*, ed. Buber, Tazriaʿ, § 12, the dictum is cited as that of R. Eleazar b. Pedat in the name of R. Joḥanan; also the conclusion of that section 'R. Joḥanan in the name of R. Simeon b. Yoḥai' etc., is quoted in *T.B. Yoma* 77a in the name of 'R. Ḥana bar Bizna in the name of R. Simeon Ḥasida'; see *Diqduqe Soferim, ibid.*, p. 239. The sentence 'the Holy One, blessed be He, did not wish to do the evil Himself, but only through an angel' is apparently an observation by the redactor of the Midrash.
9. *Tanḥuma*, ed. Buber, Tazriaʿ 11; and there is another saying *ibid.* of R. Joḥanan 'Thou art not drawn after evil, nor is evil drawn after Thee, nor does it dwell with Thee.'
10. *T.P. Qiddushin* i, 10, p. 61d; see *T.B. Shabbat* 32a; *Pesiqta Rabbati* 38b; and earlier, *loc. cit.*, the dictum of R. Menaḥem b. Jacob 'The angels of destruction come and arraign'. The admonition uttered by R. Joḥanan 'If you hear a statement of R. Leazar b. R. Jose the Galilean, perforate your ear like a hopper and listen' possibly comes to warn the listener that he must examine the words carefully, for sometimes they are transmitted in terms with which he is unfamiliar. Cf. also *T.B. Ḥullin* 89a. The author of the commentary *Yĕfē ʿÊnayim* was not quite exact in stating that in *T.P. Qiddushin* 'R. Eliezer b. R. Jose the Galilean himself said this to his listeners that they might accept his words'.
11. See above, p. 194.
12. *Lev. Rabba* xviii, 3, p. 406; see the parallels noted there. On the tasks of the angels in the hereafter as guardians of the souls of men and as executors of punishments, see above, p. 164.
13. *Megillat ha-Serakhim*, ed. J. Licht, p. 92; see *ibid.* p. 88. See *Megillat Milḥemet Bne 'or bi-Bne Ḥoshekh*, ed. Yadin, Section 19, p. 214; Yadin rightly identifies the Prince of Light with Michael on the basis of what is stated *ibid.* in Section 27. In *I Enoch*, 75, the angel Uriel is he 'whom the Lord of Glory hath set for ever over all the luminaries of the heaven, in the heaven and in the world'. On the other hand, the light is not attributed to a specific angel in Rabbinic sources. Even in the late Midrashim opposition to this view is stressed; see *Pesiqta Rabbati*, xlvi, p. 188a: 'Uriel on the left, facing Dan, who is darkness. And why is he called Uriel? On account of the Torah, Prophets, and Hagiographa, for the Holy One, blessed be He, makes atonement for him [Dan] and he gives light to Israel....' See *Num. Rabba* ii, 9, and *ʿArugat ha-Bośem*, Pt. I, p. 287.
14. *Exod. Rabba* xxxii, § 1; *ibid.* § 7; see above, p. 149.
15. *M. 'Avot* iv, 11.
16. *Tanḥuma*, Mishpaṭim, 19; see *Num. Rabba* xii, 4.
17. See *T.B. Berakhot* 6a, the Baraita in the name of Abba Benjamin; the Babylo-

nian Amoraim that speak of the number and activity of the demons are Rav Joseph, Abbaye (in the printed editions: Abbaye Rava, but see *Diqduqe Soferim*, p. 16, n. *Tāw*, and p. 17, n. *Bêt*) and Bevai bar Abbaye, who relied on his experiment to 'know' them. In the discussion there a short dictum in the name of Rav Huna is cited: 'Each one of us has a thousand on his left and ten thousand on his right'. But the MS. (see *Diqduqe Soferim* § *Gímel*) reads Ḥanina. Despite the view of R. Ḥanina that the precepts cast down the demons, and the concepts of R. Joshua b. Levi and R. Levi that on account of the merit of the precepts the Almighty assigns angels to man to guard him, and that their number is equal to that of the precepts, and that if a man 'is perfect in Torah and good deeds' the Lord guards him, the Palestinian Amoraim of the third century did not deny the existence of angels, destroying angels, and demons. They exist, but their work is non-existent, nor are they to be seen, and only if a man's sins bring it about, as R. Levi declared 'is the mask removed and the man becomes insane'. In paradoxical fashion R. Levi expressed himself similarly concerning the appearance of the angels to Abraham and to Lot: 'To Abraham, whose merit was great, they appeared in the likeness of men; but to Lot, whose merit was small, they appeared like angels' (*Gen. Rabba* l, 5, p. 517; the reading 'R. Levi' is confirmed by most MSS., see vv.ll. *ibid.*). This is preceded by an anonymous teaching: 'Here Scripture says "the angels", whereas in the other passage it says "men"! The explanation is that in the other episode, since the Shekhina was over them, (they appeared as) men; but once the Shekhina departed from them, they assumed (again) the guise of angels.'

18. *T.B. Pesaḥim* 112b; 111a; see *Num. Rabba* xii 4. It is obvious that the words ' "Thou shalt not be afraid of the terror by night" — of Igrat the daughter of Maḥalat and her chariot' etc. are not the continuation of the words of R. Simeon b. Yoḥai. On the formation of male and female spirits during the 130 years that Adam was separated from Eve, see *Gen. Rabba* xx, 11, p. 195, and cf. *T.B. ʿEruvin* 18b. Kohut's interpretation of 'Igrat the daughter of Maḥalat', *Aruch Completum*, Pt. I, p. 31, was rejected by B Geiger in the *Additamenta* to the *Aruch Completum*, p. 9. Cf. L. Ginzberg, *op. cit.*, p. 420. See also *T.B. Ḥullin* 105b concerning the angel of poverty, who has no power over one who is careful to remove the food crumbs from his house.
19. *T.B. Berakhot* 55b; see *Diqduqe Soferim*, *ibid.*, p. 305.
20. See S. Shaked, 'Some Notes on Ahreman, the Evil Spirit, and his Creation', *Studies in Mysticism and Religion*, presented to Gershom Scholem, Jerusalem 1967, English Section, pp. 227–234. He proves there, from sources of variegated character, that the view that the demons have no existence in the world apart from man also has a place in the cosmological field, and *ibid.* n. 15 he is also inclined to posit foreign influence on the dualistic concept in the Sassanian era.
21. Plotinus, *Enead*, III, ed. Creuzer, p. 140, cites the conclusion of Marsilius Ficinus: 'Daemones nostri sunt aliquid ipsius animae praesidens videlicet

potestas potestati animae, qua vivimus: itaque secundum vitae differentias in nobis daemones differentes.' See Hopfner, *ibid.*, p. 28.

22. *T.P. Rosh Hashana* i, 2, p. 56a; *Gen. Rabba* xlviii, 8, p. 485: 'R. Ḥanina said: New names were brought up by them from Babylon. R. Simeon b. Laqish said: Also the names of the angels, Michael, and Gabriel, and Raphael.' See *ibid.* Theodor's note, and on Resh Laqish's dictum, that God associated His name with those of the angels, cf. above, p. 128. A list of the names of angels was drawn up by M. Schwab, *Vocabulaire de l'Angelogie d'après les Manuscrits de la Bibliothèque Nationale*, Paris 1897. A sharp and justified criticism of this book was written by W. Bacher, *MGWJ*, XLII, 1898, pp. 525–528; pp. 570–572. See also L. Blau, *Hebr. Bibliographie*, II, p. 119. The book entitled *Mal'ăkhê ʿElyôn* [Angels of the Most High] by Reuben Margoliouth, Jerusalem 1964, contains an alphabetic list of the angels of both the right and left wings, but there is no differentiation between the earlier and later names and no explanation is offered of the appellations; nor did the author, apparently, make use of earlier writers on the subject. See *ʿArugat ha-Bośem*, Pt. IV, Index of Angels, pp. 280–281; M. Margoliouth, *Sefer ha-Rāzîm* [Book of Secrets], 1967, Index of the Names of Angels, pp. 158 ff.
23. See above, p. 745, n. 26; cf. above, p. 168.
24. *Dial. c. Tryph.*, 103; so, too, Irenaeus, *Adv. Haer.*, 21, 2.
25. *Gen. Rabba* xvii, 6, p. 157; see vv.ll. *ibid.*
26. *Ibid.* xix, 1, p. 171; the reference is probably to a Tanna of this name. He is mentioned after R. Hoshiah Rabba and before R. Simeon b. Eleazar; see *ibid.* n. 3.
27. See above, p. 155.
28. *Pirqe de-R. Eliezer* xiii, ed. David Luria [RaDaL] 31b; see notes *ibid.*
29. *Pirqe de-R. Eliezer* xiv, 33b.
30. *Ibid.* xxvii, 62b; hence he was called *Pālîṭ* ['one that had escaped'], and 'he is identified with the fugitive that told Abram about the capture of Lot (Genesis xiv 13) and with the fugitive who came to Ezekiel (XXXIII 21).
31. *Ibid.* xxii, 50b–51a.
32. *Gen. Rabba* xxvi, 5, p. 247; see *ibid.*, n. 7. The Aramaic Targumim paid heed to R. Simeon b. Yoḥai's curse and rendered the expression 'sons of the great'.
33. There is a similar motif in the *Book of Enoch* (cvi, 6): the wondrous appearance of the child Noah arouses suspicion in the mind of his father Lamech that he is not his offspring (c, 6–10) but that of the angels. In the *Genesis Apocryphon*, ed. N. Avigad and Y. Yadin, Jerusalem 1957, fol. II, line 1, Lamech says: 'Then I thought in my heart that the conception has been from the Watchers and the... from the holy ones', and she replied to him *ibid.*, line 15: 'that thine is this seed and from thee is this conception... And it is no stranger's, nor is it of any of the Watchers or of the Sons of Heav[en]'.
34. *Pirqe de-R. Eliezer* xxi, 48a. I have cited the text according to the Ginzburg

MS. 111; it is the same in MS. Parma 1203 (*ibid.*: *bā' ʿālehā* 'had intercourse with her'). MS. Warsaw 204_5: 'The Serpent had intercourse with her and made her conceive Cain... What is meant by "he knew?" He knew that she was made pregnant... and she understood and said....' The Paris MS. 710 reads: 'The Serpent came to her, lay with her, and made her conceive, and thereafter... and she prophesied and said...' The text before us is corrupt; David Luria already emended it, see *ibid.*, n. 5. It is noteworthy that the Cincinnati MS. 70 omits the words *bā'*... *naḥash* ['the Serpent came...'].

35. Targum Pseudo-Jonathan, ed. Ginzburger, iv, 1, p. 8 renders: 'And Adam knew Eve his wife that she was with child by the angel Sammael.' G. Friedlander in his English translation of *Pirqe de-R. Eliezer*, London 1916, p. 151, added the word 'Sammael' in brackets. L. Jung, *Fallen Angels in Jewish, Christian and Mohammedan Literature*, 1926, p. 78, copied Friedlander's translation without mentioning the translator, but omitted the brackets, giving the impression that Sammael's name is actually mentioned in *Pirqe de-R. Eliezer*.
36. See also *T.B. Sanhedrin* 59b, where R. Judah b. Tema declares that the serpent was envious of the honour shown by the angels to Adam. Philo explains at length why pleasure (ἡδονή) is likened to the serpent (*Leg. Alleg.*, II, 74).
37. *Soṭa* iv, 17, p. 301.
38. *Gen. Rabba* xviii, 6, p. 168; see *ibid.*, n. 7, where the parallel sources are indicated, especially *'Avot de-R. Nathan*, Version I, i. Cf. *T.B. Soṭa* 9b: 'Similarly we find in the case of the Primordial Serpent, who set his heart on something that was not due to him. What he wanted was not given him, and what he had was taken from him.'
39. *T.B. Yevamot* 103b and the vv.ll.
40. Charles, *Pseudepigrapha*, II Enoch xviii, 3 n.
41. See *ibid.* xxix, 4, 5 n; *ibid.* xxxi, 4. In the Ethiopic *Enoch*, the chief of the rebellious angels is called in Ethiopic 'Samyaz' or Samyazz (vi, 1), and he is apparently identical with ʿAzazel, who taught men both how to make weapons and the arts of cosmetics and luxury (viii, 1–2). In the Midrash, too (cited in *Yalquṭ Shimʿoni, editio princeps*, § 44, but not in *Midrash 'Avkir*, which is usually given as the source), which tells of the descent and downfall of the two angels Shamḥazzai and ʿAzael, it is stated: 'And ʿAzael was over coloured materials and over adornments of women who entice men to sinful thoughts'. In another passage of the *Book of Enoch*, compiled from various sources, there appear other rebellious and seducing angels, called ʿAzbiel [Asbeêl] and Gadriel [Gâdreêl]. The former 'imparted to the holy sons of God evil counsel, and led them astray so that they defiled their bodies with the daughters of men, and the latter led astray Eve, and showed [the weapons of death to the sons of men] the shield and the coat of mail, and the sword for battle, and all the weapons of death to the children of men' (*ibid.* lxix, 5–6). The name ʿAzbiel signifies that the angel forsook God. Also the name Gadriel has been explained as a corruption of Qaṭriel, that

is, one who conspired against God (See L. Ginzberg, *Legends*, Pt. V, p. 121); Sammael is expressly mentioned in the Greek *Apocalypse of Baruch* (iv, 9–10). There he is identical with Satan, who led Adam astray, and elsewhere it is stated there that he assumed the guise of a serpent (ix, 7). Apparently the names Saṭanel, Samyazz, and ʿAzbiel are all synonyms for the angel that stood at the head of the rebels. The name Sammael simply means 'he who made himself a god.' The etymology suggested by Kohut (*Aruch Completum*, vi, p. 68, and earlier hesitantly by Jacob Levy, *Neuhebräisches und Chaldäisches Wörterbuch*, p. 534) *sam-'El* ['poison of God'], on the basis of *ʿAvoda Zara* 20b, 'It is said of the Angel of Death that he is full of eyes and when an ailing person is on the point of dying, he stands above his head-rest with his sword drawn in his hand and a drop of gall suspended on it...', is not an improvement on the ancient homiletical exposition in the *Acts of Andrew and Matthew* 24, M. R. James, *The Apocryphal N.T.*, 1924, p. 456; see L. Ginzberg, *Legends*, *loc. cit.* Cf. below, p. 763, n. 63, that he is called Sammael because he is blind [*sûmā'*].

42. *T.B. Bava Batra* 16a, according to a MS. reading; see *Diqduqe Soferim ibid.*, p. 72, n. *Lāmed.*
43. See below, xv, § 6.
44. *T.B. Bava Batra, loc. cit.*
45. *Gen. Rabba* lvi, 4, p. 598, where he comes to prevent Abraham and Isaac from performing the act of the *ʿĂqēdā* [attempted sacrifice of Isaac; literally: 'binding']; but in *T.B. Sanhedrin* 89b, and also in *Tanḥuma*, Wa-yērā', 22 and 42, and in *Pesiqta Rabbati* 170b, Satan is the seducer. It is noteworthy that also in *Martyrium Jesaiae*, 2, 1, it is stated that Sammael made his abode in Manasseh and surrounded him.
46. *Tanḥuma*, Wa-yishlaḥ, § 8; so, too, *Zohar*, Pt. I, 35b. In *Midrash ha-Neʿelam*, Noaḥ (*ad fin.*): ' "And there wrestled a man with him" — this was Sammael, the teacher of Adam'; see *Sĕfer Ṣĕrôr ha-Môr*, Venice 1564, 44b–c.
47. *Midrash 'Avkir*, *Yalquṭ Shimʿoni*, *editio princeps*, § 132: 'or with Gabriel'; *Zohar*, Pt. II, 41b.
48. According to *Antiquities* attributed to Philo, xviii, 6, it was the angel appointed over the hymns of praise; in *Gen. Rabba* lxxviii, 1, p. 916, we learn from the words of R. Ḥelbo that it was either Michael or Gabriel, who are angels who do not interchange their praise.
49. *Gen. Rabba* lxxix, 8, p. 949. It is noteworthy that the author of *Pirqe de-R. Eliezer*, who was familiar with Sammael, preferred here this homily to others, and deduced from it that the name of the angel is Israel; see *ʿArugat ha-Bośem*, Pt. III, p. 107, and the notes there; cf. also *Tanḥuma* xcvi, § 2 (*ad fin.*).
50. Origen, *Commentarius in Joann.* IV, II, 25, published by Preuschen, *CGIS* Leipzig 1903, p. 88; the whole passage is cited by Schürer, III, p. 560, and he, too, noted the Jewish character of the Prayer of Joseph. The view of Vacher Burch, *Journal of Theol. Studies*, XX (1918), p. 20, that the prayer emanates from a Christian source is without foundation. The expression 'a

Divine name may not be erased' points to a Hebrew source. M. R. James, *The Lost Apocrypha*, London 1920, p. 29, found it difficult to translate and observed: 'The expression "inextinguishable name" I have not found elsewhere; though I believe it does exist.' However, L. Ginzberg, *Legends*, V, p. 310, already draws attention to 'Names that may not be erased', *T.B. Shavuot* 35a. Also Philo, *De Somniis*, I, § 114 speaks of βλέποντος 'Ισραήλ, but he refrains from interpreting the name as 'one that sees God'. Regarding the modern Bible scholars who have sought to explain the name Israel in a similar manner, see *Encyclopedia Biblica*, [Hebrew] III, p. 939. Now see also the detailed article of Jonathan Z. Smith, 'The Prayer of Joseph', *Studies in the History of Religions*, XIV, 1968, pp. 253–294.

51. *Gen. Rabba* lxix, 7, p. 796; on Jacob's study, see *ibid.* lxviii, 11, p. 784. *Yisrā'el sāvā'* simply means 'Israel the aged patriarch' in contradistinction to the people of Israel. R. Joshua b. Levi and R. Samuel bar Naḥman interpret the verses 'Let Israel now say' (Psalms cxxiv 1) and 'O Thou that art enthroned upon the praises of Israel' (*ibid.* xxii 4) not as referring, according to their plain meaning, to the people of Israel, but to the patriarch Jacob. Y. Baer, *Lĕ-Bērûrah shel Tòrat 'Aḥărît ha-Yāmîm bi-Yĕmê ha-Bayit ha-Shēnî'* [A Contribution to the Elucidation of the Eschatology of the Second Temple Period], *Zion*, xxii–xxiii, 1958–1959, p. 30, identifies the epithet *Yisra'el Sāvā'* with 'the image of Jacob', but the aforementioned homilists had no such idea in mind; nor is it stated in 'Rabbinic dicta that Jacob saw his image' (Baer, *ibid.*, p. 31). On the saying 'It is the Patriarchs who are the Chariot', see below, xv, § 7.

52. *Gen. Rabba* lxix, 2, p. 791, and the statement of R. Abbahu *ibid.* § 3, p. 992. H. Albeck *ibid.*, p. 796, n. 3, rightly notes that even the Rabbis who declared *ibid.*, p. 780, that the words, ' "because the sun was set" teach us that the Holy One, blessed be He, had caused the sun to set before its time in order to speak with Jacob privately', refer to the night and not to the dream. Y. Baer compares the words of the Amoraim that we have cited with Philo's observations in his work *De Somniis*, but it seems that the purpose of the Amoraim in removing the angels, for reasons that we have discussed, is antithetic to that of Philo. Even when he describes the appearance of the Unseen to the so ıls who thirst to meet Him, he uses the term θεῖος λόγος (§ 31): 'His interpretation of Jacob's dream (§ 157–158), in which he saw 'the great angel the Lord standing upon the ladder', is intended primarily to explain, according to his method, the word *niṣṣāv* ['standing'].

53. *Sifre Deuteronomy* § 305, and with a few changes in *'Avot de-R. Nathan*, Version I, p. 50. See *Sifre ibid.*, § 357, and *T.B. Soṭa* 13b. It seems that both the statement of R. Eliezer and that of Semalyon are intended to contradict the view of those who aver that Moses did not die, a view that was known to Josephus, *Ant.*, IV, § 326; see S. Rappaport, *Agada und Exegese bei Flavius Josephus*, 1930, p. 127, and cf. S. E. Löwenstamm, 'Mot Moshe' [Death of Moses], *Tarbiz*, XXVII, 1958, pp. 148 ff.

54. According to the version of *'Avot de-R. Nathan*: 'the Ministering Angels'.
55. See *Pesiqta Rabbati* xx, 96b–98a, where appear Qemuel, the angel in charge of the twelve thousand angels of destruction; Hadarniel, the angel whose every utterance consists of flashes of lightning; Sandalfon, of whose fire even Hadarniel is afraid; Rigyon, the river of fire; and Gallişur, who receives the breath of the Living Creatures; see *'Arugat ha-Bośem*, Pt. II, pp. 183, 187. This struggle is alluded to in *Sifre Deut.*, § 306, and in the Midrash before us; see below, n. 62.
56. *Deut. Rabba* xi, 9. I cite the passage according to the version of *Yalquṭ Shim'oni, editio princeps*, which is almost identical with that of *'Avot de-R. Nathan*, the Vatican MS., ed. Schechter, Addendum II, p. 156.
57. In *Deut. Rabba* the text reads: 'Has the time come when the Holy One, blessed be He, wills to renew His world?... The time has not yet arrived... to renew his world.'
58. In *Deut. Rabba* 'Zagzagel master [Rav] and scribe'. With regard to the interpretation of the name, L. Ginzberg, *Legends*, Pt. VI, p. 150, notes that in the *Book of Enoch*, *Bet ha-Midrash*, p. 116, the name Segan Zagel appears among the appellations of Meṭaṭron, and he accordingly wishes to regard Zagzagel as a corruption of 'Segan Seganniel' — 'The prince of the heavenly princes'. But it appears that Zagzagel is actually ζυγός – *'ēl*, and it recalls the name Sandalfon, Συνάδελφος. Hence the form Zagzagel and likewise that of Segan Zagel are forms expressive of transcendance.
59. *Śĕrēfā Lehāvā*, literally: 'conflagration flame'; in *Deut. Rabba* the reading is: *śarfē* 'serafim of'.
60. In *Deut. Rabba* we find the last passage from 'Said he before Him...' up to this point. On the motif of fixing an eye as a hinge for a door, see Isidore Levy, *La Légende de Pythagore*, 1927, pp. 154 ff, and *ibid.*, p. 165 and p. 142. See also S. Lieberman, *Sheqi'in*, p. 39; idem, *'Al Ḥăṭā'îm wĕ-'Ōnāshîm* ['On Sins and their Punishment]', *Jubilee Volume in honour of Louis Ginzberg*, p. 254 and p. 258.
61. From 'And [Sammael] had not yet shown...' up to this point is a kind of duplicate, parallel version.
62. Moses related to Sammael the full story of his great achievements, including 'and I ascended and I trod the way of heaven, and I took part in the war of the angels, and I received the Torah of fire [and I spoke] with Him face to face, and I conversed with Him in the heavenly entourage, and I revealed their secrets to the children of men...'. See *Sifre Deut.*, § 306. When Moses told Israel how much he had suffered for the Torah, he mentioned '...I entered among the angels and among the Living Creatures and among the Seraphim...'; see above, pp. 155–156.
63. In greater detail in the passage of *Peṭirat Moshe* [The Death of Moses] (*Bātê Midrāshôt*, Pt. I, p. 286): 'The wicked Sammael jumped up... he went immediately and found Moses, who was engaged in the study of the Torah. When he saw him, his eyes were instantly blinded, and he could not find the way.

He returned to the Holy One, blessed be He, groping his way in darkness...'; but it was not on account of this episode that he was called Sammael, see above, p. 760, n. 41. Possibly the etymology mentioned above originates in an aetiological narrative of this kind.

64. See *M. Soṭa* i, 9: 'Who is greater than Moses with whom the Omnipresent alone occupied himself?' The continuation, however, 'and not of Moses only did they say this but of all the righteous', serves to weaken the uniqueness of Moses' burial. In *Tosefta* iv, 8, p. 300, this addition is wanting, and instead it is stated 'R. Judah said: For a distance of four miles Moses was lying in the wings of the Shekhina.' In *T.B. ibid.* i, p. 17c: 'It was taught in the name of R. Juda: Were it not written, it would not be possible to say it; this teaches us that when Moses died he was lying...'. As against this, see *Sifre Num.* §34, p. 38: "'And one buried him in the valley" (Deut. xxxiv 6) — but did others bury Moses? Lo, he buried himself!'

65. 'R. Joḥanan b. Dahavai said: Four things the Ministering Angels told me...', *T.B. Nedarim* 20a. But Amemar *ibid.* 20b states: 'Who are the Ministering Angels? The Rabbis... because they are as distinguished as the Ministering Angels'; see Rashi *T.B. Qiddushin* 72a s.v. *Dômîm*; but cf. below, p. 751, n. 68. From the words of Amemar it is not to be deduced that the Halakha is always according to an angel, but only in the case under consideration — 'they are more expert in regard to the formation of the fetus'. Nevertheless, the Torah was given to human beings, and this is the significance of the dictum 'The Torah was not given to the Ministering Angels' (*T.B. Berakhot* 25b and the parallels indicated there; cf. also R. Joseph Engel, *Gilyônê ha-Shas, ibid.*) although they are capable of greater exactitude and greater care.

66. See above, p. 168. Our Midrash was used by the authors of the works *Midrash Pĕṭîrat Môshe Rabbênû, ʿālāw ha-Shālôm* [Midrash of the Death of Our Teacher Moses, Peace be upon him], Jellinek's *Bet ha-Midrash*, Pt. I, pp. 115 ff, and *ibid.*, Pt. VI, pp. 71 ff; *Midrash Gĕdûlat Moshe* or *Kĕ-Tappûaḥ ba-ʿĂṣê ha-Yaʿar* [Midrash of the Greatness of Moses or As an Apple-tree among the Trees of the Wood], Wertheimer, *Bate Midrashot*[2], I, pp. 273, and *ibid.*, p. 286. They combined themes, including descriptions of Hell and Paradise from both early and late sources, in which even the influence of Islam is discernible; see L. Ginzberg, *Legends*, Pt. V, p. 416.

67. See above, p. 174, that the Holy One, blessed be He, proclaims in all the gates of every lawcourt.

68. The word is Latin; see S. Krauss, *Lehnwörter*, p. 463; cf. also the *Additamenta* to the *Aruch Completum*, p. 328. In Greek φαμιλία occurs in inscriptions and papyri; see Liddell and Scott, 1953, p. 1914. In the lexicon of W. Bauer, *Wörterbuch zu den Schriften des N.T. und der übrigen urchristlichen Literatur*, 1958, the word does not appear at all. In the Epistle to the Ephesians (iii 15) we find πᾶσα πατριὰ ἐν οὐρανοις in the sense of the family of the angels in heaven.

69. *Sifra*, Qedoshim, i, 86d; so, too, in the parable of *Mekhilta*, Be-shallaḥ, Shira x, p. 150, and in the Baraita. 'The School of R. Ishmael taught', *T.B. Zevaḥim* 41b; see Rashi *ad loc.* s.v. *Pamalyā Shelô*: 'the assembly of the group of his counsellors, who are in agreement with his policy and to whom he confides his secrets', according to *Shiṭṭa Mequbbeṣet* § 13.
70. *Sifre Numbers* § 42, p. 47.
71. See *Mekhilta*, Neziqin, xiii, p. 295: 'and the heart of the Bet Din was stolen by them' parallels 'they sought to steal the mind of the Most High'; *Tosefta Bava Qamma*, vii, 9, 'He was stolen [i.e. deceived] by them', and also 'the Great Bet Din [High Court]'; cf. *Mekhilta de-R. Ishmael*, Wa-yissaʿ, vi, 174, 'From this we learn that the Great Bet Din is called *Maqom* ['Omnipresent']'; *Mekhilta de-R. Simeon b. Yoḥai*, p. 118, where it is inferred from the dictum of R. Todros 'Hence we learn that the Great Bet Din, blessed be He, is called *Maqom*'. R. Israel Lévi comments on this in his study *Ein Wort über die Mechilta des R. Simon*, Breslau 1886, p. 9, n. 4, and he also refers to the *Tosefta 'Oholot* (*ad fin.*), p. 617; see above, p. 717, n. 40. All this was overlooked by A. Marmorstein in his above-mentioned article, p. 49; he suggested that the text of the Mekhilta be emended to 'Hence they called the Great Bet Din Maqom', or 'the Blessed One is called Maqom'. His view that the idea of a heavenly Bet Din is not found in Tannaitic literature is likewise erroneous. Cf. now also *Mekhilta de-R. Simeon b. Yoḥai*, p. 113, cited from the Firkovich MS.: 'and from the days of the Great Bet Din, blessed be He'.
72. See *Gen. Rabba* xxxvi, 6, p. 252; regarding the reading R. Eliezer or R. Eleazar, see *ibid.*, n. 1. The first interpretation is given in *Deut. Rabba* v, 5, and the second in *Midrash Tehillim* lxxii, 2, p. 163a.
73. *Mekhilta de-R. Ishmael*, Wa-yehi, vi, p. 112; see *ibid.* n. 11. In *Canticles Rabba* i, 9, there is added after 'and all with justice': 'for it is written "I saw the Lord sitting upon a throne high and lifted up". Cf. *Yĕfē Qôl* [S. Yafe Ashkenazi], *Maharzaw* [Z. W. Einhorn] and *Ḥiddushê Harashash* [Novellae of S. Strashun], who all emend to 'upon his throne', referring to I Kings xxii 19. Instead of *ba-dîn* ['in judgement'] read *yôshēv ba-dîn* ['sitting in judgement']; cf. *Sifre Deut.* § 307.
74. *Gen. Rabba* xii, 1, p. 99; *Ecclesiastes Rabba* ii, 11, where there is the addition 'And should you say, there are two godheads, lo, it is already stated "Hath He not made thee and established thee?" ' It seems to me that the authenticity of R. Simeon b. Yoḥai's dictum is confirmed by *Sifre Deut.* § 307 '...and His ways are not to be questioned, even if the matter be of no consequence [this is the correct reading; see S. Lieberman, *Tosefta ki-Fshuṭah*, Moʿed, p. 584], 'and there is not one of them who would consider and say: If I had three eyes, if I had three hands... how beautiful it would be! Thus Scripture teaches us "for all His ways are justice"; He sits in judgement with each one and gives him...' The expression 'sitting in judgement' is the equivalent of 'sitting in the Court of Justice ['Bet Din']'.
75. *T.B. Sanhedrin* 5a; the statement by L. Ginzberg, *Ginze Schechter*, Pt. I,

p. 495, that the Baraita is Babylonian is improbable, since it is explained in *T.P. Sanhedrin* i, 1, p. 18a: 'R. Ammi entered and taught: if an expert compelled (the litigants to have their case tried by him alone) and gave judgement, his decision is valid.'

76. *T.P. Sanhedrin*, *ibid.*
77. *T.B. Sanhedrin* 38b.
78. *T.P. Sanhedrin*, *loc. cit.* In *Cant. Rabba* i, 9, the homilist connects R. Eleazar's dictum with the argument between R. Pappos and R. Akiba, and asks: 'And how does R. Eleazar explain the verse cited by R. Pappias "But He is One, and who can turn Him?" The meaning is that He signs alone for all mankind and no being signs with him.' See also *Deut. Rabba* i, 9, and *Ḥiddushe ha-RaDal*, *ibid.*
79. Above, p. 161. See *Gen. Rabba* li, 2, p. 533: ' "And the Lord caused to rain"... R. Lazar said: Wherever Scripture says "And the Lord" it means He and His Bet Din'; cf. *Exod. Rabba* xii, 4, and the parallel passages listed *ibid.*, n. 4.
80. *T.P. Sanhedrin*, *loc. cit.*, and *Gen. Rabba*, *loc. cit.*: 'R. Judah bar Simon — i.e. R. Judah b. Pazzi — "And the Lord caused to rain" this is Gabriel, from the Lord'.
81. *T.P.*, *loc. cit.*; see *Lev. Rabba* xxiv, 2, p. 551; cf. *Tanḥuma*, Exodus xviii.
82. *T.B. Sanhedrin* 67b; see Rashi *ad loc.*, s.v. *Kĕshāfīm*, and above, p. 97.
83. See W. Bacher, Die Agada der pal. Amoräer Pt. I p. 195.
84. *T.B. Sanhedrin* 99b.
85. *T.B. Berakhot* 17a. After this prayer it is stated 'At the end of his prayer, R. Alexandri said as follows... Some say that this was the prayer of Rav Hamnuna, whereas R. Alexandri on concluding his prayer said the following....' The second prayer is attributed in *T.P. Berakhot* iv, 2, p. 7d, to R. Tanḥum bar Iskolastiqa [= *Scholasticus*, 'the Pleader']; possibly the prayer of R. Alexandri is the one attributed to R. Safra.
86. *T.P. Berakhot* ix, p. 14c, where the statement is cited in the name of R. Joshua the Daromean [Southerner]. See B. Ratner, *'Ahavat Ṣiyyon wi-Yerushalayim*, p. 215; Hyman, *Toledot Tanna'im wa-'Amora'im*, p. 561. Cf. also *T.B. Makkot* 23b and *Ruth Rabba* iv, 4, where the text reads: 'R. Tanḥuma in the name of the Rabbis said: Three edicts were proclaimed by the Bet Din below and the Bet Din on high agreed with them.' The meaning is that the passage was taken from the Midrash of R. Tanḥuma, and actually it is to be found in the *Tanḥuma*, Wa-yeḥi, § 8, and in Buber's edition, § 10, but the reading there is 'and the Holy One, blessed be He, agreed with them', which is obviously a textual emendation. In *Gen. Rabba*, Shiṭṭa Ḥadasha, Wa-yeḥi, § 96, p. 1202, which emanates from the *Tanḥuma* (see *ibid.* the notes of H. Albeck, p. 1199) the reading is: 'and the Holy One, blessed be He, on high [*mi-lĕ-maʿălān*] agreed with them'; here the emender has still left the word *mi-lĕ-maʿălān*.
87. *T.P. Rosh ha-Shana* i, 3, p. 57b.
88. *T.P. Rosh ha-Shana* ii, 6, p. 58b. See Tosafot, *T.B. Sanhedrin* 10b, s.v. *She-*

kĕvār; cf. *Exod. Rabba* xv, 20; *Deut. Rabba* ii, 14; *Midrash Tehillim* iv, 4, p. 43.

89. See above, p. 72.
90. See above, p. 155.
91. *Lev. Rabba* xxix, 2, p. 673; see vv.ll. *ibid.*, and cf. *Pesiqta de-Rav Kahana*, ed. Mandelbaum, p. 337.
92. See below, the chapter on the Torah.
93. *T.B. Ḥullin* 91b; see above, p. 151. In *Midrash Tehillim* civ, 9, p. 442, the following dispute is reported with reference to the meaning of the verse 'Beside them dwell the fowl of the heaven' (Psalms civ 12): R. Akiba said 'These are the Ministering Angels.' Said R. Ishmael to him 'Cease your prating and turn to (the laws of) plagues and tents... this refers,' said R. Ishmael, 'to the birds that dwell upon the trees, from whom the praise of the Holy One, blessed be He, arises....'
94. *Gen. Rabba* lxxviii, 1, p. 916; see *ibid.* n. 1.
95. *T.B. Ḥagiga* 14a.
96. *Gen. Rabba, loc. cit.*, p. 917.
97. *Dial c. Tryph.* 128, 3–4.
98. *Tosefta Ḥullin* ii, 18, p. 503; the Leiden MS. reads: 'to Michael, the Prince' (*Tosefet Ri'shonim*, II, p. 226); note also *T.B. ʿAvoda Zara* 41b: 'to Michael, the Great Prince'. Paul, too, warns against the 'worship of angels' in Colossians ii 18; on the spread of the worship of angels, especially in the fourth century, see Th. Hopfner, *Griechisch-Ägyptischer Offenbarungszauber*, I, p. 33.
99. *T.P. Berakhot* ix, 12, p. 13a. Note *T.B. Yoma* 52a 'Beloved are Israel, for Scripture did not require them to have an intermediary', and Rashi, *ibid.*, s.v. *wĕ-Rabbî Yôsê*, comments 'but each one prays for himself'. On praying to angels in the later Halakhic literature, see the responsa *Zekher Yehosef* by R. Joseph Zechariah Stern, *'Oraḥ Ḥayyim*, § 210.

1. See M. C. Grant's essay (mentioned below, p. 756, n. 3) pp. 255 ff; cf. below, p. 204 and p. 229.

CHAPTER IX

HE WHO SPOKE AND THE WORLD CAME INTO BEING

1. See M. Cassuto, 'Shîrat hā-ʿAlîlā bĕ-Yisrā'ēl', *Keneset*, VIII (1943–1944), pp. 121–142; N. H. Ṭur-Sinai, *Ha-Lāshôn wĕ-ha-Sēfer*, vol. 'Hā-'Emûnôt wĕ-ha-Dēʿôt', Jerusalem 1956, pp. 168–173, 195–204.
2. *T.P. Ḥagiga* ii, 1, p. 77a.
3. *Gen. Rabba* i, 14, p. 12; see *ibid.* n. to line 6.
4. See M. Yoel, *Blicke*, Pt. I, p. 169, who refers to the remarks of Irenaeus, *Adv. Haer.*, I, 18, τέσσαρα οὖν ταυτα ὀνομάσας θεὸν καὶ ἀρχὴν, οὐρανον καὶ γῆν τὴν τετρακτὺν αὐτῶν ὡς αὐτοὶ λέγουσι, διετύπωσεν; cf. above, p. 76.
5. See *Tanḥuma*, ed. Buber, Bere'shit, 8. The passage there is in confusion, the words of R. Ishmael being interpolated into those of R. Akiba.
6. *Gen. Rabba* i, 15, p. 13; see the *Commentary of Z. W. Einhorn* (RaZaW) and *Ḥiddushe David Luria* (RaDaL) *ad loc.*
7. This verse is not cited in *Gen. Rabba*, but is found in *T.P. Ḥagiga* ii, 1, p. 77c–d. In *T.B. Ḥagiga* 12a, Amos ix 6 is quoted. From Isaiah the Sages deduce that 'both were created simultaneously'.
8. The words of R. Eleazar, the son of R. Simeon b. Yoḥai, in *T.P.* and in *Gen. Rabba*. On the source of the simile like 'a pot and its lid' in Babylonian cosmological conception, see G. Ben-Ammi Zarfati, 'Ha-Qosmografya ha-Talmudit [The Talmudic Cosmography]', *Tarbiz*, XXV, 1966, p. 141.
9. A similar statement is made in the Pseudo-Clementine work, *Recognitiones*, I, 27, 'cum fecisset Deus caelum et terram tamquam domum unam'; see L. Ginzberg, *Die Haggada bei den Kirchenvätern*, Berlin 1900, p. 12.
10. *Gen. Rabba* xii, 11, p. 112; in *Tanḥuma*, ed. Buber, Bere'shit, 17, the dictum of R. Simeon b. Yoḥai is attributed to the School of Hillel, but apparently there is an omission there due to homoeoteleuton.
11. *Quaestiones et Solutiones in Genesin*, I, 2; see *De Opificio Mundi*, 26–30.
12. *De Opificio Mundi*, 16–18; see H. Wolfson, *Philo*, I, p. 243, where in n. 11 he cites the simile used in *Gen. Rabba* i, 1, which we shall discuss later. Wolfson, *ibid.*, p. 271, puts in Philo's mouth an answer to the objection raised by Aristotle against Plato, namely, why could not the Almighty God

create the visible world without creating an ideal world? Philo does not expressly ask this question, but Wolfson knows what his answer would be, to wit, the simile mentioned above. God works in an analogous manner to human beings. And why does He do so? Wolfson says that Philo would have answered as did the Sages: In order to serve as an example to men. This appears to me far-fetched. Nor is the proof advanced from Philo's observations, *Quaest. in Gen.*, I, 53, on Genesis iii 21, valid, for there a moral idea is inculcated, whereas no such idea is to be found in the planning of a city by an architect. See also J. Horovitz, *Untersuchungen über Philons und Platons Lehre von der Weltschöpfung*, Marburg 1900, pp. 80–82. With regard to creation in thought, cf. *Megillat ha-Serakhim*, ed. Licht, pp. 90–92 (iv, 15–16): 'Before things came into existence He determined the plan of them; and when they fill their appointed roles, it is in accordance with His glorious design that they discharge their functions' [Translation by Th. Gaster, *Dead Sea Scrolls*] (note of Prof. D. Flusser).

13. *T.B. Tamid* 32a; I have cited the version of the Florence MS. This is also the reading of *'Aggadot ha-Talmud*, and the commentary there explains 'This matter has no solution'. In the Talmud it is objected 'But they should have said to him, Darkness was created first, for it is written "Now the earth was unformed and void, and darkness" etc., and subsequently "And God said 'Let there be light' " '; to this objection the Talmud gives the answer recorded there.
14. See J. N. Epstein, *Sifre Zuṭa*, pericope Para, *Tarbiz*, I (1930), p. 52.
15. *Gen. Rabba* i, 4, p. 8.
16. On the question of *Creatio ex Nihilo* in the apocryphal literature, see *The Wisdom of Solomon* xi, 17; the *Letter of Aristeas* 136; *II Maccabees* vii 28. So, too, Philo — cf. D. Neumark, *Toledot ha-Pilosofya be-Yisra'el*, New York 1921, pp. 60 ff; Wolfson, *op. cit.*, pp. 302 ff; and now V. Nikiprowetzky, 'Problèmes du "Récit de la Création" chez Philon d'Alexandrie', *REJ* (CXXIV) 1965, pp. 271–306; Kahn-Yashar, "ʿAl beʿāyot ha-Bĕrîʾā yēsh mēʾayin bĕ-kitvê Fîlôn' [On the Problem of *Creatio ex Nihilo* in the Writings of Philo], *Sefer ha-Shana*, the University of Bar Ilan, 1968, pp. 60–66.
17. *Gen. Rabba* ii, 4, pp. 17–18; see *Tosefta Ḥagiga* ii, 6; *T.P. ibid.* ii, 1, p. 77a; *T.B. ibid.* 15a; for the elucidation of the text of the story, see S. Lieberman, *Tosefta ki-Fshuṭah*, Moʿed, V, pp. 1292 ff.
18. 'How much Greek in Jewish Palestine?', *Biblical and Other Studies*, published by Philip W. Lown Institute of Advanced Judaic Studies, Harvard Univ. Press; 1963, XXI, pp. 135–139; cf. also *Tosefta ki-Fshuṭah, loc. cit.*
19. Lieberman, *ibid.*, cites from *Evangelium Veritatis*, 22, 13 ff and from the *Gospel of Thomas* 55. He also quotes, of course, the saying of ʿAqavya b. Mahalalel, *M. 'Avot* iii, 1, and *loc. cit.*, n. 13, he mentions the words of Seneca, *Ep.*, 82, 'sciat quo iturus sit, unde ortus' etc., to which A. Kaminka, *Meḥqarim be-Miqra u-be-Talmud*, Tel-Aviv 1951, p. 50, drew attention. I wish to add another source, the Persian work, '*Čīdag andarz ī Pōrytōkēšān*,

or *Pandnāmag ī Zurduxšt* (printed in the book by H. S. Nyberg, *A Manual of Pahlavi*, I, Wiesbaden 1964, pp. 62 ff; see the Introduction *ibid.*, p. XVII), where it is stated: 'The teachers of the Ancient Doctrine declared by virtue of what was revealed to them by religion: Every man, upon reaching the age of 15, is obliged to know the following things: 'Who am I? Whose am I? Whence do I come and whither am I going?' etc. The answers are: 'I came from another world (*mēnōg*); I was not fashioned in this world; I am created and am not eternal (*būdāg*); I belong to Ormuzd and not to Ahriman'. Of Ormuzd it is subsequently stated: 'He is the author of all the good and all the light'. The formulation of the question was thus known in various circles, and the answers were given according to the traditional conceptions; it is difficult therefore to regard the question itself as tantamount to occupying oneself with Gnosis.

20. *Derekh Ereṣ Rabba* iii, ed. Higger, p. 155; *'Avot de-R. Nathan*, Version II, xxxii, 35a.

21. According to the recension of the Tosefta, the Palestinian Talmud, and the Babylonian Talmud, Ben Zoma replied at once to R. Joshua's question 'Whence and whither' with the words 'I was contemplating the work of Creation'. It is difficult to suppose that in all three sources there is the same omission due to homoeoteleuton. We must regard them as representing a parallel version, according to which Ben Zoma answered R. Joshua's question forthwith.

22. Lieberman, *op. cit.*, p. 139, cites the teaching of the Gnostic sect, 'The Men of Seth', according to J. Doresse, *The Secret Books of Egyptian Gnostics*, New York 1960, p. 150. They declare: 'The Light was above and the Darkness below, and the Pneuma between them. This Pneuma, which was dominant in the middle, is not to be equated with a storm wind or a light, gentle breeze, but was like the fragrance that exudes from myrrh or incense'. Clearly there is no comparison between 'the hovering spirit that all but touches' of Ben Zoma and the description of the 'Sethites', which is part of a mythology in which there is a parallelism between the creation of the world, the genesis of man, and the redemption. Everything is ruled by three fundamental principles, which enshrine infinite forces. The clash between the forces generates ideas. A ray of light penetrates the darkness, which desires to hold it, together with the fragrance of the Pneuma, but the light and the Pneuma endeavour to liberate their forces, which are intermingled in the black waters. From the first clash of the disturbed forces was born the idea of heaven and earth. In this myth, which is recounted at length by Hippolytos, *Elenchos*, V, 19–22, there are interwoven Orphic, Platonic, and Iranian elements. See Bousset, *Hauptprobleme der Gnosis*, Göttingen 1907, pp. 119 ff; H. Leisegang, *Die Gnosis*, Leipzig 1924, pp. 151 ff; H. Jonas, *Die Mythologische Gnosis*, Göttingen 1954, p. 289, n. 4; H. Wolfson, *The Philosophy of the Church Fathers*, Cambridge Mass. 1956, pp. 544 ff. Actually in the Iranian element of this myth, as we know it from late works, we can find an analogy to Ben Zoma's dic-

tum. It is thus stated in *Bundahišn* 2, 12–36: 'Ormuzd was above with the Knowledge of everything, the Good and Time unbounded by Light; this is the Royal Throne and Place of Ormuzd. Some call it the Infinite Light... Ahriman was in the midst of the darkness... This darkness is the Place; some designate it Infinite. Between them is void, some call it Wind (*Wāy*)' etc. And in summary form it is stated in *Zādspram*, I, 1–2: 'The Light was above and the Darkness below; between them was empty space. Ormuzd was in the Light, Ahriman was in the Darkness.' See R. C. Zaehner, *Zurvan — A Zoroastrian Dilemma*, Oxford 1955, p. 312, and *ibid.*, p. 341.

23. See also M. Joel, *Blicke*, Pt. I, p. 163; J. Weinstein, *Zur Genesis der Agada*, Göttingen 1901, p. 199.
24. *Gen. Rabba* iv, 6, p. 30; see *ibid.* n. 1.
25. *Ibid.* xii, 11, p. 109; see *ibid.* n. 8.
26. See *Tosefta Nega'im* ix, 9; *T.B. Nidda* 69b; see S. Lieberman, *op. cit.*, p. 131.
27. *Gen. Rabba* x, 3, p. 75; see *ibid.* lxxviii, 1, p. 917, and also the story of the visit of R. Eliezer and R. Joshua to Rome, *Gen. Rabba* xiii, 9, p. 118: 'Said Hadrian to them: What are the waters of the Ocean?'
28. *Gen. Rabba* iii, 1, p. 18.
29. *Tanḥuma*, ed. Buber, *Bere'shit*, i.
30. *Tanḥuma*, ed. Buber, Wa-yaqhel, § 7; also in standard version of *Tanḥuma*, *ibid.*, § 6, with slight changes; but it is difficult to reconcile the version of the debate given there with this simile: 'R. Judah said: The Holy One, blessed be He, created the darkness first, and thereafter He created the world. And R. Nehemiah said: The Holy One, blessed be He, created the world first and subsequently the darkness.' However, in the Vatican MS. 44 of the *Tanḥuma* the text reads: 'R. Judah said: He created the light first and afterwards the world; and R. Nehemiah said: He created the darkness first.'
31. However, in *Tanḥuma*, We-yaqhel, § 6 (ed. Buber, *ibid.*, § 7) it is stated after the analogy of R. Judah: 'Even so did the Holy One, blessed be He: the world was in darkness... so He wrapt himself in light; and thereafter created the world'; but this version is only a duplication of the dictum of R. Samuel bar Naḥman *ibid.* and is not the statement of R. Judah, as Aptowitzer cited it in his article 'Zur Kosmologie der Agada', *MGWJ*, LXXII (1928), p. 363. To the question of Avnimos the Weaver [or Oenomaus of Gadara] (see, on him, Graetz, Pt. IV, p. 469), *Exod. Rabba* xiii, 1, the Sages did not reply, but referred him to Abba Joseph the Mason; see below, n. 15. to p. 259.
32. *Yalquṭ Shim'oni* to Job, § 954.
33. *Midrash Tehillim* l, 1, p. 279. Aptowitzer, *op. cit.*, p. 368, follows a different line of interpretation. In his view, R. Eliezer and R. Joshua differ in regard to the material from which the world was created, and he accordingly explains that the Sages also — i.e. R. Judah — deal with this subject. Zion symbolizes the light, and when the Rabbis declared that the world was created from

Zion, they meant that the world was created from the light. But this is merely a homiletical interpretation, and Aptowitzer arrived at it through his interpolation of Amoraic teaching into that of the Tannaim; see above, n. 31.

34. H. Grätz, *Gnosticismus und Judentum*, Krotoschin 1846, pp. 94–95; M. Joel, *Blicke*, Pt. I, p. 163; W. Bacher, *Die Agada der Tannaiten*, I, p. 333.
35. See G. Scholem, *Major Trends*, p. 51; *ibid.*, p. 357, n. 46. Cf. my observations in my essay 'Ha-Māsôrôt ʿal Tôrat ha-Sôd bi-Tĕqûfat ha-Tannāʾîm [The Traditions about Merkabah Mysticism in the Tannaitic Period]', *Studies in Mysticism and Religion*, presented to Gershom G. Scholem, Jerusalem 1968, pp. 12 ff [Hebrew Section].
36. *M. Ḥagiga* ii, 1; *Tosefta ibid.*, ii, 7; *T.P. ibid.*, ii, 1, p. 77c; *T.B. ibid.*, 11b. S. E. Loewenstamm deals with the authenticity, source, and interpretations of the version in the *Jubilee Volume in honour of Y. Kaufmann*, 1961, pp. 112–121.
37. The harmonistic interpretation of Loewenstamm, *ibid.*, p. 114, n. 3 — even though qualified by 'perhaps' — that the editor of the Mishna did not actually have mere speculation in mind, but exposition uttered aloud, is unacceptable. The verb. *histakkēl* [rendered 'meditate'] is used only in the sense of 'reflect (or, meditate)', 'know', as in 'Reflect [*histakkēl*] upon three things and you will not come within the power of sin: know whence you came' etc. (*M. 'Avot* iii, 1). Also in the *Tosefta, loc. cit.*, there is preserved the expression 'Whoever meditates [*mistakkel*]'. In the Baraita in the Babylonian Talmud it is replaced by 'One might think that a man may enquire'; the difference between the opening and concluding parts is thus annulled.
38. This is also demonstrated by the difference in style.
39. *Pesiqta Rabbati* 95a; see *ʿArugat ha-Bośem*, Pt. I, p. 242; in my reference to pericope *Ki Tiśśa'* the subject is cited in the name of *Midrash Canticles*; cf. L. Ginzberg, *ʿAl Halakha we-'Aggada* [On Halakha and Haggada], Tel-Aviv 1960, p. 243.
40. 'The Great Bundahišn', 4, 12–14; see R. C. Zaehner, *Zurvan*, p. 313.
41. In *Pesiqta Rabbati, loc. cit.*, there are found two successive answers of the Lord; but in the Parma MS. 1240, p. 186a, the text reads: 'And the Prince of Darkness resembled an ox [*Shr*]. At that time the Prince of Darkness said to the Holy One: Sovereign of the universe, what dost Thou wish to create before me? Said the Holy One to him: Depart from Me....' The comparison of the Prince of Darkness to an ox (Meir Ish-Shalom's emendation is confirmed both by *Shr* of the MS. and by the wording in Sefer Razi'el; see my remarks in *ʿArugat ha-Bośem, loc. cit.*, n. 20) deserves attention, since it is contrary to the position held by the Cosmic Ox in the Iranian religions. It is actually Ahriman who fights with the Ox, for it is the source of abundance and the good creatures. See F. Cumont, *Les Mystères de Mithra*, Paris 1913; R. C. Zaehner, *The Dawn and Twilight of Zoroastrianism*, London 1961, pp. 126–127; 262–263. The words 'And the Prince of Darkness resembles an ox' are an addition that serves to link the story of the creation

of the world with the explanation given of the signs of the Zodiac. It is obvious that this narrative is of a completely different character. The signs of the Zodiac are explained as full of omens for the destiny of man, the people of Israel, and the world. This is even more conspicuous in the parallel source to the *Pesiqta* — *Genesis Rabbati*, ed. H. Albeck, p. 10 (printed by Meir Ish-Shalom as an addition, *ibid.*, p. 203). There the beginning 'Why did the Holy One, blessed be He, create the world in Nisan?' is missing, and the Midrash commences 'When the Holy One, blessed be He, created the world, He said to the Prince of Darkness....' Only after he has heard about the constellation Gemini does it occur to the Prince of Darkness to enquire 'What is the constellation of light called? Aries. And what is his constellation named? He replied, Taurus', etc. See U. Cassuto, 'The Israelite Epic' [Hebrew], *Keneset*, VIII (1943), pp. 121–142.

42. *T.B. Ḥagiga* 12a. The saying of Resh Laqish *ibid.*, which transferred the identical wording to the sea, serves to moderate Rav's myth.
43. *Gen. Rabba* iv, 7, p. 31. The dictum is transmitted by R. Abba bar Kahana; it is preceded by 'Rav said: Fire and water'. But in the Vatican MS. this saying is cited in the name of R. Levi; see vv.ll. *ibid.*; *T.B. Ḥagiga, loc. cit.*, reads: 'In a Baraita it is taught: fire and water'.
44. *Gen. Rabba* x, 3, p. 75. R. Ḥanina differs *ibid.* and says 'four — to the four sides of heaven', and R. Ḥama says 'Six — four to the four sides, and one upward and one downward'. W. Bacher, *Die Agada der Tannaiten*, I, p. 171, n. 3, is of opinion that R. Ḥanina refers to the four elements, and R. Ḥama to the six things mentioned in the second verse. But if so, the essential point is missing, namely that the dispute concerns the number of clews and not their nature. Theodor is inclined to accept Bacher's interpretation, but it seems that the debate centres on the number of clews. According to Rav the world was created from two that were integrated, while R. Ḥanina puts a clew in each direction, and R. Ḥama adds two more. In the story about R. Joshua and Hadrian that follows, the former answers the emperor's question and explains how it was possible that God created the world from His place. R. Joshua stresses in his reply to the emperor that in a small room even a human being is able, by stretching out his arms, to reach the walls and to place something upon them. Thus he holds to his doctrine that the world was created from the sides (see above, p. 192), and the Tanna does not deal with clews. The editor of the Midrash observes that R. Joshua replied in conformity with the view of R. Ḥama — he could also have said: in accordance with R. Ḥanina — that the work of creation was carried out from all directions. See the commentary attributed to Rashi and the commentaries of David Luria (RaDaL) and Z. W. Einhorn (RaZaW).
45. *T.B. Ḥagiga* 12a, according to the text of *Haggadot ha-Talmud*, reads: 'R. Jeremiah said in the name of Rav....' Philo, *De Opificio Mundi*, § 29, enumerates seven things that were created on the first day, namely: the incorporeal heavens, the invisible earth, the idea of air and of empty space (the one

he called 'darkness' and the other 'deep'), the incorporeal element of water, of wind, and of light over all. M. Schwabe, 'Philon, 'Al Beri'at ha-'Olam' § 15, *Yedi'ot ha-Makhon le-Madda'e ha-Yahadut*, No. 2, 1925, p. 81, n. 1, states that the two traditions have a common source. If the reference is to the verses in Genesis, the statement is true, but not beyond this.

46. Our text has '*tĕnā*' [a Tanna teaches] *tōhû*', but the Munich MS. 2 omits the word *tĕnā*'; this is the correct reading. See *Diqduqe Soferim* to *Ḥagiga*, p. 34, n. *Zayin*.

47. M. Joel (*Blicke*, I, p. 142) drew attention to the fact that the figure 'and *tōhû* is a green line that surrounds the whole world' has not been explained and remains incomprehensible. He was also the first to point to the description of the diagram of the sect of Ophites *apud* Origen (*Contra Celsum*, vi, 38). A. Hönig, *Die Ophiten*, Berlin 1889, p. 30, does not discuss Origen's account of the Ophites at all, for he saw no possibility of elucidating the diagram. The explanation was clearly given, however, by H. Leisegang, *Die Gnosis*, p. 165, and he even related it to Justin's *Book of Baruch*, as is reported by Hippolytus, *Elenchos*, V, 24–26, and to the account of Irenaeus, *Adv. Haer.*, 30, where reference is made to a green (yellow) circle (line), and he comes to the conclusion 'either that the Talmudic Sages knew something about the Ophitic diagram, or that they clarified their conception for themselves by a similar representation'. An examination of Origen's observations shows that the green circle is the colour of light, and in it there is a blue circle, which is the colour of darkness. They constitute the intermediate kingdom of the soul, which is itself a mixture of light and darkness and exists between the heavenly dominion of the spirit and the earthly dominion of the Cosmos. These dominions are also represented in the form of circles. Not only does Rav's dictum regarding *tōhû* contain no references to the myth described by the Ophitic diagram, namely the power-play between the three substances — spirit, soul, and body — with the entire complex of motifs that operate this drama, but the very figure is not like the diagram. The green line encompasses the world, and from it proceeds the darkness. In the Ophitic diagram the green circle is above the cosmos and consists of light. The Greek word denoting the colour of the circle is ξανθός, i.e. yellow, whereas the green colour is χλωρός (for the antithesis yellow-green, see *T.B. Ketubbot* 103b). The description of *tōhû* as a line and of *bōhû* as stones derives from the Scriptural text of Isaiah xxxiv 11 'and He shall stretch over it the line of *tōhû* and the plummet of *bōhû*'. (See *Midrash Tadshe* ii; A. Epstein, *Mi-Qadmoniyyot ha-Yehudim* [From Jewish Antiquities], *Kitve A. Epstein*, II, p. 145, 'This is a green line that encompasses the whole world, as it is said "and He shall stretch over it the line of *tōhû*"'.) In view of the fact that *tōhû* is the material from which the darkness emanates, green, which approximates to darkness, was chosen as its colour, just as to the stones of *bōhû* was added the epithet 'slimy', which explains them to be the source of water. It is not impossible that these features stem from a mythological story, which we are unable to identify.

48. Hebrew: *mĕfullāmôt* — a verb formed from the Greek word πήλωμα 'clay', 'mire'; see Fleischer in Levy's *Wörterbuch*, III, p. 315. In keeping with Rav's view, the Aramaic translator of Job xxviii 3 rendered: 'stone of gloom and deep darkness [or: shadow of death]' by: 'slimy stones whence emanates darkness'.
49. *Genesis Rabba* i, 5, p. 3.
50. See A. Epstein, 'Recherches sur le Séfer Jecira', *REJ*, XXVIII–XXIX, 1894.
51. *T.P. Ḥagiga* ii, 1, p. 77c. In *Gen. Rabba* i, 2, p. 2, the author of the proem is given as 'R. Huna in the name of Bar Qappara', but as Theodor has already pointed out, note to line 6, only the exposition at the end of the proem belongs to R. Huna in the name of Bar Qappara, hence the whole homily is attributed to him. M. Joel, *Blicke*, I, p. 155, noted the anti-Gnostic character of the proem, but he speaks of 'an interpretation of a verse in Psalms'.
52. I omitted the interpretations that do not pertain to the essence of the dictum.
53. In *Gen. Rabba* we find 'Rav said' and in the vv.ll. *ibid.* 'the Rabbis say'. Possibly this is an interpolation, since Rav's name was omitted at the beginning. See *ibid.*, p. 3, n. 3; in the Genizah fragment printed in the 'Supplement to the Introduction' of *Gen. Rabba*, Pt. II, p. 147, the text reads: 'Rav said, May he not have "Oh how [*mā*] abundant is Thy goodness" [here the Hebrew has *mā* instead of *kĕ-mā*, as in our text]...!'
54. This is the version of *Gen. Rabba, loc. cit.*; in *P.T., loc. cit.*, this analogy is cited in the name of R. Eleazar, and it concludes: 'Thus, one who says that at first the world consisted of water in water is guilty of disparagement'.
55. Graetz, *Gnosticismus und Judentum*, p. 32.
56. Hippolytus, *Elenchos*, V, p. 102. A Gnostic work would begin with the words 'Therefore, it shall remain sealed, unexplained, and esoteric...'; see E. Haenchen 'Gibt es eine vorchristl. Gnosis?', *Zeitschrift für Theologie u. Kirche*, p. 319; cf. *Gen. Rabba* i, 1, "*Āmôn* means "covered", '*āmôn* means "hidden" ', that is, the Torah, which is also "*āmôn* in the sense of pedagogue'.
57. *T.B. Ḥagiga* 12a; the transmitter, in Rav's name, is Rav Zuṭra bar Ṭobiah. In the Munich MS. Rav's name is missing, but *Diqduqe Soferim* has already pointed out, *ibid.* 35, that this is an erroneous reading. Rav Zuṭra bar Ṭobiah also transmits in Rav's name that 'whoever learns a single thing from a Magian is deserving of death', *T.B. Shabbat* 75a.
58. G. Scholem, *Ursprung und Anfänge der Kabbala*, Berlin 1962, p. 72, is of opinion that Rav's dictum reflects the Gnostic doctrine of the aeons, and he also adduces as a parallel the dictum in '*Avot de-R. Nathan*, Version I, xxxvii, p. 110, 'Seven attributes serve before the Throne of Glory....' But in the preceding paragraph we find: '...by seven things the Holy One, blessed be He, created His world....' Only two of them, however, are identical with the attributes. In Version II of '*Avot de-R. Nathan*, xliii, p. 119, we only find the saying 'By ten things was the world created'. There are added *ibid.*: wisdom, procreation, creation. In the Cambridge MS. of the *Tanḥuma*, *Śĕrîdê Tanḥuma-Yĕlammĕdēnû*, *Qoveṣ 'al Yad*, N.S., Book VI (16) 1966,

p. 15, it is expressly stated 'With seven attributes God created His world: by creation, by making, by speaking, by spirit, by stretching, by inclusion, and by saying'. Not even one of these attributes is identical with those enumerated by Rav.

59. See above, p. 738, n. 39.
60. See *Gen. Rabba* xvii, 1, p. 151; and regarding the interpretation of the Mishna, Menaḥem b. R. Jose and R. Jacob bar Qurshai differ there.
61. See A. Epstein, *loc. cit.*, pp. 180, 198, 202.
62. See A. Aptowitzer, 'Bêt ha-Miqdāsh shel Maʿălā [The Heavenly Temple]', *Tarbiz*, II (1931), p. 36.
63. *Gen. Rabba* xii, 10, pp. 107–108, and the parallels noted there. In *T.B. Menaḥot* 29b we find כדדרש רבי יהודה בר אילעי אלו שני עולמות וכו׳ 'as R. Judah bar R. 'Ilʿai expounded: This refers to the two worlds' etc.; but the MS. reads כי הא דדריש ר״י בר׳ אלעאי 'in accordance with the exposition of *R.Y. b. R. 'Ilʿai*' (see *Diqduqe Soferim*, p. 72); possibly it is a corruption of 'R.Y. (R. Joḥanan) and R. Eleazar....' In *T.P. Ḥagiga* ii, 1, p. 77c, the homily about the two worlds is given in the name of R. Joḥanan.
64. However, in the 'Alphabet of R. Akiba', letter *Hē'*, *Bate Midrashot*, II, p. 363 we read, 'H.Y. is none other than the Ineffable Name by which the whole world was created....' The homilies on the forms of the letter *Hē'* and *Yôdh*, which give the subject an ethical complexion, are not by R. Joḥanan and R. Eleazar.
65. *M. 'Avot* iii, 14; this is the reading of the Kaufmann MS. and also of the Cambridge MS. See Ch. Taylor, *Sayings of the Jewish Fathers*, Cambridge 1897, p. 20. So, too, in *Mĕle'khet Shĕlômô* on *'Avot ibid.* as a v.l. cited by Joseph Ashkenazi. These works also lack the Biblical verses; in the Kaufmann MS. the second verse is given in the margin, but is wanting in the text. In *Sifre Deut.* § 48, R. Eliezer b. R. Zadok designates the Torah 'an instrument by which this world and the next were created'.
66. See *Encyclopedia Biblica*, III, pp. 130–131 [Hebrew].
67. See L. Ginzberg, *Perushim we-Ḥiddushim bi-Yerushalmi*, IV, 1961, p. 20.
68. *Gen. Rabba* i, 1, p. 2, and the parallels noted there. In the Addenda and Corrigenda *'Avot de-R. Nathan*, Version I, xxxi is also referred to; what we have quoted is the essential part of R. Oshaʿya's proem — see Theodor's note *ad loc.*
69. *Guide of the Perplexed*, Pt. II, ch. vi; Maimonides refers, apparently, to the saying of R. Joḥanan, *T.B. Sanhedrin* 38b: 'The Holy One, blessed be He, does naught without consulting [*nimlakh*] the Heavenly Court', and it seems that he had before him the reading *nistakkel*. See *Midrash ha-Gadol*, Bere'shit, ed. Margaliot [Margulies], p. 55, and the vv.ll. *ibid.*; cf. below, p. 205.
70. See J. Freudenthal, *Hellenistische Studien*, Pt. I, p. 73; W. Bacher, *Agada der Pal. Amoräer*, I, p. 107, n. 2; and recently Yitzhak Baer, 'Le-Berurah shel Torat Aḥarit ha-Yamim bi-Yeme ha-Bayit ha-Sheni', *Zion*, XXIII–XXIV (1958–1959), p. 142, who compares the words of Plato in *Timaeus* 28, and

concludes: 'The Torah is, therefore, a complex of eternal forms ('ideas') and forces, a model for the physical world below', but this is not stated in the Midrash. M. Joel, *Blicke*, Pt. I, p. 117, was more cautious in his day and spoke of 'the Judaization of a Platonic idea'; but even according to his view it must be admitted that the Judaization exceeds the essence of the Platonic concept.

71. *De Opificio Mundi*, 17–20.
72. See J. Horovitz, *Untersuchungen über Philons und Platons Lehre von der Weltschöpfung*, Marburg 1900, p. 80, and *ibid.* n. 2, for the parallel expressions in Plato's writings.
73. Wolfson, *Philo*, Pt. I, p. 243, noted this difference; see above, p. 768, n. 12.
74. Bacher, *loc. cit.*; see above, n. 70. Cf. also L. Wächter, 'Der Einfluss platonischen Denkens auf rabbinische Schöpfungsspekulationen', *Zeitschrift für Religions- und Geistesgeschichte*, 1962, pp. 36–56. He follows Bacher's line of interpretation. An analogy closer to that of Philo is found in a late work, *Pirqe de-R. Eliezer*, iii; it is cited there incidentally:

    > Before the world was created, only the Holy One, blessed be He, and His great name existed. When it entered the mind (maḥăshāvā; but in most MSS the text has *bĕ-maḥăshavtô*, 'His mind') to create the world, He modelled the world before Him, but it would not stand. The Sages adduced an analogy: To what can the matter be compared? To a king who wishes to build his palace. If he does not model on the ground its foundations, entrances, and exits, he does not begin to build. Thus, too, the Holy One, blessed be He, modelled the world before Him, but it did not stand until He created repentance.

    The analogy does not explain the central idea of the creation of repentance, only the fact of the modelling of the world, and apparently emanates from another source. David Luria already noted in his commentary, *ibid.* 6a, n. 13, the similarity between the language of the analogy and that of Ezekiel xliii 11.
75. See E. Urbach, *Śeride Tanḥuma-Yelammedenu*, *Qoveṣ ʿal Yad*, Book VI (16), 1966, p. 20.
76. This is also the intent of the question 'Why was (the world) created with a *Bêt*...' as it appears in *Gen. Rabba*, i, 10, p. 9, and in *T.P. Ḥagiga* ii, 5, p. 77c. See my observations in my aforementioned article, n. 60, and *ibid.* p. 10; Theodor in *Minḥat Yehuda*, *loc. cit.*, note to line 5, refers to the Book *Bārûkh she-'Āmar* [Blessed be He who said], which cites *Gen. Rabba* in the version 'Why does the Torah begin with a *Bêt*....?'
77. R. Jonah in the name of R. Levi (*Gen. Rabba* and Palestinian Talmud, *loc. cit.*) bases on the shape of the letter *Bêt* the dictum 'You have no right to inquire what is above and what is below....'
78. *Recognitiones*, II, 49.
79. Tertullianus, *Adv. Marcionem*, I, 14–17.
80. *De Opificio Mundi*, 21; see *Tim.* 29e; L. Cohn, *Die Werke Philos*, Breslau 1909, Pt. I, p. 34; H. A. Wolfson, *Philo*, Pt. I, p. 315.

81. *Sifre Deuteronomy* § 307, p. 344; see *Midrash Tanna'im*, ed. Hoffmann, p. 187.
82. This is the correct reading, and it means 'not even in the least'; see S. Lieberman, *Tosefta ki-Fshuṭah*, Moʿed, p. 583.
83. *Gen. Rabba* xii, 1, p. 98; see *Eccles. Rabba* ii, 12. A. Marmorstein, 'The Background of the Haggada', *HUCA*, 1929 (= *Studies in Jewish Theology*, 1950, pp. 7 ff) regarded this homily as an anti-Marcionite polemic, but this assertion appears to have no foundation, because the view negating the creation of the world and its nature was prevalent in most Gnostic sects.
84. Plutarch, *De Stoicorum Repugnantiis*, 21, and *ibid.* 31.
85. *T.B. Shabbat* 77b; see *T.P. Berakhot* ix, 3, p. 13c, where the dictum is transmitted in the name of R. Nehorai, and he is apparently the Amora of that name who reported a ruling in the name of Samuel, *T.B. Ḥullin* 55b; cf. A. Hyman, *Sefer Toledot Tanna'im wa-'Amoraim*, London 1910, p. 919; see also *Seder Eliahu-Rabba*, i, ed. Meir Ish Shalom, p. 6; *Shoḥer Ṭov* xviii, 12; civ 25.
86. *Gen. Rabba* v, 9, p. 38, and *ibid.* xx, 9, p. 192. There is reason to doubt, however, whether the words 'that it should produce' etc., belong to R. Nathan, for in *T.P. Kil'ayim* i, 7, p. 27b, we find only 'and it will accord with the teaching of R. Nathan: Three were tried and four went forth condemned, (for Scripture says:) "cursed is the ground for thy sake".'
87. *Gen. Rabba* x, 7, p. 79, and the parallels indicated *ibid.* in the note to line 5.
88. *Ibid.* xii, 1, p. 99; see *ibid.* xv, 5, p. 138, and *Eccles. Rabba* ii, 14.
89. H. Jonas, *Gnosis und spätantiker Geist*, dritte verb. u. vermehrte Auflage, Göttingen, Pt. I, 1964, pp. 357–358. See above, p. 183.
90. *Tanḥuma*, Wa-Yēshev, 4. R. Berechiah adds a proof: 'Because it is said, "and darkness was upon the face of the deep" — this refers to the Angel of Death, who darkens the faces of people'.
91. *Gen. Rabba* i, 3, p. 5, and *ibid.* iii, 8, p. 24; see the notes *ad loc.*
92. In *Tanḥuma*, ed. Buber, Bere'shit § 1, the text has 'that the sectarians should not say: Michael' etc.; see *ibid.* § 12. However, we find in *'Avot de-R. Nathan*, Version I, xxxi, 46a: 'R. Eliezer, the son of R. Jose the Galilean, said: Nine hundred and seventy-four generations before the world was created, the Torah was written and lying in the bosom of the Holy One, blessed be He, and was uttering song with the Ministering Angels'; but in the Epstein MS. (see *ibid.* n. 7) and in the parallel sources (*Gen. Rabba* xxviii, 4, p. 263, and *Tanḥuma*, Lekh Lĕkhā, § 11) the song of the angels is not mentioned. In the words of the Lord to Israel: 'Before I created My world the Ministering Angels used to laud Me through you and sanctified My name through you, saying "Blessed be the Lord, the God of Israel, from everlasting and to everlasting" ', 'world' is used instead of 'man', as is clear from the continuation, only the homilist forgot, in his fervour, that there were no angels before the creation of the world. The expression 'lying in the bosom of the Holy One, blessed be He', contains an implicit reply to the puzzlement expressed by R. Isaac Albarceloni in his commentary to *Sefer Yĕṣirā* [Book of Creation], p. 88, 'How is it

possible that the Torah was created before the world, for there is no created entity that does not need a location, and if the location of the world was not yet created, where was the Torah situated?' See *T.B.* *'Avoda Zara* 2a; also *ibid.* 18a and *T.B. Sukka* 41b. Cf., further, *Midrash Konen*, Bet-ha-Midrash, Pt. II, p. 23.

93. *Mekhilta*. Pisḥa, xiv, p. 50; *T.P. Megilla* i, 11, p. 74d; *T.B. ibid.* 9a; see A. Aptowitzer, 'Die rabbinischen Berichte über die Enstehung der Septuaginta', *Ha-Qedem*, II, pp. 11–12, 102–122, Petersburg 1908; *ibid.*, III, pp. 4–17, Peterburg 1912.
94. *De Opificio Mundi*, pp. 74–76: ἕτεροι τῶν ὑπηκόων.
95. On the question of the source of evil see below, p. 275.
96. *Genesis Rabba* viii, 4, p. 59; see also *ibid.* xvii, 4, p. 155, in the name of R. Aḥa.
97. *Ibid.*, pp. 60–61.
98. *Ibid.*, p. 62; see there note 1.
99. See *Śeride Tanḥuma-Yelammedenu*, which I published in *Qoveṣ 'al Yad*, Book VI, p. 25.
1. *Ibid.*, p. 63. In *T.P. Berakhot* ix, 1, p. 12d, we find in the middle of the questions put by the sectarians to R. Simlai, and before the question about 'Let us make man', the following statement: 'R. Simlai said, wherever the sectarians *pārĕqû* ['took off (the yoke)' — instead of *pāqĕrû* 'advanced an heretical interpretation'] their refutation is near at hand'.
2. *Dial. c. Tryph.*, 62c, 1–2. On the Christian exegesis of Genesis i, 26, see L. Ginzberg, *Die Haggada bei den Kirchenvätern*, Berlin 1900, pp. 19–20; R. Mc. L. Wilson, 'The Early History of the Exegesis of Gen. 1. 26', *Studia Patristica, I* (TUGAL 63), 1957, pp. 420–437; J. Jervell, *Imago Dei*, Göttingen 1960 (see the excellent critique of Morton Smith, 'On the Shape of God and the Humanity of Gentiles', *Studies in the History of Religions*, XIV, 1968, pp. 315 ff); G. T. Armstrong, *Die Genesis in der Alten Kirche*, Tübingen 1962.
3. *Ad Autolyc.*, II, 18.
4. *Adv. Haer.* IV, 20, 1, in *Pirqe de-R. Eliezer* xi; in *Midrash Aggada*, ed. Buber, p. 3. Cf. also *Zohar*, Pt. III, p. 35b.
5. *Adversus Praxean*, 12, 1–2.
6. *Hexaemĕron*, Hom. ix, 6. Ginzberg, *loc. cit.*, p. 20, n. 1, attempted to reconcile his statement with that of Justin, but the statements are irreconcilable. The view that the Holy One, blessed be He, consulted the Torah before the creation of man, is found only in late Midrashim.
7. *T.B. Ḥagiga* 12a; in *Gen. Rabba* xli (xlii), 3, p. 405, there is a similar homily to that of R. Eleazar, cited in the name of R. Judah bar Simon (see vv.ll. *ibid.*), only he bases himself on Proverbs iv 18. See *Gen. Rabba* iii, 6, p. 21 and the notes there; and *ibid.* xii, 6, p. 103 and the notes.
8. *Gen. Rabba* iii, 4, pp. 19–20.
9. See G. Scholem, *Jewish Gnosticism, Merkabah Mysticism and Talmudic Tradition*, New York 1960, p. 58, n. 10.
10. See W. Bacher, *Agada der Pal. Amoräer*, II, p. 209.

11. See the commentary to *Gen. Rabba*, attributed to Rashi: 'This is the meaning thereof: If R. Isaac had not expounded it in public, that (the verse) teaches us that He wrapped Himself' etc.
12. Apart from *Gen. Rabba*, see *Lev. Rabba* xxxi, 7, p. 725, and also *Exod. Rabba* l, 1.
13. Ed. Buber, Bere'shit § 10: Wa-yakhel § 7.
14. See A. Aptowitzer, 'Zur Kosmologie der Agada', *MGWJ*, LXXII (1928), pp. 363 ff; *ibid.*, p. 366; and his article in *Bitzaron* XI (1945), pp. 105–112; 195–203. He combines both questions in a single conversation: when the answer has been given that the world was created from the light, the second question is asked: From what was the light created? To this R. Samuel bar Naḥman gives his reply. The same line of interpretation is adopted by S. Aalen, *Die Begriffe 'Licht' und 'Finsternis' im A.T. im Spätjudentum und im Rabbinismus*, Oslo 1951, pp. 262–264, and also by G. Scholem, 'Schöpfung aus Nichts und Selbstverschränkung Gottes', *Eranos-Jahrbuch*, XXV, 1956, Zürich 1957, p. 96, n. 10. In *Pirqe de-R. Eliezer*, iii (ed. David Luria, pp. 7b ff; see n. 44 *ibid.*) the Midrash in the *Tanḥuma* is explained as follows: 'Whence were the heavens created? From the light of the garment of the Holy One, blessed be He (in the Cincinnati MS. 75: 'From the light of the garment that He wears... until He announced to them'. A similar recension is found in the Parma MS. 563), that He wears; He took some of it and spread it as a garment, and they continued to stretch until He said to them "Enough!"... and they stopped. And how do we know that it was created from the light of His garment? For it is said, "Who coverest Thyself with light as with a garment, who hast stretched out the heavens like a tent." Whence was the earth created? From the snow beneath the Throne of Glory...' (see below, n. 15; cf. *T.P. Ḥagiga* ii, 1, p. 77a; and *Gen. Rabba* i, 6, p. 4, and *ibid.* n. 3). Whilst in the *Tanḥuma* the light was created from the garment and the heavens from the curtain, here the heavens were created from the light. Clearly, we have here only an interpretation that seeks to remove the difficulty of light created from light, and we can no more learn from it the original intent of R. Samuel bar Naḥman than we can infer the meaning of his words from *Sefer Hekhalot* [Book of Palaces], as G. Scholem suggests in *Jewish Gnosticism*, p. 58.
15. When the material from which anything is created is spoken of, the question acually is 'whence?' Thus we find in *Tanḥuma*, ed. Buber, § 11, p. 8: 'Whence were the heavens created? From the curtain, as it is said "who stretches out the heavens like a curtain" (Isa. xl 22). And whence was the earth created? From a lump of snow...' (I have cited the text according to the Vatican MS. 44; the version published by Buber is corrupt and defective); see *Exod. Rabba* xiii, 1. To the question of Avnimos ha-Gardi: 'How was the earth first created?' Abba Joseph, the builder, replied: 'The Holy One, blessed be He, took earth from beneath the Throne of Glory etc., and in *Midrash ha-Gadol* to Genesis, ed. Margulies, p. 20, we read: 'The Holy One, blessed

be He, took snow-dust' (see above, n. 14). It seems to me that the text of the reply in *Tanḥuma*, Wa-yaqhel, also supports our interpretation: 'When the Holy One, blessed be He, wished to create the world, He wrapped Himself in light and created His world, as it is said "who coverest Thyself with light like a garment", thereafter "who hast stretched out the heavens like a tent".' The meaning of 'and created His world' is therefore 'thereafter He created the world'.

16. See J. Freudenthal, *Hellenistische Studien*, I, p. 71; J. Weinstein, *Zur Genesis der Agada*, p. 41; also A. Altman, 'The Rabbinic Doctrine of Creation', *JJS*, VII (1956), pp. 195 ff.
17. *De Fuga*, 110.
18. *De Opificio Mundi*, 31.
19. *Pesiqta de-Rav Kahana*, Qumi 'Ori, ed. Mandelbaum, p. 323.
20. This wording is cited also in the commentary to *Gen. Rabba* attributed to Rashi as a v.l. On the motif of the 'Robe' see Robert Eisler, *Weltenmantel und Himmelszelt*, Munich 1910, pp. 224–227; F. N. Klein, *Die Lichtterminologie bei Philon von Alexandrien und in den Hermetischen Schriften*, Leiden 1962, pp. 61–68.
21. *Pesiqta de-Rav Kahana, loc. cit.*, p. 322. Reference should be made to Philo's statement, *De Praemiis*, 45–46, where he observes that as in the case of light, which can only be seen by means of light, so, too, God is not to be conceived except through Him: 'The questers after truth are they who envisage God by means of God, light by means of light (φωτὶ φῶς)'.
22. *Gen. Rabba* iii, 7, p. 23.
23. See W. Bacher, *Agada der Pal. Amoräer*, III, pp. 160 ff.
24. *Gen. Rabba, loc. cit.*; R. Phinehas bases there the dictum of R. Abbahu on Gen. i 31.
25. *Midrash Tehillim* xc, 13, ed. Buber, p. 392. See *ibid.* cv, 3, p. 449, 'In the name of R. Samuel bar Naḥmani: 974 generations — those who should have arisen from them were blotted out in the generation of the Flood'.
26. On R. Simeon, see W. Bacher, *Die Agada der Bab. Amoräer*, Strassburg 1878, p. 77, n. 8, who regarded him as a Tanna. But see A. Hyman, *Toledot Tanna'im wa-'Amora'im*, p. 1226.
27. *T.B. Ḥagiga* 13b; see *Gen. Rabba* xxviii, 4, p. 262: 'It was the Divine intention that a thousand generations should be created. How many of them were blotted out? R. Huna in the name of R. Eliezer the son of R. Jose the Galilean (said): Nine hundred and seventy-four....' Cf. also the Introduction to *Halakhot Gedolot = Dĕrāshā bĕ-Shevaḥ ha-Tôrā* [Homily in Praise of the Torah], ed. Aptowitzer, p. 1, where note 22 refers to the commentary on *Sefer Yeṣira* by Judah Albarceloni, p. 22. Cf. further *'Arugat ha-Bośem*, Pt. II, p. 175, and my observations *ibid.*, n. 14.
28. In *Midrash Tehillim, loc. cit.*, the text has: 'What is meant by *zĕramtām* ['Thou carriest them away']? R. Joḥanan said: זרו תמו They were estranged (from the Torah), they came to an end. R. Simeon b. Laqish said: זרו מתורתך

They were estranged from Thy Torah; worms consumed them....' The gematria [i.e. the calculation of the numerical value of Hebrew letters] of the word בראשית ['In the beginning'] and the significance of the big letter *Bêt* is likewise attributed to R. Joḥanan, but in other MSS. the name is missing; see *ibid.*, n. 72. In *Eccles. Rabba* iv, 3, and in *Tanḥuma*, Lekh Lĕkhā, 11, the dictum of R. Jose the Galilean in *Gen. Rabba* — but in a different version — is transmitted by R. Joḥanan.

29. *De Aeternitate Mundi*, 4, and *ibid.* 39–44. As to whether the work belongs to Philo, see the Introduction of F. H. Colson, *Philo*, IX, 1941, pp. 172 ff; on Philo's views on the subject see H. Wolfson, *Philo*, I, pp. 295 ff.
30. *De Opificio Mundi*, 26.
31. Freudenthal, *Hellen. Studien*, I, p. 71, states generally that the idea emanated from 'Hellenistic circles'; see M. Kasher, 'Muśśag ha-Zĕman [The Conception of Time]', *Ṭalpiyyot*, XXV (1952), pp. 799 ff. Y. Baer's explanation, *op. cit.*, p. 163, 'that the order of times was fixed after the creation of heaven and earth, but before evening and morning were defined' is without foundation.
32. See H. Leisegang, *Gnosis*, pp. 281 ff, and *ibid.*, p. 290; H. Jonas, *Gnosis und spätantiker Geist*, I, pp. 362 ff, and *ibid.* p. 374.
33. *Timaeus*, 370.
34. *Timaeus*, 27–28. See S. Sambursky, 'The Concept of Time in Late Neoplatonism', *Proceedings of the Israel Academy of Sciences and Humanities*, II, 1967.
35. On the question of time in the cosmology of Origen see Jonas, *loc. cit.*, pp. 211–213, and *ibid.*, n. 1.
36. *T.B. Sanhedrin* 65b. The correct reading is 'Rav Ḥananiah'; see *Diqduqe Soferim, ibid.*, p. 186, note *Bêt.* He and Rav Hoshaiah were both Babylonians, contemporaries of Rabbah and Rava, and clearly the story concerning them, like that which follows it about Rava, is Babylonian, contrary to the view of G. Scholem, *Zur Kabbala und ihrer Symbolik*, Zürich 1960, p. 219.
37. See A. Epstein, ''Iyyûnîm bĕ-Sēfer Yĕṣîrā [Studies in the Book of Creation]', *Kitve Avraham Epstein*, II, pp. 189 ff; G. Scholem, *Major Trends in Jewish Mysticism*, pp. 74–76.
38. See N. Séd, 'La Bĕraytā dī Maʿaseh Bĕrēšīt, Une Cosmologie Juive du Haut Moyen Age', *REJ*, 123 (1965), pp. 259–305.
39. Including even Midrashic expositions like *Exod. Rabba* xv, 22, or *Śeride Tanḥuma-Yelammedenu, Qoveṣ ʿal Yad*, Book VI, pp. 15–16.
40. *M. 'Avot* v, 1; Mekhilta, Shîra X, p. 150; *Gen. Rabba* xvii, 1, p. 151; see note *ibid.*; cf. also *T.B. Rosh Hashana* 32a. With regard to formulas of benedictions, see *T.B. Berakhot* 59a; *T.B. Sanhedrin* 42b.
41. See H. Wolfson, *Philo*, I, p. 239; *ibid.*, p. 327. Even in passages where the use of Philonic terms seems certain, as in *Exod. Rabba* xv, 22 'Blessed be the Omnipresent who hewed it out and created it by a word...', which recalls λόγος τομεύς (*Quis Rer. Div. Heres*, 130; first pointed out by N. J. Weinstein, *Zur Genesis der Agada*, pp. 45–46), the text has 'the Omnipresent who hewed

it out' and not 'the word that hewed'; the Midrashic portrayal there contains no Philonic concept. Weinstein did not note this, nor did Y. Baer in his comparisons; see *Zion*, xxiii–xxiv (1958–1959), p. 162.

42. See M. Ginsburger, *Die Anthropomorphismen in den Targumim*, Braunschweig 1891, pp. 12–13. See also V. Hamp, *Der Begriff Wort in den Aramäischen Bibelübersetzungen*, Munich 1838, pp. 188–205. Jonathan Shunary, 'Avoidance of Anthropomorphism in the Targum of Psalms', *Textus*, V, 1966, pp. 133–144.

43. *T.B. Sanhedrin* 19a; see *Tosefta Yoma* i, 4; cf. A. Marmorstein, *The Old Rabbinic Doctrine of God*, 1927, p. 89. Relying on the statement of S. H. Langdon, *Sumerian and Babylonian Psalms*, Paris 1909, p. 127, Marmorstein says that the expression was discovered in a Sumerian psalm; but Dr. A. Shaeffer, who examined the source, informed me that Langdon was mistaken in his translation, and that the reference there is to the god Mu, who causes the world to tremble, and not to the creation or formation of the world. In *Enūma eliš*, Tablet iv, 21–22, the gods say to Marduk: 'Thy destiny (which thou wilt determine), O lord, shall be acceptable to the gods, to wreck or create. Say and it shall be!'

44. In the formula of the benedictions 'Blessed is the Author of creation [*bĕ-rē'shît*]', *M. Berakhot* ix, 2 (this is the reading in the Kaufmann MS., the Cambridge MS., the Naples edition, and in the Mishna of the Babylonian and Palestinian Talmuds); see the prayer *Bārûkh she-'āmar* in the prayer book of S. Baer, *'Avodat Yisra'el*, p. 58, and likewise the expression *yôṣēr bĕ-rē'shît* [the Creator of all things in the beginning] in *Môdîm de-Rabbānān* [the Rabbinic 'We give thanks'], *T.P. Berakhot* i, p. 3d. L. Ginzberg's statement, *Perushim we-Ḥiddushim bi-Yerushalmi*, p. 187, that the epithet *Yôṣēr bĕ-rē'shît* contains an allusion to *creatio ex nihilo* is unfounded. On the use of this designation in the literature of the *Hêkhālôt*, see G. Scholem, *Jewish Gnosticism etc.*, pp. 26–27; in second edition, p. 128.

45. It is so worded in the Palestinian version and in the prayer *Māgēn 'āvôt* [A Shield to our forefathers]; see J. Elbogen, *Der Jüdische Gottesdienst*,[2] 1924, p. 43, and *ibid.*, p. 517. Cf. also *Shoḥer Ṭov*, p. 163.

CHAPTER X

MAN

1. '*Avot de-R. Nathan*, Version I, xxxi, p. 46a.
2. 'Aggadat Shir ha-Shirim', ed. Schechter, *JQR*, O.S., IV (1894), p. 688 (= *Aggadat Shir ha-Shirim*, Cambridge 1896, p. 19).
3. In Yeḥezkel Kaufmann's work, *Toledot ha-Emuna be-Yisra'el*, there is no special discussion of the conception of man in the Bible. In the General Index *nephesh* is completely missing, because the starting-point of the author's study is the people, not the individual, but the book does contain, in various contexts, discussions of this subject, too. See G. Pidoux, *L'homme dans l'Ancien Testament*, *Anthropologie Religieuse*, Supplements to Numen, II (1955), pp. 155–165.
4. J. Pedersen, *Israel, its Life and Culture*, I, 1946–1947, p. 100. See also W. Hirsch, *Rabbinic Psychology*, London 1947.
5. On the Biblical attitude to the desert and the role that it plays in Biblical research, see S. Talmon, *The Desert Motif in the Bible and in Qumran Literature*; Philip W. Lown, *Studies and Texts*, Institute of Advanced Studies, III, 1966, p. 31.
6. *Sifra*, Qedoshim, iv, 12, p. 89b; *T.P. Nedarim* ix, 4, p. 41c. In the eighth and seventh centuries the kings of Assyria were called the 'image of Bel'; see S. A. Löwenstamm, '*Ḥāvîv 'Ādām she-nivrā' be-Ṣellem* [Beloved is man for he was created in the Divine Image]', *Tarbiz*, vii, 1958, pp. 1 ff. On the text of the Mishna and its interpretation see my observations in *'Arugat ha-Bośem*, Pt. IV, pp. 79–80.
7. *Tosefta Sanhedrin* viii, 4–5; *T.P. ibid.*, iv, 12–13, p. 22b; *T.B. ibid.* 38a. A different and more moderate attitude with regard to the time of Adam's creation was adopted in the days of the Amoraim; see below, p. 232.
8. In the Tosefta and *T.B. ibid.* another reason is offered for the lateness of the first man's creation: 'Another explanation is: in order that he might go into the banquet at once. It may be illustrated by the following analogy: To what can the matter be compared? To a king who built a palace and dedicated it and prepared a banquet, and thereafter he invited the guests'

(see also *Genesis Rabba* viii, 6, p. 61 and *ibid.* n. 1). This explanation was known to Philo, who devotes a long discussion to the question why man was created last. He cites at length the analogy of the preparation of the banquet and states that God desired that man, when he came into the world, should find forthwith a banquet and a most holy spectacle (ἵν' εἰς τὸν κόσμον εἰσελθὼν εὐθὺς εὕρῃ καὶ συμπόσιον καὶ θέατρον ἱερώτατον) *De Opificio Mundi*, 77–78; see also *Die Werke Philos von Alexandria*, Pt. I, Breslau 1909, where Leopold Cohn refers to Ambrosius, *Epist.*, 43, and to Gregorius da Nyssa, *De Hom. Opif.*, 2, who also cite this analogy. In his third explanation (*op. cit.* 82) Philo declares that first among the created beings God set up the heavens, the most perfect among the imperishable things, and at the end of Creation He formed the most perfect being among the transient entities, who is, as it is said in truth, 'a miniature heaven' (βραχὺν, εἰ δεῖ τἀληθὲς εἰπεῖν, οὐρανόν). This reason I found only in *Midrash Ha-Gadol* to Genesis, ed. Margulies, p. 54: 'Why was he [man] created only at the end? Because he is the seal of the creation of the Holy One, blessed be He, and it is man's nature that he invariably concludes with what he begins. So, too, the Holy One, blessed be He, first created heaven and earth... and He finished with man who is like unto heaven.' Margulies notes, *ad loc.*, 'Its source is not known; possibly it is the author's own explanation.' We have no means of determining in what way the Philonic idea found its way to the Yemenite author of the Midrash, but it is clear that he derived it from an ancient Midrash in his possession.

9. In the continuation of his statement (*op. cit.*, 87–89), Philo stresses that we must avoid the error of inferring from the fact that man was the last to be created that he is of inferior status. On the contrary, he is like the charioteers, whose place is behind the horses, but it is they who drive the steeds; or like a ship's captain, who is stationed at the end of the ship beside the helm, yet both drive and direct. Even so is man — a kind of driver or captain, who is appointed over all the creatures. The idea that we have cited in the text was thus already known to Philo, and he sought to contradict it.

10. *Mekhilta de-R. Ishmael*, Ba-ḥodesh, viii, p. 231 (there no reasons are given); *Torat Kohanim*, Qedoshim i, p. 86d; *T.B. Qiddushin* 30b (anonymous); so, too, *T.P. Pe'a* i, 1, p. 15c, and *T.P. Qiddushin* i, 7, p. 61b; but there it is stated in the name of R. Simeon b. Yoḥai: 'Great is the honour due to father and mother, for the Holy One, blessed be He, gave it precedence over His own honour.'

11. *De Specialibus Legibus*, II, 224.

12. *Ibid.*, 10; *De Decalogo*, 120. See Heinemann, *Philons griech. u. jüd. Bildung*, pp. 254 ff.

13. *T.B. Bava Meṣiʿa* 32a; *Torat Kohanim*, *loc. cit.*; in the *Antiquities* attributed to Philo 16, 4 — G. Kisch, *Pseudo-Philo's Liber Antiquitatum Biblicarum*, Notre Dame, Indiana 1949, p. 156 we read: The sons of Korah answer their father: 'Pater nos non genuit sed Fortissimus nos plasmavit' — The father did not beget us but the Almighty fashioned us.

14. *Genesis Rabba* xxxiv, 10, pp. 320–321. In *T.B. Sanhedrin* 91b the order of the questions is reversed, and the question about the soul is worded thus: 'At which stage is it [the soul] instilled in man — from the moment that the Divine decree is given [what the sperm shall become] when the embryo is formed?
15. A. Marmorstein, 'Iranische und jüdische Religion', *ZNW*, XXVI (1927), p. 242, states for some reason that the narrative is nearer to Iranian mythology. He relies on the work of R. Reitzenstein–H. Schäder, *Studien zum Antiken Synkretismus*, 1926, p. 230. But in the fourteenth chapter of the *Bundahišm* (see below, n. 52) it is stated in the name of an Avestan source: 'Ormuzd said: Effulgence was created first and afterwards the body, and it was put in the body, for thus was the purpose (*Xwēš-kārīh*, a deed for itself — a precept) created, and the body was created for the sake of the purpose.' There is no similarity between the modes of explanation adopted in the two narratives, and no interdependence whatsoever between them can be posited. On the problem of *de animatione foetus* in the world of antiquity, see S. Krauss, *Antoninus und Rabbi*, Frankfort on the Main 1910, p. 63; J. Preuss, *Biblisch-talmudische Medizin*, p. 450; H. Diels, *Doxographi Graeci*, 1958, p. 425; J. Needham, *A History of Embryology*², Cambridge University Press, 1959.
16. The identity of 'Antoninus', with whom Rabbi maintained friendly relations, has no bearing on our subject. Evidently the story refers to an emperor-philosopher. See S. Krauss, *loc. cit.*, p. 64; L. Wallach, 'The Colloquy of Marcus Aurelius with the Patriarch Judah I', *JQR*, N.S., XXXI (1940/1), pp. 259–286.
17. *T.B. Pesaḥim* 104a; *Tosafot* s.v. *Dĕlā*'; *T.B. 'Avoda Zara* 50a; see my observation in *IEJ*, IX (1959), pp. 152 ff.
18. *De Opificio Mundi* 27, and *ibid.* 66. See Wolfson, *Philo*, Pt. I, p. 390.
19. *Timaeus* 90.
20. *De Opificio Mundi*, 134–135.
21. On the problem of suicide in Josephus see the article of Yitzḥak Baer in *Sefer Dinaburg*, Jerusalem 1959, pp. 193 ff.
22. On the comparison of the soul to a bird, see A. Aptowitzer, 'Die Seele als Vogel', *MGWJ*, LXIX (1925), pp. 150–168, and *ibid.* p. 158.
23. In *Lev. Rabba* iv, 5, p. 88, this analogy is cited as a Baraita: 'R. Ishmael taught: The case may be compared to a king who had an orchard....' The whole story was given at length in the apocryphal *Book of Ezekiel.* The date of the composition of this book is not known. It was thought that there is an allusion to it in Josephus (*Antiquities* x, 5, 1). But the view of R. Marcus is to be accepted (ed. The Loeb Class. Lib., VI, p. 201, n. e) that Josephus refers to two parts of the extant Book of Ezekiel, which was regarded as divided into two. The aforementioned parable was known also to the Church Fathers. See Athenagoras on 'Resurrection' (περὶ ἀναστάσεως, ed. Ed. Schwartz, TUGAL, IV, 2). He was a contemporary of R. Judah the Patriarch, and the motif was subsequently publicized by other writers. See also L. Wallach, 'The Parable of the Blind and the Lame', *JBL* (1943), p. 333.

24. *De Gigantibus*, 12.
25. *M. 'Avot* iii, 1; see *Derekh Ereṣ Rabba* iii, ed. Higger, p. 155. On the actual formulation of the question 'whence you come' etc. — see above, p. 139.
26. *Ecclesiastes Rabba* xii, 7; for the expression 'the soul that Thou hast placed in me is pure', see *T.B. Berakhot* 60b.
27. *T.B. Nidda* 31a; *Lev. Rabba* xiv, 6, p. 309.
28. J. Preuss, *op. cit.*, p. 448.
29. *De Opificio Mundi*, 67.
30. *Ibid.*, 22; see above, p. 205.
31. See *ibid.*, 136, and 141.
32. *Lev. Rabba* xxxiv, 3, p. 776, and see *ibid.* n. 2.
33. *Tosefta Yevamot* viii, 4, p. 250. Ben ʿAzzai's dictum is placed earlier in the Vienna MS. and is cited in the name of R. Eleazar b. Azariah; see *Tosefta ki-Fshuṭah*, Pt. VI, p. 75; and cf. *Gen. Rabba* xxxiv, 12, p. 326. Theodor observes there, n. 2, that according to the reading of the *She'iltot*, pericope Noah, *ʿEn Yaʿaqov*, *Yalquṭ Shimʿoni* § 61, and *T.B. Yevamot* 63b, the second dictum likewise is by R. Akiba; this is also the case in *Haggadot ha-Talmud.*
34. *Mekhilta de-R. Ishmael*, Ba-ḥodesh, VIII, p. 233.
35. *De Opificio Mundi*, 134–142.
36. *Mekhilta de-R. Ishmael*, Wa-yehi, VI, p. 112; but this did not subsequently deter the Amora R. Judah b. R. Simon from expounding this verse in a more extreme form — 'like the Only One of the world', *Gen. Rabba* xxi, 5, p. 200; and for the parallel sources see *ibid.* nn. 6 and 7.
37. See *T.P. Berakhot* ix, 1, p. 12d; this is the exposition of R. Ishmael in *Gen. Rabba* xxii, 2, p. 206; see *ibid.* viii, 9, p. 63.
38. *T.B. Ḥagiga* 12a; *T.B. Sanhedrin* 38b; see *ibid.* the parallel dictum of R. Eleazar.
39. *Gen. Rabba* viii, 1, p. 55. In *Lev. Rabba* xiv, 1, p. 296, the hermaphrodite exposition is cited in the name of R. Samuel bar Naḥman (see the vv.ll. *ibid.*), and the interpretation of the two-faced man in the name of R. Simeon b. Laqish. In *T.B. Berakhot* 60a these Midrashic explanations are given in the name of R. Jeremiah bar Eleazar, and it is evident that this Amora, who belongs to the fourth generation, transmitted the dicta of R. Samuel bar Naḥman and of R. Simeon b. Laqish.
40. Michael Sachs, *Beiträge*, Berlin 1852, Pt. I, p. 57; Freudenthal, *Hellen. Studien*, 1879, Pt. I, p. 69. Whereas Sachs suggests the possibility that the Amora's saying implies a knowledge of the content of the Platonic dialogue, Freudenthal, without mentioning his predecessor, declares that no one could suppose that R. Jeremiah and R. Samuel bar Naḥman had read Plato's dialogue, and therefore he is of opinion that they borrowed this idea from Philo or from some other Jewish-Hellenistic source. See also Weinstein, *Zur Genesis der Agada*, pp. 51 ff. Y. Baer, *Yisra'el ba-ʿAmmim*, p. 131, accepts Reitzenstein's view that Philo and Plato drew upon an older source, and in his opinion 'this common source could only be a dictum formulated in

Hebrew'. In the light of the facts cited in our text there is no foundation for such a conjecture.

41. 189a–190a.
42. See above, p. 144.
43. *Legum Allegoriae*, II, 13.
44. *Ibid.*, I, 31.
45. Y. Baer, *Zion*, XXIII–XXIV (1958–1959), p. 23, posits, as usual, here too that Philo is dependent on 'the Hebrew Midrash', and overlooked the substantive difference between them.
46. *T.B. Ḥagiga* and *T.B. Sanhedrin, loc. cit.* In *Gen. Rabba, loc. cit.*, the conclusion is missing. See also *'Avot de-R. Nathan*, Version I, end of ch. I, p. 8: 'Another interpretation is "And laid Thy hand upon me" — when he [Adam] had sinned, the Holy One, blessed be He, took one of them away... How do we know that man was created with both His hands? For it is said 'Thy hands have made me and fashioned me' (Psalms cxix 73). Similarly we find in *Ezra IV*, iii, 4 (R. L. Bensly, *The Fourth Book of Ezra*, Cambridge 1895, p. 7), 'et ipsum figmentum manuum tuarum erat'. So, too, in the name of Aphraates the Syrian (*Homilies*, ed. W. Wright, 809, 6–16): 'By the word of the Lord were the heavens made, man alone He made with His hands'. Man was vouchsafed the greatness of being the work of God's hands and was not created by the Divine word alone. Apparently this was also the intent of the homilist in *'Avot de-R. Nathan.*
47. *Pesiqta de-Rav Kahana*, Para, ed. Mandelbaum, p. 66; see the parallel sources indicated there.
48. See now H. M. Schenke, *Der Gott 'Mensch' in der Gnosis*, Göttingen 1962, pp. 6–15. In pp. 125–130 the author cites Rabbinic dicta according to Strack-Billerbeck, especially as interpretations of Genesis i, 26, but without elucidating their significance or making clear differentiations.
49. *Gen. Rabba* viii, 9, pp. 63–64.
50. See *Śeride Tanḥuma-Yelammedenu*, which I published in *Qoveṣ 'al Yad*, Book VI (1966), p. 24, n. 13, where I have referred to the apocryphal work *Ḥayyê 'Adam* [The Life of Adam] 13–16, according to which the angel Michael enjoined the angels to prostrate themselves to Adam and he himself did so first. On the parallel in the Hermetic work *Poïmandres*, and also in The Epistle to the Hebrews i 6, see C. H. Dodd, *The Bible and the Greeks*, 1935, p. 156. See also A. Altmann, 'The Gnostic Background of the Rabbinic Adam Legends', *JQR*, N.S., 35 (1944–5), pp. 379 ff.
51. See *T.B. Sanhedrin, loc. cit.*, and *Diqduqe Soferim, ibid.*, p. 106. Cf. also Rav's dictum, *T.B. Bava Batra* 75a: 'The Holy One, blessed be He, said to Hiram, king of Tyre, I looked at you (I saw that you would rebel and make yourself a god' — Rashi), so I created many apertures in man....' On Hiram's rebellion cf. *Gen. Rabba* ix, 5, p. 70, and *Śeride Tanḥuma-Yelammedenu*, cited above, pp. 25 ff.
52. *Bundahišn*, ed. B. T. Anklesaria, Bombay 1908, 32, XIV, and in English

rendering Zand Ākāsīk, *Iranian or Greater Bundahišn*, Transliteration and Translation in English, 1956, p. 135. See also A. Christensen, *Les Types du premier homme et du premier roi dans l'histoire légendaire des Iraniens*, Pt. I, Stockholm 1917, p. 18.

53. This is not to say that all the speculations found about the Pristine Man, like those of Philo, of the Hermetic work *Poîmandres*, or of all the Palestinian Amoraim, have their origin in Iran, as was thought at the time by W. Bousset, *Hauptprobleme der Gnosis*, Göttingen 1907, pp. 215–217; R. Reitzenstein, *Das Iranische Erlösungsmysterium*, Bonn 1921, pp. 11–28, and their followers. See against this view O. G. von Wesendonk, *Urmensch und Seele*, Hannover 1924, pp. 94 ff, on Philo, and *ibid.*, pp. 121 ff, on the position in Babylon; C. H. Dodd, *op. cit.*, p. 146, n. 1; and H. M. Schenke, *op. cit.*, pp. 16–33.

54 This is the view of J. Scheftelowitz, *Die altpersische Religion und das Judentum*, Giessen 1920, p. 217. But it is incomprehensible how the developed and complex Iranian myth evolved from the isolated dictum of the Midrash. It is precisely the reverse that appears probable, namely that the solitary saying in the Midrash derived from this or another myth. Similarly, we must reject the view of Scheftelowitz, *op. cit.*, p. 218, that the saying of R. Joshua b. Qorḥa 'They went to bed two and left seven — Cain and his twin sister, Abel and his two twin sisters' (*Gen. Rabba* xxii, 2, p. 205; *ibid.*, n. 5, where the parallel dicta are recorded) influenced the Iranian myth of *Bundahišn*. It will suffice to cite the relevant passage there to show how unfounded this opinion is. This is the text of the *Bundahišn*: 'After nine months one pair was born of them — a woman and a man. Because of their sweetness the mother ate one of the children, and the father ate the other. Thereafter Ormuzd took away the sweetness of the children from the thought of the parents and left in them only what was necessary for the rearing of the children. There were born unto them six pairs of twins (so in ed. Anklesaria; in the earlier editions the reading is — seven. See Christensen, *ibid.*, p. 20), male and female, and the man always took his sister to wife'. It is noteworthy that in two sources the teaching of R. Joshua b. Qorḥa is transmitted in the name of R. Jonathan (*T.B. Yevamot* 62a) and in the name of R. Judah b. Bathyra (*'Avot de-R. Nathan*, Version I, i, p. 6, and *Midrash ha-Gadol* to Bere'shit, ed. M. Margulies, p. 133) and both liveḍ in Babylon.

55. The dictum of Resh Laqish, *Gen. Rabba* viii, 1, p. 56; see *ibid.* n. 5 by Theodor, who already rejected the observations of L. Ginzberg, *Die Haggada bei den Kirchenvätern*, Berlin 1900, pp. 5–9 (= *MGWJ*, XLII, p. 545 *apud* Theodor), which are based on the reading of the printed edition; the parallel passages are also indicated *ibid.* See the statement of R. Eleazar in *Lev. Rabba*, ed. Margulies, p. 298 and the vv.ll. *ibid.*; cf. *Gen. Rabba*, *loc. cit.*, p. 55, and *Lev. Rabba*, *loc. cit.* On the parallel Midrashic exposition of Resh Laqish in *Gen. Rabba*, ii, 4, p. 17, see below, ch. xvii.

56. *Midrash 'Avkir*, cited in *Yalquṭ Shim'oni* § 34; in *Gen. Rabba*, *loc. cit.*, R. Berechiah himself transmits the dictum 'and He created him a lifeless body'

etc. in the name of R. Eleazar. A. Aptowitzer attempted to explain the homiletical exposition of R. Berechiah in *Midrash 'Avkir* in another way; see his article 'Zur Erklärung einiger merkwürdiger Agadoth über die Schöpfung des Menschen', *Festskrift Simonsen*, København 1923, pp. 115 ff; but his observations on this subject, like his interpretation of R. Eleazar's exposition, *ibid.* p. 118, do not seem probable to me.

57. *Lev. Rabba* xi, 1, p. 220.
58. *Mekhilta de-R. Ishmael*, Wa-yehi viii, p. 144; *Mekhilta de-R. Simeon b. Yoḥai* xv, 11, p. 94. See *Midrash Samuel* v, 6, p. 59; *Midrash Tehillim* xviii, 26, p. 154, where the exposition is expanded.
59. *Mekhilta de-R. Ishmael* reads 'in the dust'; see *ibid.*, n. 6, by Horovitz.
60. *Gen. Rabba* xxxii, 5, p. 292; this is the reading of most MSS., including that of the Vatican. See *ibid.* vv.ll., and n. 6; cf. *Lev. Rabba* xxiii, 12, p. 547: 'Throughout forty days the Holy One is occupied with the form of the embryo'; also the statement in *T.B. Menaḥot* 99b 'the soul is formed in forty (days)', which Rashi explains: 'The form of the embryo (is formed) in forty days'. A. Marmorstein, in his aforementioned article, p. 241, wished to link the forty days of the formation of the embryo to the Iranian account of the creation of man, but in *Bundahišn* it is stated that the seed of Gayōmard was 40 years in the ground.
61. *M. Nidda* iii, 7. A similar differentiation made by Aristotle is noted by Preuss, *op. cit.*, p. 452. On Aristotle's theory and its influence see Erna Lesky, 'Die Zeugungs- und Vererbungslehren der Antike und ihr Nachwirken', *Abhandlungen der Akademie der Wissenschaften*, Mainz 1950, pp. 132 ff and p. 151; but apparently she did not know of Preuss's work and hence makes no mention of Jewish sources.
62. *Tosefta Nidda* iv, 17, p. 645; see also *T.B. ibid.* 30b. In the Tosefta the Sages do not dispute the proof itself; only in their view the maidservants cannot provide evidence, because they are suspected of lewdness. In the Babylonian Talmud the experiment is transmitted in two antithetic traditions. The language in which the testimony is rejected by the other side is also harsher: 'I bring you proof from the Torah, while you advance the evidence of fools'. The Talmudic discussion, which raises doubts about the experiment in order to justify the epithet 'fools', belongs to the time of Abbaye, since he concludes the debate by confirming the view of R. Ishmael. J. Needham, *A History of Embryology*[2], New York 1959, p. 65, states that when he was preparing the first edition his attention was drawn to this strange story, whose source he could not discover. Now it seems to him that it is of Talmudic origin, and he refers to the work of Preuss, p. 451. He adds that the story shows how near people can come to Bacon's conception. The substitution of the gynaecologist Cleopatra, the contemporary of Galen, for Queen Cleopatra, as Needham suggests *ibid.* p. 66, cannot be entertained for chronological reasons. It was said of R. Simeon b. Ḥalafta that 'he was an experimenter', i.e. he carried out experiments in respect to the laws of *Ṭerefa* [an animal

suffering from an organic disease] and he even wished to investigate the correctness of Prov. vi 6 concerning the régime of the ant society. However, an anonymous passage of the Talmud rejects his proof, and the conclusion is: 'Rely on Solomon's statement.' See also J. L. Katzenelson, *Ha-Talmûd wĕ-Ḥokhmat hā-Rĕfû'ā* [The Talmud and Medical Science], Berlin 1928, p. 195.

63. See Preuss, *op. cit.*, p. 649. See *T.B. Ḥullin* 77a, where Rav states 'I enquired about this of Sages and physicians'.

64. *T.B. Yoma* 85a; in *T.B. Nidda* 25a, on the other hand, we find 'Abba Saul says: The head is the first to be formed'; see also *Tosefta Nidda* iv, 10, p. 644. Cf. Lieberman, *Tosefet Ri'shonim*, Pt. III, p. 266; *Tanḥuma*, Pequde, § 3 'Just as the child born of woman begins (to develop) from its navel and extends this way and that way'.

65. The expression is found in *Tanḥuma*, Pequde, § 3.

66. *'Avot de-R. Nathan*, Version I, xxxi, 46a.

67. *De Plantatione*, 28–30, and see *ibid.* 11–13. Cf. Yitzḥak Heinemann, *Schriften der jüd- Hellenistischen Literatur*, Philos Werke, Pt. IV, Breslau 1923, p. 152, n. 2. He points there to the word φυτουργός used by Plato, *The Republic*, 597 D, and Philo's dependence on Stoic resources.

68. Y. Baer, 'Ha-Ḥăsîdîm hā-Ri'shônîm bĕ-Khitĕvê Philon û-ba-Māsôret ha-'Ivrît' [The Early Ḥăsidim in Philo's Writings and in the Hebrew Tradition], *Zion* xviii (1953), p. 104, n. 84a. But he offers no evidence from any Midrashic source whatsoever, except from *Sefer ha-Bahir*; see the next note.

69. Heinemann, *op. cit.*, p. 148, cites the statement of Hippolytus (Elenchos VI, 9), who gives the gist of Simon Magus's work, according to which the treasure-house of all material and spiritual things is the supercelestial fire, which is identical with the Great Tree. All the things that appear on the Great Tree will be destroyed by the consuming fire, and only the fruit, which is the soul of man, will be consigned to the treasure-house and not to the fire. G. Scholem has now drawn attention in his book *Ursprung und Anfänge der Kabbala*, 1962, p. 63, n. 36, to the similarity between this passage and that in *Sefer ha-Bahir* regarding the forces that constitute the Tree of the Holy One, blessed be He. By which channel the Gnostic heresy reached *Sefer ha-Bahir* it is difficult to tell, but it is clear that we must not follow Baer and discover in *Sefer ha-Bahir* an ancient Rabbinic Midrash. With regard to the Gnostic myth, mention should be made of the Iranian story — *Bundahišn*, 14 — which relates that the first human pair 'were changed from the form of a plant to that of man'. Also now, 'in like manner there grows a tree whose fruit are ten kinds of men'. The Biblical comparison of the righteous to 'a tree planted' (Psalms i 3), and of the men of Judah to 'the plant of His delight' (Isaiah v 7), as well as the 'everlasting plantation' [מטעת עולם] of the Qumran Scrolls (see Y. Licht, *Megillat ha-Hodayot*, 1957, pp. 131 ff; idem, *Megillat ha-Serakhim*, 1965, p. 168) and the expression 'everlasting life hath He planted in our midst' do not belong here.

70. *Lev. Rabba* xiv, 2, p. 302: '...even so does the Holy One, blessed be He:

people deposit with Him a whitish drop [of semen] secretly, and the Holy One, blessed be He, gives them back complete persons openly'; see above, n. 60.

71. For the general background to Plato's conception see E. R. Dodds, *The Greeks and the Irrational*, p. 208 and pp. 215 ff. On the differences between the various dialogues with regard to this subject see W. K. C. Guthrie, 'Plato's view on the Nature of the Soul', *Entretiens*, III, 1955, pp. 3–19.
72. See H. Wolfson, *Philo*, I, pp. 381 ff.
73. *Phaedo* 67.
74. *T.P. Megilla* ii, 3, p. 73b.
75. See F. C. Porter, 'The Pre-Existence of the Soul in the Book of Wisdom and in the Rabbinical Writings', *The American Journal of Theology*, XII (1908), pp. 115–153.
76. In *Poseidonios' metaphysische Schriften*, Breslau 1921, he devoted a special chapter to the Book of Wisdom of Solomon, 'Die griechische Quelle der "Weisheit Salomos" ', p. 142 (this chapter was also printed separately in *Jahresbericht d. jüd. theol. Seminars* (Breslau 1921).
77. *Mekhilta de-R. Ishmael*, Massekhta de-Wa-yehi, iii, p. 99; see also R. Meyer, *Hellenistisches in der Rabbinischen Anthropologie*, Stuttgart 1937, p. 48, n. 1.
78. *Tanḥuma*, Niṣṣavim, 3; cf. *ibid.*, Jethro, 11, in the name of R. Isaac.
79. *T.B. Yevamot* 62a; *ibid.* 63b. In *T.B. 'Avoda Zara* 5a, the dictum is cited in the name of R. Jose, but in the Spanish MS. published by Abramson, the author is given as Rav Assi; see *ibid.* 71. In *T.B. Nidda* 13b our text has R. Jose; but in the Munich MS. it is Rav Joseph. J. Klausner, *Hā-Ra'yôn ha-Meshîḥî bĕ-Yisrā'ēl mē-Rē'shîtô wĕ-'ad Ḥătîmat ha-Mishnā*[3] [The Messianic Idea in Israel from the beginning to the close of the Mishna], Tel Aviv 1950, p. 254, accepts, without qualification, the reading 'R. Jose', and regards 'the store-house of souls' in the Syriak *Baruch* xxx 2 and *IV Ezra* 5, 78–101 as corresponding to 'Gûf'. But the pseudepigraphical passages refer to the souls after death; see above, p. 238.
80. This is Rashi's gloss to *T.B. 'Avoda Zara* 5a, s.v. *'Ad*; see also *T.B. Yevamot* 63b, s.v. *Gûf* ('A Curtain that forms a partition between the Shekhina and the angels, and there are the spirits and souls...'); and *T.B. Nidda* 13b, s.v. *She-ba-Gûf* ('A chamber like a body — the name of a place specifically assigned to the souls...'); cf. *Otzar ha-Gaonim* to *Yevamot*, p. 220; *'Arukh Completum*, Pt. II, p. 335; the Supplement to the *'Arukh*, p. 128; and the commentary to *Sefer Yeṣira* by Isaac Albarceloni, p. 208.
81. *Gen. Rabba* xxiv, 4, p. 233, and *ibid.* n. 4; see *Lev. Rabba* xv, 1, p. 319.
82. *Die Agada der Tannaiten*, II, p. 65, n. 3.
83. Porter, *op. cit.*, p. 253, n. 67; R. Meyer, *op. cit.*, p. 53, n. 6. So, too, H. Bietenhard, *Die himmlische Welt im Urchristentum und Spätjudentum*, Tübingen 1951, p. 8.
84. The point is not noted in *Diqduqe Soferim*. This is also the reading in *Sefer Oṣar ha-Kavod* by R. Ṭodros ha-Levi, Satmar 1926, p. 38a.

85. In *Deut. Rabba* ii, 32, 'Rav said: There are two firmaments'; in *Shoḥer Ṭov* cxiv, 2, 'The Rabbis said: There are two firmaments... our Rabbis said: Three... R. Eleazar said: There are seven...'; see *Śeride Tanḥuma-Yelammedenu, Qoveṣ 'al Yad*, Book VI (1966), p. 17, n. 17. Only in *'Avot de-R. Nathan*, Version I, xxxvii, p. 110, we find: 'R. Me'ir says, There are seven firmaments...', but apparently the entire theme there is a late interpolation. There is no parallel passage to it in Version II; see Schechter's Introduction, p. 23. Cf. L. Finkelstein, *Introduction to Tractates Avot and Avot de-R. Nathan*, New York 1951. So, too, we find in 'Pereq Re'iyyôt Yĕḥezqē'l', Wertheimer, *Bate Midrashot*, Pt. II, p. 130: 'R. Levi said in the name of R. Jose of Maon, who said that R. Me'ir [had said]'. It is difficult to decide in favour of this tradition in the light of all the testimonies cited above, but be that as it may, the last two sources have no importance for our subject, for in *'Avot de-R. Nathan* there is no mention of the 'Storehouse of souls', while in 'Pereq Re'iyyot Yeḥezqe'l' it is mentioned subsequently on p. 133 and was obviously excerpted from the Gemara in *Ḥagiga*.
86. *Sifre Numbers*, § 139, p. 185; see also *Sifre Deuteronomy*, § 344, ed. Finkelstein, p. 401: 'These are souls of the righteous, which are enshrined in the treasure-house'.
87. *T.B. Shabbat* 152b. In the continuation the following Baraita is cited: 'It is taught: R. Eliezer said: The souls of the righteous are hidden away beneath the Throne of Glory, as it is said: "Yet the soul of my Lord... but (the souls) of the wicked continue to be muzzled...." ' R. Eliezer does not yet use the expression 'treasure-house' or 'Gûf'; see also *'Avot de-R. Nathan*, Version I, xii, p. 50. For the expression 'zooming' [*zômĕmôt*] see S. Lieberman, 'Some Aspects of After Life in Early Rabbinic Literature', *H. A. Wolfson Jubilee Volume*, Jerusalem 1965, pp. 497 ff.
88. vii 78–101, ed. Bensly, pp. 32–34. This parallel was already pointed out by F. Rosenthal, *Vier apokryphische Bücher aus der Zeit und Schule R. Akiba's*, Leipzig 1885, p. 64. See also *The* Syriac *Apocalypse of Baruch* xxi 23; xxx 2, where אוצרא 'treasure-house' is mentioned.
89. *II Enoch*, xviii, ed. Charles, *Pseudepigrapha*, p. 444 (see n. 5): 'For all souls are prepared to eternity, before the formation of the world.' Josephus' statement concerning the Essenes, *Wars* ii, 8, 11, is ambivalent on the subject. *The* Syriac *Apocalypse of Baruch* xxiii, 4 (ed. Charles, *Pseudepigrapha*, p. 495) has 'a place was prepared where the living might dwell', and in the continuation it is stated, '[For My spirit is the creator of life], and Sheol will receive the dead'. See A. Marmorstein, 'Mē-ra'yônôt hā-Gĕ'ûlā ba-Aggādat hā-'Amora'im' [Some of the Ideas of Redemption in the Aggada of the Amoraim], *Metsudah*, No. 2 (1944), pp. 94–105; and Lieberman, *op. cit.*, p. 502, n. 41.
90. See Ad. Harnack, *Lehrbuch der Dogmengeschichte*[4], 1931, pp. 797 ff.
91. *Lev. Rabba* iv, 5, p. 90: 'R. Ḥiyya taught...'; but in two MSS. the text has 'R. Levi taught'. In the *Midrash ha-Gadol* to Leviticus, ed. N. A. Rabinovitz, New York 1930, p. 86, the reading is: 'R. Levi employed the analogy....'

92. *Lev. Rabba* iv, 4, p. 87.
93. This expression does not occur either in Tannaitic sources, or in the Palestinian Talmud, or in the utterances of the early Babylonian Amoraim. In most passages it is an anonymous Talmudic formula. In *T.B. Giṭṭin* 23b, however, we find: 'Two leading authorities of their generation — R. Zera and R. Samuel bar Rav Isaac — explained the matter. One said: According to whose opinion is this? It agrees with the view of Rabbi, who ruled: If one emancipates half his slave, the latter acquires (the liberated part of himself). The other said: What is Rabbi's reason for this ruling? He is of opinion that the embryo is to be regarded as the 'thigh' [i.e. an integral part] of its mother; hence the master (in emancipating the embryo) caused her, as it were, to acquire one of her limbs.' But actually the dual expression shows that 'the embryo is its mother's thigh' is not the Amora's phrase but a formula of the Babylonian Talmud, whereas the Palestinian Amora only said 'caused her, as it were, to acquire one of her limbs', and so it is cited in the *T.P. Bava Batra* iii, 1, p. 13d: 'But if the animal was pregnant, they regarded it [the embryo] as one of his limbs.' Also in *T.B. Temura* 30b the sentence 'The embryo is its mother's thigh' is an anonymous statement of the Talmud, since three versions are transmitted in the name of Rav Naḥman of his explanation of the point of dispute between R. Eliezer and the Rabbis. From the discussion in *T.B. Ḥullin* 58a there is some indication that Rav Ashi and Amemar used the expression 'The embryo is its mother's thigh'. Also in Roman law the embryo was regarded as part of the mother; see *Digesta Iustiniani*: 'Partus enim antequam edatur, mulieris portio est vel viscerum', XXV, 4, 1. He is not looked upon as a human being; *ibid.* XXXV, 2, 9: 'Quia partus nondum editus homo non recte puisse dicitur.' See also Th. Mommsen, *Römisches Strafrecht*, 1899, p. 633.
94. See Yitzḥak Heinemann, *Philons griech. u. jüd. Bildung*, pp. 390 ff; S. Belkin, *Philo and the Oral Law*, Harvard Univ. Press, Cambridge (Mass.), 1940, pp. 130 ff.
95. *Mekhilta de-R. Ishmael*, Massekhta di-Neziqin, viii, pp. 275–276. A. Geiger's thesis, *Urschrift*, Breslau 1857, p. 437, that the view of the Septuagint is to be attributed to R. Ishmael, was already refuted by F. Pineles, *Darkāh shel Tôrā* [The Way of the Torah], Vienna 1861, p. 190; cf. S. Horowitz, *loc. cit.*, n. 3.
96. *M. 'Oholot* vii, 6. See also *Tosefta Giṭṭin* iv, 7, p. 328; *T.B. Sanhedrin* 72b.
97. Rashi's gloss to *T.B. Sanhedrin, ibid.* s.v. *Yāṣā'*.
98. *M. ʿArakhin* i, 4, *Tosefta, ibid.*, i, 4. See S. Lieberman, *Tosefet Ri'shonim*, Pt. II, p. 275.
99. *T.B., loc. cit.*, 7a; cf. *T.B. Nazir* 51a.
1. *Sifre Zuṭa*, Be-midbar, xxxv, 22, p. 334. In Greek law, however, embryos are differentiated according to the number of months of pregnancy; see J. H. Lipsius, *Das attische Recht*, Leipzig 1905–1915, pp. 608–609.
2. *T.B. Sanhedrin* 57b.

3. See the passages referred to above, notes 93, 99, 2; and cf. *T.B. Temura* 19a and *Shiṭṭa Mequbbeṣet ad loc.*
4. See Aptowitzer, 'Observations in the Criminal Law of the Jews', *JQR*, N.S., XV (1924–1925), pp. 68–75 and pp. 85–118; idem, ''Emdat hā-'ubbār bĕ-Dînê 'Onāshîn shel Yisra'el [The status of the embryo *vis-à-vis* the Jewish laws of penalties]', *Sinai*, VI (1942–1943), pp. 9–32, is only a translation, with slight changes, of the aforementioned article, although this is not expressly stated.
5. Aptowitzer, *op. cit.*, p. 106, deals at length with the words of the *Mekhilta de-R. Ishmael*, Massekhta di-Neziqin, viii, p. 275: 'Abba Ḥanin in the name of R. Eliezer said: "and hurt a pregnant woman" — why does Scripture state this? Since it says "and there is a miscarriage", we already know that she is pregnant. Why then does it say "pregnant"? — If the man smote her on her head or on any part of his body, I might have inferred that he is liable; therefore the text has "pregnant", to teach us that he is liable only when he smites her where her embryo lies'. Aptowitzer holds that this Halakha can be understood only in accordance with the view that the embryo in the body is an independent living being. This argument would be valid, if R. Eliezer mentioned, as does Philo, that a man who strikes a pregnant woman on her abdomen and hurts the embryo, whose form is already completed, shall surely be put to death (see *De Spec. Legibus*, II, 19). But R. Eliezer appears to take the extreme view that the embryo is merely a part of the mother's body, and just as one becomes liable under the law of "hand for hand, foot for foot" only if one severs a head or foot, but not for a blow on the head that causes paralysis of the hand, so he is obliged to pay for harming the embryo only if the blow was delivered 'upon it'. Similarly no connection is to be found between our question and the ruling of Rabban Simeon b. Gamaliel in *M. Bava Qamma* v, 4: 'The value of the young must be assessed and given to the husband'. The reason for this is fully elucidated in *T.P. Bava Qamma* v, 6, p. 5a; see the commentary of Israel Lewy on *T.P. Bava Qamma*, Breslau 1911, p. 143. On the view of the Early Authorities (Ri'shonim), on whom Aptowitzer attempted to base his interpretation, see I. H. Daiches, *Netivot Yerushalayim*, Bava Qamma, Vilna 1880, p. 58. Certainly there is no reason to attribute to R. Akiba the view that 'the embryo is its mother's thigh' on the basis of *M. Ḥullin* iv, 3 and *T.B. ibid.* 72a. Aptowitzer's thesis, *op. cit.*, p. 72, n. 64, contradicts all the Early Authorities that he cites; see Ramban's [Nachmanides'] novellae to *Ḥullin*, ed. S. Z. Reichman, New York 1955, pp. 139–140; Ha-Me'iri to *Ḥullin*, New York 1946, p. 270; and Tosefot Yom Ṭov, *'Oholot* vii, 4. As regards R. Jose's pronouncement in *M. Yevamot* vii, 3, 'that the embryo disqualifies [the mother from eating heave-offering], but does not bestow the right to eat [heave-offering]' — on which Aptowitzer bases himself, *loc. cit.*, and so, too, Belkin, *op. cit.*, p. 132 — R. Josah has already stated in *T.P. Yevamot* vii, 4, p. 8: 'This means that the embryo was deemed a proper being for the purpose of disqualifying,

but was not so regarded in order to bestow the right to eat'. See *T.B. ibid.* p. 72b, and the Me'iri to *Yevamot*, ed. H. Albeck, p. 252 and *ibid.* n. 53.

6. *T.B. Temura* 25a, where the parallel passages are indicated; see below, n. 16.
7. *Mekhilta de-R. Ishmael*, Shira, i, p. 120; and see *ibid.* nn. 13 and 17. There is certainly no reason to delete 'ha-Gĕlîlî [the Galilean]', as is suggested by Aptowitzer, *op. cit.*, p. 71, n. 60, merely on the ground that 'he found that R. Jose the Galilean maintains that 'the embryo is its mother's thigh'' '. Apart from the fact that in the light of our observations in the text there is no justification for the entire line of argument based on 'according to his principle', it is difficult to suppose that in all the MSS. of the *Mekhilta* and in the sources dependent on it the word 'ha-Gĕlîlî' has been interpolated.
8. *T.B. Yoma* 82b, where a similar story is also related of R. Ḥanina; in *T.P. ibid.* viii, 4, p. 45a, a parallel narrative is reported in the name of R. Ṭarfon.
9. *Gen. Rabba* lxiii, 6, p. 682, and the parallels cited there. See also *Seder Eliahu Zuṭa* xix, ed. Me'ir 'Ish-Shalom; the Appendices to *Seder Eliahu Zuṭa*, Vienna, 1904, p. 26; and *Yalquṭ Shim'oni*, Toledot, § 110, in the name of *Midrash 'Avkir*.
10. Plutarch, *De Placitis Philosophorum*, V, 15; see Z. Frankel, *MGWJ*, 1859, p. 400; Aptowitzer, *op. cit.*, p. 115. In regard to the views attributed to Plato, see K. Praechter, 'Philologus, Platon Präformist?', LXXXIII (1928), p. 18, and *ibid.* 27.
11. *T.B. Temura* 19a: 'R. Eleazar (this is the correct reading; see *Shiṭṭa Mequbbeṣet ibid.*) holds the same view as R. Joḥanan... that the embryo is not its mother's thigh'.
12. *Ibid.* 25b: 'The refutation of R. Joḥanan is upheld', and thereafter 'Shall we say that the Tannaim differ on the subject'. Indeed Rabbenu Tam deleted from his copy the word *tyuvta* ['refutation'] *ibid.*: 'And he wrote in one responsum that in the books written before 1028 *teyuvta, ibid.*, is omitted...' — *Tosefot R. Elḥanan* to *'Avoda Zara* 24b, s.v. *R. Joḥanan* (Husiatin 1901, p. 55); see Tosafot *Sanhedrin* 80b, s.v. *'ubbār* [embryo]. Cf. also *T.P. Bava Qamma* v, 6, where it is stated by R. Joḥanan — according to the correction of Jose bê R. Bon — 'Embryos are not emancipated on account of the mother's tooth or eye'. See, on the other hand, *T.B. Qiddushin* 25b, and cf. *No'am Yerushalmi, Netivot Yerushalmi*, and the commentary of I. Lewy to *T.P. Bava Qamma, loc. cit.*
13. *Tanḥuma*, Pequde, § 3; A. Jellinek, *Bet ha-Midrash*, Pt. I, pp. 153 ff.
14. *T.B. Nidda* 16b; in *Gen. Rabba* lxxxv, § 8, p. 1042, we find a saying of R. Joḥanan that speaks of 'the angel in charge of desire', and *ibid.* liii, § 6, p. 560, it is cited in the name of Rav Huna. An angel called 'Night' is also mentioned by R. Joḥanan in *T.B. Sanhedrin* 96a. For another embryological dictum of R. Ḥanina bar Papa see *T.B. Nidda* 31a.
15. *T.B. Nidda* 30b. A totally different account of the embryo's incipience is given in Abba Saul's name in *Tosefta Nidda* iv, 10; see also *T.B. ibid.* 25a.

16. In *Tanḥuma*, ed. Buber, Tazria', § 2 the text reads: 'Even so is it in the case of the child: before he emerges from his mother's womb, the Holy One, blessed be He, enjoins him: Of this shall you eat, and of this you shall not eat, "and these are they which are unclean unto you"; and after he has taken upon himself all the precepts of the Torah, while still in his mother's womb, he is born.' In *Tanḥuma*, Pequde, the angel leads the spirit, after he has introduced it into the mother's womb, and brings it to the Garden of Eden and to Gehenna and warns it concerning the observance of the commandments. The theme of Torah-study is missing there. Also when he goes forth into the atmosphere of the world, it is stated: 'Instantly the child forgets, upon emerging, all that he saw and all that he knew.'
17. Introduction to *Bet ha-Midrash*, Pt. I, p. XXVII; see M. Joel, *Blicke*, Pt. I, p. 119.
18. *The Republic*, 10, B 614 ff.
19. For the elucidation of the eschatology of the Second Temple period see *Zion*, xxiii–xxiv (1958–1959), pp. 18–19.
20. The motif of strolling in the Garden of Eden and in Gehenna also occurs in a story about two pietists [*ḥăsîdîm*] in Ashkelon in the time of Simeon b. Sheṭaḥ in *T.P. Ḥagiga* ii, 2, p. 77d, and in a narrative about R. Joshua b. Levi's tour, whose source is *T.B. Ketubbot* 77b — but it underwent many revisions (see *Bet ha-Midrash*, Pt. II, p. 48; Higger, *Halakhot wa-'Aggadot*, New York 1933, p. 142; S. Lieberman, *Sheqi'in*, pp. 34–41) — and the Christian apocryphal works, the *Apocalypse of Peter* and the *Apocalypse of Paul*. They were all influenced by Pythagorean circles, as was shown by Isidore Levy, *La Légende de Pythagore de Grèce en Palestine*, Paris 1927, pp. 87 ff, pp. 154 ff, p. 164 and p. 192. See also S. Lieberman, *Sheqi'in*, *loc. cit.*, and his article on 'Ḥaṭa'im we-'Onsham', in the *Ginzberg Jubilee Volume*, pp. 249 ff.
21. In *Tanḥuma*, Pequde, § 3, the motif of the angel's slap is missing; it is merely stated: 'and he quenches the lamp that burns over his head and brings him forth into the atmosphere of the world against his will. Thereupon the infant immediately forgets...'; but in the recension of *Bet ha-Midrash*, Pt. I, p. 154 the text reads: 'and as he [the child] emerges, he [the angel] strikes him under his nose and extinguishes the lamp.' M. Güdemann, *Religionsgeschichtliche Studien*, Leipzig 1876, pp. 9 ff, attempted to connect the motif of the burning lamp and of the slap under the nose of the child with the Egyptian myth concerning Horus-Harpocrates; see also R. Meyer, *op. cit.*, pp. 108 ff.
22. *Lev. Rabba* iv, 4, p. 86; *ibid.* n. 4 the parallel passages are noted.
23. *T.B. Berakhot* 10a, the observations of R. Joshua b. Levi to R. Simon b. Pazzi; see *Diqduqe Soferim*, p. 41, n. *Qôf.* In a fragment of the *Tanḥuma*, *apud* J. Mann, *The Bible* etc., p. 70, the dictum is in the name of R. Tanḥuma; cf. also *Lev. Rabba* iv, 8, p. 96.
24. *Gen. Rabba* xiv, 9, pp. 133–134: 'R. Joḥanan in the name of R. Me'ir'.
25. Josephus, *Wars*, vii, 8, 7.

26. *Lev. Rabba* iv, 8, p. 96; see above, n. 17.
27. *De Opificio Mundi*, 69–71; see *Die Werke Philo's*, I, p. 51, n. 2. The analogy is also found *apud* the Stoic Diogenes of Babylon, *De Piet. Philodem*, ed. Gomperz, Vienna 1891, p. 82, and *apud* Seneca, *Ep.* 24, 65. Attention was already drawn to this by J. Bergmann, 'Die Stoische Philosophie und die jüdische Frömmigkeit', in the *Hermann Cohen Jubilee Volume*, Judaica, Berlin 1912, p. 151. But his conclusion that the idea that the soul pervades the body just as the Holy One, blessed be He, fills the universe reached the Sages from popular Stoic philosophy, because it maintained God's immanence in the world, whereas the Sages of Israel did not, has nothing to support it in the light of what was stated above, pp. 39 ff.
28. *De Ebrietate*, 67; see also *De Abrahamo*, 9–11.
29. See *M. 'Avot* i, 17; iv, 6, *et al.*; cf. above, p. 227.
30. *M. Nedarim* iv, 4; *T.B. ibid.* 41b.
31. *T.B. ʿEruvin* 54a.
32. *T.B. Bava Meṣiʿa* 86a.
33. *T.B. ʿAvoda Zara* 27b; see *Tosefta Ḥullin* ii, 23; the same reading is found in *T.P. ʿAvoda Zara* ii, p. 41a.
34. Said with reference to R. Jose b. Ḥalafta, *T.P. Yoma* viii, 1, p. 44d; on the saintliness of this Tanna see *T.P. Giṭṭin* vi, 9, p. 48b. Cf. the reply of R. Eleazar b. R. Simeon's wife to Rabbi, *T.B. Bava Meṣiʿa*, 84b. See also *Gen. Rabba* xlv, 3, p. 449; where Sarai says to Hagar 'Happy art thou that art joined to a holy body'. It is true that we find in the preamble to the dialogue between Antonius and Rabbi concerning the judgement of man after his death, in the version of the *Mekhilta de-R. Ishmael*, Shira, § 11, p. 125: 'Antoninus asked our holy master: When a man dies and the body wastes away, does the Holy One, blessed be He, make him stand trial? He answered him: Rather than ask me about the body, which is impure, you should ask me about the soul, which is pure!' But apparently Rabbi answers according to the notions of Antoninus: Rather than ask me about the body, which you consider to be the part (of man) that is defiled, and consequently, when it wastes away, it cannot be judged, ask me whether the soul is pure. See above, p. 223, and also the dictum of R. Sinai in *Sifre Deuteronomy*, § 306.
35. See *Midrash Psalms* li, 2, p. 281: 'From this you learn that whoever commits a transgression is as though he were defiled by contact with a dead person (נפש מת)... Was David then defiled? Nay, it was through sin, by which the soul is slain (אלא בעון שהנפש הוא חלל)....' In the *Yalquṭ Shimʿoni*, Psalms, § 764 the text has: ...אלא העון שהוא חלל הנפש ('but sin, which is the corpse [i.e. slaying] of the soul...'). In *Yalqut Makhiri*, Psalms, *ibid.*, p. 280, we read: 'Was David then defiled by the sin of a person slain? Nay, it was through sin, by which the soul is slain.' See A. Büchler, *Studies in Sin and Atonement*, London 1928, p. 313.
36. Comparison with these sources is possible only with respect to ideas that are common to all of them, and which clearly belong to Zoroastrianism in

general, and not with reference to terms and concepts that are the subject of divergent opinions in the sources themselves. Hence the observations of Scheftelowitz, *Die altpersische Religion und das Judentum*, Giessen 1920, p. 157, regarding the influence exerted by the teaching of *Fravaši* on the dicta of the Amoraim who posit the pre-existence of the soul are no better founded than his conjecture, *ibid.* p. 158, respecting its influence on Plato, as was shown by H. W. Bailey, *Zoroastrian Problems in the Ninth-century Books*, Oxford 1943, pp. 101–119. The sources differ considerably in regard to the very meaning of the concept *fravahr* or *fravaš*. These divergences were created both by the need to translate Avestan terminology into the dialects of the writers and by the endeavours to preserve the ancient Iranian tradition, while adjusting it to speculation influenced by Greek philosophy, which had been introduced by Syrian intermediaries.

37. Page 239. On the resurrection of the dead in their garments see *T.B. Sanhedrin* 90b; on the chastity of the Persians cf. *T.B. Berakhot* 8b. The nations whose people walk naked are condemned in *T.B. Yevamot* 63b.

38. R. C. Zaehner, *The Dawn and Twilight of Zoroastrianism*, London 1961, pp. 273–279.

39. *Elenchus* v, 1, 6–v, 11, ed. Wendland, pp. 77–104.

40. See H. Schlier, 'Der Mensch im Gnostizismus', in *Anthropologie Religieuse*, pp. 60–70 (*Supplements to Numen*, II, 1955); cf. also H. Jonas, *Gnosis*, Pt. I, pp. 201 ff.

41. See the excellent note of H. L. Fleischer to Jacob Levy's *Wörterbuch*, Pt. I, p. 288, in which he rejects the latter's explanation that *bārā*' is 'a denominative of *bar* in the sense of the external' as an attempt to give to the ancient verb the signification of pantheistic immanation 'in the spirit of the philosophers, mystics and Cabbalists'.

42. J. Wiesner, *Scholien zum bab. Talmud*, Pt. III, Prague 1867, p. 10, already cited the observations of Pliny and Seneca. On the views of the sages of Greece and Rome see Yitzḥak Heinemann, *Die Lehre von der Zweckbestimmung des Menschen im griechisch-römischen Altertum und im jüdischen Mittelalter*, Breslau 1926, pp. 3 ff, and pp. 19 ff (= *Jahresbericht* of the Breslau Seminary, 1925). See W. Bacher, *Die Agada der Tannaiten*, I, p. 17; likewise Moore, *Judaism*, Pt. II, p. 285; and so, too, J. Bonsirven, *Le Judaisme*, Pt. II, p. 8 — all of them have understood the dispute to be concerned with the significance of man and his creation. Schechter and Finkelstein preferred to ignore the whole subject. A. Büchler, *Studies in Sin and Atonement*, 1928, pp. 207–211, connected the debate with a discussion on the Books of Job and Ecclesiastes, and even attempted to date it between the years 30–68, but this is no more than a conjecture. Leo Baeck in his essay 'Hat das überlieferte Judentum Dogmen?', which was included in the book *Aus drei Jahrtausenden*, Tübingen 1958, p. 24, quotes the Baraita in order to confute those who maintained that Judaism has dogmas, but nevertheless ignored this source. Baeck, of course, uses it as proof that in Judaism even 'the majority' cannot

create dogmas, but does not touch upon its interpretation and significance.

43. This is not a definite number; see Meshullam Behr, *Divre Meshullam*, Frankfort 1926, pp. 49 ff, who showed that while in Babylon a few years were indicated by the expression 'two and a half years', in the Palestinian sources we always find 'three and a half years'. Cf. S. Lieberman, *Sheqi'in*, 1939, p. 78; and now S. Abramson, 'Mi-Sîḥatam shel Běnê Ereṣ Yisra'el' [Aspects of the Speech of the Palestinians], *Sinai*, 1968, pp. 20–21. On numbers that are not necessarily in Rabbinic sources, see Joseph Zechariah Stern, *Ma'amar Tahălûkhôt ha-'Aggādôt* [Characteristics of the Agadot], Warsaw 1902, ch. xii, p. 44, and J. Bergmann, 'Die runden und hyperbol. Zahlen', *MGWJ* 1938, pp. 360–376.
44. The only echo is found in the book *Ma'ăsê Tôrā*, Warsaw 1885, § 337, and in *Ḥuppat 'Eliyyahu*, cited in *Měnôrat ha-Mā'ôr* by Israel ibn Al-Nakawa, ed. H. G. Enelow, Pt. IV, p. 456: 'Thrice every day the herald goes forth from the Holy One, blessed be He, and proclaims: It were better for man not to have been created and now that he has been created, let him examine his deeds and do the will of his Creator'; on *Ḥuppat 'Eliyyahu* see *ibid.* p. 452, n. 1.
45. *T.P. 'Avoda Zara* i, 9, p. 40a; in *T.P. Berakhot* ix, p. 13c the text has only: 'who saw a beautiful non-Jewess'. For the formula of the benediction see S. Lieberman, *Tosefta ki-Fshuṭah*, Pt. I, p. 108.
46. *Lev. Rabba* xxxv, 8, p. 828, 'R. Hiyya taught'; in *Sifra Be-ḥuqqotay*, § 5, p. 110c it is cited as an anonymous Baraita.
47. *T.B. Berakhot* 43b; *T.B. Ketubbot* 67b; *T.B. Soṭa* 10b; *T.B. Bava Meṣi'a* 59a. In *Diqduqe Soferim* to *Berakhot*, p. 231, Rabbinovicz notes that in the Munich MS. the words 'in the name of R. Simeon b. Yoḥai' are missing, but they are to be found in *T.B. Bava Meṣi'a*; see *Diqduqe Soferim* to *Bava Meṣi'a*, p. 172, and the Munich MS. *Tractate Ketubbot*.
48. *T.P. Berakhot* i, 5, p. 3b; *T.P. Shabbat* i, 5 (*ad fin.*), p. 3b; *Exodus Rabba* xl, § 1. Rava also used this phraseology: 'All those that do not carry out (the Torah precepts) for its own sake, it were better for them if they had not been created'; see above, p. 395.
49. Matthew xviii 6. See *ibid.* xxvi 24 and the First Epistle of Clement xlvi 8.
50. *T.P. 'Avoda Zara* ii, 2, p. 40d; and *ibid.* מה הוה ליה אילו מית [literally: 'What would have been to him if he had died']; correct to: נח הוה ליה ['It would have been better for him if he had died']. This is also the reading in *T.P. Shabbat* xiv, 4, p. 14d.
51. *Tanḥuma* (printed ed.) and *Tanḥuma*, ed. Buber, Balak, § 2.
52. *M. 'Avot* vi (*ad fin.*), *'Avot de-R. Nathan*, Version I, xli, p. 134. See *Tosefta Yoma* ii, 5; and S. Lieberman, *Tosefta ki-Fshuṭah*, Mo'ed, pp. 762–763.
53. *'Avot de-R. Nathan*, Version I, xxxi, p. 91.

CHAPTER XI

ON PROVIDENCE

1. *Wars* ii, 8, 14.
2. *Antiquities* xiii, 5, 9.
3. This comparison is expressly made by Josephus at the end of *The Life of Josephus Flavius* and in *Antiquities* xv, 6, 4. See the notes of Simḥoni to *Wars, loc. cit.*, p. 603 [Hebrew]; G. Foote Moore's article in *Harvard Theol. Review*, XXII (1929), p. 371, and in summary form his note to *Judaism*, III, p. 139; cf. Schürer, *Geschichte des jüd. Volkes*, II, p. 460.
4. See D. Flusser, 'Kat Midbar Yehuda we-Hashqafoteha' [The Qumran Sect and its Concepts], *Zion*, XIX (1954), pp. 96 ff; Y. Licht, *Megillat ha-Hodayot* [Scroll of the Thanksgiving Psalms], Jerusalem 1957, pp. 31 ff; idem, 'Mussag ha-Nĕdāvā bi-Khĕtāvehā shel Kat Midbar Yĕhûdā [The Concept of the Freewill-Offering in the Qumran Scrolls]' in the volume *Iyyûnîm bi-Mĕgillôt Midbar Yĕhûdā* [Studies in the Qumran Scrolls], Jerusalem 1957, pp. 77 ff. Cf. F. Nötscher, 'Schicksalsglaube in Qumran und Umwelt', *Biblische Zeitschrift*, 1959, p. 205; *ibid.* 1960, pp. 90 ff. The author endeavours to compare the standpoint of the Qumran Sect with the Catholic viewpoint (p. 107), but he concedes that it is not possible to find a general formula for the doctrine of the Sect in this sphere (p. 108). In his observations on post-Biblical Judaism he cites the views of Wochenmark on pp. 108–115.
5. The same criticism applies to the dissertation of Joseph Wochenmark, *Die Schicksalsidee in Judentum*, 1933. The author deals in his works with both the Biblical period and the philosophy of the Middle Ages; but his treatment of Rabbinic literature is entirely unsatisfactory. Lütgert's brochure, *Das Problem der Willensfreiheit in der vorchristlichen Synagoge*, 1906, devotes less than half a page to the teaching of the Sages, but his observations on the apocryphal literature and on Philo are not without interest. H. Wolfson, *Philo*, Pt. I, pp. 424–462, treats of Philo in detail.
6. 'Thou dost help and support all human beings, but me most of all... Thou art the salvation of all human beings but especially of me' (*Mekhilta de-R. Ishmael*, Shira, iii; ed. Horovitz-Rabin, p. 126). And R. Zadok said: 'At

all times He provides food for all mankind in accordance with their needs and satisfies every living thing with favour, and not for the good and righteous alone (does He provide), but also for the wicked who are idolaters' (*Mekhilta*, Amalek, i, p. 195; see the vv.ll. there, and cf. Bacher, *Die Agada der Tannaiten*, I, p. 45). See also above, p. 20.

7. See also *Sifre Deuteronomy* § xl, where Rabbi explains that the passages Deut. xi 12, Psa. cxxi 4, and I Kings lx 3, do not come to negate Providence in respect of the Gentile nations and countries, but to give primacy to God's providential care of Israel. See E. Sjöberg, *Gott und die Sünder im pal. Judentum*, 1939, pp. 86–89.
8. Gen. vi, 5; Jer. xvii 9–10; Psa. cxxxix is a hymn in praise of God's all-embracing knowledge; *ibid.* xciv 9; cf. Sirach xxiii 32. R. Pettazzoni, the historian of religions, has shown in his work, *The All-knowing God*, 1956, on the basis of copious comparative material, that the concept of an all-knowing and all-seeing god is not linked to a given form of religion. It is found in primitive, polytheistic religions, but does not occur in all developed faiths, not even in all monotheistic creeds (p. 5). This consequently renders nugatory the views of Biblical scholars like Gunkel, *Die Psalmen*, p. 586, Hempel, *Gott und Mensch im A.T.*, p. 230, who hold that the idea of God's omniscience and omnipresence came to Israel as a result of Egyptian and Babylonian influence. Pettazzoni rightly stresses that actually the concept of the Lord as Judge, as a zealous and beneficent God, implies omniscience. The doctrine, which is found among so many peoples, came into being among the Israelites with a nuance specific to their conception of God (p. 108 and p. 437); see above, pp. 52 ff.
9. See above, p. 29. The Amora R. Samuel bar Rav Isaac found statements tending towards heresy in Ecclesiastes xi 9, 'Rejoice, O young man, in thy youth... and walk in the ways of thy heart, and in the sight of thine eyes', for they are tantamount to saying 'There is neither judgement nor judge, every restraint is removed' (*Lev. Rabba*, xxviii, § 1, p. 648; see *ibid.* the vv.ll. and notes).
10. See the commentary of R. Jonah to *M. 'Avot*, *ibid.* Cf. J. Guttmann, *Philosophies of Judaism*, JPS, Philadelphia 1964, p. 40.
11. This interpretation is cited by R. Simeon b. Ṣemaḥ Duran in *Magen 'Avot* 51b, in the name of 'our teacher Solomon'. In the printed commentary ascribed to Rashi the text reads 'All that... chambers is seen by, and revealed before, the Holy One, blessed be He'; and in the commentary in *Maḥzor Vitry* the reading is 'The Holy One, blessed be He, beholds all the deeds of the children of men, as it is said "the eyes of the Lord, which range the whole earth" '. Hame'iri also explains the dictum in this way: 'He [R. Akiba] meant to say by the phrase *ha-kōl ṣāfûy* that all actions are known to Him [God]; a man cannot evade [the Almighty], as the Sages said "and all thy works are written in a Book" '. In *'Avot de-R. Nathan*, Version I, xxxix, p. 116, R. Akiba's saying is reported in this form: 'All is seen, all is revealed, and all is according

to the intention of a man'. See C. H. Taylor, *Sayings of the Jewish Fathers*, p. 59. See the commentary of R. Isaac b. R. Solomon on *M. 'Avot, loc. cit.*, Jerusalem 1965, p. 111.

12. *Tosefta Shabbat* xiii, 11; see *T.B. ʿEruvin* 43b. Cf. also *Tosefta ʿEruvin* vi, 13; *Tosefta Pesaḥim* ii, 11.
13. See Ben Yehuda's *Dictionary*, vol. XI, pp. 5579–5580; and below, the examples cited in the text.
14. This is also the signification of the dictum according to the reading *ha-kōl sāfûn*; see *Arukh Completum*, s.v. סער, vol. VI, p. 98, and *Magen 'Avot* (mentioned above), p. 55a.
15. *T.B. Sukka* 53a; on the completely new turn given to this saying in the days of the Amoraim, see above, p. 278.
16. *T.P. Berakhot* iv, 1, p. 7d; *T.B. ibid.* 27b. On the dispute in respect to ancestral merit, which continued from as long back as the time of Shemaʿya and Avtalion (*Mekhilta*, Wa-yehi, iii, p. 99), see Marmorstein, *The Doctrine of Merits in Old Rabbinical Literature*, 1920, pp. 37 ff; but the question of merit in relation to that of Providence and freewill is not discussed there at all. It will suffice to point out that the terms 'Providence', 'fate', 'freewill', and the like do not appear at all in the index of the book.
17. See the Introduction of M. H. Segal to *Sefer Ben-Sira ha-Shalem*, pp. 26–29. I very much doubt if in chapter xxiii 33–34 and in chapter xxxiii 10–13 Ben Sira intended to say that God determined that a given person should be righteous and another wicked. Segal's interpretation was influenced by the conventional meaning given to R. Akiba's statement. Cf. Büchler, *JQR*, 13 (1922–1923), pp. 318 ff.
18. This was shown by D. Flusser in his article 'Kat Midbar Yehuda we-ha-Naṣrut', *ʿIyyunim bi-Megillot Midbar Yehuda*, pp. 84 ff, and in his article 'The Dead Sea Sect and pre-Pauline Christianity', *Scripta Hierosolymitana*, V, pp. 220 ff.
19. A. Marx, 'Y a-t-il une prédestination à Qumran?', *Revue de Qumran*, iv, 1967, pp. 163–181 overlooked Flusser's observations and, needless to say, what I wrote in Hebrew in the first version of this chapter in the *Yeḥezkel Kaufmann Jubilee Volume*, Jerusalem 1961, pp. 121–148.
20. *M. 'Avot* iii, 14. On the text of this Mishna see *Magen 'Avot* of R. Simeon b. Ṣemaḥ Duran. In the Cambridge MS. (published in Taylor's ed. cited above, n. 110) the word *ḥemda* ['desirable'] is missing; cf. *Mele'khet Shelomo, ad loc.*
21. See Licht, *Megillat ha-Hodayot*, p. 36; cf. above, p. 216.
22. See above, p. 26.
23. W. Bacher, *Die Agada der Tannaiten*, I, p. 294, identifies Zonin here with Rabban Gamaliel's superintendent, who is mentioned in *Tosefta Pesaḥim* ii, 11; *T.B., ibid.*, 49a. But the style of the narration shows that a Gentile is referred to. A. Marmorstein, *Studies in Jewish Theology*, 1950, p. 79, writes: 'It is irrelevant whether the questioner was a Jew or the philosopher of the

same name, who wrote a treatise against idolatry'. As his source, he refers to P. Wendland, *Die Hellenistische-Römische Kultur*, 1912, p. 17; but there is no mention there — nor have I found any reference elsewhere — to this work. All the philosophers known by this name lived long before R. Akiba, and a definite identification is not to be sought.

24. See above, p. 114; cf. also Wendland, *op. cit.*, 110.
25. See my article in *IEJ*, IX (1959), pp. 162 ff.
26. *Deut. Rabba*, ed. S. Lieberman, p. 75. Zinon of our text becomes there 'R. Zinon, who had come to Alexandria', and he takes R. Akiba's place as het respondent; see Lieberman's note *ibid.* Celsus likewise argued, in reply to the Christian claim that Jesus healed the sick, that Aesculapius, too, performed such miracles. Origen's answer (*C. Cels*, 3, 25) is completely different from that of R. Akiba, notwithstanding the observations of J. Bergmann, *Jüdische Apologetik*, 1908, p. 12.
27. *Gen. Rabba* xxxiii, p. 299; *Lev. Rabba* xxvii, 1, p. 614; *Pesiqta de-Rav Kahana*, Sec. 9; see also *'Avot de-R. Nathan*, xxxix.
28. *Mekhilta de-R. Ishmael*, Be-shallaḥ, Massekhta de-Wa-yehi, vi, p. 112; *Gen. Rabba* xxi, 5, p. 200. See also the notes *ibid.*, and cf. above, p. 227.
29. *Gen. Rabba ibid.*; and *ibid.* viii, 10: 'R. Hoshaiah: When the Holy One, blessed be He, created the first man, the Ministering Angels mistook his identity and wished to say "Holy!" before him.' See *Pesiqta Rabbati*, addendum, ed. Meir Ish Shalom, 192b; cf. above, p. 229.
30. *De Opificio Mundi*, 148: ὁ θεὸς ἠξίου δευτερείων ὕπαρχον μὲν αὐτου τῶν δ'ἄλλων ἁπάντων ἡνεμόνα τιθείς.
31. *Leg. Alleg.*, I, 31; De Confusione Ling., 41: αἰδίον λόγος.
32. *Leg. Alleg.*, I, 90–92; see C. Siegfried, *Philo von Alexandrien*, 1878, p. 149 and p. 242. Cf. N. I. Weinstein, *Zur Genesis der Agada*, 1901, pp. 51 ff.
33. R. Bultmann, *Die Theologie des NT's*, 1953, pp. 245 ff. On the subject of Original Sin in Rabbinic sources see below, n. 39.
34. *T.P. Shevi'it* ix, 1, p. 38d; see *Gen. Rabba* lxxix, 6, p. 942 and the notes *ibid.*, and *Pesiqta de-Rav Kahana*, p. 191. A similar saying is to be found in Matthew x 29; cf. the comment of A. Aptowitzer, *HUCA*, III (1926), p. 121, n. 11. On recompense to animals see above, p. 278.
35. This is also the reading of the MS. of *Haggadot ha-Talmud* in the National Library at Jerusalem. It is noteworthy that in *'En Ya'aqov* the reading is found in the parallel dictum of R. Samuel, ' "and righteousness delivereth from death" — not from death itself but from violent death', but in *Haggadot ha-Talmud* the reading is identical. See *Diqduqe Soferim*, p. 384, note *Yôd*, where the author comments on 'this correct version' and also refers to R. Joḥanan's saying, *T.B. Bava Batra* 10a. See also *Midrash Mishle* x, 1, p. 65; the name of R. Eleazar b. R. Jose is also missing in *Yalquṭ Makhiri* to Psalms lxxxix 49, p. 80. So far as the theme itself is concerned, it seems to me that the story about R. Akiba's daughter is not authentic, and is merely a parallel narrative to that about Samuel; and Ha-Kotev in *'En Ya'aqov* has already

noted: 'I found a scholar's responsum dealing with this subject in an old book containing *novellae* on *Tractate Sanhedrin*, which offers a good explanation of this theme. I cite it here verbatim: "R. David, of blessed memory, wrote with reference to the Amoraic statement in chapter 'Four kinds of death penalty' (65b) 'and the Sages say: This refers to one who practices optical illusion; R. Akiba says: This refers to one who calculates times and hours...' And there in chapter 'If (on the eve of the Sabbath) darkness overtook a man' the Sages said: 'For the Chaldeans [i.e. soothsayers] told R. Akiba...' " Since R. David relies on what 'The Rabbi, my teacher (the All-Merciful preserve him!) wrote in answer to a question...', and the responsum is that of Moses Naḥmanides (Attributed Responsa, No. 283; *Orḥot Ḥayyim*, II, p. 620), it seems that he is R. David, author of *Ha-Mikhtam*.

36. *T.B. Yevamot* 50a; see also *Ecclesiastes Rabba* iii, 4, where reliance is placed on an incident that happened to R. Simeon b. Ḥalafta, and R. Akiba replied: 'What have we to do with the incident? I base myself not on the incident but on an explicit Scripture "The number of thy days I shall fulfil"....' The reading R. Simeon b. Ḥalafta as the hero of the episode is difficult, and Z. W. Einhorn already expressed his surprise at this in his commentary. It seems that the whole narrative is only an interpolation, but at any rate we have no reason to doubt, with him, the reading 'R. Akiba', which is confirmed by the sources. This is also the text of the MSS. of *Ecclesiastes Rabba*: Oxford 164, Vatican 291, Paris 821.

37. The comment of Rabbenu Nissim in *Megillat Setarim* (*Otzar ha-Geonim*, Yevamot, p. 125) on *Tosefta ʿEduyot* i, 15; see also S. Lieberman, *Tosefet Ri'shonim*, p. 182; the responsa of Rav Hai Gaon in *Otzar ha-Geonim, loc. cit.*, pp. 127 ff. Lewin refers *ibid.*, p. 129, n. 2, to the interpretation of Naḥmanides that I have quoted (cf. G. Weil, 'Tĕshûvātô shel Rav Hai Gaon ʿal ha-Qēṣ ha-Qādûm lĕ-Hayyîm', *Sefer Asaph*, 1953, pp. 267 ff) and see Rav Sherira's responsum, *Teshuvot ha-Geonim*, ed. Harkavy, § 348; J. N. Epstein refers to it in *Mavo' le-Nosaḥ ha-Mishna*, p. 690; cf. also H. Albeck in his Supplements to *Neziqin*, p. 478. With regard to *Karet* see *Tractate Semaḥot* iii, 8: 'If one dies under the age of fifty, it is death by *karet* (by Divine visitation).'

38. *Midrash Tannaim*, ed. Hoffmann, p. 179 and *ibid.* 18. See also *Tanḥuma*, Wa-'etḥanan § 6; *Deuteronomy Rabba*, ed. Lieberman, p. 38. With reference to the dictum 'One kingdom may not impinge upon another to the extent of a hair's breadth' see *T.B. Shabbat* 30a and the parallel passages. Regarding Ben ʿAzzai's view see above, p. 268. R. Simeon b. Yoḥai found that also Israel's sin with the calf and David's sin fulfilled a mission — *T.B. ʿAvoda Zara* 5a.

39. *T.B. Shabbat* 55a–b in the name of R. Ammi; the attempts to ascribe this opinion to Tannaim is rejected there, and the discussion concludes: 'From this is to be inferred that there is death without sin, and there is suffering without iniquity, and the refutation of R. Ammi stands.' It seems that R.

Ammi intended to negate completely the belief in original sin and to restrict the consequences of Adam's transgression just to the fact that death came into the world. For other explanations of the death of the righteous and the wicked see *Genesis Rabba* ix, 5, p. 70; *Leviticus Rabba* xxvii, 4, p. 628 and the vv.ll.; cf. *Tanḥuma*, ed. Buber, *Be-ḥuqqotay* § 39. See also R. Mach, *Der Zaddik im Talmud und Midrasch*, pp. 147 ff, but he did not fully perceive the significance of the dicta. It appears that there is a connection between the limitation of the consequences of the first man's sin and the infiltration of the notions concerning his great stature and pre-eminence into the Haggada of the Amoraim; see above, p. 230. For another way of dissociating the existence of death from Adam's sin, which is linked to the concept of fate, see above, p. 279.

40. *De Spec. Leg.*, III, 120–123; see H. Wolfson, *Philo*, 1947, Pt. I, p. 440, and *ibid.* also the earlier literature.
41. *Antiquities* xviii, 1, 3, § 13. This concept also underlies the historiographic philosophy of Josephus himself. Frequently he points out, in describing events, the combined action (συμμαχία, συνεργία) of God and man. On the other hand there are numerous accounts written in the spirit of 'Greek fatalism', and not in that of Jewish Providence — *Antiquities* viii, 418; xvi, 395; see also Lütgert, *op. cit.*, pp. 13–17.
42. J. V. Arnim, *Stoicorum Veterum Fragmenta*, 1904, No. 975, and the famous parable there of Zeno about the dog tied to the moving cart, and likewise Seneca's remarks: 'ducunt volentem fata nolentem trahunt'; cf. also Pohlenz, *Die Stoa*, I, pp. 98–106; II, pp. 55–62. Philo, too, followed in the footsteps of the Stoics in his work, *De Providentia*; see P. Wendland, *Philos Schrift über die Vorsehung*, 1892, p. 24, n. 4.
43. This interpretation also accords with the usage in late Midrashim; see below, n. 65 and n. 72. Cf. also L. Ginzberg, *Perushim we-Ḥiddushim bi-Yerushalmi*, III, p. 413.
44. *T.B. Ḥullin* 142a (see *Tosefta ibid.*, x, 16); *T.B. Qiddushin* 39b. See also below, p. 436.
45. *M. Qiddushin* i, 10; the Mishna uses Biblical phraseology 'and shall inherit the land', which means, the Land of Israel, no mention being made therein of reward in the world to come. See J. N. Epstein, *Mevo'ot le-Sifrut ha-Tanna'im*, p. 53; *T.B. Sanhedrin* 101a; *T.B. Berakhot* 61b; and see my article ''Asqezis we-Yissurim be-Torat Ḥazal', *Yittzḥak Baer Jubilee Volume*, p. 60; and my paper 'Hilkhôt Yĕrushshā wĕ-Ḥayyê 'Olām [Thè Laws of Inheritance and Everlasting Life]', *Proceedings of the Fourth World Congress of Jewish Studies*, 1967, p. 138.
46. *Midrash Mishle* xxviii 27. In the light of his saying that alms delivers from violent death, the authenticity of the dictum is not to be doubted. Although in replying to Ṭurnus Rufus — *T.B. Bava Batra* 10a — he said that charity delivers from the judgement of Gehenna, yet the one dictum does not exclude the other; see also *Tosefta Qiddushin* v, 15, the statement of R. Simeon b.

Eleazar 'I have acted evilly and thus forfeited my livelihood', and the remarks of R. Me'ir *ibid.*

47. *Tosefta Yoma* ii, 7 ('Of that which belongs to you you will be given' resembles the language of I Chron. xxix 14; in a metaphorical sense R. Simeon used this phrase in the Mishna, at the end of *'Eruvin*). In *T.B. ibid.* 38b there is added 'and one kingdom does not impinge upon another to the extent of a hair's breadth', but this sentence is wanting also in *T.P. ibid.* iii, 9, p. 41b, where the dictum is cited in the name of Ben Zoma. In *Cant. Rabba* iii, 5, the text agrees with that of the Babylonian Talmud, but it appears to be only an interpolation, for in all the other sources the saying is cited in the name of R. Joḥanan. Cf. also W. Bacher, *Die Agada der Tannaiten*, I, p. 412, n. 1, and above, n. 33. For the interpretation of the dictum, see Rashi *ibid.* and the commentary of R. Eliakim on *Yoma*, Jerusalem 1964, p. 136.
48. *Tosefta Megilla* iv, 27; *T.B. Berakhot* 47a; *T.P. ibid.* viii, 9, p. 12c. See Bacher, *op. cit.*, p. 416, and *Ḥiddushe Aggadot*, of the Maharsha [Edels] to *Berakhot, loc. cit.*
49. Plato, *Laws*, 743A shows that 'it is impossible for a man to be pre-eminent in his virtue, when he is exceedingly rich'. Celsus (*C. Cels. Orig.* VI, 16) charged that Jesus was influenced by Plato in his aphorism 'It is easier for a camel to go through the eye of a needle, than for a rich man to enter into the kingdom of God' (Matthew xix 24). See also my article 'Megammot Datiyyot we-Ḥevratiyyot be-Torat ha-Ṣedaqa shel Ḥazal', p. 17.
50. *The Zadokite Documents*, ed. Ch. Rabin, 1958, p. 7. See also L. Ginzberg, *Eine Unbekannte jüd. Sekte*, 1922, p. 235. Likewise in the *Letter of Aristeas* it is stated that the ability to do good actions is the gift of God (§ 231) and that it is impossible to acquire the attribute of temperance unless God created the requisite disposition towards this (§ 237; cf. *ibid.* § 238).
51. *T.B. Yoma* 39a; 'Yefe 'Enayim' [A. L. Yellin] *ibid.* refers to *Sifra*, Shemini, xii, according to the interpretation of 'some explain' cited in the RABaD [R. Abraham b. David of Posquieres] *ibid.* The Amoraim, R. Joḥanan and the School of R. Shila, formulated this concept in various ways. Resh Laqish limited the help to good deeds, saying: 'If a man comes to defile himself, he is allowed to do so ('and he is not prevented by Heaven and hindered' — Rashi, *ad loc.*); if he comes to purify himself, he is helped' (*T.B. Yoma* 38b; *T.B. Shabbat* 104a. See also Tosafot *ibid.* 104a, s.v. *'Ît degārsînān pāthîn lô* [Another reading is 'he is given an opening']; cf. *Diqduqe Soferim, ibid.* p. 224; S. Lieberman, *Midrashe Teman*, 1940, p. 34). His saying is closer to that of Philo, cited in the text; see also above, p. 278.
52. See Wolfson, *op. cit.*, Pt. I, pp. 448–450.
53. *Quod Deus sit immutabilis*, 47–48; see Wolfson, *op. cit.*, p. 436.
54. *De Confusione Ling.*, 179: 'Man is practically the only being who having knowledge of good and evil often chooses the worst... Thus it was meet and right that when man was formed, God should assign a share in the work to His lieutenants (τοῖς ὑπάρχοις), as He does with the words "Let

us make men", that so man's right actions might be attributable to God, but his sins to others.' See Lütgert, *op. cit.*, p. 21. See above, p. 205.

55. *Gen. Rabba* iii, 8, p. 23; *ibid.* ii, 5, p. 18, this homily is cited in the name of R. Abbahu, followed by the saying of R. Ḥiyyah Rubbah (חייה רובה), who expounded this verse differently; generally R. Yannai and R. Ḥiyya are mentioned together. See Bacher, *Agada der Pal. Amoräer*, I, p. 35.
56. *Tanḥuma*, Tazria', § 9. The saying is transmitted by R. Eleazar b. Pedat; in *Gen. Rabba* lxxiii, 6, the reading is: 'Thus said R. Eleazar'. Freudenthal, *Hellenistische Studien*, 1874, Pt. I, p. 70, discerned Philo's concept in this dictum, namely that only good can come from the absolute good, but here it is only the mention of God's name that is spoken of, as is shown also in the continuation of the dictum in *Tanḥuma, loc. cit.*
57. *Lam. Rabba* iii, 38. In the text I have cited the version of Pesaro, 1519.
58. Ed. Buber, 68a (based on the Rome MS.) reads: 'From that moment "Out of the mouth of the Most High proceedeth not evil [and good]"; but do not all benefits proceed from the mouth of the Holy One, blessed be He? Only....' Buber, *ibid.*, note 115, observes that Rashi to Lamentations, *ibid.*, reads 'R. Joḥanan'! It is noteworthy that also in the late Midrash, *Seder Eliahu Zuṭa*, iii (ed. Me'ir Ish Shalom, p. 175), which culled many ideas from external sources, we do, indeed, find the version 'Is it possible to say so? But do not bounties proceed from before Him?', in consonance with the beginning of the chapter 'The Holy One, blessed be He, created everything in His world except the quality of falsehood, which He did not create, and the quality of wickedness, which He had not wrought' (*ibid.*, p. 179). However, it resolves the problem as follows: 'That the good does not proceed to the doer of evil, and the evil does not proceed to the doer of good, but good goes towards good and evil towards evil'.
59. *Deut. Rabba* lxxxiv, 3; in *Deut. Rabba*, ed. Lieberman, p. 92, the text actually has 'R. Ḥaggai', but it is not clear if this is not a mistake. Me'iri, in his *Ḥibbur ha-Teshuva* [Book of Repentance], ed. Sofer, New York 1950, cites the dictum from *Deuteronomy Rabba* (the publisher's reference to *Lam. Rabba* is incorrect) in a different version: ' "Out of the mouth of the Most High proceedeth not evil and good" — said R. Joḥanan: From the day that the Holy One, blessed be He, said "see, I have set before thee this day life and good", evil and good have not come forth from the Holy One, blessed be He, but issue of their own accord through the acts of those who do them.'
60. Clement of Alexandria, *Strom.* I, 17, 81–87; Origen, περὶ ἀρχῶν, I, 5_2; II, 9_2. See A. Harnack, *Lehrbuch der Dogmengeschichte*[5], 1931, I, pp. 675 ff.
61. See Hans Jonas, *Gnosis und spätantiker Geist*, I, 1954, pp. 160 ff.
62. Thus far I have cited the Baraita of *Tosefta Sukka* ii, 6 (ed. Zuckermandel, p. 194; see the vv.ll. *ibid.*, and *T.B. Sukka* 29a); from now on the quotation is from *Mekhilta of R. Ishmael*, Bo', i, ed. Horovitz, p. 7. See *Tosefta, loc. cit.*, 5, and *T.B. loc. cit.* Cf. S. Lieberman, *Tosefta ki-Fshuṭah*, p. 856.
63. *Sifra*, Qedoshim vi, 2, ' "Ye shall not practise divination", e.g. those who

divine by means of a weasel, birds and stars'. The rationalistic church father, Theodore of Mopsuestia, regarded the practice of astrology, the watching of the stars, or taking note of the voice or flight of birds, as the work of the Devil. See Mingana, *Woodbroke Studies*, VI, 1933, p. 43.

64. On the biography of this Tanna see M. Hakohen, *Sinai*, xvii, p. 409. At any rate he lived round about the time of Julian — father and son — to whom the Neo-Platonists attributed the λόγια τῶν Χαλδαίων; see Hans Lewy, *Chaldean Oracles and Theurgy*, Cairo, 1956, pp. 4 ff and *ibid.*, pp. 426 ff.

65. Rav's homily, that the Holy One, blessed be He, said to Abraham 'Leave your astrological speculation' is to be compared with that of R. Eleazar of Modiʿin: ' "And the Lord had blessed Abraham in all things" — this refers to the vast astrological knowledge that our father Abraham possessed' (*Tosefta Qiddushin*, v, 17; *T.B. Bava Batra* 16b). See also the saying of this Tanna in *Mekhilta*, da-Amalek, ii, p. 198. Kings made use of a *maḥăzît* ['glass'] — apparently an astrological instrument — Moses looked through window-glass (*specularia*); see *Eccles. Rabba* i, 14: 'An astrologer who sits... people have no need to be grateful to him.' Cf. also *Gen. Rabba* x, 6, p. 79: 'R. Simon said, There is no herb in the world that has not a planet in the sky, that strikes it and says, Grow!... Pleiades [or, Draco] flavours the fruits, and Orion draws (the sap) from one joint to another... [Mazzarot is a] planet that shapes the fruits...'; see the notes *ibid.* In the *Book of Enoch* viii, 3, the teaching of astrology is ascribed to Kôkabêl, one of the angels who came down to the earth (Genesis vi 1–4), just as Shemḥazzai gave instruction in sorcery.

66. See *T.B. Shabbat* 156a–b; *T.B. Yevamot* 21b. Cf. also the letter written by R. Abraham b. R. Ḥiyya Ha-Nasi to R. Judah b. R. Barzillai regarding the consultation of Chaldeans; it was published by Zecharias Schwarz in the *Festschrift Adolf Schwarz*, p. 27, where an attempt is made to harmonize the two views; see, on the other hand, the responsum of Maimonides to the Sages of Southern France, published by A. Marx in *HUCA*, III, p. 356. See further the comments of Naḥmanides, to which I referred above, n. 35, and S. Lieberman, *Greek in Jewish Palestine*, N.Y., 1942, p. 99. He draws attention there to the statement in the *Tanḥuma*, Shofeṭim, § 10, which attributes to an astrologer the sentence 'You are Jews; astrological factors do not apply to you, for you are Jews', and he adduced an interesting parallel in the statement of the Syrian Gnostic Bardesan, who was a contemporary of R. Jonathan: 'And the Jews... nor does the star, which has authority in the clime govern them by force.' See P. Wendland, *op. cit.*, pp. 27–34; cf. n. 68.

67. *Exod. Rabba*, iii, 7; see *Mattenot Kehunna* [Baermann Ashkenazi] and Maharzaw [Z. W. Einhorn] *ad loc.*

68. See also the Geonic responsum, *Otzar ha-Geonim*, *Shabbat*, p. 160. Similarly the Valentinians asserted that, with the coming of Jesus, those who believed in him were transferred from the domain of fate to that of Providence (ἀπὸ

τῆς εἱμαρμένης εἰς τὴν ἐκείνου πρόνοιαν). See *Excerpta ex Theodoto*, § 74, ed. R. P. Casey, London 1934, p. 86; and *ibid.* § 78, p. 88 (cf. *ibid.* the notes on p. 156 and p. 158): 'Until baptism, fate is real, but after it the astrologers are no longer right.' The underlying thought is actually the same as that of the story in the Palestinian Talmud, *Shabbat*, vi, 9, p. 8d, about the proselyte who was an astrologer and said, after he had thought of using his astrological knowledge, 'Did you not join this holy people in order to abandon these practices? Let us go on our journey in the name of our Creator!' See Lieberman, *Ha-Yerushalmi Kiphshuto*, p. 116, and *Greek in Jewish Palestine, loc. cit.*, n. 32.

69. In *T.B. Bava Batra* 91b the following statement is reported in the name of Rav: 'Even a superintendent of wells (from which the fields are irrigated) is appointed by Heaven'; but in *T.B. Berakhot* the dictum is cited in the name of R. Joḥanan. For other readings see *Diqduqe Soferim, loc. cit.*, p. 328, note *Lāmed*; and *Arukh Completum*, s.v. גרגותא, p. 353.
70. See Pohlenz, *op. cit.*, pp. 197–198.
71. *Gen. Rabba* x, 7, pp. 79 ff, and the parallels indicated *ibid.*
72. *T.B. Sukka* 53a; Rashi *ad loc.* glosses: 'to the place where it was decreed upon him to die... thither his feet lead him.' In *T.P. Kil'ayim* ix, 4, p. 32c, the dictum is transmitted by R. Jonah in the name of R. Ḥama bar Ḥanina. In *Gen. Rabba* c, 4, the text reads: 'R. Jonah in the name of R. Ḥama'; see p. 1286, and the notes *ibid.*
73. *T.B. Yoma* 38b, and a similar exposition *ibid.* in the name of the School of R. Shila, see above, p. 273. Here also belongs the anonymous dictum cited several times in the Babylonian Talmud: 'Seeing that the Holy One, blessed be He, does not permit the beast of the righteous to be snared into unwitting sin, how much less the righteous themselves.' See *T.B. Ḥullin* 5b and the parallel passages cited there, and *Tosafot ibid.* s.v. *Ṣaddîqîm* ['the righteous']; cf. *T.P. Demai* i, 3, p. 21d. See also *T.P. Yevamot* i, 6, p. 3b: 'The Omnipresent guards (them), and no untoward incident has ever occurred.'
74. Wa-yeshev, § 4. The homily begins with a passage in Psalms 'This is the meaning of the verse "Come, behold..." R. Joshua b. Qorḥa said: Even the terrible (punishments) that Thou dost inflict upon us, Thou dost by pretext.' But it is clear that the continuation, which is entirely based on Amoraic dicta, does not belong to the Tanna, whose exposition is also capable of another explanation. In a new Midrash on the Torah, which was published by Jacob Mann in his book *The Bible as Read and Preached in the Old Synagogue*, 1940, Hebrew Section, p. 182, we only find 'R. Joshua said', and it is immediately followed by the homily about Moses, while that about Joseph is attributed there to R. Levi. The exposition concerning Adam is missing there; see also *ibid.*, p. 274, the dicta of the *Yelammedenu* cited from *Yalquṭ Talmud Torah*, where the whole ending is wanting and likewise the words of R. Tanḥuma. Cf. the dialogue between Rav Bevai bar Abbaye and the angel of death, *T.B. Ḥagiga* 4b–5a. The Amora accepts the answer: 'There is that

is swept away without judgement', i.e. a man dies without having committed any wrong. But even the angel of death finds it difficult to answer Rav Bevai's argument: 'One generation passeth away, and another generation cometh'!, i.e. no man dies until his allotted years are completed. In order to justify the untimely death of a woman, the angel of death admits that he does not deliver the souls of those who die before their time to the custodian of the dead, Duma, 'but they roam about with him and fly through the world, until their respective years are completed, and that is called a generation'; see Rashi, *ad loc.*, s.v. *Dĕrāʿênā* ['I shepherd them'].

75. *T.B. Sanhedrin* 67b; the RaMaH (R. Me'ir ha-Levi Abulafia) in *Yad Rama* seeks to reconcile the two views, but his remarks are grounded in his own attitude towards sorcery. But Rashi explains only the intention of the Amoraim; see the commentary on the Aggadot by RaSHBA (R. Solomon b. Abraham Adret), cited in *ʿEn Yaʿaqov* to *Ḥullin*, and see above, p. 97.
76. Rashi, *T.B. Ḥullin*, 7b, s.v. *'Ăfîlû.*
77. *T.B. Ḥullin* 7b, according to the Munich MS. In *Yalquṭ Shimʿoni* to Etḥanan, § 828, the reading is 'bruises his foot' (however, *ibid.*, Proverbs, § 959 the text has 'bruises his finger'), which is stated by *Diqduqe Soferim* to be the correct version, but the reading 'finger' is confirmed by the continuation of the Gemara and Rava's dictum, which refers to the 'thumb of the right hand'; see *Bet ha-Beḥira* by Me'iri, p. 32. The Stoics, too, stated that the εἱμαρμένη embraces both the movements of the spheres and the putting forth of a small finger. In *ʿEn Yaʿaqov* (even in the first edition) the dictum is quoted in the name of R. Eleazar, but it appears to be a mistake due to the saying that follows; likewise in *Haggadot ha-Talmud* the reading is 'R. Ḥanina'. In *Yalquṭ Shimʿoni*, Proverbs, *loc. cit.*, the second dictum is also given in the name of R. Ḥanina; see above, p. 277.
78. *T.B. Qiddushin* 62a; see *T.B. Yevamot* 52a, and *T.B. Ketubbot* 59a. But sometimes account is taken, even in civil law, of an argument resting on the ways of Providence; see *T.P. Bava Meṣiʿa* ix, 5: 'But cannot he say to him: The Holy One, blessed be He, is patient with the wicked?' Cf. *T.B. ibid.* 106a, and Rashi *ad loc.*, s.v. *Le-Nissa'*. See also *T.P. Qiddushin* i, 2, p. 59a: 'Had you been with me you would not have become sick.' See below, n. 87.
79. *T.B. Bava Meṣiʿa* 107b; *T.B. Bava Batra* 146b; *T.B. ʿAvoda Zara* 3b. In all these passages the dictum is in the name of R. Ḥanina; only in *T.B. Ketubbot* 30a the saying is quoted from a Baraita; see Rashi, *Bava Meṣiʿa, loc. cit.*; *Tosefot Ha-Rosh, ibid.*; RaSHBaM, *Bava Batra, loc. cit.*; Tosafot, *Ketubbot, loc. cit.*, s.v. *Ha-kol*; the parallel passages, and *Shiṭṭa Mequbbeṣet, loc. cit.*
80. *T.P. Shabbat* xiv, 3, p. 14c; see *Lev. Rabba* xvi, 8, ed. Margulies, p. 364; *Deut. Rabba*, ed. Lieberman, p. 80.
81. *T.B. Berakhot* 33b; see Maharsha, *Ḥiddushe Aggadot, ibid.* Rashi, *T.B. Megilla* 25a, s.v. *Ḥûṣ mi-yir'at Shāmayim*, states: 'This He left to man, that he should himself prepare his heart for this, although it is in God's power

to direct our hearts to Him, for it is written: "Behold, as the clay in the potter's hand, so are ye in My hand, O house of Israel" (Jer. xviii 6); and it is further stated: "and I will take away the stony heart out of your flesh" (Ezekiel xxxvi 26)'. See Tosafot, *T.B. Nidda* 16b, s.v. *Ha-kol*; *ibid.*, the homily of R. Ḥanina bar Papa, which is a synthesis of the exposition of Rav, cited above, and that of R. Ḥanina. Cf. *Eccles. Rabba* i, 14: 'R. Abba bar Kahana said: "I have seen all the works"... except repentance and good deeds.' But these good deeds do not necessarily influence a man's fate. In *T.P. Berakhot* i, 1, p. 2d it is stated: 'And whoever recites the Tefilla [Eighteen Benedictions] immediately after the benediction of *Ge'ula* ['Redemption'], is not accused by Satan that day.' In reply to R. Ze'ira's complaint 'I said the *Tefilla* immediately after *Ge'ula*, yet was I pressed into service to carry myrtles to the palace', the Sages replied with good humour: 'This is quite a big thing; some people pay to see the palace'. See *T.B. loc. cit.*, 9b, and above, p. 273.

82. H. F. Müller, 'Plotinos — über die Vorsehung', *Philologus*, LXXII, pp. 338–357.
83. *T.B. Mo'ed Qaṭan* 28a; see Rashi *ad loc.* Me'iri, *Bet ha-Beḥira, Mo'ed Qaṭan*, Harry Fischel Institute Publications, Jerusalem 1937, commented on Rava's statement as follows: 'Let no heed be given to the dictum here "(Length of) life, sons...", for it is the view of an individual, which the tenets of the Faith can in no respect tolerate, and the weakness of the saying can be gauged from the reason given here for the statement, namely that he (Rava) saw Rabba and Rav Ḥisda, who were equal in his eyes... and this is the cause that has led many to doubt the truth, as persons of understanding know'. But what the dogmatic approach of Me'iri, inspired by the medieval spirit, could not tolerate the Amoraim did without fear. See also Me'iri's *novellae* to *T.B. Shabbat* 156a. Cf. the comment of R. Asher of Lunel, cited by J. Lubetzky from the Guenzburg MS. in the introduction to *Sefer ha-Hashlama*, p. XII, n. 11. Even in civil law Rava decided according to the principle 'The angel of death — what difference does it make whether it is here or there?', *T.B. Bava Meṣi'a* 36b; see above, n. 77.
84. *T.B. Bava Batra* 16a; cf. Rashi *ad loc.*, and RaMaH, *Yad Rama*, *ad loc.*
85. Rava used, in his reply, the statement of the Baraita, *Sifre*, 'Eqev, § 45; see *T.B. Qiddushin* 30b and the parallels cited there; cf. *Gen. Rabba* xxii, 6, p. 212.
86. *T.P. Rosh Ha-shana* i, 3, p. 57b; in *T.B. ibid.* 17b the Baraita is anonymous and linked to the verse 'the eyes of the Land thy God are... upon it' (Deut. xi 12).
87. *T.B. Rosh Hashana* 16a, where the author of the dictum is Rav Joseph. But the Munich MS. reads 'Rava'; see *Diqduqe Soferim*, *ibid.*, p. 28; this is also the reading in *T.B. Nedarim* 49b. In the Halakha, too, the argument based on the decree issued on New Year is accepted; see *T.B. Bava Meṣi'a* 106a, and Rashi s.v. *we-tigzor-'ōmer* ['Thou dost decree a thing'], who comments: 'What you ask from the Creator is done, and I did not ask Heaven at the beginning of the year to prosper me in the barley produce but in the wheat.'

Maimonides, 'Hilkhot Śĕkhîrût' [Laws of Hiring], v, 5, does not, of course, advance this argument. See above, p. 811, n. 77.

88. The commentary of the RaN [Nissim b. Reuben Gerondi], *Nedarim*, *loc. cit.* The Gemara in *T.B. Rosh Ha-shana* resolves the question of prayer even according to the Rabbis: 'In accordance with R. Isaac, for R. Isaac said: Crying (to Heaven) is good for a man both before the pronouncement of the decree and after.' See the *Novellae* of the RaN to *Rosh Ha-shana*, where he distinguishes between a decree involving a community and that concerning an individual. A similar distinction is made by the RIṬBA [Yom Ṭov b. Abraham Ishbili], *loc. cit.*

89. *T.B. Shabbat* 88a; see *T.P. Shevi*ʿ*it* vi, 1; cf. above p. 328.

90. *Tanḥuma*, ed. Buber, Maṭṭot, § 7, pp. 159–160; see the note there, where he indicates the vv.ll. in the ordinary edition of the *Tanḥuma* and in the *Midrash Be-Midbar Rabba*.

91. On a similar distinction made in the writings of Philo, in which he defends the doctrine of Providence against its critics, who point to the prosperity of the wicked, see P. Wendland, *op. cit.*, pp. 51–54.

CHAPTER XII

THE WRITTEN AND THE ORAL LAWS

1. 'Torah', in the sense of study of the Torah, occurs in Hillel's saying 'the more Torah the more life' — *M. 'Avot* ii, 7; cf. *ibid.* ii, 2; iii, 17; and see J. Guttmann, 'Tora be-Talmud' [Torah in the Talmud], *Festschrift Adolf Schwarz*, Berlin-Vienna 1917, Hebrew Section, pp. 1 ff. See also below, ch. XVI, § 7.
2. See *M. Megilla* iii, 5; cf. L. Blau, *Zur Einleitung in die Heilige Schrift*, Budapest 1894, p. 45, and *ibid.* n. 3 (= *Jahresbericht of the Rabbinical Seminary*, Budapest 1893/94) against the view of Geiger, *Urschrift*, p. 87.
3. *Mekhilta*, Pisḥa, v, p. 15; cf. above, p. 42.
4. See also *Sirach* i, 1; xxiv 2; *The Wisdom of Solomon* ix, 9. Cf. Bousset-Gressmann, *Die Rel. des Judentums*, 1926; B. Gemser, *Sprüche Salomos*, Tübingen 1963, p. 48, and the bibliography listed there; Y. Kaufmann, *Toledot ha-'Emuna ha-Yisre'elit*, vol. II, Book II, p. 583.
5. *Sifre*, 'Eqev, § 37; *Gen. Rabba* i, 4, p. 6. In Amoraic literature we find the formulation 'The world and its fullness were created only for the sake of the Torah' — *Gen. Rabba* i, 10, p. 9, or 'The entire world was created only on account of the Torah' — *Lev. Rabba* xxiii, 3, p. 529; see *Bereshit Rabbati*, ed. H. Albeck, p. 4, and the parallels indicated *ibid.* n. 2. But *IV Ezra* vi, 55–59; vii, 11, and the Syriac *Baruch* xiv 18–19, speak of Israel, not of the Torah. Cf. below, p. 525.
6. *Sifre Deut.* §48; *M. 'Avot* iii, 14. Y. Baer, 'Lĕ-Bērûrāh shel Tôrat Aḥărît ha-Yāmîm', *Zion*, XXIII–XXIV (1958–1959), p. 142, writes: 'The first to be created in the world on high was the Torah, concerning which the well-known statements are made in Proverbs viii 21–31...'; but Proverbs speaks of Wisdom, not of the Torah. See above, p. 198.
7. See my article 'Halakha u-Nevu'a', *Tarbiz*, XVIII (1947), p. 17, notes 151–152. See further *T.B. 'Avoda Zara* 52b; *T.B. Bekhorot* 50a (the Munich MS. reads 'until he found a Biblical verse', but in *T.B. 'Avoda Zara, loc. cit.*, the Munich MS. also reads 'a verse from the Torah'); *Tanḥuma*, ed. Buber, *Re'ē*, § 13.
8. See my aforementioned article, p. 13; and cf. also the dictum of Resh Laqish,

Tanḥuma, Naśo', § 25: 'Why should I learn this from the Book of Psalms? The teaching is Pentateuchal.'

9. Romans iii 10–18; I Corinthians xiv, 21; John x 34; xii 34; xv 25. See W. G. Kümmel, 'Jesus und der jüd. Traditionsgedanke', *ZNW*, 1934, p. 111. Cf. C. H. Dodd, *The Bible and the Greeks*, London 1935, p. 35 and p. 38.
10. G. von Rad, *Theologie des A.T.*, Munich 1962, p. 90; D. Rössler, *Gesetz und Geschichte*, Neukirchen Kreis Moers 1960, pp. 15 ff. Against the latter work sharp and justifiable criticism was expressed by Andreas Nissen, *Tora und Geschichte im Spaetjudentum*, Novum Testamentum, 1967, pp. 241–277; only he, too, did not sufficiently grasp the variegated character of Rabbinic thought in relation to history and apocalypticism.
11. See S. Schechter, *Some Aspects of Jewish Theology*, p. 116. L. Baeck, *The Essence of Judaism*, New York 1948, pp. 270 ff.
12. See *op. cit.*, p. 34.
13. See *De Migratione*, § 92; cf. Yitzḥak Heinemann, *Philons griechische u. jüd. Bildung*, pp. 177–178; H. Wolfson, *Philo*, I, p. 70.
14. G. Östborn, *Tora in the Old Testament*, Lund 1945.
15. See C. H. Dodd, *op. cit.*, p. 26, from Pseudo-Demosthenes, *Contra Arystogitonem*, 774.
16. O. Schroeder, 'Νόμος ὁ πάντων βασιλεύς', *Philologus*, LXXIV (1917), pp. 194 ff; see *ibid.*, p. 204. It is difficult to refrain from mentioning here, as a curiosity, the following note of this scholar: 'This view was first expressed by the great antagonist of the French Revolution, Edmund Burke, and was subsequently repeated [dann nachgesprochen] by Woodrow Wilson, before he became the President of the United States and the enemy of Germany and the truth'!
17. As the text should read according to I. L. Seeligmann, *The Septuagint Version of Isaiah*, Leiden 1948, p. 105. On the change from singular to plural and *vice versa* in the Septuagint see S. H. Blank, 'The Septuagint Renderings of Old Testament Terms for Law', *HUCA*, VII (1930), pp. 278 ff.
18. F. Heinemann, *Nomos und Physis*, Basel 1945. See H. Koester, 'NOMOS ΦΥΣΕΩΣ', *Studies in the History of Religions*, XIV, 1968, pp. 522 ff. He holds that Philo made the most decisive contribution to the development of the concept of 'natural law'; on its relationship to 'the seven Noahide precepts' cf. *ibid.* p. 532, n. 1; and see below, p. 323.
19. *T.B. Shabbat* 31a; see J. H. Weiss, *Dor Dor we-Dorshaw*, Pt. I, p. 1, who writes: 'that later Sages put it into his mouth'; W. Bacher, *Die Agada der Tannaiten*, I, p. 76, n. 4; Y. Baer, *Zion*, XXVII (1962), p. 128, n. 22, considers this view 'unbeweisbar', but agrees with Weiss.
20. Apparently, we should read Antonius. In *Sifre Deut.*, § 351, p. 408, and in *Midrash Tannaim*, p. 215, the text has: 'The general [*hegmon*] Agrippa asked Rabban Joḥanan b. Zakkai'.
21. *'Avot de-R. Nathan*, Version I, xv, 31a. On the question of the 'dogma' of the Oral Law see J. Kaatz, *Die mündliche Lehre und ihr Dogma*, Leipzig 1922,

pp. 38–39. His assertion 'There are individual interpretations of the Tannaim and Amoraim, but individual dogmatism regarding the Oral Law is not to be found among them' is only partly true, for the author has overlooked the historical context, as we have explained it. On the Oral Law in the apocryphal literature, see R. Marcus, *Law in the Apocrypha* (*Columbia Univ. Oriental Studies*) vol. 26 (1927), pp. 59–66, and pp. 70–74.

22. 'Die Lehre vom Ungeschriebenen Gesetz im Jüdischen Schriftum', *HUCA*, IV (1927), p. 155.

23. See S. Lieberman, *Hellenism in Jewish Palestine*, p. 83.

24. B. Ritter, *Philo und die Halacha*, Leipzig 1879, p. 14, parallels Philo's statement with that in *T.B. Shabbat* 85a: 'And whence do we know that the lore of the Sages is a matter of consequence? For R. Hiyya bar Abba said in the name of R. Joḥanan: What is the meaning of the Scripture "Thou shalt not remove thy neighbour's landmark, which they of old have set"? — the landmark set by those of old you shalt not set aside.' But the Talmudic teaching *ibid.* relates to a concrete matter, as Rashi *ad loc.* explains: 'Whence do we know that Rabbinic lore with regard to the area required for the sustenance of vegetation is something to be relied upon, so that we may say: the Sages are well versed in agriculture?... "thy neighbour's landmark" — this means to plant near the boundary (of thy neighbour) so as to impoverish his land, according to the measurement laid down by the men of old.' Now the men of old, as explained in the Gemara *ibid.*, are the sons of Seir, the Horite, 'who were well versed in the cultivation of the land'. See Marcus, *op. cit.*, p. 74; and cf. *Midrash Mishle* xxii, 28: 'R. Simeon b. Yoḥai said: A custom established by your ancestors do not change'. Possibly this Midrash constituted the source for Rav Sherira Gaon, who inferred from the verse cited above, 'Whence do we know that custom is of consequence?' etc. See *Shaʿare Ṣedeq*, Pt. IV, Gate I, § 20, p. 33a. Wolfson, *Philo*, Pt. I, p. 192, n. 171, quotes Rav Sherira from *Ṭur Ḥoshen Mishpaṭ* § 368, as indicated in *Tora Temima*, Deuteronomy, *loc. cit.* Also in the *Damascus Document* i, 16, it is stated: 'diverting them from the paths of righteousness and removing the landmark set by the men of old'. It is difficult to agree with Baer's approach in the article cited earlier, pp. 126–127; and there certainly cannot be found in Philo's statement evidence of the dispute that took place among the Hellenistic Jews 'concerning the validity of the laws of the ancients that were transmitted only by word of mouth'.

25. *Auctor ad Herrenium*, II, 10, 4; Quintilian, VII, 1, 49; see B. Cohen, 'Letter and Spirit in Jewish and Roman Law', *M. Kaplan Jubilee Volume*, New York 1953, and now in his book *Jewish and Roman Law*, New York 1966, p. 32, n. 9.

26. See my article 'Ha-Dĕrāshā ki-Yĕsôd ha-Hălākhā û-Bĕʿāyot ha-Sôfĕrîm [Scriptural Exposition as a Basis of Halakha and the Problem of the Scribes]', *Tarbiz* XXVII (1958), pp. 166 ff, and *ibid.*, pp. 180–181.

27. V 18–19. It is of no consequence to our theme whether these verses are truly

anti-Paulinian or not. On the different views on the subject see W. D. Davies, *The Setting of the Sermon on the Mount*, Cambridge Univ. Press, 1964, pp. 334 ff. See also the detailed exegetical and theological discussion of the question by W. Trilling, *Das wahre Israel*, Munich 1964, pp. 167–187.

28. Boaz Cohen refers, *op. cit.*, p. 36, to *Mekhilta*, Mishpaṭim, § 17, p. 310. The correct text is *bĕ-'ôtôtehā nittĕnā Tôrā*, and although *'ôtôt* can also mean *'ôtiyyôt* ['letters'] (see *'Arugat ha-Bośem*, Pt. IV, p. 208), yet here it seems best to interpret the expression, with Horovitz (*Mekhilta, loc. cit.*), that the Torah provided 'signs' for her words; this is also the interpretation given by D. Hoffmann, *Midrash Tannaim*, p. 60. The nearest and earliest parallel is the dictum of R. Simeon b. Yoḥai, *T.P. Sanhedrin* ii, 6, p. 20c, that in answer to the complaint of the Book of Deuteronomy that Solomon wished to abstract a *Yôd* from it, the Holy One, blessed be He, declared: 'Solomon and a thousand like him shall come to nought, but no word of yours shall ever be void.' The other dicta that speak of *'ôt 'aḥat* [one letter, or tittle] are by Amoraim. See *Lev. Rabba* xix, 2, p. 402, and *ibid.* n. 3, where the parallels are given; Strack-Billerbeck, Vol. I, p. 244; cf. also *T.B. Yevamot* 79a, the statement of R. Joḥanan 'Rather let one letter of the Torah be uprooted, than the name of Heaven should be desecrated in public'; *T.B. Temura* 14b, 'R. Joḥanan and Resh Laqish... said: Rather let the Torah be uprooted than forgotten by Israel', and in the Munich MS. 'Rather let one letter of the Torah be uprooted...'; cf. *T.B. 'Eruvin* 64a.

29. See, on the other hand, *T.B. Qiddushin* 40b; nevertheless the view expressed by G. F. Moore, *Judaism*, I, p. 235, seems to be a far-fetched generalization.

30. *T.P. Qiddushin* i, 2, p. 59d. The formula is found in the dicta of Tannaim and Amoraim relative to the teachings of their predecessors: 'R. Simeon said: Four things R. Akiba used to expound that I do not interpret as he did', etc. — *T.B. Rosh Ha-shana* 18b; cf. *Tosefta* vi, 6; R. Joshua with reference to R. Ishmael 'but I do not say so' — *T.B. Bekhorot* 20a; 'R. Judah said: Me'ir used to say... but I say...' — *T.B. Ḥagiga* 19a–b; see H. J. Kosovsky, *Oṣar Leshon ha-Talmud* [Thesaurus Talmudis], V, p. 2105. All that was written by D. Daube, *The New Testament and Rabbinic Judaism*, London 1956, pp. 55–62, on our subject is without foundation. He made use of a note of S. Schechter, *JQR*, O.S. (1898), p. 11, n. 3, to the effect that 'Ηκούσατε has the meaning of the Midrashic term 'I hear', 'We have heard'. But this view was refuted already by W. Bacher, *Die Älteste Terminologie der jüd. Schrift-auslegung*, Leipzig 1899, p. 190, n. 3, who explains that the expression 'You have heard it said of former scholars' refers to actual hearing and nothing more. Daube's statement, *op. cit.*, p. 62, that 'I hear' is an abridgement of a longer formula, is pure conjecture, which does not conform to the use of the Midrashic term.

31. *T.B. Temura* 14b, according to the Munich MS., which reads: 'one letter from...' (so, too, in *Yalquṭ Makhiri* to Psalms, p. 228), but the word 'one' was struck out, and the printed editions have: 'let the Torah be uprooted'

[*tĕʿāqēr Tôrā*]. For Hillel's dictum see *Tosefta Berakhot* vii, 22, p. 17; and cf. above, p. 342.

32. On Paul's allegorical methods of exegesis in comparison with those of Philo see H. Wolfson, *The Philosophy of the Church Fathers*, 1956, I, pp. 29–75; Jean Pépin, *Mythe et Allégorie*, 1958, pp. 231–259.
33. *M. 'Avot* iii, 11; I have cited the Mishna according to the text of the Kaufmann MS.
34. The bibliography is given by A. Buechler, *Sin and Atonement*, London 1928, p. 103, n. 2. See also J. M. Guttmann, *Bĕḥînat Qiyyûm ha-Miṣwôt* [The Aspect of the Observance of the Precepts], Breslau 1931, p. 63. The translation of C. Taylor, *Sayings of the Jewish Fathers*, Cambridge, 2nd ed., 1897, p. 51, must also be cited 'and acts barefacedly against the Thorah'; he relies — *ibid.* n. 28 — on C. Buxtorf's *Lexicon*, and the sense of 'be impudent' that pertains to *galli 'anpîn* in the Elephantine Papyri (Cowley, 37, 7–8); cf. N. H. Torczyner [Tur-Sinai], *Lĕšonénu*, XII (1943), p. 271.
35. The words are wanting not only in the Kaufmann MS., but also in the Cambridge MS., and were likewise deleted by Joseph Ashkenazi — see *Mele'khet Shelomo*; they are also omitted in *'Avot de-R. Nathan*, Version I, xxvi. See Louis Finkelstein, *Introduction to Tractate 'Avot de-R. Nathan*, pp. 74, 160–161.
36. See Wolfson, *loc. cit.*; H. F. Weiss, 'Zur Frage der historischen Begegnung von Antike und Christentum', *Klio*, Vols. 43/45 (1965), pp. 307 ff.
37. *Tosefta Berakhot* iii, 25, p. 8: The "benediction" referring to the sectarians is included in that concerning those who depart from the ways of the community; see the commentary of S. Lieberman, *Tosefta ki-Fshuṭah*, I, p. 54.
38. This is the reading of the printed editions and of the Cambridge MS.; see also Taylor, *An Appendix*, 1900, p. 150, and *'Avot de-R. Nathan* (*loc. cit.*). But the Kaufmann MS. reads: 'one who gives a (wrong) interpretation and who makes void....'
39. *Tosefta Sanhedrin* xii, 9, p. 433. See *T.P. Sanhedrin* x, 1, p. 27c, and *T.P. Pe'a* p. 16b, where the Amoraim interpret the passage: 'one who gives a (wrong) interpretation of the Torah — this refers to one who says: The Torah was not given from Heaven... it refers to one who transgresses the words of the Torah publicly....' Both interpretations indicate the consequence of the action of the 'one who gives a (wrong) interpretation'.
40. Cambridge MS. of *'Avot de-R. Nathan*; *Sifre.*
41. In the printed editions it occurs before 'one who makes void the covenant of Abraham our father, peace be upon him!'; in the Kaufmann MS. (see above, n. 33) and in the *Maḥzor Vitry*, p. 512, it comes at the end.
42. M. Löwy, 'Die Paulinische Lehre vom Gesetz', *MGWJ*, 1903, pp. 322–339; 417–433; 534–544; *ibid.* 1904, pp. 267–276; 321–327; 400–416. He endeavoured to discover sources for Paul's doctrine in Rabbinic teaching, and he almost left him no original thought; but Löwy's entire thesis is merely an example of the misinterpretation of verses and of disregard for the entire historic nexus. See W. D. Davies, *Torah in the Messianic Age*, Philadelphia 1952;

idem, *The Setting of the Sermon on the Mount*, Cambridge University Press, 1964, pp. 109–190; the earlier bibliography is listed *ibid.*, to which should be added, J. M. Guttmann, *Beḥinat Qiyyum ha-Miṣwot*, pp. 75 ff. On the other hand, there is no connection between our subject and the work of S. Holdheim, *Das Ceremonialgesetz im Messiasreich*, Schwerin 1845, which Davies mentions on p. 110, but apparently did not see it.

43. *T.B. Shabbat* 151b and R. Joḥanan's statement *ibid.* 'When a man dies he is freed from (the obligation of) the precepts'; likewise the deduction of Rav Joseph, *T.B. Nidda* 61b, 'This implies that the precepts will be abolished in the Hereafter', refers to the time of the Resurrection of the Dead, since the Sages inferred this from the Baraita that states 'A garment in which *kil'ayim* [i.e. a thread of wool in a garment of flax, or *vice versa*; see Deut. xxii 11] has been lost... may be made into cerements for the dead'. The reference is not to the Days of the Messiah, a view advanced by W. Bacher, *Die Agada der bab. Amoräer*, p. 105, n. 23, and followed by L. Baeck, *The Pharisees*, New York 1947, pp. 72 ff, and other scholars listed by Davies, *op. cit.*, pp. 180–182, though he himself is hesitant about it. B. Cohen's contention, *op. cit.*, p. 33, n. 14, that Romans vii 4 is simply an inversion of R. Joḥanan's statement in *T.B. Shabbat, loc. cit.*, 'When a man dies he is freed from the precepts', is difficult to comprehend. On the question of the Hereafter and the Days of the Messiah see below, ch. XVII. Resh Laqish's dictum 'At times the annulment of the Torah is its foundation' relates to the breaking of the Tables by Moses, an act for which the Lord said to him 'You are to be congratulated for having broken them' (*T.B. Menaḥot* 99b; Rashi, *ad loc.*, s.v. *She-biṭṭulah* glosses 'One who interrupts his study of the Torah for a funeral or for a wedding actually founds it, i.e. he is rewarded as though he were sitting and founding it and occupying himself with it...'); see above, pp. 606–607.

44. *M. ʿEduyot* viii, 7, according to the Kaufmann MS.; the editions read 'dispute'.

45. See *ibid.* Mishna 3; and cf. *T.B. Qiddushin* 71a, and the *novellae* of Naḥmanides *ibid.* s.v. *Hā' dĕ'āmrînān*, and the Ritba [R. Yom Ṭov b. Abraham Ishbili], *ibid.*, s.v. *Kĕgôn 'ēllû.*

46. See A. Ehrlich, *Miqrā' ki-Fĕshûṭô*, Berlin 1901, Pt. III, p. 498.

47. This is the reading of the Erfurt MS., p. 321; the printed editions and the Vienna MS. read: *zĕhîhê* [instead of *zĕhârê*]. See *T.B. Soṭa* 47b, where Rashi explains the word to mean 'haughty'. The *ʿArukh* has *zĕhôhê ha-lēv*, and Abraham Geiger compared this expression with the Samaritan *zhwh*; see *Nachgel. Schriften*, Pt. III, p. 264, and the *Additamenta* to *Aruch Completum*, p. 169. Z. Ben-Ḥayyim, *Tarbiz*, X, p. 354, interprets *zĕhûtā* in the sense of 'folly'. Possibly the expression 'the proud [or, unruly] of heart' refers to sectarians of the type of the adherents of the Damascus Covenant, who claimed (i 10–11) 'that they sought Him [God] with a whole heart and He raised up for them a righteous teacher to guide them in the way of His heart' and they framed a Halakha of their own. In the new scroll, designated

'the Temple Scroll' they wrote the Halakhot together with Torah verses.

48. *Tosefta Pe'a* iii, 2, p. 21; cf. *Sifra*, Ṣaw, vii, and *T.B. Menaḥot* 89a.

49. *Lev. Rabba* xvi, 4, p. 354, and the parallels cited there. The story about Elisha b. Abuyah in *T.P. Ḥagiga* ii, 1, p. 77b, likewise bears witness to the circle of R. Akiba and its views on the intertwining of the verses of Torah, Prophets, and Hagiographa. See my observations in my article 'Ha-masorot 'al Torat ha-Sod bi-Tequfat ha-Tanna'im', pp. 7 ff.

50. The point was discussed by H. P. Chajes, *Torat ha-Nevi'im* [Teaching of the Prophets], ch. ii, 'Bērûr 'Eliyyāhû' [Elijah's Clarification], Zolkiew 1836, p. 4b; see also L. Ginzberg, *Eine Unbekannte Sekte*, New York 1922, p. 304, n. 1, but instead of *T.B. Pesaḥim* 70a read 34a. As an alternative explanation to the transmission by Elijah of the traditional rulings that were cited on Sabbath morning before Rav Ḥisda in Sura to the academy of Rava in Pumbeditha, the demon Joseph is mentioned (*T.B. 'Eruvin* 43a; see Rashi *ad loc.*: 'who does not observe the Sabbath').

51. In *Tosefta Soṭa* xiii, 2, this verse is glossed as follows: 'Like a man who says to his fellow: "Till the advent of Elijah", or "until the dead are resurrected" '. See *I Maccabees* iv 46, and *ibid.* xiv 41.

52. *Sifra*, Be-ḥuqqotay, xiii, and the parallel passages; see my article 'Halakha u-Nevua', *Tarbiz*, 1947, pp. 1–27, where the subject is discussed at length.

53. See R. Bultmann, *Theologie des Neuen Testaments*, Tübingen 1953, pp. 255 ff. The approach of several Catholic scholars is more critical: F. Prat, S.J., *The Theology of St. Paul*, New York 1934, II, p. 312, writes: 'In seeing Paul intent on destroying the whole edifice of the ancient Law, without appearing to think of reconstructing it, we ask with anxiety where this work of demolition is going to stop and on what foundation the obligation of the new dispensation is to rest.' See Stanislaus Lyonnet, *St. Paul, Liberty and Law*, The Bridge, 1962, pp. 229 ff.

54. *T.B. Shabbat* 116b, according to the Munich MS.; see *Diqduqe Soferim* 131a. On the dispute with 'the Gentile sages' in regard to inheritance by a daughter see *T.P. Bava Batra* viii, 1, p. 16a.

55. *Religionsgeschichtliche Studien*, 1876, pp. 76–97.

56. See also E. Hennecke, *Handbuch zu den Neutestamentlichen Apokrypha*, 1914, p. 71, who does not, however, mention Güdemann's study. Regarding the aphorism, see *Sifre Numbers* § 131, p. 173, and the n. *ibid.* Cf. Luitpold Wallach, 'The Textual History of an Aramaic Proverb', *JBL*, LX (1941), pp. 403–415. His suggestion to replace the answer that is identical with Matthew V 17 by Deuteronomy xxvii 26 appears to me an example of *furor philologicus*, the very thing with which he charges others; see *ibid.* p. 441. A distinction must be drawn between the essential motif of the story, which, as the context also shows, is a demonstration of the inconsistency of the philosopher in his attitude to the Torah and its literary form. Wallach's statement, *ibid.* p. 410, that the narrative provides an answer to the contention of the Ebionites, to whom Rabban Gamaliel's judge belonged, is

imaginary. See also S. Lieberman, *Greek etc.*, New York 1942, p. 104.

57. See R. Bultmann, *op. cit.*, p. 55, who thus describes the attitude of the early community towards the Torah, without reference to the Talmudic story. Cf. also H. F. Weiss, *Der Pharisäismus im Lichte der Überlieferung des NT* (*Sitzungsbericht der Säch. Akademie*), Berlin 1964–1966, pp. 89 ff.

58. *T.B. Pesaḥim* 118a; in this spirit the dictum was understood by the author of a late Midrash. See *Bereshit Rabbati*, p. 9.

59. *Exod. Rabba* xxviii, 6; *Tanḥuma*, Jethro, xi; see *T.B. Berakhot* 5a and *Exod. Rabba* xlii, 8. However, the desire to restrict the Revelation to a single act is already to be found in Tannaitic dicta; see *Sifre*, Be-ha'alotkha § 68; Shelaḥ § 111; *ibid.* § 133. Cf. B. J. Bamberger, 'Revelations of Torah after Sinai', *HUCA*, XVI (1941), p. 97. Although they seek to emphasize that Revelation is not a continuing process, and that the Torah that was given to Moses was given him in its entirety, yet they do not negate the special domain of prophecy; see *Shoḥer Ṭov* xc, § 4.

60. See *T.P. Pe'a* ii, 6; cf. the statement of R. Joḥanan, *T.B. Megilla*, 19b.

61. *T.B. Nedarim* 22b; *Eccles. Rabba* i, 73, where the dictum is cited in the name of R. Ḥunya.

62. *T.B. Ḥullin* 60b; see Rashi *ad loc.* s.v. *Miqra'ot* and s.v. *Wĕhēn*. In the same manner the Amoraim acted towards sayings of the Sages who preceded them; if it appeared to them that these amounted only to the determination of past facts, they asked 'But what happened happened!' [i.e. it has no further relevance; why then discuss it?]; see *T.B. Yoma* 5b; *T.B. Ketubbot* 3a; or they enquired 'What difference does it make?' — see *T.B. Sukka* 51a, and cf. also *T.B. Pesaḥim* 53a. See S. Lieberman, *Sifre Zuṭa*, New York 1968, p. 30, n. 74; and cf. *T.P. Shevi'it* i, 1, p. 33a. Cf. also Rashi, *T.B. Ḥullin* 17a 'It is a case of "Expound and receive reward!" for we must ascertain the truth even though the matter belongs to the past.'

63. *Tanḥuma*, Kî Tiśśā', § 34; Wa-yērā', § 5; see my aforementioned article, p. 7, n. 50.

64. See my article, *ibid.*, n. 57.

65. *T.P. 'Avoda Zara* ii, 8, p. 41c; *T.P. Berakhot* i, 7, p. 3b.

66. *Midrash Aggada*, Rĕ'ē, § 9; see *Gen. Rabba* lxxxii, 5, p. 981, and *Tosafot Sanhedrin* 89b, s.v. *'Eliyyāhû*.

67. *Tanḥuma*, Rĕ'ē, § 1, and ed. Buber *ibid.* In a fragment from the Genizah published by A. Marmorstein, 'Ein Fragment einer neuen Pjska zum Wochenfest und der Kampf gegen das mündliche Gesetz', *Jeschurun*, XII (1925), pp. 34 ff, it is stated: 'Thus said the Holy One, blessed be He: "Say not, the Holy One, blessed be He, gave us only the Torah at Sinai; the Prophets and Hagiographa are as dear to Me as that [the Torah] in writing." '

68. See L. Ginzberg, *Eine Unbekannte jüd. Sekte*, p. 230, and my article, cited above, p. 2, notes 17–18. Cf. A. Marmorstein, 'Judaism and Christianity', *HUCA*, X (1935), p. 226, p. 229, and p. 259. See also H. J. Schoeps, *Theologie und Geschichte des Juden-Christentums*, Tübingen, 1949, pp. 159 ff. It is extra-

ordinary that he states there, p. 168, n. 1, that Marmorstein, 'The Background of the Haggadah', *HUCA*, VI (1929), p. 197, regarded the polemic in the aforementioned Midrash as directed against the Samaritans and Sadducees, but Marmorstein observes there expressly 'Yet it is unlikely that at this stage of separation from the people of Nablus, or after the Sadducees have lost all their influence, or power, this should be the subject of homilies (similarly, *HUCA*, X, p. 226, n. 13). On the other hand, he makes no mention of the express statements of Marmorstein in the article that indicate that the homily was directed against Judeo-Christian sects, and this interpretation is explicitly given by Schoeps himself *ibid.*, p. 140, n. 1.

69. See Güdemann, *op. cit.*, p. 106. See G. Alon, *Tarbiz*, XI (1940), pp. 23 ff.
70. See *T.B. ʿEruvin* 4b, the dictum of R. Isaac and Rashi *ad loc.* s.v. *Dĕvar Tôrā*: 'Torah law: A Halakha of Moses given at Sinai in the Oral Torah.' See *T.B. Shabbat* 48b: 'Rava said: It is a Torah law that when in use they are (deemed to be) connected....' See the glosses of H. P. Chajes *ad loc.*
71. *T.B. Yevamot* 36b and the parallel passages cited there in the margin. The reason for this attitude is that 'people avoid transgressing a Scriptural law'. For the appraisal of the 'enactments of the Scribes', see below, p. 333.
72. For the concept that the Lord occupies Himself with Halakha see also *T.B. Berakhot* 8a; *ibid.* 63b; *T.B. ʿAvoda Zara* 3b; *Seder Eliahu Rabba*, pp. 62, 162.
73. See L. Ginzberg, *op. cit.*, pp. 334 ff; J. Klausner, *Ha-Raʿyon ha-Meshiḥi be-Yisraʾel*³, Tel-Aviv 1950, pp. 11 ff. Schoeps, *op. cit.*, pp. 87 ff. W. D. Davies, *op. cit.*, pp. 25 ff.
74. *T.B. Ḥullin* 137b; *T.B. Bekhorot* 58a, Rabbenu Gershom and Rashi *ad loc.*
75. *T.B. Sukka* 44a; see *T.P. ibid.*, iv, 1, p. 54b; *T.P. Sheviʿit* i, 7, p. 33b.
76. See above, n. 59.
77. *T.B. Menaḥot* 45a. It is evident that he did not know the Baraita, according to which R. Judah, too, said 'This passage Eliyah will expound', for after R. Jose had explained the passage, R. Judah said to him: 'May your mind be at ease, for you have set mine at ease'. See the annotations of *Miṣpe ʾÊtān* to *Menaḥot, ad loc.*, who raises the objection 'if so, R. Joḥanan's view accords with no Tannaitic opinion'. In the Messianic apocalypse in *Aggadat Shir ha-Shirim*, ed. Schechter, p. 38 (see *ibid.*, p. 85), it is stated that Elijah 'will produce the Book of Jashar, of which the whole of this Torah is but one line of it.'
78. *T.B. Shabbat* 151b; in *Ecclesiastes Rabba* xii, 1, the dictum is cited in the name of R. Ḥiyya bar Neḥemiah.
79. *Lev. Rabba* ix, 7, p. 185; the parallel passages are listed *ibid.* n. 6.
80. *Cant. Rabba* ii, 14, 4; *T.B. Sanhedrin* 97a the whole theme is cited as a Baraita, and there the text reads 'and the Torah is restored to its students'. See Weiss, *Dor Dor we-Dorshaw*³, Pt. I, p. 215, n. 4; Klausner, *op. cit.*, p. 204, did not understand his observations, and Klausner's remark that in *Pesiqta Rabbati* there were added the words *û-mitḥaddēsh lĕ-Yisrāʾēl* ['and renews itself unto Israel'] is incorrect, for these words occur in *Cant. Rabba*, and

they are missing in *Pesiqta Rabbati*, where the whole passage is cited in the name of 'the Rabbis'. See also *Cant. Rabba* viii, 5: 'R. Joḥanan said that she resolves [*mannaḥat*] (*'Ot 'Ĕmet* and *RaDaL* read: *matteret*) problems of the Torah and of monarchy in the time to come.'

81. *Gen. Rabba* xcviii, 9, p. 1260; see the notes *ibid.* The homily concerning the thirty pieces of silver as thirty precepts is transmitted in most sources in the name of R. Joḥanan.
82. See *Gen. Rabba* xcv, 3, p. 1190, and cf. *Tanḥuma*, Tavo', § 4: 'R. Jonah, the father of R. Mana, said in the name of R. Levi, who said it in the name of R. Abba: The Torah need not have been given to Israel in this world. Why? For all will be learning Torah from the Holy One, blessed be He, in the world to come. Why then was it given to them in this world? So that when the Holy One, blessed be He, comes to teach them in the world to come, they would know with which section He is dealing.' The intent of the homily is to stress the identity of the Torah that the Lord would teach in the future world with that of this world. Cf. *T.P. Shabbat*, end of ch. vi, p. 8d: 'The Ministering Angels ask them — the righteous — what has the Holy One, blessed be He, taught you?' and in *Deuteronomy Rabba* i, 12, 'What Halakhot did the Holy One, blessed be He, originate today?' See also *Num. Rabba* xx, 20.
83. As a separate dictum it is cited in the name of the *Yelammedenu* in *Yalquṭ Shim'oni* to Isaiah § 479: 'The Holy One, blessed be He, said: In this world Israel learns Torah from a human being, hence they forget it because it was given by Moses who was human... but in the Hereafter Israel will learn Torah only from God... and just as God lives for ever, so too does His teaching — what they will learn from Him they will never forget.' See the Targum to Canticles V 10.
84. See *Mattenot Kehunna* and the commentary of Z.W. Einhorn (*Maharzaw*) *ad loc.*
85. *Gen. Rabba* xvii, 5, p. 157; *ibid.* xliv, 17, p. 439.
86. See above p. 651.
87. *Lev. Rabba* xiii, 3, p. 278. In *'Arugat ha-Bośem*, Pt. I, p. 242, the wording of the answer is: 'R. Abba said: The Holy One, blessed be He, will say, A new Torah shall come forth from Me'.
88. See the appendices to *Eliahu Zuṭa*, ed. Meir Ish-Shalom, p. 19: 'The Torah gives life... in this world, and in the world to come, and in the days of the Messiah.'
89. *Sifra*, 'Ahare (*Mekhilta*), xiii, 10, p. 86a; *Pesiqta de-R. Kahana*, ed. Mandelbaum, p. 74.
90. See *T.B. Pesaḥim* 119a: 'What is meant by *li-mĕkhasse 'atîq* [rendered: 'for stately clothing']? This refers to one who conceals [*mĕkhasse*] the things that the Ancient ['*Atîq*] of days revealed. What are these? The reasons of the Torah.' See *Diqduqe Soferim*, *ibid.* p. 379. Of Ahijah and Jereboam it is stated in *T.B. Sanhedrin* 102a: 'that all the reasons of the Torah were revealed to them as a field'.

91. *Pesiqta de-R. Kahana*, p. 72; see *Midrash Proverbs* ii, § 1, p. 48: 'If you have succeeded in storing up [*lispôn*] the words of the Torah, I shall sate you with the stored away [*ṣafûn*] good that I have laid up [*ṣafanti*] for the Hereafter'; see the responsa of RaShBa [R. Solomon b. Abraham Adret], I, § 93.
92. See G. Scholem, 'Der Sinn der Tora in der jüd. Mystik', *Zur Kabbala und ihrer Symbolik*, Zürich 1960, pp. 56 ff.
93. From R. Ishmael's admonition to R. Me'ir, 'My son, be punctilious in your work, for your work is Heaven's work; for should you omit one letter or add a superfluous letter you will be destroying the entire universe' (*T.B. 'Eruvin* 13a), Baer infers in his aforementioned article, p. 145, 'that all that could be said in later generations concerning the nature of the Torah, be it halakhically or mystically, was dependent on the paradigmatic and cosmic power possessed by the Torah according to the view of the early Sages.' But R. Ishmael's intent is clear. He warns R. Me'ir, the disciple of R. Akiba, who expounded every letter in *scriptio plena* and *defectiva*, that since he was a scholar and a scribe (*T.B. Gittin* 67a), he should be meticulous and not be influenced by these expositions when writing. Indeed it is reported that in the scroll of R. Me'ir were found allusions to his homiletical interpretations (*Gen. Rabba* ix, 5, p. 70, and n. *ibid.*). In no way is there the slightest reference to any intention on the part of R. Ishmael to say, as Naḥmanides maintains, that the Torah is composed of Divine names. But G. Scholem, *loc. cit.*, p. 57, stressed unequivocally that the reference is to Naḥmanides' interpretation. On the other hand, he is inaccurate in stating, *ibid.* p. 110, that in *T.B. Shabbat* 116a we find that the complete Torah consisted of seven books. We are told there that the passage *Wa-yĕhî bi-nĕsôa'* ['When (the ark) journeyed'] is a book on its own, whence it follows that there are seven books; see *Sifre Numbers* § 84, '*Wa-yĕhî bi-nĕsôa'*... Rabbi said: Because it is a book on its own'. Only the Cabbalists deduced from this that the book was at one time more comprehensive and complete.
94. See G. Scholem, *Judaica*, 1963, pp. 44 ff.
95. *T.B. 'Eruvin* 21a; Rashi, Tosafot and Maharsha *ad loc.* See S. H. Kook 'Gōdel ha-Tôrā wĕ-Yaḥăsah lĕ-Gōdel hā-'Olām' [The Size of the Torah and its Relationship to the Size of the World], '*Alummaḥ*, 1936, pp. 129 ff.
96. In two Talmudic passages, *T.B. Sanhedrin* 51b and *T.B. Zevaḥim* 45a, Rav Joseph expressed surprise that a Halakha should be decided about things that are not applicable at present, and asks '(Do we have to decide) a Halakha for (the days of) the Messiah?' And Rashi explains in *Sanhedrin, loc. cit.*, 'When the Messiah comes and the dead are resuscitated, we shall ask R. Eliezer how he worded his ruling'. In *Yad Rama, Sanhedrin, ibid.*, it is explained 'and when the Messiah comes, lo, Elijah will accompany him and he will teach [i.e. decide] truly'; but elsewhere in the Talmud the Tannaim and Amoraim decided Halakhot also in instances termed 'a Halakha for (the days of) the Messiah'; see *T.B. Zevaḥim* 45b; Tosafot *ad loc.* s.v. *Halakha*; Tosafot, *Yoma* 13a, s.v. *Hilkheta.* The surprise expressed by Rav Joseph is

apparently connected with his views concerning the days of the Messiah — see above, p. 681.

97. Wherever the expression occurs in the Babylonian Talmud it is cited anonymously; see *T.B. Beṣa* 5b; *T.B. Sukka* 41a; *T.B. Ta'anit* 17b; *T.B. Bekhorot* 53b.

CHAPTER XIII

THE COMMANDMENTS

1. 'But the word is very nigh unto thee, in thy mouth, and in thy heart, that thou mayest do it' (Deuteronomy xxx 14).
2. In Psalms there occurs a synonym for *miṣwā* ['precept', 'commandment'] — *piqqûdîm* ['precepts']: 'The precepts of the Lord are right, rejoicing the heart' (Psalms xix 9 [8]). This sense of the term is expressed in the Septuagint by ἐντολή or πρόσταγμα: C. H. Dodd, *The Bible and the Greeks*, p. 27.
3. 'Because he hath despised the word of the Lord, and hath broken His commandment' (Numbers xv 31); see *Sifre Numbers* § 112, p. 118; cf. Büchler, *Sin and Atonement*, pp. 7 ff. See also above, p. 294.
4. See J. Kaufmann, *Toledot ha-'Emuna*, Pt. III, pp. 686 ff.
5. *Die Ethik des Judenthums*, Frankfurt-on-Main 1898.
6. In the critical review of Lazarus' book in *MGWJ*, XLIII (1899), which was included in the *Jüdische Schriften* of Hermann Cohen, III, pp. 1-35.
7. In his introduction to the second volume of his work, which appeared posthumously in 1911, p. XXXIX, Lazarus mentions Cohen's essay in the same breath as the criticism of 'Oberlehrer Bonhomer... im Antisemitischen Jahrbuch für 1900', without saying a word relevant to the issue itself. *Ibid.*, p. XLI, occurs the sentence: 'Only through Kant do we learn to understand the words of the Sages better'—'Erst durch Kant lernt mandie Rabbinen besser verstehen.'
8. Even Julius Guttmann, *Kant und das Judentum* (Leipzig 1908), who realizes the difference between the concept of the autonomous ethic and the ethic of Judaism, points, *ibid.* p. 226, to 'a daring Talmudic dictum', which prompts him to state: 'This fundamental conception of Kant is the type of Jewish ethical teaching.'
9. The Kaufmann MS. reads: 'So, too, you find that Abraham our father kept the Torah before it was given to the world, as it is said: "Because that Abraham obeyed My voice and kept My charge, My commandments, My statutes, and My laws".'
10. In the printed edd. and the Vienna MS., *shenitgallû* (instead of *sheniglû*), 'that were revealed'.

11. The kidneys are the source of counsel, and so, too, we find in a Baraita: 'The Rabbis taught: Man has two kidneys, one counsels him to (do) good, and the other counsels him to (do) evil... The Rabbis taught: The kidneys counsel, the heart understands...' (*T.B. Berakhot* 61a); see also *Gen. Rabba* xliii, 6, p. 420, ' "Brought forth bread and wine": R. Samuel bar Naḥman (said): He transmitted to him the laws of priesthood; the Rabbis said: He revealed Torah to him.' The reference is to Melchizedek. H. Albeck, *Das Buch der Jubiläen und die Halacha*, 1930, p. 40, n. 27, states, on the one hand, that even *Seder Eliahu Rabba* does not intend to say that the Patriarchs had no 'teachers'; but, on the other hand, he criticizes Perles for finding testimony to the spontaneous learning of the Patriarchs only in *Seder Eliahu Rabba*, and not in other Midrashim. See below, n. 64.
12. VIII, 1–7; see G. H. Box, *The Apocalypse of Abraham*, 1919.
13. *Num. Rabba* xiv, 2; see *Yalquṭ Makhiri* to Proverbs xiv, 14, in *Sefer ha-Liqquṭim* of Dr. A. Grünhut, Frankfurt-on-Main 1903, Pt. VI, p. 11; see *ibid.* n. 5.
14. In *Lev. Rabba*, ii, 10, this is a late interpolation that was added from *Seder Eliahu Rabba* and is not found in correct MSS. of *Lev. Rabba*. See ed. M. Margulies, pp. 46–49 and the vv.ll. and notes there.
15. See *Mekhilta de-R. Ishmael*, Be-shallaḥ, Petiḥta, p. 79, and the parallels cited in the note to line 13; *'Avot de-R. Nathan*, Version I, 4a, *T.B. 'Avoda Zara* 8a; *Gen. Rabba* xi, p. 95.
16. *Sifra*, Aḥare Mot, xiii, 10, ed. Weiss, p. 86a; ed. Finkelstein, p. 373; see also *T.B. Yoma* 67b.
17. Julius Guttmann, *Dat u-Madda'*, Jerusalem 1956, p. 226.
18. *Op. cit.*, Pt. I, p. 100. Without mentioning his name, Alexander Ehrenfeld, *Der Pflichtbegriff in der Ethik des Judentums*, Bratislava (the date of publication is not given, but apparently it was printed in 1931; see *Biblica*, XIII [1932], p. 101), p. 47, also states that this rendering by Onkelos clearly states that the human intellect is the source of morality.
19. See Samson Baruch Scheftel, *Be'ure Onkelos* [Commentary to Onkelos], Munich 1888, p. 8; cf. also U. Cassuto, *From Adam to Noah*, Jerusalem 1961, pp. 111 ff, who gives a similar interpretation of the plain sense of the verse, referring, for corroboration, to Deuteronomy i 39, 'and your children, who this day have no knowledge of good or evil'.
20. *Op. cit.*, p. 401, and also Felix Perles in his essay, 'Die Autonomie der Sittlichkeit im Jüd. Schriftum', in the *Hermann Cohen Jubilee Volume*, Judaica, Berlin 1912, p. 105.
21. See *Tosefta Bava Meṣi'a* iii, 25, p. 378; *Torat Kohanim*, Qedoshim, ii, 14, p. 88d; vii, 14, p. 91a; *ibid.*, Behar, vi, 2, p. 109d; *T.B. Qiddushin* 32b.
22. *T.B. Baba Meṣi'a* 58b; the point is well explained by Maharsha *ad loc.*: 'For this is a matter that people can also understand, for the one equated the honour of the servant with that of his Maker, whereas the other did not' etc.

23. *Op. cit.*, pp. 103 ff.
24. See Lazarus, I, p. 124; Ehrenfeld, *op. cit.*, p. 49.
25. See above, p. 290, and p. 815 n. 19.
26. I. Heinemann, 'Die Lehre vom Ungeschriebenen Gesetz', *HUCA*, IV (1927), pp. 149 ff.
27. See *Tanḥuma*, Mas'e, § 8; ed. Buber, *ibid.* § 6. There the verse is applied to the bull of Elijah and the ravens. Man recognizes the worth of the good qualities inherent in animals, while they themselves are unconscious of them. See *Sifre Numbers* § 119, p. 143: 'If Torah issues from a man's mouth, he is like the Ministering Angels; but if not, he is like the beasts and cattle who do not recognize their Maker.'
28. *Sifre Deut.* § 306: 'Alas for man that he has to learn from the ant...!' See also Ḥida [Ḥayyim Joseph David Azulai], 'Petaḥ 'Ênayim' to *T.B. 'Eruvin, loc. cit.*
29. On the duty of honouring parents in the Hellenistic world and on the comparison of parents to gods, see J. Heinemann, *Philons griech. und jüd. Bildung*, pp. 252 ff. On the arguments of the Cynics against honouring parents, see *ibid.*, p. 257. But the Sages also knew Gentiles whose attitude to their father was different from that of the non-Jew in Ashkelon: 'Said R. Akiba, I have seen a certain heathen bind his father and cast him before his dog, who devoured him' — *Sifre Deut.* § 81.
30. *Tanḥuma*, Tavo', 1; ed. Buber, § 3, p. 46, where the first dictum is missing. Buber, *ibid.*, n. 11, speaks of the printer's error in the Mantua ed., and failed to note that the text here contains two different dicta that also expound two different verses. The printed ed. reads 'as though it were given from Mount Sinai', but having regard to the theme and what is subsequently stated the text must be emended as I have given it.
31. The thought is already explained in Tannaitic sources — *Mekhilta de-R. Ishmael*, Massekhta da-Amalek, Jethro, ii, p. 196: 'For whoever delivers an absolutely true judgement is accounted by Scripture as though he was a partner of the Holy One, blessed be He, in the work of Creation'. See *Gen. Rabba* xliii, 7, p. 421; *'Arugat ha-Bośem*, Pt. III, p. 461; *ibid.* n. 89; and cf. *T.B. Sanhedrin* 99b, where it is stated in the name of Rav, that whoever occupies himself with the Torah for its own sake 'is deemed as though he had built the Palace [i.e. Temple] in heaven above and on the earth below, as it is said "And I have put My words in thy mouth, and have covered thee in the shadow of My hand, that I may plant the heavens, and lay the foundations of the earth" (Isa. li 16)'.
32. The commentary of *'Ĕṣ Yosef* by R. Hanoch Sündel of Bialystok on *Tanḥuma, ibid.*, states in philosophic parlance: 'He means to say, it is as though you had re-created the concept of the precepts and had understood them with your own intellect.'
33. In *Lev. Rabba* xxxv, 7, pp. 825–26, R. Ḥama b. R. Ḥinena expounds the Scripture Lev. xxvi 3 thus: 'If you have carefully observed the Torah, I account

it unto you as if you had made them [the precepts]'; and R. Ḥinena bar Papa says 'as if you make yourselves'. In *T.B. Sanhedrin* 99b R. Eleazar expounds the verse Deuteronomy xxix 8 'as though he had formed the words of the Torah'; which Rava interprets the verse 'as though he had created himself'. See below, n. 42.

34. *Mekhilta de-R. Ishmael*, Massekhta de-Ba-ḥodesh, v, p. 221; *Sifre Deuteronomy* § 343.

35. *Cant. Rabba* i, 2; this is also the opinion of the Rabbis there. They differ from R. Joḥanan only in regard to the angel and declare 'the commandment itself went round....' See my remarks in *Tarbiz* XXX (1961), p. 152; cf. also *Tanḥuma*, Wa-yiggash, § 2. See above, p. 152.

36. *T.B. Shabbat* 88a, for Rav Aḥa bar Jacob reacts to R. Avdimi's dictum, and Rav Aḥa was the disciple of Rav Huna (see *T.B. Yevamot* 64b). The words 'bar Ḥasa' are missing in the Munich MS. and in *ʿEn Yaʿaqov*, but are found in other MSS., see *Diqduqe Soferim*, p. 185, n. *Dalet*. R. Avidimi's homily is found once again in *Cant. Rabba* viii, 5: ' "Under the apple-tree I awakened thee" — Palṭion of Rome expounded and said: Mount Sinai was plucked up and tied [ונענב] (this is the reading of the Pesaro ed.; other editions read וניצבו 'and they stood') to the heavens on high and the Israelites stood beneath it, as it is said "And ye come near and stood under the mountain...." Said the Holy One, blessed be He, if you will accept the obligation of My Torah, well and good; but if not, behold I shall press down upon you this mountain and slay you — "there thy mother threatened to destroy thee [usually rendered: 'there thy mother was in travail with thee']." The homily is interrupted in the middle by other expositions; see *Ḥiddushe Ha-RaDaL* [*Novellae* of R. David Luria], § 2. The name of the homilist occurs only once more in *Midrash Tehillim* xxviii, 2 (*ibid.*: 'Palṭion of Rome'). Since we do not know when he lived, we cannot determine who received the tradition from whom.

37. *Mekhilta de-R. Ishmael*, Massekhta de-Ba-ḥodesh, iii, p. 214. It is clear that the citation in *Midrash ha-Gadol* to Exodus, ed. Margulies, p. 392, does not emanate from the *Mekhilta de-R. Ishmael*; see ed. Epstein-Melammed, p. 143, and *ibid.* n. 16; the Kaufmann MS., *ibid.* p. 246, suffices to turn the doubt into a certainty. In keeping with the spirit of *Mekhilta de-R. Ishmael* is the homily in *Cant. Rabba* ii, 1: 'Another interpretation: "I am a rose of Sharon": I am she and I am beloved, for I was concealed in the shadow of Sinai and in a little while, like a rose, I filled myself with the sap of good deeds, with hand and heart [i.e. with all my might], and I said before Him "all that the Lord hath spoken will we do, and obey" '. The words 'For He tilted the mountain over me like a cask, as it is stated "and they stood at the nether part of the mount" ' in *Midrash Tehillim* i, 20, ed. Buber, p. 20, do not fit in with the preceding text, and are really an additional interpretation of the phrase 'I am concealed in Sinai' according to the dictum of R. Avdimi. They are wanting in two good MSS., א and ו, and in *Yalquṭ Shimʿoni* to

Canticles. Without noticing the difficulty, Buber inserted the words in the text.

38. See B. M. Lewin, 'Mi-Śeride ha-Geniza, Pirqoy b. Bavoy', *Tarbiz*, II (1931), p. 395; *Tanḥuma*, Noaḥ, § 3. Cf. A. Aptowitzer, *HUCA*, VIII–IX (1931–1932), p. 416; see also *'Arugat ha-Bośem*, Pt. I, p. 177, and my note *ibid.* 8. Cf. also M. Kasher, *Torah Shelemah*, XV, p. 103, n. 224.
39. 'For if He summon them to judgement, saying "Why did you not fulfil what you undertook?" they can reply that they accepted it under coercion' (Rashi, *T.B. Shabbat* 88a). The term *môdā'ā* [translated 'protest'] signifies a declaration that nullifies an act performed under duress; see *T.B. Bava Batra* 40 a–b, and Rashbam [R. Samuel b. Me'ir] *ad loc.*
40. *T.B. Shabbat, loc. cit.*; see also *T.P. Shevi'it* vi, 1, p. 36b, the statements of R. Eleazar and R. Jose b. R. Ḥanina. R. Joseph Engel in *Gilyone ha-Shas* (Vienna 1924) on *T.B. Shabbat, loc. cit.*, refers to this passage and cites the explanation given by Maharal [R. Judah Löw b. Bezalel of Prague] in *Ḥiddushe Gur Aryeh* of Rava's dictum: 'This, it appears, is the meaning: Since they (the Israelites) accepted the obligation of reading the Megillah, thus adding a precept of their own accord, we can no longer say that they were coerced to accept the precepts, for had they accepted the precepts in the first instance under duress, why should they have added (a further precept) voluntarily?'
41. Literally, 'as though he had made himself'; see above, p. 271.
42. *T.B. 'Avoda Zara* 19a; the Spanish MS., ed. Abramson reads: 'A man should always learn eagerly [literally, 'with desire']... as it is said... Rava further said: At first it is named after the Holy One, blessed be He, but in the end after his own name, as it is said "Whose desire is in the Law of the Lord" and thereafter "and in his own Law doth he meditate" '; see *ibid.*, p. 162.
43. *T.B. 'Eruvin* 55a; see *Diqduqe Soferim*, *ibid.*, p. 219, n. *Ṭêt*. *Haggadot ha-Talmud* reads: 'Rav Avdimi bar Ḥama bar Ḥasa'; see Tosafot, *Ta'anit* 7a, s.v. *'Af* [So, too, the words of the Torah].
44. *Sifra*, Be-ḥuqqôtay, viii, p. 112c.
45. See my articles 'Halakha u-Nevua', *Tarbiz*, XVIII (1947), p. 6; 'Mashmā'ûtāh ha-Dātît shel ha-Halakha [The Religious Significance of the Halakha]', *'Erkhê ha-Yahădût* [The Values of Judaism], 1953, p. 26; and above, p. 293.
46. *T.B. Bava Meṣi'a* 30b; the correctness of the interpretation given by the Babylonian Talmud to R. Joḥanan's statement is corroborated by the Baraita *ibid.* 88a.
47. *M. Giṭṭin* iv, 4; *Tosefta Terumot* ii, 1; see S. Lieberman, *Tosefta ki-Fshuṭah*, Terumot, p. 307.
48. See *T.B. Berakhot* 45b; *T.B. Bava Qamma* 99b; *T.B. Bava Meṣi'a* 24b; *ibid.* 30b.
49. See M. Güdemann, 'Moralische Rechtseinschränkung im mosaisch-rabbinischen Rechtssystem', *MGWJ*, LXI (1917), pp. 422 ff; *ibid.* p. 431 he bases himself on R. Azariah Figo (Picho), *Bînā lĕ-'Ittîm*, § 10. See M. Eschelbacher, 'Recht und Billigkeit in der Jurisprudenz des Talmud', in *Hermann Cohen Jubilee Volume, Judaica*, pp. 501–514, who gives the gist of the story without

establishing the text; but he notes that Rav's decision is not in accordance with the law. Also M. Silberg, *Kakh Darkô shel Talmud* [This is the Way of the Talmud], Jerusalem 1962, pp. 127 ff, overlooks the variant reading.

50. It is missing the first time in MS. ה׳, *Yalquṭ*, *Halakhot Gedolot* and *R. Isaac Alfasi*; the second time in MS. מ׳, *Yalquṭ* and *Halakhot Gedolot*. See *Diqduqe Soferim, loc. cit.*, p. 235 and note. It appears that Rashi, too, did not have the word in his text; see s.v. *Bĕderekh Ṭôvîm*.

51. *T.P. Bava Meṣi'a* vi, 8, p. 11a. The commentators of the Palestinian Talmud have found the words 'R. Nehemiah taught', which precede the story, difficult, and they have assumed that a Baraita is missing before the word 'potter'; see *Nĕtîvôt Yĕrûshālayim* [The Paths of Jerusalem] to *T.P. Bava Meṣi'a*, *ibid.* and Z. W. Rabinovitz, *Sha'are Torat Ereṣ Yisra'el* [The Gates of Palestinian Learning], p. 492. It is almost certain that the narrative in the Palestinian Talmud served as a model for the Amora before whom the incident of 'certain porters' was brought for judgement. The names of the Sages in the Babylonian Talmud are not clear; instead of 'Rav' we find v.l. 'Rava', and in place of 'Rabbah bar bar Ḥanan' there occurs 'Rabbah bar bar Ḥanah' and also Rabbah bar Rav Huna — see *Diqduqe Soferim ad loc.*

52. *T.B. Bava Meṣi'a* 108a. See Rashi, *ad loc.*, s.v. *Wĕ-'aśîtā*: 'Something that you do not miss so much, for you can find land elsewhere, without causing your neighbour the inconvenience of having his estate divided into two' — a reason that is suited to all views.

53. *Sifre Deuteronomy* § 79, ed. Finkelstein, p. 145; see *Tosefta Sheqalim* ii, 2, and S. Lieberman, *Tosefta ki-Fshuṭah*, Mo'ed, p. 677.

54. See *T.B. Bava Meṣi'a* 35a: 'The law is that devaluation is always returnable (upon paymen tof the debt), because it is said "And thou shalt do that which is right and good" '. So, too, the Nehardeans decided; see Maimonides, 'Hilkhot Shekhenim [Laws of Neighbours]', xii, 5; *Ṭur Shulḥan 'Arukh*, Ḥoshen Mishpaṭ, § 175, 5.

55. This distinction is blurred in Boaz Cohen's essay 'Letter and Spirit in Jewish and Roman Law', which first appeared in the *Mordecai Kaplan Jubilee Volume*, 1953, and now in his book *Jewish and Roman Law*, New York 1966, I, p. 53. M. Silberg, *op. cit.*, pp. 99 ff, has dealt with the 'legal' character of the precept 'And thou shalt do that which is right and good', but he has made it difficult for himself and has resorted to forced explanations on account of his comparison of 'that which is right and good' with the principle of equity in English law. On the relationship of *aequum et bonum* in Roman law to ἐπιεικές, see R. Hirzel, *Themis, Dike und Verwandtes*, 1907, pp. 121 ff, and pp. 230 ff. See now the illuminating essay of E. S. Rosenthal, "Al Derekh hā-Rōv [On the Way of the Majority]', *Peraqim*, I, pp. 189 ff.

56. 'Rav Papa acted beyond the strict requirement of the law' (*T.B. Ketubbot* 97a) is not a statement of fact, but an anonymous suggestion of the Talmud, to wit, that the problem is not to be solved by the personal conduct of Rav Papa, for he may have acted as he did by going beyond the letter of the

law. The Halakha decided at the end of the Talmudic discussion 'If a man sold (some of his land) and did not (in the end) need the money, the sale may be withdrawn' is actual law, and in that case Rav Papa, too, acted strictly according to the requirement of the law.

57. Maimonides, 'Hilkhôt Gĕzēlā wa-'Åvēdā [Laws of Robbery and Lost Property]', xi 17 (see also *ibid.* 7) does indeed state: 'He who walks in the way of the good and the righteous and acts beyond the requirement of the law, restores lost property in every instance, even if it is not consonant with his dignity.' This is also the reading in ancient MSS. The text of *Maggid Mishneh*, 'He who walks in the way of the good, beyond the requirement of the law', is undoubtedly only an abridgement. Similarly Maimonides writes in 'Hilkhot Rôṣēaḥ u-Shĕmîrat ha-Nefesh [Laws concerning a Murderer and the Preservation of Life]', xiii, 4: 'And if he is a man of piety and acts beyond the requirement of the law....' But in 'Hilkhot Sekhirut' ['Laws of Hiring'] iii, 2, he overlooked the story of the porters; *Sefer Miṣwot Gadol*, positive precepts, § 89, Venice 1547, p. 172b, who quoted Maimonides on the aforementiond Halakha, added it. Also the *Ṭur*, Ḥoshen Mispaṭ, § 304, 2, states: 'Nevertheless it is meritorious to act beyond the strict letter of the law and to give him his wages, if he has nothing to eat.' The act that went 'beyond the letter of the law' performed by R. Ḥiyya (*T.B. Bava Qamma* 99b) is mentioned neither in Maimonides, 'Hilkhot Sekhirut', x, 5, nor in the *Ṭur*, Ḥoshen Mishpaṭ, § 306, 10.

58. This quality was discovered by Rav Ḥisda in *M. Bava Meṣi'a* iv, 6, and he observed: 'They have taught here the quality of piety' (*T.B. Bava Meṣi'a* 52b). He inferred this from the wording, namely that if he does not receive it (the coin) back in the times stated, (the defrauded person) has only a grievance against him (the person who gave it in exchange), *ibid.* See Maimonides, *Perush ha-Mishna*, ed. Rabbi Joseph Kapach, Jerusalem 1965, p. 66; Maimonides, 'Hilkhot Mĕkhîra [Laws of Selling]', xii, 12; and *Maggid Mishne, ad loc.* In regard to the two other matters concerning which Rav Ḥisda said 'They have taught here the quality of piety', Rava rejected his view. *T.B. Shabbat* 120a: 'Said Rava: Would pious men take payment for Sabbath (labour)? (Rashi, *ibid.*, s.v. *Ḥăsîdê*: 'Surely, if they are pious men they should forgo any benefit due to them, if the slightest suspicion of transgression attaches to it...!'). Rather said Rava: 'We refer here to a God-fearing person' (Rashi: 'The rescuer [of the food from the conflagration] is God-fearing [*yĕrē' shāmayim*], but not pious [*ḥāsîd*], so as to forgo what is due to him'). So, too, in *T.B. Ḥullin* 130b Rava objects: 'The Tanna rules "that he must pay", yet you say that they taught here the quality of piety!' Although the Talmud, anonymously, seeks to validate the view of Rav Ḥisda, nevertheless according to this explanation Rav Ḥisda introduced an innovation in the conception of the 'quality of piety', which does not find expression in the Mishna; see *Tosafot, loc. cit.*, s.v. *'Āmar* and s.v. *Tannā'*; cf. Maimonides, 'Hilkhot Mattĕnôt 'Anniyyîm [Laws of the Gifts to the Poor]', ix, 15. The

identification of 'quality of piety' with 'beyond the requirement of the law' was overlooked by Silberg, *op. cit.*, pp. 124 ff, and, by the same token, also the distinction between 'quality of piety' and 'the spirit of the Sages finds pleasure in him', which is nearer to the concept of law and enactment; see next note.

59. But in *T.B. Bava Qamma* 94b, s.v. *'Ĕn*, Rashi glosses: 'The spirit of wisdom and piety is not in him'; see *Diqduqe Soferim* (*ibid.*), p. 227, n. 2; S. Lieberman, *Tosefta ki-Fshuṭah*, Zeraʿim, p. 595, n. 63. In *T.B. Shabbat* 121b, there is a distinction made between 'the spirit of the pious' and 'the spirit of the Sages', and Rava bar Rav Huna even says there: 'And in these men of piety the spirit of the Sages finds no pleasure'; see Rashi, *ibid.*, s.v. *'Ên*.
60. In *T.P. Bava Meṣiʿa* iv, 2, p. 9d, we read: 'Rav instructed his servant: "When I tell you to give a gift to someone, if he is a poor man give it to him immediately, but if he is a rich man, consult me again." '
61. See the commentary attributed to Rashi, *T.B. Taʿanit* 10b. Cf. also *Tosefta Taʿanit* i, 7: 'R. Simeon b. Gamaliel said: Where abstinence is involved, if a man wishes to act as a *yāḥîd* [one who is exceptionally scrupulous in his observance of the precepts] he may do so, and a scholar may do so'; cf. *T.P. Berakhot* ii, 9, p. 5c–d; L. Ginzberg, *Perushim we-Ḥiddushim bi-Yerushalmi*, Pt. I, pp. 410 ff; and S. Lieberman, *Tosefta ki-Fshuṭah*, Moʿed, p. 1071. See also *T.B. Bava Qamma* 81b, where Rabbi asks R. Ḥiyya, with reference to R. Judah b. Neqosa (so in the MSS.; see *Diqduqe Soferim*, p. 183): 'Who is this person that is showing off before us?' See Rashi s.v. *Gĕdûlātô*. The matter spoken of there is one between man and man.
62. *T.B. Bava Qamma* 30a; see commentary of R. Ḥananel *ad loc.*
63. See *The Book of Jubilees* vii, 38; xxi, 10; iv, 17, 21. Cf. H. Albeck, *Das Buch der Jubiläen und die Halacha*, Berlin 1930, pp. 4–5.
64. See above, n. 11. In *Tanḥuma*, Wa-yiggash § 11, it is stated that Abraham taught his sons Torah.
65. *Gen. Rabba* xxv, 1, p. 238; see n. *ibid.* Cf. L. Ginzberg, *Legends*, Pt. V, p. 156.
66. *Gen. Rabba* lxviii, 5, p. 773; *ibid.* § 11, p. 784; *ibid.* lxxxiv, 8, p. 1010; see *Seder ʿOlam Rabba* ii, and *T.B. Megilla* 17a.
67. See above, p. 332. See also *Baraita de-Massekhet Nidda*, *Tosefta ʿAtiqta*, ed. H. M. Horowitz, Frankfurt-on-Main, 1890, p. 24: 'And who revealed it to him? None other than the Holy One, blessed be He, as it is said: "because that Abraham hearkened to My voice...." '
68. *M. Ḥullin* vii, 6; see Rashi, *T.B. Ḥullin* 100b, s.v. *ʿĀmĕrû*, who explains the view of the Sages thus: 'Up to the time of Sinai they were not prohibited, but it was written in its (due) place, after it had been enjoined at Sinai....' This is also the inference to be drawn from *Tosefta Ḥullin* iv, 8, p. 509, and from the Baraita in Ḥullin 101b. But see Maimonides, *Perush ha-Mishna*, *ad loc.*, on the fundamental principle that he expounds; and cf. my article 'Halakha u-Nevua', *Tarbiz*, XVIII (1947), p. 21, n. 179.
69. Albeck, *op. cit.*, p. 39, n. 26, discerns the doctrine of the 'autonomy of the

Patriarchs' in all the sources, and even to the expression 'were revealed to him' in the *Tosefta*, at the end of *Qiddushin*, he gives the forced interpretation of 'inner vision'. But, as we have shown, the difference between the later and earlier Midrashim is not to be annulled or blurred.

70. Perles, *op. cit.*, pp. 103 ff; Isaac Heinemann, *Philos griechische und jüdische Bildung*, p. 53, n. 1; so, too, Kaminka, *Meḥqarim*, II, Tel-Aviv 1951, p. 168.
71. See above, p. 323.
72. Possibly the position was also influenced by the trend to restrict the direct revelation to that at Sinai, a view that found expression in the words of Rav Ḥisda 'Was the Torah then given on two different occasions?' (*T.B. ʿEruvin* 21b) and in the remark of Rav Aḥa b. Rava to Rav Ashi, *T.B. Ḥullin* 101b. See below, p. 821, n. 59.
73. *Mekhilta*, Ba-ḥodesh, § 7, p. 228, where the parallels are listed.
74. *Pesiqta de-R. Kahana*, ed. Buber, p. 51b; see ed. Mandelbaum, p. 99; cf. *Lev. Rabba* xxiv, 5, p. 558.
75. *Sifra*, Ṣaw, Millu'im, i; MS. Rome, ed. Finkelstein, p. 185. The printed edition, ed. I. H. Weiss, p. 42b reads: ' "That a man may devote unto the Lord" — i.e. sacred gifts to the Temple, sacred gifts (set aside and consumed) outside Jerusalem....'
76. See Rashi, *T.B. Shabbat* 156a, s.v. *Wĕ-Ṣadqān*; cf. below, p. 348.
77. *T.B. Yevamot* 65b; see Rashi, *ad loc.*, s.v. *'Êkh 'ēlēkh.*
78. *T.P. Soṭa* viii (*ad fin.*), p. 23a; *T.B. ibid.*, 44b; R. Judah's view is reported in accordance with the explanation of R. Joḥanan in *Tosefta Soṭa* vii, 24, p. 309.
79. *T.B. Berakhot* 27b. Proof of the fact that the statement is by Samuel is to be found in *T.P. Moʿed Qaṭan* iii, 5, p. 82d.
80. This explanation is also given in a responsum of Rav Sherira in *Shĕ'ēlôt û-Tĕshûvôt Gĕonê Mizrāḥ û-Ma-ʿărāv* [Inquiries and Responsa of the Geonim of East and West], ed. Müller, Berlin 1888, p. 34, § 141: '...Because all agree — both those who hold that they are obligatory and those who maintain that they are optional — that they constitute a religious act [*miṣwā*]. For religious acts (precepts) are of two kinds: some of them are obligatory, so that one who does not perform them is guilty of transgression; and some of them are optional, so that whoever performs them receives reward... but both those that are optional and those that are obligatory constitute religious acts.' S. Lieberman commented on the statement of the Gaon in the name of H. Brody in *Tarbiz*, VI (1935), p. 111; see also Lieberman, *Tarbiz*, V, pp. 97 ff; G. Alon, 'Shĕvût, Rĕshût, Miṣwā', *Tarbiz*, VII, pp. 135 ff; and J. N. Epstein, *ibid.*, pp. 150 ff. See *T.B. Shabbat* 25b 'The kindling of the Lamp on the Sabbath is obligatory'; Maimonides, 'Hilkhot Shabbat', V, 1, and RABYaH [R. Eliezer b. Joel ba-Levi of Bonn] § 199. Cf. Tosafot, *Ḥullin* 54b, s.v. *'Ên*: ' "not permitted" means the same as "not obligated" '.
81. *T.B. Ketubbot* 91b, and Rashi, *ad loc.*, s.v. *Miṣwa*; see also Tosafot, *Bava Qamma*, 157a, s.v. *Miṣwa.*
82. *T.B. Ketubbot* 86a–b; see Rashi, *ad loc.*, 86a, s.v. *Pĕriʿat.* Tosafot, *ibid.*,

s.v. *'Āmar* observes: 'Is it not obvious that he is compelled (to repay the debt), why then should it be called a religious act [*miṣwa*]?' On the views of the other Ri'shonim and legal authorities on the nature of the obligation of paying a debt, see Menaḥem Alon, *Hêrût ha-Pĕrāṭ bĕ-Darkhê Gĕviyyat Ḥôv ba-Mishpāṭ hā-ʿIvrî* [The Freedom of the Individual in the methods of collecting debts in Hebrew Law], Jerusalem 1964, pp. 19 ff; cf. *ibid.*, p. 20, n. 44. But he, like Silberg, *op. cit.*, p. 71, did not take account of the various meanings of the term *miṣwa*.

83. Silberg, *ibid.*, states that 'There is a dispute among the Sages of the Talmud as to whether the payment of a creditor ...is a religious-moral duty... or whether it is an obligation under civil law'. M. Alon, *op. cit.*, p. 20, writes: 'According to Rav Papa it is not a legal obligation like the restoration of a robbed object or a deposit....' But the restoration of a robbed article is also not 'a legal obligation' but a positive precept; see Maimonides, 'Laws of Robbery', i, 1.
84. Hillel's analogy is found in another version in *Lev. Rabba* iii, p. 776; see above, p. 227.
85. See A. Büchler, *Types of Jewish Palestinian Piety*, London 1922, p. 15, n. 4.
86. *T.B. Beṣa* 16a; see *Diqduqe Soferim, ibid.*, p. 34; and Rashi, *ad loc.*, s.v. *Lĕshēm shāmayim*, who comments: 'trusting that a fine (animal) would come his way'. Even the Ri'shonim realized the difficulty of this interpretation. See the *Novellae* of Me'iri on *Beṣa, ibid.*, and the *Novellae* of the disciple of the RaN (R. Nissim b. Reuben Gerondi), called *Shiṭṭa Mequbbeṣet*, printed in *Naḥalat Yehoshuaʿ*, Constantinople 1731.
87. It seems that this is how R. Simon b. Ṣemaḥ Duran (RaShBaṢ) understood the statement of Hillel; see *Magen 'Avot*, p. 34a.
88. *T.B. Shabbat* 50b; see *Tosefta Berakhot* iv, 1, p. 8; see S. Lieberman, *Tosefta ki-Fshuṭah*, Zeraʿim, p. 56; and S. Büchler, *op. cit.*, p. 19, n. 1.
89. *T.B. Berakhot* 63a; see *Diqduqe Soferim*, p. 184a, § *Mêm*. It should be added that in *ʿEn Yaʿaqov, editio princeps*, the author of the dictum is given as Rav Papa. It appears that this change was influenced by the addition 'Rav Papa said: Thus people say "A thief at the entrance of the breach calls to God (the All-Merciful)" '.
90. *T.B. Nazir* 23b; *T.B. Horayot* 10b, and an anonymous Talmudic statement moderates the extremism of the statement and changes it to 'Say: Like a precept performed from an ulterior motive'.
91. *T.B. Nazir, loc. cit.*; see Tosafot, *ad loc.*, s.v. *Tāmār*: 'But her intention was for the sake of Heaven', etc. [i.e. her action was motivated by piety];
92. See Mark ii 23. The reference to David, who ate the shewbread, which it was not lawful to eat, is intended to prove that it is permissible to commit a transgression for the sake of fulfilling a precept, namely to feed a hungry person in order to sustain his life. The inference is: So, too, may his hungry disciples, who hearken to his teaching, pluck ears of corn. See *T.B. Menaḥot* 95 (*ad fin.*): 'Give him to eat — his life is in danger'; cf. Rashi, *ad loc.*, 96a,

s.v. *Mĕsukkān*. Similar arguments underlie Mark vii 1–23; Matthew xxiii 16–27. Yitzhak Baer 'Li-Bĕʿāyat Dĕmûtāh shel ha-Yahădût bĕ-'Evangelyônîm ha-Sinôpṭiyyîm [On the Problem of the Image of Judaism in the Synoptic Gospels]', *Zion*, 1966, pp. 117 ff, advances the date of all these polemical passages to the period following the Destruction, but his arguments are not convincing, and his proofs are inadequate. Jesus' teaching is in part a radicalization of views held by several of Israel's Sages.

93. *Tosefta Berakhot* vi, 24; Lieberman, *ibid.*, p. 40 (Zuckermandel *ibid.*, vii, p. 17); see also *T.P. Berakhot* ix, 8, p. 14d; *T.B.*, *ibid.*, 63a. Cf. Lieberman, *Tosefta ki-Fshuṭah*, Zeraʿim, p. 124; now also idem, *Sifre Zuṭa*, New York 1964, p. 112. On the expression 'the Torah is dear to Israel', see *T.B. Rosh ha-Shana* 4a: 'Because the Torah is as dear to Israel as is a queen [*shēgāl*] to the Gentile nations, they have merited...'; cf. *Diqduqe Soferim*, *ibid.*, p. 3.

94. See *Tosefta*, *loc. cit.*, according to the Erfurt MS. In the light of our interpretation R. Me'ir does not disagree with Hillel's statement, as Lieberman, *op. cit.*, p. 125, supposes. This is also the meaning of R. Nathan's saying — which was interpolated from the Baraita into the Mishna at the end of *Berakhot* — according to *T.P. Berakhot*, *loc. cit.*: 'Rabbi Nathan transposes the parts of the text: "They have made void Thy law — it is time to work for the Lord." ' Cf. J. N. Epstein, *Mavo' le-Nosaḥ ha-Mishna*, p. 975, and H. Albeck, the *Hashlamot* ['Supplements'] to *M. Zeraʿim*. The dictum of R. Nathan in the Babylonian Mishna reads: 'They have made void Thy law, because it is time to work for the Lord.' The change was influenced, apparently, by the dictum of Rava: 'This verse can be expounded so that the beginning explains the end, and the end explains the beginning — so that the end explains the beginning: "They have made void Thy law" — why? — Because it is time to work for the Lord" ', in accordance with Rava's view ' "In all thy ways acknowledge Him" — even where a transgression is involved'; see Rashi, *loc. cit.*, s.v. *Mi-sêfêh*.

95. The first Baraita is in the Tosefta, *loc. cit.*, and the second in the Palestinian Talmud, *loc. cit.* See *Midrash Tehillim* cxix, 57, p. 251a: 'if you have seen that the generation has neglected the Torah and become lax... at such a time do you fulfil it.'

96. Above, p. 333. The Haggadah that tells how R. Simeon b. Yoḥai left the cave ascribes to him the exclamation 'See how dear the precepts are to Israel!', *T.B. Shabbat* 33b.

97. *Tanḥuma*, Shelaḥ, § 15; ed. Buber § 28.

98. On the two hundred and forty-eight parts of the body see *M. 'Oholot* i, 8, and Preuss, *op. cit.*, pp. 66 ff.

99. The dictum of R. Judah b. R. Simon, *Pesiqta de-Rav Kahana*, ed. Mandelbaum, p. 203 (ed. Buber, p. 101); see *Midrash Mishle* xxxi, 29, ed. Buber, p. 110.

1. *Mekhilta de-R. Ishmael*, Massekhta de-Ba-ḥodesh, V, pp. 221–222, and see the vv.ll. cited there; so, too, *Sifre Deuteronomy*, § 343, and *ibid.* § 76: 'Behold, there are three hundred and sixty-five negative precepts in the Torah.'

But cf. in ed. Finkelstein, p. 141, the vv.ll. and note 5, where it is stated that in MSS. א׳ and ה׳ the text has: 'the three hundred positive precepts in the Torah'.

2. The dictum in *T.B. Makkot*, *loc. cit.*, is reported in the name of Rav Hamnuna, and in *Cant. Rabba*, i, 2, 2 we read: 'R. Azariah and R. Judah b. R. Simon, in the name of R. Joshua b. Levi, followed his view. They said: It is written "Moses commanded us a law"....' In *Pesiqta Rabbati* p. 111a the text has: R. Azariah and R. Judah be R. Simeon and R. Simeon be R. Joshua b. Levi: "Moses commanded us a law"....' But MS. Parma reads: 'R. Azariah and R. Judah bar Simeon b. Levi ציר his view'. It appears, however, that the correct reading is: 'R. Azariah and R. Judah b. R. Simon followed [תפיסו] the view of R. Joshua b. Levi and said...', that is to say, they followed the view of R. Joshua b. Levi that the first two commandments of the Decalogue were uttered by the Almighty, and thus they were able to supplement the numerical value of 'Torah' [i.e. 611 plus two commandments total 613, the number of the commandments]. Also in *Gen. Rabba* xxiv, 5, p. 234, there is a dictum about 248 positive precepts etc. in the name of R. Judah b. R. Simon; see vv.ll. *ibid.* The same dictum in *Pesiqta Rabbati* p. 99b has: 'R. Levi in the name of R. Joḥanan'. Bacher's statement, *Agada der Palästinischen Amoräer*, I, p. 558, n. 2, that Rav Hamnuna's dictum is 'in accord with the Palestinian sources of R. Joshua b. Levi', requires amendment. Since Rav Hamnuna's dictum comes after R. Simlai's homily, it seems that the reference is to Rav Hamnuna III or IV; see A. Hyman, *Toledot Tanna'im wa-Amora'im*, p. 378.
3. See Maimonides' Introduction to *The Book of Precepts* and Naḥmanides' critical remarks about his principles ['roots'].
4. Vilna 1879, p. 59a.
5. Moses Bloch's theory, *REJ*, I (1880), p. 209, concerning the polemical aim of R. Simlai's homily is improbable.
6. In *T.B. Makkot* 24a Rav Simlai's exposition is interrupted by examples and explanations, and at the end Rav Naḥman bar Isaac raises an objection and replaces the verse from Amos by Habakkuk ii 4; see W. Bacher, *op. cit.*, p. 559, n. 2.
7. R. Judah b. R. Nathan (RIBaN) (continuation of Rashi's commentary) *T.B. Makkot*, *loc. cit.*, s.v. *Wĕ-he'ĕmîdān* [and reduced them]: 'But the later generations were not so righteous... and so the whole time the generations are declining'. See, however, the comments of R. Me'ir ha-Levi (RaMaH), cited by *Ha-Kotev* in *'En Ya'aqov*; R. Solomon Edels (MaharShA) to *Makkot*, *loc. cit.*; and cf. the *Novellae* of R. Yom Ṭov b. Abraham Ìshbili (RIṬBA): 'Habakkuk came and reduced the Torah to one (precept), for in keeping it one keeps the whole Torah, provided he recites it properly with the Divine Name, accepting the One God and the yoke of His kingdom, as we are commanded in the passage of the *Shema'*, which comprises the entire Torah'.
8. *M. Makkot* iii, 15. R. Ḥanania b. 'Aqashya's dictum, *ibid.*, 16, could undoubtedly also serve as a source for Rav Simlai's teaching, only it is an

addition in *M. Makkot*; see J. N. Epstein, *Mavo' le-Nosaḥ ha-Mishna*, p. 977.

9. *T.B. Sanhedrin* 81a, and it was transferred in *T.B. Makkot* to the verse 'He who doeth these things shall never be moved.'
10. *T.B. Sevu'ot* 12b; *T.P. ibid.* i, 9, p. 33b.
11. See M. Steckelmacher, 'Etwas über die leichten und schweren Gebote', *Festschrift Adolf Schwarz*, Berlin and Vienna 1917, pp. 259 ff.
12. *Sifre Deuteronomy* § 76, p. 141. On the reading 'three hundred' see below, p. 836, n. 1.
13. *M. 'Avot* iv, 2; see above, p. 269.
14. *T.P. Pe'a* i, 1, p. 15d (*ad init.*).
15. *T.B. Menaḥot* 44a; Rashi, *ad loc.*, glosses 'just a positive commandment'. See the annotations of Samuel Strashun (*RaShaSh*).
16. *Sifre Num.*, Shelaḥ, § 115, p. 126; see *T.B. Menaḥot* 43b.
17. See Y. Yadin, *Ha-Mimṣā'îm mi-Yĕmê Bar Kôkhbā bi-Mĕ'ārat hā-'Iggĕrôt* [The Finds from the Period of Bar Kokhba in the Cave of the Letters], Jerusalem 1963, pp. 190 ff; pp. 289 ff.
18. *T.P. Berakhot* i, p. 3c, according to the version of R. Solomon Sirillo, Mainz 1878.
19. See my article 'Megammot Datiyyot we-Ḥevratiyyot be-Torat ha-Ṣedaqa shel Ḥazal', *Zion*, XVI, 1951, pp. 1–27. Cf. also in *T.B. 'Avoda Zara* 5a, the dictum of R. Samuel bar Naḥmani in the name of R. Jonathan 'If any one performs but a single precept in this world, it precedes him and goes before him to the world to come'; see *ibid.* 4b and the saying of R. Joshua b. Levi. Of the man who does not fulfil a given precept properly R. Joḥanan says that 'he is buried naked', and in the Gemara 'naked' is explained to mean 'without precepts' — *T.B. Shabbat* 14a.
20. *T.B. Qiddushin* 39b; *T.B. Ḥullin* 142a.
21. *T.B. Menaḥot* 44a. In his commentary on *M. 'Avot*, Magen 'Avot, p. 20b, R. Simeon b. Ṣemaḥ Duran explains R. Nathan's teaching psychologically: 'And I say that he expressed this view only to satisfy the mind of the general public, who run to perform the precepts so that they may receive reward for them....' At any rate these remarks are appropriate in the case of Ben 'Azzai, see above, p. 807, n. 48. But 'R. Nehorai said, I would set aside every craft in the world and would teach my son nought but Torah, whose reward a man enjoys in this world and its capital in the world to come' — *M. Qiddushin* iv, 14. The concluding clause is an addition from a Baraita (see *Tosefta, ibid.*, V, 16, p. 343) and is missing in the text of the Baraita in the Palestinian and Babylonian Talmuds. Cf. J. N. Epstein, *Mavo' le-Nosaḥ ha-Mishna*, p. 977. See also *T.B. Shabbat* 49a 'The commandments protect Israel', and the same topic *T.B. Berakhot* 53b.
22. *Tanḥuma*, 'Eqev, § 2; ed. Buber, § 3; *Tanḥuma*, Teṣe, § 2; *Pesiqta Rabbati*, xxiii–xxiv, p. 121b; and, with variations, *Deut. Rabba*, vi, 2, and *ibid.* § 7.
23. The purport of this analogy is different from that of the vineyard, Matthew xx 1–16; see Strack-Billerbeck, *op. cit.*, Pt. IV, pp. 484 ff.

24. *T.P. Pe'a* i, 1, p. 15d (*ad init.*); *T.P. Qiddushin* p. 61b (*ad fin.*); see also *Tanḥuma, loc. cit.*, and *Pesiqta Rabbati, loc. cit.*
25. *T.P. Pe'a, loc. cit.*; *T.P. Qiddushin, loc. cit.*
26. *T.B. Menaḥot* 44a (*ad fin.*); see *T.B. Shabbat* 130a.
27. *T.B. Sanhedrin* 74a; see *T.P. Shevi'it* iv, 2, p. 32a, and *T.P. Sanhedrin* iii, 6, p. 21a.
28. R. Joḥanan's statement is formulated in *Tosefta Shabbat* xv, 17, ed. Zuckermandel, p. 134, as follows: 'Nothing supersedes the duty to save life except three things: idolatry, incest and murder. When does this rule apply? When there is no religious persecution. But at a time of religious persecution, a man must give his life even for the least of the commandments, as it is said: "And ye shall not profane My holy name; but I will be hallowed among the children of Israel"; and it is further stated: "The Lord hath made every thing for His own purpose." ' The two verses are missing in the Talmud; see S. Lieberman, *Tosefta ki-Fshuṭah*, Mo'ed, p. 263. The opening sentence 'Nothing supersedes... murder' is cited in *T.B. Ketubbot* 19a, where it is introduced by the formula 'for a master said'; possibly the whole passage is only an Amoraic addition to the Tosefta. See also S. Lieberman, *Tashlum Tosefta*, p. 52; and cf. H. Albeck, *Meḥqarim be-Baraita we-Tosefta*, Jerusalem 1944, p. 101.
29. In the Palestinian Talmud, *loc. cit.*, only the distinction between *bênô lĕ-bên 'aṣmô* ['individual privacy'] and *rabbîm* ['many'] is mentioned. But the example 'like Lulianus and his brother Papus, who were given water in a coloured glass (so that it should be supposed that they were drinking *yên nesekh* ['idolatrous wine']) and they would not accept it' is also an example relating to a time of religious persecution; see G. Alon, *Toledot ha-Yehudim be-Ereṣ Yisra'el*, Pt. I, p. 260. According to the Tanna R. Ishmael, however, even the duty 'to be slain rather than transgress' in the case of idolatry applies only to public worship; cf. *T.B. Sanhedrin, loc. cit.*, and *T.B. 'Avoda Zara* 27b.
30. See Rashi, *loc. cit.*, 74b, s.v. *'Āraqtā*; but in *She'iltot*, Wa'era', § 44, ed. S. K. Mirsky, Pt. III, p. 45, it is explained thus: '(If you were ordered:) Bend down and undo your shoe-strap, so that you will not be prostrating yourself before the idol, but you will be bending down to untie your shoe-strap, only those who see you will suppose that you have prostrated yourself — this subterfuge is forbidden.' See S. Lieberman, *Tosefta ki-Fshuṭah, loc. cit.*, and H. Z. Taubes, *Otzar ha-Gaonim* to *Sanhedrin*, Jerusalem 1967, pp. 428–429.
31. *Mekhilta de-R. Ishmael*, Massekhta de-Ba-ḥodesh, vi, p. 227.
32. *T.B. Shabbat* 130a; the Munich MS. reads: 'Every precept for which they did not give their lives — for example, phylacteries — they are still lax in its observance; but every precept for which they gave themselves to destruction (read להשמד instead of להשמר) — for example, idolatry — is still scrupulously observed by them.' See *Diqduqe Soferim*, p. 151a, n. *'Ayin.*
33. *Mekhilta de-R. Ishmael*, Massekhta de-Shabbeta, i, p. 343. The Sabbath, circumcision, and ritual ablution are mentioned among the observances

prohibited by Rome — *T.B. Me'ila* 17a. In *Sifre Deut.* § 76, p. 141, the author of the dictum is given as R. Simeon b. Gamaliel, but the examples are wanting.

34. *T.B. Shabbat* 130a; see A. Büchler, 'Tôlĕdôt Birkat ha-Ṭôv wĕ-ha-Mêṭîv [The History of the Benediction "Thou art good and beneficent"]', *H.P. Chajes Memorial Volume*, Vienna 1933, p. 159; G. Alon, *op. cit.*, p. 261.

35. *T.B. Giṭṭin* 54a. On the meticulous observance of the laws of the Sabbatical year by the labourers of Sepphoris see *Tosefta Shevi'it* iv, 13; and see S. Lieberman, *Tosefta ki-Fshuṭah*, Zera'im, p. 539. On the other hand *Tosefta Demai* iii, 17, refers 'to an entire town whose inhabitants eat the produce of the Sabbatical year'. Cf. the lengthy article of S. Safrai 'Miṣwat Shĕvî'ît bi-Mĕṣî'ût she-lĕ-'aḥar Ḥurban Bayit Shēnî [The Precept of the Sabbatical Year in the Circumstances prevailing after the Destruction of the Second Temple]', *Tarbiz*, XXXV (1966), pp. 304 ff, and *ibid.* p. 323. See also S. Lieberman, *Tosefta ki-Fshuṭah*, Zera'im, p. 233.

36. See *Tosefta Shabbat* i, 14: 'R. Simeon b. Eleazar said: How far ritual purity had spread among Israel...'; on the other hand see *T.P. Berakhot* iii, 6c. This has already been noted in Tosafot, *Soṭa*, 7a, s.v. *'Āmar*: 'For we find in many places that people take a strict view of a minor transgression and fear it more than a grave transgression, as for instance in *T.B. Ketubbot* 4b, where it is stated that people observed the laws of mourning, which are only Rabbinical enactments, more strictly than those connected with a menstruant, which carry the penalty of extinction...'; and in *T.B. Beṣa* 2b it is stated: 'That which is less stringent requires greater precaution' etc.; A. Aptowitzer points to the statement of Tosafot in a note to the aforementioned article of Steckelmacher, p. 261, n. 1.

37. See *T.B. Beṣa* 2b, and *ibid.* 35b: 'It is permissible to (clear away) four or five bundles because the Sabbath is stringent and people will not come to treat it lightly, but on a festival, which is less stringent and people may come to treat it lightly, it is utterly forbidden.'

38. *T.B. 'Eruvin* 21b; see the commentaries of R. Ḥananel, Rashi, and Maharsha [R. Samuel Eliezer Edels] *ad loc.*

39. *T.P. Berakhot* i, 7, p. 3b; see *T.B. Sanhedrin* xi, 6, p. 30a. For the interpretation of the Mishna *ibid.* xi, 3, cf. F. Pineles, *Darkah shel Torah*, 1861, p. 20, referred to by H. Albeck, Hashlamot, *Seder Neziqin*, p. 459. See also *Cant. Rabba* i, 2; *T.B. Berakhot* 4b, and *T.B. 'Eruvin* 21b; cf. Rashi, *ibid.* 32, s.v. *Bĕshel.*

40. *M. Sanhedrin* x, 1. R. Joḥanan knew the original Epiqoros [Epicurean, heretic] and distinguished between a Gentile and Jewish Epiqoros; see *T.B. Sanhedrin* 38b.

41. *T.P. Sanhedrin* x, 1, p. 27d. The commentaries *Pĕnê môshe* and *Qorban ha-'Ēdā* explain אהן ספרא as 'this book', but the analogy that follows is in that case unsuitable. It is also clear that there is no disagreement here between R. Eleazar and R. Joḥanan, but only a difference of terminology, namely that one Sage uses the expression 'this Scribe', a designation for the Sages commonly used by the Minim (see my article, *Tarbiz*, XXVII [1958], p. 174;

cf. Y. Baer, *Zion*, XXXI [1966], p. 136, n. 44, who misunderstood my remarks). On the other hand, R. Eleazar used a contemptuous expression that was common among Jews who were not Minim. See *T.B. Sanhedrin* 100a; and for the meaning of the analogy see *Qorban ha-ʿEda, loc. cit.*

42. *T.B. Yevamot* 20a; see *T.B. Ḥullin* 106a.

43. *T.B. Shabbat* 23a; *T.B. Sukka* 46a; *ibid.* in the name of Rav Naḥman bar Isaac, see *Diqduqe Soferim*, Shabbat, p. 43, Sukka, p. 143. Cf. L. Ginzberg, *Perushim we-Ḥiddushim bi-Yerushalmi*, Pt. I, p. 150. He notes there the comments of R. Elijah Mizraḥi on *Sefer Miṣwot Gadol*, Hilkhot Megilla, p. 272d, who writes as follows: 'It may be said that the prohibition "Thou shalt not turn aside" applies only to one who rebels against the teaching and instruction of the Sages, and does not submit to them, like the Sadducees and Boëthusians and their congeners, but not to one who accepts their injunctions yet transgresses them. In such an instance, one who eats *nĕvēlā* [animal not correctly slaughtered] to satisfy his appetite, but admits that the Lord forbade it to Israel, is flogged under Torah law and that suffices; whereas if one eats it because he refuses allegiance to Torah law, he is executed by the sword.' But this view again equates Rabbinic enactments with Torah precepts.

44. *T.B. Berakhot* 19b. The Rav Kahana mentioned here, before whom Rav bar Shava explained the dictum, was the disciple of Rava and the teacher of Ashi; see A. Hayman, *Sefer Toledot Tanna'im wa-'Amora'im*, p. 847 and p. 1039. On the question whether the prohibition 'Thou shalt not turn aside' is really a negative precept or merely a Scriptural support, see the Introduction to Maimonides' *Sefer ha-Miṣwot* ['The Book of Commandments'], Root I, and the critical comments of Naḥmanides *ad loc.*; cf. also idem, 'Hilkhot Mamrim', i, 2; and see H. P. Chajes, 'Ma'ămar Lō-Tāsûr [The Injunction 'Thou shalt not turn aside']', *Torat ha-Nevi'im*, Zolkiew 1836, pp. 10a ff.

45. See *T.P. Berakhot*, *loc. cit.*, and *T.P. Sanhedrin* xi, 6, p. 30a; *T.P. ʿAvoda Zara* ii, 8, p. 41c; in *Cant. Rabba* i, 2, 2 both 'the college students in the name of R. Joḥanan' and R. Simeon bar Va in the name of R. Joḥanan use the expression *ḥăvîvîm* ['beloved']; in the name of R. Tanḥum b. R. Ḥiyya it is reported 'The ordinances of the Elders are weightier [*ḥămûrîm*] than those of the prophets'; in *T.P. ʿAvoda Zara* the reading is 'The ordinances of the Elders is desirable [*ḥămûdîm*]' etc.; only in *Cant. Rabba* do we find 'weightier than the ordinances of the Torah and prophecy'.

46. See *M. Tohorot* iv, 11; cf. *T.B. Shabbat* 34a and *T.B. ʿEruvin* 45b. See S. Abramson, 'Tôsāfôt wĕ-Heʿārôt li-Shĕ'ēlôt û-Tĕshûvôt hā-Rambam' [Additamenta and Notes to Maimonides' Responsa], ed. J. Blau, III, p. 171.

47. *T.P. Sanhedrin* vii, 11, 25b.

48. *Tosefta Pe'a* i, 2, ed. Zuckermandel, p. 18; ed. Lieberman, p. 41. See *T.P. Pe'a* i, 2, 15d: 'and in antithesis to them there are four things for which one is punished....' See *Tosefta ki-Fshuṭah*, Zeraʿim, p. 126.

49. *T.B. ʿArakhin* 16b, 'The School of R. Ishmael taught', which corresponds to the Tosefta; R. Joḥanan said in the name of R. Jose b. Zimra: 'Whoever

speaks slander is as one who has denied the fundamental Principle [i.e. God]'; Rav Ḥisda said in the name of Mar ʿUqba: 'Whoever speaks slander is worthy of being stoned' *et al.* See *T.P. Pe'a, loc. cit.*, p. 16a: 'The generation of David were all righteous men, but because there were informers among them, they went forth to battle and fell... but in the case of the generation of Ahab, although they were idol-worshipers, yet because they did not have informers among them, they went forth to battle and conquered'; cf. *Lev. Rabba* xxvi, 2, p. 589 and the parallel passages listed there.

50. *Lev. Rabba* xxxiii, 3, ed. Margulies, pp. 760–761. A similar statement regarding a thief occurs in *Tractate Semaḥot*, ii, 9; see vv.ll. *ibid.*

51. *Lev. Rabba* xxii, 6, pp. 512–514. See the vv.ll. and nn. *ibid.*

52. Rashi and Abraham Ibn Ezra in their commentaries to Proverbs interpret *wĕ-tāfaśtî shēm 'Ĕlōhay* [usually rendered: 'and profane the name of my God'] as an oath, and the author of *Yĕfē Tō'ar* regards the oath as an intermediate link between theft and *Ḥillûl ha-Shēm.* Z. W. Einhorn (Maharzaw) explains *Ḥillûl ha-Shēm* to inhere in theft, because the thief acts as if the Heavenly Eye does not see; but undoubtedly the expositor does not intend to differentiate between theft and robbery.

53. *Tosefta Yoma* V, 6–8, ed. Zuckermandel, p. 190; ed. Lieberman, iv, 6–8, pp. 251–252; *Mekhilta de-R. Ishmael,* Massekhta de-Ba-ḥodesh, vii, p. 228, and the other parallel passages indicated by S. Lieberman in *Tosefta ki-Fshuṭah,* Moʿed, p. 824; see *ibid.* on the reading 'If the name of Heaven was profaned by one presumptuously'; cf. below, n. 57.

54. See *Lev. Rabba, loc. cit.*, in the name of R. Eleazar or R. Ḥanina; in *T.P. Nedarim* iii, 14, p. 38b we read: 'R. Yudah bar Pazzi said: '*Ḥillul ha-Shem* is the gravest (sin) of them all. This is the meaning of the verse....' On the central position of the idea of *Qiddush ha-Shem* and *Ḥillul ha-Shem* in the prophecy of Ezekiel see Y. Kaufmann, *Toledot ha-'Emuna ha-Yisra'elit,* pp. 560 ff. In *Midrash Tehillim* xxvii, 5, ed. Buber, p. 226, we find: 'Because the Holy One, blessed be He, overlooked idolatry, incest, and murder in time of danger'. But at a time of danger due to persecution He did not overlook them.' However, according to the MS. used by Buber for his edition the reading should be 'at a time when there is no danger'; see *ibid.*, n. 43.

55. *T.B. Qiddushin* 40a. It appears that the words attributed to King David in the homily of Rav Judah transmitted in the name of Rav, 'Shall a king like me be slain by his son? Rather let me [literally, 'he', i.e. David] worship idols than that the name of Heaven should be profaned publicly' (*T.B. Sanhedrin* 107a), also refer to clandestine idolatry, for the public worship of idols certainly involves *Ḥillul ha-Shem.* However, in the commentary ascribed to Rashi *ad loc.*, s.v. *Mûṭāv* [Rather], it is stated 'and I alone shall profane the Name, but not the entire people'. See also *Yad Rama* to *Sanhedrin ad loc.*, and the Maharsha *ad loc.*

56. *T.B. Moʿed Qaṭan* 17a, according to the Munich MS.; see *Diqduqe Soferim,* p. 54; cf. also my book *Baʿălê ha-Tôsāfôt* [The Tosafists], p. 552.

57. *M. 'Avot* iv, 4. With regard to an unwitting offender and a wanton transgressor see Maimonides, *Pērûsh ha-Mishnā* [Commentary on the Mishna], and the commentary on *'Avot* in *Maḥzor Vitry*, p. 523, where the first interpretation is that of Rashbam [R. Samuel b. Me'ir]. See also the commentary of R. Isaac b. R. Solomon of Toledo, Jerusalem 1965, p. 134; R. Simeon b. Ṣemaḥ Duran, *Magen 'Avot*, i, 1; cf. above, n. 53.
58. This is also the interpretation given in *Maḥzor Vitry*, *loc. cit.*; see also the commentary ascribed to Rashi, and the commentary of R. Jonah, who limited *Ḥillul ha-Shem* in secret to transgressions that inherently consitute *Ḥillul ha-Shem*, such as idolatry and false swearing.
59. *Tosefta Yoma* v, 12, ed. Zukermandel, p. 191; ed. Lieberman, iv, 12, p. 253; *T.B. ibid.*, 86b, and Rashi *ad loc.*, s.v. *Měfarsěmîn*. In *Midrash Tehillim* lii, 3, p. 284, we read: 'And why does the Holy One, blessed be He, set an evil way before him? In order to expose his deeds to the world, for if nought befalls him on account of his transgressions, people will rail against the Divine justice'. See S. Lieberman, *Tosefta ki-Fshuṭah*, Mo'ed, pp. 827–828. See the statements of R. Ḥanina and of R. Levi in the name of Resh Laqish in *T.P. Yevamot* viii, 3, p. 9c.
60. *T.B. Ḥagiga* 16a. Against the view of R. Isaac an objection was raised *ibid.* by reference to the Baraita of R. Il'ai the Elder; so, too, in *T.B. Mo'ed* 17a, according to the version of the Munich MS., the question is asked 'But is this so? For R. Isaac said' etc.; see *Diqduqe Soferim*, *ibid.*, p. 54. Rav Joseph's dictum recalls, by its formulation, the exposition of R. Joḥanan b. Zakkai about the thief who is more iniquitous than the robber, because he did not give as much honour to his Creator as to the servant; see above, p. 371. Cf. Matthew xxiii 5.
61. *Ecclesiastes Rabba* iv, 1. Since R. Benjamin is mentioned after R. Ḥanina, it appears that the reference is to R. Benjamin bar Japhet or R. Benjamin bar Levi. See *Pesiqta Rabbati* 111b: 'What is the meaning of the verse "Thou shalt not take the name of the Lord thy God in vain"? — That you should not wear phylacteries, and don your *Tallit*, and go and commit transgressions.' Cf. also the story cited *ibid.* and in *Midrash Aggada*, ed. Buber, p. 152.
62. See above, p. 351.
63. *T.P. Bava Qamma* iv, 3, p. 4b. In *Tosefta Bava Qamma*, x, 15, ed. Zuckermandel, p. 368 we read: 'Robbing a Gentile is a graver sin than robbing a Jew, on account of *Ḥillul ha-Shem*.' See the commentary of Israel Levy on *T.P. Bava Qamma*, p. 114.
64. *T.B. Bava Qamma* 113a, according to MS. ה'. See *Diqduqe Soferim*, p. 277, n. 3; the printed editions read: 'on account of *Qiddush ha-Shem*'.
65. *T.P. Bava Meṣi'a* ii, 5, p. 8c; see *Deut. Rabba* iii, §3. The formula 'Blessed be the God of the Jews' occurs also in *T.P. Pe'a* iii, 8, p. 17d, uttered by Gentiles in Ashkelon.
66. *T.P. Sevi'it* iv, 2, p. 35b. In 'Qonderos Aḥaron [Final Addendum]' — see L. Ginzberg, *Śeride Yerushalmi*, p. 330 — we read: מאן מודע לך... אי יהודאי

או ארמאי 'Who would tell you... whether one is a Jew or an Aramaean', but the text has not accurately been copied. In *Yalquṭ loc. cit.*, the text has: או ארמאי ארמאי 'or if one is an Aramaean, let one be an Aramaean'. It appears to me that we should read: אי יהודאי יהודאי אי ארמאי ארמאי 'If one is a Jew, let one be a Jew; if one is an Aramaean, let one be an Aramaean'.

67. *T.P. Qiddushin* iv, 1, p. 65b (*ad fin.*).
68. *T.B. Yoma* 86a, and Rashi *ad loc.*, s.v. *Wĕ-lā' Yāhivnā'* [And I do not give]. R. Ḥananel, *ad loc.*, reads: רב אמר: כגון אנא, אי שקילנא מבי טבחא בישרא באתרא דלא תבעי, דאתו למימר: אנא חזיתיה לרב דשקיל בישרא בלא דמי 'Rav said: Take me, for instance: If I took meat from a butcher in a place where they do not go out to collect payment, people may say: I saw Rav taking meat without money'. It is obvious that he did not have the reading: אמר אביי: לא שנו 'Abbay said: This was taught only', nor is it found in the Munich MS. See *Diqduqe Soferim*, p. 293.
69. *T.B. Yoma, ibid.*, according to the reading of the MSS.; see *Diqduqe Soferim, ibid.* Cf. also *Yalquṭ Makhiri* on Isaiah, p. 172. The first part of the verse in Ezekiel reads: 'And when they came unto the nations, whither they came *they profaned My holy name*'.
70. *Mekhilta de-R. Ishmael*, Massekhta de-Shira, iii, p. 128; see the vv.ll. to line 16.
71. *Sifra*, Qedoshim, x, 7–8, 92d; *Sifre Deuteronomy*, § 40, p. 90.
71a. See *De Decalogo* § 19, § 154, and *De Special. Leg.*, I, § 1.
72. *Philo, Foundations of Religious Philosophy in Judaism, Christianity and Islam*[2], Cambridge (Mass.) 1948, II, p. 201.
73. J. Wohlgemuth, *Das jüd. Religionsgesetz in jüd. Beleuchtung*, II, 1919, p. 23, did not differentiate between the meanings of the dicta, but speaks in general terms of the view that the Decalogue enshrines all the precepts. See *ibid.* n. 1.
74. *M. Tamid* v, 1; see H. Albeck, Hashlamot to *Seder Qodashim*, p. 428.
75. *T.P. Berakhot* i, 5, p. 3c. See *Sifre Deut.* § 34 ' "And thou shalt teach them diligently" — these words are to be diligently repeated, but not the Ten Commandments', i.e. they are not to be recited every day. See *ibid.* § 35 ' "And thou shalt bind them" — these words are to be bound, but not the Ten Commandments', i.e. they are not to be included in the Scriptural sections of the phylacteries, but actually we know that the members of the Qumran sect incorporated the Decalogue in their phylacteries; cf. A. M. Habermann, "ʿAl ha-Tĕfillîn bi-Yĕmê Qedem' [On Phylacteries in Antiquity], *Eretz-Israel*, Book III, 1954, pp. 174 ff. Hieronymus also mentions the Decalogue in phylacteries in his commentary on Matthew xxiii 6; PL 26, 167. See now Y. Yadin, 'Tefillin shel Rosh mi-Qumran [The Head Phylacteries from Qumran], *Eretz-Israel*, Book IX, 1969, pp. 29 ff.
76. See above, p. 295; cf. J. M. Guttmann, 'Beḥinat ha-Miṣwot', p. 60, appendix to *Jahresbericht d. jüd. Theol. Seminars Breslau*, 1928.
77. Ed. H. Albeck, p. 8; see *ibid.* n. 16, where he refers to *Num. Rabba* xiii, § 16; xviii, § 21.

78. *Qoveṣ Ma'aśê Yĕdê Gĕ'ônîm Qadmônîm*, ed. Judah Rosenberg, Berlin 1856, pp. 39–53; see Judah Al-Barceloni's commentary on *Sefer Yeṣira*, p. 278.
79. *T.B. Berakhot* 5a. Rashi, *ad loc.*, s.v. *Ze miqrā'*, comments 'The Pentateuch, for it is a religious duty to read the Torah (in public).' See *Diqduqe Soferim*, Berakhot, p. 12, and *ibid.* n. *Rêsh* and n. *Shîn.*
80. *T.B. Shabbat* 87a, according to the text of the Munich MS.; see *Diqduqe Soferim*, *ibid.*, p. 184.
81. In *T.P. Ta'anit* iv, 8, p. 68c, the syllogism is cited in the following version: 'If now in the case of the passover sacrifice, which is but a single commandment, it is stated "no uncircumcised person shall eat thereof", how much more so (does the principle apply to) the Torah in which all the commandments are included'. It is clear that 'the Torah' is used here in the sense of 'the tables of the covenant' (and the phrasing in the second half of the dictum is anachronistic, or that the entire syllogism was transferred here from another context) or 'the tables of stone', and all the commandments included therein are the Ten Commandments. In *Exod. Rabba*, xix, § 3, the text reads: 'Can the Israelites, who served idols, receive the Torah?' A version most suited to the theme is found *ibid.*, xlvi, § 3: 'If now in the case of the passover offering, which is a sacrifice of a minor grade, it is stated "there shall no alien eat thereof", should the tables, which are the work of God, be used by idolaters?' etc. See also *Tanḥuma*, Tiśśa', § 30, where the syllogism is ascribed to R. Ishmael; cf. *T.P. loc. cit.* Rabbi M. Kasher, *Torah Shlemah*, XVI, pp. 203 ff, treats at length of the Decalogue and the 613 precepts without differentiating between the dicta of the Sages, on the one hand, and the observations of R. Saadia Gaon and those indebted to him, on the other; and he interpolated the views of the later scholars into those of the earlier authorities. Also J. M. Guttmann, *Beḥinat ha-Miṣwot*, p. 58, finds in *T.B. Yevamot* 47b and in *T.P. Ta'anit*, *loc. cit.*, 'that in the Decalogue all the precepts are included'. But actually comparison with *Num. Rabba* xiii, 15–16, xviii, 21, points up the difference between the homilies of the Amoraim and the teaching of the school of R. Moses ha-Darshan.
82. *Tractate Sheqalim*, ed. A. Sopher, New York 1954, p. 71.
83. See my observations in *Kirjath Sepher*, XXXI, p. 326.
84. On the differences between the two interpretations see the Introduction to *'Arugat ha-Bośem*, Pt. IV, p. 54, n. 97. With regard to the interpretation of the *T.P.* version, see *ibid.*, Pt. I, p. 223: 'Its signs, that means the crownlets on the letters'. Cf. also Pt. IV, p. 208, the 'Hôsāfôt wĕ-Tiqqûnîm' (Addenda and Corrigenda) to Pt. II, p. 55.
85. See *Sifre Num.* § 143, p. 191: 'Simeon b. 'Azzai said, Come and see: in respect of all the sacrifices of the Torah... to teach thee that He neither eats nor drinks; only He commanded and His will was fulfilled.' In *T.B. Menaḥot* 110a a different orientation is given to the words; see Rashi, *ad loc.*, s.v. *Li-rĕṣônĕkhem.*
86. *M. Makkot* iii, 16; it has also been added at the end of *M. 'Avot* VI (*Pereq*

Qinyan Tora, 'Chapter of the Acquisition of the Law') and at the end of *'Avot de-R. Nathan*. See J. N. Epstein, *Mavo' le-Nosaḥ ha-Mishna*, p. 977.

87. In MSS. and old editions his name is given as R. Ḥanina; see *Diqduqe Soferim* to *Makkot*, p. 45.

88. See Rashi, *T.B. Makkot* 23b, s.v. *Lĕzakkôt*: '...For there was no need to enjoin many precepts and many prohibitions in regard to abominable creatures and animals not properly slaughtered, which inspire loathing in every person; the purpose was therefore that they (the Israelites) should receive reward for abstaining from them.' R. Judah b. R. Kalonymos in *Sēfer Yiḥûsê Tanna'im wa-'Åmôrā'îm*, ed. R. J. L. Maimon, Jerusalem 1963, p. 410, cites Rashi's comment in the form 'All explain', and he continues 'It seems to me that "the making worthy" refers to the wide range of the Torah... and the multiplicity of precepts is also a vouchsafement of merit....'

89. This recension is found in a fragment of the Palestinian Talmud included in the Genizah writings published by S. Wieder, *Tarbiz*, XVII (1946), p. 135; it is omitted in the printed editions. See *Lev. Rabba* xxxi, 8, ed. M. Margulies, p. 727, and S. Lieberman's note *ibid.*, p. 880.

90. *Gen. Rabba* xliv, 1, pp. 424–425, and the parallels cited *ibid.* In *Tanḥuma*, Tazria', § 5, this concept is already ascribed to R. Akiba, who replied *ibid.* to Turnus Rufus: 'As for your question: Why is not (the child) born circumcised? — it is because the Holy One, blessed be He, gave the precepts to Israel only in order to refine them thereby.' It is possible that R. Akiba said this only relative to circumcision, and that it was formulated in the late Midrash in Rav's dictum as a general principle. At any rate an educational-ethical reason is given here for the precept of circumcision and not as Isaac Heinemann explains it in *Ṭa'ămê ha-Miṣwôt* [The Reasons of the Precepts], Jerusalem 1942, Pt. I, p. 23. On the version of *Midrash Samuel* iv, 1, p. 53, see A. Büchler, *Studies in Sin and Atonement*, 1928, pp. 339 ff; cf. above, p. 392.

91. *T.B. Sanhedrin* 107a; see *Yalquṭ Makhiri*, Psalms, xvii, 11, pp. 48a–b, where the text reads: ועבידנא עבידת בהדך [the substitution of עבידת 'work' for מילתא 'thing' does not change the meaning], and at the end: ... ואי זממא דפרזלא... ['If only an iron bridle...'].

92. *Mekhilta de-R. Ishmael*, Massekhta de-Shabbeta, i, p. 341.

93. *Sifre Numbers* § 115, p. 127.

94. *Mekhilta de-R. Ishmael*, Massekhta de-Kaspa, § 20, p. 320.

95. *Sifra*, Qedoshim (*ad init.*), 86c. See *T.P. Yevamot* v, 4, p. 3d; *Lev. Rabba* xxiv, 6, p. 559.

96. *Lev. Rabba* xxii, 8, p. 517; see *ibid.* n. 5, which refers to Maimonides' observations in *Guide of the Perplexed*, Pt. III, xxxii and xlvi.

97. *Tosefta Berakhot* vii, 9, ed. Zuckermandel, p. 15; S. Lieberman, *ibid.*, vi, 9, p. 36. See *T.P. Berakhot* ix, 4, 14a; *T.B. Pesaḥim* 7b.

98. *Genesis* ii 1–3; see Kaufmann, *Toledot ha-'Emuna ha-Yisre'elit*, I, Book II, p. 300.

99. See *Mekhilta de-R. Ishmael*, Massekhta de-Shabbeta, i, pp. 340–341; *ibid.*,

Mishpaṭim, iv, pp. 263–264; *Tosefta Shabbat* xv (xvi), 16–17, ed. Zuckermandel, p. 134. Cf. Lieberman, *Tosefta ki-Fshuṭah*, Mo'ed, p. 261.

1. See G. Scholem, 'Tradition und Neuschöpfing im Ritus der Kabbalisten', *Eranos Jahrbuch*, XIX, 1950, included in his work *Zur Kabbala und ihrer Symbolik*, Zürich 1960, pp. 159 ff. Cf. *ibid.*, pp. 163–164; also I. Tishby, *Mishnat ha-Zohar*, II, pp. 435 ff.
2. *T.B. Shabbat* 22a. It is indeed stated in the prayer first mentioned in *Tractate Soferim* xx 'These lights are sacred, and we are not permitted to make profane use of them', but this 'sanctity' means appointed for the performance of a precept and not for any other use.
3. *T.B. Giṭṭin* 45b; see *T.P. ibid.* iv, 6, p. 46a.
4. *T.B. Giṭṭin* 54b; see Maimonides, 'Hilkhot Tefillin [Laws of Phylacteries]', i, 15.
5. *Pesiqta de-R. Kahana* xxviii, pp. 427, 429; see above, p. 373. Even Philo, who maintained the idea of spiritual worship, remained faithful to the Temple and the sacrifices; see V. Nikiprowetzky, 'Spiritualisation et Culte Sacrificiel chez Philon d'Alexandrie', *Semitica*, XVII, 1967, pp. 97 ff.
6. *M. Menaḥot* v, 6; see *T.B. ibid.* 65a; *T.B. Sukka* 37b; cf. *Lev. Rabba* xxviii, 5, p. 659, where R. Simon reports R. Joḥanan's statement in the name of R. Joshua b. Levi.
7. *T.B. Menaḥot* 39a; the subject itself is taught in a Baraita, which begins with *tĕnā'* ['one taught'], and which is apparently later than the preceding Baraita, cited in the name of Rabbi. On Baraitot of this kind see H. Albeck, *Meḥqārîm bĕ-Bāraitā' wĕ-Tôseftā'* [Studies in Baraita and Tosefta], 1944, pp. 55 ff; regarding the seven heavens see above, p. 237.
8. *Mekhilta de-R. Ishmael*, Massekhta de-Ba-ḥodesh, xi, p. 244, and the parallels cited *ibid.*, n. 13. Similarly we find 'R. Joshua b. Levi said: Why are courts symbolically connected by *'ērûv* [a ritual act whereby community or continuity of residence is established]? For the sake of peace' — *T.P. 'Eruvin* vii, 9, p. 24c; see the Mishna *ibid.*, vii, 9, and cf. S. Lieberman, *Hayerushalmi Kiphshuto*, p. 387, and H. Albeck, Seder Mo'ed, Hashlamot, p. 439.
9. *Tosefta Bava Qamma* vii, 2, p. 357; *T.B. ibid.* 79b.
10. See below, p. 843, n. 59.
11. *Mekhilta de-R. Ishmael*, Massekhta di-Neziqin, xii, p. 292; and preceding this, *ibid.* p. 291, the statement of R. Me'ir, which is cited below.
12. *Tosefta Bava Qamma* vii, 2, p. 357.
13. See J. M. Guttmann, *Beḥinat Qiyyum ha-Miṣwot*, pp. 24 ff.
14. *Mekhilta de-R. Ishmael*, Massekhta di-Neziqin, ii, p. 253; there is another version of this homily in *Tosefta Bava Qamma, loc. cit.*, and in *T.B. Qiddushin* 22b; a further recension is found in *T.P. Qiddushin* i, 1, p. 56d. See my article 'Hilkhot 'Avadim' etc., *Zion*, XXV (1960), pp. 145–146.
15. *M. Soṭa* i, 6–7; see *Tosefta, ibid.*, iii, 1 ff, p. 293; J. N. Epstein, *Mĕvô'ôt lĕ-Sifrût ha-Tanna'im* [Introductions to Tannaitic Literature], p. 407.
16. *T.B. Soṭa* 46a (*ad fin.*); R. Joḥanan b. Saul is mentioned in *T.B. 'Eruvin*

81a, but in the MS. *ibid.*, the reading is: 'R. Menaḥem b. Saul said in the name of Rabbi'. See *Diqduqe Soferim*, *ibid.*, p. 318.

17. See *Sifra*, Meṣora', v, 43a; *Sifre Deut.* § 275; and *T.B. 'Arakhin* 15a.
18. *T.B. Yoma* 44a; see *ibid.* the statement of R. Eleazar that incense atones, and the question of the Gemara 'Does incense make atonement?' See Tosafot Yeshanim, s.v. *Yāvô' dāvār she-ba-ḥăshay* [Let that which is performed in secret].
19. *T.P. Yoma* vii, 5, p. 44b; see *T.B. Zevaḥim* 88b, where the author of the dictum is given as R. Inyani bar Sason, and R. Ḥanina is the one who explains how the principle of measure for measure applies; it is then pointed out that one interpretation of the atonement by slander contradicts the other, and the explanation is given: 'The one refers to clandestine slander — in that case incense, which is offered up secretly, atones; the other refers to public [*bĕ-qôl*] slander — in that case the sound [*qôl*] of the bells makes atonement for it' (Rashi *ibid.*).
20. *T.P. Sheqalim* i, 1, p. 45d (*ad fin.*).
21. See above, p. 378.
22. *Pesiqta de-R. Kahana*, Sec. Pārā, ed. Buber, 40b; the dictum is cited, with certain changes, in the name of R. Aibu in ed. Mandelbaum, I, p. 74.
23. *Mekhilta de-R. Ishmael*, Massekhta di-Neziqin, xiv, p. 296.
24. See *T.P. Giṭṭin* v, 1, p. 46c: 'Whence does R. Akiba deduce the rule that damages must be paid out of the best land? It is not a Torah law; it is an enactment'; cf. *T.B. ibid.* 48b.
25. See *T.P. Giṭṭin*, *loc. cit.*; *T.B. ibid.* 50a.
26. *M. Bava Meṣia'* ix, 13; *T.B. ibid.* 115a (in the text I have cited the Baraita according to the Munich MS.; see *Diqduqe Soferim*, *ibid.*, p. 342; cf. also *T.B. Sanhedrin* 21a and *Diqduqe Soferim*, *ibid.*, p. 36, n. 3). In the *Tosefta*, *ibid.*, x, 10, p. 394, R. Simeon's statement is given as follows: 'He (the creditor) may not take a pledge from a poor (widow); from a rich (widow) he may take (a pledge) and not return it, so that he should not be constantly visiting her and thus bring her into disrepute'; the same version is also found in *T.P. ibid.* ix, 16, p. 12b, except that the names of the Tannaim are interchanged, R. Me'ir taking the place of R. Simeon. But there is no difference between the text of the Tosefta, the Palestinian Talmud, and the Babylonian Talmud in respect of the clause 'from a rich (widow) he may take (a pledge), and not return it'. The meaning is 'which he does not return', and the sentence 'so that he should not be constantly' etc. gives the reason for 'He may not take a pledge from a poor (widow)'; a similar interpretation is advanced by R. Joshua Benveniste in *Śede Yehoshua'*'. But later commentators enter into far-fetched finesses; see I. H. Daiches, *Netivot Yerushalayim*, Bava Meṣia', p. 102; cf. *Sifre Deuteronomy*, § 281.
27. *T.B. Bava Meṣia'*, *loc. cit.*, according to MS. ח׳, which differs in several details from the printed edition and from MS. מ׳; see *Diqduqe Soferim*, p. 342, and the vv.ll. in *T.B. Sanhedrin* 21a.

28. *T.P. Yevamot* viii, 3, p. 9c; *T.B. ibid.*, 76b.
29. *T.B. ibid.*, 77a according to the Munich MS.; In *Sifre Deut.*, § 241, this homily is cited in the name of 'the Sages', and in *Midrash Tannaim*, ed. Hoffmann, p. 145, in the name of R. Ishmael.
30. *M. Yevamot*, *ibid.*; see *T.B. ibid.*, 77b.
31. See above, p. 98. In all the sources the story is given anonymously, and only in the Cambridge MS. of the *Tanḥuma* do we find: 'R. Zera in the name of R. Eleazar b. Pedat said: A certain Gentile....' See my article 'Śeride Tanḥuma Yelammedenu', *Qoveṣ ʿal Yad*, vi, p. 43.
32. *Tosefta Para* iii, 8, p. 632.
33. *Ibid.* iv, 7; *Sifre Num.* § 123, p. 151, and see Horovitz's notes *ibid.*, n. 13.
34. See *Sifre ibid.*; in *T.B. Menaḥot* 27a the ordinances of the Mishna *ibid.*, iii, 6, 'The three sprinklings (of the blood) of the [red] heifer can each impair the validity of the others. The seven sprinklings between the bars... can each impair the validity of the others' are provided with a Scriptural basis in the word *ḥuqqa* ['statute']. Horovitz's explanation (*Sifre Zuṭa*, p. 305, n. 19) that the difficult dictum ' "an everlasting statute" — they sprinkle from the one on account of the other', refers to 'the Haggadic homily that the heifer should come and atone for itself, that is to say, for the sin of the (golden) calf' (see above, p. 373) seems improbable. See J. N. Epstein, *Tarbiz*, I, p. 60, n. 26. I was privileged to obtain the correct interpretation from S. Lieberman in his letter to me of 26.1.1969: 'We sprinkle from this one' (from this 'everlasting statute' [Num. xix 10] from this heifer) 'only on account of this' — on account of 'this' "everlasting statute" ' mentioned below (xix 21), which follows immediately upon the verse 'But the man that shall be unclean, and shall not purify himself, that soul shall be cut off from the midst of the assembly, because he hath defiled the sanctuary of the Lord...', that is to say, the sprinkling was not an end in itself; see *Sifre*, § 189, p. 167, and *ibid.*, § 125, p. 160.
35. *Mekhilta de-R. Simeon b. Yoḥai*, p. 133; but see *Mekhilta de-R. Ishmael*, Massekhta de-Vayissaʿ, i, p. 157: ' "And wilt give ear to His commandments" — these are the decrees; "and keep all His statutes" — these are the Halakhot.' Targum Onkelos, to Exodus xii 43 also renders 'This is the statute of the passover' by 'This is *gĕzērat* ['decree of'] the passover'; but *ibid.* xiii 10, 'And thou shalt keep this statute' is translated 'and thou shalt keep this *qĕyāmā* ['law', 'covenant']'. So, too, in Num. xix 2 'This is the statute of the law' is rendered 'This is the decree [*gĕzērat*] of the law'; but *ibid.* 'for a statute for ever' is translated 'a *qĕyām* for ever'. Additional examples will be found in S. B. Sheftel, *Bĕʾûrê Onqelos* [Annotations to Onkelos], p. 85, but the distinctions he draws are far-fetched. A general injunction is termed *gĕzērā* ['decree'] and also *pisqê Bêt Dîn* [decisions of the court] (*M. Moʿed Qaṭan* iii, 3). See H. Albeck, 'Hashlamot' to *Seder Qodashim*, p. 403.
36. See S. Lieberman, *Hellenism in Jewish Palestine*, pp. 159 ff, and pp. 164 ff.
37. See the dictum of R. Akiba, *Tosefta Para* iii, 3, p. 631, and Lieberman, *loc cit.*, p. 274, n. 21.

38. See Yitzhak Baer, 'Ha-Mishna we-ha-Historiyya', *Molad*, Nos. 179–180, p. 317, and *ibid.*, n. 21. It is true that the doubts that I have raised in the text regarding the authenticity of R. Joḥanan b. Zakkai's dictum nullify the value of the tradition as evidence of the separation of the Halakha from myth for the period of this Tanna, as is pointed out by G. Scholem, 'Kabbala u. Mythus', *Eranos Jahrbuch*, and now in his book *Zur Kabbala u. ihrer Symbolik*, 1960, p. 127. But, as I have stated, there is nothing even in the Tannaitic sources treating of the red heifer that points to such a connection.

39. *Pesiqta de-R. Kahana*, ed. Mandelbaum, pp. 71–72, and see vv.ll. *ibid.*; *Tanḥuma*, Ḥuqqat 7, ed. Buber, *ibid.* § 23.

40. See *Sifre*, Ki Teṣe', § 234; *T.B. Menaḥot* 42b. Apparently R. Levi interpreted 'My statutes' as in the *Sifra*, Aḥare, ix, 85d: ' "My statutes" — these are the expositions'. The expression 'the evil inclination criticizes them' in R. Levi's saying occurs in a Baraita: ' "Mine ordinances shall ye do" — these are the laws written in the Torah that, had they not been written, reason would have required us to write them, such as the laws of robbery and incest... "and My statutes shall ye keep" — these are the laws ordained in the Torah that the evil inclination criticizes and the nations of the world criticize, like (the prohibition of) eating pig, and of wearing mingled stuff, the (ceremony of) taking off the levir's shoe, (the rite of) the purification of the leper, and (the ritual of) the scapegoat, which the evil inclination criticizes and the nations of the world criticize. Hence Scripture declares "I am the Lord", I have ordained them; you have no right to criticize them.' This Baraita which emanates from the School of R. Ishmael (*Sifra*, Aḥare, xiii, 5, 86a, known as the 'Mekhilta de-ʿArayot'; see D. Hoffmann, *Le-Ḥeqer Midreshe ha-Tanna'im*, Messilot le-Torah ha-Tanna'im, ed. A. Z. Rabinovitz, Tel-Aviv 1928, pp. 30–31; J. N. Epstein, *Mevo'ot le-Sifrut ha-Tanna'im*, p. 640. The text of the Baraita is that of the Rome MS. 66, ed. L. Finkelstein, New York 1957, p. 373) does not distinguish between laws that the evil inclination cavils at and those that are criticized by the nations of the world, but identifies the two kinds. Accordingly there is included in 'statutes' all that does not belong to the category of 'a law that, had it not been written, reason would have required us to write it', and not specifically ordinances to which the word 'statute' is applied by Scripture. It is noteworthy that R. Eleazar b. Azariah included the wearing of mingled stuff and the eating of pig, jointly with incest, among the things concerning which a man says 'I have no desire for them', and he declares: 'Whence do we learn that a man should not say: I have no desire to wear mingled stuff... but (he should say,) I do desire, but what can I do since my Father in heaven has prohibited [*gazar*] it to me' (*Sifra*, Qedoshim [*ad fin.*], 93d). It is quite clear that R. Levi, whose teaching we have cited in the text, was not acquainted with this Baraita, which was known in Babylonia, but apparently not in Eretz-Israel (see *T.B. Yoma* 67b; cf. *Diqduqe Soferim*, *ibid.*, p. 189, n. *Shîn*). The passage 'Lest you say these are absurd rites, Scripture comes to teach us "I am the Lord", I the Lord

have decreed it, and you have no right to question these laws' was, it seems, interpolated from another Baraita, which is cited in the Talmud earlier with reference to the scapegoat: 'Lest you say it is an absurd rite, Scripture comes to teach us "I am the Lord", I have decreed it and you have no right to question these laws'. In the Baraita preceding the one we have cited, the verse 'neither shall ye walk in their statutes' is expounded thus: "that you shall not follow their observances'. Among those who define the nature of the observances are R. Me'ir and R. Judah b. Bathyra, and in the continuation of the Baraita it is stated: 'And lest you say: Are there statutes for them but not for us? Therefore Scripture teaches: "Mine ordinances shall ye do, and My statutes shall ye keep" ' etc. But the evil inclination is still able to disparage and say: Theirs is superior to ours; hence Scripture teaches: "Observe therefore and do them; for this is your wisdom and your understanding" etc.' (*Sifra*, *ibid.*, 9, in accordance with the aforementioned MSS.). It appears that the conclusion agrees with R. Judah's view. While the Sages rule that the ordinance requires beheading to be performed with a sword 'as the government does' (*M. Sanhedrin* vii, 3), R. Judah states that beheading is done with an axe. To the argument of the Sages 'There is no more repulsive death than this', he replied 'Because it is said: "neither shall ye walk in their statutes' (*Tosefta*, *ibid.*, ix, 11). In the Babylonian Talmud (*ibid.* 52b) the ruling of the Sages is justified with the argument 'Sincc it is written in the Torah, we do not learn this from them', and we find allusions to beheading with a sword; but see *T.B. ʿAvoda Zara* 11a and *Tosafot ibid.*, s.v. *Wĕ-'î* [And if]. Possibly R. Levi was influenced by the conclusion of this Baraita.

41. *Pesiqta de-R. Kahana*, Para 'Adumma, ed. Mandelbaum, pp. 54–55; *Tanḥuma*, Ḥuqqat, § 3; ed. Buber, *ibid.*, § 4; see *Midrash ha-Gadol*, Numbers, ed. Z. M. Rabinovitz, Jerusalem 1967, p. 323, where the passage from the *Pesiqta* is preceded by the aforementioned passage from *T.B. Nidda* and is followed by the refrain 'Who did so? Who decreed so?' etc.
42. *Pesiqta de-R. Kahana, loc. cit.*, p. 73; see *Pesiqta Rabbati* 64b, and *ibid.*, 54b. The motif of the story recalls the words of Rav Judah in the name of Rav concerning R. Akiba in *T.B. Menaḥot* 29b; cf. also *T.B. Giṭṭin* 6b, and above, p. 267.
43. This dictum was attributed in error by W. Bacher, as well as others, to R. Jose b. R. Ḥanina (*Agada der Pal. Amoräer*, I, p. 435 n. 2, II, p. 225, n. 1). Actually this reading is found in *Tanḥuma*, Ḥuqqat § 8; ed. Buber, § 24; but as Buber observes *ibid.*, n. 240, in the excellent Rome MS. the names appear as in *Pesiqta de-R. Kahana*, ed. Buber, 39a. In ed. Mandelbaum, p. 72, we read: 'Lulianus bar Tiberius in the name of R. Isaac Qatriqi and R. Azariah — others say, R. Isaac and R. Jose bar Ḥanina — the Holy One, blessed be He, said to him...' The continuation is the same as in the text; I have chosen the version with which most MSS. agree; see also *Pesiqta Rabbati* 64a, and the Parma MS. 1240. There, too, the text reads: 'R. Luliani bar Tiburi... and R. Jose berabbi Ḥanina'. In *Yalquṭ Shimʿoni*, *editio princeps*, § 759, we read:

' "That they bring thee" — the Holy One, blessed be He, said: Moses, to you I reveal... "and his eye seeth every precious thing" — this refers to R. Akiba. "That they bring thee" — R. Jose bar Ḥanina said: There is a hint....' In regard to the interpretation of the word *qaṭrîqî*, see my article 'Lāshôn wĕ-ʿInyān [Expression and Theme]', *Lĕšonénu*, XXXII (1968), pp. 122–124.

44. *T.B. Pesaḥim*, 119a; see *Diqduqe Soferim*, p. 379, nn. *Hĕ-Wāw*, and the commentary of Rashbam *ad loc.*
45. *'Avot de-R. Nathan*, Version I, vi; Version II, xii.
46. *Pesiqta de-R. Kahana*, ed. Mandelbaum, p. 72. Although it is possible to interpret R. Aḥa's statement in the same way as we interpreted that of R. Ṭarfon, yet R. Ḥuna's homily and the context show that it was regarded as referring to the reasons for the precepts.
47. *T.B. Sanhedrin* 21b. It is reported that R. Elijah, the Vilna Gaon, wished to ascribe a similar view to R. Ishmael, who said 'How wise are the words of the Sages, who ruled: One should not read by lamplight' (*M. Shabbat* i, 3), and in the Mishna the reason is not explained, whereas in the Baraita it is (*T.B. Shabbat* xii b). See the annotations of H. P. Chajes to Shabbat, *ibid.*, who refers to *T.P. ibid.*, p. 3b, where R. Ishmael declares 'Wise are the words of the Sages, who said, Lest he forget and tilt (the lamp).' This apart, R. Ishmael uses this expression also in *Tosefta Kelim*, Third Gate, i, 2–3, as has been pointed out by S. Lieberman, *Tosefta ki-Fshuṭah*, Moʿed, p. 11.
48. *Mekhilta de-R. Ishmael*, Massekhta de-Shira, iii, p. 127, and the parallels noted *ibid.*, n. 6. See also *Seder Eliahu Rabba*, xxvii, p. 143; and cf. A. Marmorstein, 'The Imitation of God in the Haggadah', *Studies in Jewish Theology*, 1950, pp. 106 ff; H. Kosmala, 'Nachfolge und Nachahmung Gottes', *Annual of the Swedish Theological Institute*, III (1964), pp. 65 ff.
49. *T.P. Berakhot* v, 3; *ibid. Megilla* iv, 10, p. 75c.
50. *M. Berakhot* v, 3; *M. Megilla* iv, 10.
51. *T.P. loc. cit.*; *T.B. Berakhot* 33b.
52. See J. N. Epstein, *Mavo' le-Nosaḥ ha-Mishna*, p. 90.
53. Elbogen, *Der Jüdische Gottesdienst*, p. 57, holds that the formulas 'Unto a bird's nest' etc., and 'May Thy name be remembered for well-doing' were recited at the end of the benediction of 'Thanksgiving', and this view was also accepted by Jacob Mann, *HUCA*, II, p. 297; but if so the order should have been reversed, 'We give thanks,' heading the list. There are, it seems, indications that such formulations were incorporated in the benediction of the 'Tefilla', for although one of the Palestinian versions was 'Hear, O Lord our God, the voice of our prayers and speedily fulfil our request, blessed art Thou, O Lord, who hearest prayer' (Mann, *ibid.*, pp. 306–307), yet along with it there is found also the version 'Hearken to our voice and hear our prayer, and have compassion upon us, and speedily fulfil our request, for Thou art a gracious and compassionate God, blessed art Thou, O Lord who hearest prayer' (S. Asaaf, 'Mi-Sēder ha-Tĕfillā bĕ-'Ereṣ Yisrā'ēl [From the Order of the *Tefilla* in Eretz-Israel]', *Sefer Dinaburg*, 1959, p. 118). In payyetanic

adaptations and abbreviated forms of the ʿAmida prayer, which were common in Eretz-Israel and which have been preserved in the Genizah, there are to be found also unexpurgated formulations like 'Answer us, when we entreat Thee, with Thy compassion, blessed art Thou, O Lord, who hearest prayer', and 'Turn away from evil and do good; may God hear thee when thou art wrapt in prayer, blessed art Thou, O Lord, who hearest prayer'; see A. Marmorstein, 'Mitteilungen zur Geschichte und Literatur aus der Geniza', *MGWJ*, vol. 69 (1925), pp. 36, 39. Particularly in the blessing *Shômēaʿ tĕfillā* ['Thou hearest prayer'], concerning which Rav already said 'Although (the Sages) have said that a man pray for his personal needs in *Shomeaʿ tefilla*' (*T.B. Berakhot* 31a) there was reason to fear the interpolation of improper formulas.

54. This is the text of *T.P. Megilla*, and it is undoubtedly right. In *Śeride Yerushalmi*, p. 20, we find 'For they evaluate the attributes of the Holy One, blessed be He, as compassion.' It seems that the words 'For they evaluate the attributes of the Holy One, blessed be He, as compassion' are only the addition of an editor, who wished to connect in this way the dictum of R. Josa b. R. Bun with the preceding passage, but primarily the dictum of R. Josa b. R. Bun has to be construed thus: 'Those who expound... do not do right'. This is the version in *T.P. Megilla*, but in *T.B. Berakhot* the text was emended to 'and those who expound'. In *T.B. Berakhot* 33b the statement of R. Josa b. R. Bun is cited as follows: 'Because he evaluates the attributes of the Holy One, blessed be He, as compassion, but they are actually decrees', and Rashi, *ibid.*, s.v. '*Middotaw* [His attributes]', explains the term as 'His precepts'.

55. *T.B. Berakhot* 33b, according to the text of the MSS.; see *Diqduqe Soferim*, pp. 181–182; cf. *Megilla, loc. cit.* This is also the reading of Rav Hai, *Otzar ha-Geonim* to *Berakhot*, Perushim, p. 46, where the text has **ראבא**. Abbaye's question 'But we have learnt (in the Mishna) that he is to be silenced?' remains unanswered, but in the Gemara the explanation is offered 'Rabba, too, wished to sharpen Abayye's mind'. The expression 'Have pity and compassion upon us' conforms to the Babylonian version of the benediction of the 'Tefilla' (see *Siddur R. Saadia Gaon*, p. 18) and confirms our statement regarding the place where the additions were made; see above, n. 53.

56. *Lev. Rabba* xxvii, 11, p. 644, and the parallels noted there.

57. *Sifra*, Qedoshim, viii, 10, 91b.

58. *Ibid.*, Be-har, v, 4, 109c. See *ibid.*, 'Emor, ix, 6, on Lev. xxii 38: 'I brought you out of the land of Egypt conditionally, on condition that you devote yourselves to the sanctification of My name.' There, too, the continuation is found 'For whoever acknowledges' etc.; see Be-har, vi, 1, ' "For they are My servants, whom I brought forth out of the land of Egypt" — on condition that he should not be sold as a bondman'; *ibid.* ix, 4, in explanation of a similar verse, 'on condition that they shall not enslave them'. It is clear that despite the formal textual resemblance, these homilies differ in content, and

the conditions are not linked to the observance of the precepts. H. Albeck, *Untersuchungen über die hal. Midraschim*, Berlin 1927, p. 15, dealt only with the formal similarity between the homilies, but not with their substantive differences.

59. *Ibid.*, Shemini, xii, 4, 57b.
60. *Sifre*, Shelaḥ, § 115, pp. 127–128. *Sifre Zuṭa*, p. 190, like *Sifra*, Qedoshim and Be-har, reads: 'I brought you out conditionally... on condition that you accept the precepts of fringes, for whoever acknowledges the precept of fringes' etc.
61. The homilies in *Sifre Deut.* §§ 86, 90, and *Mekhilta de-R. Simeon b. Yoḥai*, ed. Epstein-Melamed, p. 146, where the text has 'Even if my sole claim upon you is that I brought you forth from the land of Egypt, it is sufficient', refer to the same idea, despite the difference of formulation.
62. *T.B. Bava Meṣia*ʿ 61b, and Ravina, following in Rava's footsteps, also applied the idea to the mention of the exodus from Egypt in conjunction with the prohibition of eating reptiles.
63. *Ibid.* 72a; the printed editions have Rav Ḥisda, but the reading we have cited is found in all the MSS.; see *Diqduqe Soferim, ibid.*, p. 201.
64. In late Midrashim of the type that emanated from the school of R. Moses ha-Darshan both concepts are combined, namely that of 'a decree, which is not to be questioned' together with that of the reasons; see *Midrash Aggada*, ed. Buber, Pt. II, p. 120: 'I ordained for you a statute, I decreed a decree, and none may question it; and although it is a decree, the precept is as important as the rest of the Torah'; then the Midrash continues to explain the reasons. Also in *Midrash ha-Gadol* to Deuteronomy (see *Midrash Tannaim*, ed. Hoffmann, p. 205): 'There is not a word in the Torah, let alone a clause, which has not a number of reasons, as it is said: For "it is no vain thing for you", and if it is vain — the fault is yours, because you did not examine it and search for its reason properly'. The attitude to such reasons was expressed by R. Ṭobiah b. R. Eliezer in *Leqaḥ Ṭov* on Numbers, 119b: 'The Holy One, blessed be He, ordained a statute, and you may not question it — to ask why and wherefore — but you may expound it as far as the mind may grasp.'
65. *De Migr. Abr.*, 93. See J. M. Guttmann, *Beḥinat Qiyyum ha-Miṣwot*, pp. 58 f; Yitzḥak Heinemann, *Philons griech. u. jüd. Bildung*, pp. 463 ff; *Taʿame ha-Miṣwot*, pp. 25 ff.
66. See above, p. 323.
67. See *De Migr. Abr.*, 86 ff; Yitzḥak Heinemann, *loc. cit.*, p. 465.
68. *Sifre Deut.* § 36, pp. 67–68.
69 *T.B. Rosh ha-Shana* 28a, and Rashi, *ad loc.*, s.v. *Lōʾ*; see also Rashi, *T.B. Ḥullin* 89a, s.v. *Wĕ-Rāvāʾ*. In regard to the opinion of Rav Judah, *T.B. Rosh ha-Shana, loc. cit.*, see the *Novellae* of R. Solomon b. Adret (*RaShbA*), ed. Ch. Z. Dimitrovsky, New York 1961, p. 152.
70. *Cant. Rabba* i, 15; see *ibid.*, iv, 1, and *Tanḥuma*, *Teṣawwe*, § 5.
71. See above, p. 336.

72. *Tanḥuma*, ed. Buber, Shelaḥ, § 28. See *Deut. Rabba*, vi, 3: 'R. Phinehas bar Ḥama said, Wherever you go the precepts accompany you....'
73. *T.B. Sanhedrin* 81a; see *Diqduqe Soferim*, p. 222.
74. The homilist seeks to answer the question 'What does Ezekiel teach us?' See Rashi, *ad loc.*, s.v. *'El he-hārîm*, and the difficulty pointed out by Maharsha.
75. See S. Lieberman, *Tosefta ki-Fshuṭah*, Zera'im, pp. 169–170.
76. *Sifre*, Ki Teṣe', § 283 (*ad fin.*), p. 300; the version in *Ruth Zuṭa* ii, 16, p. 51, referred to, *loc. cit.*, by Lieberman 'And he made on that day a great banquet and rejoiced' represents an adaptation that takes into account the circumstances prevailing after the destruction of the Temple.
77. *Mekhilta de-R. Ishmael*, Massekhta de-Ba-ḥodesh, v, p. 219.
78. *Sifre Num.* § 141, p. 187, and *Sifre Zuṭa*, p. 322.
79. *Sifra* xcvi (*ad fin.*), 43b.
80. *Lev. Rabba* xxxiv, 8, p. 790.
81. *T.B. Berakhot* 9b. See *Diqduqe Soferim*, *ibid.*, p. 38, and the Baraita *ibid.*, 31a, reads 'One must not rise to say the *Tefilla* in a melancholy mood... but in a spirit of joy resulting from the observance of a precept [שמחה של מצוה]'. But see *Diqduqe Soferim*, *ibid.*, p. 160, and *ibid.* n. *Rêsh*, which states that the reading of the Munich MS. is דבר שמחה ('matter of joy'). The text of *Bet Nathan* has שמחה של תורה ('joy of the Torah'); the Paris MS. reads שמחה של הלכה ('joy of the Halakha'); and the *Tosefta*, *loc. cit.*, iii, 21, has דברים של חכמה ('words of wisdom'). See S. Lieberman, *Tosefta ki-Fshuṭah*, Zera'im, p. 47.
82. *T.B. Shabbat* 30b. The current edition adds של מצוה ('of the precept'), but this reading is not found either in the MSS. or in the early editions; see *Diqduqe Soferim*, *ibid.*, p. 57, n. 4. See *T.B. Pesaḥim* 117a, and *Diqduqe Soferim*, p. 366, n. *Shîn*.
82a. The supplementation of the precepts was not inspired by an ascetic purpose. Palestinian Amoraim stated in the name of R. Me'ir: [God declared:] 'I have permitted you more than I have forbidden you.' Following in their footsteps, Babylonian Amoraim also sought to find something permitted to correspond to everything prohibited. See *Lev. Rabba* xxii, 10, p. 922. Cf. *T.B. Ḥullin* 109b.
83. *Tanḥuma*, Tazria', § 5; ed. Buber, § 7. The version in the text is according to the Rome MS.; see *ibid.*, § 33.
84. *Seder Eliahu Rabba*, xxvii, p. 144.
85. *T.B. Yoma* 72b; see Rashi, *ad loc.*, 'tries him with suffering'; cf. Maharsha, *ad loc.*
86. *Sifre Deut.* § 48, p. 113; *ibid.* § 41, p. 87, the text reads: 'in order that I may receive reward in the world to come' and other variant readings; see vv.ll. and the n. *ibid.*, and cf. *T.B. Nedarim* 62a.
87. *Loc. cit.*, p. 114.
88. *Sifre*, Be-ha'alotekha, § 89, p. 90; there the text has R. Dostai b. R. Jose, but see vv.ll. and *T.B. Pesaḥim* 8b, where a similar dictum occurs in the name of R. Isaac.

89. See above, p. 349, and p. 270.
90. *T.B. Berakhot* 17a; see *Diqduqe Soferim, ibid.*, and cf. Rashi, *ad loc.*, s.v. *Hā-'ôśe*; and the passages noted in the margin. See above, p. 800, n. 48.
91. *M. 'Avot* iv, 5.
92. *T.B. Yoma* 72b; see Rashi, *ad loc.*, s.v. *Tartē*, and above, p. 418.
93. In *Sifra*, Be-ḥuqqotai, i, 5, 110c, the passage is cited anonymously, but in *Lev. Rabba* xxxv, 7, p. 826, in the form 'R. Ḥiyya taught', and in the continuation *ibid.* we find in the name of R. Joḥanan: 'If one studies (Torah) without the intention to observe (the commandments), it had been better for him if his placenta had turned over upon his face, and he had never gone forth into the world.' See *T.P. Berakhot* i, 2, p. 3b; *T.P. Shabbat* i, 2, p. 3b. Cf. above, p. 253.
94. *T.B. Pesaḥim* 50b. The words שמתוך שלא לשמה ['for from doing these things from other motives'] are not found in the Munich MS., a fact not noted in *Diqduqe Soferim.* The same omission occurs in this MS. in Soṭa 22b and *ibid.* 47a; but the dictum is cited twice in its normal form, as in the printed editions, in *T.B. Nazir* 23b.
95. *T.B. Rosh ha-Shana* 28a; see *T.B. Ḥullin* 31b, and cf. Maimonides, 'Hilkhot Shofar', ii, 4, and *Maggid Mishne* and *Leḥem Mishne, ad loc.*
96. *T.B. Rosh ha-Shana* 29a; see the *Novellae of Rashba ibid.*, ed. Dimitrovsky, p. 159.
97. *T.P. Yevamot* viii, 1, p. 8d (*ad fin.*); in *T.B. 'Avoda Zara* 27a the wording of R. Jose's dictum is: 'But where do we find in the Torah that circumcision must be performed for its own sake?' according to the version of the Spanish MS., ed. Abramson; see *ibid.*, p. 173. In *Tosefta 'Avoda Zara*, iii, 13, p. 464, the text is: 'Where do we find circumcision in the Torah that is not for the sake of the covenant' [שאינה לשום ברית].
98. See also *T.B. 'Eruvin* 95b (*ad fin.*).
99. See *T.B. Pesaḥim, loc. cit.*, 'Resh Laqish said: This shows that the precepts require intent.' But the author of *Yefe 'Enayim, ad loc.*, already noted that according to the statement of Resh Laqish in *T.P. Pesaḥim* x, 3, p. 37d (*ad init.*), 'If he did not dip the first time, he must do so the second time', this does not appear to be the case.
1. See *T.B. Ta'anit* 2a, *Sifre Deut.* § 41.
2. *Tosefta Berakhot* ii, 7, p. 4; see *T.P. Berakhot* ii, 5, p. 5a.
3. *Tosefta, loc. cit.*, iii, 6, p. 6.
4. *Ibid.*, ii ,2, p. 3; *T.P., loc. cit.*, ii, 1, p. 4a–b; *T.B., loc. cit.*, 13a–b. The words in the Mishna, *loc. cit.*, ii, 1, 'If he put his mind to it', signify that he intended to fulfil his religious duty. See the commentary of RAH [R. Aaron b. Joseph ha-Levi], *Pequddat ha-Leviyyim*, p. 19. Cf. L. Ginzberg, *Perushim we-Ḥiddushim bi-Yerushalmi*, Pt. I, p. 229; S. Lieberman, *Tosefta ki-Fshuṭah*, Zera'im, p. 15.
5. *T.P. Berakhot* ii, 5, p. 5a; see *ibid.* i, 5, p. 3b. Cf. L. Ginzberg, *op. cit.*, p. 357.
6. *T.P. Megilla* ii, 2, p. 73a. The commentaries have found it difficult to resolve

the contradiction between his ruling and that of the Mishna; see *Mar'ē ha-Pānîm* and *Shĕyārê Qorbān, ad loc.*

7. *T.B. Rosh ha-Shana* 28b (*ad fin.*)–29a; see Rif (Isaac Alfasi), *ibid.*, § 947, and the *Novellae of the Rashba* [R. Solomon b. Abraham Adret] to Tractate *Rosh ha-Shana*, p. 158. Cf. *Rabyah* [R. Eliezer b. Joel ha-Levi], Pt. II, § 533, p. 214, who cites the following passage in the name of the Palestinian Talmud: 'If a man passed behind the synagogue... this proves that the precepts require intent.' See *ibid.* the note of A. Aptowitzer; he refers to other Ri'shonim who quote this text from the Palestinian Talmud, although it does not occur in the existing version; cf. also S. Lieberman, *Tosefta ki-Fshuṭah, Rosh ha-Shana*, p. 1045.
8. See Rashi *ad loc.*; cf. *'Oraḥ Mîshôr, ad loc.*
9. See above, p. 341. The teaching is not derived from the story of Tamar but from that of Jael.
10. *Mekhilta de-R. Ishmael*, Massekhta de-Wa-yehi, vi, p. 114; see S. Schechter, *Some Aspects of Rabbinic Theology*, pp. 164–165.
11. See Maimonides' commentary on *M. Makoth* iii, 16, ed. Y. Kapach, p. 247, who explains the saying of R. Ḥananiah b. 'Aqashiya concerning the multiplicity of precepts as follows: 'For on account of the multiplicity of precepts it is not possible that a man should not perform one precept in his life perfectly...'
12. *Mekhilta de-R. Ishmael,* Massekhta de-Pisḥa, ix, p. 33; see *T.B. Megilla* 6b, and Rashi *ad loc.*, s.v. *'Ên ma'ăvîrîn.*
13. *Deut. Rabba,* ed. S. Lieberman, p. 58.
14. *Lev. Rabba* xxii, 2, p. 499, and *Deut. Rabba, loc. cit.,* in the name of R. Isaac.

CHAPTER XIV

ACCEPTANCE OF THE YOKE OF THE KINGDOM OF HEAVEN
LOVE AND REVERENCE

1. *Mekhilta de-R. Ishmael*, Massekhta de-Ba-ḥodesh, vi, p. 222.
2. *Sifre Num.* § 115, p. 126. Cf. *Tanḥuma*, Balak, 14: 'They recite the *Shema'* without delay and proclaim the Holy One, blessed be He, as King'. See also Tosafot, *Menaḥot* 32b, s.v. *Hā'* [Now...], '... the reference is to the *mezuza*, which contains the fundamental truth of the Torah, for it proclaims the kingdom of heaven.'
3. *Deut. Rabba*, ed. S. Lieberman, p. 66; see *Deut. Rabba* ii, § 32, and cf. above, p. 20.

3a. D. Flusser, 'Sanktus and Gloria, Abraham unser Vater', *Festschrift für O. Michel*, 1963, pp. 138–139, believes that in *Enoch* xxxix 12 'the Lord of hosts' was understood as 'the Lord of Spirits'; and accordingly he supposes that in ch. lxi 11 'May the name of the Lord of Spirits be blessed' substitutes 'Blessed be the name of His glory'. But he overlooked the fact that in xl 3 it is stated 'They uttered praises before the Lord of glory'. Nor does the addition in the Septuagint to Daniel iii 31–32, on which he relies (*ibid.*, p. 134, n. 2), indicate the original intent of the response. The author of the hymn was not thinking of the destroyed Temple (see *Enoch*, lxi, 11) but of the heavenly Sanctuary, and accordingly he divided the response into three parts: 'Blessed be the name of Thy holy glory, blessed art Thou in the Temple of Thy holy glory... blessed art Thou upon the throne of the glory of Thy kingdom.'

4. See *Tosefta Ta'anit* i, 13, p. 226; ed. Lieberman p. 327; *T.P. ibid.* ii, 11, p. 65d; *T.B. ibid.*, 16b; cf. S. Lieberman, *Tosefta ki-Fshuṭah*, Mo'ed, p. 1074; Joseph Heinemann, *Ha-Tefilla bi-Tequfat ha-Tanna'im we-ha-'Amora'im.* Jerusalem 1964, pp. 80 ff.
5. *M. Yoma* iii, 8; iv, 2.
6. See above, p. 19; cf. Israel Levy, *MGWJ*, xxxv, p. 120, who states that this response was used in the Temple, because the Divine Name used to be pronounced there also in prayers.

7. The testimony of the men of Jericho who 'wrapped' the *Shema'* [i.e. recited it without the prescribed breaks], but were not reproved for it, *M. Pesaḥim* iv, 8, is explained by R. Judah to mean 'that they did not say "Blessed be the name of the glory of His kingdom for ever and ever" ' — *Tosefta Pesaḥim* ii (iii), 19, p. 160; ed. Lieberman, p. 157 and the parallels; cf. idem, *Tosefta ki-Fshuṭah, ibid.*, p. 542. R. Me'ir disagrees with R. Judah regarding the interpretation of the word 'wrap' (*kôrĕkhîn*); hence it is difficult to find clear evidence in the Mishna that already in Temple times it had become customary not to say the response outside the Temple precincts, just as the men of Jericho did not. R. Me'ir's statement does not imply that the men of Jericho did say the response 'Blessed be the name of the glory of His kingdom for ever and ever'. At any rate it appears that R. Judah himself, who had wide knowledge of traditional usages, knew the custom not to say 'Blessed be the name of the glory of His kingdom'.
8. On the various conjectures advanced with regard to the origin of the response and the political or religious protests that it is supposed to express, see A. Aptowitzer, '*Bārûkh Shēm Kĕvôd Malkhûtô Lĕ'ōlām Vā'ed* ['Blessed be the name of the glory of His kingdom for ever and ever'], Geschichte einer liturgischen Formel', *MGWJ*, 1929, pp. 93–118. Aptowitzer's own theory concerning the anti-Hasmonean trend in the wording of the prayer is no better grounded than the anti-Herodian-Roman protest ascribed to it by Büchler, *Priester und Cultus*, pp. 127 ff, and before him by Me'ir Friedmann (Ish Shalom), in 'Me'ir 'Ayin' on *Sifre Deut.* 72b, n. 17. Basically H. Albeck, Hashlamot ['Supplements'] to *Seder Zera'im*, p. 328, is correct, only the change is not linked with 'the pause to divide [*li-frôs*] upon the *Shĕma'*'. On the meaning of *pôrēs 'al ha-Shĕma'* or *pôrēs 'et ha-Shema'* see S. Lieberman, *Tosefta ki-Fshuṭah*, Mo'ed, pp. 1206 ff.
9. *T.B. Pesaḥim* 56a, according to the text of two Yemenite MSS. to which my attention was drawn by my friend Prof. E. S. Rosenthal, who conjectures that in other MSS. באושא was omitted on account of its similarity to בחשאי; and this was also R. Ḥananel's version, as may be inferred from his commentary *ad loc.* Aptowitzer, *op. cit.*, p. 115, being unaware of the reading of the MSS., argued that R. Ḥananel had no such reading, and he accordingly assigns a later date to the enactment, regarding it as a protest against the doctrine of the Trinity. See *ibid.*, p. 117.
10. The Christian doxologies added the name of Jesus to the Jewish formulas; see Romans xvi 27; Ephesians iii 21; Jude v. 25. For examples from later Christian liturgies see F. Heiler, *Das Gebet*[4], p. 463; A. Spanier, 'Stilkritisches zum jüdischen Gebet', *MGWJ*, 1936, p. 345; A. Baumstark, *Comparative Liturgy*, 1958, p. 62. E. Werner, 'Doxology', *HUCA*, xix (1945–46), pp. 287 ff, argues that the Minim made use of formulas similar to 'Blessed be the name of the glory of His kingdom for ever and ever', and hence he rejects the possibility that it was directed, as Aptowitzer thinks, against the views of the Minim. But Werner's explanation that the response was said in a low

voice as a sign of mourning, and that the Minim made fun of this whispering, is purely imaginary.

11. *T.P. Berakhot* i, 5, p. 3c; *T.B. ibid.*, 12a reads: מפני תרעומת המינים ['on account of the *insinuations* of the Minim'].

12. *T.B. Berakhot* 12a: 'Rabba bar Rav Huna (so in the Munich MS.; *Diqduqe Soferim*, p. 52) thought to institute it [i.e. the recitation of the Decalogue] in Sura. Said Rav Ḥisda to him: It has already been abolished... Amemar thought to institute it in Nehardea. Said Rav Ashi to him: It has already been abolished...'; but see below, p. 709, n. 99.

13. *T.B. Pesaḥim, loc. cit.*: 'And in Nehardea, where there are no Minim, they still [עד השתא] say it in a low voice'. The Yemenite MSS. read: ...עדאן. On the Christians in Babylon and the fact that the Jews took little note of them, see my article in *Tarbiz*, XX (1950), p. 121.

14. Against this background we can understand the divergences between the different versions of the Haggadah, which attributes the recitation of *Shĕma' Yisrā'el* ['Hear, O Israel'] to the sons of Jacob, and the response 'Blessed be the name of the glory of His kingdom for ever and ever' to Jacob; according to some versions Jacob alone said 'Blessed be the name of the glory of His kingdom for ever and ever' — *Sifre Deut.* § 31, p. 52. 'He, too, moved his lips and said "Blessed be the name of the glory of His kingdom for ever and ever" — *Gen. Rabba* xcviii, 3, p. 1252. Likewise in the version of the Haggadah in *T.B. Pesaḥim, loc. cit.*, it is reported in the name of Simeon b. Pazzi (see *Diqduqe Soferim, ibid.*, p. 165): 'He opened and said (פתח ואמר) "Blessed be the name of the glory of His kingdom for ever and ever" '. But *Gen. Rabba* xcvi, Shiṭṭa Ḥadasha, p. 1202, has 'began (and) said in a low voice (התחיל א׳ בלחישה) "Blessed be the name of the glory of His kingdom for ever and ever" '; so, too, in *Deut. Rabba* ii, 35. In *Ginze Schechter*, Pt. I, p. 122, the reading is: 'Jacob also mediated in his heart and said....' See *Deut. Rabba, loc. cit.*, 36; ed. Lieberman, p. 62, and the note *ad loc.*

15. It is possible that the recitation of 'Blessed be the name of the glory of His kingdom for ever and ever' in a low voice drew in its train the institution of a special benediction before the reading of the *Shema'*, a benediction that is actually found in the Palestinian versions of the liturgy before the blessing *yôṣēr*: 'Blessed art Thou, O Lord our God, king of the universe, who hast sanctified us with Thy commandments and commanded us concerning the commandment to recite the *Shema'*, to proclaim Thy sovereignty with a perfect heart and to profess Thy unity with a good heart and a willing spirit, Amen!' — J. Mann, *HUCA*, II (1925), p. 286, and *ibid.*, n. 50.

16. *Sifre Deut.* § 32.

17. *T.P. Berakhot* ix, 7, p. 14b; see *Midrash Tannaim*, p. 25.

18. Deut. vi 5, 13; x 12.

19. *Ibid.* v 9–10; iv 24; vi 15.

20. Moore, *Judaism*, II, pp. 98–99; B. J. Bamberger, 'Fear and Love of God in the O.T.', *HUCA*, XXVI (1929), pp. 39 ff; R. Sander, *Furcht und Liebe im*

pal. Judentum, Stuttgart 1935, pp. 4–24; G. Vajda, *L'amour de Dieu dans la Théologie Juive du Moyen-Age*, Paris 1957, which is a comprehensive and profound study of the subject of love in the philosophy of the Middle Ages, in German Hasidism, in the Cabbala, and in the period of the expulsion from Spain. He also added a preliminary chapter on the Bible (pp. 15–25), and on the Sages (pp. 34–61), and referred there, p. 14, particularly to the work of A. Büchler, *Studies in Sin and Atonement*, London 1928. E. L. Dietrich, 'Das Liebe des Einzelnen zu Gott in der Jüd. Frömmigkeit von der Zeit der Gaonim bis zum Auftreten der Kabbala', Oriens 1964, pp. 132 ff; on p. 134 he writes: 'Vorarbeiten für unser Thema finden sich auf jüdischer Seite nicht, auf Christlicher, meines Wissens nur Georges Vajda...'! This writer's observation on Rabbinic literature in his prefatory remarks, p. 135, is characterized by the spirit of Protestant theology in the last century.

21. This is the version of the Kaufmann MS., and Rashbaṣ [R. Simeon b. Ṣemah Duran] already noted in *Magen 'Avot*, Leipzig 1855, 6a: על מנת שלא לקבל פרס 'This is the text of the Mishna, but some emend it and read שלא על מנת לקבל פרס "not for the sake of receiving reward"... but the reading should not be altered.' See Ch. Taylor, *An Appendix to Sayings of the Jewish Fathers*, 1900, p. 135; cf. *T.B. 'Avoda Zara* 19a, and the Spanish MS., ed. S. Abramson, p. 161.
22. See the commentary of Me'iri, *Bet ha-Beḥira*, 3a. Cf. E. Bickermann, *Harvard Theol. Review*, XLIV (1951); S. Lieberman drew his attention *ibid.* to the aforementioned sources. Bickermann's conclusions are improbable, because he disregards the signification of the words *'al mĕnāt* ['for the sake of'].
23. The term is thus interpreted by Maimonides in his Commentary on the Mishna, and by Rashbaṣ, *Magen 'Avot*, *ibid.* On the etymology of the word see Löw's notes *apud* Krauss, *Lehnwörter*, p. 492.
24. Version II, x, p. 26. See *ibid.* Schechter's note 10, where another lengthy version is cited from the Halberstam MS.; he concludes: 'And strangeness and lateness — all these qualities are discernible in them; but perhaps they were written in opposition to the well-known sect, which went to extremes in this matter, to the point of casting off the yoke of the Torah and of the precepts.' In citing the Baraita in the text I have omitted the following words: 'He who acts from love inherits the life of the world to come; he, however, who serves in awe and fear inherits the life of this world, but does not inherit the life of the world to come... and they shall inherit the life of this world and the life of the world to come'. A. Büchler, *Studies in Sin and Atonement*, p. 159, n. 2, found great difficulty in understanding the words, but undoubtedly the correct version is that found in the Halberstam MS., which Schechter cites *ibid.*, n. 2: 'He who acts from love inherits the life of this world, but does not inherit the life of the world to come. He, however, who serves in awe and fear inherits the life of this world and the life of the world to come.' Just 'because of the utter strangeness' that Schechter found in the homily, the text was corrupted. But this entire subject of reward is only a

late addition, which conflicts with Antigonus' teaching. The proofs, too, are in no way relevant to reward.

25. L. Finkelstein, *Māvo' la-Massekhtot 'Avôt wĕ-'Avôt de-R. Nathan* [Introduction to the Tractates *'Avot* and *'Avot de-R. Nathan*], New York, 1951, p. 33, is correct in his criticism of Schechter's view, but he, too, did not discern the addition to the aforementioned Baraita and treated it as a unitary passage. See J. Goldin, 'Bêt Midrāshô shel Yoḥanan bèn Zakkai [The School of R. Joḥanan b. Zakkai]', *H. Wolfson Jubilee Volume*, 1965, p. 3.
26. *Sirach* vii 30–31, ed. M. H. Segal, p. 47.
27. *Ibid.* ii 16, ed. Segal, p. 8: 'They that fear the Lord will not be disobedient to His words, and they that love Him will keep His ways.' But in the continuation (*ibid.* v. 17) 'They that fear the Lord will seek His approval, and they who love Him will promote the Law.'
28. *Sirach* ii 7–9; see Büchler, *op. cit.*, p. 146; Sander, *op. cit.*, pp. 30 ff.
29. *Quod Deus Immutabilis Sit*, 60–64. See Joshua Amir, 'Dĕrāshôtāw shel Philon 'al ha-Yir'ā wĕ-'Ahăvā wĕ-Yaḥăsān lĕ-Midrĕshê 'Ereṣ Yisrā'ēl [The Homilies of Philo on Fear and Love and their Relationship to the Palestinian Midrashim]', *Zion*, XXX (1965), pp. 47 ff. It is surprising that in his article, which is a thorough study in many respects, Amir makes no mention of Antigonus' dictum, and, on the other hand, compares Philo's statement, *ibid.*, p. 51, with the saying of R. Simeon b. Eleazar in its abbreviated form: 'Greater is he that acts from love than he that acts from fear.'
30. Amir is right (*ibid.*, p. 54), when he points to the lack of system in Philo's teaching; he is tied down to Scriptures, which he expounds according to his method in order to make religious deductions. See below, p. 413.
31. *Deuteronomy* viii 5; see Philo, *loc. cit.*, 54.
32. *Ibid.* 69.
33. xvii, 1319–1320. A. Kaminka, *Meḥqarim be-Miqra u-be-Talmud*, Bk. II, 1951, p. 45, cited these lines in order to elucidate the saying of Antigonus, but did not mention the cognate statement of Philo.
34. In Letter 47 to Lucilius [*Epistulae Morales ad Lucilium*], referred to by Amir, *op. cit.*, p. 48, n. 14.
35. In Letter 18.
36. In stating this, I do not overlook the vast difference between the connotation of the concept 'God' as used in Rabbinic literature and that which it has in Seneca's writing. On this see J. N. Sevenster, *Paul and Seneca*, 1961, pp. 26 ff. All that this author had adduced as common to Seneca and Paul is at least equally common to the Bible and Rabbinic teaching, but the writer has not even bothered to raise this question, although all his efforts to discover any analogy whatsoever to Paul's distinctive teaching were fruitless. Furthermore, he overlooked all that has been written about the relationship between Seneca and Judaism, and even J. Bergmann's essay 'Die Stoische Philosophie und die jüd. Frömmigkeit', *Hermann Cohen Festschrift, Judaica*, Berlin 1912, pp. 145 ff, receives no mention.

37. As Amir, *op. cit.*, p. 48 and p. 51, maintains, and it is pointless to search for 'an unknown Stoic source common to both of them'.
38. See above, p. 414.
39. *T.B. Soṭa* 31a; but the Munich MS. and likewise *Tosefta Soṭa* vi, 1, p. 303, read 'Rabbi says'. This is also the recension in *Yalquṭ Shimʿoni*, Job, § 891 (so, too, the Oxford MS.); but in *Haggadot ha-Talmud* the text is identical with that of the printed editions of the Talmud.
40. *T.P. Berakhot* ix, 7, p. 14b; *T.B. ibid.*, 61b.
41. *Tanḥuma*, ed. Buber, Shelaḥ, § 27 (114); *Num. Rabba* xvii, 2. See *Sifre Deut.* § 313: ' "He kept him as the apple of His eye" — even if the Omnipresent had asked Abraham for the ball of his eye, he would have given it to Him, and not only the ball of his eye, but even his life he would have given him....' In *Gen. Rabba* lvi, 7, p. 603: ' "For now I know" ...now you have made Me known to all that you love Me... I account it unto you as if, had I bidden you to sacrifice yourself unto Me, you would not have denied My request'.
42. See *Gen. Rabba* xliv, 13, p. 435. Cf. my article 'Asqezis we-Yissurim be-Torat Ḥazal', *Yitzḥak Baer Jubilee Volume*, p. 59.
43. *Mekhilta de-R. Ishmael*, Massekhta de-Ba-ḥodesh, vi, p. 227. *Ibid.*, n. 5, the editors quote the annotation of R. Me'ir Ish-Shalom in his edition, p. 68b, 'Abraham, who was not enjoined'; but his interpretation is incorrect, as is evident from the continuation of the Mekhilta text: 'R. Nathan said, "Of them that love Me and keep My commandments" — this refers to the Israelites, who dwell in the Land of Israel and give their life for the commandments.' This, too, is how Naḥmanides interpreted the dictum of the *Mekhilta* in his commentary to Exodus xx 6. See *Mekhilta de-R. Simeon* b. *Yoḥai*, p. 148; *Midrash ha-Gadol* to Exodus, p. 407; *T.B. Soṭa* 31a.
44. *Cant. Rabba* i, 13.
45. *M. Soṭa* v, 5.
46. Reference should be made to Targum Pseudo-Jonathan, xv 6: 'And he had faith... and He counted it to him for merit that he did not cast reproaches against Him.'
47. See Rashi, *Soṭa* 27b, and cf. *Tif'eret Yisra'el* to the Mishna cited above (n. 45). I. Wiernikowski's dissertation *Das Buch Hiob nach der Auffassung des Talmud und Midrash*, Breslau 1902, does not deal with our question at all, and is merely a compilation of citations.
48. See above, p. 414.
49. *Tractate Semaḥot* viii; see *Midrash Tehillim* xxvi, 2, p. 215, where the name of the author of the saying is not given. But see *ibid.* n. 2, where it is stated that four MSS. read 'R. Akiba says', and there are divergences between the texts, especially in regard to the Scriptures cited. Cf. also *Midrash Tehillim* cxix, 46, p. 499, where David dissociates himself from 'the people who reflect on the fear of God as a result of their sufferings, and not from love', and he declares 'I did not perform them under duress or out of fear, but out of love.'

50. *M. ʿEduyot* ii, 10. In the *Mekhilta*, Ba-ḥodesh, x, p. 239, it seems that R. Akiba's homily extends only to the words 'I have brought sufferings upon you; be thankful!'; the continuation 'And thus David said' etc. is an editorial addition. In *Sifre Deut.* § 32 and in *Midrash Tannaim*, p. 26, we find 'And thus did David say... and thus did Job say... (as proofs 'Since Scripture enjoins "with all thy soul", "with all thy might" follows *a fortiori*); but for whichever measure (of fortune) He measures out to you....' In the *Sifre* the teaching is ascribed to R. Jacob (ed. L. Finkelstein reads עקיבה; see the note of R. Me'ir Ish Shalom in his edition), and in *M. Berakhot* ix, 5 it appears as 'another explanation'. At any rate, no proof can be derived from here for R. Akiba's view concerning Job's 'fear of God', since it is the first two chapters that are referred to and these precede Job's reproaches; and undoubtedly we cannot ascribe to R. Akiba the view that Job served God out of love, as did Büchler, *Studies* etc., pp. 128 ff. The dispute between Pappos and R. Akiba regarding the interpretation of Job xxiii 13 (*Mekhilta de-R. Ishmael*, Massekhta de-Wa-yehi, i, p. 112) is not concerned with the justification of Job. Pappos, too, does not interpret the text according to its plain sense. He uses the verse to emphasize that God is the only Judge of all mankind, and R. Akiba, on the other hand, stresses that His greatness lies in the fact that He 'judges everyone truly and everyone justly'. Akin to Pappos' view is the translation of the Septuagint, εἰ δὲ καὶ αὐτὸς ἔκρινεν οὕτως; it introduces the idea of judgement, which does not appear in the Hebrew original. See Leo Prijs, *Jüdische Tradition in der Septuaginta*, 1948, p. 32. But he refers to *Deut. Rabba* i, 9, that is to the dictum of Resh Laqish; see above, p. 178.
51. See Malachi ii 5; Psalms ciii 11, 17; *ibid.*, cxi 5.
52. See above, p. 270 and p. 416.
53. *T.B. Berakhot* 28b.
54. *M. Soṭa* v, 5, according to the Kaufmann MS. Rashi, *T.B. ibid.*, 27b, glossed 'He was the disciple of R. Akiba', but only because in a preceding Mishna R. Joshua said: 'Who will take away the dust from your eyes, O Rabban Joḥanan b. Zakkai... and has not your disciple R. Akiba now...' In *Haggadot ha-Talmud* we find 'That same day R. Eliezer b. Hyrcanus expounded: '(Job only) served... and has not R. Eliezer your disciple now...' But in the light of the accepted version in all the witnesses this is only a *lapsus calami* arising from the habit of citing the usual name. Maimonides, in his commentary on the Mishna, explains that the expression 'your disciple' is applied to R. Akiba 'on account of his greatness; hence the Mishna does not say "the disciple of your disciple", although he was the disciple of his disciple, for R. Akiba was the disciple of R. Eliezer b. Hyrcanus... However, this honour was not shown to R. Joshua b. Hyrcanus, but the Mishna says "the disciple of your disciple" as he actually was.'
55. The plain sense of the verse is that Job proclaims his refusal to admit his guilt; see Rashi *ad loc.*

56. The verse was aptly interpreted by R. Judah b. Kalonymus, *Yiḥuse Tanna'im wa-'Amora'im*, ed. J. L. Maimon, Jerusalem 1963: 'Since Scripture does not state "I shall not remove *yir'ātô* ['the fear of Him'] from me", but *tummātî* [rendered above 'my integrity'], the meaning of *tōm* being 'affection', 'love', as it is written "Thou shalt be *tāmîm* with the Lord" ' (Deut. xviii 13).

57. *Tosefta Soṭa* vi, 1, p. 303, where the text has 'R. Joshua said in the name of Ben Peṭuri', but in the printed editions and in the Vienna MS. the reading is 'R. Judah said in the name of Ben Peṭuri'. But the author of *Yiḥuse Tanna'im wa-'Amora'im* (to which S. Lieberman refers in *Tosefet Ri'shonim*, II, p. 60) cites the version 'R. Joshua said in the name of Ben Peṭuri', but he finds it difficult to assume that the reference is to R. Joshua b. Ḥananiah, for in that case the objection raised by R. Joshua in regard to the homily of R. Joshua b. Hyrcanus is hard to understand. Hence he concludes that R. Joshua, cited without further qualification in the Tosefta, refers to R. Joshua b. Hyrcanus, and infers therefrom: 'and if it be as I have explained, it is clear that Ben Peṭurin actually lived before R. Joshua, who was the teacher of R. Akiba.' He also adds: 'In an accurate version of the Tosefta the reading is as I have stated. But I found in another version of the Tosefta: "R. Joshua said in the name of R. Judah b. Peṭurin"; but this is not so accurate.' Nevertheless, it appears that it is precisely the version of the Tosefta 'that is not so accurate', which is to be relied upon. 'R. Judah b. Peṭurin' is a corruption, apparently, of 'R. Judah in the name of Ben Peṭurin', and this is the version of the Vienna MS. and of the printed editions; also in *T.P. Soṭa* V, 7, p. 20c, we find 'It is taught in the name of R. Judah'. But how is it possible that R. Joshua should report in the name of R. Judah? Now R. Samuel b. Nissim Masnuth, *Ma'yan Gannim* on Job, ed. S. Buber, Berlin 1889, p. 84, cites the dictum in the name of R. Joshua b. Levi, and it is accordingly possible that the reading in the Tosefta text referred to was 'R. Joshua b. Levi in the name of R. Judah in the name of Ben Peṭuri'. According to the *Sifra*, Be-har, V, 3, 109a, Ben Peṭuri was a contemporary — apparently a younger contemporary — of R. Akiba, and perhaps, in view of what we have stated, it is possible to validate the reading of the Erfurt MS. in *Tosefta Soṭa* V, 13, 'R. Joshua said that R. Judah b. Peṭuri expounded in the name of R. Akiba'. It is not surprising that R. Joshua b. Levi's name appears in the Tosefta, seeing that the names of R. Ḥiyya, R. Abba — that is Rav — and R. Jose b. Ḥanina also occur therein. See H. Albeck, *Meḥqarim be-Baraita we-Tosefta*, Jerusalem 1944, p. 138; J. N. Epstein, *Mevo'ot le-Sifrut ha-Tanna'im*, p. 251. It may be that the occurrence of the name of R. Joshua in the Mishna in connection with this theme resulted in the omission of 'b. Levi' in the *Tosefta*.

58. See *Tosefta Soṭa*, vi, 1, p. 303, where the passage is cited in the name of Rabbi; but in *T.B. ibid.*, 31a, it is quoted in the name of R. Me'ir, but the ending 'and so for the rest of the reproaches' is wanting there.

59. *T.B. Bava Batra* 16a; see Rashi *ibid.*, s.v. *Lahăfôkh*: 'To uproot all glory,

for he reproached and blasphemed'. See *Sifre Num.* § 112, p. 120: ' "The same blasphemeth the Lord" — R. Eleazar b. Azariah: It is analogous to a man who says to his fellow "You have scraped out (גדפת; vv.ll.: גרפתה, גרבתה, and in *T.P. Sanhedrin* vii, 11, p. 25b: גידפת; so, too, in *T.B. Keritot* 7b) the dish' etc.

60. *Tosefta Shabbat* xiii, 2, p. 128; ed. Lieberman, p. 57; *T.P. ibid.*, xvi, 1, p. 15c; *T.B. ibid.*, 115a.

61. On the Aramaic translation see W. Bacher, 'Das Targum zu Hiob', *MGWJ*, XX (1871), pp. 208–223; P. Churgin, *Targum Kathuvim* [Targum of Hagiographa], pp. 87 ff.

62. According to the view of Graetz, 'Das Zeitalter der griech. Übersetzung des Buches Hiob', *MGWJ*, XXVI (1877), pp. 83 ff. On the Septuagint translation see below, n. 65.

63. Such a translation is that of Theodotion, who at times merely transliterates the Hebrew words, for example, xxxvi 30; xxxvii 12; xxxviii 32; xxxix 13. It is difficult to come to any definite conclusions regarding the character of the fragments of the Aramaic translation of Job discovered in Qumran, cave 11. J. Van der Ploeg, *Le Targum de Job de la grotte 11 de Qumran*, Amsterdam 1962, published six lines of the Targum (xlii 10–11. Instead of ושׁ|ט|ף להון חטאיהון read ...ושׁ|ב|ק להון), but he puts forward a multiplicity of conjectures and conclusions concerning the date and character of the Targum. Having regard to the fragment that he has published and the examples that he cites in French translation, Van der Ploeg's assertion, *ibid.* p. 11, 'Le Targum... est du type simple' is not so certain. It differs from the Septuagint rendering. In the aforementioned fragment the words 'And the Lord restored the fortunes of Job' are not translated, and the rendering presupposes the text 'And the Lord accepted Job when he prayed for his friends', and thus avoids the repetition in the Septuagint translation.

64. This conjecture was adduced by N. Brüll, *Bet Talmud*, IV (1885), pp. 43 ff; and A. Büchler, *Studies* etc., p. 136, is inclined to accept it.

65. Possibly the absence of a translation of the book in Greek serves to explain the surprising fact that in rendering the words of his grandfather, *Sirach* xlix 12, the translation changed *'iyyôv* ['Job'] to *'ôyēv* ['enemy']; see M. H. Segal, *Ben Sira ha-Shalem*, p. 338. Philo mentions Job once (*De Mutatione Nominum*, 48), when quoting xiv 4 in a version that differs from the Septuagint, which, in turn, diverges completely from the original.

66. For instance ix 13; xiv 4; xvi 13–14; xix 6, and other examples given in the following works: G. Baer, *Der Text des Buches Hiob untersucht*, Marburg 1897; G. Gerleman, *Book of Job* (Studies in the Septuagint, I), Lund 1946; D. H. Gard, "The Concept of Job's Character according to the Greek Translator of the Hebrew Text', *JBL*, 72 (1953), pp. 182 ff. Additional bibliography on the problem of the Septuagint on Job in H. M. Orlinsky, 'Studies in the Septuagint of the Book of Job', *HUCA*, XXVIII (1957), pp. 53 ff. In a series of articles, which appeared in the volumes of this annual, Orlinsky com-

pletely rejects the view that the Septuagint translator was motivated, in his rendering of the Book, by any given trend, and he is at pains to prove that the many divergences in the translation are due either to a Hebrew original differing from our present text, or to the character of the translator's particular style. Although many of his arguments against his predecessors are justified, and notwithstanding that he succeeded in explaining by his method quite a number of questions, it is nevertheless not possible to accept Orlinsky's general thesis concerning the character and method of the translator. He adduces extremely forced interpretations so as to avoid admitting that the translator changed the original text and interpreted it tendentiously. See *HUCA*, XXX (1959), p. 166; XXXII (1961), pp. 245–246, 252–253; XXXIII (1962), p. 127. Orlinsky's contention that there are parallel passages where the translator neither altered nor toned down the text (see *ibid.*, XXXII, p. 259) is not valid, for such consistency is not characteristic of the ancient versions, and its absence in no way detracts from the aim underlying the changes (see *ibid.*, p. 261). Similarly Orlinsky's argument (*ibid.*, p. 254) that the rendering, in vii 21, of *we-šiḥartani* [literally, 'and Thou shalt seek me'] shows no tendentiousness, since a similar rendition is found in viii 5, is unconvincing, because in the latter passage the translation is in order, but not in vii 21. The evidence from xxxiv 5 (*ibid.*, p. 267), where 'and the Lord hath removed my judgement' is translated without change, is considered by Orlinsky to be conclusive, but in fact proves the opposite. In xxvii 2, the translator weakened the force of the indictment because it was uttered by Job himself, but he did not take the trouble to tone down the words cited in his name by Elihu, since it is natural for the accuser to aggravate the charge. Passages that are inconvenient to his contention Orlinsky is accustomed to emend; see *HUCA*, XXXV (1964), p. 67, n. 25, or to put forward a *Vorlage* (see *ibid.*, p. 69).

67. xiv 12 acquires a different meaning by the omission of the words 'nor be aroused out of their sleep'. The question (*ibid.*, v. 14) 'If a man die, may he live again?' is rendered as an affirmation 'he will live'. On 'my release' see L. Prijs. *op. cit.*, p. 71; D. H. Gard, 'The Concept of Future Life according to the Greek Translator of the Book of Job', *JBL*, LXXIII (1954), pp. 137 ff. Orlinsky's comments on xiv 14, *HUCA*, XXXII (1961), p. 245, are unconvincing. On the 'proofs' from verses, in which the translator made no substitution nor change, see above, n. 66.

68. See K. Kohler, 'The Testament of Job', *Semitic Studies in Memory of A. Kohut*, Berlin 1897, pp. 264–338, which contains the Greek text (cf. ed. A. Mai, Rome 1833, based on the Vatican MS.) with English translation and introduction; Kohler tried to prove, without any real basis for his contention, that the work had an Essene character. It was translated by Abraham Kahana into Hebrew, *Ha-Sefarim ha-Ḥiṣoniyyim* ['The Apocryphal Books'], I, pp. 515 ff, under the title *Divrê 'Iyyôv* ['The Words of Job'], after the opening words of the edition of M. R. James, *Apocrypha*, anecdota II, Cam-

bridge 1897, pp. 104–137 (he printed the text of the Paris MS. and gave the vv.ll, according to the aforementioned ed. of Mai. Now a new critical edition has appeared, which is based on additional MSS. and takes into account the Slavonic version: S. P. Brook, *Testamentum Jobi*, Leiden 1967). The view of Kahana, *loc. cit.*, p. 518, who assigns so early a date to the composition of the Testament that he regards it as the source of the addition to the Septuagint version of the Book of Job, is without any foundation. He misunderstood the observations of J. Freudenthal, *Hellenistische Studien*, Pt. II (1875), pp. 136 ff, who drew attention at the time, with reference to the identity of the Septuagint addition, to a passage from the Book of Aristeas cited by Eusebius, *Praep. Ev.*, ix, 25 (see Freudenthal, *op. cit.*, p. 231) from the work of Alexander Polyhistor. But he also stated *ibid.*, p. 139, that although Aristeas used a Septuagint version similar to our own, yet the author of the supplement made use of Aristeas, who lived in the second century B.C.E. and certainly did not use the *Testament of Job* (on the Septuagint addition as being earlier than the translation, see N. H. Torczyner [Tur-Sinai], 'Lĕ-Tôlĕdôt Sifrê ha-Miqrā [On the History of the Books of the Bible]', *A. Gulak and S. Klein Memorial Volume*, Jerusalem 1942, pp. 99 ff). Undoubtedly the work, as we have it, is based on the Septuagint version; see G. Gerleman, *op. cit.*, p. 53. M. Philonenko, 'Le Testament de Job et les Therapeutes', *Semitica*, VIII (1958), pp. 41–53, revived Kohler's conjecture, only he bases himself on a comparison with Philo's description of the Therapeutae. But all his arguments are devoid of real proofs. At any rate there is nothing of the asceticism described in *De Vita Contemplativa*, 37–40, to be found in the *Testament of Job* (see *ibid.*, ix–xi). Job is the owner of slaves who weary themselves with the cooking of savoury dishes for widows and the poor (*ibid.* xiv 2), whereas the Therapeutae regarded slavery as contrary to the law of nature (*De Vita Contemplativa*, 70).

69. In the Vatican MS. there is added ὑπερ της αγαπης του θῦ i.e. 'from love of God'; see ed. Brook, *ibid.* p. 22.
70. James, *The Testament of Abraham*, Text and Studies, II, 2, p. 96.
71. So Sander translated correctly, *op. cit.*, p. 81; see *ibid.*, n. 3, against Kohler, *JQR* XXVII (1895), p. 589, and Büchler, *op. cit.*, *Studies* etc. p. 138, n. 2.
72. Tertullian, *De Patientia*, XIV; see Gerleman, *ibid.*, p. 56, and Orlinsky, *HUCA*, XXVIII (1957), p. 57, n. 15.
73. The addition to ch. ix in Version I of '*Avot de-R. Nathan*, ed. Schechter, p. 164, was directly or indirectly influenced by the *Testament of Job*; see L. Ginzberg, *Legends*, Pt. II, p. 384, n. 39.
74. *T.P. Soṭa* V, 8, p. 20c.
75. *T.P. ibid.*, p. 20d; *Gen. Rabba* lvii (*ad fin.*), p. 618: 'One righteous man arose among the (Gentile) nations....'
76. *T.P. Berakhot* ix, 7, p. 14b; *T.P. Soṭa loc. cit.*
77. The commentators of *Gen. Rabba* have interpreted the expression אמרה פגה [rendered in the Text 'spoke dogmatically'] in the sense of 'he spoke unripe

words', basing themselves on the *Tanḥuma*, Wa-yera, § 13, ed. Buber, § 7: 'Job swallowed it as unripe fruit, but Abraham swallowed it when it was ripe'; see Theodor, *loc. cit.*, n. 2. But as I have shown (*Lĕšonénu*, XXXII, 1968, p. 124) the version of *Gen. Rabba* represents the original text. אמרה פגא really means אמרה πηγή, that is, uncompromisingly, without hesitation, and this is precisely what Job did when he said 'It is all one'. It is not fortuitous that in the Septuagint the words rendered 'It is all one' are not translated, and apparently this omission was not considered sufficient, so the words תם וישר ['the innocent and the wicked'] were changed to Μέγάν καὶ δυνάστην, and the sense of the translation is 'the wrath of the Lord destroyeth the great and mighty man'. See on the other hand Orlinsky's remarks, *HUCA*, XXXV (1964), p. 69.

78. See *Tanḥuma* ed. Buber, *loc. cit.*; *Tanḥuma*, printed edition, *loc. cit.*
79. *Quis Rerum Divinarum Heres*, 6–7. Speaking openly is akin to friendship.
80. *Ibid.* 21–28; see also *Die Werke Philos von Alexandria*, ed. Heinemann, V, p. 228, n. 2, on the dual meaning of Θαρρῶ.
81. See Philo, *Quaest in Gen.*, Supplement Loeb Classical Library, I, translated by R. Marens, p. 299 and the parallels listed there in the note on p. 300.
82. In his article, *op. cit.*, pp. 57 ff, Amir put forward the conjecture that underlying Philo's exposition is a homily of a Palestinian Sage that was delivered at Alexandria: 'Philo heard this homily... in his synagogue from a Jerusalem Sage... it stirred his soul to the depths... and since he did not understand the language of the source, he endeavoured to adapt the homily to the textual basis available to him...' (p. 59). So far it was a matter of conjecture that did not affect the issue, but when Amir seeks to reconstruct the original homily of the Jerusalem homilist, he is unable to do so except by indulging in inventions that have no foundation and by distorting the true sense of the known sources and introducing alien meanings into them. In this homily of Philo the characteristic exposition of the Divine Names is entirely absent, and it is obvious that Philo did not have two Names before him, but only δέσποτα, which he does expound (Amir admits this; see *ibid.*, n. 51 and n. 59). But what does Amir do? He simply 'invents' a Hebrew source that expounded the two Names as the two attributes and comes to the conclusion 'that the nexus between the two attributes of God and the two ways of serving Him was formerly to be found also in the teaching of Eretz-Israel' (*ibid.*, p. 60). But surely it is not fortuitous that this nexus left no trace in any of the Tannaitic and Amoraic dicta concerning the fear and love of God! To this the author also has an answer. The statement of R. Joshua b. Hyrcanus that 'Job acted from love' destroyed this connection, while the homily 'with every measure (of recompense) that he metes out to you, be it of benefit or of punishment' 'expressly withdraws love from its relationship to one of the two attributes'. However, it never occurred to Rabban Joḥanan b. Zakkai to say that Job served God out of fear because he saw a link between retribution and the attribute of justice, on the one hand, and fear of God, on

the other, but because Job rebelled when retribution came upon him; hence he thinks all Job's service of God was due only to fear, that is to say, to considerations of reward and punishment, and there is no distinction between the attribute of good and that of punishment. Contrariwise, R. Joshua did not assert that Job served from love because Job reacted to retribution with 'love', but, as we have explained (above, p. 408), because he did not regard Job's reactions and reproaches as 'rebellion'.

83. *T.B. Bava Batra*, 16a; see *Diqduqe Soferim*, p. 73, n. 3.
84. *T.B. Bava Batra, loc. cit.*; see *Diqduqe Soferim*, p. 75.
85. Sander, *op. cit.*, pp. 112 ff, adduced this explanation, but he himself admits, *ibid.*, 106, that nothing is known concerning the views of these Tannaim about the date and birthplace of Job.
86. See above, p. 408.
87. *Tosefta Bava Qamma* vii, 5, p. 358; on the text of the parallel passages see my article in *Zion*, XXV (1960), pp. 145–146; see also *Mekhilta*, Ba-ḥodesh i, p. 203, where Rabban Joḥanan b. Zakkai is reported as saying after the destruction of the Temple: 'You would not subject yourselves to Heaven, so now you are subject to the most inferior of the Arab nations. Cf. *M. 'Avot*, iii, 5, the dictum of Neḥunya b. Haqana.
88. *Tosefta Ta'anit* iv, 7–8, p. 200; see ed. Lieberman, p. 339. Our argument is unaffected by the question whether there is any historical basis to the Tosefta version 'for when the Greek kings posted guards along the roads so as to prevent (pilgrims) from going up to Jerusalem, just as Jeroboam the son of Nebat had done', or whether preference should be given to the text of *T.P. Ta'anit* iv, 7, p. 68b, which makes no mention of the Greek kingdom, or of the edict of the wicked kingdom referred to in *T.B. ibid.*, 28a, as is favoured by H. Malter in his edition of *Tractate Ta'anit*, New York 1930, p. 131, and also, apparently, by S. Lieberman, *Tosefta ki-Fshuṭah, ibid.*, p. 1141–1142, who refers to the comments of Rabbenu Jonathan and Me'iri on the subject. The final formulation of the Baraita, as we have it, did not precede the period of religious persecution, to which the expressions 'because they risked their lives for the Torah and the precepts', and 'because they gave their lives for the precepts' point; the citation of Prov. x 7 is only an imitation of *M. Yoma* iii, 11. If the words 'because they risked' etc. are an addition (they are missing in *T.B., loc. cit.*, where only the conclusion from Proverbs is cited; this also proves that the Babylonian version is independent of the Tosefta and the Palestinian Talmud, a fact that was noted by E. S. Rosenthal, *Leshonot Soferim*, 'Yuval Shay', Ramat Gan, 1958, p. 321, on the basis of the difference between פרסדיות – פרדסאות), then the text of the Baraita cannot be dated earlier than about the period of the Destruction, and it is possible that the stories were intended to encourage the pilgrimage to Jerusalem. On the vv.ll, to the expression יראי חטא שבאותו הדור ['the God-fearing of that generation'] see Malter, *loc. cit.*, n. 2.
89. *T.B. Soṭa* 22b; Rashi explains both terms negatively 'a Pharisee from love —

from love of the reward of the precepts, but not out of love for the commandments of his Creator; from fear of the punishments....' This interpretation is contrary to *T.P. Berakhot* ix, 7, p. 14b; see above, p. 412, and Tosafot, *T.B. Soṭa* 22b, s.v. *Pārûsh* [Pharisee]. Cf. also Tosafot, *T.B. Yevamot* 48b, s.v. *She-'ên* [Because they do not act out of love]; see above, p. 406.

90. See above, p. 407.
91. *T.B. Sanhedrin* 101a; see my article "Asqezis we-Yissurim be-Torat Ḥazal', *Yitzḥak Baer Jubilee Volume*, 1961, pp. 60 ff.
92. *T.B. Berakhot* 61b, and my aforementioned article, p. 60, n. 62.
93. *The Psalms of Solomon* x 2–3 [1–2]: 'Happy is the man whom the Lord remembereth with reproving, and whom He restraineth from the way of evil with strokes, that he may be cleansed from sin, and that it may not be multiplied. He that maketh ready his back for strokes shall be cleansed, for the Lord is good to them that endure chastening.' *Ibid.* 8–11 [7–10]: 'Sparingly is the righteous chastened, lest the sinner rejoice over the righteous. For He correcteth the righteous as a beloved son, and His chastisement is that of a firstborn. For the Lord spareth His pious ones, and blotteth out their errors by His chastening. For the life of the righteous shall be for ever; but the sinners shall be taken away unto destruction.' *Ibid.* xiv 1: 'Faithful is the Lord to them that love Him in truth, to them that endure His chastening.' The translation is that of Gray in R. H. Charles, *Pseudepigrapha*, pp. 643 ff.
94. Büchler, *Studies* etc., p. 170, writes: 'About one hundred and sixty years before R. Akiva, the author of the Psalms of Solomon voiced the same religious belief', but he based himself only on R. Akiba's saying concerning David, and did not interpret it in conformity with his other dicta, with the result that he does not compare the *Psalms of Solomon* with R. Akiba's opinion but with the views of other Sages; see *ibid.*, nn. 3–4.
95. *Aggadot Shir ha-Shirim*, ed. Schechter, p. 5.
96. *Aggadot Shir ha-Shirim*, p. 15; see my article 'Derashot Ḥazal u-Perushe Origines le-Shir ha-Shirim we-ha-Wikkuaḥ ha-Yehudi Noṣri', *Tarbiz*, XXX (1961), pp. 150 ff = 'The Homiletical Interpretations of the Sages and the Expositions of Origen on Canticles' etc., *Scripta Hierosolymitana*, XXII (1971), pp. 247 ff.
97. See *Mekhilta de-R. Ishmael*, Ba-ḥodesh x, p. 241, and my article "Asqezis we-Yissurim' etc., p. 61 and *ibid.* n. 66. On R. Akiba's own attitude to reward and punishment see below, chapter xv, § 2.
98. *T.B. Soṭa* 31a; the Munich MS. has 'R. Simeon' only. See my aforementioned article, n. 67.
99. *T.B. Yoma* 86a; see *Diqduqe Soferim*, *ibid.*, p. 295, n. פ and n. צ.
1. *'Avot de-R. Nathan*, Version I, xxxiii, p. 95, and *ibid.*, Version II, p. 94, as a commentary on *M. 'Avot* v, 3. Apparently the Sages interpreted the words 'to show how great was the *love* of Abraham our father' to mean, in accordance with the verses in Psalms xciv 13 and Prov. iii 12 (see above, p. 354), that he was *beloved* by the Holy One, blessed be He. See H. Albeck,

Hashlamot to *Neziqin*, p. 499. See the commentary of Rabbenu Jonah, and R. Simeon b. Ṣemaḥ Duran, *Magen 'Avot*, p. 76b.

2. See the dictum of Judah b. Tema, *'Avot de-R. Nathan*, Version I, xli, 67a 'Love Heaven, fear Heaven, tremble and rejoice at all the commandments'; cf. *Derekh Ereṣ Zuṭa* ii, 1; see also the saying of R. Ḥiyya, *Ruth Zuṭa*, ed. Buber, p. 48, concerning a proselyte 'who accepts the yoke of the Omnipresent from love and from fear'. Both Sages put love before fear. With regard to R. Ḥiyya's statement compare *T.B. Yevamot* 48b: 'Abba Ḥanan said in the name of R. Eleazar that proselytes in this generation are oppressed "because they do not act out of love but out of fear" '.
3. The author of *Seder Eliahu Rabba* xxvi, p. 140, answers the question 'What is the difference between love and fear?' with the analogy of two servants 'one of whom loves the king and fears him, while the other fears him, but does not love him'.
4. *T.B. Berakhot* 33b; see *Diqduqe Soferim, ibid.*, p. 182. Accordingly to a number of witnesses the dictum concerning the store of the fear of Heaven was transmitted by R. Joḥanan in the name of R. Eleazar b. R. Simeon; cf. *T.B. Shabbat* 31b, and *Diqduqe Soferim, ibid.*, p. 61. In the printed edition the analogy is preceded by 'For R. Ḥanina said', but in all the MSS. and in the Ri'shonim the name is omitted; it is also missing in *T.B. Megilla* 25a.
5. *T.B. Berakhot* 17a; see *Seder Eliahu Rabba* xxvi, p. 140.
6. *Sifre Deut.* § 31; Abbaye himself cites a similar Baraita in *T.B. Yoma* 86a (see above, p. 360): ' "And thou shalt love the Lord thy God" — (this means) that the name of Heaven should become beloved through you', and it appears that the continuation 'If a man studies Bible and Mishna... and his dealings with his fellow creatures are gentle. What will people say of him...?' is Abbaye's interpretation. See *T.B. Bava Batra* 88a concerning 'Rav Safra who exemplified in himself "and speaketh truth in his heart" '; cf. *T.B. Makkot* 24a, Rashi *ad loc.*, s.v. *Rav Safrā*, and *Mekhilta*, Amalek, v, p. 198: ' "Men of truth" — as for example, R. Ḥanina b. Dosa and his colleagues'.
7. *T.B. Soṭa* 31a. In the Munich MS. the words 'wholly righteous' are missing.
8. *T.B. Soṭa, ibid.*, and *Sifre, loc. cit.* The verses cited in the story of Rava are interpreted with reference to reward; see *T.P. 'Avoda Zara*, iii, 1, p. 42c; *Gen. Rabba* lxii, 4, p. 670. From the wording of the second benediction before the reading of the *Shema'* in the morning service, 'and unite our heart to love and fear Thy name... that we might in love give thanks unto Thee and proclaim Thy unity' we can learn nothing relative to our subject, not only on account of the many variant readings among the different versions (in the Siddur of Rav Amram 5a: 'and unite our heart to fear Thy name...', and at the end only 'and Thou hast brought us near to Thy great name'; but in the Siddur of Rav Saadia Gaon, p. 14: 'and unite our heart to love Thy name and to fear Thee', concluding 'and Thou hast brought us near to Thy name that we may give thanks unto Thee and proclaim Thy

unity'; in the version of Maimonides, according to the Oxford MS., ed. D. Goldschmidt, *Studies of the Research Institute for Hebrew Poetry in Jerusalem*, Book VII, 1959, p. 193: 'and unite our heart to love Thy name and reign over us... and Thou hast brought us near to Thy great name... and that we might exalt Thee and love Thy name'), but because it seems that in the time of the Amoraim this benediction did not contain more than does the second benediction before the recitation of the *Shema*ʿ in the evening service, which comprises only a blessing for Israel's election and for the gift of the Torah as a token of the Lord's love for His people. The differences between the various versions are slight, see *Siddur Rav Amram*, p. 18, and I. Ellbogen, *Der Jüdische Gottesdienst in seiner geschichtlichen Entwicklung*, p. 21; and J. Mann, *HUCA*, II (1925), p. 307. Possibly it originated already in Temple times, when the Decalogue was recited before the reading of the *Shema*ʿ, and was recited in this version in the morning service, too. At all events we cannot infer anything from the wording of the prayer 'With abounding love' regarding the nexus between the character of the Lord's service and the attributes of God; see above, p. 414.

9. This fear liberates us from another kind of fear, namely from dread of the ruling power; see *T.B.* *ʿAvoda Zara*, 65a.
10. *T.B. Berakhot* 39b; see *T.B. Shabbat* 61a.

CHAPTER XV

MAN'S ACCOUNTING AND THE WORLD'S ACCOUNTING

1. See above, p. 268, p. 349, and p. 394.
2. See Y. Kaufmann, *Toledot ha-'Emuna ha-Yisre'elit*, Pt. V, pp. 595 ff; Pt. VII, p. 554; M. Weiss, 'Mi-bĕʿāyôt "Tôrat ha-Gĕmûl", ha-Miqrā'ît [Problems of the Biblical "Doctrine of Requital"]', *Tarbiz*, XXXI (1962), pp. 236–263; XXXII (1963), pp. 1–18, where the relevant bibliography of Biblical exegetical literature is given. Important observations of a general character are to be found in G. Scholem, 'Le Mythe de la Peine dans le Judaisme', *Archivio di Filosofia*, Rome 1967, pp. 135–141.
3. On Gen. ii 17 see U. Cassuto, *From Adam To Noah* [English translation], Jerusalem 1961, p. 124 f.
4. Hosea vi 7 'But they like *'ādām* transgressed the covenant' refers to Adam only according to the Haggadic exposition — Rashi, *ad loc.*, in accordance with *T.B. Sanhedrin* 38b; see, on the other hand, the Septuagint, Targum Pseudo-Jonathan, and the commentary of David Qimḥi. Contrariwise the expression 'your first father sinned' in Isa. xliii 27 is referred by Rashi to Abraham, and by David Qimḥi to Adam; see above, p. 215.
5. *Gen. Rabba* xvii 8, pp. 159–160, and the parallels listed there.
6. *'Avot de-R. Nathan*, Version II, xlii, 7, 59a; *Gen. Rabba* ii, 5, p. 186.
7. See Israel Levi, 'Le péché originel dans les anciennes sources Juives', *Ecole Pratique des Hautes Etudes*, Paris 1907; S. Cohon, 'Original Sin', *HUCA*, XXI, 1948, pp. 275 ff.
8. This was particularly due to the words in v. 12: ἐφ' ᾧ πάντες ἥμαρτον 'because they all sinned'; the Vulgate renders: *in quo omnes peccaverunt.* In the commentary attributed to Ambrosius, which was accepted by Augustine, it is stated: *in quo, id est, in Adam omnes peccaverunt.* This interpretation was affirmed as a dogma of the Catholic Church at the Council of Trent in 1546.
9. See W. D. Davies, *Paul and Rabbinic Judaism*, London 1955, pp. 20–35; cf. Julius Gross, *Entstehungsgeschichte des Erbsündendogmas von der Bibel bis Augustinus*, 1960, pp. 48–52, while Protestant scholars argue that Paul changed

nothing of what he had received from his Jewish environment, which recognized the problem of the contradiction between the fact that death is the result of Adam's sin and the explanation of death as a punishment for the personal sin of each individual; see Gross, *ibid.*, p. 60 and p. 63, n. 67. For the position of Catholic scholars cf. Gaudel, 'Péché originel', *Dictionnaire de Théologie Catholique*, XII, pp. 308–9. See also O. Kuss, *Der Römerbrief*, pp. 241–275.

10. *Mekhilta,* Ba-ḥodesh, ix, p. 237. See *T.B. 'Avoda Zara* 5a and the Munich MS. (see *Diqduqe Soferim, ibid.*, p. 13) and the Spanish MS. (ed. S. Abramson; see *ibid.*, p. 141): 'R. Jose said... that there should not be a people or tongue over which the angel of death rules'. Possibly the first Tanna is R. Me'ir; see above, p. 429.
11. *Lev. Rabba* xviii, 3, p. 407 (see also *Tanḥuma*, 'Eqev, 8); *Cant. Rabba* viii 6 in the name of R. Judah, and it is R. Nehemiah who says 'freedom from (the dominion of) the kingdoms'; but in *Exod. Rabba* xxxii, 1; xli, 7; li, 8; *Tanḥuma*, Tissā', 16 (ed. Buber, *ibid.*, 12); Shĕlaḥ, 13, the text reads: 'R. Nehemiah said: Freedom from the angel of death'; see also *'Arugat ha-Bosém*, Pt. I, p. 176. In *Lev. Rabba* xxvii, 4, p. 627, it is R. Judah who says 'If a man say unto you that if Adam had not sinned and eaten from your tree, he would have continued to live to this day, say to him: It has already happened: Eliyah lives on for ever'. Cf. *Eccl. Rabba* iii, 15.
12. *Exod. Rabba* xxxii, 1. As regards the relationship between Adam and the Ministering Angels, see above, p. 221. In *Seder Eliahu Zuṭa*, ed. Friedmann (Me'ir Ish-Shalom), p. 179, a universal character is given to this homily: 'And what did the Holy One, blessed be He, have in mind? He had in mind that every nation and kingdom that would come and receive the Torah, would go on living for ever and ever....'
13. *T.B. Shabbat* 55b; see *Diqduqe Soferim, ibid.*, p. 113.
14. *Sifre Num.* § 137; see *T.B. Yoma* 87a, and there, too, we find only: 'Had you believed in Me, your time would not yet have come to depart from the world....'
15. *Sifre Deut.* § 339, p. 388, where a parallel homily occurs in which Moses himself argues: 'It is not good that people should say: This is Moses... for when they say he did this and that...', The Holy One, blessed be He, gave him the answer cited in our text: 'It is My decree, which is the same for all men'. See *T.B. Shabbat* 55b, where He replied to the Ministering Angels in the words of Ecclesiastes ix 2: 'There is one event to the righteous and to the wicked; to the good' etc.
16. See *Sifre, loc. cit.*, § 341: 'The Holy One, blessed be He, said to him: "but thou shalt not go thither... but thou shalt not go over thither" — neither as king nor as commoner, neither alive nor dead.' See the *Novellae* of Maharsha [Edels], *Shabbat, loc. cit.*, s.v. *'Af Moshe* [Also Moses].
17. *T.B. 'Arakhin* 17a; this is also the reading of the Munich MS.; but R. Samuel Strashun emended אלמלא [If not] to אלמלי [If].

18. L. Ginzberg, *Die Haggada bei den Kirchenvätern*, 1900, pp. 46–47, regards — but to my mind without foundation — the view that death is a Divine decree as an anti-Christian reaction, which brought about the rejection of the old concept that 'there is no death without sin'. On the conception of death as a punishment for sins in the Graeco-Roman world, see R. Hirzel, *Themis., Dike u. Verwandtes*, 1907, p. 154, n. 4, and pp. 223–225.
19. This is the opinion of Israel Levi in his aforementioned article, p. 9.
20. *T.B. Shabbat* 55b; *T.B. Bava Batra* 17a. The preceding Baraitot in *Bava Batra* on 'Over three the Evil Inclination had no dominion', on 'Over three the Angel of Death had no dominion' ('but they died with a Divine kiss'— Rashi *ad loc.*), and 'Over seven worms and maggots had no dominion' are not necessarily connected with the idea contained in the Baraita quoted in the text, and Israel Levi's observations in the article cited above, p. 9, n. 4, are improbable. Also the motif underlying the Baraita *Derekh Ereṣ Zuṭa* i, 'Nine entered the Garden of Eden in their lifetime', is different.
21. Formally the Gemara states anonymously in *T.B. Shabbat, loc. cit.*, that this Baraita holds that 'there is death without sin', on account of what has been said about the four exceptions. R. Menaḥem Me'iri, however, in *Bet ha-Beḥira* on *Tractate Shabbat*, ed. S. Lange, Jerusalem 1965, p. 204, found it necessary to comment, in accordance with his dogmatic approach, as follows: 'Do not be disturbed by the dictum concerning "four died because of the serpent". The meaning is that the fact that the penalty of death was imposed on account of the serpent and was instilled in (human) nature — this attribution to nature is more hyperbole, to minimize their iniquities to the extent that they did not merit being placed on the scales (of judgement); and this assessment is based on human estimation, but who knows the hearts of men... ?'
22. The Gemara, *T.B. Shabbat, loc. cit.*, comments on the Baraita: 'And they are all known by tradition, except Jesse', and for the latter an allusion is found in Scripture; but see *Gilyon ha-Shas* [Marginal Note] by R. Akiba Eger, who refers to the words of the *Zohar*, Genesis 17b: 'For we have learnt: There is no death without sin, except those three who passed away on account of the counsel of the primordial serpent; these are Amram, Levi and Benjamin, and some say also Jesse'. R. Aaron Worms, *Mĕ'ôrê 'Ôr*, Pt. 'Bin Nun', Metz 1924, p. 124a also mentions the words of the *Zohar*. He likewise refers to Rashi's commentary on Psalms xxvii 10 concerning Jesse's sin; possibly Chileab also came within the category of 'some say'.
23. *T.B. Shabbat* 145b–146a; see *Diqduqe Soferim, ibid.*, p. 346; *T.B. Yevamot* 103b; *T.B. 'Avoda Zara* 22b; see the Spanish MS. *ibid.* See *T.P. Rosh ha-shana* iv, 8, p. 59e, and *Cant. Rabba* iv, 4.
24. On *ṭāmē'* ['unclean'] used in an ethical sense in the Bible, see A. Büchler, *Studies in Sin and Atonement*, pp. 214 ff; on *ṭinnûf* ['filth'] and *likhlukh* ['dirt'] in Rabbinic homilies see *ibid.*, pp. 299 ff; and on the stem *zāham* [pollute] see *ibid.*, pp. 316–317. Büchler did not note the difference between

R. Joḥanan's statement and the dicta of R. Jose and R. Neḥemiah. He apparently overlooked the aforementioned article of Israel Levi, referred to above, p. 874, n. 7. On the connection between defilement and sin in the Greek world, see K. Latte, 'Schuld und Sünde in der Greich. Religion', *Archiv für Religionswissenschaft*, XX, 1920–1921, pp. 154 ff, and *ibid.*, pp. 281 ff.

25. *T.P. Yevamot* x, 7, p. 11a: 'R. Joḥanan in the name of R. Jannai (said): She only has [*'ên lāh*] contamination [i.e. is disqualified] with respect to the priesthood, but the court does not declare her contaminated'; see *ibid.* xiii, 4, p. 13d; *ibid.*: 'There is in her only [*'ên bah*] contamination with respect to the priesthood, but the court' etc. See further *T.P. Giṭṭin* ix, 10, p. 49c; *T.B. Bekhorot* 47a: [And do not say]: '... for there are some who say that... the offspring is legally fit'.
26. *T.B. Shabbat* 146a. See *Sifre Deut.* § 31: 'that unworthy offspring do not issue from him'; cf. also *T.B. Pesaḥim* 56a.
27. *Gen. Rabba* ix, 5, p. 70. On the divinity of Hiram see 'Seride Tanḥuma-Yelammedenu,' published by me in *Qoveṣ al Yad*, Book VI (1962), p. 25. Attention should be paid to the following expressions: 'Because they are but flesh and declare themselves gods, impose upon them folly, so that they know not what they do...'; 'Thou givest them a god, and in consequence they become overweening towards Thee and declare themselves gods'; *ibid.*, p. 27: '... "and man hath no pre-eminence above a beast", and if he says "I am a god" — (tell him) "yet thou art man, and not God". By your life! because you say "I am a god", I shall not even raise up against you a man to punish you, but the son of a man....'
28. *T.P. Bikkurim* ii, 1, p. 64c; *T.B. Mo'ed Qaṭan* 28a; *Tractate Semaḥot* iii, 8–10 (ed. Dov Zlotnik, p. 6, and the notes *ibid.*, p. 109); *Gen. Rabba* lxii, 2, p. 673. On the difference between *kārēt* ['extirpation', 'premature death', 'childlessness'] and death at the hands of Heaven, see *T.B. Shabbat* 25a, Rashi s.v. *Wĕ-kārēt* and Tosafot, *ad loc.*, s.v. *kārēt*; but cf. *M. Yevamot* iv, 13: 'Simeon of Teman said: [The offspring of any union] for which the participants are liable to extirpation at the hands of heaven'; this is also the reading of the Kaufmann, Cambridge, and Munich MSS. Cf. also *Mekhilta de-R. Ishmael*, Mishpaṭim, x, p. 285, and *ibid.*, n. 4.
29. *Gen. Rabba*, *loc. cit.* Preceding it is a parallel tradition: 'In R. Me'ir's Torah they found written "and, behold, it was very good" — and, behold, death is good'; see Theodor *ibid.*, n. 1 and cf. *Bereshit Rabbati*, ed. Albeck, p. 209, and *ibid.*, n. 12.
30. *Gen. Rabba*, *ibid.*, p. 71. See *T.B. Megilla* 15a: 'R. Eleazar said in the name of R. Ḥanina: When a righteous man dies, it is unto his generation that he dies....'
31. *Loc. cit.*; see the vv.ll, to line 8; the version that I have cited in the text is also that of the Genizah fragment *Ebr. Antonin* 268 B III.
32. See *T.B. Ḥagiga* 15a; and above, p. 265.

33. *T.B. Berakhot* 18a. R. Joḥanan said 'Our father Jacob did not die... just as his offspring lives so does he...' (*T.B. Ta'anit* 5b); and in *Gen. Rabba* xcvi, 4, p. 1194, Resh Laqish states that the Holy One, blessed be He, said to Jacob 'By your life! You shall be buried, but not die', and *ibid.* the Vatican MS., p. 1237: 'R. Simeon b. Lqish said: The days of the righteous die, but they themselves do not die...'; a similar dictum occurs in *Tanḥuma*, ed. Buber, *Berakha*, 7, in the name of R. Samuel bar Naḥmani. See also *Midrash Tanna'im*, ed. Hoffmann, p. 180.
34. *T.B. Shabbat* 55a; see Rashi *ad loc.*, s.v. *Bĕlō' ḥēṭ'*: and Tosafot *ad loc.*, s.v. *'En*, that death comes for unwitting, and suffering for witting, transgressions. On R. Ammi's saying, *T.B. Mo'ed Qaṭan* 28a, see below, p. 908, n. 52.
35. *Tosefta Yoma* iv (v), 6; ed. Lieberman, p. 251, where all the parallel passages are indicated; see also *Tosefta ki-Fshuṭah*, pp. 824 ff.
36. See *ibid.*, iv (5), 9; cf. Lieberman, *ibid.*, p. 825; s.v. *R. Yehuda.*
37. *Mekhilta de-R. Ishmael*, Ba-ḥodesh, p. 228. Preceding this passage there is still another proof: ' "that the iniquity of Eli's house shall not be expiated by sacrifice or offering for ever" — it shall not be expiated by sacrifice or offering, but it will be expiated by death.' See above, p. 434.
38. See *T.B. Yoma* 86a, and above, pp. 356 ff.
39. *Midrash Tehillim* lii, 3, p. 284, and 'R. Ḥiyya taught' refers to the Baraita in the *Tosefta, loc. cit.*, Halakha 12. Buber gives the reference there as Ezekiel xviii 24, but this verse does not contain the continuation 'and I lay a stumbling block before him', which is the main basis of the homily and occurs in ch. iii 20; only the Bible reads מצדקו (whereas the Midrash has מצדקתו). See *Tosefta ki-Fshuṭah, ibid.*, p. 827, s.v. *Mĕfarsĕmîn*, and *ibid.* n. 54.
40. I have emended the text according to the *Yalquṭ Makhiri* on Psalms, p. 285, which reads: 'in order to expose (them) now, for if anything happens on account of the transgressions, [people] will charge [God] with injustice....'
41. *T.P. Yoma* viii, 6, p. 45c; *T.P. Sanhedrin* x, 1, p. 27d; *T.P. Shevu'ot* i, 9, p. 33b; see 'Pene Moshe', *Yoma, loc. cit.*: 'But the view of the Sages is that the scapegoat, together with repentance, atones even for desecration of the Name'.
42. *T.B. Pesaḥim* 66b; *T.B. Nedarim* 9b; see A. Büchler, *Studies in Sin and Atonement*, pp. 416 ff.
43. *Tosefta Bava Qamma* vii, 5, p. 358. See *Sifra*, Nedava, § 5, 19c; *T.B. Horayot* 10b.
44. *Sifra*, Be-ḥuqqotay, ch. viii, 'And they shall make confession... the words refer to repentance'. See *Sifre Num.* § 2, p. 6: 'We thus know only that a sin-offering requires confession. Whence do we learn that a guilt-offering (also requires confession)? There we are taught' etc.
45. *T.B. Nedarim* 10a; cf. *Tosefta, ibid.*, i, 1, ed. Lieberman, p. 101, and *Tosefta ki-Fshuṭah, ibid.*, p. 395. See also my article "Asqezis we-Yissurim be-Torat Ḥazal', *Yitzḥak Baer Jubilee Volume*, 1961, p. 52, n. 18.
46. *T.P. Shabbat* i, 3, p. 3b; *Tosefta Shabbat* i, 13; *T.B. ibid.*, 12b.

47. *Midrash Tannaim*, p. 164. See also *T.B. Shevu'ot* 21a in the name of R. Simeon b. Yoḥai: 'The earthly court lash him and cleanse him.'
48. *Sifre Deut.* § 286.
49. *'Avot de-R. Nathan*, Version I, iv, ed. Schechter, 11a; see also my article 'Megammot Datiyyot we-Ḥevratiyyot be-Torat ha-Ṣedaqa shel Ḥazal', *Zion*, XVI (1951), pp. 6 ff.
50. *Pesiqta de-R. Kahana*, ed. Mandelbaum, p. 120; see also my article in *Yitzḥak Baer Jubilee Volume*, p. 54, n. 26.
51. *T.B. Berakhot* 17a. On the reading of the order of the sacrifices as a substitute for the sacrifices, see *T.B. Ta'anit* 27b; *T.B. Megilla* 31b, and *Tanḥuma*, Ṣaw, 14.
52. *Sifre Num.* § 2, p. 6. See *T.B. Shabbat* 32a: 'If a man falls ill and death draws near, he is told "confess, for all who are sentenced to death must make confession".' But in *Sifre Zuṭa*, p. 230, we find only: 'This obligates all who are liable to the death-penalty to confess.'
53. See *M. 'Avot* iii; *T.P. Sanhedrin* x, 1, p. 27c; and S. Lieberman, *Tosefta ki-Fshuṭah*, Pt. IV, p. 826.
54. See above, p. 279 and p. 366.
55. *T.B. Shabbat* 55b. We have already seen, above, p. 876, n. 21, that this conclusion is not inevitable on account of the objection raised in the Talmudic discussion.
56. *T.B. Sanhedrin* 46b; see also *ibid.* 101a. Cf. *Midrash Tehillim* xvi, 2, p. 120: ' "As for the holy [Saints] that are in the earth" — for the Holy One, blessed be He, does not call a righteous man "holy" until he is placed in the earth. Why? Because the Evil Inclination vexes him, and (the Lord) puts no trust in him until the day of his death. So, too, Solomon declared "For there is not a righteous man upon earth...." '
57. See my article 'Hilkhot Yerushsha we-Ḥayye 'Olam', *Papers of the World Congress of Jewish Studies*, I, 1967, p. 139; see *T.B. Shabbat* 152b, and *Midrash Tehillim* xl, p. 101; cf. above, p. 442.
58. *T.B. Rosh Hashana* 4a, where parallels are listed; see Rashi s.v. *Kan*, and below p. 890, n. 54.
59. *M. 'Avot* ii, 16. The expression 'And faithful is the Master of your work who will pay you the wages of your toil' is also found in our text *ibid.*, Mishna 14, in the dictum of R. Eleazar, but is missing in most MSS.; see *Mele'khet Shelomo*, *ibid.*, and in ed. Taylor, Cambridge 1897, p. 12; in the Kaufmann MS. there is omitted in R. Ṭarfon's saying the sentence 'And know that the giving... is in the time to come.' On the other hand, it is stated in *M. 'Avot* V, 19, in the printed texts: 'The disciples of Balaam the wicked go down to Gehinnom..., but the disciples of Abraham our father enjoy this world and inherit [*nôḥălîn*] the world to come.' In the Kaufmann MS., however, the text has 'The disciples of Abraham our father inherit the Garden of Eden [*yôrĕshîm lĕ-gan 'ēden*]'; so, too, in ed. Taylor, p. 41: *yôrĕshîn gan 'ēden*; see also my article, *Tarbiz*, xxv (1956), pp. 275 ff. Me'iri explains R.

Ṭarfon's saying as follows: 'that He will pay you the wages of the work both in this world and in the world to come.' Cf. also the *Commentary of R. Isaac b. R. Solomon of Toledo*, Jerusalem 1965, p. 78, and R. Simeon b. Ṣemaḥ Duran, *Magen 'Avot*, 38b. See further *T.P. Shabbat* vi, 9, p. 8d; *Lev. Rabba* xxvii, 2, p. 624.

60. *M. 'Avot* iii, 16, see the commentary of Maimonides, and that of R. Jonah, as well as other commentators mentioned in the preceding note.

61. *M. Shabbat* ii, 6; in the Midrash the three precepts devolving on a woman are related to Eve's sin. See *T.P. Shabbat* ii, 6, p. 5b; *'Avot de-R. Nathan*, Version II, ix; cf. above, p. 874, n. 5. This homily appears to be an explanation of R. Jose's dictum *ibid.*, this being the Baraita in *Tosefta Shabbat* ii, 10, 'There are three assistants of death [*dibqê mîtā*] and the three of them were delivered to the woman....' The reading *bidqê mîtā* ['breaches of death'] in *T.B. Shabbat* 32a and *T.B. Berakhot* 31b, seems to be in conformity with the aforementioned homily; see S. Lieberman, *Tosefta ki-Fshuṭah* iii, p. 35. On *dāvēq* in the sense of 'assistant, helper' in Palestinian Aramic, see Z. Ben Hayyim, *'Ivrit we-Aramit Nosaḥ Shômĕrôn*, III, Bk. II, 1967, p. 373; idem on 'Divqe Mita', *Lĕšonénu lā-'Am*, 1967, qonṭres 4–5, p. לט (p. 135).

62. *Tosefta, loc. cit.* and *T.B. Shabbat* 32b read: 'For the sin of (the non-fulfillment of) vows a man's wife dies', and *T.P. ibid.* has: 'One authority reads in the Baraita "girls", another reads "giving birth". He who reads "girls", teaches in the name of R. Juda: For the sin of (the non-fulfillment of) vows children die...; and the one who reads "giving birth" (teaches): From this we infer that Satan brings charges only in the hour of danger'; see J. N. Epstein, *Mavo' le-Nosaḥ ha-Mishna*, p. 121.

63. *T.B. Shabbat* 32b; see *Diqduqe Soferim*, p. 64: 'After he had heard it from R. Eleazar the son of R. Simeon bar Yoḥai and before he retracted, Rabbi said: 'Because of the sin of the neglect of the Torah'; and *T.B. loc. cit.*: 'And R. Me'ir and R. Judah disagree thereon: One said: Because of the sin of (neglecting the precept of) *Mezuza*; and the other said: Because of the sin of (neglecting the precept of) Fringes'. *Ibid.* there is also the Baraita of R. Nehemiah that I have cited in the text.

64. *T.B. Shabbat* 33a. Regarding the dicta *ibid.* of Samuel the Little and Rava, who seek to defend the righteous from the suspicion of sin, see above, p. 495.

65. *M. 'Avot* v, 8; in the Kaufmann MS. the word *lĕ-'ōlām* ['upon the world'] is missing. See *'Avot de-R. Nathan*, Version I, xxxviii; Version II, xli, 57a–58a; *T.B. Shabbat* 33a.

66. *M. Soṭa* i, 7–10, according to the Kaufmann MS. Printed editions read: 'Absalom prided himself on and gloried in [*nitgā'ā we-nitnawwā*]'; the aforesaid. MS. also reads 'Whom have we greater than Moses?'

67. *Tosefta Soṭa* iii, 6–11, p. 296; see *T.B. Sanhedrin* 108a (as regards the expression 'they spend their days in prosperity', see the margin, where Job xxxvi 11 is referred to), and *ibid.* 109a.

68. See *Gen. Rabba* ix, 11, p. 73, and the parallels noted there. The principle of 'measure for measure' — the Sages created only the concept — has been discussed by many scholars in connection with the *lex talionis*; see E. Goiten, *Das Vergeltungsprincip im Biblischen und Talmudischen Recht*, Frankfurt 1893; J. Horovitz, 'Auge um Auge', *Hermann Cohen Festschrift*, Judaica, pp. 610 ff; B. Jacob, *Auge um Auge*, Berlin 1929. This work contains much instructive material from all the sources, both legal and religious, but it is over-apologetic. See *ibid.* p. 6 on the Hebrew slave, and *ibid.* 49, n. 3, on the statement of R. Eliezer 'an eye for eye, literally'; although he stigmatizes the writings of others, *ibid.* p. 70, as 'Seichte Apologetik', he suffers from the same defect. On the concept in Hellenistic literature and especially in Philo, see Heinemann, *Philo's Griechische und Judische Bildung*, pp. 349–383. On 'measure for measure' as a homiletical principle and a poetic formula, see A. Mirsky, 'Maḥṣavtān shel Ṣûrôt ha-Piyyûṭ [The Quarry of Paytanic Forms]', *Studies of the Research Institute for Hebrew Poetry*, Book vii, 1959, pp. 34–42, and pp. 63–67.

69. xxxvii 2, ed. Margulies, p. 856. The story is entirely in Aramaic; even the sentence at the end of p. 857, נתביש לילך אצל אשתו. מה עשה? הלך לבית הכנסת ['He felt ashamed to go (back) to his wife. What did he do? He went to the Synagogue'] is found in the MSS. in Aramaic: איכסף למיזל לביתיה, אזל לגבי כנשתא. See also the vv.ll. *ibid.*, p. 858, l. 3; on p. 856, n. 4, the editor lists the adaptations of the narrative.

70. *T.P. Berakhot* ii, 8, p. 5c. See *Lev. Rabba* xxiv, 8, p. 562; *Tanḥuma*, Teṣe', § 2: *Deut. Rabba* vi, 2; *Midrash Mishle* xvi, 11 cf. Matthew xix 28–xx 16, whose aim is totally different; see also above, p. 402.

71. *T.B. Qiddushin* 39b; *Tosefta Ḥullin* x, 16, p. 512; *T.B. ibid.* 142a. R. Jacob taught: ' "That it may be well with thee" — in the day that is wholly good; and "that thy days may be long" — in the world eternal [literally, 'wholly long']'. It is Rava who defined his view by the formula 'The reward of the precept is not given in this world', and the Gemara finds it very difficult to determine whether this conclusion is to be drawn from the incident described. The Sages decide that the tragedy occurred because of a broken ladder, and that we must not rely on miracles; nor should he have relied on the precept's protection, because he might have entertained a sinful thought; therefore he was punished in this world, and the reward of the commandment was given him in the world to come. This difficult solution only teaches us that there is length of days in the world eternal, but it does not exclude the possibility of longevity as a reward for a precept in this world, too.

72. *M. Pe'a* i, 1, according to the Kaufmann MS.; see *Diqduqe Soferim, ibid.*

73. *'Avot de-R. Nathan*, Version I, V, p. 26; see L. Finkelstein, *Mavo' le-'Avot u-le-'Avot de-R. Nathan*, p. 35.

74. *Mekhilta de-R. Ishmael*, Mishpaṭim, xviii, p. 313. In the view of Halévy, *Dorot ha-Ri'shonim*, Pt. I, vol. v, p. 180, R. Simeon is R. Simeon b. ha-Sagan ['Deputy'], the son of R. Ḥanina, the Deputy High Priest. According to

another version the reference is to R. Simeon b. Gamaliel; see below, n. 75. A similar motif is to be found in a story about Naḥum of Gimzo; see below, p. 889, n. 44. Also the church father Eusebius asked the question: Why did calamity befall the Christian martyrs? His answer is that they sinned in the administration of their offices, *De Mar. Pal.*, 12; only these martyrs were required to serve idols.

75. *'Avot de-R. Nathan*, Version I, xxxviii; Version II, xli, p. 114, and also in the name of R. Simeon b. Gamaliel; see also the beginning of the story according to the Second Version, which contains the same motif as in the *Mekhilta*, and the continuation according to the First Version, which has preserved the unity of style. Historically it is difficult to determine the event, and none of the emendations of the names is of help, not even that of L. Finkelstein, *loc. cit.*, p. 101, who chose R. Simeon b. Nethanel instead of R. Simeon b. Gamaliel.
76. *Mekhilta*, *ibid.*: 'And when R. Simeon b. Gamaliel and R. Ishmael were put to death, R. Akiba said to his disciples: "Prepare yourselves for tribulation, for were good due to come in our generation, R. Simeon and R. Ishmael would have been the first to receive it....'
77. Thus Pappus and Lulianus, his brother, in Laodicia answered Trajan.
78. See my aforementioned article in the *Yitzḥak Baer Jubilee Volume*, 1961, p. 61. See also *T.B. Bava Qamma* 61a 'If any one delivers himself unto death for words of the Torah, no Halakhic ruling is said in his name'; cf. above, p. 351.
79. On the nature of the decrees see S. Lieberman, 'The Martyrs of Ceasarea', *Annuaire de l'Institut de Philologie et d'histoire orientales et Slaves*, Tome VII, 1934–1944, p. 424. My pupil Mr. M. D. Herr has shown in his doctorate thesis 'On the Roman Empire in the Talmuds and Midrashim', after a thorough investigation of all the sources, that actually in the reign of Hadrian the Jews were not forced to commit religious transgressions as in the days of Antiochus.
80. In *T.P. Berakhot* ix, 7, p. 14b there is added at the end: 'He had not finished speaking when he breathed his last'; in the text I have cited the parallel version in *T.P.* v. 7, p. 20c, where this addition is missing; see *T.B. Berakhot* 61b. On the imprisonment of R. Akiba and his death, see S. Lieberman, *ibid.*, pp. 420–421.
81. *Tractate Semaḥot* viii, 9, ed. Higger, pp. 154–155 [ed. D. Zlotnik, p. 21].
82. The reaction of Jesus, when crucified, was totally different; the portrayals of martyrdom in *II Maccabees* and *IV Maccabees* have been influenced by Greek literature and pagan martyrology, in which the main motif is the heroic one of the 'athlete and hero of the spirit' (*IV Maccabees* vi 10–11). See Joshua Guttmann, 'Hā-'ēm wĕ-shiv'at bānehā bā-'aggādā û-bĕ-sifrê ha-ḥashmônā'im II, IV' [The Mother and her Seven Sons in the Haggadah and in *II* and *IV Maccabees*], the *Yoḥanan Levi Volume*, Jerusalem 1949, pp. 29–37, and my aforementioned article in the *Yitzḥak Baer Jubilee Volume* p. 57, n. 44.

83. *Apology* 41; *Phaedo* 117; note the fate of the truly righteous person in the *Republic*, II, 361; see E. Betz, 'Der gekreuzigte gerechte bei Plato, im Neuen Testament und in der Alten Kirche', *Akademie der Wissenschaften*, Mainz 1950, pp. 31 ff. About fifty years after R. Akiba's death one of the Christian martyrs relies on the words of Plato; cf. *ibid.*, p. 38.
84. From a theoretical point of view Simeon b. ʿAzzai summed up the view of his teacher in his aphorism ' "With all thy soul" — love Him until the agony of death' (*Sifre Deut.* § 32), and in practice R. Ḥanina b. Teradion (*T.B. ʿAvoda Zara* 17a–b) and R. Judah b. Bava (*T.B. Sanhedrin* 14a) acted like him. The tradition in *Tosefta Bava Qamma* viii, 13, and the parallels, that 'He [R. Akiba] said at the time of his death "I know that I committed no sin but this" ', does not cast doubt on the first tradition (see G. Alon, *Meḥqarim be-Toledot Yisra'el*, Pt. II, p. 35, n. 83). We have here the same motif, namely that even those who offer their lives for the observance of the commandments examine themselves to see whether they have not been seized because they had stumbled and committed some sin; see above, n. 74.
85. *T.B. Sanhedrin* 101a. The story is told by Rabba bar bar Ḥanna; see above, p. 879, n. 56.
86. *Ibid.* in the Baraita 'The Rabbis taught'; in the *Mekhilta*, Ba-ḥodesh, x, p. 240, it occurs in the version 'R. Eliezer was already ill....' In the printed editions of the *Mekhilta* we find only 'Ṭarfon observed "Master, you are better to Israel than the disk of the sun"; thus you learn that suffering is precious.' Evidently the scribes shortened the passage; the differences between the MSS. in which it occurs are considerable, and there is reason to suspect that the abridgement was completed according to the recension of the Babylonian Talmud (see next note). In *Sifre Deut.* § 32 the MSS. mark the passage as 'an addition'. Rabbenu Hillel in his commentary on the *Sifre*, ed. Rabbi Koleditzky, Jerusalem 1948, p. 1, observes 'It is designated "an addition" because it is not an integral part of the theme, but since suffering is discussed here, this passage has also been included'; see A. Büchler, *Studies in Sin and Atonement*, 1928, pp. 170 ff.
87. R. Akiba's answer is: 'I expound a verse: "Manasseh was twelve years old when he began to reign, and he reigned fifty and five years in Jerusalem..." and it is written "These are also the proverbs of Solomon, which the men of Hezekiah king of Judah copied out". Did then Hezekiah king of Judah teach the whole world Torah, but not his own son? The meaning is that all the trouble and toil that he devoted to him [i.e. to his education] did not lead him to the path of rectitude, but suffering did, as it is said... "and they took Manasseh with hooks and bound him with fetters of bronze..." and it is written "And when he was in distress he entreated the favour of the Lord his God and humbled himself greatly before the God of his fathers"... Thus you learn that suffering is precious.' In the Munich MS., in *Haggadot ha-Talmud*, and in the *Yalquṭ* MS. a description of his suffering is added: 'What did they do to him? They cast him into a bronze oven....'; see *Diqduqe*

Soferim, Sanhedrin, p. 307. It seems, therefore, that this entire exposition does not belong to the original source of the narrative, which concluded with the words 'Said he [R. Eliezer] to them: "Support me that I may hear the words of my disciple R. Akiba, who said 'Suffering is precious' ".' In this way R. Eliezer showed his agreement with his remarks (from the *Mekhilta, ibid.*, one may possibly infer that the text was: 'Said he to him: "Akiba, how do you know this?" He answered "Thus have you taught me", and it is obvious that the passage from the words 'I expound a verse' is an addition derived from the Babylonian Talmud). The citation of the case of Manasseh as an explanation for the sufferings of R. Eliezer seems very strange. In the Mishna, Manasseh is one of the three kings, who have no portion in the world to come, but R. Judah seeks to except him. See the discussion *ibid.* 102–103b; the transmitter of the tradition concerning the suffering of Manasseh is the Amora R. Levi; cf. *T.P. Sanhedrin* x, 2, p. 28c.

88. See *Mekhilta, loc. cit.*; *Sifre, loc. cit.*; *T.B. Berakhot* 5a; and *Tanḥuma*, Teṣe, 2.
89. *T.B. ʿArakhin* 16b.
90. *Gen. Rabba* xliv, 13, p. 435; see my article, cited above, in the *Yitzḥak Baer Jubilee Volume*, p. 59.
91. *Sifre Deut.* § 311. A similar explanation of the sufferings inflicted upon Israel is given in *II Maccabees* vi 12–17; see above p. 526.
92. *T.B. Qiddushin* 40b; see the dictum of R. Simeon b. Yoḥai in the *Mekhilta* and *Sifre, loc. cit.*; and cf. *Lev. Rabba* xxix, 3, p. 672.
93. See G. Alon, *Toledot ha-Yehudim be-'Ereṣ Yisra'el bi-Tequfat ha-Mishna we-ha-Talmud*, Pt. II, pp. 69 ff.
94. *M. Qiddushin* iv, 14. On the argument that animals are well equipped from birth, while man is born unequipped, see Plato, *Protagoras*, 321 A–B, cf. Origen, *Contra Celsum*, iv, 78.
95. *Tosefta Bava Meṣiaʿ* iii, 25, p. 378. See *T.B. ibid.* 58b. Rava testified that Abbaye suffered from a type of dropsy that is an indication of starvation and not of sin; see *T.B. Shabbat* 33a.
96. See *T.B. Bava Meṣiaʿ* 84b–85a on the sufferings of R. Eleazar b. R. Simeon and of Rabbi. (It is narrated there that once R. Eleazar b. R. Simeon heard a scholar spoken of contemptuously without remonstrating; but see the commentary of Rivan [R. Judah b. Nathan] to *T.B. Makkot* 24a, s.v. *Kĕgôn.*) In the name of Rabbi himself it is reported: 'Whoever accepts the pleasures of this world is deprived of the pleasures of the world to come; but whoever does not accept the pleasures of this world is granted the pleasures of the world to come' — *'Avot de-R. Nathan*, Version I, xxviii, p. 85; see A. Marmorstein, *The Old Rabbinic Doctrine of God*, 1927, pp. 186 ff.
97. See *T.B. Berakhot* 5a. Thus R. Ḥiyya bar Abba in his name; but preceding this dictum the matter is disputed: 'The following subject is disputed by R. Jacob bar Idi and R. Aḥa bar Ḥanina. One said: The sufferings of love are such as do not entail interruption of study...; and the other said... such as

do not involve intermission of prayer.' In *Gen. Rabba* xcii, 1, p. 1137, it is R. Joshua b. Levi who said: 'All sufferings that do not cause him to interrupt his (study of the) Torah are sufferings of love.' In *T.B. Berakhot* 5b it is transmitted in the name of R. Joḥanan: 'Leprosy and childlessness are not sufferings of love.' It is also related there that when he fell ill and R. Ḥanina came to visit him and asked him 'Are the sufferings welcome to you?', he replied 'Neither they nor their reward.' It thus appears that we have here a different and conflicting tradition (indeed in *Cant. Rabba* ii, 15, it is R. Ḥanina who said 'I want neither them nor their reward'), for on the same page it is related that R. Joḥanan regarded the death of his sons as 'sufferings of love'; see Rashi, *ibid.* s.v. *Bîr*, and Tosafot, *ibid.*, s.v. *Wĕ-hā-'āmar*; cf. *T.B. Bava Batra* 116a, and the commentary of Rashbam, *ad loc.*, s.v. *Dên garmā.*

98. *T.B. Berakhot, loc. cit.*, and Rav Huna said: 'Even as the guilt-offering is brought willingly so too must suffering be endured willingly.' In *Gen. Rabba* ix, 8, p. 72 it is stated that these sufferings enable a man to attain to the world to come; see the notes *ibid.* In *T.B. Berakhot* 5b it is narrated that R. Huna's wine turned sour (see above, the story about R. Eliezer and R. Akiba, p. 444), and when the Sages came to visit him and told him to examine his deeds, he answered: 'Am I suspect in your eyes?' To which they replied: 'Is then the Holy One, blessed be He, suspect of executing judgement unjustly?' And in truth it subsequently emerged that his attitude to his tenant was not correct; see Tosafot, *ad loc.*, s.v. *Dînā* that 'they wished to hint to him not to do this any more.'
99. See above, n. 91, and the dictum of R. Joshua b. Levi, *T.B. Ta'anit* 8a.
1. *M. 'Avot* iii, 13; see R. Simeon b. Ṣemaḥ, *Magen 'Avot, ad loc.*
2. *T.P. Nedarim* viii, 1, p. 40d.
3. *T.B. Qiddushin* 81b. In *Sifre Deut.* § 31 it is stated that Reuben fasted for his action until Moses came and received him in penitence, but there the reference is to a transgression that he had committed. See *The Testaments of the Twelve Patriarchs*, The Testament of Reuben i, 10, where, however, it is abstinence for seven years from wine, meat, and pleasant food that is spoken of. On the fasts of other patriarchs see R. Eppel, *Le piétisme Juif dans les Testaments des douze Patriarches*, 1930, p. 182.
4. *Tosefta 'Ahilot* v, 11–12, p. 603; see *T.B. Hagiga* 22b.
5. *Tosefta, loc. cit.*, iv, 2, p. 600; see *T.B. Nazir* 52b.
6. *T.P. Shabbat* v, 4, p. 7c.
7. See my aforementioned article in the *Yitzḥak Baer Jubilee Volume*, pp. 50 ff.
8. See *ibid.*, p. 64. Regarding a man who let his hair and nails grow long in order to make himself repulsive as a penance, Rava said 'Perhaps he is only deceiving' (*T.B. Sanhedrin* 25a).
9. *T.B. Ta'anit* 11a–b; a parallel to this distinction drawn between scholars and other people is to be found in the following remarks of Chrysostom (*De Sacerdotio*, 13, 3, Migne, PG 48, 644): 'To contemn food, drink, and bed

is no hardship for many who are of a rough nature. Fasting and other self-afflictions are suited to a Nazirite who lives a solitary life. A priest, on the other hand, is obliged to train himself differently.

10. *T.P. Nedarim* ix, 1, p. 41b.
11. *T.B. Beṣa* 32b. Although we have learnt that it is also related of R. Joḥanan that when he was asked during an illness 'Are your sufferings welcome to you?', he replied 'Neither they nor their reward' (*T.B. Berakhot* 5b; see *Cant. Rabba* ii, § 16); yet it is very possible that this tradition emanates from the opponents of those who welcomed suffering, and it was their intention to show that even a Sage who professed the principle 'suffering is precious' could not stand up to the ordeal in practice. See above, p. 884, n. 97. R. Joḥanan reacted to Rav's observation regarding the eating of cooked food 'From Sabbath eve to Sabbath eve' thus: 'Abba comes from a family of robust folk; but in our case, whoever has a *peruṭa* in his pocket should run with it to the shop-keeper' (*T.B. Ḥullin* 84a).
12. *T.B. 'Arakhin* 16b; see Rashi *ad loc.*, s.v. *Takhlît yissûrîn*. Cf. also Rava's comment on R. Eleazar's dictum 'The blood of a bruise affects atonement like the blood of a burnt offering'; see above, p. 811, n. 77.
13. *T.B. Berakhot* 17a. 14. *Ibid.* 5b.
15. *M. Ta'anit* ii, 4; in regard to the date of this benediction, see H. Albeck, *Seder Mo'ed*, Hashlamot, pp. 492–493.
16. *T.P. Ta'anit* iii, 9, p. 67a; this passage was overlooked by Marmorstein, *The Old Rabbinic Doctrine of God*, 1927, p. 80; on R. Levi's dictum 'The All-Merciful does not, to begin with, destroy lives', which is incorrectly quoted there, see *Lev. Rabba* xvii, 4, p. 379, and the parallels noted there, n. 1.
17. See *Tosefta Berakhot* vi, 1, p. 14: 'For every judgement with which He judges you, be it by the attribute of good or by the attribute of retribution.'
18. *Tosefta Ṣota* iv, 1, p. 298.
19. *Mekhilta de-R. Ishmael*, Wa-Yissa', iii, p. 166; see the parallels indicated *ibid.*, n. 6.
20. See *ibid.*, Massekhta de-Pisḥa, vii, p. 24, and *ibid.* xiii, p. 46; Wa-yehi, i, p. 85. Particularly noteworthy is Massekhta de-Kaspa, xx, p. 328, ' "For I will not acquit the wicked" — now it is an argument from minor to major: If in the case of the attribute of retribution, which is scant, the Torah declared "For I will not acquit the wicked", how much more so in the case of the attribute of good, which is abundant!' The homily is linked to the preceding text 'I might have thought that just as he left your court not guilty, so he will leave My court...', and remains wholly within the realm of law and justice. See *T.B. Shabbat* 97a; and cf. *Midrash Tehillim* lxii, 4, p. 308; *Tosefta Pe'a* i, 1, and *Tosefta ki-Fshuṭah, ibid.*, p. 126.
21. *Mekhilta de-R. Ishmael*, Mishpaṭim, xviii, p. 314; see the vv.ll. In a fragment from the Genizah, Antonin 239, the text reads: 'Now it is an argument from minor to major: If in the case of the attribute of retribution, which is scant, yet when they cry out against the community [literally 'the many'],

the omnipresent hears their cry, how much more so in the case of the attribute of good, which is abundant, when many pray for an individual!' (My attention was drawn to this version by Mr. J. Weisberg). In *Mekhilta de-R. Simeon b. Yoḥai*, p. 211, the version of the homily is as follows: 'Now which attribute is the more abundant — the attribute of good or of retribution? Perforce one must say: The attribute of good. If then in the case of the attribute of retribution, which is scant, yet when the individual prays, the Omnipresent hears his prayer, it follows logically that where the attribute of good is concerned, when an individual prays, the Omnipresent hears his prayer.' But in *Mekhilta de-R. Ishmael* the passage is preceded by another syllogism: 'If when an individual cries out against an individual (Scripture declares) "I shall surely hear his cry", then how much more so when many do cry!' Under the influence of this argument *a minori ad majus* the next version follows, but according to the opening clause 'When an individual cries out against the many it is thus...' the text should continue 'when an individual prays for many...', for it does not follow logically that in the case of the attribute of good, when many pray for an individual they are heard. But see *Sifre Deut.* § xxvii: 'If in the case of an individual's prayer for many it is heard thus, how much more so is the prayer of many for an individual (heard)!'

22. See above, p. 448. On the Septuagint translation of Exodus xxxii 12, 14; Isa. liv 10, which employs passive forms of the verb ἱλάσχεσθαι in the sense of 'to forgive', see C. H. Dodd, *The Bible and the Greeks*, pp. 85–86. Nelson Glueck, in his work on the concept of *ḥesed* ['lovingkindness', 'steadfast love'] in the Bible, did stress its intimate link with the covenant between God and His people as well as its legal character, but he went too far in his differentiation between *ḥesed* and *raḥămîm* ['compassion', 'mercy']. The German book, which appeared in 1927, has now been translated into English under the title *Hesed in the Bible*, 1967, to which G. A. Larue has added a preparatory review on the studies published in the course of the last forty years on the concept '*ḥesed*'. In regard to our subject see pp. 84–85 of the work proper and the Introduction, p. 15.

23. With regard to human justice, R. Akiba said 'Compassion does not enter into law' (*M. Ketubbot* ix, 2, 3), and the Amoraim, too, were careful to differentiate, if they acted according to the principle of compassion, so that the decision should not become a fixed law. Thus it is related: 'R. Eleazar proposed to allow maintenance (for daughters) out of movable property. Said R. Simeon b. Eliakim to him: "Master, I know full well that your ruling is not based on law, but is motivated by compassion. But (there is the danger) that disciples will note it and fix it as a Halakha for all time" ' (*T.B. Ketubbot* 50b). See above, p. 444.

24. See *M. Shevu'ot* iv, 13. 'Gracious and compassionate' are epithets. *Raḥămān* ['All-Merciful'] occurs in *Tosefta Bava Qamma* ix, 30, p. 366; and the Aramaic form *Raḥmana* is common in the Talmuds and in the Tannaitic Midrashim.

25. See above pp. 460–1.
26. *Mekhilta de-R. Ishmael*, Shira, iv, pp. 129–130, and *Mekhilta de-R. Simeon b. Yoḥai*, p. 81.
27. *Sifre Deut.* § 27; see *Sifra*, 'Aḥare, ix, 85c: ' "I am the Lord your God" — I am the Lord who spoke and the world came into being; I am Judge; I am full of compassion...'
28. For this reason Onkelos invariably translated 'every Name signifying Lordship and Deity by the Tetragrammation.' See, S. D. Luzatto, *'Ôhēv Gēr*, 1830, p. 2, except where the expression 'the Lord [Tetragrammaton] God ['Elohim]' occurs.
29. *Mekhilta de-R. Ishmael*, Shira, iii, p. 128, and *Mekhilta de-R. Simeon b. Yoḥai*, p. 80.
30. *De Plantatione* 86; *De Abrahamo*, 124–125.
31. *Über den Einfluss der pal. Exegese auf die alex. Hermeneutik*, Leipzig 1851, p. 26.
32. See A. Marmorstein, *The Old Rabbinic Doctrine of God*, 1927, pp. 43–49; his view was accepted by H. Wolfson, *Philo*, I, pp. 224–225.
33. The controversy in *Mekhilta*, Mishpaṭim, xix, p. 317: ' "Thou shalt not curse *'Elohim*" — whoever it may be [i.e. God or human judges]; this is the view of R. Akiba. R. Ishmael said: The verse speaks of judges', does not indicate that the 'later' connotation *of 'Elohim* was unknown in their days, as Marmorstein avers *ibid.*, p. 44, n. 15a. The reverse is the case. That Marmorstein's remarks on 'the attribute of retribution and the attribute of good' are unfounded follows from what we have stated in the text on the signification of this pair of terms; see above, p. 449.
34. See C. H. Dodd, *op. cit.*, pp. 8 ff; and W. W. Baudissin, *Kyrios*, I, p. 17; pp. 84–86, pp. 439 ff, pp. 516 ff, pp. 600 ff; and especially II, pp. 241ff. Cf. also III, p. 107, but his conjecture, *ibid.*, p. 709, that the Rabbinic interpretation was influenced by the Alexandrian conception, which connected αἰώνιος (according to the interpretation of B.) with Κύριος, has nothing to support it.
35. See H. Wolfson, *op. cit.*, pp. 223 ff.
36. See Isa. xiv 1: כי ירחם ה' — καὶ ἐλεήσει Κύριος, and *ibid.* liv 10: מרחמך ה' — Κύριος ἵλεώς σοι, *et al.*
37. *M. Berakhot* v, 3; M. *Megilla* iv, 9.
38. *T.P. Berakhot* v, 3, p. 19c; *T.B. ibid.*, 33b. See also T.B. *Megilla* 25a, and Tosafot *ad loc.*, s.v. *mi-pĕnê*. Kalir's *piyyuṭ* accords with the homily of R. Berekhia in the name of R. Levi, *Lev. Rabba* xxvii, 11, p. 644, and of the parallels cited *ibid.*, n. 4.
39. This is evidenced by the fact that this formula recurs in the continuation of the passage in connection with 'Those who translate'; see above, p. 853, n. 54.
40. *T.B. Berakhot* 60b; see *Diqduqe Soferim, ibid.*, p. 349, n. 3.
41. *Mekhilta de R. Ishmael*, Ba-ḥodesh x, p. 239.
42. See above, p. 883, n. 87.

43. Above, p. 887, n. 23.
44. *T.B. Taʿanit* 21a, where the narrative comes to explain Nahum's title איש גמזו ['man of Gimzo', explained as though the name were גם זו]. In his understanding of suffering, this teacher of R. Akiba did not attain to his disciple's conception. He explained to his pupils that the visitations to which he was subjected were due to sin, and the motif is similar to that found in the explanation given of the death of R. Ishmael and R. Simeon (see above, p. 442). But according to the version in *T.P. Pe'a* viii, 9, p. 21b, and in *T.P. Sheqalim* v, 6, p. 49a, R. Akiba came to visit Nahum of Gimzo and said to him 'Woe unto me that I see you in this plight!', to which his teacher replied 'Woe to me that I do not see you thus!' Said R. Akiba to him: 'Why do you curse me?' Nahum answered him: 'Why do you rebel against suffering?' According to this version R. Akiba learned from his teacher Nahum not to rebel against suffering. But it appears to be a late version, which anticipates R. Akiba's end; and so far as the essential story of Nahum is concerned, the theme of sin is retained even in the text of the Palestinian Talmud.
45. *Sifre Num.* § 137, p. 184 (the verse is not quoted according to the Masoretic tradition [על אשר instead of כאשר; סין for צין]; see the vv.ll., *ibid.*, p. 183); cf. *ibid.* § 102, p. 103.
46. *Tosefta Berakhot* iv, 16–17, p. 10.
47. See the commentary of Rashi and Abraham ibn Ezra to Ḥabakkuk, *loc. cit.*
48. *Lev. Rabba* xxiv, 1, p. 549.
49. *Tosefta Bava Qamma* ix, 30, p. 366; this is also the reading in *T.P. Bava Qamma* viii, 10, p. 6c, with the addition 'If you are not compassionate, the Omnipresent will not have compassion on you.' But in *Sifre Deut.* § 96, the dictum is cited in the name of Rabban Gamaliel Berabbi; and so, too, in *T.B. Shabbat* 151b. But 'Berabbi' is missing in *Haggadot ha-Talmud* and in *Yalquṭ*; see *Diqduqe Soferim, loc. cit.*, p. 367, n. 3.
50. See *Mekhilta*, Shira, iii, p. 127, and the parallels given *ibid.*, n. 6, see above, p. 177.
51. The first dictum of R. Me'ir is taught as a Baraita in *T.P. Taʿanit* ii, 1, p. 65b. The second dictum occurs in *Pesiqta de-Rav Kahana*, p. 370. See *Sifra*, 'Aḥare, ix, 1, 85c, which is a Baraita of R. Ḥiyya, as can be seen from *Lev. Rabba* xxiii, 9, p. 535.
52. *T.P. Taʿanit* iv, 8, p. 69b; *Pesiqta de-Rav Kahana*, Lamentations, ed. Mandelbaum, p. 258, and the parallel passages indicated *ibid.*, n. 1. A man must first show his compassion; hence R. Huna, in the name of R. Simeon b. Ḥalafta, explains that the repentance of the people of Nineveh was deceitful, for 'they placed the calves inside and their dams outside... so that the former cried on the one side and the latter on the other. They said: "If He takes no pity on us, we shall have no pity on them." ' See *T.P. Taʿanit* ii, 1, p. 65b; cf. my observations in the *J.N. Epstein Jubilee Volume*, 1950, pp. 118 ff.
53. *T.P. Taʿanit* ii, 1, p. 65b. On R. Aḥa as a transmitter of R. Joḥanan's teaching see W. Bacher, *Agada der Palästinischen Amoräer*, III, p. 110, n. 2.

54. *T.P., loc. cit.* In *T.P. Sheqalim* v, 2, p. 48d, R. Aḥa's dictum is not reported in the name of R. Joḥanan, but after R. Ḥanina's statement R. Aḥa states: 'It is written "And around about Him a mighty tempest [*niś'ărā*]' — (this means that) He deals strictly with them [those around Him] to a hair's breadth (*śa'ărā*]'. So, too, in *T.P. Beṣa* iii, 9, p. 62b, where the reading is 'He deals strictly with them to a hair's point' [חוד for חוט]'. See *T.B. Bava Qamma* 50a; cf. *T.P. Qiddushin* i, 7, p. 61b: 'The Holy One, blessed be He, does not delay the bestowal of the reward due to those among the Gentiles that perform precepts'; and *Tanḥuma*, ed. Buber, Toledot, 14, p. 134: ' "So God give thee" — in accordance with justice... but to Esau, be he righteous or wicked, He will give... Why? Esau is wicked... but Jacob, who is righteous, even if he performs a precept and yet suffers affliction, he will not reproach the attribute of justice...'; see *T.B. Rosh ha-Shana* 4a, and above, p. 8h9, n. 58.
55. *Gen. Rabba* xxxiii, 3, p. 308.
56. *T.B. Rosh ha-Shana* 17a; see Rashi *ibid.*, s.v. *ma'ăvîr* [He sets aside], and s.v. *ma'ăvîrîn* [are forgiven].
57. *Gen. Rabba* viii, p. 59; see notes *ibid.* On R. Berechiah and his relationship to R. Samuel bar Naḥman, cf. W. Bacher, *op. cit.*, III, p. 348.
58. *Gen. Rabba* xii, 15, p. 112; see above, p. 274.
59. *T.B. Rosh ha-Shana* 17b, and Rashi *ad loc.*, s.v. *Û-lĕ-va-Sôf.* In *T.P. Pe'a* i, 1, p. 16b the following exposition is given: 'R. Eleazar said: "Also unto Thee, O Lord, belongeth loving kindness; for Thou renderest to every man according to his work" — and if he has none, Thou givest him of Thine. This is the view of R. Eleazar...: And He that is abundant of lovingkindness inclines (the scales of judgement) towards lovingkindness.'
60. *Midrash Tehillim* lxii 4, p. 308, in the name of 'Our teachers said'; see n. 13. It appears that two interpretations have been combined there; the analogy — 'Like a young man who is inflamed with sin and deserving of death. What does the Holy One, blessed be He, do? He suspends his sentence until he takes a wife and begets children, and the Holy One, blessed be He, takes one of his children for the transgression that he committed' — illustrates the delaying of punishment.
61. *T.B. Shabbat* 55a; so, too, *Tanḥuma*, Mishpaṭim, § 7. But *Tanḥuma*, Tazria', § 9, reads: 'Prosecution entered before the Holy One, blessed be He.' This is also the reading in ed. Buber § 13; see above, p. 205.
62. See *T.B. Megilla* 15b: 'The attribute of justice said before the Holy One, blessed be He: "Sovereign of the Universe! In what way are these different from those?" The Holy One, blessed be He, said to him: "The Israelites occupied themselves with the Torah, the Gentile nations did not occupy themselves with the Torah." He (justice) then said: "But these also reel through wine..." ' However, the words from 'He said' to 'He said' are missing in all the MSS. and in all the old printed editions. See *Diqduqe Soferim*, *ibid.*, p. 78, and cf. *T.B. Sanhedrin* 111b. See also *T.B. Sanhedrin* 94a, where the Prince of the World complains about the triumph of the attribute of justice.

63. *T.B. Sanhedrin* 97b; the beginning of the homily against those who seek to calculate the End [the advent of the Messiah] is by R. Samuel bar Naḥmani in the name of R. Joḥanan, and apparently the continuation of the homily also belongs to him. On his opinion concerning compassion see above, p. 457; the words 'will the Lord wait' is explained by Rashi, *ad loc.*, thus: 'He himself waits and longs for the coming of the Messiah.'
64. *T.B. Pesaḥim* 119a. Rashbam s.v. *Mi-pĕnê middat ha-dîn*: 'It [the attribute of justice] accuses and says "Do not receive them", but He [God] receives them secretly'. See *Diqduqe Soferim*, p. 379, n. *Ṭêt*: MS. ב reads 'on account of the attribute of justice that he should not see'. The dictum is transmitted in the name of 'Rav Kahana in the name of R. Ishmael b. R. Jose, and the Rabbis say in the name of Resh Laqish in the name of R. Judah Nesi'ah', or 'and others say that Resh Laqish' etc. (see *Diqduqe Soferim*, *ibid.*, n. 8). But it is surprising that in no version is it stated 'And Rav Kahana said in the name of R. Ishmael b. R. Jose', although previously another dictum was reported in this form; hence it appears that this entire tradition seeks only to explain the place of the dictum here. See *T.B. Pesaḥim* 118b: 'Rav Kahana said that when R. Ishmael b. R. Jose fell ill...'
65. *T.B. Sanhedrin* 103a.
66. *T.P. ibid.* x, 2, p. 28c in the name of R. Levi; *Pesiqta de-Rav Kahana*, Shuva, p. 365 in the name of R. Levi bar Ḥita; similarly in *Ruth Rabba* v, 14, and in *Deut. Rabba* ii, 4, without the name of the expositor. In *T.P. Taʿaniyyot* ii, 1, p. 65b, R. Levi, after drawing an analogy with 'a king who had two ruthless legions', said 'Thus said the Holy One, blessed be He, Anger and Wrath are angels of destruction; I shall, therefore, send them on a long journey, so that if the Israelites vex Me, then ere I send for them [Anger and Wrath] and bring them back, the Israelites will repent and I shall accept their repentance.' On Anger and Wrath see *T.B. Nedarim* 32a, and above, p. 154.
67. In the passages cited above, the Holy One, blessed be He, answers the argument of the angels thus: 'If I do not receive him back in penitence, I shall close the door to all penitents.' In *T.B.*, *loc. cit.*, this answer is paralleled by the dictum of R. Joḥanan: 'Whoever says that Manasseh has no share in the world to come, weakens the hands of the penitent.'
68. שובה in Isa. xxx 15 'בשובה ונחת תושעון' ['In sitting still and rest shall ye be saved'] simply means 'quiet' rest; see Rashi *ad loc.* Thus, too, the Rabbis inferred from this verse that 'Israel are redeemed only on account of the Sabbath', *Lev. Rabba* iii, 1, p. 58. תשובה is found in the sense of 'answer' in Job xxi 34, and in the literal meaning of returning to a place in II Sam. xi, 1, I Kings xx 22. It occurs in the same signification also in the *Scroll of the Thanksgiving Psalms*: ותשובת עפר ['to return to dust'] (xii, 26); ולעפר תשובתו ['to return to dust'] (x, 3–4); but not in the connotation of 'returning from iniquity'. Hence it is strange that s.v. ἀποστρέφω, *Theol. Wörterbuch zum NT*, VII, 1964, p. /21, Bertram states, on the basis of the aforementioned passages, 'Die Rabb. haben den Ausdruck übernommen.'

69. See E. K. Dietrich, *Umkehr und Busse im AT und im Judentum*, 1936; Y. Kaufmann, *Toledot ha-'Emuna ha-Yisre'elit*, II, pp. 285.
70. *T.P. Makkot* ii, 7, p. 31d, according to a fragment of a Genizah MS, published by S. Wieder, *Tarbiz*, xvii (1946), p. 133; see S. Lieberman, *Hilkhôt ha-Yĕrûshalmî lĕ-Rambam*, New York 1948, p. 67, n. 7, on the variant readings in this fragment; cf. *Pesiqta de-Rav Kahana*, Shuva, p. 355.
71. *Tanḥuma*, Wa-Yērā', 8; see *Pesiqta Rabbati*, Hosafa [supplement] III, 198a.
72. *Tosefta Ta'aniyyot* i, 8; ed. Lieberman, pp. 325–326; see vv.ll. and *Tosefta ki-Fshuṭah*, p. 1072, where the parallels are listed. The presumption was that when a man repents, he does so wholeheartedly. See *T.B. Ḥullin* 51a '(But if they returned them) because they repented, they would make proper repentance.'
73. *Sifre Num.* § 136, p. 183.
74. *M. Sanhedrin* x, 2; see above, n. 66.
75. *T.P. Ḥagiga* ii, 1, p. 77b; see *T.B. Ḥagiga* 15a; *Eccl. Rabba* vii, 8; *Ruth Rabba* vi, 13; *Eccl. Zuṭa*, ed. Buber, p. 110.
76. *Tosefta Yoma* iv, 11, ed. Lieberman, p. 253; see *'Avot de-R. Nathan* 60a; *T.B. Yoma* 87a.
77. See *Sifre Deut.* § 328; cf. above, p. 314.
78. See the sources listed above, n. 75.
79. On this motif see A. Büchler, 'Die Erlösung des Eliša b. Abujah's aus dem Höllenfener', *MGWJ*, 1932, pp. 412–456.
80. *T.B. Yoma* 86b.
81. *Sifre Be-midbar* § c, 34, p. 180. *Mekhilta de R. Ishmael*, Shira, v, p. 133, and the parallels listed *ibid.*, n. 16. The seven days in which the Ark was made is similarly explained also by Philo, *Quaestiones*, 13; see A. Aptowitzer, *Kain und Abel in der Agada*, Wien, 1922, p. 175, n. 344. See above, p. 439,
82. *M. 'Avot* ii, 10; in the text I have quoted the recension of *'Avot de-R. Nathan*, Version II, xxix, p. 62; see *ibid.*, Version I, xv, and *T.B. Shabbat* 153a, and *ibid.* also the parable employed by R. Joḥanan b. Zakkai in his interpretation of Ecclesiastes ix 8: 'Let thy garments be always white' (and R. Me'ir's son-in-law cited R. Me'ir's comment on this parable; see *Diqduqe Soferim*, *ibid.*, p. 374). Cf. *Midrash Psalms* xc, 16, 197a; R. Simeon b. Ṣemaḥ Duran, *Magen 'Avot*, 32b, after quoting the words of the Midrash 'It follows that he will repent today lest he die tomorrow, and thus all his days will be spent in repentance', adds: 'And there are versions of the Mishna in which this sentence is incorporated.' In *Mĕle'khet Shelomo* on *M. 'Avot*, *loc. cit.*, we find: 'R. Joseph Ashkenazi wrote: "Another reading is: But does a man know...?"' and he cites the text of *'Avot de-R. Nathan*, Version II.
83. xviii 21–22; and *ibid.* v 7–8; H. Albeck refers to this verse in his commentary on the Mishna.
84. *Sifre Num.* § 134, p. 180.
85. *Tosefta Qiddushin* i, 14, p. 337. See *Eccles. Rabba* vii, 15, and *ibid.* i, 9.
86. See 'Śeride Tanḥuma-Yelammedenu', *Qoveṣ 'al Yad*, vi, p. 9, and the notes

ibid. In *Gen. Rabba* i, 4, p. 6, the name of the Sage who adds repentance is R. 'Ahava b. R. Ze'ira; see *ibid.*, n. 9. See above, p. 287, and above p. 528.

87. *Gen. Rabba* xxii, 13, p. 220; *Lev. Rabba* x, 5, p. 206; *Pesiqta de-Rav Kahana*, Shuva, p. 359.
88. See *Lev. Rabba*, *loc. cit.*, p. 205, and *ibid.*, n. 3; *Pesiqta de-R. Kahana*, *loc. cit.*; cf. *'Arugat ha-Bośem*, II, p. 119. R. Joshua b. Levi deduces from the story of Cain that prayer accomplishes half; and that repentance accomplishes all he learnt from the men of Anathoth. In *Gen. Rabba*, *Shîṭā Ḥădāshā*, xcvii, p. 1215, we read: 'At that time the Holy One, blessed be He, said: "If I do not pardon Cain I shall lock the door before all penitents. (Hence) the Holy One, blessed be He, immediately forgave him half, but because he did not repent wholeheartedly, He did not forgive him for all his sins.' See *ibid.*, n. 6.
89. See *'Arugat ha-Bośem*, *ibid.*, and the preceding note.
90. *Tanḥuma*, ed. Buber, Bereshit, § 25; see above, n. 88.
91. *Pesiqta de-Rav Kahana*, Shuva, p. 358.
92. See my aforementioned article in the *J.N. Epstein Jubilee Volume*, pp. 121 ff.
93. *Pesiqta de-Rav Kahana*, *loc. cit.*, p. 361.
94. *T.B. Rosh Hashana* 17b. The commentators found it difficult to explain the words 'before a man sins' in the dictum of R. Joḥanan; see Rosh i, 10. But we have seen that there were Tannaim who restricted the attribute of compassion to people who had not sinned; see above, p. 456.
95. *Pesiqta de-Rav Kahana*, p. 349. See Midrash Psalms lxv, 4, p. 349.
96. *Pesiqta de-Rav Kahana*, p. 369. *'Arugat ha-Bośem*, Pt. II, p. 113.
97. See above, p. 273.
98. *Pesiqta de-Rav Kahana*, *loc. cit.*; the editor forgot to indicate that the dictum already appeared in the section 'Ha-Ḥodesh ha-Ze', p. 87, where he explained וכצוצטריות is the same as וגזווטראות, in Greek ἐξώστρα. On the other hand, in *Lev. Rabba* i, 11, p. 26, to which he refers subsequently, the reading is קאסטריאות = *castra*.
99. In Ezek. xl 1 reference is made to 'the beginning of the year, in the tenth day of the month', but the Septuagint reads in 'the first month, on the tenth of the month'; see Y. Kaufmann, *Toledot ha-'Emuna ha-Yisre'elit*, II, pp. 492 ff. On the connection between 'the day of blowing the horn' and the Day of Judgement, see also *ibid.*, p. 497 and cf. *ibid.*, III, p. 346.
1. See J. N. Epstein, *Mevo'ot le-Sifrut ha-Tanna'im*, p. 368.
2. This is the reading in the Kaufmann MS. and in other Palestinian versions; see S. Lieberman, *Tosefta ki-Fshuṭah*, p. 1022.
3. *Tosefta Rosh ha-Shana* i, 13; ed. Lieberman, p. 308.
4. See *Tosefta*, *ibid.*; *T.P. Rosh ha-Shana* i, 3, p. 57a; *T.B.*, *ibid.*, 16a.
5. *T.P.*, *ibid.*
6. *T.P.*, *ibid.*; *T.B.*, *ibid.*, 16b.
7. *T.P. Rosh Hashana* iv, 8, p. 59c; *Lev. Rabba* xxix, 12, p. 686, with reference

to the New Year, and *Pesiqta Rabbati* 169a, where a similar expression occurs with regard to the Day of Atonement. See Edmund Stein, 'Der Begriff der Palingenesie im talm. Schrifttum', *MGWJ*, vol. 83, 1939, pp. 194 ff.

8. See J. Mann, *HUCA*, II (1925), p. 310.
9. See F. C. Porter, 'The Yeçer Hara, A Study in the Jewish Doctrine of Sin', *Biblical and Semitic Studies*, 1902; U. Cassuto, *From Adam To Noah*, Jerusalem 1961, p. 303 [English translation]; Mr. M. H. Segal, *Sefer Ben-Sira ha-Shalem* [The Complete Ben Sira] xv, 14; cf. *ibid.* p. 97, xvii, 5; p. 105 and p. 137.
10. In the story of the struggle waged against the Evil Inclination by the young Nazirite, who appeared before Simeon the Just, there is found in only one version, in *Sifre Num.* § 22, p. 26, the wording ופחז לבי עלי ['and my heart became overweening'], while in all the parallels listed *ibid.*, n. 13, the reading is: פחז יצרי עלי ['my evil inclination was overweening']; cf. *Sifre*, *ibid.*, § 116, p. 127 '... the eyes follow the heart', but in *T.P. Berakhot* i, 5, p. 3c, the text has 'R. Levi said (v.l.: 'R. Isaac'; see L. Ginzberg, *Perushim we-Ḥiddushim bi-Yerushalmi*, I, p. 163): The heart and the eye are two brokers of sin.'
11. See above, p. 170 and cf. *The Testament of Asher* i, 8–9, where the doctrine of the two Inclinations is explained, and man's surrender to the Evil Inclination is termed the rule of Belial [Beliar]. It appears that the identification of the Evil Inclination with Satan underlies the dictum of Resh Laqish: 'A person does not commit a transgression unless a spirit of folly [שטות] enters into him, as it is said "If any man's wife go aside [תשׂטה]' (Num. v 12) — it is written תשׂטה [i.e. from the same stem as שטות 'folly']. On the demon that incites man to sin, see above, p. 755, n. 95; cf. also K. Latte's aforementioned article, pp. 286 ff.
12. *Sifre Deut.* § 45, p. 103; see vv.ll. *ibid.* Cf. *T.B. Berakhot* 61a, where Rav Naḥman bar Isaac states categorically that a beast has an evil inclination 'for we see that it injures and bites and kicks', but in the name of the Tanna R. Reuben b. Strobilus (*'Avot de-R. Nathan*, Version I, xvi, p. 64) it is stated 'that a beast has no evil inclination.' See above, p. 519.
13. *T.B. Qiddushin* 30b.
14. *'Avot de-R. Nathan*, Version I, xvi, p. 64.
15. *Cant. Rabba* i, 2. The verse cited does not occur in that form, but is a combination of Exod. xx 18 and Deut. v 25. This is also the case in the Parma MS. 1240, where the text reads תעשה את פריזרים בינינו but the word פריזרים should be emended to פריזבים. It is obvious that שליח ['emissary'] has been added by way of explanation. On the removal of the Evil Inclination in time to come see *T.B. Sukka* 52a; *Tanḥuma*, ed. Buber, Kî Tissā', 13; see above, p. 689.
16. *Gen. Rabba* xxii, 6, p. 216, and also *Midrash Tannaim*, ed. Hoffmann, p. 131, cite the dictum in the name of R. Akiba; in *Sifre Num.* 112, p. 120, it is anonymous; but in *T.B. Sukka* 52a it is ascribed to R. Assi, and in *T.B. Sanhedrin* 92b to R. Ammi.

17. *Gen. Rabba, loc. cit.*; in *T.B. Sukka* 52b there is a similar analogy in the name of Rava.
18. *T.P. Shabbat* xiv, 3, p. 14c. See *Lev. Rabba* xvi, 8, p. 363.
19. *'Avot de-R. Nathan*, Version I, xvi, 32a; see *Eccles. Rabba* iv, 14; cf. *ibid.*, ix, 7, on Abba Taḥana the Pious who 'imposed the sovereignty of the Good Inclination over the Evil Inclination'; see also *Midrash Tehillin* ix, 5, p. 82. Jerome heard the homiletical exposition of Ecclesiastes from his Jewish teacher in the name of R. Akiba. Cf. L. Ginzberg, 'Die Haggada bei den Kirchenvätern', *Abhandlungen zur Erinnerung an H.P. Chajes*, Vienna 1933, p. 30.
20. *M. 'Avot* iv, 1; see the citation in the name of 'the Gentile sages' *apud* R. Simeon b. Ṣemaḥ Duran, *Magen 'Avot*, 57a. Cf. Plato, Laws, 626a: τὸ νικᾷν αὐτὸν πασῶν νικῶν πρώτη τε καὶ ἄριστη ('a man's victory over himself is the primary and noblest of victories').
21. *Tosefta Bava Qamma* ix, 31, p. 366. In *T.B. Shabbat* 105b the text reads: 'For this is the way the Evil Inclination works; today he says to him [i.e. to a man] "Do this", and tomorrow he says to him "Do that", until he tells him "Go, serve idols", and the person goes and does this.'
22. *Sifre Deut.* § 187, p. 226; see *Sifre Num.* § 112, p. 120, the dictum of Rabbi; cf. *ibid.*, n. 15.
23. See above, p. 21, and cf. *T.B. 'Avoda Zara* 17a, the story of R. Ḥanina and R. Jonathan. So, too, Rava stated: 'If a Gentile harlot and Israelites were dining together, the wine is permitted, because while the desire for sexual transgression would be strong, the desire for *yên nesekh* [wine known (or suspected) to have been manipulated by an idolater] is not strong in them [*T.B. 'Avoda Zara* 69b].
24. *T.B. Yoma* 69b: 'Rav or, as some say, R. Joḥanan said'; but in the MSS.: 'R. Judah or, as some say, R. Nathan said'. See *Diqduqe Soferim, ibid.*, p. 200, n. 2. Also in *Yalquṭ ha-Makhiri* on Zechariah, ed. A. W. Greenup, London 1909, p. 55: 'Rav Judah or, as some say, Rav Nathan said', and in *T.B. Sanhedrin* 64a: 'Rav Judah or, as some say, Rav Jonathan said'; cf. *Diqduqe Soferim, ibid.* In *Cant. Rabba* i, 17: '... for R. Joḥanan said... It is I who took pains to uproot the craving for idolatry'; *ibid.*, vii, 8: 'Rav Judah said: Thus the Holy One, blessed be He, uprooted the craving for idolatry, but left that for whoring.' Nor did all the Sages wish to rely on the assurance of the cessation of lust for incest; see *T.B. Shabbat* 13a, and Tosafot, *ibid.*, s.v. *U-fĕlîgā.*
25. *Gen. Rabba* ix, 7, p. 71: 'Naḥman in the name of R. Samuel'; see vv.ll. and *ibid.*, n. 19, and the Antonin Fragment *Ebr.* III B268, which reads: 'Naḥman the son of R. Samuel bar Naḥman in the name of R. Samuel bar Menahem.' It is clear that the reading should be 'bar Naḥman'; see *'Avot de-R. Nathan*, Version I, xvi, the dictum of R. Reuben b. Strobilus.
26. *M. Berakhot* ix, 5; so, too, *Sifre Deut.* § 32, p. 55. But in *Tosefta, loc. cit.*, vi, 7, ed. Lieberman, p. 35, the dictum is cited in the name of R. Me'ir.

27. *T.P. Soṭa* v, 8, p. 20c, and there David, who slew his Evil Inclination, is presented as a contrary example, the basis for this being Psa. cix 22 'and my heart is slain [*ḥālal*] within me'; see *T.B. Bava Batra* 17a.
28. *T.B. Berakhot* 61b; see *Diqduqe Soferim, ad loc.*, p. 354.
29. *Bereshit Rabba* xxxiv, 10, p. 320; see *Sifre Deut.* § 45, p. 104, 'And if you so wish, you shall rule over it'; cf. vv.ll., *ibid.*
30. See above, p. 274.
31. *Sifre Deut.* § 33, p. 59; see vv.ll., *ibid.*, and cf. *Sifre Num.* § 88, p. 88, where it is stated that Boaz 'swore to his Evil Inclination and said to him, "As the Lord liveth, I shall not touch her!" '
32. *T.B. Berakhot* 5a. See *Diqduqe Soferim, ad loc.*, p. 12; see *Pesiqta de-Rav Kahana*, p. 352. An example of vexing the Evil Inclination is to be seen in the interpretation of R. Judah bar Pazzi, in the name of R. Joḥanan, of the verse ' "So they were shut up unto the day of their death, in widowhood, with their husband alive" (II Sam. xx 3) — this teaches us that David had their hair plaited, provided them with adornments, and had them brought in before him each day, and he said to his Evil Inclination "You desired that which was forbidden to you; by your life! I shall cause you to desire that which is permitted you' — *T.P. Sanhedrin* ii, 3, p. 20a. See below, p. 898, n. 57.
33. *T.B. Qiddushin* 30b; *T.B. Sukka* 52b; see *T.B. Yoma* 38b, and above, p. 469.
34. *T.B. Berakhot* 60b; *Diqduqe Soferim, ad loc.*
35. *T.B. Sukka* 52a. See *T.B. Qiddushin* 81a for the preventive measures taken by Amoraim to save themselves from stumbling; and the story *ibid.* concerning Rav Amram the Pious, who was overcome by his Evil Inclination and cried 'There's a fire at Amram's!' in order to summon 'the people of the neighbourhood to gather together and come and extinguish the fire, so that he might refrain from his Inclination, for he would feel ashamed before them' (Rashi *ad loc.*, s.v. *'āmar*). When the Sages said to Rav Amram 'You have made us feel ashamed', he answered them 'It is far better that you should feel ashamed of me in this world, and not be ashamed of me in the world to come.' Rav Amram put an oath upon (his Evil) Inclination and what looked like a pillar of fire issued from him. He then said 'See, you are fire and I am flesh, yet am I superior to you.' This adjuration is different from that mentioned above, p. 475; it bears a magic character.
36. *T.P. Demai* ii, 2, p. 23b; it seems that ר׳ (בי) זעירא ['R. Zeʿira'] is a corruption of דזעירא ['that Zeʿira']. On another occasion R. Zeʿira said 'Let it appear to him as if a sword were cutting his flesh', and the Sages asked, by way of comment, 'Are all people (as God-fearing) as R. Zeʿira?' — *T.P. Horayot* ii, 5, p. 46d.
37. *Gen. Rabba* 54a, p. 575; *Pesiqta de-Rav Kahana*, p. 176, where it is transmitted in the name of R. Samuel bar Naḥman with the addition 'It was said of Joḥanan, the high priest, that he served in the high priesthood eighty years; and in the end he became a Sadducee.'

38. *T.P. Shabbat* i, 3, p. 3b; see *Tanḥuma*, ed. Buber, Bereshit, xxvii, p. 20. A similar story is told about R. Ḥiyya bar Ashi in *T.B. Qiddushin* 81b, only there his wife played the role of the spirit, and it was she who disguised herself as the well-known harlot in the town, called Ḥaruta. R. Simeon b. Ṣemaḥ Duran, *Magen 'Avot*, Leipzig 1855, p. 24a, refers to this story, only he reads 'Rav Huna bar Assi', but I have not found an Amora by that name.
39. *T.B. Shabbat* 64a, where the verse Num. xxxi 50, 'And we have brought the Lord's offering', is expounded as referring to sinful thought; in *Cant. Rabba* iv, 3: 'For the sweat of the evil inclination we wish to bring a sacrifice.'
40. *T.P. Qiddushin* iv, 11, p. 66b.
41. *T.B. ibid.* 80b. See Rashi, *ad loc.*, s.v. *Wĕ-Rabbānān*; Tosafot, *ad loc.*, s.v. *Ki ha-hû maʿăse*; *Otzar ha-Gaonim* to *Qiddushin*, p. 194, and *ibid.*, p. 222; and Liqquṭe Perushe R. Ḥananel, p. 50.
42. *T.B. Sanhedrin* 107b; see Rashi, *ad loc.*, s.v. *Yēṣer* and *Yad Rama, ad loc.*; cf. also *T.B. Soṭa* 47a; Rashi, *ad loc.*, s.v. *Yeṣer.*
43. *T.B. Sukka* 52b and *T.B. Sanhedrin*, 107a.
44. *T.B. Sanhedrin* 75a; see Rashi, *ad loc.*, s.v. *Heʿĕlā libbô ṭînā*: 'Because of his great love, his mind was stupefied and he sickened.' In *T.P. Shabbat* xiv, 4, p. 14d, a similar story is narrated: 'Like a certain man who conceived a passion [*rĕḥām*] for a woman in the days of R. Eleazar and his life was in danger....' *Rĕḥēm* implies ὑστέρα, hysterical passion or pining love; on its healing in antiquity see J. Preuss, *Biblisch-Talmudische Medizin*, Berlin 1923, 3rd ed., p. 347. The Amoraim R. Jacob bar Idi and R. Samuel bar Naḥmani (in *T.P.*: R. Isaac bar Naḥman) disagree as to whether the incident concerned a married woman or spinster. To the question 'Then let him marry her' they replied 'His passion would not be assuaged... for it is said "Stolen waters are sweet, and bread eaten in secret is pleasant".' In *T.P.*, *loc. cit.*, 'The explanation is that he had set his heart on her while she was still married. Others say: She was a woman of high standing and would not marry him, and all that he would have done, he would have done unlawfully; hence he was forbidden.
45. *T.B. ʿAvoda Zara* 19a. The current version reads 'Rav Amram said in the name of Rav'. In the Spanish MS., ed. S. Abramson, there is added in the margin 'ואמרי לה א' [רב] נחמן אמ' ר[ב]' '[and some say Rav Naḥman said in Rav's name]'; see also *ibid.*, p. 201. Apparently this is also the meaning of R. Joshua b. Levi's dictum *ibid.*, 'Happy is the man who prevails over his inclination like a man'; see Rashi *ad loc.*
46. *T.B. Nedarim* 20b 'A certain woman that came before Rav...'; see *ibid.* a similar story concerning Rabbi.
47. 'Whenever Rav came to Darshis, he announced "Who will be (my spouse) for the day [יומא]?..." '; a similar story is related of Rav Naḥman in *T.B. Yoma* 18b; see Tosafot *ibid.*, s.v. *Yaḥōdê*. In *T.B. Yevamot* 37b Rashi reads ליומי ['for days'] and annotates 'Who is willing to be married (to me) for the days that I shall stay here.?' From the commentary of R. Abraham b.

Isaac of Montpellier on *Yevamot*, ed. M. Blau, New York 1962, p. 78, it appears that he read also in *Yoma* ליומיה ['for his days']; but the commentary of R. Eliakim, ed. D. Genachowski, Jerusalem 1964, p. 88, glosses 'Whoever wishes to be married for a single day only.'

48. See R. Margulies, 'Man hāwyā lĕ-yômā [Who would be (mine) for a day?]', *Sinai* XXI (1951), pp. 176–179, and S. Krauss, *ibid.*, XXII (1952), pp. 299–302. Cf. S. Lowy, *J.J.S.*, IX, 1958, pp. 124–129.
49. See *T.P. Qiddushin* iv, 12 (*ad fin.*), p. 66d: 'R. Hezekiah in the name of R. Kohen, in the name of Rav: A man will have to give account for all that his eye saw but he did not enjoy.'
50. *T.B. Yevamot* 62b; See Rashi, *ad loc.*, s.v. *Lō' niṣrĕkhā.*
51. *T.B. ibid.*; the Munich MS. reads: 'R. Tanḥum b. R. Ḥanilai.' See *Gen. Rabba* xvii, 1, p. 151, where the passage is introduced by תנ'; cf. vv.ll. and n. 11.
52. *T.B. Yoma* 67a.
53. *Lev. Rabba* xiv, 5, p. 308; see *ibid.* vv.ll. and notes. Before Rav Aḥa, R. Reuben b. Strobilus already said 'Because the first drop that a man injects into a woman is the evil inclination' — *'Avot de-R. Nathan*, Version I, xvi, p. 63. On the expression 'the most pious person [literally 'pietist of pietists']' see *T.P. Ketubbot* ii, 8, p. 25d 'Even the most pious person may not be appointed a guardian where unchastity is involved.' We do not know whether R. Aḥa, after all, included Jesse among those who died on account of the Serpent; see above, p. 427.
54. See I. Heinemann, *Philons griech. und jüd. Bildung*, p. 257, and *ibid.*, p. 265.
55. *T.B. Yoma* 18b, and parallels listed there.
56. *T.B. Bava Meṣia'* 32b, from which is derived the dictum of 'Others say': 'Who is mighty?' — 'He who turns his enemy into a friend'; see *'Avot de-R. Nathan*, Version I, xxiii, 38a; cf. *Tanḥuma*, Mishpaṭim, i; see also Matthew V 43–44.
57. *T.B. 'Avoda Zara* 17b; see *T.B. Pesaḥim* 113b concerning R. Ḥanina and Rav Hoshaiah (in *Diqduqe Soferim, ad loc.*, p. 351: Rav Haviva); and cf. the homily of R. Ḥanina, *T.B. Megilla* 15b, concerning the man who passes judgement on his inclination and the one who prevails over his inclination.
58. *T.B. Yoma* 87a, where the text has 'Rav Huna said in the name of Rav'; but none of the MSS. have 'Rav', just as it is missing in the current text, *ibid.*, 86b and in the parallels listed in the margin. See *Diqduqe Soferim*, p. 304. Cf. Rashi, *T.B. 'Arakhim* 30b, s.v. *Lō' hirgîsh*: 'If a man is not conscious or shocked so as to repent of his sin, and he continues (to transgress), it will no longer occur to him that he is committing any wrong.'

58a. The admonitions concerning robbery are numerous: see *T.B. Ḥullin* 89a regarding robbery and the completely righteous; cf. also *ibid.* 91a: 'R. Eleazar said... From this (it is learnt) that to the righteous... because they do not stretch forth their hands to robbery.'

59. *T.B. Bava Batra* 164b, where current editions read 'Rav Amram said in the

name of Rav...'; so, too, 'Rav Judah said in the name of Rav.' But there are recensions that omit 'in the name of Rav' [אמר רב] in both dicta; see *Diqduqe Soferim*, p. 439, §§ *Samekh* and *ʿAyin*. On עיון תפלה see Rashbam and Tosafot *ad loc.* The explanation of the 'Master' is that of Rabbenu Tam; see Tosafot, *Rosh ha-Shana* 16b, s.v. *We-ʿiyyûn*, whence it was taken over by *Novellae of Ramban* on *T.B. Bava Batra*, *loc. cit.*, and thence again by *Novellae of Rashba*, of *Ritba*, and of *Ran*. On the subject of 'sinful thoughts' see *T.B. Berakhot* 12b; *T.B. Shabbat* 64a; *T.B. Yoma*, 29a, and above, p. 476.

60. *T.B. Sukka* 52b.
61. *T.P. Taʿanit* iii, 4, p. 66c, where the current text has: 'R. Joshua b. Jair...', but in *Yalquṭ Makhiri* on Micah, ed. Greenup, London 1910, p. 27, the text has 'R. Joshua b. Levi.' As we do not find a Sage called R. Joshua b. Jair, it appears that the name was distorted under the influence of that of the Tanna. The story about the ass of R. Phinehas b. Jair, who did not 'sin' in error by eating fodder whose tithing was in doubt, led to the inference in the Babylonian Talmud 'If now the Holy One, blessed be He, does not allow (even) the beast of the righteous to sin in error, *a fortiori* the righteous themselves' (*T.B. Ḥullin* 7a); but already in the Talmud itself it was found difficult to reconcile this conclusion with the unwitting sins committed by the righteous; see *T.B. Yevamot* 99b, *T.B. Giṭṭin* 7a, and cf. Tosafot, *Ḥullin* 5b, s.v. *Ṣaddiqim*, and the parallels given there. See further below, n. 65.
62. *T.B. Sukka*, *loc. cit*: 'Were it not for these three verses, the feet of Israel's "enemies" would have tottered, one is the verse "And her that I have afflicted...." In *T.B. Berakhot* 32a the passage is cited in the name of R. Ḥama b. R. Ḥanina; see *ibid.*, 31b, the dictum of R. Samuel bar Rav Isaac.
63. *Exod. Rabba* xlvi, 4; I have corrected the text according to *Yalquṭ Makhiri*, *loc. cit.*
64. *T.B. Qiddushin* 81a. See *ibid.*, 81b, concerning the great precautions taken by R. Me'ir, who said 'Keep watch on me on account of my daughter', and concerning R. Ṭarfon, who said 'Keep watch on me on account of my daughter-in-law', and the story of the disciple who scoffed. On the proclamations in heaven 'Take heed of so-and-so and his Torah-learning' see *T.B. Pesaḥim* 112b; cf. above, p. 476. For the identification of 'Satan' with 'the Evil Inclination' see *T.B. Bava Batra* 16a, and see above, p. 170. When R. Zeʿira and R. Jeremiah transgressed in error, one by eating untithed produce and the other by causing someone else to eat it, the Sages drew a different deduction from that which we find in the Babylonian Talmud (above, n. 61). Against the background of the story about R. Phinehas b. Jair ('What can one do with this poor creature, for she observes the law with exceeding strictness') R. Mana reports that R. Zeʿira did not merely say 'If the earlier generations were angels, we are human beings; and if they were human beings, we are (but) asses', but added: 'even to the ass of R. Phinehas b. Jair we cannot be compared' — *T.P. Demai* i, 3, p. 21d; *T.P. Sheqalim* v, 1, p. 48d; *Gen. Rabba* lxviii, pp. 648–650; see *T.B. Shabbat* 112b.

65. See *T.P. Berakhot* iv, 2, 7d; cf. L. Ginzberg, *Perushim we-Ḥiddushim bi Yerushalmi*, III, pp. 230 ff. See also *T.B. Berakhot* 60b, and the prayer formulas *ibid.* 'And may not the Evil Inclination rule over me', 'and compel our Inclination to submit to Thee'.
66. *T.P. loc. cit.* '*R. Tanḥum* prayed...', and in *T.B.*, *ibid.*, p. 17a, a similar form of prayer is transmitted in the name of 'R. Alexandri, [who] after he prayed'; we also find *ibid.* the prayer of Mar the son of Ravina 'O My God, guard', which also contains the words 'And deliver me... from the Evil Inclination. The prayer of Jabez (I Chron. iv 10) 'that it may not hurt me' is interpreted by R. Judah the Patriarch and in the teaching of R. Nathan 'so that the Evil Inclination may not prevail over me' — *T.B. Temura* 16a; see *Mekhilta de-R. Ishmael,* Amalek ii, p. 201. On the expression 'leaven in the dough' cf. *Gen. Rabba* xxxiv 10, p. 320: 'Wretched is the dough that its (own) baker declares to be... Wretched is the leaven (see vv. ll.) that He who ferments it declares it to be....'
67. See the Baraita, *T.B. Yoma* 39a; and above, p. 807, n. 51.
68. *Lev. Rabba* xi, 5, p. 225; see *ibid.*, n. 5.
69. *Gen. Rabba* xxxiii, 3, p. 304; see *Lev. Rabba* xxxiv, 14, p. 806.
70. *Sifra*, Qedoshim, i, 86c.
71. *Lev. Rabba* xxiv, 4, p. 550.
72. *Ibid.*; see *Tanḥuma*, Qĕdôshîm, 9; *Midrash Tehillin* xx, 5, p. 175.
73. Plato, *Republic*, ii, 379, states that it lies within the nature of god to help and to be of benefit, but he adds emphatically that since the deity is good, he cannot be the cause of evils, for which other causes than god must be sought.
74. *Sifre Num.* § 11; see *Tanḥuma*, ed. Buber, Noah 7, p. 30; cf. above, p. 481.
75. *T.P. Nedarim* ix, 1, p. 41a. In *T.B. Shabbat* 105b R. Avin refers to this dictum in support of the preceding Baraita; see above, pp. 473–474, and cf. Rashi *ad loc.*, s.v. *Bĕkhā.*
76. Plutarchus, *De Stoicorum Repugnantiis*, d1048; see W. Capelle, 'Zur antiken Theodicee', *Archiv für Geschichte der Philosophie*, XX, 1907, pp. 173 ff; and cf. *ibid.*, p. 191, n. 70.
77. C. H. Dodd, *The Bible and the Greeks*, p. 43.
78. The correct reading in the Targum is נפק זכאי; see Targum pseudo-Jonathan and S. D. Luzzatto, *'Ohev Ger*, p. 52.
79. *Mekhilta*, Mishpaṭim, xx, p. 327; see *ibid.*, n. 7. The author of the homily cites, as the source of his account, the story of Judah b. Tabbai. But neither in it nor in the parallel versions (*ibid.*, n. 11) is there any connection with the verse 'and the innocent and the righteous'.
80. 'A man who does the will of his Father in heaven... a man who does not keep the Torah and does not fulfil the will of his Father in heaven' correspond to 'the righteous' and 'the wicked', which are mentioned previously — *Sifra*, Qedoshim, x, 92c. 'Those who transgress My will' in antithesis to the righteous — *Sifre Zuṭa*, Behaʿălōtĕkhā, p. 273; see *Sifre*, ʿEqev, § 47, p 105; *ibid.* § 306, p. 340; § 346, p. 403; cf. above, p. 403.

81. *Gen. Rabba* xxxiii, 1, p. 298 'R. Ishmael said: The righteous who accepted the Torah... but the wicked who did not accept the Torah....'
82. *M. 'Avot* vi, 1.
83. See *T.B. Shabbat* 156a, and Rashi, *ad loc.*, s.v. *Ṣadqan*; *Deut. Rabba*, ed. S. Lieberman, p. 36, n. 10; and my observations in my article 'Megammot Datiyyot we-Ḥevratiyyot be-Torat ha-Ṣedaqa shel Ḥazal', *Zion*, XVI, 1951, p. 25, n. 176, and *Bulletin of the Jewish Palestine Exploration Society*, XIX (1955), p. 103.
84. *Sifre Deut.* § 49, p. 114; see vv.ll. *ibid.* I have cited the version of *Yalquṭ Makhiri* to Joel, ed. Greenup, London 1913; cf. *Gen. Rabba*, Noah, ix, p. 630.
85. *Mekhilta de-R. Ishmael*, Pisḥa, xvi, p. 61; see *T.B. Yoma* 37a. A. Marmorstein, *The Old Rabbinic Doctrine of God*, 1927, p. 96, has not listed the passages that we have quoted. The dictum in *Midrash Tehillim* vii, 8, p. 67, cited there: 'From the fact that Thou triest hearts and reins we know that Thou art a righteous God', is not the oldest interpretation, and certainly not the only one, of this epithet of God, as G. Scholem supposes in his article on the Righteous One, *Von der mystischen Gestalt der Gottheit*, Zürich 1962, p. 87. On the designation 'Life of the world' see my observations in 'Śeride Tanḥuma-Yelammedenu', p. 50, n. 18. Cf. above, p. 700, n. 54. See also my remarks in *ʿArugat ha-Bośem*, Pt. III, p. 479, and in *Tûrê Yĕshûrûn*, iv (1966), p. 21. Cf. now N. Aloni, *Ha-'Egron le-Rav Saʿadya Ga'on* [The Egron (Lexicon) by R. Saadia Gaon], pp. 220–221, and p. 401.
86. See my aforementioned article in *Zion*, p. 5, n. 26; p. 9, n. 55; p. 75, n. 105.
87. *T.B. Sanhedrin* 103b.
88. *T.B. Ṣota* 4b.
89. See *The Testaments of the Twelve Patriarchs*, Asher, ii, 8: 'Another committeth adultery and fornication, and abstaineth from meats, and when he fasteth he doeth evil, and by the power of his wealth overwhelmeth many; and notwithstanding his excessive wickedness he doeth [the] commandments; this, too, hath a twofold aspect, but the whole is evil.' See *T.B. Berakhot* 61a; *T.B. ʿEruvin* 18b; *Tractate Kalla* i, 10, ed. Higger, p. 130.
90. *Midrash Mishle* xi, 21, ed. Buber, p. 69. The authenticity of the dictum is proved by the statement of R. Joḥanan, *T.B. Soṭa* 4b.
91. See *T.B. Soṭa, loc. cit.*, the dicta of Rav and the School of R. Shila; cf. the correction of Baḥ ['Bayit Ḥadash' by Joel Sirkes] § *'Alef*, whose amendment agrees with the reading of the Munich MS.: 'Any man who is filled with overweening conceit....'
92. *T.P. Berakhot* ix, 7, p. 14b; *T.P. Soṭa* v, 7, p. 20c.
93. See above, p. 475. In *T.P. ʿAvoda Zara* v, 4, p. 44d a distinction is drawn between a man who is 'master of his soul' and one whose 'soul is master of him', and the dictum is based on the verse Proverbs xxiii 1; see Targum pseudo-Jonathan *ad loc.* Cf. also *T.B. Ḥullin* 6a and *T.B. Nidda* 65b, and my observations in my essay in the *Y. Baer Jubilee Volume*, p. 68, n. 100.
94. *T.B. Qiddushin* 40a.

95. *Esther Rabba* vi, 1. See *T.B. Ketubbot* 50a; *Midrash Tehillim* cvl, 3, p. 454.
96. *Tosefta Qiddushin* i, 14, p. 3; *T.B., ibid.*, 40b.
97. *T.B. Berakhot* 7a.
98. *Ibid.* 61b; see Rashi, *ad loc.*, s.v. *Lĕ-rashshîʿē gĕmîrē*, and in several versions there, too, the author of the dictum is given as רבה; cf. *Diqduqe Soferim, ibid.*, p. 354, n. *Rêsh.*
99. See *T.B. Horayot* 10b, Rava's own statement 'Happy are the righteous who are vouchsafed (good) in this world according to the deeds of the wicked in this world.' The homily of Mari bar Mar that is reported by Rav Ḥisda in *T.B. ʿEruvin* 21a (on the identity of Mari bar Mar see *Diqduqe Soferim, ad loc.*, p. 72, n. *Qôf*) is based on the verse of Jeremiah xxiv 3 '... The good figs, very good; and the bad, very bad'; see R. Ḥananel, *ad loc.*, and Maharsha, *Ḥiddushe Aggadot, ad loc.*
1. *Mekhilta de-R. Ishmael*, Shîrā, i, p. 118; see *Gen. Rabba*, xxx, 1, p. 270.
2. *T.B. Ḥagiga* 12b.
3. *Mekhilta de-R. Ishmael*, Shîrā, ix, p. 146.
4. *Ibid.*; it is a homiletical exposition of Canticles vi 8 'There are three score queens....' The correct reading is: ד״א ששים וכו׳ זה משה. See vv.ll. and *Mekhilta de-R. Simeon b. Yoḥai*, p. 71 and p. 72.
5. *T.B. Yoma* 38b. See *T.B. Qiddushin* 72b, where the text is anonymous and simply has ללמדך ['to teach you']; cf. *Gen. Rabba*, lviii, 2, p. 619 and the notes *ibid.*
6. See *T.B. Yoma, loc. cit.*, and the dictum of R. Eleazar 'Even for the sake of one righteous man the world would have been created'; cf. above, p. 487. To the statement of R. Joḥanan there is added *ibid.* 'And R. Ḥiyya bar Abba said in his own name 'חסידיו implies two' (according to the reading of the MSS.; see *Diqduqe Soferim*, Yoma, p. 105, notes ג and ד), but 'Rav Naḥman bar Isaac said: The *Kĕttîv* is חסידו.'
7. *T.B. Ḥullin* 92a; on the meaning of בי כנישתא דאפתא see *Aruch Completum*, I, p. 246; cf. S. Krauss, *Synagogale Altertümer*, 1922, p. 303. The place where the righteous are to be found alludes, according to Abbaye, to righteous men who were 'unknown'. G. Scholem, 'Die 36 Verborgenen Gerechten in der jüd. Tradition', *Judaica*, Frankfurt 1963, p. 216, makes no mention of this dictum of Abbaye. On the number 36 see below, n. 112, and on righteous men who do not reveal themselves see above, p. 496.
8. Moses Baer, 'Li-Mĕqôrôtaw shel ha-Mispār 36 Ṣaddîqîm [On the Sources of the Number 36 Righteous Men]', Bar-Ilan, *Sefer ha-Shana le-Maddaʿe ha-Yahadut we-ha-Ruaḥ shel Universitat Bar-Ilan*, 1963, p. 176, expresses surprise that Abbaye does not react to the actual division between the righteous of Eretz-Israel and those of Babylon, but in the light of our observations in the text there is no reason for surprise. The preference for Eretz-Israel stems from the Palestinian tradition; see below, n. 9.
9. *Gen. Rabba* xcviii, 9, p. 1260; see vv.ll. of MS. 1 (Vatican) and n. 8 *ibid.* The version that I have cited in the text is based on the Genizah fragment

T.S. C2. In *T.P.* *'Avoda Zara* ii, 1, p. 40b Rav is the author of the homily ' "thirty pieces of silver" — these are the thirty commandments... but the Rabbis say: These are the thirty righteous men, whom the world never lacks; for Rabbi Naḥman said in the name of R. Mana: The world can never be with less than thirty righteous men like our father Abraham. How do we know this? (Scripture states) "Seeing that Abraham shall surely become [יהיה], and יהיה totals thirty. Sometimes the majority of them are in Babylon and the minority in Eretz-Israel; (and) sometimes the majority of them are in Eretz-Israel and the minority in Babylon, (which) is a good omen for the world.' R. Naḥman, who transmits in the name of R. Mana, belongs to the fifth generation of the Palestinian Amoraim (see Zechariah Frankel, *Mevo' ha-Yerushalmi*, 116b). This was overlooked by M. Baer, *loc. cit.*; hence his observation about 'the lessening of the opposition between Eretz-Israel and Babylon' is unacceptable.

10. *Gen. Rabba* xxxv, 2, p. 330, and see the preceding dictum *ibid.* See above, p. 491.
11. *Ibid.* xlix, 3, p. 502: R. Judan and R. Aḥa in the name of R. Alexandri. It is preceded by the same homily in the name of R. Berechiah. R. Alexandri was accustomed to transmit in the name of R. Joshua b. Levi (see W. Bacher, *Agada der Palästinischen Amoräer*, I, p. 195). In *Midrash Tehillim* v, 2, p. 52, indeed, we find that R. Joshua b. Levi said: 'הנחילות ['flutes'] is an acronym... the ל stands for thirty righteous men...'; but in two MSS. the name of R. Joshua b. Levi is missing; see Buber, *ibid.*, n. 27.
12. *T.B. Sukka* 45b; *T.B. Sanhedrin* 97b; the version in the text is that of the Munich MS. and *Haggadot ha-Talmud, loc. cit.*; see *Diqduqe Soferim*, Sanhedrin, p. 288, n. צ, and cf. *ibid.*, Sukka, p. 141, n. *Kaf.*
13. G. Scholem, in his aforementioned article, p. 218, refers to the article of Z. Ameisenowa in *Journal of the Warburg Institute*, XII, pp. 33 ff. But she was not the first to advance this theory; she merely quotes the views of Gundel on the subject; see the next note.
14. See S. Schott, 'Altägyptische Festdaten', *Akademie der Wissenschaften in Mainz*, 1950, p. 22 and p. 30; see W. Gundel, *Dekane und Dekansternbilder*, 1936, pp. 327–345.
15. See Th. Hopfner, *Griechisch-Ägyptischer Offenbarungszauber*, I, 1921, pp. 159–161; Gundel, *loc. cit.*, p. 270.
16. *Testamentum Salomonis*, PG. Migne, Vol. 122, p. 1342, and an English translation in Conybeare's article in *JQR*, XI, 1899, pp. 36–38; a German translation of the whole of ch. xviii on the 36 *decani* is to be found in Gundel, *op. cit.*, pp. 383 ff. On the influence of the *decani* and the attempt to overcome it in Paul, Galatians iv 3 and 9, see Conybeare, *op. cit.*, p. 9; Origen, *c. Celsum*, viii, 58, and H. Chadwick's notes in *Origen Contra Celsum*, Cambridge 1953, p. 496.
17. M. Baer's remarks on a certain similarity between the Persian-Zoroastrian concept and the thought expressed by Abbaye, based on the fact that 33

Amesha-Spentas are spoken of, neither explain the number 36 nor the subject itself. He also did not perceive the specific idea of this dictum of Abbaye and the difference between it and the other statement transmitted in his name, and thus he came to assume 'a radical change' in the teaching of Rav Judah, *T.B. Ḥullin, loc. cit.* 'These are the thirty righteous men on account of whom the Gentile nations exist', which is none other than the dictum of Rav in *Gen. Rabba,* see above, n. 14 This tradition, in accordance with Rav's view, is that transmitted by Rav Judah in contrast to that of Rav Huna in the Palestinian Talmud.

18. See Rashi, *T.B. Sukka* 45b, s.v. *Rā'îtî*; cf. the commentary of R. Me'ir b. Todras ha-Levi Abulafia, *Yad Rama* on *T.B. Sanhedrin* 97b, s.v. *'Amar Abbaye,* who cites 'And R. Hai Gaon, of blessed memory, explained that there are many degrees for the righteous in respect of the reward that they are given, each degree corresponding to the deeds, and R. Simeon b. Yoḥai says that with regard to the highest degree, which transcends all the others and is called *'ăliyyā,* I have seen its sons and they are but few.'
19. *Sifre Deut.* § 47.
20. This is indicated by the expression 'If they number a thousand...' and in *T.B. Sukka, loc. cit.*, an objection is raised to R. Simeon b. Yoḥai's statement by reference to Abbaye's dictum, in the form 'Are they then so few?' On the interpretation of the answer 'the one figure refers to those who enter with permission, the other to those that enter without permission' see Rashi *ad loc. Yad Ramah* on *T.B. Sanhedrin, loc. cit.*, cites the interpretation of Rav Hai Gaon: 'The righteous who enter together with their sons, who, together with their sons, are worthy of this degree like R. Simeon b. Yoḥai, who had merited this degree together with his son, are few... and it is an excellent interpretation.'
21. *Ecclesiastes Rabba* vii 15; *Midrash Yelammedenu* on Deuteronomy, ed. J. D. Wilhelm, *Qoveṣ 'al Yad*, Bk. VI, Pt. I, p. 86 and n. 12.
22. *Lev. Rabba* xxxii, 4, p. 744, where the meaning of the verse 'and when he saw that there was no man' (Exod. ii 12) is disputed by R. Judah, R. Nehemiah, and the Sages, and the latter say 'He [Moses] saw that no hope would issue either from him or his children or children's children.' See the v.l. in the Munich MS.: 'hope of righteous men', and so, too, in *Exod. Rabba* i, 33; in *Tanḥuma*, Exodus, ix, the text has: 'He investigated [התבונן] whether any of his descendants would not be converted.' Cf. *Deut. Rabba*, ed. S. Lieberman, p. 59; a similar statement occurs with reference to the people of Sodom in *Midrash ha-Gadol*, Bereshit, ed. Margulies, p. 309.
23. On the entire manifestation see R. Mach, *Der Zaddik im Talmud und Midrash*, Leiden 1957.
24. See *A Genesis Apocryphon* [Hebrew and English], ed. N. Avigad and Y. Yadin, Jerusalem 1956, col. II; cf. *ibid.*, pp. 12–15.
25. See *Gen. Rabba* xxv, 1, p. 238 and the note *ibid.*
26. *Gen. Rabba* xxv, 2, p. 239. In a later Midrash, *Tanḥuma*, Bereshit, § 11, it is

reported in the name of the teacher of R. Joḥanan, R. Simeon b. Jehozadak: 'Whence did he know that "This one shall bring us relief from our work" etc.? Was he a prophet?... They had a tradition that when the Holy One, blessed be He, said to Adam "cursed is the ground...", Adam said: "Sovereign of the universe! How long?" (God) replied: "Until a man is born circumcised." When Noah was born circumcised, Lamech immediately knew and said assuredly "This one shall bring us relief...." When Noah was born, the world reverted to its habitable condition... Furthermore, until Noah was born, people worked with their hands, therefore it is stated "and from the toil of our hands"; but when Noah was born, he made for them ploughs, scythes, mattocks, and all (other) implements of work.'

27. See *Gen. Rabba* lxiii, 1, p. 678; *ibid.* liii, 8, p. 563; *T.B. Sanhedrin* 113b.
28. *Tanḥuma*, Toledot, 2. The birth of Isaac is linked up with the creation of the world and with the redemption; see *T.B. Rosh ha-Shana* 11a. Rashi in his commentary to Genesis xvii 21 designates Isaac 'holy from the womb', on the basis of his interpretation of the wording of the benediction 'who sanctified the well-beloved [i.e. Isaac] from the womb', *T.B. Shabbat* 137b, s.v. *'Âsher*; see Tosafot *ad loc.* s.v. *Yĕdîd*, and the commentary *Da'at Zeqenim* of the Ba'ale Tosafot on Genesis *loc. cit.*
29. *Pesiqta Rabbati* 177a. In the fragment of the *Tanḥuma* in *Ginze Schechter*, I, ed. L. Ginzberg, p. 53, we find: 'And whence do we know that the Holy One augmented the sun's orb and the moon's orb and lit up [literally 'made φωτός] the world in which Isaac was born?' On the birth of the 'Divine child' see E. Norden, *Die Geburt des Kindes*, Leipzig 1924, p. 104. Following him and R. Kittel, *Die hellen. Mysterienrelig. und das A.T.*, 1924, Mach, *op. cit.*, pp. 77 ff, endeavours to show that this Haggada was influenced by the Helios cult, which has also been connected with the celebration of Ḥanukka and Christmas. The reborn sun-god was welcomed with the cry 'The virgin has given birth, the light has increased' and the festival was called αὐξίφωτος. But it is doubtful if any direct influence is to be seen here (in regard to Ḥanukka, J. Heinemann has already noted in his article 'Messianisms u. Mysterienrel.', *MGWJ*, 1925, pp. 343 ff, that the *tĕqûfā* ['solstice'] is actually called *tĕqūfat Ṭēvēt* ['the solstice of the month of Ṭevet' = the winter solstice] and is not linked to the month of Kislev), even if the phraseology used resembles that which was customary at these pagan festivals. The eulogistic expressions with which a new emperor was welcomed at the celebration of the *adventus*, or the arrival of a proconsul as a σωτήρ, such as 'Happy is the world to have such a king, happy is the world to have such a judge! The sun has shone upon us, the moon has shone upon us', served the Sages as a parable with which to explain Moses' blessing; *Sifre Deut.* § 343, p. 394. See *Midrash ha-Gadol*, Bereshit, ed. Margulies, p. 522; cf. S. Lieberman, 'Qallēs qillûsîn', *'Alê 'Ayin, Minḥat Dĕvārîm le-Sh. Z. Schocken* [*Alei Ayin*: The Salman Schocken Jubilee Volume], 1948–1952, pp. 75 ff.
30. *T.B. Soṭa* 12a. *Yalquṭ Shim'oni* § 166 has: 'When Moses was born, the whole

world was filled with light.' For parallels in general literature see Mach, *op. cit.*, pp. 66–67.

31. *Deut. Rabba* xi, 8. The phrase 'Moses the Righteous' occurs in *M. Nedarim* iii, 11.
32. On the might of Moses see *T.B. Nedarim* 38a; *T.B. Shabbat* 92a. Cf. *T.P. Ta'anit* iv, 8, p. 68c; *Tanḥuma*, 'Eqev, 11, and *ibid.*, Tissa', 21. On the beauty of the righteous and the wise see *T.B. Bava Meṣia'* 84a; *T.B. Bava Batra* 58a; for the odour of the righteous see *Tanḥuma*, ed. Buber, Toledot, 15; *Aggadat Canticles*, ed. Schechter p. 12, and *ibid.*, pp. 54–55. Parallel material is given in Mach, *op. cit.*, pp. 103–104.
33. *Midrash Shemu'el* iii, 4, p. 52.
34. *Sifre Deut.* § 38, p. 76; see *Gen. Rabba* lxxiii, 8, p. 852. Cf. *Midrash Tehillin* cxvi, 7, p. 478.
35. See *Tosefta Soṭa* x, 1–10, pp. 313–314, and *ibid.*, xii, 6, p. 318; cf. *Gen. Rabba* xxxix, 11, p. 376; lxviii, 6, p. 775.
36. *Gen. Rabba* lx, 16, p. 556. See *Deut. Rabba* vi, 2–3; *Midrash Shemu'el* xxix, 2, p. 68; *Eccles. Rabba* iii, 14.
37. *Sifre Num.* § 136, p. 182: 'R. Eliezer said: He (God) endowed Moses' eyes with the power to see from one end of the world to the other. So, too, you find in the case of the righteous, that they see from one end of the world to the other.' See *Sifre Deut.* § 47; on the miraculous shortening of a journey, cf. *Gen. Rabba* xlii (xliii), p. 418.
38. They, too, are called 'fathers' [the same word as that rendered Patriarchs]. Hillel and Shammai and the Pairs, and also R. Ishmael and R. Akiba, are called 'fathers of the world' (*M. 'Eduyot* i, 4; *T.P. Ḥagiga* ii, 2, p. 77d; *T.P. Sheqalim* iii, 1, p. 47b). R. Ṭarfon is called 'the father of all Israel' (*T.P. Yoma* i, 1, p. 38d). In *II Maccabees* xiv 37–39 it is said of Razis, one of the elders of Jerusalem, that he loved his fellow citizens and was very well thought of, and was called 'father of the Jews'. Men of piety and miracle-workers like Hilkiah, Ḥanan ha-Neḥba (*T.B. Ta'anit* 23b), Jose b. Qiṭnit (*Tosefta Soṭa* xv, 5), Hosaia of Ṭuria (*Lev. Rabba* xxx, 1, p. 690) and their like are called 'Abba' [= father]. The contention of K. Kohler ('Abba, Father, Title of spiritual leader', *JQR*, XIII, 1900, pp. 567–580) that every Abba is an Essene is unfounded.
39. See above, p. 103 and p. 117; and see *T.B. Ta'anit* 20b, the stories about Rav Ada bar Ahava.
40. *T.P. Demai* i, 1, p. 22a; *T.B. Ḥullin* 7a.
41. See *Sifre Num.* § 135, p. 182: 'The Holy One, blessed be He, said to Moses: With respect to this matter make no request to me, but in another case command Me and I shall do (your bidding).' Cf. *T.P. Ta'anit* iii, 12, p. 67a; in *T.P. Sanhedrin* x, 2, p. 28b it is stated: 'Blessed be the God of the righteous, for He fulfils the wishes of the righteous.' See also *T.B. Ta'anit* 23a; *Tanḥuma*, Wa-yērā', xix, Wā-'ērā', iii, Nāśo', xxix; *Deut. Rabba* v, 13, *Pesiqta Rabbati* 7b; cf. Jos. x 14 'And there was no day like that before it or after it, that the Lord hearkened unto the voice of a man; for the Lord fought for Israel.'

42. *Tosefta Qiddushin* i, 14, p. 336.
43. *T.B. Sukka* 56b; see Rashi, *ad loc.*, s.v. *'Oy lā-rāshā'*; cf. *M. Nega'im* xii, 60 *Sifra*, Mĕṣōrā', iv, 73c; *'Avot de-R. Nathan*, Version II, xvi, p. 36. The analogy of one who enters an apothecary's shop and one who enters a tanner's workshop, which is cited in *Midrash Mishle* xiii, 16, p. 72, to explain the verse 'He that walketh with wise men shall be wise; but the companion of fools will suffer harm' (Prov. xiii 20), is transferred in *Pirqe de-R. Eliezer* to 'one who walks with the righteous' and 'one who walks with the wicked'; the analogy is also found in Philo, *De Somniis*, I, 178.
44. *T.B. Shabbat* 55a. See *Lam. Rabba* ii, 1, ed. Buber, p. 98: When the Holy One, blessed be He, said to the angel ' "Do not touch the righteous!" Accusation rushed forward to the Holy One, blessed be He, and said to Him: "Sovereign of all the worlds! why dost Thou spare them? Which of them had his head broken for Thy sake? Which of them gave his life for Thee?" ' But it sometimes happened that the Sages themselves retreated on account of the threats to their wellbeing and honour; see *T.P. Sanhedrin* vi, 6, p. 23c: 'R. Judah b. Pazzi went up to the upper chamber of the schoolhouse and saw two men having intercourse with each other. Said they to him: "Master, remember that you are one and we are two" ', that is to say, they have the power, as two witnesses, to bear false witness against him. Cf. *T.B. Pesaḥim* 113b that 'one who observes his fellow commit an indecency and testifies against him alone' is hated by the Holy One, blessed be He, and the story of Tobias and Zigud *ibid.*
45. *Gen. Rabba* xxxiii, 3, p. 308. See *T.B. Sukka* 14a: 'The prayer of the righteous changes the intention of the Holy One, blessed be He, from the attribute of strict justice to that of compassion'; see *Exod. Rabba* xlii, 1; *Deut. Rabba*, iii, 15 and 17.
46. As Aristotle stated. *Eth. Nic*, 31, 1128a: ὁ χαρίεις οἷον νόμος ὢν ἑαυτῷ. I. Heinemann, 'Die Lehre vom ungeschriebenen Gesetz', *HUCA*, IV, 1927, p. 171, n. 52, referred to S. A. Horodetzky, *Sēfer Shivḥê ha-Beshṭ* [*Book of Praises of the Ba'al Shem Tov*], Introduction, p. 13, who states in the name of R. Naḥman of Bratslav that 'the righteous man is himself the statutes and the precepts.' This dictum is not in the writings of R. Naḥman but in *Degel Maḥane Ephrayim* (Korets 1868, p. 4a. Prof. G. Scholem kindly clarified the matter). In any case the context and meaning are different from those of Aristotle's aphorism.
47. See Eliezer Margulies, *Ha-ḥayyāvîm ba-Miqrā' wĕ-Zakkā'îm ba-Talmud û-ba-Midrashim*, London 1949, pp. 1–8; cf. *ibid.*, pp. 60 ff. On the indictment of the righteous see below, p. 505.
48. On the antinomistic trend in this approach see G. Scholem, *Shabbĕtay Ṣĕvî wĕ-ha-Tĕnû'ā ha-Shabbĕtā'ît bi-Yĕmê Ḥayyaw*, II, 1957, p. 695. On the relationship of Hasidism to this question, see Rebecca Schatz-Uffenheimer, *Ha-Ḥăsîdût kĕ-Misṭîqā*, Jerusalem 1968, pp. 51 ff.
49. *T.B. Sanhedrin* 107a. The Tanna of the School of R. Ishmael and Rava,

who said 'Bathsheba was destined for David since the six days of Creation', did not minimize the offence; see Rashi, *ad loc.*, s.v. *She-'akhālāh*; cf. *loc. cit.* the homily of R. Dosetai of Beri, and *Midrash Tehillim* xviii, 3, p. 136: 'And so you find in the case of David; until he repented from that deed, his name was not listed in the heavenly cadre and he was called 'servant of the Lord'. R. Joḥanan reported in the name of R. Simeon b. Yoḥai that the purpose of the entire episode is only to teach the way of repentance to individuals, and even R. Samuel bar Naḥmani in the name of R. Jonathan said that 'David established the world of repentance' (*T.B. ʿAvoda Zara* 4b–5a).

50. *T.P. Taʿanit* iii, 8, p. 66d and *Pesiqta de-Rav Kahana*, p. 277. A similar motif concerned with the decline of the generations is to be found in *Lam. Rabba*, Petiḥa 30, and *ibid.* iv, 12, relating to David, Asa, Jehoshaphat, and Hezekiah; but it is considerably toned down and bears a quietistic character: 'Hezekiah arose and said: "I have no strength either to kill, or pursue, or to sing praise. I shall, therefore, sleep on my bed and act Thou." Said the Holy One, blessed be He, to him: "I shall act...." ' In this form the motif found its way into the stories of the new Ḥasidism. S. Y. Agnon related it under the title 'Sippûr shel Yĕshûʿā ['A story of Salvation'] and disclosed its parallel in the Midrash. G. Scholem concluded with it the chapter on Ḥasidism in his work, *Major Trends*, p. 345.
51. See *T.P. Taʿanit* i, 4, p. 64b, and the episodes there recounted, especially the story about פנדקקא. On the reading and the meaning, see S. Lieberman, *Greek in Jewish Palestine*, p. 31. It should be noted that R. Abbahu, who was shown פנדקקא in a dream, was a contemporary of the disciple of Levi bar Sisi's disciple.
52. In *T.B. Moʿed Qaṭan* 28a it is reported in the name of R. Ammi, who learned from the juxtaposition of the sections treating of the death of Miriam and the red heifer that the death of the righteous brings atonement; but in *T.P. Yoma* i, 1, p. 38b, *Lev. Rabba* xx, 12, p. 471, and the parallels indicated *ibid.*, n. 5, the dictum is cited in the name of R. Abba bar Avina. See *T.B. Ḥullin* 7b, the saying of R. Ḥama bar Ḥanina 'The righteous are greater in their death than in their lifetime'; cf. *T.B. Sanhedrin* 47a, and *Diqduqe Soferim, ad. loc.*, p. 140.
53. See *Mekhilta de-R. Ishmael*, Massekhtā de-Wa-yĕhî, iii, p. 99.
54. *Ibid.*, Massekhta de-Wa-Yissaʿ, ii, p. 160; cf. *ibid.*, Massekhtā da-Amalek, p. 179 and p. 180.
55. *Ibid.*, Pisḥa, v, p. 14, the view of R. Mattia b. Ḥeresh; *ibid.*, xvi, p. 62, the views of R. Simeon b. Yoḥai and R. Nathan; and *ibid.*, p. 98, Siomeon of Teman and Rabbi (in *Midrash Ḥakhamim* — see vv.ll. — R. Me'ir). The opinion attributed to Rabbi, *ibid.*, p. 62, is cited in the name of 'the Sages', *ibid.*, p. 98; however, in place of 'Rabbi' there is also found the reading ד״א ['another interpretation']; see vv.ll. *ibid.*
56. See *Midrasch Tannaïm*, Mekhilta to Deut., ed. Hoffmann, p. 62.

57. The Tanna Banna'ah, who is mentioned only in the homilies of the School of Ishmael (see J. N. Epstein, *Mavo' le-Sifrut ha-Tanna'im*, p. 581) follows the view of Shema'yah, R. Eleazar b. Azariah, and R. Jose the Galilean, that on account of the merit of the precept fulfilled by Abraham the sea was divided, see *Mekhilta de-R. Ishmael, loc. cit.*, p. 98 and p. 100.
58. D. Hoffmann, *Midrasch Tannaïm, loc. cit.*, n. 9, writes: 'Schechter has rightly noted that the *Sifre* differs from the Mekhilta, for in § 96 and § 184 it is stated "all is on account of the merit of the Patriarchs", and likewise in the *Mekhilta de-R. Simeon b. Yoḥai* to Exod. xiii 5 we find that all is on account of the merit of the Patriarchs, but in the *Mekhilta de-R. Ishmael* this does not occur.' However, in *T.B. Qiddushin* 37b we read: 'The School of R. Ishmael taught: Perform this precept, for on account of it you will enter the Land.' But in *Sifre Deut.* § 55, p. 122, which represents 'the School of R. Akiba' (see D. Hoffmann, *Zur Einleitung in die hal. Midraschim*, Berlin 1888, pp. 66 ff) we find: ' "When [the Lord] shall bring thee": Accept the precept mentioned in this passage for on account of it you shall enter the Land', and see the references given by Finkelstein *ibid.*, n. 11. *Ibid.* § 184, p. 225, we find the following combination: ' "And if the Lord thy God enlarge...": Perform the precept mentioned in this passage, for on account of it the Lord your God will enlarge... "as He hath sworn unto thy fathers" — all is because of the merit of your fathers'; so, too, in the *Mekhilta de-R. Simeon b. Yoḥai*, ed. Epstein-Melamed, p. 38. Cf. *ibid.*, p. 42: ' "When [the Lord] shall bring thee"... Perform the precept mentioned in this passage... "as He hath sworn unto thee and unto thy fathers" — all is because of your merit and that of your fathers.' See H. Albeck, *Untersuchungen über die halachischen Midraschim*, Berlin 1927, p. 16.
59. *Exod. Rabba* xliv, 7. I have cited the text according to the Venice edition. In later editions the text is emended to: 'Said Moses to Him: "Sovereign of the universe..." '; see *Deut. Rabba* iii, 15; *Tanḥuma*, Tiśśa', 32.
60. *Gen. Rabba* xliv, 5, p. 429; see vv.ll. *ibid.* In *Cant. Rabba* i, 14, this homily is cited with variations in the name of 'R. Levi in the name of R. Ḥama', and it ends 'I see some great man among them who can say to the attribute of justice "Enough!" and I take him as a pledge for them.' Cf. above, p. 905, n. 45.
61. *Mekhilta de-R. Ishmael*, Wa-yĕhî, iii, p. 97; here the word *bizĕkhût* [literally 'for the merit of'] has the connotation of *bishĕvîl* ['on account of']. The statement of A. Marmorstein, *The Doctrine of Merits in Old Rabbinical Literature*, London 1920, p. 11, that in the School of R. Ishmael the term *biśĕkhar* [literally 'in reward for'] was used instead of *bizĕkhût* is unfounded; see above, notes 51–58.
62. *Mekhilta de-R. Ishmael*, Wa-yĕhî, vi, p. 112. There is no real difference between *tĕfillā* and *Tefillîn*; see vv.ll. *ibid.* and n. 3.
63. *Ibid.*, Shîrā, ix, p. 146: ' "Thou hast guided them in Thy strength" — on account of the Torah... another explanation is... on account of the dynasty

of the House of David... "To Thy holy habitation" — on account of the Temple...'

64. *Ibid.*, Wa-yĕhî, iii, p. 98; see *Midrash Tehillim* cvii, 1, p. 462.
65. *Midrash Tehillim* cxiv, 5, p. 472 (this is R. Nehemiah's view on redemption; see below, p. 998 n. 75). It is preceded by the dictum of R. Judah 'On account of the blood of the Passover sacrifice and the blood of circumcision', and it is taught anonymously in *Pesiqta de-Rav Kahana*, p. 125, which represents the opinion of R. Mattia b. Ḥeresh in *Mekhilta de-R. Ishmael*, Pisḥa, v, p. 14.
66. *Midrash Tehillim, loc. cit.*, p. 473; the last dictum is reported in the name of R. Eliezer b. Jacob. As Buber points out *ibid.*, the words 'ben Jacob' are wanting in the printed edition and in all the MSS., except MS. Parma, which is the version he used for his edition, and they are missing also in *Yalquṭ Makhiri* to Psalms, p. 195. Hence there is no reason for Marmorstein's doubt, *op. cit.*, p. 57, and it is precisely R. Eliezer b. Jacob's dictum (*Gen. Rabba* lvi, 7, p. 602, and *ibid.*, lxxiv, 3, p. 860, and in both passages the reading is confirmed; see vv.ll. and the notes *ad loc.*) 'There is not a generation in which there are not to be found men like Abraham, Jacob, Moses and Samuel' that is a complete contradiction of the saying in *Midrash Tehillim*. It seems that the author of the dictum is the Amora R. Eleazar; see his teachings on the merit of the Patriarchs and Matriarchs in *T.B. Megilla* 13b.
67. *M. ʿEduyyot* ii, 9; see above, p. 265.
68. *M. 'Avot* ii, 2. See the commentary of Rabbenu Jonah on *M. 'Avot*, ed. M. S. Kasher and J. J. Blacherowicz, Jerusalem 1966: 'Although you labour with them and their needs are furnished by you, it is not you who bring about (their achievement), but the merit of the fathers of the community aids them....' R. Menaḥem Me'iri in his commentary *M. 'Avot*, ed. Stern, Vienna 1854, 10b, states: 'And he (Rabban Gamaliel) says that the merit of their father aids them, that is to say, although the affairs of the community compel them to unburden themselves of the yoke of many commandments, the merit of their fathers aids them and combines with their own merit... and he says "merit of their fathers", because as a rule only a man who has ancestral merit is appointed'; it seems that he derived his interpretation from Maimonides' commentary to the end of the Mishnah.
69. *T.P. Berakhot* iv, 1, p. 7d; see *T.B. ibid.*, 27b; cf. L. Ginzberg, *Perushim we-Ḥiddushim bi-Yerushalmi*, Pt. III, p. 185.
70. *Gen. Rabba* xliii, 8, p. 422. In most recensions, including the Vatican MS., the dictum is reported in the name of R. Jose b. R. Nehorai, and in some of the MSS. in the name of R. Jose b. Zimra; see vv.ll. *ad loc. Ibid.*, n. 4, Theodor identifies the pegs with the three pillars on which the world rests. See *Cant. Rabba* vii, 8: 'That people swear, saying "By Him who established the world on three pillars. Some say the reference is to Abraham, Isaac, and Jacob; others say that Ḥanania, Mishael, and Azariah are meant.' On the source of the oath 'By Him who established the world on three pillars' see S. Lieberman, *Greek in Jewish Palestine*, p. 81. The theme of three

righteous men appears in late Midrashim; cf. *Num. Rabba* iii, 1, and *Midrash Tadshe'* xxi, ed. A. Epstein, p. 41 (= *Kitve Abraham Epstein*, II, p. 168). On Ḥananiah, Mishael and Azariah see above, p. 443. The homily of Rav in *T.B. Hullin* 92a on ג׳ שרי גאים [literally 'three princes of the proud'] (see Rashi *ad loc.*), and likewise the allegorical exposition in the Baraita, *ibid.*, on Gen. xl, 10, do not belong to our subject. See now B. Mazar, 'Kĕtôvet ʿal riṣpat bêt-kĕneset be-ʿÊn-Gedî [The Inscription on the Floor of the Synagogue in En-Gedi]', *Tarbiz*, xl, No. 1, October 1970, p. 20 and *ibid.*, p. 22, n. 7. It should be noted that the Amora Rav Giddel swore by 'the Torah, the Prophets and the Hagiographa', *T.B. ʿEruvin* 17a; see Rashi, *ad loc.*, s.v. *'Ôraytā'*. It resembles the oath that R. Eleazar b. Azariah was accustomed to pronounce 'By the Torah! These are the words that were said to Moses at Sinai', *Tosefta Pe'a* iii, 2, ed. S. Lieberman, p. 51. But in *T.P. ibid.*, vi, 2, p. 19b the reading is: 'By the Covenant! These are the very...'; so, too, *Tosefta Ḥalla* i, 6; *T.B. Pesaḥim* 38b. It seems that the text in *Damascus Document* xv, 1 כי אם שבועת הב[רית] באלות הברית תורת משה אל יזכר should be constructed in the light of these passages, and not as L. Ginzberg does in *Eine unbekannte Sekte*, followed by Ch. Rabin, *Zadokite Documents*, Oxford 1958, pp. 72–73. It is difficult to accept Rabin's restoration שבועת ה[סכ]ם. The author of the scroll permits swearing in the form הברית [By the Covenant!], as alluding to אלות הברית [oaths of the Covenant], but prohibits the use of התורה [By the Torah!] in oaths.

71. *Gen. Rabba* lxviii, 12, p. 786. The first dictum is reported in the name of Shelomyani, a scholar mentioned nowhere else; while the second dictum occurs three times in *Gen. Rabba*, the principal passage being lxix, 3, p. 793 (see n. 1 *ad loc.*). Y. Baer, 'Le-berurah shel torat aḥarit ha-yamim bi-yeme ha-bayit ha-sheni', *Zion*, XXIII, 1958–1959, p. 31, basing himself on the commentary *Yefe To'ar* on *Gen. Rabba* lxix, 1, and referring to Philo, *De Somniis*, 157, explains the dictum of Resh Laqish to mean that the Patriarchs 'are pre-existent beings of the highest order, who dwell in heaven with the other souls of the righteous'; but it is difficult to suppose that this was what Resh Laqish intended to convey. On the θρόνοι as angels, see Colossians i 16, Strack-Billerbeck, III, p. 581.
72. *Sifre Deut.* § 329, p. 380; see *'Avot de-R. Nathan*, Version II, xxvii, p. 54, and *Midrash Tehillim* cxlvi, 2, p. 534.
73. vii 102–105, Charles, II, Pseudepigrapha, pp. 589–590.
74. xxxiii, 4–5, ed. G. Kisch, p. 209, and *ibid.*, note *m*, the addendum from MS. A: 'Sanctorum mortuorum nulla est pro nobis intercessio.'
75. *T.P. Sanhedrin* x, 1, p. 27d; *Lev. Rabba* xxxvi, 5, p. 845.
76. *Lev. Rabba, ibid.*; see *ibid.*, notes 1–2.
77. See my article in the *Yitzḥak Baer Jubilee Volume*, pp. 60 ff.
78. See above, n. 70.
79. *Mekhilta de-R. Ishmael*, Wa-yehi, iii, p. 100; *Mekhilta de-R. Simeon b. Yoḥai*, p. 59.

80. See S. Spiegel, 'Mē-'aggādôt hā-'Âqēdā', the *Alexander Marx Jubilee Volume*, New York 1950, pp. 471 ff.

81. *Gen. Rabba* lvi, 3, p. 598; see *ibid.*, p. 603, vv. ll.: 'Father I am a young man, and I am afraid lest my body tremble... bind me, therefore, very tight....'

82. *Mekhilta de-R. Ishmael*, Pisḥa, vi, p. 24, and *ibid.*, xi, p. 24, and *ibid.*, xi, p. 38. The homily in *Gen. Rabba* lvi, 7: ' "And he said: 'Lay not thy hand upon the lad...' " Said he (Abraham) to him (the angel): Let me strangle him! The angel replied: "Lay not thy hand upon the lad". Said Abraham to the angel: Let me draw a drop of blood from him! The angel answered: "Neither do thou anything [מאומה] unto him" — make no blemish [מומה] unto him...' may be regarded as directed against the view that blood was drawn from Isaac, but it is also possible that Abraham's very readiness to sacrifice his son was interpreted as though he had drawn blood, and it was to this that the expositor alluded, when he said 'and when I see the blood'. However, in the *Mekhilta de-R. Simeon b. Yoḥai*, p. 4, 'the Notes of R. Abraham ha-Laḥmi' (see *ibid.*, Mavo', p. י"ד) we find: 'R. Joshua said "And God spoke to Moses"—the Holy One, blessed be He, said to Moses: I am faithful to pay the reward of Isaac the son of Abraham, from whom a quarter of a *log* of blood issued on the altar, and I said to Him "According to the greatness of Thy power set free those that are appointed to death" (Psa. lxxix 11).' Likewise in *Midrash ha-Gadol*, ed. Margulies, p. 91, we read 'who gave a quarter of a *log* of blood....' But it is very doubtful, if this tradition is authentic (Spiegel in his aforementioned article, *loc. cit.*, p. 493, expresses himself with great caution: 'If the dictum emanates from the *Mekhilta de-R. Simeon b. Yoḥai* and was actually said by R. Joshua b. Hananiah, the Haggada is essentially very old'). It contradicts the explicit view of R. Joshua on the question of ancestral merit; see above, p. 497. Furthermore, the tradition of the names is in doubt. In 'The Notes of R. Abraham ha-Laḥmi' R. Joshua's saying is preceded by that of R. Jose, an unusual order, and actually the editor of the *Midrash ha-Gadol* 'amended' the text, changing the reading from 'R. Jose said' to 'R. Eliezer says'. Also in *Midrash Tanḥuma*, Wa-yērā', 23, it is only stated 'and he took the knife to slaughter him until a quarter of a *log* of blood would issue....' Likewise the reading in *Bereshit Rabbati*, p. 90, 'when Isaac saw that his father's face had changed... he said to him: "Father, fear not; may it be (God's will) that every quarter *log* [of] my [blood] be accepted with favour by Him who enjoined you concerning me" ', and even the wording 'This Midrash was uttered through the Holy Spirit' (Jacob Mann, *The Bible as Read and Preached*, Hebrew Section, p. 10; this is not 'an ancient Midrash', Spiegel, *op. cit.*, p. 492; see H. Albeck, in the additions to Zunz, *Ha-Derashot be-Yisra'el*, p. 400, n. 84) and 'May it be (God's will) that this quarter *log* of my blood shall be an atonement for all Israel', do not prove that the reference is to blood actually shed, since the words were uttered before the act.

83. *Sifra*, Be-ḥuqqôtay, viii, 7, 112c. The anonymous passage of the *Sifra* is

cited in *Lev. Rabba* xxxvi, 5, p. 849 in the name of 'the Rabbis', see n. 3 *ad loc.*

84. *T.P. Ta'anit* ii, 1, p. 65a. See *Gen. Rabba* xlix, 11, p. 513, where the text reads 'one said... and the other said.' Note 4 *ad loc.* cites from a manuscript commentary on *Gen. Rabba* 'R. Samuel bar Naḥmani said: the merit of Isaac'. In *T.B. Ta'anit* 16a the names of the disputants are R. Levi bar Ḥama and R. Ḥanina; see ed. Malter, p. 59.
85. *T.B. Berakhot* 62b. R. Isaac Nappaḥa states *ibid.*: 'He beheld the money of the atonement; R. Joḥanan said: He saw the Temple.' This dispute is also reported in the name of R. Jacob bar Idi and R. Samuel bar Naḥmani.
86. *T.B. Zevaḥim* 62a; R. Samuel bar Naḥmani said 'From there [the altar's site] they smelt the odour of limbs.'
87. *Gen. Rabba* lvi, 9, p. 606. His homily is transmitted there in two versions, one by R. Yudan and one by R. Phinehas. In the *Mekhilta de-R. Ishmael*, Massekhta de-Wayehi, p. 98, and *Gen. Rabba* lv, 8, p. 594, R. Banna'ah ascribes the parting of the sea to the merit of the chopping of the wood (for the *'Aqeda*) by Abraham.
88. *Tanḥum*, Shelaḥ, § 14. See also *Midrash ha-Gadol*, Bereshit, ed. Margulies, p. 360, in the name of 'R. Eleazar b. Pedat: Although he did not die, Scripture accounts it to his credit as if he had died....' Only in the Middle Ages did they link legends woven around the motif that Isaac's soul fled in sheer terror, and that only when he heard the words 'Lay not thy hand', did it return to his body, or that the Holy One, blessed be He, restored it by means of the dew of resurrection (*Pirqe de-R. Eliezer* § 31; Leqah Tov, p. 161), to such expressions as 'the ashes of Isaac that lie'. These derive, as we have seen, from Midrashim with the opposite motif, that Isaac was willing to be slaughtered and to be burned, and thus it came about that 'the ashes of Isaac were cast upon Mount Moriah', until 'the Holy One, blessed be He' brought 'dew and revived him'; see *Shibbole ha-Leqeṭ*, on the Eighteen Benedictions, pp. 17–18; cf. S. Spiegel, *op. cit.*, p. 485 ff.
89. *T.P. Ta'anit* ii, 4, p. 65d. See L. Ginzberg, *Śeride Yerushalmi*, p. 176, and cf. *ibid.* the dictum of R. Judah be R. Simeon: 'In time to come thy children will be caught up in iniquities and become enmeshed in troubles, but in the end they will be redeemed by the horns of this ram....' In the light of R. Joḥanan's teaching we can understand the motif of the benediction of *Zikhronot* ['Remembrances'] in the *Musaf* ['Additional Prayer'] of New Year: '... Mayest Thou be mindful of the time when Abraham bound ['Aqeda] his son Isaac... suppressing his compassion... so may Thy compassion overcome....' See *Gen. Rabba* lvi, 9, p. 605; *ibid.* 10, p. 607; and cf. the parallels indicated *ibid.*
90. See above, pp. 497–9.
91. *Lev. Rabba* xxix, 6, p. 676; *Pesiqta de-Rav Kahana*, p. 339. Regarding ניקוליגוס (νικολόγους) see S. Lieberman's note *ad loc.*, p. 475.
92. *Lev. Rabba* and *Pesiqta de-Rav Kahana*, *loc. cit.*; see the notes *ad loc.* The

words 'and Thou rememberest the pious deeds of the fathers' in the benediction *'Avot* ['fathers, Patriarchs'] of the Eighteen Benedictions do not occur in the Palestinian version; see S. Schechter, *JQR*, X, p. 656, and S. Assaf, 'Mi-Sēder ha-Tĕfillā be-'Ereṣ Yisrā'el [From the Palestinian Liturgy]', *Sefer Dinaburg*, 1949, p. 117.

93. *T.P. Sanhedrin* x, 1, p. 27d; this is the view of R. Tanḥuma in the name of R. Ḥiyya. Others ascribe this view to R. Ba bar Zavda; see *Lev. Rabba* xxxvi, 5, p. 851; cf. *T.B. Shabbat* 55a and Tosafot *ad loc.*, s.v. *ŪShĕmū'ēl.*

94. *T.P., loc. cit.*; *Lev. Rabba, loc. cit.*

95. *Gen. Rabba* lvi, 11, pp. 611–612; there, of course, R. Berechiah's exposition precedes that of R. Joshua b. Levi; see *T.B. Sanhedrin* 93a.

96. *T.B. Berakhot* 10b; see Maharsha, *Ḥiddushe ha-Aggadot, ad loc.*, who emends the text to read העיר הזאת... (instead of וגנותי על אל), the reference being to II Kings xx 6. See *Diqduqe Soferim, ad loc.*, p. 44, n. 5.

97. *T.P. Ma'aśer Sheni* v, 8, 56d. The dispute concerns the interpretation of the verse 'These are the two anointed ones' (Zechariah iv 14), and it appears that it is R. Joḥanan who said that they come on the strength of the performance of precepts and good deeds, and Resh Laqish who said that they come with power — with the claim of 'merit of the fathers'.

98. *T.P., loc. cit.*; see R. Solomon Sirillo's commentary, Jerusalem 1954, p. 105a: 'And these come with power, and are far from charity, that is to say, they have no need of charity, their own merit being sufficient.'

99. See the story cited in *T.P., loc. cit.*; cf. *T.B. Berakhot* 17b and *T.B. Ḥullin* 86a.

1. See above, p. 909, n. 60.

2. This homily is not opposed to the teaching of R. Levi, who said 'In time to come Abraham will sit at the entrance to Gehenna and will permit no Israelite to descend into it. But what does he do with those who sinned excessively? He will remove the foreskin from the infants who died before they were circumcised and put it upon them and take them down to Gehenna' — *Gen. Rabba* xlviii, 8, p. 483. See also *T.B. 'Eruvin* 19b; there Abraham raises up every Israelite from Gehenna, except those who prepuce is stretched. In other parallel sources Abraham is not reported as performing a particular function. The ancient concept was apparently that the uncircumcised cannot avoid going down to Gehenna; against this view the authors of the Gospels — see Luke xvi 21–25 — polemized (but not against the idea of the merits of the fathers, as A. Marmorstein, *Merits*, p. 169, thought; as regards the expression 'the bosom of Abraham' see Strack-Billerbeck, III, p. 226; S. Lieberman, *The Martyrs of Caesarea*, p. 443, and *ibid.* p. 390, n. 73). In advocating the observance of the precept of circumcision at the time of religious persecution and danger, the Sages devoted much homiletical exposition to its power and merit. Not content with saying that the verse ' "Therefore the netherworld hath enlarged her desire, and opened her mouth without measure [*ḥoq*]" (Isa. v 14) means for those that have not kept the statute [*ḥoq*] of circumcision' — an exposition directed against the Christians, who

abolished circumcision — they added ' "And He established it unto Jacob for a statute, to Israel for an everlasting covenant" (Psa. cv 10): this means that the circumcised do not go down to Gehenna.' The Amoraim, again, who were afraid of extreme formulations in Halakha, restricted the application of this teaching, and 'R. Berechiah said: In order that the apostates and wicked of Israel should not say: "Since we are circumcized, we shall not go down to Gehenna — what does the Holy One, blessed be He, do? He sends an angel who stretches their prepuce and they descend to Gehenna' (*Exod. Rabba* xix, 4, according to the Venice edition). Incidentally we learn that it was not the custom to circumcise infants that died; see S. Lieberman, 'Some Aspects of After Life in Early Rabbinic Literature', *Wolfson Jubilee Volume*, 1965, pp. 525 ff.

3. *T.B. Shabbat* 89b; See *Diqduqe Soferim*, p. 192, n. 3. The version I have cited in the text is according to MSS. א״פ, *Haggadot ha-Talmud*, and the *Yalquṭ* MS., which do not read 'and Isaac caused them to see the Holy One, blessed be He, with their own eyes'. See *Ḥiddushe Maharsha*, who points out that the expositor explains by his homily the difference between the beginning of the verse, where it is said 'For thou art our father', and the end 'For Thou, O Lord, art our Father'; see above, n. 2.
4. *T.P. Sanhedrin* x, 1, p. 27d; see *Lev. Rabba* xxxvi, 6, p. 852, where the text has 'Go, cleave to the practice of lovingkindness [בגמילות חסדים]'; but the Münich MS. — see vv.ll. *ibid.* — has 'to lovingkindness [בחסד]', the sense being the same.
5. *T.B. Shabbat* 89b.
6. *Sifre Deut.* § 210, p. 244; see *ibid.*, notes 4–5.
7. The entire discussion is to be found in *T.B. Horayot* 6a and in *T.B. Temura* 15b; on temporary rulings see *T.P. Horayot* i, 8, p. 46b.
8. *T.P. Sanhedrin* x, 1, p. 27d. According to the addition in *M. Pesaḥim* iv, 9 (see J. N. Epstein, *Mavo' le-Nosaḥ ha-Mishna*, p. 950) Hezekiah dragged the bones of his father to win atonement for him.
9. *T.B. Sanhedrin* 104a. On Amon's wickedness see *ibid.*, 103b. The question why Jehoiakim was not included remains unanswered; see Rashi *ad loc.*, s.v. *Mi-pĕnê mā*; *Yad Rama, ad loc.*; *Ḥiddushe Maharsha, ad loc.*, attempts to explain the difficulty.
10. *T.B. Qiddushin* 31b. R. Akiba Eger refers to *M. Negaʿim* ii, 1: 'R. Ishmael said: The Children of Israel — May I be their atonement', but he has in mind his contemporaries who are alive together with him (see the Commentary of the Geonim to *Ṭohorot*, who refer to the regulations relating to the High Priest, *M. Sanhedrin* ii, 1; cf. *T.B. Yevamot* 70a and *Otzar ha-Gaonim, ibid.*, p. 269); more relevant here is the reference of R. Samuel Strashun to *T.B. Sukka* 20a, where Resh Laqish says 'May I be an atonement for R. Ḥiyya and his sons!....' See Rashi's commentary *ad loc.*, s.v. *Harênî.*
11. *T.B. Soṭa* 10b; see Tosafot *ad loc.* a.v. *Dĕ-'atyeh,* the end of the comment. See *T.B. Yoma* 87a: 'Happy are the righteous! Not only do they acquire

merit, but they bestow it on their children and children's children, to the end of all generations....' At first blush it would seem that, even in the light of the preceding discussion, the bestowal of merit is for life in the world to come, but the proof from Aaron's sons (see *Diqduqe Soferim*, *ad loc.*, p. 303, n. 5) precludes this interpretation.

12. *Pesiqta Rabbati* 95b.
13. *Shibbole ha-Leqeṭ*, ed. Buber, p. 60: 'I have heard, in the name of R. Shne'ur Kohen Tsedek, of blessed memory, that there is in the Midrash... but it does not occur in the *Sifre*.' But also in *Sefer Tashbas*, by R. Simeon b. Ṣemaḥ Duran, § 440, the author quotes the passage of the *Sifre* according to our version, and continues: 'This (homily) is cited by R. Shemariah, of blessed memory, as proof that it is an act of piety to give alms for the sake of the dead.' In *Sefer ha-Roqeah*, § 217, it is stated: 'And of what avail is it to the dead that a living person gives alms on his behalf? Only the Lord tries the hearts of the living and the dead: If this deceased person used to give charity in his lifetime, or if the deceased was poor, but his heart was well-disposed and would have given if he had the means, then it avails him somewhat, for this (living individual) can supplicate to lighten the sentence of the dead. But if he gave on behalf of a wicked man it is fruitless....' As regards Christian influence on the matter see I. Levi, 'La commémoration des morts dans le Judaisme', *REJ*, XXIX, 1884, pp. 43–60. On the Egyptian and Orphic origin of the prayer for the dead see S. Reinach, 'De l'origine des prières pour les morts', *REJ*, XLI, 1900, pp. 161 ff. The dictum of R. Joshua b. Levi: 'If anyone responds "Amen. May His great name be blessed!" with all his might, his sentence (decreed by Heaven) is torn up' (*T.B. Shabbat* 119b) refers to the prayer of thanksgiving after Torah-study, called 'Kaddish'; see Z. Jawitz, *Mĕqôr ha-Bĕrâkhôt* [Source of the Blessings], Berlin 1910, pp. 82 ff. Not till the Middle Ages did it become a mourner's prayer; see *'Or Zarua'*, Pt. II, § 50 'And so, too, my teacher R. Eleazar of Worms found in *Seder Eliahu Rabba* that when a minor recites *Yitgaddal* ['May He be magnified'], he delivers his father from punishment.' See also Me'ir Ish-Shalom (Friedmann), *Nispaḥim le-Seder Eliahu Zuṭa* [Appendices to Seder Eliahu Zuṭa], 1904, pp. 24–25; Elbogen, *Der jüd. Gottesdienst*, pp. 95–96, and p. 528. Cf. also the commentary ascribed to Rashi, *T.B. Me'ila* 10b: 'And a sin-offering whose owner has died is also left to die, for the reason that there is no atonement for the dead, for their death has made atonement for them.'
14. *Gen. Rabba* xlix, 4, p. 503, and see *Sifre Deut.* § 48, p. 113: '... "My son, if thy heart be wise, my heart will be glad, even Mine" (Prov. xxiii 15). R. Simeon b. Menasya said: This refers only to his earthly father. Whence do we learn that it applies also to his Father in heaven? Therefore Scripture states "even Mine", which includes his Father in heaven.' However, in the printed editions and in the London MS. the author of the dictum is R. Simeon b. Yoḥai, but in most MSS. and in *Yalquṭ Shim'oni*, 'Eqev, § 873,

and likewise in *Yalquṭ Makhiri* to Proverbs, the reading is 'R. Simeon b. Menasya'; it is possible, however, that his exposition followed the lines of R. Simeon b. Yoḥai's dictum. It is noteworthy that in *Gen. Rabba* lxiii, 1, p. 678, R. Simeon b. Menasya's homily is cited in the form 'For even the Holy One, blessed be He, is filled with compassion for him...' under the influence of the dictum of R. Huna in the name of R. Aḥa, which precedes it.

15. Although in a late Midrash, *Sefer Eliahu Zuṭa* xii, ed. Me'ir Ish-Shalom (Friedmann), p. 194, we read 'An ignorant person who had his son taught Scripture and Mishna, is saved by his son from the punishment of Gehenna', the proof from Isaiah xxix 22 is derived from a source in which the verse is expounded in another sense; see below, n. 19.
16. *Sirach* xxx 4–6; see my article 'Hilkhot Yerushsha we-Ḥayye ʿOlam', *Papers of the Fourth World Congress of Jewish Studies*, Jerusalem 1967, I, pp. 138 ff.
17. *Gen. Rabba* xxxv, 2, p. 329; see *ibid.* the parallel versions cited in n. 4, and cf. above, p. 452.
18. *Gen. Rabba* lxiii, 2, p. 679, in the name of R. Samuel bar Rav Isaac, but in MS. 2K the text has 'bar Naḥman'. This version is confirmed by *Aggadot Bereshit* lxv, ed. Buber, p. 130, where the passage reads 'Were it not that Jacob was due to be your descendant, you would not have gone forth from here.'
19. *T.B. Sanhedrin* 19b; our recension has only 'Rav Judah said', but see *Diqduqe Soferim*, *ibid.*, p. 40, n. ט.
20. See M. Weiss, 'Mi-beʿayot "Torat ha-Gemul" ha-Miqra'it', *Tarbiz*, XXX, 1962, p. 240.
21. *Midrash Tannaim*, p. 21: ' "Visiting the iniquity of the fathers upon the children" — when Moses heard this he was taken aback in bewilderment, until He (God) said to him: "(This applied only) when the succession is uninterrupted". But perhaps (this applies) even when the succession is interrupted? Therefore Scripture teaches "of them that hate Me" — that is a wicked man, the son of a wicked man, who is the son of a wicked man.' See *Mekhilta de-R. Ishmael*, Ba-ḥodesh vi, p. 226.
22. *T.B. Makkot* 24a. The homily in *Num. Rabba* xix, 33, is constructed according to the pattern of R. Jose b. R. Ḥanina's exposition, and under its influence the homily of the Tannaim cited above, in n. 21, was reworked as follows: 'This is one of the three things that Moses said to the Holy One, blessed be He, and He replied "You have taught Me"... When the Holy One, blessed be He, said to him: "Visiting the iniquity of the fathers upon the children", Moses said: "Sovereign of the universe, how many wicked people have begotten righteous children? And is it fitting that the righteous should be punished for the iniquity of their father? Said the Holy One, blessed be He, to him: "You have taught Me; I swear by your life that I shall revoke My words and fulfil yours, as it is said "The fathers shall not be put to death for the children"....'
23. See above, p. 436.
24. *Sifra*, Qedoshim, viii, 13, 91c; see *T.B. Shevuʿot* 39a.

25. *T.B. Pesaḥim* 112a; see G. Alon, *Toledot ha-Yehudim be-'Ereṣ Yisra'el bi-Tequfat ha-Mishna we-ha-Talmud,* Pt. I, p. 338.
26. *Sifra, loc. cit.*, 13; the exposition is anonymous and possibly belongs to R. Simeon b. Yoḥai. *T.B. Shevu'ot, loc. cit.*, reads 'Rabbi said', but the Munich MS. has 'R. Me'ir said'.
27. *Sifra, loc. cit.*, 10–11.
28. *Ibid.*: סנדריות של ישראל; I. H. Weiss draws attention there to the reading of the *Yalquṭ*: סנהדראות של שבטים. In the Rome MS. of the *Sifra*, edition of the Jewish Theological Seminary of America, New York 1957, p. 406, the reading is the same as that cited here in the text.
29. *Loc. cit.*, 8. Although this exposition refers, in the *Sifra, ibid.*, iv, 1, to 'the judge who perverts judgement', yet *ibid.* viii, 91a, it refers also to one who, 'falsified measures.'
30. *Pesiqta Rabbati* xxi, 107a; in our text we have cited the passage according to the Parma manuscript, 1240.
31. *Sifre Deut.* § 307, p. 346; see *T.B. 'Avoda Zara* 18a, where another tradition is inserted, whose motif is that even martyrs are not free from sin. See above, p. 443, and further on, p. 522.
32. *Sifre Deut., loc. cit.*
33. *T.P. Sanhedrin* vi, 12, p. 23d. The expression 'neither respect of persons nor taking of bribes' is also that used by R. Eliezer Ha-Qappar in *M. 'Avot* iv 22; and R. Simeon b. Ṣemaḥ Duran, *Magen 'Avot*, 72b, has already referred to the Biblical passage, II Chron. xix 7.
34. See *T.P. Qiddushin* iv, 1, p. 65b; *T.P. Sanhedrin* vi, 10, p. 23d (attention should be paid to the interpretation of על שאול ['for Saul'] [this is the reading in both passages of the *T.P.* and not as in our text of the Bible: אל שאול] 'because of Saul to whom you showed no lovingkindness'. Thus the Sages also found in this verse an answer to our problem, which ascribes the famine to David's sin. On the views of modern scholars, who discerned here two traditions, see M. Buber, *Darko shel Miqra'* [The Biblical Method], Jerusalem 1964, p. 231). In *T.B. Yevamot* 79a it is stated: 'At that moment David said: Three precious gifts did the Holy One, blessed be He, give to Israel: they [i.e. the people of Israel] are compassionate, bashful, and practice lovingkindness.'
35. See the sources cited above, and *Midrash Shemuel* xxviii, p. 133: 'And the Gentiles seeing them said: The Torah of these (Jews) is a fraud. It is written in their Torah "His body shall not remain all night upon the tree", but these (corpses) have been hanging seven months. It is written in the Torah that two may not be sentenced (to death) on one day, but these "(fell) all seven together" (II Sam. xxi 9)...' It is written in the Torah "The fathers shall not be put to death for the children...", but these died for their fathers' sins...' So, too, in *Num. Rabba* viii 4, only there the following dictum has been interpolated: 'R. Ḥiyya bar Abba said in the name of R. Joḥanan: Rather let a letter of the Torah be uprooted than the name of Heaven be profaned publicly', as it is found in *T.B. Yevamot, loc. cit.*

36. *Eccles. Rabba* vii, 16, according to the Pesaro edition. In the Oxford MS. 164, 2 אומר ['said'] is wanting. In *Midrash Shemu'el*, Sec. xviii, 2, p. 99 the reading is: ר' בנייה בשם רב הונא; see *ibid.*, n. 5.

37. *T.B. Yoma*, 22b. In *Cant. Rabba, loc. cit.*: 'The Rabbis said (this is also the reading in the aforementioned Oxford MS., but in the Parma MS. 541 the names of the Rabbis and the order of the dicta are changed: 'R. Banna'ah: He began to criticize [the law of] the heifer whose neck was broken... and the Rabbis said: He criticized the Holy One, blessed be He....' In the Parma MS. 616 we read: 'R. Yannai said in the name of Rava Huna: He began to speak against [the law of] the [heifer] whose neck was broken... for the Rabbis say...' In this part, too, the MS. is corrupt), He began to argue against (the law of) the heifer whose neck was broken, and said: Scripture ordains "and shall break the heifer's neck there in the valley" — he (the man) kills, yet she (the heifer) has its neck broken! If man has sinned, what crime has the beast committed? (Thereupon) a Heavenly Voice went forth and said....' This text appears truncated, for it is not relevant to Saul, and it seems that by 'the Rabbis' R. Mani—the earlier R. Mani — of the Babylonian Talmud is meant, and that after 'and said' the words 'If now in respect of one soul...' have been omitted. Also the expression 'If man has sinned, what crime has the beast committed?' is out of place in the context of the heifer whose neck was broken, for 'Scripture describes it as an atonement like sacrifices' (*T.P. Soṭa* ix, 5, p. 23d; *T.B. Megilla* 21a) and no such objection is raised against the sin offerings and other sacrifices, but only with reference to passages where the punishment of beasts is spoken of, as for example the ox that is stoned, *M. Sanhedrin* vii, 4. See also *T.B. Sanhedrin* 108a — the story of the generation of the Flood — and cf. *T.B. Sanhedrin* 44a: To the Exilarch's question in regard to Achan 'And if he sinned, did his sons and daughters sin?' Rav Huna replied 'And according to your reasoning, if he sinned, what sin did all Israel commit?... the purpose was to discipline them; similarly here, too, the object was to discipline them' (i.e. that they should see his punishment and take heed unto themselves that they should not continue to transgress). Concerning the chattels Ravina said: 'That which was fit for burning was burnt, that which was fit for stoning was stoned', and Rashi explains 'This refers to his ox and (other) beasts; this was a penalty to discipline others.' On reward and punishment for animals see A. Aptowitzer, 'The Rewarding and Punishments of Animals', *HUCA*, III, 1926, pp. 131 ff; see *ibid.* p. 138. Cf. also S. Abramson, *Ba-Merkāzîm û-ba-Tĕfûṣôt bi-Tĕqûfat ha-Ge'onim* [In the Centres and in the Diaspora in the Period of the Geonim], Jerusalem 1965, pp. 65 ff; and see above, p. 264 on Divine Providence over animals, and above, p. 849 n. 12, on the evil inclination of animals.

38. *Cant. Rabba, loc. cit.* The dictum of Resh Laqish was joined in *T.B. Yoma, loc. cit.*, to the end of the statement of R. Mani: 'And when Saul said to Doeg' etc.

39. *T.B. Yoma, ibid.* Rav Huna based himself on the verse 'Saul was a year old when he began to reign.' Rav Naḥman reacted (this is the reading in the MSS; see *Diqduqe Soferim, ad loc.*, p. 56) saying: 'Perhaps one should say like a year-old infant who is covered in mud.' The Talmud relates that 'He saw a frightening vision in his dream. (Thereupon) he said: "I beg your pardon, O bones of Saul son of Kish." Again he saw a frightening vision in his dream. (Again) he said: "I beg your pardon, O bones of Saul son of Kish, king of Israel."' See Tosefot Yeshanim, *ad loc.*, s.v. *Kĕ-ben*, where an attempt is made to defend Rav Naḥman and it is argued that he, too, intended to speak in favour of Saul, but 'he expressed himself inelegantly'. At any rate the evaluation of Saul's personality, both by the Amoraim and in the anonymous passages of the Talmud, is much more favourable than that of the Book of Samuel.
40. It is found in another context as a dictum of Rava, *T.B. Bava Qamma* 20b.
41. On the subject of David, R. Ḥananel states in his commentary on *T.B. Yoma, ad loc.*, 'Because he found grace in the eyes of God', but Maharsha [R. Samuel Eliezer Edels] in his *novellae* notes: 'The commentators have already raised the objection: But is there Divine favouritism in the matter?' (see, however, *T.P. Sanhedrin* x, p. 29a) and he rejects their explanations and declares: 'It seems to me that the problem should be explained on the basis of the Rabbinic principle that he who seeks to purify himself is helped to do so by Heaven... Because he (David) wished to purify himself and confessed his sins and accepted (the penance of) suffering, therefore he was helped by Heaven... But this was not so in the case of Saul, for we do not find that he confessed this sin before God, blessed be He...' But Saul expressly said 'I have sinned; for I have transgressed the commandment of the Lord...' (I Sam. xv 24; cf. also v. 24 and v. 30; and see the commentary of R. Isaiah *ad loc.*). The author of *Sĕfat 'Emet*, in his *novellae* to *T.B. Yoma*, notes the difficulty inherent in the Maharsha's comments, and gives the following interpretation of his own: 'For there are two categories of the righteous. There is a type of righteous man who maintains his righteousness by himself; therefore the Sages said of him that he was like a year-old infant without sin... and there is no respecting of persons in the matter; it is simply that Saul himself chose this way for himself, that he should be dealt with according to his deeds....' It seems that, like the Amoraim, he aimed in his commentary to maintain Saul's righteousness. I was aided by his observations to adopt the interpretation that I have given in the text.
42. *Midrash Tehillim* lxii, 4, p. 309; the sentence in *Pesiqta Rabbati*, ii, 7a, 'Said R. Simeon b. Yoḥai: The expression "before Me" means none other than sacrifices, as it is said "And he shall kill the bullock *before* the Lord"' is wanting in the Parma MS. 1240.
43. See S. Z. Zeitlin, 'The Legend of the Ten Martyrs and its Apocalyptic Origin', *JQR*, 1945–46, pp. 1 ff, where the early literature is listed; to this I would add the article by S. Krauss, "Asārā hărûgê malkhût [The Ten Martyrs]',

Ha-Shiloaḥ, XLIV (1925), pp. 10–22, 106–117, 221–223. Cf. also S. Lieberman, 'The Martyrs of Caesarea', *Annuaire de l'institut de Philologie et d'histoire orientales et Slaves*, VII, pp. 417 ff.

44. *Midrash Mishle* i, 13, ed. Buber, p. 45, in the name of R. Avin or R. Bon. See *ibid.* n. *'Ayin*; in MS. Vat. 76 the reading is: ר׳ אבין אמר: בכל דור עדיין החטא קיים ('R. Avin said: In every generation the sin is still unexpiated'). In MS. Vat. 92: בכל דור החטא קיים... ('In every generation the sin still exists').

45. On the connection between this Midrash and the literature of *Hekhalot*, see my article 'Ha-Masoret 'al Torat ha-Sod bi-Tequfat ha-Tanna'im', *Studies in Mysticism and Religion Presented to Gershon G. Scholem*, Jerusalem 1968, p. כה [25] n. 119; cf. also *Midrash 'Elle 'Ezkĕrā* [These I remember], A. Jellinek, *Bet ha-Midrash*, Pt. II, pp. 64 ff, and Pt. VI, pp. 36 ff; *ibid.*, in his Introduction, p. 18, he treats of the relationship of the Midrash to *Sefer Ha-Hekhalot*, but his statement there, in n. צ, that the nexus between the Ten Martyrs and the verse 'And he that stealeth a man, and selleth him... shall surely be put to death', Exod. xxi 16, is to be found in the *Mekhilta*, 'As Simeon Duran attests in his commentary on *M. 'Avot* (S. Krauss, in his aforementioned article in *Ha-Shiloah*, p. 222, follows Jellinek) is erroneous. Rashbaṣ, *Magen 'Avot*, 14a, says only, with reference to 'Simeon his son said', that he was one of the Ten Martyrs as is mentioned in the *Mekhilta*, in the section of 'And he that stealeth a man, and selleth him', and inadvertently he wrongly referred to this passage, but the story about Simeon's execution occurs in the homily on the verse 'If thou afflict them in any wise', Exod. xxii 22; see above, p. 443.

46. *Midrash Mishle, loc. cit.*, Buber cites the dictum in square brackets, in order to indicate that it is wanting in the Paris MS. 152; see *ibid.*, n. 69. But it does occur there, and likewise in MSS. Vat. 76, 92 and in the Escorial MS. 1155, and it is actually in the Parma MS. 616, which Buber claims to have used (it is, however, the worst of all the MSS.) that we find the reading לא נמסרו עשרה הרוגי מלוכה אלא על מכירתו של יוסף ('The Ten Martyrs were delivered [for execution] only on account of the selling of Joseph'), and in the oldest of the MSS., Parma 1240 (written in 1270) the reading is: א״ר יהושע בן לוי: לא נמשכו עשרה ה״ק (the word is not clear; perhaps it should be הק׳ = הקדושים ['the martyrs']) הרוגי לוד אלא בחטא מכירתו של יוסף ('R. Joshua b. Levi said: The Ten Martyrs, the slain of Lydda, were dragged to execution only on account of the sin of the selling of Joseph'). On the slain of Lydda in the ancient sources see S. Lieberman in his aforementioned article, pp. 412 ff.

47. *Bereshit Rabbati*, ed. H. Albeck, pp. 177–178; see *ibid.*, p. 176, n. 1. On the fact that the compiler of this Midrash used *Midrash Mishle* cf. the Introduction, p. 28.

48. *T.B. Berakhot* 10a; see *Diqduqe Soferim, ad loc.*, p. 42. The author of the dictum in the Babylonian Talmud is Rav Hamnuna, with whose name the

preceding homily commences. In *T.P. Sanhedrin* x, 2, p. 28c the exposition occurs anonymously in the following version: '... "For thou shalt die" in this world, "and not live" in the world to come. Said (Hezekiah) to him (Isaiah) "Wherefore?" He replied: "Because you do not wish to raise up children for yourself." He (then) said: "Why do you not wish to raise up children for yourself?" (Hezekiah) replied: "I have seen (prophetically) that I shall beget a wicked son; hence I do not wish to raise up children." Said (Isaiah) to him: "Take my daughter; perhaps from me and from you a virtuous man will be begotten. Nevertheless, an evil man arose. This is the meaning of the verse "The instruments also of the churl are evil" (Isa. xxxii 7).' From the textual aspect the narrative in the Palestinian Talmud is less drastic; in the Babylonian Talmud it is Hezekiah who suggests to Isaiah 'Give me your daughter', but the latter rejects him, saying 'It has already been decreed concerning you.' But the evaluation of Hezekiah's approach remains unaffected. In the Munich MS., *'En Ya'qov*, and *Haggadot ha-Talmud*, there is a continuation to the story in the spirit of the narrative in the Palestinian Talmud; cf. *Diqduqe Soferim, ad loc.*, p. 43, n. ע. In addition to the sources cited *ibid.*, see *Paḥad Yiṣḥaq*, § מ, 90a, which cites a different version, at the end of which it is stated 'This entire addendum from יהב ליה ברתיה וכו' ['He gave him his daughter' etc.] to the end does not occur in our texts of the Gemara, but is to be found in the Portuguese printings of the Talmud.

49. See Rashi, *T.B. Berakhot, loc. cit.*, s.v. *Kivshê.*

CHAPTER XVI

THE PEOPLE OF ISRAEL AND ITS SAGES

1. See E. Schürer, *Geschichte des jüd. Volkes* etc.,[4] III, pp. 606–608; Joshua Gutman, *Ha-Sifrut ha-Yehudit ha-Helenistit*, 1958, I, pp. 63 ff.
2. The genuine passages of Hecataeus, which have survived in the fragments of Diodorus' work, have been published in Müller, *Fragmenta historicorum Graecorum*, II, pp. 384–396. On the excerpts in Josephus, *Against Apion*, I, see Yoḥanan Levi, *'Olāmôt Nifgāshîm* [Worlds that meet], Jerusalem 1960, pp. 44 ff, and *ibid.*, p. 51.
3. *Contra Faustum*, Migne, *PL*, XLII, p. 261. A similar answer was put by R. Abba bar Kahana into the mouth of the philosopher, Avnimos [Oenomaus] of Gadara, to the question of the Gentile nations: 'Do you think that we can join battle with this people?', *Gen. Rabba* lxv, 20, p. 734, and note *ad loc*.
4. See A. Tcherikover, *Hellenistic Civilization and the Jews*, pp. 117–120.
5. This was done in so far as the *Mekhilta* is concerned in M. Kaduschin's article 'Aspects of the Rabbinic Concept of Israel', *HUCA*, XIX, 1945–46, pp. 57–96; see also his essay 'Běḥîrat Yisrā'ēl bě-Divrê Ḥazal [Israel's Election in Rabbinic Teaching]', *Proceedings of the Rabbinical Assembly of America*, VIII, 1941–44, pp. 20–25. I cannot refrain from observing, on this occasion, that I have not succeeded in perceiving the advantage of using the terminology chosen by Kaduschin to present and clarify the thought of the Sages. The notion that the absence of the term *běḥîrā* ['election'] as a noun in Rabbinic literature shows, as it were, that it is only an 'auxiliary idea' (see idem, *The Rabbinic Mind*, 1952, p. 55, and prior to that in his aforementioned Hebrew article) in no way detracts from the intrinsic importance of the theme and adds nothing to our understanding of it. The dissertation by S. W. Helfgott, *The Doctrine of Election in Tannaitic Literature*, New York 1954, does not contribute much to the elucidation of the questions that we have raised.
6. See M. Buber, *Darkô shel Miqrā'*, Jerusalem 1964, pp. 88–99.
7. *T.B. 'Avoda Zara* 4a. See Rashi, *ad loc.*, s.v. *man dě-'ît lêh*; *Diqduqe Soferim*, p. 9; and *Massekhet 'Avoda Zara Kětāv Yad Sěfārādî* [Tractate A. Z., Spanish

MS.], ed. S. Abramson, p. 199. Similar views to those of R. Abbahu are also expressed in *T.B. ʿAvoda Zara*, *loc. cit.*, by Rava; see Rashi, *ad loc.*, s.v. *ka-pîd*; cf. *Aggadot Bre'shit*, viii, p. 22.

8. See *Contra Celsum*, VIII, 69; see *ibid.*, pp. 50–51.
9. See above, p. 77, Cicero, *Pro Flacco*, 28 and 69; see further Josephus, *Against Apion*, II, 125–135; M. Joel, *Blicke in die Religionsgeschichte*, II, p. 103; cf. J. Bernays, *Gesammelte Abhandlungen*, II, p. 309; J. Levi, *ʿOlamot Nifgashim*, pp. 86–87.
10. *T.B. Ḥagiga* 5b: 'When R. Joshua b. Hananiah was at the court of Caesar, a certain sectarian showed him (by gestures) that his Lord had turned his face away from him (Israel). He indicated to him (in turn by gestures) that His hand was stretched out (in protection) over us...' Since R. Joshua understood the Min's [sectary's] sign, but the latter failed to comprehend what R. Joshua meant, the emperor ordered the *Min* to be executed. Even if we wish to find some historical background to this story, such as the beginning of the reign of Hadrian, who thought of rebuilding Jerusalem, if not the Temple (see G. Alon, *Toledot ha-Yehudim be-'Ereṣ Yisra'el bi-Tequfat ha-Mishna we-ha-Talmud* [The History of the Jews in Palestine in the period of the Mishna and Talmud], 1953, Pt. I, pp. 279, and also *ibid.*, p. 191, where the author cites our narrative, but does not connect the sections), we must concede that its purpose is to emphasize the polemical skill and sagacity of R. Joshua. This is also shown by the continuation of the passage in the Gemara, *loc. cit.*, where it is stated that after R. Joshua's death the Sages said 'What will become of us when we are harrassed by the sectarians?' (see *Diqduqe Soferim*, *ad loc.*, p. 14). The comfort that they found in the verse Jeremiah xi 7, which is interpreted to mean 'When counsel is perished from the children (of Israel) the wisdom of the Gentile peoples deteriorates', is also indicative of the contempt in which the source holds disputes of this kind. See also *T.B. Yevamot* 102b: 'A certain *Min* said to Rabban Gamaliel: (Israel) is a people for whom their Lord had drawn off (the shoe) [i.e. has severed relations with them by performing *ḥălîṣā*], for it is written "With their flocks and with their herds they shall go to seek the Lord... (He hath withdrawn Himself [*ḥālaṣ*] from them)." Said he in reply: Fool, is it written *ḥālaṣ lāhem* ['he hath performed *ḥaliṣa* unto them']? It is written *ḥalaṣ mēhem* ['He hath drawn off from them']; if brothers draw off (the shoe) of a sister-in-law, has it any validity? [Since it is she who must draw the brother's shoe off].' Needless to say, explanations of this sort could not satisfy Celsus; nor did they contribute in any way to strengthening faith in Israel's election. The derisive undertone of R. Me'ir's reply was not understood by 'a certain Samaritan', and only when he went 'to their patriarch' did the latter make the intention of 'the master of the Jews' clear to him — *Gen. Rabba* xciv, 7, p. 1178.
11. *Mekhilta*, Massekhta de-Wa-yehi, iii, p. 99; see also *Mekhilta de-R. Simeon b. Yoḥai*, p. 59, where the text reads: כבר מוזכרין הן לפני משׁשת ימי בראשׁית

'They are already remembered by Me since before the six days of creation.' This is an acceptable reading; cf. *Sifre Deut.* § 47.

12. See *The Assumption of Moses* i 12; *The Syriac Apocalypse of Baruch* xiv 18; Ephesians i 4; cf. below, note 16.

13. *M. 'Avot* iii, 14; I have cited the text according to the Cambridge MS. and the Kaufmann MS. In the latter manuscript the verses are added in the margin. See R. Simeon b. Ṣemah Duran, *Magen 'Avot* 51b: 'We do not read in our texts of the Mishna, except in a few versions, the words 'as it is said "For I give you good doctrine; forsake ye not My Law".'

14. *Sifre Deut.* § 308.

15. *Gen. Rabba* i, 4, p. 6; see above, p. 198.

16, iv Ezra vi 55–59, ed. R. Bensly, p. 25: '... quoniam dixisti quia propter nos creasti primogenitum saeculum Residuas autem gentes ab Adam natas dixisti eas nihil esse et quoniam saliuae adsimilatae sunt et sicut stillicidium de uaso similasti habundantiam. corum. Et nunc, Domine, ecce istae gentes quae in nihilum deputatae sunt dominantur nostri et deuorant nos. Nos antem populus tuus quem uocasti primogenitum, unigenitum, aemolatorem, carissimum traditi sumus in manibus eorum. Et si propter nos creatum est saeculum, quare non haereditatem possidemus nostrum saeculum? usquequo haec?'

17. *T.B. Ḥagiga* 3a and *T.B. Berakhot* 6a. In *Tosefta Soṭa* vii, 10, p. 307, printed ed., and in the Vienna MS. the reading is: '...בעוה״ז... בעוה״ב' ['... in this world... in the world to come']; but this is undoubtedly an addition. See Targum Onkelos and Targum Yerushalmi to Deut. xxvi 17–18.

18. *Mekhilta de-R. Ishmael*, Mishpaṭim, xx, p. 320; see *Sifre Deut.* § 97.

19. *Sifre Deut.* § 312, pp. 353–354. Deut. xiv 2 does not contain, in our texts, the word אלהיך ['thy God']; hence Me'ir 'Ish-Shalom (Friedman) identified the verse, in his ed., p. 134b, with Deut. vii 6, but the Septuagint and the Targums, as well as the *Sifre* itself, § 97, read 'thy God' in Deut. xiv 2. On the other hand, Deut. vii 6 has בך ['thee' instead of ובך ('and thee')].

20. The reading in the Finkelstein edition does not fit the context well: תלמוד לומר לישראל סגולתו ['Scripture teaches: to Israel his own treasure'] adds nothing to the verse כי יעקב בחר לו יה ['For the Lord hath chosen Jacob; conceivably it could also mean 'For Jacob hath chosen the Lord'] in order to solve the question of who chose whom. It seems that the version in *Midrash Tanna'im*, p. 190 (without D. Hoffmann's additions) and in *Yalquṭ Makhiri* on Psalms, p. 254, enables us to reconstruct the original text as follows: וכה״א 'כי יעקב בחר לו יה ישראל לסגולתו' ועדיין הדבר תלי ואין אנו יודעין אם הקב״ה בחר לו לישראל לסגלתו ואם ישראל בחר בהקב״ה וכשהוא אומר 'בך בחר ה' אלהיך'... הרי יה בחר ביעקב ומנין שאף יעקב בחר ביה שנ' 'לא כאלה חלק יעקב' ['And thus it says "For the Lord hath chosen Jacob unto Himself, and Israel for His own treasure." But the matter is still undecided (תלי) and we do not know whether the Holy One, blessed be He, has chosen Israel unto Himself as His own treasure or Israel has chosen the Holy One, blessed be He; but when it says "Thee the Lord thy God hath chosen...", it is evident that the

Lord has chosen Jacob. And whence do we know that Jacob has also chosen the Lord? For it is said "Not like these is the portion of Jacob"?]. It appears that the expression בדלא תלי [literally 'on that which is not dependent', i.e. undecided, ambiguous] is only a stereotyped phrase [אשגרתא] derived from the locution in the Babylonian Talmud תלי תניא בדלא תניא ['bases that which has been taught on that which has not been taught'], Shabbat 22a, where the parallels are listed (in the *Yalquṭ Shim'oni*, Jeremiah § 288, later editions read ועדיין הדבר תלי בדלא תניא ['but it still depends on that which has not been taught'] but the *editio princeps* reads בדלא תלי; however, even this textual corruption shows the power of a cliché [אשגרתא]). The reading ועדין הדבר תלי בדלא תלי is found twice — apart from its occurrence in our passage — in *Sifre Deut.* § 333 and § 342, and in *Sifre Num.* § 90, ed. Horovits, p. 91. But see vv.ll. *ibid.*; already Ch. Albeck cast doubts on the accuracy of this reading in his *Untersuchungen über die hal. Midrashim*, p. 77. In *Mekhilta de-R. Simeon b. Yoḥai*, p. 16 (*ibid* .ועד אין דבר תלוי בדלא תלי) the phrase is completely meaningless, since there is no second verse there; and although this verse is found in *Mekhilta de-R. Ishmael*, Bo', vii, p. 25, yet there the text has עדיין הדבר שקול ['the matter is still evenly balanced']; and the words עדיין הדבר תלוי ['the matter is still undecided'] only occurs as an alternative reading to עדיין הדבר חלוק ['the matter is still divided'] in *Sifre Zuṭa*, p. 253, n. 5. See Albeck *ibid.*

21. In *Yalquṭ Shim'oni*, *ibid.*, according to the *editio princeps*, the homily concludes as follows: 'And how do we know that Jacob, too, chose the Holy One, blessed be He, as it is said "Not like these is the portion of Jacob", "Jacob the lot [חבל] of His inheritance", and it is further said "The lines [חבלים] are fallen unto me in pleasant places" (Psalms xvi 6). Just as חבל [which means both 'cord' (or 'line') and 'portion' (or 'lot')] occurs three times, so was Jacob the third of the Patriarchs and concerning him it is said "and a threefold cord is not quickly broken"' (it appears that this ending was also known to the compiler of *Yalquṭ Makhiri*, only he abbreviated it). In this way the homiletical cycle was closed and its two parts were joined together. See *Gen. Rabba* xlvi 1, p. 458, and *'Arugat ha-Bosem*, Pt. III, p. 152, and *ibid.*, n. 7. Cf. Joshua xxiv 22, and *Sifre Deut.* § 306.
22. *Sifre Deut.* § 96; cf. *ibid.*, § 97 ' "For thou art a holy people unto the Lord thy God" — the sanctity that is upon you has brought this about for you', in accordance with the view of R. Ishmael above, n. 18.
23. See Isaiah xli 8–9 and Nehemiah ix 7.
24. See *The Book of Jubilees* xv 30; and *IV Ezra* iii 13–17, ed. Bensley, p. 8. Actually this fact nullifies the conjecture of Eugene Mihaly, 'A Rabbinic Defence of the Election of Israel', *HUCA*, XXXV, 1964, pp. 103–143, who sought to explain the statement of the *Sifre* as an anti-Christian polemic. See *ibid.*, pp. 108 ff, where he bases himself on the arguments of Paul, and especially of Barnabas, that the Christians, as the seed of Abraham, are the Chosen People; see *ibid.*, p. 112, n. 16. It is clear that the stress laid on the

election of Jacob is earlier than the statement of Barnabas and also of Paul. Likewise Mihaly's treatment of the continuation of the homily is a case of 'inferring the known from the unknown'.

25. *Midrash Shemu'el* viii, 2, p. 70. See *Exod. Rabba* xxxvii, 4; *Num. Rabba* iii, 2.
26. *Lev. Rabba* xxiii, 3, pp. 529–530; I have cited the conclusion according to the version of two Oxford MSS. and the Jerusalem MS. See vv.ll. *ibid.*
27. *Mekhilta de-R. Ishmael*, Massekhta de-Ba-ḥodesh, v, p. 221; see the parallels listed *ibid.*, n. 7.
28. Κατὰ Γαλιλαίων ed. Wright, published by Loeb Classical Library, 1923, III, 106c–106d.
29. See *Tosefta 'Avoda Zara* viii (ix), 4, p. 473, and *T.B. Sanhedrin* 56 a–b. This fact, to which insufficient attention has been paid, refutes the view of Schoeps, *Aus frühchristlicher Zeit*, p. 190, that the *Mekhilta, loc. cit.*, replies, as it were, to Christians of the type of Barnabas, who contended that the precepts were given to Israel as a punishment. It would in that case have been difficult to argue against Christians that they did not keep the Noachide commandments; see M. Guttmann, *Das Judentum und seine Umwelt*, 1927, pp. 105–106.
30. *Sifre Deut.* § 343; see *T.B. 'Avoda Zara* 2b.
31. See *T.P. 'Avoda Zara* ii, 1, p. 40c. On the verse Zechariah xi 12 'Ulla commented (according to another version: Rava; see *Diqduqe Soferim*, p. 125b): 'This refers to the thirty precepts that the descendants of Noah accepted, but they keep only three — (one is) that they do not write a *ketubba* for males; another is that they do not weigh the flesh of the dead in the meat-market; and yet another is that they honour the Torah' — *T.B. Ḥullin* 92 a–b. Although M. Joel, 'Einige Notizen als Ergänzungen zum zweiten Theil meiner Schrift, "Blicke in die Religionsgeschichte", *Graetz-Jubelschrift*, 1887, p. 179, n. 1, noted that the number thirty recalls the thirty pieces of silver in Matthew xxvii 9 (see above, p. 310), he did not attempt to identify the type of people against whom 'Ulla directed his remarks. M. Guttmann, *op. cit.*, p. 102, n. 2, gives the gist of Joel's observations, but whereas Joel wrote 'Sehr eigenthümlich is die Stelle...' Guttmann observes 'Merkwürdig ist die Konstatierung dass die Noachiden...' and adds in brackets: 'der Talmud kann hier bloss an den ihm nahestehenden Kreis seiner griechisch-römischen Zeitgenossen gedacht haben.' Both scholars apparently refrained from specifically naming those alluded to for apologetic reasons. It is almost certain that 'Ulla gave a dubious compliment to the Christian sectaries of his day, who accepted thirty precepts, but, unlike the pagans, kept three. M. Joel already cited the story told by Dio Cassius, 63, 13, concerning the Emperor Nero, as a parallel to the writing of a *ketubba* for males, and for 'the weighing of flesh of the dead in the meat-market' he quoted the narrative in *T.B. Menaḥot* 29b about the fate of R. Akiba. Undoubtedly the pagans did not respect the Torah, but this was not the case with the Christian sectaries.
32. *Lam. Rabba* iii, 1, ed, Buber, p. 122.

33. *Ibid.* 'It is I, and I have become accustomed to all that Thou dost bring upon me.' In the text I have cited the passage according to the recension of the *Yalquṭ Shim'oni*, Rome ed., § i, 28; in later editions there is added [יסורים ('suffering')] after דיליפנא. Buber's remarks in n. 7 are incorrect.
34. The conclusion follows the text of the *Yalquṭ*, *loc. cit.*
35. *Mekhilta de-R. Ishmael*, Mishpaṭim, xiii, p. 295; *Tosefta Bava Qamma* vii, 9, p. 358.
36. *Sifre Num.* § 67, p. 62.
37. *Mekhilta de-R. Ishmael*, Massekhta de-Pisḥa, v, p. 16. It seems that the Tannaim who gave this exposition assessed the words of the prophet more objectively than Yeḥezkiel Kaufmann in his observations on this chapter, *Toledot-ha-'Emuna ha-Yiśre'elit*, III, Bk. II, pp. 512 ff.
38. *Lev. Rabba* vii, 1, p. 147; see the vv.ll. *ibid.*, and n. 4.
39. *T.B. Berakhot* 32b; I have cited the passage according to the version of the Munich MS. See *Diqduqe Soferim, ad loc.*, pp. 172–173. Cf. *T.B. Sanhedrin* 105a.
40. *T.P. Ta'anit* ii, 1, p. 65a; *T.P. Horayot* iii, 2, p. 47c; *T.B. Yoma* 21b. See my article 'Mātay Pāsĕqā ha-Nĕvû'ā', *Tarbiz*, VI, p. 3, and *ibid.* n. 16.
41. *Pesiqta Rabbati* xxxv, 160a; *T.B. Yoma* 9b.
42. *Cant. Rabba* viii, 9, 3: רבנן פתרי קרא בעולי גולה... אם חומה היא – אלו ישראל העלו חומה מבבל לא חרב בית המקדש בההיא שעתא פעם שנית ('The Rabbis explained the verse to refer to the exiles who came up [to Eretz-Israel]... "If she be a wall": If Israel had come up like a wall from Babylon, the Temple would not have been destroyed again at that time') and there it is stated that also R. 'Ila (this is the reading in the Pesaro edition; in other editions we find 'R. Shila', but the occurrence of R. Ze'ira in this context shows that the correct reading is R. 'Ila; see Z. Frankel, Mavo' ha-Yerushalmi 75b) gave a similar exposition at the college.
43. *Cant. Rabba, loc. cit.*; *T.B. Yoma* 9b.
44. *Cant. Rabba* v, 5; see my article 'Ḳôresh wĕ-hakhrāzātô bĕ-'ênê Ḥăzal [Cyrus and his Proclamation in the view of the Sages]' *Molad*, 1961, p. 372.
45. *Deut. Rabba* vii, 8; in *Mekhilta de-R. Ishmael*, Massekhta de-Ba-ḥodesh, iii, p. 212, the dictum is anonymous, and R. Jose disputes this view, stating 'Even if there had been there [at Sinai] but two thousand and two myriads they would have been worthy of receiving (the Torah), as it is said "And when it rested, he said: Return, O Lord, unto the myriads, the thousands of Israel" ' (Num. x 36).
46. *Deut. Rabba, loc. cit.*
47. *Mekhilta de-R. Ishmael*, Massekhta de-Ba-ḥodesh, v, p. 219; see *ibid.*, n. 13, that the inference is drawn from the fact that the singular suffix is used in the verse 'I am the Lord *thy* God' [אלקיך]; cf. *ibid.*, i, p. 206. On the subject of 'overt and secret sins' see also *ibid.* Mishpaṭim, xvii, p. 311. In *T.P. Soṭa* vii, 5, p. 22a, we read: 'R. Simeon b. Laqish said: 'At the Jordan they accepted the secret (sins)... R. Levi said: At Jabneh they were released from this

responsibility; a Heavenly Voice went forth and said: Secret sins are not your concern.'

48. *Sifra*, Be-ḥuqqotay, vii, 5; see *T.B. Sanhedrin* 27b and *Sifre Num.* 156, p. 208. In the *Sifra* the reading is ערבין זה בזה (Dr. Jonah Frankel drew my attention to this), and so, too, in *T.B. Sanhedrin* 27b; nor does *Diqduqe Soferim, ibid.*, p. 72, record a different reading (in the Munich MS.: עורבין זה בזה). But in *ʿEn Yaʿqov, editio princeps*, the text has שכולם ערבים זה לזה, and this is also Rashi's recension, Lev. xxvi 37 (ed. A. Berliner, p. 24). See *Midrash Tehillim* viii 4, ed. Buber, p. 76: בשעת מתן תורה שהיו ערבין זה לזה...; cf. *Cant. Rabba* i, 3; *Tanḥuma*, Wa-yiggash, 2; *Midrash Mishle* vi, 2.

49. *Lev. Rabba* iv, 6, pp. 91–92 את מספיק עוונותיך means 'You attach your iniquities to us'; see *ibid.*, n. 3, in the name of H. Yalon, *Kunteresim* I, 1, p. 2.

50. See *Mekhilta de-R. Ishmael*, Tiśśa, i, p. 342; *Sifre Num.* § 14, p. 19, and the other parallels noted *ibid.*, n. 15; cf. Ch. Albeck, *Untersuchungen über die hal. Midraschim*, p. 4.

51. *Mekhilta de-R. Ishmael*, Massekhta de-Ba-ḥodesh, ii, p. 209.

52. *Mekhilta de-R. Simeon b. Yoḥai*, p. 139. On the proof from Achan see the commentary of R. Joseph Kara to Joshua, ed. S. Eppenstein, *JJLG*, V, 1907, p. 57: 'That is to say, although he was one man, he did not perish alone, but Scripture states in the narrative "And the men of Ai smote of them about thirty and six men" (Joshua vii 5), how much more so you, who are many'; cf. also the commentary of R. David Kimchi. The analogy of 'a scattered sheep' also occurs in *Mekhilta de-R. Ishmael, loc. cit.*, and in *Lev. Rabba, loc. cit.*, in the form 'Hezekiah taught'. See also Israel Lévi, *Ein Wort über die Mechilta des R. Simon*, Breslau 1889, p. 25; and cf. *Cant. Rabba* vi, 11: ' "I went down into the garden of nuts..." Just as a nut, if you take one of them, they all come rolling down one after the other, even so are Israel: if one is harmed, all of them suffer....' See also *Pesiqta Rabbati* 42a.

53. *T.P. Yoma* i, 1, p. 38c; *T.B. ibid.*, 9a–b; see also *Tosefta Menaḥot* xiii, 22, p. 534.

54. *Lam. Rabba* i, 20, p. 56; see below, n. 56.

55. *T.B. Sanhedrin* 44a. Current texts lack the words 'Rav said', but they are to be found in MSS.; see *Diqduqe Soferim*, p. 128 and Rashi, *ad loc.*, s.v. *Ḥāṭā'*. On the evolution of the connotation of the dictum see J. Katz "Af ʿal pî she-ḥāṭā' Yisrā'ēl hû [Even though he has sinned he is still called Israel]', *Tarbiz*, XXVII, 1958, pp. 203 ff.

56. *T.B. Menaḥot* 53b; see *Diqduqe Soferim, ad loc.*, p. 139. R. Isaac used the homily of R. Joshua b. Levi and made it the conclusion of the dialogue between the Holy One, blessed be He, and the Patriarch Abraham, when the Temple was destroyed. In *Lam. Rabba* i, 20, p. 56, the story is told in the name of R. ʿUqba, and lacks the ending of R. Isaac's homily: '... And he said to Him, perchance — Heaven forfend! — their position is irremediable? Thereupon a Heavenly Voice went forth and declared: "Leafy olive-tree..." — just as the olive-tree produces its fruit at the end, so shall Israel's (true) efflorescence come at the end.'

541 —

57. *T.B. Beṣa* 25b; see Rashi, *ad loc.*, s.v. *Shĕ-hēn ʿazzîm*; *Bet ha-Beḥira* on *Beṣa*, ed. I. S. Lange–K. Schlesinger, Jerusalem 1956, p. 154; and cf. H. P. Chajes, *Haggadot*: 'I have heard the explanation that they are 'strong' (*ʿazzim*) and worthy of receiving the Torah, because despite all the religious persecutions to which they have been subjected, they have not forsaken their heritage and destiny from Sinai.'
58. *T.B. Beṣa, loc. cit.*; see *Diqduqe Soferim, ad loc.*, p. 99. Cf. *Exod. Rabba* xlii, 9, where it is stated that Israel is the most impudent of the nations, and R. Isaac bar Redifa said in the name of R. Ammi: 'You may suppose that this is disparaging; but in fact it is laudatory — either a Jew or crucified!' In truth the experience of 'Israel in the Diaspora' was ever hard; see *Tosefta ʿAvoda Zara* iv, 6; *T.B.*, *ibid.* 8a; and my article 'Hilkhot ʿAvoda Zara we-ha-Meṣi'ut ha-'Arkhi'ologit we-ha-Hisṭorit', *Eretz-Israel*, V, 1958, p. 200, n. 101 [Translated into English *IEJ*, 1959–60]. See *T.B. Soṭa* 11b: 'This people is like an animal'; see *Gen. Rabba* xcix, 4, p. 1276, and *Cant. Rabba* iv, 7.
59. *Mekhilta de-R. Ishmael*, Mishpaṭim, p. 334, and the parallels noted *ibid.*; see also above, p. 696, n. 7.
60. See B. J. Bamberger, *Proselytism in the Talmudic Period*, Cincinnati 1939; cf. W. G. Braude, *Jewish Proselyting in the First Five Centuries*, 1940 (see the critique of G. Alon, *Kirjath Sepher*, III, 1946, pp. 37–42; *Meḥqarim be-Toledot Yisra'el*, II, p. 278), S. Lieberman, *Greek in Jewish Palestine*, pp. 68–90, and my article *Gēr*, *Encyclopaedia Hebraica*, XI, pp. 172–182. But it should be noted that the view advanced by L. H. Feldman, 'Jewish Sympathizers in classical literature and inscriptions', *Transactions Am. Phil. Assoc.*, 81 (1950), pp. 200–208, based on a comprehensive analysis of epigraphic material, to the effect that the adjective θεοσεβής does not denote pagans inclined towards Judaism, or mere sympathizers, but Jews who feared the Lord as well as proselytes who observed the precepts with similar devotion, has been corroborated by the new inscriptions found at Sardes; see L. Robert, *Nouvelles Inscriptions de Sardes*, I, Paris 1964, pp. 37–45; on 'a fearer of Heaven' who was secretly circumcised in Rome, see *Deut. Rabba* ii, 24.
61. *T.B. Pesaḥim* 87b; see *Gen. Rabba* xxxix, 14, p. 378, the dictum of R. Eleazar in the name of R. Jose b. Zimra, and *ibid.*, n. 10.
62. *T.B. Pesaḥim, loc. cit.* Current editions have R. Ḥanina, but see in *Diqduqe Soferim, ad loc.*, p. 268, n. *Rêsh*, the version that I have cited in the text according to MS.] (my friend S. Rosenthal informs me that this is also the reading in the two Yemenite MSS. of *Pesaḥim*). Cf. S. Lieberman, *Greek in Jewish Palestine*, p. 141, n. 195, who refers to *Seder Eliahu Rabba*, xi, ed. Me'ir Ish Shalom (Friedmann), p. 54. The Massoretic reading in I Kings, *loc. cit.*, is עד הכרית כל... (instead of עד אשר הכרית given in the text); see Targum Jonathan *ad loc.*
63. The same motif occurs in the story of Qeti'a bar Shalom and the emperor who hated the Jews — *T.B. ʿAvoda Zara* 10b.

64. גפא של רומי. For the many interpretations see S. Krauss, *Lehnwörter*, p. 182. S. Lieberman, *op. cit.*, p. 140, accepted the suggestion of Sachs to explain גפא as ἀγάπη, only he regards this word as an epithet of the goddess Isis. He bases himself on a papyrus according to which Isis was called in Dora-Tantura φιλία and in Italy ἀγάπη.
65. See Josephus, *Ant.* xiv, § 115–117, in the name of Strabo; Philo, *Flaccum*, § 43; § 45–48. Cf. M. Stern, 'Ahădā la-Yĕhûdîm be-Ḥûgê Senātôrîm Romiy-yîm bi-Tĕqûfat ha-Qĕsarût ha-Qĕdûmā [Sympathy for the Jews in the Circles of the Roman Senators in the Period of the Ancient Empire]', *Zion*, XXXIX, 1964, pp. 155–167.
66. See below, n. 95.
67. See A. Büchler, 'The Minim of Sepphoris and Tiberias in the Second and Third Century', *Studies in Jewish History*, London 1956, pp. 245 ff (it appeared in German in the Herman Cohen Jubilee Volume, *Judaica*, 1912, pp. 271–295); see *ibid.*, p. 252. In *Seder Eliahu Rabba, loc. cit.*, it is stated that the one who put the question to R. Judah the Patriarch was a *hegmon* [ἡγεμών, 'general']; cf. S. Lieberman, *op. cit.*, n. 196.
68. See the story about Aquila the proselyte, *Exod. Rabba* xxx, 12 and *Tanḥuma* Mishpaṭim, v; see *T.B. 'Avoda Zara* 11a (according to the version of the Spanish MS., ed. S. Abramson): "Anqelos bar Qaloniqos was converted (to Judaism); thereupon the Emperor sent a troop of Roman (soldiers) after him. He won their hearts with Scriptural verses (and) converted them...." Of Aquila himself it is said 'Were it not that R. Joshua exercised patience, even Aquila would have reverted to paganism' — *Gen. Rabba* lxx, 5, p. 803, according to the version of the MSS. in the vv.ll., *ibid.* to line 2, and n. 5 *ad loc.* Epiphanius, *De Mensuris et Ponderibus*, § 15 (see I. E. Dean, *Epiphanius' Treatise on Weights and Measures*, 1935, p. 31) further relates that at first Aquila was converted to Christianity, and that only after he had been expelled from the Church on account of his interest in astrology, did he convert to Judaism and become circumcised. Eusebius tells (*Hist. Eccl.*, VI, 12) of one called Domnus, who left the church and returned to the fold of Judaism during the period of religious persecution.
69. Like Tatian, *Oratio*. See Ad. v. Harnack, *Mission und Ausbreitung des Christentums*[3], 1915, pp. 269 ff. See J. Bergmann, *Jüdische Apologetik*, 1908, p. 47.
70. See I. Heinemann, 'Ha-Yahădût be-'ênê ha-'Olām ha-'Attîq [Judaism in the Eyes of Antiquity]', *Zion*, IV, 1939, pp. 269 ff. Cf. Joḥanan Levi, *'Olamot Nifgashim*, pp. 7 ff. In the countries of the East the rebellions of the Jews also served to intensify anti-Jewish feeling — certainly among the Roman soldiers, because of the revolt of the Jews in the reign of Trojan in Cyrene and Egypt. Cf. V. Tcherikover, *Ha-Yehudim be-Miṣrayim ba-Tequfa ha-Helenistit ha-Romit le-'Or ha-Papirologya*,[2] 1963, pp. 160–179. Cf. Alexander Fuks, 'The Jewish Revolt in Egypt in the light of the Papyri', *Aegyptus*, xxxiii, 1953, pp. 132 ff, and *ibid.*, p. 157 on the origin of the designation Ἀνόσιοι Ἰουδαῖοι.

544-545

CHAPTER XVI

71. The dictum is reported in the name of R. Jeremiah in *Sifra*, 'Aḥărê Môt, xiii, 13, = *Mekhilta*, ʿArāyôt. It does not occur in the *editio princeps*, but was added by the author of *Qorban Aharon* from the *Yalquṭ* (see J. N. Epstein, *Mevo'ot le-Sifrut ha-Tanna'im*, Jerusalem 1957), where the text reads: אפילו גוי עושה את התורה ['Even a Gentile who keeps the Torah', instead of ועוסק 'who studies']. But in the annotations on the *Sifra* in 'Tummat Yesharim', copied from another MS., the reading is אפילו ע״א ועוסק בתורה ['Even an idolator who studies the Torah']. This was also the version of R. Hillel, as can be seen from his commentary on the *Sifra*; it is likewise the reading in all the passages in which the Baraita is cited in the Babylonian Talmud, including those in which the observance of commandments by Gentiles is spoken of. It is not surprising, therefore, that the Sages were able to adduce objections from the Baraita, which praises a Gentile who studies the Torah against dicta that condemn Gentiles who observe precepts. The version ועושה את התורה ['who keeps the Torah'] in the above passage of the *Sifra* appears to be an 'emendation' that seeks to adapt the homily to the language of the verse 'which if a man do...' [see also S. Safrai 'Wĕ-Zēdîm bĕ-Yad ʿOsĕqê Tôrātĕkhā (And the presumptuous in the hand of those who occupy themselves with Thy Law)', *Tarbiz*, xxxviii, 1969, p. 190, but his remarks are inexact]. R. Jeremiah makes his statement in the name of 'Rabbenu ha-qadosh' ['Our holy teacher'] in *T.B. Megilla* 18a and *T.B. Menaḥot* 32b. On the relationship between Rabbi and Antoninus see S. Krauss, *Antoninus und Rabbi*, 1910; L. Wallach, 'The Colloquy of Marcus Aurelius and the Patriarch Judah I', *JQR*, N.S., XXXI, 1940/1, p. 259 ff.
72. See *T.B. Bava Qamma* 38a, and *Diqduqe Soferim*, *ad loc.*, p. 80, n. ג; *T.B. Sanhedrin* 59a and *T.B. ʿAvoda Zara* 3a. This is also the reading in the Spanish MS., ed. S. Abramson.
73. *T.B. Rosh Hashana* 19a. Current editions have ולא בני אם אחת אנחנו ['And are we not the children of one mother?'], but these words are missing in the MSS.; see *Diqduqe Soferim*, *ad loc.*, p. 42. See *T.B. Taʿanit 17b*, ed. H. Malter, p. 67, and *Megillat Taʿanit*, ed. Lichtenstein, *HUCA*, VIII–IX, p. 350.
74. See S. Lieberman, *Greek in Jewish Palestine*, pp. 85–86, who bases himself on the statement of Celsus, V, 25. From another point of view, J. Vogt, *Kaiser Julian und das Judentum*, 1939, p. 9, speaks of the pagan-Jewish coalition, which he regards as 'an alliance of the blind and the lame'. Cf. also M. Simon, *Verus Israel*, Paris 1948, p. 61, who likewise takes Celsus as his basis. The account of the disputation between R. Judah Nesi'a and a Min (Lieberman cited it only in connection with the expression גפה של רומי in another chapter of his book; see above, n. 64) is not in accord with this view. See also Lieberman's own statement about the attitude of the Jews to the Christian martyrs, *The Martyrs of Caesarea*, pp. 411 ff.
75. See Yitzhak Baer, ''ʿAm Yisra'el, ha-Kenesiyya ha-Noṣrit we-ha-Qesarut ha-Romit mi-Yeme Septimius Severuṣ we-ʿad Re'shit Yeme Constantinus [The Jewish People, the Church, and the Roman Empire, from the time of Sep-

545 —

timius Severus to the beginning of Constantinus' reign]', *Zion*, 1956, pp. 1–49; cf. *ibid.*, p. 203. As usual Baer explains many facts against their historic background, but it is doubtful if his own statements warrant the conclusions he reaches on p. 23: 'In this struggle Judaism found itself actually attacked together with Christianity; for the Greek (Celsus) there is no great difference between Jews and Christians.' Or *ibid.*, p. 31: 'The Jews, Christians, and polytheists were closer to one another than they admitted. All three of them were ascetics who longed for their homeland in the world on high.'

76. Largely for tactical reasons. For in their anti-Christian writings the Jews were not a party to the polemic, but served as a background thereto. This was recently demonstrated by David Rokach in his doctorate thesis 'The Jews in the Pagan-Christian Polemic in the Roman Empire'.
77. Origen in his commentary to Canticles ii 5. See my aforementioned article in *Scripta* etc., XXII (1971), p. 249, and see *ibid.*, n. 48*, my quotation from Origen; cf. also *ibid.*, p. 263. See further Origen's commentary on Psalms xxxvi (xxxvii), Migne, *PG*, 1319, as cited by Y. Baer in his aforementioned article, p. 15.
78. This task was completed comprehensively and very thoroughly by Eusebius in his works, *Preparatio Evangelica* and *Demonstratio Evangelica*. The anti-Jewish legislation commenced even before the triumph of Christianity at the Synod of Elvira in Spain. See J. Juster, *Les Juifs dans l'empire Romain*, II, 1914, pp. 35 ff, and *ibid.*, p. 46, n. 3. Cf. J. E. Seaver, *Persecution of the Jews in the Roman Empire*, Lawrance, 1952, pp. 25 ff.
79. *T.B. Sanhedrin* 97a: 'R. Nehemiah said the generation in which the son of David [Messiah] will come... the whole Empire will be converted to heresy (*mînût*) with none to rebuke them... This supports R. Isaac (who said): The son of David will not come until the whole Empire is converted to heresy' (see *Cant. Rabba* ii, 13). This is the reading in the margin of the Munich MS., but in the scribe's handwriting; see *Diqduqe Soferim*, *ad loc.*, p. 286, n. h. The addition to *Mishna Soṭa* (which is found both in the Kaufmann MS. and in the Cambridge MS.) reads: והמלכות תהא מינות ואין תוכחת ['and the Empire shall fall into heresy and there shall be none to utter rebuke']; and the Munich MS. has והמלכות תהא מינות ['and the Empire shall fall into heresy']. If the dictum attributed to R. Nehemiah is authentic, it would seem that he is referring to 'heresy' in the sense of various sects, but when the term is used by R. Isaac — at the end of the third century — it appears that he is really alluding to Christians. Eusebius was also conscious of the victory that was soon to come in favour of Christianity; see Y. Baer, *op. cit.*, p. 42. There is no room for A. Büchler's doubts expressed in his aforementioned article, p. 251, n. 3.
80. See the dictum of R. Azariah, *Cant. Rab.* ii, 13; so, too, in the Pesaro ed. Cf. *Pesiqta de-Rav Kahana*, ed. Mandelbaum, p. 97, and vv.ll, *ibid.*; see also my article, cited above.
81. See above, n. 70, and above, p. 647.

82. See above, n. 60 and n. 73. On the pious men among the nations and good Gentiles and their attributes see M. Guttmann, *Das Judentum u. seine Umwelt*, p. 139.

83. *Contra Celsum*, I, 55; *ibid.* § 54 the whole chapter of Isaiah is cited. We do not know who was the Jewish Sage. W. Bacher, 'The Church Father Origen and Rabbi Hoshaya', *JQR*, III, 1891, pp. 357–360, tried to show that there was contact between the two, but there is no proof for his contention; see above, p. 777, n. 74. He also failed to note the content of the arguments that Origen quotes in their name. Bacher repeated this conjecture in *Agada der Palastinischen Amoräer*, I, p. 92, and in his essay 'Die Gelehrten von Caesarea', *MGWJ*, 1910, XLV, pp. 298–310, without adding any evidence. Although Rav Hoshaia spoke in favour of proselytization and approved it — see *Gen. Rabba* LXXXIV, 4, p. 1006 — yet this does not prove that he was the interlocutor of Origen in the episode referred to above. See G. Bardy, 'Les Traditions juive dans l'oeuvre d'Origine', *Revue Biblique*, 1925, p. 217; *idem*, *Revue Bénédictine*, 1934, pp. 145–164.

84. See *loc. cit.*, § 46.

85. *Lev. Rabba* VI, 5, p. 142; see *ibid.*, n. 1, and also n. 4, and cf. the commentary of Z. W. Einhorn (Maharzaw) *ad loc.*

86. *T.B. Yevamot* 47a; the words בזמן הזה ['at this time'] are wanting in the Munich MS. In *Bet ha-Beḥira* of Me'iri, ed. H. Albeck, p. 196, the text reads: שישראל בזמן הזה דחופים ומטורפים בצרות ['For Israel at this time are harassed and tormented with troubles']. Our text above has: שישראל בזמן הזה דויים סחופים ומטורפים וייסורים באים עליהם.

87. *Massekhot Gerim* i, Septem Libri Talmudici Parvi Hierosolymitani, ed. R. Kirchheim, Frankfurt 1951, p. 38; it is evident that its source is not in the aforementioned Baraita in the Babylonian Talmud. Zunz, *Gottesdienstliche Vorträge*, p. 19, n. f, already noted the 'laws of proselytes' mentioned in *Ruth Rabba* ii, 12, and in *Eccl. Rabba* v, 8.

88. *Exod. Rabba* xxx, 12.

89. *Massekhet Gerim*, *loc. cit.* According to *T.B.*, *loc. cit.*, we also state, even before circumcision and ritual immersion, not only the punishment inflicted for the transgression of the precepts but also the reward vouchsafed for their fulfilment: 'He is told: Know that the world to come was made only for the righteous, and Israel at the present time are incapable of enduring either too much prosperity or too much tribulation.' Maimonides in 'The Laws of Forbidden Sexual Relations', xiv, 4–5, explained the passage thus: 'He is told: Know that the world to come is reserved only for the righteous, namely Israel, and though you see Israel in distress in this world, good is in store for them, for they cannot receive overmuch good in this world like the other nations, lest their heart become proud and they go astray and lose the reward of the world to come, as it is said "But Jeshurun waxed fat, and kicked"; and the Holy One, blessed be He, does not inflict too much punishment upon them in order that they should not perish. Thus all the

other nations come to an end, but they (Israel) endure and live long as a result of this, so as to cherish them.' Possibly the source of his conclusion is to be found in the above-cited passage of *Massekhet Gerim*.

90. *Tanḥuma*, Mishpaṭim, 5.

91. *Sifre Deut.* § 354. But even concerning the proselytes of the past R. Nehemiah said that they had to be converted 'as at the present time' ('that they should not act with a view to rising to power' — Rashi), *T.B. Yevamot* 24b. On proselytes in the days of David and Solomon and in the Messianic Era see also *ibid.* 76a, 79a, and Maimonides, 'The Laws of Forbidden Relations', xiii, 14–16.

92. *Cant. Rabba* iv, 1. On the homiletical discourses in the synagogues see Zunz, *Gottesdienstliche Vorträge der Juden*, pp. 329–332; and on 'Esau used to go behind the colleges... and steal teachings' see my article 'Megammot Datiyyot we-Ḥevratiyyot be-Torat ha-Ṣedaqa shel Ḥazal', p. 16, n. 109. The theft of ideas by Christian teachers was intended to serve their propaganda, but there were Christians who were influenced by these visits and they were attacked by the author of *Const. Ap.*, II, 61, 1; VIII, 47, 65, and, with special vehemence, by Chrysostom, *Adv. Judaeos*, MPG., vol. 48, 839, 848, 858.

93. For apologetic reasons, it seems, M. Guttmann deals but little with them in his book *Das Judentum und seine Umwelt*, p. 86. Following I. Levy, 'Le Prosélytisme juif', *REJ*, vol. L, 1905, pp. 4 ff, he mentions only the dictum of R. Ḥelbo; see the observations of G. Alon, in his aforementioned article, p. 280, on the work of W. G. Braude (see above, n. 60).

94. *T.B. Shabbat* 33b. R. Simeon b. Yoḥai's dictum was uttered in reaction to the statement of R. Judah: 'How fine are the works of this nation! They have established market-places, they have established bridges, they have installed baths.' The author of *Aggadat Shir ha-Shirim*, ed. Schechter, p. 25, did not contradict R. Judah's praise of these works of philanthropy, but found another fault with them: '... They build public baths and (private) baths, in which poor and rich can bathe; thus they bestow many benefits. What sin do they commit thereby? When they complete the structure, they say: Let us make a place for an idol. Hence their merit is vitiated.'

95. *T.B. Shabbat*, *loc. cit.*, concerning 'Judah, the son of proselytes', who went and reported the matter to the government, and *Mekhilta de-R. Ishmael*, Wa-yehi, i, p. 89 '... Thus we learn that those who feared the word of the Lord proved a danger to Israel. Hence R. Simeon b. Yoḥai used to say "The best of the heathens slay...!"'

96. *Mekhilta de-R. Ishmael*, Mishpaṭim xviii, p. 311. The homily continues in the same style as the dicta commencing 'Precious [literally, 'Beloved'] is suffering', *ibid.* x, p. 240, but this does not prove that it also belongs to R. Simeon b. Yoḥai, as S. Klein stated in the periodical *Zion*, Book I, 1926, p. 5, n. 3.

97. *Mekhilta*, *loc. cit.*, p. 312, and the same phraseology is used in *Sifre Num.* § 80, p. 76: '"And thou shalt be to us instead of eyes" — so as not to close

the door before proselytes who will come in future, that it should not be said (see vv.ll.): If Jethro, Moses' father-in-law, did not accept (the Torah), *a fortiori* other people will not.' The wording in *Sifre Zuṭa*, p. 265, makes the contemporary significance of the homily still clearer: 'That you should not focus all eyes upon us, so that the whole world would look and say: It seems that they do not wish to accept proselytes... But come and go with us and thus you will encourage proselytes to come with us and magnify the glory of the Omnipresent....'

98. *Tosefta Berakhot* vi, 2, ed. Lieberman, p. 33; see vv.ll. *ibid.* and *T.P. ibid.*, ix, 2, in the name of R. Ishmael b. Gamaliel, and *T.B. ibid.* 57a, in the name of R. Simeon b. Eleazar. Cf. *Tanḥuma*, Noah, xix, 'And the subjugation of Israel by the nations will come to an end and they (the Gentiles) will serve them (Israel) with joy....' In the continuation the words 'But the nations of the world' are a later addition that is wanting in the Cambridge MS. and in the Vatican MS.; see my article 'Śeride Tanḥuma-Yelammedenu', *Qoveṣ ʿal Yad*, Bk. VI, p. 30. Likewise the words 'and will destroy the nations before you', in ed. Buber, p. 56, are merely an interpolation and are moreover missing in the recension of the 'Yelammedenu' in *Yalquṭ Makhiri* to Zephaniah, ed. Greenup, London 1913, p. 24. Cf. *T.B. ʿAvoda Zara* 3b: 'It is taught: R. Jose said, In the time to come the nations of the world will offer themselves for conversion': see above, p. 553.

98a. R. Joḥanan was opposed to adopting a harsh attitude to apostates. When R. Abbahu recited before him: '... Minim, informers, and apostates are to be cast down and not brought up', he (R. Joḥanan) said to him: I interpret the words "with every lost thing of thy brother's" to include an apostate, yet you say: he is to be cast down. Omit apostate!' (*T.B. ʿAvoda Zara* 26b; see *Diqduqe Soferim, ad loc.*; the distinction drawn between 'an apostate who seeks to satisfy his appetite' and 'an apostate who seeks to provoke' is an anonymous Talmudic teaching based on the dispute between R. Aḥa and Ravina).

99. *T.P. Sanhedrin* x, 6, p. 29b. Although R. Joḥanan bases his teaching there on the verse 'The stranger did not lodge in the street; my doors I opened to the roadside' (Job xxxi 32), he continues 'Not as Elisha did, who thrust Gehazi aside with both hands.' Gehazi represents the Min and the seceder. It is also difficult to explain how repelling with the left hand is to be inferred from the verse in Job. Indeed, this verse is expounded as the opening of the gates without restriction; see above, p. 552. R. Joḥanan's view regarding the acceptance of proselytes is clearly to be inferred from his reply to the question 'Why was Abraham punished and his children enslaved by the Egyptians...? Because he prevented people from entering beneath the wings of the Shekhina', *T.B. Nedarim* 32a.

1. M. Guttmann, *op. cit.*, n. 83, writes on p. 86: 'Chelbo blieb, wie I. Levi nachwies, vereinzelt mit seiner Ansicht.' Although the dictum is mentioned three times in *T.B.* (*Yevamot* 47b; *ibid.* 109b; *Qiddushin* 70b; see also *T.B.*

Nidda 13b), as he himself noted, *op. cit.*, p. 55, he finds it necessary to emphasize that 'it is not mentioned in *T.P.*, notwithstanding that R. Ḥelbo lived and worked there'! Also M. Simon, *Verus Israel*, pp. 318–319, gives this dictum central and primary importance.

2. *T.B. Pesaḥim* 118a: 'The sustenance of man is more difficult....'
3. *Cant. Rabba* ii, 7; see below, p. 1001, n. 5.
4. *T.B. Yevamot* 109b; see Tosafot, *ad loc.*, s.v. *Rāʿā*, for they were conscious of the exceptional character of R. Isaac's dictum, and sought to harmonize it with the Halakha regarding the acceptance of proselytes. The words in the Gemara 'as R. Ḥelbo (said)' are merely an anachronistic comparison; see below, n. 6.
5. *T.B. ʿAvoda Zara* 3b; see *ibid.* the statement of R. Isaac.
6. *Cant. Rabba* i, 5–6; see my abovementioned article in *Scripta*, etc., XXII (1971).
7. See *Lev. Rabba* v, 7, p. 120. ' "And the elders of the congregation shall lay their hands" (Lev. iv 15): R. Isaac said: The nations of the world have none that can lay on hands....' It is possible that this statement seeks not only to deny the Gentiles the protection of the right of elders, but also the claim of the Christians that the authority to ordain was transferred to the Church. Cf. also *Esther Rabba* i, 2, 'The nations of the world have no scholars' session'; see my article 'Derashot Ḥazal ʿal 'Ummot ha-ʿOlam u-Parashat Bilʿam', *Tarbiz* XXII, 1956, p. 273, n. 3.
8. See W. Bacher, *Agada der palästinischen Amoräer*, III, p. 348.
9. *Exod. Rabba* xix, 4; see also *ibid.* xxvii, 2.
10. *Exod. Rabba* ii, 5. 552
11. *Ibid.* iii, 6; see also *Sifre Num.* § 115, p. 128, and *Sifre Zuṭa*, p. 290.
12. *T.B. Taʿanit* 3b; see ed. H. Malter, p. 7, and *ibid.*, n. 3, and cf. *T.B. ʿAvoda Zara* 10b; but it is wanting in the Spanish MS., ed. S. Abramson; see *ibid.*, p. 149, n. 3.
13. *T.B. Menaḥot* 110a; see J. Obermeyer, *Die Landschaft Babyloniens*, 1929, pp. 134–135.
14. *Pesiqta de-Rav Kahana*, ed. Mandelbaum, p. 86, transmitted by R. Iudan in the name of R. Ḥama bar Ḥanina. However, there were Haggadists who were not content until they had made the great foes of Israel, like Sisera, Sennacherib, Nebuzaradan, Haman, and the Emperor Nero, the ancestors of proselytes and of Sages like Shemáiah and Avṭalion, R. Akiba, and R. Me'ir. See *T.B. Gittin* 56a; 57b; *T.B. Sanhedrin* 96b and *Diqduqe Soferim*, *ad loc.*, p. 283; cf. W. Bacher, *Die Agada der Tannaïten*, II, p. 5, n. 6. 553
15. *Eccles. Rabba* v, 11. In *T.P. Berakhot* ii, 8, p. 5b, anonymously, and in *Cant. Rabba* in the name of R. Samuel bar Naḥman; in both these passages the reference to Antoninus is missing. On the proselytization of Antoninus see S. Lieberman, *Greek in Jewish Palestine*, p. 77.
16. *T.B. Shabbat* 146a. See *T.B. Shevuʿot* 39a, where it is stated that Moses also adjured 'the proselytes who would in future be converted'.

17. *T.B. Berakhot* 17b. From the expression of the Gemara in *T.B. Gittin* 85a, 'conversion is uncommon', no inference is to be drawn, for the passage compares it to death, and undoubtedly death is far commoner. It appears that proselytization varied in the different parts of Babylonia. Of Rabbah bar Abbuha, who lived in Maḥoza (*T.B. Shabbat* 59b; *T.B. Yevamot* 115b), it is related that he said to 'Those who came before him... Go, sell all that you have and come and be converted'; and long afterwards Rava said of Maḥoza that it was 'a place where proselytes were common', *T.B Qiddushin* 73a.
18. *M. Yoma* vii, 1; *Tosefta, ibid.*, iii, 17; *T.P., ibid.*, vii, 1, p. 44b.
19. *Tosefta Berakhot* iii, 7; see S. Lieberman, *Tosefta ki-Fshuṭah*, p. 35.
20. On the various versions see *Tosefta ki-Fshuṭah*, Mo'ed, Pt. IV, pp. 800–801; cf. J. Heinemann, *Ha-Tefilla bi-Tequfat ha-Tanna'im we-ha-Amora'im*, pp. 105–106.
21. *T.B. Berakhot* iib.
22. See S. Assaf, 'Mi-Seder ha-Tefilla be-'Ereṣ Yisra'el', *Sefer Dinaburg*, p. 123. Cf. *M. 'Avot* vi, 1, 'Blessed be He that chose them and their Mishna', and see H. Albeck, *Hashlamot le-Seder Neziqin*, p. 501, who refers to *T.P. Terumot* viii, 5, p. 45d: 'Blessed be He that chose the Sages' (in the commentary of R. Solomon Sirillo: 'them and their Mishna'), and cf. *Seder Eliahu Rabba*, pp. 96, 107. See also *T.B. Sanhedrin* 104b, where it is narrated that a non-Jewish captor, who was enthusiastic about the wisdom of a Jewish captive, pronounces the blessing: 'Blessed be He that chose the seed of Abraham and gave them of His wisdom....'
23. *T.B. Berakhot, loc. cit.*; see *Diqduqe Soferim*, p. 49. Ze'ev Yawitz, *Meqor ha-Berakhot*, 1910, p. 54, wrote as he did because he had not seen the version of the MSS. and the Early Authorities. The statement in the Baraita 'Not *'ahăvā rabbā* ['With abounding love'] but *'ahăvat 'ōlām* ['With everlasting love'] is to be said' implies that the preceding words 'The Rabbis said' refer to the Sages of Eretz-Israel in contradistinction to the Sages of Babylonia, Samuel, and R. Eleazar, who held to the Babylonian custom; and this is actually confirmed also by the Genizah fragments containing the liturgical recension of Eretz-Israel; see Jacob Mann, 'Genizah Fragments' etc., *HUCA*, II, 1925, p. 291, and cf. *Otzar ha-Gaonim* to *Berakhot*, the section of responsa, p. 29.
24. *M. Ta'anit* iv, 1.
25. *T.B. Yoma* 87b. Possibly there is a connection between 'Ulla bar Rav and 'Bar 'Ulla Ḥazzana ['superintendent'] of the Synagogue of the Babylonians', who is mentioned in *T.P. Yoma* vii, 1, p. 44a (= *T.P. Megilla* iv, 5, p. 74a), who was the contemporary of R. Josah (יוסה). If Bar 'Ulla Ḥazzana is identical with Bar 'Ulla in *T.P. Shabbat* iv, 2, p. 7a, and *T.P. Beṣa* i, 7, p. 60c, then the reference is to R. Jasa (יסא) II, the colleague of R. Jonah. A parallel to the theme of the prayer occurs in *The Book of Baruch* iii, 26–27: 'There were the giants born that were famous of old, great of stature, and expert in war.

These did not God choose, neither gave He the way of blessing unto them.' See E. Peterson, *Frühkirche, Judentum und Gnosis*, pp. 43 ff; reference is also made there to Corinthians I and to *Const. Apost.*, XXX, ed.[3] Funk, p. 224, but the explicit link with the concept of election is wanting there.

26. *T.B. Menaḥot* 53a. According to Rashi the homilist was R. Perida, who wished to placate 'R. Ezra the grandson of Avṭolos, who was the tenth generation from R. Eleazar b. Azariah, who was (in turn) the tenth generation from Ezra.' According to the commentary attributed to R. Gershon, the homilist was R. Ezra, but the difficulty is that R. Perida is mentioned in the generation of R. Judah the Patriarch. Even if we were to suppose that he was the R. Perida that asked R. Ammi a question (see A. Hyman, *Toledot Tanna'im wa-Amora'im*, p. 1033), it is still difficult to make him a contemporary of R. Ezra, who was the tenth generation from R. Eleazar b. Azariah. R. Ammi was the contemporary of R. Judah Nesi'a and one of his officers, and the latter was the seventh generation from Rabban Gamaliel II, the distinguished colleague of R. Eleazar b. Azariah.
27. See *Midrash Tehillim* xvi, 2, p. 120, where it is inferred from this verse 'that the Holy One, blessed be He, does not call the righteous "saints" until they are laid in the grave, and even the fathers of the world were not called "saints" until they were laid in the grave.'
28. The answer to this argument R. Joshua put into the mouth of the Holy Spirit that cries aloud saying ' "In the place of righteousness that wickedness was there" — in the place where I had proclaimed them righteous and said of them "Ye are godlike beings, and all of you sons of the Most High" (Psalms lxxxii 6) there was wickedness, there they went and said to the calf "This is thy god, O Israel" (Exod. xxxii 4)' — *Lev. Rabba* iv, 1, p. 77; *Eccles. Rabba* iii, 15; see above, p. 149.
29. *Sifre Num* § i, p. 4. R. Jose the Galilean and R. Simeon b. Yoḥai ennumerate the changes to which they were subject 'from the time they put forth their hands to transgression'; see *Lev. Rabba* xi, 3, p. 222, and above, p. 426.
30. See above, p. 537.
31. *Sifre Deut.* § i.
32. *Lev. Rabba* xxvii, 8, p. 641.
33. *Lev. Rabba, ibid.*, 6, p. 633; see *Pesiqta de-Rav Kahana*, p. 745.
34. *Lev. Rabba, ibid.*, 8, p. 640; this contradicts the homily in the *Sifra*, Shemini, 4, p. 43a: 'Let the ox come and atone for the episode of the ox; let the calf and make atonement for the incident of the calf'; see below, n. 36.
35. *Cant. Rabba* i, 6; see above, p. 937, n. 6.
36. *Lev. Rabba* xxvii, 3, p. 626; *T.P. Rosh ha-Shana* iii, 2, p. 58d. It is actually R. Levi that explains the underlying reason of the Halakha in the Mishna to be 'that an accuser cannot become a defender'. See *T.B. ibid.*, 26a, in the name of Rav Ḥisda and 'Ulla.
37. In *T.P. Berakhot* i, 6, p. 3d, he transmits this homily in the name of Rabbi. Z. Frankel, *Mevo' ha-Yerushalmi*, 66a, suggests that the text be emended

in accordance with *T.B. Berakhot* 49a to read 'in the name of Rav'; see *Diqduqe Soferim*, p. 258, n. ש. But I fail to understand his purpose.

38. *T.P. Sheqalim* i, 5, p. 45d.
39. *T.B. Megilla* 16a; see *Sifre Deut.* § 47: 'If Israel do the will of the Omnipresent, they are like stars, and if not they are like dust.'
40. *T.P. Sheqalim, loc. cit.*, and the current text has 'in the name of Rav'. See B. Ratner, *Ahavat Ṣiyyon wi-Yerushalayim*, p. 2, who notes that we do not find this Sage transmitting in the name of Rabbi; hence he proposes 'in the name of רב״י i.e. רבי יוחנן, R. Joḥanan'. In the Bodleian MS. and likewise in the commentary of R. Meshullam, ed. Rabbi A. Schreiber, New York, 1954, p. 3, the reading is 'R. Simeon b. Pazzi' without 'in the name of Rabbi', and R. Simeon b. Pazzi is the same as R. Simon b. Pazzi, the father of R. Judah; possibly the text should read: 'R. Judah in the name of R. Simon b. Pazzi.'
41. *Mekhilta de-R. Ishmael*, Petiḥa, p. 6.
42. *Ibid.* pp. 3–4; see the parallels noted there. On Jonah's punishment for suppressing his prophecy see *Tosefta Sanhedrin* xi, 15; *T.P. ibid.* xi, 3, p. 30c; *T.B., ibid.* 89a.
43. Luke xi 32; Matthew xii 41.
44. See *Mekhilta, loc. cit.*; *Aggadat Shir ha-Shirim*, ed. S. Schechter, p. 26: 'So, too, when the people of Nineveh repented, the iniquities of Israel were visited upon them'; see *ibid.* p. 71.
45. See my article 'Teshuvat 'Anshe Nineveh we-ha-Wikkuaḥ ha-Yehudi-Noṣri', *Tarbiz*, XX, 1946, pp. 118–122.
46. The matter is perfectly clear with regard to *Vitae Prophetarum*; see E. Nestle's introduction to this edition, Tübingen 1893; and cf. Th. Scherman, *Propheten und Apostellegenden*, 1907, pp. 116–126. He distinguishes between different parts of the work and states that the basic section of the book is not to be dated later than the first century, although he finds in the life of Ezekiel and in the life of Daniel material that is suited to the time of Trajan. He also maintains that it was originally a Hebrew book of which a Jewish Greek translation was made, and from which the other versions evolved; *ibid.* p. 132. S. Klein, ''Al Sefer Vitae Prophetarum [On the book Vitae Prophetarum]' in *The Joseph Klausner Jubilee Volume*, pp. 189–209, treats of the traditions concerning the places of the prophets.
47. *T.B. Yevamot* 49b.
48. *T.P. Sanhedrin* x, 2, p. 28b; *T.B., ibid.* 103b; and *Baraita* ed. S. Schönblum, Lemberg 1877, 45a–b.
49. On the Jewish part of the work see R.H. Charles, *The Ascension of Isaiah*, 1919.
50. See *T.P. Ta'anit* iv, 8, p. 69a; *Pesiqta de-R. Kahana*, Lamentations, pp. 257–258, and the other parallels noted. Cf. S. B. Blank, 'The Death of Zechariah in Rabbinic Literature', *HUCA*, XII–XIII, 1937–8, pp. 327–346; H. A. Fischl, 'Martyr and Prophet', *JQR*, 37, 1946, pp. 265–280, pp. 303–386; H. I. Schoeps, *Aus Frühchristlicher Zeit*, 1950, pp. 126–143.

51. Matthew xxiii 37; Luke xiii 34.
52. *Dial. c. Tryphone*, 120, 5. Origen makes similar observations in his letter to Julius Africanus: Migne, *PG*, XIII, 861, in 'Homil. in Isaiam', *ibid.* col. 223. On the views of other Church fathers on the subject see E. Tisserant, *Ascension d'Isaie*, Paris 1904, pp. 62–73.
53. *Sifre Zuṭa*, Num. xv, 23, p. 284.
54. *Exod. Rabba* xxxi, 16; see *Midrash Aggada*, ed. Buber, Num., pp. 157–158, on the death of Jeremiah, where it is stated: 'Nor is this the only prophet that they killed, but they slew many others.'
55. *Lev. Rabba* x, 2, p. 197, and the expression 'I was walking about my schoolhouse' seems to be a translation of περιπατέω in the sense of instruction and teaching.
56. *Tanḥuma*, Tazria', 9. See *Pesiqta Rabbati* 129a, where Jeremiah argues: 'Sovereign of the universe, I cannot prophesy against them. Which prophet went forth to them without their seeking to slay him....' Cf. also *Exod. Rabba* ii, 20, regarding the overseers of the children of Israel in Egypt, who were appointed prophets because they offered their lives for Israel.
57. *Cant. Rabba* i, 6. I have cited both the homily of R. Simon and that of R. Joḥanan according to the Parma MS. 1240, which differs considerably from the recension of the printed texts and appears to be more original.
58. The MS. add וגו׳ ['etc.']; but it is clear that the primary proof derives from the continuation of the verse.
59. The Bible reads נדמיתי ['I am undone']; see *T.B. Yevamot* 49b. On the subject of Moses' sin in calling the Israelites 'Rebels', see *Pesiqta de-Rav Kahana*, pp. 246–247. '... R. Reuben said: This is the expression Greeks use when they shout at a fool — μῶρος — ...yet you call my children *môrîm* ['Rebels']. A clever person has no business to go with a fool... neither you, nor your brother, nor your sister will enter the Land of Israel.' Cf. Matthew v 22; another criticism of Moses' attitude to Israel is contained in the dictum of R. Levi 'Come and see that the Holy One, blessed be He, does not act like a mortal. The Holy One, blessed be He, blessed Israel with twenty-two blessings and cursed them with eight curses... whereas Moses, our teacher, blessed them with eight blessings... and cursed them with twenty-two' — *T.B. Bava Batra* 88b. An exposition defending Moses as one who pleaded on behalf of Israel is found in *Eliahu Rabba* iv, p. 17. Characteristically this homilist uses extravagant language: 'I call heaven and earth to witness that the Holy One, blessed be He, did not enjoin Moses thus... but Moses the Righteous thought to himself, arguing from minor to major... Then Moses the Righteous arose and prayed...' It appears that the expositor knew the homily that related Moses' declaration 'Thus saith the Lord' etc. (Exod. xxxii 27) to the verse 'He that sacrificeth unto the gods... shall be utterly destroyed' (*ibid.* xxii 19). See *Mekhilta de-R. Ishmael*, Pisḥa, xii, p. 40; Targum Pseudo-Jonathan and Rashi *ad loc.*; *Yalquṭ Shim'oni*, Judges, § 43; and *Ginze Schechter*, Pt. I, p. 75.

60. Here there is an omission due to homoeoteleuton.
61. In the printed editions (including the *editio princeps*) the text reads: והיה להם יום אחד שהיו על כולן באותו היום ועובדין אותם ['And they had one day when it was obligatory for all of them on that day, and they served them']; in *Lam. Rabba*, Petiḥta, ed. Buber, p. 9: והיה להם יום אחד והיו כולן עובדין באותו יום ['And they had one day and all of them worshipped that day'], and from there it was transferred to *Yalquṭ Makhiri* on Isaiah, p. 103. In the printed editions there is added here in *Cant. Rabba*: וכולם עשו ישראל אמוניאה ועבדו אותם, שנ׳ ׳ויוספו בני ישראל לעשות הרע בעיני ה׳ ויעבדו את הבעלים ['And Israel declared all these gods one government and worshipped (all of) them, as it is said "And the children did evil again in the sight of the Lord — and they served the Baalim" '] (Jud. iii 12), but if so it is difficult to understand the argument 'instead of denouncing....' It seems that R. Isaac made the exposition of R. Joḥanan a *Petiḥa* [Introduction to a lecture] for Isaiah xliii 22 'Yet thou hast not called upon Me, O Jacob, neither hast thou wearied thyself about Me, O Israel' and omitted the passage about Elijah from באותה שעה... ['At that moment...'], inserting in its place וכולם עשו ישראל וכו׳, and that one of the copyists completed the lacuna, so to speak, in *Cant. Rabba*.
62. *T.B. Pesaḥim* 87b and *ibid.* 87a; see *Seder Eliahu Zuṭa* ix, ed. Me'ir Ish Shalom (Friedmann), p. 186. A defence of Hosea and Elijah is found in *Pesiqta Rabbati* 183a, and it is directed, apparently, against the homilies we have cited: 'It is said that Hosea and Elijah were ruthless. Heaven forfend! they were not ruthless...'; *ibid.* 183b and 184a Hosea is portrayed as transcending other prophets in his love of Israel, while in *Num. Rabba* ii, 17, it is stated: 'Hosea who was intermediate, neither loving nor hating'.
63. *Lam. Rabba* iv, 22, ed. Buber, § 22, p. 153 reads: 'Pharaoh's transfer of the ring to Joseph was more effective.' The version that I have cited in the text is also found in the Pesaro ed., 1519, but Buber has not commented on this; undoubtedly this is a scribal correction, but one that is completely unfounded. R. Samuel Jaffe, in *Yefe ʿAnaf*, has already explained that the decree is termed 'transfer of the ring' under the influence of the next homily; cf. the commentary of Maharzaw [Z. W. Einhorn] *ad loc.*
64. *T.B. Megilla* 14a. See M. Zucker 'Ha-'efshar she-Nāvî Yehěṭa'? [Is it possible for a prophet to sin?]', *Tarbiz*, XXXIX, 1966, pp. 148–173.
65. *Lam. Rabba, loc. cit.* On the 60 myriads of prophets in the days of Elijah see *Cant. Rabba* iv, 11; cf. *Tosefta Soṭa* xii, 5, p. 317, and *Seder ʿOlam Rabba* xxi, ed. D. Ratner, p. 46.
66. *Cant. Rabba* i, 6, according to the Parma MS. mentioned above. Unlike R. Joḥanan, who said 'Better is the fingernail of the former (generations) than the body [literally 'belly'] of the latter', Resh Laqish argued 'On the contrary, the latter (generations) are the better, for despite the oppression of the (Roman) government they occupy themselves with the Torah' — *T.B. Yoma* 9b.
67. In *Lev. Rabba* x, 2, p. 198, the verse 'Thou hast loved righteousness, and

hated wickedness' (Psalms xlv 8) is expounded, in the continuation of R. Judah b. R. Simon's homily, in favour of the prophet Isaiah: 'Thou hast loved — to justify my children; and hated wickedness — for you hated to condemn them.' In *Pesiqta Rabbati* 150b this homily is joined to the continuation of R. Samuel bar Naḥman's dictum; after Isaiah had been punished by receiving burns, it is stated 'And when Isaiah saw this, he began to justify Israel and to defend them.'

68. *T.B.* *'Arakhin* 16b; see *Sifra*, Qedoshim, iv, 8.
69. *T.B.* *'Arakhin, loc. cit.* See Maimonides, 'Laws of Ethics (*Dē'ot*)' vi, 7–8, and Leḥem Mishne on 8; cf. Haggahot Maymuniyyot § 5, which is based on the statement in the *Tanḥuma*, cited above in note 56.
70. *Sifra, loc. cit.*, 9, and *T.B.* *'Arakhin, loc. cit.*
71. See my article 'Mātay Pāsĕqā ha-Nĕvû'ā [When did prophecy cease?]', *Tarbiz*, xvii, 1946, pp. 1–11.
72. See B. Uffenheimer, s.v. 'Nĕvû'ā [Prophecy]', *Ha-Enṣiqlopedya Ha-Miqra'it* [Encyclopaedia Biblica], v, 1968, p. 690, and the bibliography cited *ibid.*, p. 731.
73. *T.B.* *Sanhedrin* 11a; *T.B.* *Yoma* 9b; *T.B.* *Soṭa* 48b; *Tosefta Soṭa* xiii, 2, p. 318 reads: 'The Holy Spirit ceased in Israel.'
74. *Against Apion*, I, § 41–42.
75. *Cant. Rabba* iv, 11.
76. *Pesiqta de-Rav Kahana*, Naḥamu, p. 266.
77. *T.B.* *Megilla* 14a.
78. *Cant. Rabba, loc. cit.*; *T.B.* *Megilla, loc. cit.*
79. *Seder 'Olam Rabba*, vi, ed. Ratner, p. 140; see the continuation *ibid.* (according to the *Yalquṭ* and the Rome MS., *ibid.*, note 46): 'From now on "Ask thy father, and he will declare unto thee, thine elders and they will tell thee' (Deut. xxxii 7). I might have thought this refers to old men in the street; therefore Scripture teaches "and they will tell thee". Thus you learn that זקן ['elder'] means (as an acronym) זה שקנה חכמה ['He who has acquired wisdom']. Cf. the parallels *ibid.*, note 48.
80. See above, p. 302, and p. 117.
81. Above, p. 304.
82. According to the view of many Biblical scholars since Wellhausen; Yeḥezkel Kaufmann, *Toledot ha-'Emuna ha-Yisra'elit*, iv, p. 384, note 21, lists them and rejects their arguments. He accepts the view of the Sages — as I have explained it in my aforementioned article, p. 3 — that prophecy came to an end with the destruction of the First Temple. But the explanation he offers for this opinion — *ibid.*, p. 389 — namely 'In this consciousness of God's wrath is the cessation of prophecy rooted', is purely his own theory and is not well founded.
83. Z. Frankel, *Darkhe ha-Mishna*, wrote: 'It was these generations that returned to the Lord with all their heart, and the admonishments of the prophet were wholly superfluous for them' (referred to by Y. Kaufmann, *op. cit.*, p. 385).

R. T. Herford, *The Pharisees*, 1924, pp. 140 ff, explains the phenomenon in similar fashion, but since he is more discursive he sounds less drastic. G. Foot Moore, *Judaism*, I, p. 238, links the termination of prophecy with the manifestations of its decline, as these are described in Zechariah xiii 1–6; but false prophets always existed, and Zechariah himself was a prophet.

84. See L. Finkelstein, *Ha-Perushim we-'Anshe Keneset ha-Gedola*, New York 1950, p. 51, and *ibid.* n. 144, where the entire voluminous bibliography is listed. Cf. also Y. Baer, *Yisra'el ba-'Ammim*, 1955, pp. 24 ff; G. Alon, *Toledot ha-Yehudim be-'Ereṣ Yisra'el bi-Tequfat ha-Mishna we-ha-Talmud*, II, 1956, p. 223.

85. From the dictum of the Amora R. Jeremiah 'One hundred and twenty elders, of whom more than eighty were prophets, instituted this prayer...', *T.P. Berakhot* ii, 4, p. 4d, which is transmitted in *T.B. Megilla* 17b in the version 'One hundred and twenty elders, among whom were a number of prophets, instituted....', nothing is to be inferred regarding the composition of the 'Great Synagogue'; see L. Ginzberg, *Perushim we-Ḥiddushim bi-Yerushalmi*, Pt. I, pp. 328–330.

86. This is the correct order, as is clear from *'Avot de-R. Nathan*, Versions I and II, and as L. Finkelstein pointed out in his aforementioned book, p. 54, note 151; but his emendation, 'raise up many Sages [חכמים]', is unfounded. Actually the text of the Rome MS. (ed. Schechter, Appendix, p. 154) and that of the New York MS., which is identical with it — 'Many Sages rose up and made a fence round their words' — prove that this is the end of the paragraph, 'What fence...', and it is followed by the dispute of the School of Shammai and the School of Hillel as a commentary to 'And raise up many disciples' as in Version II, iv. On 'Be deliberate in judgement', see *Sifre Deut.* § 16, p. 25, and S. Lieberman, 'He'arot le-Pereq i shel Qohelet Rabba [Notes to chapter i of *Eccles. Rabba*]', Studies ... Presented to G. Scholem [Hebrew Section], 1968, p. 168.

87. The fact that the word *kĕneset* [rendered 'Synagogue'] does not appear in the Bible (and the verb *kānas* ['to assemble'], too, occurs chiefly in late books and only once in Isaiah xxviii 20, *kĕhitkannēs* ['to stretch himself'] shows that it was coined when the institution was established. In contradistinction to *'ēdā* ['congregation'] and *qahal* ['assembly'], which denote the gathering of the whole people, the word *kĕneset* (the translation of the Aramaic *kĕnishta*) was chosen to signify 'the assembly of deputies', while *kĕneset ha-gĕdolā* ['the Great Synagogue'] connoted the 'assembly of the important — great — people.' Its roots go back to the assembly of the people that made the covenant in the Book of Nehemiah, but it differed from it constitutionally. It was not ἐκκλησία, the assembly of the whole people, but συναγωγή (in the Septuagint the two words are used interchangeably as translations of *'ēdā* and of *qāhāl*; the distinction drawn in this regard by L. Rost, *Die Vorstufen von Kirche und Synagogue in A.T.*, 1938, were rejected by W. Schrage, 'Ekklesia und Synagogue', *Zeitschrift für Theologie und Kirche*, 1963, pp. 178 ff; see also

H. Kosmala, *Hebräer, Essener und Christen*, 1959, p. 63) a gathering of elders and sages. H. D. Mantel, 'Ṭivah shel ha-Kneset ha-Gedola [The Nature of the Great Synagogue]', *Papers of the Fourth World Congress of Jewish Studies*, vol. I, 1967, p. 81, speaks of 'the Great Synagogue' as of 'an organization of the disciples of Ezra in the period of the Ptolemies' and in his opinion (*ibid.*, p. 82) 'there is no evidence that it was a governmental body', and he further concludes (*ibid.*, p. 88) 'the Great Synagogue was a federation of all branches of the Assembly.' On the one hand he ignores the few existing testimonies concerning 'the Great Synagogue', and on the other he cites — without distinguishing between concepts and dates — a great deal of material on the Synagogue members, the associations and the Pharisees, while comparing uncritically parallels from works on Hellenistic associations. This comparison is intrinsically valuable (see below, p. 584), but not in relation to the subject under discussion.

88. See W. T. Tarn, *Hellenistic Civilisation*, 3rd edition, London 1952, pp. 74 ff, p. 147, and p. 21. Cf. V. Tcherikover, *Ha-Yehudim we-ha-Yewanim ba-Tequfa ha-Helenistit*, Tel-Aviv, 1963, p. 39, and pp. 71 ff.
89. Josephus, *Antiquities* xii, § 138; cf. Tcherikover, *op. cit.*, p. 64, and the bibliography cited *ibid.*, p. 347, note 119.
90. See *T.P. Sheqalim* iv, p. 2; cf. my article 'Ha-Derasha ki-Yesod ha-Halakha u-be'ayat ha-Soferim', *Tarbiz*, XXVII, p. 17, and *ibid.* notes 24 and 25.
91. *I Maccabus* ii 29, 41.
92. *Ibid.*, xiv 28.
93. *M. Ma'aser Sheni* v, 15; on the meaning of 'He abolished the "awakeners" and the "knockers" see *Tosefta Soṭa* xiii, 10, p. 320, on the basis of which S. Lieberman, *Hellenism in Jewish Palestine*, p. 141, explained that Joḥanan the High Priest sought to abolish customs that obtained in idolatrous cults, only the statement 'until his time the hammer used to strike in Jerusalem' remains unexplained. *Ibid.*, note 13, are listed the studies in which theories in connection with our subject are advanced.
94. *M. Ma'aser Sheni, loc. cit.*; see *T.P. ibid.* v, 9, p. 56d. Cf. G. Alon, 'Le-Ḥeqer ha-Halakha shel Philon [On Philo's Halakha]', *Meḥqarim be-Toledot Yisra'el*, Pt. I, pp. 84 ff; Chaim Tchernowitz (Rav Tsair), *Toledot ha-Halakha* [History of the Halakha], Pt. IV, pp. 179–196; S. Zeitlin, 'The High Priest's Abrogation and Decrees', *Studies and Essays in honour of A. Newman*, 1962, pp. 569 ff. Alon's conjecture that all the traditions concerning the enactments of Joḥanan in regard to tithes refer to John Hyrcanus II, is without any real foundation. The tradition relating to the threefold distribution of the tithe 'A third to acquaintances among the priests and Levites, a third to the Temple treasury, and a third to the poor and "associates" who were in Jerusalem' should be compared with the command of Ptolemy Philadelphus in the year 265–4 B.C.E. that the ἀπόμοιρα (the sixth part of the produce) was not to be given to the priests but direct to the treasury, and for this purpose collectors and cashiers were appointed (see W. Otto, *Priester und Tempel*, 1905, p. 346) like the 'pairs' installed by John Hyrcanus, see *T.P. loc. cit.*

95. *Wars* i, § 68; *Ant.* xiii, § 300; he uses the expression προφητεία in the sense of telling the future; see *The Testament Levi* viii 15, *The Testaments of the 12 Patriarchs*, p. 46.
96. *Tosefta Soṭa* xiii, 5, p. 319; see *T.P. Soṭa* ix, 12, p. 24b; see *T.B. ibid.* 33a. This story is also told by Josephus, *Ant.* xiii, § 282, and here he uses the expression ἀκούσειε φωνῆς. In *Tosefta*, *T.P.*, and *T.B. Soṭa, loc. cit.*, mention is made of a Heavenly Voice that went forth from the Holy of Holies in the days of Simeon the Just; see also *Megillat Ta'anit*, ed. Lichtenstein, *HUCA*, VII–VIII, pp. 344–345. On 'a Heavenly Voice from the Holy of Holies' see also *Mekhilta*, Massekhta da-Amalek, ii, p. 200. The interpretation of A. Geiger, *Urschrift*, p. 152, that בני שותה מים refers to the Pharisees who did not eat meat or drink wine after the destruction of the Temple (*Tosefta Soṭa* xix, 11, p. 322) has no foundation in the light of the parallels cited above; cf. below, p. 950, note 36.
97. *T.B. Sanhedrin* 82a; *T.B. 'Avoda Zara* 36b. R. Dimi and Ravin cite the tradition about the 'Bet Din of the House of the Hasmoneans' (see the Spanish MS., ed. Abramson), who issued a decree regarding one who has intercourse with a Gentile woman. The nature of the decree is not sufficiently clear — this is shown by the discussion in *T.B. 'Avoda Zara, ibid.* — but it seems that its purpose was to fix the Halakha for the courts of justice on the subject; the practice during war, in this respect, was based on the rule that 'If one has intercourse with a Gentile [literally 'Aramaean'] woman, he is punished by zealots'; *M. Sanhedrin* ix, 6. See G. Alon, *Meḥqarim be-Toledot Yisra'el*, I, p. 102.
98. *T.B. Sanhedrin* 19a. Also on another occasion Simeon b. Sheṭaḥ uses the expression 'May He who knows the thoughts (of man) call that man to account'; see *Tosefta Sanhedrin* viii, 3; *T.P. ibid.* iv, 10, p. 22b; *T.B. ibid.* 37b. But in *Mekhilta*, Mishpaṭim, xx, p. 327, the dictum is quoted in the name of Judah b. Tabbai.
99. *T.P. Sanhedrin* vi, 5, p. 23a; *T.B. Ḥagiga* 16a.
1. *T.B. Shabbat* 14b; *T.B. Ketubbot* 82b.
2. *T.P. Ketubbot* viii, 11, p. 32c.
3. *T.P. Berakhot* vii, 2, p. 11b; *T.P. Nazir* v, 2, p. 54b.
4. *M. Sanhedrin* vi, 4; *T.P. Ḥagiga* ii, 2, p. 77d; *T.P. Sanhedrin* vi, 9, p. 23c.
5. *T.B. Berakhot* 48a; see above, note 3. On Elijah as 'showing honour to the king', see *Mekhilta*, Pisḥa, xiii, p. 45, and the parallels noted *ibid.*, n. 5.
6. *T.P. Bava Meṣi'a* ii, 5, p. 8c. See above, p. 358.
7. *M. Ta'anit* iii, 8; *Tosefta ibid.*, iii, 1. See S. Lieberman, *Tosefta ki-Fshuṭah*, p. 1096; *T.P. Ta'anit* iii, 11, p. 66d; *T.B. ibid.*, 23a.
8. See J. Z. Lauterbach, 'The Sadducees and Pharisees' (it first appeared in *Studies in Jewish Literature issued in honour of K. Kohler*, Berlin 1913), *Rabbinic Essays*, Cincinnati, 1951, p. 45, n. 21; he bases himself on the story in *T.B. Qiddushin* 66a and on the Gemara to *Megillat Ta'anit*. L. Finkelstein, *Ha-Pĕrushim we-'Anshe Keneset ha-Gedola* [The Pharisees and the Men of the

Great Synagogue], New York, 1950, p. 33, n. 119, also writes 'that the opponents of the Pharisaic sect began to defame them by calling them Perushim, and refers, as his authority, to the *Tosefta Berakhot* iii, 25 (see now *Tosefta ki-Fshuṭah*, Pt. I, p. 53), 'the *Minim* are included in (the benediction) referring to the Pharisees', i.e. those who secede from the community in time of trouble. However, it is clear that there are 'Perushim' of another kind; see *M. Ḥagiga* ii, 7 'The garments of an *ʿAm hā-ʾAreṣ* [literally 'people of the land', i.e. those who were ignorant of the Law and did not observe the rules of purity and impurity; they were likewise not scrupulous in setting apart the various tithes] are deemed to have *midras* — uncleanness [literally 'place of treading or pressure', denotes impurity attaching to an object upon which one who suffers a flux sits, lies, rides upon, or leans against; this is equivalent to the first degree of impurity] for Pharisees', that is to say, for those who keep away from *ʿAmme hā-ʾĀreṣ* and may even include 'a Sadducean associate' [an associate (*ḥāvēr*) is one who strictly observes the Law; the opposite of *ʿAm hā-ʾĀreṣ*] (*T.B. Nidda* 33b); see *Mishna, ibid.* iv, 2) 'The daughters of the Sadducees... if they have separated themselves and follow the ways of the Israelites... R. Jose says: They are ever considered like (the women of) the Israelites until they separate themselves and follow the ways of their fathers'. With regard to the expression 'Although they were wives of Sadducees, they were afraid of the Pharisees', which occurs in the story 'Once a Sadducee' in *T.B. Nidda, loc. cit.*, see *Tosefta, ibid.*, v, 3, p. 645 'Although we are Sadducean wives we all consult a Sage'. The Sages did not regard themselves as a sect, even though they ate unconsecrated food under conditions of Levitical purity and also professed the ideal ' "Be ye holy" — be ye Pharisees' (*Sifra*, Qedoshim, i) and consequently Finkelstein's observation (*loc. cit.*) 'The Pharisees never ceased regarding their sect as the sect of Ḥasidim' is without foundation. The Sages regarded themselves as 'Sages of Israel', and the early Ḥasidim were not viewed by them as founders of their sect but as ideal figures of corporate Israel. In debates with Sadducees they did not mind using the designation Pharisees mockingly; see *M. Yadayim* iv, 6: 'R. Joḥanan b. Zakkai said: Is this then the only thing that we have against the Pharisees?'

9. *M. Makkot* i, 6; *M. Yadayim* i, 6–8; *M. ʿEruvin* vi, 2; *Tosefta Yoma* i, 8, and *Tosefta Ki-Fshuṭah, ibid.*, p. 729. See the preceding note. A critical perusal of Josephus' Statements, *Ant.* xiii, § 410–415, shows that they do not contradict what was stated above.
10. *Tosefta Berakhot* iii, 25; *T.P. ibid.*, ii, 4, 5a; *Tosefta Shabbat* xiii, 5, and *Tosefta Ki-Fshuṭah, ibid.*, p. 206; *T.P. ibid.*, xvi, 1, p. 15c; *T.B. ibid.*, 115b. See above p. 527.
11. *T.B. Yoma* 71b. See *Diqduqe Soferim, ad loc.*, p. 208, n. 9.
12. *Tosefta Menaḥot* xiii, 20, p. 533; see *T.B. Pesaḥim* 57a. Josephus relates similar stories about the servants of the High Priest Ḥananiah, *Ant.* xx, §§ 206–207.

13. *Tosefta Zevaḥim* xi, 16 p. 497.
14. *M. Yoma* iii, 11; *T.P. ibid.* iii, 9, p. 41a.
15. *Tosefta Yoma* i, 12. The exact date of R. Zadok, in whose day the incident occurred and who said 'Listen to me, O my brethren the House of Israel... Come let us measure for whom the heifer [whose neck is to be broken] has to be brought — for the Temple or for the courts,' is not known; see *Tosefta ki-Fshuṭah*, p. 735. It appears that the criticism voiced in *The Assumption of Moses* vii, 5–10, with reference to 'the impious men... who say "Do not touch me lest thou shouldst pollute me in the place (where I stand)"' is directed against priests of the type mentioned above; see A. Büchler, *Die Priester und der Cultus*, p. 78.
16. *Tosefta Pesaḥim* iv, 13; *T.P. ibid.* vi, 1, p. 33a; *T.B. ibid.* 66a. In *T.P., loc. cit.*, we read: 'R. Abuna said: Now it is impossible for the fourteenth of Nisan not to fall on a Sabbath in the course of two Sabbatical years [i.e. fourteen years]. Why then did they forget the Halakha? In order that high office might be granted to Hillel.' The expression 'the sons of the prophets', found in *Tobit* iv 12, has a different meaning. This is not quite clear in the Greek version, but it distinctly emerges from the Itala recension: 'quoniam filii prophetarum sumus qui in veritate prophetaverunt priores. Noe prophetavit prior, et Abraham, et Isaac et Iacob.' So, too, in the Aramaic version; see A. Neubauer, *The Book of Tobit*, p. 8. Cf. *ibid.*, p. LXXIV 'For we are the sons of the prophets, since the earliest prophets were Noah, Abraham, Isaac, and Jacob, our ancestors of old...' The reference, therefore, is to ancestors who were also prophets.
17. *Tosefta Sukka* iv, 3.
18. *T.P. ibid.* v, 1, p. 55a; see *Midrash Tanna'im*, p. 99, and J. N. Epstein, *Mavo' le-Nosaḥ ha-Mishna*, pp. 320 ff.
19. *Tosefta Soṭa* xiii, 3, p. 318, שאין דורו זכאי לכך; *T.P. ibid.* ix, 13, p. 24a, where the reading is שאין הדור כדיי ['His generation is not worthy']; in *T.B. ibid.* 48b the text is the same as in the *Tosefta*; all the sources cited above give the parallel story concerning Samuel the Small in Jabneh; see below, n. 21.
20. See the dictum of R. Phinehas b. Jair that was added to the Mishna at the end of *Tractate Soṭa* (cf. J. N. Epstein, *op. cit.*, p. 949) 'and saintliness leads to (the gift of) the holy spirit'; in *T.P. Sheqalim* iii, 3 p. ,47c (*ad fin.*) proof has been added from the verse 'Then Thou spokest in vision to Thy godly ones' (Psa. lxxxix 20 [19]). But in *T.P. Shabbat* i, 3, p. 3c the reading is: 'Fear of sin (leads) to (the gift of) the holy spirit: "Then shalt thou understand the fear of the Lord, and find the knowledge of the Lord" (Prov. ii 5); the holy spirit (leads) to saintliness: "Then Thou speakest in vision to Thy godly ones"' (see S. Lieberman, *Yerushalmi ki-Fshuṭo*, p. 35; cf. the commentary ascribed to the disciple of R. Samuel b. R. Shne'ur, ed. A. Schreiber, p. 35, who writes 'and there the sequence is reversed'). In *T.B. 'Avoda Zara* 20b the text has: 'Holiness leads to the holy spirit; the holy spirit leads to resurrection,

but saintliness transcends them all'. The Munich MS. has 'Fear of sin leads to (the gift of) the holy spirit; the holy spirit leads to saintliness; saintliness transcends them all.' But the Spanish MS., ed. S. Abramson (so, too, in *Haggadot ha-Talmud*, and in the *Yalquṭ* MS.; see *Diqduqe Soferim*, to *'Avoda Zara*, p. 53, note ל reads: 'Holiness leads to fear of sin... humility (leads) to saintliness, but saintliness transcends them all, as it is said: "Then Thou spokest in vision to Thy godly ones".' The verse itself states that saintliness brings with it the holy spirit, but it appears that learned scribes completed, in various passages, whatever seemed to them to be wanting — namely the holy spirit. In *T.P. Shabbat* it is possible that two ancient traditions, which were only parallels, were combined; the one read 'Fear of sin leads to (the gift of) the holy spirit', and the other stated 'Saintliness leads to the holy spirit'; on the parallel 'fear of sin — saintliness' see below, p. 953, n. 71.

21. See *Mekhilta de-R. Ishmael*, Massekhta de-Pisḥa, xi, p. 38; *T.B. Nedarim* 38a, the statement of R. Joḥanan; *T.B. Shabbat* 92a; *ibid.* 30b; *T.B. Pesaḥim* 66b; *ibid.* 117a; and Rav already added to this dictum 'and so it is also in respect of Halakha.' On humility and prophecy see *Sifre*, Be-ha'alotekha, § 95, p. 96; cf. *Tanḥuma*, ed. Buber, Mi-qeṣ vi, p. 192. The story related there about Samuel is also found in *Liber Antiquitatum Biblicarum*, which is ascribed to Philo, lix, 2, ed. G. Kisch, p. 260.
22. E. Bass, *Die Merkmale der israel. Prophetie nach der traditionellen Auffassung des Talmud*, Kirchain (undated), is a valueless dissertation. See H. Parzen, 'The Ruah hakodesh in Tannaitic Literature', *JQR*, 1929–1930, N.S. XX, pp. 51 ff; N. N. Glatzer, 'Talmudic interpretation of Prophecy', *Review of Religion*, 1946, pp. 195 ff. With regard to the relationship between prophecy and ecstasy, see my article 'Derashot Ḥazal 'al Nevi'e 'Ummot ha-'Olam we-'al Parashat Bil'am', *Tarbiz*, XXV, 1956, pp. 278. On Philo's conception see H. A. Wolfson, *Philo*, II, pp. 22 ff, pp. 48 ff. Regarding prophecy and mysticism see the important and fundamental observations of G. Scholem, *Rel. Autorität und Mystik* (first appeared in Eranos Jahrbücher, 1949), *Zur Kabbalah und ihrer Symbolik*, 1960, pp. 18 ff.
23. *T.B. Sukkah* 28a; *T.B. Bava Batra* 134a.
24. See my article 'Ha-Māsôrôt 'al Tôrat ha-sôd bi-tĕqûfat ha-Tannā'îm [The Traditions about Merkabah Mysticism in the Tannaitic Period]', *Studies in Mysticism and Religion*, presented to Gershom G. Scholem, Jerusalem 1969, pp. 1–28.
25. See above, p. 572.
26. See above, p. 147.
27. *T.B. Bava Batra* 12a; see Rashi *ad loc.*, s.v. *Hākhî*, and *Ḥiddushe ha-Ramban, ad loc.*, s.v. *Hā'*: 'The prophecy of the prophets, which consists of vision and revelation, the prophecy of Sages, which is vouchsafed through wisdom'. Cf. Maimonides, 'Laws of the Fundaments of the Torah,' vii, 1.
28. See *Tosefta Pesaḥim* i, 27, p. 157: 'From this we learn that Rabban Gamaliel divined by the holy spirit'. Cf. *T.B. 'Eruvin* 64b, and Tosafot *ad loc.*, s.v.

She-Kiwwēn. Concerning R. Akiba see *Lev. Rabba* xxi, 8, p. 485; cf. *T.P. Shevi'it* ix, 1, p. 38d, the story about R. Simeon b. Yoḥai: 'R. Simeon b. Yoḥai saw by means of the holy spirit'; but in *Gen. Rabba* lxxix, 6, p. 944, the miracle is narrated without this expression; see the v.l. *ibid.* and the notes.

29. *T.B. Bava Batra* 12b; see the story there concerning Mar bar Rav Ashi. *Shôte* [rendered 'idiot'] means 'madman'. The phenomenon that children sometimes ask questions and make remarks that seem to delve to the depths of philosophy, and that metaphysical manifestations are to be found in the initial state of mental illness, is discussed by Karl Jaspers, *Einführung in die Philosophie*, p. 13, and he discovers a profound meaning in the saying 'Children and idiots tell the truth.' He did not know, of course, the dictum of R. Joḥanan.
30. In *T.B. Megilla* 32a, 'using a Heavenly Voice', or 'using the holy spirit' is equivalent to 'using the Express Name [i.e. the Tetragrammaton]'; see above, p. 110. Cf. S. Liebermann, *Hellenism in Jewish Palestine*, p. 249.
31. *T.P. Shabbat* vi, 9, p. 8c, where R. Eleazar expounds the verse in Isaiah to mean that 'We may follow the instruction of a Heavenly Voice.'
32. 'Ten prophesied, but did not know what they prophesied...', *'Avot de-R. Nathan*, Version II, xliii; among them are counted Laban, Pharaoh, and Gehazi, and all of them made remarks that were subsequently interpreted as an allusion to events about to happen; in this usage the expression 'the holy spirit was enkindled within them' — *Gen. Rabba* lxxxiv, 19, p. 1024, and *ibid.* xci, 7, p. 1127; *ibid.* lxxxv, 12, p. 1046, we find 'the holy spirit said.'
33. See above, p. 577, and the examples I have cited in my article 'Halakha u-Nevu'a', in the Appendix *Bat Qol* [Heavenly Voice], pp. 24–27; see also *T.B. Sanhedrin* 96b נפקא קלא ואמרה ['a Voice went forth and said']. Cf. Allegro, *QC*. V, 1968, p. 91 (Prof. D. Flusser's note).
34. See *T.B. Shabbat* 34a; *T.B. Bava Batra* 75a.
35. See 'Yerushalayim shel Maṭṭa wi-Yerushalayim shel Ma'ala' in *Yerushalayim le-Doroteha*, Jerusalem 1969, pp. 164–171.
36. See above, p. 577, and my article 'Class-Status and Leadership in the World of the Palestinian Sages', *Proceedings of the Israel Academy of Sciences and Humanities*, II, pp. 38 ff.
37. *M. 'Arakhin* ix, 4.
38. *M. Shevi'it* ix, 3; *T.B. Gittin* 36b.
39. G. Alon, *Meḥqarim be-Toledot Yisra'el*, Pt. I, Tel-Aviv 1957, pp. 26 ff. A Schalit, *Hordos ha-Melekh, hā-'Îsh u-Po'ălô* [King Herod, the Man and his work], Jerusalem 1960, p. 190, writes that, in the view of the Pharisaic party, the period of the Seleucid suzerainty 'was, without doubt, better for the Jewish people than the Hasmonean era of sovereign independence... because within the boundaries of the Seleucid kingdom the Jewish people was in no danger of being tempted to deviate from the path marked out for it by God and to engage in matters outside the sphere of a holy life...' Without

doubt the Sages held no such views, but it is strange that a historian like A. Schalit should completely ignore the simple fact that the acts of the Hellenizers and the decrees of Antiochus preceded the Hasmonean period and fell within the term of Seleucid suzerainty.

40. *T.B. Bava Batra* 3b.
41. See *T.B. Beṣa* 20a; *M. Keritot* vi, 3; above, p. 433.
42. *M. Soṭa* vii, 8; see *Tosefta, ibid.*, and *T.P. ibid.* vii, p. 7; *T.B., ibid.*, 43b. See *Lev. Rabba* iii, 5, p. 10; see above, p. 582.
43. Gen. xlix 10.
44. *T.B. Yoma* 53b.
45. *M. Yoma* i, 2.
46. See *ibid.*, i, 6: 'If he was a Sage, he expounded; if not, scholars expounded before him'; but in the Kaufmann MS. the text is: 'If he was a Sage, he expounded; and if a disciple, the Sages expounded before him.' See *Mele'khet Shelomo*, ad loc., *M. Nega'im* xii, 5; *T.P. Beṣa* i, 7, p. 60c; cf. S. Lieberman, *Yerushalmi Ki-Fshuṭo*, p. 23.
47. See *M. Sheqalim* v, 1–2; *Tosefta, ibid.*, ii, 14–15; *M. Yoma* iii, 11; *Tosefta, ibid.*, ii, 7–8, pp. 184–185.
48. Shürer, *Geschichte*,[4] Pt. II, pp. 325 ff; S. Lieberman, *Hellenism in Jewish Palestine*, pp. 257; M. Avi-Yonah, 'Bet ha-Miqdash ha-Sheni [The Second Temple],' *Sefer Yerushalayim*, 1956, pp. 392 ff.
49. *Tosefta Yoma* ii, 4–6, pp. 183–184.
50. *M. Yoma* v, 5; see *T.P., ibid.*, v, 6, p. 42d: 'Two priests fled during the war [i.e. during the siege of Jerusalem]; one said: I used to stand and sprinkle, and the other said: I used to walk and sprinkle.' Cf. *T.B. ibid.* 59a.
51. See S. Safrai, *Ha-'Aliyya le-Regel bi-Yeme Bayit Sheni* [The Pilgrimage (to the Temple) in the time of the Second Temple], 1965, pp. 181 ff.
52. *M. Kelim* i, 8–9; *Tosefta Nega'im* vi, 2, p. 625; *T.B. Bava Qamma* 82b.
53. See *M. 'Eruvin* x, 15; *M. Sheqalim* viii, 1–2; *M. Ḥagiga* iii, 5. *M. Sanhedrin* ix, 6: 'A priest who served (at the altar) in a state of impurity, was not brought by his fellow priests to the Bet Din (Court), but the young priests took him outside the Temple Court and split open his brain with clubs [or 'faggots'].' In *Tosefta Kelim* i, 6, p. 569 we read: 'Simeon the Modest [= Pious] said to R. Eliezer: "I entered between the entrance hall and the altar with unwashed hands and feet." He answered him: "Who ranks higher, you or the High Priest?" He (Simeon) remained silent. Said (R. Eliezer) to him: "Are you ashamed to say that the High Priest's dog ranks higher than you?" He (Simeon) replied: "You have said it." Said (Eliezer) to him: "By the Service! Even if the High Priest acted thus, they would split open his brain with clubs. But what are you to do, since the guardsman did not find you!" ' Mention should also be made of the Gospel fragment in papyrus Oxyrhynchus, V, 1908 (see M. R. James, *Apocryphal New Testament*, Oxford 1924, p. 29): 'And he took them to a holy place and entered the Sanctuary, when a Pharisee High Priest, called Levi(?), drew near, and approaching them said to the

saviour: "Who gave you permission to walk in this holy place and to gaze upon the holy vessels without immersion, and your disciples whose feet are unwashed?" ' In his reply Jesus negates the value of the laws of ritual purity. It is possible that the sharp reply of R. Eliezer (a similar rhetorical utterance by Ben ʿAzzai occurs in *Deut. Rabba*, ed. S. Lieberman, p. 13) was given on account of his suspicion that Simeon the Modest inclined towards Christian heresy; on R. Eliezer's arguments with sectarians see *T.B. ʿAvoda Zara* 16b. Joseph Perles (*MGWJ*, XXI, p. 252) put forward the theory that the guardsman [בעל פול] belonged to the family of the High Priest the son of Fiabi (פיאבי — Fabius is derived from *faba* = פול 'bean'; see *Aruch Completum*, II, p. 148, and *ibid.*, I, s. אפון, p. 220; S. Krauss *Lehnwörter*, p. 419). Indeed we find recensions in which the Tanna R. Eleazar b. Pila (*M. Ṭohorot* vii, 9, and *Tosefta*, *ibid.*, viii, 16, p. 696) is called R. Eleazar b. Fiabi (see *Tosefet Ri'shonim*, Pt. IV, p. 88; on the different readings בעל הפיל – בעל הפול the recensions of the Ri'shonim see *ibid.*, Pt. III, p. 3). R. Margaliot, Lĕ-Ḥēqer Shēmôt wĕ-Kinuyyîm bĕ-Talmûd [A Study of Names and Designations in the Talmud], Jerusalem 1960, p. 44, writes, as it were, 'by prophecy', without mentioning his predecessors. See also J. Jeremias, *Unbekannte Jesusworte*, 1963, pp. 50–60.

54. *T.B. Shabbat* 14b–15b.
55. *Tosefta Shabbat* i, 14; see Lieberman, *Tosefta ki-Fshuṭah*, *ibid.*, p. 12.
56. *Tosefta 'Ahilot* xviii, 3, p. 616.
57. *Sifra*, Shemini, iv, 49a; *T.B. Rosh ha-Shana* 16b.
58. *M. Yoma* iii, 3, where the text reads לעבודה [for the service]. In *T.P. ibid.* iii, 3, p. 40b: אפילו שלא לעבודה [even not for the service]. See *T.B. ibid.* 30a–b; cf. J. N. Epstein, *Mavo' le-Nosaḥ ha-Mishna*, pp. 461–463.
59. *M. Ḥagiga* iii, 6.
60. *T.P. ibid.* iii, 8, p. 79d.
61. *M. Ḥagiga* iii, 7.
62. *Tosefta ibid.*, iii, 35. *T.P. ibid.* reads: 'immerse the disk of the sun'; see *Tosefta Ki-Fshuṭah*, *ibid.*, p. 1331.
63. *T.P. ibid.*, 6. *Yalquṭ Shimʿoni*, § 703, cites: 'Yerushalmi chapter "Palm-Branch and Willow"... as we have learnt: Each day they went round the altar once. What was the order of the circuit? All Israel, old and young...' This passage from the Palestinian Talmud, which is no longer extant, is cited also by the Early Authorities; see D. Ratner, *Ahavat Ṣiyyon vi-Yerushalayim*, Sukka, p. 141, who does not, however, refer to the note of the Gaon Elijah of Vilna in his annotation to the *Oraḥ Ḥayyim* § 660, in which he cites the *Yalquṭ* and observes 'And the circuit in the Temple was performed only by the priests, for a non-priest may not come in between the entrance hall and the altar....'
64. *T.B. ʿEruvin* 69b, *T.B. Ḥullin* 5a; only an apostate and one who offered libations to idols were exceptions; see *Sifra*, Nedava, Pericope, ii, 3: 'Excepted are the apostates who do not accept the covenant.' Cf. ed. Me'ir Ish Shalom [Friedmann], Breslau 1915, p. 41.

65. *Sifra*, Shemini, iv, 9, 49a; *T.B. Rosh ha-Shana* 16b.
66. *M. Ḥagiga* ii, 7.
67. See Isidore Lévy, *La Légende de Pythagore de Grèce en Palestine*, pp. 236–263.
68. S. Lieberman, 'The Discipline in the so-called Dead Sea Manual of Discipline', *JBL*, LXXI, 1952, pp. 199–206; Ch. Rabin, *Qumran Studies*, 1957; J. Neussner, 'The Fellowship in the Second Jewish Commonwealth', *H.T.Ri.*, LIII, 1960, pp. 126–142; Jacob Licht, *Megillat ha-Serakhim*, Appendix i, pp. 294–303. See H. D. Mantel, *op. cit.* (p. 505, n. 87), p. 82.
69. See Licht, *op. cit.*, pp. 8 ff, pp. 28 ff. The statute of the penalties of the Manual of Discipline [or Rule of the Community] vi 24–vii 25, ed. Licht, pp. 153 ff, should be compared with the legal penalties appearing in the demotic papyrus; see W. Erichsen, *Die Satzungen einer Ägyptischen Kultgenossenschaft aus der Ptolemäerzeit*, Kobenhaven 1959, p. 14. The society was called *dmd* = *yaḥad*; see *ibid.*, pp. 20–21.
70. See *Tosefta 'Avoda Zara* iii, 10, p. 464: 'And who is an *'Am ha-'Areṣ*? Whoever does not eat unconsecrated food in purity — this is the view of R. Me'ir.' The Sages say: 'Whoever does not separate the tithes'; obviously R. Me'ir and the Sages did not initiate this dispute. See *M. Demai* iv, 6: 'Yet the more scrupulous [*ṣĕnu'ê*] of the School of Hillel acted according to the ruling of the School of Shammai.' Cf. *T.P. ibid.*, 5, p. 25d: 'What is meant by *ṣĕnû'ē*? The worthy ones [כשירין]. Rav Ḥisda said: Here (for כך read כאן = כן; see R. Solomon Sirillo and *Mele'khet Shelomo*) the worthy person is called *ṣānûa'*. See below, p. 957, n. 18.
71. *M. 'Avot* ii, 5; in *'Avot de-R. Nathan*, Version I, xxvi, 41b, the following dictum is reported in the name of R. Akiba: 'An *'Am ha-'Areṣ* cannot be saintly, nor a shy person learn, nor an irascible person teach.' *Ibid.*, Version II, xxxiii, 36b we read: 'A brutish person cannot be god fearing, nor can one who engages overmuch in business grow wise, nor can an *'Am ha-'Areṣ* become a saintly Pharisee'; see below, n. 76.
72. See *T.B. Berakhot* 47b.
73. *Tosefta Berakhot*, ed. Lieberman, vi, 20, p. 39; *Tosefta ki-Fshuṭah*, *ibid.*, p. 122.
74. *T.P. Berakhot* ix, 1, p. 12d.
75. See *Megillat ha-Serakhim* xi, 15; *Megillat Milḥemet Bne 'Or*, xiii, 2; xiv, 4; *Megillat ha-Hodayot* iv, 15.
76. *M. 'Avot* v, 10. On the continuation of the Mishna R. Simeon b. Ṣemaḥ Duran, *Magen 'Avot* 86a, writes: '... In old copies of the Mishna arriving from Eretz-Israel, which are vocalized, there is a more accurate recension, namely "Mine and yours is yours, is a saint; yours and mine are mine, is wicked" '; and indeed this is the reading of the Kaufmann MS. and of the Cambridge MS. (where the word 'yours' is omitted), and so R. Jehoseph Ashkenazi (see *Melekhet Shelomo*) emended the text. It appears to me that the meaning of the Mishna according to this recension is: If doubt or litigation arises as to whom something belongs in a case of 'mine and yours', the

saintly person forgoes his claim and says 'It is yours', acting beyond the strict requirements of law; on the other hand, the wicked man refuses to go to court but uses force, declaring 'Yours and mine are mine.'

77. See Licht, *op. cit.*, pp. 10–11.
78. *Tosefta Demai* ii, 13.
79. See Israel Lewy, Über Einige Fragmente aus der Mischna des Abba Saul, Berlin 1876, pp. 32 ff, on the expression 'Abba Saul says even....'
80. *M. Yoma* i, 1; *M. Middot* ii, 5. See Israel Lewy, *op. cit.*, pp. 19–21; cf. also *T.B. Zevaḥim* 88a: 'Abba Saul said: There was a knife in the Temple that caused *ṭĕrēfôt* [used here in the sense of *nĕvēlôt*, animals improperly slaughtered] and the priests decided by vote to conceal it.
81. *Tosefta Sanhedrin* iii, 4, p. 418: 'Abba Saul said: There were two ponds (reservoirs) in Jerusalem... in the lower one, which was completely holy, *ʿAmmĕ ha-'Areṣ* could eat sacrifices of a lower degree and second tithe, and Associates (could eat) sacrifices of a lower degree, but not second tithe. In the upper one, which was not completely holy, *ʿAmmê ha-'Areṣ* could eat sacrifices of a lower degree, but not second tithe, and Associates (could eat) neither sacrifices of a lower degree nor second tithe.'
82. *T.B. Bekhorot* 30b; our text reads: 'R. Joḥanan said: In the days of the son of R. Ḥanina b. Antigonus this Mishna was formulated. R. Judah and R. Jose were in doubt about a matter of levitical purity; so they sent Rabbis to the son of R. Ḥanina b. Antigonus. They went (and) asked him to look into the matter. They found him guarding levitically pure foodstuff; he seated some Rabbis of his own with them, while he arose to look into the matter. They came (back and) told R. Judah and R. Jose. Said R. Judah to them: This man's father insulted scholars....' In the Munich MS. we read: 'They sent Rabbis to R. Ḥanina b. Antigonus: Antigonus, since he was guarding levitically pure foodstuff, seated Rabbis of his own with them....' Perhaps the text should be emended to: 'In the days of R. Ḥanina b. Antigonus... They sent Rabbis to the son of R. Ḥanina b. Antigonus....' See *Sefer Yiḥuse Tanna'im wa-Amora'im*, ed. Rabbi J. L. Maimon, Jerusalem 1963, p. 430; cf. Z. Frankel *Darkhe ha-Mishna*, p. 128.
83. *Tosefta Demai* iii, 4.
84. *Ibid.*, ii, 9, and *ibid.* 3.
85. According to A. Büchler, *Der Galiläische ʿAm-ha-'Areṣ*. This view was rejected by G. Alon, 'Teḥuman shel Hilkhot Ṭohorot', *Meḥqarim be-Toledot Yisra'el*, I, pp. 158–169. We shall see further on how forced were Büchler's explanations in reconciling the sources that contradict his thesis, which seeks to refer all the laws of Associates to priests who eat heave-offering.
86. *T.P. Shabbat* i, 3, p. 3c.
87. See *Tosefta Ḥagiga* iii, 36, concerning R. Ṭarfon, who undertook — after he had heard that people were criticizing him — not to accept heave-offering from any man unless he was assured that 'it contains one fourth (of a *log*) of sacred produce'. See S. Lieberman, *Tosefta ki-Fshuṭah*, *ibid.*, p. 1333:

'Perhaps this incident occurred at the time of the Revolt of Bar Koseva, when they had already begun to set aside wine and oil in purity for the Temple.' Cf. my article ''Asqezis we-Yissurim be-Torat Ḥazal', *Jubilee Volume in honour of Y. Baer*, p. 57.

88. *T.B. 'Eruvin* 32b; see *ibid.* 32a and *T.P. Ma'asrot* ii, 1, p. 49c.

89. *T.B. Sanhedrin* 8b, where the parallel passages are cited. We already find that 'R. Ḥiyya the Elder enjoined Rav: If you are able to eat unconsecrated food in purity throughout the year, do so. But if not, eat it (in purity) seven days of the year' — *T.P. Shabbat* i, 1, p. 3c. However, it is noteworthy that in Galilee there still existed water of purification in the days of 'Ulla and R. Jeremiah (*T.B. Nidda* 6b and *T.P. Berakhot* vi, 1, p. 10a according to the recension of the Rome MS. and R. Solomon Sirillo); undoubtedly there were individuals who were meticulous about eating ordinary food in levitical purity. See *T.B. Ḥullin* 106a; *T.B. 'Avoda Zara* 36a.

90. *T.B. Bava Batra* 75a, the dictum of R. Joḥanan; they are identical with 'the Torah Associates' mentioned in *T.P. Berakhot* i, i, p. 2d. In *Tanḥuma*, Niṣṣavim, 4, Hezekiah expounded the verse in Job xl 30 — on which R. Joḥanan based his saying — with reference to 'the Torah Associates'. See W. Bacher, '*Zur Geschichte der Schulen Pal's im 3n. und 4 ten Jahrhundert*', *MGWJ*, 1899 (43), pp. 343 ff.

91. *T.B. Sukka* 20a, the statement of R. Simeon b. Laqish; it appears that he added the reference to R. Ḥiyya and his sons to a much older dictum.

92. *T.B. Berakhot* 60a; cf. *T.B. Beṣa.*

93. *T.B. Shabbat* 31a; '*Avot de-R. Nathan*, Version I, xv; Version II, xxix, ed. Schechter, pp. 61–62. The adage is found in *Tobit* iv 15: ὃ μισεῖς ἄλλῳ οὐ ποιήσεις; similarly in *Hypothetica* 6.7 (629) of Philo: ἅ τις παθεῖν ἐχθαίρει. On the sources see J. Bernays, *Gesammelte Abhandlungen*, pp. 274–275, and *ibid.*, p. 280. He inclines to the view that Philo drew upon a Judeo-Hebraic source; cf. I. Heinemann, *Philo's griech. und jüd. Bildung*, p. 354. Parallels to other dicta of Hillel in the works of Seneca, who lived after Hillel, are cited by A. Kaminka, *Meḥqarim*, Bk. II, Tel-Aviv 1951, p. 46. His view that Hillel came from Alexandria, is unfounded. Sirach xxxi 24; ed. Segal, p. 192 and his commentary p. 195. Cf. A. Dihle, *Die goldene Regel, Eine Einführing in die Geschichte der antiken und früchristl. Vulgärethik*, Göttingen 1962, p. 8, cites a free translation of the story in *Tractate Shabbat*, although he relies on Strack-Billerbeck, I, p. 460. He concludes the narrative with the words 'Das ist die Summe des Gesetzes', as a rendering of זו היא כל התורה כולה, omitting ואידך... זיל גמור [and the rest... go learn] (in the Oxford MS. and in *Sefer ha-Muṣar* [Book of Ethics] the words זו היא כל התורה כולה are missing; see *Diqduqe Soferim*, 30a, note 6). זו היא כל התורה כולה is, of course, equivalent to זה כלל גדול בתורה [This is a most important principle of the Torah], and is not to be translated *die Summe des Gesetzes*. Dihle rightly stresses, *op. cit.*, p. 10, that the positive version occurs in sources outside Christianity and that the negative formulation appears in early Chris-

tian sources. But Dihle's summation, pp. 82–84, is unsound. It is difficult to comprehend why the Scriptural sentence 'And thou shalt love thy neighbour as thyself' is less abstract than the negative or positive version of the Golden Rule; while his interpretation of the words of Sirach is forced and the Greek provides no proof for the acceptance of the version.

94. See the sources cited in the preceding note. R. Simeon b. Ṣemaḥ Duran, *Magen 'Avot*, 13b, raised the question: 'But why did Shammai the Elder not reprove himself in this respect? For he was irascible, as is mentioned in the second chapter of *Tractate Shabbat*.'

95. See *M. Sukka* ii, 5; *Tosefta Yoma* iv, 2: 'It once happened that Shammai the Elder did not wish to feed his son and the Rabbis decreed (that he should do so) and he fed him with his own hand'; see *Tosefta ki-Fshuṭah*, *ibid.*, p. 812. *Tosefta Shevi'it* iii, 10: 'As regards a field that had been well tilled [in the Seventh Year], Shammai the Elder said: Had the time been free, I should decree that it may not be sown [at the termination of the Seventh Year]. The Bet Din after him decreed that it should not be sown.' Obviously the view of Shammai was preserved in this instance, since the Bet Din after him accepted his view (see *M. Shevi'it* iv, 2), and he said on this occasion 'Had the time been free', because he did not have the power to prohibit, when his colleagues — apparently Hillel — were opposed to his view. In *Mekhilta*, Bo', xvii, p. 69, it is stated that the School of Shammai said that phylacteries never require examination, and they cite the statement of Shammai the Elder: 'And these are the phylacteries of my maternal grandfather.' But Saul Horovitz already referred to *T.P. 'Eruvin* x, 1, p. 26b, where it is stated: 'Hillel the Elder said: These are from my maternal grandfather.' See S. Liebermann, *Ha-Yerushalmi Kiphshuṭo*, p. 358. Cf. Rabbi M. Kasher, *Torah Shelemah*, Bo', § 131, who refers to *Hădar Zĕqēnim*, which cites in the name of the *Tanḥuma*: 'Shammai the Elder said: From this we learn that one's phylacteries should be examined every year; but Hillel said: My father left me phylacteries.'

96. *M. 'Eduyot* i, 1–3; *T.B. Shabbat* 15a.

97. See my article 'Ha-Derasha ki-Yesod ha-Halakha' etc., *Tarbiz*, XXXVII, 1958, p. 170.

98. *Tosefta Ketubbot* xiv, 9; see S. Lieberman, *Tosefta ki-Fshuṭah*, p. 246, where he cites the Early Authorities mentioned above.

99. In his *Novellae* to *T.B. Bava Meṣi'a* 104b, s.v. *Û-Mā*.

1. His observations are cited in the *Shiṭa Mequbbeṣet* to *T.B. Bava Meṣia'*, *ibid.*, and so, too, in the *Responsa of the Rashba*, Pt. III, § 12.

2. *M. Ḥagiga* ii, 2; see Ch. Albeck, *Seder Mo'ed*, Hashlamot and Tosafot, p. 511.

3. *Tosefta*, *loc. cit.*, ii, 11, p. 236. The wording 'He put them off with words and they went away. Forthwith the School of Shammai prevailed...' is difficult; apparently two episodes have been combined in the *Tosefta*.

4. *T.P. Ḥagiga* ii, 3, p. 78a; so, too, *T.P. Beṣa* ii, 4, p. 61d. Also in *T.B. Besa*

20a it is not stated 'Forthwith... prevailed' but 'And that day... prevailed'; and it may be explained thus: 'On the day when... prevailed.' It would seem that this Bava b. Buṭa was a descendant of the Bava b. Buṭa, who lived in the days of Herod — see above, p. 581 — or that he was one of the Sons of Bava, who fled to Edom (*Ant.* xv, §§260–264), on account of Herod's anger, and returned with the disciples of Edom to Jerusalem, see below.

5. See A. E. Halevi, 'Ha-Maḥaloqet ha-Ri'shona [The First Dispute]', *Tarbiz* xxviii, 1959, pp. 154 ff, who discusses the reasons for the dispute.
6. *Lev. Rabba* i, 5, p. 17; see *ibid.* n. 2.
7. *Tosefta Soṭa* xiii, 4; see above, p. 514.
8. *'Avot de-R. Nathan*, Version I, iii, p. 14; see *ibid.*, ix, p. 42; *Mekhilta de-R. Ishmael*, Massekhta da-Amalek, i, p. 190 and L. Finkelstein, *'Avot de-R. Nathan*, p. 21.
9. *M. Sanhedrin* iv, 2, and see *Tosefta*, *ibid.*, vii, 1. In the Sanhedrin, apparently, sat only those to whom priestly families were actually allied in marriage (see *T.B. Pesaḥim* 57a) and not those who were merely fit to do so.
10. *M. Middot* v, 4; see *Sifre* Num. §116, p. 133, where it is stated: 'There was a place behind the Veil where they investigated the genealogies of the priesthood.' See A. Büchler, *Das Synhedrion in Jerusalem*, 1902, p. 23, and S. Lieberman, *Hellenism in Jewish Palestine*, p. 172.
11. *Sifre Num.* §78, p. 73. See also A. Büchler, *Die Priester und der Cultus*, pp. 100–102; and idem, *Das Synhedrion in Jerusalem*, 1902, p. 72.
12. *Antiquities* xiii, 288.
13. See my article 'Class-Status and Leadership in the World of the Palestinian Sages', *Proceedings of the Israel Academy of Sciences and Humanities*, II, No. 4, p. 50 [13].
14. *M. Keritot* i, 7. The oath formula 'By this Temple' is also used by Bava b. Buta, *ibid.*, vi, 3, and by R. Zechariah b. ha-Qaṣṣav (The Butcher), *M. Ketubbot* ii, 9. Apparently it was current in the last years before the Destruction. The oath formula 'By the Service!' was used by R. Eliezer (*Tosefta Kelim*, Bava Qamma, i, 6) and R. Ṭarfon (*Tosefta Zevaḥim* i, 8) and by both in connection with cultic matters in the Sanctuary. Cf. also the form of oath employed by R. Ishmael 'By the robe worn by my father and the plate that he put between his eyes!' (*Tosefta Ḥalla* i, 10). The oath 'By the Service (עבודה)!' uttered by R. Joḥanan in *T.P. Qiddushin* iv, 1, p. 65c, corresponds to 'By the Temple (היכלא)!' in *T.B. ibid.*, p. 71a; see Rashi, *ad loc.*, s.v. *Hêkla*. Cf. *T.P. Bava Batra* viii, 5, p. 18a, where 'By the Service!' is said by R. Eleazar.
15. *M. Ketubbot* i, 5, and *ibid.* xiii, 1–2; *M. 'Oholot* xvii, 5; see Z. Frankel, *Darkhe ha-Mishna*, pp. 60–61.
16. *M. 'Orla* ii, 12.
17. *Tosefta Sukka* ii, 3; *T.B. Yevamot* 15b.
18. *M. Damai* vi, 6; and see *M. Kil'ayim* ix, 5–6; *T.P. Ma'aser Sheni* v, 1. The *ṣĕnu'im* [literally 'modest ones'; rendered in the text 'the more scrupulous']

denotes the meticulously observant. Cf. *Hexapla*, II, 996, to Micah vi 8; see also Sirach xvi 29 ובהצנע אחוה דעי ['And humbly shall I declare my knowledge'], for which the Greek has: Καὶ ἐν ἀκριβείᾳ ἀπαγγέλλω ἐπιστήμην.

19. *Sifre Num.* § 115, p. 124, and in the continuation *ibid.* there is a dispute between the School of Shammai and the School of Hillel regarding the prescribed limits of the fringes; cf. *T.B. Menaḥot* 41b, where the question is raised and answered: 'Does this not mean that there is no prescribed length for it at all? No, it has no maximum limit, but it has a minimum limit.'

20. The recent attempts made to show that the Zealot party had a continuous existence for generations, from the days of the Hasmoneans to Massada, as, for example, by W. R. Farmer, *Maccabees, Zealots and Josephus*, New York 1956, are without foundation. The 'Zealots' are not to be regarded as a party but as a religious or political type at various periods of strife, wars, and schisms, the like of which existed in all ages. From this point of view it seems to me that even M. Hengel, in *Die Zeloten*, Leiden 1961, the most comprehensive book from the aspect of material collected, has not succeeded in proving the existence of a Zealot movement with a fixed and definite religious ideology. See *ibid.*, pp. 5, 86, and 385. Rabban Joḥanan b. Zakkai was certainly not less 'theocratic' than the Zealots. S. G. F. Brandon, *Jesus and the Zealots*, Manchester 1967, bases himself on Hengel. He tries hard to demonstrate a close relationship between Jesus and Zealots like Judah the Galilean and his sons. The disciples of Jesus are all allegedly Zealots, and not merely Simeon ὁ Καναναῖος (Matthew x 4; it appears to me that the explanation קנאי–קנאן — see Strack-Billerbeck, I, p. 537 — which is based on the parallel Luke vi 9, ζηλωτής, is erroneous and that קנאי means 'a man of Kanah [Qānā]'; on this locality in the Lower Galilee see *Sefer ha-Yishuv*, p. 163), but even Judas Iscariot is portrayed as a סיקריון ['terrorist'] (Brandon, *op. cit.*, p. 204, n. 1, and p. 339). ליסטים ['bandits'], wherever mentioned, becomes a title of honour, and he is regarded as a freedom fighter (see *ibid.* p. 41, 55, 78). The works I have mentioned and their like (to a great extent Brandon builds on the acute but ungrounded theories of R. Eisler, ΙΗΣΟΥΣ ΒΑΣΙΛΕΥΣΟΥ ΒΑΣΙΛΕΥΣΑΣ,, Heidelberg, I–II, 1929–1930) portray the Zealots in the way other scholars have depicted the Essenes, the common denominator being that the conjectures are sheer flights of fantasy without any relationship to historical reality.

21. See Y. Yadin, 'Massada', *Israel Exploration Journal*, xxix, 1965, pp. 118–120.

22. *Wars* ii, 20, 4. See Joseph Klausner, *Historya shel ha-Bayit ha-Sheni*, v, pp. 324 ff, and especially C. Roth, *The Historical Background to the Dead Sea Scrolls*, Oxford 1958, who wished to identify the sect of the scrolls with the Zealots. On the debate aroused by these views in the literature dealing with the scrolls, see Hengel, *op. cit.*, p. 3. n. 3. The discovery of the sectarian scroll serves only to prove what was stated in the text.

23. Josephus, *Life*, 190–192; M. Stern, 'Ha-Manhigût bi-Qĕvûṣôt Lôḥămê ha-Ḥērût bĕ-sôf yĕmê ha-Bayit ha-Shēnī' [The Leadership in the Groups of

Freedom Fighters at the Close of the Second Temple Period], in the volume *Hā-'Ishiyyut wĕ-Dorah* [The Personality and his Generation] 1964, pp. 70–78.

24. *T.B. Gittin* 56a.
25. *Wars* iv, 4, 1; on Eleazar b. Hananiah see *ibid.*, ii, 17, 2. The opposition to the offering of sacrifices in honour of the emperors of Rome is explicitly mentioned in *Aggadot Shir ha-Shirim*, ed. Schechter, p. 96 (*Shir-ha-Shirim Zuṭa*, ed. Buber, p. 41). G. Alon dealt with this in his article 'Nesi'uto shel Rabban Joḥanan b. Zakkai', *Klausner Jubilee Volume*, 1933, p. 165, n. 55 (=*Meḥqarim be-Toledot Yisra'el*, I, 1957, p. 266, n. 63; see also *ibid.*, p. 44), and he observes with regard to ארחומי 'that it signifies Rome, for in Syriac it is written ܪܗܘܡܝ; *Rehumi*....'
26. *T.P. Shabbat* i, p. 3c, and *ibid.* p. 3d we read: 'The eighteen (decrees) even a greater (Bet Din) cannot abrogate, because they were ready to give their lives for them'; see *T.B. ibid.*, 17a.
27. *Wars* ii, 20, 4. See *Mekhilta de-R. Ishmael*, p. 229, where a Halakha is cited in his name according to the view of the School of Shammai; see above, p. 340.
28. *Aggadat Shir ha-Shirim*, *loc. cit.*, n. 33. For its meaning see S. Lieberman, *Greek in Jewish Palestine*, p. 179.
29. *Wars* iv, 5, 2.
30. *Sifre Zuṭa*, ed. J. N. Epstein, *Tarbiz* 1, 1930, p. 70; see *ibid.* Epstein's Introduction, p. 52.
31. *Tosefta Shabbat* i, 17; *T.P. ibid.* i, 4, p. 3c; *T.B. ibid.* 17a.
32. *M. 'Avot* iii, 2, and so, too, in the Kaufmann MS.; but the Cambridge MS. and the printed editions read בלעו. See *Magen 'Avot* 40b, which refers to *T.B. 'Avoda Zara* 4a. Also in the Spanish MS., ed. Abramson, the reading is בלענו; see the notes *ibid.*, p. 138.
33. See *Midrash Tannaim*, ed. Hoffmann, pp. 175–176.
34. See my article 'Class-Status and Leadership etc.', *Proceedings of the Israel Academy of Sciences and Humanities*, p. 54, and *ibid.* n. 36.
35. *Tosefta Para* iii, 8; *T.B. Bava Batra* 115b; *T.B. Menaḥot* 65a.
36. *Midrash Tannaim*, ed. D. Hoffmann, p. 58.
37. See Zechariah Frankel, *Darkhe ha-Mishna*[2], p. 72, the addendum. Likewise the statement of G. Alon, *Meḥqarim be-Toledot Yisrael*, I, p. 45, that R. Joḥanan b. Zakkai 'demanded unqualified subjection to the Romans' applies only to the final stage of the account.
38. *Tosefta Soṭa* xiv, 1, p. 320.
39. *Mekhilta de-R. Ishmael*, Massekhta de-Ba-ḥodesh, xi, p. 244.
40. *T.B. Giṭṭin* 56a. *Siqra* is σικάριος, and Abba was one of their leaders; S. J. Rapoport already conjectured this in *'Erekh Millin*, Prague 1852, pp. 1 ff. The charge Rabban Joḥanan levelled against him 'How long will you go on acting thus, so that you kill the people with famine?' fits the story related in the Mishna (*Makhshirin* i, 6): 'It once happened that the men of Jerusalem hid their fig-cakes in water on account of the סיקרין *sicarii* ['robbers'] (this

is also the reading in the Kaufmann MS., while in other passages of the Mishna, like *M. Giṭṭin* v, 6, *et al.*, סיקריקון are mentioned; for the meaning of this word see A. Gulak, 'Siqriqon', *Tarbiz*, V, 1934, pp. 23–27). Possibly ראש הבריונים ['Chief of the outlaws'] is only a gloss on 'Abba Siqra'. The etymology of בריון has not been properly elucidated. The various theories have been collected by Hengel, *op. cit.*, p. 55. It may merely be the diminutive of בריה ['creature'] in a derogatory sense (like ἀνδρίον from ἀνήρ, or ἀνθρωπισκος [see Liddel & Scott, p. 128 and p. 141]), הני בריוני ['these biryonim'] substituting for בריות אלו ['these creatures'].

41. See my article 'Class-Status and Leadership' etc., p. 49, n. 25, and *ibid.* p. 55.
42. *'Avot de-R. Nathan*, Version II, vii, 11a; see *Mekhilta*, Ba-ḥodesh, i, p. 203; see my article 'Megammot Datiyyot we-Ḥevratiyyot be-Torat ha-Ṣedaqa shel Ḥazal', *Zion*, XVI, 1951, p. 6.
43. *M. Rosh Ha-shana* iv, 4: see *T.B.*, *ibid.*, 29b.
44. *Tosefta 'Eduyot* i, 1.
45. *T.B. Yevamot* 16a; see my article 'Class-Status and Leadership', p. 57–58,
46. *M. 'Eduyot* v, 6.
47. In dating the incident as early as the days of Hillel and Shammai (see Z. Frankel, p. 57) the scholars concerned have not given attention to this expression; most recently S. B. Hoenig, 'New Light on Akabiah b. Mahalalel', *Studies and Essays in honour of Abraham A. Neuman*, 1962, pp. 291–298 (all that is stated there about the Divine epithet *Maqom* is unfounded; see above, pp. 66 ff), collected the views of his predecessors, and dated the episode earlier still to the time of Menaḥem's departure before the appointment of Shammai. But it seems to me that all who dealt with this subject did not pay attention to the style of the Mishna.
48. *M. 'Eduyot* vii, 7.
49. *T.B. Yevamot* 9a.
50. Its abolition is expressly mentioned in *Cod. Theod.*, 16, 8, 21. On the legal status of the Patriarchate in the Roman Empire see I. Juster, *Les Juifs dans l'empire Romain*, I, pp. 385–408; cf. G. Alon, *Toledot ha-Yehudim be-'Ereṣ Yisra'el bi-Tequfat ha-Mishna we-ha-Talmud*, II, p. 125.
51. Juster, *op. cit.*, pp. 381 ff; G. Alon, *op. cit.*, I, pp. 146–147.
52. See B. Dinaburg, 'Ha-Resqript shel Dioqlitianus li-Yehuda mi-Shenat 293 [Dioclitian's Rescript to Judea of the year 293]', *Sefer Zikkaron le-A. Gulak u-le-S. Klein* [Memorial Volume to A. Gulak and to S. Klein], 1942, pp. 82–91; and cf. H. Albeck, 'Semikha u-Minuy Bet Din [Ordination and the Appointment of the Bet Din], *Zion*, VIII, pp. 85–93.
53. R. Joḥanan b. Nuri, who was one of the poor Sages and sustained himself with gleanings (*T.P. Pe'a* viii, 1, p. 20d) relates: 'Akiba was punished by me more than four or five times in front of Rabban Gamaliel' (*Sifra*, Qedoshim, iv, 89b). Obviously this incident occurred after the appointment of R. Joḥanan b. Nuri (*Sifre Deut.* § 16), and is undoubtedly connected with the freedom

R. Akiba claimed for himself to decide against the view of the Patriarch; see *Tosefta Demai* v, 24, 'Who gave you permission?' 'Why do you involve yourself in a dispute?' (*Tosefta Berakhot* iv, 15; *Tosefta Beṣa* ii, 12); cf. also *T.P. Rosh Hashana* i, 6, p. 57b.

54. *T.P. Berakhot* iv, 1, p. 7c–d; *T.P. Ta'aniyyot* iv, 1, p. 67d; *T.B. ibid.* 27b–28a; see *M. Rosh Hashana* ii, 8–9; *T.B. Bekhorot* 31a.
55. *T.B. Sanhedrin* 32b; in *Tosefta Yadayim* ii, 16: 'R. Jose b. Durmasqit said: I was with the former Elders when they came from Jabneh to Lydda, and I came and found R. Eliezer sitting in the bakers' shop in Lydda...'
56. *Sifre Num.* § 52, pp. 53–54.
57. *Sifre Zuṭa*, pp. 252–253; *T.P. Mo'ed Qaṭan* iii, 1, p. 81c; *T.B. Bava Meṣia'* 59b; *T.B. Sanhedrin* 68a.
58. See Y. D. Gilat, *Mishnato shel R. Eliezer b. Hyrcanus* [The Teaching of R. Eliezer b. Hyrcanus], Tel-Aviv 1968, pp. 322 ff.
59. *Sifre Deut.* § 343; see *T.P. Bikkurim* iii, 3, p. 65c; *T.P. Nedarim*, end of xi, 42b; cf. my article 'Class-Status and Leadership' etc., pp. 62–63, and *ibid.*, pp. 66–67.
60. *T.B. Sanhedrin* 38a, and see G. Alon, *Toledot ha-Yehudim be-'Eres Yisra'el*, II, p. 144, and in my aforementioned article, p. 68.
61. *T.B. Ketubbot* 103b.
62. The words of the Baraita, *T.B. Horayot* 11b, 'The Exilarch in Babylonia, who rules Israel with a sceptre... the descendants of Hillel, who teach Torah to Israel in public' are applicable to the time of Rabbi, and actually they are attributed to R. Ḥiyya. See J. Neussner, *A History of the Jews in Babylonia*, Leiden 1966, II, pp. 92–125; III, 1968, pp. 41–94 and the bibliography given there; cf. my observations in *Tarbiz*, XXXXIV, pp. 156–161.
63. *T.B. Ḥullin* 7b; *T.B. Bava Batra* 8a; *T.B. Megilla* 28a; *T.B. Ḥullin* 44a, and Rashi *ad loc.*
64. See my article, 'Class-Status and Leadership' etc., p. 64, and *ibid.* n. 2.
65. *T.B. Pesaḥim* 112a, where Rashi and Rashbam gloss: 'because he is occupied with study and neglects public affairs'; see also *T.P. Pe'a* viii, 1, p, 21a: 'When they wanted to appoint R. Akiba as administrator of the community, he replied that he would consult his family... they heard the voice of one saying: Even if you are cursed, even if you are abused'; it seems that not all the heads and administrators, even if they were scholars, were prepared to accept these conditions.
66. *T.P. Bava Batra* x, 14, p. 17d.
67. *T.B. Shabbat* 32b, where the elevation of R. Judah is attributed to the favourable remarks that he made concerning the acts of the government; see above, p. 549. Possibly there is also some connection between R. Judah's good standing with the Roman authorities and his position at the Patriarch's court. This relationship, however, did not prevent R. Judah from saying — as R. Joḥanan transmitted in his name — 'Rome is destined to fall into the hands of the Persians' (*T.B. Yoma* 10a).

68. *T.P. Sheqalim* iii, 2, p. 47c; *ibid.* viii, 1, p. 51b; *T.B. Menaḥot* 104a.
69. *T.B. Horayot* 13a–14a.
70. *T.P. Sanhedrin* i, 1, p. 18a, 'Blessed be the All-Merciful that I am not learned enough to judge'. It is very possible that this blessing implies acceptance of the existing position— that he need not be a judge in view of his experiences. This is attested by his criticism of the judges; see *Gen. Rabba* xxvi, 2, p. 247. At all events, it is related that in his youth, when Rabbi Akiba came to appoint his disciples and said ' "R. Me'ir shall sit first", R. Simeon turned pale' — *T.P. Sanhedrin* i, 2, p. 19a. The view of A. Büchler, *The Political and Social Leaders of the Jewish Community of Sepphoris*, 1909, p. 24, n. 1, that the Romans compelled the Jews to give judgement according to their laws, and R. Simeon b. Yoḥai said that he did not know their laws is unacceptable; see G. Alon, *Toledot ha-Yehudim be-'Ereṣ Yisra'el*, II, p. 79.
71. *Sifre Deut.* § 13, p. 22.
72. On Rabbi see above, n. 62, and on the antagonism between Resh Laqish and R. Judah Nesi'a see *T.P. Sanhedrin* ii, 1, p. 19d, and *ibid. Horayot* iii, 2, p. 47a. Cf. *T.B. Sanhedrin* 90b, where it appears that the struggle was bound up with the question of appointing judges; cf. *T.P. Bikkurim* iii, 3, p. 65d. R. Joḥanan, who mediated between the Patriarch and Resh Laqish, is also the author of the dictum 'A generation must have one leader, not two' — *T.B. Sanhedrin* 8a. See G. Alon "Illēn de-mitmannîn be-khesef' [Those who are appointed for money]', *Meḥqarim*, II, pp. 18 ff.
73. *Tosefta Sanhedrin* vii, 8; see *T.B. Horayot* 13b: 'R. Joḥanan said: This Mishna was taught in the days of Rabban Simeon b. Gamaliel.' Cf. A. Büchler, 'Mĕfassēaʿ ʿal rā'shê ʿAm Qadosh [He that strides over the heads of the holy People]', *Dissertationes in honorem Dr. Edwardi Mahler*, Budapestini 1937, pp. 379–405; G. Alon, 'Bĕnêhem shel Ḥăkhāmîm [The Sons of the Sages]' *Meḥqarim be-Toledot Yisra'el*, II, pp. 58 ff, and see my article 'Class-Status and Leadership', p. 47, n. 49.
74. *T.B. Giṭṭin* 60a; see Rashi *ad loc.*, s.v. *Hā-Rĕ'ûyîn li-mānôt.*
75. From the statement of R. Joshua b. Levi (*T.P. Horayot* iii, 7, p. 48a; see *Śeride Yerushalmi*, p. 286, and S. Lieberman, 'Yerushalmi Horayot', *Sefer ha-Yovel le-R. Ḥanoch Albeck*, 1963, p. 299) 'In the case of a head and an elder, the head takes precedence of an elder who is not a head' it appears, on the one hand, that there is a distinction between 'heads' that are the leaders of the congregation, and 'elders', who are 'Sages'. But on the other hand, there is also the possibility of combining them — 'An elder who is a head'; see against this view, G. Alon, *Meḥqarim be-Toledot Yisra'el*, II, p. 53, n. 145. Cf. also *T.P. Berakhot*, v, 1, p. 8a, 'R. Jeremiah said: He who occupies himself with communal needs is as one who occupies himself with the study of the Torah'; cf. L. Ginzberg, *Perushim we-Ḥiddushim bi-Yerushalmi*, IV, pp. 64 ff; also S. Sirillo, Commentary on Berakhot, *loc. cit.*, refers to Maimonides, 'Hilkhot Tefilla', vi, 8. See also *T.P. Pe'a* viii, 7, p. 21a: 'When R. Ḥaggai appointed administrators he emphasized to them a Torah teaching'

namely that every position of authority stemmed from the Torah, as it is said "By me kings reign". Cf. *T.B. Giṭṭin* 62a.

76. *Deut. Rabba* v, 8. Z. W. Einhorn emended the text here according to *Esther Rabba*, Petiḥa 9, but the Oxford MS. (ed. Lieberman, p. 98) has the same reading as the current text. It is clear that R. Judah b. R. Simon formed a Petiḥa out of the homilies of R. Joḥanan and Resh Laqish (his dictum is missing in *Deut. Rabba*) with regard to Ahasuerus, whereas their homiletical interpretations of the verse 'I will set a king over me' referred originally to Jewish leaders.

77. *T.B. Shabbat* 114a, see *Diqduqe Soferim, ad loc.*, p. 254. R. Joḥanan's dictum follows upon *M. Miqwa'ot* ix, 6; cf. H. Albeck, *Seder Ṭohorot*, Hashlamot we-Tosafot, p. 581. It appears that R. Joḥanan made use of the opportunity provided by Resh Laqish's question regarding a grease stain on a saddle in order to give him his opinion about scholars — builders (on the identification of *ʿAm ha-'Areṣ* and *bôr* (uncultivated person) and the antithesis *bôr-ḥakham* ['Sage'], see above, p. 953, n. 71), which was opposed to the attitude of Resh Laqish regarding the acceptance of appointments by scholars — see *T.B. Sanhedrin* 103b: 'R. Simeon b. Laqish said... When a man becomes a head [rō'sh] below [on earth], he becomes [*rāshāʿ*] above [in the sight of Heaven]' (This is the version of the MSS. and the Early Authorities [Ri'shonim]; see *Diqduqe Soferim, ad loc.*, p. 315, and cf. *Baʿal ha-Ṭurim* to Numbers i 7: 'A man does not become an officer [*shôṭēr*] unless he becomes wicked above'); it was also intended as a reaction to his harsh remarks about the judges who were installed by the Patriarch; see above, n. 72. Possibly there was already an allusion in Resh Laqish's question to R. Josiah's dictum (*T.P. Bikhurim, loc. cit.*, n. 72) 'And the *Ṭallit* which is on him like the saddle of an ass.' But Resh Laqish also knew that 'Sometimes the annulment of the Torah is its foundation,' see above p. 819 n. 43.

78. See *T.B. Shabbat* 114a. In regard to 'Whoever (is able to answer) a *halakhic* question on any subject [בכל מקום, literally 'in any place'], see the commentary of R. Ḥananel to *T.B. Taʿanit* 10b, who reads בכלום מקום, i.e. in one place of the Talmud, even in a tractate studied by scholars who wish to expound; see *ʿArugat ha-Bośem*, I, p. 15, and *ibid.*, n. 6. But 'R. Levi said in the name of R. Simeon b. Laqish... a scholar must be well versed [literally 'wise and industrious'] in the twenty-four books of the Bible' — *Tanḥuma*, Tiśśa', 16; *Exod. Rabba* xli, 5.

79. See the dictum of Resh Laqish, cited above, n. 77. The saying of R. Simeon b. Jehozadak 'No administrator is appointed over a community unless he has a basket of reptiles hanging on his back' (*T.B. Yoma* 22b) was not encouraging, and in truth R. Zeʿira did not wish to accept an appointment until he heard that 'Also a Sage who is appointed is forgiven all his iniquities' (*T.P. Bikkurim* iii, 3, p. 65c); *T.P. Sheqalim* v, 2, p. 48d: 'When R. Jose came to Kufra, he wished to appoint administrators over them, but they would not accept the responsibilities of office (ולא קבלון עליהון — this is

the reading of the Oxford MS., ed. Abraham Sofer, New York 1954, p. 54). He began and said: ...if he, who was only appointed over the wicks [aliter: 'knouts'] was (eventually) privileged to be appointed with the great men of the generation, how much more so will you, who are appointed over vital needs, (be thus privileged)!' See *T.P. Pe'a* viii, 6, p. 21a.

80. *Exod. Rabba* vi, 5; *Tanḥuma*, Wa-'ēra', 5, where the reading is preferable to that of *Eccles. Rabba* vii, 10; see *Mattenot Kehuna* and Z. W. Einhorn (Maharzaw) *ad loc.* R. Joshua b. Levi testified regarding himself (*Eccles. Rabba*, *ibid.*, and the parallels): 'I learned eighty Halakhot from Judah b. Pedaya concerning a grave that has been ploughed over, but because I was occupied with public affairs I forgot them.'

81. See my article "Asqezis wi-yesurim be-Torat Ḥazal', *Sefer ha-Yovel le-Yiṣḥaq Baer*, pp. 65–66; cf. Moses Baer, 'Talmud Torah we-Derekh 'Ereṣ [Torah Study and Wordly Occupation]', *Bar Ilan Annual*, II, 1964, pp. 145 ff. As regards *T.P. Sanhedrin* ii, 6, p. 20c, see *Tosefta, ibid.*, iv, 8, p. 422; הדיוט ['commoner'] in *T.P.* stands in antithesis to מלך ['King']. just like שאר כל העם ['the rest of the people'] in the *Tosefta*. Possibly the entire homily belongs to R. Eleazar of Modi'im; but see *T.B. ibid.*, 22a. See also A. Marmorstein, 'Ma'alat Talmud Torah [The Status of Torah Study]', *Dr. B. M. Lewin Jubilee Volume*, 1940, pp. 160 ff.

82. R. Judah did not wish to accept a robe that was sent to him by Rabban Simeon b. Gamaliel, and he said to the messenger 'I do not wish to benefit from this world' — *T.B. Nedarim* 48b–50a; see also his dictum *T.B. Pesaḥim* 114a and the story about him and R. Jose in *T.B. Yoma* 83b in the amended version of *Diqduqe Soferim, ad loc.*, p. 277.

83. *'Avot de-R. Nathan*, Version I, xli, p. 130. Schechter emended the text according to one MS: 'The Holy One, blessed be He, has acted rightly towards you, for you left the study of the Torah and occupied yourself with worthless matters.' This is clearly an apologetic emendation, since it does not illustrate the dictum 'Toil in the study of the Torah, and do not occupy yourself with worthless things.'

84. *M. Pe'a* i, 1.

85. *T.B. Nedarim* 40a. See the commentary of the Rosh, s.v. *She-kibbedu*: 'In front of the sick person, at the injunction of R. Akiba, for one that comes to visit a sick person looks after all his needs, (thereby) sustaining him'; Me'iri, *Bet ha-Beḥira* to *Nedarim*, ed. A. Lis, Jerusalem 1965: 'And R. Akiba entered and tried to sweep and sprinkle the house before him... and some explain that they swept and sprinkled the house in honour of R. Akiba and thus benefited the sick person.' The different explanations reflect different concepts. Marmorstein, *op. cit.*, sought to discern a development in R. Akiba's approach, but in the story of R. Akiba's son in *Tractate Semaḥot* viii, 13, it is stated that 'he inquired after him through messengers'; thus he was concerned about the sick boy. R. Eliezer's question (*'Avot de-R. Nathan* xxv) 'Why did you not come and wait on me?' does not refer to visiting

the sick, but to the fact that his disciples forsook him on account of the ban.

86. *T.B. Berakhot* 31a (see *Diqduqe Soferim, ad loc.*, p. 159); it is related in the Talmud, ibid., that Resh Laqish never indulged in laughter from the time that he heard of R. Simeon b. Yoḥai's dictum from R. Joḥanan. Cf. *T.B. Nidda* 23a: 'To such an extent did R. Jeremiah seek to make R. Zera laugh, but he did not laugh'; but see *T.B. Berakhot* 30b: 'R. Jeremiah was sitting before R. Zera; he saw that he was very cheerful'; and cf. *T.B. Shabbat* 77b, where it is related that 'R. Zera found Rav Judah in a cheerful mood' and he saw that the moment was opportune for asking him questions. And Rabba 'Before commencing (his lecture) made a jocular remark and the Rabbis were amused; subsequently he sat in awe and began the discourse' (*T.B. Shabbat* 30b, where the parallels are given), in accordance with the view of Rav 'Where there is joy let there also be trembling' (*T.B. Berakhot* 30b; the current texts read: 'R. Ada bar Mattena said in the name of Rabba'; but see *Diqduqe Soferim, ad loc.*, p. 158). When two men, whom Elijah the prophet attested to be assured of the world to come, were asked what their occupation was, they replied: 'We are jesters; we cheer up those who are sorrowful (*T.B. Ta'anit* 22a). The numerous stories and proverbs in the Talmuds and Midrashim attest, more than direct declarations, the attitude of the Sages to laughter. Although most of them are not intended to amuse, yet by their closeness to life, which nullifies any gap between form and content, they made their listeners laugh, just as they make us laugh. Of course. the Sages distinguished between different kinds of laughter and said that a man's character 'can be discerned even by his laughter' (*T.B. 'Eruvin* 65b). On the laughter of the Holy One, blessed be He, see *T.B. 'Avoda Zara* 3b.

87. *T.B. Nedarim* 66b; in the Munich MS. the reading is: 'rather than that Simeon should depart from his honour [מכבודו instead of ממקומו]'. See the commentary of the Rosh [R. Asher b. Jeḥiel] *ad loc.*: 'rather than that Simeon should depart from his position to slight the honour of his Torah learning.' Cf. Me'iri, *Bet ha-Beḥira, ad loc.*, p. 246: 'rather than that Simeon should depart from his honour.' The editor rightly notes that R. Joel Sirkes (*Bayit Ḥadash, Baḥ*) emended the text according to the commentary attributed to Rashi.

88. *T.P. Soṭa* i, 4, p. 16d; see *Lev. Rabba* ix, p. 191; *ibid.*, n. 1, the late sources that cite the story are listed. In *T.B. Nedarim, loc. cit.*, it is related that a certain woman spat upon the garment of R. Simeon b. Gamaliel in order to fulfil her husband's vow, but Rabban Simeon b. Gamaliel took no active part in the matter. Cf. the account of the incident that occurred in Sidon (*Pesiqta de-R. Kahana*, śôś 'āśîś, p. 327), according to which R. Simeon b. Yoḥai advised a couple who came to be divorced because no children were born to them in the course of ten years: 'Just as you were joined in matrimony with food and drink, so you must not separate without food and drink.' The central motif of this story, 'Take him to my father's house', is found in dozens of versions of the legend about 'the wise daughter of the farmer', which is current among the Germanic, Slavic, and Rumanian peoples. In

the Jewish version there is added the prayer of R. Simeon b. Yoḥai, on account of which the barren woman was vouchsafed children.

89. The homily 'Great is peace', of which both R. Me'ir and R. Judah made use, occurs as an anonymous passage of *Sifre Num.* § 42, p. 46, on the verse 'and grant thee peace', and in *Lev. Rabba, loc. cit.*, p. 104, as 'R. Ishmael taught'; see *ibid.*, n. 6. In *Sifre Zuṭa*, pp. 248–249, totally different homilies are transmitted in the name of R. Simeon: 'Beloved is peace, for had the Holy One, blessed be He, created a more beautiful attribute than peace, he would have given it to the righteous...'; another interpretation is as follows: 'R. Simeon used to say: Great is peace, for not as the way of man is the way of the King of the kings of kings, the Holy One, blessed be He....'

90. *T.B. Ketubbot* 17a; see *T.P. Ḥagiga* 1, 7, p. 76c: 'When R. Judah used to observe a deceased person or a bride being eulogized, he looked at his disciples and said: Observance takes precedence of study.' The following two stories are related in *'Avot de-R. Nathan*, Version I, iv, p. 18: 'It once happened that R. Judah b. Il'ai was sitting and teaching his disciples, and a bride passed by, whereupon he took in his hand כדי צרכו והיה משנין בה [the text is obscure and apparently corrupt; on the basis of parallel passages it might be emended to בדין (של הדס) והיה משענן בה and rendered: 'twigs (of myrtle) and waved therewith'], until the bride passed before him. On another occasion it happened that R. Judah b. Il'ai was sitting and teaching his disciples, when a bride passed before him... he said to them: My sons, stand and occupy yourselves with the bride....' As regards משנין – משענן see the notes of Schechter *ibid.*, n. 16; the Targum translates 'And all the trees of the field shall clap their hands' by ישענון בענפיהון ['wave their branches']. See S. Lieberman, 'Qalles qillusin', "Alê 'Ayin", *Minḥat Devarim le-S. Z. Schoken*, 1948–1952, p. 80. The distinction drawn between כשאין עמו כל צרכו ['when he has insufficient people with him'] and שיש עמו כל צרכו ['when he has sufficient people with him'] (*T.B. Ketubbot, loc. cit.*, and *'Avot de-R. Nathan, loc. cit.*), or, in the language of the Rabbis of Caesarea (*T.P. ibid.*), between בשיש עמו מי שיעשה ['when he has with him one that will attend to his requirements'] and אם אין מי שיעשה ['when there is no one to attend to his requirements'] is to be regarded merely as a compromise between R. Judah's view and that opposed to it. It is clear that in the stories concerning R. Judah the reference is to cases 'where there was someone to attend to the requirements.' This is also evidenced by the version found in *Tractate Semaḥot* xi, 3: 'Whenever he observed a deceased person or a bride being eulogized [שנקלסין ובאין] (in the Oxford MS. ואת המקלסין באין 'and the eulogizers coming'). See D. Zlotnik, *The Tractate Mourning*, Yale 1966, Hebrew Section, p. 33. Not all the Amoraim accepted the compromise; thus Rav Samuel bar Isaac acted in accordance with R. Judah's view, 'for he took a branch and did honour to brides, but the Rabbis criticized him' — *T.P. 'Avoda Zara* iii, 1, p. 42c. See *T.B. Ketubbot, loc. cit.*, and cf. H. Z. Reines, *Tora u-Musar* [Torah and Ethics], pp. 71 ff.

91. *T.B. Yevamot* 62b.
92. *T.B. Sanhedrin* 20a; see *T.B. Berakhot* 63b. There he speaks in praise of 'scholars who go from city to city and from country to country in order to learn Torah.'
93. See above, n. 81.
94. See *T.B. Berakhot* 32b and *T.P. ibid.*, v, 1, p. 8d; the answer pertains to R. Isaac be R. Eleazar.
95. *T.P. Berakhot* ix (*ad. fin.*), p. 14d.
96. *M. 'Avot*, i, 13; the Kaufmann MS. reads: ודי לא יְלִיף קטלה חייב, לא יעביד קטלה קטלין, ישתמש בתגא חלף ['And he who does not study deserves death; he who does not observe is slain; he who makes wordly use of the Torah perishes']. The punctuator did not point the additional words, which I have found in no other recension. Before לא יעביד and before ישתמש he has added a siglum and in the margin there is inserted ודי, i.e. this word is to be added in both places. Accordingly, Hillel uttered the whole passage and required the combination of study, practice and worldly occupation. See S. Lieberman, "'Eśer Millin' [Ten Words], *'Eshkolot*, III, 1959, pp. 82–83.
97. In the Kaufmann MS.: סופה בטילה לְגָדֵר עוון ['comes to naught in the end amounting to sin'; לגדר replaces here גוררת of current text].
98. *T.B. Megilla* 28a; *T.P. Sanhedrin* i, 1, p. 18b; *T.B. Ketubbot* 105a.
99. *T.B. 'Avoda Zara* 17b.
1. *T.P. Bava Meṣi'a* iv, 9, p. 30d; *T.B. Shabbat* 119a; *T.B. Yevamot* 65a; *T.B. Ketubbot* 17a.
2. *T.P. Shabbat* vi, 1, p. 7d.
3. *T.P. Pesaḥim* iii, 7, p. 30b; see *Ha-Yerushalmi Kiphshuṭo*, p. 425. Cf. *Eccles. Rabba* vii, 7: 'And who is a scholar? R. Abbahu said in the name of R. Joḥanan: Whoever sets aside his business on account of his study.'
3a. Possibly this position enables us to understand the right to the priestly gifts (see R. Joseph's statement *T.B. Ḥullin* 133a; also the remarks of R. Joḥanan and Rav Ḥisda *ibid.* 132b), which the Sages claimed for themselves. At any rate we hear a shepherd, who is an *'Am ha-'Areṣ* and a priest, say of his employer 'He will not pass over a scholar and give it to me' — *T.B. Bekhorot* 35b.
4. *T.B. Menaḥot* 110a. See *Sifre Deut.* § 41: ' "And to serve Him" — this refers to study of the Torah. You say this refers to study of the Torah, but perhaps it means actual (sacrificial) service! When Scripture declares "And the Lord God took the man, and put him into the garden of Eden to serve it [לעבדה usually rendered 'to till it'] and to keep it" (Gen ii 15) — but what service was there in the past, and what keeping was there to do in the past? — thus you learn: "to serve it" means study of the Torah, "and to keep it" means the observance of the precepts; and just as the service of the altar is called "service", even so is the study of the Torah called "service".' This exposition is difficult, for it is impossible to tell why 'to serve it' should connote study of the Torah and not the service of sacrifice (and thus it is actually inter-

preted in *Gen. Rabba* xvi, 5, p. 149: ' "To serve it and to keep it" refers to the sacrifices'; see *ibid.* n. 2. With regard to the precepts observed by Adam see above, p. 320). The understandable homily that follows emphasizes this difficulty: ' "And to serve Him" — this means prayer... but perhaps it means none other than service? (Hence Scripture says) "With all your heart". Is there then service in the heart?... just as the altar-service is called "service", even so is prayer called "service".'

5. *'Avot de-R. Nathan* iv, p. 18; see the notes *ibid.*
6. *Tanḥuma*, Aḥare, 10; ed. Buber, *ibid.*, xvi, 35a.
7. See my article 'Megammot Datiyyot we-Ḥevratiyyot be-Torat ha-Ṣedaqa shel Ḥazal', *Zion*, XVI, 1951, pp. 6 ff.
8. See my article 'Asqezis we-Yissurim', *Sefer ha-Yovel le-Yitzḥak Baer*, pp. 54–56.
9. *T.B. Megilla* 16b, according to the recension of the MSS. See *Diqduqe Soferim, ad loc.*, p. 91, notes פ – ע: 'Rav Joseph taught... and R. Joseph said'; cf. *Midrash Ezra* of R. Samuel Masnut, published by Isaac S. Lange and S. Schwartz, 1968, p. 148.
10. *T.B. Soṭa* 21a; in the continuation of the discussion Rav Joseph said, with reference to 'Another explanation...', 'R. Menaḥem b. R. Jose expounded this verse as though it were taught at Sinai...'. See the note in the margin of the Talmud; the reading of the Munich MS. agrees with the recension I have cited in the text.
11. *Ibid.* in the printed editions: 'Rav and some say Rav Samuel bar Marta'; according to the Munich MS. 'Rav Isaac bar Samuel bar Marta in the name of Rav Giddal'. See also additional vv.ll, in *Diqduqe Soferim, ad loc.*, ק. Against this dictum see above, p. 538.
12. *T.B. Rosh Hashana* 18a; the printed editions read 'Rabba and Abbaye', but in the MSS. and the Early Authorities we find 'Abbaye and Rava'; see *Diqduqe Soferim, ad loc.*, p. 38, n. ל. So, too, in *T.B. Yevamot* 105a; but Isaak Halevy, *Dorot Harischonim*, II, p. 219, followed by A. Hyman, *Seder Tanna'im wa-'Amora'im*, p. 1063, adopts the reading of the printed editions that Rabba lived sixty years. Both scholars failed to consult *Diqduqe Soferim*. Cf. *T.P. Rosh ha-Shana* ii, 5, p. 58a (= *T.P. Sanhedrin* i, 5, p. 18c), where Rav Kahana states 'I am descended from the House of Eli... it is not expiated with sacrifice nor offering, but it is atoned for by prayer.'
13. *T.B. Mo'ed Qaṭan* 28a.
14. *T.B. Shabbat* 11a; see *T.P. ibid.*, i, 2, p. 3a, where R. Joḥanan declares in the name of R. Simeon b. Yoḥai: 'Such as we, who occupy ourselves with the study of the Torah, do not interrupt our studies even for the reading of the *Shema'*. Of himself, however, R. Joḥanan said: Such as we, who do not occupy ourselves with the study of the Torah, interrupt our studies even for the Prayer [Eighteen Benedictions]... R. Joḥanan, giving his own opinion said: Would that we prayed all day....' The words 'who do not occupy ourselves with the study of the Torah', coming from R. Joḥanan, are difficult,

and as S. Lieberman has pointed out, *Ha-Yerushalmi Kiphshuṭo*, p. 25, the entire passage is missing in the Leiden MS., and is merely added in the margin; in the novellae of Me'iri to *T.B. Berakhot* 10b we find only: 'R. Joḥanan said of himself: Such as we interrupt our studies even for the Prayer.'

15. See *T.B. Berakhot* 56a; *T.B. Nedarim* 55a; *T.B. Bava Meṣi'a* 73a; *T.B. Bava Batra* 149b; 153a. See my article 'Hilkhot 'Avadim ke-Maqor le-Historiya ha-Ḥevratit' etc., *Zion*, XXV, 1960, p. 186. Cf. *T.B. Ta'anit* 24b; *T.B. Bava Batra* 10b; *T.B. 'Avoda Zara* 65a; *T.B. Zevaḥim* 116b.
16. For R. Joḥanan's devotion to the study of the Torah while foregoing ephemeral life, see *Lev. Rabba* xxxi, p. 688, and cf. *T.B. Ta'anit* 21a.
17. *T.B. Shabbat* 10a; see *ibid.* also the story about R. Zera and R. Jeremiah. Cf. *T.B. Berakhot* 21b: 'When Rav Dimi came back from Eretz-Israel he said that R. Judah and R. Simeon, the disciples of R. Joḥanan, said: We do not interrupt our study of the Torah (for any response), except for "May His great name be blessed", for which, even if he is studying the Work of the Chariot he interrupts his study, but the Halakha is not in accordance with their view.' See *Diqduqe Soferim, ad loc.*, p. 102, notes ס–ע, where the author observes that we do not know who these disciples of R. Joḥanan were.
18. The homily of R. Simlai, *T.B. Soṭa* 14a. See *Ruth Rabba* ii, 8: 'R. Ze'ira said: This scroll contains no (laws of) defilement or purity, no prohibitions or laws of permission. Why then was it written? To teach you how great is the reward awaiting those who perform acts of benevolence.'
19. *T.B. Soṭa* 4b; in *T.B. Horayot* 13a the homily 'More precious... than the High Priest...' is in the name of R. Aḥa b. R. Ḥanina; Rava transmits it in his own name — see *T.B. 'Eruvin* 64a.
20. *T.B. Berakhot* 17a; I have cited the text according to the version of the Munich MS. and the Early Authorities. See *Diqduqe Soferim, ad loc.*, p. 79.
21. *T.B. Berakhot ibid.*; in *T.B. Yoma* 87b this prayer is cited as the confession of Rav Hamnuna. The Gemara observes: 'This is the regular confession of Rava, and of Rav Hamnuna Zuṭa (the Younger) on the Day of Atonement.' See *Diqduqe Soferim, ad loc.*, p. 309.
22. *T.B. Berakhot* 5a. See *T.B. Ketubbot* 62b, where Rava says that the Rabbis who rely on the opinion of Rav Ada bar Ahava and leave home [without their wives' permission] to study Torah for two or three years 'do so at the risk of their lives' ('for they are punished and die' — Rashi). Note the story there about Rav Reḥumi, who studied at the school of Rava and was accustomed to return home on the eve of the Day of Atonement, but once he was absorbed in his subject [and forgot to go home], and his wife's tears brought about his death. The entire discourse there is directed against disciples who neglect their wives and families; cf. also *T.B. Giṭṭin* 6b with regard to the letter sent by R. Abiathar to Rav Judah, and Rashi s.v. *Wa-yittĕnû.*
23. The homily is ascribed to Rava as an explanation of the fact that in the

days of Rav Judah, when they occupied themselves solely with the study of the Order of *Neziqin*, 'Rav Judah had only to take off his shoes and rain fell', whereas we teach a great deal (more)... yet no heed is taken of us...' — *T.B. Sanhedrin* 106b; see *Diqduqe Soferim*, p. 333. In *T.B. Ta'anit* 24b (ed. Malter, p. 183) a different explanation is attributed to Rava: 'What, however, can the leaders of a generation do, when their generation does not appear good (in the sight of Heaven)?', an explanation that is reminiscent of the dictum of R. Ḥanina in *T.P. Ta'anit* iii, 4, p. 66c: 'It was not R. Joshua b. Levi who brings down rain for the Daromeans nor R. Ḥanina who withholds rain from the Sepphorites; only the Daromeans [Scholars of the South] have responsive hearts, and when they hear the words of the Torah they humble themselves; whereas the Sepphorites have irresponsive hearts, and when they hear the words of the Torah they remain abdurate.' See *T.B., ibid.*, the stories about Rav Naḥman and Rav Pappa, whose prayers were accepted only after 'they felt humbled'. On the other hand, it is related there that Rava was helped by the dream of Rav Eleazar of Hagrunya to determine the propitious time (for supplication), and in another story he became a kind of Ḥoni ha-Me'aggel 'who was persistent towards Heaven' and only the fact that his father appeared to him in a dream saved him from punishment. (Cf. *T.P., ibid.*, concerning R. Ḥanina: 'Rain fell immediately and he vowed never to do this again.') See *T.B. Berakhot* 20a, and above, p. 103. The common denomination of all these explanations is the abolition of the connection between eminence in the knowledge of the Torah and the effectiveness of prayer.

24. *T.B. Yevamot* 109b; see Rashi s.v. 'He who rivets himself to Halakhic matters, saying: I shall study, but not observe' etc.; see *Exod. Rabba* xxxiv, 2; *Deut. Rabba* vii, 4; xi, 6. However, we find in *Eccles. Zuṭa* ii, 13, ed. Buber, p. 94: 'It is taught in the name of R. Me'ir that even as light transcends darkness, so study of the Torah transcends (the observance of) the words of the precepts [דברי מצות].' But in the photostat of the Parma MS. 541, according to which Buber published the text, the reading מצות ['precepts'] is not at all certain and it is also possible to read מינות ['heresy'] as in *Eccles. Rabba* ii, 13 (this is the reading in the Pesaro ed., but in the new editions the text has לדברי הבלים ['words of vanity']). Notwithstanding all the hyperbolical statements that we found in the homilies in praise of Torah in comparison with the precepts, it is difficult to assume that R. Me'ir likened the precepts to 'darkness' and to 'folly'. It appears that his homily was directed against the sectarians [Minim] who regarded their wisdom (gnosis) as light [see now S. Lieberman, *Sifre Zuṭa*, New York 1968, p. 122, n. 159], and cf. above, p. 196, and p. 189.
25. See above, p. 613.
26. *T.P. Shevi'it* ix, 1, p. 38d; *T.B. Shabbat* 34b–35a. But this narrative also concludes with the statement that he set his gaze on an elder and he became a heap of stones.

27. *T.B. Me'ila* 17a–b; there, too, it is related that he punished R. Eleazar b. R. Jose; see Rashi s.v. *'Iqqem*.
28. *Mekhilta de-R. Ishmael*, Mishpaṭim, i, pp. 246–247. See also *ibid.*, Massekhta da-Amalek, Jethro, ii, p. 196: 'Whoever renders a true judgement is accounted by Scripture as though he had become a partner of the Holy One, blessed be He, in the work of creation'; undoubtedly dicta of this kind were intended for the encouragement of the judges.
29. *T.P. Sanhedrin* i, 1, p. 18b; *T.B., ibid.*, 6b. On the view of R. Simeon b. Gamaliel, *T.P., ibid.*, and *T.B., ibid.*, 5b, see Tosafot, *ad loc.*, s.v. *Yāfe*. In *Sifre Deut.* § 17 we read: 'Rabban Simeon b. Gamaliel said If one elevates an inferior person to a great man's place and reduces a great man to an inferior man's place — this constitutes arbitration. The Sages declare: He who arbitrates actually contemns....' Cf. also *ibid.* § 144. The exposition of R. Eliezer b. Jose and R. Me'ir in *T.P.* and *T.B., ibid.*, imply that they agreed to arbitration; see *M. Sanhedrin* iii, 1. Cf. *T.P. Me'ed Qaṭan* iii, 1, p. 82a: 'And documents regarding the choice of arbiters, R. Joḥanan said: קומפרומיסון [agreement between parties to submit to arbitration; Latin *compromissum*]. See B. Cohen, *Jewish and Roman Law*, II, pp. 651 ff; cf. *ibid.*, p. 708.
30. See *T.B. Sanhedrin* 8a, the statement of Rav Kahana, and that of Rav Huna, *ibid.*, 7b: 'Fetch me the instruments of my office', etc. Prior to this it is related that 'When a case was submitted to him, he used to gather and take with him ten Rabbis from the schoolhouse. He said: So that a chip from the beam might reach each one.' *Ibid.* 'Rav used to come to court' etc. Cf. Rav's remarks about a disciple who has not attained the qualification to decide questions of law, yet gives such decisions, and about a disciple who has attained the qualification to decide questions of law, but does not do so — *T.B. Soṭa* 22a; *T.B. 'Avoda Zara* 19b.
31. *T.B. Sanhedrin* 7a.
32. *Tanḥuma*, Mishpaṭim, 2; see *Exod. Rabba* xxx, 13.
33. *T.B. Sanhedrin* 7b: 'When Rav Dimi came back (from Eretz-Israel) he said: Rav Naḥman bar Kohen expounded.' This Amora transmits in the name of R. Assi in *T.B. Ḥullin* 5b (see *Diqduqe Soferim, ad loc.*, 3b, n. 30).
34. *T.B. Sanhedrin* 8a, printed edition, reads 'R. Eleazar said in the name of R. Simlai', but this is wanting in the MSS., see *Diqduqe Soferim, ad loc.*, p. 13, n. *Bêt*. See R. Simlai's statement about Sages that 'put their words to shame before the ignorant people' — *Deut. Rabba* ii, 19; *Ruth Rabba* i, 2; *Eccles. Rabba* ix, 16.
35. *Tanḥuma, loc. cit.*; *Yalquṭ Makhiri* to Proverbs, ed. Grünhut, p. 82, reads 'It once happened that R. Ammi.' But this story does not fit what is known of R. Ammi's status. See *T.B. Giṭṭin* 44a 'R. Ammi sent back the answer: From me, Ammi bar Nathan, goes forth the rule to all Israel.' See Z. Frankel, *Mevo' ha-Yerushalmi*, p. 63. However, in *T.B. Sanhedrin* 17b both R. Ammi and R. Assi are called 'the judges of Eretz-Israel', and both were *Kohanim* [priests] (*T.B. Giṭṭin* 59b). Possibly Rav Naḥman bar Kohen was the son of

R. Assi's sister, and he delivered his homily in order to comfort his uncle, for Rav Assi was never the reigning head, only Rav Ammi. See the letter of Rav Sherira, ed. Levin, p. 80; cf. A. Hyman, *Toledot Tanna'im wa-'Amora'im*, p. 221.

36. *Tanḥuma*, Bo', 2: 'In three (Scriptural) passages we learn that a man should express his teaching when he is nearing his end... when a man is drawing close to the shadow of death, he must put his teaching in order.'
37. *Eccles. Rabba* iii, 2; see *Tosefta Nidda* vi, 6.
38. *T.B. Sanhedrin* 51b; see *T.B. Zevaḥim* 13a.
39. *Tosefta Zevaḥim* i, 8; see my article 'Ha-Derasha ki-Yesod ha-Halakha u-Beʿayat ha-Soferim', *Tarbiz*, XXVII, 1958, pp. 176 ff.
40. J. M. Guttmann, *Asmakhta*, Berlin 1962, pp. 38 ff.
41. The definition of the *'Arukh* s.v. *Halakha*; see *Arukh Completum*, iii, p. 208.
42. *T.P. Berakhot* ii, 6, p. 5b.
43. *T.P. Beṣa* ii, 1, p. 61b.
44. *T.B. Bava Batra* 130b. The Baraita *ibid.* 'The Rabbis taught: The Halakha may not be deduced either through theoretical study or from a practical decision, but only when one is told "This is the Halakha in practice". If one asked and was told "This is the Halakha in practice", he may go and act accordingly, provided he draws no comparisons' conforms to the view of R. Joḥanan. See Rashban [R. Samuel b. Me'ir], *ad loc.*, s.v. *ʿAd she-yō'mĕrû*; cf. *T.B. Nidda* 7b. See also *T.B. Giṭṭin* 19a, where R. Joḥanan replies to Resh Laqish: 'Shall we, because we hold a certain opinion, also act upon it?' So, too, *ibid.* 37a. When Rava wished to rely, in giving a practical decision, on an explanation offered in regard to two conflicting traditions of R. Joḥanan's view, Abbaye said to him: 'Shall we then rely on an explanation?' — *T.B. Bava Batra* 135a; the same argument was used by Rav Huna the son of R. Joshua against Rav Pappa — *T.B. Yevamot* 91b. When Rav Pappa repeated verbatim the explanation given by Rami bar Ḥama and only added the word *hilkhĕtā* [Halakha], the question was asked in the Gemara 'What does he wish to teach us?' and the answer is given: 'That the explanation we adduced is valid' — *T.B. Ketubbot* 98b. See also *T.B. Menaḥot* 36b: 'Ravina said: I was once sitting before Rav Ashi when it had grown dark, and he put on phylacteries. I said to him: "Does the master intend to guard them?" He replied: "Yes". But I observed that it was not his intention to guard them. He was of opinion that this was the law, but that one should not (in practice) rule thus.'
45. *T.P. Nedarim* xii, 11, p. 42d, referring to the anonymous Mishna. In *T.B. Nazir* 59b: 'Samuel said: R. Joshua said this only to sharpen the mind of his disciples.' In *T.P.*, *ibid.*, viii, 1, p. 57a: 'In order not to lock out counter-argument from the school-house.' *T.P. Terumot* ix, 4, p. 46d: 'R. Abbun said: R. Akiba asked R. Simeon b. Yoḥai in order to test his knowledge' (see *T.B. Bava Meṣiʿa* 90b). This expression is often used with reference to Amoraim; cf. *T.P. Nedarim* ii, 3, p. 36b: 'Ḥêfa wished to test his knowledge';

see also *T.P. Shevu'ot* iii, 8, p. 34d; *T.B., ibid.*, 28b; in *Lev. Rabba* xxii, 6, p. 514 we read: 'R. Eleazar asked R. Ḥanina, and some say R. Ḥanina asked R. Eleazar. But is it conceivable that the master would ask the disciple? He did so to test his knowledge.' Cf. *T.B. 'Eruvin* 76a: 'Reḥava tested the knowledge of the Rabbis'; *ibid.* 51a: 'Rav Pappa said: Rava tested our knowledge.' See the marginal note of R. Akiba Eger *ibid.*, and cf. *T.B. Berakhot* 33b: 'And Rabba also wished to sharpen the mind of Abbaye'; the parallels are cited *ibid.* See *Tosefta 'Ahilot* xvi, 8, p. 614, where it is stated of Rabban Joḥanan b. Zakkai — according to another view, of Hillel the Elder — 'Not that he did not know the answer, but he wished to stimulate the disciples.'

46. *T.P. Sukka* i, 1, p. 52a.

47. *T.B. 'Eruvin* 46b; see *ibid.* 47b: 'For Rav in fact did not accept these rules.'

48. *T.B. Pesaḥim* 27a: 'Alternatively: as a rule Samuel holds that the Halakha is according to Rabbi against his colleague, but not against his colleagues; in this case, however, even against his colleagues. Therefore he thought: I will reverse the teaching, so that the Rabbis may appear to hold the view that forbids.' See Rashi *ad loc.*, s.v. *Wĕ-'î bā'êt 'êmā*, cf. also *T.B. Pesaḥim* 30a; *T.B. Sukka* 34b.

48a. The self-confidence of a Sage — even of one like Samuel — is no assurance that the Halakha accords with his view; see *T.B. Ketubbot* 7b: 'As Samuel said to Rav Ḥanan of Bagdath (= Bagdad): Go out and fetch me ten men and I will tell you in their presence: If one assigns (property) to an embryo, it acquires it. But the law is that if one assigns (property) to an embryo, it does not acquire it. Possibly the motif here is that self-praise and self-assurance lead to the opposite results; see below, p. 979, n. 6. Cf. also *T.B. Giṭṭin* 20a and *ibid.* 29b. It is already stated in Proverbs xvi 18 'And a haughty spirit before a fall'; see also *ibid.* xv 33, xviii 12. But we likewise encounter the phenomenon that a trustworthy tradition regarding a given Halakhic decision — sometimes of as many as five Sages — is set aside by the Talmud with the words 'This is not so; the Halakha does not follow R. So-and-so.' See *T.B. Giṭṭin* 39b; *T.B. Keritot* 13b, and *Shiṭa Mequbbeṣet, ad loc.* § 14.

49. *T.B. Bava Meṣi'a* 69a; see *ibid.* Tosafot s.v. *'Ellā'*. Cf. *T.B. Bava Batra* 78a, Rashbam, *ad loc.*, s.v. *We-kulhû*, and Tosafot, *ad loc.*, s.v. *Kulhû*; *Yad Malakhi*, Kelale ha-'Ālef, § 57–59, and Kelale ha-Shîn, § 620–621. See A. Guttmann, *Decisionsmotive im Talmud*, Berlin 1938, pp. 22 ff.

50. *T.B. Bekhorot* 23b; see also *T.B. Yevamot* 91a.

51. On Rav Naḥman see *T.B. 'Eruvin* 16b; on Rava, *ibid.*, 104b, *T.B. Bava Batra* 127a, *T.B. Zevaḥim* 94b; on Rav Dimi, *T.B. Shabbat* 63b, and the parallels quoted *ibid.* Cf. also *T.B. Giṭṭin* 43a: 'Rabba bar Rav Huna appointed an *'Amora* ['public orator'] and expounded: "And this stumbling is under thy hand" — a man does not truly understand the teachings of the Torah until he has stumbled over them.'

52. See *Tosefta Terumot* iii, 12: 'R. Judah said: The Halakha is according to

the School of Shammai, but the majority follow the view of the School of Hillel'; see above, p. 590. Note also 'When R. Abbahu happened to be in R. Joshua b. Levi's locality he would move a lamp (on the Sabbath), but when he came to R. Joḥanan's locality, he did not move a lamp' etc. — *T.B. Shabbat* 46a. Cf. *T.B. Ḥullin* 18b: 'Every river has its own course'; see Rashi, *ad loc.*, s.v. *Nahara.* Cf. also *ibid.* 110a, where it is related that Rami bar Diqûli of Pumbeditha came to the Bet Din of Rav Ḥisda at Sura, and caused mounting astonishment at his behaviour, finding an explanation or authority for each act in the teaching of Rav Judah. This narrative is in the nature of a parody, and ultimately carries a sting for the men of Sura. Quite common is the explanation: 'Each master follows his local usage' — *T.B. Pesaḥim* 3a; see *Gilyon ha-Shas* (Marginal Note of the Talmud) *ibid.* Cf. A. Perls, 'Der Minhag in Talmud', *Festschrift Israel Levy*, 1911, pp. 66 ff. See also M. Guttmann, *Zur Einleitung in die Halakha*, Budapest 1913, pp. 71 ff.

53. See *T.B. Shabbat* 110a: 'Rava retracted from this view... for it is taught...'; and *ibid.* 123a: 'Rav Naḥman said the Halakha... are we to assume that he holds... but behold Rav Naḥman said... Rav Naḥman retracted...' But see *T.B. 'Eruvin*: Rabba bar Rav Ḥanin said to Abbaye: If the master had heard that which was taught... he would have retracted. But it is not so; he did hear, but did not retract.' The same expressions are used of Samuel in *T.B. Menaḥot* 109a; see J. M. Guttmann, *op. cit.*, pp. 62 ff.
54. *Sifre Deut.* § 96.
55. *Tosefta Ḥagiga* ii, 9; *Tosefta Sanhedrin* vii, 1, according to the printed edition and the Vienna MS. In the Erfurt MS. the words ונעשו שתי תורות ['and two Torahs were formed'] are wanting.
56. *Tosefta Yevamot* i, 10; see *T.P. ibid.*, i, 6, p. 3b; *T.P. Qiddushin* i, 1, p. 58d; *T.B. ibid.* 14b; cf. S. Lieberman, *Tosefta ki-Fshuṭah*, Yevamot, pp. 7 ff.
57. *M. Yevamot* i, 4; *M. 'Eduyot* iv, 8.
58. *Tosefta Yevamot, loc. cit.*, and parallels.
59. *M. 'Eduyot* i, 5; see my article 'Class-Status and Leadership', pp. 56–57.
60. *T.B. Yevamot* 14a; see *ibid.* 15a.
61. *T.B. Soṭa* 44a; see Rashi to *T.B. Ḥullin* 17a s.v. *She-hikhnîsû*: ' "Investigate and receive reward" means that we must determine the truth even though it is a matter that belongs to the past'; but see the Rosh [R. Asher b. Jehiel], *ad loc.*, i, § 23.
62. *Aggadat Shir ha-Shirim*, ed. Schechter, p. 19; see *ibid.*, p. 61.
63. *T.B. Sanhedrin* 99a: 'And it is taught: R. Me'ir used to say: He who learns Torah, but does not teach it — of him it is written "He hath despised the word of the Lord".' See *T.B. Rosh ha-Shana* 23a, and *Sefer Eliahu Rabba*, p. 94.
64. *T.B. Sanhedrin* 111b; see above, p. 625.
65. There is a great external similarity between the reactions and ways of expression of the Rabbinic Schools and the Gentile Academies, whether chron-

ologically and geographically near or distant. On Athens in the age of Plato, Isocrates, and Aristotle, see W. Jaeger, *Paideia*, III, 1945, pp. 132–155. On the professional training of the lawyers, see L. Mitteis, *Reichsrecht u. Volksrecht*, Leipzig 1891, pp. 189–203; F. Schulz, *History of the Roman Legal Science*, 1958, pp. 23 ff. On the teaching centres of rhetoric in the fourth century see P. Wolf, *Vom Schulwesen der Spätantike*, 1952; on Confucian China see Max Weber, *Gesammelte Aufsätze Zur Religionssoziologie*, 1920, pp. 395–430. However, these similarities do not diminish the distinctive character of the Sage, a type that cannot be identified either with the philosopher and the sophist, or with the rhetor and *magister iuris*, or with the Chinese *puotsche* (man full of learning).

66. *T.B. Qiddushin* 52b; *T.B. Nazir* 49b.
67. *T.B. Sanhedrin* 24a.
68. It will suffice to mention that Rav, the Babylonian, did not receive an enthusiastic welcome when he returned there. This is attested by the stories regarding his meetings with Qarna and Samuel (*T.B. Shabbat* 108a; but see *T.B. Bava Batra* 89a and *T.P. ibid.*, v, 2, p. 15b (*ad fin.*), and cf. N. Brüll, *Bet Talmud*, V, 1889, p. 146), with R. Shila (*T.B. Yoma* 20b), and with a certain elder, who was not impressed by Rav's announcement 'I am the local Ben ʿAzzai' (*T.P. Pe'a* vi, 3, p. 19c; *T.P. Soṭa* ix, 2, 29c). But see *T.B. Ḥullin* 59a, where Samuel applies to Rav the verse 'There shall no mischief befall the righteous', and Rav applied to Samuel the verse 'No secret troubleth thee.'
69. *T.B. Yevamot* 84a; but see *T.B. ʿEruvin* 53a, where Rabbi states 'When we were studying Torah under R. Eleazar b. Shammuaʿ, we used to sit six to each cubit.'
70. *T.B. Shabbat* x, 5, 12c. When Rabbi said to R. Eleazar 'I heard thus from your father', he replied to him 'I have served my father in my youth more than you have served in advanced age'. See S. Lieberman, *Ha-Yerushalmi kiphshuṭo*, p. 166, and cf. *T.B. Menaḥot* 72a.
71. *T.B. Makkot* 10a.
72. *T.B. Yevamot* 9a; it seems to me that Rabbi displays the same attitude in *T.P. Soṭa* ii, 4: 'Levi bar Sisi asked Rabbi: Does the scroll of the *soṭa* [a wife suspected of faithlessness] defile the hands? He replied: Is this a question?' Although 'Pĕnê Môshe' and 'Qorban hā-ʿEdā' take it as a statement [i.e. this is indeed a question] — apparently on the basis of Rashi's commentary to *T.B. Zevaḥim* 30b, s.v., *Zû Shĕ'ēlā* and *ibid.* 92b, s.v. *Zu She'ela* (in *T.B. Bava Qamma* 116a Rav replies 'and this is a question', but Rashi does not comment *ad loc.*) — yet it seems that at least in the Palestinian Talmud the expression has to be interpreted as a question, for the Amora R. Jose subsequently explains: 'It is not a question. Did not the Sages decree?', etc.
73. *T.B. Ketubbot* 103b.
74. *T.B. Shabbat* 63a; this dictum is transmitted by R. Jeremiah, and similar dicta are reported there in the name of R. Abba.

75. *T.B. Ḥullin* 54a.
76. *T.B. Sanhedrin* 26a.
77. *T.B. Yevamot* 72b; *T.B. Ketubbot* 25b; *T.B. Zevaḥim* 5a; *T.B. Menaḥot* 93b. This attitude is not to be ascribed purely to the Babylonian origin of R. Eleazar (see *T.B. Yoma* 9b), just as the expression 'Resh Laqish criticized the southern scholars' (*T.B. Zevaḥim* 22b) does not indicate a particularly negative attitude to the Sages of the south. When Rav Kahana immigrated to Eretz-Israel, Resh Laqish said to R. Joḥanan: 'A lion has come up from Babylonia'; see *T.B. Bava Qamma* 117a; cf. the harsh remarks made by R. Joḥanan to R. Simlai about both the southern and Babylonian scholars — *T.B. Pesaḥim* 62b. In *T.P. ibid.*, v, 3, p. 32a the speaker is R. Jonathan. See also R. Joḥanan's observations in *T.B. Yoma* 66b; *T.B. Menaḥot* 100a.
78. *T.B. Bava Batra* 81b; see *T.P. Bikkurim* i, 8, p. 64a: 'R. Jose b. Ḥanina asked... R. Eleazar replied: You are asking about matters that the Rabbis still need (to clarify) in the schoolhouse.'
79. *T.B. ʿEruvin* 15a; *T.B. Bava Batra* 84b; *T.B. Giṭṭin* 39a; *T.B. Bava Meṣiʿa* 11b.
80. *Sifre Num.* § 75, p. 70; see the parallels listed *ibid.*, n. 6. See the eulogies of R. Dosa b. Harkinas in *T.P. Yevamot* i, 6, p. 3a; of R. Akiba he said 'that he is a mighty man in the Torah'.
81. *'Avot de-R. Nathan*, Version I, xxix, p. 88. See *ibid.*, n. 28, and cf. the words of Ben ʿAzzai: 'All the Sages of Israel are esteemed by me (as little) as a husk of garlic, except yon bald head.' See Rashi and Tosafot *ad loc.*, s.v. *Ḥûṣ*, and 'Yefe ʿEnayim' *ad loc.*
82. *Ibid.* xviii, p. 68; prior to this it is stated *ibid.*, p. 66: 'Correspondingly R. Judah the Patriarch recounted the praise of the Sages....' Apparently this is the continuation of xvii, *ibid.*: 'Rabban Joḥanan b. Zakkai had five disciples; he gave them all names....' See *ibid.*, appendix I, p. 145.
83. *Ibid.*, p. 69; see *T.B. Giṭṭin* 67a.
84. *T.B. Giṭṭin, ibid.*; see *Midrash ha-Gadol Shemot*, ed. M. Margulies, pp. 386–387.
85. *T.P. Kil'ayim* ix, 4, p. 32b; *T.P. Ketubbot* xii, 3, p. 35a; see *Gen. Rabba* xxxiii, 3, p. 307. On Rabbi's attitude to R. Jose and the reaction of R. Ishmael's son cf. *T.P. Giṭṭin* vi, 9, p. 48b; *T.B. Ketubbot* 103b.
86. *T.P. Shabbat* x, 8, p. 12c; see *Eccles. Rabba* xi, 2; cf. above, p. 621.
87. *T.B. Taʿanit* 21b, ed. H. Malter, pp. 154–155; see the vv.ll., *ibid.*
88. *T.B. Giṭṭin* 41a; see *T.B. Megilla* 28b (see *Diqduqe Soferim*, p. 146). Cf. *T.B. Bava Batra* 8a; *ibid.* 36b (this figure of speech was already employed by R. Joseph; cf. *T.B. Yevamot* 45a). See also Margulies *Le-Ḥeqer Shemot we-khinnuyim be-Talmud*, p. 33; he has substituted, however, Rav Naḥman bar Jacob for Rav Naḥman bar Isaac, but it is clear that in *T.B. Ketubbot* the reference is to the latter (in the Munich MS. *ibid.*: 'Rav Naḥman said to Rava'; but read: 'Rav Huna'), and so, too, in *T.B. Qiddushin* 70a.
89. *T.B. Shabbat* 134b.
90. See *T.B. ibid.*, 111b concerning R. Ḥiyya bar Avin; and see *Gilyon ha-Shas*, *T.B. Bava Batra* 88a on R. Zera; cf. *T.B. Pesaḥim* 76a, *T.B. Yevamot* 113a,

T.B. Bava Qamma 40a, *T.B. Bava Batra* 88a. See *T.B. Zevaḥim* 43b: 'Rava said: Every Scriptural text that Rav Isaac b. R. Avudimi did not explain, and every Baraita that Rav Zeʿiri did not explain, remain unexplained.

91. *T.B. Menaḥot* 95b. This encomium, which refers to Rav Sheshet's acuteness of mind ('A Sage who had the sharpness of mind to dissect a Halakha as with steel' — Rashi), did not prevent Rav Ashi from saying 'What question is this!', but the anonymous view of the Talmud rejects his opinion — 'Rav Ashi's remark is beside the point'. In *T.P. Nidda* ii, 6, p. 50b, R. Joḥanan and Resh Laqish say of R. Ḥanina 'Wise is this elder whose tools are sharp' in the sense that he is well versed in traditions. Indeed Rav Sheshet, too, gained recognition primarily on account of his great erudition; see *T.B. ʿEruvin* 67a; *T.B. Giṭṭin* 68a; *T.B. ʿAvoda Zara* 42b; and see below, n. 94. Possibly Rava and before him Rabba (*T.B. Menaḥot, loc. cit.*) and likewise Rami bar Ḥama (*T. B. Bekhorot* 50b) praised his acuity after he became blind (*T.B. Berakhot* 58a), for R. Zeʿira remarked: 'We do not pay attention to the traditions of Rav Sheshet, for he is blind' (*T.P. Qiddushin* i, 7, p. 61a).

92. *T.B. Bava Batra* 7a; see *Gilyon ha-Shas, ad loc.*

93. *T.B. Berakhot* 50a; see *T.B. Pesaḥim* 88a; *T.B. Bava Batra* 133b, and cf. Rashbam: 'Arbitrators who are not well versed in the law... but R. Ḥananel explained חצצתא as a cemetery.' See *Aruch Completum*, Pt. III, p. 477. Cf. *T.P. Giṭṭin* i, p. 43d (and the parallel in *Tractate Qiddushin*).

94. *T.B. Bava Batra* 23b, where it is stated that he was expelled from the schoolhouse; see *T.P. Nedarim* ix, 3, p. 40d: 'Said R. Ba the son of R. Ḥiyya bar Wa: Why does he annoy them?' Cf. also *T.B. Pesaḥim* 34b; *T.B. Zevaḥim* 60b.

95. *T.B. Kettubot* 75a; see *T.B. Yoma* 57a. Similarly we find 'R. Abba said Bēha (a Sage unknown from any other source) knew how to explain this teaching, but had he not gone up there [i.e. to Eretz-Israel] he would not have known, for Eretz-Israel was the cause of it' — *T.B. Temura* 29a. On the emissary of Abbaye — Rav Safra — and R. Zeriqa's (apparently himself a Babylonian) attitude to him, see *T.B. Ḥullin* 110b–111b.

96. *T.B. Bava Meṣiʿa* 16a. See *T.B. Bava Qamma* 32b: 'Rava tapped his (Rav Shimi's) shoe' (cf. *T.B. Moʿed Qaṭan* 25a), and *ibid.*, 105b, Rabba (see *Diqduqe Soferim* p. 254) calls Rav Amram 'a confused person'; cf. *ʿAruch Completum*, p. 287. Of Rav Huna and Rav Ḥiyya bar Ashi it is related that they called each other 'orphan' — *T.B. Ḥullin* 111b, which Rashi, *ad loc.*, explains as 'without knowledge'. See *T.P. Berakhot* vii, p. 11c: 'R. Zeʿira was displeased that R. Jacob bar Aḥa called R. Ḥiyya bar Ba a caviller.' R. Zeʿira himself was inclined to praise: 'And R. Zeʿira praised him for giving a clear decision.' See also *T.P. Yoma* iii, 5, p. 40c, and so one should read in *T.P. Bava Batra* viii, 9, p. 16c: 'R. Zera praised him...' But even R. Zera used to rebuke the expounders of Haggadot, whom he termed scribe-diviners (ספרי קסמי — this is the correct reading)...' — *T.P. Maʿaśrot* iii, 10, p. 51a.

96a. Bar Qappara was annoyed with Rav Koshaʿya, who had formerly visited him frequently. After he had left him and gone over to R. Ḥiyya, Bar Qappara met him and asked him in these terms: 'What does the Babylonian say on the subject?' — *T.B. Keritot* 8a. See *Shiṭa Mequbbeṣet* § 4 'What does ʿIyya say on the subject....' Cf. the *additamenta* and *novellae*, *ibid.* § 5, and see also *T.B. Ketubbot* 5a.

97. *T.B. ʿAvoda Zara* 19a; *Gilyon ha-Shas* notes: The correct reading is דרבה ['of Rabba', instead of דרבא ('of Rava')]. But the Spanish MS. also reads דרבא. See *T.B. ʿEruvin* 53a and Tosafot *ad loc.*, s.v. *Dĕ-gāmre*. On Rav Ḥisda's anger with the elders of Nizunia for not coming to his 'discourse', see *T.B. Qiddushin* 25a. The rivalry between Sura and Pumbeditha in the days of Rav Ḥisda is alluded to in the story about Rami bar Diquli in *T.B. Ḥullin* 100a; see also above, p. 973, n. 52.

98. In *T.P. Nazir* vii, p. 56a, it is taught in a Baraita that a Kohen is permitted to defile himself in order to learn Torah. 'R. Juda said: If he has someone else from whom he can learn, he should not defile himself. R. Jose said: Even if he has someone else from whom he can learn, he may defile himself, for a man is not granted to learn from everyone.' See *'Avot de-R. Nathan*, Version I, iii, p. 16, in the name of R. Me'ir; on the other hand, *ibid.* viii, p. 36, the opposite opinion is cited in his name.

99. *T.B. Zevaḥim* 96b; see Rashi, *ad loc.*, s.v. *'Alqaftin*; *Diqduqe Soferim*, *ad loc.*, p. 185. Cf. *T.B. Nedarim* 78a.

1. *T.B. Bava Batra* 22a; see *Diqduqe Soferim*, p. 99. On the flight of students from teacher to teacher, on friction and even actual combats in the academies of the sophists at Athens and Antiochia, see P. Wolf, *op. cit.*, pp. 51–52, pp. 55–57, but the reference there is to pupils who paid their teachers fees.

2. *T.B. Ḥagiga* 14a; see *T.B. Berakhot* 32a: 'Happy is the disciple whose master concedes that he is right.'

3. *T.B. Bava Batra* 142b: 'Does the matter depend on age? It depends on reason!' The speaker is R. Jeremiah, see *Diqduqe Soferim*, *ad loc.*, p. 387, n. צ קשישותא [rendered above, 'age'] does not mean merely 'old age'. In an Aramaic inscription of the Synagogue of Dura Europos it is stated: ...בקשישותה דשמואל כהנא, i.e. In the days when Samuel acted as elder of the congregation. In a Greek inscription Samuel's title is πρεσβύτερος; see E. L. Sukenik, *Bêt ha-Kĕneset bĕ-Dura Europos* [The Synagogue in Dura Europos] Jerusalem 1947, pp. 152–152. Cf. K. Brockelmann, *Lexicon Syriacum*, 1928, p. 702.

4. *M. 'Avot* ii, 5; *Sifra*, Shemini, ii, 47d; *T.B. Zevaḥim* 101a; *'Avot de-R. Nathan*, Version I, i; see *T.B. Taʿanit* 8a. Rava declares *ibid.*: 'If you see a student who finds his study as hard as iron, it is because his teacher shows him no friendliness.' The Sages who learnt, but did not teach, were criticized by R. Me'ir (*T.B. Sanhedrin* 99a), R. Nathan (*T.B. Temura* 16a), and Rav (*T.B. Sanhedrin* 91b); cf. *Lev. Rabba* 22a, p. 498.

5. See *T.B. Berakhot* 27a; *T.B. ʿEruvin* 62b, 63a; *T.B. Yoma* 37a; *T.B. Ketubbot* 84b; *T.B. Soṭa* 22a; *M. Bava Mesiʿa* ii, 11; *T.P. ibid.*, 12, p. 8d; cf. *Lev. Rabba* § 27, p. 460.

6. *T.B. ʿArakhin* 16a. In the Munich MS. the text has: '[speak in] praise of his fellow overmuch'; in this version, too, the Rif [Isaac Alfasi], Shabbat, § 325, cites the Gemara in *T.B. ʿArakhin*, and it is also implied in Rashi's commentary *ad loc.* (Maimonides, 'Hilkhot Deʿot', vii, 4, agrees with the second explanation *ibid.*; cf. 'Kesef Mishne', *ad loc.*), but in *ʿEn Yaʿaqov*, *editio princeps*, and in *Haggadot ha-Talmud*, the reading is the same as in our text; see *T.B. Bava Batra* 162a; and *Diqduqe Soferim*, *ad loc.*, p. 439, § *Sāmekh*, notes that this version is also found in the Paris MS. According to 'Some say', it is Rav Safra that cited the dictum before his brother and indeed the praise accorded him by R. Abbahu 'as a great man' eventually led to his disparagement; see *T.B. ʿAvoda Zara* 4a. The motif that praise leads to a different result from that intended by the praiser forms the basis of several stories. See *T.P. Moʿed Qaṭan* iii, 5, p. 82d: 'R. Jose b. R. Ḥalafta once praised R. Me'ir before the men of Sephoris: "A great man, a holy man, a humble man..." said they to him: "Master, is this the man whom you praise?"' See the story about Levi bar Sisi in *Gen. Rabba* lxxxi, 2, p. 969, and the parallels indicated *ibid.* See *T.P. Kil'ayim* viii, 1, p. 31b: '... Said R. Joḥanan to him: But is this not a Mishna...? and R. Jannai praised him... Said R. Simeon b. Laqish after all these praises I can (still) interpret it....' Cf. *T.P. Yevamot* i, 1, p. 2c; *T.P. Qiddushin* iii, 5, p. 64a (but *ibid.*, 6, 64b we read: 'Said R. Joḥanan to R. Jannai: But is there a Mishna that speaks thus? He replied: Do you ask poor Jannai a matter in *Qiddushin*? R. Jannai then re-interpreted the Mishna....'); and R. Joḥanan himself said with regard to R. Ishmael's statement in the Mishna (*M. Bava Batra*, x, *ad fin.*): 'Whoever wishes to occupy himself with civil law should wait upon Simeon b. Nannas' — although R. Ishmael eulogized Ben Nannas, it was his exposition that he praised, but the law is not in accordance with the view of Ben Nannas' (*T.P. ibid.*, x, 7, p. 17d). See *T.B. Makkot* 17b: 'Rava said: May every pregnant mother bear a son like R. Simeon, and if not let her not bear (at all)! — although his argument may be refuted... But if so, why (did Rava say) 'May every pregnant mother bear a son like R. Simeon'? It is because he recasts the verse to suit his purpose....' On the other hand, Rashi, *T.B. ʿArakhin* 9a: 'And people would criticize the Rabbis, saying: They do whatever they like.'
7. See *T.B. Zevaḥim* 5a: 'Resh Laqish was lying on his stomach in the schoolhouse and he raised a question... said to him R. Eleazar... he retorted: Is this the person that is called a great man? I speak of....' Cf. above, n. 75.
8. *T.B. Moʿed Qaṭan* 17a: 'If the Rabbi is like an angel of the Lord of hosts, they should seek Torah at his mouth; but if not let them not seek Torah at his mouth.' See below, n. 16.
9. See above, n. 94 and n. 99. R. Joḥanan himself took umbrage when R. Eleazar failed to report a Halakha in his name — *T.B. Yevamot* 96b; see *T.P. ibid.*, x, 17, p. 11b. Cf. *T.B. Ḥullin* 18b, 19b; see also *T.B. Meʿila* 7b: 'R. Joḥanan

said: I have cut off the legs of the youngster' (with reference to Resh Laqish). On objections of other scholars see *T.B. Shabbat* 46a; *T.B. Qiddushin* 31b, 32a; *T.B. Bava Mesiʿa* 33a; *T.B. Bekhorot* 44a; 'R. Abbahu derided it' — *T.B. Qiddushin* 71b; see *Gilyon ha-Shas, ad loc.* 'R. Jeremiah derided it' — *T.B. ʿAvoda Zara* 35a. 'Rav cursed' — *T.B. Shabbat* 108a; see *ibid.* 120b and *T.B. Qiddushin* 33b. (Cf. *T.P. Sanhedrin* x, p. 29a '... This is the meaning of the proverbial saying: A man should be concerned about his master's curse even if it is uttered without cause'). 'Kicked him [or, 'rebuked him']' — *T.P. Shabbat* viii, 1, p. 11a; see *T.P. Sheqalim* iii, 2, p. 47b. 'Rav Sheshet blew upon his hand [a derogatory gesture]' — *T.B. Bava Batra* 134b; cf. *T.P. Maʿasrot* iii, 10, p. 51a: 'R. Zeʿira used to rebuke the expounders of Haggadot, whom he termed scribe-diviners'; and regarding the homilies of R. Ba bar Kahana and R. Levi he said: 'Turn the verse as you will, we learn nothing from it.' Note also that the praise accorded to the question of R. Jeremiah is worded: 'For it is better than nothing' (see S. Lieberman, *Greek in Jewish Palestine*, p. 168, n. 60). See *T.P. Maʿaser Sheni* i, 4, p. 53a: 'R. Ḥaggai said... he said it before R. Avina and he praised him, (but) when he said it before R. Jeremiah he rebuked him... when R. Ḥaggai left (the schoolhouse) he found a Baraita that taught... if R. Jeremiah heard this teaching he was right to rebuke me... Said R. Zeʿira to him: Don't retract, for R. Eleazar said....' See *T.P. Giṭṭin* i, 2, p. 43c: 'And R. Zeʿira looked at him...'; and cf. *ibid.*, ii, 1, p. 44a, and see *T.P. Maʿaser Sheni* iv, 6, p. 55a. Cf. above, n. 96.

10. R. Ḥiyya with reference to Rabbi, *T.B. Ḥullin* 16a; while of R. Joḥanan himself it is stated: 'Not only did he not listen to the Tanna [one who recited Baraitas before the expounding teacher], but he did not even listen to his teacher', *T.B. Yoma* 43b. See *T.P. Soṭa* i, 1, p. 16c: 'I disagree with his teacher, how much more so with him.' In *T.P. Qiddushin* iii, 2, p. 63d we find: 'The disciples of R. Jonah say... R. Jonah (however) says....'
11. See *T.B. Shabbat* 3b; *T.B. Taʿanit* 9a; *T.B. ʿEruvin* 63a. Cf. above, p. 976, n. 78.
12. See *T.P. Berakhot* vii, p. 10c; *T.P. Sheqalim* iii, 2, p. 47c; *T.P. Moʿed Qaṭan* iii, 1, p. 81b–c; *T.B. ibid.* 16a–17a.
13. *T.B. ʿAvoda Zara* 44b, where R. Ḥama bar Joseph said that R. Hoshaʿya (so in MSS.) said: 'But I say it was not fallacious'; cf. Rashi *ad loc.*, s.v. *Wa-'ănî*: 'and disagrees with R. Hoshaʿya his teacher'; see Tosafot *ad loc.*, s.v. *Tĕshûvā*, and cf. *T.B. Meʿila* 7b.
14. *T.B. Sukka* 32b; see above, p. 447.
15. *T.B. Megilla* 28a; see *Diqduqe Soferim*, *ad loc.*, p. 144; *T.B. Taʿanit* 20b. The correct reading is 'Rav Ada bar Ahava' instead of 'R. Zera'.
16. *T.B. Qiddushin* 30b; see Rashi *ad loc.*, s.v. *'Et Wāhēv*: 'War over a book leads to love in the end'. R. Ḥiyya bar Abba himself experienced such treatment on the part of R. Abbahu, *T.B. Soṭa* 40a. See *ibid.* R. Abbahu's attitude to R. Abba of Acco and of the latter's humility and unassertiveness.

17. See W. Bacher, *Tradition und Tradenten,* pp. 618 ff; B. Murmalstein, *Ma-'ămārîm le-Zikhron Ṣĕvi Pereṣ Chajes* [Essays in Memory of H. P. Chajes], Vienna 1933, pp. 223 ff. In addition to the early commentaries cited *ibid.*, see the commentary ascribed to R. Samson b. Abraham of Sens (Ha-Rash) to the *Sifra,* Negaʿim, 1, 52b: 'So, too, *ṣoreva me-rabbanan* who has completed his studies and is knowledgeable and erudite.'

17a. The saying: I am like Ben ʿAzzai in the markets of Tiberias' is also ascribed to Abbaye (*T.B. Qiddushin* 20a; *T.B. ʿArakhin* 30b) and to Rava (*T.B. ʿEruvin* 59a; see Rashi *ad loc.*, s.v. *Bĕ-shûqê*; but this epigram was said by, or attributed to, other scholars as well. Of Rav it is related: 'When he went down there, he said "I am the local Ben ʿAzzai" ' (*T.P. Pe'a* vi, 3, p. 19a; *T.P. Soṭa* ix, 2, p. 23a); likewise R. Joḥanan declared on arriving at 'a certain place': 'I am the local Ben ʿAzzai' (*T.P. Bikkurim* ii, 2, p. 65a). But in both cases the motif is that self-praise turns to disparagement. Rav was asked a question by an elder, who disagreed with his answer, and when he came to Rabbi he discovered that the elder was right. When R. Joḥanan's error was pointed out by a certain elder, he himself said 'The local Ben ʿAzzai has gone.' With this expression compare *T.P. Yevamot* x, p. 14: 'The spiced wine is gone'; in *T.B. Bava Batra* 134b: 'R. Joseph's "because" has gone.'

18. *T.B. Nedarim* 62a–b; see *ibid.* the preceding dicta against those who make use of the crown of the Torah, and the explanation 'for he was very wealthy and he should have appeased him with money.' *T.B. Shabbat* 121b; *T.B. Megilla* 28a; and see *Diqduqe Soferim, ad loc.*, p. 143.

19. *T.P. Makkot* ii, 7, p. 32a; *T.P. Sheviʿit* x, 8, p. 39d has only: 'R. Jose said: From this is to be inferred that a man who has learned' etc. See Z. Frankel, *Mevo' ha-Yerushalmi*, p. 61.

20. *T.B. Shabbat* 119a. See also the saying of Rava, *T.B. Taʿnit* 4a: 'If a *ṣoreva mē-rabanan* becomes incensed it is the Torah that inflames him.'

21. *T.B. Shevuʿot* 30–b. For the wording of Rabba bar Rav Huna's dictum see *Diqduqe Soferim, ad loc.*, p. 58.

22. While in the Baraita, *Tosefta Sanhedrin* vi, 2, p. 423 — cited in *T.B. loc. cit.*, and in *T.P. ibid.*, iv, 1, p. 35b — it is stated: 'R. Judah said: I have it as a tradition that if they wished to let them both be seated together, there is no objection.' The obligation to let them both be seated flowed from the desire to let one of them sit down. See the *Tosefta, loc. cit.*, vii, 7, p. 426, with reference to answers to questions: 'In the case of a Sage and a disciple, the Sage is attended to (first); in the case of a disciple and an *ʿAm ha-'Areṣ*, the disciple comes first.

23. He sent a message to Rav Naḥman: 'Our associate ʿUlla is a colleague in Torah and precepts'; and Rav Naḥman said: 'Why did he send me this message — to favour him?' Then he said: To deal with his case first.' Rav Joseph praised Rav Naḥman in these terms: 'Rav Naḥman expounded these verses as (though his authority came) from Sinai' — *T.B. Arakhin* 30b; cf. the expression used by R. Eleazar b. Azariah in p. 911, n. 70.

24. See *T.B. Shevuot* 30b, Tosafot, s.v. *'Ăsē di-Khěvôd Tôrā*, and the annotations of H. P. Chajes *ad loc.* See *T.B. Ketubbot* 105a–106a.
25. *T.B. Shevuot* 41a; so Rashi explained *ad loc.*, s.v. *Lo' mizdaqqěqînān lê.* But cf. the commentary of R. Ḥananel: 'We do not attend to the borrower when he demands that he should swear to him.' See Maimonides, 'Hilkhot Malwe we-Lowe [Laws of Lender and Borrower]' xiv, 2, and 'Maggid Mishne', *ad loc.*, who states that the Ramah [R. Me'ir b. Todros ha-Levi Abulafia] gives the same explanation as Rashi.
26. *T.B. Shabbat* 119a.
27. See above, p. 608 and above, p. 98; *T.P. Bava Meṣi'a* ii, 8, p. 8b; *T.B. ibid.*, 71a and *ibid.*, 78a; and cf. *T.B. Bava Batra* 52a.
28. *T.P. Bikkurim* iii, 3, p. 65d. See the Commentary ascribed to R. Samson of Sens, Jerusalem 1951, 48a. From the letter that R. Abbahu sent him (see J. N. Epstein, *Mevo'ot le-Sifrut ha-'Amora'im*, p. 609) it appears that R. Joḥanan refused to appoint him.
29. See *T.P. Nedarim* x, 10, p. 42b.
30. See S. Zuri, *R. Yose b. R. Ḥanina mi-Qisrin*, Jerusalem 1926, pp. 45 ff; *ibid.*, pp. 179 ff.
31. See above, p. 608, and on '*miṣwā – ṣědāqā*' cf. my article 'Megammot Datiyyot we-Ḥevratiyyot be-Torat ha-Ṣedaqa shel Ḥazal'; p. 25, n. 176.
32. *Gen. Rabba* lxxii, 5, p. 843; see *Lev. Rabba* xxv, 2, p. 570, and the parallels cited *ibid.*, n. 5; cf. above, p. 606 [and see M. Bär, 'Yissakhar u-Zevulun', *Shenaton Bar-Ilan* [Bar Ilan Annual] VI, 1968, pp. 167 ff].
33. *T.P. Horayot* iii, 7, p. 48a, where there are three narratives; the first refers to the time of R. Eliezer, R. Joshua, and R. Akiba 'who went up to the Harbour [Suburb] of Antiochia to raise funds for the Sages, and there was a certain Abba Judah there, who contributed liberally to charity [*miṣwa*]'. The second story concerns a son of Salluni at the academy of Tiberias in the days of R. Ḥiyya bar Abba. The third tells of Abba Judah the crafty, 'who was crafty in giving charity [*miṣwot* — i.e. he acted astutely in donating to charity]', and when Resh Laqish visited his place at Boṣra, he gave as his contribution a sum equal to that of the entire community. The editor of the narratives integrated them by the refrain 'He [the Sage] seated him next to him and applied to him the verse "A man's gift maketh room for him, and bringeth him before great men" (Proverbs xviii 16); see *Lev. Rabba* v, 4, pp. 110–113, where the other parallel passages are listed in the notes. Cf. *T.P. Pesaḥim* vii, 1, p. 34a and the parallels referring to Todos of Rome, to whom the Sages sent the message 'Were you not Todos, we should surely have put you under the ban'; and to the question 'Who is Todos? R. Ḥananiah replied that he sends (the funds for) the maintenance of the Rabbis', while in *T.B. ibid.*, 33b, R. Jose bar Avin says 'He throws the profits of merchandise into the purse of the scholars' (i.e. gives them an opportunity to gain a livelihood).
34. *T.B. Sanhedrin* 92a.
35. *T.B. Ketubbot* 111b. The theme commences there with the words of R. Eleazar

'The ignorant will not be resurrected.' When R. Joḥanan reacted 'It is not pleasirg to their Master that you speak of them thus', R. Eleazar adduced proof from Scripture; and only when he saw that R. Joḥanan was grieved, he said to him: 'Master, I have found a remedy (תקנה) for them in the Torah' (in the Munich MS.: מנוח ממקום אחר 'comfort in another passage'); and he then referred to what I have cited in the text.

36. *T.B. Sanhedrin* 52b. On R. Eleazar's refusal to accept gifts from the house of the Patriarch see above, p. 603.
37. *Lev. Rabba* xxxiv, 13, p. 800.
38. *T.B. Shabbat* 23b; see *Diqduqe Soferim, ad loc.*, p. 45. The Gaon R. Elijah of Vilna emends the text as follows: 'He who is in awe of the Rabbis... he who honours the Rabbis'; cf. Maharsha [R. Samuel Eliezer Edels], *Ḥiddushe Aggadot, ad loc.* It seems that 'to be in awe of the Rabbis' means to accept their views and identify oneself with them (which is not so with love and honour, which can find expression in support only), and these — i.e. those who are fit for it — can themselves become Sages, and if they have not the ability, Rava assures them that their words will also be listened to.
39. See my article 'Megammot Datiyyot we-Ḥevratiyyot be-Torat ha-Ṣedaqa shel Ḥazal', pp. 13 ff.
40. *T.B. Yoma* 86a; see *T.B. Pesaḥim* 113b.
41. *T.B. Berakhot* 19a; *T.B. Sanhedrin* 82a; *T.B. 'Eruvin* 63a; *T.B. Shevu'ot* 30b.
42. *Midrash Mishle* vi, 20, p. 56, where it is ascribed to Elisha b. Avuya, the teacher of R. Me'ir.
43. *Exod. Rabba* xxvii, 9; see *Midrash Tehillim* viii, 3.
44. *T.B. Ketubbot* 105b.
45. *T.B. Bava Qamma* 113b.
46. *M. Shabbat* xiv, 4; *T.P., ibid.*, xiv (*ad fin.*), p. 15a; *T.B. ibid.*, 111b; *ibid.*, 67a.
47. *T.B. Pesaḥim* 22b, where the parallels are listed. In *T.P. Berakhot* ix, 7, p. 14a: 'Nehemiah 'Imsoni attended on R. Akiba... he said to him: Him and his Torah learning.'
48. *T.B. Pesaḥim* 49b.
49. *'Avot de-R. Nathan*, Version I, xi, p. 46.
50. *Gen. Rabba* lxxxi, 2, p. 969; see *ibid.* the story about Levi b. Sisi and Rabbi, and *T.P. Yevamot* xiii, 7, p. 13a. See below, p. 986, n. 83.
51. *T.B. Ta'anit* 4a; see the edition of H. Malter, p. 17, and the notes *ibid.*
52. *Tosefta Sukka* ii, 5; *T.B. ibid.* 29a (an anonymous Baraita); so, too, *Derekh Ereṣ Rabba* ii. See *'Avot de-R. Nathan*, Version II, xxxi, p. 67, in the name of R. Joḥanan b. Zakkai (= He used to say); cf. *T.B. Ta'anit* 8b, where R. Joḥanan (!) stated: 'The rains are withheld only on account of those who subscribe to charity in public'. See also *T.P. Qiddushin* iv, 1, p. 65b: 'R. Ammi taught in the name of R. Joshua b. Levi... David said: On account of four sins... and those who subscribe to charity in public, but do not pay.'
53. See *T.P. Ketubbot* iv, 8, p. 28d: 'R. Simeon b. Laqish in the name of R. Juda bar Ḥanina said: They decided by vote in Usha that if one insults an elder

and strikes him, the latter must be indemnified for the shame in full.' Cf. *T.P. Bava Qamma* viii, 8, p. 6c, where it is related that Resh Laqish imposed a fine of a pound of gold on a man who insulted R. Judah bar Ḥanina.

54. See *T.P. Ḥagiga* i, 7, p. 76c, the statement of R. Simeon b. Yoḥai: 'If you see towns plucked up from their place in Eretz-Israel, know that they have failed to pay the wages of Bible-teachers and Mishna-teachers.' See *ibid.* the story dating from the time of R. Judan Nesi'a concerning towns in which there were no Bible-teachers nor Mishna-teachers; cf. *Lam. Rabba*, Petiḥta, ii, ed. Buber, p. 2.
55. *T.B. Berakhot* 47b; see *Diqduqe Soferim, ad loc.*, p. 250. In the text I have cited an amended version based on MSS. and Ri'shonim.
56. *T.B. Soṭa* 22a in the name of R. Me'ir, while the view of R. Joshua is cited as 'and the Sages say'; this is also the reading in the Munich MS. (*ibid.*: 'the recitation of the Shemaʿ... with its benedictions'); in *Haggadot ha-Talmud ibid.*: 'So Rabbi; but the Sages say....'
57. See *Diqduqe Soferim*, § ן; so, too, *T.B. Soṭa, loc. cit.*
58. *T.P. Demai* ii, 3, p. 23a; see *Tosefta ʿAvoda Zara* iii, 10; S. Lieberman, *Tosefet Ri'shonim*, Pt. III, p. 190, and idem, *Tarbiz*, XX, 1950, p. 110.
59. See 'Pirqa de-Rabbenu ha-Qadosh', ed. S. Schönblum, *Shelosha Sefarim Niftaḥim*, Lemberg 1877, 21b; the dictum occurs at the end of the Baraita of 'Four things are a disgrace to a scholar...' to which are joined Baraitas of *Pesaḥim*; see below, n. 61.
60. See above, p. 588.
61. *T.B. Pesaḥim* 49b; this is the reading in the printed editions and the Munich MS.: 'R. Eliezer... and R. Eliezer (further) said.' See *Diqduqe Soferim, ad loc.*, p. 139; but according to my friend S. Rosenthal the reading in the Enelow MS. is 'R. Eleazar' in both sayings (In the Yemenite MS., Columbia, the first dictum is ascribed to 'R. Eliezer' and the second to 'R. Eleazar'). 'R. Eleazar' is also found in the Rome MS., in the Oxford MS. 366, and in the Adler MS., N.Y. 850, where the text has 'The Rabbis taught: R. Eleazar said'. From the phrasing 'His disciples said to him' it would appear that the reference is to the Tanna R. Eleazar; see *Diqduqe Soferim, ad loc.*, § ש.
62. Rashi, *ad loc.*, s.v. *U-mi-gabbô*, refers to *T.B. Ḥullin* 21a; see *ibid.*
63. The wording is strange and appears to be an inadvertent repetition from the expression cited above, 'His disciples said to him: Say.' Indeed in the Oxford MS. 366 there is added: '...but now I say: "Would that I had an *ʿam ha-'areṣ* (in my power) and I would bite him like an ass." Said his disciples to him...'; it seems, however, to be a textual amendment. In the Enelow MS. and in the Yemenite MS., cited above, the reading is: ואמרת ['and did you say?'] instead of אמור ['Say!']. With regard to biting by the Sages, R. Eliezer (*M. 'Avot* ii, 10) said: 'Their bite is like that of a fox'; and on the motif of biting see E. Peterson, *Judentum und Gnosis*, Frühkirche, pp. 226 ff.
64. *T.B. Ketubbot* 103b; *T.B. Bava Meṣiʿa* 85b.

65. See *T.B. Giṭṭin* 57a: 'If anyone has heard anything about Kefar Sekhania of Egypt [מצרים], let him tell. One of them thereupon proceeded to say: It once happened... The other then said... and they investigated and found that a father and son had had intercourse with a betrothed girl on the Day of Atonement. So they were brought to the Bet Din and were stoned.' It seems that instead of מצרים one should read מינים ['sectarians'] (the צ was formed by the fusion of נ and י ; this can be seen in the Munich MS.). Kefar Sekhania was known as a place of sectarians; see *Tosefta Ḥullin* ii, 22; *T.P. ʿAvoda Zara* ii, 1, p. 40d; *T.B. ibid.*, 27b; *Eccles. Rabba* i, 8. On disgraceful acts attributed to the Minim see above, p. 535.
66. See *Tosefta Shabbat* xiii, 5, the statement of R. Ṭarfon.
67. *'Otzar ha-Gaonim*, Pesaḥim, p. 69, the responsum of Rav Sherira.
68. See *ibid.*, p. 67, the citation from *Teshuvot Ge'onim*, ed. Harkavy, § 380, pp. 197–198.
69. See *ibid.*, p. 68, and the parallels in the name of Rav Sherira.
70. *M. Qiddushin* i, 10.
71. *T.B. Qiddushin* 40b; see Rashi *ad loc.* And he is disqualified to give evidence 'for since he is uncultivated, he is not scrupulous and has no sense of shame.' Cf. Maimonides, 'Hilkhot ʿEdut', xi, 1: 'For one who has sunk so low may be presumed to commit most of the transgressions that chance his way.' See *ibid.* Halakha 2.
72. *T.B. Ḥagiga* 22a; see Tosafot *ad loc.*, s.v. *Kĕ-ma'n.* Cf. *'Otzar ha-Gao'nim*, the section of responsa, p. 45, § 33.
73. See *T.B. Bava Qamma* 119a. The Gemara there gives as the reason for the view that an informer may not be destroyed 'in case he has worthy descendants', the very reason advanced for proclaiming the lost property of an *ʿAm ha-'Areṣ*; cf. above, p. 633.
74. *M. 'Avot* ii, 11, and *'Avot de-R. Nathan*, Version I, xvi, p. 64; see *ibid.* notes 31–32. The Masoretic text of Psalms reads בתקוממיך (instead of ובמתקוממיך) ['Those that rise up against Thee'].
75. *Tosefta ʿAvoda Zara* iii, 9, p. 464.
76. In *Pirqa de-Rabbenu ha-Qadosh*, Bava de-'Arbaʿa, ed. Schönblum, 21b, there is added: 'R. Nathan said: If now he brought meat from the market, and a weasel or mouse came and took it, she is not concerned, but brings meat of an unclean animal or of an animal that has not been properly slaughtered, and gives it to him to eat. R. Judah said: An *ʿAm ha-'Areṣ* is like a non-Jew, of whom it is said "thy daughter thou shalt not give unto his son".'
77. *T.B. Pesaḥim* 49a.
78. *T.P. Terumot* viii, 4, p. 45c: 'There was a butcher in Sepphoris who supplied the Jews with meat of *nĕvēlôt* [improperly slaughtered animals] and *ṭĕrēfôt* [animals with fatal disease]. Once he drank wine on Sabbath eve and went up to the roof, and he fell, and died. Dogs began licking his blood, so people came and asked R. Ḥanina: May he be removed from them? He replied: It is written "Therefore ye shall not eat any flesh that is torn of beasts in the

field; ye shall cast it to the dogs" (Exod. xxii 30), but this fellow robbed the dogs and fed the Jews with it. He said to them: Leave them alone; they are eating what belongs to them.' See *Lev. Rabba* v, 6, p. 119. On thieves who broke into houses in Sepphoris, see *Gen. Rabba* xxvii, 3, p. 257, and the parallels cited there. Regarding those who raped virgins on the Day of Atonement in Nehardea, see *T.B. Yoma* 19b.

79. *T.B. Bava Meṣi'a* 85a; see below, n. 82.

80. *T.B. Sanhedrin* 96a, the current text reads: 'Although Rabbi Judah b. Bathyra of Nisibis sent....' See *Diqduqe Soferim, ibid.*, p. 279, n. *Yôd*, where it is stated that 'Nisibis' is wanting in the Karlsruhe MS.; in that case the reference could be just to Rav Judah (without further qualification). R. Solomon Luria [Maharshal] emends to: 'R. Joshua b. Levi.'

81. *T.B. Bava Meṣi'a* 85a. Apparently this was not a common phenomenon. To R. Osha'ya, the son of R. Ḥama, the son of R. Bisa, Rami bar Ḥama applied the verse 'And a threefold cord is not quickly broken.' We do, indeed, find Rav Shimi the son of R. Ḥiyya bar Rav; but by marriage the chain of Torah scholarship extended over many more generations, and mostly the sons-in-law appear as important members of such a family-tree. On 'Rabbana 'Uqba and Rabbana Nehemiah, the sons of the daughter of Rav' see *T.B. Ḥullin* 92a; cf. also *ibid.* 93a, 'The father of your mother', that is, R. Jeremiah b. Abba, in relation to Levi, the son of R. Huna b. Ḥiyya. Rava was the son-in-law of Rav Ḥisda, and Rav Ḥisda was the son-in-law of Rav Ḥanan bar Rava, and the latter was the son-in-law of Rav (*T.B. Ḥullin* 63a). Although the grandsons of Rava are also known — Nanai and Rava Ḥaviva b. Rav Joseph (*T.B. Yevamot* 66b and *T.B. Bava Batra* 143b) — yet it is certain that their status was not to be compared to that of Rav Ḥisda and Rava (incidentally it is not known whether Rav Joseph was the son of Rav Ḥisda's daughter). Rav Ashi said of his father-in-law's son, Rami (in the MSS. Rav Aḥi, see *Diqduqe Soferim* 151a) bar Abba: 'How presumptuous is this Rabbi' — *T.B. Ḥullin* 111b.

82. *Sifre Deut.* § 48, *Midrash Tanna'im*, pp. 212–213.

83. *T.B. Nedarim* 81a.

84. See *T.B. Bava Batra* 74a: 'Every Abba is an ass...'; see above, p. 625.

85. *T.B. Menaḥot* 53a; see *Diqduqe Soferim, ad loc.*, p. 133, n. *Mêm.* When R. Ammi was told that Rav Naḥman had said to 'Ulla: 'If R. Joḥanan had told me this himself, I should not have accepted it', he reacted: 'And even if Rav Naḥman is the son-in-law of the Exilarah, shall he lightly esteem the teaching of R. Joḥanan".' [*T.B. Ḥullin* 124a]. See above, p. 980, n. 10.

85a. Here belongs also the story concerning R. Joshua b. Hananiah, *T.B. 'Eruvin* 53b, which begins with a confession 'Never did any one get the better of me except a woman, a little boy and a little girl...' and concludes with praise: 'Happy are you, O Israel, that you are all eminently wise, both the great and small among you.'

86. *T.B. Ta'anit* 20a, ed. H. Malter, p. 80; see the parallels cited *ibid.* and the vv.ll.

87. See *The Fables of Aesop*, No. 258.
88. *Lev. Rabba* ix, 3, pp. 176–178; see the editor's notes *ibid.*
89. The reference is, apparently, to R. Jonathan, in whose name R. Samuel bar Naḥmani is accustomed to transmit dicta. The story that he narrates testifies to the results of his exhortation to disseminate Torah among the *ʿAmme ha-'Areṣ* (see above, n. 59), which did not, however, reduce his hostility to those who remained ignorant. On disputations with Samaritans see above, p. 924, n. 10.
90. *Gen. Rabba* xxxii 10, pp. 296–297; see *ibid.* n. 5.
91. See *Gen. Rabba* lxxviii, 12, p. 932: 'An *ʿAm ha-'Areṣ* once said to R. Hosea: 'If I tell you a "good word" [felicitous interpretations], will you repeat it in my name in public... He replied: "By thy life! You have said a good word; I shall tell it in your name'; on the other hand see *ibid.* lxxix, 6, p. 943.
92. Undoubtedly in this case, too, we cannot accept the view of A. Büchler, in his book *Der Galiläische ʿAm ha-'Areṣ* (see above, p. 954, n. 85), p. 184, according to which 'It is impossible to accept the reading that R. Akiba uttered the words (regarding the *ʿAmme ha-'Areṣ*, see above, p. 588). It appears that the name R. Akiba is a corruption here of another name, Akavia, Jacob....'
93. *T.B. Bava Batra* 8a.
94. *T.B. Shabbat* 63a.
95. *M. Soṭa* iii, 4,
96. *T.B. ibid.* iii, 3, 19a; *T.B. ibid.* 21b.
97. *T.B. Shabbat* 121b: 'A Tanna recited before Rava bar Rav Huna: He who kills snakes or scorpions on the Sabbath is displeasing to the pious. Said (Rava) to him: And those pietists are displeasing to the Sages.'
98. *T.B. Berakhot* 43b.
99. *T.B. Shabbat* 32a. The printed editions read 'R. Ishmael b. Eleazar', but the MSS. and the Early Authorities have the reading that I have quoted in the text: see *Diqduqe Soferim, ad loc.*, p. 64. On R. Simeon b. Eleazar's attitude to an ugly man see above, p. 640.
1. *T.B. Bava Meṣiʿa* 33b; see *Diqduqe Soferim, ad loc.*, p. 99.
2. See above, p. 467.
3. *Sifre Deut.* § 96; *ibid.* § 308; *ibid.* § 320.
4. See *T.B. Berakhot* 10a, the story about 'Certain highwaymen', where it is Beruria who said to R. Me'ir: 'Rather pray for them that they may repent.' See *Diqduqe Soferim, ad loc.*, p. 39, n. *Hē*'; cf. *Midrash Tehillim* cv, 27, p. 448. *Ibid.* R. Judah says: 'Let them become men of integrity and the wicked shall be no more.'
5. *'Avot de-R. Nathan*, Version I, xxix, p. 87; see *Derekh Ereṣ Zuṭa* ix, and above, pp. 621 ff.
6. *T.B. Ḥullin* 92a; see *Diqduqe Soferim*, 125a, § ה. Cf. *Lev. Rabba* xxxvi, 2, p. 838.
7. *Lev. Rabba* xxx, 12, p. 709, and the parallels cited there. See *T.B. Keritot* vib.

8. *Yalquṭ Shim'oni*, Deut, § 938, culled from *Deut. Zuṭa*; see *Sifre Deut.* § 345.
9. S. Zeitlin, 'The origin of the Synagogue', *PAAJR*, 1931, p. 81. Incidentally συναγωγή was also used of the Christian community, see Schrage, *Theol. WB zum N.T.*, VII, 1964, p. 839.
10. Moore, *Judaism*, I, p. 111.
11. In *Mekhilta de-R. Ishmael*, Shira, iii, p. 128: 'The Congregation of Israel said to the Holy One, blessed be He: Sovereign of the universe', but this is entirely wanting in all the MSS. and also in the *Yalquṭ*. See *ibid.* the vv.ll., and *ibid.*, Wa-yassa', iii, p. 163: 'The Holy One, blessed be He, said to Moses: What the Congregation of Israel said (מה שאמרה כנסת ישראל) is known to Me'; see the vv.ll., *ibid.* 11. The reading in the Oxford, Munich, and *Midrash Ḥakhamim* MSS. is: שאמר ישראל, and in the *Yalquṭ*: מה שישראל אמרו.
12. *Mekhilta de-R. Ishmael* iii, p. 214: 'To receive Israel like a bridegroom going forth to meet his bride'.
13. *Gen. Rabba* xi, 8, p. 94: 'It is taught: R. Simeon b. Yoḥai said... the Congregation of Israel is your match...', but in the *Yalquṭ*: 'The Holy One, blessed be He, said to it: Israel shall be your match'; in the continuation, however, we do find again 'Congregation of Israel': In *Lev. Rabba* xxviii, 6, p. 667, 'The Congregation of Israel says', but in all the MSS. and early editions: 'The Israelites said.' See *T.B. 'Avoda Zara* 35b: 'When Rabbi Dimi came (from Israel) he said: The Congregation of Israel declared...', but it is wanting in *T.P. Berakhot* i, 4, p. 3b; *T.P. 'Avoda Zara* ii, 8, p. 41c.
14. *T.B. Berakhot* 10a on Isa. liv. 1; *ibid.* 32b on Isa. xlix 14: 'His mother means none other than the Congregation of Israel' (but in the *Sifra*, Millu'im, Petiḥa, 15: 'His mother means none other than Israel'); in *T.B. Berakhot* 35b, and *ibid.* 53b and parallel passages cited there: 'The Congregation of Israel is like a dove.' On Isa. li 16 'R. Ḥanina bar Papa said: We went through the whole Bible and we did not find that Israel was called "Zion" except here' — *T.P. Ta'anit* iv, 5, p. 68d; *T.P. Megilla* iii, 7, p. 74b; *Pesiqta de-Rav Kahana* p. 309. Therefore 'Zion' is not to be regarded as the source of the concept 'Congregation of Israel'; see B. Dinaburg, 'Dĕmûtah shel Ṣiyyôn wi-Yerûshālayim bĕ-hakkārātô ha-Histôrît shel Yiśraèl' [The Image of Zion and Jerusalem in the Historic Consciousness of Israel], *Zion*, XVI, 1951, p. 4.
15. *T.B. Shabbat* 88b (on Cant. i 14), in the name of R. Joshua b. Levi; *T.B. 'Eruvin* 21b, in the name of Rava; idem in *T.B. Pesaḥim* 87a. See *ibid.* 118b in the name of Resh Laqish on the verse 'Who maketh the barren woman to dwell in her house' (Psa. cxiii 9); Israel is likened to a mother in *T.B. Sanhedrin* 105a; without any reference to verses alluding thereto, in the name of Rava, *T.B. Pesaḥim* 118b; *T.B. Megilla* 22b.
16. See Cant. i 2; ii 3; in *Ekha Rabbati* v, 11, p. 160, we find 'the Congregation of Israel', but in *Midrash Tehillim* lxxxv, 3, p. 372, 'Israel say to Thee; see *T.B. Berakhot* 53b, where to begin with we have 'Congregation of Israel' and at the end 'Israel'.
17. *T.B. Berakhot* 11b; 29b; 33b; 49b; 60b.

18. Cant. i 14.
19. *Lev. Rabba* xxvii, 7, p. 639.
20. See A. D. Nock-J. Festugière, *Le dieu, La révélation d'Hermes Trismégiste cosmique*, II, 1949, pp. 460 ff.
21. See Hermas, *Sim*, ix, 17, 4.
22. See E. Peterson, *Das Problem des Nationalismus in der alten Kirche*, in *Christentum, Frühkirche*, etc. pp. 51–63.
23. *T.P. Nedarim* iv, 12, p. 38b; see *Gen. Rabba* liii, 12; *T.B. Nedarim* 31a; *T.B. Sanhedrin* 59b.
24. Origen applies this verse to Jesus; see *C. Cels*, *I.* 60, and also Hom, in *Num.*, XXII, 7. R. Aḥa uses this verse to prove that 'Abraham's seed' means Jacob; this is acknowledged even by the Christians in their homilies. It does not seem that R. Aḥa's exposition is directed against the assent to the act of Julian the Apostate; see S. Lieberman, *The Martyrs of Caesarea*, p. 414, and cf. above, p. 689.
25. *Tanḥuma*, ed. Buber, Noah, xxviii, p. 57; see standard *Tanḥuma*, *ibid.*, xix. Cf. *Mekhilta de-R. Ishmael*, Wa-yassa', p. 171: 'And when will the kingdom of the House of David be restored and this guilty kingdom be uprooted?' See *ibid.* the vv.ll. and n. 13.

CHAPTER XVII

ON REDEMPTION

1. See *Encyclopaedia Biblica* [Hebrew], ii, s.v. *Ge'ula*, pp. 389–391, and the bibliography cited there.
2. See J. Klausner, *Ha-ra'yon ha-Meshiḥi be-Yisra'el*,[3] 1950, pp. 24–56; Judah Kaufmann [Yehuda ibn Shemu'el], *Midrĕshê Gĕ'ûlā*,[4] 1954, General Introduction. I shall indicate the abundant literature on our subject only in so far as this is required for the subjects I shall touch upon. A good collection of sources has been furnished by M. Zobel, *Gottes Gesalbter, der Messias und die Messianische Zeit in Talmud und Midrasch*, Berlin 1938. An authoritative contribution to the elucidation of the Messianic question in Judaism was made by G. Scholem in his article 'Zum Verständnis der messianischen Idee im Judentum', *Judaica*, 1963, p. 757. Not a few studies have not added anything to our knowledge, but have presented a collection of material without naming the sources; see K. Hruby, *Judaica*, Zurich 1964, pp. 6–22, 73–90, 193–212; and *ibid.* 21 (1945), 100–122.
3. G. Scholem in his brochure *Ra'yon ha-Ge'ula be-Qabbala*[2] [The Concept of Redemption in the Kabbala], 1950, p. 10, exaggerated, in my opinion, in stating that 'classical Judaism was fond of emphasizing the catastrophic aspect of redemption.' The question is, who in 'classical Judaism' was fond of this? See now his aforementioned article, pp. 10 ff.
4. See my article 'Matay paseqa ha-Nevu'a?' *Tarbiz*, XVII (1946), p. 6, and *ibid.*, n. 42.
5. Although the polemical aims are not explicitly stated in Rabbinic dicta, as for example in the remarks of Naḥmanides in *Sefer ha-Ge'ula*, ed. J. M. Aharonson, Jerusalem 1959, pp. 21–22, who declares 'that the base, falsifying people that has replaced our Torah by another...' is responsible for the fact that 'many commentators' apply to 'the subject of the future redemption only such verses as necessarily deal with it and refer to it alone', yet they are also discernible in the teachings of the Sages.
6. This is the source of the polemic centering on the words of Maimonides in

'Hilkhot Teshuva [Laws of Repentance]' viii, 2; see *'Arugat ha-Bośem*, II, pp. 254–262, and cf. *ibid.* p. 259: 'And I have already shown that there are three kinds of "worlds to come".' See *ibid.* p. 256, and my article in *Zion*, 1947, p. 149.

7. See *'Arugat ha-Bośem, ibid.*, p. 256.
8. A contrary opinion is expressed by I. Baer, 'Le-Bêrurah shel Torat 'Aḥarit ha-Yamim bi-Yeme ha-Bayit ha-Sheni', *Zion*, XXIII–XXIV (1958–1959), p. 5. His criticism that 'The representatives of Jewish philosophy in the Middle Ages, who sought to separate the inseparable, interpreted the tradition on this subject incorrectly' appears to me unjustified. See my article 'Hilkhot Yerushsha we-Ḥayye 'Olam', *Papers of Fourth World Congress of Jewish Studies*, I, 1967, pp. 138 ff; cf. also L. Finkelstein, *Mavo' le-Massekhtot 'Avot we-'Avot de-R. Nathan*, New York 1951, p. 218. On the meaning of 'end of days' in the Bible and the difference between this expression and 'End', and on the distinction between ἔσχατον and καιρός see H. Kosmala, 'At the End of Days', *Annual of the Swedish Theological Institute*, II, 1963, pp. 27–37; cf. J. Licht, 'Torat ha-'Ittim shel Kat Midbar Yehuda we-shel Meḥashsheve Qiṣṣim 'Aḥerim [The Doctrine of Times of the Qumran Sect and of other Calculators of the End]', *Eretz-Israel*, Book VIII, 1967, pp. 63–70. On the different use of 'End' in *IV Ezra*, see N. Stone, 'The Concept of the Messiah in IV Ezra', *Studies in the History of Religions*, XIV, 1968, pp. 298 ff.
9. See above, p. 436 and, p. 653.
10. On resurrection in the Bible see Y. Kaufmann, *Toledot ha-'Emuna ha-Yisre'elit*, III, pp. 191 ff, and p. 523, and on the question of the influence of the Persian religion see F. König, *Zarathustras Jenseitsworstellungen und das A.T.*, Vienna 1964. The author made use of the earlier literature, pp. 171 ff, and pp. 262 ff; his evaluations are very balanced.
11. *M. Sanhedrin* x, 1, according to the version of the Kaufmann MS. (the words *min ha-Tora* [prescribed in the Law] are wanting also in the Cambridge MS., and in Maimonides' version of the Mishna), and the opening passage 'All Israel' is missing *ibid.* R. Solomon Luria [Maharshal] in *Sefer Hokhmat Shelomo* on Rashi writes: 'Some recensions read here "All Israel have a share in the world to come"; this section does not belong to this Mishna, but is merely a Haggada and has been inserted here in order to provide the chapter with an auspicious opening...'; see *Diqduqe Soferim*, *ibid.*, p. 247. It is surprising that Finkelstein, *op. cit.*, pp. 252 ff, ignored all this; his remarks, *ibid.*, p. 227, n. 5, are unfounded. This apart, 'the resurrection of the dead' is mentioned in *M. Berakhot* v, 2, 'We make mention of "the power of rain" in "the resurrection of the dead",' that is, in the benediction for the resurrection of the dead. But see *M. Ta'anit* i, 1; *T.B. ibid.* 2a; cf. Tosafot of R. Judah Sir Leon to *T.B. Berakhot* 19b. In *M. Rosh ha-Shana* iv, 5: 'The order of the benedictions: One says "The Fathers", "Power", and "the Hallowing of the Name".' To begin with, apparently, the benedic-

tion was intended to give thanks for the Power of the Lord, and only when the need was felt to stress the belief in the resurrection was it given a central position in the benediction of Power. See L. Ginzberg, *Perushim we-Ḥiddushim bi-Yerushalmi*, Pt. IV, pp. 164–168, and *ibid.* pp. 185–198. *M. Soṭa* ix, 15, is merely an addition that is not to be found even in early printed editions (in the words of R. Phinehas b. Jair: 'the Holy Spirit leads to the resurrection of the dead' etc.); see J. N. Epstein, *Mavo' le-Nosaḥ ha-Mishna*, p. 976.

12. In his commentary on the Mishna 'Three kings and four commoners have no share in the world to come', Maimonides observes: 'It [the Mishna] mentions these on account of their high degree of wisdom. Thus it informs us that the foundations of their faith were undermined....' With regard to an 'Epicurean', who regards the world as 'self-moving (αὐτόματος)' see above, p. 28. On the question of 'the Torah is not from Heaven' — and hence is wholly subject to allegorical interpretation — see above, p. 297. With regard to one who asks 'Do the dead live?' being called a 'Min' [Sectarian] see *Exod. Rabba* xliv, 6.
13. *Wars* ii, 8, 11, and *ibid.* 14; *Ant.* xviii, 1, 3.
14. *Tosefta Sanhedrin* xiii, 1, p. 434; see *Rosh ha-Shana* 16b.
15. See *M. Ta'anit* ii, 2–4; cf. the Hashlamot of H. Albeck to Seder Mo'ed, p. 492; *Tosefta Ta'aniyyot* i, 9–11, ed. Lieberman, p. 326; see *Tosefta ki-Fshuṭah* to Mo'ed, p. 1074.
16. See Jacob Mann, 'Jewish Fragments of the Palestinian Order of Service', *HUCA*, II (1925), p. 306; S. Assaf, 'Mi-Seder ha-Tefilla be-'Ereṣ Yisra'el', *Sefer Dinaburg*, 1949, p. 117. In *Siddur Rav 'Amram* there are added the words 'for Thou art a mighty Redeemer'. In 'Seder ha-Tefilla shel ha-Rambam', Oxford MS., ed. D. Goldschmidt, *Studies of the Research Institute for Hebrew Poetry*, Book VII, 1959, p. 196: 'and hasten to redeem us for Thou art a mighty, redeeming God (and) King'. None of these versions is decisive, and only in a fragment from the Geniza published by Schechter, *JQR*, X, pp. 657, 659, do we find: 'And bring near speedily the year of the end of our redemption.' Also the words 'and bringest a redeemer to their children's children' of the first benediction do not occur in the version of Eretz-Israel, which is 'the great, mighty and revered God, the most high God, the Creator of heaven and earth, our Shield, the Shield of our fathers, our Trust in every generation, never shall they that hope in Thee be put to shame. Blessed art Thou, O Lord, Shield of Abraham.' See S. Assaf, *op. cit.*, p. 117.
17. In *T.P. Berakhot* ii, 4, p. 4d the question is raised: 'Then let (the benediction) "who healest the sick" be said first!' and the teaching of R. Aḥa is cited in reply, but originally this exposition was not given in this context.
18. Genesis xlviii 16; Job xix 25; see above, n. 1.
19. *Sifre Deut.* § 343. S. D. Luzzatto comments on the passage of the *Sifre* in his Introduction to the *Maḥzor Bnê Roma* [Festival Prayer Book of Rome], Livorno 1856, pp. 5 ff; but his conjecture that 'loosest the bound' was orig-

inally the closing formula of the seventh benediction is not necessarily correct, since the homilist does not enumerate the closing formulas of the benedictions. Many studies have been devoted to the history of the Eighteen Benedictions, and opinions are divided with regard to both its unitary character and its date. See most recently A. Mirski, 'Meqorah shel Tefillat Shemone 'Eśre', *Tarbiz*, 1964, pp. 28 ff, where all the preceding literature is recorded. The actual fixing of the number of the Eighteen Benedictions is better attested perhaps both by the wording of the *Sifre* 'The Eighteen (Benedictions) ordained by the early: Sages', and by the expression of R. Joshua b. Levi 'Also he that composed this Prayer', than by the 'tradition' concerning the 'hundred and twenty elders of whom more than eighty were prophets' (on this tradition see L. Ginzburg, *Perushim we-Ḥiddushim bi-Yerushalmi*, I, pp. 327–220), but only their themes and closing formulas were determined. Needless to say their wording was not uniform; nor was their order and number decided before the period of Jabneh (see S. Lieberman, *Tosefta ki-Fshuṭah*, Pt. I, p. 53). Even the statement in the *Sifre* 'And likewise the Eighteen Benedictions... do not begin with Israel's needs, but with the praise of the Omnipresent' is only in accordance with the view of R. Joshua (a fact that even Mirsky overlooked), 'A man should (first) say the Prayer and then ask for his personal needs, while R. Eliezer rules 'A man should (first) ask for his personal needs and then say the Prayer' (*T.B. 'Avoda Zara* 7b; *T.P. Berakhot* iv, 8, p. 8b). It is possible that 'Simeon ha-Paquli [Rashi: 'cotton dealer'] arranged the eighteen benedictions in proper order before Rabban Gamliel in Jabneh' (*T.B. Berakhot* 28b; *T.B. Megilla* 17b) following R. Joshua's sequence; see L. Ginzberg, *op. cit.*, p. 322. See now Isaac D. Gilat, *Mishnato shel R. Eliezer b. Hyrcanus u-Meqomah be-Toledot ha-Halakha*, Tel Aviv 1968, pp. 83 ff, and his reference to me *ibid.*, p. 86, n. 9. Cf. also Rav Assi's statement in *T.B. Berakhot* 34a 'The intermediate benedictions have no fixed order'; see Rashi, *ad loc.*, s.v. *'En*; Tosafot s.v. *'Emṣā 'iyyôt*; the Novellae of R. Solomon b. Abraham Adert [Rashba] on *T.B. Megilla, loc. cit.*, ed. H. Z. Dimitrovsky, p. 72, and *ibid.* n. 27.

20. See above, n. 15.
21. *T.B. Megilla* 17b; the MSS. and the Early Authorities read: R. Ḥiyya bar Abba; see *Diqduqe Soferim.*, p. 97. The view expressed by Ginzberg, *ibid.*, p. 330, is un-acceptable.
22. It is cited *in extenso* in *T.B. Sanhedrin* 97a.
23. L. Ginzberg, *op. cit.*, p. 324, overlooked this annotation of Rashi in rejecting Luzzatto's view. The plural used in the prayer for redemption is satisfactorily explained by Mirsky in his aforementioned article, *ibid.*, p. 35.
24. *M. Yoma* vii, 1; *M. Soṭa* vii, 7. I have cited the recension found in the Kaufmann MS.; current editions read 'and for the Temple separately, and for Israel separately, and for Jerusalem separately and for the priests separately.' For the text of other MSS. see *Diqduqe Soferim*, to *T.B. Yoma*, p. 195, n. נ.
25. R. 'Idi cites here a parallel version to the closing formula 'who choosest

the Temple'; this was possibly responsible for the inclusion of 'Jerusalem' into the text of the Mishna, but Jerusalem is not mentioned in the *Tosefta*, *loc. cit.*, iii, 18, ed. Lieberman, p. 247.

26. 'Hilkhot 'Avodat Yom ha-Kippurim [Laws concerning the Service on the Day of Atonement]', iii, 11.
27. 'Perush R. Yoseph Naḥmias', *JJLG*, XXVII, p. 13; see S. Lieberman, *Tosefta ki-Fshuṭah*, Mo'ed, p. 802.
28. See ed. Segal, ch. xxxvi, 225, and his notes *ad loc.*, p. 227.
29. See *ibid.*, pp. 355–356.
30. See Y. Kaufmann, *Toledot ha-'Emuna ha-Yiśre'elit*, VI, p. 376; cf. above, p. 298.
31. xlviii 11; ed. Segal, p. 330.
32. *T.B. Berakhot* 48b; *T.P. ibid.* cites the ruling 'in the name of R. Ba b. R. Aḥa in the name of Rabbi'; the Munich MS. of the Babylonian Talmud also omits 'Eliezer'. But see *Diqduqe Soferim*, p. 258, n. ע, and the statement of R. Jose b. R. Judah, *T.B. Berakhot* 49a, where the Munich MS. reads 'R. Joshua'; cf. *Diqduqe Soferim*, *ad loc.*, n. ב. R. Abba's stricture *ibid.* 'And whoever concludes with the formula "who savest Israel"... is an ignoramus' implies that some were accustomed to say this. In the Gemara, however, the statement of R. Jose is explained to mean 'who also savest Israel'.
33. On the versions of the grace after meals see L. Finkelstein, *JQR*, XIX, pp. 211–252; and S. Assaf, *Sefer Dinaburg*, p. 129. In 'The Teaching of the (Twelve) Apostles', Διδαχή, there is even found the blessing 'and gather Thy church from the ends of the earth to Thy kingdom'; G. Klein, *Der Älteste Christl. Katechismus und die jüd. Propaganda-Literatur*, Berlin 1902, did not succeed in finding a suitable parallel. H. Köster, *Synoptische Überlieferungen bei den Apostal. Vätern*, 1957, p. 194, stresses that the author of ' "The Teaching of the Twelve Apostles" did not draw upon the Synoptic Gospels (see Matthew xii 42), but upon a prayer of the community, and points to the passage of the *Musaf 'Amida* 'Bring our scattered ones among the nations near unto Thee, and gather our dispersed from the ends of the earth.'
34. E. Schürer, *Geschichte des jüd. Volkes*, I, p. 245.
35. *T.B. Soṭa* 48b; so, too, in the Munich MS. See *T.P. Qiddushin* iv, 1, p. 65b.
36. *M. Sanhedrin* ii, 2; *T.B. ibid.* 19a–b. Rav Joseph is the author of this tradition. In *T.P. Sanhedrin* ii, 3, p. 20a the Rabbis resort to forced explanations in order to reconcile, in accordance with the methods of ethical Haggada, the Mishna ruling with the verses that refer to David's judgement.
37. See *T.B. Sanhedrin* 19a, and above, p. 946, n. 98.
38. See above, p. 572.
39. *T.B. Qiddushin* 66a.
40. See above, p. 575.
41. Above, p. 581.
42. Above, p. 576.
43. See below, n. 60.

44. See *Tosefta Sanhedrin* xiii, 3, p. 434, and above, p. 652.
45. *M. ʿEduyot* viii, 7; see above, p. 298. It appears that R. Judah and the Sages only dispute the phrasing of R. Joḥanan's dictum; the wording of the Sages 'not to put away nor to bring nigh, but to make peace in the world...' fits in with the well-known homily of Rabban Joḥanan b. Zakkai concerning peace, in *Mekhilta*, Ba-ḥodesh, xi, p. 244. Only in *Pirqe de-R. Eliezer*, xliii, is the view ascribed to R. Judah that 'Israel will not repent on a large scale until Elijah, of blessed memory, comes.'
46. See 'De Praem. et Poenis' § 165: 'When they have gained this unexpected liberty, those who but now were scattered in Greece and the outside world over islands and continents will arise and post from every side with one impulse to the one appointed place, guided in their pilgrimage by a vision divine....'

    Philo echoes here the prayer for the gathering of the banished ones of Israel (see above, n. 33). On the other elements in the descriptions of 'the time to come' see H. A. Wolfson, II, pp. 408–426. It seems to me that the expression 'Messianic age' is not suited to Philo's portrayal.
47. See P. Volz, *Die Eschatologie der jüdeschen Gemeinde*,[2] 1934, pp. 26 ff; J. Klausner, *op. cit.*, pp. 158 ff, and pp. 261 ff. D. S. Russel, *The Method and Message of Jewish Apocalyptic*, Philadelphia 1964, where a detailed bibliography is given pp. 430–436. Cf. K. Hruby, 'L'influence des apocalypses sur l'eschatologie judéo-chrétienne', *L'Orient Syrien*, 1966, pp. 291–320.
48. An excellent discussion on the subject of the 'two Messiahs' is to be found in Jacob Liver, *Toledot Bet David* [The History of the House of David], Jerusalem 1959, pp. 116–140. See also A. S. Van der Woude, *Die Messianischen Vorstellungen der Gemeinde von Qumran*, Assen 1957, pp. 27 ff and also pp. 217 ff.
49. See J. Licht, *Megillat ha-Serakhim*, p. 188 and *ibid.*, 247. The Aramaic fragment found in Qumran cave 4, which describes the birth, body, and spiritual development of a boy designated 'the elect of God', produced an entire literature of Messianic exegesis. To my mind J. A. Fitzmyer, 'The Aramaic Text from Qumran Cave IV "Elect of God",' *The Catholic Biblical Quarterly*, XXVII (1965), pp. 348–372, is right in casting doubts on 'the Messianic character' of the fragment. He correctly stresses the resemblance of the type of stories concerning the birth of Noah in *Enoch*, cvi–cviii, *Jubilees* iv, 10, and *A Genesis Apocryphon*; see *ibid.*, p. 371, and cf. above, p. 492.
50. See the Introduction of Menaḥem Stein, *Ha-Sefarim ha-Ḥiṣoniyyim* [Apocrypha], ed. A. Kahana, I, p. 431. The lengthy essay of Joshua Ephron, *Zion*, 1965, pp. 1–46, which seeks to prove that the work blends with the pattern of Christian theology, is unconvincing. Cf. above, p. 694, n. 12.
51. This verse appears to me to allude to Dan. vii 18 'But the saints of the Most High shall receive the kingdom....' The Palestinian Targum to Gen. xlix 10–12 is not necessarily the parallel to Psalm xvii of *The Psalms of Solomon*, as P. Grelot, 'Le Messie dans les Apocryphes de l'AT, *Recherches Bibliques*, VI,

1962, pp. 30 ff. This author belongs to the school of 'the new study of the Targum', and he regards the above passage of the Targum as testimony to the pre-Christian period; see *ibid.*, p. 20, n. 5. However, if there is any need for further proofs in refutation of this approach, the comparison cited above can provide them. See below, n. 64.

52. See John vii 41–42: '... Shall Christ come out of Galilee? Hath not the scripture said, That Christ cometh of the seed of David.' Subsequently, the lack was supplied.
53. *T.B. Yoma* 39b.
54. See above, p. 990, n. 4.
55. *'Avot de-R. Nathan*, Version II, vii, 11a.
56. *Ibid.*, Version I, iv, 11a; see my article 'Megammot Datiyyot we-Ḥevratiyyot be-Torat ha-Ṣedaqa shel Ḥazal', *Zion*, xvi, 1951, pp. 6 ff.
57. *M. ʿEduyot* viii, 6 (see Tosafot *T.B. Ḥullin* 17a, s.v. *We-khol she-ken*); however, the statements refer to the initial period of the Second Temple. On the attempt to rebuild the Temple in the days of R. Joshua see above, pp. 672–3; on the exile and return of the Shekhina see above, pp. 55–56.
58. *'Avot de-R. Nathan* xxxi, 33b–34a.
59. *Tosefta Bava Qamma* xii, 5; *T.P. Qiddushin* i, 2, p. 59d; *T.B. ibid.* 22b.
60. See my article 'Ha-Masorot ʿal Torat ha-Sod bi-Tequfat ha-Tanna'im', *Meḥqarim ba-Qabbala u-be-Toledot ha-Datot'*, 1968, pp. 1–7.
61. *T.P. Soṭa* ix, 17, p. 24c; *T.P. ʿAvoda Zara* iii, 1, p. 42c (where it is related that his disciple R. Eliezer said 'and set a throne for R. Joḥanan b. Zakkai', but 'another view is: What his teacher saw he also saw'). In *'Avot de-R. Nathan*, Version I, xxv, 40b, the story, introduced by the words 'He used to say', is connected to another account of the passing of Rabban Joḥanan b. Zakkai, and it is similarly joined to this narrative in *T.B. Berakhot* 28b, only there and in the Oxford MS. of *'Avot de-R. Nathan* the reading is: 'for Hezekiah, king of Judah, who cometh.' On the various interpretations and conjectures that have been advanced regarding the identity of Hezekiah see J. Neussner, *A Life of Rabban Yohanan ben Zakkai*, Leiden 1962, pp. 172 ff.
62. See *T.B. Sanhedrin* 94a–b.
63. *T.B. Sanhedrin* 97b–98a; see *Diqduqe Soferim, ad loc.*, p. 288. In *T.P. Taʿanit* i, 1, p. 63d the two Baraitas have been combined and it appears that the abbreviation אל (=אלא) was erroneously changed to א״ל and interpreted as אמר לו 'he said to him', to which 'R. Eliezer' was added. Thus it came about that it was he who said: 'The Holy One, blessed be He, will appoint over them a cruel king....' The expression מה עבד לה ר׳ ליעז׳ ['What does R. Liezer do with it (i.e. the verse)?'] and likewise the interpolation of R. Aḥaʿs dictum in the name of R. Joshua b. Levi into the discussion show that the text was not formulated there by the editor. See *Tanḥuma*, Be-ḥuqqotay, 3 — the disputants are R. Judah and R. Simeon — and *Tanḥuma*, ed. Buber, *ibid.*, where R. Joshua states: 'Whether they repent or do not repent, as soon as the End arrives, they will immediately be redeemed, as it is said:

"I the Lord will hasten it in its time" '; after this the dictum about the wicked king is added in the name of R. Eleazar.

64. It is not improbable that the Septuagint rendering already is a 'theological' interpretation, although it is possibly based on a text 'And a redeemer will come to Zion and transgression shall turn away from Jacob [ושב פשע מיעקב]; similar to Hosea xiv 5 'for Mine anger is turned away from him [ושב אפי ממנו]' ὅτι ἀπέστρεψε. The *Peshiṭta* translates ואילין דמפנין עולא מן יעקב which corresponds to ושבי פשע ביעקב ['and those who turn from transgression in Jacob']. Targum pseudo-Jonathan agrees with the Septuagint ולאתבא מרודיא דבית יעקב לאוריתא; A. Sperber, *Kitvê ha-Qōdesh ba-'Ăramit* [The Scriptures in Aramaic], iii, 1962, has not indicated any vv.ll. Compare the expression *shāvê yiśra'el* in *The Damascus Document* iv, 2; vi, 5. See L. Ginzberg, *Eine unbekannte jüd. Sekte*, New York 1922, p. 18; C. Rabin, *The Zadokite Documents*, Oxford 1958, p. 13 and p. 23; G. Vermes, *Scripture and Tradition in Judaism*, Leiden 1961, p. 43. Cf. critique of J. Heinemann, *Tarbiz*, XXXV (1926), pp. 84 ff, and above, n. 51.
65. On the various interpretations of Paul's words see D. Michel, *Der Brief an die Römer*, 1966, pp. 278–283.
66. *T.B. Yoma* 86b, according to the recension of the *editio princeps* of the *'En Ya'aqov*, and *Yalquṭ Shim'oni*, Isaiah, § 498; see *Diqduqe Soferim*, *T.B. Yoma*, p. 296, n. *Qôf.*
67. *Mekhilta de-R. Ishmael*, Wa-yassa', iv, p. 169; see vv.ll., *ibid.*, n. 10, and *ibid.*, Massekhta da-Amalek, i, p. 194; cf. *Mekhilta de-R. Simeon b. Yoḥai*, p. 113, where this dictum is reported in the name of R. Joshua. See *T.B. Shabbat* 118b, and cf. *'Arugat-ha-Bośem*, Pt. III, p. 157, n. 96, and below, p. 1008, n. 57.
68. *T.B. Sanhedrin* 98b; the printed editions read 'Eleazar', but see *Diqduqe Soferim*, p. 393, n. ס.
69. *T.B. Rosh ha-Shana* 11a, where R. Eliezer says 'On Rosh ha-Shana the bondage of our ancestors in Egypt came to an end', and these words also appear in the dictum of R. Joshua, but from Tosafot, *ad loc.*, s.v. *Be-ro'sh*, it seems that there were some books in which they did not occur.
70. See *Mekhilta de-R. Ishmael*, Pisḥa, xiv, p. 52, where the text has: 'In Tishri, for it is said "Blow the horn on the new moon",' and in *T.B. Rosh ha-Shana* 11b we read: 'In one place it is written, "Blow the horn on the new moon", and elsewhere it is written "In that day a great horn shall be blown"; see Maharsha [R. Samuel Eliezer Edels] *ad loc.*
71. *Mekhilta de-R. Ishmael*, Pisḥa, v, p. 15; see below, n. 75.
72. *Gen. Rabba* lxiv, 10, pp. 710–712; see the literature listed there. Cf. G. Alon, *Toledot ha-Yehudim be-'Ereṣ Yiśra'el bi-Tequfat ha-Mishna we-ha-Talmud*, Pt. I, pp. 272 ff.
73. See *M. 'Eduyot* ii, 9; *Tosefta*, *ibid.*, i, 14 p. 456; cf. *Mekhilta de-R. Ishmael.* Pisḥa, xiv, p. 50, the statement of Rabbi.
74. See Y. Yadin, 'Maḥane IV — Me'arat ha-'Iggerot [Camp IV — the Cave

of Letters]', *Yedi'ot ba-ḥaqirat 'Ereṣ-Yiśra'el wa-'Atiqoteha*, XXVI (1962), pp. 214 ff; idem, *ibid.*, 'Ha-Mimsā'îm mi-yĕmê Bar-Kokhba bi-mĕ'ārat ha-'Iggĕrôt [The Finds from the Time of Bar Kokhba in the Cave of Letters], Nispaḥ. Ha-'Ṣiṣiyyot' [Appendix II, 'The Fringes'], p. 289.

75. *T.B. Soṭa* 11b; in the printed ed., 'R. 'Awira'. But in the Munich MS., the *Haggadot ha-Talmud*, and in *'En Ya'aqov, editio princeps*, we find 'R. Akiba'. This view is followed by the Rabbis in their homily on the verse 'Hark! my beloved! behold, he cometh, leaping upon the mountains...' in *Pesiqta de-Rav Kahana*, ed. Mandelbaum, pp. 88–89, while R. Judah explains it to mean that the Holy One, blessed be He, takes no account of the End, but 'skips over the "ends" and the calculations', and R. Nehemiah interprets the verse to signify that He 'takes no cognizance of their idolatry'. All of them speak of the deliverance from Egypt, but their words refer to the future redemption. In effect none of them makes the redemption depend absolutely either on the End or on repentance, but on the grace of the Holy One, blessed be He. R. Judah tempers the view of R. Joshua, and R. Nehemiah moderates that of R. Eliezer, apparently under the influence of the troubles of their time following the Bar Kokhba Revolt, but R. Nehemiah is not to be regarded as differing completely from the view of R. Eliezer. The sentence 'Moses our teacher, how can we be redeemed when the land of Egypt is full of the filth of our idolatry' points to the fact that the Israelites admit that they have sinned and are prepared to repent, but have not yet succeeded in removing idolatry from their midst. Moses answers them: 'Since He (God) desires your redemption, He takes no cognizance of your idolatry but skips over....' See A. Marmorstein, 'Ra'yon ha-Ge'ula ba-'Aggadat ha-Tanna'im we-ha-'Amora'im', *Sefer Zikkaron li-Khĕvod A. Marmorstein*, London 1950, p. 29. On the subject of the righteous cf. also *Cant. Rabba* ii, 2.

76. *Sifre*, *'Eqev*, § 43; *T.B. Makkot* 24a; *'Ekha Rabbati* v, 18. Ostensibly our exposition of R. Akiba's conception of redemption does not accord with the Baraita that reports the Midrashic interpretation of Dan. viii 9 ' "Till thrones were placed" — one for Him and one for David. Said R. Jose the Galilean to him: "Akiba, how long will you treat the Shekhina as profane. Rather (the meaning is:) One for justice and one for grace.' The Gemara says that R. Akiba accepted the view of R. Jose the Galilean, for in another Baraita it is stated: 'One for justice and one for grace; this is the view of R. Akiba. Said R. Eleazar b. Azariah to him: "Akiba, what have you to do with Haggada? Cease your talk and turn to (the laws of defilement through) leprosy-signs and tent-covering.' Rather (the meaning is): One for a throne and one for a stool....' (*T.B. Ḥagiga* 14a; *T.B. Sanhedrin* 38b). It should be noted that in both passages the explanation 'One for Him and one for David' is given anonymously in the Talmud, and it is corroborated by the first Baraita, which is contradicted by the second Baraita. R. Jose the Galilean's objection applies even with regard to the homily of R. Eleazar b. Azariah.

77. *Sifra*, Be-ḥuqqotay, 112b; *T.B. Sanhedrin* 110b.

78. See my article cited above, p. 996, n. 60, and *ibid.*, pp. 11 ff.

79. *M. ʿEduyot*, ii, 10. The words לעתיד לבוא ['in the time to come'] are found in the Kaufmann MS. and the Cambridge MS; the absence of לבוא in the Munich MS. (see *Diqduqe Soferim*, p. 3) makes no difference, and J. Klausner's remarks in the *Ha-Raʿyon ha-Meshiḥi*, p. 30, are not correct. See *Tosefta ʿArakhin* ii, 1, p. 544; in *T.B. ibid.* 13b we read: 'The harp of the Sanctuary had seven cords... of the Messianic era, eight... of the world to come, ten...' (in the *Tosefta* 'in the time to come, ten'). In regard to the Torah's being forgotten by and being restored to its students, see above, p. 310.

80. *T.P. Taʿanit* iv, p. 68d; see *Ekha Rabbati* ii, 4, 21a.

81. In the Septuagint שבט ['sceptre'] is rendered by ἄνθρωπος, 'man', and Targum Onkelos translated the verse: 'There shall step forth a star out of Jacob, and a sceptre shall arise out of Israel' by כד יקום מלכא מיעקב ויתרבא משיחה מישראל ['When a king arises from Jacob and the Messiah is raised up from Israel']. See the *Damascus Document* vii, 19–20, ed. Rabin, p. 31: 'And the "star" means he that expounds the Torah... the "sceptre" signifies the chief of the whole congregation.' Cf. L. Ginzberg, *ibid.*, p. 48; Vermes, ***op. cit.***, p. 59. On 'man — my servant' in *IV Ezra* see M. Stone in his aforementioned article, pp. 307 ff.

82. See above, p. 309; there is not the slightest evidence that Bar Kokhba claimed to be related to the House of David. S. Yeivin's contention, *Milḥemet Bar-Kokhba* [The Bar Kokhba War], pp. 62–66, was rightly rejected by J. Liver, *op. cit.*, p. 145.

83. *T.B. Sanhedrin* 93b; see *Diqduqe Soferim, ad loc.*, p. 165 note *Yôd.* It seems that the story is cited in corroboration of Rava's interpretation of the verse 'והריחו [usually rendered 'And his delight'] shall be in the fear of the Lord' — 'He will judge by the scent', an interpretation that is opposed to the view of R. Alexander: [It means] 'that He loaded him with precepts and sufferings as with a millstone [רחיים].'

84. *T.P. Taʿanit, loc. cit.*

85. *Mekhilta*, Wa-yassaʿ, iv, p. 169.

86. *Tosefta Menaḥot* xiii, 22, p. 533; see *T.P.*, *Yoma* i, 1, p. 38c; *T.B. ibid.* 9a.

87. *Tosefta ʿAvoda Zara* v, 3, p. 466 (see *Tosefet Riʾshonim*, Pt. III, p. 192); the conclusion 'and anyone who is buried in Eretz-Israel is as though he were buried beneath the altar' is merely an addition that found a surrogate for living in Eretz-Israel. See *T.P. Kilʾayim* ix, 4 (*ad fin.*), p. 32c — *T.P. Ketubbot* xii, 3 (*ad fin.*) p. 35b; *T.B. ibid.* 111a. The *Petiḥa* in *'Avot de-R. Nathan*, Version I, xxvi, p. 82: 'Whoever is buried in other countries is as though he were buried in Babylonia; whoever is buried in Babylonia is as though he were buried in Eretz-Israel...' nullifies the significance of burial in Eretz-Israel. As regards burial beneath the altar see S. Lieberman, *Hellenism in Jewish Palestine*, p. 269.

88. See *Tosefta, ibid.*, 4–5; *T.B. Bava Batra* 91a–b.

89. *Mekhilta de-R. Ishmael*, Massekhta de-Ba-ḥodesh, vi, p. 227.

90. *T.B. Sanhedrin* 97b.
91. See *Seder 'Olam Rabba* xxx, ed. Ratner, p. 146; cf. the notes *ibid.*
92. *T.B. Sanhedrin* 97a. The apocalyptic Mishna at the end of *Tractate Soṭa* (ix, 15) is only an addition consisting of the Baraitas in the name of R. Judah and R. Nehorai in *T.B. Sanhedrin, ibid.* (see J.N. Epstein, *Mavo' le-Nosaḥ ha-Mishna*, p. 976, and H. Albeck, 'Hashlamot' to Seder Nashim, p. 394). In *Cant. Rabba* ii, 13, they are reported in the name of Resh Laqish and that which I have cited in the text in the name of R. Joḥanan. See *Tractate Derekh Ereṣ Zuṭa*, x, and the appendices to *Seder Eliahu Zuṭa*, ed. R. Me'ir Ish Shalom, p. 11. Nevertheless scholars have not refrained from citing the Mishna in *Soṭa* as evidence of the views of its realistic and anti-mystical redactor; see G. Scholem in his aforementioned article (see above, p. 990, n. 2) p. 79, and D. Russel, p. 31.
93. The *Syriac Apocalypse of Baruch*, xxvi–xxix. See also the *Book of Enoch* xci 12–17, and ch. xciii; cf. J. Licht in his aforementioned article, pp. 66–67, who for some reason overlooked the chapters cited above from *The Apocalypse of Baruch* and the Baraita.
94. *T.B. Sanhedrin* 97a; *T.B. 'Avoda Zara* 9a. The words 'but on account of our many sins so many (years) have passed away' are a late interpolation. Not without reason Rashi added s.v. *U-shĕnê 'ălāfîm Tôrā*: 'not that the Torah would cease (to be studied) after two thousand years', for there were apocalyptic circles who conceived the Messianic era as one devoid of Torah-learning; see above, p. 311.
95. Only in *Pesiqta Rabbati* i, 4b, and in *Midrash Tehillim* xc, 17, p. 393, is the view ascribed to R. Joshua that the Messianic age would endure two thousand years. But this is clearly due to the influence of our Baraita, as is proved by the parallel Baraita *T.B. Sanhedrin* 99a. In *Tanḥuma*, 'Eqev, § 6 it is reported in the name of R. Eliezer that the Messianic era will endure a thousand years, but the whole passage, *ibid.* § 6, is an addition from the Mantua edition and is wanting in all the MSS. and in the early editions; see *Tanḥuma*, ed. Buber, 'Eqev, p. 18, n. 22. Apparently the concept emanates from *Pesiqta Rabbati*, or from a similar source, and there it is cited in the name of R. Eliezer b. R. Jose the Galilean, giving the period as 'a thousand years'; in *Mekhilta de-R. Ishmael*, Amalek, ii, p. 187, it is stated that the generation of the Messiah will be three generations. The same statement occurs anonymously in *Sifre Deut.* § 310, which corresponds to the period of one hundred years mentioned at the beginning of the *Tanḥuma, ibid.* The table given in Strack-Billerbeck, III, p. 826, and his observations *ibid.*, p. 827, are unfounded.
96. See E. Böklen, *Die Verwandschaft der jüd. christlichen mit der Parsischen Eschatologie*, Göttingen 1902, pp. 81–84, where all the parallels are listed; Bousset-Gressmann, pp. 507 ff; A. von Gall, βασιλεία τοῦ θεοῦ, Heidelberg 1926, p. 122 and p. 275; cf. Volz, pp. 143 ff. The Baraita resembles more the Iranian calculations as they are known from Plutarch, *De Iside et Osiride*,

47, on the one hand, and from the later Persian sources on the other, than the other parallels in the Jewish pseudepigraphical literature and the early Christian works. The view of I. Scheftelowitz, *Die Altpersische Religion und das Judentum*, 1920, p. 100, is unfounded, and there is no reason for not assuming here some influence of the eschatological calculations of the Iranian environment. On the question of influences see G. Widengren, *Stand und Aufgaben der iranischen Religionsgeschichte*, 1955, I, pp. [25] 39 ff, and *ibid.*, II, pp. [131] 107 ff. Regarding the apocalyptic chronology see now idem, *Die Religionen Irans*, 1965, pp. 201 ff.

97. *T.B. ʿEruvin* 43a; see the Commentary of R. Ḥananel, and Tosafot, *ibid.*, 43b, s.v. *Wĕ-'āsûr*. Cf. R. Me'ir Ish Shalom *Mavo' le-Seder Eliahu Rabba*, p. 21, n. 1.
98. *T.P. Berakhot* i, p. 2c.
99. *T.P. Shabbat* xvi, p. 15c.
1. *T.B. Rosh ha-Shana* 25a.
2. *T.P. Megilla* 1, 6, p. 70c; *T.B. ibid.* 5b.
3. *T.B. Horayot* 11b.

3a. See *T.P. Taʿanit* vii, 2, p. 68a; *Gen. Rabba* 98b, p. 1259. Cf. *T.B. Shabbat* 56a: 'Rav said: Rabbi who is descended from David seeks to defend him.'

4. See my article 'Class-Status and Leadership' etc., p. 51.
5. *Cant. Rabba* viii, 10: 'R. Simeon b. Yoḥai taught: If you see a Persian horse tied to gravestones in Eretz-Israel, await the coming of King Messiah'; see *'Ekha Rabbati* i, 1. Cf. *T.B. Sanhedrin* 98b, the dictum of R. Jose b. Qisma; *T.B. Yoma* 10a; *Gen. Rabba* xli, 4, p. 409: 'R. Eleazar b. R. Avuna said: If you see the kingdoms warring with one another, await the advent of the Messiah.'
6. *T.B. Sanhedrin* 38a.
7. *Ibid.* 98a.
8. *Ibid.*
9. *T.B. Bava Batra* 75a; see my article 'Yerushalayim shel Maṭṭa wi-Yerushalayim shel Maʿala' in *Yerushalayim le-Doroteha*, Jerusalem 1969, pp. 156 ff, and *ibid.* 169. I wish to add that the *pesher* [Qumran commentary] to Isaiah liv 11–12, published by S. M. Allegro, 'More Isaiah Commentaries from Qumran's fourth Cave', *JBL* 77, 1958, pp. 215–221, contains an allegorical interpretation of the verses referring to the existence of the congregation, which is diametrically opposed to the eschatological character both of the *Apocalypse of John* and the homilies of the Amoraim. D. Flusser, 'Pesher Yĕshaʿyā we-Raʿyôn Shĕnêm ʿAsar ha-Shĕlihîm bĕ-Rê'shît ha-Naṣrût', *Eretz-Israel*, VIII, Jerusalem 1967, p. 52, detached the number 'twelve' from its context both in the Pesher and in the *Apocalypse of John* xxi 12–14 and thereby blurred the difference between the two sources; his conclusions are also far-fetched.
10. *T.B. Sanhedrin* 99a. See *T.B. Shabbat* 63a, where there are two versions in the Gemara. According to one, R. Ḥiyya bar Abba, reporting in the name

of R. Joḥanan, had R. Eliezer b. Hyrcamus in mind, at least in respect of the prophecy 'Nation shall not lift up sword against nation'; while according to the other view he was in agreement with Samuel even in this respect. *Ibid.* 151b it is stated, even according to R. Simeon b. Eliezer, ' "And the years draw nigh, when thou shalt say, I have no pleasure in them" — this refers to the Days of the Messiah, wherein there is neither merit nor demerit. Now he disagrees with Samuel'; see *T.B. Pesaḥim* 68a. In the sources themselves the terms 'resurrection of the dead' and 'coming of the Messiah' are sometimes interchanged. In the story about R. Jeremiah in *T.P. Kila'yim* ix, 4, p. 32b, it is related that he asked to be buried in his garments at the wayside, so that 'If the Messiah comes I shall be ready.' But in the same story in *Gen. Rabba* c, 3, p. 1286, he wishes to be ready at the time of the resurrection. See S. Lieberman, *H. A. Wolfson Jubilee Volume*, English Section, p. 510.

11. *Cant. Rabba* ii, 7. See the commentary of Z. W. Einhorn [Maharzaw], who explains that the two oaths are derived from the fact that the verse is repeated in ch. iii 5. In *T.B. Ketubbot* 111a R. Jose b. R. Ḥanina is reported as referring to three oaths, the third being 'that Israel shall not go up *en masse* [literally, 'in a wall']. In *Cant. Rabba, loc. cit.*, R. Ḥelbo discerned four oaths, and R. Ḥunia said that they corresponded to 'four generations who tried to force the End to come sooner and failed.' With the renewal of Jewish immigration to Eretz-Israel these dicta attracted great interest. R. Israel of Shklov, *Pe'at ha-Shulḥan*, Laws of Eretz-Israel, § i, 3, states that the oath that Israel should not immigrate (to Eretz-Israel) *en masse* applied to the people as a whole, not to individuals. On the other hand, R. Abraham of Sochaczew states: 'We do not know the essential nature of this oath, for the term oath applies when a human being swears... and when Moses, our Teacher — peace be upon him! — adjured Israel, they accepted the oath... It is understandable that Maimonides and none of the other codifiers mention the law of the five oaths that Israel swore, because this does not appertain to Halakha...' ("Avnê Nēzer', *Yore De'a*, Pt. II, § 454, par. 42). Recently Rabbi Joel Teitelbaum renamed his anti-Zionist book 'Ma'amar Shalosh Shevu'ot' [Discourse on the Three Oaths], *Wa-Yô'el Moshe*,[2] Brooklyn 1961. See the brochure of Rabbi Mordecai Attia, *Sod ha-Shevu'a*, Jerusalem 1966.
12. *T.B. Sanhedrin* 98b; see above, p. 685.
13. *Ibid.* 106a; see *Diqduqe Soferim*, p. 329, n. ע. On the allegorical homilies to Canticles and the Jewish-Christian disputation, see my article in *Tarbiz*, XXX (1961), p. 160, and *ibid.* p. 167 (= *Scripta*, etc. XXII [1971], p. 249 and p. 263). As regards Resh Laqish's homily see my article, *Tarbiz*, XXV (1956), p. 287.
14. *T.B. Sanhedrin* 97b. Israel Lévi's explanation of the revelations vouchsafed to this Sage, *REJ*, I (1880), pp. 109 ff, does not appear to me acceptable, nor for that matter do the views of Moses Bär (*Sinai*, Shevaṭ, 1961, p. 299), who overlooked Lévi's article. It is difficult to determine the date of this Sage. On the one hand, he is engaged in discussion with Abbaye, *T.B. Shabbat*

112a, and on the other, he appears as the contemporary of Rav Huna, *T.B. Berakhot* 5b, and Rav Ḥisda explains his words *ibid.* 29b, and Rav Joseph, the son of Rav Salla the Pious, explains his view to Rav Pappa, *T.B. Ḥullin* 74b.

15. *T.B. Yoma* 19b.
16. *T.B. Sanhedrin, loc. cit.*; see *Mekhilta de-R. Simeon b. Yoḥai*, p. 27: ' "For I will go through the land of Egypt in that night" — but He did not fix the time for them, so that they should not sit thinking evil thoughts and say: "The hour has already arrived, but we have not been redeemed".' In *Derekh Ereṣ Rabba* xi there is a dictum in the name of R. Jose b. Ḥalafta 'He who declares the End has no share in the world to come.' On the attitude of this Tanna to Bar Kokhba's revolt see above, p. 676, but possibly R. Jonathan was changed to R. Jose. W. Bacher's view, *Monatschrift*, XLII (1888), pp. 298–305, who sought to find in the dictum an anti-Christian trend, was rightly rejected by Marmorstein in his aforementioned article, p. 48.
17. *T.B. Sanhedrin* 99a; Rashi *ad loc.*, s.v. *'Ên lāhem* observes: 'But the Holy One, blessed be He, will reign by Himself and redeem them alone.'
18. This is not, of course, the only description of the Messiah in the Bible; see below, p. 1004 n. 31; cf. *Tanḥuma*, Toledot, 14. The image of the Messiah is dependent, therefore, on Israel's merits.
19. *T.B. Sanhedrin* 98b. Raymond Martini, *Pugio Fidei*, p. 387, states 'but some books read "in the shadow of his ass's tail [דנבתא]" '; see S. Lieberman, *Shekiʿin*, p. 47; cf. above, p. 824, n. 96.
20. *T.B. Sanhedrin* 97b.
21. J. Klausner, *Ha-Raʿyon ha-Meshiḥi*, p. 249, and J. ibn Shmuel [Kaufman], *Midrashe Ge'ula*, p. 46, quoted the 'Baraita' according to the current text. S. Funk, *Die Juden in Babylonien*, Boskowitz, II, p. 124, did indeed translate the dictum as though it contained the name 'Rome', but the name Rav Ḥanan bar Taḥlifa, which appears nowhere else in the Talmud (see *ibid.*, n. 1), was sufficient reason for him to identify Rav Joseph with a Sabora bearing this name and arbitrarily to change the date to four thousand two hundred and sixty-one, in order to arrive at a 'historical' explanation and to reveal the events of the years 498–500. Incidentally the censor cited above served as secretary for Arabic and Persian in the Court of Venice; see *Enciclop. Cattolica*, VIII, 1952, p. 159.
22. See *Diqduqe Soferim* to *Sanhedrin*, p. 287, notes ל–מ. In the Vilna edition the text has been changed to 'Rome', in accordance with these notes.
23. *The Apocalypse of John* xx 1–6. Von Gall, p. 426, found the war of the sea-monsters in the Syriac *Apocalypse of Baruch* xxix 4, but the motif there is different, namely the preservation of Behemoth and Leviathan for the Messianic era, and these certainly did not come 'in lieu of the Persian sea-monsters.' S. Mowinkel, *He that cometh*, Oxford 1956, p. 372, n. 2, repeats the statement of Von Gall.
24. In *Haggadot ha-Talmud* it is still possible to see how the graphic error רצא–רלא came about.

25. *T.B. 'Avoda Zara* 9b. See also the dictum of R. Ḥanina *ibid.*, and the Gemara states there 'The difference between them is one of three years, the period mentioned in the Baraita being three years longer.' Funk, *op. cit.*, remained consistent, in accordance with his theory, and stated, p. 119, that the Amora R. Ḥanina lived *circa* 470; see Rashi *ad loc.*, s.v. *De-matnîtā*, and Tosafot *ad loc.*, s.v. *Lĕ-'aḥar*. Incidentally the era *anno mundi* is found nowhere in the Babylonian Talmud except in these two Baraitot.
26. In his commentary on Joel: '... ut scilicet quomodo Pharao et omnis ejus exercitus, qui per quadrigentos et triginta annos populum Dei captivum tenuit, in mari rubro submersus est, sic etiam Romani, qui eodem annorum spatio Judaeos possessuri sunt, ultione Domini deleantur.' See M. Rahmer, 'Die hebräischen Traditionen in den Werken des Hieronymus', *MGWJ*, 41 (1897), pp. 638–639, and Funk, *op. cit.*, p. 147.
27. This accords with Exod. xii 40. See *Mekhilta de-R. Ishmael*, Pisḥa, xiv, p. 50; *M. 'Eduyot* ii, 9.
28. S. Zeitlin, 'The Assumption of Moses', *JQR* xxxviii, 1947, p. 36, states that the scroll found among the archives of Rome was 'undoubtedly' the pseudepigraphical work 'The Assumption of Moses', but there is no need to refute this statement at length.
28a. On the poor Israelites sitting beside the southern gate of Rome see J. Lewy, *'Olamot Nifgashim* [Worlds Meet], pp. 197–203.
29. *T.B. Sanhedrin* 98a; see *Diqduqe Soferim, ad loc.*, p. 292, note ג. Cf. *T.P. Ta'anit* i, 1, p. 64a: 'Rabbi Aḥa in the name of Rabbi Tanḥum b. Rabbi Ḥiyya said: If Israel would repent (but) one day the son of David would come forthwith.' Also Rav Bevai bar Abbaye's dictum concerning the bird called *raḥam* — 'There is a tradition that if it settles on the ground and hisses the Messiah will come' — led to the following dialogue: 'Rav Adda bar Shimi said to Mar bar Rav Iddai: But did not (a *raḥam*) once settle on a ploughed field and hiss, when a stone fell and severed its head? He replied: That one was a liar' (*T.B. Ḥullin* 63a; see Rashi *ad loc.* 'Like a human being who is a deceiver and liar...' Cf. *Diqduqe Soferim, ibid.*, 84b, nn. ס–פ). The answer is no less ironical than the question.
30. *T.B. Sanhedrin* 97b; in the printed editions we find that it is Samuel who argues against Rav, but in the MSS. and Early Authorities R. Joshua b. Levi is expressly mentioned; see *Diqduqe Soferim, ad loc.*, p. 288, note ש. For the interpretation of the dictum see Rashi s.v. *Dayyô*, and *Yad Rama* to *Sanhedrin*, p. 169.
31. *Tanḥuma*, Wa'era', § 6; *Exod. Rabba* v, 18.
32. *T.B. Sanhedrin* 98a, where the name of the transmitter is 'R. Alexandri'. The story, cited above, about R. Joshua b. Levi and his homily on Dan. vii 11 served as a source for the author of *Aggadat Bereshit* xxiii, ed. Buber, p. 47: ' "And when ye see this, your heart shall rejoice" etc. (Isa. lxvi 14)... They will see the Messiah burgeoning from the gates of Rome and will rejoice....' But R. Aḥa expounded there, too, "your heart [לבכם] shall rejoice" —

Scripture should have said לבבבם [with *Bêt* repeated]... The reason [for the one *Bêt*] is that the Holy One, blessed be He, is destined to give the world a single heart and uproot the evil inclination of the human heart...' (this is the reading in the Bodleian MS. 2340; there the words of R. Aḥa precede and are followed immediately by the homily concerning the Messiah). See above, n. 29.

33. *Gen. Rabba* i, 3, p. 6, and the parallels given there.
34. *Die Haggada bei den Kirchenvätern*, 1900, pp. 4 ff.
35. 'Śĕride Tanḥuma-Yelammedenu', *Qoveṣ ʿal Yad*, Book VI, p. 9. Evidence that in the middle of the second century it was not yet accepted among Jews to speak of the pre-existence of the Messiah is to be found in the statement of Justin Martyr that the Jew Tryphone argued that the idea that the Messiah existed before the creation of the world was not only paradoxical but sheer nonsense (*Dial. c. Tryphone*, i, 38); see, on the other hand, p. 687. J. Klausner, *Ha-Raʿyon ha-Meshiḥi be-Yisra'el*, p. 247, follows Me'ir Ish Shalom, *Mavo' le-Seder, Eliahu*, p. 114, in stating that the name of the Messiah means the concept of the Messiah, and adds, on his own account, 'more precisely: the idea of redemption by the Messiah.' H. Wolfson, *The Philosophy of the Church Fathers*, I, 1956, p. 158, rightly rejects this definition, but his view — *ibid.*, pp. 156–157 — that the idea of the Messiah's pre-existence was current in Judaism when Christianity arose is unfounded. The passage *Enoch* xlviii 3, 6, is doubtful testimony. The Targum of Psalms lxxii 17 cited by Wolfson — 'Before the sun his name was prepared' — is conceived, of course, in the homiletical spirit. Rashi renders the verse 'His name shall be great all the days of the sun'; see the commentary of Abraham ibn Ezra.
36. *Gen. Rabba* ii, 4, p. 16. The reading משמשת [rendered 'Serve'] is the correct one; it is so also in the Geniza fragment TS 16, 322 R3. This homily is different from the cosmogonic exposition of Resh Laqish in *Gen. Rabba* viii, 1, p. 56, concerning the spirit of Adam; L. Ginzberg's remarks, *op. cit.* p. 6, are based on the text of the printed edition, but the Consensus Codicum — and now also confirmed by the Geniza fragment TS 16, 322 R3 — has the reading given above. Theodor, p. 17, n. 1 observes: 'Further on, at the beginning of section viii, the correct reading is that Resh Laqish said "And the spirit" etc. — this is the spirit of Adam' (see above, p. 241). He means to say that this is the correct recension of the passage further on, and not as Israel Lévi supposed, 'L'esprit de Dieu et l'esprit de Messie', *Simonsen Festschrift*, 1923, pp. 104–110.
37. P. Volz, *Die Eschatologie der jüdischen Gemeinde*[2], 1934, p. 176. There are parallel sources where one text has 'the name of the Messiah' and another 'King Messiah'. See *T.B. Pesaḥim* 5a: 'For the School of R. Ishmael taught: As a reward for (observing) three "firsts", they [the Israelites] were vouchsafed three "firsts"... and the name of the Messiah....' But in *Gen. Rabba* lxiii, 8, p. 687: 'R. Haggai in the name of R. Isaac said: For the merit of "And ye shall take you on the first day... and bring you the "first", namely King Messiah....' Cf. *Lev. Rabba* xxxi, 1, p. 714; *Exod. Rabba* xv, 1.

38. An exception is *Midrash Tehillim* lxxii, 6, p. 327, but this is a homily on Psa. lxxii 17; see *ibid.* xciii, 3, p. 414. According to *Sifre*, ʿEqev, § 37, 'Whoever is more beloved comes first; since the Torah is the most beloved of all, it was created before all, as it is said "The Lord made me as the beginning of His way, the first of His works of old".' In a later Midrash, *Pesiqta Rabbati* xxxiii, 152b, the two homilies are combined.
39. *T.P. Berakhot* ii, 5, p. 5a. See *'Ekha Rabbati* i, 16. In regard to the legend about the birth of the Messiah see also *'Ekha Zuṭa*, p. 133; cf. 'Derekh Ereṣ Zuṭa', Pereq ha-Shalom, ed. Higger, *Massekhtot Zeʿirot*, p. 101; see S. Lieberman, *Shekiʿin*, p. 75.
40. *T.B. Sanhedrin* 98b: 'The School of Shila said: His name is Shiloh, as it is said "until Shiloh come"....'
41. A kind of contradiction of the entire trend to reveal names is to be found in the following story of the Babylonian Talmud, *ibid.* 96b: 'Rav Naḥman said to R. Isaac: "Have you heard when Bar Naflê will come?" Said (the latter) to him: "Who is Bar Naflê?" (R. Naḥman) replied: "The Messiah." — "Do you call the Messiah 'Bar Naflê'?" He replied: "Yes, for it is written 'In that day I will raise up the tabernacle of David that is fallen [*ha-nofelet*]'."' Jacob Levy's explanation in his *Wörterbuch*, Pt. I, p. 259, 'נפילי=νεφέλη' was already rejected by W. Bacher, *Agada der babyl. Amoräer*, p. 80, n. 5, but he did not suggest another explanation in its stead. It appears to me that the remark of Rav Naḥman, whose view of the Messiah was realistic, and who said of the Messiah 'If he is of the living, he would be one like me' (*T.B. Sanhedrin* 98b), is a parody of those who search for the End and the Messiah's names. He asks the Palestinian Amora, the distinguished Haggadist, concerning the time of the Messiah's coming, but he designates him 'Bar Naflê', which arouses the protest of his interlocutor, for the term 'Ben Nefel' is a pejorative expression, like τὸ ἔχτρωμα, see W. Bauer, *Wörterbuch zum N.T.*, p. 489; cf. *T.B. Soṭa* 22a.
42. *T.B. Sanhedrin* 98b: 'And the Rabbis say: His name is 'the leper of the House of Rabbi, [*ḥiwrā*], as it is said "surely he hath borne our sicknesses...".' But Raymond Martini, *Pugio Fidei*, p. 862, reads: 'And the Rabbis say: *Ḥiwrā* [R. Raḥmon related it to the expression *ḥûr karpas* ('*white*, fine cotton'), or to 'Neither shall his face now *yeḥwarû* ('wax pale'), or to the expression *ḥûr pāthen* ('*hole* of the cobra')]. The School of Rabbi says: His name is *Ḥûlyā*, as it is said "Surely he hath borne our sicknesses [*ḥolāyênû*]".' I have found no parallel to this reading; on R. Raḥmon see S. Lieberman, *Shekiʿin*, p. 67. Regarding other connotations of the Messiah's names see above, n. 40, and below, n. 51.
43. *T.B. Sanhedrin* 93b; in the Munich MS. *kĕ-rêḥayim* ['like a millstone'] is wanting, but has been inserted in the margin.
44. *Ruth Rabba* v, 14, where we find 'six ways of exposition [*shît shiṭîn*]' in the name of Joḥanan. These have been interpolated into the Munich MS. of *Lev. Rabba*; see ed. M. Margulies, p. 788, and cf. *ibid.* the vv.ll., and note 3.

On the death of the Messiah after his manifestation see *IV Ezra* v, 28; the Days of the Messiah last there four hundred years, but he plays no role in the End of Days. A different role is ascribed to Moses in Midrash *Deut. Rabba* iii, 17: The Holy One, blessed be He, says to Moses 'Just as you have given your life for them in this world, so in the time to come, when I shall bring Elijah the prophet to them, you will both come together'; see below, n. 52, and above, p. 308.

45. *Pesiqta de-Rav Kahana*, ed. Mandelbaum, pp. 91–92, and the parallels cited there; see A. Aptowitzer, *Parteipolitik der Hasmonäer*, Vienna 1927, p. 186; cf. *'Arugat ha-Bośem*, Pt. I, p. 77.
46. R. Bultmann, *Das Evangelium des Johannes*, 10th ed., 1964, p. 522. In Matthew xxvii 34 and Mark xv 36 the episode of the vinegar is also reported differently and the reference to the fulfilment of the verse is wanting there, just as the parallel to the realization of the verse 'Neither shall ye break a bone thereof' (Exod. xii 46) is missing in John, *loc. cit.*, *vv.* 36 ff. Despite Bultmann's remarks, *loc. cit.*, n. 4, and *ibid.*, p. 524, n. 8, it cannot be doubted that the two motifs are connected through the identifications 'Jesus — the lamb — the Passover offering.' See Strack-Billerbeck, II, p. 583.
47. See A. von Harnack, *Lehrbuch der Dogmengeschichte*, 1931, I, pp. 188 ff and pp. 201 ff; cf. L. W. Barnard, *Justin Martyr*, Cambridge 1967, pp. 160 ff.
48. In Targum Pseudo-Jonathan: 'And they will beseech Me because they were exiled and they will mourn for him...', and in accordance with this interpretation Rashi annotates *ad loc.*: 'And they will look to lament because the Chaldeans had thrust them through.' In the Addendum to the Targum, ed. Sperber, p. 495: 'Thereafter Messiah, son of Ephraim, will issue forth to wage war against Gog, and Gog will slay him before the gate of Jerusalem, and they will look to Me and beseech Me...'
49. *T.B. Sukka* 52a.
50. *T.P. Sukka* v, 2, p. 55b.
51. See *Dial. c. Tryphone*, 36, 1; 68, 9; 99, 1. A. J. B. Higgias, 'Jewish Messianic Beliefs', *Novum Testamentum*, 1967, p. 298, states that, for apologetic reasons, Justin mixed together Jewish and Christian concepts and put them in the mouth of the Jew, but, as we have seen, there is nothing strange in his statements, not even in the testimony that the Messiah will be called *Adonai* ['Lord'] and will be addressed as 'Holy'. At any rate it is reported in the name of R. Joḥanan: 'There have been called by the name of the Holy One, blessed be He: The righteous, the Messiah and Jerusalem... The Messiah, as it is written "And this is the name whereby he shall be called, The Lord is our righteousness" ' (Jer. xxiii 6). R. Eleazar added: 'In time to come 'Holy' will be said before the righteous in the same way as it is said before the Holy One, blessed be He...' (*T.B. Bava Batra* 75b); see *'Ekha Rabbati* i, p. 88, and *Midrash Tehillim* xxi, 2, p. 178. From Justin we learn that there were Jews already in his time who reported these things, just as we learnt the reverse earlier, in connection with another subject, see above, p. 1005, n. 35.

52. On the various theories see J. Klausner, *Ha-Ra'yon ha-Meshiḥi be-Yisra'el*, pp. 289–295, and Volz, *op. cit.*, p. 229. It is possible that 'the Messiah of Israel' (see above, p. 663) was identified in certain circles, in contradistinction to the Messiah, son of David, with the Messiah from the tribe of Joseph, and that subsequently they attached the various images not just to two redeemers, but — like Rav Ḥana bar Bizna in the name of R. Simeon the Pious — to four: ' "And the Lord showed me four craftsmen" (Zech. ii 3): Who are they? Messiah son of David, Messiah son of Joseph, Elijah, and the Righteous Priest' (*T.B. Sukka* 52b; see Rashi *ad loc.*). Cf. *Pesiqta de-Rav Kahana*, § Ha-ḥodesh ha-ze, p. 92; in *Num. Rabba* xiv, 1 we read: 'Because there are great differences of opinion regarding the "anointed ones", some say seven... and some say eight....' See Me'ir Ish Shalom, *Mavo' le-Seder Eliahu Rabba*, p. 8. Cf. L. Ginzberg, *Eine unbekannte jüd. Sekte*, 1922, pp. 340ff; see S. Lieberman, *Sheki'in*, pp. 65–66.
53. *Pesiqta Rabbati* 161b; 162b; 163a; 164a.
54. *Ibid.* 164a; regarding the fear that there might be further servitude after the redemption, see below, p. 689.
55. *T.B. Sukka* 52a.
56. *T.P. Ta'anit* i, 1, p. 64a; *Cant. Rabba* v, 2; see above, p. 671.
57. *Gen. Rabba* xlix, 6, p. 504; cf. *ibid.* xxxviii, 9, p. 359. R. Akiba's exposition (*M. Yoma* viii, 9, which is an addition to the Mishna; see *Diqduqe Soferim*, *ibid.*, p. 290) of Ezek. xxxvi 24 leaves no doubt that he explained the words of the prophet to mean that the Holy One, blessed be He, would purify those who would come to be purified; see Tosefot Yom Tov and Mele'khet Shelomo *ad loc.* Even the conclusion of a homily of the type 'But Israel — I shall sanctify them and purify them and redeem them from among you' (*Tanḥuma* xlii, Tazria', § 16) proves nothing for our purpose, for the expositor does not tell us anything about the manner of the redemption and the purification.
58. *Mekhilta de-R. Ishmael*, Shira, i, p. 118: 'The past deliverances were followed by servitude, but the deliverance to come will not be followed by servitude'; *T.P. Shevi'it* vi, 1, p. 36b: 'Rabbi said... your ancestors, although they were redeemed were again subjugated, but you, once you are redeemed, will never again be subjugated.' See *Gen. Rabba* xliv, 17, p. 440 and *ibid.* lviii (*ad fin.*), p. 692; cf. *Pesiqta de-Rav Kahana*, Śos 'Aśiś, p. 470. See *IV Ezra* vi 9–10, and cf. above, p. 688.
59. *Midrash Tehillim* xviii, 10. On the question of the Sages' attitude to the apostate Emperor's attempt to rebuild the Temple, see S. Lieberman, *The Martyrs of Caesarea*, p. 414, and my article 'Kôresh wĕ-Hakhrāzātô be-'ênê Ḥazal [Cyrus and his Proclamation in the View of the Sages]', *Molad*, 1961, p. 373, n. 15. Cf. above, p. 1004, n. 24, and p. 989, n. 32.
60. *Midrash Tehillim* xxxi, 2. It is doubtful if it is possible to find this thought in the words of the *Sifra*, Be-ḥuqqōtay, iii, 111a: ' "And My soul shall not abhor you", for when I redeem you I shall not reject you again.'

61. See above, p. 681.
62. *Mekhilta de-R. Ishmael*, Pisḥa, xiv, p. 51. R. Samuel b. R. Isaac expounded, in the spirit of this homily, the verse 'But if ye will not hear it, my soul shall weep in secret for your pride [*gēwā*]' (Jeremiah xiii 17) — 'for the glory [*ga'ăwā*, literally 'pride'] of Israel, which has been taken away from them and given to the nations of the world' (*T.B. Ḥagiga* 5b).
63. *Midrash Tehillim* cv, 11, p. 452.
64. R. Joḥanan also wrestled with this question (*T.B. Sanhedrin* 98b) in the following homily: '"And all faces are turned into paleness" (Jer. xxx 6)... (This refers to) the heavenly entourage and the earthly entourage, when the Holy One, blessed be He, said: "These [the Gentiles] are the work of My hands and these [the Jews] are the work of My hands. How shall I destroy the former on account of the latter"?' A similar homily was apparently cited in the name of Rav: '"I see *kol gever* [E.V. "every man"] with His hands on His loins" (see *Diqduqe Soferim, ad loc.*, p. 294) — this refers to Him to whom all power [*kol gĕvûrā*] belongs', who 'is grieved... when He causes the nations to pass away before Israel' (Rashi *ad loc.*, s.v. *Mí*, and *ibid.* s.v. *Rāḥîṭ*; but see 'Yad Rama' to Sanhedrin, *loc. cit.*). In this dictum of R. Joḥanan the Talmud finds an explanation of the saying attributed to R. Joḥanan 'Let him come, but let me not see him'. However, a realistic conception of the figure of the king in the time to come is to be found in another dictum of R. Joḥanan. With regard to the Halakha that a *kohen* ['priest'] may defile himself in order to see the face of a king R. Joḥanan said: 'It is a meritorious act to see great men of the kingdom, so that when the kingdom of the House of David comes, he will be able to distinguish between (Jewish) sovereignty and (Gentile) sovereignty' — *T.P. Berakhot* iii, 1, p. 6a. In the version of R. Joḥanan's teaching in the Babylonian Talmud (*ibid.* 9b, where the parallels are cited) the kingdom of the House of David is not mentioned, but the text reads: 'Let a man make a point of running... even to meet the kings of the Gentile nations, so that if he is worthy, he will be able to distinguish between the kings of Israel and those of the Gentiles'; in this version, of course, it is cited in Maimonides' *Code*, 'Hilkhot 'Evel [Laws of Mourning]', iii, 13.
65. *Cant. Rabba* ii, 1. See *Midrash Tehillim* i, 20, p. 21, where a dictum, wanting in most MSS., has been added; see n. 277. The text there reads: 'R. Reuben in the name of R. Ḥanina', but in *Yalquṭ Shimʿoni, editio princeps*, § 692, the reading is 'R. Ḥanina in the name of R. Reuben'. His words are at all events an interpretation and continuation of those of R. Eleazar of Modiʿin.

BIBLIOGRAPHY*

CHAPTER I

1. Bacher, W., Die Agada der Tannaiten, vol. I–II, Strassburg, 1884–1890.
2. —— Die Agada der palästinensischen Amoräer, vol. I–III, Strassburg 1892–1899.
3. —— Die Agada der babylonischen Amoräer, zweite Auflage, Frankfort, 1913.
4. Bonsirven, J., Le Judaisme palestinien au temps de Jésus-Christ, Paris, 1934.
5. Bousset, W., Die Religion des Judentums im neutestamentlichen Zeitalter. Berlin, 1903.
6. —— Die Religion des Judentums im späthellenistischen Zeitalter. 3., verb. Aufl. hrsg. von H. Gressmann, Tübingen, 1926.
7. —— Volksfrömmigkeit und Schriftgelehrtentum, Berlin, 1903.
8. Burkitt, F. C., The Gospel History and its Transmission, Edinburgh, 1906.
9. Chinitz, J. M., The Elusive Revelation. Judaism, 1965, pp. 187–204.
10. Finkelstein, L., Akiba. Scholar, Saint and Martyr, New York, 1936.
11. —— The Pharisees, The Sociological Background of Their Faith, 3rd edition, vol. 1–2. Philadelphia 1962.
12. Ginzberg, L., The Legends of the Jews. vol. I–VI. Philadelphia, 1913–1928; vol. VII. Index by Boaz Cohen. Philadelphia, 1938.
13. Güdemann, M., Das Judentum im Neutestamentlichen Zeitalter. MGWJ vol. 47 (1903), pp. 38–53, 120–136, 231–249.
14. Guttmann, Julius, Die Philosophie des Judentums, München, 1933.
15. Heschel, A. J., God in Search of Man, New York, 1955.
16. Jacob, B., Im Namen Gottes, Berlin, 1903.
17. Kohler, K., Jewish Theology Systematically and Historically Considered. New York, 1928.
18. Krengel, J., Strack-Billerbeck, Kommentar zum N.T. aus Talmud und Midrasch, MGWJ vol. 68 (1924), pp. 68–82.
19. Lieberman, S., Greek in Jewish Palestine, New York, 1942.
20. —— Hellenism in Jewish Palestine, New York, 1950.

* Books and articles referred to in the notes are listed here alphabetically for each chapter and given a number. When a reference is repeated its number is given at the end of the list to the relevant chapter.

21. Moore, G. F., Judaism in the First Centuries of the Christian Era, The Age of the Tannaim. vol. 1–3. Cambridge (Mass.), 1927–1930.
22. Perles, F., Bousset's Rel. des Judentums kritisch untersucht, 1903.
23. Porter, F. C., Judaism in N.T. Times. Journal of Rel. vol. VII (1928), pp. 30–62.
24. Sandmel, S., Reflection on the Problem of Theology for Jews. The Journal of Bible and Religion 1965, pp. 101–112.
25. Schechter, S., Some Aspects of Rabbinic Theology. New York, 1909.
26. Strack, H. und Billerbeck, P., Kommentar zum Neuen Testament aus Talmud und Midrasch. vol. 1–4. München, 1922–1928. vol. V–VI. Indexes by J. Jeremias and K. Adolph. München 1961–1965.
27. Weber, F., Jüdische Theologie auf Grund des Talmud und Verwandten Schriften. 2 verb. Aufl. hrg. von F. Delitzsch und G. Schnedermann. Leipzig; 1897.
28. Wohlgemuth, J., Das jüdische Religionsgesetz in jüd. Beleuchtung, Berlin 1919.
29. אורבך, א., ביקורת על ׳דרכי האגדה׳ להיינמן. קרית ספר שנה כו (תש״י), עמ׳ 223–228.
30. אפרון, י., ׳מזמורי שלמה׳ השקיעה החשמונאית והנצרות. ציון, תשכ״ה, עמ׳ 1–46.
31. בער, י., היסודות ההיסטוריים של ההלכה. ציון ש׳ י״ז (תשי״ב), עמ׳ 1–55 ועמ׳ 173. ושם ש׳ כ״ז (תשכ״ב), עמ׳ 117–155.
32. — החסידים הראשונים בכתבי פילון ובמסורת העברית. שם ש׳ י״ח (תשי״ג), עמ׳ 91–108.
33. — ׳סרך היחד׳, תעודה יהודית נוצרית מתחילת המאה השניה לספה״נ (בצירוף דיונים על מגילת ברית דמשק). שם ש׳ כ״ט (תשכ״ד), עמ׳ 1–60.
34. — ישראל בעמים. ירושלים, תשט״ו.
35. — המשנה וההיסטוריה, מולד, תשכ״ד, עמ׳ 308–323.
36. היינמן, י., דרכי האגדה. ירושלים, תש״י.
37. השל, א. י., תורה מן השמים באספקלריה של הדורות. כ״א–כ״ב, לונדון–ניו־יורק, תשכ״ב–תשכ״ה.
38. וייס, א. ה., דור דור ודורשיו, ח״א–ח״ה, וינה–פרסבורג, 1871–1891.

Chapter II

39. Bauer, W., Rechtgläubigkeit und Ketzerei im ältesten Christentum, Tübingen, 1934.
40. Bultmann, R., Theologie des N.T., Tübingen, 1953.
41. Dodd, C. H., The Bible and the Greeks. London, 1935.
42. Harnack, A., Die Chronologie der altchristlichen Litt. Leipzig, 1897–1904.
43. Leisegang, H., Die Gnosis. Leipzig, 1924.
44. Lieberman, S., How Much Greek in Jewish Palestine. Biblical and Other Studies. Edited by A. Altman. Philip W. Lown Institute of Advanced Judaic Studies (Brandeis University). Studies and Texts. vol. 1, pp. 123–141. Harvard University Press, 1962.

45. Marmorstein, A., The Unity of God in Rabbinic Literature. HUCA 1, pp. 467–499.
46. Meyer, E., Ursprung u. Anfänge des Christentums. Stuttgart, 1924–1925.
47. Mommsen, Th., Römische Geschichte. Berlin, 1885.
48. Nilsson, M. P., Geschichte der Griechischen Religion. München, vol. 1–2, 1941–1950.
49. Nock, A. D., Conversion. Oxford, 1933.
50. Nyberg, H. S., Die Religionen des alten Iran. Leipzig, 1938.
51. Schürer, E., Geschichte des jüd. Volkes im Zeitalter Jesu. Leipzig. Vierte Auflage I–III 1907/9.
52. Shaked, S., Widengren, G., Die Religionen Irans (Review) BSOAS vol. 32 (1969).
53. Siegfried, C., Philo von Alexandria. Jena, 1875.
54. Smith, M., Goodenough's Symbols in Retrospect. JBL vol. 86 (1967), pp. 53–68.
55. Urbach, E., The Rabbinic Laws of Idolatry in the Second and Third Centuries in the Light of Archaeological and Historical Facts, Israel Exploration Journal, 1959–1960, No. 3, pp. 149 ff; No. 4, pp. 229 ff.
56. Wendland, P., Die Hellenistisch-Römische Kultur in ihren Beziehungen zu Judentum und Christentum. Tübingen, 1912.
57. Werblowsky, R. J. Z., Faith, Hope and Trust, A Study in the Concept of Bittahon. Papers of the Institute of Jewish Studies. London, 1964.
58. Widengren, G., Die Religionen Irans. Stuttgart, 1965.
59. אורבך, א., דרשות חז״ל על נביאי אומות העולם ועל פרשת בלעם. תרביץ ש׳ כ״ה (תשט״ז), עמ׳ 272—289.
60. גוטמן, יהושע, הספרות היהודית ההלניסטית. כ״א—כ״ב, ירושלים, תשי״ח—תשכ״ג.
61. הורוביץ, א., התואר הבתר מקראי ׳אדון הכול׳ והופעתו במזמור קנא מקומראן. תרביץ שנה ל״ד (תשכ״ה), עמ׳ 224—227.
62. ליברמן, ש., תוספתא כפשוטה, באור ארוך לתוספתא ח״א—ח״ז נויארק, תשטו—תשכז.
63. סגל, מ.צ., הגומא של נש. לשוננו כרך ט״ו (תש״ז), עמ׳ 27—36.
64. שטיין, מ., דת ודעת. קרקוב, תרצ״ח.

See also: 6, 19, 20.

Chapter III

65. Aalen, S., Die Begriffe Licht und Finsternis im A.T., im Spätjudentum und im Rabbinismus. Oslo, 1951.
66. Abelson, I., The Immanence of God in Rabbinical Literature. London, 1912.
67. Bacher, W., Die exegetische Terminologie der jüd. Traditionsliteratur, I 1899, II 1905.
68. Berliner, A., Der Einheitsgesang. Wissenschaftliche Beilage zum Jahresbericht des Rabbiner-Seminars zu Berlin für 1908/09. Berlin, 1910.
69. Budge, E. A. T. W., Egyptian Magic. London, 1899, reprinted. University Books, Evanston (Ill.), 1958.

70. Dölger, F. J., Sol Salutis, Münster, 1925.
71. Elbogen, I., Der Jüd. Gottesdienst. Frankfurt a.M., 1924.
72. Erman, A. — Ranke, H., Aegypten und aegyptisches Leben im Altertum. Tübingen, 1923.
73. Funk, F., Didascalia et Constitutiones Apostolorum. Paderborn, 1905 (Torino, 1962).
74. Geiger, A., Jüdische Zeitschrift für Wissenschaft und Leben. vol. XI (1875), p. 228. Hellenistische Studien (= Nachgelassene Schriften. vol. 4, p. 324. Berlin 1876).
75. Goldberg, A. M., Die spezifische Verwendung des Terminus Schekhina im Targum Onkelos als Kriterium einer relativen Datierung. Judaica vol. 19 (1963), pp. 43–61.
76. Klein, F. N., Die Lichtterminologie bei Philo von Alexandrien und in den hermetischen Schriften. (Diss.) Leiden, 1962.
77. Krauss, S., Synagogale Altertümer. Wien, 1922.
78. Landau, E., Die dem Raume entnommenen Synonyma für Gott in der neuhebräischen Literatur. Zürich, 1888.
79. Marmorstein, A., The Old Rabbinic Doctrine of God. London, 1927.
80. Moore, G. F., Intermediaries in Jewish Theology — Memra, Shekinah, Metatron. HTR 1922, pp. 41–85.
81. Murray, G., Five Stages of Greek Religion. London, 1935.
82. Peterson, E., Frühkirche, Judenthum und Gnosis. Freiburg, 1959.
83. Pohlenz, M., Die Ṣtoa. Göttingen, 1948.
84. Scholem, G., Major Trends in Jewish Mysticism. Jerusalem, 1941.
85. —— Kabbalistische Konzeption der Shechina. Eranos Jahrbuch. 1953.
86. —— Zur Kabbala und Ihrer Symbolik. Zürich, 1960.
87. Strack, H., Einleitung in Talmud und Midrasch. München, 1921.
88. Sukenik, E. L., Ancient Synagogues in Palestine and Greece. London, 1934.
89. Zimmels, H. J., Jesus and "putting up a brick". JQR (N.S.) vol. 43 (1953).
90. אלון, ג., תולדות היהודים בא״י בתקופת המשנה והתלמוד. ח״א–ח״ב. הוצאת הקיבוץ המאוחד. תשי״ד–תשט״ז.
91. אפטוביצר, א., בית המקדש של מעלה על פי האגדה. תרביץ, ש״ב (תרצ״א), עמ׳ 137–153, 257–287.
92. אפשטיין, י. נ., מבוא לנוסח המשנה. ירושלים, תש״ח.
93. גינצבורג, ל., פירושים וחידושים בירושלמי. ח״א–ח״ד, נויארק, תש״א–תשכ״א.
94. זליגמן, י. א., ΔΕΙΞΑΙ ΑΥΤΩΙ ΦΩΣ תרביץ שכ״ז (תשי״ח), עמ׳ 127–141.
95. טלמון, ש., חשבון הלוח של כת מדבר יהודה. מחקרים במגילות הגנוזות. ירושלים, תשכ״א, 77–106.
96. ליברמן, ש., מכילתא דרבי ישמעאל, הו״ל י.ב. לויטערבאך. (ביקורת) קרית ספרשנה, י״ב, עמ׳ 54–65.
97. סוקניק, א.ל., בית הכנסת של דורה אברופוס וציוריו. ירושלים, תש״ז.
98. קויפמן, י., תולדות האמונה הישראלית. ירושלים–תל־אביב, תשי״ד.

See also: 1, 16, 21, 36.

BIBLIOGRAPHY

Chapter IV

99. Baudissin, W. W., Kyrios als Gottesname im Judentum und seine Stelle in der Religionsgeschichte. (hrsg. von Otto Eisfeldt) vol. 1–4, Giessen, 1929.

100. Bloch, D., Die zweite Uebersetzung des Saadiahnischen Buches "Emunoth wedeoth", angeblich von Berechjah Hanakdan. MGWJ vol. 19 (1870), pp. 449–456.

101. Brüll, N., Jahrbücher für jüdische Geschichte und Literatur. vol. 7 (1885). Frankfurt a.M.

102. Esh, S., (הַקָּ (בָּה Der Heilige <Er sei gepriesen> Leiden, 1957.

103. Freudenthal, J., Hellenistische Studien. Jahresbericht des jüdisch-theol. Seminars. Breslau, 1874.

104. Ginzberg, L., Eine unbekannte Jüdische Sekte. New York, 1922.

105. Joel, M., Blicke in die Religionsgeschichte. Breslau vol. I, 1880.

106. Kuhn, H. W., Enderwartung und gegenwärtiges Heil in den Gemeindeliedern von Qumran. Göttingen, 1966.

107. Lewy, J., Ein Wort über die Mechilta des R. Simon. Jahresbericht des jüdisch-theol. Seminars. Breslau, 1889.

108. Nestle, E., Zu Daniel. ZAW, vol. 4 (1884). Giessen.

109. Norden, E., Agnostos Theos. Leipzig, 1913.

110. Otto, R., Das Heilige. 6th edition. Breslau, 1921.

111. Rabin, Ch., The Zadokite Documents, second edition. Oxford, 1958.

112. Reinach, Th., Textes d'auteurs grecs et romains relatifs au Judaïsme. Paris, 1895.

113. Schäder, H. H. und Reitzenstein, R., Studien zum antiken Synkretismus aus Iran und Griechenland. Leipzig, 1926.

114. Spanier, A., Die Gottesbezeichnungen המקום und הקב״ה in der frühtalmudischen Literatur. MGWJ vol. 66 (1922), pp. 309–314.

115. Weinstein, I. N., Zur Genesis der Agada. Frankfurt a.M., 1901.

116. Zaehner, R. C., The Dawn and Twilight of Zoroastrianism. London, 1961.

117. אורבך, א., שרידי תנחומא – ילמדנו. קובץ על יד. ס״ו (טז) תשכ״ו.

118. בלקין, ש., המדרש הסמלי אצל פילון. ספר היובל לכב׳ צבי וולפסון, חלק עברי. תשכ״ה.

119. בער, י., לבירורה של תורת אחרית הימים. ציון ש׳ כג–כד (תשי״ח–תשי״ט).

120. היינמן, יוסף, התפילה בתקופת התנאים והאמוראים. ירושלים, תשכ״ד.

121. ווידר, ש., קטע ירושלמי מבין כתבי הגניזה, בבודאפשט (סנהדרין – מכות). תרביץ שי״ז (תש״ו), עמ׳ 129–135.

122. ידין, י., מגילת בן סירא שנתגלתה במצדה. ירושלים, תשכ״ה.

123. ליברמן, ש., הלכות ירושלמי להרמב״ם ז״ל. נויארק, תש״ח.

124. — משהו על השבעות בישראל. תרביץ שכ״ז (תשי״ח), עמ׳ 183–189.

125. קוטשר, י., הלשון והרקע הלשוני של מגילת ישעיהו השלמה ממגילות ים המלח. ירושלים, תשי״ט.

126. שפיגל, ש., מלשון פייטנים. הדאר, תשכ״ג, גליון כ״ג, עמ׳ 398.

See also: 1, 2, 21, 26, 55, 60, 62, 64, 70, 78, 79, 84.

Chapter V

127. Bell, H. J., Cults and Creeds in Graeco-Roman Egypt. Liverpool, 1953.
128. Bergmann, I., Jüdische Apologetik. Berlin, 1909.
129. Dodds, E. R., The Greeks and the Irrational. Univ. of California Press, 1964.
130. A. M. Goldberg, Sitzend zur Rechten der Kraft, Biblische Zeitschrift 1964 pp. 284–293.
131. Grant, R. M., Miracle and Natural Law in Graeco-Roman and Early Christian Thought, Amsterdam, 1952.
132. Leeuw, Van der G., Phänomenologie der Religion. 2 Aufl. Tübingen, 1956.
133. Nilson, M. P., Greek Piety. Oxford, 1948.
134. Reinhardt, K., Kosmos und Sympathie. München, 1926.
135. Schmitz, O., Der Begriff δύναμις bei Paulus. Festgabe für A. Deissmann. Tübingen, 1927.
136. Schweizer, E., The Spirit of Power. Interpretation, 1952, pp. 259–278.
137. Wissowa, G., Religion und Kultus der Römer. München, 1912.
See also: 21, 48.

Chapter VI

138. Barb, A. A., The Survival of Magic Arts. The Conflict between Paganism and Christianity in the Fourth Century. Oxford, 1963, pp. 101–126.
139. Blau, L., Das altjüdische Zauberwesen. Jahresbericht der Landes-Rabbiner-schule in Budapest. Budapest, 1898.
140. Bloch, P., Die יורדי מרכבה die Mystiker der Gaonenzeit, und ihr Einfluss auf die Liturgie. MGWJ vol. 37 (1893), pp. 18–25, 69–74, 257–266, 305–311.
141. Bréhier, E., Les Idées philosophiques et religieuses de Philon d'Alexandrie. 1950.
142. Elbogen, I., Die Tefilla für die Festtage. MGWJ vol. 55 (1911), pp. 426–446, 586–599, vol. 58 (1914), pp. 323–325.
143. Fiebig, P., Rabbinische Wundergeschichten des neutestamentlichen Zeitalters. Bonn, 1911.
144. Guttman, A., The Significance of Miracles for Talmudic Judaism. HUCA vol. XX (1947), pp. 363–406.
145. Harnack, A., Die Mission und Ausbreitung des Christentums. Leipzig, 1924.
146. Heinemann, I., Philons griechische und jüdische Bildung. Breslau, 1932.
147. —— Die Kontroverse über das Wunder im Judentum der hellenistischen Zeit. Festschrift B. Heller. Budapest, 1914, pp. 170–191.
148. Kaduschin, M., The Rabbinic Mind. New York, 1952.
149. Mann, J., Genizah Fragments of the Palestinian Order of Service. HUCA vol. II (1925), pp. 269–338.
150. Preuss, J., Biblisch-Talmudische Medizin. Berlin, 1923.

151. Röhr, J., Der okkulte Kraftbegriff im Altertum. Philologus, Supplementband. XVIII (1923).
152. Shechter, A. J. S., Studies in Jewish Liturgy, Philadelphia, 1930.
153. Schlatter, Von A., Das Wunder in der Synagogue. 1912.
154. Tsevat, M., The Meaning of the Book of Job. HUCA XXXVII (1966), pp. 73–106.
155. Walzer, R., Galen on Jews and Christians. Oxford, 1949.
156. Wolfson, H. A., Philo, vol. I–II Cambridge (Mass.) second printing revised. 1948.
157. אורבך, א., הלכה ונבואה. תרביץ שי״ח (תש״ז), עמ׳ 1–27.
158. אסף, ש., תקופת הגאונים וספרותה. ירושלים, תשט״ז.
159. ליברמן, ש., חזנות ינייּ. סיני תרצ״ט.
160. מרגליות, מ., ספר הרזים. תל־אביב, תשכ״ז.
161. צרפתי, ג. ב., חסידים ואנשי מעשה והנביאים הראשונים. תרביץ שכ״ו (תשי״ז), עמ׳ 126–130.
162. קוק, ש. ח., עיונים ומחקרים. ירושלים, תשכ״ג.
See also: 14, 19, 47, 49, 62, 84, 98, 110, 131, 132.

Chapter VII

163. Belkin, S., Philo and the Oral Law. Cambridge (Mass.), 1940.
164. Buber, M., Königtum Gottes, Berlin, 1932.
165. Büchler, A., Die Priester und der Cultus im letzten Jahrzent des jerusalemischen Tempels. Jahresbericht der isr. theol. Lehranstalt, Vienna, 1895.
166. Gaster, M., The Sword of Moses. Journal of the Royal Asiatic Society. London, 1896, pp. 156 f. (= Studies and Texts in Folklore, Magic etc. vol. I. London, 1925, pp. 295 f.).
167. Geiger, A., Urschrift. 2 Auflg. Frankfurt a. M., 1928.
168. Grünbaum, M., Gesammelte Aufsätze zur Sprach- und Sagenkunde. Berlin, 1911.
169. Güdemann, M., Religionsgeschichtliche Studien. Leipzig, 1876.
170. Kahle, P., Die von Origens verwendeten griech. Bibelhandschriften. Studia Patristica, IV, 1961.
171. Lauterbach, J. Z., Substitutes for the Tetragrammaton. Proceedings of the American Academy for Jewish Research. vol. II (1930–31), pp. 39–67. Philadelphia, 1931.
172. Lewy, I., Ueber einige Fragmente aus der Mischna des Abba Saul. Bericht über die Hochschule für die Wissenschaft des Judenthums in Berlin, 1876.
172. Löw, L., Gesammelte Schriften. Szegedin, 1889.
174. Mann, J., Texts and Studies. vol. I, Cincinnati, 1931.
175. Perles, F., Annalekten zur Textkritik des Alten Testaments. München, 1895.
176. Preisendanz, K., Papyri Graecae Magicae. Berlin, vol. II, 1931.
177. Schoeps, H. J., Aus frühchristlicher Zeit. Tübingen, 1950.
178. Seeligmann, I. L., The Septuagint Version of Isaiah. Leiden, 1948.

179. Taylor, C., Cairo Genizah Palimpsests. Cambridge, 1900.
180. Yadin, Y., Another Fragment of the Psalms Scroll from Qumran 11. Textus, vol. V, 1966.
181. אלון, ג., גאון, גאים (מן ההיסטוריה החברתית של א״י בתקופת התנאים). תרביץ ש׳ כ״א, עמ׳ 106–111 (= מחקרים בתולדות ישראל, תשי״ז ח״א).
182. בן־חיים, ז., ההוגים השומרונים את השם באותיותיו? ספר ארץ ישראל ח״ג (תשי״ד).
183. גייגר, א., קבוצת מאמרים. ברלין, 1877.
184. ילון, ח., על מגילות ים המלח. קרית ספר כ׳ כ״ח (תשי״ב), עמ׳ 64–74.
185. ליברמן, ש., קלס קילוסין. ׳עלי עי״ן׳, ס׳ היובל לכבוד ש. ז. שוקן, ירושלים, תש״ח–תשי״ב.
186. ליונשטם, ש. א., מעתה ועד עולם. תרביץ ש׳ ל״ב (תשכ״ג), עמ׳ 313–316.
See also: 3, 12, 16, 55, 59, 62, 79, 98, 124, 146, 162.

Chapter VIII

187. Bacher, W., Schwab Moïse, Vocabulaire de l'Angélologie, MGWJ vol. 42 (1898), pp. 25–258, 570–572.
188. —— Tradition und Tradenten. Leipzig, 1914.
189. Blau, L., Schwab, M., Vocabulaire de l'angélologie etc. Zeitsch. f. Hebr. Bibliographie II (1897), pp. 82–85, 118–120.
190. Böklen, F., Die Verwandtschaft der Jüdisch-Christlichen mit der Persischen Eschatologie. Göttingen, 1902.
191. Burch, V., The Literary Unity of the Ascensio Isaiae. Journal of Theol. Studies vol. XX (1918–19), pp. 17–23.
192. Friedländer, L., Sittengeschichte Rom's. Wien. 1934.
193. Goldin, J., Not by means of an Angel and not by means of a Messenger. Studies in the History of Religions 1968, pp. 412 f.
194. Grant, R. M., Les Êtres Intermédiaires dans le Judaïsme Tardif. Studi e Materiali di Storia delle Religioni 38 (1967).
195. Harnack, A., Lehrbuch der Dogmengeschichte. 4 Auf. Tübingen, 1909/10.
196. Hopfner, Th., Griechisch-Ägyptischer Offenbarungszauber. Leipzig, 1921–24.
197. James, M. R., The Lost Apocrypha. London, 1920.
198. Jung, L., Fallen Angels in Jewish, Christian and Mohammedan Literature. Philadelphia, 1926.
199. Levy, I., La légende de Pythagore. Paris, 1927.
200. Marmorstein, A., Anges et hommes dans l'Agada. REJ vol. LXXXIV (1927).
201. Nemoy, L., Al-Qirqisani's Account of the Jewish Sects and Christianity. HUCA vol. 7 (1930), pp. 317–397.
202. Nock, A. D., Postscript. H.T.R. 34 (1941), pp. 103–109.
203. Peterson, E., Von den Engeln. Theologische Traktate. München, 1951.
204. Rappaport, S., Agada und Exegese bei Flavius Josephus. Wien, 1930.
205. Scholem, G., Jewish Gnosticism. New York, 1965.

206. Shaked. S., Some Notes on Abreman, The Evil Spirit and his Creation. Studies in Mysticism and Religion, presented to G. Scholem. Jerusalem, 1967.
207. Smith, J. Z., The prayer of Joseph. Studies in the History of Religion. vol. XVI (1968), pp. 253–294.
208. Urbach, E., The Homiletical Interpretations of the Sages and the Expositions of Origen and the Jewish Disputation. Scripta Hierosolymitana, XXXII, 1921, p. 247 ff.
209. אורבך, א., אסקיזים ויסורים בתורת חז״ל. ספר היובל לכבוד יצחק בער. ירושלים, תשכ״א, עמ׳ 48–68.
210. —— ד. גולדשמידט, הגדה של פסח מקורותיה ותולדותיה (ירושלים תש״ך) (ביקורת) קרית ספר כרך לו (תשכ״א), עמ׳ 143–150.
211. —— ירושלים של מטה וירושלים של מעלה. בספר ירושלים לדורותיה, הכינוס הכ״ה לידיעת הארץ. ירושלים, תשכ״ט.
212. אפטוביצר, א., דרשה בשבח התורה. סיני כ״ז (ת״ש), עמ׳ קעח–רכ, שפא–שפב.
213. ליברמן, ש., משנת שיר השירים. נספח עברי לספרו של ג. שלום Jewish Gnosticism. New York, 1965, עמ׳ 118–126.
214. —— על חטאים וענשם. ס׳ היובל לכבוד לוי גינצבורג. ניו־יורק, תש״ו. החלק העברי, עמ׳ רמט–רע.
215. —— שקיעין. ירושלים, תרצ״ט.
216. ליונשטם, ש. א., מות משה. תרביץ שכ״ז (תשי״ח), עמ׳ 142–157.
217. פראנקל, ז., מבוא הירושלמי. ברסלויא, תר״ל.

See also: 2, 12, 48, 58, 62, 79, 84, 92, 93, 107, 119, 156, 160, 168, 176.

Chapter IX

218. Altman, A., The Rabbinic Doctrine of Creation. JJS, VII (1956).
219. Aptowitzer, A., Zur Kosmologie der Agada. MGWJ vol. LXXII (1928).
220. —— Die rabbinischen Berichte über die Entstehung der Septuaginta. Haqedem, II, 1908, p. 11–12, 102–122; III, 1912, p. 4–17.
221. Armstrong, G. T., Die Genesis in der Alten Kirche. Tübingen, 1962.
222. Bousset, W., Hauptprobleme der Gnosis. Göttingen, 1907.
223. Cumont, F., Les Mystères de Mithra. Paris, 1913.
224. Eisler, R., Weltmantel und Himmelszelt. München, 1910.
225. Epstein, A., Recherches sur le Séfer Yecira. REJ vol. 28 (1894), pp. 95–108, vol. 29 (1894), pp. 61–78. כתבי א. עפשטיין, כ״ב, עמ׳ קעט ואילך. (= ירושלים, תשי״ז).
226. Ginsburger, M., Die Anthropomorphismen in den Targumim. Braunschweig, 1891.
227. Ginzberg, L., Die Haggada bei den Kirchenvätern. Berlin, 1900.
228. Grätz, H., Gnosticismus und Judentum. Krotoschin, 1846.
229. Hamp, V., Der Begriff Wort in den Aramäischen Bibelübersetzungen. München, 1938.
230. Hönig, A., Die Ophiten. Berlin, 1889.

BIBLIOGRAPHY

231. Horovitz, J., Untersuchungen über Philons und Platons Lehre von der Weltschöpfung. Marburg, 1900.

232. Jervell, J., Imago Dei. Göttingen, 1960.

233. Jonas, H., Die Mythologische Gnosis. Göttingen, 1954.

234. —— Gnosis und spätantiker Geist. dritte verb. u. vermehrte Auflage. vol. I, Göttingen, 1964.

235. Langdon, S. H., Sumerian and Babylonian Psalms. Paris, 1909.

236. Marmorstein, A., The Background of the Haggada. HUCA, vol. 6 (1929), pp. 141–204 (= Studies in Jewish Theology by A. Marmorstein, edited by J. Rabbinowitz and M. S. Lew. London, 1950, pp. 7–71).

237. Nikiprowetzky, V., Problèmes du 'Récit de la Création' chez Philon d'Alexandrie. REJ vol. CXXIV (1965), pp. 271–306.

238. Nyberg, H. S., A Manual of Pahlavi, vol. I. Wiesbaden, 1964.

239. Scholem, G., Schöpfung aus Nichts und Selbstverschränkung Gottes. Eranos-Jahrbuch, vol. XXV (1956). Zürich, 1957.

240. —— Ursprung und Anfänge der Kabbala, Berlin, 1962.

241. Séd, N., La Běraytā dī Ma'aseh Běrēšīt. Une Cosmologie Juive du Haut Moyen Âge. REJ vol. CXXIII (1965), pp. 259–305.

242. Shunary, J., Avoidance of Anthropomorphism in the Targum of Psalms. Textus V (1966), Jerusalem.

243. Wächter, L., Der Einfluss platonischen Denkens auf rabbinische Schöpfungsspekulationen. Zeitschrift für Religions- und Geistesgeschichte, vol. 14 (1962), pp. 36–56.

244. Wilson, R. Mc. L., The Early History of the Exegesis of Gen. 1:26. Studia Patristica. (TUGAL 63) 1957.

245. Wolfson, H. A., The Philosophy of the Church Fathers. Cambridge (Mass.), 1956.

246. Zaehner, R. C., Zurvan — a Zoroastrian Dilemma. Oxford, 1955.

247. אפטוביצר, א., חקר אגדה. בצרון כ״א (תש״ה), עמ׳ 105–112, 195–203.

248. אפשטיין, י. נ., ספרי זוטא, פרשת פרה. תרביץ שנה א׳ (תר״ץ).

249. גינצבורג, ל., על הלכה ואגדה. תל־אביב, תש״ך.

250. טור־סיני נ. ה., הלשון והספר, כרך האמונות והדעות. ירושלים, תשט״ז. מן הלויתן ומעולם הרפאים והנפילים: עמ׳ 168–173. הרקיע והשחקים: עמ׳ 195–204.

251. כהן—ישר י., על בעיית הבריאה יש מאין בכתבי פילון. ספר השנה, אוניברסיטה בר אילן, תשכ״ח, עמ׳ 60–66.

252. כשר, מ., מושג הזמן. תלפיות כ״ה (תשי״ב).

253. ליונשטם, ש. א., ׳מה למעלה ומה למטה מה לפנים ומה לאחור׳. ספר היובל לכב׳ י. קויפמן, עמ׳ קיב–קכא. ירושלים, תשכ״א.

254. נוימרק, ד., תולדות הפילוסופיה בישראל. ניו־יורק, תרפ״א.

225. סמבורסקי, ש., מושג הזמן באסכולה הניאו־אפלטונית המאוחרת. דברי האקדמיה הלאומית הישראלית למדעים כרך ב. ירושלים, תשכ״ז.

256. קאסוטו, מ. ד., שירת העלילה בישראל. כנסת ח (תש״ג–תש״ד), עמ׳ 121–142.

257. שובה, מ., פילון, על בריאת העולם. 15 . ידיעות המכון למדעי היהדות, הוב׳ ב, עמ׳ 77–86, ירושלים, תרפ״ה.

See also: 1, 2, 3, 22, 43, 44, 62, 65, 71, 76, 84, 86, 91, 93, 103, 105, 115, 116, 119, 156.

Chapter X

258. Altman, A., The Gnostic Background of the Rabbinic Adam Legends. JQR n.s. vol. 35 (1944/5).
259. Aptowitzer, A., Zur Erklärung einiger merkwürdiger Agadoth über die Schöpfung des Menschen. Festskrift Simonsen. København, 1923.
260. —— Die Seele als Vogel. MGWJ vol. 69 (1925), pp. 150–168.
261. —— Observations in the Criminal Law of the Jews, JQR n.s. XV (1924–5) pp. 68–75, 85–118.
262. Baeck, L., Hat das überlieferte Judentum Dogmen? (in Aus drei Jahrtausenden) Tübingen, 1958.
263. Bailey, H. W., Zoroastrian Problems in the Ninth-Century Books. Oxford, 1943.
264. Bergmann, J., Die Stoische Philosophie und die jüdische Frömmigkeit. Judaica. Festschrift H. Cohen. Berlin, 1912, pp. 145–166.
265. —— Die runden und hyperbol. Zahlen. MGWJ, 1938.
266. Bietenhard, H., Die himmlische Welt im Urchristentum und Spätjudentum. Tübingen, 1951.
267. Büchler, A., Studies in Sin and Atonement. London, 1928.
268. Christensen, A., Les Types du premier Homme et du premier roi dans l'histoire légendaire des Iraniens. Vol. I, Stockholm, 1917.
269. Diels, H., Doxographi Graeci. Berlin, 1958.
270. Frankel, Z., Notizen, MGWJ vol. 8 (1859), p. 400.
271. Guthrie, W. K. C., Plato's view on the Nature of Soul. Entretiens III (1955).
272. Heinemann, I., Poseidonios' metaphysische Schriften. Breslau, 1921.
273. —— Schriften der jüd.-hellenistischen Literatur, Philos Werke. Breslau, 1923.
274. —— Die Lehre von der Zweckbestimmung des Menschen im griechisch-römischen Altertum und im jüdischen Mittelalter. Breslau, 1926 (= Jahresbericht. Breslau, 1925).
275. Hirsch, W., Rabbinic Psychology, London, 1947.
276. Kisch, G., Pseudo-Philo's Liber Antiquitatum Biblicarum. Notre Dame (Indiana) 1949.
277. Krauss, S., Antoninus und Rabbi. Frankfurt a. Main, 1910.
278. Lesky, E., Die Zeugungs und Vererbungslehren der Antike und ihr Nachwirken, Abhandlungen der Akademie der Wissenschaften. Mainz, 1950.
279. Lieberman, S., Some Aspects of After Life in Early Rabbinic Literature. H. A. Wolfson Jubilee Volume. Jerusalem, 1965.
280. Lipsius, J. H., Das attische Recht. Leipzig, 1905–15.
281. Mann, J., The Bible as Read and Preached in the Old Synagogue, vol. 1. Cincinnati, 1940.

282. Marmorstein, A., Iranische und jüdische Religion. ZNW vol. 26 (1927), pp. 231–242.

283. Meyer, R., Hellenistisches in der Rabbinischen Anthropologie. Stuttgart, 1937.

289. Mommsen, Th., Römisches Strafrecht. Leipzig, 1899.

285. Needham, J., A History of Embryology, 2nd edit. Cambridge Univ. Press, 1959.

286. Pedersen, J., Israel, its Life and Culture. London, 1926.

287. Pidoux, G., Anthropologie Religieuse, l'Homme dans l'Ancien Testament. Supplements to Numen II (1955).

288. Porter, F. C., The Pre-Existence of the Soul in the Book of Wisdom and in the Rabbinical Writings. The American Journal of Theology XII (1908), pp. 115–153.

289. Praechter, K., Platon Präformist. Philologus vol. 83 (1928).

290. Reitzenstein, R., Das Iranische Erlösungsmysterium. Bonn, 1921.

291. Rosenthal, F., Vier apokryphische Bücher aus der Zeit und Schule R. Akiba's. Leipzig, 1885.

292. Sachs, M., Beiträge. Berlin, 1852.

293. Scheftelowitz, J., Die altpersische Religion und das Judentum. Giessen, 1920.

294. Schenke, H. M., Der Gott 'Mensch' in der Gnosis. Göttingen, 1962.

295. Schlier, H., Der Mensch im Gnostizismus. Supplements to Numen II (1955).

296. Talmon, S., The Desert Motif in the Bible and in Qumran Literature, Philip W. Lown Institute of Advanced Studies III, Studies and Texts, 1966.

297. Wallach, L., The Colloquy of Marcus Aurelius with the Patriarch Judah I. JQR n.s. XXXI (1940/1), pp. 259–286.

298. Wesendonk, von O. G., Urmensch und Seele. Hannover, 1924.

299. Wiesner, J., Scholien zum bab. Talmud, vol. III. Prag, 1867.

300. אברמסון, ש., משיחתם של בני ארץ ישראל. סיני, תשכ״ח.

301. בעהר, מ., דברי משלם. פרנקפורט, תרפ״ו.

302. בער, י., ספר יוסיפון העברי. ספר דינבורג. ירושלים תשי״ט, עמ׳ 178–205.

303. לוי, י., פירוש לירושלמי ב״ק Jahresbericht des Jüdisch-Theol. Seminars. Breslau 1895–1914.

304. ליברמן, ש., תוספת ראשונים. ח״א–ח״ד, ירושלים, תרצ״ו–תרצ״ט.

305. —— שקיעין. ירושלים, תרצ״ט.

306. מרמורשטיין, א., מרעיונות הגאולה באגדת האמוראים. מצודה, ח״ב (תש״ד), עמ׳ 94–105.

307. פינלש, צ. מ., דרכה של תורה. וינא, 1861.

308. פינקלשטיין, א., מבוא למסכתות אבות ואבות דר׳ נתן. ניו־יורק, תשי״א.

309. קלוזנר, י., הרעיון המשיחי בישראל מראשיתו ועד חתימת המשנה. מהדו׳ ג. תל־אביב, תש״י.

309. שטערן י. ז., מאמר תהלוכות האגדות. ווארשא, תרס״ב.

See also: 4, 21, 32, 34, 41, 55, 62, 98, 103, 113, 116, 146, 150, 156, 163, 167, 169, 195, 199, 214, 222, 227, 233, 240.

Chapter XI

310. Aptowitzer, V., The Rewarding and Punishing of Animals and Inanimate Objects. HUCA vol. III (1926), pp. 117–156.

311. Büchler, A., Ben Sira's Conception of Sin and Atonement. JQR n.s. vol. XIII (1922–23), pp. 303–335, 461–502, ibid. vol. XIV, pp. 53–83.

312. Flusser, D., The Dead Sea Sect and Pre Pauline Christianity. Scripta Hierosolymitana, vol. IV (1958), pp. 215–266.

313. Gunkel, H., Die Psalmen übersetzt u. erklärt. Göttingen, 1926.

314. Hempel, J., Gott und Mensch im Alten Testament. Studie zur Geschichte der Frömmigkeit. 2, völlig durgearb. Aufl. Stuttgart, 1936 (Beiträge zur Wissenschaft vom A. u. N. Testament, 3. Folge, Heft 2).

315. Lütgert, W., Das Problem der Willensfreiheit in der vorchristlichen Synagoge. Halle a.S., 1906.

316. Mach, R., Der Zaddik im Talmud und Midrasch. Leiden, 1957.

317. Marmorstein, A., The Doctrine of Merits in Old Rabbinic Literature. London, 1920.

318. Marx, A., Y a-t-il une prédestination à Qumran. Revue de Qumran, IV (1967).

319. Marx, A., The Correspondence Between the Rabbis of Southern France and Maimonides about Astrology. HUCA III (1956), pp. 311–358.

320. Mingana, A., vol. VI: Commentary of Theodore of Mopsuestia on the Lord's Prayer. Cambridge, 1933.

321. Moore, G. F., Fate and Free Will in the Jewish Philosophies According to Josephus. Harvard Theological Review, XXII (1929), pp. 371–389.

322. Müller, H. F., Plotinos — über die Vorsehung. Philologus, vol. 72 (1913), pp. 338–357.

323. Nötscher, F., Schicksalsglaube in Qumran und Umwelt. Biblische Zeitschrift, 1959, pp. 205–234, ibid. 1960, pp. 98–121.

324. Pettazoni, R., The All-knowing God. London, 1956.

325. Sjöberg, E., Gott und die Sünder im pal. Judentum nach dem Zeugnis der Tannaiten und der apokryphisch-pseudoepigraphischen Literatur. Stuttgart, 1938 (Beiträge zur Wissenschaft vom Alten u. Neuen Testament, 4 Folge, Heft 27).

326. Wendland, P., Philos Schrift über die Vorsehung. Berlin, 1892.

327. Wochenmark, J., Die Schicksalsidee im Judentum. Stuttgart, 1933.

328. אורבך, א., הלכות ירושה וחיי עולם. דברי הקונגרס העולמי הרביעי למדעי היהדות. כ״א, ירושלים, תשכ״ז, עמ׳ 133–141.

329. אפשטיין, י. נ., מבואות לספרות התנאים. ערוך בידי ע. צ. מלמד. ירושלים, 1957.

330. ליברמן, ש., הירושלמי כפשוטו. ירושלים, תרצ״ה.

331. ליכט, י., מושג הנדבה בכתביה של כת מדבר יהודה. בקובץ ׳עיונים במגילות מדבר יהודה׳, ירושלים, תשי״ז.

332. מרגליות, ר., מאן הויא ליומא. סיני, כ׳ כ״א (תש״ז), עמ׳ קעו–קעט.

333. פלוסר, ד., כת מדבר יהודה והשקפותיה. ציון יט (תשי״ד), עמ׳ 89–103.

334. —— כת מדבר יהודה והנצרות. בקובץ 'עיונים במגילות מדבר יהודה', ירושלים, תשי"ז, עמ' 85–103.
335. שווארץ, ז., אגרת ר' אברהם ב"ר חייא הנשיא שכתב לר' יהודה ב"ר ברזילי על שאלה בכלדיים. בס' היובל לכבוד אריה שווארץ. ברלין–ווין, 1917, עמ' 23–36.

See also: 1, 2, 14, 40, 51, 55, 56, 83, 92, 103, 104, 111, 115, 129, 156, 195, 209, 234, 281.

CHAPTER XII

336. Baeck, L., The Pharisees. New York, 1947.
337. —— The Essence of Judaism. New York, 1948.
338. Bamberger, B. J., Revelations of Torah after Sinai. HUCA vol. XVI (1941), pp. 97–114.
339. Blank, S. H., The Septuagint Renderings of Old Testament Terms for Law. HUCA, VII (1930), pp. 259–283.
340. Blau, L., Zur Einleitung in die Heilige Schrift. Budapest, 1894.
341. Büchler, A., Types of Jewish Palestinian Piety. London, 1922.
342. Cohen, B., Jewish and Roman Law. New York, 1966.
343. —— Letter and Spirit in Jewish and Roman Law. M. Kaplan Jubilee Volume. New-York, 1953.
344. Daube, D., The New Testament and Rabbinic Judaism. London, 1956.
345. Davies, W. D., Torah in the Messianic Age. Philadelphia, 1952.
346. —— The Setting of the Sermon on the Mount. Cambridge University Press, 1964.
347. Geiger, A., Zur Theologie und Schrifterklärung der Samaritaner. Nachgelassene Schriften, vol. III, pp. 255–266, Berlin, 1876.
348. Gemser, B., Sprüche Salomos. Tübingen, 1963.
349. Heinemann, F., Nomos und Physis. Basel, 1945.
350. Heinemann, I., Die Lehre vom ungeschriebenen Gesetz im Jüdischen Schrifttum. HUCA vol. IV (1927), pp. 149–172.
351. Hennecke, E., Handbuch zu der Neutestamentlichen Apokrypha. Tübingen, 1814.
352. Holdheim, S., Das Ceremonialgesetz im Messiasreich. Schwerin, 1845.
353. Kaatz, J., Die mündliche Lehre und ihr Dogma. Leipzig, 1922.
354. Koester, H., ΝΟΜΟΣ ΦΥΣΕΩΣ, Studies in the History of Religions, XIV, 1968, pp. 522–545.
355. Kümmel, W. G., Jesus und der jüd. Traditionsgedanke. ZNW, 1934.
356. Löwy, M., Die Paulinische Lehre vom Gesetz. MGWJ vol. 47 (1903), pp. 322–339, 417–433, 534–544, ibid. vol. 48 (1904), pp. 267–276, 321–327, 400–416.
357. Lyonnet S., St. Paul, Liberty and Law. The Bridge, 1962, pp. 229–251.
358. Marcus, R., Law in the Apocrypha. Columbia Univ.: Oriental Studies, vol. 26 (1927), pp. 59–66, 70–74.
359. Marmorstein, A., Ein Fragment einer neuen Piska zum Wochenfest und

der Kampf gegen das mündliche Gesetz. Jeschurum ed. Wohlgemuth XII (1925), pp. 34–53.
360. Nissen, A., Tora und Geschichte im Spaetjudentum. Novum Testamentum, 1967, pp. 241-277.
361. Östborn, G., Tora in the Old Testament. Lund, 1945.
362. Pépin, J., Mythe et Allégorie. Paris, 1958.
363. Rad, von G., Theologie des A.T. München, 1962.
364. Ritter, B., Philo und die Halacha. Leipzig, 1879.
365. Rössler, D., Gesetz und Geschichte, Neukirchen Kreis Moers, 1960.
366. Schechter, S., The Rabbinical Conception of Holiness. JQR O.S. vol. X (1898), pp. 1-12.
367. Schoeps, H. J., Theologie und Geschichte des Juden-Christentums. Tübingen, 1949.
368. Scholem, G., Zum Verständnis der messianische Idee im Judentum. Eranos-Jahrbuch vol. XXVIII (1959). Zürich, 1960, pp. 193–239 (= Judaica, Frankfurt a.M., 1963, pp. 1–74. Bibliothek Suhrkamp, Bd. 106).
369. Schroeder, O., Νόμος ὁ πάντων βασιλεύς. Philologus, vol. LXXIV (1917), pp. 194–204.
370. Trilling, W., Das Wahre Israel. München, 1964.
371. Wallach, L., The Textual History of an Aramaic Proverb. JBL, vol. LX (1941), pp. 403–415.
372. Weiss, H. F., Der Pharisäismus im Lichte der Überlieferung des N.T. Sitzungsberichte der Säch. Akademie, vol. 110. Berlin, 1964–66.
373. —— Zur Frage der historischen Begegnung von Antike und Christentum. Klio vol. 43/45 (1965), pp. 307.
374. אהרליך, א., מקרא כפשוטו. ברלין, תרס״א.
375. אורבך, א., הדרשה כיסוד ההלכה ובעית הסופרים. תרביץ ש׳ כז, עמ׳ 166–182.
376. אלון, ג., ההלכה באגרת בר נבא. תרביץ, שי״א (ת״ש), עמ׳ 23–38, 223.
377. בן־חיים, ז., פיוטים שומרוניים לשמחות. תרביץ ש״י, עמ׳ 190–220, 333–374.
378. גוטמן, י. מ., תורה בתלמוד, Festschrift Adolf Schwartz Berlin — Wien, 1917, חלק עברי, עמ׳ 1 ואילך.
379. —— בחינת קיום המצוות. Bericht des jüdisch-theologischen Seminars für das Jahr 1930. Breslau, 1931.
380. חיות, צ. ה., תורת הנביאים, פ״ב, בירור אליהו. זאלקאווא, תקצ״ו.
381. טורצ׳ינר, נ. ה., ׳גלה פנים בתורה שלא כהלכה׳, לשוננו יב (תש״ג–תש״ד), עמ׳ 272.
382. קרויס, ש., תוספות הערוך השלם (נערך ע״י ש. קרויס בהשתתפות ד. גייגר, ל. גינצבורג, ע. לעף, ב. מורמלשטיין) וינא, תרצ״ז.
See also: 19, 20, 21, 40, 41, 67, 86, 98, 104, 146, 157, 169, 177, 245, 267, 309.

CHAPTER XIII

384. Albeck, Ch., Untersuchungen über die halakischen Midraschim. Berlin, 1927.

385. —— Das Buch der Jubiläen und die Halacha. Bericht der Hochschule für die Wissenschaft des Judentums. Berlin, 1930.
386. Aptowitzer, V., Untersuchungen zur Gaonäischen Literatur. HUCA vol. 8–9 (1931–32), pp. 373–442.
387. Bloch, M., Les 613 Lois. REJ vol. 1 (1880), pp. 197–211.
388. Cohen, H., Das Problem der jüdischen Sittenlehre. Eine Kritik von Lazarus' Ethik des Judentums. MGWJ vol. 43 (1899), pp. 385–400, 433–449.
389. Ehrenfeld, A., Der Pflichtbegriff in der Ethik des Judentums. Bratislava, 1931 (?).
390. Eschelbacher, M., Recht und Billigkeit in der Jurisprudenz des Talmud. Judaica, Festschrift H. Cohen. Berlin, 1912, pp. 501–514.
391. Güdemann, M., Moralische Rechtseinschränkung im mosaisch-rabbinischen Rechtssystem. MGWJ vol. LXI (1917), pp. 422–443.
392. Hirzel, R., Themis, Dike und Verwandtes, Leipzig, 1907.
393. Hoffmann, D., Zur Einleitung in die halachischen Midraschim. Beilage zum Jahresbericht des Rabbiner Seminars. Berlin, 1888.
394. Kosmala, H., Nachfolge und Nachahmung Gottes. Annual of the Swedish Theological Institute, III (1964).
395. Lazarus, M., Die Ethik des Judentums, vol. 1–2. Frankfurt a.M., 1898–1911.
396. Marmorstein, A., Mitteilungen zur Geschichte und Literatur aus der Geniza (Fortsetzung 4). MGWJ vol. 69 (1925), pp. 150–160.
397. —— The Imitation of God in the Haggadah. Studies in Jewish Theology by A. Marmorstein, edited by J. Rabbinowitz and M. S. Lew. London, 1950.
398. Perles, F., Die Autonomie der Sittlichkeit im jüdischen Schrifttum. Judaica, Festschrift Hermann Cohen. Berlin, 1912, pp. 103–108.
399. Steckelmacher, M., Etwas über die leichten und schweren Gebote. Festschrift Adolf Schwarz. Berlin u. Wien, 1917.
400. Urbach, E., The Laws Regarding Slavery as a Source for Social History of the Second Temple, the Mishnah and Talmud. Papers of the Institute of Jewish Studies, London, vol. I, 1964 pp. 1–95.

401. אורבך, א., לשון ועניין. ׳לשוננו׳ כרך ל״ב (תשכ״ח), עמ׳ 122–128.
402. —— משמעותה הדתית של ההלכה. בתוך קובץ הרצאות ׳ערכי היהדות׳ תל־אביב, 1950, עמ׳ 24–31, (= על יהדות וחינוך. ירושלים, תשכ״ז, עמ׳ 127–139).
403. —— מגמות דתיות וחברתיות בתורת הצדקה של חז״ל. ציון שנה ט״ז (תשי״א), עמ׳ 1–27.
404. אלבק, ח., מחקרים בברייתא ותוספתא. ירושלים, תש״ד.
405. אלון, ג., שבות, רשות, מצוה. תרביץ ש״ז, עמ׳ 135–142 (= מחקרים בתולדות ישראל כ״ב, עמ׳ 111–119).
406. אלון, מ., חירות הפרט בדרכי גביית חוב במשפט העברי. ירושלים, תשכ״ד.
407. אסף, ש., מסדר התפילה בארץ ישראל. ס׳ דינבורג. ירושלים, תש״ט, עמ׳ 116–130, 422.
408. ביכלר, א., תולדות ברכת הטוב והמיטיב. מאמרים לזכרון ר׳ צבי פרץ חיות. וינא, תרצ״ג.

409. בער, י., לבעית דמותה של היהדות באבנגליונים הסינאופטיים. ציון, של״א (תשכ״ו), עמ׳ 117—152.

410. גוטמן, יוליוס, קאנט והיהדות. בקובץ מאמריו ׳דת ומדע׳. ירושלים, תשט״ו, עמ׳ 218—229.

411. גוטמן, י. מ., בחינת המצוות לפי מניינן סדורן והתחלקותן. יאהרסבריכט, ברסלאו, תרפ״ח.

412. הברמן, א. מ., על התפילין בימי קדם. ארץ ישראל, ספר ג׳, תשי״ד.

413. היינמן, י., טעמי המצוות בספרות ישראל. מהדורה חמישית. ירושלים, תשכ״ו.

414. זילברג, מ., כך דרכו של תלמוד. ירושלים. תשכ״ב.

415. ידין, י., הממצאים מימי בר כוכבא במערת האיגרות. ירושלים, 1963.

416. לוין, ב. מ., משרידי הגניזה: פרקוי בן באבוי. תרביץ ש״ב (תרצ״א), עמ׳ 383—410.

417. ליברמן, ש., תיקוני ירושלמי. רשות. תרביץ, ש״ה (תרצ״ד), עמ׳ 97—99. שם ש״ו (תרצ״ה), עמ׳ 111.

418. —— תשלום תוספתא (בראש התוספתא מהדורת צוקרמאנדל בהוצאת במברגר את וואהרמן). ירושלים, תרצ״ח, עמ׳ 5—62.

419. ספראי, ש., מצות שביעית במציאות שלאחר חורבן בית שני. תרביץ של״ה (תשכ״ו), עמ׳ 304—328. שם של״ו (תשכ״ז) עמ׳ 1—21.

420. קאסוטו, מ. ד., מאדם עד נח. ירושלים, תשי״ג.

421. רבינוביץ, ז. ו., שערי תורת ארץ ישראל. ירושלים, ת״ש.

422. רוזנטל, א. ש., על דרך הרוב, ״פרקים״, א, ירושלים, תשכ״ח, עמ׳ 183—224.

423. שעפטל, ש. ב., ביאורי אונקלוס. מינכן, תרמ״ח.

See also: 1, 2, 12, 19, 25, 26, 28, 35, 62, 79, 86, 90, 92, 93, 98, 117, 121.

Chapter XIV

424. Aptowitzer, V., Geschichte einer liturgischen Formel. MGWJ vol. 73 (1929) pp. 93–188.

425. Bacher, W., Das Targum zu Hiob. MGWJ vol. 20 (1871), pp. 208–223, 283–284.

426. Bamberger, B. J., Fear and Love of God in the O.T. HUCA vol. VI (1929), pp. 39–54.

427. Baumstark, A., Comparative Liturgy. English edition by F. L. Cross. London, 1958.

428. Beer, G., Der Text des Buches Hiob untersucht. Marburg, 1897.

429. Bickerman, E. J., The Maxim of Antigonus of Socho. HTR vol. 44 (1951), pp. 153–166.

430. Dietrich, E. L., Die Liebe des Einzelnen zu Gott in der jüd. Frömmigkeit von der Zeit der Gaonim bis zum Auftreten der Kabbala. Oriens, vol. XVII, 1964, pp. 132–160.

431. Gard, D. H., The Concept of Job's Character according to the Greek Translator of the Hebrew Text. JBL vol. 72 (1953), pp. 182–186.

432. —— The Concept of Future Life according to the Greek Translator of the Book of Job. JBL vol. 73 (1954), pp. 137–143.

433. Gerleman, G., Book of Job (Studies in the Septuagint, vol. 1). Lund, 1946.

434. Graetz, H., Das Zeitalter der griechischer Uebersetzung des Buches Hiob. MGWJ vol. XXVI (1877), pp. 83–91.

435. Heiler, F., Das Gebet. 4. Aufl. München, 1921.

436. Kohler, K., The Testament of Job. An Essene Midrash on the Book of Job, reedited and translated. Semitic Studies in memory of A. Kohut. Berlin, 1897, pp. 264–338.

437. —— The Pre-Talmudic Haggada. JQR O.S. vol. V (1892–3), pp. 339–419, ibid. vol. 7 (1894–5), pp. 581–606.

438. Lewy, I., Ein Wort über das jüdische Gebet. MGWJ vol. 35 (1886), pp. 109–121, 156–164.

439. Orlinsky, H. M., Studies in the Septuagint of the Book of Job. HUCA vols. 28–30 (1957–59), 32–33 (1961–62), 35–36 (1964–65).

440. Philonenko, M., Le Testament de Job et les Therapeutes. Semitica VIII (1958), pp. 41–53.

441. Ploeg, van der, J., Le Targum de Job de la grotte 11 de Qumran. Amsterdam, 1962.

442. Prijs, L., Jüdische Tradition in der Septuaginta. Leiden, 1948.

443. Sander, R., Furcht und Liebe im pal. Judentum. Stuttgart, 1935.

444. Sevenster, J. N., Paul and Seneca. Leiden, 1961 (Supplements to Novum Testamentum, vol. 4).

445. Spanier, A., Stilkritisches zum jüd. Gebet. MGWJ vol. LXXX (1936), pp. 339–350.

446. Vajda, G., L'amour de Dieu dans la Théologie Juive du Moyen-Âge. Paris, 1957.

447. Werner, E., The Doxology in Synagogue and Church. HUCA vol. 19 (1945–6), pp. 275–352.

448. Wiernikowski, J., Das Buch Hiob nach der Auffassung des Talmud und Midrasch. Breslau, 1902.

449. אורבך, א., תשובת אנשי נינוה והויכוח היהודי נוצרי. תרביץ ש׳ כ (תש״י), עמ׳ 118–122.

450. ברילל, נ., הערות שונות. (המשך ב.) בית תלמוד. שנה ד׳ (תרמ״ה), עמ׳ 42 ואילך.

451. גולדין, י., בית מדרשו של יוחנן בן זכאי. ספר היובל לכבוד צבי וולפסון, החלק העברי. ירושלים, תשכ״ה, עמ׳ סט–צב.

452. חורגין, פ., תרגום כתובים. ניו־יורק, תש״ה.

453. טור־סיני (טורטשינר), נ. ה., לתולדות ספרי המקרא. ס׳ זכרון לא׳ גולק ולש׳ קליין. ירושלים, תש״ב, עמ׳ 99–104.

454. עמיר, י., דרשותיו של פילון על היראה והאהבה ויחסן למדרש ארץ ישראל. ציון ש״ל (תשכ״ה), עמ׳ 47–60.

455. קמינקא, א., מחקרים במקרא ובתלמוד. ספר ב׳ ת״א, תשי״א.

456. רוזנטל, א. ש., לשונות סופרים. יובל שי, מאמרים לכב׳ ש״י עגנון. רמת גן, תשי״ח, עמ׳ 293–324.

See also: 19, 21, 70, 102, 119, 152, 208, 209, 234, 245, 329, 336, 374, 400, 401, 404, 421.

Chapter XV

457. Ameisenowa, Z., Animal Headed Gods, Evangelists, Saints and Righteous Men. Journal of the Warburg Institute, vol. XII (1949), pp. 21–45.
458. Aptowitzer, A., Kain und Abel in der Agada. Wien, 1922.
459. Betz, E., Der gekreuzigte Gerechte bei Plato, im N.T. und in der Alten Kirche. Akademie der Wissenschaften. Mainz, 1950.
460. Büchler, A., Die Erlösung des Eliša b. Abuyah's aus dem Höllenfeuer. MGWJ 1932, pp. 412–456.
461. Capelle, W., Zur antiken Theodicee. Archiv für Geschichte der Philosophie. XX (1907).
462. Cohen, S., Original Sin. HUCA vol. XXI (1948), pp. 275–330.
463. Conybeare, F. C., The Testament of Solomon. JQR XI (1899), pp. 1–45.
464. Davies, W. D., Paul and Rabbinic Judaism. London, 1955.
465. Dietrich, E. K., Die Umkehr <Bekehrung und Busse> im A.T. und im Judentum. Stuttgart, 1936.
466. Eppel, R., Le piétisme Juif dans les Testaments des douze Patriarches. Paris, 1930.
467. Ginzberg, L., Die Haggada bei den Kirchenvätern (Der Kommentar des Hieronymus zu Kohelet). Abhandlungen zur Erinnerung an H. P. Chajes. Wien, 1933, pp. 22–50.
468. Frankel, Z., Über den Einfluss der pal. Exegese auf die alex. Hermeneutik. Leipzig, 1851.
469. Glueck, N., Das Wort hesed im alttestamentlichen Sprachgebrauche. Giessen, 1927 (Beihefte zur ZAW, 47).
470. —— Hesed in the Bible. Translated by A. Gottschalk. With an introduction by G. A. Larue. Cincinnati, 1967.
471. Goiten, E., Das Vergeltungsprincip im Biblischen und Talmudischen Recht. Frankfurt, 1893.
472. Gross, J., Enstehungsgeschichte des Erbsündendogmas von der Bibel bis Augustinus, 1960.
473. Gundel, W., Dekane und Dekansternbilder. Glückstadt, 1963.
474. Heinemann, I., Messianismus und Mysterienreligion MGWJ, vol. 69 (1925), pp. 343–355.
475. Horovitz, J., Auge um Auge, Zahn um Zahn. Judaica Hermann Cohen Festschrift. Berlin, 1912, pp. 609–658.
476. Jacob, B., Auge um Auge. Berlin, 1929.
477. Kittel, R., Die hellenistische Mysterienreligion und das A.T. Stuttgart, 1924.
478. Kohler, K., Abba, Father, Title of Spiritual Leader. JQR vol. XIII (1900), pp. 567–580.
479. Kuss, O., Der Römerbrief, Regensburg 1957.
480. Latte, K., Schuld und Sünde in der Griech. Religion, Archiv für Religionswissenschaft. XX (1920–1921).
481. Levi, I., La commémoration des morts dans le Judaisme. REJ vol XXIX (1894), pp. 43–60.

482. —— Le péché originel dans les anciennes sources Juives. École Pratique des Hautes Études. Paris, 1907.

483. Löwy, S., The Extent of Jewish Polygamy in Talmudic Times. JJS, IX, 1958, pp. 124–129.

484. Lieberman, S., The Martyrs of Caesarea. Annuaire de l'Institut de Philologie et d'Histoire Orientales et Slaves. Tome VII (1939–1944). New York, pp. 395–446.

485. Norden, E., Die Geburt des Kindes. Leipzig, 1924.

486. Porter, F. C.. The Yeçer Hara, A Study in the Jewish Doctrine of Sin. Biblical and Semitic Studies, 1902.

487. Reinach, S., De l'origine des prières pour les morts. REJ vol. 41 (1900), pp. 161 f.

488. Schechter, S., Genizah Specimens (Liturgy). JQR O.S. vol. X (1895/98), pp. 654–659.

489. Scholem, G., Die 36 Verborgenen Gerechten in der jüd. Tradition. Judaica. Frankfurt a.M., 1963.

490. —— Le Mythe de la Peine dans le judaïsme. Archivio di Filosofia. Rome, 1967.

491. —— Von der mystischen Gestalt der Gottheit. Zürich, 1962.

492. Schott, S., Altägyptische Festdaten. Akademie der Wissenschaften in Mainz, 1950.

493. Stein, E., Der Begriff der Palingenesie im talm. Schrifttum. MGWJ vol. 83 (1939).

494. Zeitlin, S., The Legend of the Ten Martyrs and its Apocalyptic Origin. JQR 1945–6, pp. 1 f.

495. אברמסון, ש., במרכזים ובתפוצות בתקופת הגאונים. ירושלים, תשכ״ה.

496. אורבך, א., בשולי הידיעות. ידיעות החברה לחקירת א״י ועתיקותיה. י״ט (תשט״ו), עמ׳ 103—104.

497. — המסורת על תורת הסוד בתקופת התנאים. מחקרים בקבלה ובתולדות הדתות מוגשים לגרשם שלום. ירושלים, תשכ״ח.

498. בובר, מ., דרכו של מקרא. ירושלים, תשכ״ד.

499. בן־חיים, ז., עברית וארמית נוסח שומרון. כ״ג ס״ב ירושלים, תשכ״ז.

500. — על ׳דבקי מיתה׳. לשוננו לעם. תשכ״ז, עמ׳ 135—137.

501. בר, מ., למקורותיו של המספר ל״ו צדיקים. בר־אילן. ספר השנה למדעי היהדות והרוח של אוניברסיטת בר־אילן. תשכ״ג.

502. גוטמן, יהושע, האם ושבעת בניה באגדה ובספרי החשמונאים ב׳ וד׳. ספר יוחנן לוי, ירושלים, תש״ט, עמ׳ 29—37.

503. הלוי, י. א., דורות הראשונים. פרעסבורג – פפד״מ, תרס״א–תרע״ח.

504. וייס, מ., מבעיות ׳תורת הגמול׳ המקראית. תרביץ כל״א (תשכ״ב), עמ׳ 236—263. שם כל״ב (תשכ״ג), עמ׳ 1—18.

505. יעבץ, ז., מקור הברכות. ברלין, תר״ע.

506. לוין, ב. מ., אוצר הגאונים, כ׳ א – יב, חיפה – ירושלים תרפ״ח – תש״ג.

507. מירסקי, א., מחצבתן של צורות הפיוט. ידיעות המכון לחקר השירה העברית. ספר ז, תשי״ט.

508. מרגליות, א., החייבים במקרא וזכאים בתלמוד ובמדרשים. לונדון, תש״ט.
509. צונץ, יו״ט ל., הדרשות בישראל והשתלשלותן ההיסטורית. נערך והושלם ע״י ח. אלבעק. ירושלים, תש״ז.
510. קרויס, ש., עשרה הרוגי מלכות. השלוח כרך מד (1925), עמ׳ 10–22, 106–117, 221–223.
511. — מאן הויא ליומא. סיני כרך כב, עמ׳ רצט–שב.
512. שלום, ג., שבתי צבי והתנועה השבתאית בימי חייו. כ״א–כ״ב, תל־אביב, תשי״ז.
513. שפיגל, ש., מאגדות העקידה. ספר היובל לכבוד אלכסנדר מארכס. ניו־יורק, תש״ו.
514. ש״ץ–אופנהיימר, ר., החסידות כמיסטיקה. ירושלים, תשכ״ח.

See also: 3, 19, 20, 26, 41, 59, 71, 76, 79, 90, 92, 93, 98, 119, 121, 123, 146, 149, 150, 156, 163, 217, 227, 267, 279, 281, 308, 310, 316, 317, 328, 329, 332, 350, 393, 403, 404, 407, 420, 449.

Chapter XVI

515. Bacher, W., Die Gelehrten von Caesarea. MGWJ vol. 45 (1910), pp. 298–310.
516. —— The Church Father Origen and Rabbi Hoshaya. JQR III (1891), pp. 357–360.
517. —— Zur Geschichte der Schulen Palästinas im 3. und 4. Jahrhundert. MGWJ vol. 43 (1899), pp. 345–360.
518. Bamberger, B. J., Proselytism in the Talmudic Period. Cincinnati, 1939.
519. Bardy, G., Les Traditions Juives dans l'oeuvre d'Origine. Revue Biblique vol. XXXIV (1925), pp. 217–252.
520. —— St. Jérome et ses maîtres hébreux. Revue Bénédictine, 1934, pp. 145–164.
521. Bass, E., Die Merkmale der isr. Prophetie nach der traditionellen Auffassung des Talmud. Kirchhain (N. D.) (Diss.).
522. Bernays, J., Gesammelte Abhandlungen. hrsg. von H. Usener, 2 vol. Berlin, 1885.
523. Black, S. B., The Death of Zechariah in Rabbinic Literature. HUCA vol. XII–XIII (1937–38), pp. 327–346.
524. Brandon, S. G. F., Jesus and the Zealots. Manchester, 1967.
525. Braude, W. G., Jewish Proselyting in the First Five Centuries, 1940.
526. Büchler, A., Das Synhedrion in Jerusalem und das grosse Beth-Din in der Quaderkammer des jerusalemischen Tempels. Vienna, 1902.
527. —— Der Galilaische ʿAm-ha'areṣ, Vienna, 1906.
528. —— מפסע על ראשי עם קדוש, Dissertationes in honorem Dr. Eduardi Mahler. Budapestini, 1937, pp. 379–405.
529. —— The Minim of Sepphoris and Tiberias in the Second and Third Century. Studies in Jewish History, 1956.
530. —— The Political and Social Leaders of the Jewish Community of Sepphoris, London 1909.

531. Eisler, R., ΙΗΣΟΥΣ ΒΑΣΙΛΕΥΣ ΟΥ ΒΑΣΙΛΕΥΣΑΣ. Heidelberg, vol. I–II, 1929–30.
532. Erichsen, W., Die Satzungen einer Ägyptischen Kultgenossenschaft aus der Ptolemäerzeit, København, 1959.
533. Farmer, W. R., Maccabees, Zealots, and Josephus. New York, 1956.
534. Feldman, L. H., Jewish Sympathizers in Classical Literature and Inscriptions. Transaction Am. Phil. Assoc. vol. 81 (1950), pp. 200–208.
535. Festugière, A. M. J., La révélation d'Hermès Trismegiste (vol. II, Le Dieu cosmique). Paris, 1949.
536. Fischel, H. A., Martyr and Prophet. JQR vol. 37 (1946), pp. 265–280, 303–386.
537. Fuks, A., The Jewish Revolt in Egypt in the Light of the Papyri. Aegyptus vol. XXXIII (1953).
538. Glatzer, N. N., Talmudic interpretation of Prophecy. Review of Religion, 1946, pp. 195 f.
539. Guttmann, A., Decisionsmotive im Talmud. Berlin, 1938.
540. Guttmann, M., Das Judentum und seine Umwelt. Berlin, 1927.
541. —— Zur Einleitung in die Halakha. Budapest, 1913.
542. Helfgott, B. W., The Doctrine of Election in Tannaitic Literature. New York, 1954.
543. Hengel, M., Die Zeloten. Leiden, 1961.
544. Herford, R. T., The Pharisees. London, 1924 (= New York, 1924. Boston 1962).
545. Hoenig, S. B., New Light on Akabiah b. Mahalalel. Studies and Essays in honour of Abraham A. Neuman. Leiden, 1962.
546. Jaspers, K., Einführung in die Philosophie. Zürich (c. 1950).
547. Joel, M., Einige Notizen als Ergänzungen zum zweiten Theil meiner Schrift, "Blicke in die Religionsgeschichte", Graetz-Jubelschrift, 1887.
548. Juster, J., Les Juifs dans l'Empire Romain, vol. II. Paris, 1914.
549. Kaduschin, M., Aspects of the Rabbinic Concept of Israel. HUCA vol. XIX (1945–46), pp. 57–96.
550. Kosmala, H., Hebräer Essener und Christen. Studien zur Vorgeschichte der frühchristlichen Verkündigung. Leiden, 1959.
551. Lauterbach, J. Z., Rabbinical Essays. (The Sadducees and Pharisees) Cincinnati, 1951. (The article first appeared Studies in Jewish Literature issued in honor of K. Kohler. Berlin, 1913, pp. 176–198).
552. Levy, I., Le Proselytisme Juif. REJ vol. 50 (1905), p. 4 f.
553. Lieberman, S., The Discipline in the So-called Dead Sea Manual of Discipline. JBL vol. 71, pp. 199–206.
554. Mihaly, E., A Rabbinic Defence of the Election of Israel. HUCA vol. XXXV (1964), pp. 103–143.
555. Neussner, J., The Fellowship in the Second Jewish Commonwealth. HTR vol. 53 (1960), pp. 126–142.
556. Obermeyer, J., Die Landschaft Babylonien. Frankfurt a.M., 1929.

557. Otto, W., Priester und Tempel. Leipzig–Berlin, 1905.
558. Parzen, H., The Ruah Hakodesh in Tannaitic Literature. JQR N.S. vol. XX (1929–30), pp. 51 f.
559. Perls, A., Der Minhag in Talmud. Festschrift Israel Levy, 1911.
560. Perles, I., Miszellen zur rabbinischen Sprach- und Altertumskunde. MGWJ O.S. vol. XXI (1872), pp. 251 f.
561. Rabin, Ch., Qumran Studies. London, 1957.
562. Robert, L., Nouvelles Inscriptions de Sardes. Paris, 1964.
563. Rost, L., Die Vorstufen von Kirche und Synagogue in A.T. 1938.
564. Roth, C., The Historical Background to the Dead Sea Scrolls. Oxford, 1958.
565. Scherman, Th., Propheten und Apostellegenden, 1907.
566. Schrage, W., Ekklesia und Synagoge. Zeitschrift für Theologie und Kirche, 1963, pp. 178 f.
567. Seaver, J. E., Persecution of the Jews in the Roman Empire. Lawrance, 1952.
568. Simon, M., Verus Israel. Paris, 1948.
569. Tarn, W. T., Hellenistic Civilisation, 3rd edit. London, 1952.
570. Tisserant, E., Ascension d'Isaïe. Paris, 1904.
571. Vogt, J., Kaiser Julian und das Judentum, 1939.
572. Zeitlin, S., Johanan the High Priest's Abrogations and Decrees. Studies and Essays in honour of A. Neuman. Leiden, 1962, pp. 569–579.
573. —— The Origin of the Synagogue. PAAJR, 1931, pp. 81 f.
574. אבי יונה, מ., בית המקדש השני. ספר ירושלים, תשט״ז.
575. אופנהיימר, ב., הערך: נבואה. אנציקלופדיה מקראית כרך ה׳ (תשכ״ח).
576. אורבך, א., הערך: גר. אנציקלופדיה העברית, כרך יא, עמ׳ 172–184.
577. — כורש והכרזתו בעיני חז״ל. מולד, תשכ״א.
578. — מעמד והנהגה בעולמם של חכמי ארץ ישראל. כתבי האקדמיה הלאומית הישראלית למדעים. כרך ב׳.
579. — מתי פסקה הנבואה. תרביץ יז (תש״ו) עמ׳ 1–11.
580. אלבק, ח., סמיכה ומינוי בית דין. ציון ש״ח, עמ׳ 85–93.
581. אלון, ג., תחומן של הלכות טהרה. תרביץ ש״ט (תרצ״ח), עמ׳ 1–10, 179–195. (= מחקרים בתולדות ישראל כ״א, עמ׳ 148–176).
582. בער, י., עם ישראל הכנסיה הנוצרית והקיסרות הרומית מימי ספטימיוס סברוס ועד ראשית ימי קונסטנטינוס. ציון תשט״ז, עמ׳ 1–49.
583. בר, מ., יששכר וזבולון. שנתון בר אילן ו (תשכ״ח), עמ׳ 167 ואילך.
584. — תלמוד תורה ודרך ארץ. שנתון בר־אילן ב (תשכ״ד), עמ׳ 145 ואילך.
585. גוטמן, י. מ., מפתח התלמוד. צשאנגראד – בודאפעשט – ברסלוי. תרס״ו – תר״צ.
586. גולאק, א., סיקריקון. תרביץ ש״ה (תרצ״ד), עמ׳ 23–27.
587. דינבורג, ב., הריסקריפט של דיאוקליטיאנוס ליהודה משנת 293. ספר זכרון לא׳ גולאק ולש׳ קליין. תש״ב, עמ׳ 82–91.
588. — דמותה של ציון וירושלים בהכרתו ההיסטורית של ישראל, ציון, שט״ז, תשי״א, עמ׳ 4 ואילך.
589. היינמן, י., היהדות בעיני העולם העתיק. ציון ש״ד (תרצ״ט), עמ׳ 269–293.
590. הלוי, א. א., המחלוקת הראשונה. תרביץ שכ״ח (תשי״ט), עמ׳ 154–157.

591. ידין, י., מצדה. ידיעות החברה לחקירת א״י ועתיקותיה. שנה כט (תשכ״ה).
592. כץ, י., אף על פי שחטא ישראל הוא. תרביץ שכ״ז (תשי״ח), עמ׳ 203—217.
593. לוי, יוחנן, עולמות נפגשים. ירושלים, תש״ך.
594. ליברמן, ש., ירושלמי הוריות. ספר היובל לרבי חנוך אלבק. ירושלים, תשכ״ג, עמ׳ 283—305.
595. — ספרי זוטא. נויארק, תשכ״ח.
596. מורמלשטיין, ב., צורבא מרבנן. מאמרים לזכרון ר׳ צבי פרץ חיות. וינא, תרצ״ג, עמ׳ רכג–רל.
597. מנטל, ח. ד., טיבה של הכנסת הגדולה. דברי הקונגרס העולמי הרביעי למדעי היהדות, ח״א, עמ׳ 81—88.
598. מרגליות, ר., לחקר שמות וכינויים בתלמוד. ירושלים, תש״ך.
599. ספראי, ש., העליה לרגל בימי בית שני. תל־אביב, תשכ״ה.
600. — וזדים ביד עוסקי תורתך. תרביץ של״ח (תשכ״ט).
601. פינקלשטיין, א. א., הפרושים ואנשי כנסת הגדולה. ניו־יורק, תש״י.
602. צוקר, מ., האפשר שנביא יחטא? תרביץ, של״ט, תשכ״ו, עמ׳ 148—173.
603. צורי, ש., ר׳ יוסי בר׳ חנינא מקסרין. ירושלים, תרפ״ו.
604. צ׳ריקובר, א., היהודים במצרים בתקופה ההלניסטית הרומית לאור הפאפירולוגיה. מהדו׳ ב׳ תשכ״ג.
605. — היהודים והיוונים בתקופה ההלניסטית. ת״א, תשכ״ג.
606. קדושין, מ. י., בחירת ישראל בדברי חז״ל. Proceedings of the Rabbinical Assembly of America, vol. VIII (1941–44), pp. 20–25.
607. קלוזנר, י., הסטוריה של הבית השני. מהדו׳ ב׳ ירושלים, תשי״א.
608. קליין, ש., מאסף ציון ספר א׳ (תרפ״ו). עמ׳ 5.
609. — על ספר Vitae Prophetarum. ספר היובל לכבוד קלויזנר, עמ׳ 189—209.
610. רב צעיר, תולדות ההלכה. ח״א—ח״ג. ניו־יורק, תרצ״ה—תש״ג.
611. רוקח, ד., היהודים בפולמוס הפאגאני—נוצרי בקיסרות הרומית (דיסרטציה).
612. ריינס, ח. ז., תורה ומוסר. ירושלים, תשי״ד.
613. רפאפורט, ש. י., ערך מילין. פראג, תרי״ב.
617. שטרן, מ., אהדה ליהודים בחוגי סנטורים רומיים בתקופת הקיסרות הקדומה. ציון שכ״ט (תשכ״ד), עמ׳ 155—167.
615. — המנהיגות בקבוצות לוחמי החירות בסוף ימי הבית השני. בקובץ האישיות ודורה. תשכ״ד, עמ׳ 70—78.
616. שליט, א., הורדוס המלך, האיש ופעלו. ירושלים, תש״ך.

See also: 5, 19, 21, 26, 34, 51, 52, 55, 59, 60, 82, 90, 97, 98, 104, 105, 106, 120, 129, 145, 146, 148, 149, 156, 165, 167, 172, 177, 185, 188, 199, 208, 209, 211, 212, 262, 277, 329, 330, 342, 375, 384, 403, 407, 421, 449, 484, 497, 498, 503, 505, 506, 509.

Chapter XVII

617. Allegro, S. M., More Isaiah Commentaries from Qumran's fourth Cave. JBL vol. 77 (1958), pp. 215–221.
618. Aptowitzer, V., Parteipolitik der Hasmonäerzeit im rabbinischen und pseudoepig, Schrifttum. Wien, 1927.

619. Bacher, W., Ein polemischer Ausspruch Jose b. Chalaftha's. MGWJ vol. 42 (1898), pp. 505–507.
620. Barnard, L. W., Justin Martyr; his life and thought. Cambridge, 1962.
621. Finkelstein, L., The Birkat Hamazon. JQR N.S. vol. XIX (1928/29), pp. 211–251.
622. Fitzmyer, J. A., The Aramaic Text from Qumran Cave IV "Elect of God". The Catholic Biblical Quarterly vol. XXVII (1965), pp. 348–372.
623. Funk, S., Die Juden in Babylonien. Boskowitz, 1908.
624. Von Gall, A., βασιλεία τοῦ θεοῦ. Heidelberg, 1926.
625. Grelot, P., Le Messie dans les Apocryphes de l'AT. Recherches Bibliques vol. VI (1962), pp. 30 f.
626. Higgias, A. J. B., Jewish Messianic Belief. Novum Testamentum, 1967, pp. 298 f.
627. Hruby, K., Die Messiaserwartung in der Talmudischen Zeit, etc. Judaica vol. 20 (1964), pp. 6–22, 73–90, 193–212, ibid., vol. 21 (1965), pp. 100–122.
628. —— L'influence des apocalypses sur l'eschatologie judéo-chrétienne. L'Orient Syrien, 1966, pp. 291–320.
629. Klein, G., Der älteste Christl. Katechismus und die jüd. Propaganda-Literatur. Berlin, 1902.
630. König, F., Zarathustras Jenseitsvorstellungen und das A. T. Wien, 1964.
631. Köster, H., Synoptische Überlieferungen bei den Apostolischen Vätern. Berlin, 1957.
632. Kosmala, H., At the End of the Days. Annual of the Swedish Theological. Institute 11 (1963), pp. 27–37.
633. Lévi, I., Apocalypses dans le Talmud. REJ 1 (1880), pp. 108–114.
634. —— L'esprit de Dieu et l'esprit de Messie. Simonsen Festschrift, 1923, pp. 104–110.
635. Mariani, B., Article Marini, Enciclop. Cattolica vol VIII p. 159.
636. Michel, O., Der Brief an die Römer. Göttingen, 1966.
637. Mowinkel, S., He That cometh. Oxford, 1956.
638. Neussner, J., Life of Rabban Yohanan ben Zakkai. Leiden, 1962.
639. Rahmer, M., Die hebräischen Traditionen in den Werken des Hieronymus. MGWJ vol. 41 (1897), pp. 638–639.
640. Russel, D. S., The Method and Message of Jewish Apocalyptic. Philadelphia, 1964.
641. Stone, M., The Concept of the Messiah in IV Ezra. Studies in the History of Religions, vol. XIV (1968), pp. 298 f.
642. Vermes, G., Scripture and Tradition in Judaism. Leiden, 1961.
643. Volz, P., Die Eschatologie der jüdischen Gemeinde im neutestamentlichen Zeitalter. 2 Aufl. des Werkes "Jüdische Eschatologie von Daniel bis Akiba". Tübingen, 1934.
644. Widengren, G., Stand und Aufgaben der iranischen Religionsgeschichte. Leiden (1955) (= Numen, vol. 1–2).

645. Van der Woude A. S., Die Messianischen Vorstellungen der Gemeinde von Qumran. Assen, 1957.

646. Zeitlin, S., The Assumption of Moses. JQR N.S. vol. 38 (1947), pp. 36 f.

647. Zobel, M., Gottes Gesalbter, der Messias und die Messianische Zeit im Talmud und Midrasch. Berlin, 1938.

648. אבן שמואל, י., מדרשי גאולה. מהדו׳ ב׳. ירושלים–תל־אביב, תשי״ד.

649. אורבך, א., חלקם של חכמי אשכנז וצרפת בפולמוס על הרמב״ם ועל ספריו. ציון כ״ב (תש״ז), עמ׳ 149—159.

650. באמבערגער, מ. א. הלוי, פירוש סדר עבודה לר׳ יוסף בן נחמיאש. Jahrbruch der Jüdisch-Literarischen Gesellschaft. vol. VI (1908), pp. 1–17 Frankfurt a.M., 1909. (חלק עברי)

651. בר, מ., משהו על רב יהודה אחוה דרב סלא חסידא. סיני כ׳ מ״ח (תשכ״א), עמ׳ רצט–שא.

652. גילת, י. ד., משנתו של ר׳ אליעזר בן הורקנוס ומקומה בתולדות ההלכה. תל־אביב, תשכ״ח.

653. היינמן, יוסף, מסורות פרשניות קדומות באגדה ובתרגומים (ביקורת). תרביץ כל״ה (תשכ״ו), עמ׳ 84—94.

654. זליגמן, י.א., הערך: גאולה. אנציקלופדיה מקראית כ״ב, עמ׳ 389—391.

655. ידין, י., מחנה ד – מערת האיגרות. ידיעות בחקירת א״י ועתיקותיה. שכ״ו (תשכ״ב), עמ׳ 214 ואילך.

656. ייבין, ש., מלחמת בר־כוכבא. ירושלים, תש״ז.

657. לוצאטו, ש. ד., מבוא למחזור בני רומא. ליוורנו, תרט״ז.

658. ליוור, י., תולדות בית דוד. ירושלים, תשי״ט.

659. ליכט, י., תורת העתים של כת מדבר יהודה ושל מחשבי קצים אחרים. ארץ ישראל ספר ח (תשכ״ז), עמ׳ 63—70.

660. מירסקי, א., מקורה של תפלת שמונה־עשרה. תרביץ, תשכ״ד, עמ׳ 28 ואילך.

661. מרמורשטיין, א., רעיון הגאולה באגדת התנאים והאמוראים. ספר זכרון לכבוד א.

662. מרמורשטיין. לונדון, תש״י, עמ׳ טז – עו.

663. פלוסר, ד., פשר ישעיה ורעיון שנים עשר השליחים בראשית הנצרות. ארץ ישראל ספר ח (תשכ״ז).

664. שטיין, מ., מבוא למזמורי שלמה. הספרים החיצוניים מהדו׳ א. כהנא. כ״א, עמ׳ תלא–תלו.

665. שלום, ג., רעיון הגאולה בקבלה. מהדו׳ ב׳. ירושלים, תש״ו.

See also: 3, 5, 26, 30, 51, 58, 59, 87, 90, 92, 93, 98, 104, 111, 117, 119, 152, 156, 190, 195, 208, 209, 215, 227, 245, 279, 293, 308, 309, 328, 368, 403, 407, 415, 458, 484, 497.

GENERAL INDEX

INDEX OF RABBINIC SOURCES

(ONLY THOSE TREATED OF SUBSTANTIVELY)

* Ed. M. S. Zuckermandel, Jerusalem 1938, ed S. Lieberman 1955, 1962, 1967

* ed. S. Schechter, Vienna 1887
** ed. Horowitz-Rabin, Frankfurt 1931

* ed. Epstein-Melamed, Jerusalem 1955
** ed. Weiss, Vienna 1862

* ed. Horowitz, Leipzig, 1917
** ed. M. Friedmann, Vienna 1864, ed. Finkelstein, Berlin 1940

* ed. Hoffmann, Berlin 1909
** ed. Ratner, Vilna 1897

* ed. Theodor-Albeck, Berlin 1903–1929

INDEX OF RABBINIC SOURCES

* Venice, 1567 Rom, Vilna 1887
** ed. Margulies, Jerusalem 1953–1958
*** Pesaro, 1519, Rom, Vilna 1887

* Pesaro 1519; Rom, Vilna 1887
** ed. Buber 1899
*** Venice 1595; Mantua 1563

* ed. S. Buber, Vilna 1885
** *Kovetz 'al Yad* VI, Jerusalem 1966
*** ed. Mandelbaum, New York 1962
**** ed. M. Friedmann, Vienna 1880

* ed. Buber, Vilna 1891
** ed. Buber, Vilna 1893
*** Buber, Cracow 1893
**** ed. Warsaw 1852
***** ed. M. Friedmann, Vienna 1902
****** ed. M. Friedmann, Vienna 1904
******* ed. Schechter, Cambridge 1896
******** ed. Albeck, Jerusalem 1940
********* ed. Salonika 1521–1526; Warsaw 1826–1827

* ed. Margulies, Jerusalem, 1837–1856
** ed. Buber, Cracow 1903 *** ed. Buber, Berlin 1854
**** ed. Buber, Vienna 1894 ***** ed. Horovitz, Berlin 1889
****** *Beit ha-Midrash* ed. Jellinek, Jerusalem 1938
******* *Batei-Midrashot*, ed. Wertheimer, Jerusalem 1953
******** ed. Horvitz, Berlin

INDEX OF NON-RABBINICAL SOURCES

BIBLE VERSIONS (O. T.)

SEPTUAGINT
Gen. ii 4–5 187
Gen. xv 6 32–33
Ex. iv 24 154
Ex. xv 2 724 [23]
Ex. xxi 22–23 242
Ex. xxii 31 718 [56]
Ex. xxiii 20–22 742 [7]
Ex. xxiv 10 73; 715 [35]
Ex. xxviii 32 735 [21]
Ex. xxxii 12 887 [22]
Ex. xxxii 14 887 [22]
Lev. xxiv 16 735 [18]
Num. xxiv 17 999 [81]
Deut. vi 3 20–21
Deut. vii 11 289
Deut. xxxii 8 138
II Esdras xx 1 35
Job ix 13 411; 866 [66]
Job ix 22 869 [77]
Job xiv 4 411; 866 [66]
Job xiv 12 411; 867 [67]
Job xvi 14–15 411; 866 [66]
Job xix 6 411; 866 [66]
Job xxiii 13 864 [50]
Ps. viii 5 155; 158
Ps. lxxvii (i) 25 750 [54]
Jes. i 10 290
Jes. xiv 1 453; 888
Jes. xiv 1 453; 888 [36]
Jes. xxiv 5 290
Jes. liv 10 453; 887 [22]; 888 [36]
Jes. lix 20 670
Jes. lxiii 9 136; 741 [5]
Jer. xvi 19 724 [23]
Dan. iii 31–32 858 [3a]
Dan. vii 10 746 [40]
Hos. xiv 5 997 [64]
Hab. ii 4 35

AQUILA
Ps. xlviii 15 235

THEODOTION
Job. xxxvi 30 410; 866 [63]
Job xxxvii 12 410; 866 [63]
Job xxxviii 32 410; 866 [63]
Job xxxix 13 410; 866 [63]

HEXAPLA
Mich. vi 8 958 [18]

PESHITTA
Jes. lix 20 997 [64]

APOCRYPHA (O. T.)

I Maccabees
ii 29 569; 945 [91]
ii 41 569; 945 [91]
ii 52 32; 404
ii 56 659
ii 59 141
iii 18 69; 141; 712 [9]
iv 9 141
iv 30 141
iv 46 659; 820 [51]
vii 41–42 141
xiv 28 570; 945 [92]
xiv 41 659; 820 [51]

II Maccabees
vi 2 70
vi 12–16 526; 884 [91]
vi 17 884 [91]
vii 14 652
vii 28 769 [16]
x 29–30 141
xii 39–40 22; 697 [16]
xiv 37–39 906 [38]
xv 23 141

Tobit
iv 12 948 [16]

PSEUDEPIGRAPHA (O. T.)

* in Beit ha-Midrash, ed. Jellinek, Jerusalem 1938
** ed. Odeberg, New York 1973 (reprint of 1928 edition)
*** in Migne, PG. CXXII, Paris 1889

QUMRAN LITERATURE

*Damascus Document**
110–11 819–820 [47]
ii 12 (p. 7) 807 [50]
v 22–vi 1 (p. 21) 718 [56]
vii 19–20 (p. 31) 999 [81]
xv 1 (pp. 72–73) 911 [70]

*Genesis Apocryphon***
Col. II 493; 904 [24]
II 1 759 [33]
II 15 759 [33]

*Manual of Discipline****
iii 20 162–163; 720 [65]; 757 [13]
iii 21 162–163; 757 [13]
iv 5 260
v 17 718 [56]
v 21 718 [56]
vi 24–27 953 [69]
vii 1 587; 736 [25]; 953 [69]
vii 2–25 953 [69]
viii 13 736 [25]
viii 18 718 [56]
ix 11 259
x 12 720 [63]
xi 15 (pp. 233–235) 79; 585; 720 [63]; 755–756 [98]; 953 [75]

Pesher Isaiah
(4 *Qp Isa*$^{b\text{-}d}$)****
liv 11–12 1001 [9]

Psalm 151
696 [7]

*Thanksgiving Scroll******
i 7–8 (p. 58) 716 [39]
i 16 (p. 59) 716 [39]
i 20 (p. 60) 716 [39]
iv 15 (p. 93) 585; 953 [75]
iv 31 (p. 96) 79; 720 [63]
vii 6 (p. 133) 791 [69]
x 3–4 (p. 151) 891 [68]
x 6 (p. 151) 716 [39]
x 20 (p. 156) 716 [39]
xi 27 (p. 168) 755–756 [98]
xi 29 (p. 168) 755–756 [98]
xi 33 (p. 168) 755–756 [98]
xii 26 (p. 177) 891 [68]
xiii 7 (p. 181) 716 [39]
xiii 17 (p. 183) 260

*War of the Sons of Light etc.***1
17, [13], 2 585; 755–756 [98]; 953 [75]
19, [13], 10–11 757 [13]
19, [13], 14 742 [12]
21, [14], 4 585; 953 [75]
27, [17], 6 744 [19]; 757 [13]
27, [17], 7–8 757 [13]

2 *Q*3 *2
735 [20]

3 *Q*3 *3
735 [20]

4 *Q Mess ar*
995 [49]

11 *QPs*^{a} *4
735 [20]

* ed. Rabin, The Zadokite Documents[2], Oxford 1958
** ed. N. Avigad and Y. Yadin, Jerusalem 1956
*** in The Rule Scroll, ed. Licht, Jerusalem 1965
**** ed. Allegro, in JBL 77 (1958)
***** ed. Licht, Jerusalem 1957
*1 ed. Yadin, Jerusalem 1955
*2 in Discoveries in the Judean Desert, Vol. 3 (ed. Baillet, Milik, and DeVaux), Oxford 1962; pp. 53–55
*3 Ibid., p. 95
*4 in Discoveries in the Judean Desert, Vol. 4 (ed. Sanders), Oxford 1965; additional fragments ed. Yadin in Textus 5 (1966)

INDEX OF NON-RABBINICAL SOURCES

GREEK AND LATIN SOURCES

HOMER. *Odyssey*
xvii, 1319–1320 405; 862 [33]

AESOP, *Fables*
No. 258 987 [87]

HERODOTUS
I 131 70; 696 [4]
I 132 696 [4]

PLATO, *Apology*
41 443–444; 883 [83]

Laws
626 a 895 [20]
743 a 807 [49]
885 c 26; 698 [29]

Phaedo
67 234–235; 792 [73]
117 443–444; 883 [83]
1070 755 [95]

Protagoras
321 A–B 884 [94]

The Republic
361 883 [83]
379 900 [73]
597 D 791 [67]
614 B ff 246–248; 797 [18]
617 E 755 [95]

Symposium
189a–190a 228; 788 [41]

Timaeus
27 212; 782 [34]
28 212; 776–777 [70]; 782 [34]
29 e 777 [80]
90 221; 786 [19]
370 212; 782 [33]

ARISTOTLE
Nic. Ethics
31, 1128 a 907 [46]

STOIC VET. FRAGMENTA*
No. 975 268; 806 [42]

DIOGENES OF BABYLON, *De Piet Philodem***
p. 82 798 [27]

AUCTOR AD HERRENIUM
II, 10, 4 292; 816 [25]

CICERO, *Pro Flacco*
28 527; 924 [9]
69 527; 924 [9]

SALLUSTIUS, *Concerning the Gods and the Universe****
XV (p. 28) 51; 705 [53]

HORACE, *Satires*
I, 5 108; 727 [30]

SENECA, *Epistles*
18 405; 862 [35]
24 798 [27]
47 405; 862 [34]
65 798 [27]
82 769 [19]

QUINTILIAN
VII, 1, 49 292; 816 [25]

DIO CASSIUS
63, 13 927 [31]

DIOGENES LAERTIUS
VII, 38, 56 94; 724 [29]

PLOTINUS
*Enneads*****
III (p. 140) 165; 758 [21]

FLAVIUS VOPISCUS
Vita Saturnini
viii 27–28; 698–699 [33]

* ed. J. V. Arnim, Stuttgart 1968 (reprint of 1904 edition)
** ed. Gomperz, Vienna 1891
*** ed. A. D. Nock, Cambridge 1926
**** ed. Creuzer, Oxford 1835

***** ed. Wright, London 1923

JEWISH HELLENISTIC SOURCES

* ed. G. Kisch, Notre Dame 1949

EARLY CHRISTIAN LITERATURE

* ed. Funk, Paderborn, 1905 (Torino 1962)
** in M. R. James, The Apocryphal N. T. Oxford 1924

PATRISTIC LITERATURE

* ed. Ed. Schwartz in TUGAL IV, 2 Leipzig 1891
** in Migne, PG VII, Paris 1882
*** ed. Casey, London 1934
**** ed. Stählin, in GCS, Leipzig 1905
***** ed. Wendland, in GCS, Leipzig 1916
****** ed.Preuschen, CGIS, Leipzig 1903
*1 in Migne, PG XII, Paris 1862

*1 in Migne, PG XIII, Paris 1862
*2 ed. W. Wright, London 1869
*3 in Migne, PG XXVIII, Paris 1857
* ed. I. K. Holl in GCS, Leipzig 1915
** in Migne, PG XLVIII, Paris 1862
*** in Migne, PL XXVI, Paris 1845
**** in Migne, PL XLII, Parls 1845
***** in Migne, PL LIV, Paris 1846